Dictionary of Literary Biography

Documentary Series

Yearbooks

Concise Series

French Dramatists, 1789–1914

Dictionary of Literary Biography® • Volume One Hundred Ninety-Two

French Dramatists, 1789–1914

Edited by
Barbara T. Cooper
University of New Hampshire

A Bruccoli Clark Layman Book
Gale Research
Detroit, Washington, D.C., London

Printed in the United States of America

The paper used in this publication meets the minimum requirements
of American National Standard for Information Sciences–Permanence
Paper for Printed Library Materials, ANSI Z39.48-1984. ∞ ™

Library of Congress Cataloging-in-Publication Data

French dramatists, 1789–1914 / edited by Barbara T. Cooper.
    p. cm.–(Dictionary of literary biography; v. 192)
"A Bruccoli Clark Layman book."
Includes bibliographical references and index.
ISBN 0-7876-1847-0 (alk. paper)
1. French drama–Bio-bibliography–Dictionaries. 2. Dramatists, French–Biography–
Dictionaries. I. Cooper, Barbara T. 1944- . II. Series.
PQ501.F733 1998
842'.709'03–dc21   98-16251
                                                                          CIP

10 9 8 7 6 5 4 3 2 1

*For Wallace, who shares my love of French theater
and enriches my life in so many ways*

Contents

Plan of the Series

. . . Almost the most prodigious asset of a country, and perhaps its most precious possession, is its native literary product — when that product is fine and noble and enduring.

Mark Twain*

The advisory board, the editors, and the publisher of the *Dictionary of Literary Biography* are joined in endorsing Mark Twain's declaration. The literature of a nation provides an inexhaustible resource of permanent worth. We intend to make literature and its creators better understood and more accessible to students and the reading public, while satisfying the standards of teachers and scholars.

To meet these requirements, *literary biography* has been construed in terms of the author's achievement. The most important thing about a writer is his writing. Accordingly, the entries in *DLB* are career biographies, tracing the development of the author's canon and the evolution of his reputation.

The purpose of *DLB* is not only to provide reliable information in a convenient format but also to place the figures in the larger perspective of literary history and to offer appraisals of their accomplishments by qualified scholars.

The publication plan for *DLB* resulted from two years of preparation. The project was proposed to Bruccoli Clark by Frederick C. Ruffner, president of the Gale Research Company, in November 1975. After specimen entries were prepared and typeset, an advisory board was formed to refine the entry format and develop the series rationale. In meetings held during 1976, the publisher, series editors, and advisory board approved the scheme for a comprehensive biographical dictionary of persons who contributed to North American literature. Editorial work on the first volume began in January 1977, and it was published in 1978. In order to make *DLB* more than a reference tool and to compile volumes that individually have claim to status as literary history, it was decided to organize volumes by

From an unpublished section of Mark Twain's autobiography, copyright by the Mark Twain Company

topic, period, or genre. Each of these freestanding volumes provides a biographical-bibliographical guide and overview for a particular area of literature. We are convinced that this organization—as opposed to a single alphabet method—constitutes a valuable innovation in the presentation of reference material. The volume plan necessarily requires many decisions for the placement and treatment of authors who might properly be included in two or three volumes. In some instances a major figure will be included in separate volumes, but with different entries emphasizing the aspect of his career appropriate to each volume. Ernest Hemingway, for example, is represented in *American Writers in Paris, 1920–1939* by an entry focusing on his expatriate apprenticeship; he is also in *American Novelists, 1910–1945* with an entry surveying his entire career, as well as in *American Short-Story Writers, 1910–1945, Second Series* with an entry concentrating on his short stories. Each volume includes a cumulative index of the subject authors and articles. Comprehensive indexes to the entire series are planned.

Since 1981 the series has been further augmented by the *DLB Yearbooks,* which update published entries and add new entries to keep the *DLB* current with contemporary activity. There have also been *DLB Documentary Series* volumes which provide biographical and critical source materials for figures whose work is judged to have particular interest for students. One of these companion volumes is entirely devoted to Tennessee Williams.

We define literature as the *intellectual commerce of a nation:* not merely as belles lettres but as that ample and complex process by which ideas are generated, shaped, and transmitted. *DLB* entries are not limited to "creative writers" but extend to other figures who in their time and in their way influenced the mind of a people. Thus the series encompasses historians, journalists, publishers, book collectors, and screenwriters. By this means readers of *DLB* may be aided to perceive literature not as cult scripture in the keeping of intellectual high priests but firmly positioned at the center of a nation's life.

DLB includes the major writers appropriate to each volume and those standing in the ranks behind them. Scholarly and critical counsel has been sought in deciding which minor figures to include and how full their entries should be. Wherever possible, useful references are made to figures who do not warrant separate entries.

Each *DLB* volume has an expert volume editor responsible for planning the volume, selecting the figures for inclusion, and assigning the entries. Volume editors are also responsible for preparing, where appropriate, appendices surveying the major periodicals and literary and intellectual movements for their volumes, as well as lists of further readings. Work on the series as a whole is coordinated at the Bruccoli Clark Layman editorial center in Columbia, South Carolina, where the editorial staff is responsible for accuracy and utility of the published volumes.

One feature that distinguishes *DLB* is the illustration policy—its concern with the iconography of literature. Just as an author is influenced by his surroundings, so is the reader's understanding of the author enhanced by a knowledge of his environment. Therefore *DLB* volumes include not only drawings, paintings, and photographs of authors, often depicting them at various stages in their careers, but also illustrations of their families and places where they lived. Title pages are regularly reproduced in facsimile along with dust jackets for modern authors. The dust jackets are a special feature of *DLB* because they often document better than anything else the way in which an author's work was perceived in its own time. Specimens of the writers' manuscripts and letters are included when feasible.

Samuel Johnson rightly decreed that "The chief glory of every people arises from its authors." The purpose of the *Dictionary of Literary Biography* is to compile literary history in the surest way available to us—by accurate and comprehensive treatment of the lives and work of those who contributed to it.

The *DLB* Advisory Board

Introduction

It is often claimed that the nineteenth century in France was dominated by the novel, but the period between 1789 and 1914 was the last era in the history of French literature and culture to be marked in a significant way by drama. From the French Revolution to the dawn of World War I thousands of dramatic works, in a myriad of genres, were seen by audiences at playhouses throughout Paris and the provinces. In addition to their value as a source of entertainment for popular and elite publics, the plays audiences came to see during the *grand dix-neuvième siècle* (great nineteenth century) frequently broached serious political and social issues. For the better part of that time, however, playwrights worked under the watchful eye of the government's theater censors—a fact of life that often limited their ability to express either controversial or critical views directly. Still, audiences were quite adept at seizing upon allusions and parallels, whether these were deliberately intended by the dramatist or purposefully read into a play by its viewers.

The nineteenth century was also the era during which theater became an industry. It was a period that saw the birth of the star system, the advent of the director, the development of commercial and artistic competition, and the growing power of drama critics writing for the periodical press. It was an age marked by great advances in set, costume, and lighting design as well as by the building of new and/or more-modern performance venues. It was an epoch as notable for its frequent recourse to joint authorship—a seeming necessity in an age of changing audience demands and economic rivalries—as for its use of various forms of self-promotion and publicity, including *la claque* (paid applauders) and *l'affiche* (the playbill).

Given the visibility of the theater in the cultural marketplace and the notoriety regularly achieved by those connected with the dramatic arts, no accurate description of nineteenth-century French urban life and culture could legitimately exclude reference to the stage. Most novelists of the period appear to have understood this. Many of them used the theater as either metaphor or background for works set in Paris and featured actors, actresses, dancers, and critics as members of the social universe described in their writings. Oth-

ers, such as Prosper Mérimée, best known today for his short stories, began their careers writing drama, as did Alexandre Dumas *père,* now principally remembered for his novels. Honoré de Balzac, Eugène Sue, Gérard Labrunie (called Gérard de Nerval), Gustave Flaubert, Jules Verne, and Emile Zola likewise wrote for the theater at one time or another in their careers. So, too, did Germaine de Staël; George Sand; Philippe-Auguste, Comte de Villiers de l'Isle-Adam; and Rachilde, whose contributions to nineteenth-century French drama are described in this volume. Before he wrote *Le Rouge et le noir* (1830; translated as *Red and Black,* 1898) or *La Chartreuse de Parme* (1839; translated as *The Charterhouse of Parma,* 1895), Stendhal not only composed his celebrated treatise on drama titled *Racine et Shakespeare* (1823–1825) but also attempted, unsuccessfully, to write plays. Victor Hugo composed the influential Preface to his drama *Cromwell* (1827) and such plays as *Hernani* (1830) and *Marion de Lorme* (1831) before he wrote *Notre-Dame de Paris* (1832) or *Les Misérables* (1862). Other authors wrote theater criticism. Charles Nodier, Théophile Gautier, Jules Janin, Jules-Amédée Barbey d'Aurevilly, and Alphonse Daudet are among the best known of these literary chroniclers of the nineteenth-century French stage, but theirs are by no means the only names that have come down to the present day. Poet Stéphane Mallarmé wrote a theoretical treatise on drama titled *Crayonné au théâtre* (Notes Scribbled at the Theater, 1887). Critics such as Julien-Louis Geoffroy, Francisque Sarcey, Emile Faguet, and Gustave Larroumet also wrote influential drama reviews; these were collected later and printed in one or more volumes that capture some of the contemporary reactions to nineteenth-century French theater pieces. References to these and other appreciations of the period's dramatic productions can be found in the bibliographies appended to the individual essays included in this volume.

To understand fully the nature and importance of French drama from 1789 to 1914 one must begin by glancing back to the mid seventeenth century and the careers of Pierre Corneille, Jean Racine, and Jean-Baptiste Poquelin, known as Molière. These three playwrights, whose works shed glory on the age of Louis XIV and still serve as the finest examples of French classical dramaturgy—especially as it was articulated by Nicolas Boileau in his *L'art poétique* (Poetics) of 1674—set the standard according to which, or against which, subsequent French dramatists and their works were often judged. Corneille's and Racine's tragedies and some of Molière's comedies were written in rhymed alexandrine couplets (each line of verse contained twelve syllables). Their plays respected the so-called unities of time, place, and action, which limited each work to a single action/plotline, a period of twenty-four hours, and a single location. (Onstage there was rarely more than one set, normally unmarked by features that might distinguish it from any other work's decor. Costumes were, for the most part, likewise devoid of any historically or geographically pertinent specificity and were generally provided by the actors themselves.) In addition, when composing their plays, Corneille, Racine, and Molière accepted certain prescribed rules of *les bienséances* (aesthetic decorum) that banned the display of physical violence—some would say all nonverbal action—and the use of unseemly language from the stage. When choosing the subject matter for their works, Corneille and Racine turned principally to the history or mythology of ancient Greece and Rome or to the Bible. Molière modeled his portraits of contemporary vices on the examples found in the writings of his classical predecessors. The success of these seventeenth-century refashionings of previously treated material underscores the fact that, in this era, invention on an existing theme was prized above originality.

Subsidized by the king and other members of the royal family and the aristocracy, Corneille, Racine, and Molière saw their works staged at Versailles, in Paris, and at other elite venues and performed by actors and actresses who depended upon official patronage to underwrite their expenses. The types and repertory of works each theater troupe was allowed to produce were strictly regulated by the government and, once defined, were jealously guarded by each company. Some of the new plays that were created became the object at times of heated discussion at court, in the newly formed Académie Française, in polemical pamphlets, and in literary salons. None could be published without *privilège du roi* (royal consent). Given the many intimate connections between theater and state at the time, the significance of dramatic texts and theatrical performances within the seventeenth-century French cultural and political landscape can scarcely be overestimated and certainly far exceeded that of the nascent novel or the multivolume romance.

The extended sojourn in Paris, from 1661 to 1697, of a troupe of Italian actors also bears mentioning in this brief summary of mid-to-late-seventeenth-century French theater. Most often seen engaging in physical and verbal improvisation around a vaguely sketched-out, conventional (*canevas*) plot featuring stock characters, these practitioners of the commedia dell'arte influenced Molière's comedies and performance style—they at one time shared a theater with him—before being banished from France by the king.

Upon the death of Louis XIV in 1715 the center of French culture moved from Versailles to Paris. Initially, French dramaturgy changed little, if at all. Many playwrights continued, often less skillfully, to write comedies and tragedies in the manner of Corneille, Racine, and Molière. Gradually some changes in dramatic technique did occur. What is more, in 1716 a new troupe of Italian actors was allowed to take up residence in Paris.

François-Marie Arouet, who published his works under the pen name of Voltaire, was among the most gifted of those who continued to write plays in the classical style. In contrast to his predecessors (and his contemporary, Prosper Jolyot de Crébillon) Voltaire did occasionally introduce new subjects into his tragedies and comedies. Some of these topics were drawn from French, rather than biblical or classical, history; others were inspired by the playwright's belief in religious tolerance and other philosophical tenets. In his effort to introduce national historical subject matter into French drama Voltaire was seconded by Jean-François Hénault (called le Président Hénault), a magistrate who also wrote drama and later in the century was succeeded by Marie-Joseph Chénier, whose drama *Charles IX, ou L'Ecole des rois* (Charles IX, or The School for Kings, 1788) not only sparked considerable partisan fervor during the era of the French Revolution but also exercised some influence on the writings of early-nineteenth-century French neoclassical dramatists.

In addition to the changes he pioneered in the realm of subject matter, Voltaire encouraged the finest actors of his time—Henri Louis Cain, called Lekain, and Claire de la Tude, called Mlle Clairon—to undertake modest reforms in costume design and diction and forced the removal of aristocratic spectators from their customary seats on the stage. Although Voltaire still depended on wealthy patrons (both French and foreign) for support and often suffered the ill effects of government censorship, his international reputation and personal wealth eventually allowed him to stage performances of his works at his home in Ferney, Switzerland (where he occasionally acted in them himself). Voltaire was also among the first French playwrights to admire the dramas of William Shakespeare, dramas he later denounced as a monstrous and barbaric threat to the ideals of the French classical aesthetic. Shakespeare's plays, which in the nineteenth century would be embraced by Romantic dramatists seeking an alternative to the works of Corneille and Racine, were first translated into French by Antoine de La Place in 1745 and were again translated in 1770 by Jean-François Ducis and by Pierre Le Tourneur in 1776. None of these translations was complete or entirely faithful to the original, however. Indeed, most of the translated plays could easily have been mistaken for works written by the followers of Corneille or Racine.

Unlike tragedy, which changed little during the eighteenth century, comedy underwent some notable modification. Authors such as Jean-François Regnard and Alain-René Lesage wrote comedies of manners that denounced the unscrupulous social climbers and economic predators of the period. The eighteenth-century taste for *sensibilité* (sentimentality) was reflected in the *comédies-larmoyantes* (tearful or sentimental comedies) of Pierre-Claude Nivelle de La Chaussée, who held virtue and order in high esteem and who, most famously, condemned class-based prejudices in *Le Préjugé à la mode* (The Prejudice of the Day, 1735). The last-minute revelation of some critical bit of information (usually regarding a character's true origins) almost always brings his plays to a positive conclusion after audiences have had many opportunities to shed tears of sympathy for the long-suffering protagonist.

The sentiments examined in the prose dramas of Pierre Carlet de Chamblein de Marivaux are far more subtle than those found in Nivelle de La Chaussée's plays although Marivaux's works, too, often depend on some type of revelation to reach a conclusion. In Marivaux's plays, many of which were written for and performed by the Italian actors who had been allowed to settle in Paris after Louis XIV's death, it is often the results of unexpected emotions that are revealed in the final scenes. Marivaux, who wrote almost exclusively about the birth and surprises of love, provides audiences with keen insights into his characters' minds and emotions and endows his protagonists with wit, grace, and a refined, stylized form of speech that has come to be known as *marivaudage*. His pieces, including *Le Jeu de l'amour et du hasard* (The Game of Love and Chance, 1730) and *Les Fausses Confidences* (False Confidences, 1737), are still regularly performed today and are often said to have influenced the dramatic writings of the nineteenth-century poet and playwright Alfred de Musset.

Along with Marivaux, Pierre-Augustin Caron de Beaumarchais is without doubt the best-remembered and most influential comic dramatist of the eighteenth century. Known today primarily for *Le Barbier de Séville* (1775; translated as *The Barber of Seville,* 1776) and *Le Mariage de Figaro* (1784; translated as *The Marriage of Figaro,* 1785), the first two parts of a dramatic trilogy that concludes with *La Mère coupable* (The Guilty Mother, 1792), Beaumarchais was a man of many talents and professions. He was, for example, the founder (in 1777) of the Société des auteurs dramatiques, a professional association that sought to guarantee dramatists greater financial profit from their works. His plays, which contain biting observations on class and power, are often said to have contributed to the political ferment that led to the French Revolution. Whether or not that can be proved, the indomitable Figaro, who appears in all three plays in the trilogy and who is heir to a long succession of wily valets in the French theater, certainly does not refrain from denouncing privileges based on the "accident of birth" rather than on individual merit. Various "accidents of birth" do, however, occur in Beaumarchais's plays—accidents that, in *Le Mariage de Figaro* allow the dramatist to mock the conventions of *la voix du sang* (the call of the blood) and *la croix de ma mère* (my mother's cross) that often led to touching recognition scenes in other writers' dramas and that in *La Mère coupable* prompt an examination of the unequal punishment meted out to men and women for their marital infidelities and illegitimate children.

The touching didacticism found in *La Mère coupable* and in other plays of the eighteenth century also infuses the dramatic works of Beaumarchais's predecessor, the *encyclopédiste* Denis Diderot. The author of such *drames bourgeois* (moralizing bourgeois or domestic dramas written in prose) as *Le Fils naturel* (The Illegitimate Son, 1757), *Le Père de famille* (The Head of the Family, 1758), and *Est-il bon? Est-il méchant?* (Is He Good? Is He Wicked?, 1781), and of a treatise on acting titled *Le Paradoxe sur le comédien* (1773–1778), Diderot is frequently said to have laid the groundwork for the realistic dramas of the mid-to-late nineteenth century despite the fact that his plays were not performed during his lifetime. Like the paintings of Jean-Baptiste Greuze, which he much admired, Diderot's dramas depict pathos and virtue in an edifying middle-class environment and a relatively realistic physical decor. They use pantomime and tableaux (scenes of arrested movement) to heighten emotion and drama and are designed around the fiction of an invisible "fourth wall" (in which the audience is expected to imagine that it is looking through a wall into the home of the characters whose lives are portrayed on stage). Louis-Sébastien Mercier and Michel Jean Sedaine wrote plays in a similar vein and, like Diderot, believed in the theater's ability to educate audiences and elevate public morals. Their views ran counter to those of Jean-Jacques Rousseau, who, in his *Lettre à d'Alembert sur les spectacles* (Letter to D'Alembert on the Theater, 1758), had advanced the opinion that dramatic texts and performances could lead to social and moral corruption.

This survey of eighteenth-century French drama would be incomplete without noting some of the other forms of theatrical entertainment that lasted, in one form or another, into the nineteenth century. In addition to those troupes authorized by the Crown to perform works in elite genres at permanent playhouses, there were groups of actors, mimes, acrobats, and others who produced spectacles on temporary stages set up during annual festivals and fairs. The performers at these *théâtres de la foire* (fairground theaters) often attempted to circumvent the officially imposed limits to their repertory and in the process introduced new types of spectacles. Most notable among these innovative forms were comic operas—parodies of successful operas, tragedies, and high comedies written in what is called the genre *poissard*—a genre featuring lower-class urban characters who speak a French roughly equivalent to Cockney English; and *comédies en vaudevilles*—one- to three-act comic plays combining well-known melodies with new words, dance scenes, and passages of spoken dialogue. Pantomime dramas, sometimes including snippets of dialogue and music, were also a feature of some fairground productions. By the time of the French Revolution many of these troupes had permanent stages and openly challenged the official companies whose monopolies on certain types of performances had by then been seriously eroded. Indeed, the politicization of all aspects of life during the revolutionary period contributed significantly to the proliferation of theaters and troupes and to the development of a repertory of works responsive to and reflective of current events. While much of the circumstantial drama written during this period is said to be of little lasting merit, it did help to bring about a change in audience expectations and participation and the development of artistic competition. By 1791 circumstances were such that the privileges formerly granted to the major troupes were totally abolished.

Napoleon Bonaparte, who clearly understood the power of the theater and paid close attention to developments in the dramatic arena, eventually re-imposed limits on the number of theaters in Paris and defined the nature of the repertory to be performed at each playhouse. He also reinstituted theater censorship by the government. (With several brief lapses and varying degrees of intensity, censorship of the theater lasted until 1905 before being definitively abolished.) Napoleon's preference for tragedy and his admiration for such tragic actors as François-Joseph Talma and Marguerite Weimer, known in the theater as Mlle George, helped to prolong the life of French Neoclassical dramas both old and new but guaranteed neither the quality of contemporary compositions nor widespread audience acceptance. In their search for novelty, authors of early-nineteenth-century Neoclassical tragedies often chose to use national historical subjects in their works, but such modest innovations failed to satisfy those who craved a more resolutely "modern," post-revolutionary drama. Playwrights such as Louis-Jean-Népomucène Lemercier were thus seen as defenders of an outdated literary fashion, in contrast to the more aesthetically and politically liberal dramatists such as Casimir Delavigne who, nonetheless, did not stray far from time-honored compositional norms. The difference between the artistic visions of these two playwrights may well have been exaggerated by their ideological partisans but did, nonetheless, mark the beginnings of the battle for Romantic drama in France. At the same time that the momentum for aesthetic change was growing in elite cultural venues, the Boulevard theaters authorized by Napoleon and his successors offered melodramas, comédies en vaudevilles, parodies, pantomimes, and other types of spectacles to the public.

While some of the characteristic features of melodrama were already present in various eighteenth-century French popular entertainments, it was not until the beginning of the nineteenth century that the genre took on its distinctive aesthetic shape. Much of the popularity it quickly achieved can be attributed to René-Charles Guilbert de Pixérécourt, often called the Father of French Melodrama, and to Victor Ducange, both of whose careers are examined in essays printed in this volume. While Ducange's plays often differ considerably from Pixérécourt's, both authors' works generally include the following elements: villains who persecute or otherwise cause a virtuous young woman (or man) to suffer unjustly, attention to the moral nature of the play's outcome, some attempt to achieve "accuracy" in costuming and setting, the portrayal of actions that may cover a period of months or years and that may result from secrets not immediately revealed, and an emphasis on practicable sets and other forms of spectacle. Early melodramas also featured instrumental music which was generally used to establish a mood or to define a character's morality (and whose presence is recorded in the name of the genre: *melos* + *drama*) and dance as well as comic individuals, called *niais,* who momentarily lightened the mood of the work. These elements of melodrama were relatively quick to disappear, however, and cannot be found in the plays of mid-nineteenth-century melodramatists such as Joseph Bouchardy or Adolphe Philippe Dennery, nor even in all the plays written by Pixérécourt or Ducange.

Dissatisfaction with the Neoclassical aesthetic, together with a growing acquaintance with the works of foreign dramatists and the example of Boulevard theater stagecraft, spurred the call for the creation of Romantic dramas. Such dramas would set aside the unities, the traditional bienséances, and forgo the strict separation of comedy from tragedy; they would extend the range of subjects and introduce local color in set and costume design. Some proponents of Romantic drama, including Stendhal, wished to substitute prose for alexandrine verse; others, such as Hugo, proposed retaining poetry as the medium for dramatic speech but wanted to liberalize the rules of versification. Institutional opposition to Romanticism led the earliest Romantic playwrights, such as Prosper Mérimée, to compose closet dramas that were intended to be read rather than staged. Eventually, however, pieces such as Dumas *père*'s *Henri III et sa cour* (1829; translated as *Catherine of Cleves,* 1831); Alfred de Vigny's *Le More de Venise* (1829), a translation-adaptation of Shakespeare's *Othello* (1604); and Hugo's *Hernani* (1830) were performed at the Théâtre-Français. The source of considerable controversy in that conservative playhouse, in the press, and in the French Academy, these works ushered in an era of Romanticism in French theater that is traditionally said to have ended with the failure of Hugo's *Les Burgraves* in 1843. (As is often true in literary history, however, the dates of the "birth" and "death" of Romantic drama have been rather arbitrarily fixed and mask the evolutionary nature of aesthetic change.) Frustrated by the resistance they regularly encountered at the Théâtre-Français, some Romantic playwrights began as early as 1831 to offer their pieces to the managers of Boulevard theaters, where Marie Dorval (the stage name of Marie Delaunay), Frédérick Lemaître (Antoine-Louis Lemaître), and Bocage (Pierre Tousez) earned celebrity by starring in them. Only Alfred de Musset, who gave up writing for public performance early in his career, failed to profit from the skill these players brought to the Boulevard theater productions. Musset's armchair theater, published in 1833–1834, was composed of comedies, proverbs (a dramatic genre designed to illustrate a proverbial saying), and his *Lorenzaccio* (1834), few of which were performed during his lifetime. Now far more frequently staged than any other works of the period, Musset's plays are considered by many to be the finest examples of French Romantic dramaturgy.

With the engagement of the actress known as Mlle Rachel (née Elisabeth-Rachel Félix) at the Théâtre-Français and the creation of new Neoclassical pieces such as François Ponsard's *Lucrèce* (1843), there seemed to be a turn away from Romantic drama and a movement toward other forms of theatrical entertainment, including a brief revival of interest in tragedy. At the same time Alexandre Dumas *fils,* Emile Augier, and Octave Feuillet, among others, began composing dramas that explored the social and moral questions of the day, including such problems as prostitution, marital infidelity, money, class, and the role of religion. Their works are considered examples of realistic playwriting and generally include, in addition to recognizably contemporary settings and costumes, a moralistic message that appealed to the conservative middle class. George Sand, too, after initially writing Romantic pieces, moved in the direction of dramatic realism. Her social and political views were significantly less conservative than those of many of her playwriting contemporaries, however.

Many, though by no means all, of the realistic dramas of the midcentury are marked by a rigorous organizational design that leads, almost mechanically, to a predetermined outcome. These *pièces bien faites* (well-made plays) inherited something of their structure from the vaudevilles and other comic works of Eugène Scribe, in which obstacles and unexpected turns of events, skillfully arranged by the dramatist, first complicate and then resolve the situation posited at the beginning of the play. Comic playwrights Georges Feydeau and Eugène Labiche also inherited something of the mechanistic designs of their predecessor and, to forestall unwanted encounters, took advantage of such conventional devices as the quid pro quo and the hastily arranged hiding place to provoke laughter and heighten tension. Their witty and often saucy plays delighted theater audiences at the same time that Jacques Offenbach's operettas, whose libretti were most often provided by Ludovic Halévy and Henri Meilhac, regaled the public. All of these works continue to entertain spectators when, as often happens, they are revived today. Equally popular during the last four decades of the nineteenth century, but less enduring over time, were the plays of Victorien Sardou, which offered viewers either satires on contemporary life or lavish historical spectacles, the most renowned of which served as vehicles for the actress Sarah Bernhardt.

Whether productions were comic or serious, the increasing attention to realistic detail in the setting, costume, and, to some degree, even in the performance style adopted by the actors in the plays of the 1840s, 1850s, and 1860s set the stage for the birth of Naturalist drama in the 1870s and 1880s. Zola's dramatization of his novel *Thérèse Raquin* in 1873 and his writings on *Le Naturalisme au théâtre* (Naturalism in the Theater, 1881) were among the earliest manifestations of the Naturalist aesthetic, which held that character and behavior could be explained on the basis of scientific theory (principles regarding environment and heredity) rather than by means of individual psychology. Plays by Henri Becque, including *Les Corbeaux* (1882; translated as *The Crows,* 1912), also illustrated the genre that, at least in principle, saw drama as a "slice of life" transferred to the stage. By the end of the century, however, Eugène Brieux and Georges Courteline reverted to more-traditional forms of realism. Their works reflect many of the social concerns and issues of the day (syphilis, abortion, education for women, rigid bureaucracy, and overt injustice) and, like Becque's writings, are analyzed in detail in essays included in this volume.

While many playwrights were emphasizing the here and now—the material and social world as it might be seen outside the theater—other dramatists, including Maurice Maeterlinck, gave dramatic shape to allegory. The mood, emotion, silence, and symbolism in the works of this Belgian-born writer point to the mysterious, generally spiritual or psychological, forces that govern the universe and the lives of those who inhabit it. Thus, words such as *ineffable* and *dreamlike* are often used to describe the Symbolist plays of Maeterlinck and those of his peers who attempted to follow the principle embodied in the phrase *peindre l'effet et non l'objet* (to depict effects or mystical dimensions rather than objects or the concrete aspects of human existence). Philippe-Auguste, Comte de Villiers de l'Isle-Adam, was also fascinated by the metaphysical and spiritual dimensions of life and had hoped to make a name for himself in the theater. While he never achieved the success he dreamed of, his dramatic poem *Axël* (1890) eventually helped shape the modern French theater aesthetic. Paul Claudel, who, like Maeterlinck, began his career writing plays in the Symbolist mode, shifted to a more traditional Christian mysticism after the turn of the century and was later influenced by Eastern philosophical thought and the example of the tragic playwrights of ancient Greece. He is credited with the introduction of vers libre (free verse) in French drama. Other dramatists also avoided the mimetic representations of the world that were so prized by Naturalist playwrights. Thus, writers such as Rachilde, Jean Richepin, and Octave Mirbeau proposed decadent and perverse visions of the human experience to audiences while such late Romantics as Edmond Rostand took refuge from the present in the play of language and style. Rostand's *Cyrano de Bergerac,* which premiered in 1897, had by 1913 been performed more than a thousand times, making it one of the most successful plays of the turn of the century. Alfred Jarry's *Ubu roi* (1896; translated as *King Turd,* 1953) depicts the grotesqueness of a world without moral principles and the monstrousness and inanity of power. Jarry's work exercised greater influence on twentieth-century Surrealist and Absurdist drama than on the theater of his time.

This brief description of nineteenth-century drama hardly skims the surface of the period's varied theatrical productions and styles. Other performance genres, including grand opera, ballet, cabaret acts, and pantomime, also drew attention from audiences. Scenes from these and other spectacles are recorded in paintings by such nineteenth-century artists as Louis-Léopold Boilly, Honoré Daumier, Edgar Degas, Pierre-Auguste Renoir, and Henri Toulouse-Lautrec and in photographs by Nadar (Félix Tournachon) and others. It is often thanks to those early photographs that one is able to discover the faces of some of the principal actors and actresses of the day: Bernhardt, of course, as well as Edmond Got, Constant-Benoît Coquelin, Jean Sully (known in the theater as Mounet-Sully), and Gabrielle Réjane, among many other celebrated players whose importance to the history of nineteenth-century French drama cannot be overestimated. The epic film *Les Enfants du paradis* (Children of Paradise, 1945) by Marcel Carné likewise helps to remind one of the career of the great mime Deburau and of the audiences who flocked to the theater to see him.

The theatrical experience of nineteenth-century French audiences was further shaped by acting teachers such as Jean Mauduit-Larive, who attempted to catalogue the rules of theatrical declamation early in the century, and François Delsarte, who sought to analyze and codify gesture at a later time; by set designers from Pierre-Luc-Charles Cicéri to C. A. Cambon and Edouard Despléchin (among others); by such theater architects as Victor Louis and Charles Garnier; and by theater administrators and directors from Baron Isidore Taylor to André Antoine and Aurélien-Marie Lugné-Poë. It should be noted, too, that such little-known but nonetheless important women playwrights as Mmes Barthélemy-Hadot, Virginie Ancelot, and others created works that have yet to receive the kind of study that has begun to bring the accomplishments of nineteenth-century women novelists and poets to the attention of critics and scholars. There are many male dramatists whose theater pieces are catalogued in Charles Beaumont Wickes's listing of performances in *The Parisian Stage* that could not, for reasons of space, be treated here but whose works received popular acclaim in their day. It is also not possible to explore, in this brief introduction, publications such as *Le Magasin théâtral* (The Theatrical Storehouse), which offered readers and provincial directors inexpensive editions of new and successfully reprised plays, usually accompanied by an illustration that offered them a glimpse of the costumes, sets, and/or postures used in Parisian performances. Nonetheless, a close analysis of this and other collections of dramatic works (including examination of their cost, distribution patterns, and so forth) would certainly illuminate the scope of the theater's impact on nineteenth-century French culture, were it to be undertaken.

It is clear, then, that the essays in this volume mark only the beginning of a much needed reassessment and reexamination of the role of the theater in nineteenth-century France. There is still a great deal to be done and much to be discovered. Biographies and histories of performance and of repertories—as well as studies of publication and production records, costume, set and lighting design, acting techniques, audiences, and journalistic accounts of theater history—still need to be written. New approaches to the study of the handful of familiar plays and subjects regarding nineteenth-century French theater may also help to revive interest in a genre that has, for some time now, undeservedly slipped into the shadows cast by the novel and, to a lesser extent, by poetry. May the readers of this volume be inspired to undertake some of the many projects that remain to be done.

—Barbara T. Cooper

Acknowledgments

This book was produced by Bruccoli Clark Layman, Inc. Karen L. Rood is senior editor for the *Dictionary of Literary Biography* series. Kenneth Graham was the in-house editor.

Administrative support was provided by Ann M. Cheschi and Brenda A. Gillie.

Bookkeeper is Joyce Fowler.

Copyediting supervisor is Samuel W. Bruce. The copyediting staff includes Phyllis A. Avant, Patricia Coate, Christine Copeland, Thom Harman, and William L. Thomas Jr. Freelance copyeditors are Charles Brower, Leslie Haynsworth, and Rebecca Mayo.

Editorial associate is Jeff Miller.

Layout and graphics staff includes Janet E. Hill and Mark J. McEwan.

Office manager is Kathy Lawler Merlette.

Photography editors are Margaret Meriwether and Paul Talbot. Photographic copy work was performed by Joseph M. Bruccoli.

Production manager is Philip B. Dematteis.

Systems manager is Marie L. Parker.

Typesetting supervisor is Kathleen M. Flanagan. The typesetting staff includes Pamela D. Norton and Patricia Flanagan Salisbury. Freelance typesetters include Deidre Murphy and Delores Plastow.

Walter W. Ross, Steven Gross, and Ronald Aikman did library research. They were assisted by the following librarians at the Thomas Cooper Library of the University of South Carolina: Linda Holderfield and the interlibrary-loan staff; reference-department head Virginia Weathers; reference librarians Marilee Birchfield, Stefanie Buck, Stefanie DuBose, Rebecca Feind, Karen Joseph, Donna Lehman, Charlene Loope, Anthony McKissick, Jean Rhyne, and Kwamine Simpson; circulation-department head Caroline Taylor; and acquisitions-searching supervisor David Haggard.

Dictionary of Literary Biography® • Volume One Hundred Ninety-Two

French Dramatists,
1789–1914

Dictionary of Literary Biography

Emile Augier

(17 September 1820 – 25 October 1889)

Judith Graves Miller and Denise R. Mjelde
University of Wisconsin, Madison

PLAY PRODUCTIONS: *La Ciguë,* Paris, Second
   Théâtre Français, 13 May 1844;
Un homme de bien, Paris, Théâtre Français, 18 No-
   vember 1845;
L'Aventurière, Paris, Théâtre de la République, 23
   March 1848;
L'Habit vert, by Augier and Alfred de Musset, Paris,
   Théâtre des Variétés, 23 February 1849;
Gabrielle, Paris, Théâtre Français, 15 December
   1849;
Le Joueur de flûte, Paris, Comédie Française, 19 De-
   cember 1850;
La Chasse au roman, by Augier and Jules Sandeau,
   Paris, Théâtre des Variétés, 20 February 1851;
Sapho, Paris, Opéra, 16 April 1851;
Diane, Paris, Théâtre Français, 19 February 1852;
Philiberte, Paris, Gymnase, 19 March 1853;
La Pierre de touche, by Augier and Sandeau, Paris,
   Théâtre Français, 23 December 1853;
Le Gendre de Monsieur Poirier, by Augier and Sandeau,
   Paris, Gymnase, 8 April 1854;
La Ceinture dorée, by Augier and Edouard Foussier,
   Paris, Gymnase Dramatique, 3 February 1855;
Le Mariage d'Olympe, Paris, Théâtre du Vaudeville,
   17 July 1855;
La Jeunesse, Paris, Second Théâtre Français, 6 Feb-
   ruary 1858;
Les Lionnes pauvres, by Augier and Foussier, Paris,
   Théâtre du Vaudeville, 22 May 1858;
Un Beau Mariage, by Augier and Foussier, Paris,
   Gymnase Dramatique, 5 March 1859;
L'Aventurière, Paris, Comédie Française, 10 April
   1860;
Les Effrontés, Paris, Théâtre Français, 10 January
   1861;

Emile Augier

Maître Guérin, Paris, Théâtre Français, 29 October
   1864;
La Contagion, Paris, Théâtre de l'Odéon, 17 March
   1866;

Paul Forestier, Paris, Théâtre Français, 25 January 1868;

Le Post-Scriptum, Paris, Théâtre Français, 1 May 1869;

Lions et Renards, Paris, Théâtre Français, 6 December 1869;

Jean de Thommeray, by Augier and Sandeau, Paris, Théâtre Français, 29 December 1873;

Madame Caverlet, Paris, Théâtre du Vaudeville, 1 February 1876;

Le Prix Martin, by Augier and Eugène Labiche, Paris, Théâtre du Palais Royal, 5 February 1876;

Les Fourchambault, Paris, Théâtre Français, 8 April 1878.

BOOKS: *La Ciguë* (Paris: Furne, 1844);

Un homme de bien: comédie en trois actes et en vers (Paris: Furne, 1845);

L'Aventurière (Paris: Hetzel, 1848); translated as *The Adventuress: A Comedy in Four Acts* (New York: Rullman, 1888);

L'Habit vert, by Augier and Alfred de Musset (Paris: Michel Lévy frères, 1849); translated by Barrett H. Clark as *The Green Coat: A Comedy in One Act* (New York: Samuel French, 1914);

Gabrielle (Paris: Michel Lévy frères, 1850);

Le Joueur de flûte (Paris: Blanchard, 1851);

La Chasse au roman, by Augier and Jules Sandeau (Paris: Michel Lévy frères, 1851);

Sapho (Paris: Michel Lévy frères, 1851); edited and translated by Manfredo Maggioni as *Saffo: A Grand Opera in Three Acts,* libretto adapted by Fontana (London: Brettell, 1852?);

Diane (Paris: Michel Lévy frères, 1852);

Les Méprises de l'amour (Paris: Michel Lévy frères, 1852);

Poésies complètes (Paris: Michel Lévy frères, 1852);

Philiberte (Paris: Michel Lévy frères, 1853);

La Pierre de touche, by Augier and Sandeau (Paris: Michel Lévy frères, 1854);

Le Gendre de Monsieur Poirier, by Augier and Sandeau (Paris: Michel Lévy frères, 1854); translated by Clark as *M. Poirier's Son-in-Law,* in *Four Plays,* by E. Augier (New York: Knopf, 1915); translated by Clark as *The Son-in-Law of M. Poirier,* in *The Chief European Dramatists* (Boston: Houghton Mifflin, 1916);

La Ceinture dorée, by Augier and Edouard Foussier (Paris: Michel Lévy frères, 1855);

Le Mariage d'Olympe (Paris: Michel Lévy frères, 1855); translated by Clark as *The Marriage of Olympe: A Play in Three Acts, The Drama: A Quarterly Review of Dramatic Literature,* 19 (August 1915); translated as *Olympe's Marriage,* in *Four Plays,* by E. Augier (New York: Knopf, 1915);

Les Pariétaires, poésies (Paris: Michel Lévy frères, 1855);

Discours de M. Emile Augier, prononcé à sa réception à l'Académie française, le 28 janvier 1858 (Paris: Michel Lévy frères, 1858);

Institut impérial de France: Discours prononcés dans la séance publique par l'Académie française pour la réception de M. Emile Augier, le 28 janvier 1858 (Paris: Firmin Didot frères, 1858);

La Jeunesse (Paris: Michel Lévy frères, 1858);

Les Lionnes pauvres, by Augier and Foussier (Paris: Michel Lévy frères, 1858);

Un Beau Mariage, by Augier and Foussier (Paris: Michel Lévy frères, 1859);

L'Aventurière (Paris: Michel Lévy frères, 1860);

Les Effrontés (Paris: Michel Lévy frères, 1861); translated by Frederic Lyster as *Faces of Brass: Comedy* (New York: Rullman, 1888);

Le Fils de Giboyer (Paris: Michel Lévy frères, 1863); translated by Benedict Papot as *Giboyer's Son,* in *Drama,* 4 (1911): pp. 27–137;

La Question électorale (Paris: Michel Lévy frères, 1864);

Maître Guérin (Paris: Michel Lévy frères, 1865);

La Contagion (Paris: Michel Lévy frères, 1866);

Paul Forestier (Paris: Michel Lévy frères, 1868); translated as *Paul Forrester: A Play in Four Acts* (New York: New York Printing, 1871);

Le Post-Scriptum (Paris: Michel Lévy frères, 1869); translated by Clark as *The Post-script: A Comedy in One Act* (New York: French, 1915);

Lions et Renards (Paris: Michel Lévy frères, 1870);

Jean de Thommeray, by Augier and Sandeau (Paris: Michel Lévy frères, 1874);

Madame Caverlet (Paris: Calmann-Lévy, 1876);

Le Prix Martin, by Augier and Eugène Labiche (Paris: Dentu, 1876);

Les Fourchambault (Paris: Michel Lévy frères, 1878); translated by Clark as *The House of Fourchambault* (New York & London: Samuel French, 1915);

Théâtre complet de Emile Augier (Paris: Calmann-Levy, 1879);

Institut de France: Discours prononcés le 17 avril 1883, aux funérailles de M. Jules Sandeau, de l'Académie française (Paris: Firmin Didot frères, 1883);

Œuvres diverses (Paris: Calmann-Lévy, 1883)—comprises *Les Pariétaires, Les Méprises de l'amour, La Question électorale, Discours de réception à l'Académie française, Réponse de M. Lebrun, Discours de réception de M. Emile Ollivier, Réponse à M. Emile Ollivier;*

Paroles prononcées sur la tombe d'Amaury-Duval au cimetière Montmartre, le 28 décembre 1885 (Paris: Quantin, 1886).

OTHER: *Théâtre complet de Eugène Labiche,* volume 1, preface by Augier (Paris: Calmann-Lévy, 1878);

L. P. Laforêt, *La Femme du comique,* preface by Augier (Paris: Giraud, 1885).

Emile Augier inherited Denis Diderot's commitment to serious drama and Honoré de Balzac's dream of capturing in his art the ugliness and exaltation of a specific moment in French history. Like his younger compatriot Emile Zola, Augier wanted to make theater more "truthful." His brand of truthfulness, however, struck the fiery Zola as pretentious and cheaply moralizing. Augier may have taken Molière as his model, but his social dramas, unlike Molière's, were so relentlessly anchored in their own period as to be limited by it. Nevertheless, his attention to the concerns of the bourgeois public and his skillful grasp of the mechanics of Eugène Scribe's well-made play made him, in his lifetime, one of France's most respected playwrights. Nineteen of his works are still in the repertory of the Comédie Française, and the House of Molière has sponsored more than thirty-two hundred performances of his plays.

Born on 17 September 1820 to a solidly bourgeois family in Valence, Augier could claim a genealogical connection to one of the seventeenth-century Calais bourgeois later immortalized in a massive sculpture by Auguste Rodin. This proudly independent and antiroyalist ancestor apparently prepared the way for a later forebear of Augier's, eighteenth-century playwright and Voltairean revolutionary Pigault-Lebrun (Charles-Antoine-Guillame Pigault de l'Epinoy), whom Augier enjoyed citing as his most illustrious "uncle." With such an impeccably republican and middle-class pedigree, it is unsurprising that as a child Augier became best friends with the son of the future bourgeois king, Louis-Philippe. The boys met at the renowned Parisian high school Henri IV, where Augier began his studies about 1829 shortly after his family moved to the French capital. During this time, encouraged by the success of his schoolboy pastiches of Sir Walter Scott's melodramas and inspired by Voltaire's exhortations regarding the stage, he decided to pursue a life in the theater.

Despite parental pressure to study law, Augier continued to consider himself a writer, and in 1844, after a brief career as a law student, he made his rather inauspicious theatrical debut with *La Ciguë* (Hemlock), a verse drama in two acts portraying the tribulations of a repentant debauchee. *La Ciguë* shows the marked influence François Ponsard and his *ecole du bon sens* (school of good sense) had on

Augier, who wrote ten more verse dramas on social themes. Following Ponsard's model, Augier in these early verse plays countered the romantic playwright's championing of passion and individual ego, praising instead the conventionally moral citizen's duties to family and community. Indeed, what became Augier's realism was directly disproportional to Victor Hugo's notion of the real. Augier, like the Second Empire bourgeoisie for whom he wrote his most important works, wanted theater to mirror social life, specifically the social life of the shifting ruling classes. Unlike the romantics, he was not interested in celebrating life lived on the edge of the abyss. His thirty plays, in both verse and prose, invest members of the bourgeoisie with the status of legitimate theatrical subjects and treat their concerns as topics appropriate to the stage.

The Revolution of 1848 gave Augier the impetus to transform what he considered a dominant theater of consumption into a theater of contestation. He proclaimed this goal in the column he wrote during his short-lived stint from July to September 1848 as drama critic for *Le Spectateur républicain.* After 1850 he and Alexandre Dumas *fils,* both indebted technically to Scribe's formula for effective dramatic action, spearheaded the first truly postromantic school of French drama, castigating in their plays social and political corruption, marital infidelity, adventuresses and social climbers, and the obsessive race for money and power. According to Augier's defensive preface to his 1858 play *Les Lionnes pauvres* (The Impoverished Lionesses), the theater was potentially the most powerful contemporary vehicle for critical thought. In *Les Lionnes pauvres* he wished to demonstrate how an inordinate fondness for luxury could turn a respectable married woman into a predatory kept woman, kept, furthermore, by her dear friend's husband. This play's "impoverished lioness" nearly destroys two families in her hunt for a more elegant hat. Attuned to the fascination exerted by the social types and the situations that Augier purported to criticize, Charles Baudelaire wondered if Augier really meant his plays primarily to provoke serious thought. He speculated that Augier's literary ennobling of money and material pleasure was the true reason that the newly rich and growing richer Parisian audiences were fascinated by Augier's work.

Augier seems, in fact, to have carefully constructed his Second Empire career so as never to be on the wrong side of those in or out of power. He contrived, for example, to represent all sides in his treatment of class issues. Thus in 1854, in his most often performed play, *Le Gendre de Monsieur Poirier* (translated as *M. Poirier's Son-in-Law,* 1915), written with Jules Sandeau, Augier criticized both the outsized ambitions of the successful bourgeois businessman Poirier and the opportunism of his aristocratic son-in-law, Gaston, the Marquis de Presles. In this play virtue proves to be not an issue of class but rather of heart. In his most notorious piece, *Le Mariage d'Olympe* (1855; translated as *Olympe's Marriage,* 1915), Augier responds vehemently to what he felt was Dumas's pandering in *La Dame aux Camélias* (1848; translated as *Camille,* 1856) to the unsavory place of courtesans in nineteenth-century society. Thus, the worthy Marquis de Puygiron saves his family's honor by murdering the lower-class prostitute who has nefariously married his nephew. This avenging crime, however, also condemns him, the aristocrat, to death. All crimes, those on and off the books, are punished, and only the concept of honor rules in the end.

In play after play the marriages that take place toward the end of the action become the true unions of kindred souls they were meant to be; these marriages occur after one or the other of the lovers has lost his or her money, thereby establishing financial equality with the more virtuous but poorer partner, as in *La Ceinture dorée* (The Golden Belt, 1855), *Un Beau Mariage* (1859), *Les Effrontés* (1861; translated as *Faces of Brass Comedy,* 1888), and *Les Fourchambault* (1878; translated as *The House of Fourchambault,* 1915). In none of these plays, however, are the characters reduced to dire and irremediable poverty. Social mobility and love always make possible recovery from financial ruin. In Augier's theater love becomes the ultimate crossover mechanism that unites one class to another, conquering at the last moment all opposition and abolishing any concern over which social group better exemplifies moral values and common sense.

So successful was Augier in straddling political positions and thereby reflecting nineteenth-century society in its attempts at creating a feeling of cohesiveness that he was elected without contest in 1858, at age thirty-eight, to the Académie Française. He even began writing on political matters, calling for the establishment of parliamentary government in an 1864 pamphlet written precisely at the time in which the Second Empire was heading toward parliamentarism. When Augier retired to Croissy in 1869, he was rich, admired, and considered an elder statesman of French letters. He became a generous patron of younger playwrights, a key figure in the growing Wagnerian society, and the friend and collaborator most responsible for prompting Eugène Labiche to publish his complete works. His enthusiastic support helped launch a rethinking of Labiche

as one of the major playwrights of the last half of the nineteenth century.

Writing from the perspective of his own, audience-centered criticism, Francisque Sarcey, the leading theater critic of the latter 1800s, placed Augier among the greatest playwrights of the period. He especially appreciated the logic and clarity of Augierian construction and the popular reception of his plays among audiences well situated to receive their message. Nevertheless, it is precisely this combination of meticulous plotting and strict appeal to specific audiences that now makes Augier's plays seem artificial and dated. To give them due credit, however, they can be read as remarkable documents of that process of the blending and melding of social classes that dominated the second half of the turbulent century in which they were written.

Augier's particular kind of theatricality can be seen in his most accomplished and intriguing plays: *Le Gendre de Monsieur Poirier, Le Mariage d'Olympe, Les Lionnes pauvres, Les Effrontés, Le Fils de Giboyer* (1863; translated as *Goboyer's Son,* 1911), and *Les Fourchambault.* These plays, on close analysis, prove to be built upon fundamental unresolved tensions. On first inspection these works appear to represent Augier's complacent dramatic nod to the reigning social codes and values; in fact, they thoroughly explore those very codes and values by probing the profound oppositions between virtue and money, social hierarchy and individual worth, and married love versus other forms of bonding.

As is true of all plays adopting the Scribean dramatic formula for the well-made play, Augier's precisely oiled theatrical machines seem to imply a perfectly contained and balanced society, an "outside" world both graspable and controllable. Certain standard recurring elements, contributing to this sense of self-sufficiency, can be found throughout Augier's work. His use of spatiality and temporality, his character types, his weaving and knitting of plots, and his often sparkling dialogue presented to his audiences an ordered and appealing social field.

Both the fictional time and the actual running time of Augier's plays correspond to a nineteenth-century bourgeois sense of real and/or plausible time. His plays begin at "the beginning," with the particular dramatic problem, or problems, posed. In *Le Mariage d'Olympe* the problems, or questions, include: Will the parvenu Baudel achieve the social status to which he aspires? Will the ruined Baron Montrichard milk Baudel to obtain the money he needs to marry young Geneviève de Puygiron? Will Henri de Puygiron recover his health? Will Pauline Morin (alias Olympe Taverny), newly married to

Sketches of two characters from Augier's Les Effrontés, *his 1861 play about Parisian social climbers (nineteenth-century illustration from an issue of* Journal amusant)

Count Henri de Puygiron, convince his aristocratic family to take her, a "poor farm girl," into the fold? Will the truth about Pauline's past be learned by the Puygirons and her dissembling character be understood by Henri? These questions are addressed and resolved in the course of five acts, each act corresponding exactly to the fictional time inscribed therein. All these questions are framed in act 1 of *Le Mariage d'Olympe,* where they appear in a series of impromptu meetings of guests at an Austrian watering hole, their comings and goings mimicking the real time of the same type of encounters at a fancy resort. By the end of the play all the questions are answered, all the problems neatly resolved, with nothing left dangling to disturb the symmetry.

Time passes between the acts in an Augier play, but it is never more than a few months, most often only a few hours; and the passage from one act to the next is effortless. Nothing happens between acts that might surprise the audience. Well prepared through hints and innuendos through the course of the play, the audience is keenly attuned to the unfolding events on the stage, even set up through temporal dimensions and plotting devices to know more than the characters themselves do. This sense of

control and the comfort of a familiar world that Augier's plays creates is reinforced by his spatial organization. His set requirements always detail richly appointed sitting rooms as the locus of the action. *Les Effrontés,* for example, takes place mainly in the plush, sumptuously decorated salon of banker Charrier. *Le Gendre de Monsieur Poirier* is centered in Poirier's charming drawing room, with only a glimpse of the garden through the window suggesting a space outside the hothouse of the family. This beckoning window is a frequent element in Augier's plays; but it is never more than a promise. It is the family space, the recognizable center of bourgeois life, that envelops almost all of the action.

The power balance in an Augier play usually shifts to whomever's drawing room takes center stage or closes the play. Thus, in *Le Fils de Giboyer* the play begins in the scheming Marquis d'Auberive's personal salon but ends in the drawing room of the wealthy bourgeois Maréchal, who finally bests the marquis at his own game. Often the fourth act takes place at a ball, as in *Les Effrontés* and *Le Fils de Giboyer,* but always in the small salon that leads into the ballroom. This allows Augier to present, in rapid exchanges between passing characters, the social constraints that seem to determine his characters' fates. It also permits a heightening of the intermingling of social classes that prevails in each act. By holding within a set of four walls a mixture of aristocratic and bourgeois characters, Augier indicates that the world that "counts" is located in the confines of this opulent intimacy. His nineteenth-century audiences would recognize the place evoked, and their recognition would be furthered by the realistic and lavish contemporary costumes in which the characters appeared. Perhaps the audiences would also acknowledge their own aspirations toward a blending of classes and greater material comfort.

Augier's characters are drawn both from the aristocracy and the bourgeoisie. Moreover, neither class is solely heinous nor wholly morally heroic: disreputable and admirable types are found in both. Class-based tastes, such as the high-art painting and popular music-hall songs in *Le Gendre de Monsieur Poirier,* are given equal time and value. Few real villains exist, the characters being more flawed than evil. The only characters of whom the playwright clearly disapproves are the occasional unrepentant aristocrats, such as the stuffy Rastiboulois in *Les Fourchambault,* who cannot mingle with people outside their milieu.

Moreover, all Augier's characters are tightly bound within a family structure, a structure quite prepared to open up and swallow new members, thereby metamorphosing them to a different class status. In *Les Effrontés* Clémence Charrier, the rich banker's daughter, eventually marries de Sergine, the aristocratic but impoverished muckraking journalist, after she, too, loses her fortune through her father's noble decision to pay back business debts he has owed for many years. What the family loses in money it gains in honor and righteousness. This poor but honorable status constitutes, in effect, yet another class, one that transcends both bourgeois and aristocratic boundaries. Furthermore, within these expanding families there are specific types, such as the cynical manipulator, who always remains an outsider. This character, disenchanted by his own historical situation, as is the Marquis d'Auberive in *Les Effrontés* and again in *Le Fils de Giboyer,* effects dangerous encounters merely to see what will happen as a result. While he serves as a sort of dramatic incarnation of the omniscient narrator, his ambitions to wreak havoc are always defeated by a morally superior character who affirms the prevailing middle-class values.

This latter type is frequently a devoted father or father substitute, such as Verdelet, the godfather of Antoinette Poirier in *Le Gendre de Monsieur Poirier,* or less frequently, an upright son, such as M. Bernard in *Les Fourchambault.* His position of moral superiority usually finds an echo in one or several other characters. For example, Augier creates a host of valiant female characters, mostly daughters, such as Antoinette Poirier (*Le Gendre de Monsieur Poirier*), Fernande Maréchal (*Le Fils de Giboyer*), and Blanche Fourchambault and Marie Letellier (*Les Fourchambault*). This type of female character is by no means the passive victim of melodrama. Although other characters often plot against her, they cannot make the playwright's surprisingly independent young woman act against her will.

This doubling, sometimes even tripling, of the "voice of virtue" has the effect of obliterating the notion of a central character in Augier's drama. The protagonist more often takes the shape of a group; and opposing this group in many of the plays is the scheming, opportunistic female, such as Olympe Taverny in *Le Mariage d'Olympe* or Séraphine Pommeau in *Les Lionnes pauvres.* Again, this character, like the virtuous daughter, frequently fleshes out Augier's best scenes, as happens, for instance, in Olympe's performance in the drunken revelry in *Le Mariage d'Olympe.* Layered, strong, holding their own against the male characters, Augier's proto-feminist female characters suggest how robust women challenge the prevailing power structure.

A final character who is omnipresent in Augier's plays is the parvenu, the bourgeois who has become rich but seeks even greater prestige. Successful entrepreneurs Monsieur Poirier (*Le Gendre de Monsieur Poirier*) and Charrier (*Les Effrontés*) both want peerships. Vernouillet (*Les Effrontés*), a fictional precursor to the Rupert Murdochs and William Randolph Hearsts of the twentieth century, still hopes to marry above his station. The well-to-do Maréchal (*Le Fils de Giboyer*) aspires to a government position. Their maneuverings always take the form of a marriage to be made or unmade, a new family to be formed, which, as a result, changes the power balance among all the characters present at the outset of the action.

Marriage, then, provides the through line of each Augier play, the spring for its forward movement. Yet to say that the playwright's plots are essentially marriage plots is clearly to oversimplify his work. The many opposing projects and plans of all the characters complicate the path to conjugal union or even re-union (as is the case in *Les Lionnes pauvres* and *Le Gendre de Monsieur Poirier*). What holds the audience's attention is the suspenseful pitting of various interests against each other. In *Les Effrontés,* for example, the audience becomes caught up in the unscrupulous Vernouillet's takeover of a respected newspaper and his attempt to marry Clémence Charrier; in Albert de Sergine's internal combat over his continuing employment with such an immoralist and his conflicting attachments to his mistress, the Marchioness d'Auberive, and the woman he loves, Clémence Charrier; in banker Charrier's attraction to a peership that gets in the way of his loyalty to his family; in the Marchioness d'Auberive's potential loss of reputation, which will surely result if she helps her beloved goddaughter, Clémence Charrier, marry the man who has been her own official lover; in Clémence Charrier's inability to read her situation and her father's adamant opposition to her marriage to an impoverished newspaperman.

One watches the ups and downs of these various struggles and their impact on the central marriage question through a piling up of fortunate meetings and minor revelations (from letters intercepted, secret gifts discovered, and the like), and through a forestalling of the final, most crucial revelation, which will at last necessitate closure. This final revelation immediately follows a spectacular *scène à faire,* the obligatory scene in which the most crafty character turns the tables on the others. The Marchioness d'Auberive, for instance, in act 4, scene 14 of *Les Effrontés,* foils the attempt to defame her by showing up at the grand ball with her husband at her side. He promptly challenges Vernouillet to a duel because of the newspaper's gossipy insinuations about the marchioness. This gesture of marital solidarity frees her lover, de Sergine, to propose marriage to Clémence Charrier.

The tortuous imbrications of stories, the rapidity of revelations, new obstacles and reversals, and the showstopping scenes all tend to bury or shove aside the large issues embedded in Augier's plays. Class warfare, greed, and political machinations seem to take second place to the working out of his complex plots. As in Scribe's *Le Verre d'eau* (The Glass of Water, 1842), in which the fate of a nation depends on who asks for a glass of water, so in Augier's plays, the question of who serves a cup of tea (*Le Fils de Giboyer*) can determine whether Monarchists or Republicans will win the next election. Augier's lively, witty dialogue, the delightful sparring between well-bred opponents, enhances the sense of a cohesive and ultimately civil world, a world that works through compromise and cleverness.

Despite Augier's steadfast and apparently successful theatrical attempts at order and coherency through spatiotemporal dimensions, characterization, and plotting, his works nevertheless ooze contradictions. His obsessive concerns and leitmotivs

Caricature of Augier by Fabritzius

require that his characters pass through potent social and political minefields. What appear to be the acceptable myths of his theater—the natural progression of history, money as the new blasphemous religion, and romantic love as redemption—are in reality destabilized by the playwright's contradictory portraits of the powerful and the loving. Such tensions prompt one to ask what Augier might really intend to be saying, for example, about French global expansionism, strategies of conquest, and married love.

Indeed, several of his characters serve or are about to serve in the French war of subjugation in North Africa. But this brand of patriotism proves for Henri Charrier in *Les Effrontés* mainly to be a way of making up for his father's shady business deals. Through the character of the duke in *Le Gendre de Monsieur Poirier,* one is encouraged to see that military service and imperialist attitudes may in fact become substitutes for previously held positions of authority. There is little in these characters' motivations that speaks for the glory of the "Motherland."

Augier even more obviously criticizes various other forms of jockeying for power and power brokering. The partisan press, opportunistic marriages, and sexual liaisons are directly targeted. Yet none of these targets is portrayed in an exclusively harsh light. Vernouillet, the press magnate of *Les Effrontés,* is finally neither punished nor destroyed. Like Balzac's Vautrin, he instead appears indomitable, ready to surge forward admirably despite the scorn heaped upon him. Likewise, the many mistresses who inhabit Augier's theater, while always defeated in their role as barriers to the good marriage, show themselves to be among the most compelling of his characters. One senses the playwright's great ambivalence about these plucky ladies, even to the extent of giving the most vital scenes in *Le Mariage d'Olympe* to the very character he means to chastise. Moreover, if money appears to be the root of all evil and the motivating force behind all the unworthy characters, it is also true that those who have it know how to enjoy it. Wonderful scenes of lush menu planning (*Le Gendre de Monsieur Poirier*), of cotillions (*Les Effrontés, Le Fils de Giboyer*), and of charitable giving (*Le Mariage d'Olympe, Le Gendre de Monsieur Poirier*) abound. And while those monied interests who attempt to influence political decisions often appear cold and calculating, they also are the only characters who have any ideas about defending capitalism, the sine qua non of the new political order.

Finally, although the marriage plot provides the skeleton upon which all other intrigues are hung, perhaps Augier's most urgent emotional bondings are those between parent and child. Every one of the plays under discussion concludes not only with the promise of marriage (or a better marriage) but also with the recognition of legitimate paternity. Like other nineteenth-century writers, Augier seems to be caught up in the trope of fatherhood. Thus, in examining certain codes and behaviors of the time, his plays also construct the "good father" as the starting point for a new France. This good father is a man not only devoted to his children but also committed to a set of values and moral codes. The latter codes, rather than the biological connection, confer upon him the status of legitimate parent. In *Le Gendre de Monsieur Poirier* it is therefore Verdelet, family friend and altruistic, forward-looking mentor, who is the true father figure to Antoinette as well as to her husband, Gaston de Presles. In *Les Fourchambault* a repentant Monsieur Fourchambault finally becomes the good father he should have been by recognizing his illegitimate son, Bernard, himself a good father figure for his half sister, Blanche. In *Le Fils de Giboyer,* the most far-fetched and effervescent of all of Augier's dramas, the bohemian writer Giboyer, a classless floater, at last admits to fathering the brilliant scholar Max; because of this admission, Max can marry Fernande, the biological daughter of the Marquis d'Auberive, who has been passed off as the daughter of wealthy bourgeois Maréchal. In allowing, even promoting, this union all three fathers in *Le Fils de Giboyer* become positioned as good fathers. The ensuing marriage, as is true of all of Augier's marriages, effects a remarkable amalgam of aristocratic and bourgeois blood, of illegitimacy newly sanctioned as legitimacy, and of a total slippage of class status, with class of origin becoming irrelevant to the worthiness of the children who will be born of these unions.

Considered in this way, Augier's theater gives form and substance to the concept of social mobility. His theatrical world may be seen to represent both a utopian truce between competing class interests and a fantasy of legitimate descent for postrevolutionary France. It is reasonable to assume that, enlightened by Sarcey's evaluation, Augier's contemporaries, at least the bourgeois theatergoers among them, were content to sweep the tensions subtending his theater under the carpet of its happy endings. They did not dwell on the muddy logic of, for example, Giboyer's final, fence-sitting philosophical proclamation in *Le Fils de Giboyer:* "Equality on earth is the most important thing there is, but social hierarchy is legitimated through each individual's differing contributions." For the most part, they were apparently satisfied to bask in Augier's images of upward mobility, transcendent virtue, and raw energy.

Biography:

Paul Morillot, *Emile Augier* (Grenoble: Grattier, 1901).

References:

Francis Ambrière, "Augier et son théâtre," *Annales,* 230 (1969): 32–49;

François d'Argent, "L'Aphroessa de Gobineau jugée par Emile Augier," *Revue d'histoire littéraire de la France,* 66 (1966): 700–701;

Ewa Baranska, "D'Antony à Gabrielle ou la faillite du héros romantique," *Roczniki Humanistyczne: Annales de Lettres et Sciences Humaines,* 37–38, no. 5 (1989–1990): 41–50;

Philippe Baron, "Une pièce sur l'ascension d'un commerçant: Le Gendre de M. Poirier de Augier," in *Commerce et commerçants dans la litté-*

rature: *Actes du colloque international organisé par le Département techniques et Commercialisation de l'IUT "A", Université de Bordeaux-I (25–26 Septembre 1986),* edited by Jean-Marie Thomasseau (Bordeaux: Presses Universitaires de Bordeaux, 1989), pp. 171–179;

Frank Wadleigh Chandler, *The Contemporary Drama of France* (Boston: Little, Brown, 1920), pp. 1–23;

René Doumic, *De Scribe à Ibsen: Causeries sur le théâtre contemporain* (Paris: Delaplane, 1893), pp. 71–80;

Doumic, *Portraits d'écrivains* (Paris: Delaplane, 1892), pp. 57–96;

Henry Gaillard de Champris, *Emile Augier et la comédie sociale* (Paris: Grasset, 1910);

P. R. Grover, "Henry James and the Theme of the Adventuress," *Révue de littérature comparée,* 47 (1973): 586–596;

Léopold Lacour, *Trois Théâtres: Emile Augier, Alexandre Dumas fils, Victorien Sardou* (Paris: Calmann-Lévy, 1880), pp. 3–86;

Yannic Mancel, "Autopsie d'un triomphe: Augier," *Comédie-Française: Les Cahiers,* 7 (1993): 101–110;

J. Brander Matthews, *French Dramatists of the 19th Century* (New York: Scribners, 1880; London: Remington, 1882), pp. 105–135;

Alfred Poizat, *Les Maîtres du théâtre, d'Eschyle à Curel,* volume 2 (Paris: La Renaissance du livre, 1923), pp. 61–77;

Albert Sonnenfeld, "Théâtre de moeurs: A Reappraisal," *Kentucky Foreign Language Quarterly,* 13 (1966): 156–164;

Thomas F. Van Laan, "The Ending of *A Doll House* and Augier's *Maître Guerin,*" *Comparative Drama,* 17 (1983): 297–317.

Papers:
Some of Augier's manuscripts are in the *Bibliothèque nationale* in Paris.

Henry Becque
(18 April 1837 – 12 May 1899)

Lynn R. Wilkinson
University of Texas, Austin

PLAY PRODUCTIONS: *Sardanapale,* libretto by Henry Becque and music by Victorin Joncieres, Paris, Théâtre Lyrique, 8 February 1867;

L'Enfant prodigue, Paris, Théâtre du Vaudeville, 6 November 1868;

Michel Pauper, Paris, Théâtre de la Porte Saint-Martin, 15 June 1870;

L'Enlèvement, Paris, Théâtre du Vaudeville, 18 November 1871;

La Navette, Paris, Théâtre du Gymnase, 15 November 1878;

Les Honnêtes Femmes, Paris, Théâtre du Gymnase, 1 January 1880;

Les Corbeaux, Paris, Comédie-Française, 26 February 1882;

La Parisienne, Paris, Théâtre de la Renaissance, 7 February 1885.

BOOKS: *Sardanapale: opéra en trois actes et cinq tableaux, imité de Lord Byron* (Paris: Michel Lévy, 1867);

L'Enfant prodigue (Paris: Michel Lévy, 1868);

Michel Pauper (Paris: A. Lacroix, Verboeckhoven et Cie, 1871);

La Navette (Paris: Tresse, 1878); translated by Freeman Tilden as *The Merry-Go-Round* in *The Vultures, The Woman of Paris, The Merry-Go-Round: Three Plays by Henry Becque* (New York: Kennerley, 1913), pp. 231–266;

Les Honnêtes Femmes (Paris: Tresse, 1880);

Les Corbeaux (Paris: Tresse, 1882); translated by Benedict Papot as *The Crows* in *Drama* (February 1912): 14–126; translated by Tilden as *The Vultures* in *The Vultures, The Woman of Paris, The Merry-Go-Round: Three Plays by Henry Becque* (New York: Kennerley, 1913), pp. 1–151; translated by David Walker as *The Scavengers* (Blairgowie, Scotland: Lochee, 1986);

Le Frisson, fantaisie rimée (Paris: Tresse, 1884);

La Parisienne (Paris: Calmann-Lévy, 1885); translated by Tilden as *The Woman of Paris* in *The*

Henry Becque

Vultures, The Woman of Paris, The Merry-Go-Round: Three Plays by Henry Becque (New York: Kennerley, 1913), pp. 153–229; translated by Jacques Barzun as *The Woman of Paris* in *The Modern Theater,* volume 1, edited by Eric Bentley (Garden City, N.J.: Doubleday/Anchor, 1955), pp. 57–107;

Molière et l'Ecole des femmes, conférence (Paris: Tresse et Stock, 1886);

Sonnets mélancoliques, anthologie contemporaine des écrivains français et belges, fourth series, no. 45 (Brussels: Librairie nouvelle, 1887–1888);

Querelles littéraires (Paris: E. Dentu, 1890);

Souvenirs d'un auteur dramatique (Paris: Bibliothèque artistique et littéraire, 1895).

Editions: *Théâtre complet,* 2 volumes (Paris: G. Charpentier, 1890);

Théâtre complet, 3 volumes (Paris: Bibliothèque artistique et littéraire, 1898);

Oeuvres complètes, 7 volumes (Paris: Crès, 1924–1926).

SELECTED PERIODICAL PUBLICATIONS–
UNCOLLECTED: *Le Domino à Quatre, La Vie parisienne,* 20 March 1897; translated by Sheila Harris as *The Quiet Game* (Madison, Wis.: Play Book, 1913);

Les Polichinelles [Reproduction of unfinished manuscript], *L'illustration théâtrale,* 8 October 1910.

Henry Becque is best known as the author of two controversial plays staged in Paris in the 1880s: *Les Corbeaux* (1882; translated as *The Crows,* 1912) and *La Parisienne* (1885; translated as *The Woman of Paris,* 1913). These works, it is often said, broke with the conventions of the well-made play and paved the way for new developments in French and European drama. They are nevertheless difficult to place in French dramatic tradition. Beginning with Jules Lemaître, some critics have seen the two as links between Molièresque comedy and the development in the late nineteenth century of *la comédie rosse,* bitter comedy. Others have characterized Becque's plays as the products of keen observation in the realist tradition; still others have seen them as realized examples of Emile Zola's theories concerning naturalism in the theater. While there is some truth to each view, all overlook the extent to which Becque and his work represent anomalies in French theatrical life and literary tradition. Furthermore, some of the most radical tendencies of his plays point forward to the work of playwrights outside of France, such as Henrik Ibsen, August Strindberg, Anton Chekhov, Arthur Schnitzler, and Bertolt Brecht.

In addition to *Les Corbeaux* and *La Parisienne* Becque oversaw the staging of five other of his plays and also an opera, for which he wrote the libretto. He also published five short plays, which he called *saynètes* (playlets), and two volumes of journalism. When he died, he left an unfinished manuscript for a five-act play titled *Les Polichinelles* (The Puppets, 1910). The edition of his collected works published from 1924 to 1926 by his nephew includes some po-

etry and a collection of aphorisms as well as a selection of his letters. Much of this work, however, is as little known at present as the life of its author.

Henry-François Becque was born in Paris on 18 April 1837 to Alexandre-Louis Becque, a bookkeeper, and Jeanne Martin Becque. Never marrying, Becque remained close to his immediate family for most of his life, and he characterized his background as "petit-bourgeois." In 1848 he entered the Lycée Bonaparte, later known as the Lycée Condorcet, leaving in 1854 without attempting to pass the baccalaureate. That year he began working for the Chemins du fer du Nord, the Northern Railroad Company, at the first of many jobs he would hold only briefly. In 1860 he worked several months at the chancellery of the Legion of Honor, then tried earning his living as a stockbroker and a tutor. In 1865 he became secretary to the Polish Count Potocki, and from this time on he was engaged in Parisian theatrical life, writing plays and reviewing theatrical productions but earning little money from either endeavor.

He served in the army during the Franco-Prussian war, then returned to a succession of jobs that included stockbrokering and journalism until finally in 1894 he was awarded a government pension of Fr 1,200. After the success of *Les Corbeaux* and *La Parisienne,* Becque became a popular guest in Parisian society. His friends found that the witty and elegant figure he cut in various salons contrasted grotesquely with the austere shabbiness of his own quarters. On two occasions in the 1890s he was an unsuccessful candidate for the Académie Française. In April 1899 he fell asleep while smoking in bed and the resulting fire left him homeless. Becque died on 12 May 1899.

It was while he was a secretary for Count Potocki that Becque met the musician Victorin Joncières, and the two decided to collaborate on an opera. Becque's libretto for their work, *Sardanapale* (1867), is based on the play by George Gordon, Lord Byron, *Sardanapalus* (1821). In this version of the Sardanapalus legend the tyrant is an enlightened ruler who rescues the Greek slave Myrrha from priests about to sacrifice her to Baal. At the moment of his overthrow by rebels led by the high priest and the governor of Media, Sardanapalus wins Myrrha's heart, and she chooses to die with him at the end of the drama. *Sardanapale* opened in Paris at the Théâtre Lyrique on 8 February 1867 and ran for sixteen performances. Critics found the opera a mediocre work, reserving their praise for the Swedish soprano Christine Nilsson, who played Myrrha.

Becque's interest in the character of Sardanapalus may have been spurred in 1856 when the Paris

Opera had presented *Le Corsaire,* a ballet-pantomime based on Byron's work, and both Becque and Joncières were presumably familiar with Eugene Delacroix's celebrated painting, *Sardanapale.* Perhaps the appeal of the subject lay in the political implications of the spectacle of the destruction of an absolute ruler, especially one who saw himself as eminently benevolent and just.

Becque's next work also drew on the musical theater, but this time it was the vaudeville tradition. A family member had recently enjoyed a certain success in this field: in 1852 Becque's uncle, Martin Lubize, had successfully collaborated with Eugène Labiche in writing *Le Misanthrope et l'Auvergnat* (The Misanthropist and the Man from Auvergne). In Becque's *L'Enfant prodigue* (The Prodigal Son, 1868) a naive young provincial, Théodore, comes to Paris, where he takes as his mistress a concierge's daughter known to him as Clarisse, but known to the other men in the play as Amanda, Agathe, Madame de la Richardière, and La Princesse Valentino. The climax of the play occurs when young Théodore learns that Clarisse has also been the mistress of his father; since she presents his father to him as her father, he presumes the worst—that their relations have been incestuous. Théodore soon learns the contrary, however, and the play ends with the separation of Théodore and Clarisse and her request that he return her photograph, an object that has also circulated from lover to lover.

The action of this farce is interrupted by several songs, the most representative of which is "les pauvres p'tit's femmes" (the poor little things), sung by Clarisse at the end of the second act, which has as its refrain:

> Eh! quéqu'ça t'fait, ma chère,
> Laiss'-les donc se distraire,
> La femme a son tour
> A la fin du jour.

> (And what of it, my dear,
> Let them have their cheer,
> Women should play
> At the end of the day.)

The plot of *L'Enfant prodigue,* focusing on a promiscuous woman who juggles various relationships, is essentially the same plot in two of Becque's better-known plays, *La Navette* (1878; translated as *The Merry-Go-Round,* 1913) and *La Parisienne.* Several passages in this early play, however, make explicit a theme that underlies not only these three works, but all of Becque's dramas: that of the impersonality of all social relations. As young Théodore comments: "Voilà l'amour; la femme passe, la dette reste"

(Such is love: women come and go, but debts stay with you). Clarisse replies to a lover who laments the end of their relationship: "Console-toi. Avec une autre ça aurait été exactement la même chose" (Cheer up. With someone else, it would have been exactly the same). All of Becque's plays share this courtesan's perspective: his characters are almost always functions, flat types, rather than rounded individuals.

The story of the naive young provincial who comes to Paris and is sharply disabused of his illusions is, of course, one of the master plots of the nineteenth-century French novel. Becque's next play, *Michel Pauper* (1870), also explores this theme. The title character echoes the hero of an early novel by Honoré de Balzac, *La Recherche de l'Absolu* (1834; translated as *The Search for the Absolute*). Both Michel Pauper and Balthazar Claës seek to manufacture diamonds out of carbon. Balzac's protagonist, however, is a member of the Flemish bourgeoisie who dies because of his invention, which has almost destroyed his family. Michel Pauper, in contrast, dies because of his marriage, destroying his invention in an act of rage against the bourgeois woman who, to his horror, proves, on their wedding night, not to be a virgin. Balzac's novel opposes science and modernity to the traditions of the Flemish bourgeoisie and demonizes the former. Becque's play demonizes women and the bourgeoisie, both of whom exploit and deceive the small-time entrepreneur.

As the play opens, Michel Pauper enters the home of Henri de la Roseraye to demand money owed to him. De la Roseraye, however, who is on the brink of financial ruin, offers him Fr 3,000, which Michel Pauper says he will accept if his debtor will promise him the hand of his daughter, Hélène, with whom he has fallen in love. De la Roseraye refuses to barter his daughter but offers to introduce Michel Pauper into the household. Hélène, however, is in love with a so-called friend of the family, a count who refuses to lend money to her father to save him from bankruptcy. The count's refusal precipitates the final action. Ruined, de la Roseraye commits suicide. Hélène lets herself be seduced by the count and, when he refuses to marry her, accepts the proposal of marriage by Michel Pauper. On their wedding night she makes the mistake of telling him of her affair with the count, however, and he beats her and turns her out. Overwrought, Hélène goes to live with the count, where, as a servant tells her, an apartment has been waiting for her. Michel Pauper begins to drink excessively and dies of alcohol poisoning at the end of the fifth act, having destroyed his invention and failing to recognize his wife when she comes to beg his forgiveness.

Michel Pauper makes explicit what later plays by Becque, such as *Les Corbeaux,* suggest. One character, another friend of the family and relative of the heartless count, the Baron von-der-Holweck, serves mainly as a *raisonneur,* a commentator on the action. The other characters also make long speeches that reflect on the events where livelier dialogue and action would be more effective.

Michel Pauper is sometimes characterized as a socialist play, but its perspective is petit bourgeois rather than working class. It opposes the interests of a thoroughly corrupt bourgeoisie and aristocracy, for whom money and pleasure are the highest goods, and those of the petit bourgeois entrepreneur, who nevertheless longs to have the kind of private life that resembles that of the classes in power. Michel Pauper's position bears a certain resemblance to that of many late-nineteenth-century European writers, including Becque himself. In contrast to many successful bourgeois writers of the first part of the century, Victor Hugo, for example, these writers had no family fortune to draw on and were unable to support themselves by their work. Under the circumstances marriage and a family became all but impossible. Some late-nineteenth-century writers—such as Becque and Strindberg—seem at times to have blamed women, especially those of the more privileged classes, for their personal plights as artists.

Michel Pauper was originally accepted at the Odéon, but when that theater failed to stage it within what Becque considered a reasonable time, he put it on at his own expense at the Théâtre de la Porte Saint-Martin in June and July of 1870. The play was moderately successful, primarily because the author had engaged the popular actor Taillade to play the main role. Unfortunately, a heat wave, the approaching war with Germany, and Becque's lack of funds caused the play to close after fifteen performances, leaving Becque with a considerable debt.

His first play after the Franco-Prussian War targeted the contemporary institution of marriage. A thesis play, *L'Enlèvement* (The Abduction, 1871) argues for the legalization of divorce. At its beginning Emma de Sainte-Croix has taken refuge in the country from her profligate husband, Raoul, who is about to visit from Paris. He wants a reconciliation, mostly for the sake of his career, and his mother, who has been living with Emma, argues his case incessantly.

The play turns on a series of coincidences worthy of the most hackneyed well-made play. Just before Raoul's arrival Emma receives a declaration of love from a neighbor, who turns out to be the un-

happy and abandoned husband of her husband's mistress, Antoinette, who has followed her lover from Paris. At the end of the play Emma, realizing that her situation is impossible, runs away with her husband's mistress's husband. The play thus suggests a rearrangement of couples on the basis of natural inclination rather than decree. As Johann Wolfgang von Goethe suggested in his graceful if cynical novel, *Die Wahlverwandtschaften* (1808; translated as *Elective Affinities,* 1963), human sexual arrangements sometimes resemble chemical processes: under certain circumstances two compounds, AB and CD, will break up and form into new combinations, such as AC and BD. Becque, as well as Goethe, emphasized that sexuality had little to do with individual will or indeed individuality.

But if Becque's plot was mechanical and his characters flat types, the play's depiction of the circumstances of this couple's unhappiness is grounded in the facts of French society at the time. Emma married too young and was ignorant of what marriage entailed. She matured into what her husband sees as a bluestocking—and he finds intellectual women unbearable. In words that evoke the Alving marriage in Ibsen's *Ghosts* (1881), Raoul comments: "Je me consolerais facilement d'être un homme ordinaire, si je n'avais pas une femme supérieure. Vous me trouvez fort ennuyeux, n'est-ce pas?" (I could live with being an ordinary man if I didn't have a superior wife. You find me very annoying, don't you?). Emma wants an amicable separation within marriage; her husband refuses. Like Ibsen's Mrs. Alving, Emma leaves. It is possible to read *Ghosts* as a sequel to *L'Enlèvement:* if Emma returns, she, too, may produce a syphilitic child, unwitting evidence of the rottenness of the parents' relations.

L'Enlèvement was hissed at when it was performed at the Théâtre du Vaudeville in 1871, and it lasted only five performances. Becque later partly disavowed the work, claiming that he wrote it too quickly, mainly for money. The failure of this play marked a setback in his theatrical career; not until 1878 was another of his plays staged in Paris.

In November 1878 the Théâtre du Gymnase mounted a production of Becque's one-act play *La Navette.* A second, *Les Honnêtes Femmes* (Respectable Women), also in one act, followed at the same theater in January 1880. Both plays are admirably constructed. Despite superficial differences in theme, both use the short form with great success to suggest both the inseparability and the impersonality of amorous and financial interests in late-nineteenth-century Paris.

La Navette is often compared to Becque's more celebrated *La Parisienne,* but it also harks back to his early vaudeville *L'Enfant prodigue*. Here, as well, the focus is on a courtesan's simultaneous affairs with several men. If in the earlier play the lovers were types regarded as interchangeable by the woman they share, in *La Navette* they are scarcely distinguishable. The similarity of the names of all five characters in this short work—all begin with the letter *A*—suggests their virtual equivalence. In fact, each lover moves through a series of roles in relation to Antonio: the clandestine lover, the one who pays, the jealous lover who is about to be cast off, and, finally, the former lover. The moral of the play is that bourgeois morality, with its idealization and cloistering of women, has no place here. Love and money must circulate freely: "Sois fidèle à l'amour" (Be faithful to love).

Les Honnêtes Femmes portrays a different milieu, but the message is essentially the same. A young man visits a married woman in her home, hoping to make her his mistress. She, however, persuades him to court the marriageable daughter of a friend of hers, arguing that what her young suitor had hoped to enjoy clandestinely in her home he can possess legitimately in his own. Make your own home, she, Madame Chevalier, advises him. She will not be there, but his own wife will. "C'est la même chose, nous nous ressemblons toutes" (It's the same thing, we're all alike).

When Becque began work on his most celebrated play, *Les Corbeaux,* is unknown. He began submitting it to theaters around Paris in the late 1870s, but it was rejected everywhere. His break came unexpectedly from the summit of French theatrical life. Becque's publisher showed the play to Edouard Thierry, former administrator of the Comédie-Française, who recommended it to the current director of the theater, Perrin, and the play was accepted.

Les Corbeaux stirred interest, indignation, and admiration among the critics, but, in its first run in the fall of 1882, it did not attract large audiences and closed after sixteen performances. The play itself stands somewhat apart from Becque's other theatrical productions. Its focus is much broader—the fortunes of a nuclear family and their immediate associates—and the development much more extensive: the four acts of the play span months in the life of the Vigneron family, taking them from the luxuriously furnished apartment suitable for members of the *haute bourgeoisie* to, in the end, their final, shabby lodgings. In some ways the characters seem more rounded than those in Becque's other works although they, too, seem completely determined by circumstances. If the thematic focus has shifted in *Les Corbeaux* from sex to money, there is neverthe-less an underlying continuity in the representation of human beings as being subject to forces beyond their control.

Each of the four acts depicts a moment in the life of the Vigneron family. The first act introduces them at home on the evening of the father's unexpected death. Invited to dinner are characters, such as the father's unscrupulous business associate, Teissier, who later helps strip the widow and her children of all their property, and the mother of the young aristocrat to whom one daughter, Blanche, is engaged. None of the guests is particularly sympathetic. Even before the death of the father, the happiness of this family seems fragile.

Acts 2 and 3 take place in the same setting, mirroring each other as they represent two episodes in the family's rapid decline. In the second act Madame de Genlis comes to postpone the wedding of Blanche and her son until the family's affairs are settled, and Teissier and a notary, Bourdon, conspire to dupe Madame Vigneron. In the third act Madame de Genlis cancels the wedding and Bourdon and Teissier succeed in stripping the family of most of their inheritance. There are two added humiliations: Teissier offers to keep Marie, the youngest daughter, as his mistress; and Blanche, who begs Madame de Genlis to allow the marriage to take place since she has already been intimate with her fiancé, goes mad when her entreaties are ignored.

The fourth act finds the family disillusioned, depressed, and apparently much older, in their new lodgings. The son has left to enter the army. The middle daughter, Judith, summons her music teacher, who in the first act had spoken in flattering terms of her talent, to ask if she might support the family by performing in public or even by teaching herself; she is told bluntly that she has no prospects whatsoever. A well-known mute scene shows the family in their miserable interior, drinking tea together, a far cry from the group at the sumptuous dinner of the first act. Bourdon arrives to convey a proposal of marriage, Teissier's, to Marie, who finds the old man utterly repulsive. The play ends with her acceptance of Teissier's proposal.

It is sometimes argued that *Les Corbeaux* breaks with the conventions of mid- and late-nineteenth-century French theater by offering a realistic portrayal of contemporary life based on careful observation. But although the play lacks the multiple climaxes and dramatic reversals of the well-made play, it is nevertheless extremely tightly constructed. As in a well-made play, the individual acts mirror the structure of the whole. The ending, which indicates a forthcoming marriage between Teissier and Marie, seems a dark version of the typical conclusion of a comedy. Furthermore, if the characters of *Les Corbeaux* are more individualized than those of many of Becque's other works—it is, for example, possible to tell the daughters apart—they are still clearly divided into two camps: predators and victims. Becque himself at one time referred to the play as a melodrama. He also called it a "comédie," a "comédie-drame," and simply a play in four acts. The version included in his *Oeuvres complètes* (1924–1926) bears the subtitle "comédie en quatre actes" (a comedy in four acts).

Some critics were eager to see *Les Corbeaux* as a naturalist play, and the intellectual context of naturalism was evidently important to the play's representation of the Vignerons' plight. In act 4, for example, Bourdon refers to the survival of the fittest: "Vous avez subi la loi du plus fort, voilà tout" (You have fallen prey to the law of the strongest: that's all). More generally, the title of the play, whose significance the maid makes explicit at the beginning of act 4, reflects the common comparison of the social and animal worlds in the nineteenth-century novel. But if, like *L'Enfant prodigue* and *Michel Pauper, Les Corbeaux* owes much to the realist novel, here again, Balzac rather than Zola figures as the dominant influence. The three Vigneron daughters resemble no novelistic heroine so much as Eugénie Grandet.

But the title of the play also points beyond nineteenth-century realism and naturalism to twentieth-century avant-garde and expressionist drama. The black birds evoked by the title suggest not only the vulturelike nature of Bourdon and Teissier but also a whole invisible dimension of forces that permeate and control the lives of the characters onstage, another scene entirely, only intimated in their apparently natural actions and words. As Alfred Hitchcock demonstrated in his movie *The Birds* (1963), predatory birds are the stuff of nightmares. Some of Strindberg's post-1900 plays make this association quite explicit, as in *The Ghost Sonata* (1907), in which a particularly rapacious character speaks and acts like a parrot. But it was evident as early as Ibsen's nearly contemporaneous *The Wild Duck* (1884), in which the petit-bourgeois interior of the Ekdahls is split into visible and invisible components, the invisible attic being the home of the ill-fated wild duck.

Despite the impact that *Les Corbeaux* made in French theatrical circles, Becque's next play, *La Parisienne,* was rejected by the Comédie-Française by a vote of six to three. It was also rejected by the Vaudeville before being accepted by the Théâtre de la Renaissance. In *La Parisienne* Becque turns again to a plot centered on a woman who manages simultaneous relationships, but this time she is an elegant *grande bourgeoise* who juggles a complacent and perhaps knowing husband and two lovers. As in *L'Enfant prodigue* and especially *La Navette,* the characters are virtually interchangeable. What counts is their arrangement, rather than their individual identities. *Veuve!* (Widowed!, 1897), a short sequel to *La Parisienne,* makes this theme even more explicit. Confronted with a possessive lover after the death of her husband, Clotilde sighs and wishes it had been the lover, not the husband, who had died.

La Parisienne was staged several times during Becque's lifetime. On 7 June 1888 it was performed at the salon of Madame Aubernon with Réjane as Clotilde and André Antoine as Lafont; it was revived at the Vaudeville with Réjane in the lead role in 1893 and in 1899 at the Théâtre Antoine with Antoine again taking the part of Lafont.

Veuve! was one of five short plays that Becque published in 1896 and 1897 in the *Revue de Paris* and *La Vie parisienne.* Except for *Le Départ* (The Departure), all these plays are extremely short, evoking the implications of an aspect of contemporary urban life. *Le Domino à Quatre* (Dominoes, 1897; translated as *The Quiet Game,* 1913) is perhaps the most typical. The playlet's four scenes show the effects of Parisian café life on four friends: one by one they die off, until only the sickliest and most cautious is left. Life in the city is lethal, it seems. That is also the message suggested by *Une Exécution* (An Execution), the short scenes of which show a mayor sending his son, a talented rival, off to Paris. *Le Départ* is somewhat longer than the other pieces and harks back to earlier work by Becque. It focuses on the plight of a young female factory worker who, unable to support herself on her wages, is forced to seek a male protector. The factory owner's son wants to marry her, but his father not only opposes the union but even tries to seduce the young woman himself. A fellow worker proposes marriage, but the final scene shows the young woman writing to a baron, offering to become his mistress. The fifth short play in the series published in 1896, *Madeleine,* was a scene from Becque's *Les Polichinelles,* which he worked on intermittently for the last decade of his life but left unfinished at his death.

The manuscript of *Les Polichinelles* was first published in *L'illustration théâtrale* in 1910. Although Becque had sketched out five acts, only the first was substantially complete at his death. It was performed at the Odéon in 1924. The rest of the work suffers from an impossible proliferation of characters, as well as a tension between the schematic implications of the title and the play's totalizing ambitions: Becque seems to have aimed at capturing the totality of what he viewed as the twin underworlds of Parisian finance and prostitution, a project that both harked backward to the novel cycles of the nineteenth century and pointed forward to the work of Brecht, particularly his *Threepenny Opera* (1928). What is certain is that this last work required a different set of theatrical conventions from those that governed Becque's plays of the 1880s.

In 1890 Becque published a collection of his journalism on literary and theatrical topics, *Querelles littéraires* (Literary Quarrels), followed in 1895 by a second volume, *Souvenirs d'un auteur dramatique.* The title *Querelles littéraires* captures the tone and substance of most of the articles assembled in the two collections: of topical interest, they express Becque's resentment at the difficulties he faced as a playwright out of step with the conventions of his time. The difficulties were not imaginary: as he himself emphasized, at the time he began writing, the commercial theaters in Paris were all but closed to new works by unknown authors. As Marvin Carlson notes in *The French Stage in the Nineteenth Century* (1972): "Despite Becque's eventual success, the difficulties he had in attaining it guaranteed that few of his contemporaries would follow his example." In 1867 Hilarion Ballande formed a Société du patronage des auteurs dramatiques inconnus (Society for the Advancement of Unrecognized Playwrights) that sponsored matinee performances of the works of unknown authors. Ballande's venture was a predecessor of the new theaters that sprang up alongside the established, commercially successful Parisian theaters, the new theaters such as the Renaissance, which first staged *La Parisienne;* André Antoine's Théâtre-Libre, which also supported Becque's work; Paul Fort's Théâtre d'Art; and Aurélien-François Lugné-Poe's Théâtre de l'Oeuvre. Often the small theaters preferred shorter works, and Becque's turn toward one-act and short plays reflected his awareness that the briefer forms might be easier to stage than longer, more traditional plays.

Although Becque's plays present striking thematic and formal parallels to the work of many contemporary European playwrights, notably Ibsen and Strindberg, it is impossible not to infer his direct influence on Schnitzler, the celebrated Viennese playwright. Schnitzler's *La Ronde* (written 1896–1897; published 1903) is a cycle of ten erotic dialogues in which unindividualized types—the young man, the "sweet young thing," "the wife"—pass from one to the other; it obviously owes much to Becque's *La Parisienne,* perhaps also to *La Navette* and *L'Enfant prodigue.* While Schnitzler's work is often seen as epitomizing the erotically charged atmosphere of turn-of-the-century Vienna, what the juxtaposition of his play and Becque's plays makes even clearer is that new dramatic forms were emerging that reflected shifting sexual and social identities of people in late-nineteenth-century European urban centers.

During the last decade of his life Becque—the man, rather than his plays—was closely associated with the avant-garde theater in Paris. André Antoine acted in two productions of *La Parisienne* and strongly encouraged Becque to complete *Les Polichinelles.* But Becque's principal works antedate the theatrical avant-garde in Paris in the 1890s. Indeed, their harsh realism and unconventional perspectives helped make that avant-garde theater possible.

Letters:

Selected letters in Becque's *Oeuvres complètes,* volume 7, edited by Jean Robaglia (Paris: Crès, 1926), pp. 186–244.

Biographies:

Alexandre Arnaoutovitch, *Henry Becque,* 3 volumes (Paris: Presses Universitaires de France, 1927);

Paul Blanchart, *Henry Becque* (Paris: Nouvelle revue critique, 1930);

Maurice Descotes, *Henri Becque et son théâtre* (Paris: M. J. Minard, 1962).

References:

André Antoine, *Mes souvenirs sur le Théâtre-Libre* (Paris: Fayard, 1921); translated by Marvin Carlson as *Memories of the Théâtre-Libre* (Coral Gables, Fla.: University of Miami Press, 1964);

Marvin Carlson, *The French Stage in the Nineteenth Century* (Metuchen, N. J.: Scarecrow Press, 1972);

Lois Boe Hyslop, *Henry Becque,* Twayne World Author Series (New York: Twayne, 1972);

Jules Lemaître, "Les Corbeaux," in *Impressions de théâtre,* volume 10 (Paris: Société française d'imprimerie et de librairie, 1898), pp. 303–307;

Lemaître, "Henry Becque: une représentation de *La Parisienne,*" in *Impressions de théâtre,* volume 3 (Paris: Société française d'imprimerie et de librairie, 1900), pp. 219–230;

Jean Robaglia, "Henry Becque," preface to Becque's *Oeuvres complètes,* 7 volumes (Paris: Crès, 1924–1926), pp. 1–87;

Edmond Sée, *Henry Becque ou Servitude et grandeur dramatiques* (Paris: V. Rasmussen, 1926).

Joseph Bouchardy

(March 1810 – 25 May 1870)

John McCormick
Trinity College, Dublin

PLAY PRODUCTIONS: *Le Fils du bravo,* by Bouchardy and Eugène Deligny, Paris, Ambigu-Comique, 7 February 1836;

Hermann l'ivrogne, by Bouchardy and Deligny, Paris, Ambigu-Comique, 11 June 1836;

Gaspardo le pêcheur, Paris, Ambigu-Comique, 14 January 1837;

Un (petit) Coup de vin blanc, by Bouchardy and Deligny, Paris, Ambigu-Comique, 26 March 1837;

Le Spadassin, by Bouchardy, Charles Alphonse Brot, Adolphe Dennery, and Eugène Grangé, Paris, Saint-Antoine, 6 October 1837;

Longue-Epée le Normand, Paris, Ambigu-Comique, 1 December 1837;

Le Sonneur de Saint-Paul, Paris, Gaieté, 2 October 1838;

La Femme de ménage, by Bouchardy, Félix Auguste Duvert, Adolphe Théodore de Lauzanne, and Joseph Xavier Boniface, Paris, Palais Royal, 7 March 1839;

Christophe le Suédois, Paris, Ambigu-Comique, 29 October 1839;

L'Union fatale, by Bouchardy, Brot, and Edmond Burat de Gurgy, Paris, Saint-Marcel, 2 November 1839;

Lazare le pâtre, Paris, Ambigu-Comique, 11 November 1840;

Pâris le bohémien, Paris, Porte-Saint-Martin, 18 April 1842;

Les Enfants trouvés, Paris, Ambigu-Comique, 2 April 1843;

Les Orphelines d'Anvers, Paris, Ambigu-Comique, 30 October 1844;

La Soeur du muletier, Paris, Gaieté, 11 October 1845;

Une Fille terrible, by Bouchardy and Deligny, Paris, Variétés, 16 December 1846;

Bertram le matelot, Paris, Gaieté, 3 March 1847;

Léa, ou La Soeur du soldat, by Bouchardy and Paul Foucher, Paris, Gaieté, 6 August 1847;

La Filleule à Nicot, by Bouchardy and Deligny, Paris, Variétés, 18 September 1847;

La Roue de la fortune, by Bouchardy and Deligny, Paris, Variétés, 24 April 1848;

La Famille Thureau, by Bouchardy and Alcide Lorentz, Paris, Ambigu-Comique, 20 May 1848;

Un Vendredi, Paris, Variétés, 7 April 1849;

La Science du sommeil, Paris, Gaieté, 15 December 1849;

La Croix de Saint Jacques, Paris, Gaieté, 15 December 1849;

Jean le cocher, Paris, Ambigu-Comique, 11 November 1852;

Le Secret des Cavaliers, Paris, Ambigu-Comique, 24 December 1856;

Micaël l'esclave, Paris, Gaieté, 18 April 1859;

Philodor, Paris, Gaieté, 3 January 1863;

L'Armurier de Santiago, Paris, Châtelet, 30 September 1868.

BOOK: "Biographie de Monsieur Saint-Ernest, premier sujet du théâtre de l'Ambigu à Paris"; "Francisque Aîné"; and "Mélingue," in *Galerie des artistes dramatiques* (Bordeaux: Veuve V. Duviella, 1853).

SELECTED PERIODICAL PUBLICATIONS—UNCOLLECTED: "Deux épisodes de la vie d'un grand acteur," *Le Monde Dramatique,* 1 (1835): 233, 267;

"Une vocation et un coup de poing," *Le Monde Dramatique,* 1(1835): 347, 377;

"Théâtre chinois: *Un Héritier,*" *Le Monde Dramatique,* 1 (1835): 60;

"Les Comédiens chinois," *Le Monde Dramatique,* 1 (1835): 171;

"Théâtre chinois: *Les Malheurs de Han,*" *Le Monde Dramatique,* 1 (1835): 172;

"Le Pantomime chez les Chinois," *Le Monde Dramatique,* 2 (1836): 70;

"Garrick médecin," *Le Monde Dramatique,* 2 (1836);

"Bouchardy would have untangled Chaos, if God hadn't been there to save him the trouble," Jacques Arago wrote in his *Physiologie des foyers de tous les théâtres de Paris* (1841). Joseph Bouchardy, whose name was a byword for a certain type of melodrama with an extremely complicated plot, was one of the most popular dramatists of the late 1830s and the 1840s. His output was not prolific (he seldom wrote more than one major drama a year), but his three most popular plays, *Gaspardo le pêcheur* (Gaspardo the Fisherman, 1837), *Le Sonneur de Saint-Paul* (The Bell Ringer of Saint Paul's, 1838), and *Lazare le pâtre* (Lazarus the Shepherd, 1840), all had an initial run of nearly a whole season; in so doing, they helped change theater production from a standard repertoire system to the idea of the long-run play. These plays also continued to be revived regularly, and long after Bouchardy was out of fashion in Paris, they were performed in the suburban theaters and the provinces. They were also translated into various languages and were especially popular in Spain. According to Eugène Deligny, who collaborated with Bouchardy on several plays, the Ambigu-Comique theater made some Fr 200,000 from the first run of *Le Sonneur*.

Born in Paris in March 1810, Joseph Bouchardy belonged to a family of painters and engravers who originally lived in Lyons. His biographical details are relatively scarce. His initial training was as an engraver, working with copperplate and aquatint. Two of his major pieces are "Joan of Arc" (from a picture by Paul Delaroche) and "The Young Monk" (after Lorentz, which was published in *L'Artiste*. He is also credited with having invented or developed a form of pantograph, or "physionotrace," for the scale down of portraits for engravings. He learned at least a part of his craft from the English engraver S. W. Reynolds, who had produced large plates "à la manière noire" (in the somber manner) of Théodore Géricault's *Raft of the Medusa* and *Mazeppa*. Bouchardy probably met Reynolds in 1828, when the latter was in Paris with the renowned English actor Edmund Kean, whom Bouchardy met in Reynolds's company.

The young Bouchardy also associated with the Romantic generation of 1830, notably with a group, the Cénacle, that gathered around the poet and novelist Pétrus Borel, who referred to Bouchardy as a "soul of saltpetre." At this period Théophile Gautier described him as the typical young Romantic, with long hair, beard, moustache, and a hatred of the bourgeoisie. He was admitted to the Cénacle as an artist rather than as an aspiring dramatist.

When *Le Monde Dramatique* was founded in 1835, Bouchardy was part of the team, and his contributions to the publication ranged from articles on Chinese theater to anecdotal accounts about such English actors as George-Frederick Cooke and Kean. The latter articles are interesting not for their information or accuracy but for the descriptions and the development of scenes and characters that show something of the dramatist to come.

In 1836 Bouchardy teamed up with another young man, Eugène Deligny, to write for the theater, and this combination produced three short plays for the Ambigu-Comique in Paris. These were *Le Fils du bravo* (The Son of the Bully, 1836); *Un (petit) Coup de vin blanc* (A Drop of White Wine, 1837), also known as *Pierre et Jérôme;* and a more serious short drama, *Hermann l'ivrogne* (Hermann the Drunkard, 1836). *Le Fils du bravo,* though only a light comedy, and *Hermann* both give an indication of Bouchardy's subsequent skill in the handling of plot in the historical drama. The critic of *Le Monde dramatique* praised *Hermann* for its shortness, which made it different from most other dramas of the time (he was not aware that Bouchardy's audiences often staggered out of the theater after four or five hours of an exceptionally complicated plot). Bouchardy collaborated with Deligny again a decade later with three short comedies, or vaudevilles, for the Théâtre des Variétés: *Une Fille terrible* (A Frightful Girl, 1846), *La Filleule à Nicot* (Nicot's Goddaughter, 1847), and *La Roue de la fortune* (The Wheel of Fortune, 1848). Otherwise, with a few minor exceptions, he wrote his plays alone.

In 1836, presumably on the strength of *Le Fils du bravo,* Bouchardy was admitted to the Society of Authors. On 12 April 1840 he was elected to the management committee of the society and also became one of the two secretaries, a position he held until 1842. One piece of business that concerned him personally was an attempt by Séveste, licensee for the suburban theaters, to give performances of *Lazare* during the first successful run of the play at the Ambigu-Comique. *Lazare* had opened on 11 November 1840, and legally no other production could take place until after 7 January 1841. Séveste had announced the show for the Théâtre Montparnasse on 18 December. The matter was finally resolved with Séveste paying a fine of Fr 100 to the emergency fund of the society.

After this Bouchardy's biography seems to be virtually that of his plays, and few if any details of his personal life emerge readily. Following his brilliant beginnings he tended to repeat the formulas that had served him so well, and, allowing for changes of period, setting, and costume, all his plays have a strong family resemblance. By 1847 Jules Janin, writing in the *Journal des Débats* about *Bertram le matelot* (Bertram the Sailor, 1847), spoke of Bouchardy as someone who had been overtaken by younger talents. The play ran for two months but

Contemporary illustration of a scene from Joseph Bouchardy's 1852 play, Jean le coucher

was not a great success. Audiences clearly felt that this play simply provided more of what they had already had. Even the title evoked a familiar pattern with the name of the eponymous hero and his profession. Nine of Bouchardy's dramas have this sort of title, and another seven consist either of the profession of the central figure, as in *L'Armurier de Santiago* (The Armorer of Santiago, 1868), or some aspect of their situation, as in *Les Orphelines d'Anvers* (The Orphan Girls of Antwerp, 1844).

The last Bouchardy play that could be described as a success was *Jean le cocher* (John the Coachman) in 1852. By this time he was living in virtual retirement, possibly because of the death of his daughter. By the 1860s he was virtually forgotten. His output, which had seldom been more than one major play a year, dropped to the occasional piece. *Le Secret des Cavaliers* (The Cavaliers' Secret), despite a long and enthusiastic review by Jules Janin, opened at the Ambigu-Comique on 24 December 1856 and closed a month later. *Micaël l'esclave* (Michael the Slave, 1859) and *Philodor* (1863) failed to last a month, and his final play, *L'Armurier de Santiago,* had to be removed from the stage of the Châtelet in 1868 after ten days.

Bouchardy's style and notoriety were sufficient for at least two of his plays, *Le Sonneur* and *Jean le cocher,* to be the subjects of parodies: *Le Carillonneur de Saint-Paul* (The Bell Tinkler of Saint Paul's), a parody-vaudeville in one act by Cléophas-Reimbold Dautrevaux and Eugène Vanel, was staged at the Théâtre du Temple on 12 January 1839; and *Jean le*

porcher (John the Highwayman), "vaudeville comique et non-ambigu en un acte et sans prologue, par Bouche-Hardie (Anon)" (a comic but unambiguous vaudeville in one act without a prologue, by Bouche-Hardie [Goldmouth]), opened at the Théâtre Lazary on 30 April 1853.

Gautier, a friend and early associate of Bouchardy, had been quick to observe his literary deficiencies but also commented on his ability to handle a complicated plot at breakneck speed, leaving little room for analysis of character or emotion and even less for poetry or fantasy. In 1842 he wryly called him "the Aeschylus, the Euripides, the Sophocles of the boulevard." The rather less critical Deligny preferred to compare him with William Shakespeare, Johann Wolfgang von Goethe, and Friedrich Schiller.

Bouchardy's great model was Victor Hugo, and his intention was to be a writer of the Romantic drama. Unfortunately, despite his undoubted theatrical craftsmanship, his literary talents were almost nonexistent. With the exception of a handful of vaudevilles, mostly written in collaboration for the Théâtre des Variétés, his plays were full-scale dramas. The critic Francisque Sarcey described Bouchardy's melodrama as the "cousin of vaudeville" because of the emphasis on situations and constant *coups de théâtre*. The early vaudeville, *Le Fils du bravo,* is virtually a short historical drama with a comic plot and already shows Bouchardy's mastery of stagecraft. Murder is treated in a comic vein as the hired assassin imprisons in two cupboards the two rivals who have employed him to kill each other, and he then departs in his gondola (in Renaissance Venice) with the lady both desired. *Un Vendredi* (1849) is closer to the modern drama. Its action revolves around dubious business dealings and embezzlement. Since it is a vaudeville, the situation is saved by a stroke of good luck.

Bouchardy called his plays dramas, not melodramas, and one of the features of his work is its almost unrelieved seriousness. The mixture of genres, typical of the early melodrama and advocated by Hugo, is seldom found. Bouchardy lacked the breadth of vision of Hugo and had none of his literary qualities. If anything, the main influence on Bouchardy may have been the elder Alexandre Dumas's *La Tour de Nesle* (The Tower of Nesle, 1832), with its astounding sense of theater and of the theatrical situation. In this lay Bouchardy's primary appeal. There is little sense of an analysis of the society of his day, but the plays constantly express a populist message that audiences would have recognized. *Gaspardo,* for example, was only allowed by the censors with some modifications. Its basic theme of the successful revenge of three men of the people on the evil and powerful Visconti, Duke of Milan, who is eventually dethroned in a popular revolt, echoes feelings that were current in the 1830s (Joseph Fieschi, who had attempted to assassinate Louis Philippe, was executed about a month after the opening of *Gaspardo,* and some six thousand soldiers were present to quell any popular uprising). The theme of the weak against the strong is a constant one in Bouchardy's plays, and this theme is always coupled with the final triumph of the weak after they have endured a series of impossible situations. Libertarian sentiment was more than evident in *Micaël l'esclave,* with such declarations as "quand on a respiré dans un pays libre, on devient meilleur" (when one has breathed the air of a free country, one becomes a better person). However, even a rave review in *Entr'acte* and a fashionable Russian setting could not save this play.

Bouchardy's villains are all public figures, tyrants, or abusers of power. The innocent are caught up in a web of treachery and often framed to look as if they have committed crimes. In *Gaspardo* and *Lazare* tyranny is opposed by virtuous popular leaders. Elsewhere Bouchardy exploits the already existing sympathy for popular historical figures such as the Stuarts, in *Le Sonneur* and *Bertram le matelot.* The idea of peoples struggling for independence from a foreign power of course turns the representatives of that power into villains (*Christophe le Suédois* [Christopher the Swede], 1839).

Like an historical novelist, Bouchardy generally places real historical figures, such as King Charles II, in secondary roles. The plays are written with the idea of the average stock company in mind, and virtually all the characters fall into the category of existing types, or *emplois.* The two key roles in the plays are the mature male lead and the "heavy." The male lead appears again and again in the role of Providence as the avenger of crime and the protector of his offspring, who remain unaware of his true identity until late in the action. Bouchardy wrote splendid parts for such actors, and his interpreters included Francisque aîné, Guyon, Mélingue, and even Frédérick Lemaître. Francisque aîné was described as an energetic popular actor, in his place on the boulevard but only there. It was he who created John, the bell ringer of Saint Paul's, a role that demanded much interesting mime because of the blindness of the character for much of the play. In *Lazare* Mélingue, another great favorite of the Boulevard, played the part of a supposed mute for much of the play, and he too had to express himself through mime. Later Mélingue went on to make his name in the plays of Frédéric Soulié and created the part of Edmond Dantès, Count of Monte Cristo, for Dumas in 1848. Bouchardy gave Lemaître an ideal part for his flamboyant personality in *Pâris le bohémien* (1842).

Rene-Charles Guilbert de Pixérécourt, with *L'homme à trois visages* (The Man with Three Faces, 1801), created the melodrama in which the whole action hinges on recognition or nonrecognition of the main character, who appears in different guises in different scenes of the play. Dumas's Buridan in *La Tour de Nesle* is in this mold and provided a pattern for many of Bouchardy's protagonists. Pâris, whose identity has to remain concealed from the evil Galéas, appears as a rambunctious captain and later as a Venetian general, Leonessa, whom Gautier described as an "old master" come to life; a caricature of a Jew (which the audience seems to have enjoyed); and a slave who is supposedly poisoned, but who, at the last moment, reaches up to seize by the throat Galéas, who has come to contemplate his agony.

The clear Manichaean division of characters into good and bad, with all the appropriate signifiers, left the audience in no doubt as to where they stood. From the first line of *Lazare,* Sylvio shows concern for two young children (a clear indication that he is virtuous), and soon after the appearance of Lazare himself, the audience learns from another character that:

La nuit passée, j'avais bu un peu plus que ma part, je m'étais laissé choir en chemin, et je m'étais endormi au bord d'un précipice où je serais tombé sans doute à mon réveil, sans Lazare qui me réveilla en me traînant loin du gouffre[.]

(Last night I drank more than I should. I collapsed on the way home and fell asleep on the edge of a cliff, from which, no doubt, I would have fallen on waking up, had it not been for Lazare, who awakened me and dragged me away from the abyss[.])

Judaël de Medicis, the villain, is first mentioned as being rejected by his family as a thief, and then someone adds, "Judaël! et qu'est donc devenu ce Judas?" (Judaël! What's that Judas doing now?), thus associating him with Judas Iscariot. When Judaël, inevitably, comes onstage a few minutes later, he is masked and in search of a *spadassin* (hit man).

Bouchardy's style was fully presentational. His complicated plots demanded absolute clarity and had to be well projected to the six hundred denizens of the gallery of the two-thousand-seat Ambigu-Comique. Everything had to be explicit, and for this he often used not only rather crude techniques of exposition but also asides, either to show the reaction of a character to a particular situation or turn in the action, or else to explain motivation. Thus, the doctor Albinus casually leaves a volume on his father's cataract operations in Saint Paul's cathedral and informs the audience: "Je savais bien que ce livre oublié dans les mains d'un aveugle m'amènerait à causer avec lui" (I knew that if I left this book behind in the hands of a blind man, that would give me a chance to talk to him).

When a character says "Quel est cet homme?" (Who is this man?), this is not a question to the audience but an indication that the speaker is startled or alarmed. The aside is constantly used to indicate what is really going on in a character's mind and often to show that all is not well. This device is much used by Bouchardy in his prologues. It is also much employed by villains, sometimes with risible effects for a later audience: "Va! Charles deux, dicte ta sentence, fais dresser l'échafaud; tu ne tiens pas encore William Smith et le Sonneur de Saint-Paul n'est pas sauvé. . . . tu ne sais pas, toi, roi d'Angleterre, que tu as nommé William Smith gouverneur de la Tour de Londres!" (Go ahead, Charles II, pronounce your sentence and set up the scaffold. You haven't caught William Smith yet, and the Bell-ringer of Saint Paul's hasn't been saved. . . . King of England, you don't know that you have appointed William Smith to be governor of the Tower of London!).

Bouchardy's plays were performed in theaters capable of lavish, spectacular productions, but he seldom required more than the stock sets of the Romantic period and did not rely on spectacle for his effects. There are no earthquakes, natural disasters, or great conflagrations, and modern technology is never a source of dramatic interest; the closest he comes to anything vaguely topical is in his 1849 play *La Croix de Saint-Jacques* (The Cross of Saint Jacques), where he introduces hypnotism but keeps his action firmly in the twelfth century. He did not subscribe to the scenic effects of the sensation melodrama but, in his own way, remained remarkably classical. None of the plays is built around a grand spectacular scene, and this may be another reason why his plays dropped out of favor once spectacular theater became the rage. One of his biggest effects was probably to bring a hackney cab onto the stage in *Jean le cocher,* but this hardly compared with the most insignificant effects of the Cirque Olympique.

Bouchardy's settings draw on the conventional scenic vocabulary of the early melodrama. Characters, costumes, periods, and settings are almost interchangeable from one play to the next. His whole interest lies in the dramatic situations created. As in many melodramas the settings also relate to the characters or situation. The cottage, fisherman's cabin, or similar scene, which opens most of the plays, is the abode of the poor man and his virtuous family. This setting will be interrupted by the arrival of evil. A series of large palace scenes or similar scenes depicts the triumph of the villain, whose wealth and position usually depend on a crime carried out in the first act or prologue.

If local color were a relatively minor concern, however, the practical nature of the set was every bit as important as in a good farce or vaudeville. Doors and windows are crucial to Bouchardy's dramaturgy (as they are in *La Tour de Nesle*). They serve not only for entrances and exits. Doors can be locked, opened unexpectedly, or used for overhearing. Windows also may give access to characters but receive their fullest significance as places from which offstage action can be observed: Gaspardo addresses the people of Milan in revolt from a window; Lazare gazes eagerly out of a window, awaiting the putting of a light in a facing window, which will indicate that his nephew Juliano is alive. It is in his use of space and the set that Bouchardy's sense of the possibilities of theater is most evident.

There are comparatively few open-air scenes in Bouchardy's plays. He prefers a constant sense of enclosure and containment and uses this to build up a feeling of menace. His closed sets often consist of large public rooms in palaces. These can be extended in the last act by the opening of a set of double doors upstage or the pulling back of a curtain, effective devices to suggest that the claustrophobic atmosphere of most of the play has finally been dispelled with the triumph of right. Alternating with such scenes are smaller environments where the characters suffer the oppression of poverty or else are imprisoned. The concentration of the physical space becomes an important dramatic signifier. The claustrophobic effect of such scenes is important. The palace/prison ambivalence is fundamental to *Gaspardo, Le Sonneur,* and *Lazare.*

In play after play the main role is that of a parent who watches over the life and fate of his offspring and acts as a hidden deus ex machina. The action is generally set up in a prologue that occurs some twenty years before the main action, and this allows a mislaid infant to grow up unaware of his or her true identity, which will, of course, be revealed at the end. It has been suggested that the prologue was designed to appeal to the more popular sections of the audience, who tended to come to the theater earlier than the middle classes. Certainly most of the events shown in the prologue are referred to later as further exposition is fed to audiences. It is not immediately obvious when the first act of the play begins that a certain middle-aged man, last seen as a young man, is the father, biological or adoptive, or uncle of one of the young people who were either infants or only barely conceived in the prologue. The initial crime occurs in the first act or prologue, and the rest of the play is concerned with its consequences. In the prologue of *Gaspardo* Catarina stabs herself onstage to avoid the sexual advances of Visconti. John, the Scottish hunter (alias John the Royalist London tavern keeper), is shot by William Smith in the prologue to *Le Sonneur.* In the rest of the play John appears as the bell ringer of Saint Paul's and William as the duke of Bedfort. In the best classical manner the audience is shown the result, but not the action itself, as John staggers onto the stage in a bloody shirt, apparently dying, as the prologue ends. Various murders happen offstage during the prologue to *Lazare;* one person is poisoned onstage, and Lazare himself (alias Raphael Salviati) collapses as the result of poison.

Where the Romantic drama was generally amoral, Bouchardy saw himself as profoundly moral and kept sexual passion well out of his plays. He could never have written a play such as Hugo's *Marion Delorme* (1831), let alone the latter's *Lucrèce Borgia* (1833). Bouchardy's plays are based on a clear opposition of good and evil, but the good characters are placed in situations of extreme peril and are generally weak. Ultimately, however, it is always the simple man of the people who overcomes the rich and powerful villain or tyrant.

Bouchardy was writing in the mode of the historical melodrama of Pixérécourt and others. It is often said that he believed in his stories and characters, and it was this belief, devoid of any sense of irony, that carried his audiences with him through a labyrinth of complications. Only in *Micaël l'esclave,* perhaps, is there a sense that he too was aware of the absurd complexity of his plots, when Prince Faustus Sémoloff rushes onto the stage in the last scene declaring: "Et vous croyez que je ne déchirerais pas les pages de ce roman d'aventure que vous avez préparé tous ensemble?" (Do you really think I shan't tear up the pages of this adventure novel which you have all concocted together?).

Bouchardy added complication and seriousness to the older historical melodrama (now called a "drame") but did not lead it toward the psychological melodrama of Victorien Sardou, the spectacular drama of Adolphe Dennery and others, or the more serious issue-based modern drama. Ultimately, the mechanics of plot were more important than the subject, and this is probably another reason why his plays provided such good vehicles for actors, but contained such basically unmemorable characters otherwise. At least one of his plays was a major source for a great success of the latter part of the century, Dennery's *Les deux Orphelines* (The Two Orphans, 1874), whose basic situation is remarkably similar to Bouchardy's *Orphelines d'Anvers.* Bouchardy puts onstage a pair of female orphans, one of them blind, but later cured, after a murder attempt. They have been separated from their parents for eighteen years and eventually turn out to be the daughters of William of Orange. Dennery's career paralleled that of Bouchardy, but he was a much more versatile writer and was able to adapt in a way that Bouchardy could not. He provides a useful yardstick by which to measure Bouchardy since he began his career shortly before him but continued successfully into the 1880s. He wrote *féeries* (fairy plays) and opera libretti. His social plays attempted a degree of analysis, as opposed to Bouchardy's usually rather crude juxtaposition of rich and poor. He also drew on a much wider variety of sources and moved into the adaptation of successful novels with Jules Verne. Bouchardy had less recourse to popular fiction and drama as his sources and, once the novelty had worn off, came to be seen as a man whose great strength lay in writing one type of play.

Bouchardy existed in the fantasy land of the early-nineteenth-century melodrama. The central obsession is the avenging of a crime, and the concern is less with any moral values than with the satisfaction of that obsession, however many years it takes. The paraphernalia of melodrama—letters, documents, poison, disguises—exist for this one end. Recognition scenes are a crucial part of his dramaturgy, but this recognition invariably takes two forms, the recognition of parents by children (and sometimes vice versa) and the unmasking of the villain. After an early scene of conjugal happiness, about to be clouded, and ongoing parental concern for the well-being of children, love has little to do in these plays. The romantic interest of *Le Sonneur* revolves around Henri and Marie, but Marie herself is abducted at the end of act 1, never allowed a love scene, and does not reappear until four lines before the end. *Le Secret des Cavaliers* is one play that gives a more interesting role to an actress. Its sorely tried heroine, Ketty, is one of the best able to look after herself, even being prepared to feign madness to defeat the machinations of the wicked Lord James. Most of the more mature female characters, who have been young in the prologue, suffer and hold secrets but have little possibility of passing to a more active role. Ultimately the plays boil down to a struggle between the villain and the protagonist, who takes on the role of Providence and whose identity remains a secret from the villain until late in the action. During the penultimate act the forces of good come together, and the downfall of the villain is set in motion. Bouchardy's last acts are short—in some cases they amount to little more than a couple of pages of script—but wind up loose ends and provide the excuse for a final confrontation and tableau.

Bouchardy is a good example of a growing phenomenon in nineteenth-century theater, the professional dramatist whose main income was from his plays. Royalties for *Le Sonneur* from October 1838 to February 1839 amounted to Fr 8,192 at a fixed rate of Fr 64 a night (the average daily wage for an unskilled worker at this period was about Fr 2). In 1852–1853, with his last major success, *Jean le cocher,* which had a three-month run, he received Fr 4,828, allowing for the deduction for the Society of Authors, for the month of December (this royalty was calculated on a percentage of the takings rather than a fixed fee). Even his second-to-last play, *Philodor* (1863), which lasted a bare three weeks, netted him Fr 2,671.55, which was still a respectable sum despite the general increase in wages and cost of living. A closer study of the registers of the Society of Authors reveals that, despite a decline in popularity after 1850, Bouchardy was able to live off his plays during a retirement of nearly twenty years.

Bouchardy died at Châtenay, near Paris, on 25 May 1870. The event passed all but unnoticed, and a representative of the Society of Authors, summoned in haste, pronounced only the sketchiest of funeral orations. By this time Parisian audiences could only smile at Bouchardy's plays when they were revived, and he was regarded as a survivor of an extinct race. Indeed, few dramatists have been as completely forgotten within their own lifetimes as Bouchardy. His name survived in a street near le boulevard du Temple that was named after him in 1875, but it was replaced by that of the illusionist Robert Houdin in 1938.

References:

Peter Brooks, *The Melodramatic Imagination* (New Haven: Yale University Press, 1976);

Théophile Gautier, *Histoire de l'art dramatique en France depuis vingt-cinq ans* (Brussels: Hetzel, 1858–1859);

John McCormick, "Joseph Bouchardy: A Melodramatist and His Public," in *Performance and Politics in Popular Drama,* edited by David Bradby, Louis James, and Bernard Sharratt (Cambridge: Cambridge University Press, 1980), pp. 33–48;

Armand Praviel, "Une célébrité populaire oubliée—Joseph Bouchardy—à propos du cinquantenaire de sa mort," *Le Correspondant* (Paris), 279, 1920, pp. 534–542;

Jean-Marie Thomasseau, *Le Mélodrame* (Paris: Presses Universitaires de France, 1984).

Eugène Brieux
(19 January 1858 – 6 December 1932)

Marvin Carlson
The Graduate School and University Center, The City University of New York

PLAY PRODUCTIONS: *Bernard Palissy,* by Brieux and Gaston Salandri, Paris, Théâtre Cluny, 21 December 1879;

Stenio (opéra-comique), music by F. Le Rey, Rouen, Théâtre des Arts, 16 April 1881;

Ménages d'artistes, Paris, Théâtre-Libre, 21 March 1890;

La Fille de Duramé, Rouen, Théâtre-Français, 25 March 1890;

Corneille à Petit-Couronne, Rouen, 1890;

Blanchette, Paris, Théâtre-Libre, 2 February 1892; revised version, Comédie-Française, 9 October 1903;

M. de Réboval, Paris, Théâtre de l'Odeon, 20 September 1892;

La Couvée, Paris, Coopération des idées, Université populaire du Faubourg Saint-Antoine, 9 July 1893;

L'Engrenage, Paris, Théâtre de la Comédie Parisienne (Cercle des Escholiers), 16 May 1894;

Chacun chez soi, Rouen, 1894;

La Rose bleue, Geneva, Grand-théâtre, 26 July 1895;

Le Soldat Graindor, Marseilles;

Les Bienfaiteurs, Paris, Théâtre de la Porte Saint-Martin, 23 October 1896;

L'Evasion, Paris, Comédie-Française, 7 December 1896;

Les Trois Filles de M. Dupont, Paris, Théâtre du Gymnase, 8 October 1987;

L'Ecole des belles-mères, Paris, Théâtre du Gymnase, 25 March 1898;

Résultat des courses, Paris, Théâtre-Antoine, 10 December 1898;

Le Berceau, Paris, Comédie-Française, 15 December 1898;

La Culla, Milan, Teatro Olimpio, 9 August 1905;

La Robe rouge, Paris, Théâtre du Vaudeville, 15 March 1900; revised version, Comédie-Française, 23 September 1909;

Les Remplaçantes, Paris, Théâtre-Antoine, 15 February 1901;

Eugène Brieux

Les Avariés, Liege, Théâtre du Gymnase, 6 March 1902; Brussels, Théâtre du Parc, 7 March 1902; Paris, Théâtre-Antoine, 22 February 1905;

La Petite Amie, Paris, Comédie-Française, 3 May 1902;

Maternité, Paris, Théâtre-Antoine, 9 December 1903;

La Déserteuse, by Brieux and Jean Sigaux, Paris, Théâtre de l'Odeon, 15 October 1904;

L'Armature, Paris, Théâtre du Vaudeville, 19 April 1905;

Les Hannetons, Paris, Renaissance, 3 February 1906;

La Française, Paris, Théâtre de l'Odeon, 18 April 1907;

Simone, Paris, Comédie-Française, 13 April 1908;

La Foi, Monte Carlo, Théâtre de Monte-Carlo, 10 April 1909; produced in England by Herbert Beerbohm Tree in September, 1909;

Suzette, Paris, Théâtre du Vaudeville, 28 September 1909;

La Femme seule, Paris, Théâtre du Gymnase, 22 December 1912;

Bianchina, Rome, Teatro Argentina, 22 August 1913;

Le Bourgeois aux champs, by Brieux and Salandri, Paris, Théâtre de l'Odeon, 11 February 1914;

Les Américains chez nous, Paris, Théâtre de l'Odeon, 9 January 1920;

Trois bons amis, Paris, Théâtre de l'Odeon, 7 May 1921;

L'Avocat, Paris, Vaudeville, 22 September 1922;

L'Enfant, Paris, Vaudeville, 20 September 1923;

La Famille Lavolette, Paris, Théâtre des Nouveautés, 11 September 1926;

Puisque je t'aime, Paris, Comédie-Française, 6 May 1929.

BOOKS: *Bernard Palissy,* by Brieux and Salandri (Paris: Tresse, 1880);

Le Bureau des divorces, by Brieux and Salandri (Paris: L. Vanier, 1880);

Le Crédit agricole tel que le veulent les paysans (Rouen: Nouvelliste de Rouen, 1888);

Stenio, by Brieux, music by Frédérick Le Rey (Paris: Calmann-Lévy, 1881);

Corneille au Petit-Couronne (Rouen: Augé, 1889);

La Fille de Duramé (Rouen: C. F. Lapierre, 1890);

Ménages d'artistes (Paris: Tresse et Stock, 1890); translated by Barret H. Clark as *Artists' Families,* introduction by J. R. Crawford (Garden City: Doubleday, Page, 1918);

Blanchette (Paris: Tresse et Stock, 1892); translated by Frederick Eisemann in *Blanchette and The Escape; Two Plays by Brieux,* preface by H. L. Mencken (Boston: Luce, 1913);

Mi-Ka-Ka (Le Havre: Lemale, 1893);

La Couvée (Paris: Tresse et Stock, 1893);

L'Engrenage (Paris: Tresse et Stock, 1894);

La Rose bleue (Paris: Tresse et Stock, 1895);

L'Evasion (Paris: P.V. Stock, 1897); translated by Eisemann as *The Escape,* in *Blanchette and The Escape; Two Plays by Brieux,* preface by Mencken (Boston: Luce, 1913);

Les Bienfaiteurs (Paris: P. V. Stock, 1897);

Le Berceau (Paris: P. V. Stock, 1898);

L'Ecole des belles-mères (Paris: P. V. Stock, 1898);

Résultat des courses (Paris: P. V. Stock, 1898);

Les Trois Filles de M. Dupont (Paris: P. V. Stock, 1899); translated by St. John Hankin as *The Three Daughters of M. Dupont* in *Three Plays by Brieux* (London: A. C. Fifield, 1911);

La Robe rouge (Paris: P. V. Stock, 1900); translated by F. O. Reed as *The Red Robe;* in T. H. Dickinson, *Chief Contemporary Dramatists* (Boston: 1915); translated by Homer Saint-Gaudens as *The Letter of the Law* (N.p., 1915?); translated by A. Bernard Miall as *The Red Robe,* in *Woman on Her Own, False Gods and the Red Robe: Three Plays,* introduction by Brieux (New York: Brentano's, 1916);

Les Remplaçantes (Paris: P. V. Stock, 1901);

Les Remplaçantes, by Brieux and Marcel Luguet (Paris: Jules Rueff, 1902);

Les Avariés (Paris: P. V. Stock, 1902); translated by John Pollock as *Damaged Goods,* in *Three Plays by Brieux* (London: A. C. Fifield, 1911);

La Petite Amie (Paris: P. V. Stock, 1902);

La Déserteuse, by Brieux and Jean Sigaux (Paris: P. V. Stock, 1904);

Maternité (Paris: P. V. Stock, 1904); translated by Mrs. Bernard Shaw as *Maternity,* in *Three Plays by Brieux* (London: A. C. Fifield, 1911);

L'Armature (Paris: P. V. Stock, 1905);

Les Hannetons (Paris: P. V. Stock, 1906); translated by Arthur Hornblow Jr. as *Morals and Men* (New York: 1922?);

La Française (Paris: P. V. Stock, 1907);

Simone (Paris: P. V. Stock, 1908);

Suzette (Paris: P. V. Stock, 1909);

La Plus Forte (Paris: Illustration, 1909);

Voyage aux Indes et en Indo-Chine (Paris: Delagrave, 1910);

Discours de réception à l'Académie Française prononcé le 12 mai 1910 (Paris: 1910);

La Foi (Paris: P. V. Stock, 1912); translated by J. F. Fagan as *False Gods,* in *Woman on Her Own, False Gods and the Red Robe: Three Plays,* introduction by Brieux (New York: Brentano's, 1916);

Tunisie (Vincennes: Arts Graphiques, 1912);

Algérie (Vincennes: Arts Graphiques, 1912);

La Femme seule (Paris: P. V. Stock, 1913); translated by Mrs. Bernard Shaw as *Woman on Her Own* in *Woman on Her Own, False Gods and the Red Robe: Three Plays,* introduction by Brieux (New York: Brentano's, 1916);

Au Japon, par Java, la Chine, La Corée (Paris: Delagrave, 1914);

Deux Lettres aux combattants (Paris: 1915);

Nos soldats aveugles (Paris: Delagrave, 1916); translated by Gladys Gladding Whiteside as *Our Blinded Soldiers* (Baltimore: Red Cross Institute for the Blind, 1918);

Lettres aux soldats blessés aux yeux (Paris: Delagrave, 1918);

L'Avocate (Paris: P. V. Stock, 1922);

L'Enfant—Pierrette et Galaor (Paris: P. V. Stock, 1923);

La Famille Lavolette (Paris: P. V. Stock, 1926).

Editions and Collections: *Four Plays of the Free Theatre,* edited by Barrett Clark, preface by Brieux (Cincinnati: Stewart & Kidd, 1915);

Théâtre complet de Brieux, 9 volumes (Paris: Stock, Delamain, Boutelleau, 1921–1930) volume 1 (1921)–comprises *Ménages d'artistes, Blanchette, M. de Réboval, L'Ecole des Belles-Mères;* volume 2 (1922)–comprises *Les Bienfaiteurs, L'Evasion, La Robe rouge;* volume 3 (1922)–comprises *Les Trois Filles de M. Dupont, Résultat des courses;* volume 4 (1922)–comprises *L'Engrenage, Les Remplaçantes, Maternité;* volume 5 (1923)–comprises *Le Berceau, Simone, Suzette;* volume 6 (1923)–comprises *Les Avariés, Les Hannetons, La Petite Amie;* volume 7 (1924)–comprises *La Femme seule, Le Bourgeois aux champs, Les Américains chez nous;* volume 8 (1928)–comprises *La Foi, L'Avocat, Trois bons amis;* volume 9 (1930)–comprises *Pierrette et Galaor, Puisque je t'aime, La Régence.*

Edition in English: *Three Plays by Brieux (Maternity, The Three Daughters of M. Dupont, Damaged Goods),* with a preface by Bernard Shaw (London: A. C. Fifield, 1911).

OTHER: "Lettre-Préface" to *L'Insexuée,* by Paul Bru (Paris: n.d.);

"Introduction" to *Les Avariés,* adapted into a novel by Maurice Landay (Paris: 1904).

SELECTED PERIODICAL PUBLICATIONS–
UNCOLLECTED: *Le Bourgeois aux champs,* by Brieux and Gaston Salandri, *La Petite Illustration,* 62 (9 May 1914);

Les Américans chez nous, La Petite Illustration Theatrale, new series 11 (7 February 1920);

"Emile Augier, chevalier de la bourgeoisie," *Revue des Deux Mondes,* 61 (1921): Part I, 49–83; Part II, 297–323;

"Confidences d'un auteur dramatique," *Revue de France,* 35 (1923): 837–845;

La Régence, Les Oeuvres Libres, 67 (1 January 1927);

Puisque je t'aime, La Petite Illustration Théâtrale, new series 169 (1929); translated by V. Vernon as *Because I Love You,* in V. Vernon and F. Vernon, *Modern One-Act Plays from the French* (New York: S. French, 1933).

Eugène Brieux became the best known of the remarkable generation of French playwrights introduced by André Antoine at his experimental Théâtre-Libre in Paris, and Brieux's work typifies certain central concerns and techniques of that theater. In a striking and, for many, shockingly realistic style, he portrayed current social problems that he believed demanded attention and reform. Given these concerns, it is not surprising that he attracted the warm support of Bernard Shaw, one of his most enthusiastic champions, who considered Brieux the greatest French writer since Molière. Brieux's reputation has not stood the test of time well, but his major works are still occasionally revived, and he is still remembered as the leading creator in France of the engaged social drama that marked a new direction in theater at the end of the nineteenth century.

Brieux was born on 19 January 1858 in the working-class Parisian suburb of St.-Antoine and worked as an apprentice cabinetmaker in his father's shop. Although he had only an elementary-school education, he dreamed of a literary career, spending his meager earnings on books, studying Latin and Greek on his own, and attending night classes. An orphan at fourteen, he began working in a bank and writing plays that he submitted, in vain, to various Parisian theaters. With Gaston Salandri he created a verse comedy, *La Vielle fille* (The Old Girl, 1877), that they submitted to the leading French critic of the time, Francisque Sarcey, hoping to gain his interest and support, but Sarcey jokingly dismissed their efforts. Finally in 1879 the two young authors managed to get another one-act verse play, *Bernard Palissy,* accepted for presentation in Paris in a series of matinees of unpublished scripts at the minor Théâtre Cluny. This single performance created no further interest, however. At about this time the French Parliament was discussing a repeal of the ban on divorce in France, in place since Napoleon, and Brieux and Salandri wrote a satire anticipating the consequences of repeal, *Le Bureau des divorces* (The Divorce Office, 1880), assuming its topicality would guarantee interest, but they were disappointed. Brieux, who had had a few articles accepted by the Parisian journal *Patrie,* decided to put aside his theater ambitions for a time and pursue a career in journalism. He first worked on a newspaper in Dieppe; then he joined the staff of the provincial *Nouvelliste de Rouen,* first serving as secretary, then in six years rising to editor in chief.

Soon after his arrival in Rouen in 1881, Brieux had a comic opera, *Stenio,* produced at the local opera house, but he still dreamed of having his work produced in Paris and continued to submit manuscripts to leading literary figures such as Emile Augier and Emile Zola, receiving no encouragement from them. Brieux's situation was not unusual in France at this time. A few established dramatists ruled the theaters, and managers were rarely interested in work by unknown young writers. It was largely in reaction to this situation that in 1887 André Antoine founded his Théâtre-Libre in Paris and actively sought out new playwrights. Antoine visited Brieux in Rouen and in the spring of 1890 produced his *Ménages d'Artistes* (translated as *Artists' Families,* 1918) at the Théâtre-Libre. The play, satirizing the claim that artists must sacrifice domestic happiness for their art, drew upon Brieux's knowledge of journalistic circles but was almost universally condemned by the critics, who much preferred its companion piece, Jean Jullien's darker *Le Maître* (The Master, 1890).

Although *Ménages d'Artistes* was not particularly successful, it nevertheless marked a turning point in Brieux's career since it introduced him to Antoine and encouraged him to continue his dramatic writing. *Blanchette* (1892), Brieux's second work for Antoine, established him as a major new dramatist. It became one of the mainstays of the Théâtre-Libre, being given more than one hundred times in Paris and on tour, and Antoine chose it to open his Théâtre-Antoine season in 1897. In 1903 it entered the repertoire of the Comédie-Française, and although later works enjoyed an even greater French and international reputation, Brieux was still generally referred to as the author of *Blanchette.*

Blanchette treats a concern common in the French theater (found, for example, in Molière's *Le Bourgeois Gentilhomme* [The Would-Be Gentleman, 1670]) but particularly important in the rapidly shifting social conditions of the nineteenth century: the subject is the tension created by someone who moves outside of his expected social class, what the French call a déclassé. Brieux's play deals with a peasant girl whose education raises false hopes in her of an elegant upper-class Parisian life. In the version presented at the Théâtre-Libre, noted for its cynicism, Blanchette finally settles for a fine carriage and financial security as mistress of the elderly County Counselor, but at the urging of Sarcey and others, Brieux subsequently created a more positive ending in which Blanchette rejects this compromise and marries the son of the local blacksmith but keeps her faith in education for her children.

After the success of *Blanchette* Brieux gave up his editorship of the *Nouvelliste de Rouen* and returned to Paris to pursue a career as a dramatist. He maintained his connections with the world of journalism, however, contributing articles on literary and social subjects to the *Figaro,* the *Patrie,* and the *Gaulois* and serving from 1893 to 1899 as dramatic and musical critic of *La Vie contemporaine.* The success of *Blanchette* opened to Brieux the more prestigious Odéon, where his *M. de Réboval* was presented 20 September 1892. Again the sufferings of an idealistic daughter form the heart of the play, here the daughter of a manipulative senator who keeps a mistress in Paris. The successful social comedy of the first two acts was well received, but not the melodrama of the third, when the daughter falls in

André Antoine, who produced several of Brieux's plays at his Théâtre-Libre, an experimental theater in Paris

love with a heroic young man who turns out to be the son of her father's Parisian mistress. The play was not a great success, nor were the next several efforts by Brieux though the continuing popularity of *Blanchette* guaranteed him a hearing. *La Couvée* (The Brood, 1893), another comic study of parent-child relationships, focused on life in a provincial town and was appropriately premiered at a private club in Rouen. *L'Engrenage* (The System), a satire showing an honest man drawn into the corruptions of contemporary politics, premiered on 16 May 1894 at the Cercle des Escholiers, a minor rival of the Théâtre-Libre, and attracted sufficient attention to inspire a revival a few weeks later at a regular commercial stage, the Théâtre des Nouveautés, but its run there was short. Sarcey gave the work qualified praise but judged that Brieux's work to that date had proved that he was "born for the theater."

La Rose bleue (The Blue Rose, 1895), an amusing one-act play, is uncharacteristic of Brieux. It is a light anecdote about a young woman who puts on her worst manners for the visit of a relative from Paris so that she can stay with her father in the country. More typical was *Les Bienfaiteurs* (The Benefactors, 1896), a grimly amusing satire on contemporary organized charity and the idle volunteers (mostly women) who run it. The two directors of the Théâtre de l'Odéon disagreed about accepting the play, so Brieux took it to the Théâtre de la Porte Saint-Martin. But thesis and social dramas were not suited to the taste of the public of this popular theater, and it had only a short run in October 1896. Soon after, however, Brieux had his first play presented by the Comédie-Française, *L'Evasion* (translated as *The Escape*, 1913), on 7 December 1896. The play satirizes the virtual replacement of religion by science as a guiding life belief; it does so through the figure of Doctor Bertry, who functions rather like the classic obsessive fathers in Molière, interfering with the love and happiness of all about him by intruding his obsession, here a belief in the infallibility of science and the power of heredity to predict an individual's fate. Although the play is not well focused, it was well received, and in fact was honored by the Académie Française and awarded a prize as the best Comédie play of the year.

Brieux's career has been divided by several critics, among them Barrett H. Clark in a 1913 essay on Brieux in *The Drama,* into three periods, the first ending with *L'Evasion.* In the plays of this first period a sense of comedy, though it is often grimly ironic, as was true of much Théâtre-Libre writing, predominates over the militant seriousness that is implied by Brieux's social critiques. In the next period, which Clark and others call Brieux's Storm and Stress period, this lighter element gives way to much more unrelieved and often quite pessimistic attacks on contemporary social problems. All of these plays seem to call for reform, although not by showing the triumph of a better order, but rather by depicting in darkest tones the present evil. The first work of this period is also one of Brieux's best, *Les Trois Filles de M. Dupont* (translated as *The Three Daughters of M. Dupont,* 1911), and it enjoyed a strong run beginning on 8 October 1897 at the Théâtre du Gymnase, long associated with social drama. The central concern of the drama is negotiations over the dowry of M. Dupont's youngest daughter, Julie, but the two other daughters, Angèle, a courtesan in Paris, and Caroline, a bitter spinster, are also caught in the social web of financial speculation. The final bleak encounter of Brieux's three sisters somewhat suggests the conclusion of Anton Chekhov's *Three Sisters* (1901) but is distinctly darker and more hopeless.

The Gymnase followed this success with the presentation on 25 March 1898 of a much lighter one-act comedy by Brieux, *L'Ecole des belles-mères* (the School for Mothers-in-law), reworked from the final act of his earlier *La Couvée,* which had never been professionally produced. To gather authentic details for his next play, *Résultat des Courses* (The Result of the Races, 1898), which depicts a Parisian worker who destroys himself and his family by an addiction to gambling, Brieux disguised himself as a workman and spent some time in a Parisian bronze-working shop, then invited his fascinated fellow workers, to whom the theater was an alien world, to the premiere. The play premiered on 10 December 1898 at the Théâtre-Antoine with Antoine playing the leading role. It was his first Brieux premiere since *Blanchette,* with which Antoine had opened his new theater and which had now been given by him more than one hundred times in Paris and on tour.

Brieux's next play, *Le Berceau* (The Cradle), premiered only five days later, 15 December 1898, at the Comédie-Française and explored the popular subject of divorce. Brieux, who had poked fun at France's proposed new divorce law in his unproduced early comedy with Salandri, *Le Bureau des divorces,* returned to the subject with a much darker view now that the law had been in effect for more than a decade. As usual, Brieux champions the family and particularly the children, so often the victims of the errors made by their parents and their society. The pivot of the action is the highly emotional near-death of the unhappy child of a first marriage scorned by his righteous stepfather.

La Robe rouge (translated as *The Red Robe,* 1915), first staged at the Théâtre du Vaudeville on 15 March 1900 and revived at the Comédie-Française in 1909, is one of Brieux's best-known works, hailed as a masterpiece by critics of the time and honored by the Académie Française. In it Brieux moves from condemnation of a particular law, that of divorce, to a broader attack on the workings of the judicial system itself, the "red robe" being that traditionally worn by a French presiding judge. Brieux's harrowing drama tells how a provincial family in Southern France is destroyed by the passion of a prosecuting attorney who needs a murder conviction to gain a coveted promotion to the position of judge.

For his next two plays Brieux focused again on the family and on more-intimate and thus potentially more-shocking social concerns. Fittingly, he also returned to Antoine, still the Paris theater director most receptive to controversial work. *Les Remplaçantes* (The Substitutes), presented by Antoine on 15 February 1901 and regularly revived for several years after, dealt with the subject of wet nursing. A village peasant girl goes to Paris to become a wet nurse and, as a result, nearly loses her own child, who is seized by con-

Brieux's inscription in a presentation copy of La Française, *his comedy about misconceptions of France and French people (from Simone de la Souchère Deléry and Gladys Anne Renshaw, eds.,* La Française, *1927)*

vulsions in her absence. As usual in Brieux, the child is the central victim, but both the peasant girl and her Paris masters are shown as having been corrupted by this system. The play is one of Brieux's most didactic, featuring even a lengthy direct address to the audience about the evils of wet nursing by the author's spokesman, a country doctor named Richon.

Les Avariés (translated as *Damaged Goods,* 1911), dealing with the much more disturbing subject of syphilis, was rehearsed at the Théâtre-Antoine in the fall of 1901 but prohibited by the censor before it could be presented. Antoine arranged a private reading on 1 November 1901, just after the ban, for an audience composed largely of public officials and doctors, who praised the work but were unable to get the decision reversed. It was thus presented first in Belgium, in Liége and Brussels, in 1902. It became, however, one of the key dramas discussed in the parliamentary debates over dramatic censorship, at which Antoine and others testified and which resulted, not long after, in the ending of censorship. The way was thus finally cleared for a Paris premiere at the Antoine in February 1905. Before the performance Antoine made a brief speech in front of the curtain: "This play studies the subject of syphilis in its relationship with marriage. It contains nothing scandalous, not a single obscene word. Is it therefore necessary that women be foolish and ignorant in order to be virtuous?"

The play is built upon familiar Brieux characters and relationships. Against the advice of his doctor a man infected with syphilis marries and bears an infected child. The wet nurse, discovering the truth and fearing infection, informs the horrified mother. Thanks to an understanding and omniscient doctor, who, like Richon in *Les Remplaçantes,* loses no opportunity to lecture other characters and the audience, tragedy is averted and the marriage saved. The work is far from Brieux's best, but thanks to its notoriety it is one of his best known, and for many the author formerly associated with *Blanchette* now became better known for *Les Avariés.*

La Petite Amie (The Little Friend), which premiered at the Comédie-Française on 3 May 1902, returns to favorite themes of Brieux: unfeeling, socially ambitious parents and victimized children. The owner of a fashionable Parisian shop plans for a wealthy marriage for his son, who instead falls in love and runs off with a poor but honest girl in the shop. When she becomes pregnant and they cannot support themselves, they commit suicide. *Maternité* (translated as *Maternity,* 1911), the final play in Brieux's Storm and Stress period, was premiered at the Théâtre-Antoine on 9 December 1903 and was selected by Bernard Shaw as one of the three plays to introduce the author he called "the greatest French dramatist since Molière" to the English-speaking public. The other two works were

Les Avariés and *Les Trois Filles de M. Dupont.* Shaw's choices were clearly based more on the seriousness of the social questions discussed than upon the literary or dramatic quality of the work since *Maternité* is a scattered and unfocused play dealing with a failed abortion and the trial of the midwife who performs the abortion. Brieux recognizes the problem of undesired children and the importance of population control, but he is equally uneasy about the dymanics of abortion, and so the trial, and the play, ends in some confusion, not resolved even when Brieux produced a second version.

La Déserteuse (The Deserting Woman), presented at the Odéon on 15 October 1904 and written with Jean Sigaux, returns to the themes of *Le Berceau.* A mother, having deserted her husband and daughter, returns after many years to struggle with a devoted new wife for her daughter's affections. Brieux then undertook what was for him an unusual task in *L'Armature* (The Framework, 1905), adapting this novel by Paul Hervieu for the stage. The concerns of Hervieu's story, involving an unfaithful wife and the moral corruption of money-seeking, are familiar ones to Brieux and explain his attraction to this material; but the adaptation was not a popular one, and it had only a brief run at the Théâtre du Vaudeville in April 1905.

Les Hannetons (translated as *Morals and Men,* 1922?) was far more successful in February of the following year of 1906 at the Renaissance and enjoyed successful revivals in other countries, including England and the United States. It is unique among Brieux's works, a successful, well-constructed, low comedy bordering on farce. The domestic quarrels, the separation, and the eventual reuniting of the ill-matched, free-loving couple, Pierre and Charlotte, constitute the action; and although Charlotte plans suicide, nothing serious occurs, perhaps because there are no children, who always arouse Brieux's artistic sympathy.

On a Scandinavian trip in 1905 Brieux was struck by foreign misconceptions of the French, derived mostly from popular and often semi-pornographic novels. This experience inspired a spirited and amusing defense of his countrymen and women, *La Française,* which enjoyed a respectable run at the Odéon, now under the direction of Antoine, beginning on 18 April 1907. In it two Americans, Charles and his guardian, Bartlett, full of misconceptions about France, arrive to visit Charles's French father. Eventually they come to understand and admire their hosts; Charles finds a French wife, and Bartlett enters into a French partnership. After this brief excursion into comedy, Brieux returned to darker themes and to his continuing concern with children suffering from the marital mistakes of their parents. *Simone,* premiered at the Comédie-Française on 13 April 1908, begins in the

style of a murder mystery. Sergeac and his wife are discovered shot in their home. The wife is dead, but Sergeac recovers and eventually confesses to killing his wife for having committed adultery. Although French law excuses this crime, Simone, the daughter of the marriage, refuses to do so when she learns about the crime many years later. In the original version she rejects her devoted father, but audiences found this so grim a conclusion that Brieux reworked it and showed her forgiving her suppliant father on his knees.

In *Suzette,* which premiered at the Vaudeville on 28 September 1909, Brieux returned to one of his favorite themes, divorce and its effect upon the children of the marriage. Urged on by a disapproving mother-in-law, a husband seeks a divorce, and the daughter, the title character of the play, becomes the pawn in a protracted and bitter legal battle for custody. Finally, rather than see her suffer further, the mother resolves to give her up, a sacrifice that moves her husband to a reconciliation.

Brieux's national and international fame was by now well assured. He had become a major literary figure, connected with the Department of Public Instruction, a chevalier of the Legion of Honor, and recipient of many awards. His literary career was crowned in 1910 by his acceptance into the Académie Française. Three years later he was offered the directorship of the Comédie-Française, but he refused, being more interested in working on his own plays than in producing those of others.

Foreign travel again inspired Brieux's next play, *La Foi* (1909; translated as *False Gods,* 1916). His extensive travels at this time took him to India, Egypt, and Japan, and the visit to Egypt crystallized a long-standing interest in writing a play dealing with religious belief. This drama, set in ancient Egypt, tells of a young idealist in the Middle Kingdom who attempts to free his countrymen from their superstitious belief in miracles only to realize that in undermining their spiritual faith he has undermined their happiness and hope as well. In *La Femme seule* (translated as *Woman on Her Own,* 1916) in 1912 Brieux returned to the themes of money and marriage, depicting a heroine whose dowry is embezzled and who is forced to enter the competitive workplace and endure masculine discrimination and harassment in her attempt to gain some control over her own destiny. *Le Bourgeois aux champs* (The Bourgeois in the Country, 1914) shows the foolish Cocatrix, a socialist lawyer with echoes of a Molière character, who goes to the country full of book knowledge about farming and social justice; he is regularly duped and taken advantage of by the peasants there and almost ruins his daughter's happiness in the process.

After the outbreak of World War I, Brieux put aside his dramatic writing to devote himself full-time to the reeducation and rehabilitation of French soldiers blinded in the war. The former "author of *Blanchette* and *Les Avariés*" now became better and more affectionately known throughout France as "the father of the blind."

He continued to write occasional pieces for the *Figaro,* the *Gaulois,* and the *Illustration.* In his later years he spent his summers in Paris and his winters in Nice, where he died on 6 December 1932.

Although Shaw considered Brieux the greatest writer of his generation, his reputation has steadily declined since his death. His plays are no longer produced, even in France, and he is now primarily remembered as the most successful French writer of dramas of social commentary in the early years of this century.

Bibliographies:

E. Woodruff, "Reading List on Eugène Brieux," *Bulletin of Bibliography,* 8 (1914): 5–6;

Edmund F. Sana Vicca, *Four French Dramatists* (Metuchen, N.J.: Scarecrow Press, 1974).

Biographies:

Adrien Bertrand, *Eugène Brieux, biographie critique* (Paris: Sansot, 1910);

A. Presas, *Brieux; portrait psychologique* (Paris, 1930);

Malcolm Porter Byrnes, *Eugène Brieux: humanitaire et patriote méconnu* (London: Editor Continental, 1967).

References:

P. D. de Bâcourt and J. Cunliffe, eds., *French Literature during the Last Half Century* (New York: Macmillan, 1927);

G. P. Baker, "The Plays of Eugène Brieux, *Atlantic Monthly,* 90 (July 1902): 79–86;

Antoine Benoist, *Le Théâtre de Brieux* (Toulouse: Privat, 1907);

Barrett Clark, "The New Brieux," *Drama,* 11 (1913): 138–144;

W. L. Courtney, "Eugène Brieux, moralist," *Fortnightly Review* (1918): 561–575;

Claire DePratz, "Brieux and His Works," *Contemporary Review,* 81 (March 1902): 33–57;

Maurice Donnay, "Eugène Brieux," *Revue de France,* I (1936): 167–174;

René Doumic, "Eugène Brieux et François de Curel," *Revue des Deux Mondes,* 9 (June 1902): 922–934;

F. Falgos, "Les Moeurs judiciaires, à propos de la Robe rouge d'Eugène Brieux," *Revue Philatomique de Bordeaux,* 4 (1934): 145–169;

William Dean Howells, "Plays of Eugène Brieux," *North American Review,* 201 (March 1915): 402–411;

Laurence Irving, "Eugène Brieux," *Forum,* 43 (June 1910): 628–632;

Jean Jullien, "Brieux," *Revue d'Art Dramatique,* 1 (1897): 309–315;

Armand Kahn, *Le Théâtre social en France* (Lousanne: Fatio, 1907);

W. Küchler, "Eugène Brieux," *Germanisch-Romanische Monatsschrift,* volume 2 [Heidelberg] (1910): 483–504;

Léopold Lacour, "Le Théâtre de Brieux," *Revue de Paris,* 1 (1 January 1904): 209–224;

John F. MacDonald, "French Life and the French Stage," *Fortnightly Review,* 77 (1905): 327–340;

Amy Millstone, "French Feminist Theater and the Subject of Prostitution, 1870–1914," in *The Image of the Prostitute in Modern Literature,* edited by Pierre Horn and Mary Beth Pringle (New York: Ungar, 1984);

Guenter Moeller, *Henry Becque und Eugène Brieux. Das naturalische und das Thesendrama* (Breslau, 1937);

Claire de Pratz, "M. Brieux and His Works," *Contemporary Review,* 81 (March 1902): 33–57;

Albert Prieur, "La Science au théâtre," *Mercure de France,* 40 (December 1901): 653–676;

A. and M. R., *Les glorieux mutilés de la France. Le drame social et la guerre et Eugène Brieux* (Paris: Meynial, 1916);

Revue des Visages, special issue on Eugène Brieux (July 1929);

William H. Scheifley, *Brieux and Contemporary French Society* (New York: Putnam, 1917);

Temple Scott, "Brieux," *Forum,* 47 (April 1912): 403–418;

K. E. Shedd, "Florencia Sànchez's Debt to Eugène Brieux," *Studies in Philology,* 33 (July 1936): 417–426;

Albert-Emile Sorel, "M. Eugène Brieux," *Grande Revue,* 29 (15 February 1904): 277–289;

Eric M. Steel, "The French Writer Looks at America," *Antioch Review,* 4 (Fall 1944): 414–431;

P. V. Stock, "Brieux anecdotique," *Mercure de France,* 293 (1939): 306–350;

P. Vaughan Thomas, *The Plays of Eugène Brieux* (Boston: Luce, 1915);

Jon Van Eerde, "Brieux's Realism," *College Language Association Journal,* 2 (December 1958): 111–127;

A. B. Walkley, "Drama with a Mission," *Forum,* 66 (December 1921): 489–495;

Cora Westland, *Eugène Brieux* (The Hague: Weldt, 1915).

Marie-Joseph Chénier

(28 August 1764 – 10 January 1811)

Marvin Carlson
The Graduate School and University Center, The City University of New York

PLAY PRODUCTIONS: *Edgar ou le Page supposé,* Paris, Comédie-Française, 14 November 1785;

Azémire, Fontainebleau, 4 November 1786;

Charles IX, Paris, Comédie-Française, 4 November 1789;

Henri VIII, Paris, Théâtre-Français rue de Richelieu, 27 April 1791;

Jean Calas, ou l'Ecole des juges, Paris, Théâtre-Français rue de Richelieu, 6 July 1791;

Caïus Gracchus, Paris, Théâtre-Français rue de Richelieu, 9 February 1792;

Le Camp de Grand-Pré ou Le Triomphe de la République, Paris, Théâtre National de l'Opéra, 27 January 1793;

Fénélon, Paris, République, 9 February 1793;

Timoléon, music by Etienne-Nicolas Méhul, Paris, République, 11 September 1795;

Cyrus, Paris, Comédie-Française, 8 December 1804;

Tibère, Paris, Théâtre-Français, 15 December 1843.

BOOKS: *Azémire* (Paris: Moutard, 1787);

La Mort du duc de Brunswick (Paris: Monsieur, 1787);

Poëme sur l'Assemblée des notables (N.p., 1787);

Epître à mon père (Paris, 1787);

Dialogue du public et de l'anonyme (Paris: Bagnol, 1788);

Dénonciation des inquisiteurs de la pensée (Paris: Lagrange, 1789);

Dithyrambe sur l'Assemblée nationale (Paris: Du Croisi, 1789);

Courtes réflexions sur l'état civil des Comédie Françaisens (Paris: Monsieur, 1789);

Epître au roi (Paris: Monsieur, 1789);

Lettre aux auteurs du "Journal de Paris" (N.p., [1789]);

De la liberté du théâtre en France (N.p., 1789);

Idées pour un cahier du tiers-état de la ville de Paris (N.p., 1789);

Discours de M. de Chénier, auteur de la tragédie de Charles IX, à l'assemblée genérale des représentants de la Commune de Paris (Paris: Hérissant, 1789);

Charles IX, ou l'Ecole des rois (Paris: Bossange, 1790);

Discours pour la rentrée du théâtre de la Nation, en 1790 (N.p.: 1790?);

Portrait of Marie-Joseph Chénier, above a scene from Charles IX, *his 1789 play criticizing the French monarchy*

Rapport de Chénier sur l'Opéra (Paris: P.F. Didot, 1790);

Hymne pour la fête de la Fédération, le 14 juillet 1790 (Paris: Bossange, 1790);

Défense des Comédie Françaisens français, contre les auteurs dramatiques (Paris: Laillet et Garnéry, 1790?);

Lettre de M. de Chénier aux auteurs de la "Chronique de Paris" (N.p., 1790);

Lettre du club des Capucins . . . 1790 (N.p.: 1790?)

Lettre à M. le comte de Mirabeau (N.p.: 1790?);

Ode sur la mort de Mirabeau (Paris: P. F. Didot, 1791);

Hymne à l'Etre suprême (Paris: Galletti, n.d.);

Adresse de la ville de Paris à l'Assemblée nationale pour demander la déchéance du roi (Paris: Imprimerie nationale, 1792?);

Strophes qui seront chantées au Champ de la Fédération, le 14 juillet 1792, music by François-Joseph Gossec (N.p.: Imprimerie de la municipalité, 1792?);

L'Hymne du 10 août, music by Charles-Simon Catel, (Paris: Magasin de musique, 1792?);

Eloge funèbre des citoyens morts pour la défense de la liberté et de l'égalité, le 10 août 1792 (Paris: Imprimerie nationale, n.d.);

Pétition à l'Assemblée nationale, du 24 août 1792 (Paris: Imprimerie nationale, n.d.);

Brutus et Cassius, ou les derniers Romains (N.p.: n.d.);

Jean Calas (Paris: Moutard, 1793);

Henri VIII (Paris: Moutard, 1793);

Le Triomphe de la République, ou le Camp de Grand-Pré, music by Gossec (Paris: Baudouin, 1793);

Caïus Gracchus (Paris: Moutard, 1793);

Fénélon, ou les Religieuses de Cambrai (Paris: Moutard, 1793);

Timoléon, music by Méhul (Paris: Moutard, 1793);

Hymne sur la translation du corps de Voltaire (Paris: Bossange, 1794);

Hymne à la Liberté (Paris: Rue Saint-Fiacre, 1794);

Office des décades (Paris: Dufart, 1794);

Strophes, sur l'air de l'Hymne des Marseillais (Paris: Imprimerie nationale, 1794?);

Le Chant du départ (Paris: Imprimerie nationale, 26 messidor, 1794);

Ode à la calomnie (Paris: Langlois, 1794);

Convention nationale. Rapport sur la fête des Victoires . . . le 27 vendémiaire l'an III (Paris: Imprimerie nationale, 1795);

Rapport et décrets sur le prompt jugement des émigrés . . . (Paris: Imprimerie de la République, 1795);

13 fructidor l'an IV (Paris: Imprimerie nationale, 1796);

Discours de Marie-Joseph Chénier sur la presse. Séance du 27 ventôse an IV (Paris: Imprimerie nationale, 1796);

Rapport fait par Marie-Joseph Chénier sur la translation des cendres de René Descartes au Panthéon. Séance du 18 floréal an IV (Paris: Imprimerie nationale, 1796);

Rapport fait par Marie-Joseph Chénier sur les fêtes du 14 juillet et du 10 août. Séance du 8 thermidor (Paris: Imprimerie nationale, thermidor, 1796);

Discours prononcé par Marie-Joseph Chénier, président du Conseil des Cinq-Cents. Séance du 26 messidor (Paris: Imprimerie nationale, 1797);

Discours prononcé par M.-J. Chénier . . . à la cérémonie funèbre célébré au Champ de Mars (Paris: Laran, 1797);

Epître sur la calomnie (Paris: Didot, 1797);

Le Docteur Pancrace (Paris: Laran, 1797);

Message du Directoire exécutif relatif aux victoires de l'armée française en Suisse (Paris: 1797);

Motion d'order faite par Chénier (sur les ci-devant nobles et anoblis). Séance du 29 vebdémiaire an VI (Paris: Imprimerie nationale, 1797);

Motion d'ordre par Chénier sur les théâtres. Séance du 26 brumaire an VI (Paris: Imprimerie nationale, 1797);

Opinion de Marie-Joseph Chénier sur la loi d'amnistie. Séance du 13 fructidor l'an IV (Paris: Imprimerie nationale, 1797);

Poésies lyriques (Paris: P. Didot, 1797);

Opinion de Marie-Joseph Chénier sur la liberté de la presse. Séance du 27 prairial an VII (Paris: Imprimerie nationale, 1798);

Discours sur les progrès des connaissances en Europe et de Le Vieillard d'Ancenis (Paris: Laran, 1798);

Fête de la fondation de la République. Programme (Paris: République, fructidor, 1798);

Pie VI et Louis XVIII (Paris: Laran, 1798);

L'enseignement public en France (Paris: Didot jeune, 1800);

Les Nouveaux saints (Paris: Dabin, 1801);

Amende honorable d'An . . . à Saint-Roch (Paris: Dabin, 1802);

Discours en vers sur les poëmes descriptifs (Paris: Dabin, 1805);

Epître à Eugénie (N.p.: 1805?);

Epître d'un journaliste à l'Ampereur (Paris: Rue de la Harpe, 1805?);

Discours prononcé à l'Athénée de Paris, le 15 décembre 1806 (Paris: Dabin, 1806);

Epître à Voltaire (Paris: Dabin, 1806);

La Retraite (Paris: Dabin, 1806);

Epître aux mânes de Voltaire (N.p.: 1806?);

Discours de M. Chénier . . . prononcé aux funérailles de M. Le Brun (Paris: Dabin, 1807);

Discours adressé à Sa Majesté impériale en son Conseil d'Etat (Paris: Dabin, 1808);

Hommage à une belle action (Paris: Dabin, 1809);

Rapport historique sur l'état et les progrès de la littérature depuis 1789 (Paris: Imprimerie royale, 1815);

La Promenade à Auteuil (Paris: Delaunay, 1817);

Tibère (Paris: Ponthieu, 1819);

Chant de victoire (Paris: Rouanet, 1833);

Nous sommes citoyens, music by Méhul (Paris: Mie, 1833);

Le Chant du départ (Noyon: Cottu-Marlay, 1848).

Collections: *Théâtre de M.-J. Chénier,* 2 volumes (Paris: P. Didot, 1797);

Oeuvres diverses et inédites de M.-J. Chénier (Brussels: Weissenbruch, 1816);

Théâtre de M.-J. de Chénier with *Théâtre posthume*, 3 volumes (Paris: Foulon, 1818);

Poésies diverses de Marie-Joseph de Chénier (Paris: Maradan, 1818);

Oeuvres de M.-J. Chénier, 8 volumes (Paris: Guillaume, 1823–1827).

TRANSLATIONS: Thomas Gray, *Le Cimetière de campagne, élégie anglaise* (Paris, 1805);

Horace, *L'Art poétique* (Paris, 1818).

The name Chénier for most contemporary readers evokes the young poet, André Chénier, whose brilliant career, like that of so many others, ended tragically by the guillotine. At the time of the French Revolution, however, and during the early nineteenth century, André was much less well known and less celebrated than his younger brother, Marie-Joseph Chénier, the foremost revolutionary poet and playwright, a champion of freedom of the stage, a central figure in the organization of the great revolutionary festivals, a vigorous political pamphleteer, and an active and influential member of the National Convention. No playwright is more closely associated with the stage during the French Revolution than Marie-Joseph Chénier, particularly with his best-known play, *Charles IX,* first produced in 1789.

Marie-Joseph Chénier was born on 28 August 1764 in Constantinople. His father was the diplomat and historian, Louis de Chénier, author of several books on Morocco and Turkey, where he served in the post of French representative. At an early age Marie-Joseph and his elder brother, also born in Constantinople, were sent to live with an aunt and begin their schooling at the family home in Montfort, Languedoc. At seventeen Marie-Joseph entered a military school; despite an undistinguished school record, he dreamed of becoming a playwright, studied literature during his first garrison assignment, and two years later resigned the service to join his parents, who had returned to Paris. There his mother, a striking and highly intelligent Greek woman named Santi-l'Homaka, had established one of the capital's most brilliant salons, frequented by the painter Jacques-Louis David, the chemist Antoine-Laurent Lavoisier, and leading literary figures such as Ponce-Denis Ecouchard Lebrun, Vittorio Alfieri, and Charles Palissot de Montenoy, who became the young Chénier's patron.

In this stimulating Parisian environment Chénier began writing plays, much under the influence of Voltaire, whose works were the dominant model for young dramatists of this era. Four such works were soon completed: *Edgar ou le Page supposé* (Edgar or the Presumed Page), *Oedipe mourant* (Oedipus Dying), *Brutus et Cassius, ou les derniers Romains,* and *Azémire.* The first of these was a two-act comedy in verse dealing with a totally fictitious tenth-century love affair between a disguised king of England and a commoner. Sponsored by Palissot, it was accepted at the Comédie-Française and presented in 1785; it was a complete failure, hissed from its opening moments. Undeterred, Chénier won support for another attempt from the duchesse d'Orléans. She arranged for a presentation of the much more ambitious *Azémire* before the court at Fontainebleau in November 1786. This Voltairean tragedy concerning a Muslim queen who falls in love with a crusader who is her prisoner was also a failure. Ordinarily, the presence of the king at a play prevented much outward show of disapproval, but so overwhelming was the rejection of Chénier's piece that it was hissed throughout. A few days later the play was attempted again at the Comédie-Française. The actors used a subterfuge employed from time to time with a new play about which they had some misgivings, announcing a familiar piece (here Voltaire's distinctly similar *Zaïre* [1732]) and then announcing a last-minute substitution due to "illness." Nevertheless, the play was again roundly rejected, and the playwright, though not defeated, thought it best to withdraw from the public eye for a time. He spent the next three years studying his craft and working on a new play that would in fact establish his reputation, *Charles IX* (1789).

Royalist enemies of Chénier later claimed that his republicanism grew out of his anger at the court for rejecting *Azémire,* while his supporters claimed that his championship of the new order came from objective conviction. Whatever the motivation, Chénier at this time dropped his aristocratic coat of arms, ceased signing himself as the aristocratic "chevalier de Chénier" (knight of Chénier), and in a pamphlet, *De la liberté du théâtre en France* (On the Liberty of the Theater in France), dated 15 July 1789, claimed that the "sole glory" to which he aspired was to be the first to write "a truly national tragedy." Chénier's *Charles IX, ou l'Ecole des rois* (Charles IX, or the School for Kings, 1790), written in this spirit, dealt with the Saint Bartholomew's Day Massacre of the French Protestant Huguenots in 1572. This subject had been treated in a variety of previous works by Voltaire and others, but while the *philosophes* had seen in this event primarily an example of religious fanaticism, Chénier saw it also as a failure of royal authority, holding Charles IX and Catherine de Medici as much responsible for the massacre as the cardinal of Lorraine. In addition to the popular patriotic sentiments with which the play was liberally sprinkled, two scenes in particular were lauded for their dramatic power: one at the end of the fourth act just before the massacre, when the cardinal blesses the swords of the soldiers while the bell heralding the coming carnage sounds in the background; and one in the final act where the weak and impressionable young king, played by François-Joseph Talma in one of his first leading roles, suffers a vision of his bloody victims appearing before him. At a period when the writings of William Shakespeare, in the neoclassic adaptations of Jean-François Ducis, were first gaining a significant French following, several reviewers remarked on the Shakespearean quality of these two scenes.

Despite its revolutionary tone, the play was read and accepted by the Comédie-Française actors. While awaiting clearance from the public authorities, Chénier sought to build support for the play, as Pierre-Augustin Caron de Beaumarchais had done with his politically charged *Le Mariage de Figaro* (1784) by arranging readings at aristocratic gatherings. Palissot organized one before the duke and duchess of Orleans in January 1789, but Chénier's work was found boring by many and offensive by others; no groundswell of support developed. Chénier then made the fateful decision of turning for support to the newly emerging revolutionary political forces, Georges-Jacques Danton, Fabre d'Eglantine, Camille Desmoulins, Collot-d'Herbois, and others, who interrupted a Comédie-Française performance on 19 August 1789 to demand that Chénier's work be presented, with or without the approval of the censor. This was the first time since the revolution began that a political faction demanded the performance of a play, and it thus initiated an era of politically oriented drama, with Chénier at its center.

Despite the resistance of the monarchist mayor of Paris, Jean-Baptiste-Antoine Suard, the royal censor, and conservative members of the Comédie-Française itself, the revolutionists forced the performance of Chénier's play and hailed him as the new national poet. Danton observed, "If *Figaro* destroyed the aristocracy, *Charles IX* will destroy the monarchy." Chénier became the subject of merciless attacks by the conservatives and of adulation by the revolutionists, but his play had an exceptional run and its publication a prodigious sale. Chénier added to his political reputation by beginning to publish highly popular patriotic songs and pamphlets. He was also a central figure in drawing up the legislation of 13 January 1791 that provided protection for authors and abolished many of the privileges of the national stages, including, most important, exclusive rights to certain genres and to the classic repertoire.

This new legislation allowed the Comédie-Française company, split by the revolution into liberal and conservative camps, to split in fact since the dissident liberals, led by Talma, were able to establish a rival theater of their own (the Théâtre Français rue de Richelieu, later called the République) without giving up the repertoire they had played at the older house, including Chénier's *Charles IX*. They also premiered Chénier's next tragedy, *Henri VIII* (1791), based on events leading to the death of Anne Boleyn and portraying her as a victim of court intrigue and royal despotism. Allusions to deceitful and manipulative courtiers fill the play, but Henri himself is no better, insisting that the most important consideration is that his authority be respected, whether this is achieved by duplicity, force, or terror. Anne Boleyn undergoes his tyranny expressing more concern for her suffering fellow subjects than defiance, but others, particularly the outspoken Norris, confront Henri directly, predicting a happier age when abusive power will be replaced by freedom and equality. The play's opening performances were stormy since Chénier's supporters and foes were both well represented in the audience, but even though it lacked the theatrical power of *Charles IX*, *Henri VIII* enjoyed a respectable run.

Chénier returned to the manner and interests of Voltaire with *Jean Calas ou l'Ecole des juges* (Jean Calas or the School for Judges, 1791), the subtitle of which suggests its author's intention to offer another attack on entrenched abuses in the manner of *Charles IX*; but though Chénier's supporters remained enthusiastic, the play was presented only four times. Its relative failure was not surprising. The text was much weaker than the texts of its two predecessors, and its political allusions were less obvious. Several other Calas plays had been presented in late 1790 and early 1791, and, perhaps most important, judicial reforms since the beginning of the revolution and the declaration of the Rights of Man had removed most of the sources for the kind of abuse Chénier's play considered. In terms of Chénier's development as a dramatist, however, the play demonstrated an interest in exploring the domain of the *drame,* or middle-class tragedy, and thus anticipated the main line of development of serious drama in the following century. He returned to this approach with more success in his subsequent *Fénélon* (1793).

Despite the disappointment of *Jean Calas,* Chénier enjoyed other consolations. Beginning with the celebration marking the transfer of Vol-

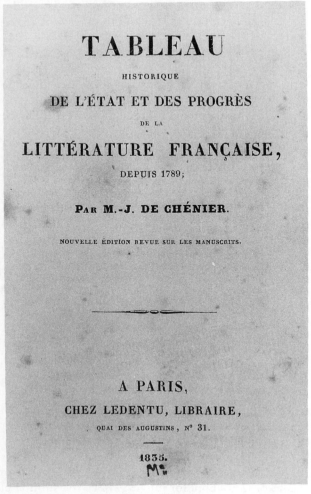

TABLEAU

HISTORIQUE

DE L'ÉTAT ET DES PROGRÈS

DE LA

LITTÉRATURE FRANÇAISE,

DEPUIS 1789;

PAR M.-J. DE CHÉNIER.

NOUVELLE ÉDITION REVUE SUR LES MANUSCRITS.

A PARIS,

CHEZ LEDENTU, LIBRAIRE,

QUAI DES AUGUSTINS, N° 31.

1855.

Title page for Chénier's history of French literature since the French Revolution

helped to subsidize the aristocratic faction. The play, Chénier's most radical work, pitted the plebian Gracchi, who demanded the distribution of the national goods to all, against the patrician senators, who wished to keep the spoils of their military conquests for the enrichment of their own class. The inflammatory rhetoric of the drama, its condemnation of tyranny and calls for revolt against tyranny and class privilege delighted Chénier's revolutionary supporters, and even though the call for the distribution of goods by the character in Chènier's play specifically involved only conquered land and not the property of any Roman citizens, a correlation to the new laws concerning the property of emigrants was obvious to all. Even so, a moderate note was struck on the subject of revolt, and when Chénier's heroes called for "Des lois, et non du sang" (Laws and not blood) or observed that "liberty does not mean license," they were enthusiastically applauded by conservatives as well. As a result the play, despite its strongly political tone, was generally well received by a wider audience than any other of Chénier's dramas.

Chénier still remained the literary figure most associated with the revolutionary cause, and within a few weeks after the opening of *Caïus Gracchus* a play by Pierre Léger was presented at the royalist Théâtre de la Vaudeville; it was called *L'Auteur d'un moment* (The Author of the Moment, 1792) and created much delight among its conservative audiences by poking fun at Chénier's vanity, his dramas, and his claims to be the national playwright. This naturally aroused patriotic protest and soon led to legislation from the Committee of Public Instruction banning "unpatriotic" works for their tendency to stimulate violence and disorder. Thus stage censorship was reestablished in France only thirteen months after its abolition. Léger's satire was one of the last attempts by the royalists to express their opinions openly on the stages of Paris.

Less than a month after these events, in March 1792, conservatives and revolutionaries clashed even more openly in Paris over patriot plans for honoring some recently released Swiss soldiers, imprisoned for revolting against abusive superior officers two years before in Metz. David, Chénier, and other revolutionary leaders submitted the petition, which was stoutly opposed by Chénier's brother, André, who called the Swiss rebels, murderers, and public enemies. The Fête de la Liberté (Feast of Liberty) nevertheless took place on 15 April with the usual triumvirate of David, Gossec, and Marie-Joseph Chénier as organizers. Chénier's patriotic lyrics for this occasion were among his most popular and were repeated in many later celebrations.

taire's remains to the Pantheon on 12 July 1791, Chénier regularly collaborated with the painter David and the musician François-Joseph Gossec as a triumvirate responsible for the organization of the great civic festivals of the revolution. His *Charles IX* and *Henri VIII* were performed so regularly at the revolutionary Théâtre-Français rue de Richelieu that the newspaper *Le Consolateur* began referring to it as the "Théâtre-Chénier." Here Chénier's next play, *Caïus Gracchus,* premiered on 9 February 1792. The occasion was highly charged. Two days before, Austria and Prussia had joined forces against France, and the day of the premiere a decree was passed confiscating the property of the aristocrats who had fled the country. Both revolutionary and conservative forces looked upon Chénier's new play as an occasion to test their power, and representatives of rival factions dominated the audience. The queen herself was reported to have

André published on the day of the ceremony a sarcastic "Hymn on the Triumphal Entry of the Chateauvieux Swiss," mockingly lauding the butchery and theft of the Swiss soldiers.

The Chateauvieux celebration exposed a long-simmering feud between the Chénier brothers, who in the later months were generally recognized as the poetic spokesmen for the bitterly opposed Feuillants, who generally favored a constitutional monarchy somewhat on the British model, and the Jacobins, who wished to eliminate royalist and aristocratic influence altogether. During the spring of 1792 the brothers exchanged emotional attacks on and defenses of the Jacobin Party in pamphlets and in the pages of the most widely read paper of the period, the *Moniteur*. Several more-popular patriotic songs were created by Marie-Joseph in the summer, but he also became much more directly active in the political process itself. He was appointed the representative of his Parisian district, Poissonnière, and when forty-seven out of the forty-eight districts voted in July to declare the throne vacant, Marie-Joseph was appointed to draw up a petition to this effect to be presented to the Legislative Assembly, the *Adresse de la ville de Paris . . . pour demander la déchéance du roi* (Address of the City of Paris . . . To Demand the Dethroning of the King, 1792). This petition, widely distributed by the Jacobins, served as a model for many others.

Under the pressure of these petitions the National Assembly set aside a week for deliberating the future of the monarchy, but when that week passed without a decision, the revolutionary forces in Paris arose in revolt on the night of 9 August. Once again the divided Chénier brothers reflected the surrounding civil strife, André participating in the ultimately unsuccessful attempt to defend the royal family in the Tuilleries and Marie-Joseph leading rebellious patriot forces in the populist Faubourg Saint-Antoine. On the day following the uprising Marie-Joseph was elected president of the Bibliothèque district of Paris, but the more extreme revolutionaries now coming to power, such as Jean-Paul Marat, continued to suspect him of less than total dedication to the revolution. Nevertheless, Chénier continued to function as the unofficial poet laureate of the revolution, delivering the principal oration at the official funeral ceremony held by the Paris Commune on 26 August to honor the "victims of despotism" killed defending the revolutionary cause on 10 August. The Legislative Assembly printed this speech and distributed it throughout France and to the armies.

When the National Convention was formed in September as France's new governing body, Chénier sought election as a Paris representative. With the increasingly radical orientation of the city he received few votes, but his national reputation as a champion of the revolution still served him, and he was appointed a departmental deputy from Seine-et-Oise. Despite the suspicions of Marat and others in the radical Montagnard Party, Chénier was never a consistent supporter of their more-moderate rivals, the Girondists; but Chénier was unquestionably disturbed by the increasingly violent turn the revolution was taking, especially after the September Massacres, when fear of internal subversion led to the breaking open of the jails and the murder of politically suspect prisoners.

In December 1792 Chénier published an appeal calling for the king to be heard before the National Convention, but the appeal essentially assumed Louis XVI's guilt, and, indeed, when the vote was finally taken on the fate of the king, Chénier voted with the majority for immediate execution, although with a statement expressing his regret for this "painful duty." Only three days after this momentous vote Chénier was drawn back into the more familiar and surely more comfortable role of orchestrating a major festival. One of the deputies who had voted for the king's execution was Michel Le Pelletier de Saint-Fargeau, a former nobleman with great wealth who had enthusiastically embraced the revolutionary cause, held high offices in the assembly and the convention, and gained the hatred of other aristocrats who saw him as a traitor to his class. His vote on the king's death sealed his fate, and he was assassinated by a guardsman at a restaurant in the Palais-Royal. Almost immediately, Chénier presented a report to the convention in the names of the Committees of Inspectors and Public Instruction calling for Le Pelletier to be given a state funeral and to be entombed in the Pantheon as the "first martyr of the Republic." The report was adopted, and Chénier himself naturally supervised the funeral celebration, with his usual collaborators David and Gossec. The celebration had many of the characteristics of state funerals of the past, but with statues of Liberty and banners of the Bill of Rights replacing the trappings of Catholicism. In an apparent attempt to reach out to his own political adversaries Chénier ended the report by asking his countrymen to bury along with Le Pelletier "the deadly partisanship that divides us." The convention considered Chénier's ceremony so stimulating to the revolutionary spirit that copies were distributed throughout France, and many towns and departments presented the service as a civic celebration, even in the absence of any Le Pelletier to entomb.

In January 1793 a new dramatic work by Chénier premiered, *Le Camp de Grand-Pré ou Le Triomphe de la République* (The Camp of the Grand-Pré, or The Triumph of the Republic), an operatic spectacle with music by Gossec. This was Chénier's first attempt at an opera and his first production at the Théâtre National de l'Opéra, a former stronghold of aristocratic sympathy that was oriented under the new order toward republican celebration. The work included new songs as well as hymns Chénier had created the previous year for the Festivals of Liberty and the Federation. Recent victories in the Low Countries and a declaration of war against England made this military celebration of French recruits departing for the front and returning in victory both topical and attractive. At the conclusion the Goddess of Liberty descended from Heaven to make France her abode, but the commanding general promised that France should not enjoy her reign alone, but that her soldiers would in time free all peoples of the globe, beginning with Savoy, Brabant, Belgium, Rome, and Vienna.

Chénier had been working on a major new play, *Fénélon,* since the completion of *Caïus Gracchus,* but his intense involvement in civic celebrations and politics had delayed its completion. Even as he was involved in the preparations for its opening on 9 February 1793, he took time to seek help in the convention on behalf of a suffering fellow playwright, Carlo Goldoni. Goldoni had come to Paris in 1762 to write for the Comédie Française Italienne and had retired with a royal pension that was terminated by the revolution. When Chénier heard of the penury of the Italian dramatist and his wife, he successfully petitioned the convention to restore the pension.

In the early years of the revolution "convent plays" were a highly popular genre in Paris, catering to anticlerical feelings via melodramatic depictions of young women incarcerated against their will in these establishments. Although the Catholic Church remained among the feared enemies of the revolution, the abolition of all religious orders and the closing of convents and monasteries in February 1790 removed this particular concern and essentially ended the brief vogue of such drama. Chénier's play was thus rather an anomaly, recalling topical pieces of several years before. The subject is a typical one and is based on an anecdote involving another cleric with no actual relationship to the historic Fénélon, a cleric who used his authority to free a suffering novice who had been shut away in a miserable prison by her superior for becoming pregnant. To increase the emotional impact and expand the work to five acts, Chénier gives to the suffering Héloïse, his imprisoned heroine, a daughter, Amélie, who has been terrorized into making forced vows that have entrapped her, too, in a convent.

The somewhat dated subject of the play proved an advantage since it aroused less partisan feelings than a more contemporary subject would have, and most spectators agreed that Chénier's language and treatment of this familiar subject was far superior to that of his predecessors. Like *Jean Calas,* the play dealt with middle-class characters even though Chénier insisted that it still merited the designation of tragedy. His "Discours préliminaire" (Preliminary Discourse) to the published version of *Fénélon ou les Religieuses, de Cambrai* (1793) puts him squarely among those champions of bourgeois tragedy that include George Lillo in England, Louis-Sebastien Mercier and Mme Anne-Louise-Germaine de Stael in France, Gotthold Ephraim Lessing in Germany, and more recently Arthur Miller, and his arguments closely resemble theirs:

> I believe that it would be ridiculous to respond seriously to those who assert that tragedies can only be based on the adventures of kings, princes, conquerers, or heads of states. It seems to me unquestionable that the nature of dramatic poems, of whatever genre, is quite independent of the rank that their characters hold on the world stage. When the tone is pathetic, simple, and majestic, when the characters act in a dignified manner, when the aim of the author is clearly to stimulate tears, the work is a tragedy.

In addition to developing the concept of a non-aristocratic tragedy Chénier was at least equally concerned with writing a play that would champion sympathy, tolerance, and humanity (all qualities represented to Chénier by such enlightenment heroes as Voltaire, and, indeed, Fénélon) in opposition to the extremism represented by figures such as Marat and events such as the September Massacres. Indeed, the "Discours préliminaire" specifically claims that the play was written to bring back to the drama a "voice of humanity" lost "in these dark and stormy days when evil citizens openly preach pillage and murder" and when "true Republicans" mourn the public morality "sullied by the September crimes." At a time when Montagnard deputies were denouncing *Caïus Gracchus* for preaching moderation in such lines as the now-renowned "Des lois, et non du sang" (Laws and not blood), Chénier accepted their challenge by publishing the play with that line as an epigraph.

By such actions, and by proposing legislation that would penalize "incitement to murder or violation of property rights" by any faction, liberal or conservative, Chénier increasingly antagonized the

Montagnards, who were steadily growing in power. Regarded by them as a moderate and as a sympathizer with the now-proscribed Girondists, Chénier saw his political influence rapidly slip away. After the publication of *Henri VIII* and *Jean Calas* in June 1793, he stopped working with the Committee of Public Instruction and did not again speak in the National Assembly until October. Chénier's political fortunes were clearly waning during the summer of 1793. He had been appointed in February by the Committee of Public Instruction to prepare a report on the current status of literary and artistic property rights, a subject dear to his heart and with which he had been closely associated since the beginning of the revolution, but during the summer he was replaced as spokesman for this study by Lakanal, a Montagnard delegate. Surely an even greater blow to Chénier's pride was his replacement that summer as one of the planners for the Festival of 10 August, a celebration of the fall of the monarchy surpassing every previous revolutionary festival in elaborateness and expense. He contributed not a single lyric or inscription to the 10 August celebrations. This task was given to a quite unknown poet, Varon, and Chénier had only the small consolation of having his earlier lyric, the "Chant du 14 juillet" (Song for the Fourteenth of July), sung in the much more modest 14 July celebrations.

Even Chénier's plays, previously so closely associated with the revolutionary cause, now came under open attack. *Fénelon* was attacked in the Montagnard press as a reactionary, proclerical work because of its sympathetic portrayal of a prelate and an aristocrat. Even *Caïus Gracchus,* which the convention had recently listed along with Voltaire's *Brutus* (1730) and Antoine-Marin Lemierre's *Guillaume Tell* (William Tell, 1766) as a play so imbued with revolutionary spirit that it should be presented once a week at public expense, even this play was not spared. Early in October the celebrated line (laws and not blood) drew its accustomed applause, but it also drew a violent protest from a Montagnard deputy, throwing the audience into an uproar. The evening ended peacefully, but Chénier's piece was not presented again at the République. Only a month before, the entire company of the rival Nation (the former Comédie-Française) had been placed under arrest and were now under the threat of execution for their performance of what the Committee of Public Safety considered to be reactionary and antipatriotic works, and in this atmosphere Chénier's drama became too much of a risk.

Chénier does not seem to have been much intimidated by running political risks, but he was surely concerned by the threat of a declining artistic visibility. During the fall of 1793 he became involved in projects that once again put him in the public eye. Although he, along with other suspected moderates, was dropped from the Committee of Public Instruction on 6 October 1793, he presented just before his departure a much-praised and highly influential report in the name of the committee to the convention calling for the placement of the remains of René Descartes in the Pantheon; he also used the occasion to ridicule the ignorance and superstition of the Catholic Church and to condemn its robbing of the poor to build lavish altars and tombs. This widely circulated speech doubtless contributed to a wave of vandalism against churches, libraries, and other sites associated with religion and aristocracy during October and November, and Chénier felt it necessary to make an impassioned speech in the convention calling (successfully) for a cessation of this wanton destruction of treasures of national art and culture.

Although no longer a member of the Committee of Public Instruction, Chénier continued to exercise considerable influence in this domain. Proposals that he had made before his departure continued to shape public discussion, and one of his most renowned and influential orations, the *Discours sur l'instruction publique* (Discourse on Public Education), given 5 November, called for a complete system of public education stressing both civic and scholastic instruction. Chénier continued to be called upon for a variety of major projects in the civic domain. He was a member of the committee that created the new republican calendar, and, at least according to some historians, he was the originator of the poetic names for the new months—*vendémiaire, brumaire, frimaire, nivôse, pluviôse, ventôse, germinal, floréal, prairial, messidor, thermidor,* and *fructidor.* Immediately following his speech on public education Chénier was ordered to prepare a report on a series of civic holidays to replace religious ones. The first such celebration was the well-known Feast of Reason held in Notre-Dame and including Chénier's "Hymne à la liberté" (Hymn to Liberty). An equally popular "Hymne à la raison" (Hymn to Reason) was written for a subsequent Feast of Reason in the Church of Saint Roch in Paris. Chénier even participated indirectly in the celebrations honoring his old enemy Marat after Marat's assassination by Charlotte Corday. His "Chant du 14 juillet" was sung at the ceremony unveiling busts of Marat and Le Pelletier at the Opéra, and three Chénier songs, including one composed especially for the occasion, accompanied the burial of Marat in the Pantheon on 21 September 1793.

The recapture of the city of Toulon from the British on 9 December 1793 provided another occa-

FÉNELON,

OU

LES RELIGIEUSES DE CAMBRAI,

TRAGÉDIE EN CINQ ACTES,

Par MARIE-JOSEPH CHÉNIER, Député à la Convention
Nationale;

Représentée pour la première fois à Paris, sur le Théâtre
de la République, le 9 Février 1793, l'an II de la
République Françaife.

Prix, 1 livre 10 fols.

A PARIS,

Chez MOUTARD, Libraire-Imprimeur, rue des
Mathurins, hôtel de Cluni, N°. 334.

1793.

*Title page of Chénier's 1793 play, which was attacked by his
fellow radicals for its sympathetic portrayal of a priest*

sion for Chénier to add to his patriotic credentials. He collaborated again with his former colleague David and with the young composer Charles-Simon Catel, a student of their past collaborator Gossec, to create a new festival devoted to the Victories of the Republic, held 30 December 1793. Chénier's new hymn for this occasion, "La Reprise de Toulon" (The Recapture of Toulon), was criticized by some radical journals for its references to God and to antiquity, and one of its verses was expunged as too radical when it was published under the Bourbon Restoration; but for most of the French public of its era, the song, like the "Hymne à la liberté" and the "Hymne à la raison," precisely expressed contemporary concern with the ideals of patriotism and republicanism. Festivals of Liberty, Reason, and Victory were celebrated all over France, and almost all utilized Chénier's popular and accessible songs,

which were widely circulated in journals and collections of patriotic music.

Doubtless encouraged by these successes, Chénier again turned his attention to the drama, writing a play that revived all the worst suspicions of his enemies and placed him in the greatest political danger of his career. *Timoléon* (1795), drawn from a narrative in Plutarch, tells of a failed attempt in Corinth to seize dictatorial power. While Timoléon is absent on a military campaign, his brother Timophane plots to gain control of the republic of Corinth. The triumphant general unexpectedly returns, and one of Timophane's followers attempts unsuccessfully to convert popular enthusiasm for Timoléon into political support for his brother's cause. Timoléon himself denounces such a scheme, and Timophane appears to give up his ambition, but he continues to plot. When Timoléon discovers this, he denounces Timophane and delivers him to the people's judgment and to death.

Although the play was full of praise for republican virtue and wars in the name of freedom and equality, lines such as "Terror, as we know, produces slaves" and "Does every tyrant wear a diadem?" could hardly be tolerated by Maximilien-Françoise Marie-Isidore de Robespierre and his party. The play, submitted to the police administrator for approval, was forwarded to Robespierre with advice that it be banned as presenting bad examples to the public. Chénier, unaware of or defiant of such resistance, had his play announced the day of the execution of Georges-Jacques Danton, one of his first strong supporters, and proceeded with rehearsals at the République. At the dress rehearsal on 8 May 1795 a member of the Committee of Public Instruction arose during the performance, denouncing the play as an affront to the French people and denouncing Chénier as a counterrevolutionary. The performance was stopped, audience and actors fled, and Chénier realized that he was on the brink of joining his brother André, who had been in prison since March, facing judgment by the Revolutionary Tribunal. Chénier appealed to friends on the Committee of General Security, who advised him to burn the manuscript in their presence. This done, the committee issued a certificate witnessing to the dramatist's patriotic conduct and removed him from immediate danger.

An occasion for Chénier to regain something of his threatened reputation was offered by the next great festival, Robespierre's Fête de l'Etre Suprème (Festival of the Supreme Being). The National Institute of Music, established the previous November at the recommendation of Chénier to provide music for patriotic occasions, was naturally called upon to participate in this festival, and it called upon Chénier to provide the songs. Informed of this decision, Robespierre demanded that another poet be selected, but this was done so late that several papers printed Chénier's text as the official one, and two other Chénier lyrics, one of them the popular "Chant du 14 juillet," were still included in the ceremony and enthusiastically received by a public that had no inkling of the poet's present difficult political status.

The notorious law of 22 Prairial (22 June 1794), which included among "enemies of the Revolution" not only the usual emigrants, refractory priests, and royalists but also anyone who sought to mislead or corrupt the people or to corrupt public instruction, caused many public figures who disagreed with Robespierre to leave their homes to avoid arrest. Chénier took refuge at the National Institute of Music, but he continued to attempt to prove his patriotism through his art. His best-known song, the "Chant du départ" with music by Méhul, was written at this dark time and first performed at the great victory of France's Northern Army at Fleurus on 26 June 1794. The chant was first performed in Paris by the National Institute on 4 July along with Chénier's "Dithyramb sur la Fédération" (Dithyramb on the Federation) to celebrate French victories at Ostend and Tournai and was so successful that it was repeated at the following Bastille Day celebrations. Chénier's political enemies were not won over by these successes, but they were unable to act in the face of his continued public support. His brother André, less in the public eye and more openly associated with antigovernment positions, was not so fortunate. He was guillotined on 25 July 1794, one of the last victims before the Thermidorian reaction two days later toppled Robespierre from power and ended the Reign of Terror.

The actress Mme Apolline Baldassare Vestris (doubtless at Chénier's suggestion) had preserved a copy of the condemned play *Timoléon*. It was at once put into rehearsal and announced eleven days after Robespierre's fall. The production on 11 September 1794 was a political if not an artistic triumph since the weakness of the play was overlooked by audiences eager to read it as an attack on the extremism now associated with Robespierre.

Chénier lost no time in involving himself in the new political order. Six days after the premiere of *Timoléon* he provided hymns and choruses for the festival placing in the Pantheon the remains of Marat (whose reputation had not yet suffered from the rapidly changing political situation). Chénier now turned almost exclusively to political concerns, rapidly becoming one of the most influential and

outspoken members of the post-Thermidorian Convention and, in time, its president. When the convention gave way to the directory in November 1795, he became an influential member and eventually president of one of the new legislative bodies, the Council of Five Hundred.

The presumed topicality of *Timoléon* was not sufficient to keep this weak drama on the stage, and in the period after the Thermidorian reaction *Fénélon* was the major Chénier work represented, primarily by the original actors headed by Talma and Mme Vestris, who in these turbulent days performed in several different venues. The scattering of actors of talent among the multitude of theaters now operating in Paris and the instability of most of these ventures led Chénier in 1797 to propose a modification of the prerevolutionary monopoly, limiting the total number of theaters and providing special support for certain ones whose work was considered most beneficial for public education. Although not enacted at that time, these proposals anticipated the theatrical reforms enacted by Napoleon in 1807, establishing the system of state-supported and private stages that still exists, with many modifications.

Chénier produced a few elegies and occasional pieces during his service on the Council of Five Hundred, but almost all of his energy went into political matters until his opposition to the growing power of Napoleon lost him his position. Even during his final year in the government he began to turn again to literature, his long-standing anticlericalism aroused by Napoleon's growing closeness to the Catholic Church. In June 1801 he published the satire *Les Nouveaux saints,* condemning the "fanatics" and their long-standing opposition to "philosophy." He also began work on a new tragedy, "Philippe II," dealing with that favorite target of Enlightenment authors, the Spanish Inquisition. Spain being now an ally of France, however, the consulate censors banned the play. *Charles IX* and *Henri VIII,* popular for their condemnations of royalty, were occasionally performed, along with the even more popular *Fénélon,* but Chénier's political past continued to haunt him. He was increasingly accused of being a political opportunist, of attacking royalty and religion when that was fashionable, or resisting extremists such as Marat, but in supporting Marat's apotheosis when that was advantageous. Chénier published several public defenses, but even the popular *Fénélon* began to lose its supporters. When it was revived in 1802, the République had presented no Chénier play in almost two years, and *Fénélon* itself was given its final performance the following March.

In 1804 Chénier turned forty and was thus eligible to serve in the French senate. The necessary cost of this continued involvement in the political scene was an acceptance of Napoleon, declared heredity emperor this same year, but Chénier, like many former Revolutionaries, convinced himself that Napoleon could carry on the work of the revolution. He composed a new tragedy, *Cyrus* (1804), in honor of the imperial coronation. The discreet balance that Chénier attempted in this work between allegorical praise of the new emperor and a continued glorification of the values of liberalism and constitutional power created an awkward blend that pleased no one, neither the public nor Napoleon. The play was given only once, on 8 December 1804, and was immediately withdrawn. *Henri VIII* was revived the following February but replaced after a single performance upon a request from the emperor, by Pierre Corneille's *Le Cid* (1637).

With Chénier's political and literary fortunes again on the wane, his enemies grew bolder. Julien-Louis Geoffroy, the leading dramatic critic of the era, attacked him as a mediocre follower of Voltaire, and indeed went so far as to attack Voltaire himself as an inferior artist in the tragic style. This attack on his idol was infuriating to Chénier, who published in response one of his best-known literary statements, the *Epître à Voltaire* (Letter to Voltaire), at the beginning of 1806. Here Chénier returned to an unqualified defense of his fundamental principles, the championship of liberty and tolerance, represented by Voltaire and his philosopher friends, against tyranny and arbitrary power of all sorts. The *Epître* rehabilitated Chénier in liberal circles but infuriated the emperor and resulted in the loss of most of Chénier's remaining political power. Deprived of any official position and with considerable debts, Chénier appealed to the emperor, who to his credit accorded him an annual pension and a commission to continue an official history of France begun by Jean Millot.

After the single revival of *Henri VIII* early in 1805, Chénier's stage career was finished. Political drama of any sort was discouraged under Napoleon, and from the spring of 1806 onward the Ministry of Police had to approve all plays, and it enforced this ban strictly. Moreover, there was a ban on the depiction of any church figures on stage, which in itself would have eliminated the three Chénier tragedies most likely to be revived: *Charles IX, Henri VIII,* and *Fénelon*. Chénier did write one more tragedy, *Tibère,* in the early years of the nineteenth century, but it was not staged in his lifetime nor indeed even submitted for consideration to any company. Clearly Chénier realized that this study of the power and duplicity of a tyrant, even in a Roman setting, was unacceptable during the Empire. Without giving up his political ideals, he turned his talents in other directions. In 1806 he undertook an epic poem, the *Bataviade,* in which he returned to the subject of his unperformed tragedy *Philippe II* to condemn religious and political oppression; in his poem he traces the story of the struggle for independence of the United Provinces against that monarch. Of this he completed the first book and most of a second. He also began a course of public instruction on French literature, several lectures of which survive, and participated in a study, commissioned by the emperor, on French literature since 1789, which was Chénier's major occupation for the remainder of his life. He treated the authors studied, many of them still living, with commendable impartiality, and for himself made only the modest claim of being the author of the popular *Fénelon*.

In declining health and spirits since 1802, Chénier died on 10 January 1811. His manuscripts were left to his friend and fellow author Pierre-Claude Danou, who published a posthumous collection in 1818. Here the tragedies *Cyrus, Philippe II,* and *Tibère* appeared for the first time, along with two tragedies predating *Charles IX* (*Oedipe mourant* and *Brutus*), an adaptation of Sophocles's *Oedipus Rex* written during the consulate, and a three-act drama in verse called *Ninon,* based on Gotthold Ephraim Lessing's *Nathan the Wise* (1779). In addition to these completed plays there were several fragments—one of an *Electre* based on Sophocles and two of verse comedies, one based on Richard Brinley Sheridan's *The School for Scandal* (1777), the other on Voltaire's *Le Dépositaire* (The Guardian, 1772). Also included were his unfinished *Bataviade* and the first of four sections of a Horatian didactic poem, *Les Principes des arts* (Principles of the Arts), along with several other completed literary essays too liberal or oppositional to be published under the Empire.

Although the publication of his work was permitted under the Bourbon Restoration, Chénier remained banned from the stage. The Revolution of 1830 removed such censorship, and both *Tibère* and *Charles IX* were presented, but without arousing great interest. Chénier, like most of the prominent figures of the revolution, remained a controversial and debated figure, but his dramas had lost their appeal. Their classic form and subject matter were far from the taste of the Romantic period, and although *Tibère* and *Henri VIII* were revived again at midcentury, they gained little success. Not surprisingly, there were minor revivals of *Charles IX,* the play that established Chénier as the poet laureate of the revolution, in 1889 and 1989 as part of the centennial and bicentennial celebrations. From the beginning of his career Chénier defined himself as a national and a political poet, and it is in that context that his work is now remembered.

Biographies:

Dominique Garat, *Notice sur la vie et les ouvrages de M.-J. De Chénier* (Paris: Dabin, 1812);

Charles Labitte, "Marie-Joseph Chénier, sa vie et ses écrits," *Revue des Deux Mondes*, I (1844): 240–324;

Pierre Claude Daunou, *Notice sur la vie et les ouvrages de M.-J. de Chénier* (Paris: Dabin, 1911);

Alfred Jepson Bingham, *Marie-Joseph Chénier, Early Political Life and Ideas* (New York: Privately printed, 1939).

References:

Antoine Vincent Arnault, *Lettre sur M.-J. Chénier* (Paris: Didot, 1826);

H. C. Ault, "*Charles IX, ou l'école des rois,* tragédie nationale," *MLR,* XLVIII (1953): 398–406;

J. A. Bleuet, *Catalogue des livres de la bibliothèque de feu M. Marie-J. Chénier* (Paris, 1811);

Théodore Delmont, *Marie-Joseph Chénier, poète dramatique* (Arras: Sueur-Charruey, 1903);

Charles-Marie de Féletz, "Théâtre de Marie-Joseph Chénier," *Mélanges,* II (1828): 123–154;

Louis Gallois, "Marie-Joseph Chénier," in *Histoire des journaux et des journalistes de la Révolution française* (Paris: Société de l'industrie fraternelle, 1846), II: 503–510;

Gérard Gley, *Etude littéraire sur Tibère* (Epinal: Collot, 1886);

Charles His, *Parallèle entre M. de Chateaubriand et M.-J. De Chénier* (Paris: Schoell, 1812);

Walther Küchler, *Marie-Joseph Chéniers dramatische und lirische Dichtung* (Leipzig: Noske, 1900);

Louis-Jean-Népomucène Lemercier, "Théâtre de Marie-Joseph Chénier," *Revue encyclopédique,* I (1810): 111–134, 298–307, 497–502;

Adolphe Liéby, *Etude sur le théâtre de Marie-Joseph Chénier* (Paris: Société française d'imprimerie, 1901);

Joseph Lingay, *Eloge de M.-J. Chénier* (Paris: Rosa, 1814);

Charles Palissot de Montenoy, *La critique de la tragédie de Charles IX, Comédie Française* (Paris: Duchesne, 1790);

Félix Pyat, *Marie-Joseph Chénier et le Prince des Critiques* (Paris: Leriche, 1844).

Papers:

Chenier's papers are held at the Bibliothèque Nationale in Paris, collection NAF, 6852.

Paul Claudel
(6 August 1868 – 23 February 1955)

Bettina L. Knapp
Hunter College of The City University of New York

PLAY PRODUCTIONS: *L'Annonce faite à Marie,* Paris, Théâtre de l'Oeuvre, December 1912;

L'Otage, London, Scala Theater, 1913; Paris, Théâtre de l'Oeuvre, June 1914;

L'Echange, Paris, Théâtre du Vieux-Colombier, 15 January 1914;

Protée, music by Darius Milhaud, performed by Groningen students in Dutch, Groningen, 1914;

La Nuit de Noël 1914, read by Eve Francis, Paris, Université des Annales, March 1915;

Tête d'Or, Paris, Théâtre du Gymnase, 30 May 1919;

Le Pain dur, act 2, scene 2, read by Eve Francis and Jean Hervé, Paris, Théâtre du Gymnase, 30 May 1919;

L'homme et son désir, music by Milhaud, Rolf de Maré's Swedish Ballet, Paris, Théâtre des Champs-Elysées, 6 June 1921;

Partage de Midi, Paris, Groupe Art et Action, 12 November 1921;

La Femme et son ombre, Tokyo, Imperial Theater of Tokyo, 16 March 1923;

La Ville, Paris, reading at "Palais de Bois," 1926; Paris, Théâtre National Populaire, 1955;

Sous le rempart d'Athènes, Paris, Palais de l'Elysée, 26 October 1927;

Le Père humilié, Dresden, Schauspielhaus, 26 November 1928;

Le Repos du septième jour, Warsaw, Théâtre Nadorow, 1928;

Le Livre de Christophe Colomb, music by Milhaud, Berlin, Staatsoper Unter den Linden, 30 June 1930;

Aeschylus, *Agamemnon,* translated and directed by Claudel, music by Milhaud, Brussels, Théâtre de la Monnaie, 27 and 28 March 1935;

La Danse des morts, music by Arthur Honegger, Paris, Claudel's home, 2 February 1939;

Jeanne d'Arc au bûcher, music by Honegger, Orléans, Théâtre municipal d'Orléans, 6 May 1939;

Le Soulier de Satin, Paris, Comédie-Française, 23 November 1943;

Paul Claudel

La Jeune Fille Violaine, Paris, Salle Iéna, 1944;

L'Histoire de Tobie et de Sara, Roubaix, Francs-Alleux Troupe, February 1947;

L'ours et la lune, Algiers, 1948;

Le Festin de la sagesse, music by Milhaud, Rome, 15 February 1950;

La Cantate à trois voix, Marseille, Groupe Théâtral Universitaire d'Aix-Marseille, 27 May 1955;

Aeschylus, *Oresteia, Agamemnon, Les Euménides, Les Choéphores,* translated by Claudel, music by Milhaud, Berlin, Berlin Opera, 1963.

BOOKS: *Tête d'Or,* anonymous (Paris: Librairie de l'Art indépendant, 1890); translated by John

Strong Newberry (New Haven: Yale University Press, 1919);

La Ville, anonymous (Paris: Librairie de l'Art indépendant, 1893); translated by Newberry as *The City* (New Haven: Yale University Press, 1920);

Vers d' exil (Paris, n.p., 1895);

La Jeune fille Violaine (Paris: L'Arbre, 1901);

L'Echange (Paris: Mercure de France, 1901);

Le Repos du septième jour (Paris: L'Arbre, 1901);

Partage de Midi (Paris: Bibliothèque de l'Occident, 1906); translated by Wallace Fowlie as *Break of Noon* (Chicago: Regnery, 1960);

Connaissance de l'Est (Paris: Société de Mercure de France, 1907); translated by Teresa Frances and William Rose Benét as *The East I Know* (New Haven: Yale University Press, 1914);

L'Otage (Paris: Nouvelle revue française, December 1910, January 1911); translated by J. Heard as *The Hostage* (Boston: J. W. Luce, 1944);

L'Annonce faite à Marie (Paris: Nouvelle revue française, December 1911, January–April 1912); translated by Wallace Fowlie as *The Tidings Brought to Mary* (Chicago: Regnery, 1960);

Protée (Paris: Nouvelle revue française, April–May 1914); translated by Newberry as *Proteus, a Satiric Drama in Two Acts* (Rome: Broom, 1921-1922);

Le Pain dur (Paris: Editions de la Nouvelle revue française, 1918);

Le Père humilié (Paris: Nouvelle revue française, September–October 1919);

L'Ours et la Lune (Paris: Editions de la Nouvelle revue française, 1919);

La Femme et son ombre, in *L'Oiseau noir dans le Soleil levant* (Paris: Excelsior, 1927);

Sous le rempart d'Athènes (Paris: Nouvelle revue française, December 1927);

Le Soulier de satin (Paris: Gallimard, 1928–1929); translated by the Reverend Father John O'Connor as *The Satin Slipper* (New York: Sheed & Ward, 1955);

Le Livre de Christophe Colomb (Paris: *Commerce,* Autumn 1929); translated by Claudel and Agnes Meyer as *The Book of Christopher Columbus* (New Haven: Yale University Press, 1930);

La Sagesse ou la Parabole du Festin (Paris: Editions de la Nouvelle revue française, 1939);

Jeanne d'Arc au bûcher, music by Arthur Honegger (Paris: Editions de la Nouvelle revue française, 1939); translated by Dennis Arundell as *Joan of Arc at the Stake* (Paris: Salabert, 1947);

L'Histoire de Tobie et de Sara (Paris: Gallimard, 1942); translated by Mother Adele Fiske as *Tobias,* in *Port-Royal and Other Plays* (New York: Hill & Wang, 1962);

Accompagnements (Paris: Gaillard, 1949);

La Lune à la recherche d'elle-même (Paris: Pléiade, 1949).

Collections: *Oeuvres complètes,* 26 volumes (Paris: Gallimard, 1950–1970)

Oeuvres poètique (Paris: Bruges, 1957);

Théâtre, volume 1, edited by Jacques Madaule and Jacques Petit (Paris: Bruges, 1957);

Cahiers de Paul Claudel, 12 volumes (Paris: Gallimard, 1959–1984);

Oeuvres en prose, edited by Petit and Charles Galpérine (Paris: Pléiade, 1965);

Théâtre, volume 2, edited by Jacques Madaule and Petit (Paris: Pléiade, 1965);

Mes idées sur le théâtre, edited by Petit and Jean-Pierre Kempf (Paris: Gallimard, 1966);

Journal, 2 volumes, edited by François Varillon and Petit (Paris: Pléiade, 1968, 1969);

Mémoires improvisés (Paris: Gallimard, 1969).

TRANSLATIONS: Aeschylus, *Oresteia,* music by Darius Milhaud, trilogy includes *Agamemnon* (Fou-Tchou: Rosario, 1896); *Les Choéphores* (Paris: Nouvelle revue française, 1920); *Les Euménides* (Paris: Nouvelle revue française, 1920).

SELECTED PERIODICAL PUBLICATIONS–UNCOLLECTED: "Fragment d'un drame," *Revue indépendante* (May 1892);

La Nuit de Noël 1914, Le Correspondent (10 April 1915);

L'Homme et son désir, Danse (June 1921);

La Parabole du Festin, Revue des Jeunes (January 1926);

Le Ravissement de Scapin, Opéra (January 1952).

The plays of Paul Claudel are unique. Neither a naturalist nor a realist, Claudel veered away from the kind of theater found in the work of Henri Becque, Eugène Brieux-Georges de Porto-Riche, and Gerard Hauptmann. His plays did not conform to Maurice Maeterlinck's theater of silence, stasis, darkness, and dream or to the Boulevard productions typified by the witty and brash comedies of Georges Feydeau, Henri Meilhac, and Ludovic Halévy. Claudel created his own genre, which was poetic, but unlike the outpourings of Victor Hugo; religious, but with greater amplitude, depth, and vigor than the litanies of Henri Ghéon; symbolic, but reaching more deeply into the elemental world than the plays of Henrik Ibsen or Jean-Marie Mathias Philippe-August Comte de Villiers de l'Isle Adam. Claudel was tormented by sexual problems, but his were different from those plaguing August Strindberg. If comparisons are to be made, one might liken Claudel's dramatic dirges and dithyrambs to the works of Jean Racine and Aeschylus. They reach into the core of human nature and flesh out its agonies. They deal with collective beings and collective problems; his theater is archetypal in dimension.

The protagonists of Claudel's sensual and erotic dramas are earthly beings lusting for heaven, bodies obsessed with spirit, dark beings longing for light. Perpetual turmoil rages in the hearts and minds of the playwright's split and chaotic souls. Each character in his own way seeks to liberate himself or herself from egotism and arrogance in a search for altruism, humility, and godliness. Claudel's creatures are pagans clothed in Catholic vestments; they are hedonists yearning to be ascetics.

Claudel was born on 6 August 1868 in the town of Villeneuve-sur-Fère-en-Tardenois in the Aisne region. His early years were spent moving from one town to another, wherever his father's job as conservator of mortgages took the family. In 1881 Claudel's favorite sister, Camille, a talented sculptor, decided to pursue her studies in Paris, first at the Colarossi atelier, then with Auguste Rodin. The family separated, the mother moving to Paris with the children. Claudel's student years at the Lycée Louis-le-Grand in Paris were marred by the emotional aftereffects of his parents' separation. His exposure to the scientific determinism of Hippolyte Taine and the relativist, historical works of Ernest Renan did nothing to relieve his tormented soul.

The year 1886 became a momentous one for Claudel when he made a discovery that opened up "the supernatural world" to him: Arthur Rimbaud's *Les Illuminations* (The Illuminations, 1886). This slim volume of poems became a seminal force in his life. Rimbaud, the Promethean, the rebel, the adolescent who fought society, God, and himself, made Claudel aware of his own turmoil and dissatisfactions and the growing chaos within his psyche. The year 1886 was also of extreme importance because it brought Claudel the answer to his metaphysical anguish. During the Christmas Mass at Notre Dame Cathedral in Paris, he was so shaken by the experience of divinity that he converted, so to speak, to Catholicism, thereby returning to the faith of his fathers.

Other influences profoundly marked Claudel's life. In 1887 he began attending Stéphane Mallarmé's Tuesday gatherings in the poet's apartment on rue de Rome, along with such men as Maeterlinck, Henride Régnier, René Ghil, and Villiers de l'Isle Adam. From Mallarmé, Claudel learned to sound out the quintessential value of words—their impact, logic, and sensuality as visual and intellectual instrumentalities, as solitary entities, and as connecting links within the poem's ensemble of dynamic forces.

At this juncture in his development Claudel chose the drama as the best vehicle for his creative urge. His three-act play *Tête d'Or* (Golden Head, 1890) dramatically relates the violent and cruel crisis of youth undergoing spiritual and psychological dismemberment. Each of the protagonists—or antagonists—is an energy charge, tormented and twisted, lusting for power and yearning for love. Simon Agnel, known as Tête d'Or, was a conqueror and fire principle. So great was his drive for power that it placed him beyond the human sphere in an extratemporal time scheme. As the play opens, he is in the process of burying the woman with whom he had lived and whom he had loved. But he had left her in order to travel, to see new lands, to cut through the confines of his circumscribed world so that he could discover his essence. His guilt, however, is ferocious. Upon his return to his lover, just prior to her death, he happens upon an old friend, Cébès, a weak man who forever laments his hopeless fate. A shadow figure, Cébès symbolizes that factor in Simon that he rejects, that cannot be assimilated into his psyche. Cébès dies later from battle wounds.

Act 2 of *Tête d'Or* takes place in a king's palace. Rather than being strong and wise, Claudel's king is old, feeble, and fearful that his kingdom will be conquered by the enemy at the gates. His daughter, the Princess, solitary and courageous, comforts and nurtures by her very presence. Tête d'Or, victorious in battle, claims the aged king's throne. Because the monarch refuses to yield his kingdom to the conqueror, Tête d'Or kills the senescent figure, thus symbolically slashing all that is archaic, unregenerate, and fallow within himself. The unforgiving Princess is banished.

Act 3 is set in the Caucasus, the divide between East and West. It is here that Prometheus had been chained to the rock, that his liver had been torn out nightly by an eagle. A creature covered with animal skins crouches on the side of the stage. The once exalted Princess has regressed to her primitive nature. A Deserter walks onstage, recognizes the Princess whom he despises, seizes her, and nails her to a tree. Suspended motionless, she takes on the value of a cosmic emanation. Neither earthly nor celestial, she hovers between two destinies.

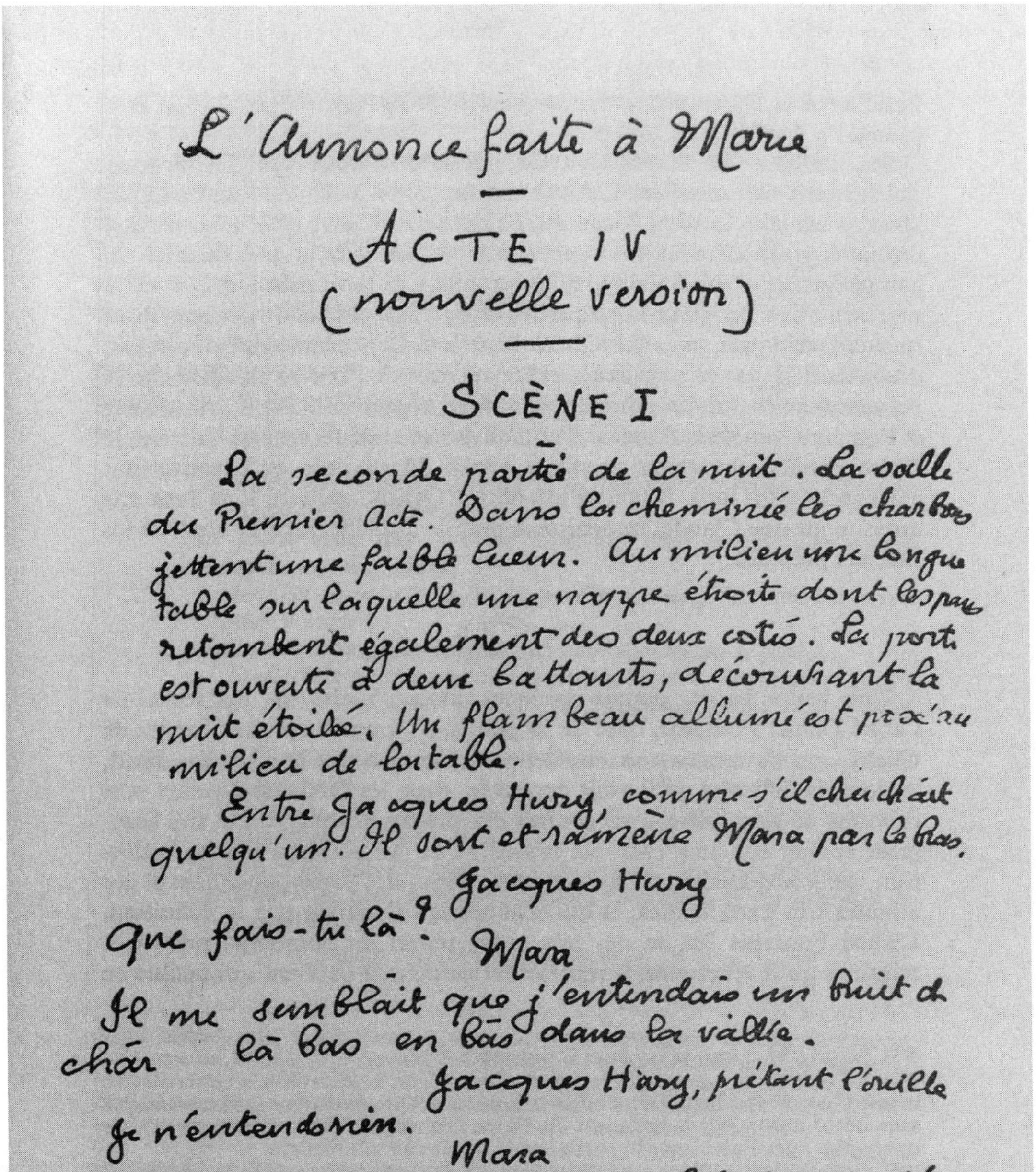

L'Annonce faite à Marie

ACTE IV
(nouvelle version)

SCÈNE I

La seconde partie de la nuit. La salle du Premier Acte. Dans la cheminée les charbons jettent une faible lueur. Au milieu une longue table sur laquelle une nappe étroite dont les pans retombent également des deux côtés. La porte est ouverte à deux battants, découvrant la nuit étoilée. Un flambeau allumé est près du milieu de la table.

Entre Jacques Hury, comme s'il cherchait quelqu'un. Il sort et ramène Mara par le bras.

Jacques Hury

Que fais-tu là?

Mara

Il me semblait que j'entendais un bruit de char là-bas en bas dans la vallée.

Jacques Hury, prêtant l'oreille

Je n'entends rien.

Mara

C'est vrai, tu n'entends rien. Mais moi, j'ai l'oreille vivante et le jas de l'œil ouvert

Page from the manuscript for Claudel's most popular play, which explores religious issues through its focus on the Virgin Mary (from Louis Chaigne, Vie de Paul Claudel et genèse de son oeuvre, *1961)*

Meanwhile, Tête d'Or, wounded during a battle, is carried onstage. He who had once sought to seize the earth is now dying. He sees the Princess. In a moment of extreme heroism he rises to pull out the nails from her limbs with his teeth. Bloodied but still strong, the unleashed Princess now carries him to his mortuary bed. She wishes it had been he who had nailed her to the cross; then she would have experienced true ecstasy. The Princess leans over Tête d'Or to kiss him on the mouth, thereby cementing their union. Although one of Claudel's early plays, *Tête d'Or* explodes with talent and power and still holds contemporary audiences enthralled.

La Ville (1893; translated as *The City,* 1920) is naive in its ideations and heavily emotional in its poetics. It is the drama of a seared soul: a young man who, prior to his conversion, lies gasping for want of air, starving for need of food, parched in his desire for water. The work of an adolescent—far more so than *Tête d'Or,* which is an art piece—*The City* is a thesis play. Rigid in its ideas and simplistic in its answers, it dramatizes the conflict between the individual and society: the city emerges as a monstrous force, crushing and lacerating the young man, bringing stagnation and the obliteration of his creativity. The poet/protagonist struggles to discover new values amid a disintegrating bourgeoisie and a soulless proletariat whose powers are misguided. Claudel's descriptions are brutal and his expressions rough-hewn; his epithets are sequences of strident cacophonies. Claudel's city is necessarily destroyed in the end: constrictions vanish as the life-sapping enclave is reduced to rubble.

In 1889 Claudel enrolled at the School of Political Science, but a year later he changed to the School for Oriental Languages in Paris. After passing the competitive examination required for foreign service, he began his brilliant career as world traveler and diplomat. The powerful feelings of nostalgia and melancholia that overcame him in the United States (1893–1894) during a consular assignment there were set into a dramatic framework in *L'Echange* (The Exchange, 1901). Claudel was utterly isolated in the new land, in a different culture; he did not feel any more at home in France, where he returned the following year. *L'Echange,* although directed by such notables as Jacques Copeau, Georges Pitoëff, and Jean-Louis Barrault and Madeleine Renaud, remains one of Claudel's poorest plays. Revolving around adultery, materialism, and death, it nevertheless subsumes themes to which he later returned.

Claudel's next port of call was China, from 1895 to 1900, which left him with even stronger feelings of displacement than he had known in the United States. Although he made the effort to open his mind to foreign ways and to accept the spiritual offerings of other peoples and lands, in *Connaissance de l'Est* (1907; translated as *The East I Know,* 1914), an "intimate diary" or "interior itinerary," his anti-Buddhist prejudices and intolerance were evident. Although Claudel's attitude modified over the years, it never left him.

During Claudel's stay in China he wrote *Vers d'Exil* (Poems of Exile, 1895), poems expressing feelings of disquietude and isolation, and a play, *La Jeune fille Violaine* (The Young Violaine, 1901). The latter was the forerunner of his most popular dramatic production, *L'Annonce faite à Marie* (1911–1912; translated as *The Tidings Brought to Mary,* 1960), first directed by Aurélien-François Lugné-Poë at his Théâtre de l'Oeuvre in Paris in 1912. A religious mystery, its dominant theme is the spirit of sacrifice as a means of gaining access to heaven. *Le Repos du septième jour* (Rest on the Seventh Day, 1901), a complex theological drama set in China, where the cult of the dead is important, undertakes to isolate the notion of Evil. The dead invade the domain of the living, with the result that the latter can neither eat, drink, nor sleep, so possessed are they by hovering invisible forces.

Claudel, having decided to enter a church order, returned to France in 1900. He sought to sacrifice his worldly condition to God: to surrender life in favor of spirit, sensuality in favor of sublimity. To this end, he went into retreat at Solesmes and then entered the Benedictine monastery of Ligugé. In September that year he experienced a religious crisis, which he expressed in "Muses," the first of his celebrated odes. Because his great "sacrifice" was unacceptable to his religious superiors, perhaps because of his innate pride and arrogance and sense of spiritual superiority, Claudel was compelled to return to the world.

Sent again on assignment to China in 1901, he remained there until 1905. Aboard the ship the *Ernest-Simmons,* returning him to the Orient, Claudel met the beautiful Polish blond Rose Vetch, a wife and mother. His great passion for her was reciprocated. Despite the commandments of his religion and the fact that only months prior to the traumatic love affair he was on the verge of taking the vows of chastity, the man of flesh was unleashed. Claudel's liaison, which involved the birth of a child, lasted for several years. Few know the reasons for its conclusion. It has been suggested that Rose gave him up, weary of his bouts of remorse and then his élan toward God. Others believe he yielded to the advice of his superiors at Quay d'Orsay: they stated categorically that if he wished to pursue a successful government career he would have to live a more conventional existence. Whatever the reason for the end of their relationship, he expressed his pain in many poems, including "Ténèbres."

Claudel's grief and turmoil were transmuted into his greatest dramatic work—one of the great dramatic works in literature—*Partage de Midi* (1906; translated as *Break of Noon,* 1960), a play that he alluded to as a "deliverance," a work so personal and so traumatic that he refused to allow it to be staged in its entirety until 1948, when Jean-Louis Barrault was awarded this singular honor. *Partage de Midi* centers around adultery: a wife, a husband, and two lovers. Every word breathes with Dionysian fervor and jubilation. *Partage de Midi* is a giant cosmic awakening in which the four Aristotelian elements (sun, moon, water, earth) activate and energize what happens on the stage. Each element, in consort with the protagonists, participates in the drama that unfolds in act 1 aboard a ship sailing on the Indian Ocean to China, in a cemetery in Hong Kong in act 2, and in a colonial-style house in a port town in southern China in act 3. An animistic world is brought to life, which allows the four characters to bathe in primitive powers and to experience viscerally the mysterious and inexorable forces that are to decide their fate.

The blond, beautiful, sensual, and proud Ysé (wife, mother, and mistress) needs to be loved and longs for affection. Although she does not love her husband, De Ciz, she is drawn to him sexually, and when he looks at her in a certain way, she feels shame. She knows that he does not love her. But she is not weak. Although until now only her senses have been aroused—not her soul—her unfulfilled existence has made her consider herself a stranger to the world at large and imprisoned in superficiality. De Ciz, on the other hand, is weak, irresponsible, cut off from himself and the world at large; he follows a path leading to intriguing business ventures.

Mesa, the character who most closely resembles Claudel and who becomes Ysé's lover, is given to passionate extremes. Searching for beatitude, longing to give his life to God, but prevented from doing so by his superiors, he has been thrust into a world of temptation. Immoderate in his thoughts, feelings, and deeds; perpetually dissatisfied; egotistical; self-centered; and inflated with feelings of spiritual superiority, he is chaos striving to become cosmos. Given Mesa's inability to give himself wholeheartedly to Ysé, she leaves him and takes Amalric as her lover and protector. Amalric, driven by a passion for life and a need for conquest, encompasses a world and, like Atlas, is able to bear the heaviest burden on his shoulders. It is he who cares for the child born to Ysé and Mesa. At the play's conclusion he alone emerges alive from the ordeal.

Le Soulier de satin (1928–1929; translated as *The Satin Slipper,* 1955), which concludes Claudel's so-called Rose cycle, dramatizes the Sacrament of Penance and Sacrifice. It illustrates a spiritual flagellation and psychological humiliation, a prolonged test of humankind's will to transcend the flesh, to battle matter and the Devil in order to experience God in his plenitude. It is the most involved, ambiguous, and lengthy play of Claudel's career. Written when he was in his early fifties, older and wiser, it is devoid of the whirlwind passion and the frenetic tempo that are the fiber of *Partage de Midi.* An intellectual and global construct in which Orient and Occident, Africa and the Americas participate, *Le Soulier de Satin* resembles a baroque cathedral in which every area is overly illuminated, overly detailed. More than a hundred characters inhabit the stage. Some play significant roles; some appear only once; and others are occasional walk-ons. Some are essences, appearing as visions or flesh-and-blood beings acting as devices to contrast or harmonize with the prevailing mood. The two main characters, Prouhèze and Rodrigue, weave their web throughout the globe, crossing continents and communicating by means of waterways. At the outset of the play a prayer is said for the hero so that he may attain his goal of experiencing divinity and not be bogged down in matter, entrapped in flesh. The hero's way may be circuitous, Claudel indicates, so let it be: "and if he does not go toward you by means of his own clarity, let him seek you through obscure ways; if not through direct paths, then by indirect ways."

A giant conglomeration of disparate and fragmented byroads and sideroads, *Le Soulier de Satin* may be viewed as networks of involutions and convolutions, an aggregate of genres and feelings, a storehouse of irony, comedy, tragedy, whimsy, parody, burlesque, and satire—almost unending riches, which a febrile imagination puts to good use. Were the play to be given in its entirety, it would take nine hours. Barrault cut it extensively in his 1943 production, dividing it into two performances given on consecutive evenings. What is lacking in this bulbous drama, in this gargantuan panoramic vision, is the fulgurating murmur of the heart. The mind predominates. Structure is all-important, as is theology in all of its syllogistic array. Its mystery is dead, with feelings banished and melody missing.

Claudel returned to Paris in 1905, took the advice of his superiors, and after consulting with his father confessor married Reine Sainte-Marie Perrin in 1906. Three days after the wedding the couple left for Peking. Theirs was an ultraconservative

Catholic household in which they eventually raised five children. In 1909 Claudel and his family returned to France, only to leave for Prague six months later.

Claudel's four-act drama *L'Annonce faite à Marie,* situated in fifteenth-century France, is one of his most popular and most accessible works. The prologue opens in front of a large barn on a vast countryside at Combernon. Pierre de Craon, mason, builder of churches, devotes his life to spiritual concerns, namely, the building of Saint Justitia at Rheims. During his stay at Combernon, however, he had strayed from the straight and narrow path when he noticed his host's daughter, Violaine, beautiful, young, pure in all ways. He had desired her carnally: her body, her softness, and all the vigor of burgeoning womanhood. Attempting to take by force this first woman whom he had ever touched, he used his knife to make a slight cut on her arm in a moment of passion. Suddenly, the Devil seized him, he explained, taking advantage of the moment. It was on that very day that he was struck down with leprosy. A year had passed since the incident, during which Pierre de Craon had experienced the meaning of anguish. When he saw the first spots of leprosy on his body, he understood that the disease fulfilled a dual purpose: it was a form of chastisement as well as an incitement to a more positive God-oriented goal of accomplishing something worthwhile in life.

Upon his return to Combernon he is stopped by Violaine, who darts out from the darkness. The matins sound from the convent nearby; the two recite their prayers. Violaine pardons Pierre de Craon, then questions him about Saint Justitia, in whose honor he was building the cathedral at Rheims. To help further the construction of the cathedral, she donates the ring given to her by Jacques Hury, her fiancé, who had found it in the earth when plowing. Violaine's perfection, both spiritual and physical, was not to be wasted in human involvements. It had to be consecrated to higher matters—that is, to God's works. Prior to his departure, Pierre de Craon shakes Violaine's hand. She, however, bends over to kiss him on the face. Unbeknown to them, Violaine's sister, Mara, hiding behind the barn, sees the kiss.

The following acts depict Violaine's family. Her father, prior to his journey to the Holy Sepulchre, seeks to settle earthly matters. Violaine, the "angel," the "Immaculate One," his favorite daughter, is to marry Jacques Hury and inherit the land. The two love each other. Mara, "the black one," an appellation stemming from the blackness of her hair and which serves to describe her character, will also

be given a percentage of the farm. Mara, in love with Jacques, threatens suicide if Violaine marries him. Just before her wedding, Violaine discovers on her body the first spot of leprosy. Jacques is aghast. Having been informed by Mara that she had seen Violaine kissing Pierre de Craon, he furiously rejects his fiancée.

Eight years pass. Violaine has withdrawn into the Chrevroche forest, where she lives in isolation, penance, and prayer. Mara, dressed in black and carrying a small bundle in her arms, asks the peasants the whereabouts of Violaine, the leper. They point the way. A woman emerges from the forest, veiled, small. She is carrying a little bell. One of the peasants casts a piece of bread her way. She stoops to retrieve it. The black form withdraws. Mara follows it. A clearing in the forest becomes visible. The Leper takes Mara into her cave. Violaine is blind and does not know it is her sister, who has come to visit her. Mara identifies herself, then tells Violaine that their mother has died and that she is married to Jacques. She now hands Violaine the bundle she is carrying. It is her dead little girl. Violaine takes her cold body, her stiff limbs, holds her close, covers the baby with her cloak. Return the baby to me alive, Mara orders. Violaine protests. It is not in her power to resuscitate the dead. Mara pleads.

Jacques does not know the child has died. If he finds out, he might never love her again. Mara cannot bear more children. Violaine asks Mara to read from her prayer book—the Christmas prayer, Isaiah's prophecy. Voices of angels become audible; a choir is heard chanting in Latin. The first rays of dawn become visible. Mara looks at Violaine. Something beneath her cloak seems to be stirring. A little foot is moving about. The baby is crying. She kneels before her sister. Mara is filled with wonderment. The child's eyes are blue, the color of Violaine's. A drop of milk is visible on the baby's lips. Violaine is the instrument of Grace for Claudel. As Aeschylus had written in his fifth-century B.C. *Les Choéphores,* which Claudel had translated, the world is nourished from the earth; Mother Earth gives of herself—soil and water—so that humanity may implant the seed and turn plant into food. Whether as Great Goddess of Vegetation, as Hesiod's Gaia, or the Christians' Virgin Mary, nature is fruitful and abundant; its presence, therefore, is sacred.

Violaine's father, returning from his journey and finding her nearly lifeless body, carries her to Jacques Hury's home. Violaine confesses her innocence: she kissed Pierre de Craon so that she could fill him with her joy and rapture for life, nothing more. "If you had believed in me / Who knows if you would not have healed me?" she tells Jacques.

Claudel, circa 1955

The two declare their love for one another. Life is ebbing as Violaine discloses Mara's secret visit to the forest and the miracle of resuscitation. Violaine dies. Pierre de Craon enters and carries her dead body into the shed her father had built for the poor. Mara confesses her feelings of jealousy, then questions: Was the love Jacques had for Violaine any better, or Pierre de Craon any purer? How did they react to her leprosy? Jacques threw her out of the house. Pierre de Craon did not aid her in any way. Who is the purer of the two? Mara's confession liberates her and gains her sanctification. She feels reborn, the poisons of jealousy, anger, and dissatisfaction having been exorcised from her system. Violaine told her that she had been the only one who had really believed in her, the only one to possess true faith.

Claudel's trilogy, often called the Coûfontaine cycle, consists of *L'Otage* (1910–1911; translated as *The Hostage,* 1944), *Le Pain dur* (1918; translated as *Stale Bread,* 1944), and *Le Père humilié* (1919; translated as *The Humiliated Father,* 1944). Claudel, now fifty-one years of age and with considerable diplomatic experience, understandably made the world of compromise, concession, and arbitration the fo-

cus of these dramas. He knew the behind-the-scenes machinations that dominate the promulgation of laws and the writing of pacts. As a diplomat he was part of an international organization into whose very structure were built false appearances, hypocrisy, accommodation, and deception. Politics was a game, the winner being the clever individual or nation, the manipulating and conniving force. The Coûfontaine cycle, which deals with the period beginning in 1813 and concluding in 1871, juxtaposes the ancien régime, with its absolute monarchy, its union of church and state, and the postrevolutionary period in France, the Napoleonic era, the Restoration, and the creation of modern Italy. The setting off of opposites is Claudel's dramatic method: past as opposed to present, the ideal to the real, illusion to reality, good to evil, Godlessness to a God-filled world. The inner conflict fleshed out in the cycle of plays also mirrors Claudel's own emotional and spiritual concerns: his view of sacrifice and his perpetual struggle to maintain some semblance of purity of soul. Love relationships never really ripen in the trilogy. They come into being only to be extinguished suddenly and brutally under allegations of sin or evil. Feelings are forever thwarted and twisted; yearnings are punished. Wedlock is presented as a scourge, marked with pain, despair, and martyrdom. Discord between man and woman is the rule of the day. Unlike the great religious dramas—*Tête d'Or*, *Partage de Midi*, and *L'Annonce faite à Marie*—the Coûfontaine cycle is more a philosophical tract than a drama, but one that nonetheless brings to the stage the political and religious antagonisms that mark a changing society.

Max Reinhardt had commissioned Claudel and Darius Milhaud to write an opera. *Le Livre de Christophe Colomb* (1929; translated as *The Book of Christopher Columbus*, 1930) resulted, a strange and haunting play about a hero figure journeying along his global trajectory. Not only does the work combine Claudel's religiously oriented themes, intensely cruel love episodes, and poetics based on powerful images, rhythmic breathing techniques, and stylized gestures; it is also, technically speaking, adventuresome. His application of some of the techniques of Japanese Bunraku and No theater adds another elusive dimension to the play. By combining the rhythmics of Emile Jacques-Dalcroze and the film-projection techniques of Erwin Piscator, as well as by using the vast scenic spaces in spectacularly new ways as suggested by Max Reinhardt, Claudel succeeded in injecting into the play an otherworldly climate. He looked upon music as a means to accentuate and prolong both lyrical and dramatic moments, to emphasize words and gestures, and to reinforce the composition of scenic design. Milhaud's music sustained the action, but it also counteracted it, creating excitement and heightening tension. It injected into the stage happenings irritating and brash sonorities as well as tremulously moving tones, thereby creating a contrapuntal impression.

The periods of protracted silence accentuated the play's fearful and awesome sides, adding to its sacrality. *Le Livre de Christophe Colomb* is in some ways a reworking of Claudel's favorite themes, subsumed in *Tête d'Or*, the Coûfontaine cycle, *Partage de Midi*, and *Le Soulier de satin*: that of the adventurer, the discoverer who is misunderstood, rejected, and vilified. Certainly Claudel identified with this kind of creative spirit, which he looked upon as the prototype of the poet: a demiurge whose overwhelming ambition encourages him to break ties with family and friends, as well as with his land. Compelled by a dream, he forges ahead into an unknown, untraveled world of mystery and terror; there he bears his solitude, living out his torment playing his sacrificial role.

Always active, Claudel was named ambassador to the United States in 1927 and ambassador to Belgium in 1933. He was elected to the French Academy in 1946. Nor was his pen ever stilled—until 22 February 1955, when, reading a book about Rimbaud, the poet who had had the greatest influence on Claudel's creative life, he suffered a fatal heart attack.

Action in Claudel's theater, whether it be in *Tête d'Or*, *La Ville*, *Partage de Midi*, *L'Annonce faite à Marie*, or the Coûfontaine cycle, follows a pattern: the situation is descanted at the outset in slow, architecturally balanced scenes; gesture and attitude are not only paced in a rhythmic flow, intensifying the emotional climate, but they are also shorn of any extraneous elements and simplified to the extreme. The bare necessities are projected upon, elaborated, and then descanted. Expressed in a glance, a turn of the wrist, an arched hand, a sign, a moan or giggle, each gesture indicates a mood and sets the tone for the protagonists' lowly or superior spiritual encounter.

The characters in Claudel's more complicated dramas, such as *Le Soulier de satin* and *Le Livre de Christophe Colomb*, may be seen as mirror images: they are paradigms of greater forces living out their workaday and spiritual existences in contrapuntal blocks. Frequently Claudel's characters are featured as double (the sisters in *L'Annonce faite à Marie*) or as terrestrial and celestial aspects of the same characters (as in *Le Livre de Christophe Colomb*). Each echoes and responds to the other, transmitting clusters of feelings, sensations, and analogies. These become all the more powerful because of Claudel's special use of stichomythia: a form of dialogue used in ancient Greek theater in which alternating lines, frequently of antithetical nature, point up the divisiveness of the characters onstage, thus emphasizing anxiety and heightening emotion. Similarly, Claudel fashions universal antitheses, whose signs, mysteriously and imperiously revealed, are fraught with cosmic repercussions.

The trajectory of Claudel's characters is cyclical, beginning with a crime and concluding with a punishment. The protagonist, at least one in each play, is instinctually drawn toward a mate and commits the sin of concupiscence. Claudel, quoting Saint Augustine's renowned *etiam peccata* (even sinners), similarly believes that sin serves a purpose. Once the protagonist has bathed in sin, he seeks punishment: ascetic practices, flagellation, deprivation, or prayer. Redemption and forgiveness are then earned. The notion of sacrifice lies at the heart of Claudel's theater: the final acts are always "bloody," he writes in *Réflections sur la poésie* (Reflections on Poetry, 1963), but "always magnificent," for "Religion not only place[s] drama in daily life, but also at its end, in Death, the highest form of drama which, for all true disciples of our Divine Master, is *sacrifice*."

Claudel's theater encapsulates saint and sinner, penitents and flesh-ridden beings, the virginal creatures whose lives are unlived as well as the sick in heart and soul. Impurity coexists with purity, murderous desires with feelings of beatitude, jealousy, anger, revenge, or deception along with an insatiable need for God. Creator of a deeply personal theater, Claudel lives out his own dramas in projection, combining excoriating guilt with a need for punishment in what could be called a sadomasochistic round.

It is through the word that Claudel distills raw pain, humanizes matter, or descants brutalities. Subtle correspondences radiate in structured sequences, in blocks, placed one upon the other, and en masse, assuming the power and stature of a cathedral, its foundations dug deep in the subsoil and its spires soaring toward divinity. The protagonists are all tainted with their opposites, bearing within themselves a spark of the Divine as well as a spark of Luciferian Light and Delight.

Letters:

Correspondances avec Jacques Rivière, 2 volumes, edited by Henri Alain Fournier (Paris: Gallimard, 1948);

Correspondances avec André Suarès, edited by Robert Mallet (Paris: Gallimard, 1951);

Correspondances avec Francis Jammes et Gabriel Frizeau, edited by André Blanchot (Paris: Gallimard, 1952);

"Correspondances avec Maurice Pottecher," in *Cahiers de Paul Claudel,* volume 1, edited by Pierre Moreau (Paris: Gallimard, 1959), pp. 60–111;

"Correspondances avec Darius Milhaud," in *Cahiers de Paul Claudel,* volume 3, edited by Jacques Petit (Paris: Gallimard, 1961);

"Correspondances avec Lugné-Poë," in *Cahiers de Paul Claudel,* volume 5, edited by René Farabet (Paris: Gallimard, 1964);

"Correspondances avec Jacques Copeau, Bourdet, Dullin, Jouvet," in *Cahiers de Paul Claudel,* volume 6, edited by Petit and Henri Miciolo (Paris: Gallimard, 1966);

Correspondances avec André Gide, edited by Mallet (Paris: Gallimard, 1969);

Correspondances avec Marthe Bibesco, Echanges avec Claudel (Paris: Mercure de France, 1972);

Correspondances avec Eve Francis, Un autre Claudel (Paris: Grasset, 1973);

Correspondances avec Louis Massignon, edited by Michel Malicet (Paris: Desclée De Brower, 1973);

"Correspondances avec Jean-Louis Barrault," in *Cahiers de Paul Claudel,* volume 10, edited by Michel Lioure (Paris: Gallimard, 1974).

Bibliographies:

Bibliographie de la littérature française, volume 3 (Paris: Editions de la Chronique des Lettres françaises, 1931), pp. 146–160;

Benoist-Méchhin et Blaizot, *Bibliograpie des Oeuvres de Paul Claudel* (Paris: Auguste Blaizot, 1931);

S. Dreher, *Bibliographie de la littérature française de 1930 à 1938* (Geneva: Droz, 1948), pp. 95–96;

R. Rancoeur, *Bibliographie littéraire de la Revue d'Histoire littéraire de la France* (Paris: Colin, 1953–);

M.-L. Drevret, *Bibliographie de la littérature française de 1940 à 1949* (Geneva: Droz, 1955), pp. 145–150;

Jacqueline de Labriolle, *Claudel and the English Speaking World* (London: Grant & Cutler, 1973).

Biographies:

Daniel Rops, *Claudel tel que je l'ai connu* (Strasbourg: Editions F.-X. Le Roux, 1957);

Henri Mondor, *Claudel plus intime* (Paris: Gallimard, 1960);

Louis Chaigne, *Vie de Paul Claudel par lui-même* (Paris: Seuil, 1961);

Paul-André Lesort, *Paul Claudel par lui-même* (Paris: Seuil, 1963).

References:

André Alter, *Paul Claudel* (Paris: Seghers, 1989);

Louis Barjon, *Paul Claudel* (Paris: Editions universitaires, 1953);

Jean-Louis Barrault, *Nouvelles réflexions sur le théâtre* (Paris: Flammarion, 1959);

Cahiers de la Compagnie Madeleine Renaud-Jean-Louis Barrault, 25ᵉ (Paris: Julliard, 1958), pp. 3–38;

Georges Cattaui and Jacques Madaule, eds., *Entretiens sur Paul Claudel* (Paris: Mouton, 1968);

René Farabet, *Le Jeu de l'acteur dans le théâtre de Claudel* (Paris: Lettres modernes, 1960);

Wallace Fowlie, *Paul Claudel* (London: Bowes & Bowes, 1957);

Eve Francis, *Temps héroïques: théâtre, cinéma, préface de Paul Claudel* (Paris: Denoël, 1949);

Stanislas Fumet, *Claudel* (Paris: Gallimard, 1958);

Henri Gouhier, "La trilogie," in *Paul Claudel, IV, l'Histoire* (Paris: Minard, 1967), pp. 31–42;

Richard Griffiths, ed., *Claudel: A Reappraisal* (London: Rapp & Whiting, 1968);

Henri Guillemin, *Claudel et son art d'écrire* (Paris: Gallimard, 1955);

Bettina L. Knapp, *Paul Claudel* (New York: Ungar, 1982);

James R. Lawler, "Claudel's art of provocation," *Essays in French Literature*, 1 (November 1964): 30–55;

Michel Lioure, *L'esthétique de Paul Claudel* (Paris: Armand Colin, 1971);

Aurélien Lugné-Poë, *Dernière pirouette* (Paris: Editions du Sagittaire, 1946);

Jacques Madaule, *Claudel et le langage* (Paris: Desclée De Brower, 1968);

Madaule, *Le Drame de Paul Claudel* (Paris: Desclée De Brower, 1964);

Michel Malicet, *Lecture psychanalytique de l'oeuvre de Claudel,* 3 volumes (Besançon: Annales littéraires de l'Université de Besançon, 1978–1979);

Gabriel Marcel, *Regards sur le théâtre de Paul Claudel* (Paris: Beauchesne, 1964);

Marianne Mercier-Campiche, *Le Théâtre de Claudel* (Paris: Pauvert, 1968);

Jacques Petit and Jean-Pierre Kemp, *Claudel on the Theatre* (Coral Gables, Fla.: University of Miami Press, 1972);

Henri Peyre, "Le Classicisme de Paul Claudel," *Nouvelle Revue française* (1 September 1932): 432–441;

Georges Poulet, "Oeuf, semence, bouche ouverte, zéro," *Hommage à Paul Claudel, Nouvelle Revue Française* (1 September 1955): 445–466;

Jean Rousset, "La Structure du drame claudélien: l'écran et le face à face," in *Forme et signification* (Paris: Corti, 1964), pp. 171–189;

Joseph Samson, *Paul Claudel poète-musicien* (Geneva & Paris: Editions du Milieu du Monde, 1947);

Marie-Louise Tricaud, *Le Baroque dans le théâtre de Paul Claudel* (Geneva: Droz, 1967);

André Vachon, *Le Temps et l'espace dans l'oeuvre de Paul Claudel* (Paris: Seuil, 1965);

François Varillon, *Claudel* (Paris: Desclée De Brower, 1967);

Harold Watson, *Claudel's Immortal Heroes* (New Brunswick, N.J.: Rutgers University Press, 1971).

Papers:
Claudel's papers are held in the Fonds de la Bibliothèque littéraire Jacques Doucet and the Archives de la société Paul Claudel (13, rue Pont-Louis-Philippe, Paris).

Georges Courteline

(25 June 1858 – 25 June 1929)

Judith Graves Miller and Denise R. Mjelde
University of Wisconsin–Madison

PLAY PRODUCTIONS: *Lidoire,* Paris, Théâtre-Libre, 8 June 1891;

Les Joyeuses commères de Paris, by Courteline and Catulle Mendès, Paris, Nouveau Théâtre, 16 April 1892;

Boubouroche, Paris, Théâtre-Libre, 27 April 1893;

Emilienne aux quatr'z'arts, by Courteline and Louis Marsolleau, Paris, Folies-Bergères, 9 December 1893;

Les Grimaces de Paris, by Courteline and Marsolleau, Paris, Théâtre des Nouveautés, 26 October 1894;

La Peur des coups, Paris, Théâtre d'Application, 14 December 1894;

Les Gaietés de l'escadron, by Courteline and Edouard Norès, Paris, Théâtre de l'Ambigu-Comique, 18 February 1895;

La Cinquantaine, Paris, Théâtre du Carillon, 22 November 1895;

Petin, Mouillarbourg et Consorts, Paris, Théâtre du Carillon, 5 May 1896;

Le Droit aux étrennes, Paris, Théâtre-Salon, 13 May 1896;

Un Client sérieux, Paris, Théâtre du Carillon, 24 August 1896;

Hortense! couche-toi, Paris, Grand-Guignol, 15 March 1897;

Monsieur Badin, Paris, Grand-Guignol, 13 April 1897;

L'Extra-Lucide, Paris, Théâtre du Carillon, 17 May 1897;

Une Lettre chargée, Paris, Théâtre du Carillon, 10 June 1897;

Théodore cherche des allumettes, Paris, Grand-Guignol, 10 October 1897;

Gros chagrins, Paris, Théâtre du Carillon, 2 December 1897;

La Voiture versée, Paris, Théâtre du Carillon, 2 December 1897;

Les Boulingrin, Paris, Grand-Guignol, 7 February 1898;

Le Gendarme est sans pitié, Paris, Théâtre-Antoine, 27 January 1899;

Georges Courteline

L'Affaire Champignon, by Courteline and Pierre Veber, Paris, Théâtre de la Scala, 8 September 1899;

Blancheton père et fils, by Courteline and Veber, Paris, Théâtre des Capucines, 26 October 1899;

Panthéon-Courcelles, Paris, Grand-Guignol, 1 November 1899;

Le Commissaire est bon enfant, by Courteline and Jules Lévy, Paris, Théâtre du Gymnase, 16 December 1899;

L'Article 330, Paris, Théâtre-Antoine, 11 December 1900;

Les Balances, Paris, Théâtre-Antoine, 26 November 1901;

Victoires et conquêtes, Paris, Théâtre des Mathurins, 15 April 1902;

La Paix chez soi, Paris, Théâtre-Antoine, 26 November 1903;

La Conversion d'Alceste, Paris, Théâtre Français, 15 January 1905;

Les Mentons bleus, by Courteline and Dominique Bonnaud, Paris, Boîte à Fursy, 1 January 1906;

J'en ai plein le dos de Margot (later retitled *La Cruche*), by Courteline and Pierre Wolff, Paris, Théâtre de la Renaissance, 27 February 1909.

BOOKS: *Les Gaietés de l'escadron* [play] (Paris: Marpon et E. Flammarion, n.d. [1886?]);

Le 51e chasseurs (Paris: Marpon et E. Flammarion, n.d. [1887?]);

Les Femmes d'amis (Paris: Marpon et E. Flammarion, n.d. [1888?]);

Le Train de 8 h. 47: La Vie de caserne (Paris: Marpon et E. Flammarion, n.d. [1888?]);

Madelon, Margot et Cie (Paris: Marpon et E. Flammarion, n.d. [1890?]);

Potiron (Paris: Marpon et E. Flammarion, n.d. [1890?]);

Les Têtes de bois (Paris: Strauss, 1890);

Lidoire (La Vie de caserne) (Paris: E. Flammarion, 1891);

Les Joyeuses commères de Paris, by Courteline and Catulle Mendès (Paris: Charpentier et Fasquelle, 1892);

Les Facéties de Jean de la Butte (Paris: E. Flammarion, n.d. [1892?]);

Les Meilleurs contes de Catulle Mendès et Georges Courteline (Paris: Marpon et E. Flammarion, n.d. [1892?]);

Lidoire et La Biscotte (Paris: E. Flammarion, n.d. [1892?]);

Messieurs les ronds-de-cuir, tableaux-roman de la vie de bureau (Paris: E. Flammarion, n.d. [1893?]); translated by Eric Sutton as *The Bureaucrats* (London: Constable, 1928);

Boubouroche [play] (Paris: Charpentier et Fasquelle, 1893);

Boubouroche [novel] (Paris: E. Flammarion, n.d. [1893?]);

Ah! Jeunesse!... (Paris: E. Flammarion, n.d. [1894?]);

Ombres parisiennes (Paris: E. Flammarion, n.d. [1894?]);

La Vie de caserne (Paris: Magnier, 1894);

La Peur des coups (Paris: Charpentier et Fasquelle, 1895);

La Cinquantaine (Paris: Librairie du Carillon, 1895);

X . . . , roman impromptu, by Courteline, George Auriol, Tristan Bernard, Jules Renard, and Pierre Veber (Paris: E. Flammarion, n.d. [1895?]);

Le Droit aux étrennes (Paris: Charpentier et Fasquelle, 1896);

Pétin, Mouillarbourg et Consorts (Paris: E. Flammarion, n.d. [1896?]);

Monsieur Badin (Paris: Ollendorff, 1897);

Un Client sérieux [play] (Paris: E. Flammarion, 1897);

Un Client sérieux [novel] (Paris: P. V. Stock, 1898);

La Voiture versée (Paris: P. V. Stock, 1898);

Hortense! couche-toi, music by Charles Levadé (Paris: P. V. Stock, 1898);

Les Boulingrin (Paris: P. V. Stock, 1898);

Gros chagrins (Paris: P. V. Stock, 1898);

Théodore cherche des allumettes (Paris: P. V. Stock, 1898);

Une Lettre chargée (Paris: P. V. Stock, 1898);

Monsieur Badin and *L'Extra-Lucide* (Paris: E. Flammarion, n.d. [1899?]);

Le Gendarme est sans pitié, by Courteline and Edouard Norès (Paris: E. Flammarion, n.d. [1899?]); translated by H. Isabelle Williams as *The Pitiless Policeman* (Boston: R. G. Badger, 1918);

Le Commissaire est bon enfant, by Courteline and Jules Lévy (Paris: E. Flammarion, n.d. [1900?]);

L'Article 330 (Paris: L'Illustration, 1900);

Les Balances (Paris: E. Flammarion, n.d. [1901?]);

Sigismond, followed by *Panthéon-Courcelles* [two one-acts] (Paris: Juven, 1901);

Victoires et conquêtes (Paris: P. V. Stock, 1902);

La Paix chez soi (Paris: L'Illustration, 1903); translated by Leroy James Cook as *Peace at Home: A Comedy in One Act* (Boston: R. G. Badger, 1918);

La Conversion d'Alceste (Paris: L'Illustration, 1905);

Les Gaietés de l'escadron [novel], by Courteline and Norès (Paris: P. V. Stock, 1905);

Les Mentons bleus, by Courteline and Dominique Bonnaud (Paris: P. V. Stock, 1906);

La Cruche; ou, J'en ai plein le dos de Margot, by Courteline and Pierre Wolff (Paris: Charpentier et Fasquelle, 1910);

La Philosophie de Georges Courteline (Paris: E. Flammarion, 1917).

Collections and Editions: *Les Marionnettes de la vie,* includes *Lidoire, Boubouroche, Monsieur Badin, La Peur des coups, Les Boulingrin, Théodore cherche des allumettes, Un client sérieux, Hortense, couche-toi!, Le Droit aux étrennes, Le Gendarme est sans pitié, Le Commissaire est bon enfant,* et *L'Article 330* (Paris: E. Flammarion, n.d. [1901?]);

Oeuvres Complètes, 3 volumes (Paris: F. Bernouard, 1925–1927);

Théâtre, 3 volumes (Paris: E. Flammarion, 1929);

Contes et nouvelles, 2 volumes (Paris: Librairie de France, 1930–1931);

The Plays of Georges Courteline, adapted into English by Albert Bermel and Jacques Barzun (London: Heinemann, 1961);

Théâtre complet (Paris, 1961).

OTHER: Préface, in *Mes Campagnes, album militaire inédit,* by Albert Guillaume (Paris: Simonis-Empis, n.d. [1896]);

Préface, in *L'Art au théâtre,* volume 1, by Catulle Mendès (Paris: Charpentier et Fasquelle, 1897);

L'Affaire Champignon, adaptation by Courteline and Pierre Veber of *Tribunaux comiques* by Jules Moinaux (Paris: E. Flammarion, n.d. [1899?]);

Préface, in *Tours pittoresques,* by P. Suzanne (Tours: Lelièvre, 1899);

Blancheton père et fils, adaptation by Courteline and Veber of *Tribunaux comiques* by Jules Moinaux (Paris: E. Flammarion, n.d. [1900]);

Préface, in *Main droite et main gauche,* by Eugène Domicent Bertol-Graivil (Paris: Simonis-Empis, 1902).

The caricaturist B. Colomb (1849–1909), better known as "Moloch" for his devastating cartoons, shows Georges Courteline sweeping up with his pen the five categories of "vermin" that inhabit his plays. In Moloch's celebrated caricature policemen, judges, army officers, bureaucrats, and manipulative women tumble about at Courteline's feet, while the chronicler and playwright gazes out at the world, weary, knowing, and complicitous. This stance and these five subjects characterize the entirety of Courteline's dramatic production: some twenty-eight plays, almost all adapted from weekly newspaper columns he contributed from 1880 to 1896 to Parisian dailies, notably *L'Echo de Paris* and the literary supplement to *Le Journal.* Courteline's style, a combination of social commentary, slapstick depictions of systems gone awry, delightful portraits of a vivacious capital city, and reluctant tenderness for human folly, has made him one of France's most popular playwrights. Both during his lifetime and after his death innumerable editions of his works were published and quickly sold. In 1884, for example, a gift of Courteline's collected stories was used as a lure to promote the newspaper *Les Petites Nouvelles.* Fifty thousand copies flew from the newsstands the first day. In 1945 city street workers proved they had not forgotten the man whom Edmond de Goncourt tagged as "belonging to the race of skinny cats." A group of them surprised the widowed Mme Courteline by restoring to her the writer's bronze bust. They had spirited it away from its outdoor perch on the Avenue de St. Mandé and kept it hidden during the Occupation so that the German army would not melt it down for cannons.

Courteline's plays, having entered after 1913 into the repertory of the Comédie-Française, are regularly produced there. Movie fans of all ages still laugh uproariously at the film versions of *Le Commissaire est bon enfant* (The Cop's a Good Sport, 1913), *Les Ronds-de-cuir* (The Bureaucrats, 1937), and *Les Gaités de l'Escadron* (The Joys of the Squadron, 1932). If he is less performed in France at present than his contemporary and friend Georges Feydeau, it may be because the compactness and tidiness of Courteline's plays—almost all one-acts—do not lend themselves as well as Feydeau's to the extravagant mise-en-scenes that hallmark post-1970s theatrical production. Courteline's underlying grimness and the nightmarish quality of his dramatic situations can certainly be interpreted as prescient of the world gone mad of a Samuel Beckett, an Arthur Adamov, or a Eugène Ionesco. Nevertheless, in his refusal to succumb to an ambience of victimization, in his characters' capacities to best the system and not only be bested by it, in his resolute concentration on society and not metaphysics, Courteline remains anchored in a tradition of deriding those social institutions and conventions that can be understood as founding daily life in the West.

Born Georges Moinaux into a bourgeois family on 25 June 1858, Courteline, who took on a pseudonym to protect his job as a bureaucrat, spent his early years in Tours. His maternal grandmother took charge of the solitary and unhappy boy while his parents pursued a living in Paris. His father, Jean Moinaux, led a successful double career as court reporter and vaudeville librettist. When finally summoned to Paris for school, Courteline was overwhelmed and overjoyed by the theatrical crowd that passed in and out of his parents' home. Psychologically, he never left that creative and intensely garrulous environment.

During the Commune uprising of 1870 Courteline's family fled to Meaux. A painful but also crucial sojourn at the Collège de Meaux capped Courteline's formal education. There his teachers encouraged both his writing and his efforts at play production, specifically his work on Eugène Labiche's farces. Spending more time writing and observing than studying, Courteline failed his baccalaureate exam. He consequently had no choice but to honor his military obligation.

Courteline tried fruitlessly at first to obtain a medical discharge from the horse guards, in which he served seven months from 1879 to 1880. His distaste for military hierarchy, his highly critical and gleefully funny look at life in the barracks, at the mess hall, or on giddy leave from army discipline eventually constituted one of the major segments of his newspaper chronicles and, later, his dramatic sketches. In *Le Train de 8 h. 47* (The 8:47 Train, [1888?]) or *Lidoire et La Biscotte* (Lidoire and The Sugar Cookie, 1892), his acute ear for army slang and colloquial speech sets before his readers a whole gamut of slovenly, senseless, and pitiable soldiers. The disrespect he displays for protocol in his 1895 play *Les Gaietés de l'escadron,* adapted from the 1886 chronicle and performed during the era of the Alfred Dreyfus controversy and the mounting cries for military reform, earned him the ire of censors. However, fellow critics of the military, such as Emile Zola, were glad to count him among their numbers, even if his form of criticism was much more tongue-in-cheek than theirs.

When Courteline at last escaped from the rigors of military life, his by then well-known father used his influence to procure him a place in the Ministry of Church Affairs. Assigned in 1880 to the Bureau of Gifts and Inheritances, Courteline undertook a spurious fourteen-year career as a bureaucrat, during which time he paid a colleague to do half his work. This allowed him sufficient leisure to pursue his chief passions: playing cards, drinking, and palavering in Montmartre's cafés during the day, partaking in the bohemian arts life of Montmartre's burgeoning cabarets at night, and writing at odd moments in-between. He frequented Stéphane Mallarmé's salon, was befriended by Théodore de Banville and the Daudet family, and on 1 June 1885 had the singular honor of being one of twelve poets chosen to carry Victor Hugo's casket through the streets of Paris.

The groundbreaking and short-lived poetry journal *Paris-Moderne,* which he launched in 1881; the incisive and witty features that he published from March 1884 in *Les Petites Nouvelles;* and the patronage of Catulle Mendès, whom he joined in the Parnassian art-for-art movement, brought Courteline both recognition and protection. Thus, although in such pieces as *Messieurs les ronds-de-cuir, tableaux-roman de la vie de bureau* (1893; translated as *The Bureaucrats,* 1928) and *Monsieur Badin* (Monsieur Badin, 1897) he scathingly denounces the laxness, stupidity, and calculated cruelty of "nincompoop" bureaucrats creeping about the recesses of Parisian ministries, his own position at the Ministry of Church Affairs was never imperiled. Not only did

Courteline have an indulgent supervisor who appreciated his craft as a writer, but he also piled up a stack of satirical columns so biting and pointed that his superiors, fearful of being accused of spitefulness, dared not fire him.

Courteline took sick leave in 1894, but he kept his salary until the end of his life. He apparently experienced throughout his stint at the Ministry of Church Affairs the same conundrum as the protagonist of *Monsieur Badin:* unable to go to work because it bores him, Badin cannot stay home because he is terrified of losing his job. His recourse is to insist on receiving a raise. It would appear that such skewed logic left bosses—in Courteline's life as well in his literary works—openmouthed with admiration.

The irony of his own position helped fuel Courteline's wit. The chronicles and dramatic sketches he wrote during his years as a bureaucrat abound with characters enmeshed in a labyrinth of cheerful, if amoral, self-interest and relentlessly haywire legal, social, or professional structures. In his La Brige series, for example, the eponymous La Brige wages desperate campaigns against the legal establishment. In *L'Article 330* (Article 330, 1900) La Brige lands in jail for proving to the justice system that the crime he has committed is not, in fact, a crime. However, in *Hortense! couche-toi* (Go to Bed, Hortense!, 1897), accompanied by his nine-months pregnant wife, La Brige counters a nasty, evicting landlord by invoking the inviolable rights of the ready-to-give-birth to remain domiciled in whatever they are renting. In the latter sketch La Brige turns the law in his favor and for once experiences a moment of revenge.

In all of his plays Courteline's characters operate in a lose-lose system. In *Le Commissaire est bon enfant* (1899), written with Jules Lévy, the commissioner dismisses a legitimate complaint, imprisons an honest man, and then goes crazy after being locked up by the criminal he would not take seriously in the first place. If Courteline's characters sometimes "win," it is because they accept the logic of their own contradictions, most often with wacky consequences, less frequently with potentially tragic ones. For instance, in *La Paix chez soi* (Peace at Home, 1903), one of Courteline's comic rants against marriage, a mediocre man attempts to control a birdbrained woman. The wife, a tearful shrew, and the husband, a petty tyrant, end up forgiving each other as a means of restoring the balance of power to their couple. Throughout their irrational negotiations Courteline shows, nevertheless, that power is always unbalanced by the very structure of marriage itself.

This unresolvable tension running through all of Courteline's work—both his newspaper chronicles and later his dramatic sketches—is what originally attracted the attention of young theater director André Antoine. In 1890 Antoine first sought out the writer to contribute a play to his budding and controversial Théâtre-Libre. For Antoine, Courteline concocted *Lidoire* (1891), a farce about a soldier whose role in the platoon is to act as the Saint Bernard of drunks. This first taste of theater proved decisive. The director's staging innovations, which included naturalizing the acting style and stressing the material reality of the set, fixed Courteline's social commentary in a recognizable modernity, his characters taking on quirky and consequently individualistic contours. Courteline and Antoine, similarly restless, searching, and courageous, collaborated five more times after *Lidoire,* with Antoine showcasing Courteline's plays for three to four evenings, after which they would be immediately picked up by small Boulevard houses for a longer run. Of all their productions, their 1893 collaboration on *Boubouroche* reaped the most rewards. *Boubouroche* is now considered to be Courteline's masterpiece, a social satire that equals the best of Molière's *comédies de caractère.*

Intrigued and seduced by the world opened to him through Antoine's theater, Courteline chose occasionally to take on secondary roles in his own plays. After 1906, when he more or less stopped writing for the stage, he still toured the provinces and abroad, often introducing and commenting on his plays as a form of curtain raiser. His successive wives, Suzanne Berty and Marie-Jeanne Brécourt, both actresses, respectively toured with him and managed his theatrical career. The first Mme Courteline, who died of tuberculosis in 1902, created in *La Peur des coups* (Fear of Blows, 1894) the prototype of Courteline's dazzling, impish, and wily young brides who outwit or outperform their narcissistic and bilious husbands. The second Mme Courteline helped him keep track of the royalties and honors that kept pouring in even after he abandoned the stage to travel. These included sums of more than Fr 300,000 for Léo Marchès's 1910 adaptation of *Le Train de 8. h 47,* promotion to the rank of commander in the Légion d'Honneur in 1921, and election to the Académie Goncourt in 1926. With most of his plays written between 1890 and 1900, Courteline settled after the turn of the century into a pattern of collaborations; or he simply gave permission to others to adapt his stories and chronicles. He did take the time to cull two tomes of maxims from his already published pieces (*La Philosophie de Georges Courteline,* 1917 and 1928) and to edit meticulously his fifteen-volume collected works, *Oeuvres Complètes* (1925–1927).

Courteline's last important play, *La Conversion d'Alceste* (Alceste's Conversion, 1905), written on request for the Comédie-Française to celebrate Molière's birthday, reimagines Alceste, Célimène, and Philinte six months after the story contained in Molière's *Le Misanthrope* (1666) has arrived at its unhappy conclusion. In perfect alexandrine verse, Courteline proposes an Alceste come to his senses, married to Célimène, and controlling his emotions. Unfortunately, Célimène finds this newly reformed man boring and, as a result, accedes to his best friend's assiduous courting. In the Courteline version Molière's *honnête homme* Philinte is thus treacherous and disloyal, while the unfortunate Alceste, having won his court case against the bad poet Oronte, is now more lost than if he had lost. As in Molière's play, Alceste again decides in the end to exile himself, seeking in the forest the company of wolves less cruel than the ones who surround him.

Courteline's grumpy Alceste foreshadows the growing disgust the playwright felt as France headed into World War I. He eventually withdrew to Marseilles in strong disapproval of the war. Back in Paris in 1927, he died two years later, on 25 June 1929, of complications from a second leg amputation due to diabetes. To his final moments he never lost his mordancy. Asked about how he felt when his first leg was amputated in 1925, Courteline responded that every day he woke up hoping the leg would have grown back, and every day he was disappointed for the next twenty-four hours.

All Courteline's plays were comedies, but his humor is not always the same, and his targets of ridicule vary from rigid, illogical, or incompetent systems to people's soft, complacent, and self-contradictory attitudes. Corresponding to this difference in target is also a degree of difference in the madness undergirding each play. The social satires frequently create a feeling of out-and-out insanity, stage action evolving, as in the case of *Les Boulingrin* (The Boulingrin Family, 1898), into carefully orchestrated bedlam. Courteline's romantic triangles, on the other hand, evoke *la folie douce* (sweet insanity), the tacit understanding that living together brings about its own form of craziness.

Most often Courteline's comic sense is that of the *farceur:* taking broad aim at situations that expose how human beings have been transformed into bowling pins, ready to be knocked down by the next ball thrown by life. In this type of play, as for example in *Le Commissaire est bon enfant,* characters cannot make figures of authority hear what they are saying. No matter how many good arguments they muster in their favor, no matter how many of them protest against the system in place, they are repeatedly beaten down by the powerful who, themselves, are seen to be simple robots of a system no one seems to govern. Hence, in *Le Commissaire est bon enfant* a parade of outraged citizens attempt to enlist the help of the police commissioner, whose only real interest lies in not being bothered. In the commissioner's tautological reasoning the police exist in order to exist—not in order to combat crime or protect people. He consequently confiscates the gun of a man who needs a weapon to protect himself, kicks out a woman who claims her husband is crazy, and jails an honest person who brings back to the police headquarters a watch he has found in the street. The insane husband eventually works his way in, picks up the gun forcibly taken from the first man, and jails the commissioner. In this upside-down world no one is safe, and personal security is an impossible fantasy.

Farces such as *Le Commissaire est bon enfant* depend on quick pacing, lightning exits and entrances, rapid-fire rejoinders, and a strong dose of physical comedy. Characters fall off their chairs, mug for the double audience of other characters and spectators, throw tantrums, and get shoved into closets. Sometimes the spiraling pace creates a sense of nightmare, with one scene dissolving into the next and resolutions taking the shape of conflagrations. In the most violent of these sorts of plays characters are reduced to cartoon figures, capable of bouncing back to life, even drinking champagne, after having been shot, set afire, and drowned, as is the house guest, Des Rillettes, in *Les Boulingrin*. In fact, in *Les Boulingrin* one might say that through the fate of the protagonist Des Rillettes, Courteline advances the notion that if the institution of marriage does not kill one, bourgeois formalities might just do the trick.

Courteline also creates a much less physical farce, as in his La Brige comedies. While the pacing is not less fast, the speed is maintained through verbal pileups of examples of absurd reasoning or self-contradictory rules and regulations. The effect thus achieved is mental: a dizzying psychological holding pen from which there is no escape. In each play in which he appears, for example, La Brige, a middle-class Figaro, demonstrates his case with gusto and wit. But he rarely frees himself of the incredible institutional practice or ridiculous ordinance that has ensnared him. In *Les Balances* (The Scales of Justice, 1901) he explains to his lawyer how he is damned if he fixes up his house and damned if he does not. One code will not allow him to touch the old stones until they fall down. Another requires him to align his house with all others on his street. Trapped in a catch-22 legal system, La Brige is guilty because he cannot be proclaimed innocent.

In *L'Article 330,* the most convoluted of all the La Brige plays, La Brige, in a last effort to redress the wrong done to him by the World's Fair planners, has mooned 13,687 fairgoers who have rolled by his apartment on the brand-new electric sidewalk taking them to the fair. After suing unsuccessfully every possible agency for invasion of privacy, La Brige has resorted to exposing himself in order to expose the indecency of the justice system. If the judge he harangues seems sympathetic to La Brige's plight, he ultimately condemns him to a year of hard labor because, to paraphrase him, there is nothing more dangerous to a legal system than a smart citizen who points out its weaknesses.

In others of Courteline's plays, which might be more accurately termed comic character studies with farcical elements, Courteline tempers his sarcasm with an undercurrent of nostalgia for the dream of romantic love. Most of his triangular or bedroom farces, such as *La Paix chez soi, La Peur des coups,* and *Boubouroche,* fit this description. As is true of all his plays, the comic action has already begun before the curtain opens. This type of attack means that Courteline's pieces begin at a point of high energy, the problem exposed in the first lines of the play. The young husband of *La Peur des coups,* for example, yelps out a curse word that foregrounds his rage, rage that will carry the wife into spicy battle—marked as always by clever repartee—over her supposed infidelities. The surprise ending, another of Courteline's favorite devices, displaces the rage and even the question of infidelity onto the absent players: the mother-in-law, the maid, and the cat. The play suggests that the couple will hold together somehow. But it also airs the quagmire of bad faith and noncommunication on which their marriage flounders. In his romantic farces Courteline delivers up to public scrutiny over and over again two lovers who cannot stand to be together nor bear to be apart. This paradox exposes the gaping hole propping up romantic love. Love both exists and does not, surviving in the fierce desire of its survival, despite the demonstrated terrors of married life.

The bittersweet quality and paradoxical message of Courteline's triangles find their richest expression in *Boubouroche.* In this two-act play Boubouroche, *bonne poire*—patsy, good egg, and sweet jerk—risks that most difficult of human experiences: bottoming out. Contented with his nightly card game and mooching friends, charmed by his eight-year liaison with Adèle, who is so "proper" she does not allow him to have a key to the apartment he pays for, Boubouroche confronts a grim messenger. An old man, neighbor to Adèle and habitué of Boubouroche's favorite café, tells him at last that Adèle has had another lover for as long as Boubouroche has bought her favors.

A furious Boubouroche charges over to Adèle's to discover the truth. When after a panicked search he finds André hidden in the armoire, the situation, instead of clarifying itself, becomes more muddled. Consummate actress Adèle creates a melodramatic smoke-screen around André's presence: his honor, she claims, is her secret. She alone is privy to a tragedy she cannot reveal. Undone by Adèle's alternating scenes of fury and contrition, Boubouroche, in the end, begs her to forgive him. In a textbook scene of displacement, he then beats up the old messenger for telling such a lie.

Wonderfully comic in its depiction of Boubouroche's naiveté, Courteline's farce might also be considered sad and morally ugly. Yet Boubouroche, in choosing to believe Adèle, has opted to gloss over the horror, to refuse to live in the madness of failed love affairs and infidelities in order to live in the madness of human solidarity and commitment. He has, after all, only one song in his repertory, "Le Forgeron de la Paix" (The Blacksmith of Peace), and he sings, as he says, what he knows.

This final acquiescence to a sense of civic order and community is what distinguishes Boubouroche from that other *poire* of the turn of the century, King Ubu, the focal character of almost all of Alfred Jarry's work. Jarry, whose work Courteline disliked, also structures his dramatic world with tropes of social machines run amok. However, in Jarry the loss of control is total; appetites are completely unbridled; and man, in any recognizable humanistic sense, is missing. By privileging on stage what he felt were man's baser and more-fundamental instincts, Jarry turned away from the material reality that grounds Courteline's theater. In *Boubouroche* the unwitting hero had, indeed, truly savored his card game and his beer before heading off to Adèle's. In the Ubu farces Ubu eats and plays, but all his activities become another permutation of the *merdre* (a term that encompasses a plethora of scatological shocks) that for Jarry constitutes existence. It may be that a healthy attitude toward sensual pleasures and beautiful things saved Courteline, and consequently his plays, from complete despair. He remains a playwright of "gay Paris": frustrated, perhaps, but also solidly tasting of the here and now, ready to do honor to life, still seen as a game worth playing.

Letters:

Albert Dubeux, ed., "Lettres à Siegfried Trebitsch," *Biblio,* 8 (1949);

"Lettres à Siegfried Trebitsch," *Europe,* 36, no. 350 (1958): 31–42;

Henri Mitterand, ed., "Deux Lettres inédites de Courteline à Emile Zola (1898)," *Les Cahiers naturalistes* (1958): 471–473.

Bibliographies:

Albert Dubeux, "Bio-Bibliographie de Georges Courteline," *Europe,* 36, no. 350 (1958): 43–48;

"Essai de bibliographie," *Livres de France,* 9, no. 9 (1958): 9–11.

Biographies:

Roger Lebrun, *Georges Courteline* (Paris: Sansot, 1906);

Roland Dorgelès, *Georges Courteline: enfant de Tours, moineau de Paris* (Tours: L'artiste, 1958);

Albert Dubeux, *La Curieuse Vie de Georges Courteline* (Paris: Gründ, 1949);

Emmanuel Haymann, *Courteline* (Paris: E. Flammarion, 1990).

References:

Marcel Achard, "Le Centenaire de Courteline," *Historia,* 23 (1958): 605–611;

Edo Bellingeri, "Courteline," in *I Contemporanei: Letteratura francese,* edited by Massimo Colesanti and Luigi de Nardis (Rome: Luciani Lucarini, 1976), pp. 248–258;

Théodore Beregi, "Courteline ou la philosophie du rire," *Sur le chemin de l'immortalité, vol. 1: Littérature et art en France* (Cosne-sur-Loire: Art et Poésie, 1986);

Isabelle Bernard, *Le Théâtre de Courteline* (Paris: Larousse, 1978);

Jean-Jacques Bernard, "Le Masque de Courteline," *Annales,* 94 (1958): 49–50;

Pierre Bornecque, "A la recherche d'un monde disparu: Courteline," *Annales de la Faculté des Lettres et Sciences Humaines de Yaoundé,* 6 (1975): 60–84;

Bornecque, "Le Capitaine Hurluret: Type courtelinesque," in *De Jean Lemaire de Belges à Jean Giraudoux: Mélanges d'histoire et de critique littéraire offerts à Pierre Jourda, Doyen honoraire de la Faculté des Lettres et des Sciences humaines de Montpellier, par ses collègues, ses élèves et ses amis* (Paris: Nizet, 1970), pp. 389–411;

Bornecque, "Notes pour un portrait de Courteline," *Annales de L'Université de Madagascar, Série Lettres et Sciences Humaines,* 2 (1964): 115–152;

Bornecque, *Le Théâtre de Georges Courteline* (Paris: Nizet, 1969);

Robert Carlier, "Courteline: La Fascination de la folie," *Magazine littéraire,* 288 (1991): 55–57;

"Courteline chez lui," *La Rumeur* (13 October 1928);

Pierre Descaves, "La Composition de Courteline," *Les Nouvelles littéraires* (30 June 1960): 1–2;

Descaves, "Mon Collaborateur Courteline," in *Mémoire de ma mémoire* (Paris: Wesmael-Charlier, 1960), pp. 96–120;

Mariangela Mazzocchi Doglio, "Courteline: Peintre de la médiocrité humaine," *Cahiers de l'Association internationale des études françaises*, 43 (1991): 183–200;

Roland Dorgelès, "Courteline," in his *Images* (Paris: Michel, 1975), pp. 47–71;

Dorgelès, "L'incroyable fonctionnaire que fut Courteline," *Le Figaro littéraire* (14 June 1958): 1, 11–12;

Albert Dubeux, "Courteline: Peintre du vrai," *Livres de France: Revue littéraire mensuelle*, 9, no. 9 (1958): 4–6;

Florica Dulmet, "Voici cinquante ans mourait Courteline," *Ecrits de Paris*, 392 (1979): 51–59;

Jean Dutourd, "Courteline," in his *Le Fond et la forme: Essai alphabétique sur la morale et le style* (Paris: Gallimard, 1958), pp. 37–40;

Béatrice Elliot, *Georges Courteline: l'homme, le comique, le conteur et l'humoriste, le satiriste et le critique* (Edinburgh: Nelson, 1928);

Europe, special issue on Courteline, 36, no. 350 (1958): 3–63;

Olivier Frebourg, "Courteline: Le Pessimiste sous l'humoriste," *Le Figaro littéraire* (2 April 1990): 8;

Pierre Gaxotte, "Une Cure de Courteline," *Le Figaro littéraire* (25 March 1961): 1–2;

Roger Gouze, "Courteline dans un fauteuil," in his *Les Bêtes à Goncourt: Un Demi-siècle de batailles littéraires* (Paris: Hachette, 1973), pp. 103–108;

Solange Guberman, "Le Comique de Labiche, Feydeau, Rostand et Courteline," *Culture française: Rassegna di lingua, letteratura e civiltà francese*, 26 (1979): 69–73;

Dominique Guerrini, ed., *Théâtre à lire, théâtre à jouer* (Paris: Ecole des loisirs, 1984);

La Herse, special issue on Courteline (December 1921);

Charles Henry Hirsch, "L'Arithmétique de Courteline," *Candide* (25 July 1929);

Jean-Jules Lafont, *La Medicine mentale dans les oeuvres de Georges Courteline* (Paris: Baillière / Toulouse: Dirion, 1914);

Pierre-Robert Leclercq, "Moinaux alias Courteline," *Magazine littéraire*, 276 (1990): 85;

Frédéric Lefevre, *Une heure avec . . . 1re série* (Paris: Nouvelle Revue française, 1924);

Livres de France, special issue on Courteline, 9, no. 9 (1958): 3–11;

Jaroslav Minár, "Courteline," *Casopis pro moderní fililogii*, 40 (1958): 242–243;

Jean Portail, *Georges Courteline: L'Humoriste français* (Paris: E. Flammarion, 1928);

Henri Rabine, "A Richelieu: Courteline en lever de rideau," *Comédie-Française*, 54 (December 1976–January 1977): 14–16;

Robert Rey, "Courteline," *Les Nouvelles littéraires* (26 June 1958): 1–2, 6;

Marguerite L. Richards, *Le Comique de Courteline* (Montreal: St. Joseph, 1950);

Jacques Robichez, "Maris Jaloux et prudents chez Labiche et Courteline," in *D'Eschyle à Genet: Hommage à Francis Pruner*, edited by Jean-Pierre Collinet (Dijon: UER Lettres et Philosophie, Université de Dijon, 1986), pp. 267–273;

André Roussin, "Farce et vaudeville," *Cahiers de la Compagnie Madeleine Renaud*, 32 (1960): 61–72;

Marcel Schwob, "Le Rire," in his *Spicilège: Postface de Maurice Saillet* (Paris: Mercure de France, 1960), pp. 153–159;

André Thérive, "A propos d'un centenaire," *La Table ronde*, 129 (1958): 186–190;

Guy Thuillier, "Courteline bureaucrate," *Revue administrative*, 28 (1975): 21–26;

François Turpin, *Georges Courteline* (Paris: Editions de la Nouvelle Revue critique, 1925);

Fernand Vanderem, *Le Miroir des lettres* [M. Georges Courteline à l'Académie Goncourt] (Paris: E. Flammarion, 1929);

Jacques Vivent, *Les Inspirations et l'art de Courteline* (Paris: La Maison française d'art et d'édition, 1921).

Papers:

Courteline's papers are held in the following locations: some of his letters are held in the Archives of the Bibliothèque municipale (Municipal Library) of Tours; the letters and objects were donated by Marie-Jeanne Georges-Courteline; in the Bibliothèque-musée (Museum and Library) of the Comédie-Française in Paris are letters to Béatrix Dussane; Archives of the Académie Goncourt, Nancy; Archives nationales, manuscrits des pièces soumises à la censure, dossiers de la Direction générale des cultes (Paris); Archives of Mme Roland Dorgelès (Paris); Bibliothèque nationale, département des manuscrits et département des arts du spectacle (Paris); Société des auteurs et compositeurs dramatiques (Paris); Société des gens de lettres, file on Courteline (Paris).

Jean-François Casimir Delavigne

(4 April 1793 – 11 December 1843)

Binita Mehta
The Graduate School and University Center, The City University of New York

PLAY PRODUCTIONS: *Les Comédiens,* Paris, Théâtre de l'Odéon, 6 January 1820;

Le Paria, Paris, Théâtre de l'Odéon, 1 December 1821;

L'Ecole des Vieillards, Paris, Théâtre-Français, 6 December 1823;

La Princesse Aurélie, Paris, Théâtre-Français, 6 March 1828;

Marino Faliero, Paris, Théâtre de la Porte Saint-Martin, 30 May 1829;

Louis XI, Paris, Théâtre-Français, 9 February 1832 (or 11 February 1832);

Les Vêpres Siciliennes, Paris, Théâtre-Français, 22 June 1832;

Les Enfants d'Edouard (Les Fils d'Edouard), Paris, Théâtre-Français, 18 May 1833;

Don Juan d'Autriche ou La Vocation, Paris, Théâtre-Français, 17 October 1835;

Une Famille au temps de Luther, Paris, Théâtre-Français, 19 April 1836 (or 12 April 1836);

La Popularité, Paris, Théâtre-Français, 1 December 1838;

La Fille du Cid, Paris, Théâtre de la Renaissance, 27 March 1840;

Le Conseiller Rapporteur, by unknown author with prologue in verse by Delavigne, Paris, Théâtre-Français, 17 April 1841;

Charles VI, Opera, by Delavigne and Germain Delavigne, music by F. Halévy, Paris, Théâtre de l'Académie Royale de Musique, 15 March 1843.

BOOKS: *Trois Messéniennes, élégies sur les malheurs de la France,* as Casimir Delavigne (Paris: Ladvocat, 1818; revised edition, par M. Casimir Delavigne (Paris: Ladvocat, 1819);

Deux Messéniennes, ou Elégies sur la vie et la more de Jeanne d'Arc (Paris: Ladvocat, 1819);

Les Vêpres Siciliennes, précédée du discours d'ouverture du second Théâtre français (Paris: J. N. Barba, 1819; revised and corrected, 1829);

Les Comédiens: précédée d'un prologue en prose (Paris: J. N. Barba, 1820);

Le Paria (Paris: J. N. Barba, 1821);

Casimir Delavigne (portrait by Ary Scheffer; from M. Fauchier-Delavigne, Casimir Delavigne, *1907)*

Messéniennes, 4 volumes in 1 (Paris: Ladvocat, 1822–1824);

Nouvelles Messéniennes, as M. Casimir Delavigne (Paris: Ladvocat, 1822);

Poésies diverses, précédés d'un poème sur la vaccine, as M. Casimir Delavigne (Paris: Chez Ladvocat, 1823);

Discours d'inauguration, pour l'ouverture de la salle de spectacle du Havre, prononcé le dimanche 24 août 1823 (Le Havre: Chapelle, 1823);

Théâtre et poésies diverses, 4 volumes (Bruxelles: M. Hayez, 1824–1827);

Messénienne sur Lord Byron, as Casimir Delavigne (Paris: Ladvocat, 1824);

Messenian on Lord Byron, as M. Casimir Delavigne (Marseilles: A. Ricard, 1824);

L'Ecole des Vieillards (Paris: J. N. Barba, 1823; revised edition, Paris: Ladvocat, 1824);

Discours prononcé dans la séance publique tenue par l'Académie française pour la réception de M. Casimir Delavigne, le 7 juillet 1825; par le récipiendaire de L. S. Auger (Paris: F. Didot, 1825);

Discourse prononcé par M. Casimir Delavigne, le jour de sa réception à l'Académie française, suivi de la réponse de M. Auger (Paris: Ladvocat, 1825);

Sept messéniennes nouvelles, as M. Casimir Delavigne (Paris: Chez Ladvocat, 1827);

La Princesse Aurélie (Paris: Ladvocat, 1828);

Discours en l'honneur de Pierre Corneille (Rouen: Baudry, 1829);

Marino Faliero (Paris: Dondey-Dupré, 1829);

Nouvelle Messénienne, as M. Casimir Delavigne. . . . *Une semaine de Paris* (Paris: A. Mesnier, 1830);

Louis XI (Paris: J. N. Barba, 1832); translated into English blank verse, with a biographical sketch and historical notes, by Frank Horridge as *Louis XI; a tragedy in five acts* (London: H. J. Drane, 1909);

Les Enfants d'Edouard (Paris: Dondey-Dupré, 1833);

Don Juan d'Autriche, ou La Vocation (Paris: J. N. Barba, 1836);

Une Famille au temps de Luther (Paris: H. L. Delloye & V. Lecou, 1836);

L'Ecole des Vieillards (Paris: J. N. Barba, 1838);

La Popularité (Paris: H. Delloye, 1839);

Le Retour, nouvelle Messénienne, as M. Casimir Delavigne (Paris: Perrotin, 1840);

Messéniennes et chants populaires, as M. Casimir Delavigne (Paris: Furne, 1840);

Poésies messéniennes, chants populaires, poésies diverses, et oeuvres posthumes (Paris: F. Didot et Cie, 184–?);

Messéniennes, chants populaires et poésies diverses, as M. Casimir Delavigne (Paris: Charpentier, 1840);

La Fille du Cid (Paris: C. Tresse, 1840);

Le Conseiller rapporteur, by an unknown author, with a prologue in free verse by Delavigne (Paris: 10, rue d'Enghien, 1841);

Charles VI: opéra en cinq actes, libretto by Delavigne and Germain Delavigne, music by F. Halévy (Paris: M. Schlesinger, 1843; New Orleans: Printed by J. F. Sollee, 1847) [French and English in parallel columns];

Marino Faliero (Paris: Impr. de l'aîné, 1843), pp. 403–435;

1823–1844. Deux discours d'inauguration du théâtre du Havre, by Delavigne and Ancelot (Le Havre: J. Morlent, 1844);

Mort de Jeanne d'Arc, as C. Delavigne (Béziers: Impr. de J. Fuzier, 1879);

Les Messéniennes, by Casimir Delavigne (Paris: H. Gautier, 1887);

Poésies, messéniennes, chants populaires, poésies diverses, Oeuvres posthumes, dernier chants, poèmes et ballades sur l'Italie (Paris: Garnier, 1895).

Editions and Collections: *Théâtre et poésies diverses* (Brussels: M. Hayez, 1824–1827);

Théâtre de M. C. Delavigne . . . avec des examens critiques par E. Dumoulin, Duviquet et Etienne, 4 volumes (Paris: Ladvocat et Duféy, 1825–1834); revised and republished as *Théâtre de M. C. Delavigne* (Paris: Duféy, 1834);

Théâtre (Paris: Ladvocat, 1826);

Translations into verse from comedies of Molière and Casimir Delavigne, preceded by a cursory view of French dramatic literature, to which are added original poems, imitations, school exercises, and the magic lantern, a satire, as E. F. (Paris: A. & W. Galignani, 1829);

Oeuvres complètes de C. Delavigne (Brussels: Laurent, 1831);

Oeuvres complètes de Casimir Delavigne, 3 volumes (Brussels, 1832);

Oeuvres de C. Delavigne, 4 volumes (Brussels: L. Haumann, 1832); republished as *Oeuvres de M. C. Delavigne,* 6 volumes (Paris: Furne, 1833–1838); republished again as *C. Delavigne,* 8 volumes (Paris: Furne, 1833–1845);

Oeuvres complètes de Casimir Delavigne, introduction by Delavigne (Paris: H. L. Delloye et V. Lecou, 1836);

Oeuvres complètes de Casimir Delavigne: Théâtre, poésie, oeuvres posthumes (Paris: Librarie Garnier Frères, 1845);

Oeuvres complètes, 6 volumes, with a notice by Germain Delavigne (Paris: Didier, Librarie-Editeur, 1846); revised and enlarged as *Oeuvres complètes de Casimir Delavigne* (Paris: Didier, 1855);

Théâtre et poésies de Casimir Delavigne, 4 volumes, nouvelle édition, seule complète, de l'Académie Française (Paris: Didier, 1854);

Théâtre de Casimir Delavigne, 3 volumes, Nouvelle édition, Edition Charpentier completée (Paris: Didier et Cie, 1859);

Oeuvres complètes, 4 volumes (Paris: F. Didot, 1870).

OTHER: "Discours prononcé dans la séance publique du 7 juillet en venant prendre à la place de M. Le Comte Ferrand," in *Recueil de discours lus dans les séances de l'Académie Française, 1820–1829* (Paris: Firmin-Didot, 1843).

Jean-François Casimir Delavigne, a highly popular and successful dramatist of the early nineteenth century, gained fame from his series of patriotic poems, the *Messéniennes* (The Messinian Women, 1818), and particularly from "Waterloo," which praises the glory of France under Napoleon Bonaparte. Although committed to classical theater, Delavigne wrote tragedies and comedies that reflect the transition from Classicism to Romanticism. Considered by some a better writer than Victor Hugo and Alexandre Dumas *père* and, according to Patrick Berthier in *Revue d'histoire du théâtre* (1993), "un précieux rempart contre l'excès romantique" (a valued rampart against the excesses of romanticism), he has been virtually eclipsed by his more-durable contemporaries.

Born in Le Havre on 4 April 1793, Delavigne was the son of a well-to-do businessman. He was trained in the classics at the Lycée Napoleon, later Henri IV, which he attended with his older brother and sometime artistic collaborator, Germain, as well as the playwright Eugène Scribe. Two essays, one on antiquity and the other on a subject from French history, caught the attention of Count François de Nantes, who found the young Casimir a position in his administration. After the success of *Les Messéniennes,* he was appointed librarian at the Chancellery, and later to the Duke d'Orléans, future King Louis Philippe. Twice rejected by the Académie Française, Delavigne was finally elected to that body in 1825.

Part of a group of dramatists sometimes called pseudoclassicists, Delavigne wrote plays that were Classical in style and Romantic in content. His subjects were taken from European history rather than antiquity. Although his early plays used alexandrine verse and followed the classical unities of time, place, and action, his later plays included elements of Romantic drama—historical tableaux, exotic locales, a mixture of tragic and comic tones, and innovations in versification. As did many playwrights of his generation, Delavigne used the devices of temporal and spatial distances to critique his own society and simultaneously to circumvent censorship laws of the period. Politically, Delavigne opposed the Bourbon restoration and remained nostalgic for France's glory under the Empire. His plays reflect his anticlerical, antimonarchical, liberal, nationalistic stance. Like Voltaire's drama, Delavigne's plays often carried political, moral, and philosophical messages. They were highly successful among the emerging *bourgeoisie d'argent* (the moneyed bourgeoisie) rivals of the "emigrés," or newly returned French aristocracy.

During the first phase of his dramatic career, Delavigne's plays adhered closely to Classical rules. These include the tragedies, *Les Vêpres Siciliennes* (Sicilian Vespers, 1819) and *Le Paria* (The Paria, 1821) and the comedies, *Les Comédiens* (The Actors, 1820), *L'Ecole des Vieillards* (The School for Graybeards, 1823) and *La Princesse Aurélie* (Princess Aurelia, 1828).

Les Vêpres Siciliennes, a five-act tragedy, depicts the thirteenth-century Sicilian revolt against the country's French conquerors. Reminded of their country's occupation by foreign armies after Napoleon's defeat, the spectators identified with the oppressed Sicilians rather than the French invaders. Initially refused by the Théâtre-Français, it was successfully produced at the Odéon. In *Les Vêpres Siciliennes,* possibly the most classical of his plays, Delavigne breaks the rules of decorum when the Sicilian Lorédan stabs himself and dies onstage.

Although *Le Paria,* a five-act tragedy, is written in Classical verse and follows the unities of time, place, and action, Delavigne adds local color by setting the play in Benares, India, on the banks of the River Ganges. *Le Paria* recounts the love story of Idamore, an untouchable (disguised as a soldier), and Néala, a Brahman. Strict caste rules forbid their union. The arrival of Zarès, Idamore's father, enrages Néala's father, Akébar, the high priest, who orders Zarès's death. Idamore is forced to reveal his caste and persuades Akébar to spare his father and kill him instead. In a surprising *coup de théâtre,* Néala abandons her Brahman father and embraces Zarès, thus choosing the life of an untouchable. Despite its Indian setting, the play reflects the political, social, and religious concerns in France during the Restoration. Akébar symbolizes the "emigrés," while Idamore, the pariah/soldier, represents the military might under Napoleon. Delavigne uses the Hindu caste system and untouchability not only to avoid censorship laws but also to denounce superstition, religious intolerance, and inequality.

Delavigne shifts gears with his *L'Ecole des Vieillards* (1823), a five-act comedy that explores the repercussions that result from the marriage between a wealthy sixty-year-old widower/businessman, Danville, and twenty-year-old Hortense, the daughter of an old friend. When the play opens, Danville, played by the eminent actor Talma, has just arrived in Paris from Le Havre. Announcing his marriage to his friend Bonnard, he makes a strong case for married life to the confirmed bachelor. Hortense, meanwhile, has been enjoying the pleasures of high society. She has made the acquaintance of the young and handsome Duke of Elmar, who is notorious for falling in love with beautiful young wives and then asking his minister uncle to offer titles to their husbands. Danville, who loves his wife, becomes jealous of the duke and challenges him to a duel. Only later does he learn that his wife has been faithful to him all along. Happily reconciled, they leave the pleasures of Paris for a quieter life in Le Havre.

Delavigne's comedy is a reworking of Molière's *L'Ecole des femmes* (The School for Women, 1662) but with a twist. Although reference is made to Molière in the play, Delavigne turns the cuckold theme on its head by representing the old man Danville, Molière's Arnolphe, as intelligent and admirable rather than grotesque and comic. Hortense, unlike Agnès, remains faithful to her aging husband. Charles-Augustin Sainte-Beuve, in *Portraits Contemporains* (1846), comments: "Sur ce thème, qui semble usé, du mariage, le poëte avait su trouver un comique nouveau, un pathétique sérieux et nullement bourgeois, une morale pure et non vulgaire" (On this hackneyed theme of marriage, the poet has found a new comic angle, a genuine pathos, not in the least bourgeois, and an honest and uncommon moral). More a morality play than a comedy, *L'Ecole des Vieillards* critiques the class structure. Unlike Hortense, who is dazzled by the nobility, Danville is quite comfortable in his social milieu.

Delavigne's theatrical career entered its second phase after his trip to Italy, where *Marino Faliero* (1829) took shape. This work was closely followed by *Louis XI* (1832) and *Les Enfants d'Édouard* (Edward's Children, 1833). Although Delavigne respects the classical unities, Romantic influences led him to include a variety of characters from all social classes—nobles, bourgeois, peasants—as well as different registers of language and variations in verse. This is expressed in the preface to *Marino Faliero,* where Delavigne hopes to open "une voie nouvelle" (a new path). Delavigne explains that although it is of little importance whether *Marino Faliero* is a classical or a romantic play, he respects the "belle et flexible" (beautiful and supple) language of the masters.

Basing his plot on an episode from Venetian history and a tragedy on the same subject by George Gordon, Lord Byron, Delavigne's *Marino Faliero* is a five-act tragedy set in fourteenth-century Venice. Marino Faliero, the doge of the Republic of Venice, is an old man whose honor is violated when a young noble accuses his young wife, Eléna, of being unfaithful to him. The culprit Sténo is found and sentenced to only a month in prison. This infuriates Marino Faliero, who, with a few conspirators, plots the downfall of the patricians. Betrayed to Lioni, a member of the Council of Ten, Faliero is arrested for treason and killed. While in the original story and in Lord Byron's adaptation the wife is innocent, in Delavigne's version Eléna is in fact unfaithful, and this fact lends poignancy to the tragedy. Faliero learns of his wife's infidelity with his young nephew, Fernando. Fernando dies in a duel, attempting to defend Faliero, who ultimately forgives Eléna before he, in turn, is murdered. In *Marino Faliero* Delavigne indirectly critiques the Bourbon monarchy. As Maurice Souriau observes in *Histoire du Romantisme en France* (History of Romanticism in France, 1927): "Au premier acte nous avons l'impression d'entendre des conspirateurs bonapartistes sous la Restauration, plutôt que des conjurés vénitiens de 1355" (In the first act we have the impression that we are hearing Bonapartist conspira-

tors during the Restoration, rather then Venetian plotters in 1355). The tragedy stresses the need for a state where wealth is earned and not inherited. Faliero comments:

> D'un Etat incertain, république ou royaume.
> . . . .
> Formons un Etat libre où régneront les lois,
> Où les rangs mérités s'appuieront sur les droits,
> Où les travaux, eux seuls, donneront la richesse;
> Les talents, le pouvoir; les vertus, la noblesse.
>
> (From an unstable state, republic or kingdom,
> . . . .
> Let us form a free State where law reigns,
> Where ranks merited rely on the law,
> Where work alone yields wealth;
> Talent begets power; virtue, nobility).

This melodrama encapsulates many of the recurring themes throughout Delavigne's oeuvre: generational conflicts, duty to country, the importance of the law in upholding liberal rule, the condemnation of autocratic monarchy.

Delavigne's *Louis XI,* a five-act tragedy, focuses on the evils of absolute power embodied by the fifteenth-century French monarch Louis XI. The tragedy is inspired by the memoirs of the chronicler Commines (a character in the play) and Walter Scott's *Quentin Durward* (1823). Here Delavigne describes the last day of Louis XI, the usurper of power. Echoes of Louis XIV pervade the play as the old tyrant remarks, "Mais mon peuple, c'est moi; mais le dernier d'entre eux" (But I am my people; down to the last of them). Yet, influenced by the revolution of 1830, the overthrow of the Bourbons, and the coronation of the "bourgeois" monarch Louis Philippe, the play underscores Delavigne's denunciation of absolute power. The Dauphin comments: "La France c'est le roi; mais c'est le peuple aussi" (France is the king; but it is also the people). With his dying breath Louis XI advises his son to be a benevolent monarch, and in the final lines of the play the saintly François de Paule advises the new king, "Et n'oubliez jamais sous votre diadème / Qu'on est roi pour son peuple et non pas pour soi-même" (And never forget that under your diadem / One is king for one's people and not for oneself).

A complex, tortured figure ("Lui-même est le bourreau de ses nuits et de ses jours" [he alone is the executioner of his nights and days]), the dying Louis XI appears in act 2 and thereby breathes life into the play. Jules Lemaître, in *Impressions de théâtre* (1895), describes Delavigne's depiction of Louis: "Quel incroyable et pourtant très vivant mélange d'égoïsme féroce et de sentiment d'un devoir supérieur, de superstition inepte et de haute intelligence, d'hypocrisie et de franchise, . . . de grotesque et de grandiose!" (What an incredible and yet vivid mixture of ferocious selfishness and superior sense of duty, of useless superstition and great intelligence, of hypocrisy and frankness, . . . of the grotesque and the grandiose!). The once virile king is now a pathetic figure, haunted by death. The language used by both Louis and his enemy, the Duke of Nemours, to express their terror mirrors the literary vogue for the gothic and the fantastic during the period. Pleading with François de Paule to prolong his life, the king confesses his dastardly crimes of patricide and fratricide, but to no avail. Louis's death occurs only after he has repented and given up his crown as *fausse grandeur* (false grandeur).

While *Louis XI* is reminiscent of William Shakespeare's tragic histories, in *Les Enfants d'Édouard,* a tragedy in three acts, Delavigne focuses on a single episode of Shakespeare's *Richard III.* The action of the play is minimal as character and plot are closely intertwined. The play depicts the doomed sons of Edward IV imprisoned and killed by their uncle, the regent Duke of Gloucester and future Richard III. The rightful heir, Edward V, represents Delavigne's image of a benevolent monarch, loved by his people. Like Shakespeare, Delavigne also links internal perversity with an externally grotesque appearance. Gloucester's deformity accentuates his evil nature while the youthful beauty of the princes highlights their vulnerability and innocence. Gloucester exclaims: "O marâtre nature! / En comblant tous les miens, tu fis de leur beauté / Un sarcasme vivant pour ma difformité" (O cruel Mother Nature! / By showering my family with all that they could wish for, you turned their beauty / Into a living sarcasm for my deformity).

In a completely different vein, Delavigne's *La Popularité* (Popularity, 1838) is a political comedy that stresses the ideals of a democratic society—freedom of the press, the importance of public opinion, honor in politics. The play's title refers to the ephemeral nature of popularity in political life. Set in England during the rule of the Orange dynasty, protagonist Edward Lindsey is an orator who basks in the admiration of his people. Forced to make a moral choice between maintaining his popularity and safeguarding his honor, Edward chooses the latter. His popularity wanes, and he is abandoned by his friend Mortins and Lady Stafford, the woman he loves. His father sums up the moral of the play, personifying popularity as a fickle mistress: "Ne l'aime pas pour elle; aime-la pour le bien / Et reste indifférent quand elle t'abandonne" (Do not love it for itself; love it for the good that it brings / And remain indifferent when it abandons you).

The well-known actor Talma as Danville in Delavigne's comedy L'Ecole des Vieillards *(1823)*

Among Delavigne's other plays are a five-act comedy in prose, *Don Juan d'Autriche* (1836); *Une Famille au temps de Luther* (A Family in the Time of Luther, 1836), a one-act tragedy that explores the religious struggles in Germany; a three-act tragedy, *La Fille du Cid* (The Daughter of the Cid, 1840), a continuation of Pierre Corneille's *Le Cid;* and a three-act comedy in prose, *Le Conseiller Rapporteur* (The Reporter Counsellor, 1841). The year he died he wrote an opera, *Charles VI,* in collaboration with his brother Germain and the composer Jacques François Fromental Élie Halévy. En route to Montpellier for health reasons, Delavigne died in Lyon on 11 December 1843, leaving behind an unfinished tragedy, "Mélusine."

Delavigne received mixed reviews from his contemporaries. While Sainte-Beuve praised his style and lyricism, Théophile Gautier called him a writer devoid of imagination, a lesser Shakespeare, Byron, Scott, Corneille, Bernardin de Saint-Pierre. Lemaître, however, described Delavigne as a "useful" dramatist, saying, "qu'il est donc, dans le développement de notre littérature dramatique, une *utilité* de premier ordre" (that his usefulness in the development of our dramatic literature is first-rate). In his later reassessment Gustave Lanson wrote, "Toute la vogue de ce dramaturge est venue de son prosaïsme renforcé" (This dramatist's popularity derives from his very mundaneness). More recently, Berthier asserted that Delavigne is "un fabricateur plus habile et plus régulier que bien d'autres, comme le témoin précieux d'une attitude de modération, de prudence" (a cleverer and more consistent fabricator than many others, a valuable testimony to moderation and prudence).

Writing during a time of great political upheaval and literary innovation, Delavigne remained politically committed to liberal ideals while aesthetically clinging to the bygone rules of classical theater. Through the course of his career, however, he incorporated several elements of Romantic drama into his work. He remained popular throughout the nineteenth century as his plays were performed, translated into several European languages, and parodied. His complete works were edited every ten years after his death until 1880, and he served as an important stepping-stone for future dramatists.

Letters:

Alphonse de Lamartine, *Sa lettre à Casimir Delavigne qui lui avait envoyé "L'Ecole des Vieillards"* (Paris: Audin, 1824);

Louis Fournier, *Lettres inédites de Casimir Delavigne, Ancelot, Jules Janin à Joseph Morlent, bibliothécaire de la ville du Havre* (Beaume: Impr. de A. Batault, 1897);

"Casimir Delavigne intime, from unpublished letters of his father and other relatives in France to his uncle residing in Louisiana," edited by A. Fortier, *Modern Language Association of America*, 28 (1913): 140–158.

Biographies:

Germain Delavigne, *Notice sur Casimir Delavigne* (Paris: Furne, 1845);

F. Vaucheux, *Casimir Delavigne, étude biographique et littéraire* (Le Havre: Dumoulin, 1893);

M. Blanadet, *Casimir Delavigne, Notice biographique suivie d'un essai bibliographique des ses parodies* (Le Havre: Godefroy, 1894);

A. Favrot, *Etude sur Casimir Delavigne* (Paris, 1894; Bern: Körber, 1895);

Marcelle Fauchier-Delavigne, *Casimir Delavigne intime, d'après des documents inédits,* foreword by Victorien Sardou (Paris: Société française d'imprimerie et de librairie, 1907).

References:

L. S. Auger, *Réponse de M. Auger, Directeur de l'Académie Française, au discours de M. C. Delavigne* (Paris: Firmin-Didot, 1825): 13–24;

Patrick Berthier, "Casimir Delavigne et ses parodistes: de Louis XI à Louis Bronze (1832)," *Revue d'histoire du théâtre,* 178–179 (1993): 61–72;

Joseph L. Borgerhoff, ed., *Nineteenth Century French Plays* (New York: Appleton-Century-Crofts, 1959), pp. 61–65;

François Coppée, *Discours prononcé au Havre le 4 Avril 1893 à l'occasion du centenaire de Casimir Delavigne, Institut de France, Académie Française* (Paris: Firmin-Didot, 1893);

Dessalles-Régis, "Casimir Delavigne," *Revue des Deux Mondes,* 2 (1840): 287–321;

Emile Faguet, *Notes sur le théâtre contemporain* (Paris: Lecène-Oudin, 1889);

Théophile Gautier, *Histoire de l'art dramatique en France depuis 25 ans,* 6 volumes (Paris: Hetzel, 1858–1859; Geneva: Slatkine Reprints, 1968), 2: 42–45; 3: 43;

Charles le Goffic, *Le Centenaire de Casimir Delavigne (1793–1893)* (Le Havre: Lemale, 1893);

Victor Hugo, "L'Heure glorieuse de Casimir Delavigne" in *Anthologie de l'Académie Française,* edited by Paul Gautier (Paris: Delagrave, 1921);

Hugo, *Réponse au discours de réception de Sainte-Beuve, à l'Académie Française, le 27 février 1845* (Paris: Firmin-Didot, 1845), pp. 23–38;

Gustave Lanson, *Histoire illustrée de la littérature française,* 2 volumes (Paris: Librarie Hachette, 1923), 2: 256, 262, 291, 292, 428;

Jules Lemaître, *Impressions de théâtre,* 8e série (Paris: Lecène-Oudin, 1895), pp. 87–100;

Pierre Martino, *L'Epoque romantique en France: 1815–1830* (Paris: Hatier, 1944), pp. 67–74;

Charles-Augustin Sainte-Beuve, *Eloge de Casimir Delavigne* (Paris: Didier, 1845);

Sainte-Beuve, *Portraits Contemporains,* volume 5 (Paris: Michel Lévy, 1846), pp. 169–192, 469–486;

Martha Hale Shacford, "Swinburne and Delavigne," *Modern Language Association,* 33 (1918): 85–95;

Maurice Souriau, *Histoire du Romantisme en France* (Paris: Editions Spes, 1927), pp. 236–249;

Souriau, *Moralistes et Poètes: Pascal, Lamartine, Casimir Delavigne . . .* (Paris: Vuibert et Nony, 1907);

Jean Vidalenc, "Un Orléaniste oublié: Casimir Delavigne (1793–1843)," in *Histoire et littérature. Les Ecrivains et la politique* (Paris: PUF, 1977), pp. 105–121;

R. Weitzeg, *Studie uber die Tragödien C. Delavigne* (Leipzig, 1901).

Papers:

Many documents pertaining to Casimir Delavigne's family and career can be found in the National Archives in Paris.

Adolphe Philippe Dennery

(17 June 1811 – 25 January 1899)

Mario Hamlet-Metz
James Madison University

PLAY PRODUCTIONS: *Le Voyage de la mariée,* by Dennery, Adolphe de Leuven, and Julien de Maillan, Paris, Théâtre des Variétés, 12 September 1829;

La Monnaie de singe, ou, Le Loyer de la danseuse, by Dennery and Maillan, Paris, Théâtre des Nouveautés, 22 November 1830;

Emile, ou, Le Fils d'un pair de France, by Dennery and Charles Desnoyer, Paris, Théâtre des Nouveautés, 6 September 1831;

Un Soufflet, by Dennery and Desnoyer, Paris, Théâtre de l'Ambigu-Comique, 22 March 1834;

L'Apprenti, ou, L'Art de faire une maîtresse, by Dennery, Théodore Cognard, and Achille d'Artois, Paris, Théâtre des Variétés, 15 May 1834;

La Marchesa, ou, La Courtisane de Rome, by Dennery and Alfred [pseudonym], Paris, Théâtre de l'Ambigu-Comique, 3 June 1834;

L'Idée du mari, by Dennery and Edouard Cormon, Paris, Théâtre de l'Ambigu-Comique, 12 July 1834;

L'Ile des bossus, by Dennery and Desnoyer, Paris, Théâtre de l'Ambigu-Comique, 6 December 1834;

La Victime du corridor, by Dennery and Edonard Déaddé, Paris, Théâtre de la Gaîté, 1 January 1835;

Changement d'uniforme, Paris, Théâtre des Variétés, 2 June 1835;

Les Voisines du cinquième étage, Paris, Théâtre de l'Ambigu-Comique, 26 July 1835;

La Femme qui se venge, Paris, Théâtre des Variétés, 14 November 1835;

L'Honneur de ma fille, Paris, Théâtre de l'Ambigu-Comique, 17 December 1835;

Tiburce, ou, Qui veut de ma vie, by Dennery and Phillipe Dumanoir, Paris, Saint-Antoine, 23 December 1835;

1814, ou, Le Pensionnat de Montereau, by Dennery and Cormon, Paris, Théâtre de l'Ambigu-Comique, 19 January 1836;

L'Avocat Pathelin, by Dennery and Octave de Cès-Caupenne, Paris, Théâtre de l'Ambigu-Comique, 10 April 1836;

Silvia, by Dennery and Alfred Legoyt, Paris, Théâtre de l'Ambigu-Comique, 3 September 1836;

Dolores, Paris, Théâtre de la Gaîté, 3 November 1836;

Trois Coeurs de femmes, by Dennery, d'Artois, and Edmond Burat de Gurgy, Paris, Théâtre des Variétés, 17 November 1836;

Les Petits Souliers, ou, La Prison de Saint-Crepin, by Dennery and Eugéne Grangé, Paris, Théâtre Panthéon, 3 December 1836;

Un Bulletin de la Grande Armée, by Dennery and B. A. Tilleul, Paris, Théâtre du Palais Royal, 21 December 1836;

L'Homme qui se range, by Dennery and Cormon, Paris, Théâtre des Variétés, 25 February 1837;

Le Portefeuille, ou, Deux familles, by Dennery and Anicet Bourgeois, Paris, Théâtre de la Porte Saint-Martin, 7 March 1837;

La Sentinelle, ou, Huit ans de faction, by Dennery and Gustave Lemoine, Paris, Théâtre de la Gaîté, 14 May 1837;

Le Tour de faction, by Dennery and Grangé, Paris, Théâtre des Variétés, 20 July 1837;

L'Hôtel des haricots, ou, Il vaut mieux monter sa garde, by Dennery and Dumanoir, Paris, Théâtre du Palais Royal, 9 August 1837;

Le Spadassin, by Dennery, Alphonse Brot, and Grangé, Paris, Saint-Antoine, 6 October 1837;

Les Finesses du coeur, by Dennery and Grangé, Paris, Saint-Antoine, 28 October 1837;

Une Femme de lettres, by Dennery and Grangé, Paris, Folies Dramatiques, 14 November 1837;

Gras et maigre, by Dennery and Grangé, Paris, Théâtre du Palais Royal, 25 February 1838;

Femmes et pirates, by Dennery and Cormon, Paris, Théâtre de l'Ambigu-Comique, 19 March 1838;

Le Mariage d'orgueil, by Dennery and Déaddé, Paris, Théâtre du Vaudeville, 23 March 1838;

Madame et Monsieur Pinchon, by Dennery, Bayard, and Dumanoir, Paris, Théâtre des Variétés, 5 April 1838;

Gaspar Hauser, by Dennery and Bourgeois, Paris, Théâtre de l'Ambigu-Comique, 4 June 1838;

Raphael, ou, Les Mauvais Conseils, by Dennery, Cormon, and Grangé, Paris, Théâtre de l'Ambigu-Comique, 30 June 1838;

La Reine des blanchisseuses, by Dennery, B. de Rougemont, and Grangé, Paris, Théâtre des Variétés, 25 September 1838;

La Zambinella, by Dennery and Grangé, Paris, Théâtre de l'Ambigu-Comique, 22 October 1838;

Le Dernier élève de maître Everard, by Dennery and Grangé, Paris, Théâtre des Variétés, 10 November 1838;

Pierre d'Arezzo (L'Arétin), by Dennery, Louis Arétin, and Dumanoir, Paris, Théâtre de l'Ambigu-Comique, 28 November 1838;

Jeanne Hachette, ou, Le Siège de Beauvais sous Louis XI, by Dennery and Bourgeois, Paris, Théâtre de l'Ambigu-Comique, 7 January 1839;

1840, ou, La Guerre des saisons, by Dennery, Grangé, and Ernest Bourget, Paris, Théâtre de la Gaîté, 29 December 1839;

Le Tremblement de terre de la Martinique, music by M. Béancourt, Paris, Théâtre de la Gaîté, 23 January 1840;

Le Dernier Oncle d'Amérique, by Dennery and Grangé, Paris, Théâtre Panthéon, 1 February 1840;

Les Enfants d'Adam et d'Eve, by Dennery and Grangé, Paris, Folies Dramatiques, 18 April 1840;

Les Garçons de recette, by Dennery and Elie Berthet, Paris, Théâtre de l'Ambigu-Comique, 23 May 1840;

La Grisette au vert, Paris, Théâtre de l'Ambigu-Comique, 8 July 1840;

Toby le sorcier, by Dennery and Bourgeois, Paris, Théâtre du Palais Royal, 4 October 1840;

L'Amour en commandite, by Dennery, Leuven, and Léon Lhérie, Paris, Théâtre du Palais Royal, 8 November 1840;

La Grâce de Dieu, by Dennery and Gustave Lemoine, Paris, Théâtre de la Gaîté, 15 January 1841;

La Dette à la bamboche, Paris, Folies Dramatiques, 29 January 1841;

Potichon le Champenois, Paris, Théâtre du Vaudeville, 17 June 1841;

Les Bains à quatre sous, by Dennery and Edouard Brisebarre, Paris, Théâtre de l'Ambigu-Comique, 10 July 1841;

Le Moulin de la Galette, Paris, Folies Dramatiques, 31 July 1841;

La Citerne d'Albi, Paris, Théâtre de la Gaîté, 21 September 1841;

Les Pupilles de la garde, by Dennery and Lemoine, Paris, Théâtre de l'Ambigu-Comique, 2 November 1841;

Feu Peterscott, by Dennery and Grangé, Paris, Théâtre des Variétés, 24 December 1841;

Le Feuilleton, by Dennery and Louis-François Clairville, Paris, Théâtre de l'Ambigu-Comique, 26 December 1841;

Saint-Lundi, by Dennery and Clairville, Paris, Théâtre de l'Ambigu-Comique, 13 January 1842;

La Nuit aux soufflets, by Dennery and Dumanoir, Paris, Théâtre des Variétés, 23 March 1842;

Amour et amourette, by Dennery and Grangé, Paris, Folies Dramatiques, 12 April 1842;

La Journée d'une jolie femme, by Dennery and Cormon, Paris, Théâtre du Vaudeville, 7 July 1842;

Paris la nuit, by Dennery and Grangé, Paris, Théâtre de l'Ambigu-Comique, 13 July 1842;

La Dot d'Auvergne, by Dennery and Grangé, Paris, Théâtre du Palais Royal, 21 August 1842;

Fargeau le nourrisseur, by Dennery and Dumanoir, Paris, Théâtre des Variétés, 18 October 1842;

Ma maîtresse et ma femme, by Dennery, Dumanoir, and Paul Siraudin, Paris, Théâtre des Variétés, 25 November 1842;

Halifax, by Dennery and Alexandre Dumas *père,* Paris, Théâtre des Variétés, 30 November 1842;

Pauvre Jeanne, by Dennery and Grangé, Paris, Folies Dramatiques, 30 March 1843;

La Perruquière de Meudon, by Dennery and Bourgeois, Paris, Théâtre des Variétés, 22 July 1843;

Les Nouvelles à la main, by Dennery and Clairville, Paris, Théâtre des Variétés, 8 August 1843;

Les Bohémiens de Paris, by Dennery and Grangé, Paris, Théâtre de l'Ambigu-Comique, 27 September 1843;

Le Capitaine Roquefinette, by Dennery and Dumanoir, Paris, Théâtre des Variétés, 27 October 1843;

Les Mémoires de deux jeunes mariées, by Dennery and Clairville, Paris, Théâtre du Palais Royal, 10 December 1843;

Paris dans la comète, by Dennery, Dumanoir, and Clairville, Paris, Théâtre des Variétés, 22 December 1843;

Marjolaine, by Dennery and Cormon, Théâtre des Variétés, 18 January 1844;

La Grisette de qualité, by Dennery and Grangé, Paris, Folies Dramatiques, 2 May 1844;

Paris voleur, by Dennery, Dumanoir, and Clairville, Paris, Théâtre du Palais Royal, 16 July 1844;

Pulcinella, by Dennery and Théodore De Villeneuve, Paris, Théâtre des Variétés, 27 July 1844;

Don César de Bazan, by Dennery and Dumanoir, Paris, Théâtre de la Porte Saint-Martin, 30 July 1844;

Les Sept Châteaux du diable, preceded by *Prologue Le boudoir de Satan,* by Dennery and Clairville, Paris, Théâtre de la Gaîté, 9 August 1844;

Suzette, by Dennery, Dumanoir, and Jean-François Alfred Bayard, Paris, Théâtre du Vaudeville, 27 September 1844;

La Dame de Saint Tropez, by Dennery and Bourgeois, Paris, Théâtre de la Porte Saint-Martin, 23 November 1844;

La Mazurka, by Dennery and Dumanoir, Paris, Théâtre des Variétés, 23 November 1844;

Colin-Tampon, by Dennery and Michel Delaporte, Paris, Théâtre des Variétés, 24 December 1844;

Le Bal d'enfants, by Dennery and Dumanoir, Paris, Théâtre de la Gaîté, 21 January 1845;

L'Ile du prince Toutou, ou, Le Royaume des veuves, by Dennery and Edouard Louis Brisebarre, Paris, Folies Dramatiques, 1 February 1845;

Parlez au portier, by Dennery and Aristide Letorzec, Paris, Théâtre du Palais Royal, 2 March 1845;

Le Porteur d'eau, by Dennery and Charles Albert, Paris, Théâtre du Vaudeville, 7 March 1845;

Paris et la banlieue, by Dennery and Clairville, Paris, Théâtre de l'Ambigu-Comique, 8 August 1845;

La Vie en partie double, by Dennery and Bourgeois, Gymnase-Dramatique, 19 August 1845;

Noémie, by Dennery and René Clément, Paris, Gymnase-Dramatique, 31 October 1845;

Marie-Jeanne, by Dennery and de Maillan, music by M. Auguste Pilati, Paris, Théâtre de la Porte Saint-Martin, 11 November 1845;

La Pluie et le beau temps, by Dennery and Albert Hostein, Paris, Gymnase-Dramatique, 2 December 1845;

V'là c'qui vient de paraître, by Dennery and Clairville, Paris, Théâtre du Vaudeville, 30 December 1845;

La Mère de famille, Paris, Gymnase-Dramatique, 21 January 1846;

Les Compagnons, ou, La Mansarde de la Cité, by Dennery and Cormon, Paris, Théâtre de la Gaîté, 14 February 1846;

Le Roman comique, by Dennery, Cormon, and Romain Chapelain, Paris, Théâtre du Vaudeville, 4 April 1846;

L'Etoile du berger, by Dennery and Bourgeois, Paris, Théâtre de l'Ambigu-Comique, 17 May 1846;

Les Ouvriers de la cité, prologue followed by *Le Marché de Londres,* by Dennery and Paul Féval, Paris, Théâtre de l'Ambigu-Comique, 6 July 1846;

Le Temple de Salomon, by Dennery and Bourgeois, Paris, Théâtre de la Gaîté, 8 September 1846;

L'Angelus, by Dennery and Jean-Baptiste Pierre Lafitte, Paris, Théâtre de la Gaîté, 10 November 1846;

L'Article 213, ou, Le Mari doit protection, by Dennery and Lemoine, Paris, Gymnase-Dramatique, 16 November 1846;

Epoux libre, by Dennery and Bourgeois, Paris, Théâtre du Vaudeville, 10 December 1846;

L'Amour au village, by Dennery and Felix Dutertre de Véteuil, Paris, Délassements Comiques, 19 January 1847;

La Duchesse de Marsan, Paris, Théâtre de l'Ambigu-Comique, 17 April 1847;

Les Infortunes conjugales, by Dennery and Clairville, Paris, Folies Dramatiques, 6 May 1847;

Le Mari anonyme, by Dennery and Lafitte, Paris, Gymnase-Dramatique, 31 July 1847;

Les Foyers d'acteurs, by Dennery, Grangé, and Clairville, Paris, Théâtre des Variétés, 16 August 1847;

Mlle Agathe, by Dennery and Cormon, Paris, Gymnase-Dramatique, 19 August 1847;

Les Paysans, by Dennery, Cormon, and Grangé, Paris, Théâtre de l'Ambigu-Comique, 16 November 1847;

Gastibelza, ou, Le Fou de Tolède, by Dennery and Cormon, music by Louis Aimé Maillart, Paris, Cirque Olympique, 16 November 1847;

Royal Pendard, ou L'Amour d'un roué, by Dennery and Paul Foucher, Paris, Gymnase-Dramatique, 20 March 1848;

Les Trois Révolutions, by Dennery and Clairville, Paris, Théâtre de l'Ambigu-Comique, 28 March 1848;

Pauvre aveugle, by Dennery and Lafitte, Paris, Théâtre du Palais Royal, 20 April 1848;

Le Maréchal Ney, by Dennery, Charles Dupeuty, and Bourgeois, Paris, Théâtre de la Porte Saint-Martin, 25 May 1848;

La Comtesse de Sennerey, by Dennery and Bayard, Paris, Gymnase-Dramatique, 11 September 1848;

Le Chemin de traverse, by Dennery, Dumanoir, and Clairville, Paris, Théâtre du Vaudeville, 30 September 1848;

Les Sept Péchés capitaux, by Dennery and Bourgeois, Paris, Théâtre de l'Ambigu-Comique, 23 October 1848;

Cadet la Perle, by Dennery and Lafitte, Paris, Théâtre du Vaudeville, 4 November 1848;

La Poule aux oeufs d'or, by Dennery and Clairville, music by Alexandre Charles Fessy, Paris, Cirque National, 29 November 1848;

Le Dernier des Rochegune, Paris, Gymnase-Dramatique, 29 January 1849;

Le Bouquet de violettes, by Dennery and Dumanoir, Paris, Gymnase-Dramatique, 7 April 1849;

Bernerette, ou, Les Prodigalités, by Dennery and Grangé, Paris, Folies Dramatiques, 3 May 1849;

Mauricette, ou, Un Mariage pour l'autre monde, by Dennery and Michel Masson, Paris, Gymnase-Dramatique, 31 July 1849;

Le Marquis de Carabas et la princesse Franfreluche, by Dennery and Adolphe Choler, Paris, Théâtre des Variétés, 7 August 1849;

Le Petit Pierre, by Dennery and Adrien Decourcelle, Paris, Théâtre des Variétés, 6 October 1849;

La Mariée de Poissy, by Dennery, Grangé, and Charles de la Rounat, Paris, Théâtre des Variétés, 6 March 1850;

L'Echelle de femmes, Paris, Gymnase-Dramatique, 18 July 1850;

Paillasse, by Dennery and Marc Fournier, Paris, Théâtre de la Gaîté, 9 November 1850;

Mercadet le faiseur, by Dennery and Honoré de Balzac, Paris, Gymnase-Dramatique, 24 August 1851;

La Paysanne pervertie, by Dennery and Dumanoir, Paris, Théâtre de la Gaîté, 18 October 1851;

La Croix de Marie, music by Maillart, Paris, Opera-Comique, 19 July 1852;

Si j'étais roi, by Dennery and Jules Brésil, music by Adolphe Charles Adam, Paris, Théâtre Lyrique National, 4 September 1852;

La Bergère des Alpes, by Dennery and Desnoyer, Paris, Théâtre de la Gaîté, 31 October 1852;

La Case de l'oncle Tom, by Dennery and Dumanoir, music by Amédée Artus, Paris, Théâtre de l'Ambigu-Comique, 18 January 1853;

Le Vieux Caporal, by Dennery and Dumanoir, Paris, Théâtre de la Porte Saint-Martin, 9 May 1853;

Les Mémoires de Richelieu, Paris, Théâtre de la Porte Saint-Martin, 15 May 1853;

Un Ménage à trois, by Dennery and Decourcelle, Paris, Gymnase-Dramatique, 1 June 1853;

Sept merveilles du monde, by Dennery and Grangé, music by M. Gondois, Paris, Théâtre de la Porte Saint-Martin, 29 September 1853;

La Prière des naufragés, by Dennery and Edouard Dugué, Paris, Théâtre de l'Ambigu-Comique, 20 October 1853;

La Bonne Aventure, by Dennery, Foucher, Prosper Parfait Goubeaux, and Eugène Sue, Paris, Théâtre de la Gaîté, 21 April 1854;

Les Oiseaux de proie, music by Fossy, Paris, Théâtre de la Gaîté, 16 October 1854;

Un Système conjugal, by Dennery and Charles Gabet, Paris, Théâtre des Variétés, 24 October 1854;

Les Cinq Cents Diables, by Dennery and Dumanoir, Paris, Théâtre de la Gaîté, 25 November 1854;

Le Muletier de Tolède, by Dennery and Clairville, music by Adam, Paris, Théâtre Lyrique National, 16 December 1854;

A Clichy, by Dennery and Grangé, music by Adam, Paris, Théâtre Lyrique National, 24 December 1854;

Le Médecin des enfants, by Dennery and Bourgeois, Paris, Théâtre de la Gaîté, 25 October 1855;

Les Lavandières de Santarem, by Dennery and Grangé, music by François Auguste Gévaert, Paris, Théâtre Lyrique National, 25 October 1855;

Le Donjon de Vincennes, by Dennery and Grangé, Paris, Cirque National, 8 November 1855;

L'Habit de noce, by Dennery and Louis Bignon, music by Paul Cuzent, Paris, Théâtre Lyrique National, 29 December 1855;

Le Paradis perdu, by Dennery and Dugué, Paris, Théâtre de l'Ambigu-Comique, 24 March 1856;

La Jeunesse de Bourgachard, ou, Un Filleul de l'Empereur, Paris, Gymnase-Dramatique, 18 June 1856;

Une Femme qui déteste son mari, by Dennery and Mme Emile de Girardin, Gymnase-Dramatique, 10 October 1856;

La Fausse Adultère, music by Fossey, Paris, Théâtre de la Gaîté, 29 December 1856;

Les Princesses de la rampe, by Dennery, Lambert Thiboust, and Léon Beauvallet, Paris, Théâtre des Variétés, 26 February 1857;

Les Orphélines de la charité, by Dennery and Brésil, Paris, Théâtre de l'Ambigu-Comique, 7 March 1857;

L'Aveugle, by Dennery and Bourgeois, Paris, Théâtre de la Gaîté, 21 March 1857;

Les Chevaliers du brouillard, by Dennery and Bourgeois, music by A. Artus, Paris, Théâtre de la Porte Saint-Martin, 10 July 1857;

Le Fou par amour, by Dennery and Bourgeois, Paris, Théâtre de la Gaîté, 5 November 1857;

Les Fiancés d'Albano, by Dennery and Constant Mocquard, Paris, Théâtre de la Gaîté, 23 January 1858;

Germaine, by Dennery and Henri Crémieux, Paris, Théâtre de la Gaîté, 3 April 1858;

Faust, music by Artus, Paris, Théâtre de la Porte Saint-Martin, 27 September 1858;

Amour et lauriers, by Dennery and Jules Arnould, Paris, Théâtre des Variétés, 29 October 1858;

Cartouche, by Dennery and Dugué, Paris, Théâtre de la Gaîté, 29 December 1858;

Le Naufrage de la Pérouse, Paris, Théâtre de la Porte Saint-Martin, 7 May 1859;

Le Savetier de la rue Quincampoix, by Dennery and Crémieux, Paris, Théâtre de la Gaîté, 5 November 1859;

Le Marchand de coco, by Dennery and Dugué, music by Artus, Paris, Théâtre de l'Ambigu-Comique, 28 December 1859;

L'Histoire d'un drapeau, music by Alex de Groot, Paris, Cirque National, 17 January 1860;

L'Escamoteur, by Dennery and Brésil, Paris, Théâtre de la Gaîté, 12 October 1860;

Le Sacrifice d'Iphigénie, Paris, Gymnase-Dramatique, 13 February 1861;

La Prise de Pékin, by Dennery and Mocquard, Paris, Cirque National, 27 July 1861;

Les Chercheurs d'or, prologue followed by *Le Lac de Glenaston,* by Dennery and Dion Boucicault, Paris, Théâtre de l'Ambigu-Comique, 17 October 1861;

Valentine Darmentière, by Dennery and Dumanoir, Paris, Théâtre de la Gaîté, 9 November 1861;

La Fille du paysan, by Dennery and Bourgeois, Paris, Théâtre de la Gaîté, 8 January 1862;

Rothomago, by Dennery, Clairville, and Albert Monnier, Paris, Cirque National, 1 March 1862;

La Chatte merveilleuse, by Dennery and Dumanoir, music by Albert Grisar, Paris, Théâtre Lyrique National, 18 March 1862;

Le Château de Pontalec, by Dennery and Dugué, Paris, Théâtre de la Gaîté, 3 September 1862;

Marengo, Paris, Châtelet, 28 February 1863;

Aladin, ou, La Lampe merveilleuse, by Dennery and Crémieux, Paris, Châtelet, 3 October 1863;

L'Aïeule, by Dennery and Karol Edmund Chojecki, Paris, Théâtre de l'Ambigu-Comique, 17 October 1863;

Les Drames du cabaret, by Dennery and Dumanoir, Paris, Théâtre de la Porte Saint-Martin, 19 October 1864;

Maria de Mancini, by Dennery and Dugué, Paris, Théâtre de l'Ambigu-Comique, 29 December 1864;

Les Mystères du vieux Paris, Paris, Châtelet, 21 January 1865;

Les Amours de Paris, by Dennery and Thiboust, Paris, Théâtre de l'Ambigu-Comique, 17 October 1866;

Le Premier Jour de bonheur, by Dennery and Cormon, music by Daniel François Esprit Auber, Paris, Opéra-Comique, 15 February 1868;

Le Dompteur, by Dennery and Chojecki, Paris, Théâtre de l'Ambigu-Comique, 29 October 1869;

Rêve d'amour, music by Auber, Paris, Opéra-Comique, 20 December 1869;

Le Centenaire, by Dennery and Edouard Plouvier, Paris, Théâtre de l'Ambigu-Comique, 18 October 1872;

Les Deux Orphelines, by Dennery and Cormon, Paris, Théâtre de la Porte Saint-Martin, 29 January 1874;

Marcelle, by Dennery and Brésil, Paris, Théâtre du Vaudeville, 6 October, 1874;

La Comtesse de Lerins, by Dennery and L. Davyl, Paris, Théâtre Historique, 25 October 1874;

La Fiancée du roi de Garbe, by Dennery and Henri Chabrillat, music by Henri Litolff, Paris, Folies Dramatiques, 29 October 1874;

Le Tour du monde en quatre-vingts jours, by Dennery and Jules Verne, music by Jean-Jacques Débillemont, Paris, Théâtre de la Porte Saint-Martin, 7 November 1874;

Une Cause célèbre, by Dennery and Cormon, Paris, Théâtre de l'Ambigu-Comique, 4 December 1876;

Les Enfants du capitaine Grant, by Dennery and Verne, Paris, Théâtre de la Porte Saint-Martin, 26 December 1878;

Michel Strogoff, by Dennery and Verne, music by Artus, Paris, Châtelet, 17 November 1880;

Diana, by Dennery and Brésil, Paris, Théâtre de l'Ambigu-Comique, 15 December 1880;

Le Tribut de Zamora, by Dennery and Brésil, music by Charles Gounod, Paris, Opera, 1 April 1881;

Voyage à travers l'impossible, by Dennery and Verne, Paris, Théâtre de la Porte Saint-Martin, 25 November 1882;

L'Amour, by Dennery and Davyl, Paris, Théâtre du Vaudeville, 27 October 1884;

Le Cid, by Dennery, Louis Gallet, and Edouard Blau, music by Jules Emile Frédéric Massenet, Paris, Opera, 30 November 1885;

Le Mari d'un jour, by Dennery and Armand Silvestre, Paris, Opéra-Comique, 4 February 1886;

Martyre, by Dennery and Edmond Joseph Louis Tarbé, Paris, Théâtre de l'Ambigu-Comique, 4 March 1886;

L'Escadron volant de la reine, music by Henry Litolff, Paris, Opéra-Comique, 14 December 1888;

Le Talisman, by Dennery and Paul Burani, music by Jean-Robert Planquette, Paris, Théâtre de la Gaîté, 20 January 1893;

Le Trésor des Radjahs, by Dennery and P. Ferrier, Paris, Châtelet, 3 February 1894.

BOOKS: *Le Voyage de la mariée,* by Dennery, A. de Leuven, and J. de Mallian (Brussels: Bureau du répertoire, 1829);

La Monnaie de singe, ou, Le Loyer de la danseuse, by Dennery and Mallian (Paris: Riga, 1831);

L'Apprenti, ou, L'Art de faire une maîtresse, by Dennery, Théodore Cognard, and Artois (Paris: Marchant, 1834);

L'Idée du mari, by Dennery and Cormon (Paris: Barba, 1834);

La Marchesa, ou, La Courtisane de Rome, by Dennery and Alfred [pseudonym] (Paris: Barba, 1834);

Un Soufflet, by Dennery and Desnoyer (Paris: Marchant, 1834);

La Femme qui se venge (Paris: Barba, 1835);

L'Honneur de ma fille (Paris: Barba, 1836); revised as *La Maison des fous* (Paris: Barba, 1850);

Les Petits Souliers, ou, La Prison de Saint-Crepin (Paris: Nobis, 1836);

Tiburce, ou, Qui veut de ma vie, by Dennery and Dumanoir (Paris: Marchant, 1836);

1814, ou, Le Pensionnat de Montereau, by Dennery and Cormon (Paris: Marchant, 1836);

Trois coeurs de femmes, by Dennery, A. d'Artois, and Edmond Burat (Paris: Nobis, 1836);

Dolores (Paris: Marchant, 1837);

Une Femme de lettres, by Dennery and Grangé (Paris: Dondey-Dupré, 1837);

L'Homme qui se range, by Dennery and Cormon (Paris: Barba, 1837);

L'Hôtel des haricots, ou, Il vaut mieux monter sa garde, by Dennery, Dumanoir, and de Leuven (Paris: Barba, 1837);

Le Portefeuille, ou, Deux familles, by Dennery and Bourgeois, in *La Bibliothèque dramatique,* third series, volume 11 (Paris: N.p., 1837);

La Sentinelle, ou, Huit ans de faction, by Dennery and Lemoine (Paris: Morain, 1837);

Le Tour de faction, by Dennery and Grangé (Paris: Marchant, 1837);

Gras et maigre, by Dennery and Grangé (Paris: Marchant, 1838);

Changement d'uniforme (Paris: Barba, 1838);

Femmes et pirates, by Dennery and Cormon (Paris: N.p., 1838);

Gaspard Hauser, by Dennery and Bourgeois (Paris: Marchant, 1838);

Jeanne Hachette, ou, Le Siège de Beauvais sous Louis XI, by Dennery and Bourgeois (Paris: Marchant, 1838);

Madame et Monsieur Pinchon, by Dennery, Bayard, and Dumanoir (Paris: Marchant, 1838);

Le Mariage d'orgueil, by Dennery and Déaddé (Paris: Marchant, 1838);

Pierre d'Arezzo (L'Arétin), by Dennery and Dumanoir (Paris: Marchant, 1838);

Raphael, ou, Les Mauvais Conseils, by Dennery, Cormon, and Grangé (Paris: Marchant, 1838);

La Reine des blanchisseuses, by Dennery, de Rougemont, and Grangé (Paris: Marchant, 1838);

Suzette, by Dennery, Dumanoir, and Bayard (Paris: Didot, l'aîné, 1838);

1840, ou, La Guerre des saisons, by Dennery, Grangé, and Eugène Bourget (Paris: Miflier, 1839);

Le Tremblement de terre de la Martinique, music by M. Béancourt (Paris: Marchant, 1840);

Le Dernier Oncle d'Amérique, by Dennery and Grangé (Paris: Bureau Central, 1840);

Les Enfants d'Adam et d'Eve, by Dennery and Grangé (Paris, 1840);

Les Garçons de recette, by Dennery and Elie Berthet (Brussels, 1840);

La Grisette au vert (Paris: Lacombe, 1840);

Toby le sorcier, by Dennery and Bourgeois (Paris, 1840);

L'Amour en commandite, by Dennery, Leuven, and Lhérie (Paris, n.d.);

La Grâce de Dieu, by Dennery and Lemoine (Paris, 1841);

La Dette à la bamboche (Paris, 1841);

Les Bains à quatre sous, by Dennery and Brisebarre (Paris, 1841);

Le Moulin de la Galette (Paris, n.d.);

La Citerne d'Albi, by Dennery and Lemoine (Paris, 1841);

Les Pupilles de la garde, by Dennery and Lemoine (Paris: Tresse, 1841);

Feu Peterscott, by Dennery and Grangé, *La Bibliothèque dramatique,* third series, volume 71 (Paris, 1841);

Amour et amourette, by Dennery and Grangé (Paris: Marchant, 1842);

La Nuit aux soufflets, by Dennery and Dumanoir, in *La Bibliothèque dramatique,* fourth series, volume 79 (Brussels, 1842);

La Journée d'une jolie femme, by Dennery and Cormon (Paris, 184?);

La Dot d'Auvergne, by Dennery and Grangé (Paris: Marchant, 1842);

Fargeau le nourrisseur, by Dennery and Dumanoir (Paris, 1842);

Ma Maîtresse et ma femme, by Dennery, Dumanoir, and P. Siraudin (Paris, 1842);

Halifax, by Dennery and Dumas *père* (Brussels: Meline, Cans et Cie, 1843);

Pauvre Jeanne, by Dennery and Grangé (Paris: Marchant, 1843);

La Perruquière de Meudon, by Dennery and Bourgeois (Paris: Lacombe, 1843);

Les Nouvelles à la main, by Dennery and Clairville (Paris: Detroux, 1843);

Les Bohémiens de Paris, by Dennery and Grangé (Paris: Marchant, 1843); translated by Pierre Basté as *The Bohemians of Paris* in "Plays," volume 878 (London, n.d.);

Le Capitaine Roquefinette, by Dennery and Dumanoir (Paris: Detroux, 1843);

Les Mémoires de deux jeunes mariées, by Dennery and Clairville (Paris: Marchant, 1844); translated by William Robertson as *My Wife's Diary* (London: S. French, 1843);

Paris dans la comète, by Dennery, Dumanoir, and Clairville (Paris: Detroux, 1843);

La Grisette de qualité, by Dennery and Grangé (Paris: Marchant, 1844);

Marjolaine, by Dennery and Cormon (Paris: Marchant, 1844);

Paris voleur, by Dennery, Dumanoir, and Clairville (Paris: Marchant, 1844);

Pulcinella, by Dennery and Théodore Ferdinand de Villeneuve, in *La Bibliothèque dramatique,* third series, volume 89 (Paris, 1844);

Caesar de Bazan, by Dennery and Dumanoir (London: W. Barth, 1844; New York: S. French, 1844); translated by Edwin Booth as *The Comedy of Don César de Bazan* (Paris: Dondey-Dupré, 1844);

Les Sept Châteaux du diable, preceded by prologue, *Le Boudoir de Satan,* by Dennery and Clairville (Paris: Marchant, 1844);

La Dame de Saint Tropez, by Dennery and Bourgeois (Paris: Typ. Walder, 1844);

Colin-Tampon, by Dennery and Michel Delaporte (Paris: Boulé, 1844);

Le Bal d'enfants, by Dennery and Dumanoir (Paris: Tresse, 1845);

L'Ile du prince Toutou, ou, Le Royaume des veuves, by Dennery and Brisebarre (Paris: Beck, 1845);

Parlez au portier, by Dennery and Letorzec (Paris: Marchant, 1845);

Le Porteur d'eau, by Dennery and Albert (Paris: Appert, n.d.);

Paris et la banlieue, by Dennery and Clairville (Paris: Marchant, 1845);

La Vie en partie double, by Dennery and Bourgeois (Paris, 1845);

Noémie, by Dennery and René Clément (Paris: Tresse, 1845); translated by William Robertson as *Ernestine* (New York: De Witt, 1845) and by Robertson as *Noémie* (New York: S. French, 1856);

Marie-Jeanne, by Dennery and J. de Mallian, music by M. Pilati (Paris: Calmann Lévy, 1845); translated as *Marianne, A Woman of the People* (New York: Academy of Music, n.d.);

La Pluie et le beau temps, by Dennery and Albert Hostein (Paris, n.d.);

V'là c'qui vient de paraître, by Dennery and Clairville (Paris: Beck, 1846);

La Mère de famille (Paris: Calmann Lévy, 1846);

Les Compagnons, ou, La Mansarde de la Cité, by Dennery and Cormon (Paris: Tresse, 1846);

Le Roman comique, by Dennery, Cormon, and R. Chapelain (Paris, 1846);

L'Etoile du berger, by Dennery and Bourgeois, in *La Bibliothèque dramatique,* third series, volume 34 (Paris, 1846);

Les Ouvriers de la cité, prologue, followed by *Le Marché de Londres,* by Dennery and Paul Féval (Paris: Boulé, 1846);

Le Temple de Salomon, by Dennery and Bourgeois (Paris: Boule, 1846);

L'Angelus, by Dennery and Lafitte (Paris: Boulé, 1846);

L'article 213, ou, Le Mari doit protection, by Dennery and Lemoine (Paris: Imprimerie de Dubuisson, 1846);

Le Mari anonyme, by Dennery and Lafitte (Paris, 1847);

Mlle Agathe, by Dennery and Cormon (Paris, 1847);

Les paysans, by Dennery, Cormon, and Grangé (Paris: Tresse, 1847);

Gastibelza, ou, Le Fou de Tolède, by Dennery and Cormon, with music by Maillard (Paris: Dondey-Dupré, 1847);

Le Maréchal Ney, by Dennery, Charles Dupeuty, and Bourgeois (Paris: Dodey-Dupré, 1848);

La Comtesse de Sennecey, by Dennery and Bayard (Poissy: G. Olivier, 1848);

Le Chemin de traverse, by Dennery, Dumanoir, and Clairville (Paris: Dondey-Dupré, 1848);

La Duchesse de Marsan (Paris: Boulé, 1849);

Le Bouquet de violettes, by Dennery and Dumanoir (Paris: Dondey-Dupré, 1849);

Mauricette, ou, Un Mariage pour l'autre monde, by Dennery and Michel Masson (Paris, 18??);

Le Marquis de Carabas et la princesse Franfreluche, by Dennery and Adolphe Choler (Paris: Beck, 1849);

Le Petit Pierre, by Dennery and Adrien Decourcelle (Paris, 1849);

La Mariée de Poissy, by Dennery, Grangé, and Charles de la Rounat (Paris: Beck, 1850);

L'Echelle de femmes (Paris: Dondey-Dupré, 1850);

Paillasse, by Dennery and Fournier (Paris, 1850); translated by C. Webb as *Belphegor, the Mountebank, or, Woman's Constancy* (London: T. H. Lacy, 1850; New York: S. French, 187?);

Mercadet le faiseur, by Dennery and Balzac (Paris: Librairie théâtrale, 1851);

La Paysanne pervertie, by Dennery and Dumanoir, in *La Bibliothèque dramatique,* third series, volume 49 (Paris, 1851);

La Croix de Marie, music by Maillart (Paris: Lévy, n.d.);

Si j'étais roi, by Dennery and Brésil, with music by Adam (Paris: Calmann Lévy, n.d.);

La Poule aux oeufs d'or, by Dennery and Clairville, music by Alexandre Charles Fessy (Paris:

Beck, 1852; London: Co-Operative Printing and Stationery, 18??);

La Bergère des Alpes, by Dennery and Desnoyer (Paris: Calmann Lévy, 1852);

La Case de l'oncle Tom, by Dennery and Dumanoir, music by Artus (Paris: Lévy, 1853);

Les Sept Péchés capitaux, by Dennery and Bourgeois (Paris: Lévy, 1853);

Le Vieux Caporal, by Dennery and Dumanoir (Paris: Lévy, 1853);

Les Mémoires de Richelieu (Clermont [Oise]: Daix, 1853);

Un Ménage à trois, by Dennery and Decourcelle (Clermont [Oise], 1853);

Sept Merveilles du monde, by Dennery and Grangé, music by Eugène Gondois (Paris: Lévy, 1853);

La Prière des naufragés, by Dennery and Dugué (Paris: Calmann Lévy, 1853); translated as *The Sea of Ice, or The Prayer of the Wrecked* (London: T. H. Lacy, 185?);

Les Oiseaux de proie, music by Fossey (Paris: Lévy, 1854);

Un Système conjugal, by Dennery and Charles Gabet (Clermont [Oise], 1854);

Les Cinq Cents Diables, by Dennery and Dumanoir (Paris: Calmann Lévy, 1854);

A Clichy, by Dennery and Grangé, music by Adam (Paris: Calmann Lévy, 1854);

La Bonne Aventure, by Dennery, Foucher, Goubeaux, and Sue (Paris: Calmann Lévy, 1855);

Le Muletier de Tolède, by Dennery and Clairville, music by Adam (Paris: Calmann Lévy, 1855); translated by John Maddison Morton as *The Muleteer of Toledo, or, the King, Queen and Knave* (London: T. H. Tracy, 185-);

Le Médecin des enfants, by Dennery and Bourgeois (Paris: Calmann Lévy, 1855);

Les Lavandières de Santarem, by Dennery and Grangé, music by François Auguste Gévaert (Paris: Lévy, 1855);

Le Donjon de Vincennes, by Dennery and Grangé (Paris: Lévy, 1855);

L'Habit de noce, by Dennery and Louis Bignon, music by Paul Cuzent (Paris: Lévy, 1856);

Le Paradis perdu, by Dennery and Dugué (Paris: Lévy, 1856);

Une Femme qui déteste son mari, by Dennery and Girardin (Paris: Lévy, 1857);

La Fausse Adultère, music by Fossey (Paris: Lévy, 1857);

Les Princesses de la rampe, by Dennery, Lambert Thiboust, and Léon Beauvallet (Paris: Lévy, 1857);

Les Orphélines de la charité, by Dennery and Brésil (Paris: Lévy, 1857);

L'Aveugle, by Dennery and Bourgeois (Paris: Lévy, 1857);

Le Fou par amour, by Dennery and Bourgeois (Paris: Lévy, 1857);

Les Chevaliers du brouillard, by Dennery and Bourgeois, music by Artus (Paris: Lévy, 1858); translated by Frédéric Boyle as *London Bridge 150 Years Ago, or The Old Mint* (London: S. French, 1876);

Les Fiancés d'Albano, by Dennery and Constant Mocquard (Paris: Lévy, 1858);

Germaine, by Dennery and Crémieux (Paris: Lévy, 1858);

Faust, music by Artus (Paris: Lévy, 1858);

Amour et lauriers, by Dennery and Jules Arnould (Paris: Librairie théâtrale, 1858);

Le Naufrage de la Pérouse (Paris: Lévy, 1859);

Le Savetier de la rue Quincampoix, by Dennery and Crémieux (Paris: Lévy, 1859);

Cartouche, by Dennery and Dugué (Paris: Lévy, 1860); translated by W. R. Waldron as *Cartouche; the French Robber* (London: N.p., 185-);

Le Marchand de coco, by Dennery and Dugué, music by Artus (Paris: Lévy, 1860);

L'Histoire d'un drapeau, music by Alex de Groot (Paris: Lévy, 1860);

L'Escamoteur, by Dennery and Brésil (Paris: Lévy, 1860); translated by T. W. Robertson as *Jocrisse* (London: T. H. Lacy, 186-?);

Le Sacrifice d'Iphigénie (Paris: Lévy, 1861);

Les Chercheurs d'or, prologue followed by *Le lac de Glenaston,* by Dennery and Boucicault (Paris: Lévy, 1861);

La Prise de Pékin, by Dennery and Mocquard (Paris: Lévy, 1861);

Valentine Darmentière, by Dennery and Dumanoir (Paris: Lévy, 1862);

Rothomago, by Dennery, Clairville, and Albert Monnier (Paris: Lévy, 1862);

La Chatte merveilleuse, by Dennery and Dumanoir, music by Albert Grisar, in *La Bibliothèque dramatique,* no. 228 (Paris, 1862);

Le Château de Pontalec, by Dennery and Dugué (Paris: Lévy, 1862);

Marengo (Paris: Lévy, 1863);

La Fille du paysan, by Dennery and Bourgeois (Paris: Lévy, 1863);

Aladin, ou, La Lampe merveilleuse, by Dennery and Crémieux (Paris, 1863);

L'Aïeule, by Dennery and Chojecki (Paris: Lévy, 1864); translated by Tom Taylor as *The Hidden Hand* (London: S. French, 1864);

Les Drames du cabaret, by Dennery and Dumanoir (Paris, 1865);

Maria de Mancini, by Dennery and Dugué (Paris: Lévy, 1865);

Les Mystères du vieux Paris (Paris: Lévy, 1865);

Les Amours de Paris, by Dennery and Thiboust (Paris: Lévy, 1867);

Le Premier Jour de bonheur, by Dennery and Cormon, music by Daniel François Esprit Auber (Paris: Tresse, 1868);

Rêve d'amour, music by Auber (Paris: Lévy & Léon Escudier, 1868);

Le Dompteur, by Dennery and Chojecki (Paris: Lévy, 1870);

Le Centenaire, by Dennery and Edouard Plouvier (Paris: Lévy, 1873);

Le Prince de Moria (Paris: Lévy, 1873);

Les Deux Orphélines, by Dennery and Cormon (Paris: Tresse, 1874); translated by Augustus Kazauran as *The Two Orphans* (New York, 1874);

La Fiancée du roi de Garbe, by Dennery and Henri Chabrillat, music by Henri Litolff (Paris: Bathlot, 1874);

Le Tribut de Zamora, by Dennery and Brésil, music by Gounod (Paris: Tresse, 1881);

Diana, by Dennery and Brésil (Paris: Tresse, 1884);

Une Cause célèbre, by Dennery and Cormon (Paris: Tresse, 1885); translated by Augustus Kazauran as *A Celebrated Case* (New York: S. French 18??);

Le Cid, by Dennery, Louis Gallet, and Edouard Blau, music by Massenet (Paris: Tresse, 1886);

Le Mari d'un jour, by Dennery and Silvestre, music by Arthur Coquard (Paris: Tresse & Stock, 1886);

Les Deux Orphelines [novel] (Paris: Rouff, 1887);

L'Escadron volant de la reine, music by Henry Litolff (Paris: Ollendorf, 1888);

Le Remords d'un ange (Paris: Rouff, 1889);

Martyre, by Dennery and Edmond Joseph Louis Tarbé (Paris: Tresse & Stock 1893);

Le Talisman, by Dennery and Paul Burani, music by Robert Planquette (Paris: Bathlot & Joubert, 1893);

Seule! (Paris: Rouff, 1896);

Markariantz (Paris: Ollendorf, 1896);

Jacqueline (Paris: Flammarion, 1899);

Voyage à travers l'impossible, by Dennery and Verne (Paris: Jean-Jacques Pauvert, "La Vue," 1981).

Collection: *Les Voyages au théâtre,* by Dennery and Verne—includes *Le Tour du monde en 80 jours, Les Enfants du capitaine Grant,* and *Michel Strogoff* (Paris: Hetzel, 1881).

On 26 January 1899 *The New York Times* printed, on its front page, the cable announcing the death of Adolphe Dennery, "one of the most prolific playwrights of the century." After mentioning in particular his *A Celebrated Cause,* which had caused a great impact in New York during the 1877 season, the notice states that "in 1862 and 1863 it several times happened that no fewer than five plays from his pen were being presented simultaneously at as many Parisian theaters. He wrote comedies, vaudeville sketches, dramas, and spectacular reviews with equal facility." This recognition was accorded to an author who, in spite of his literary flaws, had enjoyed a tremendous popularity among theatergoers in France and throughout Europe and the United States for more than two-thirds of the nineteenth century. Writing mostly in collaboration, he was particularly successful in the creation of melodramas (a genre he revitalized and perpetuated) dealing with domestic situations based on well-known scandals or popular social concerns, all filled with pathos and high emotional charge. Although his name means little to modern literary critics and audiences, his presence in the world of the performing arts can still be felt, thanks to contemporary melodrama as seen on stages and on screens, big and small.

Born in Paris on 17 June 1811, the son of modest Jewish parents, Adolphe Philippe Dennery began working at an early age as a shop assistant, then worked as a clerk in a notary's office while at the same time taking painting lessons and writing articles for newspapers—all rather unfulfilling activities for the assiduous theatergoer he had already become. Still in his teens, he signed up for the Sunday evening claque at the Théâtre de l'Ambigu and soon discovered that theater was his true passion. Having left his paternal home on the rue du Temple and being penniless at the time, he struggled to survive, began writing for the theater, and befriended Charles Desnoyer, a former actor turned vaudevillian, with whom he wrote his first moderately successful play, *Emile, ou, Le Fils d'un pair de France* (Emile, or the Son of a French Peer, 1831) at age twenty. (His first plays were signed Philippe, Philippe D., then Philippe Dennery, adopting his mother's maiden name as a pseudonym. In 1858, by imperial decree, he was authorized to use the *particule* and began signing his name as d'Ennery. In English listings he is frequently cited as Ennery.)

In the 1830s Dennery wrote abundantly until notoriety came, first at the national level in 1838 with the premiere of *Gaspard Hauser,* and then worldwide in 1841, thanks to *La Grâce de Dieu* (The Grace of God). Between *Emile* and 1894, the year of the premiere of his last piece, *Le Trésor des Radjahs* (The Treasure of the Radjahs), he wrote more than 250 plays for practically every Boulevard theater in Paris. For the most part, these were melodramas (he

A scene from Adolphe Philippe Dennery's Marie-Jeanne, *with Marie Dorval in the title role (from* L'Illustration,
22 November 1845)

called them *drames*) and vaudevilles (he called them *comédie-vaudevilles*), but he also ventured into the more complex world of the lyric theater (operetta, opera-comique, and opera libretti) and scored huge popular successes with his spectacular productions of *féeries* (fairy scenes of spectacular proportions), *à propos* (short, one-act comic plays), *folies* (follies), *épisodes* (sketches), *prologues, revues* (farces), *drames militaires et nationaux* (military and nationalistic plays), and, of course, with his adaptations for the theater of some of the novels of Jules Verne.

Dennery became director of the short-lived Théâtre Historique in 1850 but resigned from this position after a fortnight, arguing that he intended to open his own new theater, to be called Théâtre du Peuple or Théâtre du Prince Impérial, a project that never came to fruition. As a reward for his popularity he was made chevalier, then officer, and eventually commander of the Legion of Honor. Along with success came material wealth: by the 1870s he had left his apartment on the Boulevard Saint-Martin and moved to more-luxurious quarters on the avenue d'Eyleau and on the avenue du Bois de Bou-

logne, where he and his wife, Clémence, entertained on Sundays: Henri Meilhac, Ludovic Halévy, Daniel-François-Esprit Auber, Alexandre Dumas *fils,* Jules Verne, Charles Gounod, Paul Siraudin, and journalists from *Le Figaro* were among his regular guests. As he grew older he also spent much time at the "Paradou," a property he had acquired on the Cap d'Antibes, and it was here that he worked with Verne in the 1870s and 1880s. Although he was active in the theater and continued to write until the end of his life (his last novel, *Jacqueline* [1899], was published posthumously), he isolated himself from many of his former acquaintances in the artistic milieu during his last years. Nevertheless, he enjoyed the company of some Parisian colleagues and admirers who had remained loyal to him throughout his career, and he gladly accepted the many official distinctions, awards, and signs of appreciation from the most remote corners of the world.

Fellow dramatics, critics, and historians, the same ones who usually expressed consideration and appreciation for Dennery the man, were implacable in judging Dennery the writer, whose works they invariably treated with considerable contempt. First, there was the question of authenticity: because he worked mostly in collaboration, Dennery was often accused of signing but having little to do with the actual writing and staging of his plays. Indeed, from the outset of his career he cosigned his works with other playwrights, all of them just as prolific and knowledgeable of things theatrical as he. His most frequent collaborators included such familiar names (at that time) as Anicet-Bourgeois, Gustave Lemoine, Edouard Dugué, Eugène Grangé, Philippe Dumanoir, Henri Crémieux, Edouard Cormon, Louis-François Clairville, and Jules Brésil, a former actor who had made a career in villainous melodrama roles. He also had successful collaborative ventures with the composers Amédée Artus, Louis Aimé Maillart, François Auguste Gevaert, Adolphe Charles Adam, Daniel-François-Esprit Auber, Charles Gounod, and Jules Massenet; and, on four occasions, with Verne. Also worth mentioning are his single collaborations with Alexandre Dumas *père,* Honoré de Balzac, and Mme Delphine Gay de Girardin. Dennery and the elder Dumas cosigned *Halifax* (1843), a comedy in three acts that proved to be one of the few disastrous premieres for both. Considerably less talented than Balzac as a writer, Dennery nevertheless had a better knowledge of the practice of the theater than the principal author of *Mercadet le faiseur* (1851). A first reading of this play was done in private as early as 1841, and Théophile Gautier reacted to it with enthusiasm; but the five-act play, verbose and dramatically ineffective in its original form, could only be performed after Dennery rearranged it at the request of Balzac himself. Dennery left the original idea intact but reduced it to three acts and brought out more strikingly its comic and sentimental elements. Through the intervention of Dennery, Balzac's nineteenth-century speculator became a more tender, more humane, more honest character than Turcaret, his direct ancestor, which accounts for the success (posthumous, for Balzac) of the play when it opened at the Gymnase in 1851. In 1868 *Mercadet le faiseur* was revived at the Comédie-Française, where the reception was lukewarm at best. In any case, this was as close as Dennery, king of the Boulevards, would get to the preeminent French theater. Mme de Girardin, the well-known woman of letters, also called Dennery to her rescue once, on the occasion of the imminent premiere of her comedy *Une Femme qui déteste son mari* (A Woman Who Detests Her Husband, 1856). Rearranged, the piece became dramatically acceptable and opened at the Gymnase to more popular than critical acclaim.

Admittedly, without his collaborators it would have been practically impossible to see four or five of Dennery's plays being performed simultaneously in Paris, which happened frequently, or even better, to have two of them premiere on the same day, as was the case with *Les Paysans* and *Gastibelza, ou, Le Fou de Tolède* on 16 November 1847 and *Le Médecin des enfants* and *Les Lavandières de Santarem* on 25 October 1855. However, in reading Félix Duquesnel's *Souvenirs littéraires* (1922) one gets the distinct impression that the accusation of frivolity or negligence in regard to his works is truly uncalled-for. Duquesnel, who knew Dennery intimately, described him as a conscientious writer, one who after listening carefully to the ideas and suggestions made by his collaborators understood immediately what needed to be eliminated or added to the plot to make it work onstage and subsequently did the actual writing with enthusiasm. Duquesnel also wrote that it was the collaborators who were constantly knocking on his door, not vice versa, and that it was Dennery who made all the final decisions and assumed all responsibilities concerning the structure of the piece as well as its staging and performance. In fact, a look at the precise and detailed instructions found in Dennery's printed plays (for example, *La Poule aux oeufs d'or* [29 November 1848], *Si j'étais roi* [4 September 1852], *Une Cause célèbre* [4 December 1876], and *Michel Strogoff* [17 November 1880]) proves that he must have been a meticulous stage director/producer; it is also clear that Dennery was extremely demanding in the selection of actors. Many of his works were conceived for certain artists whom he knew well (he was particularly fond of Dumaine, Taillade, the Lacressonnières, Lesueur, Angèle Moreau, and Marie Laurent) or whose talent was unquestionable, notably Marie Dorval and Frédérick Lemaître. Dorval's riveting interpretation of Marie-Jeanne accounted almost exclusively for the enormous popularity of the homonymous play. Her distressed outcry, "Rendez-moi mon enfant!" (Give me back my child!), entered the annals of French theater. Gautier said in his review that Dorval's portrayal of maternity was definitive and that in the midst of a deluge of tears his own continuous sobbing was giving him chest pains and preventing him from watching the performance through his opera glasses. The charismatic Lemaître ensured the success of at least three Dennery works, plays written expressly for him: *Don César de Bazan* (where he had to recite and sing, 30 July 1844), *La Dame de Saint Tropez* (The Lady of Saint Tropez, 23 November 1844), and *Paillasse* (Belphegor, the Mountebank and His Wife, 9 November 1850). Gautier could hardly find enough superlatives to describe these performances. In his review of *Don César de Bazan* he criticized the play while praising Frédérick, who was so convincing in his elegant delivery of a poorly written part that the spectators were (falsely) led to believe that there actually was some style in the work. In *La Dame de Saint Tropez,* inspired by a well-known social scandal, Frédérick's acting was considered inspired; and in *Paillasse* the actor portrayed the despair of the heartbroken abandoned husband through simple gestures that suggested total emotional exhaustion.

Dennery was also criticized for the haste with which his works were produced and for their lack of genuine literary value. Granted, Dennery's lighter pieces (vaudevilles and comedies, which constitute about one-half of his total production) were written and produced expeditiously; but it is also true that when it came to the more serious or spectacular ones (his best melodramas, féeries, operas, and the adaptations of Verne's novels), the actual writing time was longer, and the premieres took place only when the preparation was complete: *Michel Strogoff,* the grandest of the Dennery spectacles, had a rehearsal period of an entire year. As for pure literary criticism, the condemnation was unanimous, for in the eyes of noted critics this was an author who repeatedly proved to be more concerned with immediate and lucrative success than with obtaining literary fame through serious contributions to French drama. Francisque Sarcey nicknamed Dennery "the Shakespeare of the people" and qualified his prose as *méchante* (miserable); Auguste Vacquerie said that he could not be seriously considered as a true man of letters; Jules Lemaître said that in going against all forms and ideas expressed in major nineteenth-century works and literary movements he was really making antiliterature; Gautier repeatedly praised the visual aspects of the Dennery imaginative productions but never failed to denounce their poor language and style. Emile Zola advised young playwrights to get from Dennery the knowledge of what works in theater and specifically how to construct a melodrama, but, at the same time, implored them not to follow his example in the use of the French language and not to deal with simplistic, trivial stories. Charles Félix Lenient was even harsher, calling Dennery a literary practitioner, a drama carpenter, and a simple *arrangeur* (adapter).

An adapter he almost had to be, given the sheer volume of his plays and the fast pace at which they were being produced: he used, among others, Paul Scarron's *Roman comique* (1651–1657), Johann Wolfgang von Goethe's *Faust,* Jean Nicolas Bouilly and Joseph Pain's *Fanchon la vielleuse* (Fanchon, the Hurdy-Gurdy Player, 28 January 1803), Victor

Hugo's *Ruy Blas,* Edmond About's *Germaine* (1857), and, of course, the Paris of Balzac, Henri Murger, Eugène Sue, and Dumas *fils.* However, these adaptations do not necessarily constitute the majority of his works; a close look at the titles of Dennery's plays and novels reveals that he was just as comfortable working with notorious *faits divers* (news items) and with his own sharp (serious or comical) observations of the behavior, attitudes, concerns, and tastes of the Parisians. From the beginning of his career he was fond of dealing with social issues that were being debated at all levels of society, from modest households to the Chambre des Députés: suffering and misery, especially when they were caused by the abuse of the honest working class by greedy landlords, merchants, bankers, or industrialists; education and access to property ownership by the poor; abandoned, lost, or found children and the responsibility or guilt of their biological or adoptive parents; the consequences of sexual misconduct, especially in the case of libertine aristocratic young men or well-to-do "fallen" young women; groups who lived on the fringe of society; outcasts; and, in general, all victims of prejudice, harassment, and unfair prosecution. In other words Dennery knew how to identify and exploit those topical questions that interested and moved the ordinary people for whom he was writing. In *L'Honneur de ma fille* (My Daughter's Honor, 1836) a loving father, who discovers his wife's adultery by chance, feigns madness to save the honor of his daughter; in *La Comtesse de Sennecey* (The Countess of Sennecey, 1848) a forced marriage leads the heroine to conjugal infidelity. In *Les Bohémiens de Paris* (The Bohemians of Paris, 1843), which premiered shortly after the publication of Sue's *Les Mystères de Paris* (1842), the spectators witness the monstrosity of underworld life—it was also in this, the most popular play of 1843 (the year of the failure of Victor Hugo's *Les Burgraves*), that Dennery revealed himself as a master of melodramatic suspense.

Dennery had the talent to conceive ideas and develop plots that gradually grew in complexity and increased in pathos and emotional charge. The emotion was usually produced by means of sympathy for a fragile, naive, helpless, unsophisticated victim often handicapped by temporary paralysis, blindness, deafness, speech impediments, or loss of memory. Such handicaps were generally caused by the excruciating physical or moral pain inflicted on the victims by cruel villains, whose gloating did not end until the last scene, when justice was finally done. Understandably, the sympathetic Boulevard audiences never stopped shedding tears during the Dennery melodramas—first out of compassion, then out of joy. Dennery was not the first playwright to use handicaps for dramatic purposes, but he made good use of them beginning with his *Gaspard Hauser,* which tells the story of an eighteen-year-old man who has spent his life in prison, has never really spoken with anyone, and consequently does not know how to communicate with others adequately.

La Grâce de Dieu, the melodrama that brought Dennery international fame, has rightly been called one of the great tearjerkers of the nineteenth century. Based on an 1803 comedy-vaudeville by J. N. Bouilly and J. Pain titled *Fanchon la vielleuse,* it idealized even more the already idealized true story of a rather dissolute woman known as Fanchon, who had become a legend in the cabarets of the Boulevard du Temple and the Faubourg Saint-Antoine. In the 1803 comedy Fanchon was transformed into an innocent creature who leaves her native Savoy for Paris, where she makes a living by singing in cabarets. She manages to keep her virtue intact and falls in love with and marries a young man with whom she returns home; the couple lives happily thereafter on a piece of land that she has purchased with her savings. In Dennery's play, subtitled *La Nouvelle Fanchon,* the young woman, now called Marie, inherits the innocence and the candor of her model, but she has become a character of melodrama, which means that the circumstances that force her to leave her parents' home in Savoy as well as those surrounding her Parisian experience are somewhat different.

The piece had all the ingredients to justify its enormous success. First, there were the visual components, with varied and eye-catching sets that took the audience from the purity of the Rousseauesque Alpine landscapes to Marie's modest Parisian quarters, then on to the elegance at the sumptuous home of the marquise—landlady, enemy, and future mother-in-law of the young woman—and finally, before returning to Savoy, to Marie's refuge, where André had installed her with a double purpose: hiding her from the lecherous commander, his uncle and rival, and making of her an educated, sophisticated young lady. The play was also filled with social commentaries, directly addressed to the minds and hearts of Boulevard audiences, about the involuntary migration of poor provincial youngsters to Paris in search of work and money for the eventual purchase of property upon their return home; the dangers and the temptations of the city, to which some succumb; the opposition between the opulence of the rich and the misery of the poor; and the contemptuous and cruel treatment to which the lower class is constantly subjected.

Actor Frédérick Lemaître, for whom Dennery wrote three of his plays (lithograph by Léon Noël)

In addition to these easily identifiable social commentaries, the piece is filled with melodramatic situations that made emotions run high. These involved the despair of the loving parents forced to let their child leave to protect her from the commander; the trials and tribulations of Marie in Paris; the visit of her father, who has come to her door as a beggar looking for his lost daughter and wishing to take her home to his dying wife, followed by his (unjust) outrage and curse when he believes Marie to be a kept woman. There are also scenes of the young woman's subsequent delirious madness, which makes all those around her cry, including her father; the dramatic return home; Marie's mental and her mother's physical recoveries; and, of course, the arrival of André, who has come back to marry her. Furthermore, the presence of Pierrot, an original character (a simpleton who constantly comes to the rescue of the heroine), and especially the musical component of the play contributed greatly to its success. "A la grâce de Dieu" (To the Grace of God), a leitmotiv chanson poignantly sung first by Marie's mother and used later each time the girl is in danger, was certainly an asset, and so was the third act's "La dot d'Auvergne" (The Dowry of Auvergne), both composed by the well-known Loïse Puget, wife of Gustave Lemoine, the co-author of this play.

A revival of *La Grâce de Dieu* later on in the century was a complete fiasco in spite of the efforts made by Dennery, who had supervised the rehearsals personally and had engaged the celebrated Hortense Schneider for the singing role of Pierrot; he had also added a ballet, enlarged the stage, and doubled the number of extras. Dennery would have liked to prove that his works were timeless but was bitterly disappointed to learn the contrary. And yet, his *Les Deux Orphelines* (1874), a melodrama that has the same story line of *La Grâce de Dieu,* gave Dennery enormous satisfaction: not only did it reinforce his popularity, but, above all, it reinvigorated a genre that for most of the people was well on its way to extinction.

Everything seems amplified by two in *Les Deux Orphelines*. The naive Henriette and Louise, her blind sister by adoption, are forcefully separated upon arrival in Paris and victimized by a pair of quite different villains: the debauched Marquis de Presles and La Frochard, a monstrous female beggar. Henriette is saved from de Presles by her suitor, the Chevalier de Vaudrey, whose uncle, the Count of Linières, in charge of the police office, has other plans for him, so that the troubles of the young girl continue. Constantly prevented from finding her sister, she ends up in the Salpêtrière and is almost sent into exile to Guyane, while her truthful chevalier is, in turn, imprisoned at the Bastille. He is saved by a ruse of his servant Picard; the young woman is also saved by a grateful woman whom she had dissuaded from committing suicide and who takes her place when the names are called for departure. In the meantime Henriette's blind sister is a precious prey for La Frochard, who uses her to sing and beg on the streets of Paris, especially at church doors, where on one occasion her own mother, the countess of Linières, saw and pitied her, not knowing her true identity.

There are more characters in this particular play than in others by Dennery, but they are well balanced and their existence is well justified, which accounts for its better-than-normal structure. The count has his spy (Marest) and a family victim, as well as his increasingly secretive and withdrawn wife; La Frochard has a mean, abusive son (Jacques, her favorite) and a good-hearted one (the limping knife grinder Pierre, secretly in love with Louise). The chevalier has his loyal Picard; and even the doctor has his counterpart, Sister Geneviève, who is in charge of the Salpêtrière and who is persuaded by him to tell a once-in-a-lifetime pious lie to save the innocent Henriette. In the end they are all brought back together in happiness thanks to the intervention of the doctor, who, after meeting the two girls under different circumstances, became their protector and savior. The two orphan sisters are finally reunited, and the count, who, having learned his wife's secret, is now ready to forgive her and allow the chevalier to marry the girl he truly loves. The countess has recovered from her weakening melancholy, and her daughter is no longer blind; this good doctor heals bodies and souls.

Les Deux Orphelines was praised unanimously, even by Dennery's foes; it was the melodrama of all melodramas—a well-constructed, moralistic tearjerker that touched upon many popular social issues and had a variety of characters, situations, and familiar Parisian sites, some of them renowned or legendary, such as Saint-Sulpice, the Salpêtrière, and the Bastille. It attracted thousands of spectators, first to the Théâtre de la Porte Saint-Martin, then to other theaters in Paris and around the world, for more than fifty consecutive years. The play was immediately translated and later made into movies in 1915, 1922, 1933, and 1955, the most celebrated being the 1922 *Orphans of the Storm,* directed by D. W. Griffith, with Lillian and Dorothy Gish as the two orphans. Dennery also made a more extended version of it, putting it in novel form in 1887; its last edition was published by Garnier in its Popular Literature series as recently as 1979.

Encouraged by the overwhelming acclaim of this play, Dennery conceived the equally successful *Une Cause célèbre* (A Celebrated Cause, 4 December 1876) in which, once more, he tells the story of two girls, best friends, who grow up not knowing exactly who they are: one, Adrienne, adopted by a noblewoman, is in reality the daughter of an unjustly convicted soldier; the other, Valentine, is a simple girl who turns out to be the daughter of a count. Written in the late 1870s, this play contains all the characteristics of modern violent melodramas, of which it undoubtedly is a forerunner: Lazare, the villain/impostor, tortures Adrienne's defenseless mother, forces the woman to tell her little daughter (who is listening to the screams from outside) that she is with her father, and then brutally murders her onstage. The gory sight causes the girl to lose her memory for a time.

In the late 1840s, when Dennery was already a seasoned playwright, he conceived a new type of play, one that would overwhelm the eyes with sumptuous sets and costumes, hundreds of extras, animals (horses, especially), ballets, exotic or diabolical rites, miracles, and apparitions. The genre was called Féerie, and it instantly attracted crowds first to the Gaîté, the Cirque, the Porte Saint-Martin, and later to the Châtelet, whose modern stage was immediately put to task after its inauguration on 1 March 1862 with Dennery's *Rothomago. Les Sept Châteaux du diable* (The Seven Châteaus of the Devil, 9 August 1844), in a prologue and three acts, tells the saga of two couples who want to go on a pilgrimage to Notre-Dame-de-Bon-Secours and are forced by Satan to take a detour that leads them to seven châteaus inhabited by the seven deadly sins. In the eighteen tableaux the spectators are taken on an illusory trip through the interior of the châteaus and through snowy mountains and dark forests that spring up from the ground or are swallowed by it. Reserved for the grand finale is a Christian church in which a huge, starry globe with descending angels is seen against the rays of light coming through the multicolored stained-glass windows.

La Poule aux oeufs d'or (The Goose of the Golden Eggs, 1848), in a prologue and three acts, is about two nutty brothers who, with the help of magic eggs, go searching for a princess. Their journey and nonsensical plight are but an excuse for an elaborate series of twenty-four fantastic tableaux, among them a snow-covered landscape that turns into a Chinese town and another one showing Harmony Island, where an optical illusion is created by a palace in the middle of a lake, ships, exotic palm trees, and an army, all of which are in reality the instruments of a gigantic orchestra.

To this same category of colossal spectacles belongs his eight-act loose adaptation of Harriet Beecher Stowe's *Uncle Tom's Cabin* (1852), which was titled *La Case de l'oncle Tom* (The Case of Uncle Tom, 18 January 1853). There were also *Marengo* (1863), *L'Histoire d'un drapeau* (The History of a Flag, 1860) (*drames militaires*), and *La Prise de Pékin* (The Capture of Peking, 1861), in five acts and eleven scenes during which the delighted audiences of the Cirque and the Châtelet were treated to a colorful view of the Orient and a complex plot dealing with the issue of exploitation of the poor by colonialists and the dangerous consequences of opium, a social problem of increasing significance in the Paris of the 1860s.

The great appeal of these extravagant stagings must have motivated Dennery's incursion into the world of the lyric theater and into science fiction in his collaborations with Jules Verne. Dennery's experience in vaudeville writing as well as his ability to create strong melodramatic characters, and his knowledge of the powerful impact that music can have on audiences, accounted for a series of successes as a librettist of comic and serious operas beginning in 1847. Authorized to open a third opera house in Paris, the Opéra-National, the composer

Actress Marie Dorval, whose performance was credited with making Dennery's Marie-Jeanne *(1845) a success*

Antoine Adam inaugurated it with the Dennery/Edouard Cormon/Louis Aimé Maillart *drame lyrique* in three acts, *Gastibelza, ou, Le Fou de Tolède* (The Fool of Toledo, 1847), inspired by a Victor Hugo ballad. Set in the Spanish countryside and at court, it has eight characters in search of happiness and justice: two candid peasants, two villains, the king of Spain and Count Mendoza (unjustly accused of murder), his daughter Sabine, and her suitor, Count Gastibelza, who goes mad out of despair when he thinks Sabine has betrayed him. In the height of the mad scene that precedes the predictable happy finale, Gastibelza's words have a distinctly Romantic ring, reminiscent of Hernani's, as he states that everything he touches withers; everything that loves him is hopelessly lost; and everything he loves is dishonored. In fact, the entire libretto reads like an impoverished version or a parody of a Romantic drama, the kind of play that had long lost its initial popularity and that by 1847 was acceptable only as an opera libretto.

With Gounod, Dennery collaborated on the *Le Tribut de Zamora* (Zamora's Tribute, 1881), which drew the crowds to the Palais-Garnier for some fifty-odd performances before falling into oblivion.

The setting is in Moorish-dominated Spain; the orphaned maiden Xaïma, in love with Manoel, is victimized by the villain Ben Saïd, who takes her prisoner, and by the madwoman Hermosa, a vindictive woman also in captivity. In this typical Dennery plot Hermosa eventually learns that she is Xaïma's mother, kills the villain, recovers her sanity, and sees to the happiness of her daughter and Manoel. Curiously enough, the best and most interesting lines in the libretto and in the music are not those of young Xaïma but of Hermosa, whose motherly feelings, vindictive madness, and patriotic fervor stirred up the emotions of a cheering opening-night audience that included President Jules Grévy, Léon Gambetta, and other Third Republic dignitaries. Finally, Dennery wrote with Edouard Blau and Louis Gallet the libretto for Jules Massenet's *Le Cid* (1885). The opera, in four acts and ten scenes, constituted a truly serious effort on the part of the librettists to maintain the nobility of the Pierre Corneille play, both thematically and linguistically, with no simplistic tearjerking scenes or street jargon. The 1885 opera had reached its one-hundredth performance by the end of the century, and although it never became anyone's favorite, it has never been completely dropped from the repertory.

Verne, a populist writer whose novels were eagerly devoured by the masses, got along marvelously with Dennery. To see what appeared to be the actual landscapes and the natives that Philéas Fogg encounters in his voyage around the world, the Patagonia and the Australian shores described in the adventures of the children of Captain Grant, and the Urals and Siberian steppes in *Michel Strogoff* fulfilled the dreams of many uneducated spectators of the Parisian Boulevards who were convinced that they had learned valuable lessons in geography and science.

Le tour du monde en quatre vingts jours (1874) is a free adaptation, in five acts and fifteen tableaus, of Verne's novel of the same title, published in 1873 and translated in 1874 as *A Tour of the World in Eighty Days*. When it finally opened at the Porte Saint-Martin, it played during the entire 1874–1875 season, and its revival, for the Exhibition of 1878, was just as successful. By 1900 it had been performed fifteen hundred times. The play continued to be performed in the twentieth century, and its star-studded 1956 movie version has become a classic.

Les Enfants du capitaine Grant (The Children of Captain Grant, 26 December 1878), in five acts and thirteen tableaux, tells the saga of two children who leave Glasgow on an adventurous voyage across the sea to rescue their father and younger brother, abandoned on Balker Islet. This is perhaps the most unbelievable of the Dennery/Verne stories; indeed, the plot seems nothing but a pretext for the staging of shipwrecks, whale fishing, huge birds of prey capable of carrying human beings, storms, earthquakes, sliding slopes, South American Indian celebrations, cavalcades in the Australian forests and marshes, and the midnight sun on the South Seas. Aside from Captain Grant, his children, and Lord Glenarvan (the Scottish owner of the ship), the characters are stereotypical and caricatured but provide for a good bit of healthy humor. Humor is also provided by the allusions to geography and biology; Grant's first SOS message is found in the stomach of a shark, the second on a harpoon stuck in an escaped whale; horses die because of Gastrolobium.

Michel Strogoff, "pièce à grand spectacle," in five acts and sixteen tableaux, is certainly Dennery's greatest extravaganza. The colossal production cost about Fr 300,000; it had fifty dancers performing in two grand ballets choreographed by A. Fuchs, 350 extras, and twelve hundred costumes, as well as horses, Russian and Tartar armies, and military bands. It took the spectators all the way from the New Palace in Moscow across the Urals to Kolyvan, to the borders of the Angara, to Irkutsk, in Siberia; it showed battle scenes of Turks and Tartars at war. The story is simple but somewhat more plausible than that of Captain Grant, with the exception of Strogoff's blindness, which never existed because the blinding red iron, dried by his tears, never hurt the eyes. In this piece many melodramatic situations are provided by the two female characters: Marfa Strogoff, played by Marie Laurent, and Nadia, the young girl in search of her exiled princely father. There are also two colorful traitor-villains, the Russian Ivan Ougareff and the Emir Féofar. A touch of welcome lightness and humor is offered by the rivalry between the French (Jollivet) and the British (Blount) journalists, who travel the same route as Strogoff and always compete to surpass and outdo each other. *Michel Strogoff* had 386 consecutive sold-out performances, but its huge success could not be repeated with the two authors' last (unpublished) collaboration, "Voyage à travers l'impossible" (Travels across the Impossible), where one could see the center of the world and the Nautilus. By 1882, when this play opened, the immediate interest of the audiences of the secondary Parisian stages seemed to have shifted toward a different, more realistic kind of spectacle.

Gautier ended his tongue-in-cheek review of *La Grâce de Dieu* with one short statement: "The play was a success and made women weep abundantly." This patronizing conclusion, if applied to the ensemble of the Dennery works, would hardly provoke a dissenting remark among experts. And yet it would be unfair to refuse a place in the annals of French literary history to a playwright who, without being a genius, was undoubtedly a master of his craft. It is to his credit to have intuitively known and delivered exactly what pleased and moved the uneducated, highly emotional Boulevard audiences who filled the theaters for much of the nineteenth century. A self-taught, skillful man with a pragmatic mind, Dennery seemed to enjoy his lasting popular success while enduring with humorous cynicism the unrelenting condemnation of the linguistic and stylistic shortcomings of his writings.

In response to all critiques, past, present, and future, he wrote his one-act comedy *Le Sacrifice d'Iphigénie* (The Sacrifice of Iphigenia, 1861), in which he used some of the same words that he must have frequently read in the reviews of his works and ironically stated his philosophy of theater and authorship. M. Daubray has become an affluent banker after having tried his luck as a playwright; he and his nephew Charles, suitor of his daughter and aspiring playwright himself, have something in common–they have both submitted a play titled "Le Sacrifice d'Iphigénie" to the reading committee at the Théâtre-Français, the uncle twenty years earlier, the nephew recently. The notary Villiers gives advice to the two men. First he tells the young man that in order to prove that the career of a playwright is honorable and be accepted as the future husband of his cousin, Charles must sacrifice his "Iphigénie" (which has been approved and is already in rehearsal) and rearrange it so as to make his uncle believe that it is his version that has been approved. Then the notary persuades Daubray to let go of his version because his credibility as a banker would disappear if it became known that he is a playwright. Now that he has tasted the sweet flavor of success in the theater, Daubray is satisfied, and all ends well. In the midst of their discussion about theater the practical-minded Villiers explains to the aspiring playwright the differences between a poet/stylist and a drama-carpenter/stage-trickster. The use of a simple, natural speech as well as the use of a universal language by characters from all social classes for the expression of feelings and emotions do not make a writer a stylist. If success is found through an ingenious combination of light/comical and serious/moving situations, one becomes a drama-carpenter. If euphemisms and paraphrases are not used, one will be a stage-trickster and never be ranked among poets: only the public will be on your side. Dennery repeated these ideas more seri-

ously in real life during a conversation with Duquesnel, to whom he confessed that his was a theater of action, that he wrote as one speaks, and that he did not consider himself a true writer, just a crafty playwright. That is indeed how he is remembered among serious litterateurs. Having begun his career at a time when melodrama in its original Guilbert de Pixerécourt manner was coming to an end, he managed to fill this eminently popular type of play with renewed vigor and energy by making it less idealized (more believable), more modern, more moving, and certainly more eye-catching. Current and future generations of melodrama readers or watchers, on screens silver or small, should be grateful to Dennery for having ensured not only the survival but also the perpetuation of their favorite and much-maligned genre.

References:

Archives biographiques françaises (London & New York: K. G. Saur, 1988);

Henri Beaulieu, *Les Théâtres du Boulevard du Crime* (Paris: H. Dragon, 1905);

Félix Duquesnel, "Adolphe Dennery," in *Souvenirs littéraires* (Paris: Plon-Nourrit, 1922);

Théophile Gautier, *Histoire de l'art dramatique en France depuis vingt-cinq ans,* volumes 1–6 (Paris: Hetzel, 1859);

James Harding, *Gounod* (New York: Stein & Day, 1973);

Jules Lemaître, *Impressions de théâtre* (Paris: Boivin, 1880), pp. 356–359;

John McCormick, *Popular Theatres of Nineteenth-Century France* (New York: Routledge, 1993);

Brigitte Nerlich, "Voyage à travers l'impossible, pièce fantastique: essai d'interprétation fantastique," *La Revue des lettres modernes,* 812–817 (1987): 117–130;

Frank Rahill, *The World of Melodrama* (University Park: Pennsylvania State University Press, 1967);

Francisque Sarcey, *Quarante ans de théâtre,* volume 4 (Paris: Bibliothèque des Annales politiques et littéraires, 1901), pp. 331–356;

Jean-Marie Thomasseau, *Le mélodrame* (Paris: Presses Universitaires de France, 1984);

Emile Zola, "Nos auteurs dramatiques," in his *Oeuvres complètes,* volume 35 (Paris: Fasquelle, n.d), pp. 249–259.

Papers:

Dennery willed his collections to the state. They are now at the Musée Dennery in Paris. His papers are at the Bibliothèque Nationale in Paris.

Victor Ducange
(24 November 1783 – 26 October 1833)

Marie-Pierre Le Hir
Case Western Reserve University

PLAY PRODUCTIONS: *Palmérin, ou Le Solitaire des Gaules,* Paris, Théâtre de l'Ambigu-Comique, 11 February 1813;

Pharamond, ou L'Entrée des Francs dans les Gaules, Paris, Théâtre de l'Ambigu-Comique, 10 November 1813;

La Folle Intrigue, ou Les Quiproquo, Paris, Théâtre de l'Ambigu-Comique, 21 June 1814;

L'An 1835, ou L'Enfant d'un cosaque, Paris, Théâtre de l'Ambigu-Comique, 23 March 1815;

Adolphe et Sophie, ou Les Victimes d'une erreur, Paris, Théâtre de l'Ambigu-Comique, 23 March 1816;

Les Deux Valladomir, Paris, Théâtre de l'Ambigu-Comique, 23 March 1816;

La Bague de fer, Paris, Théâtre de la Porte Saint-Martin, 25 April 1818;

La Cabane de Montainard, ou Les Auvergnats, Paris, Théâtre de la Porte Saint-Martin, 26 September 1818;

La Tante à marier, Paris, Théâtre de la Porte Saint-Martin, 2 February 1819;

La Maison du Corrégidor, ou Ruse et malice, Paris, Théâtre de la Porte Saint-Martin, 10 July 1819;

Hasard et folie, Paris, Théâtre de l'Ambigu-Comique, 3 August 1819;

Le Prisonnier vénitien, ou Le Fils géolier, Paris, Théâtre de l'Ambigu-Comique, 6 October 1819;

Le Mineur d'Auberwald, Paris, Théâtre de l'Ambigu-Comique, 25 April 1820;

Le Colonel et le soldat, ou La Loi militaire, Paris, Théâtre de l'Ambigu-Comique, 11 July 1820;

Calas, Paris, Théâtre de l'Ambigu-Comique, 20 November 1820;

Thérèse, ou L'Orpheline de Genève, Paris, Théâtre de l'Ambigu-Comique, 23 November 1820;

La Sorcière, ou L'Orphelin écossais, Paris, Théâtre de la Gaîté, 3 May 1821;

La Suédoise, Paris, Théâtre de l'Ambigu-Comique, 11 August 1821;

La Bataille de Nancy, Paris, Théâtre de l'Ambigu-Comique, 10 January 1822;

Elodie, ou La Vierge du monastère, Paris, Théâtre de l'Ambigu-Comique, 10 January 1822;

Lisbeth, ou La Fille du laboureur, Paris, Théâtre de l'Ambigu-Comique, 18 November 1823;

Léonide, ou La Vieille de Suresne, Paris, Théâtre du Vaudeville, 17 January 1824;

Le Diamant, Paris, Théâtre de l'Ambigu-Comique, 6 November 1824;

Le Banqueroutier, Paris, Théâtre de la Gaîté, 29 April 1826;

Mac-Dowel, Paris, Théâtre de la Gaîté, 12 October 1826;

Trente ans, ou La Vie d'un joueur, Paris, Théâtre de la Porte Saint-Martin, 19 June 1827;

L'Artiste et le soldat, Paris, Théâtre des Nouveautés, 9 November 1827;

Le Bourgmestre de Blackscharz, ou Les Trois Manteaux, Paris, Théâtre de la Porte Saint-Martin, 18 February 1828;

La Fiancée de Lammermoor, Paris, Théâtre de la Porte Saint-Martin, 25 March 1828;

Polder, ou Le Bourreau d'Amsterdam, Paris, Théâtre de la Gaîté, 15 October 1828;

Les Sept Heures, Paris, Théâtre de la Porte Saint-Martin, 23 March 1829;

Les Deux Raymond, ou Les Nouveaux Ménechmes, Paris, Théâtre de la Porte Saint-Martin, 27 August 1829;

Macbeth, Paris, Théâtre de la Porte Saint-Martin, 9 November 1829;

Le Couvent de Tonnington, ou La Pensionnaire, Paris, Théâtre de la Gaîté, 12 May 1830;

Le Jésuite, Paris, Théâtre de la Gaîté, 4 September 1830;

Malmaison et Sainte-Hélène, Paris, Théâtre de la Gaîté, 13 January 1831;

L'Oiseau bleu, Paris, Théâtre de la Gaîté, 13 January 1831;

Agathe, ou L'Education et le naturel, Paris, Théâtre des Variétés, 13 June 1831;

Il y a seize ans, Paris, Théâtre de la Gaîté, 20 June 1831;

La Vendetta, ou La Fiancée corse, Paris, Théâtre de la
    Gaîté, 27 October 1831;
Richard Darlington, Paris, Théâtre de la Porte Saint-
    Martin, 10 December 1831;
Le Testament de la pauvre femme, Paris, Théâtre de la
    Gaîté, 1 September 1832;
Clète, ou La Fille d'une reine, Paris, Théâtre de la
    Gaîté, 17 January 1833;
Plus de jeudi, Paris, Théâtre des Variétés, 2 Septem-
    ber 1835;
Le Baron de Montrevel, Paris, Théâtre de la Porte
    Saint-Martin, 20 September 1837.

BOOKS: *Essai sur la campagne de Bonaparte en Italie*
    (N.p., n.d);
Palmérin, ou Le Solitaire des Gaules, music by Adrien
    Quaisain and Frederic Lanusse (Paris: Dentu,
    1813);
Pharamond, ou L'Entrée des Francs dans les Gaules
    (Paris: J.-N. Barba, 1813);
La Folle Intrigue, ou Les Quiproquo (Paris: Fages,
    1814);
Adolphe et Sophie, ou Les Victimes d'une erreur, music by
    M. Amédée and Quaisin (Paris: Fages, 1816);
    republished as *Drame en trois actes* (Paris: Mi-
    chel Lévy frères, 1860);
L'An 1835, ou L'Enfant d'un cosaque (Paris: Fages,
    1816);
Les Deux Valladomir: mélodrame en trois actes, by Du-
    cange and Marie-Adélaïde Barthélémy-Hadot
    (Paris: Fages, 1816);
Le Prince de Norvège, ou La Bague de fer (Paris: Barba,
    1818); republished as *La Bague de fer* (Paris:
    Michel Lévy frères, 1861);
La Cabane de Montainard, ou Les Auvergnats, by Du-
    cange and Frédéric Dupetit-Méré (Paris:
    Fages, 1818);
Calas (Paris: J.-N. Barba, 1819);
Hasard et folie (Paris: Quoy, 1819);
La Maison du corrégidor, ou Ruse et malice (Paris: J.-N.
    Barba, 1819);
Le Prisonnier vénitien, ou Le Fils géôlier (Paris: J.-N.
    Barba, 1819);
La Tante à marier (Paris: J.-N. Barba, 1819);
Albert, ou Les Amants missionnaires, 2 volumes, Paris:
    J.-N. Barba, 1820); republished as *Albert,* 1 vol-
    ume (Paris: G. Barba, 1852);
Le Colonel et le soldat, ou La Loi militaire (Paris: J.-N.
    Barba, 1820);
Thérèse, ou L'Orpheline de Genève (Paris: J.-N. Barba,
    1820);
Le Mineur d'Auberwald, by Ducange and Dupetit-
    Méré (Paris: J.N. Barba, 1820);
Valentine, ou Le Pasteur d'Uzès, 3 volumes (Paris: J.-N.
    Barba, 1820); revised edition with a notice by

Victor Ducange

Ducange about the trial of Valentine in *Oeuvres
    complètes* (Paris: G. Barba, 1833);
La Suédoise (Paris: J.-N. Barba, 1821; Paris);
La Sorcière, ou L'Orphelin écossais, by Ducange and
    Dupetit-Méré (Paris: Quoy, 1821);
*Elodie, ou La Vierge du monastère, imité du solitaire de
    D'Arlincourt; précédé de la bataille de Nancy,
    prolologue en un acte* (Paris: Pollet, 1822);
Léonide, ou La Vieille de Surènes, 5 volumes (Paris:
    Pollet, 1823);
Thélène, ou L'Amour et la guerre, 4 volumes (Paris:
    Pollet, 1824);
Le Diamant (Paris: Pollet, 1824);
La Luthérienne, ou La Famille morave, 6 volumes (Paris:
    Pollet, 1825);
Le Médecin confesseur, ou La Jeune emigrée, 6 volumes
    (Paris: Pollet, 1825);
Mac-Dowel, music by M. Alexandre (Paris: Quoy,
    1826);
Les Trois filles de la veuve, 6 volumes (Paris: A. Marc,
    1826);
L'Artiste et le soldat, ou Le Petit Roman (Paris: Pollet,
    1827);
Trente ans, ou La Vie d'un joueur, by Ducange and
    Dinaux, as Jacques-Felix Beudin and Pros-
    per-Parfait Goubaux, music by Alexandre
    Piccini (Paris: Barba, 1827);
*La Fiancée de Lammermoor: imitée du roman de Sir Wal-
    ter Scott* (Paris: Bouquin de La Souche, 1828);
Polder, ou Le Bourreau d'Amsterdam, by Ducange and
    Charles René Guilbert de Pixerécourt (Paris:

Pollet, 1828); republished as *Drame en trois actes* (Paris: Tresse, 1840);

Macbeth: imitation libre de Shakespeare, by Ducange and Auguste Anicet-Bourgeois (Paris: Quoy, 1829);

Les Sept Heures, by Ducange and Anicet-Bouregois (Paris: Bezou, 1829); republished as *Sept Heures, ou Charlotte Corday* (Paris: Tresse, 1844);

Les Deux Raymond, ou Les Nouveaux ménechmes, by Ducange, Joseph-Mathurin Brisset, and M. Ruben (Paris: Quoy, 1829);

Le Couvent de Tonnington, ou La Pensionnaire, by Ducange and Anicet-Bourgeois (Paris: Boulland, 1830);

Isaurine et Jean-Pohl, ou Les Révolutions du château de gît-au-Diable, 4 volumes (Paris: Lecointe et Pougin, 1830);

Ludovica, ou Le Testament de Waterloo, 6 volumes (Paris: Lecointe, 1830);

Marc-Loricot, ou Le Petit Chouan de 1830, 6 volumes (Paris: Lecointe et Pougin, 1830);

Agathe, ou L'Education et le naturel (Paris: Riga, 1831);

Il y a seize ans (Paris: Riga, 1831);

La Vendetta, ou La Fiancée corse (Paris: Riga, 1831);

Richard Darlington, by Ducange and Dinaux as Jacques-Felix Beudin and Prosper-Parfait Goubaux (Paris: J.-N. Barba, 1832);

L'Oiseau bleu, by Ducange and Pixerécourt (Paris: Hardy, 1832);

Le Testament de la pauvre femme (Paris: Barba, 1832; Paris);

Clète, ou La Fille d'une reine, by Ducange and Anicet-Bourgeois (Paris: Marchant, 1833);

Joasine, ou La Fille du prêtre, 5 volumes (Paris: Gosselin, 1835);

Plus de jeudi, by Ducange and Anicet-Bourgeois (Paris: Marchant, 1835);

Le Jésuite: drame en trois actes et en six tableaux, stage adaptation of *Les Trois filles de la veuve,* by Ducange and Pixerécourt (Brussel: N.p., 1835; Paris: Tresse, 1840);

Lisbeth, ou La Fille du laboureur (Paris: J. N. Barba, 1840);

Agathe, ou Le Petit viellard de Calais; Thérèse ou l'Orpheline de Genève, Bibliothèque pour tous illustrée (Paris: G. Harvard, 1858).

Editions and Collections: *Oeuvres complètes,* 10 volumes (Paris: G. Barba, 1833–1838); volumes 1–2: *Agathe, ou Le Petit Vieillard de Calais;* volumes 3–6: *Albert, ou Les Amants missionnaires;* volumes 7–10: *Valentine, ou Le Pasteur d'Uzès;*

Les Moeurs, contes et nouvelles, 2 volumes (Paris: Lecointe et Pougin, 1834).

**SELECTED PERIODICAL PUBLICATION–
UNCOLLECTED:** *Le Diable rose, ou Le Petit courrier de Lucifer,* 12 April–19 July 1822.

Known to posterity as the third king of the French melodrama, Victor Ducange was a playwright of striking originality who brought important innovations to the French stage. Between 1813, the year he began to write, and 1833, the year he died, Ducange wrote more than forty plays. Thirteen were written in collaboration with other playwrights, a common practice at the time, and all were produced in Paris on the so-called minor stages—*les petits théâtres.*

Ducange wrote many comedies, but the genre in which he excelled, and to which he devoted more than two-thirds of his writings for the stage, was the melodrama. Often disparaged for stereotypical characters, lack of realism, and grandiloquent rhetoric, the melodrama prolongs the tradition of revolutionary oratory, but does so only formally. In the plays of the first two kings of melodrama, Louis-Charles Caignez and René-Charles Guilbert de Pixerécourt, revolutionary rhetoric was emptied of its political content. Ducange differs from his predecessors precisely on that point. His melodrama brings to the stage the ethical and political concerns of a public-minded citizen in postrevolutionary France, where democracy had failed but where it still remained, for many people, a precious ideal. In his lifetime Ducange enjoyed all the glory of a fashionable playwright, a passing glory of which little is left today: there is no complete edition of his works, and his name is rarely mentioned in anthologies of drama. Several contemporaries published biobibliographical notices about him and his work as a dramatist and novelist, but no true biography exists even now.

Given the scarcity of known archival material on Ducange, at least in France, such a work may never be written. A veil of mystery shrouds all aspects of his private life, including his name. The family name was apparently Brahain, sometimes spelled *Brahin* but also, as some documents in the French National Archives indicate, *Bréchaire* or *Brachaire.* In 1793 Victor's father, Pierre Auguste, signed a pamphlet he had written with the name "dit Ducange" (known as Ducange), thereby indicating that Ducange was not his real name but that it was the name he commonly used. With the exception of a few reference works that use the name Brahain Ducange, biographical dictionaries usually list him under "Ducange."

The same uncertainty also exists with regard to his family's nationality. When Victor Henri Joseph Brahain Ducange was born on 24 November 1783, the family lived in The Hague, Netherlands. His father, Pierre Auguste Brahain Ducange, was a *secrétaire d'ambassade* (diplomat), apparently attached to the French embassy. But if he was French, he also referred to himself as a Batavian patriot during the French Revolution. Although no documented evidence supports this claim, the family was most likely one of French Protestant origins that had found refuge in Holland from religious persecution. This personal background would account for the lack of biographical information available about the family in France: records of vital statistics of Protestants, kept at the Hôtel de Ville in Paris since the revocation of the Edict of Nantes, were destroyed in a fire in 1871. The religious-refugee status of Ducange's family would also explain several leitmotivs in Victor Ducange's work: his passionate denunciation of all forms of intolerance, his enduring fight for the democratic ideals of liberty and justice, and the recurrent presence of Protestant characters (the Calas family in *Calas* [1820], Pastor Egerthon in *Thérèse, ou L'Orpheline de Genève* [1820]), Pastor Blumfield in *Lisbeth, ou La Fille du laboureur* [1823], in his novels and plays.

Ducange's father was also a journalist for *La Gazette de Leyde,* and he wrote several books that, in the absence of other biographical data, provide useful insights into the playwright's family background. The first book, *Les Oeuvres du sieur Hadoux, commentées et rendues intelligibles* (Sir Hadoux's Works, Made Intelligible through Commentary), was published in 1783. Described by a critic, who obviously failed to appreciate Pierre Auguste's sense of humor, as "an incredible monument testifying to the poor style and the atrocious spelling of this Franco-Dutch author," the work was a parody of scholarly publications, probably intended as a practical joke. It contained, apart from the commentaries announced in the title, two comedies: the one-act *Le Dragon vert* and *Le Petit Câbret.* But there was, of course, no sieur Hadoux, and the scholar presenting his learned critique of the two comedies was also the author of the comedies: André Rhiba d'Acunenga—an anagram for Brahain Ducange—a self-described *professor omni genere* (professor of all genres). The publication place, "Criticopolis," and publication date, "the Year of the Muses"—indicated on the cover—sufficiently attest to the nonsensical, farcical character of the work.

Pierre Auguste's first published work might reveal him to be more of a trickster than a serious playwright. It is nonetheless also proof of Victor's father's interest in drama, of a knowledge and appreciation of the comic genre strong enough to moti-vate and enable him to write plays. At the same time, through the displacement of the comic focus from the plays to the satire of academic writings about comedy, the work also exemplifies the kind of farcical, almost Rabelaisian humor that later reemerges in most of Victor's novels and comedies.

Written in a much more serious register, Pierre Auguste's second publication is also helpful in understanding another important facet in his son's writings, their political nature. Pierre Auguste is known to have been an ardent supporter of the French Revolution. His second piece of writing is a political pamphlet published in 1793 under the title *Pièces remises au Comité de correspondance du Club des Jacobins par le citoyen Ducange, patriote batave* (Papers Handed Over to the Jacobin Club's Committee of Correspondence by Citizen Ducange, a Batavian Patriot). Apart from the evidence it provides of the elder Ducange's ability to write flawless French, the document also highlights the political role Victor's father played in 1792 and 1793. Focused on a particular issue, the necessity and the means of exporting the French Revolution to the Netherlands, the pamphlet documents the elder Ducange's success in convincing the French revolutionary government to support Franco-Dutch citizens such as himself—Batavian patriots who embraced the ideal of the French Revolution in their efforts to establish the Batavian Republic, which was created three years later.

Moreover, the pamphlet provides insights into what the French Revolution meant not only for the elder Ducange but also for his son: a universal fight for democracy against "aristocracies of all kinds." Recalling the Dutch Stadhouder's attempts to prevent France from providing support to the American patriots during the American War of Independence, Pierre Auguste assured the members of the National Convention, in an address reprinted in the pamphlet, that they were right "to separate the cause of the people from that of the tyrants that oppress them. . . . Liberty, equality," he concluded, "these are the divinities Reason offers to humanity."

But if Pierre Auguste wholeheartedly embraced the emancipatory ideal of the French Revolution, he also condemned the pernicious derailments that occurred during the Reign of Terror. Predictably enough, his name is listed in 1795 among those of individuals who were suspected of antirevolutionary sentiments and wanted by the Committee of General Safety. Victor's passionate denunciation of the Reign of Terror in his drama *Les Sept Heures* (Seven O'Clock, 1829) doubtless originates in his personal recollections of this traumatic period.

Pierre Auguste's early political influence on his son is perhaps best documented in Victor's first publication, a student essay written in 1798, when he was fifteen years old. That young Victor would choose Napoleon Bonaparte's campaign in Italy as his topic and celebrate its success should hardly come as a surprise. For father and son, Napoleon embodied the continuation of the good French Revolution, as well as the end of the bad one, the Reign of Terror. More than a matter of personal political convictions, Napoleon's regime considerably changed the lives of families like the Ducanges. During the Empire the meritocratic administrative system put in place by Napoleon gave concrete realization to the rights of citizenship granted in 1791 to religious minorities. Based on the revolutionary principle of equality, the Napoleonic state was open to all (male) citizens willing to serve it, according to their abilities but, just as important, without regard to their fortune or religious creeds. For members of religious minorities who had been previously excluded from participating in public affairs, or had been forced to exile, this meant full-fledged citizenship.

From 1805 to 1815 Victor Ducange was a public servant in two of the administrations newly created by the Napoleonic regime, first for the Office of Land Survey and later for the Ministry of Manufacturing and Commerce. As was suitable for a young man working for a public administration, Victor began his literary career under the pseudonym M. Victor, a pen name he used for about ten years. When his first play, a melodrama titled *Palmerin, ou Le Solitaire des Gaules,* was produced at the Théâtre de l'Ambigu-Comique on 11 February 1813, Ducange had apparently no plans to give up his administrative position, and for two years he had two careers. But historical events forced him to abandon the first. The restoration of Louis XVIII to the throne of France brought the suppression of the office of manufacturing and commerce, and Ducange lost his job. Well documented in his later writings, his opposition to the royalist politics of the new regime is certainly related to these personal circumstances, to the hardships Ducange and his family endured after he was deprived of this regular source of income.

Two years earlier the thirty-year-old Ducange, who lived in rue Saint-Honoré at the time, had wed Marie Anne Colombier on 26 April 1813. Apart from the fact that Marie Anne survived her husband's death in 1833, nothing conclusive is known about her. In the archives of the Bibliothèque Protestante de France, however, there is documentation about a Colombier family, Calvinist pastors from Geneva who settled in the area of Nîmes in 1797.

Since a novel Ducange published in 1820, *Valentine, ou Le Pasteur d'Uzès* (Valentine, or the Pastor of Uzès), attests to his personal knowledge of persecutions endured by Protestants of that area during the Restoration, it is not unreasonable to assume that Marie Anne might have been related to this Colombier family.

Fear of persecution might also explain an otherwise mysterious episode in Ducange's life. Shortly after losing his position at the ministry of manufacturing and commerce, Ducange moved to England, in one of his biographer's words, "with the intention of settling down permanently there." Exile seems quite a radical cure to unemployment, so there must be some other explanation for his decision to leave France. Ducange might have feared persecution by the new regime as a Protestant since the return to France of the king also meant the restoration of political power to the Catholic Church. He might have been afraid of retaliation for his role as a public servant of the previous government. But pure disappointment might have spurred his departure from France, a nation that was no longer the one he loved.

How long Ducange remained in England is uncertain, but when he returned to Paris, he had made up his mind to devote himself entirely to his career as a playwright and as a novelist. Truthful to the ethical and political convictions he had acquired at a young age, he became one of the most outspoken opponents of the Restoration regime. His plays, novels, and the periodical he briefly published in 1822 are a testimony to the steadfastness of his convictions, to the courage he showed in defending what he believed was right, and to the price he paid for his steady critique of royalist politics: exile (to Belgium this time), heavy fines, and jail.

During his eventful and often dramatic life Ducange seems to have kept his sense of humor. His comedies, written as if to help him forget the serious problems of the world, are pure farce, sheer laughter, and joy. But most lack the very element that makes his melodramas and dramas so original—the critical confrontation with the social world. *La Folle Intrigue, ou Les Quiproquo* (A Bold Plot, or the Comedy of Errors, 1814), *La Maison du corrégidor, ou Ruse et malice* (The Magistrate's House, or Ruse and Malice, 1819), and *Hasard et folie* (Hazard and Folly, 1819) all center around a similar plot, the obstacles two young people in love must overcome to obtain permission to marry. What stands in the way of marriage is usually folly: their own when they break the law (by a duel) or the rules of proper behavior (hiding one's loved one in one's bedroom), but it may also include the folly of parents too strict, too blind, or too old to remember what love is. Ducange thus develops a theme omnipresent in Molière's comedies, but unlike Molière he places it at the center of his comic plots. In Molière's comedies, as in those of Ducange, young people always know what their hearts desire, but in Molière's plays children are reasonable and their parents are not. For Molière the focus is clearly on the parents' follies (Harpagon's greed, M. Jourdain's vanity), and children must usually trick their parents to reach their goals. Ducange's parents have no particular vices; they always end up understanding everything; and their power is never really contested. Therefore, Ducange's comedies tend to lack the astute depiction of character types and of social milieus characteristic of high comedy; if they have any philosophical depth, it does not originate in a deep reflection on the contradictions of human nature but rather in a Rabelaisian appreciation of life as a "comédie-folie-carnaval." They are a frank celebration of youth as the age of folly and laughter, where the most common comic situations are linked to mistaken identities.

Ducange's early attraction to a genre glorifying self-denial and renunciation, the melodrama, appears somewhat paradoxical. By 1813, the year Ducange began to write melodramas, Caignez and Pixerécourt had already brought the genre to its full perfection. Their melodramas rest on a dramaturgy of strict rules and conventions with regard to themes, characters, language, and production. The theme of persecution provides the main plot. In the first act the arrival of an evil, sly, and powerful man, the traitor, perturbs the life of a happy community, usually busy celebrating some festive occasion. The traitor's power rests on his knowledge of secrets that can destroy the life of his victim, a young, pretty, honest, and usually passive woman, or her father, a poor, old, invalid, and helpless man who totally depends on her. During the second and much of the third act the traitor persecutes the heroine, blackmails her, and chases her until she is completely cut off from the community and sometimes cursed by her father while the man she loves, the passive hero, does nothing to help. Only Providence can. In the last scenes chance provides the proofs that the traitor's accusations are false. The evil traitor is expelled; virtue triumphs; and peace and happiness are restored in the community.

Based on this structure, two kinds of melodrama coexisted during the first two decades of the century—historical and bourgeois melodrama. In bourgeois melodrama the plot centers around family-related matters involving either love or money, often both: daughters are seduced and kidnapped;

fathers lose their honor and curse their children; secret marriages are celebrated; children are born mysteriously with uncertain identities; family property is stolen; and inheritances are appropriated by clever thieves. Even though these themes can also be found in historical melodramas, the latter are more closely related to the epic. They usually feature historical characters—renowned or mythical kings, queens, and valiant knights—and tell of their feats: the more unusual the adventure (battle, voyage of discovery), the more spectacular the natural catastrophe (earthquake, volcanic eruption), the better.

The success of this type of melodrama can be explained by examining the encounter of a new public and a new genre. Compared to the prerevolutionary period, the number of theatergoers increased considerably during the first two decades of the nineteenth century, and the social makeup of theater audiences also changed. The melodrama appealed to people who had just left the lower class to climb up the social ladder and who were not as well educated. As such, it directly participated in the general process of democratization characteristic of the period. Yet it would be wrong to view the melodrama as a strictly "popular" genre because it was not primarily addressed to members of the lower classes but rather to the new social elites who had the means and the time to go to the theater.

If the melodrama comforts its spectators in their new social prerogatives, it also relates to their cultural preferences more readily than does classical theater. A cathartic ritual, the melodrama has a soothing, unifying effect on audiences eager to find political stability and reassurance about the future. Like the characters in the plays they are watching, spectators are willing to suspend judgment and reason and to believe, instead, that, like them, the characters onstage form a unified social community that accepts evil as a fatality and does not ask about its origin.

Written during the Empire, Ducange's first melodrama, *Palmérin, ou Le Solitaire des Gaules* (1813), already breaks with this type of melodrama. Set in England in the Middle Ages, it is a tale of love and honor much more reminiscent of Pierre Corneille's *Le Cid* (1637) than of Pixerécourt's plays. Although many melodramatic elements are present, such as mysterious births and written confessions, Ducange's characters move in a moral universe tailored for human beings. In all of Ducange's plays evil is produced by people, and it is unacceptable. More developed than Pixerécourt's, Ducange's characters therefore refuse to be helpless victims. Even when appearances are against them, they put their faith in justice; they believe, as the king says in this play, "in the free exercise of reason's lights."

With *Pharamond, ou L'Entrée des Francs dans les Gaules* (Pharamond, or the Frankish Invasion of Gaul, 1813) Ducange distances himself from the traditional historical melodrama, where history usually serves as a pretext for displaying lavish, exotic sets. Conceived as a commemoration of the birth of France, *Pharamond* is set in Trier in 418. The play recalls the defeat of Clodibaud, a Roman ruler of Gaul, at the hands of Pharamond, a Frankish prince who becomes, thanks to this victory, the founder of the future French nation. The preface to the play, a well-documented notice on the historical figures who give their names to his characters, testifies to Ducange's ambition of "sticking as closely as possible to history," as he puts it, of producing a true national historical drama. Pharamond was still considered a real historical figure when Ducange wrote the play, but even then Clovis would have seemed a more fitting candidate for the historical role of "founder of the French monarchy." Unlike Clovis, however, Pharamond is not known as the first king of the Franks to have converted to Catholicism. Thanks to him, Ducange can dissociate church and state and indirectly assert that France was not the elder daughter of the church. In this early example of Romantic historiography Ducange retells the past, Pharamond's story, to better account for the present, to celebrate the grandeur of a regime based on the separation of church and state.

That Ducange's next play, *L'An 1835, ou L'Enfant d'un cosaque* (1835, or the Cossack's Child, 1815), should celebrate the return of Louis XVIII to the throne of France as a welcome event is therefore puzzling. Using the technique of the flashback, Ducange has his characters look back to 1815 and measure the progress accomplished during the reign of the king. But whether Ducange was being sincere or sarcastic, his support for the new regime did not last long. One year later exactly, in 1816, a second version of this melodrama was produced, *Adolphe et Sophie, ou Les Victimes d'une erreur* (Adolphe and Sophie, or the Victims of an Error), in which Ducange, probably counting himself among the "victims of a deceptive error," deleted all compliments to the new king.

At the beginning of the Restoration the political landscape changed considerably in France. In this new historico-cultural context Pixérecourt's melodrama lost its wide appeal. Although censorship regulations continued to be as strict as they were during the Empire, a new type of melodrama emerged: liberal melodrama. Ducange's drama is by far not as homogeneous as Pixerécourt's, and it is

therefore difficult to classify a dramatic corpus as wide and multifaceted under a single label. Nonetheless, "liberal melodrama" is certainly the term that best characterizes his work. Its main characteristic is perhaps less a style or a dramaturgy than a commitment to the Enlightenment and a willingness to reconnect with the political vocation of the genre.

By substituting Enlightenment conceptions of good and evil for those of his predecessors, Ducange destroys the melodrama's Manichaean universe and diverts it from its original, quasi-ritualistic function. For Denis Diderot, Voltaire, and Ducange virtue is not an abstract metaphysical concept but a social one. Virtue is what leads people to happiness. Intelligence and common sense (reason) replace blind faith as positive values in Ducange's moral universe.

Produced in 1820, *Calas* represents Ducange's first real breakthrough as a playwright. It is said that in the nineteenth century more French people learned about the renowned Calas Affair through Ducange's play than they did through Voltaire's account of it. More directly than any other of his plays, perhaps, *Calas* exemplifies Ducange's eagerness and ability to present central ideas of the Enlightenment (happiness, tolerance, freedom) in a lively and unforgettable way. It also illustrates how the distinction between historical and bourgeois melodrama tends to lose its meaning in Ducange's plays. *Calas* is both. As often in Ducange's plays, the first scenes are devoted to a depiction of the Calas family's household by the servants, Jacob, his daughter Jeannette, and her fiancé Laurent. Through these characters, devoted to the Calases, the audience learns about the impending wedding of Miss Calas to her fiancé, Edouard, and also about the enemies Mr. Calas has in Toulouse because of his Protestant creed. By having young Jeannette introduce the central theme of the play, religious freedom, in her own simple but colloquial way, Ducange presents tolerance as a natural attitude, something within the reach of anyone. Jeannette, a Catholic, conveys the author's message: matters of faith are everyone's private business. The chief justice in Toulouse (le Capitoul), she says, should make sure all trials are fair for everyone, whatever their opinions or faith.

The object of slander in town, the Calas family is nonetheless well-off and happy, except for Antoine Calas. Antoine has fallen madly in love with a young Catholic girl, Hortense, and he wants to marry her without renouncing his faith. His "friend" Ambroise, who serves as a messenger between the two lovers, is actually his worst enemy. Unwittingly, Antoine's father has made him lose a fortune in an illegal commercial deal, and Ambroise has vengeance in mind. What would hurt the Calas family most, he thinks, what would destroy its unity and harmony, would be for Antoine to recant his Protestant faith in order to marry Hortense. Besides, "separating one of the Calases from the proselytes from Geneva" would also bring Ambroise the support of the Capitoul, who likes nothing better than conversions. Ambroise's plan falters, however.

Like Ducange, Antoine is the victim of a *mal du siècle* that has a precise origin—religious persecution. The military career to which he aspired, the law career he then thought of embracing, were not open to him, a Protestant. Incapable of renouncing either his love for Hortense or his religion, he commits suicide. At the beginning of act 2 the Calas family, already devastated by the death of a dearly beloved son, must face an additional dilemma: how to bury him. Because victims of suicide are denied a regular sepulchre—and according to the play, abandoned to the furor of the mob—Edouard makes secret arrangements with the pastor. Ambroise, who has followed him to the temple, realizes that vengeance will be beyond his reach once Antoine is laid to rest. He accuses Calas of the murder of his son, setting off panic and despair in the Calas household. The supreme justice arrives, accompanied by physicians who perform an autopsy and declare that Antoine died a violent death. Ambroise comes in, talks to the Capitoul, and produces a letter Antoine wrote to Hortense: "You demand that I give up my fathers' faith. If only I could listen solely to my heart [. . .] but I can't. I would draw upon me my father's wrath, a death sentence for me." Calas is thrown in jail, and the family receives house arrests. Edouard, the loyal fiancé, starts his battle to prove Calas's innocence.

The third act is set in Toulouse's city hall, where the courthouse is also located. Edouard appeals in vain to Ambroise's conscience and, confounded by his hatred, ends up offering him money if he changes his deposition. Ambroise runs back into the courthouse to tell a judge of Edouard's attempt to buy a witness. Meanwhile, Madame Calas, her daughter, and servants arrive at the courthouse, where the trial is about to begin. They are allowed to talk to Calas, to whom they bring the news that half the town is up in arms, that poor people and workers who know him, convinced he will not receive a fair trial, are making plans to free him. All they need is a leader. Against the advice of the family, Edouard volunteers right away and leaves. Calas, who has done his best to oppose Edouard's plan, is then led inside the courtroom. The judges have deliberated, and the verdict is about to be read. The

Capitoul asks Calas whether he persists in denying his crime. Calas responds that no crime has been committed. A guilty verdict is read, and Calas is sentenced to death. Because the authorities are fearful of riots, the execution is to take place immediately. Calas is torn away from his sobbing wife and daughter. As they are about to leave, a messenger brings a letter that is first intercepted by Ambroise, then by Edouard. The letter is Antoine's farewell to his family, and it contains the proof of Calas's innocence. But it arrives too late; Calas, the innocent victim, has already been executed.

The ending of *Calas* clearly shows that liberal melodrama can sometimes be closer to tragedy than to the traditional melodrama. One of the most compelling melodramas ever written, it illustrates Ducange's admiration for Voltaire and his role as a politically committed thinker. A play with an obvious and clear message in favor of tolerance and against bigotry, *Calas* also contains a more subtle declaration of faith in liberal economics and politics: let the best (merchants, judges, priests even) do the work, and let those who have the capacity and the vision (those who see beyond their immediate personal interest, like Calas and unlike Ambroise) compete; it will be for the benefit of the people.

In that respect Calas's death sentence is unfair but just. The judges are not venal; they have used the evidence available to them and judged accordingly. Calas's outcry when Edouard decides to take justice into his own hands expresses Ducange's view that the justice system, even when it dramatically fails, is always preferable to arbitrariness. In the play the people's riots are just as responsible as bigotry for the failings of the justice system, since immediate execution of a sentence prevents the accused from appealing. Edouard, then, is also responsible for Calas's death. These ideas, and Ducange's zeal in presenting them in different forms, make him an outspoken proponent of democracy, a strong defender of law and order.

As *Calas* also illustrates, Ducange expands the family unit in his melodramas. Unlike the traditional melodrama, where the family is usually reduced to a father and a daughter, Ducange's plays also include mothers, brothers, and current lovers, additional characters who have a destabilizing function for the traditional melodrama structure. Young people's love for each other, a minor theme in Pixerécourt's plays, is central in Ducange's. The father's role also changes considerably. The focus is no longer on his rights (to be obeyed blindly, to curse his children) but on his love. Ducange's plays make the filiation from Diderot's *drame bourgeois* to Napoleon's *Code Civil* visible: both reaffirm the central role of the father; both define it as a title to which a job description is attached. Fatherhood means love and commitment to responsibilities with which old-regime fathers did not concern themselves.

In Ducange's melodramas the real father, the one who sees and accepts his responsibilities, is frequently a pastor rather than the biological father, sometimes even when the latter is present in the play. In *Thérèse, ou L'Orpheline de Genève* (Thérèse, or the Orphan of Geneva), Ducange's second triumph, Pastor Egerthon is not Thérèse's real father, but he brings her the love, moral support, and material help of a good father. He is the one who fights for her, who makes justice triumph in the end. In terms of plot, structure, and to a lesser degree character distribution, *Thérèse* is probably the most traditional melodrama in Ducange's repertoire even though the similarities with *Calas* are obvious. Like Calas, Thérèse is the victim of false accusations; like him, she has been unable to prove her innocence and has been sentenced. But if both plays are about the misfortunes of justice, *Thérèse* begins where *Calas* ends. It illustrates the tragic consequences of bypassing the justice system. Unlike Calas, Thérèse has escaped, upon the advice and with the help of Valther, her adoptive mother's corrupt lawyer. Valther has made Thérèse an outlaw so that she will marry him and he can thereby inherit her fortune. A true traditional traitor because of his unrelenting persecution of the young woman, Valther nonetheless differs from Pixerécourt's traitors to the extent that he does not look like a traitor. He is a respected member of Geneva's society; he has an important position and a good career. What he lacks are professional ethics. Even in a traditional-looking melodrama such as this one, Ducange's notions of good and evil belong to the contemporary world, where evil can be fought and vanquished by men because it is manmade. The pastor wins over the lawyer here, not because his trade is religion (there are many bad priests in Ducange's plays) but because he does his job well, unselfishly, and intelligently while Valther does not. Ducange's good professionals (fathers included) are leaders who are convinced that the way they accomplish their task is of primary importance for the well-being of society and who have the generosity and the intelligence to understand that the common good takes precedence over private gain. What Ducange's melodramas propagate, then, is the modern and very French concept of "public service."

An interesting anecdote related to *Calas* and *Thérèse* illustrates how, as a professional, Ducange practiced in real life what he preached in his plays.

The American playwright John Howard Payne recalled how one day, when locked in a debtor's jail in London, he received a parcel from France. The parcel contained "two productions of M. Victor, *Calas* and *Thérèse*," but no letter of explanation. Ducange simply gave Payne his two plays, his best to that point, and asked for nothing in return. His generosity toward Payne was likely motivated by the personal conviction that everyone deserves a fresh start in life. According to Honoré de Balzac in *Les Illusions perdues* (Lost Illusions, 1837), the success of *Calas* in France had helped Ducange get back on his feet after being plagued by debts largely caused by the legal fees and fines he had to pay for being too outspoken in his writings. Ducange probably thought his plays could do the same for Payne, and in fact they did. The adaptation of *Thérèse* that Payne wrote in a few days while still in prison enabled him to get out of debtor's jail. For Payne's biographer, Gabriel Harrison, the mysterious parcel marked a turning point in Payne's career and life.

Even if Ducange had expected money in exchange for his plays, chances are he would not have gotten any. Copyright legislation was lax at the time, and playwrights all over Europe were accustomed to borrowing their plots from novels or from plays already produced in another language and country. In the 1820s Ducange himself adapted two novels by Walter Scott into plays, *Guy Mannering* (1815) (produced under the title *La Sorcière, ou L'Orphelin écossais*, 1821) and *The Bride of Lammermoor* (adapted as *La Francée de Lammermoor*, 1828); a bestselling novel by the French Vicomte d'Arlincourt, *Le Solitaire* (1821), which became *Elodie, ou la Vierge du Monastère* (Elodie, or the Virgin of the Monastery, 1822); and William Shakespeare's *Macbeth* (1606).

By 1823, the year Ducange gave up his pseudonym, M. Victor, he had already made much more money with his plays and novels than he would ever have made as a civil servant. But the legal battles these writings were also bringing him had taken a financial toll on him. On the one hand, adapting historical works written by others enabled Ducange to stay out of political trouble while bringing in muchneeded cash. These plays might therefore appear less innovative than his previous work since they are adaptations instead of original works. On the other hand, there was never a clear phase during which Ducange devoted himself solely to the adaptation of romantic historical novels. All along, he also continued to write his own liberal melodramas, *La Suédoise* (The Swedish Girl, 1821), the year he adapted *Guy Mannering*; *Lisbeth, ou la Fille du laboureur* (Lisbeth, or the Farmer's Daughter) a year after *Elodie* (1823). For Ducange, to adapt Scott's historical novels for the stage was not radically different from writing his own plays because novelist and playwright shared the same romantic conception of history. In each of Ducange's historical melodramas, *Palmérin, Pharamond,* or *Elodie,* history provides food for thought for the present and shows which stumbling blocks society has put in the path of human progress.

To the extent that music plays an important role in Ducange's historical melodramas, they are still melodramas. But they are also romantic plays for a variety of reasons. Unlike Pixerécourt's melodramas, they do not respect key principles of classical dramaturgy, the unities of time and action, the rule of *bienséances* (propriety). Liberal melodramas are labeled "romantic" and considered an inferior genre precisely because they fail to respect the rules of classical theater. Furthermore, many of them, such as *Calas* or *Elodie,* have a tragic ending. The society presented in these plays is no longer the homogeneous community of Pixerécourt's melodramas that can that be restored to its original unity by simply excluding the traitor. On the contrary, these romantic melodramas focus on a specifically romantic problem, the lack of a future for society's youth. In Ducange's plays this conflict is represented by the stumbling blocks society puts in the way of young lovers' unions and their failure to find happiness. Elodie and Charles die at the end of *Elodie;* Lucie and Edgar drown at the end of *La Fiancée de Lammermoor.*

In terms of dramaturgy and aesthetics the romantic melodrama influenced by Scott and by the historical novel brought important changes. Thanks to new techniques and machines, the art of stagecraft improved, making the rapid changing of sets possible. No longer the snapshot imitations of paintings they once were, tableaux provided the organizing structure of these melodramas. It became customary to have up to seven or eight acts instead of the original three. Celebrated artists such as Pierre-Luc-Charles Ciceri or Louis-Jacques-Mande Daguerre designed expensive and beautiful sets that greatly contributed to the success of the genre.

Ducange's romantic melodramas are an early manifestation of the new modern, national, and popular drama Stendhal and Victor Hugo called for, Stendhal in 1823 in *Racine et Shakespeare,* Hugo in 1830 in the preface of *Hernani.* As such, they provide evidence that the influence of romanticism on the French stages was felt about ten years earlier than is usually acknowledged. But toward the end of the 1820s Ducange's drama became more visibly modern and political, in part because of its new focus on recent instead of distant history, in part because of

the social issues it more directly addressed. His plays are civic plays—they fulfill the educational function of showing how improving laws and making them work better require a strong sense of ethics and commitment on the part of citizens. Ducange's conception of the modern citizen is based on the notion of social contract: society's role is not to stand in the way of human progress but is to contribute to that progress through fair legislation.

Set in contemporary France, *Le Banqueroutier* (Banking on Bankruptcy, 1826) offers a critique of laws that encourage dishonest business practices. *Polder, ou Le Bourreau d'Amsterdam* (Polder, or the Executioner of Amsterdam, 1828) denounces the ancient and cruel custom that forces members of designated families to practice the trade of executioner against their will and to be socially ostracized as well. Refusing the fatality that makes him a headsman, Polder, who opposes the death penalty, has fled Amsterdam. He has made his fortune on the island of Java before returning to Holland. On a little Dutch island he has built a factory and thereby improved the lives of all the islands' inhabitants. A condemnation of the death penalty, the play offers a clear defense of individual human rights and an illustration of the benefits society can draw from respecting them. But the society Ducange describes in *Polder* has not reached that stage yet. If Ysel and Frédérick do not die at the end of the play, they nonetheless have to pay a high price for their happiness: exile.

Trente ans, ou La Vie d'un joueur (Thirty Years, or a Gambler's Life, 1827) illustrates in a powerful and extremely realistic manner other obstacles laid by society on the path of social progress. Marvelously performed by Frédérick Lemaître and Marie Dorval, the play was a tremendous success in 1827 and was frequently produced until the end of the century. In terms of dramatic structure, *Trente ans* anticipates Emile Zola's notion of presenting a "slice of life." Each of the three acts depicts a day in Georges de Germany's life, first in 1795, then 1805, and finally 1815. *Trente ans* also offers strikingly realistic decor, from the Paris gambling house of the opening scenes to the desolate hut of the last ones. The ideas developed in *Trente ans* are essentially those of Ducange's other plays: love should be the foundation of marriage and the family; fathers and husbands should act as unselfish, responsible citizens. *Trente ans* vividly illustrates the tragic consequences of men's failure to live up to their duties. Gambling is Ducange's choice illustration of such irresponsible behavior here, but it is presented as a social rather than an individual problem. What this more than four-hour-long melodrama dramatically points to is society's responsibility in the downfall of the gambler's family: the laws do not protect women like Amélie but simply sacrifice them. Beyond the critique of a particular vice, gambling, *Trente ans* addresses a range of feminist issues, the ones George Sand focused on several years later in *Indiana* (1832). The play condemns arranged marriages, rape, marital abuse, and the double standards for men and women in cases of marital infidelity; it criticizes the absolute power marriage grants to men; and it favors women's rights to marry according to their hearts, to preserve their dignity as women, and to divorce.

Interpreting *Trente ans* as a simple demonstration of gambling's evils, the censors only objected to the ending of the play, Georges's suicide, insisting that it should not be presented as such. By contrast, *Les Sept Heures,* first performed in 1829 at the Théâtre de la Porte Saint-Martin, was a much more controversial play. In 1829 censorship regulations prohibited plays on and even references to the French Revolution on the Parisian stages. Some censors on the committee, however, shared Ducange's liberal views and moved to authorize *Les Sept Heures* in spite of its politically sensitive and illegal topic: the murder of Jean-Paul Marat by Charlotte Corday during the Reign of Terror in 1793. Their compromise was to respect the word of the law but not its spirit. The action was said to take place in 1750; the names Marat or Charlotte Corday could not be used; and the mysterious title gave no clue about the play's topic, except perhaps an indication that it had been truncated by censors—since the melodramas' titles usually followed the same regular pattern. *Les Sept Heures* was in fact the first part of the original title, the one the play regained later, *Sept Heures, ou Charlotte Corday.* On the other hand, censors, journalists, actors, and audiences knew what the topic of the play was. There were clear giveaways, either purposefully allowed by censors or out of their reach to control: the heroine's name, Melle d'Armans, for instance, since Charlotte Corday's real name was Charlotte Corday d'Armans; the costumes that journalists described as those of 1793, not of Old Regime France; and, of course, the plot.

Les Sept Heures was hailed by some critics as an historical event, the first play of the nineteenth century about the French Revolution. By other critics it was severely criticized for presenting Marat as a mere melodrama villain instead of as a political leader and thereby for stripping an important historical event of its political dimension. The latter were probably justified in criticizing Ducange for the liberties he took with his historical material. In *Les Sept Heures,* for instance, Marat's murder does not take place in Paris but in Normandy; Charlotte Corday lives with her father and mother, which is also historically inaccurate. Ducange, however, had his own conception of faithfulness to history. In an attempt to re-create what it was like to live in 1793, his play therefore combines public and private history, an historical event, Marat's murder, and historical footnotes.

The plot of *Les Sept Heures* can actually be found in an actual footnote in Jules Michelet's *Histoire de la Révolution française* (History of the French Revolution, 1847–1853). Michelet recalls how a young woman, whose father had been sentenced to death, begged Marat to save her father's life. Marat promised to save him, but only if she sacrificed her virtue to him. In Michelet's anecdote Marat then meets with her, but, moved by her tears, saves her father without forcing her to fulfill her part of the deal. Focusing on this happy ending, Michelet presents this anecdote as an illustration of Marat's goodness, thereby overlooking the immoral, sadistic aspect of Marat's personality it reveals. For Ducange, unlike Michelet, Marat's perversity stands out as yet another example of men's failure to behave ethically and to live up to their responsibilities. In *Les Sept Heures* Charlotte Corday plays the role of the young woman in Michelet's anecdote, but she is unwilling to surrender to blackmail. She comes to her meeting with Marat (Marcel, in the play) determined to murder him, to rid France of this monster, and she does so at precisely seven o'clock.

As a political evaluation of the Revolution, *Les Sept Heures* is structured around the opposition between 1789 and 1793. Set in Corday's hometown, the play begins with an idyllic evocation of the Revolution's achievements: in this harmonious, peaceful community, parents are good and grateful, children respectful, and servants happy. An enlightened mayor and a fair judge, embodiments of the civil and political liberties gained in 1789, ensure law and order. The real subject of *Les Sept Heures,* however, is the degeneration of this revolution: with Marat's arrival, all that had been achieved crumbles. Suspicion replaces fraternity; denunciations mark the end of liberty; and arbitrariness replaces justice. Such is the primary plot of *Les Sept Heures.* The story of Charlotte's rape is secondary to this one, but it provides the crucial metaphor Ducange needed to articulate his political message: Marat embodies the Reign of Terror; the Reign of Terror is a rape. The rape metaphor is spun throughout the play to illustrate the violation of private life by spies; the destruction of the foundational unit of society, the family; the imposition of Parisian rule in the provinces; and the substitution of terror for justice. Ducange's casting of Marat as a rapist is not mere political demagoguery but rather an expression of his political priorities. The sexual anarchy unleashed by the Reign of Terror represents for him the worst undermining of the Revolution's social order, a society based on the institution of marriage and the family.

Deemed undeserving of historical scrutiny for a long time, the sexual terror (orgies, rape) unleashed during the French Revolution is now considered by feminist historians as a vital component of this historical period. Seen in that light, Ducange's tale of sex and politics sounds as if it were an early piece of feminist analysis. Drawing from women's experience of the Revolution, *Les Sept Heures* powerfully recalls the excessive violence committed against them. But it is a feminist play to that extent only. The focus remains on men's role in public life; Marat is the central character in the play, not Corday. In *Les Sept Heures* Corday does not rebel against Marat for political reasons. She kills Marat for sending her fiancé to the guillotine, for depriving her of a husband—in short, for preventing her from fulfilling her destiny as a woman. In *Les Sept Heures* women's exclusion from the public sphere is presented as an invariable factor in the processes of history. Cut off from the public realm, deprived of political thoughts and motivations, Corday shows what Ducange's 1789 revolution had in store for women: a family romance, a love plot. Still, *Sept Heures* is neither bizarre nor absurd, as some critics have argued. It is a political play written by a playwright committed to democratic ideals.

The themes of power abuse and rape appear together again in the two plays Ducange wrote in 1830, *Le Couvent de Tonnington* (Tonnington Convent) and *Le Jésuite* (The Jesuit). Set in England at the time of Henri VIII, *Le Couvent de Tonnington* centers on the cruel scheme to which two charming, intelligent young people, Tom and Héléna, fall prey. Both orphans, they have placed themselves under the protection of powerful members of the court: the lord-duke, who neglects his political duties for his perverse pleasures, and a dubious but ambitious couple, Lady Windsor and Lord Dudley, who serve his every wish. When the lord-duke sets his eyes on Héléna, Lady Windsor and Lord Dudley find a way to help the duke seduce Héléna and save appearances as well. Tom Lowe is suddenly made a colonel and offered a large sum of money and a beautiful wife, Héléna. The young people fall in love and are married, but before the wedding ceremony is over, Tom receives orders to join his regiment. In the last act Tom returns to learn about his wife's rape. At the convent where Héléna has found refuge after

losing her mind, he sees her one more time before she dies.

With Henri VIII's divorce from Catherine of Aragon looming in the background, *Le Couvent de Tonnington* celebrates the sanctity of love marriages and highlights the civilizing function of marriage. Marriage teaches men to accept their responsibilities. Men who do not respect this institution have not learned that lesson; as the play suggests, they are still beasts. In this play Ducange's position on divorce appears more rigid than in *Trente ans*. Divorce is acceptable in extreme cases, such as Amélie's in *Trente ans,* but not when its primary purpose is to satisfy men's selfish urges.

An adaptation of Ducange's novel *Les Trois filles de la veuve* (The Widow's Three Daughters, 1826), *Le Jésuite* focuses on the issue of education for young women. Mme Joannin, the widow of an artist, is too poor to raise her three daughters. Two of her sisters, one married to a rich Parisian businessman, the other to an aristocrat, have each raised one of their nieces. Césarine, who has grown up with her aunt in the fashionable district of the Chaussée d'Antin, has turned into a polite but empty-headed young woman, mainly preoccupied with her busy social life. Mme. Joannin has raised Cécile in her modest household. She has taught her to become a good housewife but also encouraged her to develop her own talents. Cécile earns a living as an artist. Dorothée lives with Madame de Saint-Aure, a rich but narrow-minded religious bigot entirely devoted to her father-confessor, Judacin.

The comparison among these three social settings reveals Ducange's preference for the modest, hardworking household of Mme Joannin and for the type of education it provides. Cécile grows to become an assertive, self-reliant young woman with clear judgment and solid moral principles. At the end she marries the young lawyer she loves, Edouard. Because of its instability and its privileging of material above moral values, the capitalist milieu of the Chaussée d'Antin reveals itself as an inappropriate breeding ground for any of those qualities. As for the outdated aristocratic world of Madame de Saint-Aure, it leaves no space for education at all.

In *Le Jésuite* the enemy of Enlightenment, the villain who misuses his position to satisfy his personal needs, is no longer a political figure but Judacin, the Jesuit priest. Already the widowed aunt's lover, he seduces young Dorothée, who ends up committing suicide. As stereotypical as Judacin appears here, the central female characters are human and engaging. Both widowed, the mothers of Cécile and Edouard are the model educators Judacin should be. They represent a new type of mature, independent, and responsible woman hitherto absent from the melodrama. This new woman is a teacher (Lady Worcester in *Le Couvent de Tonnington,* Amélie in *Il y a seize ans* [1831] and an artist (Suzanne in *L'Artiste et le Soldat* [1827], Sophie and Cécile in *Le Jésuite*) but also a seamstress (Pauline in *Le Testament de la pauvre femme* [1832]).

After the Revolution of 1830 Ducange's romantic liberal melodrama started losing its appeal. While former liberals, now in power, favored Eugène Scribe's comedies over Ducange's somber plays, a new generation of romantic playwrights was emerging, headed by Hugo and Alexandre Dumas *père.* Approaching fifty years of age, Ducange realized that the new political regime was more interested in economic profit than in the social and political changes for which he fought. In spite of his disillusion he remained convinced that "one day all inhabitants of France will know how to read, think and see clearly," as he writes in *Les Moeurs.* But the time has not come. In *La Vendetta, ou La Fiancée corse* (1831) the past still catches up with the present. The play shows the old Corsican traditions and superstitions winning over love and Albert's new democratic values. For Ducange the struggle between the past and the present is primarily a "moral," not a "physical," struggle. The road to democracy is paved by education, not violent revolutions. As long as people are uneducated, their revolutions are doomed to failure.

This uneducated lower class appears for the first time in Ducange's drama in the second act of *Il y a seize ans* as a group of homeless people roaming the countryside. Degraded by their misery, deprived of any type of education, they set farms on fire to earn a few coins. These destitute people certainly express Ducange's bourgeois fear of the dangerous lower class. But their presence in this play nonetheless illustrates his belief that "moral education" is the key to democracy: for those who have absolutely nothing, distinguishing between good and evil, even understanding the meaning of the word *criminal,* is a luxury. Here again, the real criminals are the leaders, those who willingly exploit the people's misery and ignorance.

The poor also appear in *Le Testament de la pauvre femme* but are working-class people this time. In this play Ducange emphasizes the social and cultural differences among workers, bourgeois, and aristocrats, and, as in *Le Jésuite,* the people in the lower class are presented with a strong sense of human dignity. Jules Janin, who criticized *Le Testament de la pauvre femme* for its stereotypical characters—the bad aristocrat and the good worker—seems at first to

have a point: here again the powerful one, Théodore de Préval, seduces the powerless one, Pauline. What complicates the plot, however, is the love they feel for each other. Pauline, who knows Théodore as Edouard, a clerk, falls in love with him first. Théodore, who only meant to have a brief affair with the pretty seamstress, slowly realizes how much Pauline means to him. Truly torn between his duty (marrying rich Léonie to save his family from bankruptcy) and his love for Pauline, Théodore changes his mind three times before proposing to Pauline. Overjoyed at first, Pauline's heart breaks when she realizes that she cannot marry him. She ends up rejecting Théodore, convinced that the financial sacrifice would put too heavy a burden on their future. Théodore, who marries Léonie a few days later, has lost the best part of himself, his ability to live according to his heart. He therefore appears as the victim of a society that places too much emphasis on material instead of human values. In *Le Testament de la pauvre femme* Ducange also corrects the stereotype of the aristocratic monster in the case of Baroness Delaunay, Léonie's mother. Forced to abandon her illegitimate child (who turns out to be Pauline) and to marry according to her father's will, she is as much a victim of the social system as the child she has abandoned.

Like Pauline and Théodore, the young lovers in *Clète, ou La Fille d'une reine* (1833) and *La Vendetta* belong to different social classes, and the gap between them is too wide to be overcome. There are no more happy endings; violent deaths end these plays. The heroine of *La Vendetta,* Rosa, is killed by shotgun on the steps of the church just before her wedding. Clète, the illegitimate daughter of the queen, is murdered; Urbain, the young peasant she loved, is decapitated. The romantic theme of the failed union between young lovers takes on a particular twist in Ducange's last plays. The obstacle to their union is no longer religious prejudice, as in *Calas,* or political oppression, as in *Les Sept Heures,* but rather the division of society into classes. No longer a model, the bourgeoisie is absent from these plays.

When Ducange died on 26 October 1833, he was still known as "the famous Victor Ducange." For a period of two months Parisian theaters and actors honored his memory by performing some of his greatest plays, *Calas* and *Il y a seize ans* at the Théâtre de la Gaîté, *Trente ans* at the Théâtre de l'Odeon. But except for the small popular theaters, where lower-class audiences continued to appreciate him, interest in his work declined rapidly. Similarly, when his plays were reedited in the second half of the century, they appeared in popular, often illustrated, drama series only. An acute observer of society, a committed participant in the political and cultural struggles of time, Ducange cared more about ideas than style. Nonetheless, his plays represent an interesting and important phase in the history of French theater, the transition between the early melodrama and romantic drama.

Biographies:

J. P. R. Cuisin, *Dictionnaire des Gens de Lettres vivants par un descendant de Rivarol* (Paris: Gaultier-Laguionie, 1826): 106–107;

Auguste Imbert, "Victor Ducange," in *Biographie des condamnés pour délits politiques depuis la restauration des Bourbons en France* (Amsterdam: Van Tetroode, 1827; Paris: L'Huillier, 1828);

"Ducange, Victor," in *Dictionnaire général de biographie et d'histoire,* volume 1, edited by Dezobry, Bachelet, and Theodore (Paris: Delagrave, 1829), p. 899;

Jules Janin, *Le Journal des Débats,* 4 November 1833;

"Ducange," in *Biographie universelle et portative des contemporains,* volume 2, edited by Alphonse Rabbe, Vieilh de Boisjolin, and Sainte-Preuve (Paris: Levrault, 1834);

Frédéric Lock, "Ducange (Victor-Henri-Joseph-Brahain)," in *Nouvelle biographie générale,* volume 14 (Paris: Didot, 1868), p. 915;

"Ducange, Victor," in *Grand Dictionnaire universel,* volume 6 (Paris: Larousse, 1890), p. 1325;

Louis Bethleem, "Victor Ducange, 1783–1833," in *Les Pièces de théâtre* (Paris: Revue des Lectures, 1924);

Charles Durozoir, "Victor Ducange," in *Biographie universelle ancienne et moderne,* volume 11 (Paris: C. Desplaces, 1955; Graz: Akademische Druck- und Verlaganstalt, 1966);

"Ducange," in *Dictionnaire des auteurs* (Paris: Laffont-Bompiani, 1956);

Y. Destianges, "Du Cange," in *Dictionnaire de biographie française,* volume 11 (Paris: Roman d'Amot et Limouzin-Lamothe, 1967);

"Ducange, Victor," in *Dictionnaire des Lettres Françaises XIXe,* volume 1, edited by Georges Grente (Paris: Fayard, 1971), p. 334;

Danile Couty, "Ducange, V.H.J. Brahain, dit," in *Dictionnaire des Littératures de langue française,* volume 1 (Paris: Bordas, 1987), pp. 730–731;

Jacob Abraham Van der Aa, *Biographisch Woordenboek der Nederladen, bevattende levensbeschrijvingen van zoodamige personen, die zich op eenigerleiwijze in ons vaderland hebben vermaard gemaakt* [. . .] (Harlem: J. J. Van Breddrode, n.d.).

References:

L'Almanach des Spectacles (Paris: Janet, 1818);

Annuaire dramatique, 17 volumes (Paris: Imprimerie d'Everat, 1804–1822);

Honoré de Balzac, *Illusions Perdues,* volume 5 in *La Comédie humaine,* edited by Roland Chollet (Paris: Gallimard, 1977); pp. 1–732; 1113–1411);

Pierre Barbéris, *Balzac et le mal du siècle,* 2 volumes (Paris: Gallimard, 1970);

Michel Baude, "Un Théâtre populaire: Le Théâtre du Montparnasse d'après le journal inédit de P. H. Azaïs," *Romantisme,* 38 (1982): 25–32;

Charles Bird, *The Rôle of Family in Melodrama [1797–1827]* (Visalia, Cal.: Josten's, 1976);

Peter Brooks, *The Melodramatic Imagination* (New Haven, Conn.: Yale University Press, 1976);

Brooks, "The Text of Muteness," *New Literary History* (1973–1974): 549–564;

Barry Daniels, "Mélodrame: La Musique," *Revue d'Histoire du Théâtre,* 33 (1981): 167–175;

David Owen Evans, *Le Drame moderne à l'époque romantique* (Geneva: Slatkine, 1974);

Claude Gével and Jean Robot, "La Censure théâtrale sous la Restauration," *Revue de Paris,* 120 (November–December 1913): 339–362;

Paul Ginisty, *Le Mélodrame* (Paris: Michaud, 1910);

Gabriel Harrisson, *The Life & Writing of John Howard Payne* (Albany, N.Y.: John Munsell, 1875);

F. W. J. Hemmings, "Co-authorship in French Plays of the Nineteenth-Century," *French Studies,* 41, 1 (January 1987): 37–51;

Hemmings, "The Playwright as Preacher: Didacticism and Melodrama in the French Theater of the Enlightenment," *Forum for Modern Language Studies,* 14 (April 1978): 97–115;

William D. Howarth, "Tragedy into Melodrama: The Fortunes of the Calas Affair on the Stage," *Studies on Voltaire and the Eighteenth Century,* 174 (1978): 121–150;

Auguste Jal, "Les Partis et la littérature militante sous la Restauration" in *Souvenirs d'un homme de lettres (1795–1873)* (Geneva: Slatkine, 1973), pp. 420–475;

Jules Janin, *Critique dramatique,* 4 volumes (Paris: Librairie des Bibliophiles, 1877), p. 1286;

Janin, *Histoire de la littérature dramatique,* 4 volumes (Paris: Michel Lévy, 1854), pp. 4305–4306;

Odile Krakovitch, *Les Pièces de théâtres soumises à la censure [1800–1830]* (Paris: Archives Nationales, 1982);

Marie-Pierre Le Hir, "La Représentation de la famille dans le mélodrame du début du dix-neuvième siècle: de Pixerécourt à Ducange," *Nineteenth-Century French Studies,* 18 (Fall–Winter 1989–1990): 15–24;

Le Hir, *Le Romantisme aux Enchères: Ducange, Pixerécourt, Hugo* (Amsterdam: John Benjamins, 1992);

Edith Melcher, *Stage Realism in France between Diderot and Antoine* (Bryn Mawr, Pa.: Russell, 1976);

Lucian Weld Minor, "French Melodrama: That Literary Social Climber," *Journal of Popular Culture,* 10 (1976–1977): 760–765;

Minor, *The Militant Hackwriter: French Popular Literature 1800–1848, Its Influence, Artistic and Political* (Bowling Green, Ohio: Bowling Green University Press, 1975);

Minor, "Victor Henri Ducange: A Participant in French Restoration Life and Its Interpreter," dissertation, Boston University, 1961;

George C. C. Odell, *Annals of the New York Stage,* volumes 2–3 (New York: Columbia University Press, 1927–1928);

Alexandre Pigoreau, *Petite bibliographie romancière, ou dictionnaire des romanciers,* 3 volumes (Paris: Pigoreau, 1821–1828);

Julia Przybos, "La Conscience populaire et le mélodrame en France dans la première moitié du dix-neuvième siècle," *French Review,* 58 (February 1984): 300–308;

Przybos, *L'Entreprise mélodramatique* (Paris: Corti, 1987);

Przybos, "Melodrama as a Social Ritual," *French Literature Series,* 15 (1988): 86–95;

Przybos, "Le Mélodrame, ou le spectateur mystifié: Etude sur le mélodrame en France de 1800 à 1830," dissertation, Yale University, 1977;

Przybos, "Le Tribun, ou le Comédien de l'échafaud: mélodrame révolutionnaire," *L'Esprit Créateur,* 29 (Summer 1989): 16–25;

Jean-Marie Thomasseau, "Bibliographie du mélodrame (1970–1986)," *Europe,* 703–704 (November–December 1987): 109–112;

Thomasseau, *Drame et Tragédie* (Paris: Hachette, 1995);

Thomasseau, *Le Mélodrame* (Paris: PUF, 1984);

Thomasseau, "Le Mélodrame et la censure," *Revue des Sciences Humaines,* 162, 2 (1976): 171–182;

Thomasseau, *Le Mélodrame sur les scènes parisiennes de Coelina à l'Auberge des Adrets* (Lille: Service de Reproduction des Thèses, 1976);

Jules Truffier, "*Trente ans, ou la vie d'un joueur,*" *Conferencia,* 7 (20 April 1932): 450–462;

Anne Ubersfeld, "Les Bons et le méchant," *Revue des Sciences humaines,* 162, 2 (1976): 193–203;

Ubersfeld, "Le Mélodrame," *Manuel d'histoire littéraire de la France* (Paris: Editions sociales, 1972): 669–675;

Ubersfeld, *Le Roi et le bouffon* (Paris: Corti, 1974);

Nicole Wild, *Dictionnaire des Théâtres Parisiens au XIXe Siècle* (Paris: Aux Amateurs de Livres, 1989).

Papers:

The Archives de France in Paris hold handwritten copies of most of Ducange's plays (F^{18} series) as submitted to the Censor's Bureau, as well as the censor's reports (F^{21} series). The Bibliothèque de l'Arsenal in Paris has one autograph note signed by Ducange (ms13463/24).

Alexandre Dumas *fils*

(27 July 1824 – 27 November 1895)

John A. Degen
Florida State University

PLAY PRODUCTIONS: *La Dame aux camélias,* Paris, Théâtre du Vaudeville, 2 February 1852;

Diane de Lys, Paris, Théâtre du Gymnase, 15 November 1853;

Le Demi-monde, Paris, Théâtre du Gymnase, 20 March 1855;

Le Bijou de la reine, Paris, Théâtre de l'hôtel Castellane (private performance), 1855;

La Question d'argent, Paris, Théâtre du Gymnase, 31 January 1857;

Le Fils naturel, Paris, Théâtre du Gymnase, 16 January 1858;

Un Mariage dans un chapeau, by Dumas *fils* and Eugène Vivier, Paris, Théâtre du Gymnase, 5 February 1859;

Un Père prodigue, Paris, Théâtre du Gymnase, 30 November 1859;

L'Ami des femmes, Paris, Théâtre du Gymnase, 5 March 1864;

Le Supplice d'une femme, adapted by Dumas *fils* from a manuscript of a play by Emile de Girardin, Paris, Théâtre-Français, 20 April 1865;

Héloïse Paranquet, adapted by Dumas from *Mademoiselle de Breuil,* by Armand Durantin, Paris, Théâtre du Gymnase, 20 January 1866;

Les Idées de Madame Aubray, Paris, Théâtre du Gymnase, 16 March 1867;

Le Filleul de Pompignac, adapted by Dumas *fils* as Alphonse de Jalin from a manuscript by Alphonse François, Paris, Théâtre du Gymnase, 7 May 1869;

Une Visite de noces, Paris, Théâtre du Gymnase, 10 October 1871;

La Princesse Georges, Paris, Théâtre du Gymnase, 2 December 1871;

La Femme de Claude, Paris, Théâtre du Gymnase, 16 January 1873;

Monsieur Alphonse, Paris, Théâtre du Gymnase, 26 November 1873;

Les Danicheff, adapted by Dumas *fils* as Pierre Newski from "M. de Corvin" [Petr Korvin-

Alexandre Dumas fils *in 1864*

Krukovski], Paris, Théâtre de l'Odéon, 8 January 1876;

L'Etrangère, Paris, Théâtre-Français, 14 February 1876;

La Comtesse Romani, adapted by Dumas *fils* as Gustave de Jalin from a manuscript by Gustave Fould, Paris, Théâtre du Gymnase, 16 November 1876.

La Princesse de Bagdad, Paris, Théâtre-Français, 31 January 1881;

Denise, Paris, Théâtre-Français, 19 January 1885;

Francillon, Paris, Théâtre-Français, 17 January 1887.

BOOKS: *La Dame aux camélias* (Paris: D. Giraud & J. Dagneau, 1852);

Diane de Lys (Paris: D. Giraud, 1853);

Le Demi-Monde (Paris: Michel Lévy, 1855); translated by Mrs. E. G. Squire as *The Demi-*

Monde: A Satire on Society (Philadelphia: Lippincott, 1858);

La Question d'argent (Paris: Charlieu, 1857); translated by students of Tufts and Jackson Colleges as *The Money Question,* published in *Poet Lore* 26, 2 (1915): 129–227; reprinted (Boston: R. G. Badger, 1915);

Le Fils naturel (Paris: Charlieu, 1858); translated by T. Louis Oxley (London: Kirby & Endean, 1879);

Un Père prodigue (Paris: Charlieu, 1859); preface translated by Barrett H. Clark as "The Technic [*sic*] of Drama," *Drama* (February 1917): 117–128; reprinted as "Preface to A Prodigal Father," in *European Theories of the Drama,* edited by Clark, revised again (New York: Crown, 1965): 371–376.

L'Ami de femmes (Paris: A. Cadot, 1864);

Le Supplice d'une femme, by Emile de Girardin (Paris: Michel Lévy, 1865);

Héloïse Paranquet, by Armand Durantin (Paris: Librairie Centrale, 1866);

Les Idées de Madame Aubray (Paris: Michel Lévy, 1867);

Le Bijou de la reine (Paris: Michel Lévy, 1868);

Le Filleul de Pompignac, as Alphonse de Jalin (Paris: Michel Lévy, 1869);

Une Visite de noces (Paris: Michel Lévy, 1872);

La Princesse Georges (Paris: Michel Lévy, 1872); translated anonymously (New York: F. Rullman Theatre Ticket Office, 1881);

La Femme de Claude (Paris: Michel Lévy, 1873); translated by Charles Albert as *Claude's Wife* (New York: F. Rullman Theatre, Ticket Office, 1905);

Monsieur Alphonse (Paris: Michel Lévy, 1874); translated by and adapted by Augustin Daly (New York: Privately printed, 1886);

L'Etrangère (Paris: Calmann-Lévy, 1877); translated by Frederick A. Schwab as *The Foreigner* (New York: Chickering, 1880; New York: F. Rullman Theatre Ticket Office, 1880);

La Comtesse Romani, by Gustave Fould (Paris: Calmann-Lévy, 1877);

Les Danicheff, as Pierre Newsky (Paris: Calmann-Lévy, 1879); adapted by Arthur Shirley as *The Danicheffs; or, Married by Force* (New York & London: S. French, 188?);

La Princesse de Bagdad (Paris: Calmann-Lévy, 1881);

Denise (Paris: Calmann-Lévy, 1885);

Francillon (Paris: Calmann-Lévy, 1887); first act translated by L. T. Sheffield in *Theatre* (21 March 1887): 14–25.

Few major playwrights in world literature are as well known by reputation but so little known for their actual works as Alexandre Dumas *fils.* Indeed, when asked to name the plays of Dumas *fils,* few people could come up with a single title after *La Dame aux camélias* (The Lady of the Camellias, 1852), better known in English (through the agency of Matilda Heron and Greta Garbo) as *Camille,* despite the fact that it is perhaps his least characteristic major play. If asked his historical importance as a dramatist, students might produce the standard textbook answers—that he was important in introducing social realism into nineteenth-century French theater and that he was the father of the *pièce à thèse* (thesis play)—although hardly anyone today actually reads his thesis plays (most of which are unavailable in English), and virtually no one produces them. Yet Dumas *fils* was a playwright whose historical importance was recognized in his own day, who was a member of the Académie Française, whose last plays were introduced by the Comédie-Française, and whose works toured the world at the turn of the twentieth century in the repertoires of the greatest actresses of the day.

Alexandre Dumas *fils* was born on 27 July 1824, the illegitimate son of Alexandre Dumas *père* and a lower-class seamstress named Marie Catherine Labay. Only the mother's name appeared on his birth certificate; the elder Dumas, not yet renowned and in precarious financial circumstances, took little responsibility for the boy, who for the first seven years of his life was raised by his mother and barely saw his father. The love and gratitude Dumas *fils* felt for his mother appeared throughout the corpus of his work in his fond depiction of motherhood, especially the plight of unwed mothers.

In 1831 Dumas *père,* now wealthy and celebrated, took the necessary steps to recognize his son, giving him his name and taking responsibility for his upbringing. Marie Labay, reluctant to give up her son, sued to retain custody, but the father's rights (despite the fact that the law of the time did not require paternal responsibility toward illegitimate children and actually forbade such children legal pursuit of paternity) prevailed. Taking responsibility for the child's education, the elder Dumas sent him off to boarding school. While the son's first experiences at school were positive, the years at his second school, the Pension Saint-Victor, were a living hell, as he was taunted for his illegitimacy and relentlessly persecuted by his schoolmates. His bitterness over this experience stayed with him; he referred to it several times in his later writings, and it contributed to his lifelong reformist attitudes.

After leaving the Pension Saint-Victor in 1839, he had only two more years of formal schooling before entering, at age seventeen, the bohemian world of his father. Freed from authority and following the example of his extravagant, hedonistic father, he resolved to experience life to the fullest and threw himself into what he later called the "paganism" of the Parisian demimonde. It was during this period, when he was twenty, that he met and fell in love with Marie Duplessis, the courtesan whom he immortalized as Marguerite Gautier in *La Dame aux camélias*. The result of his period of youthful dissolution was that by the time he was twenty-four he was Fr 50,000 in debt.

In an attempt to relieve his debts, young Dumas had followed the example of his father and turned to writing, cranking out novels and poems that, while hardly distinguished, still had some success, in part because, as Henry James noted, "he was so loudly introduced by his name." Many of the novels were at least partly autobiographical, and his collection of poems was titled, appropriately, *Les Péchés de jeunesse* (Sins of Youth). From this same period came his first attempt at playwriting, a one-act in verse titled *Le Bijou de la reine* (The Queen's Jewel), which would not be produced until 1855, after he had made his name as a dramatist.

In 1849, again in need of quick money, Dumas *fils* sought production for a dramatization–composed, by his own admission, in eight days–of his most successful novel, *La Dame aux camélias,* which he wrote in 1847. He finally found a producer in Hughes-Désiré Bouffé, who had taken a lease on the Vaudeville, but production was held up by censorship until 1852, and even then a license was granted only because of a personal appeal to the censor by Eugénie Doche, the actress who was to play Marguerite Gautier. During this period Dumas *fils* managed to carry out yet another affair that would be evoked in yet another novel, *Diane de Lys* (1853). But when *La Dame aux camélias* was finally produced on 2 February 1852, with Charles Fechter as Armand and Doche as Marguerite, its success brought young Dumas enough money to pay off his debts.

The stage version of *La Dame aux camélias,* dispensing with a good deal of the horror and the sexuality of the novel, still chronicles the relationship between young Armand Duval (note the initials) and the courtesan Marguerite Gautier, who gives up her opulent lifestyle and sells her belongings to support an idyllic suburban life with her young lover. Forced by the implacable logic of Armand's father to see the relationship as impossible, she manufac-

tures a breakup and ultimately dies, forgiven and adored by Armand and his father alike. The play caused great debate; many were moved to tears, but others saw the play as an apologia for the courtesan and declared it immoral, a word that would be applied to Dumas *fils*'s plays even during his most moralistic period.

The play is certainly uncharacteristic of the later Dumas. Much of it harkens back to the Romantic drama of his father, and its emotional appeals are those of an unashamed tearjerker. There is no thesis put forward, despite accusations from some corners that Dumas was calling for the rehabilitation of the prostitute. But for all its romanticism, the play anticipates the realism of Dumas's later work, and far from canonizing courtesans in general, it is clear that Marguerite is an exception, separated from the debauchery of her world by her pure love for an innocent young man. And those who suggest that Dumas is glorifying the demimonde need only look at the first and fourth acts, in which the society from which Marguerite tries to extricate herself is most clearly painted, a world in which she is first seen toying with the infatuated Armand. Here are such highly realistic figures as Prudence, a telling example of the desperate courtesan whose charms have faded; the empty-headed Olympe; and the pathetic St.-Gaudens. If the story relies a bit too much on coincidence, Dumas shows clear dramaturgical skill. Events are made probable with careful setups, and parallel characters provide perspective (as in the case of the rival jealousies of the young, passionate Armand and the more worldly Varville).

Whatever its virtues and defects, the play was a resounding success, and of all Dumas *fils*'s plays it is the only one to have held the stage outside France. Many who do not know the play or its film versions are familiar with its operatic manifestation, Giuseppe Verdi's *La Traviata*. Its reception made Dumas an overnight success in the theater, but his debts consumed much of the profits, and Dumas quickly turned his hand to dramatizing another of his partly autobiographical novels. *Diane de Lys,* which was again initially held up by censorship, is not an important play, but it does mark the first association between Dumas and the Théâtre du Gymnase, the theater that would premiere most of his work. The manager, Montigny, and his wife, actress Rose Chéri, became vital to Dumas's career.

Diane de Lys tells the story of Paul Aubry, a poor artist who is introduced by a friend to Diane, unhappily married to the Comte de Lys. He falls madly in love with her, even following her when her husband takes her overseas. Although their relationship is pure, the Comte is increasingly angry, warning that if he ever sees them together again, he will kill Paul. Paul's love persists, and when he sees Diane again, the count appears—and fatally shoots Paul dead.

The ending was a shocking coup de théâtre. Dumas *fils* says that Montigny implored him to provide a happier curtain, but Dumas insisted that logic demanded the play end as he wrote it. Audiences were confused. Where was the romantic thrust of *La Dame aux camélias?* Was Dumas now condemning illicit love even when it was never consummated? If he was expounding a moral point, an antithesis of *La Dame aux camélias,* the point was murky, especially as the "wronged" husband was hardly an exemplary character. If the play was an antiadultery statement looking forward to the thesis plays, it was less than effective, and it was not popular.

It was the next play, *Le Demi-monde* (1855), that cemented Dumas's reputation as a playwright. This cautionary comedy depicts the social netherworld whose name Dumas *fils* coined in this play, a world Dumas knew well from his youth. It is a substratum of society, teeming with those who are seeking to climb to the top and those who have fallen from respectability, like Mme de Santis, who calls herself a widow after her husband threw her out because of her adultery. The key principals are two visitors to the demimonde—Raymond de Nanjac, returning to France after years abroad, and his friend Olivier de Jalin, who is as knowing about this world as Raymond is innocent—and a former lover of Olivier, Suzanne d'Ange, who sees marriage to the honorable Raymond as her ticket to respectability. Much of the play consists of the war between Suzanne and Olivier for the soul of the smitten Raymond, who learns the truth about Suzanne only after she expresses willingness to go away with Olivier when she assumes that Raymond has been killed.

Many have seen *Le Demi-monde* as the flipside of *La Dame aux camélias.* Here the courtesan has no hope of redemption, although it should be noted that Marguerite's love is honest and unselfish, where Suzanne's is duplicitous and self-serving. Once again the social netherworld is depicted in detail, though without the overarching sentiment that drew the focus in *La Dame aux camélias,* and this time Dumas puts himself not in the person of the young lover but of the more practical Olivier, who becomes the first of his great *raisonneurs* (or philosophical mouthpieces). While still writing in the style of his earliest period, Dumas is clearly looking forward to the moral crusader who will warn France about the dangers of the predatory female Beast.

Dumas's next play was another satirical social comedy, *La Question d'argent* (1857; translated as *The Money Question,* 1915). It tells the story of unscrupulous Jean Giraud, who has made a fortune by playing the stock market. Giraud, the son of a gardener, wants to climb the social ladder, and he wheedles his way into the circle of M. Dureau, for whom he offers to invest money. He seeks to marry the daughter of a friend of Dureau's, a ruined nobleman, who agrees for her father's sake. She calls off the marriage when she discovers that Giraud has passed off a huge sum as her dowry so that he can mask it from his creditors should his luck change. Exposed, he disappears, and Dureau and his friends assume that he has absconded with their money. Giraud returns, announcing that his disappearance was just a ruse enabling him to make another financial killing. But his deceitfulness leads everyone to withdraw their money from his keeping and kick him out of their circle. Giraud will have no place in a society where honor matters more than money.

In some ways Giraud is a male Suzanne d'Ange, but Dumas was clearly less at home in the world of finance than he was in the world of romantic and sexual intrigue. Although the play found an audience, the richness of the subsidiary characters is missing, and *La Question d'argent* was soon superseded by a more substantial play.

In *Le Fils naturel* (The Illegitimate Son, 1858), Dumas tells us in his 1868 preface to the play, "for the first time, I sought to develop a social *thesis,* something more than a picture of manners and characters." This preface serves, in fact, as something of a manifesto of his thesis plays. "Let us inaugurate," he writes, "*useful* theater, at the risk of hearing howls from the apostles of 'art for art's sake,' words absolutely devoid of meaning. All literature which does not seek to perfect, to moralize, to promote the ideal—in short, to be useful—is a stunted and unhealthy literature, born dead." He suggests that he expects to meet opposition because society does not like to see its natural order of things upset. "In short, I write for those who think as I do. It is useless to fight against the opinions of others; one sometimes succeeds in winning an argument, but never in winning a *convert.* Fixed opinions are like nails; the more you hammer against them, the more deeply embedded they become. All our power boils down to saying what seems to us to be the truth." This preface, which forms the rallying cry not only of *Le Fils naturel* but also most of his subsequent plays, became his credo.

In *Le Fils naturel* the central question is the fate of the illegitimate child, an issue obviously close to Dumas's heart. The first act forms a sort of prologue. Clara Vignot, a seamstress clearly modeled after Dumas's mother, is awaiting a visit from Charles Sternay, the wealthy young man who seduced her and fathered her illegitimate child. Sternay, however, has come to tell her that he is leaving; later she finds out from her friend, a lawyer named Aristide Fressard (the raisonneur of the play), that he has left to marry a wealthy young woman. Crushed, she turns her attentions to aid a dying young man who, the audience later learns, will leave her his fortune.

The rest of the play is set twenty years later. Clara's son Jacques is in love with Hermine, who is the ward of Charles Sternay. Jacques does not know that Sternay is his father, nor Sternay that Jacques is his son. Sternay and his mother, both social climbers, are concerned about the status of their family, and they will not allow the marriage of Jacques and Hermine without knowing Jacques's heritage. Aristide, at Jacques's urging, tells Jacques his true history, and Jacques confronts Sternay, who refuses to recognize him. Jacques, who under the law is prevented from pressing his claim, uses his connections to achieve an important diplomatic post in which he becomes a huge success. Now that Jacques is famous, Sternay is eager to recognize him, but Jacques refuses, "because not having a name, I made one for myself, and I'm perfectly happy with it." The shamed Sternay admits, "You have avenged yourself nobly, Jacques. But even if you don't want to call me your father, would you be willing to let me call you my son?"

This immensely satisfying play avoids any imprecation of melodrama through its wit and charm, despite the fact that many of the characters (the angelic mother, the selfish father) are melodramatically one-dimensional. The lesson is clear as well: the man who brings a child into the world and refuses responsibility for him is shameful and deserving of social opprobrium. And by extension the law that does not require fathers to take care of their illegitimate children and forbids illegitimate children to pursue their paternity should be changed. To critics who suggested that Jacques, with his wealth and his abilities, hardly represented the typical illegitimate child, Dumas replied that if Jacques had been a typical illegitimate child, he would have had to spend five acts depicting his hero's struggle against the hunger and cold that accompany poverty, which no audience would want to see.

After his first venture into the thesis play Dumas returned once more to the social comedy of his earlier days in *Un Père prodigue* (A Prodigal Father, 1859). The widowed Comte de la Rivonnière, whom Dumas drew in some aspects from the model

Aimée Desclée, an actress who inspired four plays by Dumas fils

of his father, has a son, André, whom he raised in an environment of lavish decadence. As an adult André wants his father to settle down and get married. The Comte sets his sights on young Hélène, but she prefers André; André and Hélène are married, and the count moves in with them. When the count treats Hélène with what André considers overfamiliarity, André and Hélène go abroad. The count invites into his house a courtesan, an old friend who looks after him and the house. When André learns of this, he is furious and threatens to evict his father. The father prepares to leave, but he discovers that the husband of one of his son's former liaisons is seeking André. The father pretends to be the lover of the aggrieved husband's wife and agrees to a duel, in which he wounds the husband and settles the matter. André, awed by his father's selfless act, is repentant—and the Comte advises André not to raise his own son as he had been raised.

This is clearly not a thesis play, unless one assumes a moral suggesting that a son raised amid licentiousness will ultimately become prudish (which would assume a great deal of self-realization and foresight on Dumas's part). The biographical references to Dumas *père* certainly delighted a contemporary audience, and an intriguing tale, plus an assemblage of entertaining characters such as the Comte and the courtesan Albertine de la Borde, made the play, if something of a return to an earlier style, a commercial success.

This should have been a prolific period for Dumas *fils,* now an established dramatist with sufficient income to live the good life. He had proven himself a master of dramatic technique, an issue he later addressed in the 1859 preface to *Un Père prodigue,* when he praised Eugène Scribe, the master of the "well-made play," even while he faulted Scribe for not putting his talents to more substantial use: "high-mindedness and sincerity are lacking in M. Scribe's work. . . . He didn't want to teach or to moralize or to correct people; he wanted to amuse them." Thus his celebrated conclusion to the preface: "the dramatist who understood *mankind* like Balzac and the *theater* like Scribe would be the greatest dramatist who ever lived." Dumas had displayed his technical skill, and he had begun his campaign to teach and to moralize. But now personal concerns intervened. He was troubled by illness, and he began a liaison that produced his own illegitimate child, although he later married the child's mother. With all these distractions it would be five years before Dumas *fils* brought forth a new play.

The new play, *L'Ami des femmes* (Women's Friend, 1864), was Dumas's first utter failure. The central character, de Ryons, an independently wealthy man who has made the study of women and their foibles the central focus of his life, rather arrogantly takes it upon himself to help women out of their difficulties. In the play his case study is Jane de Simerose, who, unaware of the details of intimacy, was so shocked by her brutish husband on her wedding night that she has separated from him. De Ryons saves her from falling into indiscretion with another man and ultimately restores her to her repentant husband. Audiences and critics alike were appalled by de Ryons, and Dumas even tried to save the play by softening his leading character, who is clearly a mouthpiece for the author. In his lengthy 1864 preface he blames the failure of the play on his having broken convention by refusing to bow down "before the omnipotence of Woman." In his bitterness over the play's failure Dumas in the preface comes across as insufferably paternalistic, almost misogynistic, in his attitude toward women. Having failed to draw a clear thesis or to please his audience, Dumas nearly drowns in his defensive rhetoric—and his attitude toward women will ever after be ambivalent and controversial.

In the wake of the failure of *L'Ami des femmes* there was another period during which Dumas wrote no plays under his own name, although he did adapt two plays written by others for production. The most successful was *Le Supplice d'une femme* (A Wife's Torment, 1865), in which Dumas not only cut and honed Emile de Girardin's original text but also changed the ending, infuriating Girardin. The bitterness between the two authors was such that throughout its successful run the play bore the name of neither author. During this same period Dumas returned to the novel with *L'Affaire Clemenceau* (1866), much of it pointedly autobiographical. After three years he returned to the Théâtre du Gymnase with a new play, this time a success.

Les Idées de Madame Aubray (Madame Aubray's Notions, 1867) is nearly as reminiscent of a biblical parable as of a thesis play. The title character, who many have noted is inspired by Dumas's friend George Sand, embodies the Christian notion of forgiveness. Mme Aubray has raised her son Camille to follow her example and asks that her friends do the same, urging her friend Barantin (the raisonneur of the piece) to take back the wife who abandoned him years before. Her latest project is Jeannine, an unmarried young woman with a child who (like all of Dumas's saintly unmarried mothers) has fallen through misguided love rather than through lust. Forgiving Jeannine her fault, she tries to marry her off to young Valmoreau, but her *idées* are tested when it is instead Camille who wants to marry Jeannine. Initially she refuses her consent, but when Jeannine tries to kill Camille's love by telling him about a string of fictitious lovers, Mme Aubray's conscience forces her to allow the marriage. The female characters here are drawn with a superiority that suggests an intentional antidote to the weak women of *L'Ami des femmes.* If such is the case, it worked, for the play was a resounding success.

Following *Les Idées de Madame Aubray,* however, Dumas took another extended leave from the theater. During the next four years one pseudonymous collaboration was his only effort in playwriting. This was a particularly traumatic period in Dumas's life. He had barely finished writing the prefaces to his earlier plays for the first edition of the *Théâtre complet* (1868) when his beloved mother died. Two years later his father died. In addition to these personal shocks, Dumas also saw in the year of his father's death the fall of the Second Empire and France's humiliating defeat in the Franco-Prussian War, which had a profound effect on him. In this emotional climate Dumas fell ever more under the influence of Henri Favré, a physician but also a mystic and a social polemicist and pamphleteer, whom Dumas had first met through Sand in 1866. Favré's influence is apparent in the prefaces and notes that first appeared in the early volumes of the *Théâtre complet* and were subsequently written for each play.

The combination of these events had several results. Dumas's playwriting began to assume—sometimes overtly, sometimes subtly—a more mystic, symbolic quality. His moralizing tendencies extended beyond his playwriting to a series of controversial social/political pamphlets—the infamous *L'Homme-femme* (Man-Woman, 1872), *La Question du divorce* (The Matter of Divorce, 1879), *Les Femmes qui tuent et les femmes qui votent* (Women Who Kill and Women Who Vote, 1880), and *La Recherche de la paternité* (Pursuit of Paternity, 1883). But perhaps most notably, his dramatic moralizing came to focus (more even than on the plight of the illegitimate child and the unwed mother) on a new issue: the twin dangers of adultery and prostitution, which he felt had undermined the social fabric of France and must be eradicated if a new age, built on the foundation of the nuclear family, was to be built.

Dumas's first play of the 1870s was a bittersweet one-act on the subject of adultery, *Une Visite de noces* (The Newlyweds Come Calling, 1871). Lydie de Morancé, a young widow, has never been able to get over the man, de Cygneroi, with whom she had once had an affair. Through the agency of Lydie's friend Lebonnard (the raisonneur), de Cygneroi comes to visit with his wife, whom he married more than a year earlier (lending the title a lovely irony). When Lydie and de Cygneroi (another irony, as the name means "swan king") are alone, she admits that he was but one of a long string of lovers. This story arouses in de Cygneroi not only jealousy but passion, and soon he is planning to leave his wife and run away with Lydie. But it is then revealed that Lydie's story was a lie, crafted by Lebonnard, intended to have exactly the effect it had. Lydie is now disgusted with the man she once loved, and Lebonnard removes de Cygneroi by telling him the truth, that Lydie is not wanton but eminently respectable. His passion quenched, de Cygneroi leaves; if he is to have a respectable woman, he will keep his wife. It is for Lebonnard to voice that moral: "And so it [adultery] ends, with the woman's hatred and the man's scorn. So where's the good in it?"

This little piece was an important transitional work for Dumas, and it stirred up a great deal of controversy, particularly toward its bitter quality. It was also the first play Dumas wrote for Aimée Desclée, an actress whom Dumas discovered in Belgium and who became his greatest inspiration since the death of Rose Chéri in 1861. She also created the leading roles in his next two plays, although she died before she could play the fourth role he wrote for her.

Dumas's next play also dealt with adultery. *La Princesse Georges* (1871) is the nickname of the central character, Séverine de Birac, married to a prince who has become involved with a married woman, Sylvanie de Terremonde, the model for Dumas's latter-day predatory adulteresses. The long-suffering Séverine is almost tempted to see the faithless prince shot by his mistress's husband, but her love forces her to plead with him not to go see Sylvanie when the husband is lying in wait. Nonetheless, the prince goes. A shot is heard, and the audience is surprised to learn that the victim is not the prince but an innocent young man who is also infatuated with Sylvanie. The curtain falls as the chastened prince, his eyes now opened by his brush with death, hesitates, not knowing if he dares take the hand that Séverine holds out to him.

In his preface Dumas explains that he pointedly rejected the melodramatic device of having the prince killed as punishment for his misdeeds. He preferred to leave open the possibility of reconciliation. Ultimately, his focus was not on the adulterers but on the suffering of their victims—not only Séverine but also the young man and the Comte de Terremonde—especially the wife with no legal recourse who must suffer not only the shame of her husband's adultery but also the conflict between her love and her desire for revenge for her suffering.

In Dumas's next play, the first written after France's defeat in the Franco-Prussian War, the tables are turned and the husband of an adulterous wife is the sufferer without recourse. *La Femme de Claude* (1873; translated as *Claude's Wife*, 1905) was written to elaborate a point raised in Dumas's controversial pamphlet *L'Homme-femme*. In arguing for the legalization of divorce (forbidden under the Napoleonic Code) Dumas hypothesized that if he had a son married to an utterly contemptible woman who not only sullied his name but stood in the way of his work, and if all attempts to reform her had failed, the only recourse he could suggest to that son, in the absence of the possibility of divorce, would be "Kill her!" It was a rhetorical device, but it generated outrage in many circles. So in response Dumas dramatized his situation.

Claude Ruper (the name alludes to the Roman emperor Claudius, who was married to the hopelessly corrupt Messalina) is an engineer who has invented a weapon so powerful that its very existence would deter aggressors from warfare. He has been deserted by his wife Césarine, who has run off with

Costumes designed for L'Ami des Femmes *(Women's Friend, 1864), a play whose failure embittered*
Dumas fils *(Collection of the Comédie-Française)*

a lover, stolen money, and (although Dumas could not state it overtly) clearly aborted her lover's child. Abandoned, she returns and tries to reinsinuate herself into Claude's life. She meets a foreign agent (who could not, in occupied France, be openly declared German) who offers her a fortune to sell him Claude's invention. To get it she seduces Claude's young, smitten assistant. As she is on the verge of handing the plans over to the German agent, Claude discovers her, and when she will not let go of the plans, he shoots her down like an animal—and calmly returns to his work.

The play, which gave Desclée in Césarine the role of a lifetime, was theatrically effective but just as controversial as the pamphlet. Claude is even more melodramatically pure than Séverine in *La Princesse Georges,* and the contrast between his purity and Césarine's unrepentant evil is emphasized by the presence of Rebecca, a young Jewish woman who loves Claude deeply, with whom he agrees that under the circumstances love on the temporal plane will be impossible. But it is vital that Claude be utterly pure, or he would lose the moral authority to deal with Césarine, after all other routes have been tried, as he ultimately does.

In the lengthy preface, one of the most important he ever wrote, Dumas elaborated on his point in the play. To him Césarine embodied the essence of the adulteress/prostitute who had sapped the moral lifeblood of France and led to its fall. He equates her to the Beast in the biblical Book of Revelation, "the filthy, whoring, child-killing Beast who

is undermining society, breaking up the family, sullying love, tearing apart the country, weakening man, dishonoring woman." *La Femme de Claude* is, according to Dumas, "an entirely symbolic work," offered as a warning to a weakened, morally lax nation to guard against its internal as well as its external foes.

Despite (or because of) its symbolic and patriotic pretensions, *La Femme de Claude* was a failure, and in his next play Dumas returned to the well-made thesis play of his earlier period with *Monsieur Alphonse* (1873). He also returned to two of his favorite earlier subjects: the plights of the illegitimate child and the unwed mother. A young roué, Octave, had twelve years earlier impregnated another of Dumas's innocent young women, and the child had been sent to live with peasants. The mother, Raymonde (written for Aimée Desclée but played by her rival, Blanche Pierson, after Desclée's death), has always visited the child in her own guise, but Octave is known to the child only as "M. Alphonse." Raymonde has married an older man who knows nothing of her indiscretion. In the play Octave has become engaged to a wealthy lower-class widow, from whom he wants to keep all knowledge of his illegitimate child. He tells Raymonde that the child must either live with her and her husband or be sent overseas. Raymonde's husband agrees to adopt the child, still not knowing she is the mother, but the widow, having wrenched a confession from Octave, also tries to adopt the child. Raymonde is fearful, but her husband, guessing the truth, forgives Raymonde everything and freely gives the child his name. Octave's deceits infuriate the widow, who breaks off the match, leaving him with nothing.

Equally as satisfying as *Le Fils naturel, Monsieur Alphonse* was a hit with the public. In the preface Dumas again argued for a law allowing unwed mothers and illegitimate children the legal right to pursue paternity—and excoriated a legal system that rewards the irresponsible seducer while punishing the woman he seduced and their innocent offspring. But however serious the underlying issues, the play's success came from the fact that it sugarcoated the moral pill.

At the age of fifty Dumas *fils* had become a major literary figure, and in 1874 he was elected to the Académie Française. Later that year *Le Demi-monde* was the first of several of Dumas's earlier plays to be taken into the repertoire of the Comédie-Française. The "House of Molière," so long associated with the classics, was seeking contemporary plays, and they prevailed upon Dumas to write his next play for them. Despite reservations, Dumas ended his exclusive association with the Théâtre du Gymnase, for which he had written every play produced under his own name since 1853, and his next play, *L'Etrangère* (1876; translated as *The Foreigner,* 1880), was premiered by the Comédie at the Théâtre-Français on 14 February 1876. His final four plays all made their first appearance there.

In *L'Etrangère* Dumas returned to the symbolist bent that had marked *La Femme de Claude.* The play featured Dumas's most convoluted, least comprehensible plot. The basic circumstance is that Catherine, daughter of an extremely wealthy merchant eager for a title, has been sold in marriage to a bankrupt, dissolute nobleman, the duc de Septmonts, although Catherine loves Gérard, the son of her governess. The title character is an American, Mistress Clarkson, a quadroon who has escaped American discrimination and come to Europe, where she manipulates men in high places. Women, however, shun her, and she offers to donate Fr 25,000 if Catherine will invite her to a social event. Catherine says she will do so only if the foreigner can find a man to take her among the wives—and Catherine's husband, a former lover of Mistress Clarkson's, is the only one who will do so. Catherine is humiliated, but she soon finds solace in the arms of Gérard. The duke ultimately challenges Gérard to a duel, but the day is saved by Mr. Clarkson, who kills the duke before he can kill Gérard, freeing Catherine to marry her true love.

This simplified synopsis suggests the melodramatic nature of the plot, but it omits the contrasting elements of high social comedy. It also ignores the

mystical element and the ostensible thesis, which lies in the theory of the vibrion, an invidious destructive parasite of which the duke is a human example. Implicit in this is another plea for the possibility of divorce, since only through the duke's death can Catherine be freed from such a plague.

This odd play, with its reliance on outrageous coincidence, its confusing story, and its surprising set pieces (as in act 3, when Mistress Clarkson tells the extraordinary story of her life), outraged the critics, but their outrage made the play controversial and actually helped draw an audience. That audience was also attracted by an astounding cast, including Constant Coquelin as the duke, Sophie Croizette as Catherine, and Sarah Bernhardt as Mistress Clarkson. If the play cannot really be called a success, it was certainly an interesting curiosity. Still, the reception did not please Dumas, and he turned his attention to other efforts, notably pamphlets. It would be five years before a new Dumas play appeared.

Curious, too, was that new play, *La Princesse de Bagdad* (The Princess of Bagdad, 1881). This time symbolic mysticism joins with moralistic fairy tale. Lionette, the pampered illegitimate daughter of an Arabian prince, has married Jean, who is now deeply in debt after squandering his fortune on her. A rich young man, Nourvady, who is also in love with Lionette, offers a house and a chest of gold if she will run away with him. She repulses him, but he still pays all of Jean and Lionette's debts, which incurs Jean's jealousy. Furious at Jean's mistrust, she decides to leave him, determined to sell herself to Nourvady. But as she is preparing to leave, her six-year-old son begs her to stay. The impatient Nourvady pushes the child to the floor, and Lionette's maternal love causes her to attack Nourvady. Jean arrives, and, as he is finally convinced of her innocence, there is a reconciliation.

This is another adultery play, but the adultery never happens. The thesis is clearly that only maternal love will bring responsibility and save an impetuous, spoiled young woman from dishonor. But the moral lines are blurred, as Jean (the potential wounded party) is hardly admirable; he fritters away his fortune on Lionette and then falls prey to unreasonably abusive jealousy. Dumas confesses that he wrote the play in a single feverish week, and the lack of craftsmanship is apparent. The play was actually hissed on its opening night, although Dumas blamed this on the unpopularity of his pamphlet *La Question du divorce* among segments of the audience. But the press reaction was uniformly hostile, and Dumas swore that he would write no more for the Comédie-Française.

That vow lasted four years. When Dumas returned with his next play, *Denise,* in 1885, it seemed that he had learned a lesson. Gone were the mystical flights of symbolic fancy, and in its place was something closer to the realism of his earlier plays. André de Bardannes wants to marry the beautiful but profoundly sad Denise Brissot. Denise's former fiancé, Fernand, wants to marry André's sister Marthe, fresh from the convent, but André refuses his permission. Fernand's mother, who wanted the match for financial reasons, casts veiled aspersions on Denise's purity. André asks Fernand about this, but Fernand denies that he and Denise were lovers. André, reassured, gives his permission for Marthe to marry Fernand, but Denise refuses André, without telling him why. Only when Denise hears that Fernand is to marry Marthe does she confess her secret—she had in fact been Fernand's lover and had borne a child, though it had died. Denise's father, shocked, insists that Fernand marry Denise, and the distraught André does not object. Marthe, suggesting that both she and Denise are shamed by their love of Fernand, proposes that both join the convent. Denise agrees, but as they are leaving, André's love overtakes his hurt, and he calls Denise back to his arms.

Denise clearly recalls *Les Idées de Madame Aubray* and even *Monsieur Alphonse,* and it certainly returns to the old Dumas thesis about the need to forgive the otherwise virtuous unwed mother. It also brings back full-bore the raisonneur in the form of André's friend Thouvenin, who is always ready to dispense logic in the face of emotionalism. But the play is also a tearjerker, *La Dame aux camélias* with a happy ending. Given a splendid production by the Comédie-Française, it was a rousing success. Toward the end of his career Dumas had found again his popular stride.

His final play, *Francillon* (1887), was in the same backward-looking vein, and it was also successful. Lucien de Riverolles, a notorious ladies' man, has married Francillon, but he continues to play around after their marriage and refuses to take his wife out, as it would limit his amorous chances. Francillon threatens that if he is unfaithful to her, she will reciprocate. Following him one evening, she sees him dining with a courtesan; she in turn picks up a young man and dines in the same place, her eye on her husband. The next day she tells Lucien that she has carried out her threat, and given the detail she provides about his activity, he believes her. None of his friends has sympathy for him, and none believes that Francillon did what she said, although they cannot shake her story. Only when the young man happens on the scene and confesses that their

encounter was purely civil is the truth out. Francillon is forced to admit her fabrication, and Lucien, shamed, asks her forgiveness—which she suggests will come later.

While the basic story recalls aspects of *La Princesse Georges* and even *La Princesse de Bagdad,* this play is clearly far superior to the latter. The familiar thesis about the double standard between men and women is back in force, but more important is the gallery of secondary characters, who amplify and deepen discussion of the issue of male/female relationships. Like *Denise,* it marks a return to an earlier style, but it has a dramatic richness and philosophical depth that its predecessor lacks. The reception was enthusiastic; Dumas *fils* still knew how to write a cracking good play.

He worked during his final years on another play, "La Route de Thèbes" (The Road to Thebes), a modern version of the meeting of Oedipus and the sphinx, for the Comédie-Française, but he never finished it. His wife ill, he entered in 1887 his final affair (which effectively ended his marriage), and when his wife died in 1895, he married his mistress two months later. But in another five months he himself was dead. He was buried several meters away from the tomb of Marie Duplessis in the Montmartre cemetery.

Dumas's thirty-year career in the theater had been stormy and frequently controversial. He had had brilliant successes and resounding failures, and the appearance of a new Dumas play was a news event of major proportions. Yet a year after his death a survey of young writers and critics as to the importance of Dumas *fils* produced a rash of invective, much of it dismissing him as irrelevant. And it is true that, despite the fact that many of his plays remained in the repertoire of the Comédie-Française well into the twentieth century (including the first successful production of *L'Ami des femmes*), his plays were not commonly revived.

Why did such a major figure so quickly leave the stage? Much of the reason has to do with Dumas's insistence on dealing with contemporary issues, which—despite the vitality of characters and plots—tied the plays to their historical moment. No one has better articulated this problem than William Archer, trying to explain why "in English-speaking countries the name of Dumas *fils* is more widely known than his works": "Plays which . . . are aimed point-blank at some social institution or prejudice tend to become obsolete in direct ratio to their immediate effectiveness. If they have not some more enduring principle of vitality, they will probably be found lying inert, like spent cannon-balls, in the breach they have created." And it is clear that the immediacy of Dumas's evangelism was dulled by its effectiveness. The demimonde of his early plays died with the Second Empire. Other issues were dated by legislation. A law permitting divorce in France was passed in 1884, and other laws in the early twentieth century alleviated the problems of the illegitimate child, culminating in a 1912 law permitting the child to pursue his or her paternity legally.

Dumas himself acknowledged this possibility. In the late 1860s he was already proclaiming that he was willing for his plays to disappear along with that against which they are fighting. Still, his parochial concern with immediate social and political issues—and particularly French issues—helps to explain why his plays (*La Dame aux camélias* always excepted) have been so rarely produced in other countries. True, many of his plays toured the world into the early years of the century in the repertoire of great international actresses, performing roles that Dumas had written for his own favorite actresses. Eleanora Duse toured *La Dame aux camélias, Une Visite de noces,* and *La Femme de Claude;* Sarah Bernhardt did likewise, not only with Marguerite Gautier and Césarine but also with *La Princesse Georges* and *L'Etrangère.* But it was the stars, performing in their native languages, and not the plays, which were the attraction, and when the age of the great touring stars ended, so largely did Dumas's presence on foreign stages.

Another reason for the fact that Dumas's plays are not widely known in English-speaking countries is that he has not fared well by translators. Many of his plays have never been translated into English, and many of those that have have been "adapted." Several plays are available in English only in copies sold in theaters during French touring productions, with the French text facing an often excruciatingly literal English translation that reflects the particular stage versions of the plays with their cuts. Other translations were made for English-language productions. Perhaps the most translated has been the most produced, *La Dame aux camélias,* though never without changes. Even the rare "academic" translations rarely do the plays justice. The earliest of these, a turgid translation, "with the author's sanction," of *Le Fils naturel* by T. Louis Oxley in 1879, actually uses *thee* and *thou* in rendering the second-person singular from the French.

Other problems attach to the production of Dumas *fils* today. His treatment of women, equivocal and problematic even in his own times, can be seen as offensive and condescending in the current age. While there is some balance in his treatment of women in the early plays, the thesis plays tend to

Dumas fils *at his home in Paris, 1891*

paint women according to a melodramatic dichotomy between the saintly and the venal (with the latter his most theatrically effective). And while there are exceptions (such as Madame Aubray and Lydie de Morancé), his "good" women tend to be painted as submissive helpmates, a reflection of his view, borrowed from Favré, that the nuclear family is the cornerstone of a healthy society and the adulterer its bane (despite his own lifelong indulgence in the same adultery that his plays were condemning).

If Dumas *fils* soon ceased to be a living presence in the theater, what then is his enduring importance? As the history books suggest, it is extraordinary. In many ways he stands in relation to French drama in much the same position as Honoré de Balzac, whom he so admired, does to the French novel. Both men were credited with introducing realism to their respective forms, in essence turning away from Romanticism (the influences of which neither entirely escaped) and substituting observation for imagination, with a sharp focus on the social environment. Dumas's admiration for Balzac's model was summed up in his well-known ending to the prologue of *Un Père prodigue*—"the dramatist who understood *mankind* like Balzac and the *theater* like Scribe would be the greatest dramatist who ever existed."

This sentence also testifies to his admiration of Scribe's dramaturgical skill, although he vigorously objected to what he considered the amorality of Scribe's plays, a criticism that refers not only to Scribe's use of such subjects as adultery as comic devices but also to his refusal to use his skill for any purpose beyond mere entertainment. Part of Dumas's contribution to dramatic theory lies in his insistence on debating the very purpose of the theater, whether it was simply to amuse or to inform and instruct. Arguing that the greatest dramatists (Molière was his most common exemplar) always had a point to make in their plays, Dumas insisted that the function of the theater was to be useful—in short, to make a moral point. It is in terms of this moralizing aim that Dumas is set apart from his playwriting contemporaries in the field of social realism. For Dumas social satire like that of Emile Augier was insufficient. He sought not only to depict social problems but also to suggest their solutions. But he recognized repeatedly that if an audience is to listen to an author's preachments, that audience must be entertained as well, and it is in that regard that he so admired Scribe's abilities.

Dumas often spoke of the importance of logic in the construction of his plays, especially if the denouement, in which the ultimate point of the play lies, is to be convincing. He first addressed this issue in depth in the 1868 preface to *Une Père prodigue,* and he returned to it repeatedly. He suggested it again in the 1867 preface to *Les Idées de Madame Aubray:* "the theater is as inexorable as arithmetic. If I didn't want to come to that denouement, or rather that mathematical result, it was up to me not to treat that subject." And in the 1872 preface to *La Princesse Georges* he said that it was his practice to begin the writing of his plays with the denouement so that he could be certain that the construction of the play led inevitably to the point that he wished to make. The point of each play was also reinforced by his habitual use of a raisonneur, and he used this character with more regularity and dexterity than any dramatist since Molière. Dumas considered himself a realist in the tradition of Balzac, and he spoke of the importance of observation to the writing of effective social drama. Indeed, he saw one aspect of his art as parallel to the journalist—or perhaps more precisely the editorial writer. But as the theories of naturalism developed, Dumas pointedly stressed that he was not a naturalist, an issue that he addressed directly in the 1879 preface to *L'Etrangère.* Naturalism, he said, was appropriate to the novel but not to the theater, where the ability to depict life in accurate detail is limited both by the scope available to its few brief hours and by what a general audience was willing to sit through. He further objected to the literal transcription of life on artistic grounds, claiming that it was more useful to depict the significance that lies behind everyday detail. He emphasized this point in a remark in his speech on the occasion of his reception into the Académie Française: "Le théâtre n'existe que d'exceptions" ("Theatre exists only in the exceptions").

Despite his antipathy toward naturalism, his critical reception was often similar to that of the naturalists. His moralizing notwithstanding, he was often accused of immorality. Evelyn Jerrold called him "a moral charlatan trading in unclean curiosity under the cloak of an evangelist," and Emile Montégut said, "He has a marvelous understanding of the worst instincts of his audience." Even the venerable Francisque Sarcey, in a review that Dumas quoted in his preface to *Une Visite de noces,* wrote: "Dumas' plays deal on the stage with things that, in the moral sphere, have an effect on the imagination which is . . . well, laxative. Alright, people do take laxatives in the course of their private lives, but my God! they don't gather together 1,500 people to tell them about the results."

Still, the next generation of playwrights, the naturalists included, professed little admiration for Dumas *fils.* Emile Zola himself began a lengthy essay on Dumas by admitting, "I am not very fond of M. Alexandre Dumas' abilities"—and then proceeded to claim his irrelevance. But despite the disdain of the new wave, Dumas's example was vital to their development.

Dumas had, by the mid 1860s, firmly established the theater of ideas and an acceptance for social-problem plays that was picked up not only by the naturalists and the authors of the Théâtre-Libre (all of whom denied any debt to Dumas) but also by Henrik Ibsen. Despite the fact that Ibsen denied that he had learned anything from Dumas except to avoid duplicating his errors in dramatic form, a large body of French, English, and even Scandinavian critics have observed convincingly that Dumas's plays anticipate Ibsen in many ways. The major difference is, as Oliver Bodington eloquently expressed it in his 1927 essay, "The Social Gospel of Alexandre Dumas *fils,*" that Ibsen and his followers:

draw no moral; they express no personal opinion; they are merely pathological. They offer no solution to the problem that they place before us. . . . But not so Dumas. Bold as he was in introducing those problems upon the stage at that time, he was still bolder in attempting to solve them. He invariably makes this attempt.

In this regard one might suggest that he anticipates Bernard Shaw as much as Ibsen.

In terms of French drama Dumas's influence is palpable. Several of his plays, such as *Une Visite de noces,* look forward to Henri Becque, although Becque said that he hated not just thesis plays but Dumas's work in general. But Dumas's influence is perhaps most sharply seen in the plays of Eugène Brieux, whose thesis plays clearly reflect the form (although they widen the concerns) of Dumas's, and Paul Hervieu, who not only pursued social agendas with the logic of Dumas but utilized his model of the raisonneur as well. To perhaps a lesser extent Dumas's model can be seen in the plays of François de Curel and Georges de Porto-Riche.

But the influence that Dumas *fils* had on future generations of playwrights pales next to the importance he had to the theater of his own day. Seizing the theater from the grip of the Romantics and the facile entertainments of Scribe, he made the theater a social issue of tremendous importance, generating controversy and discussion. Indeed, this vital contribution was neatly articulated by Emile Faguet in 1899: "C'est celui qui laisse derrière lui, partout il se passe, une longue, une puissante, peut-être une féconde excitation d'esprit public" (He was the one who left behind him, wherever he went, an enduring, powerful, perhaps fertile stimulation of the mind of the nation).

Biographies:

André Maurois, *Les Trois Dumas* (Paris: Hachette, 1957); translated by Gerard Hopkins as *The Titans: A Three-Generation Biography of the Dumas* (New York: Harper, 1957); and as *The Three Musketeers: A Study of the Dumas Family* (London: Cape, 1957);

Yves-Marie Lucot, *Dumas, père et fils* (Woignarue: Vague verte, 1997).

References:

William Archer, "Dumas and the English Drama," *Cosmopolis* (February 1896): 363–372;

Neil C. Arvin, *Alexandre Dumas fils* (Paris: Presses universitaires de France, 1939);

Oliver E. Bodington, "The Social Gospel of Alexandre Dumas *fils,*" in his *"Quiseen" and Other World Thoughts* (London: Richards, 1927), pp. 49–69;

Mabel Thérèse Bonney, *Les Idées morales dans le théâtre d'Alexandre Dumas fils* (Paris: Quimper, 1921);

Paul Bourget, *Essais de psychologie contemporaine* (Paris: E. Plon, Nourrit, 1899), pp. 273–326;

Jules Claretie, *A. Dumas fils* (Paris: A. Quantin, 1882);

Réné Doumic, "Alexandre Dumas fils et la guerre de 1870," *Revue des deux mondes* (15 August 1915): 923–934;

Doumic, *Portraits d'écrivains* (Paris: Delaplane, 1892), pp. 1–56;

Doumic, *De Scribe à Ibsen: Causeries sur le théâtre contemporain* (Paris: Delaplane, 1893), pp. 59–71;

Emile Faguet, *Propos de théâtre,* fourth series (Paris: Société française d'imprimerie et de librairie, 1899), pp. 48–63;

Augustin Filon, *De Dumas à Rostand: Esquisse du mouvement dramatique contemporain* (Paris: Armand Colin, 1898), pp. 1–35; translated by Janet E. Hogarth as *The Modern French Drama: Seven Essays* (London: Chapman & Hall, 1898), pp. 5–43;

Octavian Gheorghiu, *Le Théâtre de Dumas fils et la société contemporain* (Nancy: Société d'impressions typographiques, 1931);

Jules Guillemot, "Les Préfaces de Dumas fils et quelques préfaces dramatiques de XIXe siècle," *Le Correspondant* (25 October 1909): 227–257;

Henry James, "Dumas the Younger" (1895), in *Notes on Novelists, With Some Other Notes* (New York: Scribners, 1914), pp. 362–384;

Evelyn Jerrold, "Alexandre Dumas *fils,*" *Temple Bar,* 51 (1877): 392–408;

Emmanuelle Klausner, "Alexandre Dumas fils dans la cité des femmes," *L'Avant-Scène Théâtre,* 782 (15 January 1986): 4–9;

Léopold Lacour, "Dumas et Ibsen," *Revue de Paris* (15 October 1894): 881–894;

Pierre Lamy, *Le Théâtre d'Alexandre Dumas fils* (Paris: Presses universitaires de France, 1928);

Tore Linge, *La Conception de l'amour dans le drame de Dumas fils et d'Ibsen* (Paris: Librairie Ancienne Honoré Champion, 1935);

Jules Marsan, *Théâtre d'hier et d'aujourd'hui* (Paris: Editions des cahiers libre, 1926), pp. 51–73;

Brander Matthews, *French Dramatists of the 19th Century,* fifth edition (New York: Scribners, 1919), pp. 136–171;

L'Abbé Paulin Moniquet, *Les Idées de M. Alexandre Dumas fils à propos du divorce et de l'homme-femme* (Paris: Société Générale de Librairie Catholique, 1888);

Emile Montégut, "Le Théâtre réaliste," review of *Le Fils naturel, Revue des deux mondes* (1 February 1858): 701–716;

Felix Moreau, *Le Code civil et le théâtre contemporain: M. Alexandre Dumas fils* (Paris: L. Larose et Forcel, 1887);

Pierre Moreau, "De Dumas père à Dumas fils," *Revue des deux mondes* (1 June 1923): 683–697;

Carlos M. Noel, *Les Idées sociales dans le théâtre d'Alexandre Dumas fils* (Paris: Albert Messein, 1912);

Paul Saint-Victor, *Le Théâtre contemporain: Emile Augier, Alexandre Dumas fils* (Paris: Calmann-Lévy, 1889);

Francisque Sarcey, "Alexandre Dumas," *Cosmopolis* (January 1896): 171–183;

Sarcey, *Quarante ans de théâtre (feuillitons dramatiques),* volume 5 (Paris: Bibliothèque des Annales, 1901);

Edith Saunders, *The Prodigal Father: Dumas Père et Fils and "The Lady of the Camellias"* (London: Longmans, Green, 1951);

H. Stanley Schwarz, *Alexandre Dumas* fils, *Dramatist* (New York: New York University Press, 1927);

Ernest Seillière, *La Morale de Dumas fils* (Paris: Librairie Félix Alcon, 1921);

Hugh Allison Smith, *Main Currents of Modern French Drama* (New York: Holt, 1925), pp. 122–150;

Maurice Spronck, "Alexandre Dumas fils: l'auteur dramatique et le moraliste," *Revue des deux mondes* (1 April 1898): 610–646;

Spronck, "Alexandre Dumas fils: ses origines et ses débuts," *Revue des deux mondes* (15 March 1898): 403–427;

Frank A. Taylor, *The Theatre of Alexandre Dumas fils* (Oxford: Clarendon Press, 1937).

M. S. Van de Velde, "Alexandre Dumas *fils* and His Plays," *Fortnightly Review,* 65 (January 1896): 94–103;

Bernard Weinberg, "Contemporary Criticism of the Plays of Dumas *fils,* 1852–1869," *Modern Philology,* 37 (February 1940): 293–308;

Jean-Jacques Weiss, *Le Théâtre et les moeurs,* third edition (Paris: Calmann-Lévy, 1889), pp. 17–66;

Jules Wogue, "Les Thèses d'Alexandre Dumas fils," *La Revue du mois,* 1 (June 1906): 692–719;

Emile Zola, *Nos Auteurs dramatiques* (Paris: Bibliothèque-Charpentier, 1901), pp. 113–194.

Alexandre Dumas *père*

(24 July 1802 – 5 December 1870)

Barbara T. Cooper
University of New Hampshire

See also the Dumas entry in *DLB 119: Nineteenth-Century French Fiction Writers: Romanticism and Realism, 1800–1860.*

PLAY PRODUCTIONS: *La Chasse et l'amour,* Paris, Théâtre de l'Ambigu-Comique, 22 September 1825;

La Noce et l'enterrement, Paris, Théâtre de la Porte Saint-Martin, 21 November 1826;

Henri III et sa cour, Paris, Théâtre-Français, 11 February 1829;

La Cour du Roi Pétaud, Paris, Théâtre du Vaudeville, 28 February 1829;

Stockholm, Fontainebleau et Rome, Paris, Théâtre de l'Odéon, 30 March 1830;

Napoléon Bonaparte, ou Trente Ans dans l'histoire de France, Paris, Théâtre de l'Odéon, 10 January 1831;

Antony, Paris, Théâtre de la Porte Saint-Martin, 3 May 1831;

Charles VII chez ses grands vassaux, Paris, Théâtre de l'Odéon, 20 October 1831;

Richard Darlington, by Dumas, Prosper-Parfait Goubaux, and Jacques-Félix Beudin, Paris, Théâtre de la Porte Saint-Martin, 10 December 1831;

Teresa, Paris, Théâtre de l'Opéra-Comique, 6 February 1832;

Le Mari de la Veuve, Paris, Théâtre-Français, 4 April 1832;

La Tour de Nesle, Paris, Théâtre de la Porte Saint-Martin, 29 May 1832;

Le Fils de l'émigré, Paris, Théâtre de la Porte Saint-Martin, 28 August 1832;

Angèle, Paris, Théâtre de la Porte Saint-Martin, 28 December 1833;

Catherine Howard, Paris, Théâtre de la Porte Saint-Martin, 2 June 1834;

Don Juan de Maraña, ou La Chute d'un ange, Paris, Théâtre de la Porte Saint-Martin, 30 April 1836;

Alexandre Dumas père *(photograph by Nadar)*

Kean, ou Désordre et génie, Paris, Théâtre des Variétés, 31 August 1836;

Piquillo, Paris, Théâtre de l'Opéra-Comique, 31 October 1837;

Caligula, Paris, Théâtre-Français, 26 December 1837;

Paul Jones, Paris, Théâtre du Panthéon, 8 October 1838;

Mademoiselle de Belle-Isle, Paris, Théâtre-Français, 2 April 1839;

L'Alchimiste, Paris, Théâtre de la Renaissance, 10 April 1839;

Un Mariage sous Louis XV, Paris, Théâtre-Français, 1 June 1841;

Lorenzino, Paris, Théâtre-Français, 24 February 1842;

Halifax, Paris, Théâtre des Variétés, 2 December 1842;

Les Demoiselles de Saint-Cyr, Paris, Théâtre-Français, 25 July 1843;

Louise Bernard, Paris, Théâtre de la Porte Saint-Martin, 18 November 1843;

Le Laird de Dumbiky, Paris, Théâtre de l'Odéon, 30 December 1843;

Les Mousquetaires, Paris, Théâtre de l'Ambigu-Comique, 27 October 1845;

Une Fille du Régent, Paris, Théâtre-Français, 1 April 1846;

Hamlet, prince de Danemark, by Dumas and Paul Meurice, Saint-Germain-en-Laye, Théâtre de Saint-Germain, 14 September 1846;

La Reine Margot, by Dumas and Auguste Maquet, Paris, Théâtre-Historique, 20 February 1847;

Intrigue et amour, Paris, Théâtre-Historique, 11 June 1847;

Le Chevalier de Maison-Rouge, Paris, Théâtre-Historique, 3 August 1847;

Monte-Cristo, première soirée, Paris, Théâtre-Historique, 3 February 1848;

Monte-Cristo, deuxième soirée, Paris, Théâtre-Historique, 4 February 1848;

Catalina, Paris, Théâtre-Historique, 14 October 1848;

La Jeunesse des Mousquetaires, Paris, Théâtre-Historique, 17 February 1849;

Le Chevalier d'Harmental, Paris, Théâtre-Historique, 26 July 1849;

La Guerre des femmes, Paris, Théâtre-Historique, 1 October 1849;

Le Testament de César, Paris, Théâtre-Français, 10 November 1849;

Le Comte Hermann, Paris, Théâtre-Historique, 22 November 1849;

Le Cachemire vert, Paris, Théâtre du Gymnase, 15 December 1849;

Trois entr'actes pour l'amour médecin, Paris, Théâtre-Français, 15 January 1850;

Urbain Grandier, Paris, Théâtre-Historique, 30 March 1850;

L'Auberge de Schawasbach, Paris, Théâtre de la Gaîté, 30 March 1850;

La Chasse au chastre, Paris, Théâtre-Historique, 3 August 1850;

Les Frères corses, Paris, Théâtre-Historique, 10 August 1850;

Le Comte de Morcerf, 3e partie de Monte-Cristo, Paris, Théâtre de l'Ambigu-Comique, 1 April 1851;

La Barrière Clichy, Paris, Théâtre National (former Théâtre imperial du Cirque), 21 April 1851;

Villefort, quatrième soirée de Monte-Cristo, Paris, Théâtre de l'Ambigu-Comique, 8 May 1851;

Le Vampire, Paris, Théâtre-Historique, 20 December 1851;

Romulus, Paris, Théâtre-Français, 13 January 1854;

La Jeunesse de Louis XIV, Brussels, Théâtre du Vaudeville, 20 January 1854;

Le Marbrier, Paris, Théâtre du Vaudeville, 22 May 1854;

La Conscience, Paris, Théâtre de l'Odéon, 4 November 1854;

L'Orestie, Paris, Théâtre de la Porte Saint-Martin, 5 January 1856;

La Tour Saint-Jacques, Paris, Théâtre impérial du Cirque, 15 November 1856;

Le Verrou de la reine, Paris, Théâtre du Gymnase-Dramatique, 15 December 1856;

L'Invitation à la valse, Paris, Théâtre du Gymnase-Dramatique, 18 June 1857;

L'Honneur est satisfait, Paris, Théâtre du Gymnase-Dramatique, 19 June 1858;

Le Roman d'Elivre, Paris, Théâtre impérial de l'Opéra-Comique, 4 February 1860;

L'Envers d'une conspiration, Paris, Théâtre du Vaudeville, 4 June 1860;

Le Gentilhomme de la montagne, Paris, Théâtre de la Porte Saint-Martin, 12 June 1860;

La Dame de Monsoreau, Paris, Théâtre de l'Ambigu-Comique, 19 November 1860;

Le Prisonnier de la Bastille, fin des Mousquetaires, Paris, Théâtre impérial du Cirque, 22 March 1861;

Les Mohicans de Paris, Paris, Théâtre de la Gaîté, 20 August 1864;

Les Gardes forestières, Paris, Grand Théâtre parisien, 28 May 1865(?);

Gabriel Lambert, Paris, Théâtre de l'Ambigu-Comique, 16 March 1866;

Madame de Chamblay, Paris, Théâtre de la Porte Saint-Martin, 31 October 1868;

Les Blancs et les bleus, Paris, Théâtre du Châtelet, 10 March 1869;

Ivanhoë, Dieppe, Théâtre du Casino de Dieppe, 14 May 1966.

BOOKS: *La Chasse et l'amour,* by Dumas as Davy, Pierre-Joseph Rousseau (James Rousseau), and Adolphe (Adolphe de Leuven) (Paris: Duvernois, 1825);

La Noce et l'enterrement, by Dumas as Davy, [Hippolyte] Lassagne, and Gustave (Alphonse Vulpian) (Paris: Bezou, 1826);

Nouvelles contemporaines (Paris: Sanson, 1826);

Henri III et sa cour (Paris: Vezard et Cie, 1829); translated by Lord Francis Leveson Gower as *Catherine of Cleves* (London: J. Andrews, 1831);

Stockholm, Fontainebleau et Rome, trilogie dramatique sur la vie de Christine (Paris: Barba, 1830); republished as *Christine, ou Stockholm, Fontainebleau et Rome* (Paris, 1834);

Napoléon Bonaparte, ou Trente Ans dans l'histoire de France, by Dumas and Etienne-C.-H. Cordellier-Delanoue (Paris: Tournachon-Molin, 1831);

Antony (Paris: Auguste Auffray, 1831); translated by Frederick Schwab (New York: F. Rullman, 1880);

Charles VII chez ses grands vassaux (Paris: C. Lemesle, 1831); translated by Dorothy Trench-Bonnet as *Charles VII at the Homes of His Great Vassals* (Chicago: Noble Press, 1991);

Richard Darlington, by Dumas and Dinaux (pseud. Jacques-Félix Beudin and Prosper-Parfait Goubaux) (Paris: Barba, 1831);

Teresa (Paris: Barba, 1832);

Le Mari de la veuve, by Dumas, Auguste Anicet-Bourgeois, and Eugène Durieu (Paris: A. Auffray, 1832);

La Tour de Nesle, by Dumas and Frédéric Gaillardet (Paris: Barba, 1832); translated by George Almar as *The Tower of Nesle; or, The Chamber of Death* (London: J. Cumberland, 185?); translated by Adam L. Gowans as *The Tower of Nesle* (London & Glasgow: Gowans & Gray / New York: Frederick A. Stokes, 1906);

Gaule et France (Paris: U. Canel & Guyot, 1833); translated anonymously as *The Progress of Democracy; Illustrated in the History of Gaul and France* (New York: J. & H. G. Langley, 1841);

Impressions de voyage: En Suisse, volume 1 (Paris: Guyot, 1834); volume 2 (Paris: Charpentier, 1835); volumes 3–5 (Paris: Dumont, 1837); translated by Mrs. W. R. Wilde as *The Glacier Land* (Belfast: Simms & McIntyre / London: J. W. S. Orr, 1852);

Angèle (Paris: Charpentier, 1834);

Catherine Howard (Paris: Charpentier, 1834); translated and adapted by William Suter as *Catherine Howard; or, The Throne, the Tomb, and the Scaffold* (New York: R. M. De Witt, 187?);

Chroniques de France. Isabel de Bavière, 2 volumes (Paris: Dumont, 1835); translated by William Barrow as *Isabel of Bavaria; or, The Chronicles of France for the Reign of Charles VI* (London: Bruce & Wild, 1846);

Kean, ou Désordre et génie (Paris: Barba, 1836); translated anonymously as *Edmund Kean, or The Genius and the Libertine* (London: Vickers, 1847);

Don Juan de Maraña, ou La Chute d'un ange (Paris: Marchant, 1836; revised edition, Paris: Michel Lévy, 1864);

Piquillo, by Dumas and Gérard de Nerval (Paris: Marchant, 1837);

Caligula (Paris: Marchant, 1838);

Paul Jones (Paris: Marchant, 1838); translated by William Berger (Philadelphia: Collins, 1839);

La Comtesse de Salisbury, 6 volumes (Paris: Dumont, 1839); translated anonymously as *The Countess of Salisbury; A Chronicle of the Order of the Garter* (New York: Stringer & Townsend, 1851);

Mademoiselle de Belle-Isle, by Dumas and Count Waleski (Paris: Marchant, 1839); translated anonymously as *The Lady of Belleisle, or, A Night in the Bastille* (London: T. H. Lacy, n.d.);

L'Alchimiste, by Dumas and Gérard de Nerval (Paris: Dumont, 1839); translated by Henry Bertram Lister as *The Alchemist* (San Francisco: Bohemian Club, 1940);

Crimes célèbres, 8 volumes (Paris: Administration de librairie, 1839–1840); translated anonymously as *Celebrated Crimes* (London: Chapman & Hall, 1843);

Un Mariage sous Louis XV (Paris: Marchant, 1841); translated and adapted by Sydney Grundy as *A Marriage of Convenience* (London, 1897?);

Impressions de voyage: Le Midi de la France, 3 volumes (Paris: Dumont, 1841); translated anonymously as *Pictures of Travel in the South of France* (London: Offices of the National Illustrated Library, n.d.);

Une Année à Florence, 2 volumes (Paris: Dumont, 1841);

Excursions sur les bords du Rhin, 3 volumes (Paris: Dumont, 1841);

Le Chevalier d'Harmental, 4 volumes (Paris: Dumont, 1842); translated by P. F. Christin and Eugene Lies as *The Chevalier d'Harmental; or, Love and Conspiracy* (New York: Harper, 1846); original adapted as a drama by Dumas and Maquet (Paris: Cadot, 1849);

Le Speronare, 4 volumes (Paris: Dumont, 1842); translated by Katharine Prescott Wormeley as *Journeys with Dumas; The Speronara* (Boston: Little, Brown, 1902);

Le Capitaine Aréna, 2 volumes (Paris: Dolin, 1842);

Lorenzino (Paris: Marchant, 1842);

Halifax (Paris: Marchant, n.d. [1842]);

Les Demoiselles de Saint-Cyr (Paris: Marchant, 1843); translated and adapted anonymously as *The Ladies of Saint-Cyr, or The Runaway Husbands* (London: T. H. Lacy, 1870);

Georges, 3 volumes (Paris: Dumont, 1843); translated by G. J. Knox as *George; or The Planter of the Isle of France* (Belfast: Simms & McIntyre / London: J. W. S. Orr, 1846);

Le Corricolo, 4 volumes (Paris: Dolin, 1843); translated by A. Roland as *Sketches of Naples* (Philadelphia: E. Ferrett, 1845);

Louise Bernard (Paris: Marchant, 1843);

Cécile, 2 volumes (Paris: Dumont, 1844); also published as *La Robe de noces* (Brussels: Méline Cans et Cie., 1844); translated by Eugene Plunkette as *Cecilia; or, Woman's Love* (New York: Jarrett, 1846);

Le Château d'Eppstein, 3 volumes (Paris: L. de Potter, 1844); translated anonymously as *The Spectre-Mother; or, Love after Death* (London: C. H. Clarke, 1864); translated by Alfred Allinson as *The Castle of Eppstein* (London: Methuen, 1903);

Fernande, 3 volumes (Paris: Dumont, 1844); translated anonymously as *Fernande; or, The Fallen Angel. A Story of Life in Paris* (New York: Stringer & Townsend, 1849);

Le Laird de Dumbiky (Paris: Marchant, 1844);

Sylvandire, 3 volumes (Paris: Dumont, 1844); translated anonymously as *Sylvandire; or, The Disputed Inheritance* (New York: Harper, 1846);

Les Trois Mousquetaires, 8 volumes (Paris: Baudry, 1844); translated anonymously as *The Three Musketeers* (London: G. Vickers, 1846); translated by William Barrow as *The Three Musketeers; or, The Feats and Fortunes of a Gascon Adventurer* (London: Bruce & Wyld, 1846); translated by Park Benjamin as *The Three Guardsmen* (Baltimore: Taylor, Wilde, 1846);

Une Fille du régent (3 volumes, Brussels: Méline Cans et Cie., 1844; 4 volumes, Paris: Cadot, 1845); translated by Charles H. Town as *The Regent's Daughter* (New York: Harper, 1845); original adapted as a drama (Paris: Marchant, 1846);

Le Comte de Monte-Cristo, 18 volumes (Paris: Pétion, 1844–1845); translated anonymously as *The Count of Monte-Cristo* (London: Chapman & Hall, 1846); original adapted as a drama by Dumas and Maquet (Paris: Tresse, 1848); translated anonymously as *Monte-Cristo* (London: T. H. Lacy, 1850);

La Bouillie de la comtesse Berthe (Paris: J. Hetzel, 1845); translated anonymously as *Good Lady Bertha's Honey Broth* (London: Chapman & Hall, 1846); translated by Mrs. Cooke Taylor as *The Honey Stew of Lady Bertha* (London: Jeremiah How, 1846);

Les Frères corses, 2 volumes (Paris: Souverain, 1845); translated by a pupil of Mons. G. J. Sanders as *The Corsican Brothers* (Philadelphia: G. B. Zieber, 1845);

Les Mousquetaires, by Dumas and Auguste Maquet (Paris: Marchant, 1845);

La Reine Margot, 6 volumes by Dumas and Maquet (Paris: Garnier frères, 1845); translated as *Marguerite de Valois* (London: David Bogue, 1846); translated by Frederick Gilbert as *Queen Margot; or, Marguerite de Valois* (London: John Dicks, 1885); original adapted as a drama by Dumas and Auguste Maquet (Paris: Michel Lévy, 1847);

Simples lettres sur l'art dramatique (Brussels: Société de librairie, 1845);

Vingt ans après, 10 volumes (Paris: Baudry, 1845); translated by Barrow as *Twenty Years After; or, The Further Feats and Fortunes of a Gascon Adventurer* (London: Bruce & Wyld, 1846);

La Guerre des femmes, 8 volumes (Paris: L. de Potter, 1845–1846); translated by Samuel Springer as *The War of Women; or, Rivalry in Love* (New York: Stringer & Townsend, 1850); original adapted as a drama by Dumas and Maquet (Paris: Cadot, 1849);

Le Chevalier de Maison-Rouge, 6 volumes (Paris: Cadot, 1845–1846); translated anonymously as *Marie Antoinette; or, The Chevalier of the Red House* (London: G. Peirce, 1846); translated by Henry W. Herbert as *Genevieve; or, The Chevalier of Maison Rouge* (New York: Williams, 1846); original adapted as a drama, *Le Chevalier de Maison-Rouge, épisode du temps des Girondins* (Paris: Michel Lévy, 1847); translated by Colin Hazlewood as *The Chevalier of the Maison Rouge; or, The Days of Terror!* (London: T. H. Lacy, 1859);

La Dame de Monsoreau, 8 volumes (Paris: Pétion, 1846); translated anonymously as *Diana of Meridor; or, The Lady of Monsoreau* (New York: Williams Bros., 1846); translated anonymously as *Chicot, the Jester* (London: T. Hodgson, 1857); original adapted as a drama by Dumas and Maquet (Paris: Michel Lévy frères, 1860);

Les Deux Diane, 10 volumes (Paris: Cadot, 1846–1847); translated by Plunkette as *The Two Dianas: or, The Son of a Count and the Daughter of a King* (New York: Williams Bros., 1848); original adapted as a drama (Paris: Librairie internationale, 1865);

Le Bâtard de Mauléon, 9 volumes (Paris: Cadot, 1846–1847); translated anonymously as *The Bastard of Mauléon* (London: E. Appleyard, 1848); translated by L. Lawford as *The Half Brothers, or The Head and the Hand* (London: Routledge, 1858);

Mémoires d'un médecin: Joseph Balsamo, 19 volumes (Paris: Cadot, 1846–1848); translated anonymously as *The Memoirs of a Physician* (London: T. Hodgson, 1848);

Intrigue et amour (Poissy: G. Olivier, 1847);

Hamlet, prince de Danemark, by Dumas and Paul Meurice (Paris: Dondey-Dupré, 1847);

De Paris à Cadix, 5 volumes (Paris: Garnier frères, 1847–1848);

Les Quarante-Cinq, 10 volumes (Paris: Cadot, 1847–1848); translated anonymously as *The Forty-Five Guardsmen* (London: E. Appleyard, 1848);

Catalina, by Dumas and Maquet (Paris: Veuve Dondey-Dupré, n.d. [1848]);

Le Vicomte de Bragelonne, ou Dix ans plus tard, 26 volumes (Paris: Michel Lévy frères, 1848–1850); translated anonymously as *The Vicomte de Bragelonne; or, Ten Years Later* (London: Routledge, 1857);

Le Véloce, ou Tanger, Alger et Tunis, 4 volumes (Paris: Cadot, 1848–1851); translated by Richard Meade Bache as *Tales of Algeria, or Life Among the Arabs* (Philadelphia: Claxton, Remsen & Heffelfinger, 1868);

La Jeunesse des Mousquetaires, by Dumas and Maquet (Paris: Dufour & Mulat, 1849);

Les mille et un fantômes, une journée à Fontenay-aux-Roses, 2 volumes (Paris: Cadot, 1849); translated by Alfred Allinson as *Tales of the Supernatural* (London: Methuen, 1907);

Le Comte Hermann (Paris: Firmin Didot frères, 1849);

Le Cachemire vert, by Dumas and Eugène Nus (Paris: Dondey-Dupré, n.d. [1849]);

Le Collier de la reine, 11 volumes (Paris: Cadot, 1849–1850); translated anonymously as *The Queen's Necklace; or The Secret History of the Court of Louis XVI* (New York: W. F. Burgess, 1850; Philadelphia: T. B. Peterson, 1853);

L'Auberge de Schawasbach (Paris: Librairie théâtrale, 1850);

La Chasse au chastre (Paris: Librairie théâtrale, 1850);

La Femme au collier de velours, 2 volumes (Paris: Cadot, 1850); translated by Mary Stuart Smith as *The Woman with the Velvet Necklace* (New York: G. Munro's Sons, 1897);

La Tulipe noire, 3 volumes (Paris: Baudry, 1850); translated by Fayette Robinson as *The Black Tulip* (New York: W. F. Burgess, 1850);

Urbain Grandier, by Dumas and Maquet (Paris: Librairie théâtrale, 1850);

Ange Pitou, 8 volumes (Paris: Cadot, 1851); translated by Thomas Williams as *Six Years Later; or, The Taking of the Bastille* (Philadelphia: T. B. Peterson, 1851); translated as *Ange Pitou, or The Taking of the Bastille* (New York: President & MacIntyre, 1859);

La Barrière Clichy (Paris: Librairie théâtrale, 1851);

Olympe de Clèves, 9 volumes (Brussels: A. Lebègue, 1851–1852; Paris: Cadot, 1852); translated in two parts by H. L. Williams Jr. as *Olympia of Cleves; or, The Loves of a King of France* and *The Count of Mailly* (Philadelphia: F. A. Brady, 1864);

Mes Mémoires. Souvenirs de 1830 à 1842, 22 volumes (Paris: Cadot, 1852–1854); translated by E. M. Waller as *My Memoirs* (London: Methuen, 1907–1909);

La Comtesse de Charny, 19 volumes (Paris: Cadot, 1852–1855); translated anonymously as *The Countess of Charny; or, The Fall of the French Monarchy* (Philadelphia: T. B. Peterson, 1853);

Isaac Laquedem, 2 volumes (Paris: Marchant, 1853); translated anonymously (New York: Bunnell & Price, 1853);

Ingénue, 7 volumes (Paris: Cadot, 1853–1855); translated by Julie de Marguerittes as *Ingénue; or, The First Days of Blood* (Philadelphia: Lippincott, Grambo, 1855);

Aventures et tribulations d'un comédien (Brussels & Leipzig: Kiessling, Schnée & Cie, 1854); translated by Robert Singleton Garnett as *A Life's Ambition; Being the Adventures and Tribulations of an Actor* (London: S. Paul, 1924);

La Conscience, by Dumas and Lockroy (Joseph Philippe Simon) (Paris: Tarride, 1854);

La Jeunesse de Louis XIV (Brussels: Tarride, 1854);

Le Marbrier (Paris: Michel Lévy, 1854);

Romulus (Paris: Librairie théâtrale, 1854);

Les Mohicans de Paris, 19 volumes (Paris: Cadot, 1854–1855); translated anonymously as *The Mohicans of Paris* (Philadelphia: T. B. Peterson, 1859); original adapted as a drama (Paris: Michel Lévy, 1864);

La Dernière Année de Marie Dorval (Paris: Librairie nouvelle, 1855);

L'Orestie (Paris: Librairie théâtrale, 1856);

La Tour Saint-Jacques, by Dumas and Xavier de Montépin (Paris: Librairie théâtrale, 1856);

L'Invitation à la valse (Paris: Beck, 1857);

Le Meneur de loups, 3 volumes (Paris: Cadot, 1857); translated by Allinson as *The Wolf-Leader* (London: Methuen, 1904);

Les Compagnons de Jéhu, 7 volumes (Paris: Cadot, 1857–1858); translated anonymously in two parts as *Royalists and Republicans; or, the Companions of Jehu* and *The Guillotine: or, the Death of Morgan* (London: E. D. Long, 1861); original adapted as a drama (Paris: Beck, 1857);

Black, 4 volumes (Paris: Cadot, 1858); translated by Alma Blakeman Jones as *Black, The Story of a Dog* (New York: Croscup / London: Dent, 1895);

Le Capitaine Richard, 3 volumes (Paris: Cadot, 1858); translated anonymously as *The Twin Captains* (London: C. H. Clarke, 1861); translated by H. L. Williams as *The Twin Lieutenants; or, The Soldier's Bride* (Philadelphia: T. B. Peterson, 1862);

L'Honneur est satisfait (Paris: Librairie théâtrale, 1858);

Contes pour les grands et les petits enfants, 2 volumes (Brussels: Méline Cans et Cie., 1859);

Les Louves de Machecoul, épisodes de la guerre de Vendée en 1832, 10 volumes, by Dumas and G. de Cherville (Paris: Cadot, 1859); translated in two parts by Williams as *The Royalist Daughters* and *The Castle of Souday* (New York: Dick & Fitzgerald, 1862); translated anonymously as *The She-Wolves of Machecoul* and *The Last Vendée* (New York: G. Munro, 1894);

Le Caucase (Paris: Librairie Théâtrale, 1859);

Causeries, 2 volumes (Paris: Michel Lévy frères, 1860; enlarged edition, Paris: Calmann-Lévy, 1885);

La Dame de Monsoreau, by Dumas and Maquet (Paris: Michel Lévy frères, 1860);

L'Envers d'une conspiration, by Dumas and Lockroy (Paris: Michel Lévy, 1860);

Le Gentilhomme de la montagne, by Dumas and Lockroy (Paris: Michel Lévy, 1860);

De Paris à Astrakan, 3 volumes (Paris: A. Bourdillart, 1860); revised as *Impressions de voyage: En Russie,* 4 volumes (Paris: Michel Lévy Frères, 1865); extracts translated anonymously as *Celebrated Crimes of the Russian Court* (London: Hurst & Blackett, 1906);

Le Roman d'Elvire, by Dumas and Leuven (Paris: Michel Lévy, 1860);

La Route de Varennes (Paris: Michel Lévy frères, 1860);

Bric-à-brac, 2 volumes (Paris: Michel Lévy frères, 1861);

Les Garibaliens, révolution de Sicile et de Naples (Paris: Michel Lévy frères, 1861); translated by Edmund Routledge as *The Garibaldians in Sicily* (London: Routledge, Warne & Routledge, 1861);

Le Prisonnier de la Bastille, fin des Mousquetaires (Paris: Michel Lévy, 1861);

I Borboni di Napoli, 10 volumes (Naples, 1862–1864);

Les Mohicans de Paris (Paris: Michel Lévy, 1864);

Les Gardes forestières (Paris: Michel Lévy, 1865);

Le Comte de Moret (New York: Mareil, 1866); translated by H. L. Williams Jr. as *The Count of Moret; or, Richelieu and His Rivals* (Philadelphia: Peterson, 1868);

Gabriel Lambert, by Dumas and Amédée de Jallais (Paris: Michel Lévy, 1866);

Histoire de mes bêtes (Paris: Michel Lévy frères, 1867); translated by Allinson as *My Pets* (London: Methuen, 1909);

Une Aventure d'amour (Paris: Michel Lévy, 1867);

Etude sur Hamlet et sur W. Shakespeare (Paris: Michel Lévy, 1867);

Les Blancs et les bleus, 3 volumes (Paris: Michel Lévy, 1867–1868); translated by Wormeley as *The First Republic; or, The Whites and the Blues* (London: Sampson Low, Marston, 1895); original adapted as a drama (Paris: Michel Lévy, 1874);

La Terreur prussienne, 2 volumes (Paris: Michel Lévy frères, 1868); translated by R. S. Garnett as *The Prussian Terror* (London: Stanley Paul, 1915);

Souvenirs dramatiques, 2 volumes (Paris: Michel Lévy frères, 1868); republished as *Souvenirs dramatiques et littéraires* (Paris: Tallandier, 1928);

Madame de Chamblay (Paris: Michel Lévy, 1869);

Création et rédemption, 4 volumes (Paris: Michel Lévy frères, 1872)—includes *Le Docteur mystérieux* and *La Fille du marquis;*

Grand Dictionnaire de cuisine (Paris: Lemerre, 1873); translated by A. & J. Davidson as *Dumas on Food. Selections from "Le Grand Dictionnaire de cuisine"* (Charlottesville: University of Virginia Press, 1982; New York & London: Oxford University Press, 1987);

Propos d'art et de cuisine (Paris: Michel Lévy frères, 1877);

La Cour du Roi Pétaud, by Dumas as M. Alexandre and M. Henri (Auguste Cavé, Ferdinand Langlé, and Adolphe de Leuven) (Paris: Lettres Modernes-Minard, 1994);

Le Fils de l'émigré (Paris & Arles: Actes Sud, 1995).

Editions and Collections: *Œuvres complètes d'Alexandre Dumas, Théâtre,* 6 volumes (Paris: Charpentier, 1834–1836; revised edition, Paris: C. Gosselin, 1841);

Théâtre d'Alexandre Dumas. Œuvres nouvelles, 3 volumes (Paris: Passard, 1846);

Œuvres complètes d'Alexandre Dumas, 17 volumes (Paris: Bureau de Siécle, 1850–1857);

Œuvres complètes d'Alexandre Dumas, 225 volumes (Paris: Michel Lévy frères, 1860–1865);

Théâtre complet d'Alexandre Dumas, 15 volumes (Paris: Michel Lévy, 1863–1874);

Œuvres complètes, 38 volumes, edited by Gilbert Sigaux (Lausanne: Editions Rencontre, 1962–1967);

Œuvres complètes (Paris: Calmann-Lévy, 1869–1889);

Théâtre complet, edited by Fernande Bassan (Paris: Lettres Modernes-Minard, 1974–);

The Great Lover and Other Plays, adapted, with an introduction, by Barnett Shaw (New York: Ungar, 1979)—includes *Mlle de Belle-Isle, Kean, La Jeunesse de Louis XIV,* and *Trois entr' actes pour l'amour médecin;*

Préludes poétiques, edited by Claude Schopp (Paris: Editions Champflour, 1989);

A propos de l'art dramatique, edited by Schopp (Paris: Mercure de France, 1996);

L'Invitation à la valse, edited by Jean Thibaudeau (Paris: Merenre de France, 1996).

OTHER: Marceline Desbordes-Valmore, *Les Pleurs,* preface by Dumas (Paris: Charpentier, 1833);

Mémoires de F.-J. Talma, edited and compiled by Dumas (Paris: Souverain, 1849–1859);

Mémoires de Garibaldi, translated by Dumas (Paris: Michel Lévy, 1860); translated by William Robson as *Garibaldi, An Autobiography,* edited by Dumas (London: Routledge, Warne, Routledge, 1860).

SELECTED PERIODICAL PUBLICATIONS–
UNCOLLECTED: *Le Volontaire de '92,* in *Le Monte-Cristo,* second series (25 April 1862–3 October 1862) and *Le Mousquetaire,* second series (23 February 1867–11 March 1867); translated anonymously as *Love and Liberty; or, A Man of the People* (Philadelphia: T. B. Peterson, 1874); republished as *Les Mémoires de René Besson, témoin de la Révolution* (Paris: Editions Champflour, 1989).

The dramatic writings of Alexandre Dumas *père,* long absent from publishers' booklists and often granted little more than *la portion congrue* (an extremely small place) in critical assessments of his literary corpus, seem today to be experiencing something of a renaissance. To be sure, the extent of contemporary interest in Dumas's plays is modest at best and scarcely apparent on theater playbills. Still, new editions of *Antony* (1831; translated, 1880), *Don Juan de Maraña; ou La Chute d'un ange* (1836), *Les Mousquetaires* (The Musketeers, 1845), *La Jeunesse des Mousquetaires* (The Musketeers' Early Years, 1849), and *L'invitation à la valse* (Invitation to the Waltz, 1857) as well as the first editions of *La Cour du Roi Pétaud* (The Court of King Pétaud, 1994) and *Le Fils de l'émigré* (The Emigrant's Son, 1995) are currently available in French bookstores. So, too, are the slowly emerging fascicles of what promises to be the most comprehensive edition yet

published of Dumas's complete dramatic works. Moreover, studies of selected Dumas plays, his drama criticism, his parodists, his censors, and his relationship with his collaborators figure prominently in recent volumes, including two works published under the auspices of the Société des Amis d'Alexandre Dumas (*Cent cinquante ans après* [One Hundred Fifty Years Later, 1995]; *Œuvres et critiques: La Réception critique de Dumas père* [Works and Critiques: The Critical Reception of Dumas *père,* 1996]). Thus, it would seem that the time for a new appraisal of the playwright's contributions to nineteenth-century French drama may finally have come.

Thanks, in part, to works such as *Henri III et sa cour* (1829; translated as *Catherine of Cleves,* 1831), *Antony, La Tour de Nesle* (1832; translated as *The Tower of Nesle; or, The Chamber of Death,* 185?), and *Kean, ou Désordre et génie* (1836; translated as *Edmund Kean, or The Genius and the Libertine,* 1847), Alexandre Dumas *père* can justifiably lay claim to a place among the founding fathers of French Romantic drama. What is more, Dumas's sense of stagecraft, his ability to flesh out compelling characters caught in dramatic situations, his indefatigable energy, and his personal relationships with many of the most important actors and directors of his time make him a major figure among those of his contemporaries who sought fame and fortune in the theater. A drama critic and theater-license holder as well as a playwright, Dumas earned, and lost, substantial sums of money from the various theatrical ventures he undertook during his lifetime. Why, then, are his contributions to French drama so often considered to be less important than those made by Victor Hugo, Alfred de Vigny, or Alfred de Musset? Several possible explanations come to mind.

First, unlike Hugo, whose "Preface" to *Cromwell* (1827) stands out as the foremost pronouncement on and definition of French Romantic drama, or Vigny, whose "Lettre à Lord ***" establishes his views on the relationship between the artist and society, Dumas wrote no treatise that might have helped to establish his bona fides as a *chef de file romantique* (leader of the Romantic movement). In the preface to the 1863 edition of his *Charles VII chez ses grands vassaux* (1831; translated as *Charles VII at the Homes of His Great Vassals,* 1991), the playwright explained his unwillingness to expound a theory of drama:

> Le théâtre est, avant tout, chose de fantaisie; je ne comprends donc pas qu'on l'emprisonne dans un système. . . . accordez liberté entière à tous, . . . et alors chaque individu flairera ce qui convient le mieux à son organi-

sation, amassera ses matériaux, bâtira son monde à part, soufflera dessus pour lui donner la vie, et viendra, au jour dit, avec un résultat sinon complet, du moins original, sinon remarquable, du moins individuel.

(Theater is, above all, a thing of the imagination; I therefore cannot understand imprisoning it within a system. Grant complete freedom to everyone and then each individual will sense what best suits his nature, will collect his materials, build his separate world, breathe life into it, and arrive, on the appointed day, with a work that, if not complete, will at least be original, if not remarkable, at least individual.)

Dumas's emphasis on personal vision, his rejection of the notion that all dramatic writing must conform to specific codes and conventions, is consonant with the early-nineteenth-century idea of Romanticism as liberalism in literature. Such opinions do not, however, serve as a rallying point for a cadre of disciples or mark one's place in the canon as a foundational thinker.

The relative eclipse of Dumas's theatrical works may also be explained by the fact that he composed plays in a variety of genres and styles, often with the aid of one or more collaborators. The abundance and diversity of Dumas's dramatic productions no doubt helped to keep the playwright's name before nineteenth-century theater audiences; since that time, however, the sheer number of his plays has made it difficult for critics to assess his work. A quick glance at the bibliography appended to the end of this study indicates that, until recently, most scholars have elected to focus on plays written during the first fifteen or so years of a theatrical career that spanned more than four decades and have neglected those dramas Dumas derived from his novels. But by narrowing the scope of their investigations, critics have inevitably distorted the picture they present of Dumas's life in the theater. They have also failed to recognize that Dumas's adaptation of narrative texts into dramatic works required significant skill. When audiences came to the theater to "see" a story they already knew, they not only came armed with certain preconceived notions of plot and character but also brought with them clear expectations of the ways in which those works ought to be presented onstage. Dumas almost never failed to satisfy his public's desires and provide new thrills.

Not content with restricting their analyses to a scant fraction of the playwright's works, some scholars have also argued that Dumas's texts lack the linguistic virtuosity, poetic tenor, and philosophical or psychological depth that inspire their admiration for the Romantic dramas of Hugo, Vigny, and Musset.

Their biases make it impossible for these critics to appreciate and account for the power of Dumas's dramatic language to electrify his nineteenth-century audiences. Captured in a well-known drawing by Alfred Johannot, the curtain line from *Antony*—"Elle me résistait, je l'ai assassinée!" (She resisted me, so I killed her!)—is, even today, one of the best-known phrases in all of French Romantic drama. When, on one occasion, Bocage (Pierre-Martinien Tousez), playing the role of Antony, left the stage without uttering this patent falsehood designed to save his mistress's reputation, the audience nearly rioted until Adèle, played by Marie Dorval, "came back from the dead" to declare: "Je lui résistais; il m'a assassinée" (I resisted him, so he killed me). The thunderous applause that followed her declaration not only attests to the auspiciousness of Dorval's solution but also highlights Dumas's skill in writing dialogue that plays on the public's emotions.

Dumas was, moreover, highly conscious of the importance of dramatic pacing and tension, of carefully measured and deliberately postponed revelations that alternately thrill and terrify characters and audiences alike. Quickly mastering the nascent art of mise-en-scène (stagecraft, directing), he understood the importance of such elements as setting, costume, music, and blocking and would shorten intermissions whenever necessary to keep spectators on the edge of their seats. Generally well served by actors and actresses whose energy and thespian skills were perfectly suited to his needs, Dumas filled his dramas with violence and passion; explored issues of gender, class, and identity in modern as well as historical settings; and employed what are now called "special effects" whenever they served his purposes. Whether he borrowed his subject matter from history books or the world around him, from his own novels or the works of other dramatists, or from his personal life, he almost always seemed to know what the public wanted. Thus, in contrast to Hugo, whose monumental drama *Les Burgraves* (1843) failed to win audience approval, Dumas was able to persuade spectators to spend long hours at the theater on two consecutive nights for the performance of the first and second halves of his dramatization of *Monte-Cristo* (1848). Unfortunately, such successes are often viewed as proof of the playwright's commercial rather than artistic acumen and have served to justify critical disdain of his works.

Dumas's collaboration with other dramatists has likewise been held against him. Like the adaptation of novels for the stage, joint authorship was a common practice in nineteenth-century French theater. Thus, in a defense of Eugène Scribe reprinted with other writings in his *Souvenirs dramatiques* (Recollections of Drama, 1868), Dumas declared: "Le collaborateur, c'est un passager intrépidement embarqué dans le même bâtiment que vous et qui vous laisse apercevoir petit à petit qu'il ne sait pas nager, que cependant il faut soutenir sur l'eau au moment du naufrage, au risque de se noyer avec lui, et qui, arrivé à terre, va, disant partout que, sans lui, vous étiez perdu" (A collaborator is a passenger [who has] fearlessly embarked on the same boat as you have and who gradually lets you see that he does not know how to swim; whom you must nonetheless help to stay afloat when the ship sinks even though [in so doing] you risk drowning with him; and who, once back on land, goes about telling everyone that without him, you would have been lost). Dumas was no doubt speaking from personal experience. Over the course of his career he rescued many plays only to be attacked by the very individuals whose texts garnered attention and box-office receipts as a direct result of Dumas's collaboration.

Alexandre Dumas was born on 24 July 1802 in Villers-Cotterêts (Aisne). His mother, Marie-Louise-Elisabeth Labouret, and maternal grandparents, Claude and Marie-Josephe (née Prévost) Labouret, were also natives of Villers. His father, Thomas-Alexandre Dumas Davy de la Pailleterie, had been born in Haiti (known then as Saint Domingue) to the Marquis Antoine-Alexandre Davy de la Pailleterie, a minor French nobleman from the province of Normandy, and Marie-Céssette Dumas, a black slave woman who worked in the marquis's Caribbean plantation house. A young dragoon in the French Revolutionary army, Thomas-Alexandre Dumas met his future wife when he was billeted at the Labouret family inn in August 1789. The couple married in Villers-Cotterêts on 28 November 1792 and subsequently had three children: Alexandrine-Aimée (called Aimée), born in September 1793; Louise-Alexandrine, who lived for only a year following her birth in February 1796; and Alexandre, who was baptized in the local church on 12 August 1802. The boy was not yet four years old when his father, then an ailing, involuntarily retired general, died at the Hôtel de l'Epée in Villers on 26 February 1806. The family's financial circumstances, already straitened prior to Thomas-Alexandre's death, never significantly improved, and by 1816 Mme Dumas was obliged to tell her son to look for work. In August of that year the youth was hired as an errand boy by Maître Mennesson, a family friend and local notary.

In June 1819 Dumas met Adolphe Ribbing de Leuven, a young Swedish nobleman who spent part

Mlle Mars (Anne Boutet) as the Duchesse de Guise in Dumas's Henri III et sa cour

of each year in Villers-Cotterêts and the rest in Paris. It was Leuven, destined to become Dumas's lifelong friend and occasional literary collaborator, who first stimulated the future playwright's love of the theater. In October, Dumas attended a performance of Jean-François Ducis's 1769 adaptation of William Shakespeare's *Hamlet* (circa 1600–1601) in the subprefectoral town of Soissons. Overwhelmed by the experience, the youth purchased a copy of the text and learned the titular role by heart. When Leuven returned to Villers in March 1820, after a five-month stay in Paris, he and Dumas set to work on their first collaborative efforts: "Le Major de Strasbourg" (The Major from Strasbourg), "Un Dîner d'amis" (A Dinner with Friends), and "Les Abencérages" (The Abencérages). No trace remains of these early pieces, which the authors tried unsuccessfully to have produced in Paris. The manuscript of another early work, *Ivanhoë,* which Dumas wrote after reading the novel by Sir Walter Scott, has survived. Its discovery in a library in Dieppe led to its tardy premiere in 1966.

Dumas made a brief trip to Paris in November 1822, a few short months after beginning to work as a second clerk in the law offices of Maître Lefèvre in Crépy-en-Valois. During his stay he attended a performance of Etienne de Jouy's *Sylla* and met the play's star, the celebrated tragedian François-Joseph Talma, whose *Mémoires* he later edited (1849–1850). Upon his return from the French capital Dumas was dismissed from his post, which he had left without asking permission from his employer.

Dumas next returned to Paris in late March 1823 determined to find a job. Having no marketable talents, he seemed destined to fail in that endeavor. Then, Gen. Maximilien Foy discovered the young man's skills in penmanship and recommended him for a position on the secretarial staff of Louis-Philippe, Duc d'Orléans. On 10 April 1823 Dumas began working in the staff offices located in the Palais Royal. There, under the supervision of Jacques-Parfait Oudard, the young man copied correspondence to be sent out under official signature. He was soon befriended by Oudard's assistant, Hippolyte Lassagne, who directed him to read works by modern and classical dramatists, novelists, and memorialists, and who later collaborated with Dumas and Alphonse Vulpian to write a vaudeville titled *La Noce et l'enterrement* (The Wedding and the Burial). The play opened at the Théâtre de la Porte Saint-Martin on 21 November 1826 and was published the same year.

It was also in 1823 that Dumas unexpectedly met Charles Nodier at a performance of Nodier's melodrama *Le Vampire* (1820). Dumas grew extremely fond of the Arsenal librarian and later frequented his literary salon. Dumas's own similarly titled play of 1851 is best read alongside the older man's fantastical text and may be considered one of several literary testaments to their friendship.

From 8 April 1823 until 20 February 1824 Dumas lived in a building at 1, place des Italiens (today Place Boïeldieu). There he met Marie-Catherine-Laure Labay, a seamstress whose lodgings were across the hall from his; she soon became his mistress. On 27 July 1824 Labay gave birth to Dumas's son, whom she named Alexandre. Although the baby's parents remained lovers for a time, they never married, and Dumas did not legally recognize the child's existence until March 1831.

On 11 September 1827 Dumas again attended a performance of *Hamlet,* this time performed in English by a visiting troupe of actors including Fanny Kemble, Edmund Kean, William Charles Macready, and Harriet Smithson. The experience left him spellbound, and he immediately began studying the playwriting techniques of Shakespeare, Johann Wolfgang von Goethe, Friedrich Schiller, and Pedro Calderón de la Barca. Essaying his hand at those techniques led Dumas to compose an adaptation of Schiller's *Fiesque* (1783), a five-act historical drama in prose titled "Fiesque de Lavagna" [1827]. The play was never performed, but Dumas did reuse parts of it in his *Lorenzino* (1842). In 1847 he adapted yet another Schiller play, *Intrigue et amour* (Intrigue and Love, 1784).

Once Dumas was transferred to the Duc d'Orléans forestry office in February 1828 and given permission to write what he pleased after completing his official assignments, his studies began to bear fruit. Urged on by Mélanie Waldor, a minor poetess and literary-salon hostess who had become his mistress in September 1827, Dumas set to work on a five-act verse tragedy based on the life of Queen Christine of Sweden. His play was accepted by the reading committee of the Théâtre-Français on 4 August 1828. It was rehearsed but not immediately performed despite the *tour de faveur* (priority status) it was granted in September. When Dumas learned that the premiere of *Christine* would be postponed by the performance of Louis Brault's *Christine de Suède* (Théâtre-Français, 25 June 1829) and by Frédéric Soulié's play on the same subject (Théâtre de l'Odéon, 13 October 1829), he set to writing another drama.

Within the space of two months he had composed a five-act historical drama in prose, *Henri III et sa cour.* Accepted by the Théâtre-Français's reading committee on 17 October 1828 and then granted the tour de faveur previously attributed to *Christine,* the new play quickly went into rehearsal. Soon Dumas began to neglect his secretarial duties in order to oversee preparations for the performance of his piece and was forced to resign his post. He nonetheless invited the Duc d'Orléans and his dinner guests to attend the premiere of the play on 11 February 1829. With François Firmin cast as Saint-Mégrin and Mlle Mars (Anne Boutet) in the role of the Duchesse de Guise, the work was a triumph. It was the first Romantic drama to succeed at the Théâtre-Français, which, until then, had been considered an almost inviolable bastion of aesthetic conservatism.

What distinguished Dumas's drama from those works typically performed at the Théâtre-Français was not only its prose (rather than verse) text, its violation of the unities of time and place, its emphasis on local color, and its use of staging tech-

Caricature of Dumas and Victor Hugo, leading playwrights of the Romantic movement, being
chased from the Théâtre-Français, a bastion of Classicism

niques more commonly associated with Boulevard theaters, but also its "unseemly" (from a neoclassical perspective) display of physical violence. Thus, although Saint-Mégrin does die out of sight of the audience—a bow to the *bienséances* (decorous restraint) prescribed by the conventions of neoclassical dramaturgy—the public is allowed to witness the Duc de Guise's brutal treatment of his wife. In act 3, for example, the duke crushes his wife's arm with his iron gauntlet as he compels her to write a letter of assignation meant to trap Saint-Mégrin. In act 5 he drags the duchess to the window, forcing her to watch Saint-Mégrin be strangled with a handkerchief bearing her coat of arms. Such scenes of physical (rather than verbal) aggression toward women were not normally tolerated at the Théâtre-Français; they did, however, reappear in other dramas by Dumas.

Inspired by passages from Louis-Pierre d'Anquetil's *L'Esprit de la Ligue* (The Spirit of the League, 1767) and Pierre de L'Estoile's *Mémoires pour servir à l'histoire de France* (Memoirs Intended to Serve as a Basis for the History of France, 1719), *Henri III et sa cour* features a seemingly ineffectual sixteenth-century French king, Henri III; his conniving, power-hungry mother, Catherine de Médicis; his political rival, the Duc de Guise; and a handsome

young nobleman—one of the king's favorites, Saint-Mégrin—who is secretly in love with the Duchesse de Guise. As the play begins, the Queen Mother, worried that her influence over her son and over matters of state is on the wane, sets out to weaken both the growing political powers of the Duc de Guise and the affection that binds Henri to Saint-Mégrin. Using the duchess as an unwitting pawn, Catherine adroitly provokes a series of confrontations between the duke and the king's minion. After several twists and turns, including Henri's unexpected success in supplanting Guise as the head of the Holy Catholic League and Saint-Mégrin's treacherous assassination, the Queen Mother's powers and the king's reign seem, for the moment, to be solidly reestablished.

Many of what became the standard features of Dumas's dramatic writing are clearly in evidence in this first successful piece. In *Henri III,* as in several subsequent plays, one finds a visually compelling, historically suggestive picture of a society caught in the midst of a political conflict: real people and places used as a backdrop for an invented tale of passion and ambition, masterfully crafted dialogues and bits of stage business that lead to powerfully dramatic conclusions, lovers who are separated by death, women who are portrayed as either angels or devils, profound and meaningful friendships between men, practicable sets (including secret passages, open windows, and barricaded doors) that play a critical role in the action, and fantastical and/or occult beliefs and practices that darken the atmosphere of the drama and complicate its outcome. The success of *Henri III* was signaled in typical Parisian fashion by the creation of four parodies—one of which, *La Cour du roi Pétaud,* Dumas himself helped to pen.

Though suddenly a successful playwright, Dumas resumed working for the Duc d'Orléans and was soon assigned a position as assistant librarian at the Palais Royal. Later, in 1831, he resigned that post on political grounds. Before that time, however, a revised version of *Christine* opened at the Odéon (30 March 1830), where it met with only limited success.

In June 1830 Dumas began a liaison with the actress Belle Krelsamer, known in the theater as Mélanie Serre. Soon pregnant with his child, she forced Dumas to break with Mélanie Waldor. Belle gave birth to a daughter, Marie-Alexandrine, on 5 March 1831, and two days later Dumas legally recognized the child as his. Dumas's complicated love life did not prevent him from participating in the July Revolution in 1830 or from continuing to write for the theater. His *Napoléon Bonaparte, ou Trente Ans dans l'histoire de France* (Napoleon Bonaparte, or Thirty Years in the History of France) opened at the Odéon on 10 January 1831. The action of that drama, produced during the brief postrevolutionary demise of theatrical censorship, spans the period from 1793 to 1821 and focuses on six critical moments in Napoleon's career. The eponymous hero is presented as a man of destiny who is simple, devoted to France and its people, and willing to share their suffering but who is, in defeat, abandoned by those whose fortunes he made. The title role was played by Frédérick Lemaître; the unnamed spy who reappears in each of the drama's six acts and who alone remains faithful to the end was played by Lockroy (Etienne-Auguste-Edouard Simon).

Although originally destined for the Théâtre-Français, Dumas's next work, *Antony,* was first performed at the Théâtre de la Porte Saint-Martin on 3 May 1831. The most personal of Dumas's plays, this five-act verse drama is loosely based on Dumas's relationship with Mélanie Waldor, and some of the dialogue is borrowed from the lovers' correspondence. This piece, which, by virtue of its contemporary setting and costumes and its superior but outcast hero, has been called the first modern social drama, became an even greater triumph than *Henri III* and went on to mark another milestone in the history of French Romanticism. Dumas ordered that intermissions be shortened to sustain the work's heightened emotions, and the audience, moved to a fever pitch of excitement by the performances of Bocage and Dorval, responded with frenzied applause when the celebrated curtain line drew the play to a close.

A modern drama of adultery set in the faubourg Saint-Honoré, *Antony* focuses on the tensions between the individual and society in contemporary Paris. Although a man of exceptional merit, Antony had some years earlier been denied the right to wed his beloved Adèle because his parentage was unknown. Embittered and alienated from society, he has just returned to the French capital after a long absence and is determined to pursue the woman he still loves. Adèle, in the meantime, has been obliged by her family to marry Colonel d'Hervey and has borne him a child. When she learns of Antony's impending arrival, Adèle, whose husband is temporarily stationed in Strasbourg, attempts to flee. The horses drawing her carriage bolt, however, and Antony is seriously wounded in a successful effort to stop them. Taken into Adèle's home, he tells the young woman of his undying love for her and of the suffering he has endured as a result of society's cruelty to those of illegitimate birth. Later Adèle, whose feelings for Antony are clearly in conflict with her duty as a wife and mother, quits Paris and rushes toward her husband's billet, hoping the colonel will save her from herself. Surprised and infuriated by her departure, Antony rushes after her and secures all the horses and all the rooms at the last inn before Strasbourg. When Adèle arrives, she is forced to spend the night in a room which, unbeknownst to her, shares a balcony with Antony's quarters. He breaks into her room and makes her his mistress. The lovers do not live happily ever after, however. At a social event in Paris some months later, Adèle, whose affair with Antony is known and a source of scandal, is publicly insulted. The young woman's despair is heightened when it is learned that her husband is en route back to Paris and should arrive at any moment. To save her reputation and her daughter's future, Antony stabs Adèle to death as her husband breaks down the door to her apartments. He then tells d'Hervey: "Elle me résistait, je l'ai assassinée!" (She resisted me, so I killed her!).

Antony's black frock coat and dagger, superiority and passion, illegitimate birth and social ostracism clearly identify him as a modern Romantic hero. Adèle's conflicted emotions, victimization, despair, and death likewise mark her as a Romantic heroine. Interestingly, Dumas appears to have re-

A scene from Dumas's Monte-Cristo *(1848), the melodrama he adapted from his 1844–1845 novel*

fashioned *Antony* in a much later work, a one-act comedy titled *L'Honneur est satisfait* (Honor Is Satisfied, 1858). Not only does the title of this later play echo Adèle's preoccupation with honor, but the pursuit of the heroine, Edmée, by a man who wishes to impose his attentions on her, and her frustrated attempt to rejoin her brother (a military officer) are also clearly reminiscent of Adèle's situation in *Antony*. This time, however, the young woman, who is unmarried, cannot immediately leave the hotel to which she has been followed because there is no train available until evening. Luckily, her brother, who had earlier checked out of the same hotel, has missed his train due to a carriage accident and soon returns to the inn. After Edmée refuses the offer of marriage made by the English nobleman (an orphan) who has been pursuing her, he is challenged to a duel by her brother. The young woman soon changes her mind about her suitor, however. Edmée's brother fires his weapon into the air, and "honor is satisfied." Set in an even more modern era than *Antony* and given a much less "melodramatic" ending, the play can be read as a comic revision of the playwright's youthful work.

Before arriving at that point in his career, however, Dumas wrote many other pieces fully imbued with Romantic and/or melodramatic excesses. His next major work after *Antony* was a five-act verse tragedy titled *Charles VII chez ses grands vassaux* (Charles with His Great Vassals, 1831), a play whose subject he claimed to have drawn from Alain

Chartier's medieval *Chronique du Roi Charles VII* (Chronicle of King Charles VII). Set against the background of the Hundred Years' War, in a gothic-style castle in le Berry, the play features a captured Saracen, Yaqoub, who has been enslaved and made the property of Count Charles de Savoisy; the count's barren wife, Bérengère, whom the cruel vassal of Charles VII divorces so he can marry a younger woman and sire an heir; as well as a host of other figures, including Agnès Sorel and her lover, the pleasure-seeking monarch whose name appears in the title of the piece. In the end Yaqoub, a tool of Bérengère's jealousy and desire for vengeance as much as of his own hatreds, kills the count. Despite everything, however, Bérengère still loves her husband, and so she poisons herself. As the play concludes, Yaqoub, told that he had been granted his freedom by the count, leaves for his homeland, and Charles VII decides to renounce his life of idle pleasures to fight the English for possession of his realm. Dumas was not, by nature, especially adept at writing verse drama, and thus, despite several interesting features and an extravagant mise-en-scène that included live animals, *Charles VII* cannot be counted as one of his best works.

The year 1831, which began with the opening of *Napoléon Bonaparte* at the Théâtre de l'Odéon, concluded with the premiere of *Richard Darlington* at the Théâtre de la Porte Saint-Martin. A three-act prose drama with prologue, written by Dumas, Prosper-Parfait Goubaux, and Jacques-Félix Beudin, the play is set in eighteenth-century England and starred Frédérick Lemaître in the title role. Like Antony, Richard was abandoned at birth by parents who never publicly recognized his existence. Richard, however, is not totally excluded from society. Raised by a doctor, whose daughter he quietly marries, he obtains a moderate income and becomes a member of the House of Commons. Then he is offered great wealth and a marriage that will elevate him to the rank of lord if he agrees to support a bill in Parliament. Eager to accept this proposition that will satisfy his political and social ambitions, Richard kills his wife, who has lived a discreet existence in the provinces and who, because she loves him, was unwilling to grant him a divorce. Denounced by his birth father—the Crown's executioner—who has seen him commit this crime, Richard does not profit from his heartless, cynical deed.

Tragic deaths and romantic conflicts are also at the heart of Dumas's next play, *Teresa,* which premiered at the Théâtre de l'Opéra-Comique on 6 February 1832 with Ida Ferrier, Dumas's most recent mistress, in the role of Amélie Delaunay. The play's star-crossed lovers, the eponymous Teresa and Arthur de Savigny, first meet during a dramatic eruption of Mount Vesuvius in Naples in 1805 but then lose track of each other. Some months later they find themselves living in the same household in France since Teresa has recently married Baron Delaunay and Arthur is engaged to Amélie, the baron's daughter from his first marriage. Although Arthur marries Amélie, he still loves Teresa, who shares his feelings. The two continue to see each other in private whenever possible and regularly write passionate love letters to one another. Delaunay eventually discovers their liaison but withdraws his challenge to a duel after learning that Amélie, who knows nothing of her husband's affair, is pregnant. The baron then dispatches Arthur and Amélie to Saint Petersburg, where the young man has diplomatic responsibilities, and orders him to keep silent about his relationship with Teresa. Teresa's feelings of despair on being separated from her lover lead her to commit suicide. Her servant, Paolo, who helps her to die and who has long loved her in silence, then kills himself rather than remain alone in France.

On 29 May 1832 *La Tour de Nesle,* a five-act historical drama loosely inspired by legends surrounding Marguerite de Bourgogne's nightly orgies in the Nesle Tower, opened at the Théâtre de la Porte Saint-Martin with Frédérick Lemaître in the role of Captain Buridan and Mlle George (Marguerite Weimar) as Marguerite. Based on a manuscript by Frédéric Gaillardet, the play had been significantly revised by Dumas, who was asked to undertake the task by the Théâtre de la Porte Saint-Martin's manager, Charles-Jean Harel. Dumas added a new opening tavern scene, a prison scene in act 3, and several dramatic twists. In the end only the core of Gaillardet's plot remained, and even though Dumas had requested that his name not be mentioned, Harel leaked word of Dumas's collaboration and announced the play as the work of "MM. *** and F. Gaillardet." After bitter lawsuits, exchanges in the press, and even a duel between the two writers, Gaillardet in 1861 gave formal consent for Dumas's name to appear on a play that Dumas had already published as his own work.

Set in Paris in 1314, the darkly dramatic events of this tale of passion and ambition, crime and punishment turn on the secrets that the enigmatic Captain Buridan (whose real name is Lyonnet de Bournonville) shares with the debauched queen. Will his knowledge of her past and present transgressions make his fortune (he wishes to be named prime minister) or result in his death? As the play progresses, each of these protagonists triumphs momentarily over the other. In the end, after the queen has unwittingly assassinated both of the couple's illegitimate twin sons (who were supposed to have been done away with as infants), Marguerite and Buridan die together, victims of their lust for power and of the moral conventions of melodrama. The success of this dark drama was so great that three decades later, when Paul Féval sought to give his *Cœur d'acier* (Heart of Steel, 1866)—a novel whose action is set in Paris in 1832—a grounding in history and local color, he elected to have his principal characters disguise themselves for Mardi Gras in costumes inspired by those worn by the protagonists in Dumas's play.

Following their success in *La Tour de Nesle,* Lemaître and George played the leads in *Le Fils de l'émigré* (The Emigrant's Son, 1832)—Dumas's next dramatic work at the Théâtre de la Porte Saint-Martin. The original idea for the play was suggested by Auguste Anicet-Bourgeois, who wrote the final act and was to have been the work's publicly acknowledged author. As in the case of *La Tour de Nesle,* however, Harel again put Dumas's name forward. The prologue to the piece, set at the time of the French Revolution, is followed by four acts that take place in 1815. It is revealed that the play's titular character, although raised as the eldest child of a humble and generous arms merchant, was in fact conceived after his mother was raped by a nobleman. The personality and behavior of the boy's perverse and hateful biological father, Edouard de Bray, is set in contrast to the integrity, dignity, and affection Dumas suggests is typical of the modest class of people among whom the child is raised. The drama's provocative political thesis (it paints a highly negative portrait of the vengefulness and tyranny of the upper class) and the use of the banned revolutionary anthem, "La Marseillaise," in the prologue led to virulent attacks in the royalist press. The hostile reception of the piece briefly caused Dumas to cease writing for the stage. He even excluded the text from editions of his complete dramatic works.

Politics figure, too, in *Angèle,* the drama that marked Dumas's return to the Théâtre de la Porte Saint-Martin in late 1833 and which he again wrote in collaboration with Anicet-Bourgeois. This time, however, the action takes place in 1830 and is set against the backdrop of a more recent change in political regimes (the last Bourbon king is replaced by his Orléans cousin–the very Louis-Philippe d'Orléans for whom Dumas had once worked). In the play the unprincipled Alfred d'Alvimar seduces the young Angèle de Gaston, whom he briefly considers marrying in order to advance his political career. However, soon he abandons Angèle for her widowed mother, believing that she will serve his ambition even more effectively. On the day Alfred prepares to wed Angèle's mother, the young woman, who unbeknownst to him is pregnant with his child, arrives unexpectedly and asks him to send for a doctor. Dr. Muller, who has long loved Angèle, does not initially recognize the masked woman whose baby he delivers, but he soon discovers the truth. When Alfred attempts to flee his responsibilities, Muller challenges the callous nobleman to a duel, kills him, and then marries Angèle to protect her honor and give her child a name. Bocage played Alfred; Lockroy played the fatally ill Muller, who suffers from tuberculosis; Ferrier played Angèle; and Serre played Ernestine, the mistress Alfred leaves at the opening of the play because of her connections to the Bourbons. The play's moralistic conclusion–a slap in the face to egotism and the exploitation of women to advance one's career–greatly contributed to the drama's success, as did the relative absence of romantic excesses.

Womanizing and ambition, along with excess, were very much the order of the day in two subsequent pieces by Dumas: *Don Juan de Maraña, ou La Chute d'un ange* (Don Juan de Maraña, or An Angel's Fall, 1836) and *Kean, ou Désordre et génie.* On 30 April 1836 Dumas's *Don Juan* opened at the Théâtre de la Porte Saint-Martin with music composed by Louis-Alexandre Piccini. Dumas qualifies the play as a *mystère,* using a term associated with medieval religious drama, and in it he shows good and bad angels fighting for possession of Don Juan's soul. Inspired by Prosper Mérimée's short story *Les Âmes du purga-*

Ida Ferrier, the actress whom Dumas married in 1840 (lithograph by A. Constant)

toire (Souls in Purgatory, 1834), which Dumas had read, the work starred Bocage in the title role and Ferrier in the dual role of the Good Angel/Sister Marthe. The play, which capitalizes on the romantic fascination with Don Juan and the theme of fallen angels, was applauded by Charles Nodier as the first French drama that, like Shakespeare's *Tempest* or Goethe's *Faust,* used fantastical elements to serious effect. Such elements here include raising Don Juan's father from the dead so that he can legally recognize the titular character's illegitimate elder brother, Don Josès, as his heir, and appearances by the Virgin Mary and a host of good and bad angels. In Dumas's piece Don Juan makes conscious choices; he moves from crime to repentance, then returns to a life of debauchery, and in the end is damned despite the intervention of an angel who gives up her soul and her place in heaven to save him. In an 1864 revised version of the play Don Juan is saved in the end. *Don Juan* is a luridly romantic work with spectacular stage effects and prose as well as verse passages. It is a work that surely deserves to be better known. While not entirely representative of Dumas's writings for the stage, it does share certain characteristics with his early dramas and with at least one later one: *Urbain Grandier* (1850).

In July 1836 Dumas became drama critic for *La Presse*–a job he held while continuing to create original works. *Kean, ou Désordre et génie,* the best-known drama Dumas wrote during this period, opened at the Théâtre des Variétés on 31 August 1836. A revised and expanded version of a work originally written by Marie-Emmanuel Théaulon de Lambert and Frédéric de Courcy, the play was published under Dumas's signature alone. The titular character, a celebrated English actor who is depicted as a known womanizer and drunkard living beyond his means, was played by Frédérick Lemaître, whose performance greatly contributed to the work's success. In Dumas's play Kean is shown to be the darling of the upper class and the frequent companion of the licentious Prince of Wales, as long as he remembers his place. When he presumes to forget that he is nothing more than a *saltimbanque* (clown, mere entertainer), he is quickly reminded of his true status. Dumas uses his "portrait" of Edmund Kean as a means to discuss the nature of art and the place of the artist in society just one year after Vigny used the figure of Thomas Chatterton for a similar purpose in his *Chatterton*. Each playwright, in his own fashion, proposes his view of the artist as genius and social outcast.

In 1837 Dumas and Victor Hugo obtained government authorization to open a new theater, the Théâtre de la Renaissance, where they planned to produce works in the Romantic vein written by themselves and others. Their endeavor was short-lived, however. Financial failure, due to mismanagement by the director they hired to run the day-to-day operations, quickly forced them to close the theater.

In 1839, working in collaboration with Gérard de Nerval, Dumas wrote *L'Alchimiste* (translated as *The Alchemist,* 1940) a play that opened at the Théâtre de la Renaissance on 10 April and whose paternity was attributed solely to Dumas. On 16 April of that same year *Léo Burckart,* also written with Nerval and attributed to him, opened at the Théâtre de la Porte Saint-Martin. (Controversy still rages over the authorship of this latter work, which was recently reprised at the Comédie-Française for the first time since 1839.) Two weeks earlier, on 2 April, Dumas's five-act drama (later labeled a comedy) *Mademoiselle de Belle-Isle,* possibly written with Count F.-A. J. Wale[w]ski, opened at the Théâtre-Français. The title role was composed for Mlle Mars, who at age sixty still played ingenue parts and who contributed greatly to the play's success. Firmin played the Duc de Richelieu, grandnephew of the cardinal and a man known for his many love affairs. The action, which takes place at the Marquise de Prie's castle in Chantilly in 1726, turns on Richelieu's boastful wager that he will spend the night with the first woman he sees. Chance designates Gabrielle de Belle-Isle, the fiancée of Raoul d'Aubigny (played by Lockroy), as his victim. After sending Gabrielle off through a secret door to visit her imprisoned father, Prie takes the young woman's place in bed. Both Richelieu and d'Aubigny are fooled by this stratagem, and Gabrielle, who has sworn not to reveal her whereabouts on the evening in question, fears her reputation and her future are forever compromised. Later, however, the truth is divulged and Gabrielle is free to marry her beloved Raoul. Mistaken identities, secret passages, and questions of honor are, as has been noted, frequent in Dumas's dramas; here, for once, the resulting confusion and conflicts are resolved happily.

On 5 February 1840, much to the dismay of Alexandre *fils,* Dumas married Ida Ferrier. Deeply in debt, the couple left almost immediately for Florence, where they hoped to live more cheaply. While in Florence, Dumas worked on several projects, including a comedy, *Un Mariage sous Louis XV* (1841; translated as *A Marriage of Convenience,* 1897), and a five-act drama, *Lorenzino* (1842). Inspired by the same events as those depicted in Musset's *Lorenzaccio, Lorenzino* opened at the Théâtre-Français on 24 February 1842. Dumas reduced the number of characters and settings and modified the duration of the action and the relationships among some of the protagonists found in Musset's piece. Thus while the once pure and studious Lorenzino (played by Pierre-François Beauvallet) still debauches himself in order to deceive and then assassinate his cousin Alexandre de Médicis, Duke of Florence (played by Firmin), in Dumas's reworking of the play the young man is engaged to Luisa Strozzi, daughter of the republican leader Philippe Strozzi. In Dumas's drama Lorenzino uses Luisa to lure his cousin to his doom. Because the young woman mistakenly believes that her fiancé truly intends to prostitute her to the duke, she drinks poison. Although she later learns of Lorenzino's true purpose, she cannot be saved and dies soon after Alexandre is killed. Despite Dumas's efforts to adapt the play to standard performance practices and contemporary aesthetic expectations, his play had only seven performances. Some critics have blamed its failure on the fact that Dumas did not closely supervise the production himself; others have held that the work was an inferior piece. Whatever the exact cause of its poor showing, Dumas's drama at the least allows us to see just how unusual Musset's theatrical project was for its time.

Dumas's next dramatic work, *Les Demoiselles de Saint-Cyr* (1843; translated as *The Ladies of Saint-Cyr, or The Runaway Husbands,* 1870), premiered at the Théâtre-Français on 25 July 1843. It is a light comedy whose action is set in the year 1700. Young Roger de Saint-Hérem has fallen in love with Charlotte de Mérian, whom he has seen performing in Jean Racine's *Esther* (1689) at Saint-Cyr. Hoping to seduce her, he proposes a nocturnal assignation in an isolated pavilion on that convent school's grounds. When she agrees to meet him, he decides to bring along his friend Hercule Dubouloy to occupy Charlotte's inseparable companion, Louise Mauclair. Louise, however, reveals the arrangement to the school's founder and headmistress (and Louis XIV's morganatic wife), Mme de Maintenon, who catches the young couples together and tells the men that they must either marry her "dishonored" charges or go to prison. The two youths begrudgingly agree to marriage and then leave for Spain without their spouses. The abandoned women follow them there and, after a series of events that spark their husbands' jealousy, are reconciled with the young men and return with them to France. Some critics were shocked by the "immoral" character of this work, which is set in one of France's most respectable boarding schools for young women, but the play, to which Leuven and Léon Lhérie both contributed, was nonetheless a success.

During the next decade Dumas's theatrical career centered on the adaptation of his novels. Written most often in association with Auguste Maquet, whom he had met through Nerval in 1839 and with whom he had collaborated in writing the novels, these dramatizations extended Dumas's fame and popular success. They were marked by elaborate and at times innovative staging and sets, and by the association of Dumas and the actor Etienne Marin Mélingue, who performed the leading roles in such plays as *Monte-Cristo* (1848) and *Les Mousquetaires.*

Not all of Dumas's writings for the theater were drawn from his own novels, however. On 14 September 1846 Dumas and Paul Meurice's *Hamlet, prince de Danemark,* a five-act verse drama based on Shakespeare's play, premiered at the Théâtre de Saint-Germain with Dumas's current mistress, Béatrix Person, playing Ophelia and Philibert Rouvière as Hamlet. The piece, which Dumas had composed from a draft by Meurice in 1842 and which he continued to revise over a period of years, reopened in Paris on 15 December 1847 at the Théâtre-Historique. Written in verse, the composition significantly modified parts of Shakespeare's text. It

Château de Monte-Cristo, the lavish residence that Dumas had built in Port-Marly during the mid 1840s

was, nonetheless, a vast improvement over Jean-François Ducis's late-eighteenth-century adaptation of the play and eventually became the standard version of Shakespeare's tragedy performed at the Théâtre-Français well into the twentieth century.

After an extended trip to Spain for the marriage of the Duc de Montpensier to the Infanta Luisa Fernanda and to North Africa to negotiate for the release of some French prisoners of war, Dumas returned to Paris in time for the opening, on 20 February 1847, of his and Maquet's adaptation of their novel *La Reine Margot* (1845; translated as *Marguerite de Valois,* 1846) at the Théâtre-Historique. Dumas had obtained the patent for this theater, which was to be dedicated to the performance of his own works, thanks to the influence of Montpensier, who was his friend and the fifth son of King Louis-Philippe. The success of several of his pieces notwithstanding, poor management practices and excessive production costs as well as the outbreak of the Revolution of 1848 and other circumstances led to the closing of the Théâtre-Historique on 16 October 1850. Forced into bankruptcy in December, Dumas and his latest mistress, Isabelle Constant–a young actress who had studied with Mlle George–moved to Brussels a year later to avoid his creditors.

Before their departure *Urbain Grandier* and *La Chasse au chastre* (Hunting the Chastre) had opened at the Théâtre-Historique on 30 March and 3 August 1850, respectively, and the third and fourth parts of Dumas and Maquet's adaptation of *Monte-Cristo* premiered at the Théâtre de l'Ambigu-Comique (on 1 April and 8 May 1851, respectively). It would be almost three years, following his return from exile, before Dumas would produce a new work on the Parisian stage. In 1857 Maquet sued Dumas for back wages and royalties but lost; the relationship between the two men had been strained since 1848, and this suit permanently ended their collaboration, which had already all but ceased by the time Dumas left for Belgium.

Ida Ferrier died in Genoa on 11 March 1859; Dumas had been legally separated from her since October 1844 and shed no tears on learning of her death. The final years of Dumas's life were marked by a brief liaison with the American actress Adah Isaacs Menken and by the publication of the weekly paper *Théâtre-Journal* from 5 July 1868 to March 1869. Dumas's dramatization of his novel *Les Blancs et les bleus* (1867–1868; translated as *The First Republic; or, The Whites and the Blues,* 1895), which opened at the Théâtre du Châtelet on 10 March 1869, was the last work to be staged during his lifetime. In September 1870 Dumas moved to Dieppe to live with Alexandre *fils;* he died at his son's home on 5 December of that year. His body was transferred to its final resting place in Villers-Cotterêts in 1872.

There is much that remains to be written about Dumas's theatrical career. The most prolific and successful (when measured by nineteenth-century audience response) of the French Romantic dramatists, his work continues to be ignored or dismissed as puerile and passé by critics and theater directors alike. A man of the theater in every sense of the phrase–playwright, director, license holder, drama critic–Dumas may have had no declared disciples. It is, however, impossible to imagine that his long and generally auspicious career in the theater failed to have any impact whatsoever on the evolution of nineteenth-century French drama. What is more, while Dumas's plays at times lack the refinement and stylistic elegance that critics of his and the present era

frequently take as a sign of literary excellence, they are not without interesting insights into the preoccupations and the sociopolitical structures of his age. Dumas's work for the theater is rich and complex and deserves to be rescued from the dismissive opinions and limited dimensions to which it has so long been confined.

Letters:
Lettres d'Alexandre Dumas à Mélanie Waldor, edited by Claude Schopp (Paris: Presses universitaires de France, 1982);
Narcisse et Hyacinthe. Correspondance amoureuse avec Hyacinthe Meinier, edited by Schopp (Paris: Eds. François Bourin, 1991);
Frères d'armes de la révolution romantique: Lettres d'Alexandre Dumas au Baron Taylor et à Adrien Dauzats, edited by Schopp (Paris: Fondation Taylor, 1993);
Claude Schopp, "Correspondance générale d'Alexandre Dumas pour 1844," in *Cent cinquante ans apres,* edited by Fernande Bassan and Schopp (Marly-le-Roi: Eds. Champflour, 1995), pp. 233–271;
Alexandre Dumas, ses fills et leurs mères, edited by Schopp, *Cahiers Alexandre Dumas,* no. 24 (1997): 5–149.

Bibliographies:
Frank Wilde Reed, *A Bibliography of Alexandre Dumas père* (London: J. A. Neuhys, 1933);
Douglas Munro, *Alexandre Dumas père: A Bibliography of Works Translated into English to 1910* (New York & London: Garland, 1978);
Munro, *Dumas père: A Bibliography of Works Published in French, 1825–1900* (New York & London: Garland, 1981);
Munro, *Alexandre Dumas père: A Secondary Bibliography of French and English Sources to 1983, with Appendices* (New York & London: Garland, 1985);
Réginald Hamel and Pierrette Méthé, *Dictionnaire Dumas* (Montreal: Editions Guérin, 1988);
Fernande Bassan and Claude Schopp, "Orientation bibliographique sur Dumas. . . ," in *Œuvres et critiques,* 21, no. 1 (1996): 157–164.

Biographies:
A. Craig Bell, *Alexandre Dumas: A Biography and a Study* (London: Cassell, 1950);
Henri Clouard, *Alexandre Dumas* (Paris: Albin Michel, 1955);
André Maurois, *Les Trois Dumas* (Paris: Hachette, 1957); translated by Gerard Hopkins as *The Titans: A Three-Generation Biography of the Dumas* (New York: Harper, 1957); also published as

The Three Musketeers: A Study of the Dumas Family (London: Cape, 1957);

Jean de Lamaze, *Alexandre Dumas père* (Paris: Pierre Charon, 1972);

Richard S. Stowe, *Alexandre Dumas père* (Boston: Twayne, 1976);

F. W. J. Hemmings, *The King of Romance: A Portrait of Alexandre Dumas* (London: Hamish Hamilton, 1979);

Michael Ross, *Alexandre Dumas* (London: David & Charles, 1981);

Jean Thibaudeau, *Alexandre Dumas, le prince des Mousquetaires* (Paris: Hachette, 1983);

Claude Schopp, *Alexandre Dumas: Le Génie de la vie* (Paris: Editions Mazarine, 1985); translated by A. J. Koch as *Alexandre Dumas: Genius of Life* (New York & Toronto: Watts, 1988); revised edition of French original (Paris: Fayard, 1997);

Christian Biet, Jean-Paul Brighelli, and Jean-Luc Rispail, *Alexandre Dumas, ou les Aventures d'un romancier* (Paris: Gallimard, 1986);

Daniel Zimmermann, *Alexandre Dumas le grand* (Paris: Julliard, 1993);

Yves-Marie Lucot, *Dumas père et fils* (Woignarue: Vague verte, 1997).

References:

A. O. Aldridge, "The Vampire Theme: Dumas père and the English Stage," *Revue des langues vivantes,* 39 (1973): 312–324;

Marie-Antoinette Allevy, as Akakia Viala, *Edition critique d'une mise en scène: Henri III et sa cour* (Paris: Droz, 1938);

Michel Autrand, "*Les Trois Mousquetaires* au théâtre–*La Jeunesse des Mousquetaires*," in *Cent cinquante ans après,* edited by Fernande Bassan and Claude Schopp (Marly-le-Roi: Editions Champflour, 1995), pp. 9–20;

Philippe Baron, "La Parodie d'*Angèle*," *Œuvres et critiques,* 21, no. 1 (1996): 105–111;

Baron, "*La Reine Christine* d'Alexandre Dumas à Strindberg," in *Cent cinquante ans après,* pp. 200–207;

Fernande Bassan, "L'Accueil fait à *Richard Darlington*," *Œuvres et critiques,* 55–61;

Bassan, "Les Adaptations théâtrales du *Comte de Monte-Cristo*," in *Cent cinquante ans après,* pp. 94–101;

Bassan, "Le Cycle des *Trois Mousquetaires*–du roman au théâtre," *Studia Neophilologica,* 57 (1985): 243–249;

Bassan, "Dumas père et l'histoire: A propos du drame *La Reine Margot*," *Revue d'Histoire du Théâtre,* 39, no. 4 (1987): 384–392;

Bassan, "Histoire de *La Tour de Nesle* de Dumas père et Gaillardet," *Nineteenth-Century French Studies,* 3, nos. 1–2 (1974–1975): 40–57;

Bassan, "L'*Hamlet* d'Alexandre Dumas père et Paul Meurice: Evolution d'une adaptation de 1846 à 1896," *Australian Journal of French Studies,* 19, no. 1 (1982): 11–31;

Bassan, "La Meilleure Comédie de Dumas père: *Kean, ou Désordre et génie*," *Revue d'Histoire du Théâtre,* 29, no. 1 (1977): 71–78;

Bassan and Sylvie Chevalley, *Alexandre Dumas et la Comédie-Française* (Paris: Lettres Modernes-Minard, 1972);

Michel Brix, "Nerval et l'auteur des *Trois Mousquetaires*," in *Cent cinquante ans après,* pp. 82–93;

Pierre Campion, "*Antony* d'Alexandre Dumas on la scène de l'évidence," *Revue d'Histoire du Théâtre,* no. 4 (1996): 407–430;

Michel de Certeau, "Qui proquo. Le Théâtre historique," *L'Arc,* no. 71 (1978): 29–33;

Marie-Françoise Christout, "Les Adaptations théâtrales et chorégraphiques des *Trois Mousquetaires* dans les spectacles récents," in *Cent cinquante ans après,* pp. 21–30;

Christout, "Kean ou désordre et génie," *Œuvres et critiques,* 62–72;

Barbara T. Cooper, "The Backward Glance of Parody: Author-Audience Complicity in a Comic Reduction of Dumas' *Henri III et sa cour*," *Essays in Literature,* 13, no. 2 (1986): 313–325;

Cooper, "Parodie et pastiche: La Réception théâtrale d'*Antony*," *Oeuvres et critiques,* 112–131;

Edith Covensky, "Les Débuts d'Alexandre Dumas père au théâtre: *Henri III, Antony* et *La Tour de Nesle*," *Revue d'Histoire du Théâtre,* 35, no. 3 (1983): 329–337;

François Germain, "Dumas et *La Tour de Nesle*," in *D'Eschyle à Genet. Hommage à Francis Prunier* (Dijon: Université de Dijon, 1986), pp. 175–181;

Jennifer R. Goodman, "To Display a Clearly Romantic Talent," *Harvard Library Bulletin,* 26, no. 2 (1978): 133–145;

Charles Grivel, "Le Cinéma-théâtre d'Alexandre Dumas," *Oeuvres et critiques,* 150–156;

Odile Krakovitch, "Alexandre Dumas et la censure théâtrale ou la comédie de *Qui perd gagne*," in *Cent cinquante ans après,* pp. 165–187;

Krakovitch, "Manuscrits des pièces d'Alexandre Dumas et procès-verbaux de censure de ces pièces. . . ," *Revue d'Histoire Littéraire de la France,* 82, no. 4 (1982): 638–646;

Maija Lehtonen, "La Vérité historique de *Christine*," *Oeuvres et critiques,* 73–90;

Renée Lelièvre, "*Don Juan* d'Alexandre Dumas," in *Missions et démarches de la critique,* edited by René Maraché and Henri Le Moal (Paris: Klincksieck, 1973), pp. 537–550;

Louise Fiber Luce, "Alexandre Dumas's *Kean*: An Adaptation by Jean-Paul Sartre," *Modern Drama,* 28, no. 3 (1985): 355–361;

Hippolyte Parigot, *Le Drame d'Alexandre Dumas* (Paris, 1899);

Eric-Emmanuel Schmitt, "Lorsque Dumas inventait le cinéma," in *Le Grand Livre de Dumas,* edited by Charles Dantzig (Paris: Belles Lettres, 1997), pp. 186–195;

Claude Schopp, "Dumas et le comte de Monte-Cristo à l'opéra," in *Cent cinquante ans après,* pp. 134–147;

Schopp, "Dumas critique dramatique," *Nineteenth-Century French Studies,* 18, nos. 3–4 (1990): 348–362;

Anne Ubersfeld, "Alexandre Dumas père et le drame bourgeois," *Cahiers de l'Association Internationale des Etudes Françaises,* 35 (1983): 121–139;

Ubersfeld, "Désordre et génie," *Europe* (1970): 107–119;

Ubersfeld, "Structures du théâtre d'Alexandre Dumas père," *Littérature et linguistique,* special issue of *Nouvelle critique* (1969): 146–156;

W. van Maanen, "*Kean,* From Dumas to Sartre," *Neophilologus,* 56, no. 2 (1972): 221–230;

Jacqueline Villani, "Sculpter dans l'éphémère. Quelques remarques sur le manuscrit d'*Antony,*" *Romantisme,* no. 99 (1998): 89–103;

Vladimir Volkenshtein and Daniel Gerould, "Volkenshtein on Dumas père's *Tour de Nesle:* A Russian Formalist Analysis," *New York Literary Forum,* 7 (1980): 241–245;

Jean-Claude Yon, "Du roman-feuilleton à la scène. Les cas de Dumas et de Scribe, à propos des *Trois Mousquetaires,*" in *Cent cinquante ans après,* pp. 61–66;

Yon, "*Mlle de Belle-Isle* face à la critique ou le retour équivoque de l'enfant prodigue," *Oeuvres et critiques,* 91–104.

Papers:

Some of Dumas's papers and manuscripts can be found at the Bibliothèque Nationale de France, the Archives Nationales de France, and the library of the Comédie-Française (all in Paris); others are located at the Château de Monte-Cristo in Port-Marly (France).

Octave Feuillet
(11 August 1821 – 29 December 1890)

Marcia G. Parker
University of Wisconsin—Stevens Point

PLAY PRODUCTIONS: *Un Bourgeois de Rome,* Paris, Théâtre de l'Odéon, 15 November 1845;

Echec et mat, Paris, Théâtre de l'Odéon, 23 May 1846;

Palma, ou la Nuit du Vendredi Saint, Paris, Théâtre de la Porte Saint-Martin, 24 March 1847;

La Vieillesse de Richelieu, Paris, Théâtre de la République, 2 November 1848;

York, Paris, Théâtre du Palais Royal, 1 July 1852;

Le Pour et le contre, Paris, Gymnase-Dramatique, 24 October 1853;

Romulus, Paris, Théâtre-Français, 13 January 1854;

La Crise, Paris, Gymnase-Dramatique, 7 March 1854;

Péril en la demeure, Paris, Théâtre-Français, 19 April 1855;

Le Village, Paris, Théâtre-Français, 2 June 1856;

La Fée, Paris, Théâtre du Vaudeville, 26 August 1856;

Dalila, Paris, Théâtre du Vaudeville, 29 May 1857;

Le Roman d'un jeune homme pauvre, Paris, Théâtre du Vaudeville, 22 November 1858;

Les Portraits de la Marquise, Palais de Compiègne, 13 November 1859; Paris, Théâtre-Français au Trocadéro, 2 May 1882;

Le Cheveu blanc, Paris, Gymnase-Dramatique, 16 March 1860;

La Tentation, Paris, Théâtre du Vaudeville, 19 March 1860;

Rédemption, Paris, Théâtre du Vaudeville, 19 October 1860;

Montjoye, Paris, Gymnase-Dramatique, 24 October 1863;

La Belle au bois dormant, Paris, Théâtre du Vaudeville, 17 February 1865;

Le Cas de conscience, Paris, Théâtre-Français, 9 January 1867;

Julie, Paris, Théâtre-Français, 4 May 1869;

L'Acrobate, Paris, Théâtre-Français, 18 April 1873;

Le Sphinx, Paris, Théâtre-Français, 23 March 1874;

La Clé d'or, music by Eugène Gautier, Paris, Théâtre National Lyrique, 11 September 1877;

Octave Feuillet

La Fée, music by Hémery, Paris, Opéra-Comique, 14 June 1880;

La Partie de dames, Paris, Théâtre de la Porte Saint-Martin, 23 April 1882; Paris, Gymnase-Dramatique, 28 May 1883;

Un Roman parisien, Paris, Gymnase-Dramatique, 28 October 1882;

Le Voyageur, Paris, Opéra-Comique, 9 June 1885;

Chamillac, Paris, Théâtre-Français, 9 April 1886;

L'Urne, Paris, Salle d'Horticulture, 26 February 1889;

Le Divorce de Juliette, Brussels, 7 December 1889.

BOOKS: *Un Bourgeois de Rome* (Paris: Masgana, 1845);

Alix, volume 22 (Paris: Revue des Deux Mondes, 1846), pp. 160–201;

Echec et mat, by Feuillet and Paul Bocage (Paris: Jérôme, 1846);

Vie de Polichinelle et ses nombreuses aventures (Paris: J. Hetzel, 1846); adapted as *The Life and Adventures of Punchinello* (London: Chapman & Hall, 1846); translated by J. Harris Gable as *The Story of Mr. Punch* (New York: Dutton, 1929);

Palma, ou, la Nuit du Vendredi Saint, by Feuillet and Bocage (Paris: Michel Lévy frères, 1847);

Théâtre (Paris: Lévy, 1847–1887); comprises as volume 1–*Palma, Le Roman d'un jeune homme pauvre, La Vieillesse de Richelieu;* as volume 2, *La Crise, Julie, Dalila;* as volume 3, *Rédemption, La Tentation;* as volume 4, *Le Sphinx,* and *Montjoye;*

La Vieillesse de Richelieu, by Feuillet and Bocage (Paris: Michel Lévy frères, 1848);

Bellah (Brussels: Méline, Cans, 1850; Paris: Michel Lévy frères, 1852); translated by Mary Neal Sherwood as *Bellah, a Tale of Brittany* (Philadelphia: T. B. Peterson, 1881); translated as *The Officer's Bride: A Tale of the French Revolution* (New York: Hurst, 1900?);

Scènes et proverbes (Paris: Michel Lévy frères, 1851)–includes *Le Fruit défendu, La Crise, Rédemption, Le Pour et le contre, Alix, La Partie de dames,* and *La Clef d'or,* translated by Nathanial Greene (Boston, 1872); comprises *Forbidden Fruit, The Crisis, Redemption, For and Against, Alix, The Chess Party,* and *The Golden Key;*

York, by Feuillet and Bocage (Paris: Michel Lévy frères, 1852);

Le Pour et le contre (Paris: Michel Lévy frères, 1853);

La Crise (Paris: Michel Lévy frères, 1854);

Scènes et comédies (Paris: Michel Lévy frères, 1854)–includes *Le Village, Le Cheveu blanc, Dalila, L'Ermitage, L'Urne,* and *La Fée;*

Péril en la demeure (Paris: Michel Lévy frères, 1855);

Le Village (Paris: Michel Lévy frères, 1856);

La Fée (Paris: Michel Lévy frères, 1856); translated by Barrett H. Clark as "The Fairy," in *The World's Best Plays, by Celebrated European Authors,* edited by B. H. Clark (New York: S. French, 1915), pp. 3–27;

Dalila (Paris: Michel Lévy frères, 1857);

La Petite Comtesse, Le Parc, Onesta (Paris: Michel Lévy frères, 1857); translated by Mary Neal Sherwood as *The Little Countess* (Philadelphia: T. B. Peterson, 1880); translated by James D. McCabe as *Onesta: A Story of Venice* (New York: G. Munro, 1880);

Le Roman d'un jeune homme pauvre (Paris: Michel Lévy frères, 1858); translated by Henry J. Macdonald as *The Romance of a Poor Young Man* (New York: Rudd & Carleton, 1859); adapted from the French by Pierrepont Edwards and Lester Wallack as *Honour before Wealth: or, The Romance of a Poor Young Man* (London: S. French, circa 1859);

Le Cheveu blanc (Paris: Michel Lévy frères, 1860);

La Tentation (Paris: Michel Lévy frères, 1860);

Rédemption (Paris: Michel Lévy frères, 1860);

Histoire de Sibylle (Paris: Michel Lévy frères, 1862); translated by M. H. Toland as *The Story of Sibylle* (Boston: J. R. Osgood, 1872);

Les Portraits de la Marquise (Paris: Imprimerie Impériale, 1862);

Discours prononcés dans la séance publique tenue par l'Académie Française pour la réception de M. Octave Feuillet, le 26 mars 1863 [eulogy of Alexis de Tocqueville] (Paris: Firmin-Didot, 1863);

Discours de M. Octave Feuillet, prononcé à sa réception à l'Académie Française le 26 mars 1863 (Paris: Michel Lévy frères, 1863);

Montjoye (Paris: Michel Lévy frères, 1863);

La Belle au bois dormant (Paris: Michel Lévy frères, 1865);

Le Cas de conscience (Paris: Michel Lévy frères, 1867);

Monsieur de Camors (Paris: Michel Lévy frères, 1867); translated by George B. Ives (Philadelphia: G. Barrie & Son, 1900); also translated under the titles *Camors, or, Life Under the New Empire* (New York: Blelock, 1868), *The Count of Camors. The Man of the Second Empire* (Philadelphia: T. B. Peterson, 1879), *Camors, A Love Story,* 1870, and *A Man of Honor,* 1871;

Julie (Paris: Michel Lévy frères, 1869);

Julia de Trécoeur, with *Circé: Scène parisienne* (Paris: Michel Lévy frères, 1872);

L'Acrobate (Paris: Michel Lévy frères, 1873);

Le Sphinx (Paris: Michel Lévy frères, 1874); translated by Frederick A. Schwab as *The Sphinx* (New York: F. Rullman, 1880);

Un Mariage dans le monde (Paris: Michel Lévy frères, 1875); translated by Celia Logan as *A Marriage in High Life* (New York: J. W. Lovell, 1876);

La Clé d'or, by Feuillet and Louis Gallet, music by Eugène Gautier (Paris: Calmann-Lévy, 1877);

Les Amours de Philippe (Paris: Calmann-Lévy, 1877); translated as *The Amours of Phillippe* [sic]: *A History of "Phillippe's* [sic] *Love Affairs"* (New York: American News, 1877); translated by Mary Neal Sherwood (Philadelphia: T. B. Peterson, 1877); translated by Eliot Leigh as *Philippe's Love Story: A Tale of Fashion and Passion in France* (New York: American News, 1877);

Le Journal d'une femme (Paris: Calmann-Lévy, 1878); translated as *The Diary of a Woman* (New York: Appleton, 1879);

Circé: Scène parisienne (Saint-Germain: E. Heutte et cie, 187?);

Histoire d'une Parisienne (Paris: Calmann-Lévy, 1881); translated by Charles Ripley as *The History of a Parisienne* (Philadelphia: T. B. Peterson, 1881); translated by Jacob Abarbanell as *Jeanne: or, The History of a Parisienne* (New York: G. Munro, 1881);

La Partie de dames (Paris: Calmann-Lévy, 1883);

Un Roman parisien (Paris: Calmann-Levy, 1883); translated as *A Parisian Romance* (Philadelphia: T. B. Peterson, 1883);

La Veuve; Le Voyageur (Paris: Calmann-Lévy, 1884); *La Veuve* translated by Gustave Beauseigneur as *The Widow* (Chicago: Morrill, Higgins, 1893);

La Morte (Paris: Calmann-Lévy, 1886); translated by J. Henry Hager as *Aliette* (New York: Appleton, 1886);

Chamillac (Paris: Calmann-Lévy, 1888);

Charybde et Scylla, with preface and notes by Alphonse N. Van Daell (Boston: L'Echo de la semaine, n.d.); edited by Rena A. Michaels (Evanston, Ill.: U.P., 1888);

Le Divorce de Juliette, Charybde & Scylla, Le Curé de Bourron (Paris: Calmann-Lévy, 1889);

Honneur d'artiste (Paris: Calmann-Lévy, 1890);

Théâtre complet (Paris: Calmann-Lévy, 1892–1893); comprises as volume 1–*Un bourgeois de Rome, Le Pour et le contre, La Crise, Péril en la demeure, Le Village, La Fée,* and *Le Roman d'un jeune homme pauvre;* as volume 2–*Le Cheveu blanc, La Tentation, Rédemption,* and *Montjoye;* as volume 3–*La Belle au bois dormant, Le Cas de conscience, Julie, Dalila,* and *L'Acrobate;* as volume 4–*Le Sphinx, Les Portraits de la marquise, Un Roman parisien, La Partie de dames,* and *Chamillac;* as volume 5–*Echec et mat, Palma: ou, La Nuit du vendredi saint, La Vieillesse de Richelieu,* and *York.*

SELECTED PERIODICAL PUBLICATIONS—
UNCOLLECTED: "La Crise," *La Revue des Deux Mondes,* 15 October 1848, pp. 177–215;

"Le Pour et le contre," *La Revue des Deux Mondes,* 1 July 1849, pp. 76–91;

"La Partie de dames," *La Revue des Deux Mondes,* 15 June 1850, pp. 1,112–1,127;

"L'Ermitage," *La Revue des Deux Mondes,* 15 September 1851, pp. 1,071–1,099;

"Le Cheveu blanc," *La Revue des Deux Mondes,* 1 May 1853, pp. 417–433

"Dalila," *La Revue des Deux Mondes,* 1 September 1853, pp. 841–919;

"La Fée," *La Revue des Deux Mondes,* 15 April 1854, pp. 375–402;

"La Petite Comtesse," *La Revue des Deux Mondes,* 1 January 1856, pp. 5–70;

"Le Roman d'un jeune homme pauvre," *La Revue des Deux Mondes,* 1858, pp. 5–64, 241–305;

"Julia de Trécoeur," *La Revue des Deux Mondes,* 1 March 1872, pp. 5–57;

"Un Mariage dans le monde," *La Revue des Deux Mondes,* 1 September 1875, pp. 5–29; 15 September 1875, pp. 241–263; 1 October 1875, pp. 481–522;

"Les Amours de Philippe," *La Revue des Deux Mondes,* 1 July 1877, pp. 5–33; 15 July 1875, pp. 241–264; 1 August 1875, pp. 481–524;

"Le Journal d'une femme," *La Revue des Deux Mondes,* 15 July 1878, pp. 241–294; 1 August 1875, pp. 481–519;

"Histoire d'une Parisienne," *La Revue des Deux Mondes,* 1 April 1881, pp. 491–515, 721–763;

"La Veuve," *La Revue des Deux Mondes,* 1 December 1883, pp. 481–512, 721–748;

"Le Voyageur," *La Revue des Deux Mondes,* 1 January 1884, pp. 5–28;

"La Morte," *La Revue des Deux Mondes,* 15 December 1885, pp. 721–749; 1 January 1886, pp. 5–42; 15 January 1886, pp. 241–283.

Lauded by the theatergoing public and many critics during the period of France's Second Empire, Octave Feuillet now appears in nineteenth-century theater history as a secondary playwright after Alexandre Dumas *fils,* Emile Augier, and Victorien Sardou. An acclaimed writer of novels as well, Feuillet adapted some of these works for the stage after first presenting both novels and plays to the public in the review titled *La Revue des Deux Mondes.* Theater critics praised the moral lessons taught through his plays: the importance of marriage as an institution and the value of religious faith. His portrayal of high-society women and their elegant world attracted readers and audiences. According to reviewers, Alfred de Musset, George Sand, and Alexandre Dumas *père* all influenced Feuillet's writing, which exhibited both realist and idealist tendencies. American theaters continued to perform translations and adaptations of Feuillet's work into the twentieth century, and French theaters revive his plays from time to time.

Born in Saint-Lô on 11 August 1821, Feuillet remained attached to Normandy throughout his life. Many of his characters and settings explicitly evoke people and places of Normandy or Brittany,

Feuillet in his study, circa 1890

where the writer often traveled to find inspiration for his work. Jacques Feuillet, the widowed patriarch of the Feuillet family, himself a lawyer and politician, had destined his older son, Eugène, to the world of finance and Octave to diplomacy. An excellent student at the Lycée Louis le Grand, Octave was assured a bright future as a diplomat. When he approached his father concerning his desire to write for the stage, he found himself without approval and without financial support. Returning to Paris, he and Paul Bocage, a former classmate, wrote plays together while living with Bocage's family: *Echec et mat* (Checkmate, 1846), *Palma, ou la Nuit du Vendredi Saint* (Palms or the Night of Good Friday, 1847), *La Vieillesse de Richelieu* (Richelieu's Old Age, 1848). Bocage's uncle was a recognized actor who agreed to act in two of their plays and secured the Odéon theater for them. Feuillet also worked with Alexandre Dumas *père*. Although the early plays are not valued as Feuillet's best work, they supported him and launched his career in the theater world. After three years Feuillet's father reinstated the yearly pension, which allowed Feuillet to live independently and write.

In 1850 Feuillet returned to Normandy to care for his ill father. During this time he courted and married his cousin, Valérie Dubois, and had three sons, the first of whom died at an early age. For ten years Feuillet wrote in Normandy, allowing his brother to handle most of the business details of producing the plays in Paris. At the death of his father Feuillet moved back to Paris but continued to spend part of each year in Normandy. From his wife's memoirs and in other references to Feuillet's lifestyle it is clear that the playwright enjoyed both the calm of country life and the excitement and movement of Paris, but neither for long. Until the later years of his life when he moved from Normandy to Paris to Switzerland and finally to Versailles, most of his life was spent in or near Saint-Lô.

Several one-acts and some longer plays featured Feuillet's theory behind the reason some wives had crises at about the age of thirty. Through his characters Feuillet accused many husbands of spending excessive time on business or with friends, which in turn created boredom and temptation for their wives. In his plays Feuillet usually blamed the husband's neglect for the wife's difficulties and generally rescued the situation just before "the fall." The audience invariably learned that a husband should remain attentive to his wife and that she should remain faithful to her husband. With variations, *La Crise* (The Crisis, 1854), *Péril en la demeure* (Peril at Home, 1855), *Le Cheveu blanc* (The White Hair, 1860), and *La Tentation* (Led Astray, 1860) follow this theme.

Other plays also deal with the topic of marriage (fidelity, love, honor, equity). One of Feuillet's successful novels adapted into a play, *Le Roman d'un jeune homme pauvre* (The Romance of a Poor Young Man, 1858), takes place in Brittany. A young marquis learns he has no money when his father dies, decides to sacrifice his pride in order to earn a living to provide a dowry for his younger sister, and finds a job managing the estate of a wealthy family in Brittany. The headstrong daughter in the family falls in love with this man but is suspicious of all men, believing their interest lies only in her possessions. The marquis, who hides his love for her, knows there can be no marriage because of his financial situation. Usually Feuillet's leading men are not as chivalrous and sensitive as this character; rather, his women characters draw more interest and empathy from the audience. The denouement provides one of his convenient twists of fortune that allows the two young people to marry.

Another play concerned with love of a future partner rather than love of wealth and power, *Un Bourgeois de Rome* (A Bourgeois from Rome, 1845), employs the technique of disguising one's identity to test love. A prince adopts the role of his secretary in order to learn about a young woman he loves and to ask for her hand in marriage for the prince. She passes the test by falling in love with the "secretary" and agreeing to elope with him rather than marry the prince. In *Rédemption* (1860) a celebrated actress prefers to be respected than adored by the many wealthy admirers who want to marry her for her beauty and fame. A young "honest" man who has resisted loving her continues to do so even when she claims she will give up all her wealth and glory for a respectable life. Only when she drinks a poison, which he has replaced with water, does he believe her and know he can love her. In her final words in the play she declares her belief in God—a declaration predicted by a priest who said the actress would gain such a belief when she found an honest man to love her. Here Feuillet combined the theme of respect in marriage with religious faith.

Other lessons can be found in dialogues between husbands and wives, through which it was suggested to the audience how to maintain a more harmonious family life. *Charybde et Scylla* proposes an education for a wife, but one regulated by the husband. The story suggests that a mother should be responsible for the moral upbringing of a daughter, and that the husband should oversee the daughter's literary education so that he does not end up with a "femme savante" (bluestocking) as in Molière's plays.

A recurring character in Feuillet's plays is an older, wise woman who helps young people through difficult situations, either with counsel or direct manipulation of situations. In this play the mother-in-law gently teaches the husband that a wife still sees him as superior when he becomes her teacher, and this process creates a lasting bond between them. The dialogue between husband and wife in *Le Pour et le contre* (For and Against, 1853) makes the case that the crime is greater when a husband commits adultery than when a wife follows his example. Feuillet's argument proposes that a husband, who has many more distractions than does a wife, premeditates his unfaithfulness. A wife's affair usually occurs when the husband has strayed first and would not occur if he were attentive to her.

La Fée (The Fairy, 1856) once again reinforces the wisdom of an older woman, but in this play the elder character has died before the play begins. A mother has chosen a young provincial woman to be her son's wife in order to remove him from the vices of Paris. However, the son never returns to his native Bordeaux, even when his mother dies. Preferring women in Paris, he continues his dissolute lifestyle until he no longer finds joy in it and decides to commit suicide. To honor her future mother-in-law's dying wish to save her son, the young woman writes a mysterious letter to the son about meeting a fairy in Merlin's forest in Brittany. Disguised as an old woman with powers of a fairy, the young woman shows the count the importance of other duties in life, such as helping less fortunate people. The count experiences a peaceful feeling in her presence. As he shows a real affection for her, she appears to grow younger, until she finally reveals her true identity. As in the setting in *Le Roman d'un jeune homme pauvre,* the dark skies and storms of Brittany play an important role in this play, giving both plays a melodramatic atmosphere. Feuillet's teaching of morals, sometimes by borrowing his techniques from melodrama, found a receptive audience during the second half of the nineteenth century.

Critics during Feuillet's time and after frequently draw attention to a one-act play, *Le Village* (1856), one which they see as being different from most of Feuillet's works. The play still stresses the importance of a positive and equitable relationship in marriage, but this time the couple is quite old and bourgeois. A dilemma arises when an old friend and former classmate of the husband visits. While relating his life of adventures and travel, the husband begins to regret his uneventful, provincial married life and eagerly accepts when the friend invites him to spend two years traveling together. Upon learning of the travel plans, the wife wisely refuses to dissuade her husband, though she is sad when he leaves and worries about his age and health. Having only told of the marvels of travel, the friend begins to understand the advantages of the couple's calm life and relates a painful story of an illness during which, near death, he looked around the room at the doctor and innkeeper and realized there was no one in the world who cared if he lived or died. The husband then sees the value of his own lifestyle and invites the friend to stay with them. The play supports Feuillet's belief in the importance of communication, respect, and equity in a marriage but approaches the theme from the perspective of a modest provincial couple near the end of their lives.

Three plays often cited as his most successful works simultaneously drew high praise and severe criticism from theater critics: *Dalila* (1857), *Montjoye* (1863), and *Julie* (1869). Mme Octave Feuillet, along with many critics, felt *Dalila* was the playwright's greatest play. The public supported a long theater run, and its revival in 1870 was hailed a great success. Although Barbey d'Aurevilly admitted the success of the play, he claimed Feuillet committed a serious error in making Samson an artist; a gifted artist, he believed, would not ruin his life for a worthless woman. He also attacked the language used by Feuillet, implying it was dated. The talented composer in this play, torn between two women, allows himself to be swept away by the princess, who then changes her mind and loses interest in him. Meanwhile, the young, pure daughter of his music teacher dies from a broken heart. *Montjoye* and *Julie,* different from his earlier plays, provoked stronger contradictory reactions in the press. Hailed as a masterpiece by some, others admitted *Montjoye* had strengths but failed in its denouement. Montjoye, a totally base character throughout the play, corrects the errors of his entire life in one final scene. A critic in *La Petite Presse* told his readers that if one ignored the ending, which ruined the play, *Montjoye* was one of the most beautiful theatrical works. While lauding the third act and recognizing the success with the audiences, one critic called *Julie* a poor copy of the Dumas *fils* play *Supplice d'une femme* (A Woman's Punishment, 1865), and another said it brought nothing new to the theater, had no moral value, and should not be seen by young women. A third simply called it mediocre and said that Feuillet should have continued to write plays more like his early work, as this piece was banal. Other critics gave opposite reports: a strongly written and cleverly developed play, a delicate depiction of the characters, a great success for the author, a poignant drama that their readers should see. Julie has been married for seventeen years to a man who pays little attention to her,

does not grant her wish to bring their daughter home from school, and plans to introduce his mistress to his wife. When their good friend M. de Turgy fails to convince the husband to change his ways, he turns to Julie to declare his love for her. Julie commits adultery and decides to run off with her lover. Before she can leave, the husband changes his mind and brings their daughter home to be company for his wife, and the daughter confides in her mother that she loves M. de Turgy and would like to marry him. Julie stays home, and M. de Turgy leaves abruptly for Egypt. A year later, just as M. de Turgy is returning for a visit, the husband learns from the daughter that his wife had told her she could not marry Turgy; he surmises the reason and finagles a confession from his wife. Under his cruel interrogation she loses consciousness; the lover enters to a death threat from the husband; and Turgy discovers that Julie is dead. The play enjoyed a great success with the audiences of 1869.

After the triumph of the first run of *Julie* and the revival of *Dalila* came the end of an era for France and for Feuillet with the war of 1870 and the beginning of the Third Republic. Feuillet had been one of the few intellectuals who supported the Second Empire. Napoleon III and the empress often invited him to Compiègne, attended and praised his plays, and named him the librarian at Fontainebleau. In addition to enjoying a successful writing career and being in favor with the court, Feuillet received the honors of the Légion d'honneur and in 1862 won election to the Académie Française. At the outset of the war he sent his wife and children to Jersey and stayed in Saint-Lô to help protect the village. After the war he maintained contact with the Napoleon family and was saddened by the death of the former emperor in 1873.

Feuillet's next major play, *Le Sphinx* (1874), received mixed reviews from theater critics, of whom some claimed its success resulted from the fine acting by Sophie Croizette and Sarah Bernhardt. The production of this play also captured the attention of critics and the public for its emphasis on realism—both in the lighting and in the death scene, for which the actress had studied the physical effects of poison. Feuillet's strong women characters no longer exhibited the idealism of the early plays. Blanche, whose husband is at sea as a naval officer, is interested in many other men but sets her sights on her close friend's husband. He resists her advances but raises the suspicions of his wife. In the final confrontation between the two women Blanche pours the poisonous contents of her sphinx ring into a glass of water for her friend but at the last moment decides to drink the poison herself. When *Le Sphinx* opened at the Théâtre-Française, critic Jules Clare-tie observed with regret that Feuillet's theater had changed; his new plays lacked the moral lessons of his earlier style. According to Mme Feuillet's memoirs, each of her husband's plays stressed his nerves to the point that he needed rest afterward to maintain his health but none more than this play, which was plagued by constant problems between Bernhardt and Croizette.

One of his last plays, *Le Divorce de Juliette* (Juliette's Divorce, 1889), seems to return to Feuillet's earlier style, giving the audience a heroine above reproach while showing once again the importance of a marriage in which both partners are faithful and interested in each other. A young wife who adores her husband learns that he had an affair with the friend who introduced them and encouraged their marriage in order to disarm the suspicions of her own jealous husband. Upon discovering the continuation of that liaison, Juliette confronts her husband. He does not defend himself, telling her he will do whatever she wishes. Juliette contacts a friend who is a lawyer (and had courted her before her marriage) to ask for help in planning a divorce, one in which the identity of the mistress is not revealed. Realizing that Juliette still loves her husband and that the husband does indeed love Juliette, the lawyer tricks them into thinking the divorce is final before it actually is, giving the husband the opportunity to reveal his true feelings to his wife without her believing they are insincere. Thinking they are divorced, he tells her he no longer loves his mistress, that he had grown to love and respect his wife during their brief marriage, and he asks for forgiveness before she leaves. Juliette demonstrates that she still loves him; the lawyer enters to inform them of the ruse; and the marriage is saved. Once again the moral lessons show that a husband and wife must tell each other of their love, that honor must be maintained, and that a pure, noble young wife can save her husband through love and forgiveness.

Feuillet's health deteriorated in the last years of his life. Because he suffered increasingly from deafness, he could no longer attend rehearsals of his plays. When replacing Feuillet at the Académie Française in 1892, Pierre Loti (Julien Viaud) explained in his address that Feuillet left the theater forever after the premiere of his final play in the spring of 1889 due to his deafness and ill health. He wrote a final novel and died not long after the death of his older son.

After Feuillet's death Mme Feuillet published two books in which she recalled the events of their life together, praised his work, and described the difficulties her husband endured while writing for the theater, which included the possibility of poor reviews from critics, problems with actors during rehearsals, and the constant risks associated with putting a play before the public, not knowing how the play would be received. At the same time she portrayed a man who was dedicated to the theater and who thrived on the positive reception he earned. Mme Feuillet proudly pointed to the praise and friendship her husband earned from such colleagues as George Sand and Emile Augier, as well as from the emperor, by including letters from them in her books. Feuillet enjoyed both celebrity and financial success during his lifetime.

Although now relegated to the ranks of minor playwrights of the nineteenth century, Feuillet's name has not disappeared. Scholars studying Henry James come across references to Feuillet's works, including the assumption by James that readers would immediately picture an elegant, ideal woman in any reference to a typical Feuillet female character. Those researching George Sand's work discover letters between Sand and Feuillet that provide interesting comparisons between their views of women and relationships. Earlier-twentieth-century books on theater history often included an entire chapter treating Feuillet's work. More-recent historical works assign a paragraph or a few lines to Feuillet. Almost all contend that if one wishes to study the upper-class society of the Second Empire, the plays and novels by Feuillet offer excellent sources. The playwright's outmoded language and the general lack of interest in old-fashioned morality lessons in the theater prevent a resurrection of Feuillet's plays. Early in the twentieth century, theater historians suggested that plays written by Feuillet would find only a reading audience in the future, a prediction that seems accurate today. Currently, those readers are predominantly theater historians.

Letters:

"Lettres de Compiègne et de Fontainebleau," *Revue de Paris,* 2 (1894): 1–41.

Biographies:

Jules Claretie, *Célébrités contemporaines* (Paris: Quantin, 1883);

Jules Lemaître, *Les Contemporains,* third series (Paris: Lecène et Oudin, 1887), pp. 5–35;

Anatole France, *La Vie littéraire* (Paris: Calmann-Lévy, 1890–1891), second series, pp. 341–348; third series, pp. 368–378;

Pierre Loti (Julien Viaud), *Discours de réception de Pierre Loti: Séance de l'Académie Française du 7 avril 1892* (Paris: Calmann-Lévy, 1892);

Mme Octave Feuillet (Valérie Marie Elvire Dubois), *Quelques années de ma vie* (Paris: Calmann-Lévy, 1894);

Mme Feuillet, *Souvenirs et correspondances* (Paris: Calmann-Lévy, 1896);

Henry Bordeaux, *La Jeunesse d'Octave Feuillet (1821–1890); d'après une correspondance inédite* (Paris: Librairie Plon, Plon-Nourrit et Cie, 1922).

References:

Jules Barbey d'Aurevilly, *Le Théâtre contemporain (1869–1870),* volume 3 (Paris: P.-V. Stock, 1909), pp. 1–12, 243–257;

Antoine Benoist, *Essais de critique dramatique: George Sand, Musset, Feuillet, Augier, Dumas fils* (Paris: Librairie Hachette et Cie, 1898), pp. 133–188;

Marvin Carlson, *The French Stage in the Nineteenth Century* (Metuchen, N.J.: Scarecrow Press, 1972);

"Ces messieurs du lundi," *L'Entr'acte,* 5 April 1870;

Frank Wadleigh Chandler, *The Contemporary Drama of France* (Boston: Little, Brown, 1920), pp. 15–20, 333–334, 356;

Th. Charpentier, "Les Feuilletons du lundi," *L'Entr'acte,* 12 May 1869;

Jules Claretie, *La Vie moderne au théâtre: Causeries sur l'art dramatique,* first series (Paris: Georges Barba, 1869), pp. 17–18;

Claretie, *La Vie moderne au théâtre: Causeries sur l'art dramatique,* second series (Paris: Georges Barba, 1875), pp. 81–88, 347–358;

David Du Closel, "Nouvelles," *L'Entr'acte,* 14 February 1870;

Emile Faguet, *Notes sur le théâtre contemporain,* second series (Paris: Librairie H. Lecène et H. Oudin, 1890), pp. 305–312;

Augustin Filon, *De Dumas à Rostand: Esquisse du mouvement dramatique contemporain* (Paris: Armand Colin et Cie, 1898);

Théophile Gautier, *Histoire de l'art dramatique en France depuis vingt-cinq ans,* volumes 4–6 (Leipzig: Edition Hetzel, 1859);

Christian Genty, *Histoire du Théâtre National de l'Odéon (Journal de Bord), 1782–1982* (Paris: Librairie Fischbacher, 1981), pp. 80, 138;

Arsène Houssaye, *Behind the Scenes of the Comédie-Française and Other Recollections,* translated by Albert D. Vandam (New York: Benjamin Blom, 1971), pp. 128–129, 457–462, 483–486;

B. Jouvin, "Théâtres: Comédie-Française–*Julie,*" *La Presse,* 10 May 1869;

Brander Matthews, D.C.L., *French Dramatists of the 19th Century* (New York: Scribners, 1919);

Catulle Mendès, *L'Art au théâtre* (Paris: Bibliothèque-Charpentier, 1897), pp. 223–224, 239, 304–313;

Tony Révillon, "Comédie-Française: Dalila," *La Petite Presse,* 31 March 1870, pp. 1–2;

Alberic Second, "Dalila au Vaudeville," *L'Entr'acte,* 28 March 1870;

Albert Soubies, *Almanach des spectacles: Coup d'oeil d'ensemble, 1871–1891,* volume 15 (Paris: Librairie des Bibliophiles, 1893), pp. 147–149;

"Théâtres," *Le Français: Journal du Soir,* 10 May 1869;

Jean Valmy-Baysse, *Naissance et vie de la Comédie-Française: Histoire anecdotique et critique du Théâtre Français, 1402–1945* (Paris: Librairie Floury, 1945), pp. 251, 258, 272, 293–294;

Simone Vierne, "George Sand and Octave Feuillet ou les facettes du Second Empire," *George Sand Studies,* 9 (1988–1989): 16–28;

Pierre A. Walker, "The Princess Casamassima's 'Sudden Incarnation' and Octave Feuillet," *Texas Studies in Literature and Language,* 31, no. 2 (1989): 257–272;

Jean-Jacques Weiss, *A propos de théâtre: Trois années de théâtre, 1883–1885* (Paris: Calmann-Lévy, 1893), pp. 239–324;

Emile Zola, *Nos auteurs dramatiques* (Paris: Bibliothèque-Charpentier, 1893), pp. 360–366.

Georges Feydeau
(8 October 1862 – 5 June 1921)

Norman R. Shapiro
Wesleyan University

PLAY PRODUCTIONS: *Par la fenêtre,* Paris, Cercle des Arts Intimes, 1 June 1882;

Amour et piano, Paris, Théâtre de l'Athénée-Comique, 28 January 1883;

Gibier de potence, Paris, Cercle des Arts Intimes, 1 June 1883;

Fiancés en herbe, Paris, Salle Kriegelstein, 29 March 1886;

Tailleur pour dames, Paris, Théâtre de la Renaissance, 17 December 1886;

La Lycéenne, music by Gaston Serpette, Paris, Théâtre des Nouveautés, 23 December 1887;

Un Bain de ménage, Paris, Théâtre de la Renaissance, 13 April 1888;

Chat en poche, Paris, Théâtre Déjazet, 19 September 1888;

Les Fiancés de Loches, by Feydeau and Maurice Desvallières, Paris, Théâtre du Vaudeville, 27 September 1888;

L'Affaire Edouard, by Feydeau and Desvallières, Paris, Théâtre des Variétés, 12 January 1889;

C'est une femme du monde, by Feydeau and Desvallières, Paris, Théâtre de la Renaissance, 10 March 1890;

Le Mariage de Barillon, by Feydeau and Desvallières, Paris, Théâtre de la Renaissance, 10 March 1890;

Monsieur Nounou, by Feydeau and Desvallières, Brussels, Théâtre du Vaudeville, 25 April 1890;

Madame Sganarelle, Spa, Belgium, Le Casino, 31 August 1891;

Monsieur chasse, Paris, Théâtre du Palais Royal, 23 April 1892;

Champignol malgré lui, by Feydeau and Desvallières, Paris, Théâtre des Nouveautés, 5 November 1892;

Le Système Ribadier, by Feydeau and Maurice Hennequin, Paris, Théâtre du Palais Royal, 30 November 1892;

Un Fil à la patte, Paris, Théâtre du Palais Royal, 9 January 1894;

Notre futur, Paris, Salle de Géographie, 11 February 1894;

Georges Feydeau

Le Ruban, by Feydeau and Desvallières, Paris, Théâtre de l'Odéon, 24 February 1894;

L'Hôtel du Libre-Echange, by Feydeau and Desvallières, Paris, Théâtre des Nouveautés, 5 December 1894;

Le Dindon, Paris, Théâtre du Palais Royal, 8 February 1896;

Les Pavés de l'ours, Versailles, Théâtre Montpensier, 26 September 1896;

Séance de nuit, Paris, Théâtre du Palais Royal, 29 March 1897;

Dormez, je le veux!, Paris, L'Eldorado, 29 April 1897;

La Bulle d'amour, music by Francis Thomé, Paris, Théâtre Marigny, 11 May 1898;

La Dame de chez Maxim, Paris, Théâtre des Nouveautés, 17 January 1899;

Le Billet de Joséphine, by Feydeau and Jules Méry,
music by Alfred Kaiser, Paris, Théâtre de la
Gaîté, 23 February 1902;

La Duchesse des Folies-Bergère, Paris, Théâtre des Nouveautés, 3 December 1902;

La Main passe, Paris, Théâtre des Nouveautés, 1
March 1904;

L'Age d'or, by Feydeau and Desvallières, music by
Louis Varney, Paris, Théâtre des Variétés, 1
May 1905;

Le Bourgeon, Paris, Théâtre du Vaudeville, 1 March
1906;

La Puce à l'oreille, Paris, Théâtre des Variétés, 2
March 1907;

Occupe-toi d'Amélie, Paris, Théâtre des Nouveautés,
15 March 1908;

Feu la mère de Madame, Paris, Théâtre de la Comédie
Royale, 15 November 1908;

Le Circuit, by Feydeau and Francis de Croisset,
Paris, Théâtre des Variétés, 29 October 1909;

On purge Bébé, Paris, Théâtre des Nouveautés, 12
April 1910;

"Mais n' te promène donc pas toute nue!," Paris, Théâtre
Femina, 25 November 1911;

Léonie est en avance, ou Le Mal joli, Paris, Théâtre de la
Comédie Royale, 9 December 1911;

Je ne trompe pas mon mari, by Feydeau and René Peter,
Paris, Théâtre de l'Athénée, 17 February 1914;

Hortense a dit: "Je m'en fous!," Paris, Théâtre du
Palais Royal, 14 January 1916.

BOOKS: *Notre futur,* in *Théâtre de campagne,* volume
8, edited by Ernest Legouvé (Paris: Ollen-
dorff, 1876–1883), pp. 263–287; translated by
Norman R. Shapiro as *Ladies' Man,* in *Feydeau,
First to Last: Eight One-Act Comedies* (Ithaca,
N.Y.: Cornell University Press, 1982);

La Petite Révoltée (Paris: Ollendorff, 1880);

Le Mouchoir (Paris: Ollendorff, 1881);

Un Coup de tête (Paris: Michaud, 1882);

J'ai mal aux dents (Paris: Michaud, 1882);

Un Monsieur qui n'aime pas les monologues (Paris: Ollendorff, 1882);

Trop vieux (Paris: Ollendorff, 1882);

Aux Antipodes (Paris: Ollendorff, 1883);

Patte-en-l'air (Paris: Michaud, 1883);

Le Petit Ménage (Paris: Ollendorff, 1883);

Le Potache (Paris: Ollendorff, 1883);

Les Célèbres (Paris: Ollendorff, 1884);

Le Volontaire (Paris: Ollendorff, 1884);

Gibier de potence (Paris: Ollendorff, 1885); translated
by Caryl Brahms (pseudonym of Doris Caro-
line Abrahams) and Ned Sherrin as *Before We*

Were So Rudely Interrupted, in *Ooh! La-la* (Lon-
don: W. H. Allen, 1973); translated by
Shapiro as *Fit to Be Tried, or Stepbrothers in
Crime,* in *Feydeau, First to Last: Eight One-Act
Comedies;* translated by J. Paul Marcoux as
Brothers in Crime (Woodstock, Ill.: Dramatic
Publishing, 1993);

Le Billet de mille (Paris: Ollendorff, 1885);

Le Colis (Paris: Ollendorff, 1885);

L'Homme économe (Paris: Ollendorff, 1885);

Les Réformes (Paris: Librairie Théâtrale, 1885);

Fiancés en herbe (Paris: Librairie Théâtrale, 1886);
translated by Barnett Shaw as *Budding Lovers*
(New York: S. French, 1969);

L'Homme intègre (Paris: Ollendorff, 1886);

Les Enfants (Paris: Ollendorff, 1887);

Par la fenêtre (Paris: Ollendorff, 1887); translated by
Shapiro as *Wooed and Viewed,* in *Four Farces by
Georges Feydeau* (Chicago: University of Chi-
cago Press, 1970);

Amour et piano (Paris: Librairie Théâtrale, 1887);
translated by Brahms and Sherrin as *Call Me
Maestro,* in *Ooh! La-la;* translated by Shapiro as
Romance in A Flat, in *Feydeau, First to Last: Eight
One-Act Comedies;* translated by Reggie Oliver
as *The Music Lovers* (New York: S. French,
1992);

Tailleur pour dames (Paris: Librairie Théâtrale, 1888);
translated by Shaw as *A Gown for His Mistress*
(New York: S. French, 1969); translated by Pe-
ter Meyer as *Fitting for Ladies* (London: British
Broadcasting Corporation, 1974); translated
by Shapiro as *A Fitting Confusion,* in *Classic
Comedies,* edited by Maurice Charney (New
York: New American Library, 1985), pp.
368–485; translated by Marcoux as *Love by the
Bolt* (Chicago: Dramatic Publishing, 1984); re-
titled *The Dressmaker,* in *Five by Feydeau* (New
York: Peter Lang, 1994);

La Lycéenne (Paris: Ollendorff, 1888); piano score
and libretto (Paris: Choudens, 1887);

Les Fiancés de Loches (Paris: Ollendorff, 1888);

Un Bain de ménage (Paris: Librairie Théâtrale, 1889);

L'Affaire Edouard (Paris: Ollendorff, 1889); translated by Shaw as *The Edouard Case* (Dallas:
Shaw, 1972);

C'est une femme du monde (Paris: Ollendorff, 1890);
translated by Shapiro as *Mixed Doubles,* in *Feydeau, First to Last: Eight One-Act Comedies;*

Le Mariage de Barillon (Paris: Ollendorff, 1890);
translated by Shapiro as *On the Marry-Go-
Wrong,* in *Four Farces by Georges Feydeau;* translated by Marcoux as *All My Husbands,* in
Georges Feydeau, Three Farces;

Tout à Brown-Séquard (Paris: Ollendorff, 1890);

Monsieur chasse (Paris: Ollendorff, 1896); translated by Mawby Green and Ed Feilbert as *13 rue de l'Amour* (New York: S. French, 1972); translated by Shaw as *The Happy Hunter* (New York: S. French, 1973); translated by Brahms and Sherrin as *The Chaser and the Chaste*, in *After You, Mr. Feydeau* (London: W. H. Allen, 1975); translated by Ray Barron as *A-Hunting We Will Go* (London: New Playwrights' Network, 1976);

Le Juré (Paris: Librairie Théâtrale, 1898);

Un Fil à la patte (Paris: Ollendorff, 1899); translated by Shapiro as *Not by Bed Alone*, in *Four Farces by Georges Feydeau;* translated by John Mortimer as *Cat Among the Pigeons* (New York: S. French, 1970); translated by Frederick Davies as *Get Out of My Hair*, in *Three French Farces* (Baltimore: Penguin, 1973); translated by Brahms and Sherrin as *On a String*, in *After You, Mr. Feydeau;*

Un Monsieur qui est condamné à mort (Paris: Ollendorff, 1899);

Le Billet de Joséphine, piano score and libretto (Paris: Choudens, 1902);

La Main passe (Paris: Librairie Théâtrale, 1906); translated by Suzanne Grossmann and Paxton Whitehead as *Chemin de Fer* (New York: S. French, 1968); translated by Walter Bruno as *Feydeau's Hand to Hand* (Toronto: Playwrights Canada, 1983);

Le Bourgeon (Paris: Librairie Théâtrale, 1906);

La Puce à l'oreille (Paris: Librairie Théâtrale, 1909); translated by Shaw as *A Flea in Her Rear* (New York: S. French, 1966); translated by Mortimer as *A Flea in Her Rear* (London: S. French, 1968); translated by Carol Johnson as *A Flea in Her Rear* (Chicago: Dramatic Publishing Company, 1968); translated by Brahms and Sherrin as *Caught in the Act*, in *After You, Mr. Feydeau;* translated by Frank Galati as *A Flea in Her Rear* (New York: Dramatists Play Service, 1989); translated by Graham Anderson as *A Flea in Her Rear* (London: Oberon Books, 1993); translated by Shapiro as *A Flea in Her Rear, or Ants in Her Pants*, in *A Flea in Her Rear, or Ants in Her Pants, and Other Vintage French Farces* (New York: Applause Theatre Books, 1994), pp. 303–434;

On purge Bébé, in *L'Illustration Théâtrale*, 20 August 1910, pp. 1–24; translated by Shapiro as *Going to Pot*, in *Tulane Drama Review*, 5 (Autumn 1960): 127–168; revised in *A Flea in Her Rear, or Ants in Her Pants, and Other Vintage French Farces;* translated by Peter Barnes as *The Purging*, in *The Frontiers of Farce* (London: Heine-

mann, 1977), pp. 3–40; translated by Peter Meyer as *Take Your Medicine Like a Man,* in *From Marriage to Divorce* (London: Oberon Books, 1997);

Occupe-toi d'Amélie, in *L'Illustration Théâtrale* (25 March 1911): 1–64; translated by Brainard Duffield as *Keep an Eye on Amélie*, in *Let's Get a Divorce! and Other Plays* (New York: Hill & Wang, 1958); translated by Noel Coward as *Look After Lulu* (New York: S. French, 1959); translated by Brahms and Sherrin as *Keep an Eye on Amélie*, in *Ooh! La-la;* translated by Marcoux as *That's My Girl!* in *Georges Feydeau, Three Farces;* translated by Robert Cogo-Fawcett and Braham Murray as *Keep an Eye on Amélie* (London: S. French, 1991); translated by Kenneth McLeish as *Mind Millie for Me* (London: Absolute Press, 1996);

"Mais n' te promène donc pas toute nue!," in *L'Illustration Théâtrale*, 17 February 1912; translated by C. Ostergren as *Don't Walk Around Stark Naked*, in *Yale/Theater*, 5 (Fall 1973): 66–107; translated by Don Tappan as *Don't Run Around in the Nude* (Schulenburg, Tex.: I. E. Clark, 1987); translated by Reggie Oliver as *Put Some Clothes On, Clarisse!* (New York: S. French, 1990); translated by Peter Meyer as *Don't Walk About with Nothing On*, in *From Marriage to Divorce;*

La Dame de chez Maxim (Paris: Librairie Théâtrale, 1914); translated anonymously as *The Girl from Maxim's* (Boston: Lincoln, 1900); translated by Gene Feist as *The Lady from Maxim's* (New York: S. French, 1971); translated by Mortimer as *The Lady from Maxim's* (London: Heinemann, 1977); translated by Brahms and Sherrin as *St. Shrimp*, in *Ooh! La-la;*

La Complainte du pauvre propriétaire (Paris: Librairie Théâtrale, 1916);

Léonie est en avance, ou Le Mal joli (Paris: Librairie Théâtrale, 1919); translated by Shapiro as *The Pregnant Pause, or Love's Labor Lost* (New York: Applause Theatre Books, 1985); translated by Peter Meyer as *One Month Early*, in *From Marriage to Divorce;*

Je ne trompe pas mon mari (Paris: Librairie Théâtrale, 1921);

Feu la mère de Madame, in *La Petite Illustration* (7 April 1923): 1–16; translated by Brahms and Sherrin as *A Good Night's Sleep*, in *Ooh! La-la;* translated by Meyer as *Better Late* (London: S. French, 1976); translated by Michael Pilch as *Night Errant* (London: S. French, 1990);

Champignol malgré lui (Paris: Librairie Théâtrale, 1925); translated by Meyer as *A Close Shave*

(London: British Broadcasting Corporation, 1974);

L'Hôtel du Libre-Echange (Paris: Librairie Théâtrale, 1928); adapted by George Grossmith and Arthur Miller as *A Night Out,* lyrics by Clifford Grey, music by Willie Redstone (London: B. Feldman, 1920); translated by Peter Glenville as *Hotel Paradiso* (New York: S. French, 1958); translated by Mortimer as *A Little Hotel on the Side* (London: S. French, 1984); translated by Nicholas Rudall as *Paradise Hotel* (Chicago: I. R. Dee, 1990);

Collections: *Théâtre complet,* 9 volumes (Paris: Le Bélier, 1948–1956)–volume 1 comprises *Occupe-toi d'Amélie, L'Affaire Edouard, Amour et piano, Fiancés en herbe,* and *Hortense a dit: "Je m'en fous!";* volume 2 includes *Chat en poche, Le Système Ribadier, Le Dindon, Séance de nuit,* and *Les Pavés de l'ours;* volume 3 includes *La Main passe, On purge Bébé, Je ne trompe pas mon mari,* and *Dormez, je le veux!;* volume 4 includes *Par la fenêtre, C'est une femme du monde, L'Hôtel du Libre-Echange, La Puce à l'oreille,* and *Léonie est en avance, ou Le Mal joli;* volume 5 includes *Le Mariage de Barillon, Monsieur chasse,* and *Le Circuit;* volume 6 includes *Gibier de potence, Champignol malgré lui, Un Fil à la patte, Notre futur, Cent millions qui tombent;* volume 7 includes *Un Bain de ménage, Les Fiancés de Loches, La Dame de chez Maxim, Feu la mère de Madame,* and *On va faire la cocotte;* volume 8 includes *La Lycéenne, "Mais n' te promène donc pas toute nue!," Le Ruban,* and *La Duchesse des Folies-Bergère;* volume 9 includes *Tailleur pour dames, Le Bourgeon,* and *L'Age d'or; Hortense a dit: "Je m'en fous!,"* translated, with an introduction, by Shapiro as *Hortense Said "No Skin Off My Ass!,"* in *Comedy: New Perspectives, New York Literary Forum,* 1 (Spring 1978); translated by Shapiro as *Tooth and Consequences, or Hortense Said "No Skin Off My Ass!"* (New York: S. French, 1979); translated by Marcoux as *Nothing But the Tooth,* in *Five by Feydeau; Chat en poche,* translated by Eric Conger as *A Frog in His Throat* (New York: SoHo Service Corporation, 1988); translated by Kenneth McLeish as *Pig in a Poke* (Bath, U.K.: Absolute Press, 1996); *Le Système Ribadier,* translated by Kenneth McLeish as *Now You See It* (Bath, U.K.: Absolute Press, 1996); *Le Dindon;* translated by Suzanne Grossmann and Paxton Whitehead as *There's One in Every Marriage* (New York: L. Kroll, 1970); translated by Brahms and Sherrin as *Paying the Piper* (London: Davis-Poynter, 1972); translated by Peter Meyer as *Sauce for the Goose* (London: British

Broadcasting Corporation, 1974); translated by Shaw as *The French Have a Word for It* (New York: S. French, 1983); translated by Nicki Frei and Peter Hall as *An Absolute Turkey* (Bath, U.K.: Absolute Press, 1994); *Séance de nuit; Les Pavés de l'ours,* translated by Brahms and Sherrin as *A Little Bit to Fall Back On,* in *Ooh! La-la;* translated by Shapiro as *The Boor Hug,* in *Feydeau, First to Last: Eight One-Act Comedies; Dormez, je le veux!,* translated by Shapiro as *Caught with His Trance Down,* in *Feydeau, First to Last: Eight One-Act Comedies;*

Quatre pièces pour rire (Paris: Club des Libraires de France, 1956)–comprises *Le Dindon, Feu la mère de Madame, On purge Bébé,* and *"Mais n' te promène donc pas toute nue!";*

Du mariage au divorce, edited by M. Perrin (Paris: Club du Meilleur Livre, 1959)–comprises *Feu la mère de Madame, Léonie est en avance, ou Le Mal joli, On purge Bébé, "Mais n' te promène donc pas toute nue!,"* and *Hortense a dit: "Je m'en fous!";*

Théâtre complet, 4 volumes, edited by Henry Gidel (Paris: Garnier, 1988–1989)–includes, in addition to the plays in the Le Bélier *Théâre complet,* all Feydeau's extant plays and monologues; the previously unpublished plays *L'Amour doit se taire, L'Homme de paille, Deux coqs pour une poule, A qui ma femme?,* and *Monsieur Nounou;* the monologues *Madame Sganarelle* and *Saute, marquis!;* and the short story *"La Mi-carême";*

Théâtre, edited by Bernard Murat (Paris: Omnibus, 1994)–comprises *Tailleur pour dames, Chat en poche, Monsieur chasse, Un Fil à la patte, L'Hôtel du Libre-Echange, Le Dindon, La Dame de chez maxim, La Puce à l'oreille, Occupe-toi d'Amélie, Feu la mère de Madame, On purge Bébé,* and *"Mais n' te promène donc pas toute nue!"*

SELECTED PERIODICAL PUBLICATIONS–UNCOLLECTED: "Courrier des théâtres" (a daily theatrical column), in *Le XIXème siècle,* 16 March 1885–1 March 1886;

"Comment Feydeau devint vaudevilliste," *Le Matin,* 15 March 1908;

"Lettre d'avant-première à Serge Basset," *Le Figaro,* 10 May 1911;

"Lettre d'avant-première," *Le Figaro,* 8 December 1911;

"De la rue Biot à *La Dame de chez Maxim,*" unidentified press clipping [Arsenal, R. F. 58.679], 26 April 1912;

Letter to *Le Figaro,* 3 June 1919;

"Lettre à Serge Basset: le vaudeville et le mélodrame sont-ils morts?," unidentified press clipping [Arsenal, R. F. 58.692].

The names of few French writers are as synonymous with their genres as is Georges Feydeau with his. Perhaps his only serious rival in this regard is the incomparable Jean de La Fontaine, whose name, for three hundred years, has virtually meant "the French verse fable." Feydeau's name, over the past five decades since his "rediscovery," has similarly meant "French farce." While dozens of his contemporaries in the genre have disappeared quietly back into the card files and databases of academic libraries, Feydeau continues actively to enjoy a reputation he would not have imagined possible in his lifetime. His work is now widely produced in France and wherever Western theater is staged; it is read and, indeed, seriously studied. All this has happened despite the prognostication of his elder colleague, poet-playwright Catulle Mendès, who predicted at the height of Feydeau's career that no one would ever read Feydeau's plays. One doubts moreover, that any of Feydeau's contemporaries, many of whom were no less celebrated than he in their day—Alfred Capus, Romain Coolus, Albin Valabrègue, Ernest Grenet-Dancourt, Edmond Gondinet, Léon Gandillot, or Julien Berr de Turique—will suddenly arise, resurrected from the obscurity of the theater specialists' shelves to achieve their own posthumous celebrity, on page or stage, and to challenge Feydeau's preeminence.

The rebirth of Feydeau's popularity in the early 1940s probably owed much, in the humor-starved Paris of the Occupation, to a certain nostalgia for the frothy frivolities of the Belle Epoque and its laughter without afterthought; for the extravagant, often "naughty," madcap postprandial romps of what the French dubbed the "digestive comedy" of the unofficial (not government subsidized) popular theaters of the Boulevard. But Feydeau had not been alone in confecting such easy-to-watch, easy-to-laugh-at farces. What distinguishes the best of his constructions—and they are just that in an architectural sense—is the very possibility of afterthought: in the post–World War II existentialist years of Jean-Paul Sartre, Albert Camus, and others, it was tempting, and intellectually comforting, to find in the meticulously crafted complexities of Feydeau, with their basically innocent heroes (or antiheroes) victimized by his relentless whimsy, a metaphor of the human condition. One could chortle to one's heart's and gut's content, with a certain satisfying philosophical justification, at the outrageous imbroglios—small, usually insignificant causes woven into great, monstrous ef-

Scene from Feydeau's L'Hôtel du Libre-Echange *at the Théâtre des Nouveautés, where it opened on 5 December 1894*

fects—that enmeshed his typical protagonists. Puppets in an arbitrary (if not actually malicious or even mischievous) universe, they afforded the serious-minded spectator the luxury of a cerebral rationale for a welcome visceral reaction.

Indeed, perfect and seemingly effortless as is the logical construction of the typical clockworklike Feydeau farce (or almost perfect: for all his reputation as the consummate craftsman, even he has occasional technical lapses), he might have been merely the best in the legion of forgotten fin-de-siècle disciples spawned by Eugène Scribe, talented but transient adepts of the cult of the "well-made play," clever practitioners of the intricate, well-oiled plot, with its variations on the time-proven themes of seduction, infidelity, and cuckoldry, enlivened with bits of social satire, racy innuendo, ebullient dialogue, and linguistic playfulness. Feydeau might have been just the best among the forgotten many, that is, were it not for the particular Feydeau brand of delectable madness. Innocent folly, absurdity, creative lunacy, capriciousness run amok, rampant dementia—whatever it is called, it is this madness that pervades and electrifies his theater and that sets him apart, and above, all the rest.

Feydeau's madness—the theatrical, not the clinical variety that was to beset him at the end of his too-brief life—comes in many shapes and sizes. On the most elementary level is the absurdity of the isolated remark, always perfectly true and logical in the abstract, but hilariously, often bizarrely, inappropriate in its context. Examples abound. Consider, for one, the observation voiced by Ursule, the bumptious domestic in *Le Mariage de Barillon* (1890; translated as *On the Marry-Go-Wrong,* 1970). The protagonist, in characteristic Feydeau fashion, has accidentally married his prospective mother-in-law. But Jambart, the latter's sailor husband, long disappeared and given up for drowned, suddenly returns, and the bigamous ménage à trois, to escape the taunts that their unorthodox situation attracts in the city, flee to the country while awaiting the promised annulment. When Ursule gives her notice, objecting that her family, concerned for her reputation, disapproves of her serving in a household whose morals are so obviously suspect, a scandalized Madame Jambart/Barillon reproaches the maid, telling her that she is no one to talk, and reminding her that she herself, after all, has been known to have a pair of romantic affairs going on at once. Ursule's reply is classic in its folly: "C'est possible, Madame, mais les miennes étaient illégitimes" (Yes, madame, but mine weren't both legal).

Similarly absurd, albeit more desperately motivated, is the offhand explanation that Feydeau puts into the mouth of Bois-d'Enghien, in *Un Fil à la patte* (1894; translated as *Not by Bed Alone,* 1970). When his lover, Lucette, whom he has been trying to ditch gently, unexpectedly appears at the home of his bride-to-be the evening of his marriage contract celebration, he has no recourse but to take refuge in the closest closet. Lucette, as the rules of any proper farce dictate, finds him cowering there, unwilling and unable to explain the reason for his presence, except by muttering the truism that "quelquefois, dans la vie, on a besoin de sisoler" (there are times when a man just feels like being alone). It is an observation that no one can deny, but quite logically askew, given the circumstances.

Again, note one of the many frustrating remarks uttered by Julie, wife of the harried Follavoine in *On purge Bébé* (1910; translated as *Going to Pot,* 1960), whose disheveled dress on the morning of an important business luncheon drives the latter to distraction. To quiet her husband's carpings Julie proceeds to use some of the elastic bands on his desk to hold up her sagging stockings. When Follavoine, be-

side himself, complains that they are elastic bands, not garters, Julie counters: "Ce n'est pas des jarretières, parce qu'on n'en fait pas des jarretières; mais puisque j'en fais des jarretières, ça devient des jarretières" (They're not garters because no one uses them as garters. But if I'm using them as garters, then they *are* garters). Who can argue with her impeccable, yet absurd, logic?

Feydeau's theater is rich in such examples. Equally so in those moments, similar but rather more complex, when a character about to be caught in flagrante delicto in some peccadillo or other is obliged to hide behind a fabricated bizarre explanation—usually buttressed by the facile prestige of would-be science—to save himself from the ensuing chagrin and mortification of discovery. Witness the many situations in which Doctor Moulineaux, victim of Feydeau's madcap whimsy in his first full-length comedy *Tailleur pour dames* (1886; translated as *A Fitting Confusion,* 1985), calls upon science—in pseudoscientific guise to be sure—to provide him with the spur-of-the-moment explanations that temporarily extricate him from certain disaster on many occasions during the action. Returning home early one morning from a failed amorous rendezvous of the evening before, Moulineaux is confronted by Yvonne, his suspecting wife. When he protests that he has been spending the night with a desperately ailing patient, Madame notes that he is in evening dress. Summoning a dubious medical science to the rescue, the doctor explains that it was necessary for him and his specialist colleagues to stage a mock soiree at the dying man's bedside to bolster his emotional well-being and shield him from the awful truth. When, a moment later, the "dying" man in question unexpectedly arrives on the scene, Moulineaux attempts to allay Madame's mounting suspicions by assuring her that the patient's impending death is a "chronic" condition—he could go on being about to die any minute for years—and that she should not be fooled by his appearance of perfect health. If she remains unconvinced, it is not for lack of a strong dose of absurdity in the wayward husband's explanation.

Undaunted, Moulineaux continues to fabricate similar bits of folly, as needed, within the web of circumstances that Feydeau mercilessly weaves about him—circumstances that, throughout the play, oblige him to indulge in the charade of playing a lady's fancy couturier. He does so to explain why, at the frenetic end of act 2, Yvonne had found him with a strange woman fainted dead away in his arms. (It was, in fact, a former inamorata, but that is beside the point.) When he can get her to listen, he claims that he had merely been called in as a specialist to study the woman's "curious pathology." Indeed, he would be happy to explain in greater detail, but "it's science," and she simply would not understand without years of rigorous study. Similarly, moments later, as Yvonne has begun to relent, Moulineaux's ingenuity is again tested. When the husband of his current would-be mistress inquires about the gown that he is supposed to be creating for her, and when Yvonne—unaware of her husband's pretended identity—asks "What gown?," the doctor replies unflinchingly, in a whisper, that it is a therapeutic garment: "une robe homéopathique . . . avec de l'électricité dedans" (a homeopathic gown . . . with electricity in it). He confirms the validity of his ridiculous assertion with the assurance, ex cathedra, that it too is "more science."

As is the case with the bizarre isolated remark, these absurd explanations, for all their folly, maintain a link with logic, at least in the minds of those intellectual unsophisticates to whom they are proffered. Mad as they are, there is a ring of credibility about them. They cannot be rejected out of hand; all the less so since they have the cachet and backing of Science with a capital *S,* that turn-of-the-century *nouvelle idole* worshiped by those who knew little or nothing of its workings and who could generally be counted on to bow down unquestioningly before it. Moulineaux's wife is somewhat atypical in this regard, taking longer than most to be convinced.

Much more usual is the gullibility of Madame Petypon, in *La Dame de chez Maxim* (1899; translated as *The Girl from Maxim's,* 1900), whose doctor husband, abetted by his colleague Mongicourt, perpetrates what is perhaps the prototypical example of many such devices in Feydeau's theater. Waking one morning after a night of unaccustomed and wholly innocent revelry, Petypon finds that he has apparently brought home a notorious cabaret performer, Môme Crevette. Apparently, that is, because she has been sleeping in his bed; a fact that he, understandably, wishes to conceal from his wife. When Petypon's unexplained panic arouses the latter's concern, Mongicourt, an early-morning visitor, comes to the rescue with an impressive-sounding medical diagnosis. Monsieur, he assures her, is suffering from a case of the dreaded "gueula lignea": a glorified Latinization of the French *gueule de bois,* or hangover. Moments later the pseudoscientific explanation is compounded as Petypon, amid his feverish attempts to get rid of "La Môme" while Madame is out of the room, is surprised by his wife's sudden approach. In a selfless effort to save the day, faithful friend Mongicourt convinces La Môme to get down on all fours, flings a rug over her, and sits down as casually as possible on the improvised pouf just as Madame returns. To distract her attention, the pan-

icking Petypon affects another attack of his gueula lignea, calling again on the prestige of science to save himself. "Tourne-moi au nord!" (Turn me toward the north!) he shouts at his flustered wife. "Tourne-moi au nord!" He adds, as if it were a perfectly well-established medical principle: "Dans ces crises, il faut tourner au nord!" (In attacks like this you always turn the patient toward the north!). Properly awed by the prestigious explanation, Madame Petypon complies, thus sparing her husband his mortification for a time. But of course, not for long. None of the legion of similarly mad explanations that Feydeau lets the victims of his whimsy confect is capable of conferring more than momentary salvation.

No less a product of the author's mad fancy than the absurd remarks and fantastic explanations he puts into the mouths of his characters are many of those characters themselves, for reasons both physical and behavioral. Undeterred by what is now termed "political correctness," Feydeau was quite willing to make gentle sport of mild physical irregularities, especially if they were bizarre enough to remove them from the everyday reality of an authentic, unfunny, disability. Thus there is a stammerer, Mathieu, in *L'Hôtel du Libre-Echange* (1894; translated as *Hotel Paradiso,* 1958), whose speech problem, no laughing matter in real life, affects him only when it rains. Lapige, in *La Main passe* (1904; translated as *Chemin de Fer,* 1968), is an emotional misfit whose timidity not only makes him quite inarticulate under pressure but even makes him bark like a dog at the most inappropriate moments. Needless to say, the plots of the plays in question are amply served by these anomalies. Occasionally, Feydeau cuts a little closer to the bone and exceeds the bounds of good taste, but never simply to indulge in mean-spirited, gratuitous mockery. In the case of young Camille, the Chandebises' cleft-palated nephew in *La Puce à l'oreille* (1907; translated as *A Flea in Her Rear, or Ants in Her Pants,* 1994), the absurdity of his role stems not from his physical impairment, which is eventually rectified by a miracle prosthesis, but rather from the flood of seeming gibberish that comes streaming from his lips, utterly incomprehensible except to his aunt, for whom it is somehow as clear as crystal.

The absurd nature of other characters lies not in their physical but in their behavioral eccentricities, which are especially marked in the impressive array of foreigners—English men and women, Latins, assorted Germanics and others—who people his comedies and add immeasurably to their delicious folly; characters (or caricatures) whose unorthodox social, amorous, and especially linguistic comport-

Scene from act 2 of La Main passe, *Feydeau's 1904 comedy about marital disillusion, at the Théâtre des Nouveautés*

ment, eccentric by definition, according to French standards, by simple virtue of their non-Frenchness, is rendered even more akin to madness by Feydeau's exaggerated treatment of them. Thus one revels, as the author himself must have done, in the portrayals of the randy brothel client Rugby in *La Puce à l'oreille* and his compatriot Maggy in *Le Dindon* (1896; translated as *There's One in Every Marriage,* 1970), undaunted in her trans-Channel escapades by a rudimentary knowledge of French; the irascible and hot-blooded General Irrigua in *Un Fil à la patte* and his brother-under-the-skin, the gun-toting Homenidès de Histangua, in *La Puce à l'oreille;* the lumpish Flemish domestics Elie in *Dormez, je le veux!* (1897; translated as *Caught with His Trance Down,* 1982) and Bretel in *Les Pavés de l'ours* (1896; translated as *The Boor Hug,* 1982); the big-hearted but naive Van Putzeboum in *Occupe-toi d'Amélie* (1908; translated as *Keep an Eye on Amélie,* 1958); the veritable Slavic menagerie in *La Duchesse des Folies-Bergère* (The Duchess of the Folies-Bergère, 1902); and others of their ilk, all going to provide a multiethnic counterpoint to Feydeau's main-theme French bourgeoisie, but whose presence is intended as anything but an idealization of diversity.

Strongly dosed with madness, too, are the nonverbal devices that Feydeau uses to unleash the laughter of his spectators: the visual, blatantly farcical effects that require no linguistic or analytical acumen to evoke appreciation and reaction. Overly serious theatergoers must have felt in his day—and, along with some theater-readers, must still feel in the present—a kind of artistic guilt at allowing themselves to be affected by such direct and intellectually undemanding visceral humor, a trifle ashamed at letting themselves be manipulated against their will and better critical judgment. But Feydeau probably did not care much then, nor would he care much today. Belly laughs, like sneezes, can neither be forced nor commanded not to happen; and it is the laughter of this "belly" variety—as opposed to the smile, the chuckle, the controlled guffaw at witty repartee and the more cerebral brand of humor—that Feydeau serves up in his spate of visual effects: the trained seal that Jambart, in *Le Mariage de Barillon,* brings home and that spontaneously barks out its "Papa! Maman!" to add to the general confusion; the sudden catalepsy of the unsuspecting victims of Doctor Petypon's "entrancing" *fauteuil extatique* in *La Dame de chez Maxim;* Monsieur Chouilloux's headlong flight out the nearest door after accidentally swallowing the laxative meant for Toto in *On purge Bébé;* and the hypnotically induced apelike antics of Monsieur Boriquet, and his sister's grotesque fandango, in *Dormez, je le veux!* or the titanic "hypnoduel" between his unscrupulous domestic and his prospective father-in-law in the same comedy. Nor are all of Feydeau's essentially visual effects seen directly. Some of the most hilarious duels in his extensive repertory—Alcibiades's duel with hand drills, Brazilian-style, in *Par la fenêtre* (1882; translated as *Wooed and Viewed,* 1970), or Petypon's with scalpels, in *La Dame de chez Maxim,* to cite but two—exist in the mind's eye alone. While they never actually take place, they are discussed and easily imagined, no less hilarious for their folly than if they were seen in action.

Visual, too, though more abstract in nature, is the madness intrinsic to the very fabric of farce and Feydeau's stock-in-trade: the relentless progress of the action, with its jack-in-the-box entrances and precipitous exits, all timed to perfection like the cogged wheels of a diabolical machine, mounting in crescendos against the background of slamming doors and the desperate interjections of those caught up in its gears. For, delectable in their lunacy as are all the elements of the typical Feydeau farce, they are ancillary to the basic madness of his theater—the madness inherent in those wild situations into which, with the perverse pleasure and abandon of a god-turned-mischief-maker, he plunges his luckless victims, who thrash about in their folly-ridden nightmares wondering "Why me, Lord?" or an appropriate equivalent thereof until Feydeau charitably frees them with a plot-resolving flourish. It is a truism that every playwright is in a power relationship with his characters. But in Feydeau's case the power often borders on cruelty, or would do so were one not constantly aware that this is comedy, after all. Played in a different key, many of his typical farces could almost be worthy of Antonin Artaud.

This suffering that Feydeau visits on his characters, whether the consequence of a modest peccadillo or wholly gratuitous and undeserved, is usually a torment of only emotional dimensions. In many cases, however, it can be painfully physical as well. A classic example is that of Champignol, in *Champignol malgré lui,* not to blame in the slightest for his fate but who, while doing his military service, eventually has his head shaved down to the skin with sandpaper to conform to regulations, all because of a mistaken identity that confuses him with his wife's long-tressed aspiring lover. More uncomfortable still is the situation of innocent-victim-once-removed Vildamour, in Feydeau's last play,

Hortense a dit: "Je m'en fous!" (1916; translated as *Hortense Said "No Skin Off My Ass!,"* 1978). At the comedy's tempestuous conclusion, virtually bound and gagged in dentist Follbraguet's chair, with his mouth full of apparatus, he is left to suffer alone as the latter, fed up with his wife's maddening behavior, storms out of his office in a frenzy, leaving the scene of marital bedlam behind.

The emotional torment that Feydeau's fancy makes so many of his victims suffer, while less painful to their flesh, is no less painful to their psyche. One could cite examples of these unfortunates in almost every one of his comedies, from the early to the late, including Barillon, whose grotesque marital nightmare is the result of no comic flaw whatever on his part, but merely of a drunken civil servant's clerical error; and the Doctors Moulineaux and Petypon, each of whom must struggle against a fate brought on by a social indiscretion, but a modest one by objective standards. For others, such as Bouzin in *Un Fil à la patte* and Tournel in *La Puce à l'oreille,* the emotional punishment they are called on to endure while entangled in the consequences of similarly petty transgressions—Bouzin for a bit of harmless pretense, Tournel for pure lust, but a lust unfulfilled—is compounded by the fear of a punishment worse even than Champignol's as they are stalked like frightened prey by their respective fire-breathing Latin antagonists in a frenzy of chases and the ever-present slamming doors.

But none of these characters in Feydeau's semilunatic universe, driven in varying degrees toward the brink of madness by his almost sadistic caprice, suffers as intensely as the husbands in the late one-act plays of domestic discord—victims, like Follavoine and Follbraguet, not of a vast mechanical imbroglio constructed with geometric precision but simply of the down-to-earth, desperate incompatibility of two spouses, a Strindbergian duo that reappears throughout the five plays of the series in a variety of situations. There are no slick-shaven heads here, no frenetic attempts to escape from the clutches of jealous, wild-eyed Latins, or to break free from the monstrous effects of some absurd but perfectly understandable misunderstanding. There is only the unspeakable frustration, increasing from play to play, of middle-class husbands trapped in the maelstrom of wife-induced chaos. That these plays reflect Feydeau's own conjugal difficulties is clear from his biographical facts; but these facts represent only his side of the story. What might Madame Feydeau, his "inspiration" in these seriocomic slices of married life, have written had she, too, been a playwright? These late plays of Feydeau's confirm the truism that it is an ill wind that blows no good, which is especially true in art, where artistic delight can result from the storm of the creative artist's personal angst and his sublimation of it.

Likewise as regards Feydeau's own personal dementia. It is supremely ironic, and would be farcical in itself were it not humanly tragic, that this master of theatrical madness, after several years of declining physical and mental health and the deterioration of his marriage, ended his days insane, a flesh-and-blood victim pushed over that same edge of sanity that his fictional creatures had all so perilously been skirting.

It is customary to divide Feydeau's career into four periods. His earliest plays were a natural outgrowth of the Parisian society that lionized him in his youth. Son of the socially prominent intellectual Ernest Feydeau and Léocadie (Lodzia) Zelewska, a Polish beauty rumored to have had a liaison with Napoleon III (and, eventually, son-in-law of society portraitist Carolus Duran), the young Feydeau, fresh from the Collège Sainte-Barbe and already a talented actor, quickly became known for his witty dramatic monologues in prose and verse; examples of a genre that spread like an epidemic during the last two decades of the century, along with other unassuming little playlets by the known and less known, tailored to the dimensions of the fashionable drawing room.

Feydeau's first three plays, each in one act—*Notre futur* (1882; translated as *Ladies' Man,* 1982), *Par la fenêtre* (1883; translated as *Wooed and Viewed,* 1970), and *Amour et piano* (1883; translated as *Romance in A Flat,* 1982)—fit squarely into this tradition. Apart from a few youthful attempts *Par la fenêtre* is usually considered his first extant *saynète* (playlet), a genre a little more ambitious than the monologue. The date given by the most reliable sources for its initial performance is 1 June 1882, and the place, a small Parisian venue, with a subsequent performance shortly thereafter in a resort town near Dunkerque. But the modest *Notre futur,* seldom accorded any importance by Feydeau critics, must also date from this early period. Although not mentioned by any sources as being performed until 1894, and supposedly left unpublished until its appearance decades later in *Théâtre complet* (1952), the playlet did, in fact, appear in print in 1882 (in the company of works by many better-known contemporaries), in a popular *saynète* collection of the period. This leads to the speculation that it may indeed have been Feydeau's first, though admittedly not by much. The playlet's very nature seems to confirm this hypothesis. Looked at with hindsight, it is clearly not "typical Feydeau." For all its charm, and even with its "surprise" denouement—a rich young gentleman's jilting of two rivals for his affection to marry a third—it is written in a much more sentimental vein than his later work. Few of Feydeau's later heroines give way to outbursts of authentic tears as poor Valentine does in her first disillusioning foray into romance. They cry crocodile tears, or tears of spite, anger, even of rage, but seldom, if ever, of sorrow or remorse. Feydeau's typical females become a more cynical lot, much more like Valentine's social-butterfly cousin, Henriette. It is as if, after a first tentative venture into sentimental comedy, Feydeau quickly realized, even if only intuitively, that delicate emotion was not to be his forte, that the robust humor of mad, absurd imbroglio, albeit tempered with wit and frequent social wisdom, was where his talents lay. *Par la fenêtre,* also a duologue, put him squarely on that track with its heroine's unorthodox request that her neighbor make love to her by an open window to excite the jealousy of her supposedly philandering husband across the way. *Amour et piano* followed, essentially a delicate little pas de deux, based on mistaken identity and provincial pretensions, though with the further development of an added minor character.

It is clear that this trio of early endeavors was conceived with salon audiences in mind. Even the piano in *Amour et piano*—a rather cumbersome prop for a twenty-minute trifle—suggests a ready-made drawing-room decor. In content each piece is essentially one-situational, developing variations on the theme of mistaken identity or mistaken motive. In technique, too, each exploits the unrealistic conventions of monologue and aside, dramatic devices common to their period in general, and to salon comedy in particular, in which the inherent intimacy of the situation—the proximity of an audience sympathetically predisposed, almost by definition—makes it all the more tempting to ignore the "fourth wall."

Still, limited and unambitious as these early playlets are, they contain here and there the seeds of things to come. *Par la fenêtre* introduces several Feydeau themes and characters in germ. The women stand out especially, as they do through all his theater: both the onstage Emma and the hero Hector's offstage wife, whose jealous wrath he fears should she learn of his bizarre encounter. The latter, though never seen, prefigures the many willful heroines of later plays, especially those at the end of Feydeau's career. As for Emma, Hector's tempestuous next-door neighbor, who has come to give her allegedly wayward husband visible tit for tat, she is only the first of many emancipated Feydeau females bent on avenging their husbands' peccadillos, real or imagined.

The men of the playlet—both the seen and the unseen—are equally prototypical of many future Feydeau characters. Hector, the butt of his wife's groundless suspicions as well as of Emma's unusual demand, matures into the several harassed husbands of the later plays, of whom Follbraguet in *Hortense a dit: "Je m'en fous!,"* the last, is the ne plus ultra, literally as well as figuratively. And Emma's Brazilian spouse, the fiery Alcibiades, whose jealousy sets the comedy in motion, though only a bodiless allusion in *Par la fenêtre,* later takes on the concrete form of General Irrigua in *Un Fil à la patte* and Homenidés de Histangua in *La Puce à l'oreille.* There he blusters across the stage, the incarnation of the swaggering Latin *rastaquouère,* soldier of fortune (and of lady's boudoir), a common figure in French society and literature since the Second Empire. Here he, in the wings, and Emma, onstage, are only the first of the legion of foreigners to parade through Feydeau's theater, which reflected the fact that Paris was becoming an increasingly cosmopolitan center.

But if *Par la fenêtre* prefigures many of Feydeau's later comedies, it is not only for its foreshadowing of certain characters and its occasional modest attempts at passing social commentary but also for the absurdity of its premise. (Where but in the universe of a Feydeau-type farce, with its special rules of logic and its own mad brand of cause and effect, will strange ladies—strange in both senses of the word—appear and ask their neighbors to make love to them in full view?) The same may be said of *Amour et piano.* All its characters appear again in different guise and in different circumstances. Lucile, the well-bred ingenue in her first brush with romance, but—like Valentine in *Notre futur*—not quite ready to blossom into womanhood, appears frequently in Feydeau's repertory. Her inept domestic, Baptiste, fresh from the country, agog at Parisian ways and properly malapropistic, develops into the boor of *Les Pavés de l'ours,* a well-meaning bull in his master's amorous china shop, as well as into less destructive, but typical, domestics, male and female. As for the would-be roué, Edouard, the fatuous provincial dandy seeking to add his ripple to the social whirl of Paris, no less agog but more adept, he, too, has many future Feydeau incarnations. At this early stage of Feydeau's career he appears as the philandering Latin professor in *Gibier de potence* (1883; translated as *Fit to Be Tried, or Stepbrothers in Crime,* 1982), less of a dandy but no less the provincial, and, like Edouard, in quest of that surefire badge of worldly success, a Parisian actress-mistress. His kind continues—developed, expanded, and nuanced—through Feydeau's theater: the provincial, of both sexes, dazzled by the social and intellectual prestige of Paris.

But contemporary allusion and stock characters aside, as with *Par la fenêtre,* what strikes one most in *Amour et piano* as "typical Feydeau" in germ is the folly of the imbroglio: mistaken identity compounded and giving rise, before the inevitable disentangling, to a series of comically suggestive double entendres, tame by any standards but titillating in their implied naughtiness, especially given the virginal innocence of the sweet young thing entangled; tame, especially, for a Feydeau who does not shrink, later in his career, from placing his boudoir adventurers and adventuresses into bed together. Clearly Feydeau was no prude. What has come to be known as bedroom farce was no genre for the bluenose. But neither was he a pornographer. He would stretch good taste to the limit at times, but never beyond. (A possible exception might be made for the late three-act play *Le Circuit,* a collaboration in 1909 with the young Francis de Croisset, parts of which are in extremely dubious taste; but Feydeau's contribution was probably minimal.) It may even be argued that much of his broadest, most explicit bedroom farce is essentially moralistic. After all, those who lust illicitly, in the mind or in the flesh, are usually plunged into a variety of infernal mortifications—emotional at least and even physical on occasion—to reap the wages of their sins, if only temporarily. Still rather timid in this regard in an early trifle such as *Amour et piano,* Feydeau is content to imply and let his spectators infer. Certainly in the context of this doubly youthful opus—both by and about the young—an ounce of inference is worth a pound of explicitness.

Another early one-act play, *Gibier de potence,* represents an important transition in Feydeau's stagecraft. *Tailleur pour dames,* his first ambitious three-act comedy, was not performed until 1886. An immediate success, it marked the beginning of Feydeau's second period, his emergence as a budding comic dramatist. *Gibier de potence* clearly points the way. His first multicharacter comedy, it is longer and already far more complex in plot and structure than its slender one-act predecessors and far richer in what later became his typical comedic devices. Unlike its more impressive successor, *Tailleur pour dames,* it shows a fledgling Feydeau still clinging to the security of the one-act nest but clearly maturing for more ambitious flight. Conventional monologues, asides, and sly confidences to the audience have not vanished from his technique, nor do they, all at once, though they become less evident as he develops a more realistic stagecraft, perhaps influenced in the 1890s by André Antoine's dramatic verism. The opening scene of the hapless Lemercier

Scene from Feydeau's 1910 farce On purge Bébé, *at the Théâtre des Nouveautés*

is a long monologue that still smacks of the salon, much as did Henriette's in *Notre futur,* Hector's in *Par la fenêtre*, and Edouard's in *Amour et piano.* As for the customary asides and the remarks to the complicitous audience, the action would be virtually impossible without them.

In other respects, however, *Gibier de potence* marks a definite advance. Its expanded cast of characters develops some types only lightly sketched in the preceding playlets, or left altogether invisible in the wings, and introduces others as yet unmet. Lemercier is a fleshed-out, middle-aging Edouard, though no less the fatuous provincial (for all his Latin), and no less intent on paying court to a Parisian actress. An ingenuous bungler and innocent butt, he foreshadows the luckless Bouzin, suffering antihero of *Un Fil à la patte,* whose only transgressions are his pretentious advances to actress Lucette Gautier, flesh-and-blood sister to Edouard's unseen actress. Pépita is something of a Lucette-in-the-making, not yet quite the toast of the Paris stage. Feydeau developed her later into the notorious Môme Crevette of *La Dame de chez Maxim,* whose brash, flamboyant, but lovable vulgarity made her

name a Parisian household word for more than a decade. Pépita, considerably more reserved than La Môme and certainly more domesticated, needs no excuse, such as Emma's unorthodox vengeance, to indulge her extramarital fancy. She too has many descendants, liberated Feydeau ladies for whom marriage is no guarantor of morals.

The other major characters in *Gibier de potence* all make their first bow, but certainly not their last. Plumard, the cuckold, spawns a hearty lineage. Given the preponderance of the cuckold in French farce from the Middle Ages on, it was inevitable that Feydeau eventually portrayed him—frequently, and with considerable nuance. For, if Plumard suspects Pépita's probable involvement, other horned husbands are less aware; Chouilloux, for example, in *On purge Bébé,* who learns of his wife's infidelity only in time for the traumatic revelation to rebound, as expected, on the innocent Follavoine. Nor do they all react in the same way. Some, such as Chouilloux, give vent to their rage, demanding the redemption of their honor at swords' points; while others, such as Savinet, the wine merchant in *Le Système Ribadier* (1892; translated as *Now You See It,* 1996), accept their horns docilely, less concerned for their blemished manhood than for their professional prestige. Still another, Chanal, the congenial bourgeois of *La Main passe,* reacts, after the first shock, with rare good sense and good humor, evoking sympathy rather than derision. Plumard, the first, is a curious case. Astute enough to have his eyes opened to Pépita's liaison (by watching a performance of *Othello,* no less), he is still too blind to see how she had hoodwinked him into a marriage of convenience in the first place. But without his awareness there would be no plot: intent upon revenge, he sets in motion a plan that will have unforeseen results—unforeseen in the ordinary scheme of things but perfectly logical in the folly of Feydeau's emerging universe. The rather bland Taupinard, Pépita's lapdog lover, is Feydeau's first "other man," but he has many descendants, all as varied as the husbands they so blithely wrong. As for Dubrochard, the grocer-cum-cop, he too is a Feydeau first. A caricature of the former military man imperfectly turned civilian, he is probably a projection of the young author's anticipation of his upcoming army service. The character develops full-blown almost a decade later into the assorted army types of *Champignol malgré lui* (1892; translated as *A Close Shave,* 1974), the immensely successful Feydeauesque nightmare that portrays the tribulations, corporeal and spiritual, of a would-be philanderer and his almost-cuckold victim enmeshed in the mindlessness of military authoritarianism. In *Gibier de potence* Dubrochard, for the few moments he bellows about as a surrogate police chief, relives the dubious glories of his military past with a dogmatic, monolithic devotion to duty. At the same time he cannot forget that he is a grocer. On the contrary, he plies his civilian trade at the most inappropriate moments, in the midst of chaos, embodying that kind of professional rigidity, single-minded and mechanical, that characterizes a variety of Feydeau obsessives: a Marollier, the "professional second" in *La Dame de chez Maxim,* for whom the protocol of the duel is more important than either its cause or its result; a Planteloup, the insistent police chief in *La Main passe,* determined to solve a nonexistent crime; Lemercier, the professor, inopportunely spouting his Latin as if by reflex; and, to a lesser extent, poor Plumard, the wronged husband.

For Plumard, the herb doctor with a puffed-up opinion of the value of his calling, prefigures many other professionals rather similarly inclined—such as the antimicrobian Doctor Paginet, hero of *Le Ruban* (1894), who covets a decoration for his misguided efforts, and, in a less scientific realm, Follavoine, manufacturer of chamberpots in *On purge Bébé,* imbued with an idealized conception of the product of his labors. As one would expect, Feydeau has Plumard's self-important notions properly deflated, not only by Pépita's sarcastic taunts but also by the audience's own recognition of his obvious simplicity. The good "doctor," after all, is scientifically naive enough to see a medical miracle in his own premature paternity. He also provides Feydeau with an opportunity for another jab at contemporary pretension: the mania for unmerited decoration. Just as Emma's reference to the duel in *Par la fenêtre* is only the first of many, so too the allusions here to the decoration craze rampant in fin-de-siècle France, where no end of bourgeois pretenders to distinction yearned to sport an imposing ribbon on their lapels. If none of the several domestic honors was within reach, there was always recourse to a seemingly endless array beyond the borders. Plumard, ashamed of his naked button hole, mumbles that his wife, after all, does know a Rumanian prince. The implication, to Feydeau's audience, would be clear; and all the more ironic since the naive Plumard does not seem to realize what services she will be called upon to perform to get him his medal (like the heroine of the late farce *Occupe-toi d'Amélie,* whose father is promised an impressive decoration in return for securing her *services exceptionnels* to the lecherous Slavic prince). Those affected by the decoration mania suffer varying degrees of Feydeau's good-natured ridicule. Doctor Paginet in *Le Ruban* embodies it to the fullest and is reminiscent of Molière's miser Harpagon in his willingness to sacrifice even his family to his obsession. By a delightfully ironic twist he finally sees himself decorated, but only by mistake.

In sum, then, although *Gibier de potence* is slighted, if not ignored altogether, by most Feydeau critics, it is surely a significant link in his development. It is hard to imagine the leap from *Amour et piano* to *Tailleur pour dames* without a *Gibier de potence* or its like in-between; not primarily for the characters it develops or introduces or for the modest social allusions—all common to many a humorist of the period—nor for the expanded punning and wordplay, promise of things to come, but rather for the burgeoning complexity of its structure. Pépita's affair, Plumard's revenge, and Lemercier's ambition all become entwined in a case of multiple mistaken identities, a mad imbroglio typical of the mature Feydeau. Lemercier's and Taupinier's extravagant mutual fabrication is already a masterpiece, appropriately absurd, of contrived deceit growing more and more involved and entangling its inventors. Feydeau's theater later became rich in such protracted prevarications.

As a result one is not surprised to find in his later, "well-made" Scribean constructions—*Champignol malgré lui, La Dame de chez Maxim, La Puce à l'oreille*—an abundance of unabashed physical action. In postclassical theater it is difficult to ensnare a helpless character in nothing more than words and ideas, however powerful—at least until the theater of Samuel Beckett. As the ultimate examples of such mechanistic farce, Feydeau's extravaganzas, as suggested in earlier paragraphs, become visual in the extreme, prototypes of what one unsympathetic critic—his own stepfather, Henry Fouquier— disparagingly termed, citing one of Feydeau's elders, "Hennequin's theater of a hundred doors." It is not the wordy, sociocerebral comedy of a Bernard Shaw or the equally wordy, poeticophilosophical comedy of a Jean Giraudoux. Despite the frequent, irrepressible glints of wit, the *mots,* the unforgettable characters, the barbs of social commentary that distinguished Feydeau's farces from the strictly mechanistic, action is still paramount in all its mad frenzy. It is a comedy for the eye as much as, or more than, for the ear, a complex collaboration of meaning and motion. With action there is "business"; with "business" there are props; and with props there is more action, as his precise, often intricate stage directions attest. These directions became an integral part of the mechanism, making the director of a typical Feydeau farce as much a choreographer as an interpreter of lines, and oftentimes more. *Gibier de potence* is rather modest in this respect. With its physical confrontations, sight gags, and props—Lemercier's puppy, his coat, his recalcitrant umbrella (foreshadowing the luckless Bouzin's in *Un Fil à la patte*)—Feydeau takes a giant step toward the visual comedy that became his hallmark for the next quarter-century, through the height of his career.

The period inaugurated by the heady success of *Tailleur pour dames* had its ups and downs for the young Feydeau. Enough downs to lead him, some four years later, to a brief hiatus, a two-year "exile" from the stage for artistic introspection. During this period he devoted himself to the study of three comic masters in an attempt to hone his own technique: Alfred Hennequin, father of one of his future collaborators, Eugène Labiche—acknowledged "king of the Boulevard"—and Henri Meilhac, little known today but much admired in his time. Meanwhile, immediately after the warm reception of *Tailleur pour dames* by both public and critics, he tried his hand at several more three-act plays and even an operetta libretto, *La Lycéenne* (1887), exploiting the then novel (and topical) subject of female public education. He also continued to compose his witty monologues, as well as two one-act plays, a genre to which he had clearly become attached.

One of the latter, *C'est une femme du monde* (1890; translated as *Mixed Doubles,* 1982), an early collaborative effort with Maurice Desvallières and one of a double bill produced on the eve of his "exile," deserves more attention that it is usually given. With this one-act play Feydeau seems to be retreating to security, as if he felt the need to retrench from an overextended technique beginning to run wild. Not that Feydeau was about to abandon the comedy of complexity, already his trademark, or that, indeed, he was to return to the intimate sentimental genre abortively attempted in *Notre futur.* On the contrary, *Le Mariage de Barillon,* the three-act comedy that joined *C'est une femme du monde* in a double bill, is a veritable romp through a bizarre marital nightmare. But it is a romp more tightly constructed, more rigorously logical in its mechanistic development than the several preceding near "flops." Perhaps it was intended to satisfy the demands of those critics, such as straightlaced Auguste Vitu of the *Figaro,* who had called for more "logic" from the playwright in the fabrication of his "ludicrous entanglements." As a pair, these two plays seem to signal Feydeau's efforts to convince the critics that *Tailleur pour dames* had been no flash in the pan: the one, by polishing and tightening his flamboyant technique; the other, by discreetly retreating from it to the comfort of a more conservative one-act play. This is not to say that *C'est une femme du monde* lacks the expected Feydeau complexity, but its complexity is on a smaller scale, situational, not slapstick, with no sight gags, no essential visual business, no slamming of doors pounding out their counterpoint to the confusion (unlike its partner, *Le Mariage de Barillon,* to which it provided an appropriate counterpoise). It is one of those rare Feydeau comedies that can be enjoyed in the reading almost as much as in the seeing. Its structure, easily appreciated on the page, is admittedly rather contrived and predictable: not the conventional lovers' triangle, but a neat "lovers' square," a naughty chiasmus.

Like most other light comedies of the period, Feydeau's included, *C'est une femme du monde* offers several social insights. Obviously its raison d'être is not as a social document. Still, it seems that the element of social sport—"satire" would be too ambitious a term—is more important in this play than in its predecessors. The reason is in the very predictability of the plot. For all their passing social allusions and caricature, such playlets as *Par la fenêtre* and *Gibier de potence* are more notable for the absurdity of their plots and resolutions. One is never quite certain just how they will turn out. Even *Amour et piano,* simple as it is, is not wholly predictable. By contrast, in *C'est une femme du monde* Feydeau seems hardly to be trying at all to conceal the denouement, even from the beginning. One suspects the relationships among all the characters, and feels little surprise when, at the end, suspicions are confirmed.

The interest and humor lie, rather, in the sketches of certain social fauna and their interactions, and, by implication, of the milieu that produced them. This comedy offers Feydeau's most explicit tableau to that point in his career, of the contemporary world of Parisian easy virtue. True, his earlier efforts had (implicitly, at least) already portrayed individuals of dubious conventional morality. Emma's amorous request of Hector, in *Par la fenêtre,* is not for innocent amusement; Edouard, in *Amour et piano,* has not come seeking his actress for a game of checkers; clearly Pépita and Taupinier, in *Gibier de potence,* are no saints; and mistresses, lovers, wronging husbands, and wronged wives weave through the fabric of the comedies that followed as early as *Tailleur pour dames,* but nowhere in such a concentrated dose. A society in microcosm, *C'est une femme du monde* presents a tableau of infidelity rampant: two braces of heroes and heroines, mistresses blithely cuckolding their no-less-blithely two-timing lovers—cads and cadesses all, albeit unbound by the bonds of matrimony, which in any event, would certainly not have stopped them. (Their humorous antics later sound a more serious echo in the elaborate mate-swapping of *La Main passe.*) In this comedy Feydeau plays no favorites, spoofing both the demimonde would-be society ladies, as well as their respectable bourgeois lotharios. The former, cocottes turned coquettes, awkwardly struggling through a maze of verbose affectation to keep their masks from slipping, are clearly the principal butts of his humor. But their men obviously amuse him too: self-important, convinced of their irresistible charms, sure that in their private dining-room love nest (backdrop for many later Feydeau adventures) they will easily wear down the resistance of their "society ladies." Paturon is even more the roué than Gigolet, yearning for the spice of danger and challenge to excite his jaded romantic palate and feed his self-image. But both lovers deserve the mortification of their egos, and to their credit both accept it gracefully in the end, convinced that a good meal is worth even more than a good affair—at least until the next time.

C'est une femme du monde is also the first of several Feydeau comedies to reflect another social phenomenon: divorce. After many years of agitation and debate, civil divorce was reestablished in France in 1884. Society quickly felt the results. As for the theater of the period, serious and comic, before and long after, it is filled with theses on the one hand, imbroglios on the other, and a host of passing allusions, light and heavy. Playwrights were adding a new string to their bows. Their characters no longer had to suffer infidelity in silence or resort to adultery, comic or dramatic. In this play, true to the spirit of the Boulevard humorists, Feydeau's allusion to divorce, while essential to the machinations of the plot, is properly lighthearted, providing a topical twist to the denouement. It will be so, too, in others of his plays. Only with *La Main passe,* a more serious comedy of marital disillusion (and, indeed, dissolution), does it take on a much less frivolous dimension at a time when the author's own domestic difficulties were beginning to project themselves onto his creations. Eventually the specter of divorce hovers over the five late plays of conjugal discord as well.

Feydeau's subsequent two-year absence from the boards—his voluntary "exile"—came to an end with a bang in 1892 with the production of no less than three successful comedies. From that point on success followed success virtually unabated. To list the plays produced during that third period of his career is, with few exceptions, to name all the best-known "machines" that were building his reputation then and that confirm it today: *Champignol malgré lui, Un Fil à la patte, L'Hôtel du Libre-Echange, Le Dindon*—all triumphs in their own time and no less so today. By the end of the century his most ambitious play was the celebrated *La Dame de chez Maxim.* It was also his most unqualified success. Critics were to vie with one another for superlatives as the comedy quickly became the classic of the genre, spreading Feydeau's name far and wide. But Feydeau, whose laziness had become legendary, did not, by his own admission, give birth to his progeny without a painful labor; and his chef d'oeuvre did not see the light of day—or of the footlights—until January 1899, though conceived and largely completed two years before. Having produced *Le Dindon* in February 1896, to critical and public acclaim, and already addicted to the sweet smell of success (and the no-less-sweet smell of cash, for his growing financial obligations and speculations), Feydeau was not about to let the public lose sight of him for three years while he reworked, finished, and polished his magnum opus. Several one-act plays were called upon to fill the gap.

Two of these, *Les Pavés de l'ours* and *Dormez, je le veux!,* deserve special mention, presenting a coherent and contrasting pair. Both are rich in Feydeau's verbal humor and his typical situational inventiveness. But while both are variations on the age-old master-servant theme, the second, exploiting the then-current rage of hypnotism, is basically a visual comedy: the cagey servant Justin's character and stratagem—his ability to have his employer, Boriquet, do all the housework—are essential, but they really exist only to provide an excuse for the zany physical antics of his unsuspecting victims and his eventual "hypno-duel" with his outraged antagonist. The first, on the other

Actress Madeleine Renaud as Amélie in a revival of Feydeau's 1908 farce, Occupe-toi d'Amélie

hand, though not without its visual moments and its less-than-subtle touches—Madame Prévallon's provocative stammer, for example, typical of many another Feydeauesque physical imperfection—is more a character study, if such a high-sounding term can be used in this context. The results of Bretel's boorish good intentions are themselves less important than the foibles that precipitate them. Whereas Justin is the product of a transient fad, Bretel is an unforgettable type. The one provokes belly laughs; the other, a more reflective chuckle.

The two contrast also in their embodiment of the venerable master-servant theme; a theatrical staple in which a social inferior—a kind of archetypal *puer* vis-à-vis the symbolic *senex*—compensates for his low social status by his presence of mind and intellectual resourcefulness, usually by abetting his inept master's amours and satisfying his own ego thereby. If Justin is a distant descendant of Molière's prototypical Scapin, it is, however, only because of his inferior station, his superior wit, and his efforts at compensatory self-

aggrandizement, certainly not because of any desire to serve his master's needs. Quite the contrary. In this he is spiritually closer to the scurrilous likes of Alain-René Lesage's Crispin and Frontin, reflections of early-eighteenth-century rumblings of upward social mobility. Bretel is his opposite in practically every respect. Justin is the cynical, ingenious Parisian; Bretel, the dim-witted, ingenuous provincial. If Justin thinks only of manipulating Boriquet to serve his own ends, well-meaning Bretel is selfless to a fault. His sole concern is to serve his new master. The results of their adventures are likewise symmetrically opposite. Boriquet is trying to marry his fiancée, and despite Justin's efforts to scuttle his love life, he wins in the end (though not by his own doing). Bretel's employer Lucien, on the other hand, is trying to shed his mistress; but through Bretel's misguided altruism his best-laid plans go awry. Justin's failure is Boriquet's success while Bretel's apparent success—he thinks, ironically, that he has put everything to rights—is Lucien's debacle, as the servant succeeds only in wreaking ultimate havoc. The nasty Justin may be mildly satanic, but at least his damage is undone before the curtain falls, and he will suffer for it. Poor lovable Bretel, on the other hand, paves his road with the best of intentions and never even realizes the damage he has caused. It will, no doubt, eventually be righted in some postcurtain future, but not before much tearing of hair and gnashing of teeth on the part of his master.

Lucien's minihell is nothing, however, compared to the torments suffered by the characters in the Feydeau extravaganzas typical of this third period: the Champignols, the Bouzins, the Bois-d'Enghiens, the Petypons. Feydeau's theater is cruel when stripped of its surface humor. Creator of a self-contained little universe, he seems to delight almost sadistically in playing a kind of cosmic cat-and-mouse with his creations. To some extent all farce portrays its characters as victims, from the anonymous, fifteenth-century *Pathelin* to Eugène Ionesco and beyond, with Charlie Chaplin and the Keystone Kops thrown in: victims of something or someone, whether brickbats or bullies, one's adversaries or oneself, comic quid pro quos or cosmic misadventures. Feydeau's theater, from beginning to end, is no exception. From his earliest farces—with the exception of *Notre futur*—it presents an array of hapless victims whose suffering—sometimes deserved, more often gratuitous—runs the gamut from mere embarrassing misunderstanding to physical discomfort, panic, and unbridled, unspeakable, mad frustration.

Nowhere in Feydeau's theater is this victimization, with all its attendant madness, more concentrated, more intense than in the late one-act plays that mark his final period. There is a curious irony here. For if the characters trapped in Feydeau's mechanistic imbroglios are victims of his whimsy, if he plunges them into absurdly grotesque situations and lets them suffer (though seldom in silence) in a crescendo of desperation until he decides to pluck them free in an exercise of sheer authorial power, he himself, in these final plays, is obviously the victim. It bears restating that the parallel between these tableaux of marital misadventure and his own domestic life, even to certain specific details, is a well-documented fact, not mere hypothesis. (It seems undeniable, for example, that his son Jacques—himself later to become a theater figure of some repute—was the inspiration for the frustratingly recalcitrant little Toto of *On purge Bébé*.) His own divorce and subsequent mental breakdown are clearly no coincidence. Perhaps this is why, of all his plays, these are the only ones in which the victimization remains not only unresolved but also with little or no hope of ultimate postcurtain resolution. The curtain that falls on Follbraguet, the last of the Feydeau incarnations, has not solved his, or their, problem. Perhaps, too, this personal dimension helps explain why, after such resounding triumphs as *La Dame de chez Maxim,* he chose to turn again to the modest one-act play, though this time with less farcical, and even serious, overtones.

There are several plausible reasons: Feydeau's celebrated laziness (hard though that may be to reconcile with his meticulous craftsmanship), a single act being easier to concoct than three—or five, if one recalls his sequel to *La Dame de chez Maxim,* the gargantuanly casted, seldom performed tour de force (and *de farce*), *La Duchesse des Folies-Bergère;* or his awareness that "Hennequin's theater of a hundred doors" was falling into disrepute with the critics, among them, even his stepfather, Henry Fouquier; or a midlife desire for artistic renewal; or, indeed, his need for something of a sublimation, a kind of therapeutic working-out of his own domestic problems. In any event Feydeau's move to a more serious form of comedy was not wholly unprepared. Even before *La Dame de chez Maxim,* as early as 1894, with *Le Ruban,* he (and Desvallières) had attempted to portray characters more at home in so-called higher comedy, even considered worthy—though not without many a raised eyebrow at the time—of the conservative Odéon, one of the state-subsidized Parisian theaters. Also after *La Dame de chez Maxim,* two other plays pointed in the same new direction: *La Main passe,* with its semiserious treatment of divorce, and *Le Bourgeon* (The Sprout, 1906), a curious mixture of farce and drama, delicately handling the difficult theme of a young seminarian's struggle with the devil in the flesh. The change in direction was not abrupt, however. Two other farces, among them his

broadest and most successful—*La Puce à l'oreille* in 1907 and *Occupe-toi d'Amélie* in 1908—proved that he was still fully in command of his intricate Chinese-puzzle technique when and if he chose to use it.

Of the five conjugal comedies, *Feu la mère de Madame* (1908; translated as *A Good Night's Sleep,* 1973) was the first. Whatever the reasons for the change in style, the warm reception by audiences, and especially by prestigious critics, determined what was left of Feydeau's career. Aside from two generous collaborations with youthful protégés and a pair of farces left unfinished, his last productive years were devoted to these painful reflections of his own disintegrating marriage and psyche. Marital love, clearly, is hardly an issue in most of Feydeau's theater, except as a prelude to the inevitable infidelities and attendant escapades. It plays little active role. But in the late conjugal comedies it plays an important role indeed, albeit negatively, by its very deterioration. *Hortense a dit: "Je m'en fous!"* shuts the door on it altogether with Follbraguet's final slam and departure. In Feydeau's earliest playlets young love is felt as a positive presence despite the none-too-serious obstacles that stand in its way. In *Notre futur* one may assume that, after her initial adolescent disillusionment, Valentine will meet a nice young gentleman—perhaps one of the guests at Henriette's posh soiree. In *Par la fenêtre,* if Hector's jealous spouse prefigures Follbraguet's shrewish wife Marcelle, it is only the dimmest of foreshadowings. At that early point in Feydeau's career theirs is only a minor spat: they will doubtless kiss and make up after the curtain, when he tells her, no doubt, of Emma's absurd request. One can even imagine that Edouard and Lucile, the young couple of *Amour et piano,* will meet again under less accidental circumstances and that their budding romance will take its course. In *Hortense a dit: "Je m'en fous!,"* however, there is no room for such optimism. It is Feydeau's parting shot, his final cynical statement about the poor potential for marital bliss. Perhaps he had not actually meant it to be quite the last word. It is known that he had planned, at least vaguely, to incorporate the late plays in a series to be titled "Du mariage au divorce" (From Marriage to Divorce). Maybe one more was intended to complete the cycle and portray the couple's actual breakup, yet further literary and dramatic revenge against the insufferable spouse. If so, it was not to be. But Feydeau, in his theater as well as in his life, had already amply illustrated colleague Alfred Capus's dictum that "there's nothing like marriage to separate so many husbands and wives."

In these five plays the author's double is no less entrapped than are the unfortunate heroes of his broad masterpieces of imbroglio; in the network of his wife's frustrating logic and irrationality in the former, and in the mesh of absurd events in the latter. In both cases the essential Feydeau perspective shows through clearly, producing a stylized interpretation of real life, exaggerated for comic effect, but not enough to obscure the fact that real life is quite similar indeed—or could be, given the appropriate mad twists of circumstance. One does not have to scratch far below the surface of a typical Feydeau comedy to find a fatalistic vision of the human condition and, along with it, an undercurrent of pessimism not out of place in an author who was destined to go mad in the last years of his life.

Not all Feydeau's characters, however, are wholly innocent and undeserving of their fate. Often it is a comic flaw on their part that brings about, as a sort of punishment, the situation in which they find themselves. Doctor Paginet, in *Le Ruban,* is a prime example, suffering as he does for his excessive egotism and pride in his would-be scientific achievements. In such a case it is human nature itself that Feydeau ridicules rather than the abstract human condition in an unpredictable universe. The affected, the overreaching, the unself-critical and unrealistic are tweaked and twitted for their sins. In some instances they are made to suffer their mortification within the very fabric of the comedy: a Paginet, for instance, sees his monomania painfully thwarted until the very last moment (unlike his modest wife, incidentally, who, also decorated—a delicious irony—accepts her medal with regret rather than vanity). In others they proceed blithely along their merry way, unmindful that spectators or readers, and the author, of course, are laughing at their expense. But laughing they are all the same; and it is in his ridicule of certain less than down-to-earth characters whom he often leaves unpunished for their excesses—pseudonobles, "duelophiles," social climbers of varying stripe—that he asserts his realistic perspective.

Happily, Feydeau is always careful to maintain a judicious balance in that down-to-earth perspective, one that prevents his theater from even coming close to losing its comic character. On the one hand, his fatalism and pessimism, if pushed to extremes, might well have resulted in more deeply philosophical appraisals of the human condition not unworthy of tragedy or drama, all things being equal; as for the victimized husbands of his last plays, it is easy to picture them in the very uncomic ambience of a late-nineteenth-century *pièce rosse*. On the other hand, had he dwelt more heavily on social absurdities he might well have produced thesis plays à la Alexandre Dumas *fils* and Emile Augier. But neither extreme won out over the comedian. Feydeau is neither a philosopher nor a social reformer: to play the commentator on Man's lot or the theatrical arbiter of his morals would

have appeared to him a ridiculous affectation, no less so than those he derides with pleasure. He never forgets that his function is to make people laugh. That his mad inventions, with all the attendant drollery of their linguistic wit and skewed social wisdom, continue to do so in the present, as they did so well in his own time, is proven almost daily in theaters throughout the world.

Biographies:

Norman R. Shapiro, "Introduction," in *Four Farces by Georges Feydeau* (Chicago: University of Chicago Press, 1970);

Jacques Lorcey, *Georges Feydeau* (Paris: La Table Ronde, 1972);

Henry Gidel, *Georges Feydeau* (Paris: E. Flammarion, 1991).

References:

Marcel Achard, "Georges Feydeau, notre grand comique," *Conferencia, Journal de l'Université des Annales* (15 April 1948): 133–149; (15 May 1948): 214–220;

Achard, *Rions avec eux, les grands auteurs comiques* (Paris: Fayard, 1957), pp. 83–123;

Jacques Bainville, *Une Saison chez Thespis* (Paris: Editions Prométhée, 1929), pp. 213–217;

Stuart Eddy Baker, *Georges Feydeau and the Aesthetics of Farce* (Ann Arbor: University of Michigan Research Press, 1981);

Jean-Louis Barrault, "Feydeau, ou sur le rire et l'observation," *Cahiers de la Compagnie Madeleine Renaud–Jean-Louis Barrault,* 32 (December 1960): 74–75;

Barrault, *Souvenirs pour demain* (Paris: Seuil, 1972), pp. 201–203;

Jacqueline Blancart-Cassou, "L'irréalisme comique de Feydeau," *Cahiers de l'Association Internationale des Etudes Françaises,* 43 (May 1991): 201–216;

Michael R. Booth, "Feydeau and the Farcical Imperative," in *Farce,* edited by James Redmond (Cambridge: Cambridge University Press, 1988), pp. 148–152;

Adolphe Brisson, *Portraits intimes,* volume 5 (Paris: Colin, 1901), pp. 10–17;

Jean Cassou, "Le génie systématique de Feydeau," *Cahiers de la Compagnie Madeleine Renaud–Jean-Louis Barrault,* 15 (January 1956): 55–61; also in *Parti pris: Essais et colloques* (Paris: Albin Michel, 1964);

Claude Cézan, "Le culte de Feydeau," *Les Nouvelles Littéraires,* 2099 (23 November 1967): 13;

Jacques Charon, "Le théâtre de Georges Feydeau," *Les Annales,* 69 (July 1962): 23–34;

Sylvie Chevalley, "Feydeau à la Comédie-Française," *Comédie-Française,* 73 (November–December 1978): 30–32;

Jean Cocteau, "C'était Feydeau . . . ," *Cahiers de la Compagnie Madeleine Renaud–Jean-Louis Barrault,* 15 (January 1956): 53–54;

Gilles Costaz, "Femmes humiliées," *Magazine Littéraire,* 286 (March 1991): 12;

Claude Damiens, "Georges Feydeau, le maître du naturalisme absurde," *Paris-Théâtre,* 150 (1959): 2–3;

Maureen Devine, "Acceptable Madness in Georges Feydeau's *Going to Pot (On purge Bébé),*" *Thalia: Studies in Literary Humor,* 9 (Spring–Summer 1986): 22–30;

Robert Dieudonné, "En souvenir de Georges Feydeau," *Le Figaro* (9 June 1921): 1;

Guy Dumur, "Des pantins et des monstres," *Nouvel Observateur* (29 November–5 December 1967): 43–44;

"L'espace dans *Hortense a dit: 'Je m'en fous!'* de Georges Feydeau," *Organon,* 78 (1978): 7–23;

Manuel A. Esteban, *Georges Feydeau* (Boston: Twayne, 1983);

Yves-Alain Favre, "Le Comique de Feydeau," *Revue des Sciences Humaines* (April–June 1973): 239–247;

Alain Feydeau, "Georges Feydeau," *Jours de France* (25–31 October 1986);

Michel Feydeau, "Mon père, auteur gai," *L'Intransigeant* (3 December 1937);

Elena Fioreli, "Feydeau, cinquante ans après," *Culture Française* (Bari), 18 (1971): 263–268;

Robert de Flers, "Georges Feydeau," *Le Gaulois* (6 June 1921);

Henry Fouquier, "Le Krach du théâtre," *Le Figaro,* 18 November 1891, p. 1;

André Frank, "Feydeau, Kafka, Adamov," *Cahiers de la Compagnie Madeleine Renaud–Jean-Louis Barrault,* 10 (1955): 126–127;

"Georges Feydeau," *Cahiers du théâtre,* edited by Jacques Lorcey, numéro spécial 8 (1973): 273;

Gilbert Ganne, *Bernanos, Giraudoux, Barrès, Claudel, Matisse, Maurras, Fromentin, La Varende, Feydeau, Loti: tels que les voient leurs héritiers* (Paris: Plon, 1972);

Michel Georges-Michel, *Un Demi-siècle de gloires théâtrales* (Paris: Editions André Bonne, 1950);

Georges-Michel, "L'époque Feydeau," *Candide* (4 January 1939);

Henry Gidel, *La Dramaturgie de Feydeau,* 2 volumes (Paris: Champion, 1978);

Gidel, "La Dramaturgie de Feydeau," *L'Information Littéraire,* 31 (1979): 209–212;

Gidel, *Le Théâtre de Georges Feydeau* (Paris: Klincksieck, 1979);

Régis Gignoux, "Georges Feydeau," *Le Figaro,* 6 June 1921, p. 1;

Sanda Golopentia, "Eh! Allez donc! C'est pas mon père!," *Romanic Review,* 83 (November 1992): 463–500;

Golopentia, "Female Kynics in Feydeau's Plays," *Romance Languages Annual,* 4 (1992): 64–69;

Golopentia, "Proust, Feydeau, et les ready-made de la Belle Epoque," *Bulletin d'Informations Proustiennes,* 23 (1992): 29–41;

Nöelle Guibert, "Feydeau chez les Comédiens français," *Comédie-Française,* 139–140 (May–June 1985): 31–33;

Philippe Hériat, "Le style d'Amélie," *Cahiers de la Compagnie Madeleine Renaud–Jean-Louis Barrault,* 32 (December 1960): 74–75;

A. Ferdinand Hérold, "Les Théâtres," *Mercure de France* (March 1899): 797–798;

Henri Jeanson, "Notes sur Georges Feydeau," *Cahiers de la Compagnie Madeleine Renaud–Jean-Louis Barrault,* 15 (January 1956): 62–70;

P. Labracherie, "Les décors psychologiques de Feydeau," *Cahiers de la Compagnie Madeleine Renaud–Jean-Louis Barrault,* 15 (January 1956): 55–61;

Hervé Lauwick, "Georges Feydeau, distrait, souriant et mélancolique," in *D'Alphonse Allais à Sacha Guitry* (Paris: Plon, 1963), pp. 79–96;

Daniel Malbert, "Surprendre," *Le Français dans le Monde,* 241 (April 1991): 17–19;

Pierre Marcabru, "Ionesco a trouvé sa place entre Labiche et Feydeau," *Arts,* 813 (15–21 March 1961): 5;

J. Paul Marcoux, "Georges Feydeau and the 'Serious' Farce," in *Farce,* edited by James Redmond (Cambridge: Cambridge University Press, 1988), pp. 131–143;

Renaud Matignon, "Feydeau, un drame en costume de vaudeville," *Le Figaro Littéraire* (18 February 1991): 5;

Thierry Maulnier, "Les grands comiques," *Revue de Paris,* 69 (1962): 150–153;

Maulnier, "La querelle du *Dindon,*" *Combat* (9 March 1951): 2;

Catulle Mendès, *"La Dame de chez Maxim,"* *Le Journal* (18 January 1899);

Didier Méreuze, "Abécédaire," *Comédie-Française,* 139–140 (May–June 1985): 34–43;

Paul-Louis Mignon, "L'Accessoire, deus ex machina, ou la fatalité dans le théâtre de Feydeau," *Cahiers de la Compagnie Madeleine Renaud–Jean-Louis Barrault,* 15 (January 1956): 72–78;

Robert Nahmias, *Tout l'humour de Feydeau* (Paris: Grancher, 1995);

Jacques Nerson, "Lire: Le monsieur de chez Maxim's," *Figaro Magazine,* 555 (9 February 1991): 136;

Peter F. Parshall, "Feydeau's *A Flea in Her Rear:* The Art of Kenesthetic Structure," *Theatre Journal* (October 1981): 355–364;

Michel Perrin, "Feydeau l'impitoyable," *Revue de Paris,* 70 (1963): 85–92;

Jean-Pierre Peter, "Feydeau à corps et à cris," *Comédie-Française,* 139–140 (May–June 1985): 4–6;

Peter, "Feydeau à corps et coeur perdus, ou le rire meurtrier de soi-même," *Communications,* 56 (1993): 115–123;

Jean-Paul Pierozzi, "Répétitions interruptions silences: Notes sur le comique verbal du théâtre de Feydeau," *Studi Urbinati,* 56 (1983): 177–208;

Jacques Porel, *Fils de Réjane* (Paris: Plon, 1951–1952), pp. 202–204;

Leonard Cabell Pronko, *Eugène Labiche and Georges Feydeau* (London: Macmillan, 1982);

Pronko, *Georges Feydeau* (New York: Ungar, 1975);

Monique Prunet, "Orton et Feydeau, ou le vaudeville travesti," *Coup de théâtre,* 9 (December 1989): 25–35;

Gaston Rageot, "Le triomphe de la technique: Rostand, Feydeau, Cocteau," *Revue Politique et Littéraire: Revue Bleue,* 77, no. 1 (1939): 33–35;

Kurt Ringer, "La vie est pleine de surprises. Aspects de la dramaturgie de Feydeau dans *L'Hôtel du Libre-Echange,*" in *D'Eschyle à Genet: Etudes sur le théâtre en hommage à Francis Pruner,* edited by Francis Claudon and others (Dijon: Editions Universitaires, 1986), pp. 261–266;

Marcel Schneider, "Huysmans, Alphonse Allais, Feydeau. Les délires 'fin de siècle,'" *Figaro Littéraire,* 13638 (4 July 1988): iii–iv;

Philippe Sénart, "Revue théâtrale. Labiche, Feydeau: la bourgeoisie au pinacle ou au pilori?," *Revue des Deux Mondes* (September 1988): 242–247;

Norman R. Shapiro, "Georges Feydeau et le fauteuil extatique," *Revue d'Histoire Littéraire de la France,* 60 (October–December 1960): 557–559;

Shapiro, "Georges Feydeau: Master of the Mad," *Midway,* 10, no. 4 (1970): 77–93;

Shapiro, "Georges Feydeau: Une date essentielle corrigée," *Revue d'Histoire du Théâtre,* 14 (1962): 362–364;

Shapiro, "Note sur deux énigmes résolues," *Revue d'Histoire Littéraire de la France,* 80 (January–February 1980): 90–93;

Shapiro, "Suffering and Punishment in the Theatre of Georges Feydeau," *Tulane Drama Review,* 5, no. 1 (1960): 117–126;

Arlette Shenkan, *Georges Feydeau* (Paris: Seghers, 1972);

Shenkan, "Georges Feydeau: simple amuseur?," *Bulletin de la Société des Professeurs Français en Amérique* (1978): 73–88;

Terje Sinding, "Des portes qui claquent," *Comédie-Française,* 139–140 (May–June 1985): 45–46;

Roger J. Steiner, "The Perennial Georges Feydeau," *Symposium,* 15 (Spring 1961): 49–54;

Jean-Marie Thomasseau, "Feydeau et la dramaturgie de la scie," *Europe LXXII,* 786 (1994): 81–90;

Léon Treich, *L'Esprit de Georges Feydeau* (Paris: Gallimard, 1927);

Kenneth Tynan, "Putting On the Style," *New Yorker* (14 March 1959): 80–83;

John Van Druten, "A Gem from the French Crown," *Theatre Arts* (March 1958): 19–21;

Louis Verneuil, *Rideau à neuf heures* (New York: Editions de la Maison Française, 1944);

Renée Winegarten, "Théâtre du printemps," *New Criterion,* 9 (June 1991): 40–44.

Papers:

Manuscripts not in private hands can be found in three libraries: the Bibliothèque Nationale, the Bibliothèque de l'Arsenal, and the Bibliothèque de la Société des Auteurs Dramatiques. The Bibliothèque Nationale has manuscripts of *La Dame de chez Maxim, La Puce à l'oreille,* and *Mais n' te promène donc pas toute nue!* and also three letters addressed to Raymond Poincaré. The Bibliothèque de l'Arsenal has eleven letters addressed to playwright Albin Valabrègue and two letters addressed to journalist Jules Huret. The Bibliothèque de la Société des Auteurs Dramatiques houses manuscripts of "Les Maris des deux pôles" (original title of *L'Hôtel du Libre-Echange*), "On va faire la cocotte" (only one act of which was completed), and *L'Age d'or.*

Ludovic Halévy

(1 January 1834 – 8 May 1908)

Diana R. Hallman
University of Kentucky

PLAY PRODUCTIONS: *Entrez, messieurs, mesdames,* by Halévy and François Méry, music by Jacques Offenbach, Paris, Bouffes-Parisiens, 5 July 1855;

Une Pleine eau, music by d'Osmond and J. Costé, Paris, Bouffes-Parisiens, 28 August 1855;

Madame Papillon, music by Offenbach, Paris, Bouffes-Parisiens, 3 October 1855;

Ba-ta-clan, music by Offenbach, Paris, Bouffes-Parisiens, 29 December 1855;

L'Impresario, by Halévy and Léon Battu, music by Wolfgang Amadeus Mozart, Paris, Bouffes-Parisiens, 20 May 1856;

Le Docteur Miracle, by Halévy and Battu, music by Georges Bizet and Charles Lecocq, Paris, Bouffes-Parisiens, 8 April 1857;

L'Opéra aux fenêtres, music by Léon-Gustave-Cyprien Gastinel, Paris, 5 May 1857;

Le Cousin de Marivaux, by Halévy and Battu, music by [Victor] Massé, Paris, Salons du Conservatoire, 22 August 1857;

Rose et Rosette, Paris, Théâtre des Folies Dramatiques, 8 May 1858;

Orphée aux enfers, by Halévy and Hector Crémieux, music by Offenbach, Paris, Bouffes-Parisiens, 21 October 1858;

Voici le jour, music by Ward, Lyon, Grand Théâtre de Lyon, 2 March 1859;

Le Carnaval des revues, by Halévy, Eugène Grangé, and Philippe Gille, music by Offenbach, Paris, Bouffes-Parisiens, 10 February 1860;

Le Souper du mardi-gras, by Halévy, Grangé, and Gille, Paris, Bouffes-Parisiens, 10 February 1860;

Titus et Bérénice, by Halévy and Fournier, music by Gris, Bouffes-Parisiens, 12 May 1860;

Ce qui plaît aux hommes, by Halévy and Henri Meilhac, Paris, Théâtre des Variétés, 6 October 1860;

Le Mari sans le savoir, by Halévy and Léon Halévy, music by Comte Saint-Remy (Morny), Paris, Bouffes-Parisiens, 31 December 1860;

Ludovic Halévy

Les Deux Buveurs, by Halévy and Crémieux, music by Léo Delibes, Paris, Bouffes-Parisiens, 26 January 1861;

La Chanson de Fortunio, by Halévy and Crémieux, music by Offenbach, Paris, Bouffes-Parisiens, 5 January 1861;

Le Pont des soupirs, by Halévy and Crémieux, music by Offenbach, Paris, Bouffes-Parisiens, 23 March 1861;

Les Eaux d'Ems, by Halévy and Crémieux, music by Delibes, Paris, Bouffes-Parisiens, 9 April 1861;

Le Menuet de Danaë, by Halévy and Meilhac, Paris, Théâtre des Variétés, 20 April 1861;

La Baronne de San-Francisco, by Halévy and Crémieux, music by H. Caspers, Paris, Bouffes-Parisiens, 27 November 1861;

Le Roman comique, by Halévy and Crémieux, music by Offenbach, Paris, Bouffes-Parisiens, 10 December 1861;

Une Fin de bail, by Halévy and Crémieux, music by Pierre-Joseph-Alphonse Varney, Paris, Bouffes-Parisiens, 29 January 1862;

Les Moulins à vent, by Halévy and Meilhac, Paris, Théâtre des Variétés, 22 February 1862;

Jacqueline, by Halévy and Crémieux, music by Offenbach, Paris, Bouffes-Parisiens, 14 October 1862;

Les Brebis de Panurge, by Halévy and Meilhac, Paris, Théâtre du Vaudeville, 24 November 1862;

La Clé de Métella, by Halévy and Meilhac, Paris, Théâtre du Vaudeville, 24 November 1862;

Le Brésilien, by Halévy and Meilhac, Paris, Théâtre du Palais Royal, 9 May 1863;

Le Train de minuit, by Halévy and Meilhac, Paris, Théâtre du Gymnase, 15 June 1863;

Néméa, ou l'Amour vengé, by Halévy, Meilhac, and A. St.-Léon, music by M. Minkous, Paris, Académie Royale de Musique, 11 July 1864;

La Belle Hélène, by Halévy and Meilhac, music by Offenbach, Paris, Théâtre des Variétés, 17 December 1864;

Le Photographe, by Halévy and Meilhac, Paris, Théâtre du Palais Royal, 24 December 1864;

Le Singe de Nicolet, by Halévy and Meilhac, Paris, Théâtre des Variétés, 29 January 1865;

Les Méprises de Lambinet, by Halévy and Meilhac, Paris, Théâtre des Variétés, 3 December 1865;

Barbe-bleue, by Halévy and Meilhac, music by Offenbach, Paris, Théâtre des Variétés, 5 February 1866;

La Vie parisienne, by Halévy and Meilhac, music by Offenbach, Paris, Théâtre du Palais Royal, 31 October 1866;

La Grande-Duchesse de Gérolstein, by Halévy and Meilhac, music by Offenbach, Paris, Théâtre des Variétés, 12 April 1867;

Tout pour les dames!, by Halévy and Meilhac, Paris, Théâtre des Variétés, 8 September 1867;

Le Château à Toto, by Halévy and Meilhac, music by Offenbach, Paris, Théâtre du Palais Royal, 6 May 1868;

Fanny Lear, by Halévy and Meilhac, Paris, Théâtre du Gymnase, 13 August 1868;

La Périchole, by Halévy and Meilhac, music by Offenbach, Paris, Théâtre des Variétés, 6 October 1868;

Le Bouquet, by Halévy and Meilhac, Paris, Théâtre du Palais Royal, 23 October 1868;

La Diva, by Halévy and Meilhac, music by Offenbach, Paris, Bouffes-Parisiens, 22 March 1869;

L'Homme à la clé, by Halévy and Meilhac, Paris, Théâtre des Variétés, 11 August 1869;

Froufrou, by Halévy and Meilhac, Paris, Gymnase-Dramatique, 30 October 1869;

Les Brigands, by Halévy and Meilhac, music by Offenbach, Paris, Théâtre des Variétés, 10 December 1869;

Tricoche et Cacolet, by Halévy and Meilhac, Paris, Théâtre du Palais Royal, 6 December 1871;

Madame attend Monsieur, by Halévy and Meilhac, Paris, Théâtre des Variétés, 8 February 1872;

Le Réveillon, by Halévy and Meilhac, Paris, Théâtre du Palais Royal, 10 September 1872;

Les Sonnettes, by Halévy and Meilhac, Paris, Théâtre des Variétés, 15 November 1872;

Le Roi Candaule, by Halévy and Meilhac, Paris, Théâtre du Palais Royal, 9 April 1873;

L'Été de la Saint-Martin, by Halévy and Meilhac, Paris, Théâtre Français, 1 July 1873;

Toto chez Tata, by Halévy and Meilhac, Paris, Théâtre des Variétés, 25 August 1873;

Pomme d'Api, by Halévy and William Busnach, music by Offenbach, Paris, Théâtre de la Renaissance, 4 September 1873;

La Petite Marquise, by Halévy and Meilhac, Paris, Théâtre des Variétés, 13 February 1874;

La Mi-Carême, by Halévy and Meilhac, Paris, Théâtre du Palais Royal, 2 April 1874;

L'Ingénue, by Halévy and Meilhac, Paris, Théâtre des Variétés, 24 September 1874;

Madame l'Archiduc, by Halévy and Albert Millaud, music by Offenbach, Paris, Bouffes-Parisiens, 31 October 1874;

La Veuve, by Halévy and Meilhac, Paris, Gymnase-Dramatique, 5 November 1874;

La Boule, by Halévy and Meilhac, Paris, Théâtre du Palais Royal, 24 November 1874;

Carmen, by Halévy and Meilhac, music by Georges Bizet, Paris, Opéra-Comique, 3 March 1875;

Le Passage de Vénus, by Halévy and Meilhac, Paris, Théâtre des Variétés, 4 May 1875;

La Boulangère a des écus, by Halévy and Meilhac, music by Offenbach, Paris, Théâtre des Variétés, 19 October 1875;

La Créole, by Halévy and Millaud, music by Offenbach, Paris, Bouffes-Parisiens, 3 November 1875;

Loulou, by Halévy and Meilhac, Paris, Théâtre du Palais Royal, 31 March 1876;

Le Prince, by Halévy and Meilhac, Paris, Théâtre du Palais Royal, 25 November 1876;

La Cigale, by Halévy and Meilhac, Paris, Théâtre des Variétés, 6 October 1877;

Le Fandango, by Halévy, Meilhac, and Louis Mérante, music by Gervais Bernard Gaston Salvayre, Paris, Académie Nationale de Musique, 26 November 1877;

Le Je ne sais quoi, by Halévy and Meilhac, Paris, Théâtre de la Renaissance, 21 January 1878;

Le Petit Duc, by Halévy and Meilhac, music by Charles Lecocq, Paris, Théâtre de la Renaissance, 25 January 1878;

Le Mari de la débutante, by Halévy and Meilhac, Paris, Théâtre du Palais Royal, 5 February 1879;

Le Petit Hôtel, by Halévy and Meilhac, Paris, Théâtre-Français, 21 February 1879;

La Petite Mademoiselle, by Halévy and Meilhac, music by Charles Lecocq, Paris, Théâtre de la Renaissance, 12 April 1879;

Lolotte, by Halévy and Meilhac, Théâtre du Vaudeville, 4 October 1879;

La Petite Mère, by Halévy and Meilhac, Paris, Théâtre des Variétés, 6 March 1880;

Janot, by Halévy and Meilhac, music by Lecocq, Paris, Théâtre de la Renaissance, 22 January 1881;

La Roussotte, by Halévy, Meilhac, and Millaud, Paris, Théâtre des Variétés, 28 January 1881.

BOOKS: *Ba-ta-clan* (Paris: L. Escudier, 1856);

L'Impresario (Paris: G. Brandus, Dufour, 1856);

Le Docteur Miracle (Paris: Michel Lévy, 1857);

Une Maladresse: nouvelle (Paris: Bonaventure et Ducessois, 1857);

L'Opéra aux fenêtres (Paris: Michel Lévy, 1857);

Rose et Rosette (Paris: Michel Lévy, 1858);

Un Scandale (Paris: A. Bourdilliat, 1860);

Le Mari sans le savoir (Paris: A. Bourdilliat, 1861);

La Chanson de Fortunio (Paris: Librairie nouvelle, 1861);

Le Pont des soupirs (Paris: A. Bourdilliat, 1861);

Les Eaux d'Ems (Paris: A. Bourdilliat, 1861);

Le Menuet de Danaë (Paris: A. Bourdilliat, 1861);

La Baronne de San-Francisco (Paris: Michel Lévy, 1862);

Le Roman comique (Paris: Michel Lévy, 1862);

Les Moulins à vent (Paris: Michel Lévy, 1862);

Les Brebis de Panurge (Paris: Michel Lévy, 1863);

La Clé de Métella (Paris: Michel Lévy, 1863);

Le Brésilien (Paris: Michel Lévy, 1863);

Le Train de minuit (Paris: Michel Lévy, 1863);

Marcel (Paris: A. Lainé et J. Havard, 1864);

Néméa, ou l'Amour vengé (Paris: Michel Lévy, 1864);

La Belle Hélène (Paris: Michel Lévy, 1865); translated by Charles Lamb Kenney as *Fair Helen* (London: Chappell, 1871);

Le Photographe (Paris: Michel Lévy, 1865);

Le Singe de Nicolet (Paris: Michel Lévy, 1865);

Les Méprises de Lambinet (Paris: Michel Lévy, 1866);

Barbe-bleue (Paris: Michel Lévy, 1866);

La Vie parisienne (Paris: Michel Lévy, 1867);

La Grande-Duchesse de Gérolstein (Paris: Michel Lévy, 1867); translated by C. L. Kenney as *The*

Grand Duchess of Gerolstein (London: Boosey, 1868);

Tout pour les dames! (Paris: Michel Lévy, 1867);

Le Château à Toto (Paris: Michel Lévy, 1868);

Fanny Lear (Paris: Michel Lévy, 1868);

La Périchole (Paris: Michel Lévy, 1868); translated and adapted by Alfred Murray (London: Boosey, [1897]);

Le Bouquet (Paris: Michel Lévy, 1868);

La Diva (Paris: Michel Lévy, 1869);

L'Homme à la clé (Paris: Michel Lévy, 1869);

Froufrou (Paris: Michel Lévy, 1870); adapted and translated by Thomas Hailes Lacy as *Frou-Frou* in *Lacy's Acting Edition of Plays, Dramas, Extravaganzas, farces etc.* (London: T. H. Lacy, 1870);

Les Brigands (Paris: Michel Lévy, 1870); translated by H. S. Leigh as *The Brigands* (London: Boosey, [1884]);

Tricoche et Cacolet (Paris: Michel Lévy, 1870);

L'Invasion: Souvenirs et récits (Paris: Calmann-Lévy, 1872);

Madame attend Monsieur (Paris: Michel Lévy, 1872);

Madame et Monsieur Cardinal; Le Rêve; Le Cheval du trompette; Le Dernier chapitre; Quand on attend ses messes; Histoire d'une robe de bal; Antoinette; Niniche; La Petite caille plucheuse; L'Insurgé; Mistingue et Lenglumé (Paris: Michel Lévy, 1872);

Le Réveillon (Paris: Michel Lévy, 1872);

Les Sonnettes (Paris: Michel Lévy, 1872);

Le Roi Candaule (Paris: Michel Lévy, 1873); translated by W. S. Gilbert as *The Realm of Joy* (London, 1969);

L'Été de la Saint-Martin (Paris: Michel Lévy, 1873); translated by Barrett H. Clark as *Indian Summer* (New York: S. French, [1913]);

Toto chez Tata (Paris: Michel Lévy, 1873);

Pomme d'Api (Paris: Tresse, 1873);

La Petite Marquise (Paris: Michel Lévy, 1874);

La Mi-Carême (Paris: Michel Lévy, 1874);

L'Ingénue (Paris: Michel Lévy, 1874);

La Veuve (Paris: Michel Lévy, 1875); translated by C. Clarke as *The Widow* (London, 1875);

La Boule (Paris: Michel Lévy, 1875);

Carmen (Paris: Michel Lévy, 1875); translated and adapted by Henry Hersee (London: C. Dickens & Evans, 1880?);

Le Passage de Vénus (Paris: Michel Lévy, 1875);

La Boulangère a des écus (Paris: Michel Lévy, 1875); translated as *La Boulangère* (London: J. B. Cramer, [1881]);

Madame l'Archiduc, partially translated by Henry B. Farnie (London: J. B. Cramer, 1876);

La Cigale (Paris: Châtillon-sur-Seine, 1877); adapted and translated by John Hollingshead as *The*

Grasshopper (London: Woodfall & Kinder, 1877);

Les Petites Cardinal; Madame Canivet; Le Programme de M. Cardinal; Pauline Cardinal; Virginie Cardinal; Le Feu d'artifice; La Pénélope; Pendant l'émeute; Régénérés; Un budget parisien; La Boule noire; À l'Opéra (Paris: Calmann-Lévy, 1880);

Un Mariage d'amour; Mariette; Les Trois séries de Madame de Châteaubrun; Le Maître de danse; Le Député de Gamache; L'Héritage; Souvenirs de théâtre; L'Ambassadeur chinois; Le Défilé; Le Petit Max (Paris: Calmann-Lévy, 1881); *Un Mariage d'amour* translated by A. van den Bogaerde and Robert A. Newill as *A Marriage for Love* (Stamford: Bookes, 1885); *Le Maître de danse* translated by Edith V. B. Mathews as *The Dancing Master . . .* in *Parisian Points of View* (New York: Harper, 1894); *Le Député de Gamache* translated by Annie W. Ayer and Helen T. Slate as *The Deputy of Gamache* (New York: A. L. Burt, 1895);

L'Abbé Constantin (Paris: Calmann-Lévy, 1882); translated by Katherine Sullivan as *The Abbé Constantin* (New York: J. W. Lovell, 1882);

Criquette (Paris: Calmann-Lévy, 1883); translated by Myron A. Cooney (New York: F. Tousey, 1884);

Deux mariages: un grand mariage, un mariage d'amour (Paris: Calmann-Lévy, 1883);

La Famille Cardinal (Paris: Calmann-Lévy, 1883); translated by Georges B. Ives as *The Cardinal Family* (Philadelphia: G. Barrie, 1897);

Discours de M. Ludovic Halévy prononcé le jour de sa réception à l'Académie française, 4 février 1886 (Paris: Calmann-Lévy, 1886);

Trois coups de foudre (Paris: L. Conquet, 1886);

Princesse; Un Grand mariage; Les Trois coups de foudre; Mon Camarade Mussard (Paris: Calmann-Lévy, 1887); *Princesse* translated by Mary K. Ford as *Catherine Duval: Sketches of Paris Life* (Boston: L. C. Page, 1899);

Notes et souvenirs, 1871–1872 (Paris: Calmann-Lévy, 1889);

Karikari; Un Tour de valse; Tom et Bob; La Plus belle; Noiraud; Guignol; Deux cyclones (Paris: Calmann-Lévy, 1892);

Mariette (Paris: L. Conquet, 1893);

Discours sur les prix de vertu (Paris: Calmann-Lévy, 1894);

Le 4 septembre 1870: Séances du Corps législatif et du Sénat (Paris: H. Daragon, 1904);

Trois dîners avec Gambetta (N.p.: Grasset, 1929);

Carnets (Paris: Calmann-Lévy, 1935).

Collection: *Théâtre de Meilhac et Halévy,* 8 volumes (Paris: Calmann-Lévy, 1900–1902).

SELECTED PERIODICAL PUBLICATIONS–UNCOLLECTED: "La Millième Représentation de *Carmen,*" *Le Théâtre,* 145 (1905);

"Carnets (1872–1883)," *Revue des Deux Mondes,* (15 January 1937): 296–323; (1 February 1937): 540–565; (15 February 1937): 817–843; (15 December 1937): 810–843; (1 January 1938): 95–126; (15 January 1938): 375–403; (1 February 1938): 589–613.

With the hurriedly written libretto of *Entrez, messieurs, mesdames,* a one-act work marking the opening of the Bouffes-Parisiens in 1855, Ludovic Halévy launched a twenty-six-year Parisian theatrical career that brought him prosperity, a name beloved by the Second Empire bourgeoisie, and entry into the prestigious Académie Française in 1884. The longevity and success of Halévy's career as playwright and librettist were built on collaboration, the essence of theatrical creation, and his dramatic contributions cannot be disassociated from the composer Jacques Offenbach, with whom he wrote *Entrez* as well as more than twenty *opérettes* and *opéras bouffes* in the course of his career, and from Henri Meilhac, his colibrettist in ten Offenbach works and cowriter of nearly forty *comédies* for the nonlyric stage. With Offenbach and Meilhac, Halévy became a key figure in the theater of the Second Empire through their rollicking mockery and satire of French institutions, traditions, and social mores. Halévy and Meilhac arose as enfants terribles for whom nothing was too sacred to be dramatized and ridiculed. For their irreverence and their attacks on and portrayals of subjects and characters generally considered immoral or taboo, Halévy and Meilhac were both despised and beloved. Critics such as Edmond and Jules de Goncourt condemned them for their cynicism and ruthlessness, yet audiences flocked to their openings, and Parisian society feted them nightly. From early to late in the career of these cowriters, their work was seen as a reflection, and even a reconstruction, of contemporary Paris. Just as Abel-François Villemain called Eugène Scribe "a historian in spite of himself" for the realistic portrayals of Restoration society found in his *comédies,* so Jules Lemaître viewed Halévy and Meilhac as historians of the "frivolous and elegant society" of the Second Empire and, later, of the early years of the Third Republic.

Although the art of Halévy and Meilhac was not completely original–techniques and devices were inherited from comédie, vaudeville, opéra comique, and opera buffa of the eighteenth and early nineteenth centuries–it is lauded today for its high technical craftsmanship, and many works have been viewed as outstanding expressions of popular genres: at least six opéra bouffe libretti are acknowledged masterpieces. Yet the historical significance of Halévy's creation lies beyond his theatrical pieces. His short stories and novels were widely read: the first printing of a book typically numbered thirty-five thousand copies, and many works went through multiple editions. His most popular novel, *L'Abbé Constantin* (1882; translated as *The Abbé Constantin,* 1882), appeared in fifty-three editions by 1883, a year after its first publication. Halévy's fifty-six volumes of *carnets* (journals), dating from 1862 to 1906, have long been recognized as invaluable documentation of fin-de-siècle Parisian life. The acute observational skills evident in Halévy's theatrical and prose works come through sharply in these chronicles, portions of which were published (some portions, however, were destroyed by the author).

As *homme du théâtre* (man of the theater) and *homme de lettres* (man of letters) Halévy continued and enlarged on the talents and prestige of a literary and artistic family. Matrilineally, he was the grandson of Hippolyte Lebas, the famed architect of Notre-Dame-de-Lorette, winner of the Prix de Rome, and curator of the Institut de France; patrilineally, the writer was the grandson of Élie Halévy. Élie, a Talmudic scholar and nationally renowned Hebrew poet, carved a place for himself in Jewish history as secretary-translator of the Parisian Consistoire Central and cofounder of *L'Israélite français,* the first Jewish journal published in France. Ludovic was the son of Léon Halévy and nephew of Fromental Halévy, brothers who remained lifelong intimates and ideological comrades. Born a little more than a decade after Élie's immigration to France from Bavaria and after the granting of Jewish civil liberties in 1791, they were among the first generation of Jews to reap the benefits of education in the distinguished institutions from which Jews had previously been excluded. Léon attended the Lycée Charlemagne, where he won honors in the *concours général;* he was appointed adjunct professor of literature at the Ecole Polytechnique in 1831 and a few years later began a clerical position at the Ministry of Public Instruction. It was as writer and thinker that Léon worked most passionately and productively: as essayist, historian, translator of classic literature, dramatist, librettist, and an important early articulator of the social philosophy of the Saint-Simonian movement, particularly enriching Claude-Henri de Rouvroy Saint-Simon's view of the social role of art. He contributed to the Saint-Simonian publication *Opinions littéraires, philosophiques et industrielles* (Literary, Philosophical, and Industrial

Henri Meilhac, who collaborated with Halévy on ten operettas and nearly forty comedies

Opinions, 1825), published histories of the Jewish people in 1825 and 1828, and presented several socially resonant dramas. His older brother Fromental entered the Paris Conservatoire at age ten and after winning the Prix de Rome in 1819 went on to a multiple-duty career as Conservatoire professor, *chef du chant* (master of singing) at the Opéra-Comique and the Paris Opéra, and, most illustriously, as composer of opera for the Paris Opéra and the Opéra-Comique and *sécretaire-perpetual* of the Académie Française. Of his thirty opéras comiques and grand operas that premiered in Paris, *La Juive* (The Jewess, 1835) became one of the most successful operas of the nineteenth century.

Aware of the achievements of family members and surrounded by their ambitious, creative activity and the illustrious artistic circles in which they moved, Ludovic Halévy seemingly followed an inevitable course. His childhood haunts were the halls of the Palais de l'Institut, habituated by his father and maternal grandfather, and the wings of the Paris Opéra, frequented by his uncle. Yet in his early years Ludovic seemed to share none of his family's ambitions. After his 1845 entry to the lycée Louis-le-Grand, whose alumni included Voltaire and Molière, he proved an undistinguished and unfocused student prone to daydreaming. His attraction to and flair for the dramatic did emerge in his school years, however: at age fourteen (when through his family he was on the free-pass list of all Parisian theaters) he converted class notes on a historic battle into a drama. In his early years after graduation in 1852, when he held a clerical post in the Ministry of State following a failed effort at law school, he completed a play titled "La Fille d'un Mécène" (A Patron's Daughter), which did not elicit the interest of Parisian directors. His professional theatrical break, the 1855 collaboration with Offenbach on *Entrez,* came shortly after this attempt through the recommendation of his uncle Fromental, who was a mentor of Offenbach. Fearful of the outcome of this initial foray and the negative effects it might have on his official position, Ludovic adopted the pseudonym Jules Servières. He quickly discarded it, however, when the play's success gave him a place in the Société des auteurs dramatiques (Society of Dramatic Authors) and led to work with Offenbach on *Ba-ta-clan,* a one-act chinoiserie. From its premiere in December 1855 this work became popular for the composer's witty rhythms and melodies as well as for its multitargeted satire, including the lofty genre of grand opera. Centered on a tyrannical ruler of a small country, *Ba-ta-clan* mocks despotism, a favored theme of grand opera, as it parodies the genre's vocal style and quotes passages from Jacques Meyerbeer's *Les Huguenots* (1836).

By the early 1860s Halévy had become a seasoned librettist of operetta. He continued to work with Offenbach, but he also collaborated with the librettist Hector Crémieux on several operettas and with his father on the opéra comique titled *Le Mari sans le savoir* (The Husband, Unwittingly, 1860). One Offenbach libretto for which he was not officially credited is that of *Orphée aux enfers* (Orpheus in Hell, 1858). Halévy wanted his contributions to *Orphée* kept secret, again because of the potential threat to a governmental post: in early 1858 he was asked to fill the position of *chef du bureau* (chief clerk) of the Ministry for Algeria and the Colonies, a job that his family viewed as more desirable and prestigious than theater work. After having completed the libretto's first act and part of the second, he pulled himself off the project with the intention of severing his ties to the Bouffes-Parisiens, despite Offenbach's protests. The composer turned to Crémieux to finish the work, but when the librettist worked too slowly, he again appealed to Halévy, who—already disillusioned with his official post—consented to complete the libretto anonymously.

The balance between Halévy's work as writer and bureaucrat continued until 1865, when he gave up public service to devote himself exclusively to the theater. A few years prior, in 1861, he had taken the less demanding position of *secrétaire-rédacteur* (secretary-editor) of the Corps législatif, partly to allow more time for writing, but it was the beginning of his creative relationship with Meilhac in 1860

that undoubtedly led to the renunciation of governmental work. Schoolboy associates at Louis-le-Grand, the two writers renewed their friendship after agreeing to work together on *Ce qui plaît aux hommes* (What Pleases Men, 1860), a parody of a François Ponsard comédie. It was a strange pairing by all accounts: Halévy appeared an elegant, punctilious intellectual with an air of superiority while Meilhac was an unaffected, ebullient, but somewhat unmannered individual. Yet as friends and collaborators they found a consummate rapport that was built on respect and sympathy for the talents, differences, and personal eccentricities of the other. They worked together until 1881, when Halévy turned his attention fully to prose.

The nature of their collaboration was a central topic among nineteenth-century literati. Alexandre Dumas *fils* remarked on the uncanny ability of these two men to write as one: "Ils se mettent à deux pour faire des pièces à un personnage" (The two of them work together to create plays with one character). Although the writers themselves never offered detailed accounts of their working methods, many critics sought to break down their union, speculating about the exact division of labor. In his address to the Académie Française in 1899, Henri Lavedan elaborated on the artistic results of their different temperaments and approaches:

> We will not see again for a long time so marvelous a combination of two such contrasts: whimsy and wisdom, prudence and rashness, the locust and the ant, excess and directness, the first try and the erasure, the school for truants and the military academy. Meilhac improvised the victory, and Halévy organized it.

(translated by Eric C. Hansen, in *Ludovic Halévy: A Study of Frivolity and Fatalism in Nineteenth-Century France,* p. 57)

The majority view of late-nineteenth-century and twentieth-century analysts is that the more creatively imaginative Meilhac constructed the plots of their works while the more observant, meticulous Halévy refined them with crafted, witty language and infusions of realism and irony. Many have determined that Meilhac wrote at least the first-draft dialogue of plays, but James H. Olander suggests that the two worked on dialogue jointly after Meilhac blocked out the plot and that in lyric works Halévy wrote the vast majority of the verse. In collaborations with Offenbach, however, the composer also contributed to the libretto. From the partnership came clever, direct, and natural dialogue that crackled with humorous puns and colloquialisms; simple, cogent plots of quick action; skillfully rhymed and energetically paced libretti that included varied solos and ensembles; and engaging, lifelike—often anachronistic—characters. Eric C. Hansen, in his biography of Halévy, characterizes the Meilhac-Halévy oeuvre as "a combination of opposites—fantasy and realism, irony and directness, detail and simplicity" that gently satirized while refraining from propaganda.

Often deemed a masterpiece among the Meilhac-Halévy-Offenbach operettas is *La Belle Hélène* (1864; translated as *Fair Helen,* 1871), a work that brought profit and critical venom for its parody of Greek mythology, as had the earlier Crémieux-Halévy work, *Orphée.* In *Journal des Débats* the leading critic Jules Janin had called *Orphée* a desecration of "holy and glorious antiquity" for its cynical twists on the beloved myth. Orpheus, for example, appears as a conservatory professor and unfaithful husband who is relieved that his equally unfaithful wife Eurydice is taken to the underworld by her disguised lover Pluto. In reaction to *La Belle Hélène* Janin condemned the perfidy of the collaborators, and Théophile Gautier found it "nearly blasphemous." Such critiques spurred Ludovic's father, a translator of classic writings, to publish a defense of his son's work as a valid reinterpretation of classic tradition. The operetta held onto the Greek idea of fate as it playfully and anachronistically modified Greek characters, presenting Orestes as a roguish, unheroic dandy; Achilles as dim-witted, immature, and petulant; Paris as a deceptive, clever seducer; and Helen as a bored, stylish coquette of the Second Empire. It alluded to the court of Napoleon III in the characterization of the vacillating King Agamemnon and in the charades and rhyming games that were common entertainments of the French court, allusions strengthened by Offenbach's music.

Other successful Meilhac-Halévy-Offenbach collaborations include the opéras bouffes *Barbe-bleue* (Bluebeard, 1866), based on the medieval legend later treated by Paul Dukas and Béla Bartók; *La Vie parisienne* (1866), set in contemporary Paris; *La Grande-Duchesse de Gérolstein* (1867), written for the 1867 Paris Exposition; and *La Périchole* (1868), a parody of Gaetano Donizetti's grand opera *La Favorite* (1840). The Meilhac-Halévy lyric work that remains in the active repertoire today is *Carmen* (1875), an opéra comique written with Halévy's cousin-in-law Georges Bizet that initially scandalized audiences with its stark presentation of onstage murder. A few years earlier *Froufrou* (1869) won critical acclaim for the heightened realism presented in the anguish and death of a respectable character. In these works, as well as other theater pieces and prose by Halévy, social and political themes parallel the writer's own personal fears that

Composer Jacques Offenbach, who provided the scores for more than twenty of Halévy's operettas, many of which satirized contemporary French institutions

materialism, corruption, licentiousness, and over-extended militarism would spell the decay of France, as revealed in his correspondence and chronicles. With these in mind, the sexual immorality featured in *La Belle Hélène* (and many other works) and the mockery of diplomatic and Napoleonic military figures in *La Grande-Duchesse de Gérolstein,* for example, appear as contemporary critiques.

Throughout his life Halévy remained close to his family, including his wife, Louise Breguet, whom he married in 1868; his sons, Élie and Daniel; and his father and uncle. Two other family members who figured prominently were his half brother, Anatole Prévost-Paradol, and his cousin Geneviève Halévy. Prévost-Paradol, the illegitimate son of Léon Halévy and the actress Lucinde Paradol, was never publicly acknowledged as Léon's son although he was adopted into his father's household following his mother's death. He shared a deep fraternal bond with Ludovic, and

Poster for the 1869 comic opera on which Halévy collaborated with Meilhac and Offenbach

later as writer for *Journal des Débats,* politician, and diplomat he grew to be his literary and political mentor. Geneviève, the daughter of Fromental Halévy and Léonie Rodrigues-Henriques and wife of Fromental's pupil Bizet, hosted a brilliant salon that attracted artistic, political, and social leaders, and she was immortalized by Marcel Proust and Guy de Maupassant as a central character in their works. Through contacts made in Geneviève's salon, his own home, and the theater Halévy established enduring friendships with a wide circle of Parisian aristocrats, authors, scholars, and artists, including Edgar Degas. (Degas dined and sketched at Halévy's house biweekly, but their diametrically opposed views of the Alfred Dreyfus affair turned them into bitter enemies.)

Despite Halévy's artistic and financial successes, his intimate associations, his adoration of Parisian life, and the joie de vivre that permeates his work, the writer was plagued by depression and nervousness, which would intensify with personal losses and political tensions. The deaths of his uncle Fromental in 1862 and his father in 1883, the suicide of Prévost-Paradol in 1870, and the Franco-Prussian War of 1870–1871 exacted immense emotional tolls on Halévy. But the author's recurring melancholia was rooted in family traits as well as generational pessimism. The psychological conflict in both father and uncle, linked in part to divided identities as elite Jews within a predominantly Catholic France, persisted unresolved in Halévy. Reveling in Parisian gaiety and aristocratic elitism as he despaired over manifestations of France's moral and political decline, Halévy endured stark contradictions in himself and in the Parisian society that he re-created on the stage.

Letters:

"Actualités: Une Lettre de M. Ludovic Halévy," *Les Archives israélites: Recueil politique et religieux,* 44 (27 September 1883): 310;

"Lettre à M. Isidore Cahen," in *La Gerbe: Etudes, souvenirs, lettres, pensées, publiées à l'occasion du cinquantenaire du recueil hebdomadaire, Les Archives israélites-politiques, 1840–1890* (Paris: Au Bureau des Archives Israélites, 1890), p. 37.

Biographies:

Jules Claretie, *Ludovic Halévy* (Paris: A. Quantin, 1883);

Eric C. Hansen, *Ludovic Halévy: A Study of Frivolity and Fatalism in Nineteenth Century France* (Lanham, Md., & London: University Press of America, 1987);

Henri Loyrette, ed., *Entre le théâtre et l'histoire: La Famile Halévy (1760–1960)* (Paris: Fayard & Réunion des musées nationaux, 1996).

References:

Maurice Barrès, "M. Ludovic Halévy à l'Académie," *Revue contemporaine,* 4 (February 1886): 236–241;

Pierre Berton, *Souvenirs de la vie de théâtre* (Paris: P. Lafitte et Cie, 1914);

Michèle Bo Bramsen, *Portrait d'Élie Halévy* (Amsterdam: B. R. Grüner, 1978);

Auguste Cartault, "MM. Henri Meilhac et Ludovic Halévy," *Revue politique et littéraire; Revue des cours littéraires,* 3 (28 May 1881): 673–683;

Myrna Chase, *Élie Halévy: An Intellectual Biography* (New York: Columbia University Press, 1980);

J. E. Chasles, "Ludovic Halévy," *La Grande revue,* 10 (1935);

Jules Claretie, "Lud. Halévy," *Célébrités contemporaines,* 31 (1883);

Claretie, "M. Ludovic Halévy," *Revue politique et littéraire,* 6 (4 August 1883): 137–142;

Simone Monnier Clay, "Henri Meilhac-Ludovic Halévy: Des Bouffes-Parisiens à l'Opéra-Comique," dissertation, University of California at Davis, 1987;

François de Croisset, *La Vie parisienne au théâtre,* twelfth edition (Paris: Grasset, 1929);

Mina Curtiss, *Bizet and His World* (New York: Knopf, 1958);

Alain Decaux, *Offenbach: Roi du Second Empire* (Paris: Perrin, 1975);

Robert De Flers, "La Société sous le Second Empire. Meilhac et Halévy: Leur vie et leur carrière (I)," *Conferencia,* 18 (15 September 1924): 281–297;

Robert Dreyfus, "Ludovic Halévy," *Pages libres,* 15 (9 May 1908): 554–556;

Félix Duquesnel, "Les Débuts de Ludovic Halévy," *Annales Politiques et littéraires,* 50 (17 May 1908): 465–466;

Jacques Du Tillet, "Théâtre de Meilhac et Halévy," *Revue politique et littéraire: Revue bleue,* 15 (12 January 1901): 60–64;

Alex Faris, *Jacques Offenbach* (New York: Scribners, 1981);

Charles Le Goffic, "(Ludovic) Halévy," in *Le Grande Encyclopédie,* volume 19 (Paris: H. Lamirault, n.d.), pp. 756–757;

Tamina Groepper, *Aspekte der Offenbachiade: Untersuchungen zu den Libretti der grossen Operetten Offenbachs* (Frankfurt am Main & New York: Peter Lang, 1990);

Maurice Guillemot, "Grands et petits: Ludovic Halévy," *Panurge: Journal parisien illustré,* 2 (21 January 1883): 3;

Daniel Halévy, *Regards sur l'affaire Dreyfus: Textes réunis et présentés par Jean-Pierre Halévy* (Paris: Editions de Fallois, 1994);

Léon Halévy, *F. Halévy: Sa Vie et ses oeuvres* (Paris: Paul Dupont, 1862);

Halévy, *La Belle Hélène: Épitre à mon ami Paul Duport* (Paris: Michel Lévy, 1865);

Victor Hallays-Dabot, *La Censure dramatique et le théâtre: Histoire des vingt dernières années (1850–1870)* (Paris: E. Dentu, 1871);

Diana R. Hallman, "The French Grand Opera *La Juive* (1835): A Socio-Historical Study," dissertation, City University of New York, 1995;

Eric C. Hansen, *Disaffection and Decadence: A Crisis in French Intellectual Thought, 1848–1898* (Washington, D.C.: University Press of America, 1982);

Siegfried Kracauer, *Jacques Offenbach on le secret du Second Empire,* translated by Lucienne Astrue (Paris: Bernard Groasset, 1937);

Kracauer, *Jacques Offenbach und das Paris seiner zeit* (Amsterdam: A. de Lange, 1937); translated by Gwenda David and Eric Mosbacher as *Orpheus in Paris: Offenbach and the Paris of His Time* (New York & London: Constable, 1937);

Henri Lavedan, and Costa de Beauregard, Marquis Charles-Albert, *Discours prononcés dans la séance publique tenue par l'Académie française pour la réception de M. Henri Lavedan, le jendi 28 décembre 1899* (Paris: Firmin-Didot et Cie, 1899);

Jules Lemaître, "Le Théâtre de Meilhac et Halévy," *Les Annales* (17 May 1908);

James H. Olander, "The Halévy-Meilhac Libretti for Offenbach," dissertation, University of Wisconsin, 1963;

Robert Pouvoyeur, *Offenbach* (Paris: Seuil, 1994);

Marcel Proust, *Correspondance avec Daniel Halévy: Texte établi, présenté et annoté par Anne Borrel et Jean-Pierre Halévy* (Paris: Editions de Fallois, 1992);

Christopher Smith, "Ludovic Halévy," in *The New Grove Dictionary of Opera* (New York & London: Macmillan, 1992), pp. 600–601;

Albert Thibaudet, *Histoire de la littérature française de 1789 à nos jours* (Paris: Stock, Delamain et Boutelleau, 1936).

Papers:

Halévy's papers are held in various institutions that include the Archives Nationales in Paris: legal papers and correspondence of the Halévy family (Minutier central, Dossier CXVII, 1058); the Bibliothèque de l'Institut de France in Paris: correspondence and papers (Mss. 4476–4500); the Bibliothèque Nationale, in Paris; and the Bibliothèque de l'Arsenal: correspondence and papers. Other papers are held in the Bibliothèque de l'Opéra: Fonds Halévy; and the Département des Manuscrits, Nouvelles acquisitions françaises includes papers of the families Halévy, Bizet, and Straus (NAF 14345–14355, NAF 14383–14386), manuscripts of works (NAF 19801–19805), journal (NAF 19806–19848), notebooks (NAF 19861–19901), and correspondence (NAF 14603, 14695, 14826, 19902, 19905, and so forth). Other papers are in the Alexandre Bixio Collection and the Rothschild Collection in the Département de la Musique, which has Lettres autographes. The J. Pierpont Morgan Library in New York City has a collection of correspondence.

Victor Hugo
(26 February 1802 – 22 May 1885)

John J. Janc
Mankato State University

See also the Hugo entry in *DLB 119: Nineteenth-Century French Fiction Writers: Romanticism and Realism, 1800–1860.*

PLAY PRODUCTIONS: *Amy Robsart,* Paris, Théâtre de l'Odéon, 13 February 1828;

Hernani, Paris, Comédie-Française, 25 February 1830;

Marion de Lorme, Paris, Théâtre de la Porte Saint-Martin, 11 August 1831;

Le Roi s'amuse, Paris, Comédie-Française, 22 November 1832;

Lucrèce Borgia, Paris, Théâtre de la Porte Saint-Martin, 2 February 1833;

Marie Tudor, Paris, Théâtre de la Porte Saint-Martin, 6 November 1833;

Angelo, tyran de Padoue, Paris, Comédie-Française, 28 April 1835;

La Esmeralda, Paris, L'Académie Royale de Musique, 14 November 1836;

Ruy Blas, Paris, Théâtre de la Renaissance, 8 November 1838;

Les Burgraves, Paris, Comédie-Française, 7 March 1843;

Les Deux Trouvailles de Gallus, Paris, Le Cercle des Arts Intimes, 21 January 1882 (only *Margarita*); *Margarita* and *Esca,* Paris, Comédie-Française, 1 June 1923;

Sur la lisière d'un bois, Paris, Théâtre d'Art, Salle Duprez, May 1889;

Les Gueux, Paris, Théâtre d'Art, Salle Duprez, 18 November 1890;

La Grand'mère, Paris, Théâtre de l'Odéon, 6 May 1898;

L'Epée, Paris, Théâtre de l'Odéon, 25 February 1902;

Mangeront-ils?, Brussels, Théâtre du Parc, 26 March 1907;

La Forêt mouillée, Paris, Comédie-Française, 22 February 1930;

Torquemada, Paris, Nouvelle Comédie, 8 May 1936;

Mille francs de récompense, Metz, Théâtre municipal de Metz, 14 April 1961;

Victor Hugo, circa 1853

L'Intervention, Paris, theatrical troupe of Louis-le-Grand High School, Salle de Spectacles du Lycée Louis-le Grand, 10 March 1964;

Les Jumeaux, Coussac-Bonneval, festival, 1970.

BOOKS: *Ode sur la naissance de Son Altesse Royale monseigneur le duc de Bordeaux* (Paris: Boucher, 1820);

Odes et poésies diverses (Paris: Pélicier, 1822);

Odes (Paris: Persan, 1823);

Han d'Islande, anonymous, 4 volumes (Paris: Persan, 1823); translated anonymously as *Hans of Iceland* (London: J. Robins, 1825);

Nouvelles Odes (Paris: Ladvocat, 1824);

Odes et ballades (Paris: Ladvocat, 1826; enlarged edition, Paris: Hector Bossange, 1828);

Bug-Jargal (Paris: Urbain Canel, 1826); translated as *The Slave-King* (Philadelphia: Carey, Lea & Blanchard, 1833);

Cromwell (Paris: E. Flammarion, 1827);

Ode à la colonne de la place Vendôme (Paris, 1829);

Les Orientales (Paris: Gosselin et Bossange, 1829);

Le Dernier Jour d'un condamné, anonymous (Paris: Gosselin et Bossange, 1829); translated by Sir P. Hesketh Fleetwood as *The Last Days of a Condemned* (London: Smith, Elder, 1840);

Hernani, ou l'Honneur castillan (Paris: Mame et Delaunay-Vallée, 1830); translated anonymously as *Hernani; or, The Honour of a Castilian* (London: W. Sams, 1830);

Notre-Dame de Paris, 2 volumes (Paris: Gosselin, 1831; enlarged edition, Paris: Renduel, 1832); translated by A. L. Alger as *The Hunchback of Notre Dame* (Boston: Estes & Lauriat, 1833);

Marion de Lorme (Paris: Charpentier, 1831);

Les Feuilles d'automne (Paris: Renduel, 1831);

Le Roi s'amuse (Paris: Eugène, Renduel, 1832); translated anonymously as *The King's Fool* (London: J. Clements, 1841);

Lucrèce Borgia (Paris: Eugène Renduel, 1833); translated by W. T. Haley as *Lucretia Borgia, a Dramatic Tale* (London: J. Clements, 1842);

Marie Tudor (Paris: Eugène Renduel, 1833);

Claude Gueux (Paris: Everat, Imprimeur, 1834);

Littérature et philosophie mêlées, 2 volumes (Paris: Renduel, 1834);

Angelo, Tyran de Padoue (Paris: J. Hetzel, 1835); translated by Charles Reade as *Angelo* (London: T. H. Lacy, 1851);

Les Chants du crépuscule (Paris: Renduel, 1835); translated by George W. M. Reynolds as *Songs of Twilight* (Paris: French, English and American Library, 1836);

La Esmeralda, music by Mlle Bertin (Paris: Marice Schlésinger, 1836);

Les Voix intérieures (Paris: Renduel, 1837);

Ruy Blas (Paris: H. Delloye, 1838); translated anonymously as *Ruy Blas: A Romantic Drama* (London: T. H. Lacy, 1860);

Le Retour de l'empereur (Paris: Furne et Cie, n.d.);

Les Rayons et les ombres (Paris: Delloye, 1842);

Le Rhin, 2 volumes (Paris: Delloye, 1842); translated by D. M. Aird as *The Rhine* (London: D. Aird, 1843);

Les Burgraves, trilogie (Paris: E. Michaud, 1843);

Œuvres oratoires de Victor Hugo, 2 volumes (Brussels: Tarride, 1852);

Napoléon-le-petit (Brussels: Tarride, 1852);

Les Châtiments (Brussels: Henri Samuel et Cie, 1853);

République universelle, démocratique et sociale. Anniversaire de la révolution de 1848. 24 féurier 1855 (Jersey: Imprimerie universelle, 1855);

Les Contemplations, 2 volumes (Brussels: Pierre-Jules Hetzel, 1856);

La Légende des siècles, 2 volumes (Brussels: Hetzel, Mèline Cans et Cie, 1859); translated by George S. Burleigh as *The Legend of the Centuries* (New York, 1874); enlarged as *La Légende des siècles, Nouvelle série,* 2 volumes (Paris: Calmann-Lévy, 1877); enlarged as *La Légende des siècles, Tome cinquième et dernier* (Paris: Calmann-Lévy, 1883);

Les Misérables, 10 volumes (Brussels: Lacroix, Verboeckhoven et Cie, 1862); translated by Lascelles Wraxall (London: Hurst & Blackett, 1862);

Inez de Castro (Brussels: A. Lacroix, Verboeckhoven et Cie, 1863);

William Shakespeare (Brussels: Lacroix, Verboeckhoven et Cie, 1864); translated by A. Hailot (Boston: Estes & Lauriat, 1864);

Les Travailleurs de la mer, 3 volumes (Brussels: Lacroix, Verboeckhoven et Cie, 1866); translated as *The Toilers of the Sea,* 2 volumes (Boston: Dana Estes, 1866; enlarged French edition, Paris: J. Hetzel et A. Quantin, 1880–1889);

La Voix de Guernesey (Guernsey: T. M. Richard, 1867);

L'Homme qui rit, 4 volumes (Brussels: Lacroix, Verboeckhoven et Cie, 1869); translated as *The Man Who Laughs* (Boston: Dana Estes, 1869);

L'Année terrible (Paris: Michel Lévy, 1872);

Actes et paroles I. Avant l'exil (Paris: Michel Lévy, 1872);

Actes et paroles II. Pendant l'exil (Paris: Michel Lévy, 1875);

Actes et paroles III. Depuis l'exil, 1870–1876 (Paris: Calmann-Lévy, 1876);

Histoire d'un crime, déposition d'un témoin (Paris: Calmann-Lévy, 1877); translated by T. H. Joyce and A. Locker as *The History of a Crime; The Testimony of an Eye Witness* (New York: Hurst, 1877);

L'Art d'être grand-père (Paris: Calmann-Lévy, 1877);

Le Pape (Paris: Calmann-Lévy, 1878);

La Pitié suprême (Paris: Calmann-Lévy, 1878);

Religions et religion (Paris: Calmann-Lévy, 1879);

L'Ane (Paris: Calmann-Lévy, 1879);

Les Quatre Vents de l'esprit, 2 volumes (Paris: J. Hetzel et A. Quantin, 1881);

Torquemada (Paris: Calmann-Lévy, 1882);

L'Archipel de la Manche (Paris: Calmann-Lévy, 1883).

Collections: *Œuvres de Victor Hugo,* 20 volumes (Paris: E. Renduel, 1832–1842);

Œuvres de Victor Hugo, 16 volumes (Paris: Furne et Cie, 1841);

Dramas, translated by T. Sterling (Boston: Aldine, 1882?);

Dramas of Victor Hugo, translated by Frederick L. Slous and Mrs. Newton Crosland (New York: President Publishing, n.d.);

Œuvres inédites de Victor Hugo: Théâtre en liberté—includes *Le Prologue, La Grand'mère, L'Épée, Mangeront-ils?, Sur la lisière d'un bois, Les Gueux, Être aimé, La Fôret mouillée* (Paris: J. Hetzel, A. Quantin, 1886);

Dramatic Works of Victor Hugo, translated by Slous and Crosland (London: G. Bell & Sons, 1887);

Œuvres inédites de Victor Hugo—includes *Amy Robsart, Les Jumeaux* (Paris: J. Hetzel & Cie et Maison Quantin, 1889);

Œuvres complètes de Victor Hugo. Drame, volume 5—includes *Torquemada, Amy Robsart, Les Jumeaux* (Paris: J. Hetzel, A. Quantin, 1889?);

Œuvres complètes de Victor Hugo, 45 volumes, edited by Paul Meurice, Gustave Simon, and Lècile Daubray (Paris: Ollendorf, Albin Michel, 1902–1951);

Œuvres complètes de Victor Hugo, Théâtre VI, Théâtre de jeunesse, Mille francs de récompense, Plans et projets—includes *Irtamène* and *A.Q.C.H.E.B.* (Paris: Ollendorff, 1934);

La Légende des siècles, La Fin de Satan, Dieu, edited by Jacques Trachet (Paris: Gallimard, 1950);

Les Misérables, edited by Maurice Allen (Paris: Gallimard, Bibliothèque de la Pléiade, 1951);

Œuvres poétiques, 3 volumes (Paris: Gallimard, 1964);

Œuvres complètes, édition chronologique, 18 volumes (Paris: Le Club Français du Livre, 1967–1969);

Notre-Dame de Paris and *Les Travailleurs de la mer,* edited by Jacques Seebacher and Yves Gohin (Paris: Gallimard, Bibliothèque de la Pléiade, 1975);

Œuvres complètes, 15 volumes (Paris: Laffont, Collection Bouquins, 1985–).

SELECTED PERIODICAL PUBLICATION—
UNCOLLECTED: *L'Intervention,* "Une Comédie inédite de Victor Hugo," edited by Henri Guillemin, *La Revue des Deux Mondes,* nos. 22–23 (15 November, 1 December 1950): 193–210, 385–404.

Victor Hugo, one of France's most prolific nineteenth-century authors, wrote novels, poems, and dramatic works. His career as a playwright began in 1816 and ended almost sixty years later. The dramas and prefaces that he wrote between 1826 and 1843 constitute his most important contribution to the history of French theater. Literary critics and historians consider Hugo to be one of the most influential theorists and practitioners of the Romantic movement as it affected the French stage. *Hernani,* whose premiere took place in 1830, ushered in the new direction that the French stage was to take during the next decade. Although Hugo did not in-

vent the historical drama, he perfected it. He also created some of the most memorable characters in the history of French theater and wrote some of the most eloquent prose and verse to have ever been spoken by a French actor or actress.

Victor-Marie Hugo was born in Besançon, France on 26 February 1802. Unlike his older brothers, Abel and Eugène, the newborn Hugo was small and weak. His health worried both of his parents. His father, Léopold Hugo, was a military officer who spent much of his time living abroad. In 1807 Sophie Hugo, Victor's mother, visited her husband, who was stationed in Naples. The trip through the war-torn Italian countryside made a deep impression on the young Hugo. Unable to get along with her husband, Sophie returned to France while her husband was sent to Spain, where he was promoted to general in 1809. A year later King Joseph granted him the title of count and, in recognition of his bravery, named him governor of two Spanish provinces. During the summer of the following year Sophie and the three sons joined the general in Madrid. The names of two cities that they visited while en route, Ernani and Torquemada, became titles for two of the future playwright's dramas.

When once again the parents could not reconcile their differences, Sophie and the children returned to Paris in the spring of 1812. During the next few years Victor pursued his studies, first at the boarding school Cordier, then at the Parisian high school Louis-le-Grand, where he wrote his first play in 1816. In 1819 he received a prestigious award for an ode that he had composed. Toward the end of that year he and his brothers founded the *Conservateur littéraire,* a royalist review that enjoyed considerable success until March 1821, when it ceased publication. In addition to contributing articles to the *Conservateur littéraire,* Hugo continued to write plays and poetry.

In October 1822 Hugo married Adèle Foucher, the daughter of family friends. The writer Alfred de Vigny was his best man. During the next six years Hugo and Adèle had five children, the first of whom died shortly after birth. It was also during this period that the aspiring author developed friendships with such writers as François Auguste-René de Chateaubriand and Charles Nodier. The young Hugo spent much of his time writing plays, poems, and his first novels, *Han d'Islande* (1823; translated as *Hans of Iceland,* 1825) and *Bug-Jargal* (1826; translated as *The Slave King,* 1833). During the 1830s he wrote the Romantic dramas for which he is primarily remembered in French theatrical history. He also continued to compose poetry and finished *Notre-Dame de Paris* (1831; translated as *The*

Engraving of the uproar created by the first performance of Hugo's Hernani *(1830), at which Hugo's Romanticist supporters fought with jeering Classicists*

Hunchback of Notre Dame, 1833). Meanwhile, Adèle began her relationship with the writer Charles-Augustin Sainte-Beuve, and Hugo began his with the actress Juliette Drouet. He and Drouet traveled not only in France but also to Belgium, Switzerland, and Germany. Many of France's literary figures, including Alphonse de Lamartine, Alfred de Musset, and Gérard de Nerval, frequented Hugo's home. In 1841 Hugo was elected to the Académie Française after several unsuccessful nominations. In 1843 his play *Les Burgraves* (The Burgraves) failed at the Comédie-Française, and he stopped writing for the stage for many years. *Les Burgraves* was the last of his plays to be staged in his lifetime.

In September 1843 Hugo was struck by tragedy when his beloved daughter Léopoldine and her husband drowned in an accident in the Seine. In 1845 Hugo was named a peer of France. During this time he had several love affairs and continued to write, beginning work on what later became the

novel *Les Misérables* (1862; translated, 1862). After the fall of Louis-Philippe in February 1848, Hugo became politically active. In June he was elected to the National Assembly and in 1849 to the Legislative Assembly. When his son Charles was imprisoned for having written an article critical of the death penalty, Hugo did not hesitate to oppose Napoleon openly. After the latter's coup d'état on 2 December 1851, Hugo, fearing for his life, disguised himself as a worker and fled France for Brussels. His stay was short-lived because he wrote a pamphlet titled *Napoléon-le-petit* (Napoleon the Little, 1852) that angered the new emperor. Hugo and his family sought refuge on the island of Jersey, where they lived until 1855. While on Jersey, Hugo and those close to him held seances during which they claimed to communicate with the dead. The family finally settled on the island of Guernsey, where Hugo purchased a residence, Hauteville-House. Juliette moved in next door. From 1851 to 1870 Hugo continued to write plays, poems, critical works, and novels. He also wrote many letters, corresponding with people such as Théodore de Banville, Charles Baudelaire, Gustave Flaubert, and Paul Verlaine. He remained politically active, opposing Napoleon III and his repressive policies whenever the opportunity arose. He and Juliette traveled to Belgium, Luxembourg, and Germany. In 1868 Adèle died. During 1869 Hugo was busy writing plays and overseeing the publication of *L'Homme qui rit* (translated as *The Man Who Laughs,* 1869).

After the fall of the emperor, Hugo ended his long exile on the island of Guernsey and returned to Paris on 5 September 1870. He was elected to the National Assembly the next year but resigned for political reasons. His son Charles died in 1871; another son, François-Victor, died in 1873. Hugo was elected to the Senate in 1876. During this time his relationship with Juliette was often compromised because of his interest in other women. She died in 1883. After his return to France, Hugo never stopped writing. Many of his theatrical works from the 1830s were staged again with great success in Paris. On 22 May 1885 Victor-Marie Hugo died. The National Assembly and the Senate voted to honor him with a period of national mourning. His body lay in state under the Arc de Triomphe on 31 May and 1 June before being accompanied by two million admirers to the Panthéon for burial.

Hugo's writings for the theater fall into three basic groups: the plays of his youth, written from 1816 to 1819; his Romantic dramas, created from 1827 to 1843; and his post-Romantic works, composed from 1854 to 1873. He actually began writing for the stage in 1812, at the age of ten. Two unfinished works, *L'Enfer sur terre* (Hell on Earth) and *Le Château du diable* (The Devil's Castle) date from that year.

From July to December 1816, while still in high school, Hugo wrote his first complete play, a five-act tragedy, *Irtamène* (1934). Its 1,508 lines of poetry relate how Zobéir, king of Egypt, regains his throne. Given the political climate of the time and the young author's devotion to the monarchy, it is not surprising that Hugo depicted a dethroned sovereign who, with the support of his devoted subjects and officers, returns to power. Although *Irtamène* remains faithful in many ways to the classical tradition of theater, it contains elements of what eventually typify Hugo's dramatic productions: characters with little psychological development; improbable, if not unbelievable, situations; cavalier treatment of the rules of dramatic composition governing place and time; long monologues and speeches; and the use of hyperbole.

During the months of September, October, and November 1817, Hugo, still a student at the Parisian high school Louis-le-Grand, wrote two acts of a second tragedy, "Athélie, ou les Scandinaves" (Athélie, or the Scandinavians). After abandoning this work he began and completed another play in December, a comic opera or vaudeville called *A.Q.C.H.E.B.* (*A quelque chose hasard est bon*) (1934). In twenty-four acts, or "scenes," the reader is treated to a typical love story with all its complications: a young couple unable to wed because of a marriage arranged by the girl's father, a hero unaware of his family background, and the unexpected discovery that the two suitors are in fact brothers. The dialogue is regularly interrupted by songs and duets.

The final work of this initial period of dramatic creativity is a melodrama, probably written in 1819, *Inez de Castro.* This work fits the mold of the genre to which it belongs: it dramatizes a fight between good and evil, with the triumph of the former; it contains disguises, chains, poison, and murder; and it has a prison, a crypt with a casket, and a ghost accompanied by angels. In 1822 Hugo submitted his melodrama to a theatrical company that decided to produce it, but the royal censors, offended by the portrayal of a weak king, forbade its production. For the next six years the young author devoted his time to writing poems and two novels, *Han d'Islande* and *Bug-Jargal.* In 1825 he composed the first four scenes of *Corneille,* a five-act play that was never completed.

In early 1822 Alexandre Soumet, a well-known poet and dramatist, asked Hugo to co-author a play based upon Sir Walter Scott's novel *Kenilworth* (1821). Hugo was to write the first three acts, Soumet the last two. When Hugo read his contribution to Soumet, the latter did not find it to his liking and abandoned the project. Hugo also set aside the work, which was titled *Amy Robsart,* until either 1826 or early 1827, when he finally finished it. To give an impetus to the literary career of his brother-in-law, Paul Foucher, Hugo agreed that the play should bear the younger man's name. The premiere at the Théâtre de l'Odéon on 13 February 1828 was a disaster. The beautiful costumes designed by Eugène Delacroix and the fine acting of a gifted cast of actors could not save the play that spectators began booing before the curtain went up. *Amy Robsart* was withdrawn from the bill after one performance. The critics attacked the work for its story line, which too closely imitated Scott's; for its style, which was seen as being in bad taste; and for the dramatic principles upon which it was based, the French public viewing the latter as contrary to current theatrical practice.

Juliette Drouet, an actress who was Hugo's mistress for nearly fifty years (lithograph by Léon Noël)

Because Hugo borrowed the plot of *Amy Robsart* from Scott, it is of little interest to summarize it here. It is useful to note, however, various dramatic, thematic, and stylistic elements found within the play that characterize much of Hugo's later Romantic theater. The historical setting of the play is comparatively recent, the action taking place in sixteenth-century England. The theme is quite simple: Amy and Count Leicester, who are secretly married, love one another, but various characters around them are opposed to this union and will stop at nothing to destroy it. Queen Elizabeth, the reigning monarch, wields ultimate power but does not control the world around her. She is duped more than once by those who are supposed to serve her. The development of the plot depends upon secrets, misunderstanding, lies, treachery, and murder. The costumes and stage settings are described in some detail. Instead of evolving psychologically, the characters remain static; they represent ideas and principles. As for the style, Hugo used a rich and varied

vocabulary. Metaphors, similes, and lengthy developments of thoughts and images are abundant.

During the first eight months of 1826 Hugo spent considerable time thinking about what became his first great historical drama, *Cromwell* (1827). In keeping with what became his regular practice, he did extensive research, taking notes whenever necessary. He wrote the first four acts from August to October. The fifth act, begun on 28 October, was not finished until the end of September 1827, almost one year later, during which time he wrote an important preface. In spite of the length of *Cromwell* (more than sixty-seven hundred lines, more than three-and-one-half times that of Hugo's regular plays in poetic form) and its impressive list of characters (more than ninety), the play is readable. Its plot is straightforward: will Oliver Cromwell be crowned king before his enemies succeed in killing him? All subplots are of minor importance. Hugo makes ample use of traditional theatrical devices associated with the comic and melodramatic genres, which include eavesdropping, a stolen letter, a letter accidentally given in the place of another, disguises, a sleeping potion, and mistaken identities. Local color plays a preponderant role in this historical drama. Hugo, a consummate set and costume designer, re-creates the period in question through detailed stage directions. Moreover, his role as director is clearly evident. He never hesitates to let the actors know how he expects a scene to be played.

Stylistically, *Cromwell* contains much of the best and the worst of Hugo the poet. He regularly satisfies his penchant for rare, unfamiliar proper names, for alliterations that are occasionally a bit cacophonous, and for rhymes that shock the ear. The copious use of asides reduces the dramatic quality of many scenes. While no speech equals in length the one delivered by Don Carlos in the fourth act of *Hernani* (1830), there are five in *Cromwell* that are longer than seventy lines. To his credit it must be noted that Hugo makes every attempt to liberate the alexandrine from its classical constraints, dividing it into four, five, even six separate exchanges of dialogue. Unwilling to remain within the limits imposed upon the use of language by his classical predecessors, he introduces all sorts of vocabulary heretofore unheard in serious works on the French stage, ranging from the most common terms to the most erudite. Anaphore, antithesis, and enjambment assume their rightful place in his stylistic repertory. Songs are interspersed throughout the play. Comic relief abounds. Humor is found not only in the judicious use of language but also in the discerning juxtaposition of characters and situations. For the first time Hugo mixes amusing and serious subject matter. The success of entire scenes depends upon what he calls in his preface the "theory of the grotesque," which involves combining comic and tragic elements in the same work.

Cromwell is far from being a perfect play. It does merit, however, careful analysis because it is Hugo's first original historical drama, because it amply illustrates many of the basic principles of his great works, and because it deals with themes that recur in his later writings. Hugo knew that no theater director would produce *Cromwell*. In its preface he admits that the current literary and political climate, and the play's length, make its staging impossible. To this day *Cromwell* has never been acted.

The *Préface de Cromwell,* written mainly in October 1827, is an important and integral part of Hugo's theatrical production. It was published at a critical moment in the battle for the heart and soul of the French stage, a battle being waged by the traditionalists and the Romantics. When the preface appeared on 5 December 1827, writers such as Alessandro Francesco Tommaso Antonio Manzoni, Friedrich von Schlegel, Mme Anne-Louise-Germaine Necker de Staël, and Stendhal had already published books dealing with theatrical reform, works that Hugo had read and used as sources for his own preface.

The most original concept developed in the *Préface* is Hugo's "theory of the grotesque." He sees "the grotesque" as the basis of all comedy and uses several words to explain the term, including "the deformed," "the horrible," "the ugly," "the comical," "the farcical," "the ridiculous," and "the depraved." Characters who embody the "grotesque" are many: gluttons, hypocrites, lechers, misers, meddlers, and phonies. The *beau,* or sublime, the opposite of the grotesque, is what is good in the human spirit. It is characterized by all that is charming, graceful, and beautiful. According to Hugo, the grotesque and the sublime had never been portrayed together in any French theatrical work. Since both are found in nature and since all that is in nature should be in art, an author should be able to present both side by side in a play. Herein lies the beauty and the originality of Romantic drama as Hugo imagined it.

In the *Préface* Hugo categorically rejects the classical unities of place and time. By limiting the scene of the action to one place, an author is forced to relegate important parts of the play to the wings, to rely on *récits* (narratives) and descriptions to inform the spectator as to what has happened. Historically accurate stage settings are "silent" witnesses. By limiting a drama to one place an author writes an incomplete play. The unity of time is seen as ridiculous because all events cannot be reduced to a twenty-four-hour period. Hugo does plead in favor of the unity of action, warning the reader not to confuse it with simplicity. A play can have subplots as long as they remain subordinate to the main story line. Hugo condemns those who copy others because imitation can only result in mediocrity. He defines "local color" as that which is "characteristic" or "typical" and believes that drama must be bathed in it. The alexandrine, rhyme, and the choice of subjects need to be freed from the limits placed on them by the classical tradition. While Hugo prefers plays written in poetic form, he states that the choice between verse and prose is of secondary importance. Finally, he acknowledges that language constantly evolves, that seventeenth-century French is not the same as nineteenth-century French. Ideas need to be expressed in such a language that contemporary audiences can understand.

After *Cromwell* Hugo did not begin another play until the summer of 1829. Two different periods (Spain in the early sixteenth century and France

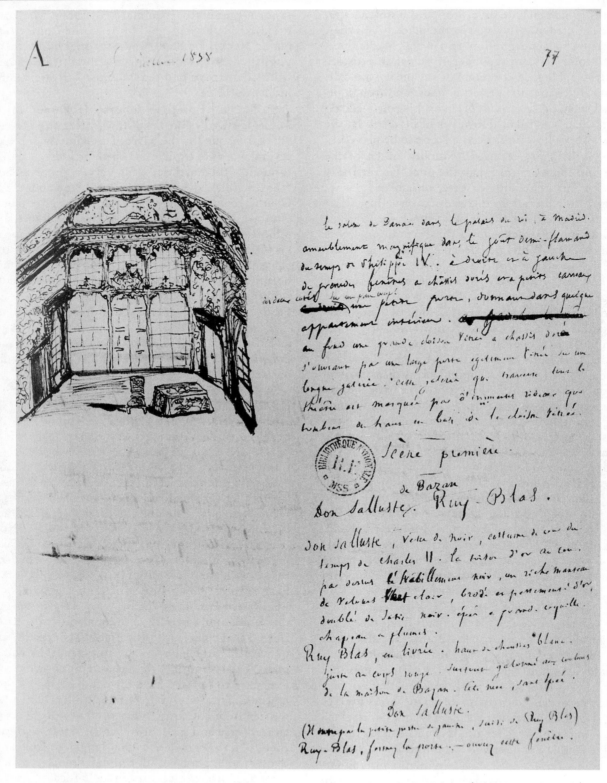

Page from the manuscript for Ruy Blas, *with Hugo's sketch of a set design for the first act (Bibliothèque Nationale)*

during the reign of Louis XIII) and two different characters (Hernani and Marion de Lorme) occupied his thoughts. He finally opted in favor of a drama set in France and, as usual, researched the lives of the characters. He also drew upon his previous readings, finding inspiration in Scott's *Kenilworth* (1821) and Vigny's novel *Cinq-Mars* (1826). He began to write "Un Duel sous Richelieu" (A Duel under Richelieu), the first title of the play later called *Marion de Lorme,* on 2 June and finished it more than twenty days later on 26 June. This play was the first one to be written after the *Préface de Cromwell* and the first one that had any chance of being a theatrical success. A privileged few were invited to Hugo's home for a reading on 2 July 1829. Honoré de Balzac, Delacroix, Alexandre Dumas *père,* Prosper Mérimée, Alfred de Musset, Sainte-Beuve, and Vigny were present. The Théâtre de la Comédie-Française, Théâtre de la Porte Saint-Martin, and Théâtre de l'Odéon pleaded with the author to allow them to stage the drama. Hugo finally chose Comédie-Française, which submitted the text to the government censors. Their reaction was categorical: without major changes the play would never be staged. Hugo acquiesced and made the necessary alterations. In spite of the modifications, the play was ultimately banned by the minister of the interior. Hugo went so far as to request and obtain an audience with Charles X, who refused to overrule his minister.

Marion de Lorme was not a typical love story. After having been the mistress of many Parisian aristocrats, Marion has sought refuge at Blois, where she has changed her name because she is in love with Didier, a young man who knows little about his own past and nothing about hers. Didier abhors courtesans, and therein lies the problem. In the second act he is condemned to death for having killed a man in a duel. So deep is his disappointment when he learns about Marion's earlier life that he hands himself over to the authorities, who imprison him. Marion does everything possible to obtain his freedom, including submitting to the amorous advances of the one person who can liberate the man whom she loves. When Didier learns what she has done, he rejects her; however, just before he is to die, he relents, admits his love for her, and pardons her. In the character of Marion, Hugo creates the first example of what became a regular figure in literature, the rehabilitated prostitute. Didier portrays yet another dramatic type who appeared in Hugo's later writings; he represents the fanatic who is ready to sacrifice everything, even the woman whom he loves, to remain faithful to his beliefs. Louis XIII continues the line of manipulated monarchs. Riche-

lieu inaugurates the line of éminences grises. L'Angely picks up where the four jesters in *Cromwell* left off. In this historical drama Hugo deals with several themes that he treats in later works: the absolute monarchy, the death penalty, personal integrity, fanatical devotion to one's principles, and love and all that a person will do to protect and preserve it.

From a technical point of view *Marion de Lorme* was the first of Hugo's plays whose plot depends upon an ever increasing number of coups de théâtre, of people recognizing people whom they are seeking, of individuals being in the right or wrong place at the appropriate or inappropriate time. Faithful to the principles put forth in the *Préface de Cromwell,* Hugo ignored the unities of time and place while respecting the unity of action. He mixed the grotesque and sublime in various ways and continued to liberate the alexandrine by dividing it among various characters. Local color was present in the settings, costumes, themes, and attitudes expressed by the actors.

With *Marion de Lorme* banned from the stage, Hugo did not hesitate to start another historical drama. Begun on 29 August 1829, *Hernani* was finished less than a month later, on 24 September. Hugo drew his inspiration for this play from a variety of sources. In 1811 he, his brothers, and his mother had traveled to Spain to be with his father, General Hugo. Although Hugo lived in Madrid for only nine months, the color, history, and people of this country made a deep and lasting impression on his young mind and imagination. Spain played a role in later works, including *Ruy Blas* (1838) and *Torquemada,* written during the year 1869. As usual, Hugo also drew heavily upon his reading and borrowed from English, French, German, and Spanish books and plays. He also did new research.

Hernani has two subtitles that indicate major themes of the play. In the manuscript one reads "Tres para una" ("Three for One"). Doña Sol is betrothed to her elderly uncle, Don Ruy Gomez de Silva. At the same time she has been secretly seeing a young outlaw named Hernani. Unbeknownst to doña Sol, King Carlos is in love with her. This triangle dominates the action of the drama. The second subtitle, "L'Honneur castillan" (Castilian Honor), is found in the first edition. At one point in the play don Ruy Gomez grants asylum to Hernani. When the king demands that he hand the young man over, he refuses to do so. At the end of the play, when Hernani has the choice between death and breaking his word, he chooses the former. Yet another important theme in the play is political in nature. At the beginning of *Hernani* the king is an unscrupulous monarch who will stop at nothing to attain his goals.

During the fourth act, when he becomes emperor of the Holy Roman Empire, he suddenly changes. He becomes a caring, generous, magnanimous sovereign who pardons his enemies and renounces his love for doña Sol.

After reading the play to an audience made up of many of those who had heard *Marion de Lorme* a month or so earlier, *Hernani* was submitted to the Comédie-Française, where the actors accepted it with great pleasure. The play then had to be sent to the government censors. Charles Brifaut, responsible for the interdiction of *Marion de Lorme,* wanted to avoid the same problems encountered earlier. He therefore charged a commission of dramatists with the task of approving or disapproving Hugo's latest dramatic work. While they criticized the play for many reasons, they felt that it should be played without changing a single word so that the public would be able to reject it. Baron Trouvé, who headed the Interior Ministry's office dealing with literature, theaters, and newspapers, did not agree and demanded modifications and deletions. Hugo naturally protested, both in writing and in person. After he begrudgingly made many of the changes, authorization was forthcoming during the last two weeks of February.

Even before permission to produce the drama had been granted, the Comédie-Française began rehearsals of *Hernani* in the fall. Some of the best-known actors of the period were in the play, including Mademoiselle Mars as doña Sol, Firmin as Hernani, Joanny as don Ruy Gomez, and Michelot as don Carlos. The premiere took place on 25 February 1830. Because Hugo did not want *claqueurs* (paid professionals) to applaud his play and thus assure its success, his wife and friends had to orchestrate the event carefully. To ensure that Hugo's supporters would have access to the theater, they were given red pieces of paper with the word *Hierro* (Spanish for iron) written on them. The doors were opened more than four hours before the play began. During this time Hugo's partisans ate, drank, laughed, and sang songs. When the play finally started the two warring factions, Hugo's admirers and those who despised him and the new Romantic movement, were prepared for the fight. Throughout the premiere the author's disciples made every attempt to drown out the laughter and jeers of the opposition. At the end the play was definitely a success; it remained on the bill until 21 November 1830.

The battle that had begun with the censors and had been continued during the premiere and its subsequent performances was also taken up by the press. Classical critics condemned *Hernani* while Romantics heaped praise upon it and its author. The critical question asked in 1830 and still discussed today remains: was the play's triumph passing in nature or truly significant in the history of French theater? Opinion remains divided. A distinction must be made between the play itself and the political, social, and literary context in which it was produced. As a drama *Hernani* is filled with contradictions. It illustrates the worst and the best of Hugo. On the one hand, the plot, with all its twists and turns, is filled with inconsistencies that often make it dramatically untenable. Characters do not evolve; they are driven by an excessive devotion to principle or duty, to an idea or a passion. They express themselves most eloquently; however, this eloquence is divorced from the action of the play, taking on a life of its own that relegates the dramatic development to the background. And yet this same eloquence is one of the play's major strengths. It is the powerfully poetic vehicle used by don Ruy Gomez to voice his anger, pain, and pride; by don Carlos to state his hopes and fears; and by doña Sol and Hernani to express their love for each other. The play is also noteworthy for its depiction of honor and generosity, for its sympathetic treatment of the love of an old man for a young girl, for the important role given to the readers' imagination, and for the dramatic power of the fifth act.

Other plays by Romantic authors had enjoyed considerable success in 1829: Dumas's *Henri III et sa cour* (Henry the Third and His Court) in February and Vigny's *Othello* in October. They did not, however, generate the interest, the passion, and the debate that were to surround *Hernani*. This play was Hugo's first work to be produced not only under his name but also at the Comédie-Française. It was viewed as the long-awaited "slap-in-the-face" to almost two centuries of theatrical tradition. The young Romantics identified with it because of its poetic and stylistic strength and beauty, because of the local color that brought another world to the stage in a most spectacular fashion, and because of the devotion to principle exemplified by Hernani, a hero, an *homme fatal* with whom they could identify. They also liked *Hernani* because it put on the stage an outlaw who dares challenge a king and because the unprincipled monarch becomes a benevolent emperor. They were not concerned with the play's imperfections. They needed a rallying point, and *Hernani* provided it. Did this play usher in a new direction for the French stage? While it did not accomplish this alone, it was the major impetus. *Hernani* represented the decisive battle in a literary war that opened the doors to more theatrical productions of a similar nature.

Caricature of Hugo in triumph, circa 1850, with his right foot resting on the Théâtre-Français and his left foot on the Academie Française (from Le Charivari)

After the success of *Hernani* Hugo waited until 1831 before deciding to allow Théâtre de la Porte Saint-Martin to produce *Marion de Lorme*. In the meantime Charles X had been replaced by Louis-Philippe, and theaters were once again free to stage plays without fear of government censorship. In the preface to *Marion de Lorme* Hugo explained that he had withheld his drama because he did not want its eventual success to be political in nature. Marie Dorval, one of the leading actresses of the time, played the role of the heroine. Acceding to the criticisms formulated by some of his friends, Hugo rewrote the end of the play, changing his hero from the unyielding, unreasoning zealot into an understanding, pardoning lover. The premiere took place on 11 August 1831. As was the case with *Hernani,* the critics were divided in their opinions. *Marion de*

Lorme was produced by the Comédie-Française in 1838 and became a standard part of its repertory. As was the case with all of Hugo's plays, it could not be staged during the reign of Napoleon III. It did not reappear on the bill until 1873. In 1885, at Théâtre de la Porte Saint-Martin, Sarah Bernhardt played the role of Marion.

During the spring of 1832 Hugo was already thinking about his next play, *Le Roi s'amuse* (1832; translated as *The King's Fool,* 1841). He read books about his new subject and, as had become regular practice, took notes. He wrote the drama between 3 June and 23 June 1832. In July he wrote *Lucrèce Borgia* (1833). Rehearsals for *Le Roi s'amuse* began in September while Hugo was on vacation. Unlike works at private theaters, plays staged at the Comédie-Française could be reviewed by the government because it was a state-subsidized theater. When Monsieur d'Argout, the minister in charge of the supervision of theaters, heard about the subject of *Le Roi s'amuse,* he asked for a copy of it. Hugo refused to give him one. During a meeting with the minister, Hugo defended his play, stating that he was not attacking Louis-Philippe through his portrayal of Francis I. The matter was dropped, and the premiere took place on 22 November 1832. Many of the best-known authors, journalists, and actors, as well as the elite of Parisian society, were in attendance. In spite of the fact that Hugo had given free seats to many of his friends and admirers, the play was seen as a disaster; it was what some critics would call a "scandal," a "rout," the "Waterloo of Romanticism." The audience was shocked not by the political nature of the drama but rather by the preponderant role played by the grotesque. The next day the director of the Comédie-Française informed Hugo that the performances of *Le Roi s'amuse* had been suspended by the government. The play was officially banned from the stage on 10 December because it was considered an attack on public morality.

Although Hugo regularly eschewed the political arena, he felt that he had no choice. To make the government accountable for what it had done, Hugo brought suit against the Comédie-Française, with which he had signed a contract. He knew that he would never win, but he felt that he had to defend the fundamental liberties that were being threatened by Louis-Philippe's ministers. Before the trial began he wrote a preface to *Le Roi s'amuse* that was published with the text of the play on 3 December 1832. The preface, whose tone is clearly political, is an attack on the government. Hugo describes the minister's decision as "unbelievable," "unheard of," and "arbitrary." For Hugo the theater is a form of publication and therefore cannot be censored. Also, according to the Charter of 1830, the state no longer has the right to confiscate anything that belongs to its citizens. By banning this play the government has stolen property not only belonging to the author, but also to the public. Hugo accuses the state of having a hidden agenda because it fears future revolutions. He goes so far as to say that the next step would be to put him in the Bastille. He defends *Le Roi s'amuse* as a work of art, saying that there is nothing immoral in it. When Hugo arrived in court on 10 December, he was greeted by a round of applause. Neither his lawyer nor he could convince the judges to rule in his favor, but by speaking out as he did, Hugo forced the government to wait two years before officially reinstating the censorship of theatrical works. *Le Roi s'amuse* was not staged again until

22 November 1882, exactly fifty years after its premiere.

The plot of *Le Roi s'amuse* is somewhat complicated. King Francis I has seen a young lady whom he would like to seduce. His court jester, Triboulet, is hated by many aristocrats because they are often the butt of his jokes. When they discover that Triboulet might have a mistress, they decide to kidnap her in order to get even. What they do not know is that the young person in question, Blanche, is Triboulet's daughter and the young woman who has attracted the king's attention. The king forces himself upon Blanche, who falls in love with him. A month goes by during which Blanche remains with Francis and during which Triboulet pretends to have pardoned his master. In fact, the jester has been carefully preparing his revenge. He proves to his daughter that the king does not love her, that he is merely using her. Triboulet has hired an assassin, Saltabadil, whose sister, Maguelonne, is the latest object of Francis's desires. Saltabadil is to kill the king and place his body in a sack that Triboulet will throw into the Seine River. Blanche, who witnessed the king's declaration of love to Maguelonne earlier in the day, returns to the tavern that Maguelonne and her brother run and where the king is spending the night. Blanche overhears the two discussing how Francis is to be assassinated. Maguelonne does not want her brother to kill him, so he agrees to slay the first person who passes in the street. In order to save her father, who would be denounced by Saltabadil, and the king, whom she still loves, Blanche enters the inn and is stabbed. Triboulet arrives, drags the sack to the water's edge, and prepares to throw it in. When he hears the king's voice in the street, he opens the sack and discovers Blanche, who dies a few minutes later.

The play, written in verse form, contains many of the stylistic, thematic, and dramatic elements found in Hugo's earlier historical dramas. He increases the number of stage directions that are designed to tell the actors how to play their roles. And for the first time he presents a tragic jester and a deflowered virgin as principal characters. Yet *Le Roi s'amuse* was a theatrical failure. After the premiere Hugo, who had seen and heard the public's reaction, and had undoubtedly spoken with the actors, made several corrections the next day that did not fundamentally alter what had so shocked the audience—the role of the grotesque, of the ugly. He modified some expressions and eliminated certain lines, but he could not rewrite the basic story line, nor could he change the characters of the protagonists. The press was brutal in its assessment of the play. *Le Roi s'amuse* was said to be "unworthy of the stage," a "monstrous play." The grotesque was manifest in too many ways and to too much of an extreme. Reviewers criticized the liberties taken with the French language, the despicable portrayal of the monarchy and the aristocracy, the cavalier treatment of history, the choice of a mean-spirited jester as the representative of fatherly love, the unbelievably cruel denouement, and the harsh depiction of reality and of human nature. Not only was Hugo's talent as a dramatist openly questioned, but also his conception of Romantic drama. Although *Le Roi s'amuse* contained many beautiful lines and a few sympathetic characters, nothing could save it. Some of Hugo's supporters wondered whether any of his dramatic works would ever be played again.

While preparing to write *Le Roi s'amuse,* Hugo was also thinking about another play, "Le Souper à Ferrare" (Dinner at Ferrara). He saw the dramas as twin works. In the preface to "Le Souper à Ferrare" he says that the idea for the two plays came to him at the same time. In *Le Roi s'amuse* he wanted to show paternal love, the purest emotion that can exist in a man, in the ugliest person possible occupying the lowest rung of the social ladder. As the action unfolded, the deformed person would become beautiful. In "Le Souper à Ferrare" he wanted to do just the opposite. He placed in a morally deformed but physically beautiful woman belonging to the highest level of society the noblest feeling that a woman can ever experience—maternal love. He began writing what was eventually called *Lucrèce Borgia* on 9 July; he completed it on 29 July. For the first time since *Amy Robsart* he wrote in prose. Instead of dividing his new work into five acts, he chose to write three, the first two of which were separated into two parts. Even before it was known whether or not Hugo would win his case against the Comédie-Française, the director of the Théâtre de la Porte Saint-Martin asked the author to allow him to stage his new work. Hugo did not hesitate; he signed the contract on 29 December. The rehearsals began with a cast that included the talented actress Mademoiselle George as Lucrèce and the gifted actor Frédérick Lemaître as Gennaro. Mademoiselle Juliette (Drouet) was to play the role of Princess Negroni. It was decided that music would be added. Hugo drew the plans for the stage settings. As was the case with all of Hugo's plays, people began discussing *Lucrèce Borgia* before its first performance. Classicists and Romantics alike were scandalized by the thought of an historical drama written in prose. Having given their all for *Hernani* and *Le Roi s'amuse,* Hugo's closest supporters had their doubts and asked to attend a reading of the play. Reassured by what they heard, they prepared themselves for another battle. The pre-

miere took place on 2 February 1833. The play was a resounding theatrical and financial success. The sixty-two performances that took place during the months of February, March, and April earned Hugo close to Fr 11,000, a veritable fortune for the period.

Why did the public and the critics react so favorably to *Lucrèce Borgia* after having so vehemently rejected *Le Roi s'amuse* a few months earlier? The story line of the former play is simple. Gennaro, who lives in Ferrara, is a young soldier of fortune who is going to Venice with several of his close friends because they have been ordered to do so by their government. Lucrèce has come to Venice incognito because she wants to be near Gennaro, who does not know that she loves him. Gennaro, who is unaware of his family origins, speaks of the mother whom he has never met in eloquent terms. His friends unmask Lucrèce and insult her in Gennaro's presence. The site of the action moves to Ferrara where Lucrèce has already decided how she will get even with the five young men who offended her. Gennaro, who expresses his hatred for Lucrèce's family, uses his knife to remove the letter *B* from the name *Borgia,* which is carved on the palace wall. Furious, Lucrèce demands that her husband, the ruler of Ferrara, put to death the guilty party. Convinced that Gennaro is his wife's lover, he is more than happy to oblige. When Lucrèce discovers that she has been tricked by her husband, she pleads with him to spare Gennaro, but to no avail. Her husband offers her a choice: either she pours the poisoned wine that Genarro is to drink or one of his aides will kill him. She gives him the wine and, after her husband has left the room, produces the antidote, which he drinks. Instead of leaving Ferrara, Gennaro goes to a party with his friends, who are all poisoned by Lucrèce. When she learns that Gennaro is at the banquet, she tries to persuade him to drink the antidote, but this time he refuses to do so. As he stabs her, she tells him that she is his mother.

The grotesque plays an important role in this play. At the end there is both an infanticide and a matricide. Motherly love is found in the heart of a heroine accused of the most heinous of crimes. Violence is present as is talk of murder, incest, and revenge. Rulers are portrayed as unscrupulous individuals who will stop at nothing to achieve their ends. Monks singing hymns appear onstage during an orgy that turns into a massacre of innocents. A quick perusal of the remarks made by the critics explains the reasons for which this play was such a success. First, the drama is almost classic in its execution. The plot is simple, subplots nonexistent. The development of the action is logical. The spectator is presented with a series of scenes dramatically linked by cause and effect. Fate, which plays such an important role in classical plays, takes center stage in *Lucrèce Borgia.* Instead of taking Hugo to task for abandoning the poetic form, the press praises his prose. It is an excellent vehicle that allows his characters to express their feelings without shocking the audience. By skillfully portraying the struggle between Lucrèce the loving mother and Lucrèce the unprincipled woman, Hugo redeems his monstrous heroine. She becomes dramatically acceptable. It should not be assumed that *Lucrèce Borgia* was universally praised by the critics. Some saw it as an immoral melodrama that should be banned from the stage. Such was not the case, however, and reviewers who questioned Hugo's ability as a dramatist a few months earlier now recognized his maturing skill.

When Harel, the director of the Théâtre de la Porte Saint-Martin, decided to replace *Lucrèce Borgia* with another play at the end of April, Hugo became angry. Harel reminded him that he was in charge of his theater and that he was waiting for Hugo's next work. The author said that he had never promised the Théâtre de la Porte Saint-Martin another drama. On 1 May 1833 the two men were ready to fight a duel. Harel convinced Hugo that the death of either one of them would serve no purpose. He agreed to continue staging *Lucrèce Borgia,* and Hugo agreed to give him his next play. During the rehearsals and performances of *Lucrèce Borgia* Hugo had become enamored with Mademoiselle Juliette. Mademoiselle George was equally interested in the author. Hugo knew that he had to write a play with two important female roles. He had already taken many notes dealing with the history of England, so he did no additional research. Borrowing from the sources that he had studied, from other plays that he had read, and from his own historical dramas, he spent much of the month of August writing "Marie d'Angleterre" (Mary of England), finishing it on 1 September 1833. He decided to use prose and, in keeping with the Spanish Renaissance theatrical tradition, to divide the play into three *journées* (days), instead of five acts. For various personal and professional reasons, several individuals did everything possible to assure the failure of *Marie d'Angleterre,* whose name had been changed to *Marie Tudor.* Nodier, Mademoiselle George, Alexandre Dumas *pere,* and several of the actors were members of the cabal. In spite of their machinations and a last-minute attempt to replace Juliette Drouet by Ida Ferrier, Dumas's mistress and a fine actress, the play was ready for its premiere, which took place on 6 November. As had been the case with *Lucrèce Borgia,* Hugo had to allay the fears of some of his closest supporters, this time by inviting them to a rehearsal. As expected, the theater was filled with the author's friends and enemies. Opinion as to the success or failure of the premiere is divided. Parts of the play won the approval of the audience, while others were wildly booed. Drouet's acting was so bad that, beginning with the second performance, she was replaced by Ferrier. The drama was staged a total of forty-two times from November to March. Financially, the work was a moderate success.

With *Marie Tudor* Hugo once again wrote a play whose plot depends on many *coups de théâtre,* or fortunate discoveries and events. Gilbert, who is thirty-four, is in love with Jane, whom he intends to marry in a week. Jane is a seventeen-year-old orphan whom Gilbert has raised from infancy. Their friend Joshua is a jailer at the Tower of London. Queen Mary is in love with Fabio Fabiani, upon whom she has bestowed many titles and to whom she has given certain estates, including those belonging to the deceased Lord Talbot. During the first part of the play Jane admits that she does not love Gilbert, that she loves another, Fabiani. The public learns that Jane is the daughter of Lord Talbot and that Fabiani has seduced her to make sure that he will be able to keep the property given to him by the queen. Fabiani stabs a character who knows the whole truth. Just before he dies, he tells Gilbert everything that he has learned. Gilbert helps Fabiani dispose of the body in exchange for a purse filled with money.

At this point Fabiani tells Gilbert that he is going to visit his mistress, who happens to be the latter's fiancée. Simon Renard, an influential foreign ambassador, promises to help the brokenhearted Gilbert get revenge in exchange for his life. The second day's activities take place at the royal palace. Renard introduces Jane to the queen, who learns that Fabiani has seduced the teenager. Gilbert, who has heard Jane's confession, sets a trap for the queen. He will do anything that Mary asks of him if she promises to give all the titles and estates belonging to Lord Talbot to his rightful heir and to force Fabiani to marry her. When the queen realizes that she has been duped, it is too late. To rid herself of Fabiani, she accuses Gilbert of trying to kill her. He plays along with her and offers the purse given to him earlier as proof that Fabiani had hired him to assassinate Mary. The third day takes place one month later in two different rooms in the Tower of London. Jane admits that she really loves Gilbert and, with Renard's help, arranges for his escape. Mary has put off Fabiani's execution, but the people revolt and demand his death. He is to be beheaded, wearing a veil that will completely cover him. One of the jail keepers tells the queen that Gilbert has fled. She orders that he be captured and put in Fabiani's place. Renard, who has done everything to guarantee Fabiani's demise, interferes with the queen's plans and, at the end of the drama, Mary is informed that Fabiani has died.

The press reacted as it had in the past, praising or criticizing *Marie Tudor* for the same weaknesses and strengths that had been perceived in Hugo's other dramas. While few reviewers spoke about the grotesque, many complained that the characters did not evolve and that the success of the play depended too much on spectacle, on extravagant stage settings such as the one in the last scene when all of London is illuminated.

Busy with other literary endeavors, Hugo did not write for the stage for more than a year. Angry with Harel and those who had worked so hard to make *Marie Tudor* a failure, he left the Théâtre de la Porte Saint-Martin for the Comédie-Française. He had written his next work, *Angelo, tyran de Padoue* (Angelo, the Tyrant of Padua) from 2 February to 19 February 1835. Once again he had composed an historical drama in prose that required the talents of two extremely gifted actresses. Mademoiselle Mars accepted the role of La Tisbe and Madame Dorval that of Catarina. The premiere, which took place on 28 April, was a resounding theatrical triumph, with the two actresses being called back for many encores. It was a great financial success as well.

As was the case with all his plays since *Cromwell,* Hugo situated the action in the not too distant past, this time in sixteenth-century Italy. The plot is uncomplicated. La Tisbe, an actress and courtesan, loves Rodolfo, who is in turn in love with and loved by Catarina, the wife of the ruler of Padua, Angelo. Angelo has led everyone to believe that he has been having an affair with La Tisbe. He is extremely jealous of his wife and decides to punish her when he learns of her feelings for Rodolfo. Homodei seeks to harm Catarina because she rejected his advances; he helps Rodolfo because the latter saved his life. All of the peripetia depend upon the nature of the relations of each woman with the three men. The play's appeal was in large part due to the successfully artistic combination of various dramatic traditions. Because of the reduced number of characters, the relative simplicity of the story line, the clarity of the prose, and the respect of two of the unities (those of time and action), the play is classical in nature. The grotesque and melodrama play important roles in the work. The political and historical dimensions of *Angelo* are reduced in favor of the moving portrayal of jealousy and love, of revenge and pardon, and of selfishness and sacrifice.

After *Notre-Dame de Paris* appeared in 1831, many composers asked Hugo to transform it into an opera. He began work on the libretto in 1832, finishing it in 1836. Hector Berlioz directed the rehearsals. The premiere of *La Esmeralda,* which took place on 14 November of the same year, was reasonably well received by the public. During subsequent productions, however, the spectators became more and more critical of the opera, as did the press. The opera was staged nineteen times between 1836 and 1839.

Angry with the directors of the Théâtre de la Porte Saint-Martin and the Comédie-Française, Hugo knew that he had to look elsewhere if his dramatic works were to enjoy any success. Between 1835 and 1838 he did not write a single play; he did, however, devote time to looking for a new site where he and others could stage dramas free from the constraints with which they had been dealing. After receiving government authorization to open a new playhouse, one was found and rented in December 1837; it was baptized the Théâtre de la Renaissance (the Renaissance Theater). In addition to all the notes that he had been taking over the years dealing with Spain, Hugo consulted many other works before writing *Ruy Blas* from 8 July to 11 August 1838. While Hugo busied himself with designing the sets and giving advice about the costumes, he also directed the rehearsals. The premiere took place on 8 November, with Frédérick Lemaître in the role of Ruy Blas. The play was an outstanding success both onstage and at the box office.

Ruy Blas was successful for several reasons. Hugo's period of experimentation was over, and the playwright chose to return to the dramatic and stylistic principles stated in the *Préface de Cromwell,* applied in some preceding works and neglected in others. While ignoring the unities of time and place, he respected the unity of action. The plot is simple and develops in an uncomplicated manner. Ruy Blas, a valet, loves the queen. His master, don Salluste, has offended the queen, who has in turn ordered his exile. Before he leaves, he gives Ruy Blas a new identity, that of his cousin, don César, whom he manages to send secretly abroad. Don Salluste wants revenge; he is aware of Ruy Blas's feelings for the queen and believes that he will end up her lover. The entire plot of the play is based upon don Salluste's hatred and the young couple's love. At the end of the play Ruy Blas kills don Salluste and then kills himself because the queen will not pardon him for having concealed his true identity. Prose has given way to polished poetry. The grotesque is omnipresent; however, it does not manifest itself as pathetically as in *Le Roi s'amuse* nor as violently as in *Lucrèce*

Borgia. When necessary, the tools of melodrama are used, yet not really abused. In the stage directions Hugo again reveals his talent as set and costume designer and as director. History and politics play a role, but not an overwhelming one. The weak king is never seen onstage; the queen is a prisoner of court etiquette; the dishonest ministers are ridiculed and dismissed; and the representative of the arrogant aristocracy is killed. He who shows courage, intelligence, and sensitivity comes from the lower class. His death at the end results not from politics but rather from fate. Inextricably interwoven with the theme of love is that of the role of the masses, of the people, represented by Ruy Blas. His demise is Hugo's pessimistic assessment of society as seen from the points of view of the individual, the social and the political. Any reader of *Ruy Blas* will find weaknesses in the work. Hugo did, however, manage to write a play that illustrated the best aspects of Romantic historical drama, and this explains in large part its success both in the nineteenth century and today.

The project for Hugo's next play dates from 1830. He had listed as a possible topic for a drama the story of the man in the iron mask. He actually began writing the play, which would be called "Les Jumeaux" (The Twins), at the end of July 1839. He stopped work on it on 23 August after having completed just three acts. Tired, sick, and lonely, he left on a trip that took him to Germany, Switzerland, and southern and eastern France. He published a collection of poems in May 1840. After another trip to Germany during the fall of that year he returned home filled with ideas for his last Romantic play, *Les Burgraves.* "Les Jumeaux" was never finished although there are subsequent references to the drama in other writings by Hugo.

After spending most of the first seven months of 1842 working on *Le Rhin,* Hugo began writing *Les Burgraves* in August, finishing it on 19 October. Although two months may seem a relatively short period for writing a drama that is nineteen hundred lines long, it was the most time that he had spent on the actual composition of any play. The action of *Les Burgraves* is situated in twelfth-century Germany. Emperor Frédéric Barberousse has been missing for twenty years. During his absence anarchy and decadence have replaced order and honor in Germany. Against this historical background Hugo develops the love between Regina and Otbert, the hatred and thirst for revenge of Guanhumara, and the generational and political conflicts that pit Job and his son Magnus against the latter's son, Hatto. In order to restore the country to its former greatness and to resolve the conflicts that are destroying its inhabi-

tants, a savior, a messiah, is needed. It is only the surprise return of Frédéric Barberousse that guarantees a positive denouement. It is he who pardons his former enemies, liberates the slaves, imprisons the guilty, and restores hope in the future. Rehearsals for the new play went well. Considerable sums of money were spent on the settings and the costumes. The premiere took place on 7 March 1843. The public's reaction was not enthusiastic. Theatergoers were tired of the experimentation that had gone on during the 1830s; they clearly preferred classical tragedy to Romantic drama. Six weeks after the premiere Francis Ponsard's tragedy *Lucrèce* (1843) was staged for the first time, and the public abandoned *Les Burgraves.* After thirty-three performances, its run ended.

Although some critics praised the beauty of the play's poetry and dialogue, most of them attacked it with vehemence. They felt that it was "unplayable," that it was chaotic, unbelievable, and incomprehensible. They viewed Hugo's attempt at combining the lyric, the epic, the melodramatic, the satiric, and the dramatic as a total failure, as a "literary error." The press failed to understand that Hugo was not attempting to write an historical drama like *Ruy Blas,* that he was in fact trying to create something new and different. Unfortunately he was not sure of the direction that he wanted to take, and the public was not willing to wait for him to find it. As a result *Les Burgraves* was a failure, and Hugo stopped writing for the stage for many years; moreover, none of his later plays was staged during his lifetime. The failure of *Les Burgraves* brought to a close the second period of his life associated with the theater. He had set as a goal the creation of a new dramatic form, the historical drama. He had hoped to revolutionize the stage by freeing it from the classical sclerosis that had imposed upon French theaters pale imitations of the great dramatists of the seventeenth century. It took him years and many attempts to define what he believed the new genre to be, to write *Ruy Blas,* a play that illustrated the idea well and that pleased the public. He and other writers did produce many fine works during the 1830s; they did not, however, succeed in imposing their new genre on a fickle public that had finally decided that it preferred other forms of theatrical expression.

The third period during which Hugo wrote plays covers the years between 1854 and 1873. While fragments and sketches of theatrical works written before 1854 exist, it was during this year that he wrote *La Forêt mouillée* (The Wet Forest, 1930), his first complete play since 1842. Some critics refer to the works written during this period as

Le Théâtre en liberté because a collection of plays bearing that title was published posthumously in 1886, because Hugo wrote most of them while living in exile, because the theme of liberty is often featured, and because the author did not feel limited by traditional theatrical constraints. This term is something of a misnomer, however, because not all of the plays written during these years were included in the volume that appeared in 1886. Les Deux Trouvailles de Gallus (Gallus's Two Discoveries), Welf, ou le castellan d'Osbor (Welf, or the Lord of Osbor), Torquemada (1882), Mille francs de récompense (The One-Thousand-Franc Reward, 1934), and L'Intervention (1950), were published separately. Théâtre en liberté did include Le Prologue, La Grand'mère (The Grandmother), L'Épée (The Sword), Mangeront-ils? (Will They Eat?), Sur la Lisière d'un bois (On the Edge of a Woods), and La Forêt mouillée. While many of the plays contain elements of his earlier dramatic writings, some of them are a startling departure from them. Many are quite short, ranging from 96 to 805 lines in length. The reader's imagination is given free reign, especially in La Forêt mouillée, where the plants and animals talk. Light humor and wit are evident throughout many of the works. Several plays produced during this period deserve special attention either because of their serious nature or because they have often been staged in the twentieth century.

Mille francs de récompense, which dates from 1861, is unique in Hugo's theatrical production. Written in prose and set in early-nineteenth-century Paris, it depicts contemporary society with many of the ills that affected it. Cyprienne, a young girl in love with Edgar Marc, lives with her mother and her elderly grandfather. The latter, a music teacher and the sole source of income for the family, has become ill. The loss of his students has brought about tremendous financial hardship. Since he cannot pay his bills, all of the family's possessions are to be sold at auction. Rousseline, the official in charge of the sale, has stolen money belonging to the grandfather. If Cyprienne agrees to marry him, he will stop the sale and return the funds that he has hidden. At the end of the play a former convict named Glapieu saves the day. In this one work Hugo puts on stage many characters not found in his earlier dramas. He depicts the plight of the unwed mother (Cyprienne's mother, Etiennette) who has been forced to hide the truth about her past. Glapieu was imprisoned at the age of sixteen for stealing "douze sous" (twelve cents). During his long and unfair incarceration he learned how to break into safes. Now that he is free, he is pursued by the police as a former convict. Rousseline represents the seamy side of the financial

Hugo (photograph by Nadar)

world. Guilty of a white-collar crime, he will stoop as low as necessary to achieve his ends. Mille francs de récompense was first published in 1934 and staged in 1961. It is a part of the repertory of the Comédie-Française, which produced it as recently as 1995.

Mangeront-ils?, finished in the spring of 1867, is written in verse form and is 1,582 lines in length. Lady Janet and Lord Slada, both relatives of the King of Man, have sought refuge in a cloister, where they have gotten married. As is often the case in Hugo's theater, the monarch also desires the young woman. He dares not touch the newlyweds because they are protected by the right of asylum. Their situation, however, is quite precarious because there is nothing to eat or drink within the cloister and because no religious person has the right to bring them succor. Their fate lies in the hands of two most interesting characters, Zineb, a one-hundred-year-old witch, and Aïrolo, a less-than-honest, fairylike inhabitant of the forest. The former sets a trap for the unsuspecting monarch, who becomes subservient to the latter. In the end the King of Man abdicates, and Lord Slada replaces him on the throne. In addition to being a well-written play with some fascinating characters, Mangeront-ils? treats several themes and situations seen in previous dramas in different and sometimes novel ways. It is the first time in Hugo's theater that a head of state is forced to obey a religious figure. In a message to the abbot of the cloister, the local bishop warns that he will deprive the King of Man of his throne if he attacks the church: "S'il touche à ton église, on touchera son trône" (If he touches your church, we will touch his throne). Neither of the lovers dies. The monarch, who represents all that is corrupt and abject, abdicates at the end, marshaling in a new order.

Les Deux Trouvailles de Gallus, a diptych based on the fable about the cock who, while looking for grain to eat, finds a pearl, was written during the first three months of 1869. In *Margarita,* the first of the two plays, Duke Gallus discovers a charming peasant woman whom he tries to seduce. Nella resists his advances, preferring George, a poor student who, without knowing it, happens to be the duke's nephew. At the end of the play Gallus abdicates in his favor. In *Esca,* the second of the works, Gallus once again comes upon a peasant girl who this time succumbs to his charm. He takes Zabeth to Paris, where she leads the life of a courtesan. She has a beautiful home, wealth, superb clothes, and many admirers, but she lacks what means the most to her: Gallus's respect and love. After decrying her humiliating lifestyle and revealing her love to the duke, Zabeth drinks poison and dies. Gallus in turn declares his love for her. In both works the women are in fact pearls. While *Les Deux Trouvailles de Gallus* constitutes a return to the melodramatic tradition of earlier plays, the dramas are written in beautiful poetic form and are a delight to read.

Hugo spent much of May, June, and July of 1869 writing what was his last great drama, *Torquemada* (1882). King Ferdinand fancies an adolescent named Rose, whom he has seen in a convent in the company of a young man named Sanche, to whom she is betrothed. The king discovers that Sanche is a distant relative who is a pawn in a political plot to get control of part of his realm. At the beginning of the play Torquemada is a simple monk who is condemned to death for his extreme views about man, his sinful state and his need to repent, or suffer and die. After being rescued by Rose and Sanche he goes to Italy, where he obtains pontifical approval to start anew the Inquisition. During the play he becomes the most powerful person in Spain. Not only does he put to death large numbers of Spaniards found guilty of religious crimes, but he also prevents the king from abducting Rose and from saving the Jews from exile. From a dramatic point of view *Torquemada* is on a par with Hugo's Romantic works. The main plotline, the rise to power of

Torquemada and his subsequent use of his position, is carefully orchestrated. All subplots exist to develop it in one way or another: the love of Rose and Sanche, Ferdinand's lust for the young girl, the attempt to deprive the king of part of the country, the discovery by the Marquis de Fuentel that he is the grandfather of Sanche, and the Jews' desire to remain in Spain. As has always been the case with Hugo's theater, the characters incarnate ideas and principles and act accordingly. Poetically speaking, *Torquemada* contains passages that can only be described as some of the poet's finest writing. As for its principal theme, this play is Hugo's most eloquent description and condemnation of fanaticism. In reaction to the persecution of Russian Jews, *Torquemada* was published for the first time in May 1882.

This third period of dramatic composition brings to an end almost seventy years of writing for the stage. The inexperienced high-school dramatist who became a consummate dramatist after spending many years perfecting his craft never really closed the door on the theater. The plays written during the Romantic period constitute the most important part of what can be called a truly remarkable theatrical career.

Critics have never agreed on Hugo's exact place in the history of French theater. His ardent admirers view the *Préface de Cromwell* as the critical basis upon which all Romantic theater is founded. If he is not indeed the father of a new genre, the historical drama, he is without a doubt the one who perfected it. In their eyes *Hernani* occupies a place as important in the history of French theater as that of Pierre Corneille's *Le Cid* (1637). His poetry and prose surpass anything ever heard on the French stage. His fiercest detractors have little positive to say about his theatrical production. They lambaste his historical and geographical inaccuracies, his theory of the grotesque, his tendency to exaggerate, his pompous style, and his robotlike characters. For them his plays are little more than glorified melodramas.

While Hugo may never have been the undisputed leader of the Romantic period, he certainly was one of its guiding stars, both as theorist and practitioner. Many of his works served as lightning rods, attracting the reactions of the censors and the press, which in turn drew attention to the new movement and its writers, ideas, and plays. While attempting to hone and perfect his concept of the historical drama, Hugo wrote plays that merited criticism from the stylistic, technical, and dramatic points of view. He was, however, one of the first serious dramatists to recognize the importance of costumes, stage settings, and music, making every effort possible to grant them a central role in his works. He also recognized the importance of good acting. He regularly indicated how he expected his actors and actresses to play the scenes that he had written. While his characters are not depicted in great psychological detail like those of Corneille and Jean Racine, they are more than lifeless, one-dimensional representations of theatrical types and ideas. They function at various levels within the plays. Central characters such as Hernani and don Carlos or Ruy Blas and don Salluste are meant to incarnate entire social groups and classes. The sometimes complicated story lines put them in situations that serve to reveal the conflicts that exist between them. When they clash they come to life as individuals whom Hugo depicts with talent and insight. With unquestionable ability, he uses an arsenal of literary devices that allow his characters to express clearly and eloquently their hopes and fears, their joys and sorrows, their hatred and love. He paints their souls and all that troubles them. No one can deny that Hugo created some of the most memorable characters to have been seen on the French stage and wrote some of the most beautiful prose and verse passages to have been spoken by an actor or actress. While not all of his plays have aged well, many have done so with grace and continue to be applauded by audiences throughout the world.

Letters:

Victor Hugo intime: mémoires, correspondances, documents inédits (Paris: Marpon & E. Flammarion, 1885);

Œuvres posthumes de Victor Hugo. Lettres à la fiancée. 1820–1822;

Correspondance. 1815–1882 (Paris: Librairie du Victor Hugo Illustré, n.d.);

Correspondance, 1836–1882 (Paris: Michel Lévy, 1898);

Lettres à la fiancée 1820–1822 (Paris: Jules Rouff & Cie, 1899–1902?);

Œuvres posthumes de Victor Hugo. Lettres à la fiancée, 1820–1822 (Paris: E. Fasquelle, 1901);

Victor Hugo. Correspondance familiale et écrits intimes, 1802–1828, volume 1, edited by Jean Gaudon, Sheila Gaudon, and Bernard Leuilliot (Paris: Robert Laffont, 1988);

Victor Hugo. Correspondance familiale et écrits intimes, 1828–1839, volume 2, edited by Jean Gaudon, Sheila Gaudon, and Leuilliot (Paris: Robert Laffont, 1991).

Bibliographies:

Maximilien Rudwin, *Bibliographie de Victor Hugo* (Paris: Les Belles Lettres, 1926);

Erwin Schneider, "Victor Hugo's *Hernani* in der Kritik eines Jahrhunderts (1830–1930)," *Romanische Forschungen,* 47 (1933): 1–146;

Elliott M. Grant, *Victor Hugo: A Select and Critical Bibliography,* University of North Carolina Studies in the Romance Languages and Literatures, no. 67 (Chapel Hill: University of North Carolina Press, 1967);

Ruth Lestha Doyle, *Victor Hugo's Drama. An Annotated Bibliography. 1900–1980* (Westport, Conn.: Greenwood Press, 1981);

Patricia A. Ward, Bernadette Lintz Murphy, and Michel Grimaud, "Victor Hugo. Œuvres et critique. 1981–1983," in *Les Carnets bibliographiques de La Revue des Lettres Modernes,* 1992.

Biographies:

Adèle Hugo, *Victor Hugo raconté par un témoin de sa vie avec œuvres inédites de Victor Hugo, entre autres un drame en trois actes: Inez de Castro* (Brussels & Leipzig: A. Lacroix, Verboeckhoven & Cie, 1863);

Edmond Biré, *Victor Hugo avant 1830* (Paris: J. Gervais, 1883);

Biré, *Victor Hugo après 1830,* volume 1 (Paris: Perrin & Cie, 1891);

Biré, *Victor Hugo après 1830,* volume 2 (Paris: Perrin & Cie, 1891);

Biré, *Victor Hugo après 1852. L'exil, les dernières années et la mort du poète* (Paris: Perrin & Cie, 1894);

Juana Richard-Lesclide, *Victor Hugo intime* (Paris: F. Juven, 1903?);

André Maurois, *Olympio, ou la Vie de Victor Hugo* (Paris: Hachette, 1954);

Pierre Flottes, *L'Éveil de Victor Hugo. 1802–1822,* Collection Vocations, volume 5 (Paris: Gallimard, 1957);

Hubert Juin, *Victor Hugo, 1802–1843,* volume 1 (Paris: E. Flammarion, 1980);

Alain Decaux, *Victor Hugo* (Paris: Perrin, 1984);

Juin, *Victor Hugo,* 1844–1870, volume 2 (Paris: E. Flammarion, 1984);

Alfred Morera, *La Vie de Victor Hugo* (Toulouse: D. Briand, 1985);

Juin, *Victor Hugo,* 1870–1885, volume 3 (Paris: E. Flammarion, 1986);

Graham Robb, *Victor Hugo* (New York: Norton, 1998).

References:

Charles Affron, *A Stage for Poets: Studies in the Theatre of Hugo and Musset* (Princeton: Princeton University Press, 1971);

Pierre Albouy, *La Création mythologique chez Victor Hugo* (Paris: J. Corti, 1963);

Georges Ascoli, *Le Théâtre romantique,* Fasicule II–V (Paris: Tournier & Constans, 1936?), pp. 55–60; 92–106; 141–154; 170–186;

Charles Baudoin, *Psychanalyse de Victor Hugo* (Genève: Editions du Mont-Blanc, 1943; with introduction and bibliography by Pierre Albouy (Paris: Armand Colin, 1972);

Paul Berret, *Victor Hugo,* Nouvelle édition revue et corrigée (Paris: Garnier Frères, 1939), pp. 275–325;

M. André Blanchard, *Le Théâtre de Victor Hugo et la parodie* (Amiens: A. Picard, 1903);

Ferdinand Brunetière, *Victor Hugo. Leçons faites à l'École Supérieure par les élèves de deuxième année (lettres). 1900–1901,* volume 2 (Paris: Hachette, 1902);

Samia Chahine, *La Dramaturgie de Victor Hugo* (Paris: Nizet, 1971);

Barbara T. Cooper, "Parodying Hugo," *European Romantic Review,* 2, no. 1 (1991): 23–38;

Maurice Descotes, *Le Drame romantique et ses grands créateurs (1827–1839)* (Paris: Presses Universitaires de France, 1955?);

Georges Froment-Guieysse, *Victor Hugo,* volume 1 (Paris: Editions de l'Empire Français, 1948), pp. 179–206);

Jean Gaudon, *Victor Hugo et le théâtre: stratégie et dramaturgie* (Paris: Ed. Surger, 1985);

Paul Glachant and Victor Glachant, *Un Laboratoire dramaturgique. Essai critique sur le théâtre de Victor Hugo. Les Drames en prose. Les Drames épiques. Les Comédies lyriques (1822–1886)* (Paris: Hachette, 1903);

Paul Glachant and Victor Glachant, *Un Laboratoire dramaturgique. Essai critique sur le théâtre de Victor Hugo. Les Drames en vers de l'époque et de la formule romantiques (1827–1839)* (Paris: Hachette, 1902);

Elliott M. Grant, *The Career of Victor Hugo,* Harvard Studies in Romance Languages, volume 21 (Cambridge: Harvard University Press, 1945);

Richard B. Grant, *The Perilous Quest: Image, Myth and Prophecy in the Narratives of Victor Hugo* (Durham, N.C.: Duke University Press, 1968);

Fernand Gregh, *L'Œuvre de Victor Hugo* (Paris: E. Flammarion, 1933);

Clayton M. Hamilton, "The Plays of Victor Hugo," *Sewanee Review,* 11 (April 1903): 169–186;

John P. Houston, *Victor Hugo,* Twayne's World Author Series (New York: Twayne, 1974);

William D. Howarth, *Sublime and Grotesque: A Study of French Romantic Drama* (London: Harrap, 1975);

Hermann Hugi, *Les Drames de Victor Hugo expliqués par la psychanalyse* (Solothurn: Buch und Kunstdruckerei Vogt-Schild, 1930);

Victor Hugo, *Les Deux Trouvailles de Gallus,* critical edition, edited by John J. Janc (New York: University Press of America, 1983);

Hugo, *Mangeront-ils?,* Cahiers Victor Hugo, volume 8, critical edition edited by René Journet and Guy Robert (Paris: E. Flammarion, 1970);

Hugo, *Ruy Blas,* critical edition, edited by Anne Ubersfeld (Paris: Les Belles Lettres, 1971);

Hugo, *Torquemada,* critical edition edited by Janc (New York: University Press of America, 1989);

Odile Krakovitch, *Hugo censuré. La Liberté au théâtre au XIXe siècle* (Paris: Calmann-Lévy, 1985);

Arnauld Laster, *Pleins feux sur Victor Hugo* (Paris: Comédie-Française, 1981);

Maria Ley-Deutsch, *Le Gueux chez Victor Hugo* (Paris: Droz, 1936);

Henry Lyonnet, *Les "Premières" de Victor Hugo* (Paris: Delagrave, 1930);

Anne Nicolas, "*Le Théâtre en liberté.* Un nouveau théâtre?" in *Manuel d'histoire littéraire de la France, De 1848–1917,* edited by Pierre Abraham and Roland Desne, volume 5 (Paris: Editions Sociales, 1977), pp. 196–201;

William D. Pendell, *Victor Hugo's Acted Dramas and the Contemporary Press,* Johns Hopkins Studies in Romance Literatures and Languages, volume 23 (Baltimore: Johns Hopkins University Press, 1974);

Paul de Saint-Victor, *Victor Hugo* (Paris: Calmann-Lévy, 1884);

Maurice Souriau, *La Préface de Cromwell. Introduction, texte et notes,* fourth edition (Paris: Société Française d'Imprimerie et de librairie, n.d.);

Anne Ubersfeld, *Le Roi et le bouffon. Étude sur le théâtre de Hugo de 1830 à 1839* (Paris: Librairie José Corti, 1974);

Ubersfeld, *Le Roman d'Hernani* (Paris: Mercure de France, 1985).

Papers:

The manuscripts, copies of the plays, and other handwritten documents relating to Hugo's dramas are to be found at the Bibliothèque Nationale, Paris, France. The manuscript of *Hernani* is held by the Bibliothèque-Musée de la Comédie-Française, Paris. Some documents and papers are housed at the Maison de Victor Hugo, also in Paris.

Alfred Jarry

(8 September 1873 – 1 November 1907)

Rhona Justice-Malloy
Central Michigan University

PLAY PRODUCTIONS:*Ubu Roi,* Paris, Nouveau Théâtre at the Théâtre de l'Œuvre, 10 December 1896;

Ubu sur la Butte, Paris, Guignol des Gueules de Bois at the Théâtre des Quatz'arts, 10 November 1901;

Ubu Enchaîné, Paris, Comédie des Champs-Elysées, 22 September 1937;

Ubu Cocu, Rheims, Chambre de Commerce, 21 May 1946;

Ubu à l'Opéra, Avignon, Théâtre de l'Est Parisien, 1974;

Ubu aux Bouffes, Paris, Centre International de Créations Théâtrales at Théâtre des Bouffes du Nord, 1977.

BOOKS: *Les Minutes de sable mémorial* (Paris: Mercure de France, 1894);

César-Antéchrist (Paris: Mercure de France, 1895); translated by James Bierman as *Caesar-Antichrist* (Tucson, Ariz.: Omen Press, 1971);

Ubu Roi (Paris: Mercure de France, 1896); translated by Barbara Wright as *Ubu Roi* (London: Gaberbocchus Press, 1951); translated by Beverly Keith and George Legman as *King Turd,* in *King Turd, King Turd Enslaved, and Turd Cuckolded* (New York: Boar's Head Books, 1953); translated by David Copelin as *Ubu Rex* (Vancouver: Pulp Press, 1973);

Les Jours et les nuits, roman d'un déserteur (Paris: Mercure de France, 1897); translated by Alexis Lykiard as *Days and Nights: Novel of a Deserter* (London: Atlas Press, 1989);

L'Amour en visites (Paris: Pierre Fort, 1898);

Almanach du Père Ubu, illustré (Paris: Privately printed, 1899);

L'Amour absolu (Paris: Mercure de France, 1899);

Ubu Enchaîné and *Ubu Roi* (Paris: Editions de la Revue Blanche, 1900); translated by Keith and Legman as *King Turd Enslaved,* in *King Turd, King Turd Enslaved, and Turd Cuckolded* (New York: Boar's Head Books, 1953);

Alfred Jarry, 1896 (photograph by Nadar)

Almanach illustré du Père Ubu [XXe siècle] (Paris: Ambroise Vollard, 1901);

Messaline, roman de l'ancienne Rome (Paris: Editions de la Revue Blanche, 1901); translated by Louis Coleman as *The Garden of Priapus* (New York: Black Hawk Press, 1936); translated by John Harman as *Messalina: a Novel of Imperial Rome* (London: Atlas Press, 1985);

Le Surmâle, roman moderne (Paris: Editions de la Revue Blanche, 1902); translated by Barbara Wright as *The Supermale, a Modern Novel* (London: Jonathan Cape, 1968);

Par la taille (Paris: Sansot, 1906); translated by Emylou Spears de Alvarez as *Par la taille,* in *Library Chronicle of the University of Texas,* 38–39 (1987): 40–75;

Ubu sur la Butte (Paris: Sansot, 1906);

Albert Samain Souvenirs (Paris: Victor Lemasle, 1907);

Le Moutardier du Pape (Paris: Private subscription edition, 1907);

Pantagruel, by Jarry and Eugene Demolder, music by Claude Terrasse (Paris: Société d'éditions musicales, 1910);

Gestes et opinions du docteur Faustroll, pataphysicien, and *Spéculations* (Paris: Fasquelle, 1911);

Gestes et opinions du docteur Faustroll, pataphysicien, and *Paralipomènes d'Ubu* (Paris: Editions du Sagittaire, 1921);

La Dragonne (Paris: Gallimard, 1943);

Ubu Cocu (Geneva: Editions des Trois Collines, 1944); translated by Keith and Legman as *Turd Cuckolded,* in *King Turd, King Turd Enslaved, and Turd Cuckolded* (New York: Boar's Head Books, 1953);

La Revanche de la nuit, poèmes retrouvés, edited by M. Saillet (Paris: Mercure de France, 1949);

Commentaire pour servir à la construction pratique de la machine à explorer le temps (Paris: Collège de 'Pataphysique, 1950);

Visions actuelles et futures (Paris: Collège de 'Pataphysique, 1950);

Autour d'Ubu (Paris: Collège de 'Pataphysique, 1951);

Les Alcoolisés (Paris: Collège de 'Pataphysique, 1952);

Les Nouveaux timbres (Paris: Collège de 'Pataphysique, 1952);

L'Objet aimé, edited by Roger Shattuck (Paris: Editions Arcanes, 1953);

L'Ouverture de la pêche (Paris: Collège de 'Pataphysique, 1953);

Le Futur malgré lui (Paris: Collège de 'Pataphysique, 1954);

Tatane (Paris: Collège de 'Pataphysique, 1954);

Soleil de printemps, with drawings by Pierre Bonnard (Paris: Collège de 'Pataphysique, 1957);

Etre et vivre (Paris: Collège de 'Pataphysique, 1958);

Le Temps dans l'art (Paris: Collège de 'Pataphysique, 1958);

Album de l'Antlium (Paris: Collège de 'Pataphysique, 1964);

Les Antliaclastes (Paris: Collège de 'Pataphysique, 1964);

Saint-Brieuc des Choux, edited by Saillet (Paris: Mercure de France, 1964);

Ontogénie (Paris, n.p., 1964);

Peintures, gravures et dessins d'Alfred Jarry, edited by Michel Arrivé (Paris: Collège de 'Pataphysique et Le Cercle français du livre, 1968);

La Chandelle verte, lumières sur les choses de ce temps, edited by Saillet (Paris: Le Livre de Poche, 1969);

Réponses à des enquêtes (Paris: Collège de 'Pataphysique, 1970);

Le Manoir enchanté et quatre autres oeuvres inédites, edited by Noel Arnaud (Paris: La Table ronde, 1974);

Léda, edited by Arnaud and H. Bordillon (Paris: Christian Bourgois, 1981).

Collections: *Oeuvres Complètes,* 8 volumes, edited by R. Massat (Monte Carlo: Editions du Livre, 1948);

Tout Ubu, edited by Saillet (Paris: Le Livre de Poche, 1962);

Selected Works, edited by Shattuck and Simon Watson-Taylor (London: Methuen, 1965);

The Ubu Plays, includes *Ubu Roi,* translated by Cyril Connolly and Watson-Taylor as *Ubu Rex; Ubu Cocu,* translated by Connolly as *Ubu Cuckolded;* and *Ubu Enchaîné,* translated by Watson-Taylor as *Ubu Enchained* (New York: Grove Press, 1969);

Oeuvres Complètes, volume 1, edited by Arrivé (Paris: Gallimard, Bibliothèque de la Pléiade, 1972);

Ubu, edited by Arnaud and Bordillon (Paris: Gallimard, Collection Folio, 1978).

The life and work of Alfred Jarry, both of which are enigmatic, complex, and at times undecipherable, mark a watershed in French theatrical history. Jarry's best-known play, *Ubu Roi* (1896; translated as *Ubu Roi,* 1951), was a revolutionary work that introduced the character of Ubu, and the Jarry/Ubu identity has defined the directions of contemporary theater for much of the twentieth century. While there are three plays in the Ubu cycle—*Ubu Roi, Ubu Enchaîné* (1900; translated as *King Turd Enslaved,* 1953), and *Ubu Cocu* (1944; translated as *Turd Cuckolded,* 1953)—there is in essence only one Ubu, whose identity is entwined with the Jarry mystery and mythology. The importance of Jarry and his writing owes much to the writers and artists who came after him, such as Guillaume Apollinaire and the Surrealists, Antonin Artaud and Roger Vitrac, and those whom theater critic and historian Martin Esslin named the Absurdists, as well as the members of the *College de 'Pataphysique* (College of 'Pataphysics), a group of scholars and thinkers deeply indebted to Jarry's groundbreaking work.

The Jarry myth is a continuously evolving narrative that adds and deletes information to serve the culture in which it thrives. From his writings one can imagine Jarry would be delighted with his success in appearing to the present time as being at once mysterious and monstrous, with his ability to conceal facts about his life and personality, and with the distortions and mystifications of meaning in his writing. Jarry was a true subscriber to what he himself dubbed "'Pataphysics," which was a scientific "discipline" that he created not only as a form of science but also as a philosophy of life to be fully enacted. In *Gestes et opinions du docteur Faustroll, 'pataphysicien* (Exploits and Opinions of Doctor Faustroll, 'Pataphysician) which he wrote in 1898 but which was not published until 1911, Jarry described the principles of 'Pataphysics, principles implicit not only in all his writings but in his attitude to life:

> La pataphysique est la science de ce qui se surajoute à la métaphysique. . . . Elle étudiera les lois qui régissent les exceptions et expliquera l'univers supplémentaire à celui-ci; ou moins ambitieusement décrira un univers que l'on peut voir et que peut-être l'on doit voir à la place du traditionnel, les lois que l'on a cru découvrir de l'univers traditionnel étant des corrélations d'exceptions aussi, quoique plus fréquentes, en tous cas de faits accidentels qui, se réduisant à des exceptions peu exceptionnelles, n'ont même pas l'attrait de la singularité.
> DEFINITION: *La pataphysique est la science des solutions imaginaires, qui accorde symboliquement aux linéaments les propriétés des objets décrits par leur virtualité.*

> ('Pataphysics is the science of the realm beyond metaphysics. . . . It will study the laws which govern exceptions and will explain the universe supplementary to this one; or, less ambitiously, it will describe a universe which one can see—must see perhaps—instead of the traditional one, for the laws discovered in the traditional universe are themselves correlated exceptions, even though frequent, or in any case accidental facts which, reduced to scarcely exceptional exceptions, don't even have the advantage of singularity.
> Definition: 'Pataphysics is the science of imaginary solutions, which symbolically attributes the properties of objects, described by their virtuality, to their lineaments.)

In both his life and his art Jarry embraced ambiguity, abstraction, and imagination. This made him very attractive to the Symbolists and all the other antirealists who followed. Like all great myths, Jarry's life is the story of fact and imagination twined in a double helix. Jarry lived what appears to be an intentionally monstrous and self-destructive life. Dead at the age of thirty-four after years of physical abuse and neglect, he remains an enigma. He wrote plays, criticism, satire, poetry, and fiction. Most of his works were published in the reviews *La Plume, La Revue Blanche,* and the *Mer-*

Jarry's woodcut portrait of his character Ubu, first published in Le Livre d' Art *(April 1896)*

cure de France. But a significant portion of his writing was not published until after his death, and little was translated into English until well into the twentieth century. Jarry lived to see *Ubu Roi,* his most important work, given only two performances onstage with live actors. Even so, he profoundly influenced the modernist transformation in theater.

Alfred-Henry Jarry was born in Laval on 8 September 1873. His father, Anselme Jarry, was a successful partner in a Laval linen factory; he married Caroline Quernest in 1868. Quernest's family was wealthy, but their social standing was somewhat tainted by a family history of insanity. Caroline's behavior was at times rather eccentric and included dressing in unusual clothes and wearing exotic hairstyles and makeup. Shortly after Alfred's birth Anselme Jarry's business began to fail, and in 1879 Caroline left her husband, moving her son and his older sister, Charlotte, to Saint-Brieuc, France. There Jarry entered the lycée and began to compose his first writings, later collected as *Ontogénie* (Ontogenesis, 1964).

In 1888 Jarry enrolled in the lycée in Rennes and began one of the most important periods of his life. He became friends with Charles and Henri Morin, who initiated him into the schoolboy mythology that had been created around Professor Félix Hébert, the school's pitiful, ineffectual teacher of physics. It was this teacher who became the prototype of Père Ubu (Pa Ubu). Professor Hébert had been the subject of schoolboy pranks and sarcasm for generations at the Rennes lycée. Jarry took the tomfoolery and harassment to a new level. His tormenting of Professor Hébert became legendary, and soon Jarry and Henri Morin began collaborating on a play, the chief character of which was a caricature of the hapless professor. Actually the Morin brothers had written an early version of the play, "Les Polonais" (The Polish), a schoolboy satire. When Jarry began working on the play, however, Hébert was transformed into a truly monstrous character, Père Héb, with an enormous *gidouille* (belly) ringed by concentric circles to accentuate his greed and gluttony. The boys gave their first performance of "Les Polonais" in the Morins' attic in Rennes in December 1888, using marionettes. Thus Ubu was born. Later that year the boys staged in their marionette theater "Onésime ou les Tribulations de Priou" (Onanism; or, The Tribulations of Priou), the original version of *Ubu Cocu*.

In the fall of 1891 Jarry entered the Lycée Henri IV in Paris to prepare for the competitive exam for acceptance to the Ecole Normale Supérieure. Jarry sat for the exam three times, each time failing to gain entry into the prestigious school. It was at this time that the seventeen-year-old began to develop the eccentric and witty behavior that later won him entrance into the Tuesday soirees of the *Mercure de France,* which were sponsored by Alfred Vallette and his wife, Marguerite Eymery, a novelist and playwright who wrote under the pseudonym Rachilde. Vallette and Rachilde became Jarry's lifelong friends and patrons. By 1893 Jarry was the irresistibly outlandish darling of the Parisian literati. At Vallette's gatherings he was courted by many of the greatest writers, artists, and composers of the time, including Catulle Mendès, Félix Fénéon, Henri de Régnier, Paul Fort, Paul Valéry, Pierre Louÿs, Gustave Kahn, Franc-Nohain, Rémy de Gourmont, André Gide, Toulouse-Lautrec, Paul Gauguin, Paul Sérusier, Henri Rousseau, and Maurice Ravel. Indeed, Jarry became acquainted with representatives of nearly every conceivable theory and artistic movement. He also became known for his unusual appearance. The poet Régnier described him in 1933 as:

> A short stocky man, with a large head and broad shoulders, planted on bowlegs. In a pale face, with fine contracted features and a thin brown moustache, brilliant eyes shone with a metallic glare. At the bottom of knee-breeches, calves ringed in garters ended in feet shod in rubber-soled shoes. . . . His pockets bulged with cycling tools, among which one could see the butt of an old revolver, at once sordid and disquieting.

A few years later Jarry's eccentric behavior had become monstrous. In his recollections of this period Gide believed that Jarry had succeeded in destroying his innate personality and adopting in its place a totally and all-consuming fictitious persona, as unique as it was mesmerizing: "Ce Kobold, à la face plâtrée, accoutré en clown de cirque et jouant un personnage fantasque, construit, *résolument factice et en dehors de quoi plus rien d'humain ne se montrait,* exerçait au *Mercure* (en ce temps) une sorte de fascination singulière" (This Kobold [*sic*], his face plastered white, got up as a circus clown, and playing a fantastic, fabricated, resolutely artificial role outside of which no human characteristics could any longer be seen, exercised [at that time] a kind of weird fascination at the *Mercure*). It was also in 1893 that Jarry suffered a terrible bout of influenza and that his mother died of the same ailment. Her death seems to be an event from which Jarry never fully recovered.

As he was courted by the artistic representatives of the time, including the celebrated poet Stéphane Mallarmé (whose attention he particularly relished), Jarry became special friends with the young writer and poet Léon-Paul Fargue. Fargue and Jarry wrote and lived together off and on until 1895. Jarry's play "Haldernablou" was written in 1894 and presents allegorically a homosexual affair between a man and a servant. The biographical relevance of this play is questionable, but some insinuated that the two male lovers in "Haldernablou" were actually Jarry and Fargue and that the play was an interpretation of their relationship.

In November 1894 Jarry was drafted into the French army. After a disastrous few months of army life and a self-administered dose of picric acid, which turned his skin yellow, Jarry was discharged and returned to Paris. Soon after Jarry and Fargue broke off their friendship; Jarry's father died in Laval; and *César-Antéchrist* (1895; translated as *Caesar-Antichrist,* 1971) was pub-

Program for the first performance of Ubu Roi, *which opened at the Théâtre de l'Œurve in Paris on 10 December 1896 (lithograph by Jarry; from* La Critique, *1896)*

lished as a complete play. This complex, symbolic work embraces many themes, including the death of God.

The year 1896 was the "Year of Jarry." At twenty-three the writer was about to change the course of theatrical art. He was also embarking on a way of life characterized by heavy drinking and poverty, a way of life that would ultimately shatter his personality. But on the brink of destruction he created his masterpiece, *Ubu Roi.* In Ubu, Jarry created one of the most monstrous, blundering characters in literature. He then deliberately set out, if not to become, then certainly to imitate in self-abuse, his own creation. Not only did Jarry make a profession of eccentricity, but he also effectively "unlived his life," as Roger Shattuck put it in *The Banquet Years: The Arts in France, 1885–1918* (1958).

Ubu Roi stands at the turning point of modern theater. Although Jarry wrote three plays for the Ubu cycle, *Ubu Roi* emerged as his most important work for the stage. The story of *Ubu Roi* is one of the traditional *guignol,* or puppet theater, that Jarry loved. Indeed, *Ubu* was first meant for the marionette stage. In the guignol theater, plot tends to be anecdotal; psychology is rudimentary; and charac-

ters are stylized while the action is free from the limitations of time, space, and logic. Guignol presents a stylized, fantasy world with only a minimal pretension to being a copy of the actual world. So it is with *Ubu Roi.*

Ubu Roi contains six acts that have little relation to traditional theatrical illusion, causal logic, or customary ideas of coherence. The argument of the play revolves around Ubu's destruction of virtually all the power structures of Poland with his "debraining" machine. He is encouraged in his murderous ways by Mère Ubu (Ma Ubu), his Lady Macbeth–like wife. Ubu assassinates the royal family of Poland; betrays his coconspirators; exterminates the nobility, the judiciary, and the bankers; and then sets about the countryside to collect taxes, which, under his rule, have doubled and tripled. Chaos increases as Ubu is forced to lead the Polish army to war against the Tsar (the thought of whom causes Ubu literally to defecate in his pants). As the play progresses, any sense of unified action or linear narrative disappears as Ubu and his wife somehow meet in the wilderness, where Ubu is attacked by a bear. They manage to escape not only the bear but also what is left of the Polish nobility, and the play ends with the two would-be despots sailing off to France to begin some new adventure.

Ubu Roi is filled with elements of spoofing and parody, especially of the works of William Shakespeare, but it is not good-natured jest: the overall effect is one of all-embracing derision. What made the play so compelling, at least for Jarry's audience, was not the events of the play but the avoidance of logic and coherence and any sense of identification with individual characters or a specific locale. Ubu himself is Jarry's vision of Everyman, and a terrifying vision it is. He is primitive, monstrous, grotesque, greedy, vulgar, sadistic, cruel, aggressive, violent, treacherous, merciless, and incapable of love, compassion, or even lust. Despite all the obscenities, the scatological references, the endless schoolboy vulgarities, and the "mot d'Ubu" (word of Ubu) that resounds throughout, there is nothing in the play intended to make the audience laugh.

If Ubu is the universal Everyman, then the Poland that Jarry refers to as "Nowhere" is by the same principle a universal Everywhere. Facts and events in the play that seem contradictory or incongruous essentially cancel each other out, creating a kind of void that Jarry equated with universality. This universality is not unlike the stylized fantasy world of the guignol or the imaginary world of the Symbolists, where the complex phenomenon called "imagination" or "fantasy" is located just this side of chaos. It follows then that in the unstageable *Ubu Cocu* Père Ubu is what Jarry called "l'anarchiste parfait" (the perfect anarchist). He is a "porcupine hunched up against humanity." With his servants, the Palotins, he continues his work of impaling and disembraining, at times consulting his conscience, which he keeps in a case covered with spiders' webs. The theme of the whole piece is "Fear and dread the Master of Phynances." The deliberately incoherent plot concerns the cuckolding of Père Ubu and his revenge against his adulterous wife and her lover. The play has no apparent internal coherence, logic, or action. In *Ubu Cocu* Jarry so successfully eliminated the conventions of traditional theater that the play is widely regarded as unpresentable.

One is tempted in the beginning of *Ubu Enchaîné* to believe that Père Ubu has reformed. He refuses to use the "mot d'Ubu," *merdre,* Ubu's often repeated and untranslatable variation on the word *merde* (shit). He also declares his intention of becoming a slave. However, the audience discovers that the so-called free men are men who use their freedom only to be able to disobey, and since they always disobey, they are no longer free. Slavery becomes a state of security for Ubu. He well knows that the free men will want to join it; when they ask

to be made slaves, he is once more master. This play is a mirror image of *Ubu Roi*. Rather than seeking power, Ubu decides to become a slave and forces himself on a master. He does not terrorize as in the first play but is imprisoned and condemned of his own volition. He is sent to the galleys, where he refuses to take command. The play ends with Ubu sailing to Turkey as he declares, "Je n'en suis pas moins veste Ubu enchaîné, esclave, et je ne commanderai plus. On m'obeit bien davantage" (I am still Ubu bound, a slave and I am not giving orders ever again. That way people will obey me even more promptly).

Though all three plays have shaped the Ubu character, it is *Ubu Roi* that has dominated Jarry's contribution to contemporary theater. There is, however, little critical agreement as to just what sort of play *Ubu Roi* is and how it is to be interpreted in production. It may be regarded as a farce or satire, or as Aurélien-François Lugné-Poë suggested, a tragedy. Then there is the question of the character of Ubu. What is he and what is he intended to mean? He has been seen as an embodiment of political anarchism, a satire upon the bourgeois, and the representation of various totalitarian dictators. Practitioners have interpreted the piece as expressing an absurd view of the universe.

But the real originality and importance of the play lie in its being an experiment in a radically new conception of dramatic form and technique. French theater prior to *Ubu Roi* was mainly an urban phenomenon and almost exclusively a bourgeois institution. Although there was always a radical element in French theater, the mainstream theater primarily provided entertainment. House lights were left on during the performance, and audience members were free to arrive and leave as they wished. With the exception of the plays of Maurice Maeterlinck and Jean-Marie Mathias Phillipe-Auguste, Comte de Villiers de L'Isle-Adam, it was a "realist" theater that followed the tradition of the well-made play. It portrayed characters whose actions were psychologically plausible in behavior and motivation, as the bourgeois audience understood these ideas. These characters existed in a concrete social and historical environment surrounded by local authenticating details. Plots revolved around a coherent, linear set of actions that resembled episodes of so-called real life. Sets endeavored to re-create convincingly the illusion of the world outside the theater. This was essentially a realistic, psychological, local, and linear form of narrative that sought to create the illusion of reality.

Jarry's aims, as stated in his suggestions for the staging of *Ubu Roi,* express a desire for a theater based on abstraction, universality, extreme simplification, and eternal and even universal themes. His theater was primarily visual rather than narrative and psychological. He was interested in characters who represented archetypes rather than individuals. In his letter to Lugné-Poë on 8 January 1896 Jarry clearly outlined his plan for the production of *Ubu Roi.*

Il sereit curieux, je crois, de pouvoir monter cette chose (sans aucun frais du reste) dans le goût suivant:

1. Masque pour le personnage principal, Ubu, lequel masque je pourrais vous procurer au besoin. . . .

2. Une tête de cheval en carton qu'il se pendrait au cou, comme dans l'ancien théâtre anglais, pour les deux seules scènes équestres, tous détails qui étaient dans l'esprit de la pièce, puisque j'ai voulu faire un 'guignol.'

3. Adoption d'un seul décor, ou mieux, d'un fond uni, supprimant les levers et baissers de rideau pendant l'acte unique. Un personnage correctement vêtu viendrait, comme dans les guignols, accrocher une pancarte signifiant le lieu de la scène. (Notez que je suis certain de la supériorité 'suggestive' de la pancarte écrite sur le décor. Un décor, ni une figuration ne rendraient 'l'armée polonaise en marche dans l'Ukraine'.)

4. Suppression des foules, lesquelles sont souvent mauvaises à la scène et gênent l'intelligence. Ainsi, un seul soldat dans la scène de la revue, un seul dans la bousculade où Ubu dit: 'Quel tas de gens, quelle fuite, etc.'

5. Adoption d'un 'accent' ou mieux d'une 'voix' spéciale pour le personnage principal.

6. Costumes aussi peu couleur locale ou chronologiques que possible (ce qui rend mieux l'idée d'une chose éternelle), modernes de préférence, puisque la satire est moderne; et sordides, parce que le drame en paraît plus misérable et horrifique.

(It would be curious, I believe, to produce this play [and at little expense really] in the following manner.

1. A mask for the principal role, Ubu, which I could do for you if necessary. But then I believe you have yourself been involved with this business of masks. . . .

2. A horse's head of cardboard, which he could have around his neck as in the old English theater, for the only two equestrian scenes—both these suggestions being in the spirit of the play, since I intended to write a "guignol."

3. Only one set, or better yet, one catchall backdrop, eliminating raising and lowering the curtain. A suitably costumed person would come in, as in puppet shows, to put up signs indicating the scene [You see, I am sure that writ-

ten signs are more "suggestive" than sets. No set or contrivance could portray the Polish army on the march in the Ukraine.]

4. The elimination of crowds, which are often bad on stage and have no intelligible effect. Thus, a single soldier in the review scene, and only one in the great scuffle when Ubu says: "What a hoard of people, what a flight, etc."

5. The adoption of an "accent" or better yet, a special "tone of voice" for the principal character.

6. Costumes with as little local color and historical accuracy as possible [it gives the best idea of something eternal]; modern ones preferably, since satire is modern; and sordid costumes because they make the action more wretched and repugnant.])

Jarry's writings on the theater are essential reading for anyone who wishes fully to understand his aims. Two articles published in the months preceding the December 1896 performance were intended to prepare the audience for the event. They are "De l'inutilité du théâtre au théâtre" (On the Futility of the Theatrical in the Theater) in the *Mercure de France* and "Les Paralipomènes du Ubu" (The Paralipomena of Ubu) in the *Revue Blanche.* In "Questions de théâtre" (Theater Questions), in the *Revue Blanche* in January 1897, Jarry replied to his critics. Also in his complete works is the text of his speech to the audience at the premiere of *Ubu Roi* and the program notes written by him, which were published by the review *La Critique.*

There is some confusion about the actual dates of the first two performances of *Ubu Roi* that Lugné-Poë staged at the Théâtre de l'Oeuvre. It is known that these performances took place at the Nouveau Théâtre. Shattuck places the premiere on 11 December 1896. In *Jarry: Ubu Roi* (1987) Keith Beaumont describes a dress rehearsal on 9 December and the actual premiere on 10 December. He also rightly points out that these distinctions (like much of what is known of Jarry) are frequently blurred in the memories of those participants who later recalled the scene (including Lugné-Poë) and have been perpetuated by many writers on the subject. One can, however, form a general picture of the event from a variety of sources and spectators.

The public dress rehearsal took place before a packed house. It was primarily an invited audience of friends and critics, representing all artistic factions, all well prepared for a scandal by recent publications of the play and commentary. Literary Paris was primed for the event.

Before the curtain rose a table was brought out. Jarry appeared, his face painted dead-white, dressed as a homeless person. He addressed the audience in his most flat, clipped, Ubuesque tones. He spoke for about ten minutes, referring briefly to the guignol theater and mentioning the masks the actors would wear and the fact that the first three acts would be performed without intermission. He concluded:

> Nous aurons d'ailleurs un décor parfaitement exact, car de même qu'il est un procédé facile pour situer une pièce dans l'Éternité, à savoir de faire par exemple tirer en l'an mille et tant des coups de revolver, vous verrez des portes s'ouvrir sur des plaines de neige sous un ciel bleu, des cheminées garnies de pendules se fendre afin de servir de portes, et des palmiers verdir au pied des lits, pour que les broutent de petits éléphants perchés sur des étagères.

> (In any case we have a perfect décor, for just as one good way of setting a play in Eternity is to have revolvers shot off in the year 1000, you will see doors open on fields of snow under blue skies, fireplaces furnished with clocks and swinging wide to serve as doors, and palm trees growing at the foot of a bed so that little elephants standing on bookshelves can browse on them. . . . As to the orchestra, there is none. Only its volume and timbre will be missed, for various pianos and percussion will execute Ubuesque themes from backstage. The action, which is about to begin, takes place in Poland, that is to say: Nowhere.)

Before the play had even begun Jarry upset his audience the best way he knew: by challenging their sense of theatrical propriety.

Jarry vanished with his table, and the curtain went up on the set—a collaboration between Jarry and Pierre Bonnard, Edouard Vuillard, Henri Marie-Raymond de Toulouse-Lautrec, and Paul Sérusier. In 1906, in "A Symbolist Farce," Arthur Symons, one of the few Englishmen present, described the backdrop:

> The scenery was painted to represent, by a child's conventions, indoors and out of doors, and even the torrid, temperate, and arctic zones at once. Opposite you, at the back of the stage, you saw apple trees in bloom, under a blue sky, and against the sky a small closed window and a fireplace . . . through the very midst of which . . . trooped in and out the clamorous and sanguinary persons of the drama. On the left was painted a bed, and at the foot of the bed a bare tree and snow falling. On the right there were palm trees . . . a door opened against the sky, and beside the door a skeleton dangled. A venerable gentleman in evening dress . . . trotted across the stage on the points of his toes between every scene and hung the new placard on its nail.

For all its obscenity the play proceeded without incident until act 3, when the now infamous and often repeated word *merdre* drew protest from the audience. The ultimate assault on the audience came later when one of the actors "became" a castle-door opening. Pandemonium followed. For at least fifteen minutes the theater was in an uproar, with some in the audience, those who approved the play and those who disapproved, at the point of exchanging blows. Firmin Gémier (playing Père Ubu) restored order by dancing a jig. The audience cheered, and the performance resumed in relative peace.

While there is some dispute among scholars, it seems that it was at the actual premiere the following evening that the real explosion occurred. There is further disagreement as to whether Gémier wore the heavy, pear-shaped mask Jarry designed for him, but he was no doubt imposing in the enormous cardboard belly that was his costume. In rehearsal director Lugné-Poë suggested Gémier imitate Jarry's own staccato voice and jerky, stylized movements. In performance Gémier pronounced his first word, which was an obscenity Jarry had appropriated to himself by adding the letter *r* to the French word *merde* (shit). "Merdre," Gémier said. The house went into an uproar. It then reacted violently each time the word was repeated. Gémier tried to silence the audience by blowing a tramway horn. The lighting designer, Fernand Hérold, stood in the wings and alternately plunged the theater into total darkness or startled the audience to silence by turning up the house lights and catching people with their fists raised or standing on their seats.

In the audience that night sat Edmond Rostand, Henri Fouquier, Francisque Sarcey, Mallarmé, and Henry Bauer. Also in the house was a young Irishman, William Butler Yeats. Despite his limited knowledge of French, Yeats was understandably shaken by the experience. In *Autobiographies* (1955) he concludes his recollections of that evening with the following remarks:

> Feeling bound to support the most spirited party, we have shouted for the play, but that night at the Hôtel Corneille I am very sad, for comedy, objectivity has displayed its growing power once more. I say: After Stéphane Mallarmé, after Paul Verlaine, after Gustave Moreau, after Puvis de Chavannes, after our own verse, after all our subtle colour and nervous rhythm, after the faint mixed tints of Conder, what more is possible? After us the Savage God.

In 1896 Jarry and his actors had created an event in the theater that involved themselves and the audience in direct confrontation. They were not reenacting an illusion or a situation that might have actually occurred. They assaulted the audience's artistic taste, and their performance fit no previous

Jarry in 1897

convention. Ubu was at once clown, comic, and monster. He fit no convention and, above all, was not meant to be humorous. Much has been written about *Ubu Roi,* which is often referred to as the first work of the Theater of the Absurd. By labeling the Ubu cycle as "Theater of the Absurd," scholars have placed Jarry's plays firmly within a theatrical convention. That convention was created long after Jarry's death, but it took its defining theme from *Ubu Roi.* It was Jarry himself who best expressed his intentions regarding the impact of the play. After the first performance he explained in his essay "Questions de théâtre" (1897):

> J'ai voulu que, le rideau levé, la scène fût devant le public comme ce miroir des contes de Mme Leprince de Beaumont, où le vicieux se voit avec des cornes de taureau et un corps de dragon, selon l'exagération de ses vices; et il n'est pas étonnant que le public ait été stupéfait à la vue de son double ignoble, qui ne lui avait pas encore été entièrement présenté; fait, comme l'a dit excellemment M. Catulle Mendès, « de l'éternelle imbécillité humaine, de l'éternelle luxure, de l'éternelle goinfrerie, de la bassesse de l'instinct érigée en tyrannie; des

pudeurs, des vertus, du patriotisme et de l'idéal des gens qui ont bien dîné ». Vraiment, il n'y a pas de quoi attendre une pièce drôle, et les masques expliquent que le comique doit en être tout au plus le comique macabrè d'un clown anglais ou d'une danse des morts. Avant que nous eussions Gémier, Lugné-Poe savait le rôle et voulait le répéter *en tragique.* Et surtout on n'a pas compris—ce qui était pourtant assez clair et rappelé perpétuellement par les répliques de la Mère Ubu: « Quel sot homme! . . . quel triste imbécile » —qu'Ubu ne devait pas dire « des mots d'esprit » comme divers ubucules en réclamáient, mais des phrases stupides, avec toute l'autorité du Mufle!

(I intended that when the curtain went up the scene should confront the public like the exaggerating mirror in the stories of Madame Leprince de Beaumont, in which the depraved saw themselves with dragons' bodies, or bulls' horns, or whatever corresponded to their particular vice. It is not surprising that the public should have been aghast at the sight of its ignoble other self, which it has never before been shown completely. This other self, as Monsieur Catulle Mendès has excellently said, is composed "of eternal human imbecility, eternal lust, eternal gluttony, the vileness of instinct magnified into tyranny; of the sense of decency, the virtues, the patriotism and the ideals peculiar to those who have just eaten their fill." Really, these are hardly the components for an amusing play, and masks demonstrate that the comedy must at the most be the macabre comedy of an English clown, or of a Dance of Death. Before Gémier agreed to play the part, Lugné-Poë had learned Ubu's lines and wanted to rehearse the play as a tragedy. And what no one seems to have understood—it was made clear enough, though, and constantly recalled by Ma Ubu's continually repeated: "What an idiotic man! . . . What a sorry imbecile!'—is that Ubu's speeches were not meant to be full of witticisms, as various little ubuists claimed, but of stupid remarks, uttered with all the authority of the Ape.)

Critics called the play vulgar and obscene. Some condemned the performance as an act of anarchist-inspired subversion; others viewed the event not as a serious piece of theater but simply as a gigantic hoax. After the premiere of *Ubu Roi* Jarry ended his relationship with the Théâtre de l'Oeuvre. His relationship with director Lugne-Poë was strained because of the uproar created by the performance and the significant production costs the play required. In various writings, however, and indeed in developing his own rebellious lifestyle, the playwright continued to elaborate on his creation, but only twice more, both times as puppet theater, did the play see production during Jarry's lifetime.

Jarry continued to write, but his active participation in the theater was essentially over. He made several attempts at creating puppet theater, including a production of *Ubu sur la Butte,* his adaptation of *Ubu Roi.* This work was staged at the Guignol des Gueules de Bois in 1901, but, like his other puppet theater attempts, it failed after only a few nights. Yet he enjoyed a unique notoriety in the literary world of Paris and was already admired by a new generation, the most important among whom were several young writers just beginning to publish: Apollinaire, André Salmon, and Max Jacob. They sought out Jarry in his macabre and bizarre living quarters and drew the alcoholic, malnourished, ether-addicted writer into their revelries and discussions. Jarry was a frequent visitor to Montmartre and exercised a special fascination over Pablo Picasso. The painter even adopted Jarry's eccentric habits, including carrying a pistol, and later acquired a valuable collection of Jarry's manuscripts. Jarry was a genuine and powerful influence on the emergence of modernism and cubism.

In late 1907 friends of Jarry's found him semiconscious in his apartment. He was gravely ill after years of physical abuse and neglect and months of declining health. He died the next day, on 1 November 1907. In 1908 *Ubu Roi* was revived briefly by Gémier, but otherwise the play was essentially forgotten for two decades, until Jarry's rediscovery in 1927. In that year Artaud and Vitrac founded the Théâtre Alfred Jarry. They proposed "to contribute by strictly theatrical means to the ruin of the theatre as it exists today in France. . . . As to the spirit which directs [the company], it partakes of the unsurpassed humoristic teachings of *Ubu Roi* and of the rigorously positivist method of Raymond Roussell." Through Artaud and his pupil Jean-Louis Barrault, Jarry's dramatic theories survived into the theater of the 1930s and 1940s after earlier plays by Apollinaire, Jules Romains, Tristan Tzara, and Jean Cocteau had celebrated the continuing tradition of *Ubu Roi.* In 1945 the writer Cyril Connolly dubbed Père Ubu the "Santa Claus of the Atomic Age," and modern scholars have continued to be fascinated with Ubu and the Jarry mythology.

Letters:

Rachilde (pseudonym of Marguerite Eymery), *Alfred Jarry; ou le Surmâle des lettres* (Paris: B. Grasset, 1928);

Correspondance avec Félix Fénéon (Société des Amis d'Alfred Jarry, 1980).

Bibliography:

L. F. Sutton, "An Evaluation of the Studies on Alfred Jarry from 1894–1963," dissertation, University of North Carolina at Chapel Hill, 1970.

Biographies:

Paul Chauveau, *Alfred Jarry; ou La Naissance, la vie et la mort du Père Ubu, avec leurs portraits* (Paris: Mercure de France, 1932);

Noël Arnaud, *Alfred Jarry d'Ubu Roi au Docteur Faustroll* (Paris: La Table Ronde, 1974);

Keith Beaumont, *Alfred Jarry: A Critical and Biographical Study* (New York: St. Martin's Press, 1984);

Nigey Lennon, *Alfred Jarry: The Man with the Axe* (Los Angeles: Panjandrum, 1984);

Patrick Besnier, *Alfred Jarry* (Paris: Plon, 1990);

Christian Soulignac, *Alfred Jarry: Biographie 1906–1962* (Paris: Fourneau, 1995).

References:

Michel Arrivé, *Les Langages de Jarry. Essai de sémiotique littéraire* (Paris: Klincksieck, 1972);

Arrivé, *Lire Jarry* (Paris: Presses Universitaires de France, 1976);

Keith Beaumont, *Jarry,* Ubu Roi (London: Wolfeboro, 1987);

Beaumont, "The Making of Ubu: Jarry as Producer and Theorist," *Theatre Research International,* 12 (1972): 139–154;

Henri Béhar, *Jarry Dramaturge* (Paris: Nizet, 1980);

Béhar, *Jarry, le monstre et la marionnette* (Paris: Larousse, 1973);

Edward Braun, *The Director and the Stage: From Naturalism to Grotowski* (London: Methuen, 1982);

François Caradec, *A la Recherche d'Alfred Jarry* (Paris: Seghers, 1974);

Charles Chassé, *Dans les coulisses de la gloire: d'Ubu Roi au douanier Rousseau* (Paris: Editions de la Nouvelle revue critique, 1947);

Judith Cooper, "Ubu Roi: An Analytical Study," *Tulane Studies in Romance Languages and Literature,* 6 (1974);

Brunella Eruli, *Jarry: i mostri dell'immagine* (Pisa: Pacini, 1982);

Martin Esslin, T*he Theatre of the Absurd* (Harmondsworth, U.K.: Penguin, 1961);

Europe, revue littéraire mensuelle, 623–624 (1981);

Maurice Marc La Belle, *Alfred Jarry: Nihilism and the Theatre of the Absurd* (New York & London: New York University Press, 1980);

André LaBois, *Alfred Jarry l'irremplacable* (Paris: Le Cercle du Livre, 1950);

Jacques-Henri Levesque, *Alfred Jarry* (Paris: Seghers, 1951);

Le Magazine Littéraire, 48 (1971);

Claude Schumacher, *Alfred Jarry and Guillaume Apollinaire* (New York: Grove, 1985);

Roger Shattuck, *The Banquet Years: The Arts in France, 1885–1918* (New York: Harcourt, Brace, 1958; revised edition, London: Jonathan Cape, 1969);

Linda K. Stillman, *Alfred Jarry* (Boston: Twayne, 1983);

Michael Zelenak, "Ubu Rides Again: The Irondale Project and the Politics of Clowning," *Theater,* 18, 3 (1987): 43–45.

Papers:

The chief repository of Jarry's works and critical studies is the Collège de 'Pataphysique in Paris. The college has published many critical studies in its *Cahiers du Collège de 'Pataphysique* (1950–1957), *Dossiers acénonètes du Collège de 'Pataphysique* (1957–1965), *Subsidia Pataphysica* (1965–1974), and the *Organographes du Cymbalum Pataphysicum* (1975–), together with the articles in the more recent *L'Etoile–Absinthe,* published from 1979 onward by the Société des Amis d'Alfred Jarry.

Eugène Labiche
(6 May 1815 – 22 January 1888)

Janice Best
Acadia University

PLAY PRODUCTIONS: *La Cuvette d'eau,* by Labiche, August Lefranc, and Marc-Michel, Théâtre du Luxembourg[?], 1837[?];

M. de Coyllin, ou L'Homme infiniment poli, by Labiche, Marc-Michel, and Lefranc, Paris, Théâtre du Palais Royal, 2 July 1838;

Le Capitaine d'Arcourt ou la fée du château, by Labiche, Marc-Michel, and Lefranc, [theater unknown], 1838[?];

L'Avocat Loubet, by Labiche, Lefranc, and Marc-Michel, Paris, Théâtre du Panthéon, 28 August 1838;

La Forge des châtaigniers, by Labiche, Lefranc, and Marc-Michel, Paris, Théâtre Saint-Marcel, 4 April 1839;

La Peine du talion, by Labiche, Lefranc, and Marc-Michel, Paris, Théâtre du Luxembourg, June 1839;

L'Article 960 ou la donation, by Jacques-Arsène Ancelot and Paul Dandré (Dandré is a collective pseudonym for Labiche, Lefranc, and Marc-Michel), Paris, Théâtre du Vaudeville, 20 August 1839;

Le Fin Mot, by Dandré, Paris, Théâtre des Variétés, 21 July 1840;

Bocquet père et fils ou le chemin le plus long, by Labiche, Paul Laurencin, and Marc-Michel, Paris, Théâtre du Gymnase, 17 August 1840;

Le Lierre et l'ormeau, by Labiche, Lefranc, and Albert Monnier, Paris, Théâtre du Palais Royal, 25 December 1840;

Les Circonstances atténuantes, by Labiche, Charles Mélesville, and Lefranc, Paris, Théâtre du Palais Royal, 26 February 1842;

L'Homme de paille, by Labiche and Lefranc, Paris, Théâtre du Palais Royal, 12 May 1843;

Le Major Cravachon, by Labiche, Lefranc, and Paul Jessé, Paris, Théâtre du Palais Royal, 15 February 1844;

Deux Papas très-bien ou la grammaire de Chicard, by Labiche and Lefranc, Paris, Théâtre du Palais Royal, 16 November 1844;

Eugène Labiche (© Collection Viollet)

Le Roi des Frontins, by Labiche and Lefranc, Paris, Théâtre du Palais Royal, 28 March 1845;

L'Ecole buissonnière, by Labiche and Lefranc, Paris, Théâtre du Palais Royal, 23 July 1845;

L'Enfant de la maison, by Labiche, Charles Varin, and Eugène Nyon, Paris, Théâtre du Gymnase, 21 November 1845;

Mademoiselle ma femme, by Labiche and Lefranc, Paris, Théâtre du Palais Royal, 9 April 1846;

Rocambolle le bateleur, by Labiche and Lefranc, Paris, Théâtre des Folies Dramatiques, 22 April 1846;

Frisette, by Labiche and Lefranc, Paris, Théâtre du Palais Royal, 28 April 1846;

L'Inventeur de la poudre, by Labiche, Lefranc, and Nyon, Paris, Théâtre du Palais Royal, 17 June 1846;

L'Avocat pédicure, by Labiche, Gustave Albitte, and Lefranc, Paris, Théâtre du Palais Royal, 24 April 1847;

La Chasse aux jobards, by Labiche and Lefranc, Paris, Théâtre des Folies Dramatiques, 18 May 1847;

Un Homme sanguin, by Labiche and Lefranc, Paris, Théâtre du Gymnase, 15 August 1847;

L'Art de ne pas donner d'étrennes, by Labiche and Lefranc, Paris, Théâtre du Gymnase, 29 December 1847;

Un Jeune Homme pressé, Paris, Théâtre du Palais Royal, 4 March 1848;

Le Club champenois, by Labiche and Lefranc, Paris, Théâtre du Palais Royal, 8 June 1848;

Oscar XXVIII, by Labiche, Adrien Decourcelle, and Jules Barbier, Paris, Théâtre des Variétés, 29 July 1848;

Le Baromètre ou la pluie et le beau temps, by Labiche, Lefranc, and Marc-Michel, Paris, Théâtre du Vaudeville, 1 August 1848;

Une Chaîne anglaise, by Labiche and Saint-Yves, Paris, Théâtre du Palais Royal, 4 August 1848;

A Moitié chemin, by Labiche, Lefranc, and Marc-Michel, Paris, Théâtre Beaumarchais, 12 August 1848;

Histoire du rire, by Labiche and Saint-Yves, Paris, Théâtre du Gymnase, 13 August 1848;

Agénor le dangereux, by Labiche, Adrien Decourcelle, and Karl, Paris, Théâtre du Palais Royal, 16 September 1848;

Une Tragédie chez M. Grassot, by Labiche and Lefranc, Paris, Théâtre du Palais Royal, 12 December 1848;

A bas la famille ou les banquets, by Labiche and Lefranc, Paris, Théâtre du Gymnase, 16 December 1848;

Madame veuve Larifla, by Labiche and Adolphe Choler, Paris, Théâtre des Variétés, 25 January 1849;

Les Manchettes d'un vilain, by Labiche, Lefranc, and Saint-Yves, Paris, Théâtre du Palais Royal, 3 February 1849;

Un Monsieur qui pose, by Labiche, Lefranc, and Philippe de Marville, Paris, Théâtre des Folies Dramatiques, 6 February 1849;

Une dent sous Louis XV, by Labiche and Lefranc, Paris, Théâtre du Palais Royal, 15 February 1849;

Mon ours, by Labiche and Choler, Paris, Théâtre des Variétés, 17 February 1849;

Trompe-la-balle, by Labiche and Lefranc, Paris, Théâtre du Palais Royal, 8 April 1849;

Exposition des produits de la République, by Labiche, P. F. Dumanoir, and Louis Clairville, Paris, Théâtre du Palais Royal, 20 June 1849;

Rue de l'homme-armé no 8 bis, by Labiche and Nyon, Paris, Théâtre des Variétés, 24 September 1849;

Pour qui voterai-je?, by Labiche and Choler, Paris, Théâtre des Variétés, 1 December 1849;

Embrassons-nous, Folleville, by Labiche and Lefranc, Paris, Théâtre du Palais Royal, 6 March 1850;

Traversin et couverture, parody of *Toussaint Louverture,* by Labiche and Charles Varin, Paris, Théâtre du Palais Royal, 26 April 1850;

Un Garçon de chez Véry, Paris, Théâtre du Palais Royal, 10 May 1850;

Le Sopha, précédé de Schahabaham XCIV, by Labiche, Mélesville, and Charles Desnoyer, Paris, Théâtre du Palais Royal, 18 July 1850;

La Fille bien gardée, by Labiche and Marc-Michel, Paris, Théâtre du Palais Royal, 6 September 1850;

Un Bal en robe de chambre, Episode de la vie du grand monde, mêlé de couplets, by Labiche and Marc-Michel, Paris, Théâtre du Palais Royal, 12 October 1850;

Les Petits Moyens, by Labiche, Gustave Lemoine, and Decourcelle, Paris, Théâtre du Gymnase, 6 November 1850;

Les Prétendus de Gimblette, by Labiche, Paul Dandré, and Charles Matharel de Fiennes, Paris, Théâtre de la Gaîté, 24 November 1850;

Une Clarinette qui passe, by Labiche and Marc-Michel, Paris, Théâtre des Variétés, 4 January 1851;

La Femme qui perd ses jarretières, by Labiche and Marc-Michel, Paris, Théâtre du Palais Royal, 8 February 1851;

On demande des culottières, by Labiche and Marc-Michel, Paris, Théâtre du Palais Royal, 2 March 1851;

Mam'zelle fait ses dents, by Labiche and Marc-Michel, Paris, Théâtre du Palais Royal, 9 April 1851;

En Manches de chemise, by Labiche, Lefranc, and Nyon, Paris, Théâtre du Palais Royal, 8 August 1851;

Un Chapeau de paille d'Italie, by Labiche and Marc-Michel, Paris, Théâtre du Palais Royal, 14 August 1851;

Maman Sabouleux, by Labiche and Marc-Michel, Paris, Théâtre du Palais Royal, 13 March 1852;

Un Monsieur qui prend la mouche, by Labiche and Marc-Michel, Paris, Théâtre des Variétés, 25 March 1852;

Soufflez-moi dans l'oeil, by Labiche and Marc-Michel, Paris, Théâtre du Palais Royal, 1 May 1852;

Les Suites d'un premier lit, by Labiche and Marc-Michel, Paris, Théâtre du Vaudeville, 8 May 1852;

Le Misanthrope et l'Auvergnat, by Labiche, P. M. Lubize, and Paul Siraudin, Paris, Théâtre du Palais Royal, 10 August 1852;

Deux Gouttes d'eau, by Labiche and Auguste Anicet-Bourgeois, Paris, Théâtre des Variétés, 22 September 1852;

Piccolet, by Labiche, Lefranc, and Montjoie, Paris, Théâtre du Palais Royal, 30 September 1852;

Edgard et sa bonne, by Labiche and Marc-Michel, Paris, Théâtre du Palais Royal, 16 October 1852;

Le Chevalier des dames, by Labiche and Marc-Michel, Paris, Théâtre du Palais Royal, 16 December 1852;

Mon Isménie, by Labiche and Marc-Michel, Paris, Théâtre du Palais Royal, 17 December 1852;

Une Charge de cavalerie, by Labiche, Eugène Moreau, and Alfred Delacour, Paris, Théâtre du Palais Royal, 31 December 1852;

Un Ami acharné, by Labiche and Alphonse Jolly, Paris, Théâtre des Variétés, 19 January 1853;

On dira des bêtises, by Labiche, Delacour, and Raymond Deslandes, Paris, Théâtre des Variétés, 11 February 1853;

Un Notaire à marier, by Labiche, Marc-Michel, and Arthur de Beauplan, Paris, Théâtre des Variétés, 19 March 1853;

Un Ut de poitrine, by Labiche and Lefranc, Paris, Théâtre du Palais Royal, 2 May 1853;

La Chasse aux corbeaux, by Labiche and Marc-Michel, Paris, Théâtre du Palais Royal, 25 June 1853;

Un Feu de cheminée, by Labiche and Beauplan, Paris, Théâtre du Palais Royal, 31 July 1853;

Deux profonds scélérats, by Labiche and Varin, Paris, Théâtre du Palais Royal, 24 February 1854;

Un Mari qui prend du ventre, by Labiche and Marc-Michel, Paris, Théâtre des Variétés, 8 April 1854;

Espagnolas et Boyardinos, by Labiche and Marc-Michel, Paris, Théâtre du Palais Royal, 7 June 1854;

Les Marquises de la fourchette, by Labiche and Choler, Paris, Théâtre du Vaudeville, 31 August 1854;

Otez votre fille, s'il vous plaît, by Labiche and Marc-Michel, Paris, Théâtre du Palais Royal, 24 November 1854;

La Perle de la Canebière, by Labiche and Marc-Michel, Paris, Théâtre du Palais Royal, 10 February 1855;

Monsieur votre fille, by Labiche and Marc-Michel, Paris, Théâtre du Vaudeville, 2 March 1855;

Les précieux, by Labiche, Marc-Michel, and Lefranc, Paris, Théâtre du Palais Royal, 7 August 1855;

Les Cheveux de ma femme, by Labiche and Léon Battu, Paris, Théâtre des Variétés, 19 January 1856;

En Pension chez son groom, by Labiche and Marc-Michel, Paris, Théâtre du Palais Royal, 2 February 1856;

Monsieur de Saint-Cadenas, by Labiche and Marc-Michel, Paris, Théâtre du Palais Royal, 20 February 1856;

La Fiancée du bon coin, by Labiche and Marc-Michel, Paris, Théâtre du Palais Royal, 16 April 1856;

Si jamais je te pince!, by Labiche and Marc-Michel, Paris, Théâtre du Palais Royal, 9 May 1856;

Mesdames de Montenfriche, by Labiche and Marc-Michel, Paris, Théâtre du Palais Royal, 14 November 1856;

Un Monsieur qui a brûlé une dame, by Labiche and Anicet-Bourgeois, Paris, Théâtre du Palais Royal, 29 November 1856;

Le Bras d'Ernest, by Labiche and Hippolye Leroux, Paris, Théâtre du Palais Royal, 26 January 1857;

L'Affaire de la rue de Lourcine, by Labiche, Monnier, and Edouard Martin, Paris, Théâtre du Palais Royal, 26 March 1857;

La Dame aux jambes d'azur, by Labiche and Marc-Michel, Paris, Théâtre du Palais Royal, 11 April 1857;

Les Noces de Bouchencoeur, by Labiche, Monnier, and Martin, Paris, Théâtre du Palais Royal, 10 June 1857;

Le Secrétaire de Madame, by Labiche and Marc-Michel, Paris, Théâtre du Palais Royal, 5 October 1857;

Un Gendre en surveillance, by Labiche and Marc-Michel, Paris, Théâtre du Gymnase, 11 December 1857;

Je Croque ma tante, by Labiche and Marc-Michel, Paris, Théâtre du Palais Royal, 14 February 1858;

Le Clou aux maris, by Labiche and Eugène Moreau, Paris, Théâtre du Palais Royal, 1 April 1858;

L'Avare en gants jaunes, by Labiche and Anicet-Bourgeois, Paris, Théâtre du Palais Royal, 1 May 1858;

Deux merles blancs, by Labiche and Delacour, Paris, Théâtre des Variétés, 12 May 1858;

Madame est aux eaux, by Labiche and Vilmar (pseudonym of Philippe de Marville), Paris, Théâtre du Palais Royal, 30 June 1858;

Le Grain de café, by Labiche and Marc-Michel, Paris, Théâtre du Palais Royal, 3 November 1858;

Le Calife de la rue Saint-Bon, Scènes de la vie turque, mêlées de couplets, by Labiche and Marc-Michel, music by Sylvain Mangeant, Paris, Théâtre du Palais Royal, 7 December 1858;

En avant les Chinois! Revue de 1858, by Labiche and Delacour, Paris, Théâtre du Palais Royal, 24 December 1858;

L'Avocat d'un grec, by Labiche and Lefranc, Paris, Théâtre du Palais Royal, 9 January 1859;

L'Amour, un fort volume, prix 3F50-c, by Labiche and Martin, Paris, Théâtre du Palais Royal, 16 March 1859;

L'Ecole des Arthur, by Labiche and Anicet-Bourgeois, Paris, Théâtre des Variétés, 30 April 1859;

L'Omelette à la Follembuche, by Labiche and Marc-Michel, Paris, Théâtre des Bouffes-Parisiens, 8 June 1859;

Le Baron de Fourchevif, by Labiche and Jolly, Paris, Théâtre du Gymnase, 18 June 1859;

Les Petites Mains, by Labiche and Martin, Paris, Théâtre du Vaudeville, 28 November 1859;

Voyage autour de ma marmite, by Labiche and Delacour, Paris, Théâtre du Palais Royal, 29 November 1859;

Le Rouge-gorge, by Labiche and Choler, Paris, Théâtre du Vaudeville, 9 December 1859;

J'invite le colonel!, by Labiche and Marc-Michel, Paris, Théâtre du Palais Royal, 16 January 1860;

La Sensitive, by Labiche and Delacour, Paris, Théâtre du Palais Royal, 10 March 1860;

Les Deux Timides, by Labiche and Marc-Michel, Paris, Théâtre du Gymnase, 16 March 1860;

Le Voyage de M. Perrichon, by Labiche and Martin, Paris, Théâtre du Gymnase, 10 September 1860;

La Famille de l'horloger, by Labiche and Raimond Deslande (Raymond Deslandes), Paris, Théâtre du Palais Royal, 29 September 1860;

Un Gros Mot, by Labiche and Léon Dumoustier, Paris, Théâtre du Palais Royal, 29 September 1860;

J'ai compromis ma femme, by Labiche and Delacour, Paris, Théâtre du Gymnase, 13 February 1861;

Les Vivacités du capitaine Tic, by Labiche and Martin, Paris, Théâtre du Vaudeville, 16 March 1861;

L'Amour en sabots, by Labiche and Delacour, music by J. Nargeot, Paris, Théâtre des Variétés, 3 April 1861;

Le Mystère de la rue Rousselet, by Labiche and Marc-Michel, Paris, Théâtre du Vaudeville, 6 May 1861;

La Poudre aux yeux, by Labiche and Martin, Paris, Théâtre du Gymnase, 19 October 1861;

La Station Champbaudet, by Labiche and Marc-Michel, Paris, Théâtre du Palais Royal, 7 March 1862;

Les Petits Oiseaux, by Labiche and Delacour, Paris, Théâtre du Vaudeville, 1 April 1862;

Le Premier Pas, by Labiche and Delacour, Paris, Théâtre du Gymnase, 15 May 1862;

Les 37 sous de M. Montaudoin, by Labiche and Martin, Paris, Théâtre du Palais Royal, 30 December 1862;

La Dame au petit chien, by Labiche and Dumoustier, Paris, Théâtre du Palais Royal, 6 February 1863;

Permettez, madame!, by Labiche and Delacour, Paris, Théâtre du Gymnase, 21 February 1863;

Célimare le bien-aimé, by Labiche and Delacour, Paris, Théâtre du Palais Royal, 27 February 1863;

La Commode de Victorine, by Labiche and Martin, Paris, Théâtre du Palais Royal, 23 December 1863;

La Cagnotte, by Labiche and Delacour, Paris, Théâtre du Palais Royal, 22 February 1864;

Moi, by Labiche and Martin, Comédie-Française, 21 March 1864;

Un Mari qui lance sa femme, by Labiche and Deslandes, Paris, Théâtre du Gymnase, 23 April 1864;

Le Point de mire, by Labiche and Delacour, Compiègne, Théâtre de la Cour, 4 December 1864;

Premier prix de piano, by Labiche and Delacour, Paris, Théâtre du Palais Royal, 8 May 1865;

L'Homme qui manque le coche, by Labiche and Delacour, Paris, Théâtre des Variétés, 31 October 1865;

La Bergère de la rue Monthabor, by Labiche and Delacour, Paris, Théâtre du Palais Royal, 1 December 1865;

Le Voyage en Chine, by Labiche and Delacour, music by Françoise Bazin, Paris, Théâtre de l'Opéra-Comique, 9 December 1865;

Un Pied dans le crime, by Labiche and Choler, Paris, Théâtre du Palais Royal, 21 August 1866;

Le Fils du brigadier, by Labiche and Delacour, music by Victor Massé, Paris, Théâtre de l'Opéra-Comique, 25 February 1867;

La Grammaire, by Labiche and Jolly, Paris, Théâtre du Palais Royal, 28 July 1867;

La Main leste, by Labiche and Martin, Paris, Théâtre des Bouffes-Parisiens, 6 September 1867;

Les Chemins de fer, by Labiche, Delacour, and Choler, Paris, Théâtre du Palais Royal, 25 November 1867;

Le Papa du prix d'honneur, by Labiche and Théodore Barrière, Paris, Théâtre du Palais Royal, 6 February 1868;

Le Corricolo, by Labiche and Delacour, music by Fernand Poise, Paris, Théâtre de l'Opéra-Comique, 27 November 1868;

Le Roi d'Amatibou, by Labiche and Edmond Cottinet, music by Hervé, Paris, Théâtre du Palais Royal, 27 November 1868;

Le Petit Voyage, Paris, Théâtre du Vaudeville, 1 December 1868;

Le Dossier de Rosafol, by Labiche and Delacour, Paris, Théâtre du Palais Royal, 20 March 1869;

Le Choix d'un gendre, by Labiche and Delacour, Paris, Théâtre du Vaudeville, 22 April 1869;

Le Plus Heureux des trois, by Labiche and Edmond Gondinet, Paris, Théâtre du Palais Royal, 11 January 1870;

Le Cachemire X.B.T., by Labiche and Eugène Nus, Paris, Théâtre du Vaudeville, 24 February 1870;

Le Livre bleu, by Labiche and Ernest Blum, Paris, Théâtre du Palais Royal, 15 July 1871;

L'Ennemie, by Labiche and Delacour, Paris, Théâtre du Vaudeville, 17 October 1871;

Il est de la police, by Labiche and Louis Leroy, Paris, Théâtre du Palais Royal, 7 May 1872;

La Mémorie d'Hortense, by Labiche and Delacour, Paris, Théâtre des Variétés, 15 November 1872;

Doit-on le dire?, by Labiche and Alfred Duru, Paris, Théâtre du Palais Royal, 20 December 1872;

29 degrés à l'ombre, Paris, Théâtre du Palais Royal, 9 April 1873;

Garanti dix ans, by Labiche and Philippe Gille, Paris, Théâtre des Variétés, 12 February 1874;

Brûlons Voltaire!, by Labiche and Leroy, Paris, Théâtre du Gymnase, 7 March 1874;

Madame est trop belle, by Labiche and Duru, Paris, Théâtre du Gymnase, 30 March 1874;

La Pièce de Chambertin, by Labiche and Jules Dufrenois, Paris, Théâtre du Palais Royal, 1 April 1874;

Les Samedis de Madame, by Labiche and Duru, Paris, Théâtre du Palais Royal, 15 September 1874;

Les Trente Millions de Gladiator, by Labiche and Gille, Paris, Théâtre des Variétés, 22 January 1875;

Un Mouton à l'entresol, by Labiche and Albéric Second, Paris, Théâtre du Palais Royal, 30 April 1875;

La Guigne, by Labiche, Eugène Leterrier, and Albert Vanloo, Paris, Théâtre des Variétés, 27 August 1875;

Le Prix Martin, by Labiche and Emile Augier, Paris, Théâtre du Palais Royal, 5 February 1876;

Le Roi dort, by Labiche and Delacour, Paris, Théâtre des Variétés, 31 March 1876;

La Cigale chez les fourmis, by Labiche and Ernest Legouvé, Comédie Française, 23 May 1876;

La Clé, by Labiche and Duru, Paris, Théâtre du Palais Royal, 5 January 1877; three-act version, Paris, Théâtre du Palais Royal, 1877.

BOOKS: *M. de Coyllin ou l'homme infiniment poli,* by Labiche, Marc-Michel, and August Lefranc (Paris: Marchant, 1838);

L'Avocat Loubet, by Labiche, Lefranc, and Marc-Michel (Paris: Musée dramatique L. Michaud, 1838);

La Clef des champs (Paris: Gabriel Roux, 1839);

L'Article 960 ou la donation, by Jacque-Arsène Ancelot and Paul Dandré (Paris: Marchant, 1839);

Le Fin mot, by Dandré (Paris: Marchant, 1840);

Bocquet père et fils ou le chemin le plus long, by Labiche, Paul Laurencin, and Marc-Michel (Paris: Marchant, 1840);

Le Lierre et l'ormeau, by Labiche, Lefranc, and Albert Monnier (Paris: Beck, 1840);

Les Circonstances atténuantes, by Labiche, Charles Mélesville, and Lefranc (Paris: Beck, 1842);

L'Homme de paille, by Labiche and Lefranc (Paris: Beck, 1843);

Le Major Cravachon, by Labiche, Lefranc, and Paul Jessé (Paris: Beck, 1844);

Deux papas très-bien ou la grammaire de chicard, by Labiche and Lefranc (Paris: Beck, 1844);

Le Roi des Frontins, by Labiche and Lefranc (Paris: Beck, 1845);

L'Enfant de la maison, by Labiche, Charles Varin, and Eugène Nyon (Paris: Beck, 1845);

Mademoiselle ma femme, by Labiche and Lefranc (Paris: Beck, 1846);

Rocambolle le bateleur, by Labiche and Lefranc (Paris: Michel Lévy frères, 1846);

Frisette, by Labiche and Lefranc (Paris: Michel Lévy frères, 1846);

L'Avocat pédicure, by Labiche, Gustave Albitte, and Lefranc (Paris: Beck, 1847);

La Chasse aux jobards, by Labiche and Lefranc (Paris: Beck, 1847);

Un Homme sanguin, by Labiche and Lefranc (Paris: Beck, 1847);

L'Art de ne pas donner d'étrennes, by Labiche and Lefranc (Paris: Beck, 1847);

Un Jeune Homme pressé (Paris: Michel Lévy, 1848);

Le Club champenois, by Labiche and Lefranc (Paris: Beck, 1848);

Oscar XXVIII, by Labiche, Adrien Decourcelle, and Jules Barbier (Paris: Beck, 1848);

Une Chaîne anglaise, by Labiche and Saint-Yves (Paris: Beck, 1848);

Histoire du rire, by Labiche and Saint-Yves (Paris: Beck, 1848);

Agénor le dangereux, by Labiche, Decourcelle, and Karl (Paris: Beck, 1848);

A Bas la famille ou les banquets, by Labiche and Lefranc (Paris: Beck, 1848);

Madame veuve Larifla, by Labiche and Adolphe Choler (Paris: Beck, 1849);

Les Manchettes d'un vilain, by Labiche, Lefranc, and Saint-Yves (Paris: Beck, 1849);

Une Dent sous Louis XV, by Labiche and Lefranc (Paris: Michel Lévy frères, 1849);

Trompe-la-balle, by Labiche and Lefranc (Paris: Beck, 1849);

Exposition des produits de la République, by Labiche, P.-F. Dumanoir, and Louis Clairville (Paris: Michel Lévy, 1849);

Rue de l'Homme-armé no 8 bis, by Labiche and Eugène Nyon (Paris: Beck, 1849);

Embrassons-nous, Folleville, by Labiche and Lefranc (Paris: Michel Lévy frères, 1850);

Traversin et couverture, parody of *Toussaint Louverture,* by Labiche and Charles Varin (Paris: Michel Lévy, 1850);

Un Garçon de chez Véry (Paris: Michel Lévy, 1850);

Le Sopha, preceded by *Schahabaham XCIV,* by Labiche, Mélesville, and Charles Desnoyer (Paris: Michel Lévy frères, 1850);

La Fille bien gardée, by Labiche and Marc-Michel (Paris: Beck, 1850);

Un Bal en robe de chambre, by Labiche and Marc-Michel (Paris: Beck, 1850);

Les Petits Moyens, by Labiche, Gustave Lemoine, and Decourcelle (Paris: Beck, 1850);

Les Prétendus de Gimblette, by Labiche, Dandré, and Senneif (Charles Matharel de Fiennes) (Paris: Michel Lévy frères, 1850);

Une Clarinette qui passe, by Labiche and Marc-Michel (Paris: Michel Lévy frères, 1851);

La Femme qui perd ses jarretières, by Labiche and Marc-Michel (Paris: Michel Lévy frères, 1851);

On demande des culottières, by Labiche and Marc-Michel (Paris: Michel Lévy frères, 1851);

Mam'zelle fait ses dents, by Labiche and Marc-Michel, (Paris: Beck, 1851);

En Manches de chemise, by Labiche, Lefranc, and Nyon (Paris: Michel Lévy frères, 1851);

Un Chapeau de paille d'Italie, by Labiche and Marc-Michel (Paris: Michel Lévy frères, 1851); translated by William Schwenk Gilbert as *The Wedding March* (London: S. French, 1873);

Maman Sabouleux, by Labiche and Marc-Michel (Paris: Michel Lévy frères, 1852);

Un Monsieur qui prend la mouche, by Labiche and Marc-Michel (Paris: Michel Lévy frères, 1852);

Soufflez-moi dans l'oeil, by Labiche and Marc-Michel (Paris: Michel Lévy frères, 1852);

Les Suites d'un premier lit, by Labiche and Marc-Michel (Paris: Michel Lévy frères, 1852);

Le Misanthrope et l'Auvergnat, by Labiche, P.-M. Lubize, and Paul Siraudin (Paris: Michel Lévy frères, 1852);

Deux Gouttes d'eau, by Labiche and Auguste Anicet-Bourgeois (Paris: Michel Lévy, 1852);

Piccolet, by Labiche, Lefranc, and Montjoie (Paris: Michel Lévy frères, 1852);

Edgard et sa bonne, by Labiche and Marc-Michel (Paris: Michel Lévy frères, 1852);

Le Chevalier des dames, by Labiche and Marc-Michel (Paris: Michel Lévy frères, 1852);

Mon Isménie, by Labiche and Marc-Michel (Paris: Michel Lévy frères, 1852);

Une Charge de cavalerie, by Labiche, Eugène Moreau, and Alfred Delacour (Paris: Michel Lévy frères, 1852);

Un Ami acharné, by Labiche and Alphonse Jolly (Paris: Michel Lévy frères, 1853);

On dira des bêtises, by Labiche, Delacour, and Raymond Deslandes (Paris: Beck, 1853);

Un Notaire à marier, by Labiche, Marc-Michel, and Aurthur de Beauplan (Paris: Michel Lévy frères, 1853);

Un Ut de poitrine, by Labiche and Lefranc (Paris: Michel Lévy frères, 1853);

La Chasse aux corbeaux, by Labiche and Marc-Michel (Paris: Michel Lévy frères, 1853);

Un Feu de cheminée, by Labiche and Beauplan (Paris: Michel Lévy frères, 1853);

Deux profonds scélérats, by Labiche and Varin (Paris: Michel Lévy frères, 1854); translated by T. W. Robertson and T. H. Lacy as *Two Gay Deceivers; or, Black, White and Grey* (London: T. H. Lacy, 18—); translated by Robertson (New York: De Witt, [n.d.]);

Un Mari qui prend du ventre, by Labiche and Marc-Michel (Paris: Michel Lévy frères, 1854);

Espagnolas et Boyardinos, by Labiche and Marc-Michel (Paris: Michel Lévy frères, 1854);

Les Marquises de la Fourchette, by Labiche and Choler (Paris: Michel Lévy frères, 1854);

Otez votre fille, s'il vous plaît, by Labiche and Marc-Michel (Paris: Michel Lévy frères, 1854);

La Perle de la Canebière, by Labiche and Marc-Michel (Paris: Michel Lévy frères, 1855);

Monsieur votre fille, by Labiche and Marc-Michel (Paris: Michel Lévy frères, 1855);

Les Précieux, by Labiche, Marc-Michel, and Lefranc (Paris: Michel Lévy frères, 1855);

Les Cheveux de ma femme, by Labiche and Léon Battu (Paris: Michel Lévy frères, 1856);

En Pension chez son groom, by Labiche and Marc-Michel (Paris: Michel Lévy frères, 1856);

Monsieur de Saint-Cadenas, by Labiche and Marc-Michel (Paris: Michel Lévy frères, 1856);

La Fiancée du bon coin, by Labiche and Marc-Michel (Paris: Michel Lévy frères, 1856);

Si jamais je te pince!, by Labiche and Marc-Michel (Paris: Michel Lévy frères, 1856);

Mesdames de Montenfriche, by Labiche and Marc-Michel (Paris: Michel Lévy frères, 1856);

Un Monsieur qui a brûlé une dame, by Labiche and Anicet-Bourgeois (Paris: Michel Lévy frères, 1856);

Le Bras d'Ernest, by Labiche and Hippolye Leroux (Paris: Michel Lévy frères, 1857);

L'Affaire de la rue de Lourcine, by Labiche, Monnier, and Edouard Martin (Paris: Michel Lévy frères, 1857);

La Dame aux jambes d'azur, by Labiche and Marc-Michel (Paris: Michel Lévy frères, 1857);

Les Noces de Bouchencoeur, by Labiche, Monnier, and Martin (Paris: Michel Lévy frères, 1857);

Le Secrétaire de Madame, by Labiche and Marc-Michel (Paris: Michel Lévy frères, 1857);

Un Gendre en surveillance, by Labiche and Marc-Michel (Paris: Michel Lévy frères, 1857);

Je croque ma tante, by Labiche and Marc-Michel (Paris: Michel Lévy frères, 1858);

Le Clou aux maris, by Labiche and Moreau (Paris: Michel Lévy frères, 1858);

L'Avare en gants jaunes, by Labiche and Anicet-Bourgeois (Paris: Michel Lévy frères, 1858);

Deux merles blancs, by Labiche and Delacour (Paris: Michel Lévy frères, 1858);

Madame est aux eaux, by Labiche and Vilmar (Philippe de Marville) (Paris: Michel Lévy frères, 1858);

Le Calife de la rue Saint-Bon, by Labiche and Marc-Michel, music by Sylvain Mangeant (Paris: Charlieu, 1858);

En Avant les Chinois! Revue de 1858, by Labiche and Delacour (Paris: Librairie nouvelle, A. Bourdilliat et Cie, 1858);

L'Avocat d'un grec, by Labiche and Lefranc (Paris: Librairie nouvelle, A. Bourdilliat et Cie, 1859);

L'Amour, un fort volume, prix 3F50-c, by Labiche and Martin (Paris: Librairie nouvelle, 1859);

L'Ecole des Arthur, by Labiche and Anicet-Bourgeois (Paris: Michel Lévy frères, 1859);

L'Omelette à la Follembuche, by Labiche and Marc-Michel (Paris: Librairie théâtrale, 1859);

Le Baron de Fourchevif, by Labiche and Jolly (Paris: Tresse, 1859);

Les Petites Mains, by Labiche and Martin (Paris: Librairie nouvelle, 1859);

Voyage autour de ma marmite, by Labiche and Delacour (Paris: Michel Lévy frères, 1859);

Le Rouge-gorge, by Labiche and Choler (Paris: Librairie théâtrale, 1859);

J'invite le colonel!, by Labiche and Marc-Michel (Paris: Michel Lévy frères, 1860);

La Sensitive, by Labiche and Delacour (Paris: Michel Lévy frères, 1860);

Les Deux Timides, by Labiche and Marc-Michel (Paris: Michel Lévy frères, 1860); translated by Julian Magnus as *A Trumped Suite, Comedy in One Act for 3 Males and 2 Females,* in *Comedies for Amateur Acting,* edited by J. B. Matthews (New York, 1880); translated by Barrett H. Clark as *The Two Cowards: A Comedy in One Act* (New York: S. French, [1915]);

Le Voyage de M. Perrichon, by Labiche and Martin (Paris: Librairie nouvelle, 1860); translated by Matthew (H) and (ATHOL) as *Mont Blanc, A Comedy . . . Part of the plot derived from "Le Voyage de M. Perrichon* (n.p., n.d.); translated by Herman Charles Merivale as *Peacock's Holiday: A Farcical Comedy in Two Acts Founded on the "Voyage de M. Perrichon"* (London: S. French, 187–[?]);

La Famille de l'horloger, by Labiche and Deslande (Paris: Librairie nouvelle, 1860);

Un Gros Mot, by Labiche and Léon Dumoustier (Paris: Michel Lévy frères, 1860);

J'ai compromis ma femme, by Labiche and Delacour (Paris: Michel Lévy frères, 1861);

Les Vivacités du capitaine Tic, by Labiche and Martin (Paris: Michel Lévy frères, 1861);

L'Amour en sabots, by Labiche and Delacour, music by J. Nargeot (Paris: Michel Lévy frères, 1861);

Le Mystère de la rue Rousselet, by Labiche and Marc-Michel (Paris: Librairie nouvelle, 1861);

La Poudre aux yeux, by Labiche and Martin (Paris: Michel Lévy frères, 1861); translated by R. M. George as *The Bluffers or Dust in the Eyes* (New York & London: S. French, 1912[?]);

La Station Champbaudet, by Labiche and Marc-Michel (Paris: Michel Lévy frères, 1862);

Les Petits Oiseaux, by Labiche and Delacour (Paris: Dentu, 1862); translated by Horace W. Fuller as *Bad Advice* (N.p., 187?); translated by S. Grundy as *A Pair of Spectacles, A Comedy in Three Acts* (London: Lacy, 1899);

Le Premier Pas, by Labiche and Delacour (Paris: Dentu, 1862);

Les 37 sous de M. Montaudoin, by Labiche and Martin, (Paris: Dentu, 1862);

La Dame au petit chien, by Labiche and Dumoustier (Paris: Dentu, 1863);

Permettez, madame!, by Labiche and Delacour (Paris: Dentu, 1863);

Célimare le bien-aimé, by Labiche and Delacour (Paris: Dentu, 1863);

La Commode de Victorine, by Labiche and Martin (Paris: Dentu, 1863);

La Cagnotte, by Labiche and Delacour (Paris: Dentu, 1864);

Moi, by Labiche and Martin (Paris: Dentu, 1864);

Un Mari qui lance sa femme, by Labiche and Deslandes (Paris: Dentu, 1864);

Le Point de mire, by Labiche and Delacour (Paris: Dentu, 1864);

Premier prix de piano, by Labiche and Delacour (Paris: Dentu, 1865);

L'Homme qui manque le coche, by Labiche and Delacour (Paris: Dentu, 1865);

La Bergère de la rue Monthabor, by Labiche and Delacour (Paris: Dentu, 1865);

Le Voyage en Chine, by Labiche and Delacour, music by Françoise Bazin (Paris: Dentu, 1865);

Un Pied dans le crime, by Labiche and Choler (Paris: Dentu, 1866);

Le Fils du brigadier, by Labiche and Delacour, music by Victor Massé (Paris: Librairie dramatique, 10, rue de la Bourse, 1867);

La Grammaire, by Labiche and Jolly (Paris: Dentu, 1867); translated by F. Berger as *La grammaire, Comédie par E. Labiche et A. Jolly (pseud.)* (New York: Appleton, 1883); translated by Clark as *Grammar: A Comedy in One Act* (New York: S. French, 1915);

La Main Leste, by Labiche and Martin (Paris: Dentu, 1867); adapted and translated into English by Norman R. Shapiro as *A Slap in the Farce,* in *A Slap in the Farce & A Matter of Wife and Death,* edited by Shapiro (New York: Applause Theatre Book Publishers, 1988);

Les Chemins de fer, by Labiche, Delacour, and Choler (Paris: Dentu, 1867);

Le Papa du prix d'honneur, by Labiche and Théodore Barrière (Paris: Michel Lévy frères, 1868);

Le Corricolo, by Labiche and Delacour, music by Fernand Poise (Paris: Librairie dramatique, 1868);

Le Petit Voyage (Paris: Dentu, 1868);

Le Dossier de Rosafol, by Labiche and Delacour (Paris: Librairie dramatique, 1869);

Le Choix d'un gendre, by Labiche and Delacour (Paris: Dentu, 1869);

Le Plus Heureux des trois, by Labiche and Edmond Gondinet (Paris: Dentu, 1870); translated by Frederick Davies as *The Happiest of the Three,* in *Three French Farces* (Harmondsworth, U.K.: Penguin, 1973);

Le Cachemire X.B.T., by Labiche and Eugène Nus (Paris: Dentu, 1870);

Le Livre bleu, by Labiche and Ernest Blum (Paris: Dentu, 1871);

L'Ennemie, by Labiche and Delacour (Paris: Dentu, 1871);

Il est de la police, by Labiche and Louis Leroy (Paris: Dentu, 1872);

La Mémorie d'Hortense, by Labiche and Delacour (Paris: Dentu, 1872);

Doit-on le dire?, by Labiche and Alfred Duru (Paris: Dentu, 1872);

29 degrés à l'ombre (Paris: Dentu, 1873); translated by Emanuel Wax as *90° in the Shade: A Play in One Act* (London: S. French, 1962);

Garanti dix ans, by Labiche and Philippe Gille (Paris: Dentu, 1874);

Brûlons Voltaire!, by Labiche and Leroy (Paris: Dentu, 1874);

Madame est trop belle, by Labiche and Duru (Paris: Dentu, 1874);

La Pièce de Chambertin, by Labiche and Jules Dufrenois (Paris: Dentu, 1874);

Les Samedis de Madame, by Labiche and Duru (Paris: Dentu, 1874);

Les Trente Millions de Gladiator, by Labiche and Gille (Paris: Dentu, 1875);

Un Mouton à l'entresol, by Labiche and Albéric Second (Paris: Dentu, 1875);

Le Prix Martin, by Labiche and Emile Augier (Paris: Dentu, 1876);

La Cigale chez les fourmis, by Labiche and Ernest Legouvé (Paris: Dentu, 1876); translated by Anna Louise Barney as *The Grasshopper at the Home of the Ants* (San Francisco: Banner Play Bureau, 1930[?]);

La Clé, by Labiche and Duru (Paris: Dentu, 1877); translated as *Artful Cards, a Translation as the Act Directs of a Clé, Comedy in Four Acts and in Prose* (London: 1877);

La Lettre chargée, in *Théâtre de campagne,* second series (Paris: Ollendorff, 1877); adapted and translated by Shapiro as *A Matter of Wife and Death,* in *A Slap in the Farce & A Matter of Wife and Death*;

L'Amour de l'art, in *Théâtre de campagne,* fourth series (Paris: Ollendorff, 1878).

Editions and Collections: *Théâtre complet,* 10 volumes, preface by Emile Augier (Paris: Calmann-Lévy, 1878–1879);

Un Coup de rasoir, in *Saynètes et monologues,* third series (Paris: Tresse, 1881);

Oeuvres complètes de Labiche, 8 volumes, preface by Marcel Achard, edited and annotated by Gilbert Sigaux (Paris: Club de l'Honnête Homme, 1966);

Une Tragédie chez M. Grassot, by Labiche and Auguste Lefranc, in *Oeuvres complètes de Labiche,* volume 2 (Paris: Club de l'Honnête Homme, 1966), pp. 93–96;

Le Grain de café, by Labiche and Marc-Michel, in *Oeuvres complètes de Labiche,* 5 (Paris: Club de l'Honnête Homme, 1966), pp. 94–126;

Eugène Labiche, Théâtre, 2 volumes, edited and annotated by J. Robichez (Paris: Robert Laffont, 1991);

Labiche, Théâtre, 3 volumes, introduction, chronology, bibliography, and notes by Henry Gidel, "Les Classiques Garnier" (Paris: Bordas, 1991–1992).

Considered by some the master of the "well-made play," by others the precursor of Surrealism and the Theater of the Absurd, Eugène Labiche was one of the great innovators of vaudeville theater. The son of a wealthy industrialist, Jacques-Philippe-Marin Labiche, Eugène-Marin Labiche was born in Paris on 6 May 1815. Labiche began his writing career as did many young men of his century—by studying law in Paris. Although he obtained his degree from the Ecole de Droit, he never practiced law. His earliest publications—souvenirs of his travels in Italy and Switzerland, short stories, and theater reviews—date back to 1834 when he began writing for *Chérubin,* the *Revue de France,* and the *Revue du théâtre.* With Auguste Lefranc, Marc-Michel, Albéric Second (all of whom later collaborated with Labiche on many plays), Edouard Thierry (future administrator of the Comédie-Française), A. Seville, J. Belin, and G. d'Avrigny, Labiche wrote a novel, *Le Bec dans l'eau* (High and Dry), which was published serially in *La Revue du théâtre* from July to September 1837. His début in theater came that same year with *La Cuvette d'eau* (The Washbasin), a play written in collaboration with Lefranc and Marc-Michel. It was probably produced at the Théâtre du Luxem-

bourg, but the play was not published; no manuscript is known; and neither Labiche nor his collaborators ever spoke of it later. The following year the same trio wrote *M. de Coyllin, ou L'Homme infiniment poli* (Mr. De Coyllin, or the Infinitely Polite Man), a vaudeville in one act performed at the Théâtre du Palais Royal in Paris.

Thus began a long and prolific career of successful collaboration. Of Labiche's 173 plays, many of which were one-acts, 166 were written with one or more of his 46 different collaborators. Marc-Michel and Lefranc were not only the first of Labiche's collaborators but also the most frequent—Marc-Michel for 48 plays and Lefranc for 36. Among his other principal collaborators were Alfred Delacour (25 plays), Edouard Martin (12 plays), Adolphe Choler (6 plays), and Albert Monnier (5 plays).

The role of these collaborators was certainly important, but it is difficult to define. Neither Lefranc nor Marc-Michel left any record of their work with Labiche, and Labiche himself, in his *Théâtre complet* (1878–1879), simply thanked those who had worked with him without naming them. The practice of collaboration was a common one in nineteenth century France—so common that, according to Henry Gidel in his preface to Labiche's *Un Chapeau de paille d'Italie* (An Italian Straw Hat, 1851; translated as *The Wedding March,* 1873), when one of the most celebrated vaudevillists of the century, Eugène Scribe, was elected to the Académie Française, one of his enemies exclaimed that it was not a chair he needed, but several benches. The theater public in the nineteenth century was much smaller than it is today; plays generally ran for shorter periods, and playwrights were constantly being pressured by theater directors to produce new plays. The mixed genre of vaudeville—which combined spoken passages with couplets (or "vaudevilles") sung by the actors to popular tunes of the day—further encouraged writers to work in collaboration.

The term *vaudeville* itself, according to the *Petit Robert,* comes from *Vaul de ville* (1507), an alteration of *vaudevire* (fifteenth century), "chanson de circonstance," and a Norman term, probably *vauder,* to turn, and *virer.* The *Encycopédie du spectacle* gives a slightly different origin: the term originally designates the songs of the "compagnons gallois" (the gallic journeymen) of the town of Vire, in Normandy, known by the name of "chansons des Vaux de Vire." Whatever its origin, the word appeared toward the end of the fifteenth century and designated popular songs that were transmitted orally and whose irreverent texts were often linked to current events. The genre grew rapidly and was extremely popular in the seventeenth century. Around the end of the seventeenth century, vaudeville made its appearance on the stage. Because the Comédie Française had a monopoly on tragedy and the Opéra on musical productions, other theaters had to specialize in mixed genres. Satirical songs naturally found their place in popular theater. The law of 1792, which granted more freedom to theaters, allowed this new genre called "comédie mêlée de couplets" (comedy mixed with couplets) or "comédie à vaudeville" (comedy with vaudevilles) to flourish, at the new Théâtre du Vaudeville, as well as at such theaters as the Palais Royal, the Variétés, and the Gymnase.

Along with popular tunes to which authors added their own verses, the genre was known for its comedy based on surprises, ambiguities, and *quiproquos* (misunderstandings). Complicity with the public was an essential ingredient. By about 1850 or 1860, however, the couplets and the music began to take a less dominant place. In the works of such authors as Pailleron, d'Ordonneau, and Georges Feydeau, for example, they disappear entirely from the genre although the term *vaudeville,* or *comédie-vaudeville,* continued to be used to designate any situational comedy.

Labiche's work is situated at this frontier although when he began writing he did so without any pretentions of being an innovator. He and his first collaborators, Lefranc and Marc-Michel, chose to write a vaudeville because it was the type of play that theater directors were most willing to accept. In fact, their play was accepted by the first director they approached, Charles Dormeuil at the Palais Royal. Encouraged by this early success, Labiche soon began to turn out several plays each year. His marriage in 1842 to Adèle Hubert did little to slow down his productivity. After the Revolution of 1848 and his defeat in the elections for the Assemblée Constituante, Labiche, a *républicain de la veille* (Republican of the day before, a term used to differentiate those who were Republicans before the 1848 Revolution from those who became Republicans after, mainly for opportunist reasons, and who were called *républicains du lendemain,* that is, Republicans of the day after), considered retiring to the countryside in Sologne. However, to buy the property where he intended to live he needed to write several successful plays. Between 1848 and 1852 Labiche wrote forty-four plays, among which was his first major success, *Un Chapeau de paille d'Italie,* first produced on 14 August 1851. In1853 Labiche

Caricature by Honoré Daumier of Labiche and Alphonse Jolly, who collaborated with Labiche on three plays (© Collection Viollet)

bought the château de Launoy at Souvigny, near Lamotte-Beuvron, in Loir-et-Cher, which included nine hundred hectares of land. For the remainder of his life he resided a part of the year at his country home, farming the land himself. The château still exists and has remained in Labiche's family.

Un Chapeau de paille d'Italie marked Labiche's first success at a full five-act play. His only other attempt, *Rue de l'homme-armé no 8 bis* (Street of the Armed Man, Number 8b, 1849), had been a failure. The director of the Palais Royal, Dormeuil, hesitated before accepting this new attempt and arranged for the play to open in August, at a time when theater crowds were generally small and a failure would not entail as great a financial loss as during the winter season. Neither Labiche nor Dormeuil were present for the opening, fearing an almost certain disaster. The play was, however, an immediate success and ran for seventy-seven performances (not three hundred, as has sometimes been claimed). For many critics it marked the creation of a new genre—a "vaudeville of movement" rather than situation, according to Francisque Sarcey, or a "vaudeville-nightmare," to quote René Clair.

Un Chapeau de paille d'Italie offers one of the best illustrations of Labiche's technique of the quiproquo. Linked in this play to the motifs of initiation and quest, the quiquopros place the audience in a position of knowing more than any of the characters, including the hero Fadinard himself. The action of the play is limited to one twenty-four-hour period—the day of Fadinard's wedding to Hélène Nonancourt, daughter of a rich nurseryman from Charentonneau. The initial object of Fadinard's quest is simply to enter into the "paradise in rosewood" he has prepared for his bride. Labiche places two obstacles in his path. The first is Fadinard's future father-in-law, Nonancourt, whom he calls a "porcupine" and who, at each obstacle or delay, threatens to call off the wedding and give his daughter to her cousin, Bobin. The second obstacle is an Italian straw hat that Fadinard's horse, Cocotte, ate earlier that day in the bois de Vincennes. The owner of the hat, Anaïs, and a man identified as her "cousin" Emile Tavernier, an army lieutenant, demand that Fadinard replace the hat with another exactly like it. Anaïs's husband is extremely jealous and is certain to imagine things if he sees her without her hat, so she and Emile decide to remain hidden in Fadinard's apartment. It is this situation that Fadinard must conceal from his father-in-law while, at the same time, procuring a new hat. The search for a straw hat thus replaces Fadinard's initial quest, constituting a series of quasi-initiation trials through which he must pass and mistakes he must expiate before he can become worthy of his bride.

Fadinard's mission takes him first to a milliner's boutique where the proprietor turns out to be his former mistress, Clara, whom he had abandoned six months earlier. His wedding guests, who have followed him with their eight hired carriages, soon arrive. For the rest of the play they follow Fadinard everywhere, seeing in each of the various places his quest takes him another stage in the normal course of events of a wedding day. The dual nature of Fadinard's quest thus imposes a duality on the places he visits. The milliner's boutique becomes the mayor's office for the wedding guests, and they take the store clerk, Tardiveau, who appears with an order of tri-colored sashes, for the mayor. The clerk, on the other hand, supposes that they are a group from the provinces and tries to take their order. As his guests, like a parody of a Greek chorus, follow Tardiveau around the boutique, Fadinard placates Clara by promising to marry her.

His search next leads Fadinard to the salon of a baronness to whom Clara had sold a hat similiar to the one eaten by Cocotte. The baronness, however, mistakes Fadinard for a celebrated Italian tenor, "Nisnardi of Bologne," who is known for his eccentric requests for objects such as shoes as payment for his services. Fadinard, who has managed to get married thanks to a traffic jam, has left his guests waiting in the courtyard. Believing that they are parked in front of the restaurant, the "Veau-quitête," where the wedding dinner is to take place, they make their way to the dining room and set about devouring the dinner intended for the baronness's guests. The baronness is quite willing to give her hat to Fadinard, thinking his request just another of the Italian tenor's eccentricities. It turns out, however, that the baronness has given away the hat Fadinard wants to her goddaughter, Madame de Beauperthuis. Upon learning this, Fadinard escapes, leaving his wedding guests to fend for themselves.

By the time Fadinard arrives at the home of Madame de Beauperthuis in act 4, it is ten o'clock at night. Her husband, who has been awaiting his wife's return since seven minutes to nine that morning, mistakes Fadinard for a thief and pursues him with a pistol in each pocket. Nonancourt and the other wedding guests, who have managed to follow Fadinard once again, believe that they have arrived at his apartment for the night. Nonancourt places the myrtle bush he has been carrying with him throughout the play in what he takes to be the nuptial chambers and makes a speech. When the guests realize that they are in the home of a complete stranger, Nonancourt decides to call off the wedding once again. In desperation Fadinard explains the entire situation to Beauperthuis, who realizes that the woman hidden in Fadinard's apartment is none other than his wife.

Instead of ending with the substitution of one thing for another, the play seems to conclude with a return to the point of departure and a reversal of the conventional function of the quiproquo. During four acts Fadinard has been attempting to replace the original hat with a different one but, in fact, all he has done is retrace the road that led this hat to the Bois de Vincennes and its unfortunate encounter with Cocotte. Pursued by Beauperthuis, who, by putting on Nonancourt's shoes, seems to have taken his place, Fadinard is now the one who runs after his wedding guests. He arrives only to discover them taking his wedding gifts out of the window of his apartment. The guests are arrested for robbery and thrown into jail, but not before the package containing the gift brought by Uncle Vézinet comes open,

Authorization by Labiche for an 1873 production of L'Affaire de la rue de Lourcine, first staged in Paris in 1857 (courtesy of the Lilly Library, Indiana University)

revealing an Italian straw hat, complete with poppies.

When he sees his wife with the hat, Beauperthuis has no choice but to believe her innocent. Nonancourt, who has learned the story from Fadinard's groom ("Ton groom nous a conté l'anecdote! . . . c'est beau, c'est chevalersque! c'est français!" [Your groom told us the anecdote! . . . It's beautiful, it's chivalrous! It's French!"]), decides to forgive Fadinard. He returns his daughter and the gifts to him. The wedding guests are released from jail; Anaïs and Beauperthuis return home; and Fadinard can at last invite his bride into the rosewood paradise that he has prepared for her.

As Michael Issacharoff has remarked, substitution is the principal motor of farce in general and of Labiche's plays in particular. In *Un Chapeau de paille d'Italie,* places, objects, and people are constantly taken for something other than what they are. A mannequin's head, for instance, suddenly becomes a bust of Marianne, the quasi-official symbol of

France. This chain of substitutions begins and ends with the hat itself. For, as Gidel noted, the entire plot is set in motion by the actions of Fadinard's horse, which mistook a straw hat for some hay, and is only resolved by a similar misunderstanding. Beauperthuis believes his wife's story because he takes the new hat she is wearing to be the same one with which she left home that morning.

Chance encounters and coincidences drive the plot forward, yet, at the same time, render it curiously static. Stories are begun, interrupted, and never finished. Like Uncle Vézinet, who is deaf and never understands anything, the characters all live in separate worlds, defined by the object of their personal quest. It is precisely the static nature of Fadinard's quest that prompted René Clair to call this play a nightmare vaudeville.

This combination of frantic yet static motion is repeated in many of Labiche's plays. In *La Cagnotte* (The Nest Egg, 1864), for example, a small troupe of provincials goes on an excursion to Paris to spend

Bust of Labiche by Daumier (© Collection Viollet)

Club), first produced on 8 June 1848. In this play Labiche takes the conventional plot structure of vaudeville, defined by Dadard in *Un Jeune Homme pressé* (A Young Man in a Hurry, 1848) as "l'art de faire dire *oni* an papa de la demoiselle qui disait *non* . . . " (the art of making the father of the daughter who says *no* say *yes*), and sets it during the elections of 1848. Pontcharrat, mayor of Vitry-le-Brûlé in the Champagne region and uncle of Henriette, plans to marry his niece to the local schoolteacher, Gindinet. Henriette, on the other hand, is in love with her cousin, Cassagnol, an actor. When his niece points out that he approves of everything the new government does, just as he did with the previous government, he replies "C'est mon devoir, je suis fonctionnaire" (It is my duty, I am a civil servant). Pontcharrat has been ordered by the proconsul to create a political club "pour propager les idées démocratiques" (to propagate democratic ideas) and is in danger of losing his position (and perhaps his head) if he does not succeed in holding a candidates meeting. Unfortunately, no one in the region is interested in the club, much less in becoming a candidate. In desperation he offers to marry his niece to whichever of her suitors can persuade the most candidates to come to the meeting. Cassagnol wins the day by playing the role of three different candidates—Jean-Louis, a worker; Grand-Bagout, an economist who is opposed to work; and Chauvinancourt, a renowned general under Napoleon Bonaparte who forgets that the new government is a republic and proclaims: "Vive l'Empereur!" (Long live the Emperor!). Pontcharrat's political career is thus saved, and Henriette can marry the man she loves.

Henri Meilhac, Labiche's successor at the Académie Française, claimed that there were no women in Labiche's plays and no love. Although neither women nor love are absent from his work, they are never the principal motors of the plot but serve more generally as the pretext that brings out the vanity, greed, or selfishness of the main characters. In *Le Voyage de M. Perrichon,* for example, it is because Daniel and Armand truly love Henriette and wish to marry her that they seek to gain favor with her father, Perrichon. Similarly, in *La Poudre aux yeux* (1861; translated as *The Bluffers or Dust in the Eyes,* 1912) Emmeline Malingear and Frédéric Ratinois hope that their parents will agree to their wedding. Difficulties arise when each family tries to impress the other by pretending to greater wealth and a higher social status than they have. Both fathers end up offering far more dowry than they can possibly afford to pay and are on the point of breaking off the engagement. It is only when Uncle Robert

the money they have collected by betting on card games. Once again, each member of the party has a different goal—one wants to buy a shovel; another is shopping for her wedding; two others have secret meetings with a marriage broker. They, too, are taken to be thieves and arrested but manage to escape and eventually return home, where they continue to argue about the best way to spend what remains of their nest egg. *Le Voyage de M. Perrichon* (The Voyage of Monsieur Perrichon, 1860) also ends where it began, with Perrichon embarking on another trip to Switzerland where he must make amends for an insult committed on his first trip.

Labiche mocks the bourgeoisie, yet even in his plays that deal with political issues (such as *Oscar XXVIII* [1848], or *A bas la famille, ou les banquets* [Down with the Family, or the Banquets, 1848]) he does not seek to undermine the social order. He ends his plays at their point of departure, thereby preserving the status quo. It is in fact the bourgeois penchant for the status quo that Labiche satirizes in plays such as *Le Club champenois* (The Champagne points out that the two families are sacrificing their children's happiness to their own vanity that they finally agree to stop posing and admit their true status.

As noted in the preface to *Oeuvres complètes de Labiche* (1966), Labiche's characters are almost exclusively bourgeois. They are generally seeking to marry off an only child, or are themselves an only child attempting to be married. Not as wealthy as characters in plays by Scribe, they are mainly parvenus and cowards who are self-centered and pretentious. Their main motivators are money, vanity, and selfishness. In *Un Jeune Homme pressé,* for instance, Pontbichet does not hesitate to renege on his promise to marry his daughter to her cousin Colardeau when a wealthier suitor appears on his doorstep one night. He justifies his action: "Je t'ai donné ma parole, mais je la reprends, comme tout galant homme doit le faire" (I gave you my word, but I take it back, as any gallant man should do). Nonetheless, these characters love their families and are relatively honest and only superficially mean. Labiche often juxtaposes the more mean-spirited of his characters with more-redeeming ones, such as Uncle Robert in *La Poudre aux yeux* or Blandinet in *Les Petits Oiseaux* (Little Birds, 1862; translated as *Bad Advice,* 187?) who, unlike his brother François, continues to believe it is better to close one's eyes and open one's heart than constantly to mistrust people. Generally these characters are able to make their point, and the plays end with a recognition of error and a promise to reform. Monsieur Perrichon, for example, realizes the dangers of his vanity when he overhears Armand explaining how he pretended to fall into a crevasse so that Perrichon could save him and then boast of his heroic action.

Comedies of situation generally leave little room for character development; nonetheless, Labiche manages to create characters who are more than simple marionnettes. For instance, the myrtle bush that Nonancourt carries with him—a bush that he planted the day Hélène was born—characterizes his pompous but genuine affection for his daughter, as much as his tight shoes signify his irascibility. Labiche's plays also contain much verbal humor derived from absurd logic. When Armand learns in *Le Voyage de M. Perrichon* that an employee of his company is deaf, he exclaims: "Tiens! Il est sourd, notre correspondant? C'est donc pour ça qu'il ne répond jamais à nos lettres" (So! our correspondent is deaf, is he? That must be why he never answers our letters). In the dialogue in *Un Chapeau,* where Fadinard explains that his mistress cannot come to his wedding because "elle est en deuil" (she is in mourning), his father-in-law replies "En robe rose?" (In a pink

dress?). Fadinard answers: "Oui, c'est de son mari" (Yes, it's for her husband). As these examples show, Labiche's plays seem at times to be pure Theater of the Absurd. The often intriguing titles (such as *Je croque ma tante* [I'm Munching My Aunt, 1858], *La Femme qui perd ses jarretières* [The Woman Who Loses Her Garters, 1851], or *J'ai compromis ma femme* [I Compromised My Wife, 1861]) present a riddle to spectators which the action often solves in surprising and humorous ways. It is, for example, not the aunt who is being eaten, but the inheritance she left.

Labiche continued to produce plays at a rate of several per year until 1877. After the failure of *La Clé* (The Key) in 1877, Labiche gave up writing for the theater and turned his attention to the publication of his *Théâtre complet,* containing 57 of his 173 plays, which he completed in 1879. Chevalier of the Légion d'honneur since 1861, Labiche was elected to the Académie Française in 1880, where he replaced Samuel Silvestre de Sacy. He did not entirely abandon politics after his defeat in the elections of 1848 and was later elected mayor of Souvigny, in Sologne. In 1870, during the Prussian occupation, he refused to leave his post, staying in order to protect his citizens, and was later commended for his bravery. In 1885 Labiche became ill, and on 22 January 1888 he died of heart disease at the age of sixty-seven at his home in Paris.

Although Labiche ceased to write for the theater after 1877, his plays continued to be produced. Between 1878 and 1914 not a month went by without at least one, and often several, appearing in theaters across Paris and in the provinces. Two of his plays were produced at the Comédie-Française during his lifetime (*Moi* [Me] in 1864 and *La Cigale chez les fourmis* [The Cicada at the Aunt's House] in 1876) and several later entered the repertoire, starting with the important revival of *Un Chapeau de paille en Italie* in 1938. Despite the advice of former minister of culture André Malraux, who was apparently horrified by the success of plays such as *Les Trente Millions de Gladiator* (Gladiator's Thirty Millions, 1875) and *La Poudre aux yeux* at the Comédie-Française and "recommended" they be withdrawn from the billboard as soon as possible, Labiche's plays continue to figure in the repertory of the Comédie-Française.

Letters:

A. Benet, "Eugène Labiche et la Commune de Paris. Deux lettres inédites," *Correspondance historique et archéologique* (1901);

Jean Montval, "Eugène Labiche débutant, auteur de la Comédie-Française et académicien. Lettres inédites," *Revue de France,* 2 (1918): 492–505;

Paul Blanchart, "Dix-neuf lettres inédites d'Eugène Labiche," *Revue d'Histoire du Théâtre,* 4 (1959);

Oeuvres complètes de Labiche, volume 8 (Paris: Club de l'Honnête Homme, 1966), pp. 363–396.

Biographies:

Jules Clarétie, *Eugène Labiche* (Paris: Quantin, 1883);

Phillipe Soupault, *Eugène Labiche: Sa vie, son oeuvre* (Paris: Sagittaire, 1945; revised and expanded edition, Paris: Mercure de France, 1964);

Emmanuel Haymann, *Labiche et l'esprit du Second Empire* (Paris: Olivier Orban, 1988).

References:

Jacqueline Autrusseau-Adamov, *Labiche et son théâtre* (Paris: L'Arche, 1971);

Fernande Bassan, "Eugène Labiche et la comédie de boulevard au XIXe siècle," *Cahiers de l'Association Internationale des Etudes françaises* (1991): 169–181;

Janice Best, "Quiproquos et mondes possibles dans *Un Chapeau de paille d'Italie," Nineteenth Century French Studies,* 19 (Summer 1991): 554–565;

Jean-Pierre Collinet, "Labiche et La Fontaine," *Travaux de Littérature,* 3 (1990): 191–202;

Michel Corvin, "La Ville-piège des bourgeois de Labiche," in *Paris au XIXe siècle: Aspects d'un mythe littéraire,* edited by Bellet-Roger (Lyon: Presses universitaires de Lyon, 1984), pp. 123–133;

Henry A. Garrity, "René Clair Interprets Labiche: Comic Language on the Silent Screen," *Proceedings of the Fifth Annual Conference on Film, Kent State University, April 7–8, 1987,* in *Transformations: From Literature to Film,* edited by Douglas Radcliff-Umstead (Kent, Ohio: Romance Languages Department, Kent State University, 1987), pp. 2–7;

Pierre Haffter, "Labiche et la rhétorique," *Revue d'Histoire du Théâtre,* 24 (1972): 46–57;

Haffter, "Les Noms des personnages de Labiche," *Revue d'Histoire du Théâtre,* 24 (1972): 58–66;

Michael Issacharoff, "Labiche et l'intertextualité comique," *Cahiers de l'Association Internationale des Etudes Françaises,* 35 (1983): 169–182;

Issacharoff, "Quand le référent est roi (*Un Chapeau de paille d'Italie*)," in *Le Spectacle du discours* (Paris: José Corti, 1985), pp. 129–139;

Francis L. Lawrence, *Le Misanthrope Reprised: Four Versions of Molière's Theme* (Jackson: University Press of Mississippi, 1975);

Linda Klieger Stillman, "The Absent Structure of Farce: Ça biche," *Romantic Review,* 76 (November 1985): 405–414.

Papers:

The papers of Eugène Labiche can be found in several different collections: those of the family of Eugène Labiche, of the Bibliothèque de la Comédie-Française, the Bibliothèque de l'Arsenal, the Bibliothèque Nationale, and the Archives Nationales, all in Paris.

Louis-Jean-Népomucène Lemercier

(21 April 1771 – 7 June 1840)

Barbara T. Cooper
University of New Hampshire

PLAY PRODUCTIONS: *Méléagre,* Paris, Théâtre-Français, 29 February 1788;

Clarisse Harlowe, Paris, Théâtre-Français, April 1792;

Le Tartuffe révolutionnaire, Paris, Théâtre Français de la République, 9 June 1795;

Le Lévite d'Ephraïm, Paris, Théâtre Français de la République, April 1796;

Agamemnon, Paris, Théâtre Français de la République, 24 April 1797;

La Prude, Paris, Théâtre Français de la République, 4 December 1797;

Ophis, Paris, Théâtre Français de la République, 23 December 1798;

Pinto, ou La Journée d'une conspiration, Paris, Théâtre Français de la République, 22 March 1800; Paris, Théâtre de la Porte Saint-Martin, 19 November 1834;

Isule et Orovèse, Paris, Théâtre-Français, 23 December 1802 (incomplete performance);

Plaute, ou La Comédie latine, Paris, Théâtre-Français, 20 January 1808;

Christophe Colomb, Paris, Théâtre de S. M. l'Impératrice [Théâtre de l'Odéon], 7 March 1809;

Charlemagne, Paris, Théâtre-Français, 29 June 1816;

Le Frère et la sœur jumeaux, Paris, Théâtre de l'Odéon, 7 November 1816;

Le Faux Bonhomme, Paris, Théâtre-Français, 25 January 1817 (incomplete performance);

Le Complot domestique, ou Le Maniaque supposé, Paris, Théâtre de l'Odéon, 16 June 1817;

Agar et Ismaël, ou L'Origine du peuple arabe, Paris, Théâtre de l'Odéon, 23 January 1818;

La Démence de Charles VI, Paris, Théâtre de l'Odéon, 25 September 1820 (banned prior to scheduled performance);

Frédégonde et Brunehaut, Paris, Second Théâtre-Français [Théâtre de l'Odéon], 27 March 1821;

Louis IX en Egypte, Paris, Second Théâtre-Français [Théâtre de l'Odéon], 5 August 1821;

Louis-Jean-Népomucène Lemercier

Le Corrupteur, Paris, Second Théâtre-Français [Théâtre de l'Odéon], 26 November 1822;

Richard III et Jeanne Shore, Paris, Théâtre-Français, 1 April 1824;

Camille, ou Le Capitole sauvé, Paris, Théâtre de l'Odéon, 3 December 1825;

Baudouin, empereur, Paris, Théâtre de l'Odéon, 9 August 1826;

Les Deux Filles spectres, Paris, Théâtre de la Porte Saint-Martin, 8 November 1827;

Clovis, Paris, Théâtre-Français, 7 January 1830;

Les Serfs polonais, Paris, Théâtre de l'Ambigu-Comique, 15 June 1830;

Richelieu, ou La Journée des dupes, Paris, Théâtre-Français, 16 March 1835;

L'Héroïne de Montpellier, Paris, Théâtre de la Porte Saint-Martin, 7 November 1835.

BOOKS: *Agamemnon* (Paris: Barba, 1797); revised editions (Paris: 1800, 1804, 1818);

Ophis (Paris: Fayolle, 1798);

Pinto, ou La Journée d'une conspiration (Paris: Huet, 1800);

Ismaël au désert, ou L'Origine du peuple arabe (Paris: Les Marchands de nouveautés, 1801); reprinted as *Agar et Ismaël, ou L'Origine du peuple arabe* (Paris: Nepveu, 1818);

Isule et Orovèse (Paris: Barba, 1803);

Plaute, ou La Comédie latine (Paris: L. Collin, 1808);

Baudouin, empereur (Paris: L. Collin, 1808);

Christophe Colomb (Paris: L. Collin, 1809);

Discours prononcé dans la séance publique tenue par la classe de la langue et de la littérature françaises de l'Institut de France, le 5 septembre 1810, pour la réception de M. Lemercier [texts by Lemercier and Merlin] (Paris: Baudouin, 1810);

Charlemagne (Paris: Barba, 1816);

Le Frère et la sœur jumeaux (Paris: Barba, 1816);

Le Complot domestique, ou Le Maniaque supposé (Paris: Barba, 1817);

Cours analytique de littérature générale, tel qu'il a été professé à l'Athénée de Paris, 4 volumes (Paris: Nepveu, 1817);

Le Faux Bonhomme (Paris: Barba, 1817);

Du Second Théâtre-Français, ou Instruction relative à la déclamation dramatique (Paris: Nepveu, 1818);

La Panhypocrisiade (Paris, 1819);

La Démence de Charles VI (Paris: Didot l'aîné, 1820);

Clovis (Paris: Baudouin frères–Barba, 1820);

Frédégonde et Brunehaut (Paris: Barba, 1821);

Louis IX en Egypte (Paris: Barba, 1821);

Le Corrupteur, précédé de Dame Censure (Paris: Barba, 1823);

Richard III et Jeanne Shore (Paris: Firmin-Didot, 1824);

Les Martyrs de Souli, ou l'Epire moderne (Paris: U. Canel, 1825);

Camille, ou Le Capitole sauvé (Paris: U. Canel, 1825);

Les Deux Filles spectres (Paris: Barba, 1827);

Comédies historiques, includes *Pinto, ou La Journée d'une conspiration; Richelieu, ou La Journée des dupes; L'Ostracisme, ou La Comédie grecque* (Paris: Dupont, 1828);

Caïn, ou Le Premier Meurtre (Paris: Constant-Chantpie, 1829);

Les Serfs polonais (Paris: R. Riga, 1830);

Alminti, ou le mariage sacrilège, roman physiologique (Paris, 1834);

L'Héroïne de Montpellier (Paris: Didot l'aîné, 1835);

Variantes sur le rôle de Christol, dans la tragédie Les Martyrs de Souli (Paris: Firmin-Didot, 1839).

OTHER: "Analyse raisonnée du théâtre de Chénier," in *Œuvres choisies de M.-J. de Chénier* (Paris: Baudouin, 1821), I: i–lxvii; preface in-

cludes parts of the "Analyse de Tibère" originally published in the *Revue encyclopédique* in 1819;

"Remarques sur les bonnes et mauvaises innovations dramatiques," *Revue encyclopédique*, 26 (April 1825): 26–40; published separately (Paris: Rignoux, 1825);

"Notice sur Talma, lue à l'Académie Française . . . ," *Revue encyclopédique*, 35 (August 1827): 289–310; published separately (Paris: Rignoux, 1827);

Principes et développements sur la nature de la propriété littéraire (Paris: Pillet aîné, 1826);

"Drame," in *Encyclopédie moderne, ou Dictionnaire abrégé des sciences, des lettres et des arts*, volume X, edited by Eustache Courtin (Paris: Mongie aîné, 1827), pp. 502–513.

An author, lecturer, journalist, and member of the French Academy, Louis-Jean-Népomucène Lemercier is barely remembered today, yet in his own time Lemercier's works were widely discussed and often sparked considerable controversy. Some of the ups and downs of the poet-playwright's career seem inseparable from early-nineteenth-century political and aesthetic upheavals and can best be understood in the context of that transitional period in French history and letters. Other impediments to his success appear to stem from Lemercier's misuse of his own talents.

A staunch defender of political liberties, Lemercier often found himself at odds with the Napoleonic and Bourbon regimes. He so strongly opposed the establishment of the empire, for example, that he returned his Legion of Honor medal on the eve of Napoleon I's coronation in 1804. Expressions of the dramatist's republican beliefs were not limited to such noteworthy acts, however. Denunciations of tyranny, political ambition, vice, and deceit can also be found in many of his writings. As a result government officials viewed Lemercier's theater pieces with suspicion and more often than not postponed, prohibited, or otherwise impeded their performance. The playwright responded by attacking his censors in works such as *Dame Censure* (Dame Censorship, 1823), a one-act tragicomedy not intended for the stage, and in a section of the preface to *Les Martyrs de Souli, ou l'Epire moderne* (The Martyrs of Souli, or Modern Epirea, 1825) titled "De l'ancienne liberté du théâtre" (On the Former Freedom of Drama).

But if Lemercier's politics were liberal, his literary convictions were decidedly conservative. In his public lectures on tragedy and comedy, published in 1817 as part of his *Cours analytique de littéra-*

Costume designs by Eugène Giraud for Lemercier's Frédégonde et Brunehaut *(Collection of the Comédie-Française)*

ture générale (Analytical Course on Literature), in articles such as his "Remarques sur les bonnes et mauvaises innovations dramatiques" (Remarks on Good and Bad Dramatic Innovations), published in the *Revue encyclopédique* in 1825, and in his dramatic parody, *Caïn, ou le Premier Meurtre* (Cain, or The First Murder), of 1829, Lemercier repeatedly heralded his opposition to Romanticism. The "Remarques," which Lemercier read at a meeting of the French Academy in April 1825, and his 1827 entry on "[Le] Drame" (Drama) in the *Encyclopédie moderne* underscore the playwright's firm rejection of foreign theatrical models, of prose tragedy, and of works that mix comic and tragic elements.

At times, however, Lemercier deliberately violated the very artistic principles he publicly espoused. His departures from the norms of French Neoclassical dramaturgy are most apparent in *Chris-*

tophe Colomb (Christopher Columbus, 1809) and in *Richard III et Jeanne Shore* (Richard III and Jane Shore, 1824), where he admitted to violating the unities of time and place and to adapting (but not adopting) a "Shakespearean" aesthetic. While these and other dramatic innovations shocked and outraged conservative critics, they struck other reviewers as unduly timid. In the end the playwright, who stubbornly refused the title of precursor some innovators wished to bestow upon him, found himself with few defenders in either the Romantic or the Neoclassical camps. Had he chosen to align his aesthetic practices with his liberal political beliefs and wholeheartedly embraced the cause of artistic "modernism," Lemercier might not only have made better use of his talents but might also have earned a more enduring place for himself in the pantheon of theatrical history.

Born in Paris on 21 April 1771 to Louis Lemercier and his wife, Marguerite-Ursule Pigory de Lavault, Louis-Jean-Népomucène Lemercier was baptized at the Church of Saint Eustache the following day. The baby's mother immediately sent him out to be wet-nursed and, when he returned to the family home, gave him over to the care of a governess-housekeeper. Later, Louis-Jean and his younger brother (who died while still a child) both attended the Collège de Lisieux, where they had their own private tutor. Lemercier also studied painting for a time with Jacques-Louis David but had to give up serious hopes of an artistic career because of the partial paralysis of his right arm that resulted from an accident when he was three or four years old.

At age sixteen Lemercier composed a five-act verse tragedy on a mythological subject, *Méléagre* (Meleagros, 1788), which he submitted to the reading committee of the Théâtre-Français. Finding it difficult to believe that the young man was the author of so polished a work, the committee members asked Lemercier to revise parts of the text on the spot, which he did. Finally persuaded that the play was indeed his, they accepted it for their repertory. Still, the work most likely would never have been produced were it not for the intervention of Lemercier's godmother, the princesse de Lamballe, who successfully urged Queen Marie-Antoinette to order its performance. Thus, on 29 February 1788 the youth was able to watch the production of his piece from a seat in the royal box and to receive the audience's accolades. He then withdrew the play, saying that he intended to revise it. While the text was never published or performed again, the work's single performance did help the adolescent author achieve a measure of celebrity and launched him in literary and salon society.

In April 1792 Lemercier's *Clarisse Harlowe*, a five-act verse drama based on Samuel Richardson's novel of 1748, was performed at the Théâtre-Français. In this work, sometimes called *Lovelace*, Richardson's infamous seducer, played by Fleury (Abraham-Joseph Bénard), used opium to have his way with his female victims. The success of the play, which was never printed, earned it a parody at the Théâtre du Vaudeville. Under repeated attack from novelist and playwright Louis-Sébastien Mercier, who worried that the similarity in their names might prompt an unfortunate confusion between them, the youthful dramatist began signing his works Népomucène rather than Louis-Jean Lemercier.

It was also during 1792 that Lemercier, whose family ranked among the minor nobility and whose connections to the aristocracy put him at some risk, decided to leave Paris for Bagnères-de-Bigorre, a small town in the Pyrenees where he hoped to escape the revolutionary turmoil. While there, he saved several nonjuring priests from mob violence and enabled them to cross into Spain unharmed. He then almost immediately began his return trip to Paris. En route he was briefly detained in Tours for refusing to drink to the death of aristocrats. After escaping from jail, he retreated to Etampes, and then to Maisons-Alfort, before returning to Paris in November 1794.

In June 1795 Lemercier's five-act verse comedy, *Le Tartuffe révolutionnaire* (The Revolutionary Tartuffe), was performed at the Théâtre Français de la République with Nicolas Anselme Baptiste in the title role. The play, modeled on Molière's comic denunciation of religious hypocrisy in *Le Tartuffe* (1664–1667), satirized the political charlatanism and terror of the day. Because it struck those in power as too true to life, *Le Tartuffe révolutionnaire* was banned from the stage after just five performances. The first of several of Lemercier's texts to suffer a similar fate, it was never published.

Lemercier's next dramatic production, *Le Lévite d'Ephraïm* (The Levite of Ephraim, 1796), was a three-act tragedy with a biblical subject and setting. Offering François-Joseph Talma his first starring role as the eponymous Levite (priest), the play, which may have been written as early as 1794, opened at the Théâtre Français de la République in April 1796. It marked the beginning of a long association between the actor and author. After a brief run the play was withdrawn from the repertory as a result of objections expressed by Maximilien Robespierre. Like Lemercier's previous plays, it was never published.

Lemercier's next piece, a five-act verse tragedy titled *Agamemnon,* was based on a more traditional subject: the assassination of the king of Argos by his wife, Clytemnestra, and her lover, Ægisthus. Performed at the Théâtre Français de la République in April 1797, with Talma in the role of Ægisthus, the twenty-six-year-old playwright's work was a great success and was later hailed by the French Academy as the best French tragedy in thirty years. It was revived on many occasions and was the first of Lemercier's dramas to be printed.

In *Agamemnon* Clytemnestra, who hates her husband for having sacrificed their daughter Iphegenia to the gods, has fallen in love with Ægisthus who, to avoid recognition, has taken to calling himself Plexippe. When Agamemnon finally returns from the Trojan Wars after a ten-year absence, the queen does not know what to do. Should she follow

Ægisthus, who, having revealed his true identity to Agamemnon, has been banished from Argos, or should she seek a reconciliation with her husband? Before she can decide, Ægisthus escapes from his guards and returns to her side. He persuades Clytemnestra to kill Agamemnon, telling her that he is motivated by love when in truth what he wants is to avenge his father's death and to become king of Greece. The queen does as she is asked but then is horrified by her crime and by Ægisthus's announcement that he means to have her son Orestes imprisoned. Warned by Cassandra, a Trojan priestess who arrived in Argos with Agamemnon, Orestes manages to escape before he can be arrested. Cassandra, who is subsequently poisoned by Ægisthus, dies after predicting that one day Orestes will return to punish the criminal couple.

In December 1797 Lemercier's next dramatic work, a five-act verse comedy titled *La Prude* (The Prude), was performed by the Comédie-Français with Mlle Louise Contat in the title role. In *La Prude* a libertine rapes a young woman and then abandons her. When he meets her again twenty years later, he fails to recognize his former victim and decides that the conquest of such a paragon of virtue is a challenge worthy of his skill. His efforts to overcome her resistance are forestalled when the woman's son, who as it happens is also his, forces him to marry her. The drama, which enjoyed a succès de scandale due to its depiction of contemporary manners and dress, had only a brief run. This time it was Lemercier who withdrew his work rather than make any changes to it. The piece was never published.

The portrait of the abandon, license, and excesses of Directory society offered in *La Prude* may well have been based on Lemercier's own observations of life in the salon of Joséphine de Beauharnais, whom the young dramatist soon convinced to marry his friend, Gen. Napoleon Bonaparte, and that of Thérésa de Cabarrus (later Mme Tallien). It was also in these salons that the young Népomucène met the poet Jacques Delille, playwright Marie-Joseph Chénier, and the novelist and naturalist Jacques-Henri Bernardin de Saint-Pierre, with whom he became friends.

Lemercier's next play, *Ophis,* a five-act verse tragedy set in ancient Egypt, opened at the Théâtre Français de la République in December 1798 and enjoyed a succès d'estime, in part because it coincided with Napoleon's military campaign in Egypt. The title role in that work was played by Auguste-Alexandre Damas; the role of his brother and rival, Tholus, was created by Talma. Like *Agamemnon, Ophis* features a character ambitious for power and willing to commit any crime to achieve his goal.

Here, however, the would-be usurper (Tholus) is set beside a legitimate monarch who agrees to pardon his antagonist and renounce the throne rather than provoke a civil war. Unfortunately, Ophis's generosity and abnegation do not have the desired effect; in the end both brothers die, and the country is plunged into chaos.

Questions of political legitimacy and insurrection are also at the heart of Lemercier's *Pinto, ou La Journée d'une conspiration* (Pinto, or The Day of a Conspiracy), which opened at the Théâtre Français de la République on 22 March 1800. The work, composed in a mere twenty-two days, was written in response to a challenge to prove that it was still possible to invent a new dramatic genre after Pierre-Augustin Caron de Beaumarchais's *Mariage de Figaro* (1784). A five-act historical comedy in prose, the play depicts the Portuguese struggle for independence from Spain. While serious, the subject is treated with a mixture of levity and solemnity; the characters are not uniformly noble, nor is their language.

The only one of Lemercier's dramas to have been reprinted in the twentieth century, *Pinto* is held to be the playwright's finest, most original work. It has been seen by some critics as a "proto-romantic" piece whose titular character (played by Talma) is often described as a successor to the Figaro of Beaumarchais's *Barbier de Séville* (1775) and the precursor of the eponymous hero of Victor Hugo's *Ruy Blas* (1838). This innovative piece, which later prompted Stendhal to declare "Notre nouvelle tragédie ressemblera beaucoup à Pinto, le chef-d'œuvre de M. Lemercier" (Our new [romantic] tragedy will strongly resemble Lemercier's masterpiece, *Pinto*), had only twenty performances before Napoleon, by then first consul and said to be displeased with the work's depiction of the restoration of a legitimate heir to the throne, granted multiple leaves of absence for its actors, thereby ending its run.

Pinto recounts the efforts of a lowborn man who is determined to reestablish his country's independence by orchestrating a revolt against a tyrannical foreign power. Secretary to the duc de Bragance, the patriotic Pinto must not only find the ways and means to overthrow the reigning Spanish government but must also persuade his employer, who is the heir to the Portuguese throne, to accept his birthright and rule over the country. Although not eager for power, the duke ultimately agrees to join the rebels. The conspirators—including the duke's ambitious wife, a lubricious monk, a wealthy Jew, a mute servant, and other comical collaborators—eventually prevail, thanks in part to the unwitting support of Pinto's vivacious mistress, Madame

Dolmar, who is the Spanish vice-reine's lady-in-waiting. In the end Pinto is named prime minister of Portugal and makes clear his desire to work as a power behind the throne to guarantee his countrymen's liberties.

Lemercier's next work, a tragedy titled *Isule et Orovèse* (Isule and Orovèse), opened at the Théâtre-Français on 23 December 1802 and failed to receive a single complete performance. The play tells the story of a Gallic druid, Orovèse, who, unable to overcome his "criminal" feelings for Isule, has chosen to expiate his sin by living a solitary life in a sacred forest. When Orovèse learns that Isule is about to be married to his rival, he uses his religious authority to declare that the young woman must be sacrificed to the gods. Had Lemercier not ripped the manuscript from the prompter's hands at the beginning of the third act, the audience would have discovered that Isule loved Orovèse and would have seen the two lovers kill themselves on the sacrificial altar in the final moments of the play. When he published his text, which he dedicated to Joséphine Bonaparte, Lemercier explained that he interrupted the performance of his play because of the audience's vociferous objections to its "depraved" language and "immoral" conduct. He saw this response as the work of a cabal and claimed that it was unjustified.

It was also around 1802 that Lemercier read his tragedy *Charlemagne* (1816) at Joséphine's home, La Malmaison, located just outside of Paris. Napoleon, who was already making plans to become emperor, reportedly admired the work but sought to convince Lemercier to change the ending so that Charlemagne would be offered the title of Holy Roman Emperor. The playwright refused and then wrote an epistle to Napoleon warning him of the dangers of ambition. The play was not performed until after the Bourbon Restoration and even then with only limited success.

There can be no doubt that Lemercier's persistent opposition to the empire negatively affected his dramatic career. Although he continued to write for the theater between 1804 and 1814–1815, few of his plays were actually staged during this period, and those that were often had only brief runs. The dramatist's three-act comedy *Plaute, ou La Comédie latine* (Plautus, or Latin Comedy), which opened at the Théâtre-Français on 20 January 1808, provides a case in point. The play, which starred Talma and Joanny (Jean-Bernard Brissebarre), suggests that events in Plautus's life served as the inspiration for the works the father of Roman comedy would later write. Although seemingly innocuous, the production was nonetheless shut down following Napole-on's attendance at its seventh performance. Apparently the emperor saw the titular character's complaint that he had been robbed by a prince as a veiled allusion to his government's expropriation of the Lemercier family's property several years earlier and therefore ordered a halt to the work's performance.

By this time Lemercier already had a reputation (thanks to *Pinto*) for semantic and syntactical "bizarreries." Negative opinions regarding his dramas gained further strength when his *Christophe Colomb* opened at the Théâtre de l'Odéon on 7 March 1809. The three-act historical comedy (written in verse rather than prose) provoked riots in the theater that cost one spectator his life and resulted in the injury of several others. The disturbances, said to be the equal of those later sparked by Hugo's *Hernani* (1830), apparently resulted from the playwright's failure to observe the unities of time and place—two of the three unities (the other being the unity of action) traditionally considered essential to the composition of French tragedy and comedy. So great was the turmoil occasioned by this play that its run ended after just twelve performances. Lemercier acknowledged the "irregularity" of his work, which he called "Shakespearean," but claimed that his violation of the rules was required by the subject matter and was not meant to serve as an example for others. Today the dramatist's artistic license seems minimal at best. In the eyes of his contemporaries, however, his break with conventional aesthetic practice created a dangerous precedent. Indeed, feelings surrounding this work were so intense that when asked to consider reviving the play in 1824, the director of the Odéon refused to do so on the grounds that it might prompt renewed riots.

The play presents Columbus as a maligned, misunderstood genius (no doubt something like Lemercier himself). Covering a period of months and moving from the explorer's home in Pinos, Spain, in act 1 to Isabel's palace in Granada in act 2 to the spot in the ocean where Columbus first sights land in act 3, the work highlights the many obstacles and indignities the navigator must overcome before he achieves success. Moments of some pathos and danger are relieved by comic scenes animated primarily by Columbus's wife's cousin Salvador, who is a chaplain, and by a doctor named Pharmacos. The two men argue, before and during the voyage, as to whether the explorer is possessed or mentally ill, and in their obtuseness and obduracy seem to announce the priest and the tutor in Alfred de Musset's *On ne badine pas avec l'amour* (1834; translated as *Perdican and Camilla*, 1924). In the end, however, Columbus finds words of praise for these representatives of religion and science who rejoice (albeit for reasons of their own) in his discovery of a new world. When the play ends, the explorer expresses confidence that God and future generations will reward him for his efforts.

For a while it seemed as if the playwright too would have to wait until a later date to be recognized and appreciated for his genius, but then, in 1810, Lemercier was elected to the prestigious French Academy. His election, which was controversial on both political and artistic grounds, came only after Lemercier wrote an "Ode à l'hymen" (Ode to Marriage) in honor of Napoleon's marriage to Marie-Louise of Austria. The poem, set to music by Luigi Cherubini, was designed to placate the emperor, who had the right to veto any candidate's election to the academy.

In his response to Lemercier's inaugural speech the academician Philippe-Antoine Merlin did not hesitate to chastise the new "Immortal" (as members of the Academy are called) for his radical and inappropriate innovations in drama—innovations that the playwright had already pledged never to repeat. Still, when Lemercier, then newly married to the daughter of a Parisian *notaire,* began giving public lectures on French literature at the Athénée in Paris in order to support himself and his family (a daughter, Népomucénie, was born the following year), people came expecting to hear the "extravagant" views of the author of *Christophe Colomb.* Instead they found themselves listening to someone whose opinions on tragedy, comedy, and poetry were both perfectly traditional and expressed in perfect French.

Lemercier's election to the academy and his aesthetically conservative lectures did not guarantee that his plays would be produced, however. His *Baudouin, empereur* (Emperor Baudouin), although published in 1808, was not performed until August 1826. *Camille, ou Le Capitole sauvé* (Camille, or The Capitol Preserved), which the playwright claimed had been accepted by the reading committee of the Théâtre-Français in 1811, was given a single performance—in 1825. *Le Corrupteur* (The Corruptor), composed in 1812, was first performed at the Odéon in November 1822. Its brief run came to an end when a government official complained of being personally maligned by the work.

Lemercier continued to find himself at odds with the censors even after the restoration of the monarchy. The most egregious example of the Bourbon government's obstruction of Lemercier's theatrical career involves *La Démence de Charles VI* (The Madness of Charles VI), a five-act Neoclassical tragedy purportedly written in 1806 and set for

performance at the Odéon in September 1820. Deeply disturbed by the work's portrayal of a mad king and the conflicts surrounding his succession, the censors refused to grant the necessary authorization for its production even though Lemercier protested that his aim in writing the play was entirely patriotic and monarchical. Viewed in the context of the assassination of the duc de Berry, heir apparent to the Bourbon throne, their initial rejection of the piece perhaps made some sense. The censors' refusal took on an air of persecution, however, when they authorized the production of a competing play on the same subject yet maintained the ban on Lemercier's piece. Believing himself a victim of plagiarism as well as governmental bias, Lemercier printed his drama with all its offending passages and argued his case in the press. An aesthetically conservative piece not without moments of beauty and power, *La Démence* was both condemned and praised by clearly partisan literary critics. Reviewers were, however, unanimous in their belief that Queen Isabelle de Bavière's political ambitions and lubriciousness were detrimental to the nation's integrity and deserved the denunciation they received in Lemercier's play.

Although *La Démence* was never performed during the Restoration years, other plays by Lemercier were. Neither *Le Frère et la sœur jumeaux* (The Twin Brother and Sister), which opened at the Odéon in November 1816, nor *Le Faux Bonhomme* (The Falsely Good-Natured Man), which had a single showing at the Théâtre-Français in January 1817, nor even *Le Complot domestique, ou Le Maniaque supposé* (The Domestic Plot, or The Alleged Maniac), which premiered at the Odéon in June 1817, did much to enhance the dramatist's reputation, however, and may be passed over quickly, as can the somewhat more interesting and financially successful *Agar et Ismaël, ou L'Origine du peuple arabe* (Hagar and Ishmael, or The Origins of the Arab People), performed at the Odéon in January 1818. Lemercier's association with the Odéon also yielded a polemical treatise titled *Du Second Théâtre-Français, ou Instruction relative à la déclamation dramatique* (On the Second Théâtre-Français, or Lessons on Dramatic Declamation, 1818), in which the playwright explained his belief in the value of competition among authors and actors in the French capital and outlined his thoughts on the art of declamation.

Lemercier's next play, *Frédégonde et Brunehaut,* a five-act tragedy that premiered at the Odéon in March 1821, was, by all accounts, his most successful of the Restoration era. Set in the Middle Ages, the play describes the political rivalry and personal animosity between two queens, one of whom is the

The Théâtre-Français and the Théâtre de l'Odéon, the Paris playhouses where most of Lemercier's plays had their premieres

second wife of King Chilpéric and the other of whom has wed Chilpéric's son Mérovée without the king's consent. As in *Baudouin* and *La Démence,* the women in this play are villainous and ambitious for power, and their crimes are the source of civil disorder. But if, like those earlier works, this piece underscores the nefarious effects of women's participation in affairs of state, it differs from them by allowing the queens to go unpunished for their misdeeds. Still, the play offered viewers and readers ample opportunity to feel terror and pity. (Mérovée's death, secretly ordered by a stepmother who wishes to see her own children inherit the throne, is one source of such feelings.) While critics deplored the queens' crimes and the weakness of their husbands, they nonetheless felt that Lemercier's tragedy was, overall, worthy of their praise. Given the positive reception of his play and its increasingly rare performance at the Odéon, Lemercier decided in October 1827 to withdraw the work from that theater and to offer it to the Théâtre-Français. The piece was accepted with some hesitation and did not open at that theater until 1842. Even then, despite Rachel's skills as a tragic actress, there would be only six performances of the play.

In August 1821 Lemercier's *Louis IX en Egypte* (Louis IX in Egypt), a five-act tragedy written much earlier, was performed at the Odéon with moderate success. Critics complained that Lemercier's depiction of Louis IX's imprisonment in Egypt during the Crusades was marred by the inclusion of a distracting romantic subplot. They also declared that the piece did not sustain comparison with Jacques Ancelot's *Louis IX* (Théâtre-Français, 1819). The playwright's hope that his positive portrayal of a revered

Bourbon ancestor might win him permission to produce *La Démence* was therefore quickly dashed.

Lemercier's next significant theatrical text was *Richard III et Jeanne Shore,* a five-act historical drama inspired by plays by William Shakespeare and Nicholas Rowe. Sometimes simply referred to as *Jeanne Shore,* the piece opened at the Théâtre-Français on 1 April 1824 with Talma playing Richard and first Mlle Duchesnois (Catherine-Joséphine Rafin) and then Mme Anne-Catherine-Lucinde Paradol as Jane. Unfavorably compared by contemporary critics to P. C. Liadières's five-act tragedy, *Jane Shore,* which premiered at the Odéon the following day, the work was only moderately successful. Today it is difficult to imagine why *Jeanne Shore,* with its condemnation of political ambition and abuses of power, its dramatic reversals and revelations, and its defense of the poor and the oppressed failed to achieve greater success. In many ways a precursor to Hugo's *Marie Tudor* (1833) and *Marion Delorme* (1831) and to the historical dramas of Alexandre Dumas *père,* it is a work that reveals something of the romantic and melodramatic side of Lemercier's genius and suggests what he might have become had he chosen to rebel against his own conservative tastes.

Lemercier's subsequent attack on political oppression took shape in his tragedy *Les Martyrs de Souli, ou l'Epire moderne,* which was inspired by the Greek war for independence from the Turks. In that drama, which was never performed because Lemercier refused to submit it to the government's theater censors, people of all colors, nationalities, and religions join forces to fight against tyranny. Given Lemercier's passion for Greek culture and for liberty, it is not surprising that he wrote such a piece. The fact that he wrote a variant text for the part of the African colonel Christol in 1839 would seem to indicate that even at that late date he held out some hope for the eventual performance of this work.

A former French combatant in another war for independence is one of the characters in Lemercier's *Les Deux Filles spectres* (The Two Girl Ghosts), a three-act melodrama performed at the Théâtre de la Porte Saint-Martin in November 1827 and then printed on presses owned by Honoré de Balzac. The play, which incorporates virtually every melodramatic cliché and convention, concerns family politics rather than national politics, however. It also denounces social inequalities and the unequal punishment meted out to those who commit crimes. In the preface to the work Lemercier defended his incursion into the world of melodrama by claiming that, when suitably composed and performed in appropriate theaters, any theatrical genre could come to occupy a legitimate place in the repertory.

The year 1828 saw the publication of Lemercier's *Comédies historiques* (Historical Comedies), a single-volume work including *Pinto; Richelieu, ou La Journée des dupes* (Richelieu, or The Day of the Dupes); and *L'Ostracisme, ou La Comédie grecque* (Ostracism, or Greek Comedy). *L'Ostracisme,* which some saw as a companion piece to *Plaute,* was never performed. There were, however, three performances of *Richelieu* at the Théâtre-Français in March 1835; six more were given in 1837. The work, originally written in 1804, had been accepted immediately by the reading committee of the Théâtre-Français. Had it been performed in 1804 with the originally proposed cast (Talma as Richelieu, Saint-Phal as Louis XIII, Caroline Talma as Anne d'Autriche, and Mlle Contat as Marie de Médicis), this boldly original historical comedy might have changed the course of Lemercier's career. By the 1830s, however, the work had lost its novelty, and the playwright's career had already foundered.

Much like *Henri III et sa cour* (Henri III and His Courtiers, 1829) by Dumas *père* but with a decidedly less tragic bent, *Richelieu* describes a power struggle at the French court. Cardinal Richelieu is the king's prime minister and most trusted adviser. However, the king's mother, Marie de Médicis, and his wife, Anne d'Autriche, as well as a few ambitious nobles at court, are jealous of the power and influence the cardinal wields and hope to precipitate his fall from grace. Although momentarily successful, in the end those who believed they could topple the cardinal are themselves disgraced or exiled, hence the subtitle, The Day of the Dupes.

As the temporal reference in the subtitle indicates, on this occasion Lemercier did respect the unity of time, just as he had in *Pinto*. And, as he had in *Pinto,* he confined the work's single action to one (albeit generously expanded) place. But whereas in *Pinto* the playwright limited what Hugo would later call the "grotesque" to secondary characters, in *Richelieu* it is not only such characters as the cardinal's confidant, Father Joseph, or the Queen Mother's doctor, or the Jewish astrologer who are ridiculous. Here, even the king, Richelieu, Anne, and Marie are at times shown to be comically self-absorbed, alternately ludicrous and odious. All told, the play is a fine example of political derision and daring that might well garner favorable reviews were it properly performed today.

Like *Richelieu,* Lemercier's *Clovis* was written early in the century, published decades later, and finally performed with limited success at the Théâtre-Français in January 1830. The five-act tragedy, set in King Sigebert's palace in Cologne, tells the story of a royal prince who learns too late that he has been cruelly manipulated by Clovis, a Frankish king who uses religion and false modesty to disguise his successful plan to usurp the throne. Given that Clovis was often associated with the founding of the French monarchy and the establishment of Catholicism as the French state religion, it is not surprising that the government's censors had long objected to the play's performance.

Six months later, in June 1830, the playwright's *Les Serfs polonais* (The Polish Serfs) opened at the Théâtre de l'Ambigu-Comique. Characterized by deliciously thrilling tableaux and dramatic *chutes de rideau* (curtain falls), this three-act melodrama sets such virtues as humanity and principle opposite jealously and pettiness. It denounces all abuses of power and calls for the abolition of servitude and the recognition of individual merit. Although the first act is exceedingly long (it occupies roughly one-half of the volume), the local color somewhat thin, and the text replete with virtually every cliché of the genre, this work affords another interesting glimpse at that side of his talent that Lemercier generally refused to exploit. Of his three excursions into melodrama (the third was *L'Héroïne de Montpellier* of 1835), this work, fueled by Lemercier's passionate support of the Poles in their war for independence, is the one that perhaps most deserves to be read.

During the July Monarchy, Lemercier made two unsuccessful bids to participate in politics. In 1833 he unsuccessfully sought nomination to the chair in literature at the Collège de France. Then in 1834 he published his only novel, *Alminti, ou le mariage sacrilège, roman physiologique* (Alminti, or The Sacrilegious Marriage, A Physiological Novel).

The playwright's final theatrical text was *L'Héroïne de Montpellier* (The Heroine from Montpellier), which opened at the Théâtre de la Porte Saint-Martin in November 1835. The play describes an attempt to ruin the reputation of Judith de Néville, the marriageable daughter of an elderly general, as well as the consequences of the duel that the young woman fights (in male disguise) to avenge the insult to her honor. Condemned by a court of law for violating the injunction against dueling (the action takes place at the end of the reign of Louis XIV) and for killing her opponent, Judith, who was set to be wed, is about to be beheaded on the public square. At the last minute, however, the heroine is pardoned by the king, and the populace rejoices. The play contains statements against torture and a discussion of the justice system and underscores Judith's unwillingness to be victimized by calumny. Once again Lemercier's liberal politics are evident, but this time with a hint of protofeminism.

From 1835 until his death on 7 June 1840, Lemercier spent time both in Paris and at the home he purchased in Normandy. When in Paris he occupied himself with the work of the French Academy, where he continued to proclaim his opposition to Romanticism. Although he fought hard to keep Hugo from being admitted to membership in the academy, it was Hugo who, upon Lemercier's death, was elected to the playwright's seat and required to give a speech on the life and works of his predecessor. Lemercier died at his Paris home two hours after having written his own epitaph: "Il fut homme de bien et cultiva les lettres" (He was a man of virtue and cultivated literature).

While some of Lemercier's tragedies—most notably *La Démence*—are still readable today and certainly worth studying as examples of an aesthetic in transition and the shift to national historical subjects, the playwright's most interesting contributions to nineteenth-century French drama may be found in those works where he violated the rules of Neoclassical composition he so doggedly attempted to defend. With their mixture of comic and serious characters and language, *Pinto, Richelieu,* and *Jeanne Shore* offer important insights into the origins of French Romanticism and deserve greater attention than they have received to date.

The playwright's melodramas—*Les Deux Filles spectres, Les Serfs polonais, L'Héroïne de Montpellier*—which he and his contemporaries thought of as works of minor import, also deserve to be reconsidered. While these pleasant entertainments would not have earned Lemercier election to the French Academy and do not display as much originality as some of his other pieces, they merit examination in light of our current interest in popular theater and gender studies. What is more, these texts, like the historical comedies cited above, help one to see Lemercier as something more than a narrow-minded literary ideologue. They allow one to recognize that while he never abandoned his belief in the superiority of the Neoclassical dramatic aesthetic, Lemercier was at times willing to test new ideas and to explore other options. The creator of *Agamemnon,* a perfectly traditional example of French tragic dramaturgy on a classical Greek subject, was, after all, also the author of *Les Martyrs de Souli,* a modern Greek tragedy of a quite different sort. He was likewise a strong proponent of the use of national historical subjects as a means of reviving French tragedy. Lemercier's failure to achieve celebrity in his own time can no doubt be attributed both to artistic and political causes; his disappearance from later histories of nineteenth-century French drama may in part be explained by the "victory" of Romanticism over Neoclassicism and by the general lack of availability of his texts.

Letters:

Maurice Souriau, *Népomucène Lemercier et ses correspondants* (Paris: Vuibert & Nony, 1908).

Biographies:

Charles Labitte, "Poètes et romanciers modernes de la France. Népomucène Lemercier," *Revue des Deux Mondes,* 21 (February 1840): 445–488; reprinted in his *Etudes littéraires* (Paris: Joubert, 1846), II: 176–228;

Sanson de Pongerville, *Biographie de Népomucène Lemercier* (Marseilles: Veuve M. Olive, 1859);

Gabriel Vauthier, *Essai sur la vie et les œuvres de Népomucène Lemercier* (Toulouse: A. Chauvin & Fils, 1886);

F. Chaffiol-Debillement, "Népomucène Lemercier," *Revue des Deux Mondes,* 1 (1968): 53–64.

References:

E. Abry, "Lemercier et la comédie historique," *Revue d'art dramatique et musical,* 14 (1903): 214–231, 240–254;

Ch[artier]-P[hilibert], *La Vérité sur M. Lemercier et ses ouvrages* (Paris: Palais Royal, 1827);

Barbara T. Cooper, "Censorship and the Double Portrait of Disorder in Lemercier's *La Démence de Charles VI,*" *Orbis Litterarum,* 40.4 (1985): 300–316;

Cooper, "The Queen as Other in Three French Restoration Tragedies," *Romance Quarterly,* 34.3 (1987): 275–283;

Michèle H. Jones, "Népomucène Lemercier: Un Promoteur du théâtre national," in her *Le Théâtre national en France de 1800 à 1830* (Paris: Klincksieck, 1975), pp. 56–89;

Ernest Legouvé, *Soixante Ans de souvenirs* (Paris: Hetzel, 1886–1887);

Jules Lemaître, *Théories et impressions* (Paris: Société française d'imprimerie, 1903);

Pierre Marie Michel Lepeintre-Desroches, ed., *Suite du Répertoire du Théâtre-Français,* volume 10, includes "Notice sur Lemercier" and the texts of *Agamemnon, Charlemagne, La Démence de Charles VI, Louis IX en Egypte,* and *Clovis* (Paris: Veuve Dabo, 1822);

Albert Le Roy, *L'Aube du théâtre romantique* (Paris: Société d'éditions littéraires et artistiques, 1904);

Antoine-M.-T. Métral, *De la liberté des théâtres, dans ses rapports avec la liberté de la presse, à l'occasion de l'analyse de* La Démence de Charles VI, *tragédie de M. Lemercier* (Paris: Barba, 1820);

Alfred Michiels, *Histoire des idées littéraires en France au dix-neuvième siècle,* volume 2 (Paris: W. Coquebert, 1842), pp. 44–68;

Norma Perry, ed., *Pinto,* by Lemercier (Exeter: University of Exeter Press, 1976);

Laurier Gérard Rousseau, *Népomucène Lemercier et Napoléon Bonaparte* (Mayenne: Floch, 1958);

Rousseau, *Le PINTO de Népomucène Lemercier et la Censure. Contribution à l'histoire de la Censure dramatique en France de 1789 à 1836* (Mayenne: Floch, 1958).

Papers:
Lemercier's manuscripts and letters can be found in the municipal library of Bayeux, France, in the library of the Comédie-Française in Paris, and in the Archives Nationales in Paris.

Maurice Maeterlinck
(29 August 1862 – 6 May 1949)

Lynn R. Wilkinson
University of Texas at Austin

PLAY PRODUCTIONS: *L'Intruse,* Paris, Théâtre d'Art, 21 May 1891;

Les Aveugles, Paris, Théâtre d'Art, 7 December 1891;

Pelléas et Mélisande, Théâtre des Bouffes parisiens, 16 May 1893;

Annabella, Paris, Théâtre de l'Oeuvre, 6 November 1894;

Intérieur, Paris, Théâtre de l'Oeuvre, 15 March 1895;

Aglavaine et Sélysette, Paris, Théâtre de l'Odéon, 14 December 1896;

Monna Vanna, Paris, Théâtre de l'Oeuvre, 17 May 1902; Comédie-Française, 22 December 1903;

Joyzelle, Paris, Théâtre du Gymnase, 20 May 1903;

Le Miracle de Saint-Antoine, Geneva, 1903; Brussels, 1903;

La Mort de Tintagiles, with music by Nouguès, Paris, Théâtre des Mathurins, 28 December 1905;

Ariane et Barbe-bleue, Paris, Opéra-Comique, March 1907;

L'Oiseau bleu, Moscow, Moscow Art Theater, 30 September 1908; Paris, Théâtre Réjane, 2 March 1911;

La Tragédie de Macbeth, nouvelle traduction, Saint-Wandrille, Maeterlinck's private theater, 28 August 1909;

Soeur Béatrice, New York, New Theater, 14 March 1910;

Marie Magdaleine, Nice, Casino Municipal, 18 March 1913; Paris, Théâtre du Châtelet, 28 May 1913;

Le Bourgmestre de Stilemonde, Buenos Aires, 1918; Paris, Théâtre Moncey, 1919;

Les Fiançailles, performed in translation as *The Betrothal,* New York, Schubert Theater, 18 November 1918;

La Princesse Isabelle, Paris, Théâtre de la Renaissance-Cora, 8 October 1935.

BOOKS: "Le Massacre des innocents," as Mooris Maeterlinck, *La Pléiade,* 1886; reprinted in *Maurice Maeterlinck,* edited by Gerard Harry (Brussels: Ch. Carrington, 1909), pp. 85–107; reprinted again in Maurice Maeterlinck, *Les Dé-*

Maurice Maeterlinck (photograph by Dover Street Studios)

bris de la guerre (Paris: Fasquelle, 1916), pp. 129–147; translated by Alfred Allinson as *The Massacre of the Innocents* (London: Allen & Unwin, 1914; New York: Duffield, 1915);

Serres chaudes, poèmes (Paris: Vanier, 1889);

La Princesse Maleine (Ghent: Louis van Melle, 1889); translated by Harry as *The Princess Maleine* (London: Heinemann, 1890); translated by Richard Hovey as *The Princess Maleine* (New York: Dodd, Mead, 1894);

Les Sept Princesses (Brussels: P. Lacomblez, 1891); translated by William Metcalfe as *The Seven Princesses* (London: Gowans & Gray, 1909);

Pelléas et Mélisande (Brussels: P. Lacomblez, 1892); translated by Erving Winslow as *Pelléas and Mélisande* (New York: Crowell, 1894); translated by Laurence Alma Tadema as *Pelléas and Mélisanda*, in *Pelléas and Mélisanda, and The Sightless. Two Plays* (London: Walter Scott, 1895); translated by Richard Hovey as *Pelléas and Mélisande*, in *Pelléas and Mélisande, Alladine and Palomides, Home* (New York: Dodd, Mead, 1896);

Le Trésor des humbles (Paris: Mercure de France, 1896); translated by A. Sutro as *The Treasure of the Humble* (London: George Allen, 1897);

Aglavaine et Sélysette (Paris: Mercure de France, 1896); translated by Sutro as *Aglavaine and Sélysette* (London: Grant Richards, 1897);

Douze chansons (Paris: Stock, 1896); translated by Martin Schütze as *Songs* (Chicago: Ralph Fletcher Seymour, 1912);

La Sagesse et la destinée (Paris: Fasquelle, 1898); translated by Sutro as *Wisdom and Destiny* (London: George Allen, 1898);

Serres chaudes, suivies de quinze chansons (Brussels: P. Lacomblez, 1900); translated by Martin Schütze as *Songs* (Chicago: Ralph Fletcher Seymour, 1912);

La Vie des abeilles (Paris: Fasquelle, 1901); translated by Sutro as *The Life of the Bee* (New York: Dodd, 1901);

Monna Vanna (Paris: Fasquelle, 1902); translated by A. I. Du P. Coleman as *Monna Vanna* (New York: Harper, 1903); translated by Sutro as *Monna Vanna: A Drama in Three Acts* (London: G. Allen & Sons, 1904);

Joyzelle (Paris: Fasquelle, 1903); translated by Alexander Teixeira de Mattos (London: George Allen, 1906);

Le Double Jardin (Paris: Fasquelle, 1904); translated by de Mattos as *The Double Garden* (London: George Allen, 1904);

L'Intelligence des fleurs (Paris: Fasquelle, 1907); translated by de Mattos as *Life and Flowers: Twelve Essays* (London: G. Allen & Sons, 1907); also published as *Intelligence of the Flowers* (New York: Dodd, Mead, 1907);

L'Oiseau bleu (Paris: Fasquelle, 1909); translated by de Mattos as *The Blue Bird: A Fairy Play in Five Acts* (London: Methuen, 1909);

La Mort (Paris: Fasquelle, 1913); translated by de Mattos as *Death* (London: Methuen, 1911);

Marie Magdaleine (Paris: Fasquelle, 1913); translated by de Mattos as *Mary Magdalene, A Play in Three Acts* (London: Methuen, 1910);

Les Débris de la guerre (Paris: Fasquelle, 1916); translated by de Mattos as *The Wrack of the Storm* (London: Methuen, 1916);

L'Hôte inconnu (Paris: Fasquelle, 1917); translated by de Mattos as *The Unknown Guest* (London: Methuen, 1914);

La Belgique en Guerre. Album illustré, text de Maeterlinck, Cyriel Buysse, etc. (Brussels & Le Havre: E. Van Hammée, 1918);

Deux Contes: Le Massacre des innocents, Onirologie (Paris: Crès, 1918);

Le Miracle de Saint-Antoine (Paris: Edouard Joseph, 1919); translated by Ralph Roeder as *A Miracle of Saint Anthony*, in *A Miracle of Saint Anthony and Five Other Plays* (New York: Boni & Liveright, 1917), pp. 11–43; translated by de Mattos as *The Miracle of Saint Anthony* (London: Methuen, 1918);

Le Bourgmestre de Stilemonde (Paris: Edouard Joseph, 1919); translated by de Mattos as *The Burgomaster of Stilemonde. A Play in Three Acts* (London: Methuen, 1918; New York: Mead, 1919);

Les Sentiers dans la montagne (Paris: Fasquelle, 1919); translated by de Mattos as *Mountain Paths* (New York: Dodd, Mead, 1919);

Le Grand Secret (Paris: Fasquelle, 1921); translated by Bernard Miall as *The Great Secret* (London: Methuen, 1922);

Les Epîtres de Sénèque (Lyons: Lardanchet, 1921);

Les Fiançailles (Paris: Fasquelle, 1922); translated by de Mattos as *The Betrothal; or The Blue Bird Chooses. A Fairy Play in Five Acts. Being a Sequel to The Blue Bird* (London: Methuen, 1919);

Pages choisies, 2 volumes (Paris: Crès, 1924);

Le Malheur passe (Paris: A. Fayard, 1925);

La Puissance des morts (Paris: A. Fayard, 1926);

Berniquel (Paris: Candide, 1926);

En Sicile et en Calabre (Paris: S. Kra, 1927);

Marie Victoire (Paris: A. Fayard, 1927);

La Vie des termites (Paris: Fasquelle, 1927); translated by Sutro as *The Life of the White Ant* (London: Allen & Unwin, 1927);

La Vie de l'espace (Paris: Fasquelle, 1928); translated by Miall as *The Life of Space* (London: Allen & Unwin, 1928; New York: Dodd, Mead, 1928);

En Egypte (Paris: Chronique des lettres françaises, 1928); translated by Sutro as *Ancient Egypt* (London: Allen & Unwin, 1925);

Juda de Kérioth (Paris: A. Fayard, 1929);

La Grande Féerie (Paris: Fasquelle, 1929); translated by Sutro as *The Magic of the Stars* (London: Allen & Unwin, 1930; New York: Dodd, Mead, 1930);

La Vie des fourmis (Paris: Fasquelle, 1930); translated by Miall as *The Life of the Ant* (London: Cassell, 1930);

L'Araignée de verre (Paris: Fasquelle, 1932); translated by Miall as *Pigeons and Spiders* (London: Allen & Unwin, 1934);

La Grande Loi (Paris: Fasquelle, 1933); translated by K. S. Shelvankar as *The Supreme Law* (London: Rider, 1935);

Avant le grand silence (Paris: Fasquelle, 1934);

La Princesse Isabelle, pièce en 20 tableaux (Paris: Fasquelle, 1935);

Le Sablier (Paris: Fasquelle, 1936); translated by Miall as *The Hour-Glass* (London: Allen & Unwin, 1936);

L'Ombre des ailes (Paris: Fasquelle, 1936);

Devant Dieu (Paris: Fasquelle, 1937);

La Grande Porte (Paris: Fasquelle, 1939);

L'Autre Monde ou le cadran stellaire (New York: Editions de la maison française, 1942; Paris: Fasquelle, 1942);

Jeanne d'Arc, pièce en 12 tableaux (Monaco: Editions du Rocher, 1948);

Bulles bleues (souvenirs heureux) (Monaco: Editions du Rocher, 1948; Brussels: Club du livre du mois, 1948).

Editions and Collections: *L'Intruse, Les Aveugles* (Brussels: P. Lacomblez, 1890); translated by Mary Vielé Washington as *Blind, The Intruder* (N.p.: W. H. Morrison, 1891); translated as *The Sightless*, in *Poet-Lore* (1893): 159–163, 218–221, 449–452; translated as *The Intruder* (London & Glasgow: Gomans & Gray, 1913);

Alladine et Palomides, Intérieur, et La Mort de Tintagiles, trois petits drames pour marionnettes (Brussels: Collection du Réveil, 1894); translated by A. Sutro and William Archer as *Alladine and Palomides* [Sutro], *Interior* [Archer], and *The Death of Tintagiles* [Sutro], in *Three Little Dramas for Marionettes,* with an introduction by G. Granville Barker (London & Glasgow: Gowans & Gray, 1911);

Théâtre I (Brussels: P. Lacomblez, 1901)–comprises *La Princesse Maleine, L'Intruse and Les Aveugles*;

Théâtre III (Brussels: P. Lacomblez, 1901)–comprises *Aglavaine et Sélysette, Ariane et Barbe-Bleue,* and *Soeur Béatrice*;

Théâtre II (Brussels: P. Lacomblez, 1902)–comprises *Pélléas et Mélisande, Alladine et Palomides, Intérieur,* and *La Mort de Tintagiles*;

Théâtre de Maurice Maeterlinck, 3 volumes, with preface by Maeterlinck (Brussels: Deman, 1902)–comprises *La princesse Maleine, L'Intruse, Les Aveugles, Pélléas et Mélisande, Alladine et Palomides, Intérieur, La Mort de Tintagiles, Aglavaine et Sélysette, Ariane et Barbe-bleue,* and *Soeur Béatrice*;

The Plays of Maurice Maeterlinck, translated by Richard Hovey (Chicago & New York: Herbert S. Stone, 1905)–comprises *Princess Maleine, The Intruder, The Blind,* and *The Seven Princesses*;

The Plays of Maurice Maeterlinck, second series, translated by Hovey (Chicago & New York: Herbert S. Stone, 1905)–comprises *Alladine and Palomides, Pélléas et Mélisande, Home,* and *The Death of Tintagiles*;

Morceaux choisis, with introduction by Georgette Leblanc (Paris: Nelson, 1910);

Théâtre, 3 volumes (Paris: Fasquelle, 1919)–volume 1 comprises: *La Princesse Maleine, L'Intruse, Les Aveugles;* volume 2 comprises: *Pélléas et Mélisande, Alladine et Palomides, Intérieur, La Mort de Tintagiles;* volume 3 comprises: *Aglavaine et Sélysette, Ariane et Barbe-bleue, Soeur Béatrice*;

Théâtre inédit: L'abbé Sétubal, Les trois justiciers, Le jugement dernier (Paris: Del Duca, 1959).

TRANSLATIONS: Jan van Ruysbroeck, *L'ornement des noces spirituelles de Ruysbroeck l'admirable,* translated from the Flemish, with an introduction, by Maeterlinck (Brussels: P. Lacomblez, 1891); translated by Jane T. Stoddart as *Ruysbroeck and the Mystics. With Selections from Ruysbroeck* (London: Hodder & Stoughton, 1894);

John Ford, *Annabella,* translated and adapted from *T'is a Pity She's a Whore, for the Théâtre de l'Oeuvre* (Paris: Ollendorf, 1895);

Novalis, *Les Disciples à Saïs et les fragments de Novalis,* translated, with an introduction, by Maeterlinck (Brussels: P. Lacomblez, 1895);

William Shakespeare, *La Tragédie de Macbeth, traduction nouvelle avec introduction et notes* (Paris: Fasquelle, 1910).

A Belgian of Flemish descent who wrote in French and spent most of his life in France, Maurice Maeterlinck had a powerful effect on the theatrical world of the late nineteenth century. In a prolific career that extended into the ninth decade of his life, he published twenty-eight plays, two collections of poetry, two short stories, many volumes of popularizing essays on philosophical, occult, and scientific subjects, and an autobiography. But literary historians generally agree that his most innovative and influential works were the plays that he wrote in the 1890s and early 1900s. In 1891 Paul Fort's avant-garde Théâtre d'Art produced *L'Intruse* (1891; translated as *The Intruder,* 1891) and *Les Aveugles* (1891; translated as *Blind,* 1891); Aurélien-François Lugné-Poë's troupe staged *Pelléas et Mélisande* (1893; translated as *Pelléas and Mélisande,* 1894) and *Intérieur* (1895; translated as *Interior,* 1911). Maeterlinck's plays were, in fact, among the few French texts that suited the avant-garde repertory of these theaters.

In 1908 the production of Maeterlinck's *L'Oiseau bleu* (1908; translated as *The Blue Bird: A Fairy Play in Five Acts,* 1909) at the Moscow Art Theater was a milestone in the development of symbolist and avant-garde theater in Russia. Indeed, Maeterlinck's early plays were especially influential outside France and formed an integral part of the repertory of the Russian director Vsevolod Meyerhold and the German director Max Reinhardt. The early dramas of Chekhov, as well as the plays of William Butler Yeats and the late plays of August Strindberg all draw on and develop aspects of Maeterlinck's early work.

But Maeterlinck's early plays represent only a small part of his creative output, which grew increasingly remote from any kind of avant-garde art. Always a solitary figure, Maeterlinck withdrew in his later years to a series of country estates, settling at last into Orlamonde, his palatial residence on the French Riviera that he decorated in art nouveau style and where he played the roles of the country gentleman and reclusive man of letters. Although he continued to write plays after World War I, Maeterlinck was best known in the last four decades of his life for his popularizing essays and his courtly lifestyle.

Mauritius Polydorus Maria Bernhardus Maeterlinck was born in Ghent, Belgium, on 29 August 1862. His parents were Polydore Maeterlinck, a prosperous retired notary, and Mathilde Colette Françoise Van den Bossche, the daughter of a lawyer. The family was bilingual and divided its time between a town house in Ghent and a country estate at Oostacker, where Maeterlinck's father raised bees and devoted himself to gardening. Maeterlinck was educated at a convent school, the private Institut Central in Ghent, and the Jesuit Collège Sainte-Barbe, where he met and became friends with the future poet Charles Van Lerberghe. From 1881 to 1885 Maeterlinck studied law at the University of Ghent. At the successful completion of his law studies the young man persuaded his father to send him to Paris for several months, ostensibly to study French law, but Maeterlinck spent his time there in literary circles, meeting writers such as Saint-Pol-Roux, Catulle Mendès, Stéphane Mallarmé, and, most importantly, Phillipe-Auguste Villiers de l'Isle-Adam. Returning to Ghent, Maeterlinck practiced law until 1889, "failing brilliantly," in the words of his first biographer, Gerard Harry.

During these years, however, the young writer saw the first publication of his work: in 1886 La Pléiade published his short story "Le Massacre des innocents" (translated as "The Massacre of the Innocents," 1914), and in 1887 twelve of his poems appeared in Le Parnasse de la jeune Belgique. In 1889 Maeterlinck published his translation of Jan van Ruysbroeck's fourteenth-century mystical treatise, Adornment of Spiritual Marriage, in La Revue générale; a volume of poetry, Serres chaudes, and a play, La Princesse Maleine, at his own expense.

Except for La Princesse Maleine, Maeterlinck's early works were unnoticed by the critics. When, however,

Maeterlinck at age fifteen

Maeterlinck sent a copy of La Princesse Maleine to Mallarmé, the influential poet, much impressed, gave the play to Octave Mirbeau. On 24 August 1890 Mirbeau published a highly enthusiastic review of the play in Le Figaro, thereby launching Maeterlinck's career as a playwright and man of letters. During the next five years Maeterlinck wrote the plays for which he is best known in literary and theatrical history. La Princesse Maleine was followed by L'Intruse, Les Aveugles, Les Sept Princesses (1891; translated as The Seven Princesses, 1909), Pelléas et Mélisande, Alladine et Palomides (1894; translated as Alladine and Palomides, 1911), Intérieur (1895), and La Mort de Tintagiles (1894; translated as The Death of Tintagiles, 1911).

In the 1890 review that brought La Princesse Maleine and its author to the attention of the literary world, Mirbeau celebrated Maeterlinck's play by comparing it to the work of Shakespeare. In fact, Maeterlinck's play has more in common with the symbolist interpretations of Shakespeare, such as are found in Mallarmé's Igitur (1869), than it does with Shakespeare's work. Set in a northern kingdom in an unspecified feudal past, the five acts of La Princesse Maleine present the events that lead to the death of the innocent young princess of the title, who is ultimately killed by the evil and powerful Danish queen, Queen Anne. In the first act Queen Anne, who has seduced the feeble old king of the land, Hjalmar, is determined to marry her daughter, Uglyane, to the young prince, also called Hjalmar. But Anne must first get rid of the young prince's betrothed, Maleine. Early in the play Maleine escapes from the tower in which she has been imprisoned; later, however, she is recaptured and imprisoned again; finally, in the last act, she is strangled by Anne.

The vague northern setting of the play and the plight of the young prince recall Shakespeare's *Hamlet* (1603) in general terms: certainly young Hjalmar's family is as dysfunctional, and his kingdom in as much chaos, as are Hamlet's. Several crowd scenes provide a glimpse of disorder outside the castle; young Hjalmar, too, dies at the end of the play. But he dies by his own hand when he discovers the corpse of Maleine, whose death has been caused by his mother, not by his words or actions. Hjalmar's father is still alive at the end of the play, a symbol, perhaps, of a decadent order unable to renew itself. Unlike Gertrude, his Danish consort is purely evil. *La Princesse Maleine* shifts the focus of the Hamlet legend away from the young male heir and to the women of the castle: what ensues is a struggle between the acquiescent victim, Maleine, and an active and intelligent queen consort who is demonized.

This struggle has at least two dimensions. Like the two Hjalmars, Anne and Maleine seem in some respects doubles, but in the world of Hjalmar's castle they are necessarily at odds with each other. The doubling in the play suggests a psychological allegory in which different aspects of the self cannot be reconciled. At the same time, however, the action of the play suggests the acknowledgment and the deploring of the emergence of women as powerful agents in politics and culture: murder, even if it targets the weak and helpless rather than the principal offenders, seems to be the solution to cultural decadence and the decline of male authority proposed here.

In its representation of the power-hungry and murderous Queen Anne, *La Princesse Maleine* also draws on *Macbeth* (1606), which Maeterlinck translated in 1910. But perhaps the play's most important echoes are of the unperformable dramas of Mallarmé. The beautiful princess in the tower at the beginning of the play recalls Mallarmé's virginal Hérodiade in his fragment by that name. And Maeterlinck's highly psychological and vague treatment of the Hamlet theme also suggests Mallarmé's *Igitur*, which transforms the Hamlet theme into a single soliloquy and a drama of consciousness confronting nothingness. Ironically, it seems that Maeterlinck's first readers hailed the play because it seemed to represent a performable version of symbolist theater. The play, however, was not performed in the 1890s. Paul Fort tried to get permission to stage it at his Théâtre d'Art, but Maeterlinck refused, ostensibly because he preferred to give it to André Antoine, who may have flirted with the idea of putting it on but recognized in the end that *La Princesse Maleine* was fundamentally at odds with the naturalist aesthetic of his theater and its repertory.

Maeterlinck's first produced play was his next, *L'Intruse*, which opened in Paris on 21 May 1891 at the Théâtre d'Art. With a subject matter quite different from that of *La Princesse Maleine*, its single act takes place in a "dark room in a rather old castle," where members of a family have gathered. As the play opens, a child has just been born, and the mother is apparently recovering in a room offstage. Only the blind grandfather, waiting with the other family members, fears the worst; but at the end of the play his fears are confirmed. Silently, the nun who has been tending the new mother appears in the doorway. The old blind man has been able to sense what the others have not. *L'Intruse* represents the first of Maeterlinck's celebrated and revolutionary *drames statiques* (static dramas), relatively plotless works in which a small group of characters focus on a metaphysical or psychological presence that cannot be represented in visible terms.

Maeterlinck's third play, *Les Aveugles*, also premiered at the Théâtre d'Art, where it opened on 7 December 1891. In this play all the characters are blind, thereby emphasizing to an even greater degree than *L'Intruse* the evocation onstage of invisible forces. The characters in *Les Aveugles* are a group of blind patients who wander in the woods to which they have been taken on an outing by a priest; as they talk, it becomes clear that they are unaware that the priest has quietly died during the outing; it is also clear that there is a storm approaching. The play ends with the patients wandering and lost. The representation of vision and its absence in this short work is given an ironic twist since the play harks back to sixteenth-century paintings and engravings, especially to Pieter Brueghel the Elder's *The Parable of the Blind*, in which blind people lead other blind people. In *Les Aveugles*, in contrast to *L'Intruse*, the blind flail about rather than merely listen for intimations of mortality. This is not the first time that Maeterlinck turned to Flemish painting for the subject of a literary piece. His early prose piece, "Le Massacre des innocents," is a literary transposition of the Brueghel painting by the same name.

In the single act of Maeterlinck's *Les Sept Princesses* an aging king and queen live in an isolated and chilly castle with seven sleeping princesses. Outside a crowd is about to embark on an ocean voyage. Through the windows come their shouts of jubilation.

The death of Pelleas in Maeterlinck's Pelléas et Mélisande

The long-awaited prince arrives to claim one of the princesses, but although he manages to awaken six of the seven frail and languorous young women, one of them has died as he and the royal couple have stood discussing them. She is, of course, the one who had most attracted him. The play ends with the old queen's lamentations and the group's discovery that all doors and windows of the castle are locked. *Les Sept Princesses* turns back to and reworks familiar motifs from folktales and fairy tales. The plight of the princesses echoes that of Snow White, as well as innumerable royal children who have fallen under an evil spell and must be rescued. The allusion to the swans outside the castle at the beginning of the play suggests the princesses' association with the beautiful birds that, particularly in late-nineteenth-century European culture, were associated with sexuality, death, and transcendence. In Maeterlinck's early plays the possibility of a physical or sexual awakening inevitably leads to death.

Maeterlinck's fourth play, the ethereal *Pelléas et Mélisande* also turns to fairy tales for its subject. But its evocation of a vaguely northern kingdom ruled by an aging and ineffectual king also recalls *La Princesse Maleine*. Here, as well, a young and innocent princess must die, as well as her beloved, whose death she also helps bring about. The plot is simple. Golaud, the middle-aged son of the aging King Arkel, who reigns over a vaguely Germanic kingdom called Allemonde, comes across beautiful Mélisande sitting by a fountain in a forest. She has lost her crown. He finds it for her and proposes marriage. Back in the castle, Melisande finds his younger half brother, Pelléas, more attractive. When they meet in the forest, Golaud, now her husband, comes upon them and stabs Pelléas. In the fifth act Mélisande gives birth to a girl, but she dies, unable to accept motherhood or to answer Golaud's questions concerning the nature of her love for Pelléas. But where *La Princesse Maleine* drew very generally on the plots of *Hamlet* and *Macbeth*, *Pelléas et Mélisande* is a vague distillation of the plots of innumerable folktales and fairy tales. Settings and characters alike are emptied of all individuality. What is left is longing, a musical suggestiveness that Claude Debussy exploited in his musical version of the play in 1907.

Maeterlinck's next three plays were published together in 1894 as "trois petits drames pour marionnettes" (three little dramas for marionettes). As Maeterlinck himself admitted, the first, *Alladine et Palomides*, represents little more than a reworking of *Pelléas et Mélisande*. The second, *Intérieur*, also turns back to an earlier work but brilliantly transcends its model. Like *L'Intruse*, *Intérieur* presents the dilemma of a family forced to confront the death of one of its members. Here, however, they are seen from the outside, through the windows of their home, as a procession approaches in the foreground, led by an old man who knows of the death by drowning of a daughter. The crowd debates how to break the news. Finally the old man enters the household and informs the family. Their reactions, seen through the windows of their house, are mimed only. The audience hear no words. *Intérieur* offers a stunning example of a self-conscious representation of the symbolic setting of turn-of-the-century theater, representing a split stage, an interior within the interior, as well as a representation within the representation. Here, as in other early plays by Maeterlinck, some characters inhabit an isolated structure threatened by forces that come from outside. But in this play the threat is given concrete representation in the form of the old man and his followers, who also participate in the catastrophe. The two settings, one incorporating darkness and language, the other light and silence, suggest a third, ineffable presence.

La Mort de Tintagiles, the last of the three dramas, is also the sparest. Its four acts are extremely short, evoking in impressionistic fashion moments in the decline of the young boy, Tintagiles, and his family, who are represented here by his two sisters, Ygraine and Bellangère, and his aged father, who like the old king of *La Princesse Maleine* has become involved with a powerful queen anxious to do away with the children of his first marriage. In this play, however, the new queen's ascent to power and designs on the children are linked to political changes outside the castle: a crowd surges around its walls, anxious to participate in the change of regimes. By the end of the play Ygraine and Tintagiles have fled to a remote part of the castle, and Ygraine has managed to shut herself up in a fortified room. Unfortunately, she succeeds so well that when Tintagiles also seeks refuge there she cannot open the door to let him in. At the end of the play we hear him die, the victim of an invisible presence whose nature is ambiguous: death, the crowd, or the new queen herself.

Alladine et Palomides, Intérieur, et La Mort de Tintagiles marked the end of the first phase of Maeterlinck's theatrical production. At the beginning of 1895 he met Georgette Leblanc, who became his companion and collaborator and for whom he was to write a series of plays incorporating, but by no means entirely affirming, a feminist perspective. But less personal factors also played a role in Maeterlinck's turning to a different style of drama. Audiences noted a certain repetition in his plays, and symbolist plays did not bring in the kind of revenues that sustained an independent theater. In 1897 Lugné-Poë, whose Théâtre de l'Oeuvre had been the major venue for symbolist plays, turned to other kinds of theater, ostensibly because there were so few suitable French plays in this style. Maeterlinck's

plays, moreover, were far more influential abroad than in France, where they were rarely staged in the 1890s.

The year 1895 marked a turning point in Maeterlinck's life and literary production. That year, following the five plays considered his most important works for the theater, he published his translations of *The Disciples at Sais* (1802) and *Fragments* (1802), both by the German Romantic writer Novalis. Maeterlinck's translations from Novalis were followed by essays on other writers and on philosophical, scientific, and theosophical subjects; he turned at this time to writing plays intended for Leblanc, plays that center on the presence of a strong "new woman," whose sexuality, initiative, and frequent exhibitionism place her at odds with her surroundings. In 1897 he and Leblanc set up house in Paris, but they were often apart; from 1907 to 1914 they spent summers in the abandoned Benedictine abbey of Saint-Wandrille in Normandy. Plays such as *Aglavaine et Sélysette* (1896; translated as *Agalaine and Sélysette,* 1897), *Monna Vanna* (1902; translated, 1903), and *Ariane et Barbe-bleue* (1907) point to an obvious collaboration between the playwright and the actress, and Leblanc claimed to have contributed to the essays Maeterlinck published during this period, as well.

The last play he wrote specifically for her to perform was *Marie Magdaleine* (1913), begun in 1908, but the culmination of their theatrical collaboration was the single performance of his translation of Shakespeare's *Macbeth* at Saint-Wandrille in 1909. Leblanc apparently hoped to turn Saint-Wandrille into a French version of Richard Wagner's Bayreuth in Germany. The following summer saw a well-received production of *Pelléas et Mélisande* at the same location, but Maeterlinck's objections to having his privacy disturbed by rehearsals stopped plans to stage *Hamlet* and *La Princesse Maleine* there.

In 1896 Maeterlinck moved from his native Belgium to France and published two works, each of which marked a new departure in his authorship. *Le Trésor des humbles* (1896; translated as *The Treasure of the Humble,* 1897), which includes essays on Novalis, Ralph Waldo Emerson, and Ruysbroeck as well as on the aesthetics of the theater, was the first of what became his many volumes of popularizing prose. *Le Trésor des humbles* contains one of the playwright's most influential essays, "Le tragique quotidien" (The Tragic in Everyday Life), a statement of the aesthetics informing his dramas of the 1890s. Traditional theater, Maeterlinck argues, focuses too much on events and superficial dialogue, evoking an atavistic world in which violence predominated. Modern theater, in contrast, should emphasize the spiritual dimension of human existence.

Il ne s'agit plus ici de la lutte déterminée d'un être contre un étre, de la lutte d'un désir contre un autre désir ou de l'éternel combat de la passion et du devoir. Il s'agirait plutôt de faire voir ce qu'il y a d'étonnant dans le fait seul de vivre. Il ssagirait plutôt de faire voir l'existence d'une âme en elle-même, au milieu d'une immensité qui n'est jamais inactive.

(It goes beyond the determined struggle of man against man, and desire against desire: it goes beyond the eternal conflict of duty and passion. Its province is rather to reveal to us how truly wonderful is the mere act of living, and to throw light upon the existence of the soul, self-contained in the midst of ever-restless immensities.)

This aesthetic has much in common with the evocative poetics of symbolist poetry; however, it also points the way to a reinterpretation of dramatic tradition. In this view Shakespeare and Ancient Greek tragedy appear as important ancestors of *le tragique quotidien,* but it is Isben who, in his late dramas, emerges as the first truly modern dramatist. Concerning *The Master Builder* (1892) Maeterlinck writes: "Hilde et Solness sont, je pense, les premiers héros qui se sentent vivre un instant dans l'atmosphère de l'âme, et cette vie essentielle qu'ils ont découverte en eux, par delà la vie ordinaire, les épouvante" (Hilda and Solness are, I believe, the first characters in drama who feel, for an instant, that they are living in the atmosphere of the soul; and the discovery of this essential life that exists in them, beyond the life of every day, comes fraught with terror). The dialogue of this "drame somnambulique" (somnambulistic drama) leaves what is most important unsaid.

Aglavaine et Sélysette, Maeterlinck's other important work in 1896, was his first play to incorporate a strong female lead—one who could be played by the playwright's new companion, Georgette Leblanc. In fact, the inclusion of such roles distinguishes most of the plays Maeterlinck published between 1896 and 1913. *Aglavaine et Sélysette, Ariane et Barbe-bleue, Soeur Béatrice* (1910), *Monna Vanna, Joyzelle* (1903; translated, 1906), and *Marie Magdaleine* (1913) all revolve around a central character who resembles Leblanc's image of herself as a new woman proud of her sexuality and not afraid to flout conventions, especially those surrounding marriage. In her memoirs the actress emphasizes her role as collaborator in all of her companion's writing while they were together. The plays certainly bear witness to her influence, but they do so ironically. Maeterlinck was never a feminist and seems never to have taken this first extended relationship seriously.

Georgette Leblanc as the title character in Monna Vanna, *the play Maeterlinck wrote for her in 1902*

Aglavaine et Sélysette recalls Henrik Ibsen's *Rosmersholm.* In both plays a rival uses the powers of suggestion to lead the wife of the household to commit suicide. In Maeterlinck's play, however, the new woman (and future wife) is older, and if the husband and outsider lament the suicide of the young Sélysette, *Aglavaine et Sélysette* nevertheless suggests the inevitability and desirability of their relationship in a way that is foreign to Ibsen's ambiguous and complex presentation of the situation of Rosmer and Rebecca West. As in Maeterlinck's early plays, in *Aglavaine et Sélysette* a powerful and sexually attractive older woman is responsible for the death of a virginal younger one, but here the emphasis has shifted. In Maeterlinck's production as a whole, this play seems to represent a transitional piece that bids farewell to the pale virgins of his first dramas by having one give way to the sexual and maternal older woman. Yet, as in the early plays, female strength is still allied with murder.

Maeterlinck's *Joyzelle,* another play written for Leblanc, echoes Shakespeare's *The Tempest* (1611). Together with his magical assistant, Ariel, Merlin inhabits an island, on the shores of which a young man, Lanceor, and a young woman, Joyzelle, meet. Both have been promised in marriage to partners they shun. Merlin appears and tests their love, but the two young lovers prevail. The old ruler/magician turns out to be the father of Lanceor, and at the end of the play the three affirm their intention to live together on the island as a new family. The play premiered at the Théâtre du Gymnase on 20 May 1903 but was a failure. French critics were to be increasingly critical of Maeterlinck's plays. Another play in 1903 was *Le Miracle de Saint-Antoine,* first performed at Geneva and Brussels. It describes an unlikely miracle that takes place in a town in the Netherlands and is Maeterlinck's only comedy.

In *Ariane et Barbe-bleue* the central character sets out to rescue the imprisoned wives of Blue-Beard, making speeches along the way on the importance of feminine solidarity and freedom, only to be undermined at the end by the wives' refusal to leave: feminine autonomy, it seems, pales in contrast to the cruel charms of the strong male. Interestingly, the wives all bear names from previous plays by Maeterlinck: Sélysette, Mélisande, Ygraine, Bellangère, and Alladine. In *Soeur Béatrice* the central character takes on the shape of a statue of the Virgin Mary and also leaves the convent for a lifetime of sin. In the end, however, her choice is affirmed: she returns to the convent, and the statue appears as it had before she left. The other nuns, now quite old, mourn her as a saint.

Monna Vanna was probably the most successful of the plays written for Leblanc. This play transposes the theme of Judith and Holofernes to Renaissance Italy. Prinzivalle, captain of the Florentine army surrounding the city of Pisa, promises to lift the siege if Guido Colonna, the commander of the Pisan garrison, sends his wife to him, naked under her cloak. After discussing the issue with her father-in-law, Giovanna Colonna goes to Prinzivalle's tent, but this Renaissance Judith is never faced with the choice between submitting to the unwanted sexual advances of a barbarian invader and murder. It turns out that Prinzivalle knew her when they were children. He saw her sitting, Mélisande-like, by a fountain but never dared to declare his feelings since he was of humble origins. Nothing transpires but their conversation and a chaste kiss on Giovanna's forehead, but she realizes she has never really loved her husband and resolves to help Prinzivalle escape from his enemies, who now sur-

round his encampment. Returning to Pisa, Giovanna proclaims herself untouched, but when her jealous husband refuses to believe her and proposes to kill Prinzivalle, she reverses herself, lying that he raped her, but demanding the key to his prison. The play ends with her words: "C'était un mauvais rêve. . . . Le beau va commencer . . . Le beau va commencer . . . " (It was a bad dream. . . . The beautiful is going to begin . . . The beautiful is going to begin . . .).

As Bernard Shaw pointed out, the central scenes of the play, in which the threat of rape and dishonor gives way to Giovanna's recognition that the man who has lured her there is a childhood friend and a decent person, have a false ring about them. But the play is an interesting dramatization not only of feminist ideals of heroism, according to which the courageous woman learns that she has nothing to fear from sexuality but everything from convention, but of the male reception of such notions. Two threats are deflected here: rape and beheading/castration. But the reference to the dream at the end of the play calls into question the effectiveness of Giovanna's or Prinzivalle's actions.

In 1907 Maeterlinck wrote *L'Oiseau bleu,* one of his best-known plays and, with *Pelléas et Mélisande,* his most often performed. According to Leblanc, the play was first commissioned as a Christmas piece. It premiered at the Moscow Art Theater in 1908 in a production directed by the renowned Russian director Konstantin Stanislavsky. Three years later Leblanc, who had studied the Russian production, produced the work in Paris.

Set in a poor woodcutter's cottage, *L'Oiseau bleu* is an allegory that follows two children, Tyltyl and his sister Mytyl, on their dream quest for the blue bird of happiness. On the way they visit a fairy's palace; the land of memory, where the dead live on; the palace of the night, where sleep and death coexist; a dark forest in which plants and animals talk to them; and the land of the light, where the souls of the unborn await their entry into human life. The blue bird has much in common with the blue flower Novalis had written about in *Heinrich von Ofterdingen* (1802), and the dream-adventure plot recalls J. M. Barrie's *Peter Pan* (1904), to which Maeterlinck acknowledged his debt. But the pirates of the English work give way in Maeterlinck's play to symbolic figures that suggest a neoplatonic allegory with very young protagonists.

In fact, *L'Oiseau bleu* is an unusually lighthearted and light-handed example of the station drama, in which a character wanders through the world in search of identity, understanding, or happiness. Its cheerfulness stands in stark contrast to the mostly gloomy Scandinavian and German examples in this genre: Strindberg's *A Dream Play* (1901), for example, or the plays of the German Expressionists. What they share, however, is a belief that the phenomena of everyday experience are meaningful and point beyond themselves. In 1918 an English version of a sequel to *L'Oiseau bleu* was performed at the Schubert Theater in New York. Here Tyltyl has become an adolescent, and his fairy-mentor leads him on a second quest for love.

In 1911 Maeterlinck was awarded the Nobel Prize in literature. Other official honors followed: the Belgian government sponsored an official "Festival Maeterlinck" and presented the writer with the insignia of Grand Officier de l'Ordre de Léopold. In 1913, however, Maeterlinck's essay *La Mort* (translated as *Death,* 1911) was placed on the Index by the Catholic Church. In response he quipped that his publisher would be delighted at this "prehistoric phenomenon of no importance" although elsewhere he complained, incorrectly, that he had been excommunicated for no real reason.

In 1913 Maeterlinck wrote *Marie Magdaleine,* his last play for Leblanc. This play, like the others written for the actress, represents a woman whose strength lies in her unconventional sexuality. The heroine of *Marie Magdaleine,* however, makes a distinction between sexuality and love, refusing to sleep with the Roman who loves her devotedly and falling passionately in love with Jesus. Because of its unorthodox treatment of biblical material, the play was censored in Britain and first produced at the Casino Municipal at Nice in 1913.

During World War I Maeterlinck wrote several propagandistic pieces, including *Le Bourgmestre de Stilemonde* (1918; translated as *The Burgomaster of Stilemonde,* 1918). In this play a brutal German officer demands the death of a citizen of a Belgian town for a minor offense. The work is remarkable principally for the anti-German sentiments that later served as a pretext for Maeterlinck's emigration to the United States.

In 1919 Maeterlinck married Renée Dahon, a young woman whom he had met at a rehearsal of the French production of *L'Oiseau bleu* in 1911 and to whom he dedicated *Les Fiançailles* (1918; translated as *The Betrothal,* 1918), a sequel to *L'Oiseau bleu.* In *Les Fiançailles* one of the woodcutter's children, now a young man, goes off in search of true love. Maeterlinck and his wife moved to the south of France, where he continued to write, producing *Le Grand Secret* (1921; translated as *The Great Secret,* 1922), a history of the occult sciences, and, between 1927 and 1942, twelve volumes of essays.

In 1920, during a lecture tour in the United States, Maeterlinck accepted a commission by producer Samuel Goldwyn to write film scripts. Apparently three scenarios were completed although none was filmed. Of one, nothing is known; of the second,

only the title, "The Blue Feathers," is known. Maeterlinck transformed the third, "The Power of the Dead," into a play that he published as *La Puissance des morts* in 1926.

Although his popular accounts of the lives of bees, termites, flowers, and other nonhuman inhabitants of the natural world sometimes lapse into allegorical accounts of ideal forms of social organization, Maeterlinck made few direct political statements during his life, either as a writer or private citizen. At the turn of the century he expressed socialist views, but after World War I his sympathies turned increasingly to fascism, although never to the Germans. He became a friend of the Portuguese dictator Antonio de Oliveira Salazar and, in a conversation with Gratien Candace, apparently approved of the Italian invasion of Ethiopia. Maeterlinck's politics are most disturbing in their thoughtlessness. One passage in *La Sagesse et la destinée* (1898; translated as *Wisdom and Destiny,* 1898) seems particularly ominous in its complacency:

Il n'y a pas longtemps, pour ne citer qu'un seul de ces problèmes que l'instinct de notre planète est appelé à résoudre, il n'y a pas longtemps, on eut, paraît-il, l'intention de demander aux penseurs de l'Europe s'il faudrait considérer comme un bonheur ou un malheur qu'une race énergique, opiniâtre et puissante, mais qui nous semble, à nous autres Aryens, en vertu de préjugés trop aveuglément acceptés, inférieure par l'âme ou par le coeur, la race juive, en un mot, disparût ou devînt prépondérante. Je suis persuadé que le sage peut répondre, sans qu'il y ait dans sa réponse ni résignation ni indifférence répréhensibles: "Ce qui aura lieu sera le bonheur."

(Not long ago—to cite only one of the problems that the instinct of our planet is invited to solve—a scheme was on foot to inquire of the thinkers of Europe whether it should rightly be held as a gain or a loss to mankind if an energetic, strenuous, persistent race, which some, through prejudice doubtless, still regard as inferior to the Aryan in qualities of heart and of soul—if the Jews, in a word, were to vanish from the face of the earth, or to acquire preponderance there. I am satisfied that the sage might answer, without laying himself open to the charge of indifference or undue resignation, "In what comes to pass will be happiness.")

Of greatest interest among Maeterlinck's later works for the theater was his 1935 play, *La Princesse Isabelle,* in which Renée Dahon-Maeterlinck performed in the title role. *La Princesse Isabelle* is remarkable for its framing of the fairy-tale motifs so common in Maeterlinck's early plays: here the "princess" inhabits a psychiatric hospital.

In 1940 Maeterlinck settled in the United States and remained there until the end of World War II. He and his wife lived briefly in New York before moving to Florida. In 1945 the couple returned to Orlamonde,

Maeterlinck and his second wife, Renée, arriving in New York in 1940

their estate in the south of France. Although Maeterlinck continued to write plays after World War II, he had little to do with theatrical life, and his later plays were seldom performed.

The aged writer died from a heart attack on 6 May 1949. The most theatrical aspect of Maeterlinck's work in the last decades of his life was his playing of the somewhat anachronistic role of the isolated sage and man of letters, but such a staging of the self had always characterized his authorship, as it had that of so many turn-of-the-century writers and actors. Leblanc's account of her arrangement of their first meeting—she wore a Pre-Raphaelite costume—is especially illuminating on this aspect of their relationship.

Paradoxically, the work that made Maeterlinck famous in Paris, *La Princesse Maleine,* was never staged there in the 1890s. There were four extremely important productions of his plays in Paris during that decade, however. *L'Intruse* and *Les Aveugles* were both staged at the Théâtre d'Art in 1891, and *Pelléas et Mélisande* and *Intérieur* were performed by Lugné-Poë's troupe in 1893 and 1895, respectively. As Frantisek Deak points out in *symbolistTheater: The Formation of an Avant-Garde* (1993), the theaters of these two men are

often seen as the successors and antithesis of Antoine's Théâtre-Libre, which emphasized a naturalist repertory, but in reality the programs of both the Théâtre d'Art and the Théâtre de l'Oeuvre challenged a clear distinction between the two styles. Maeterlinck's plays appeared in the company of works by Ibsen, Strindberg, Gerhart Hauptmann, and other dramatists, whose dramas combined elements from both. As Maeterlinck's own remarks on Ibsen's *Master Builder* in *Le Trésor des humbles* show, the distinctive mixture of realism and symbolism in the Norwegian's late plays were particularly attractive to playwrights, theater directors, and audiences alike in Paris in the early 1890s.

Yet in Maeterlinck's plays the realist dimension is reduced to the vague evocation of spooky northern settings or timeless bourgeois interiors in which families await a fate that is unrelated to specific actions or social conditions. Atmospheric realism has given way to atmosphere. The interiors represented onstage are mostly psychological in significance. The characters are flat, unindividuated, more like voices in a single psyche than rounded representations of human agents. Maeterlinck's early dramas are prototypes of the chamber theaters of Max Reinhardt and Strindberg and thus of the dramatic genres of the chamber play and chamber movie. As embodied in Strindberg's five *Chamber Plays* (1907–1908), chamber plays involve a kind of performance akin to chamber music, in which dramatic characters interact like the elements in a musical ensemble and in which the borderline between psychological and architectural interiors tends to dissolve. The highly repetitive dialogue of Maeterlinck's early plays, in which the voice of one character picks up, repeats, and transforms the words of another, points especially to this kind of musical interplay. It was also admirably suited to the kind of incantatory delivery that Fort and Lugné-Poë encouraged in their actors.

If Maeterlinck's plays were only seldom staged in the 1890s in France, they were nevertheless far more suited to theatrical performance than other contemporary pieces associated with the symbolist movement, Villiers de l'Isle Adam's *Axel,* for example, or the dramatic fragments of Mallarmé. One suspects that the initial appeal of Maeterlinck's dramas to admirers of and participants in the symbolist movement lay in their superficial resemblance to Mallarmé's work. The pale, death-bound princesses of the Belgian's early plays recall the frigidly beautiful and deadly Hérodiade, although in this stage of Maeterlinck's production the murderous aspect of the chaste princess has been deflected onto an aging stepmother-queen. But the language in Maeterlinck's plays is strikingly different from that in Mallarmé's work. Where the French poet's language is complex, economical,

and rife with ambiguities and intersecting resonances, the dialogue of Maeterlinck's plays is loose
and repetitive. It harks back to the plaintive refrain
of Edgar Allan Poe's "The Raven" (1845) "Nevermore, nevermore"–rather than to the concern with
literary form and meaning associated with Poe's essay "The Philosophy of Composition" (1846). One
sees in Maeterlinck's early plays the tendency to
popularize, represented more obviously in his many
books of essays. These plays translate the esoteric
language and mythic abstractions of late-
nineteenth-century French poetry into the forms of
fairy tales. If the poetry of writers such as Charles
Baudelaire and Mallarmé invites comparison with
the evocation of the ineffable in the writings of mystics, Maeterlinck's essays expound the ideas of writers in the mystic tradition. The language of Maeterlinck's early plays emphasizes orality over textual-
ity; its silences are highly meaningful; it fills in the
gaps, the white spaces, of the texts of Mallarmé and
other poetic turn-of-the-century authors.

The legacy of Maeterlinck is double-edged. On
the one hand he was one of the most innovative
dramatists of fin-de-siècle Europe. His plays point forward to the intimate theater of Strindberg, Reinhardt,
and other major twentieth-century playwrights and directors. They played a crucial role in the development
of Russian symbolism. The early plays influenced
William Butler Yeats, and their emphasis on myth and
sacrifice also points forward to the dramatic theories
and practice of Antonin Artaud. Maeterlinck himself
was capable of taking up and transforming a new form
in the theater, such as the station drama. But on the
other hand his writing, especially his popularizing essays, sometimes lapses into clichés and apolitical complacency. At his worst he warns of the dangers of New
Age philosophy. At his best he reminds one of the necessary relationship between good theater and the unknown.

Bibliographies:

Maurice Lecat, *Bibliographie de Maurice Maeterlinck: littérature–science–philosophie* (Brussels: Ancienne librairie Castaigne, 1939);

Annales de la fondation Maurice Maeterlinck (Ghent:
1955–1980; 1989–);

Raymond Renard, "Maurice Maeterlinck en Italie,"
Annales de la fondation Maurice Maeterlinck, 4 (1958):
75–95;

Carlo Bronne, "Un bilan de l'année Maeterlinck," in *Le
centenaire de Maurice Maeterlinck* (Brussels: Palais
des Académies, 1964), pp. 299–305;

R. Brucher, *Maurice Maeterlinck. L'Oeuvre et son audience.
Essai de bibliographie 1883–1960* (Brussels: Palais
des Académies, 1972);

Jean Warmoes, "La Bibliographie de Maurice Maeterlinck," *Annales de la fondation Maurice Maeterlinck,* 18
(1972): 33–66.

Biographies:

Gerard Harry, *Maurice Maeterlinck* (Brussels: Carrington, 1909);

Georgette Leblanc, *Souvenirs: My Life with Maeterlinck,*
translated by Janet Flanner (New York: Dutton,
1932);

W. D. Halls, *Maurice Maeterlinck: A Study of His Life and
Thought* (Oxford: Clarendon Press, 1960).

References:

Jean-Marie Andrieu, *Maurice Maeterlinck* (Paris: Editions
universitaires, 1962);

Rogert Bodart, *Maurice Maeterlinck* (Paris: Seghers,
1962);

Gaston Compère, *Maurice Maeterlinck* (Paris: La Manufacture, 1993);

Compère, *Le Théâtre de Maurice Maeterlinck* (Brussels:
Palais des Académies, 1955);

Frantisek Deak, *symbolistTheater: The Formation of an
Avant-Garde* (Baltimore: Johns Hopkins
University Press, 1993);

Guy Donneux, *Maurice Maeterlinck* (Brussels: Palais des
Académies, 1961);

Paul Gorceix, *Les Affinités allemandes dans l'oeuvre de
Maurice Maeterlinck* (Paris: Presses Universitaires
de France, 1975);

Bettina Knapp, *Maurice Maeterlinck,* Twayne World
Author Series (Boston: G. K. Hall, 1975);

Aurélien François Lugné-Poë, *La Parade,* 3 volumes
(Paris: Gallimard, 1930–1933);

Stéphane Mallarmé, "Planches et feuillets," in *Crayonné
au théâtre, Oeuvres complètes,* Editions de la Pléiade,
edited by Jean Aubry and Henri Mondor (Paris:
Gallimard, 1945), pp. 324–330;

Alex Pasquire, *Maurice Maeterlinck* (Brussels: Renaissance du livre, 1965);

Marcel Postic, *Maeterlinck et le symbolisme* (Paris: Nizet,
1970);

Debora L. Silverman, *Art Nouveau in Fin-de-Siècle France:
Politics, Psychology, and Style* (Berkeley: University
of California Press, 1989);

Peter Szondi, *Theory of the Modern Drama,* translated by
Michael Hays (Minneapolis: University of Min-
nesota Press, 1987), pp. 351–363;

Una Taylor, *Maurice Maeterlinck* (London: Taylor,
1914);

Edmund Wilson, *Axel's Castle: A Study in the Imaginative
Literature of 1870–1930* (New York: Scribners,
1931).

Prosper Mérimée

(28 September 1803 – 23 September 1870)

Daniel Gerould
The Graduate School and University Center, The City University of New York

See also the entry on Mérimée in *DLB 119: Nineteenth-Century French Fiction Writers: Romanticism and Realism, 1800–1860.*

PLAY PRODUCTIONS: *L'Amour africain,* Paris, Théâtre des Nouveautés, 11 July 1827; Geneva, Salle Communale de Plainpalais, 20 April 1918; Paris, Théâtre des Arts, 12 May 1926;

Le Carrosse du Sacre-Sacrement, Paris, Théâtre Français, 13 March 1850; New York, Vieux Colombier at the Garrick Theatre, 5 December 1917; Paris, Vieux Colombier, 5 March 1920;

Une Charade, Compiègne, Château de Compiègne, 15 November 1857; Moscow, Theatre Korsh, 1922;

Le Cor au pied, Compiègne, Château de Compiègne, 24 November 1863;

Les Mécontents, Paris, Cercle des Arts (les Castagnettess) at Salle Duprez, early 1880s;

Monsieur l'Inspecteur Général (translation of *The Inspector General* by Nikolai Vaselyevich Gogol), Paris, Théâtre de l'Oeuvre, 8 January 1898;

Une Femme est un diable, ou La Tentation de Saint Antoine, Paris, Théâtre de l'Odéon, 30 April 1898; presented as *Comedies of Mérimée,* along with *Le Ciel et l'enfer* and *Le Carrosse du Saint-Sacrement,* Moscow, Vakhtangov Studio, 19 September 1924;

La Jaquerie, adapted by G. N. Frolov with prologue and epilogue by Vadim Shershenevich, Moscow, Experimental Heroic Theatre, 18 November 1921; adapted by Georges Arest, Paris, Théâtre Charles de Rochefort, 13 November 1952;

L'Occasion, Paris, Théâtre de l'Atelier, 1 April 1922;

Le Ciel et l'enfer, Moscow, Vakhtangov Studio, 19 September 1924; presented as *Comedies of Mérimée,* along with *La Femme est un diable* and *Le Carrosse du Saint-Sacrement,* Moscow, Vakhtangov Studio, 19 September 1924; Paris, Théâtre de Paris, 19 November 1940;

Prosper Mérimée, 1868

Le Carrosse du Saint-Sacrement, Moscow, Vakhtangov Studio, 19 September 1924;

Inès Mendo, Paris, Théâtre Charles de Rochefort, 10 February 1940;

Les Espagnols en Danemark, Paris, Comédie-Française, 5 May 1948.

BOOKS: *Théâtre de Clara Gazul, comédienne espagnole,* as Clara Gazul (Paris: A. Sautelet & Cie,

1825)–comprises *Les Espagnols en Danemark, Une Femme est un diable, ou La Tentation de Saint Antoine, L'Amour africain, Inès Mendo ou Le Préjugé vaincu, Inès Mendo ou Le Triomphe du préjugé,* and *Le Ciel et l'enfer;* translated anonymously as *The Plays of Clara Gazul, a Spanish Comedian* (London: George B. Whittaker, 1825)–comprises *The Spaniards in Denmark, A Woman Is a Devil, African Love, Inès Mendo* (first part), *Inès Mendo* (second part), and *Heaven and Hell;* revised edition (Paris: H. Fournier jeune, 1830)–includes *Le Carrosse du Saint-Sacrement,* translated by L. A. Loiseaux as *The Coach of the Holy Sacrament* (Paris & New York: Collection du Vieux Colombier, 1917), and *L'Occasion;*

La Guzla, ou Choix de poésies illyriques recueillies dans la Dalmatie, la Bosnie, la Croatie et L'Herzégovine, anonymous (Paris: F.-G. Levrault, 1827);

La Jacquerie, scènes feodales, suivies de La Famille de Carvajal (Paris: Brissot-Thivars, 1828);

1572. Chronique du temps de Charles IX (Paris: Alexandre Mesnier, 1829); republished as *Chronique du regne de Charles IX* (Paris: H. Fournier jeune, 1832); translated as *1572. A Chronicle of the Times of Charles the Ninth* (New York: G. & C. & H. Carvill, 1830);

Mosaique (Paris: H. Fournier jeune, 1833); translated by Emily Waller and Mary Dey as *The Mosaic* in *The Novels, Tales and Letters of Prosper Mérimée* (New York: Frank Holby, 1905);

La Double méprise (Paris: H. Fournier, 1833); translated by William Arnold as *The Double Mistake* in *The Novels, Tales and Letters of Posper Mérimée;*

Les Mécontents in *Mosaique* (Paris: H. Fournier jeune, 1833); translated anonymously as *The Conspirators* in *The Works of Prosper Mérimée,* volume 2 (New York: Bigelow, Brown, 1905);

Notes d'un voyage dans le midi de la France (Paris: Fournier, 1835);

Notes d'un voyage dans l'ouest de la France (Paris: Fournier, 1836);

Notes d'un voyage en Auvergne (Paris: Fournier, 1838);

Notes d'un voyage en Corse (Paris: Fournier jeune, 1840);

Essai sur la guerre sociale (Paris: Firmin-Didot frères, 1841);

Colomba (Paris: Magen & Comon, 1841); translated anonymously (Boston: Phillips, Sampson, 1856)–comprises *Les Ames du purgatoire* and *La Venus d'Ille,* translated by Oliver Palmer and Waller as *Souls in Purgatory* and *The Venus of Ille* in *The Novels, Tales and Letters of Prosper Mérimée;*

Etudes sur l'histoire romaine, 2 volumes (Paris: Victor Magen, 1844);

Notice sur les peintures de l'église de Saint-Savin (Paris: Imprimerie royale, 1845);

Carmen (Paris: Michel Lévy frères, 1846); translated by Thomas Diven (Chicago: Donnelly, Grasset, Loyd, 1878)–comprises *Arsène Guillot* and *L'Abbé Aubain,* translated by Mary Loyd and Edmund Thompson in *The Novels, Tales and Letters of Prosper Mérimée;* enlarged as *Nouvelles* (Paris: Michel Lévy frères, 1852);

Monuments historiques (Paris: Imprimerie royale, 1846);

Histoire de Don Pédre I roi de Castile (Paris: Charpentier, 1848); translated as *The History of Peter the Cruel, King of Castile and Leon* (London: Richard Bentley, 1849);

Episode de l'histoire de Russie. Les Faux Démétrius (Paris: Michel Lévy frères, 1853); translated by Andrew R. Scoble as *Demetrius the Imposter: An Episode in Russian History* (London: Richard Bentley, 1853);

Les Deux Héritages; L'Inspecteur général et les débuts d'un aventurier (Paris: Michel Lévy frères, 1853);

Melanges historiques et littéraires (Paris: Michel Lévy frères, 1855);

Architecture gallo-roamine et architecture du moyen-âge: Instructions du Comité historique des arts et monuments, by Mérimée, Albert Lenoir, August Leprévost, and Charles Lenormant (Paris: Imprimerie impériale, 1857);

Les Cosaques d'autrefois (Paris: Michel Lévy frères, 1865);

Dernières nouvelles (Paris: Michel Lévy frères, 1873); translated by Waller and Louise Paul in *The Novels, Tales and Letters of Prosper Mérimée;*

Portraits historique et littéraires (Paris: Michel Lévy frères, 1874);

Etudes sur les arts au Moyen Age (Paris: Michel Lévy frères, 1875);

Mémoires historique (Paris: Bernouard, 1927);

Histoire du règne de Pierre le Grand suivie de L'Histoire de la fausse Elisabeth II, edited by Henri Mongault and Maurice Parturier (Paris: Conard, 1947);

Théâtre de Clara Gazul, Romans, Nouvelles (Paris: Gallimard, Bibliothèque de la Pléiade, 1978).

OTHER: Théodore-Agrippa d'Aubigné, *Aventures du baron de Fæneste,* edited by Mérimée (Paris: P. Jannet, 1855);

Pierre de Bourdeille, Seigneur de Brantôme, *Œuvres complètes,* edited, with an introduction, by Mérimée (Paris: P. Jannet, 1858–1895);

Ivan Turgenev, *Pères et enfants,* preface by Mérimée (Paris: E. Fasquelle, 1863);

Turgenev, *Nouvelles moscovites,* translated by Mérimée and Turgenev (Paris: J. Hetzel, 1869);

Turgenev, *Fumée,* preface by Mérimée (Paris: J. Hetzel, n.d.).

SELECTED PERIODICAL PUBLICATION—
UNCOLLECTED: *Le Cor au pied, L'Information*
    Compiègne, Château de Compiègne, 24 November 1863.

Prosper Mérimée is little known as a playwright and is chiefly remembered for his novella *Carmen* (1846), which provided the basis for Georges Bizet's celebrated 1875 opera. Yet Mérimée began his literary career in 1825, when he was twenty-one, with a collection of plays that pioneered Romantic drama in France several years before Victor Hugo or Alexandre Dumas *père.* Rarely performed in the nineteenth century, Mérimée's plays had to wait nearly a hundred years until changes in sensibility after 1917 gave them a second life in France and Russia. Jacques Copeau and his disciples Louis Jouvet and Charles Dullin revealed the theatricality of Mérimée's dramas to French audiences, while in the Soviet Union the plays were promoted by Communist repertory committees and performed by avant-garde companies. Marginal to the mainstream of nineteenth-century French drama, Mérimée's works for the theater, like those of Georg Büchner, are twentieth-century discoveries.

Born in Paris on 28 September 1803, Prosper Mérimée was, by birth and education, at odds with his age. His father, Léonor Mérimée, was a teacher and administrator at the School of Fine Arts. His mother, Anne Morean, was a talented portraitist and taught art to young ladies. His well-to-do bourgeois family was committed to the anticlerical and rationalistic ideas of Voltaire and the French Enlightenment, and he was probably never baptized. Under paternal pressure to follow in his grandfather's footsteps, Prosper studied law at the University of Paris from 1819 to 1823, but he preferred the visual arts, hoping to be a painter like his father. A gifted linguist fascinated by other cultures, he spoke English fluently and quickly mastered Greek and Spanish. Under the influence of Stendhal, whom he met at the literary and artistic salons that he frequented, the young man turned to literature.

In 1822 the eighteen-year-old Mérimée made his debut as a writer with *Cromwell* (text now lost), an historical tragedy which the young author read to a group of friends that included Stendhal. His first publications, appearing in 1824, were four unsigned articles on Spanish drama in the newly founded liberal periodical, *Le Globe.* In these articles the young writer praises the great Spanish drama-

tists Pedro Calderón de la Barca, Lope de Vega, Tirso de Molina, and Leandro Fernández de Moratin for their lifelike dialogue and use of modern historical subjects. Although he did not visit the Iberian peninsula until 1830, the Spain of Mérimée's reading and imagination was the inspiration for his early writing.

Mérimée's major collection of plays, the *Théâtre de Clara Gazul, comédienne espagnole* (1825; translated as *The Plays of Clara Gazul, a Spanish Comedian,* 1825), pretended to be a French translation of the work of a Spanish actress. In the early 1820s foreign plays began to be widely translated and published in France. Friedrich von Schiller's works had appeared in 1821, followed by *Les Chefs-d'Oeuvres des Théâtres Etrangers* (The Masterpieces of the Foreign Theaters) in 1823. To make the hoax doubly deceptive, Mérimée assigned his pseudonymous book to a nonexistent series, *Collection des Théâtres Etrangers* (Collection of Foreign Theaters). A few volumes intended for friends contained a portrait of Mérimée as Clara Gazul, dressed in a woman's gown, head covered by a mantilla. In an even more limited number of copies, this portrait was preceded by another, showing a man's head and shoulders, cravat and jacket, with the face cut out so that when superimposed on Clara Gazul, Mérimée appeared. The hoax distanced the creator from his own creation, perplexing critics as to the writer's seriousness. But trickery, dual vision, sudden metamorphosis, and playing with an audience's perceptions were integral to Mérimée's romantic irony. His double game consisted of dressing as a passionate Spanish actress while remaining a jacketed and cravated French bourgeois—a form of transvestism that permitted his writing Romantic drama while simultaneously mocking it.

The *Théâtre de Clara Gazul* contains a hoax within a hoax—a fictitious translator and commentator named Joseph L'Estrange provides a brief biography of the actress-author, enabling Mérimée to interpret his own invented persona. According to L'Estrange, Clara Gazul, niece of a Spanish guerrilla commander hanged by the French and daughter of a fortune-teller, claimed to have been born under an orange tree by the side of road in the kingdom of Granada. After escaping from a convent where she had been held against her will, she went on the stage and soon became a celebrated actress and playwright. By birth, race, sex, profession, and temperament an outsider, the rebellious young woman was forced to flee to England after all her works were put on the Index by the Royalists.

The persona of Clara Gazul served Mérimée as both manifesto and mask, enabling him to adopt a radical new aesthetic that challenged neoclassical rules of decorum, propriety, and probability. By imitating the naive, fast-paced action of archaic Spanish drama, with its primitive characters and exotic settings, Mérimée cultivated a theatrical style that exemplified the theoretical ideas of his older friend and mentor, Stendhal, who, in *Racine and Shakespeare* (1823), proposed a modern dramatic art in prose, not verse, that would disregard the rules, mix comedy and tragedy, and countenance onstage violence.

In 1823 Spain was a topical issue. To restore the monarchy in Spain, the reactionary French government had undertaken a Spanish expedition. For a French author to invent Clara Gazul at such a time was an act of defiance, but Mérimée's dissent was ironic and guarded. In the playwright's covert system of political allusion Clara's native land plays a dual role as both oppressor and victim. As home of the Inquisition and an empire savagely colonizing indigenous peoples, Spain becomes a coded metaphor for France, but as a country assailed by brutal French troops of occupation, it stands for freedom menaced.

Les Espagnols en Danemark (1825; translated as *The Spaniards in Denmark,* 1825) opens with a prologue in Clara Gazul's loge where the actress-author, following Stendhal's ideas, attacks the unities of time and place and defends the use of a subject from recent history. The play, based on historical documents, is an irreverent spy thriller debunking the still-taboo imperial legend; it tells the story of General de la Romana, who in 1808 commands fifteen thousand Spaniards in Denmark in the service of the emperor against the English. When he learns of Napoleon Bonaparte's plans to place his brother on the Spanish throne, the general secretly leads his troops back to Spain. Although death and destruction are constant threats, the melodramatic *Les Espagnols en Danemark* ends happily for the sympathetic Spaniards, who outwit the powerful but morally ugly and inept French. By treating satirically the Napoleonic army of occupation and siding with the victims of French aggression, Mérimée adopted a subversive stance.

The French governor of the Danish island of Fionie, where the action unfolds, engages two spies, the beautiful Mme de Coulanges and her scheming, corrupt mother, Mme de Tourville, to keep an eye on Romana. Mme de Tourville discovers that Romana is planning a clandestine return to his country to fight for national independence. Meanwhile, Lieutenant Charles Leblanc of the Imperial Guard—brother and son to the two spies—arrives on a mission to "neutralize" the Spaniards by inviting

Romana and his staff to a banquet where they will be executed.

But Mme de Coulanges falls in love with Romana's aide, the dashing Colonel Diaz, after witnessing his bravery in rescuing a drowning seaman (actually an English secret agent come to help the Spaniards escape). Changing allegiances, the reformed Mme de Coulanges warns Diaz of the danger he faces and shamefacedly refuses his offer of marriage. Forewarned of the plot, the Spaniards foil the French and escape for Spain, taking with them Mme de Coulanges dressed as a Spanish cadet.

Defending France's enemies, Mérimée celebrates a romantic national hero in Diaz, who, free of class prejudices, dares love a commoner without family or money. The play's racy language and amusing characters (based on known historical figures) combine with suspenseful action and colorful spectacle to create a lively drama in an idiom popularized by René-Charles Guilbert de Pixérécourt.

A short play in three scenes designed to shock, *Une Femme est un diable, ou La Tentation de Saint Antoine* (1825; translated as *A Woman Is a Devil,* 1825) takes place in Granada during the War of the Spanish Succession in a dimly lit hall of the Inquisition, with instruments of torture looming in the background. Two cynical inquisitors, Rafael and Domingo, await their new superior, Fray Antonio, an anguished young ascetic obsessed with sensual visions of a diabolical woman waiting to ensnare him. When Mariquita is brought in to be tried as a sorceress, Antonio recognizes the beautiful young prisoner as his temptress and, unable to surmount his desires, proposes that they flee together.

When Rafael enters the cell and finds them embracing, Antonio demands that the priest bless his union with Mariquita: "Marie-moi, on je te tue!" (Marry me, or I'll kill you!). After a struggle in which her lover stabs Rafael, Mariquita puts on the dead monk's robe to facilitate their flight. "En une heure, je suis devenu fornicateur, parjure, assassin" (In an hour, I have become fornicator, perjurer, and murderer), Antonio exclaims. The "comedia" ends with the overt theatricality of the old Spanish stage. Antonio and Mariquita step forward to address the audience directly, announcing the conclusion of the play and giving its title and subtitle, as they ask for the audience's indulgence.

Inspired by Calderón's *El magico prodigioso* (Prodigious Magician, 1637), from which the play's epigraph is derived, Marimèe uses lurid details about the Inquisition from Matthew Gregory Lewis's *The Monk* (1795) and Ann Radcliffe's *The Italian* (1797). Mérimée imbues his sensational

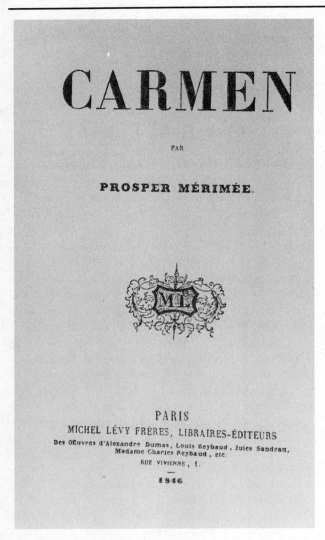

Title page for Mérimée's best-known work, the novella on which Georges Bizet based his 1875 opera, Carmen

gothic drama of sex and violence with Voltairean anticlerical malice.

In *L'Amour africain* (1825; translated as *African Love,* 1825), an even shorter one-act *comedia* that takes place at Cordoba, Mérimée extracts picturesque local color from a North African setting and dramatizes exotic Moorish customs and manners, pitting cruel codes of honor and vengeance against passionate feelings of love and friendship. Here, as elsewhere, the author provides notes to explain foreign words and strange practices, citing learned authorities to substantiate authenticity. The public is invited to perceive the world of the other from an anthropological and historical perspective although, in fact, Mérimée often invents his sources and documents.

In a beautiful enclosed garden the rich Moor, Hadji Nouman, lavishes presents on his beloved Mojana, a lovely young slave newly purchased. His wild Bedouin friend Zein appears in a state of great agitation, ready to sell everything he owns, except his horse, to buy a beauty recently on display at the slave market. Unaware that the two girls are one, Hadji agrees to lend his friend the money needed since the Bedouin once saved his life in the desert. But when Zein sets eyes on Mojana in Hadji's garden, he feels himself betrayed by his friend and attacks the Moor. Forced to kill his friend to defend himself, the aggrieved Hadji vents his rage on the cause of the tragedy by stabbing Mojana.

As Hadji stands over the bodies of his friend and lover, whose blood he has just spilled, his servant enters and announces, "Seigneur, le souper est prêt et la pièce finie" (My lord, supper is served and the play is over). To which Nouman replies, "Ah! cela est différent" (Oh, that's a different matter), whereupon the corpses arise and Mojana delivers the epilogue to the audience. The murdered heroine comments on the relativity of cultural values, ironically pointing out that if the author had wanted to conform to the taste of the public, she should have given her Bedouin more Spanish sentiments. But the geographical location demanded otherwise. "Leur amour se ressent de la chaleur du Sahara" (Their love partakes of the heat of the Sahara), Mojana explains. By undermining theatrical illusion, Mérimée plays with dramatic convention as freely as he does with social and moral conventions.

The two parts of *Inès Mendo*—*Inès Mendo ou Le Préjugé vaincu* (Inès Mendo or Prejudice Vanquished, 1825) and *Inès Mendo ou Le Triomphe du préjugé* (Inès Mendo or The Triumph of Prejudice, 1825)—form a cautionary diptych. In the first, liberal telling of the tale, love overcomes prejudice, with marriage across class barriers producing a happy ending. In the second, revisionist account, when the curtain goes up again on the progress of the marriage, a tragic about-face reveals prejudice triumphant. Mérimée sees double, superimposing over romantic optimism, hardheaded good sense, and disabused psychology.

As the epigraphs to each of the parts indicate, the central idea for *Inès Mendo* comes from Miguel de Cervantes's *Don Quixote, Part Two* (1615), chapter 5, where Sancho Panza and his wife, Theresa, discuss whether their daughter should marry above her station or within her class. The first play bears out Sancho's contention, the second his wife's.

Like an old ballad, *Inès Mendo ou Le Préjugé vaincu* revolves around a duel, a murder, a trial, an executioner who cuts off his own hand, and a king who arrives at the last moment with a pardon. The characters suddenly find themselves placed in impossible and terrifying circumstances not of their own making that threaten their sanity and well-being in a manner reminiscent of Heinrich Wilhelm von Kleist's tales.

The drama takes place in Montlar, a small town in Galicia in 1640. Juan Mendo, son of the former executioner forced to continue a despised hereditary profession, has been able to keep his secret even from his daughter because no crimes are committed in the village. But Mendo tells the priest his recurring nightmares in which he sees a young man lying at his feet as the mayor hands him the fatal ax. Mendo's beautiful, innocent, and naive daughter Inès is in love with Don Esteban, who seeks her hand in marriage. His father, Don Luis de Mendoza, a wealthy nobleman and friend of Mendo, approves of the match, considering himself a *philosophe,* free of class prejudices, who sees no difference between a Mendoza and a Mendo except for the *za.*

The scrupulous Mendo discloses his shameful calling to his daughter, forcing her to renounce Esteban, who refuses to abandon her. The honorable young man has, however, in the meantime killed a friend, Don Carlos, son of the village mayor, for making insulting remarks about Inès and planning to seduce her. Esteban is arrested, put in prison, and condemned to death at the hands of the executioner, Mendo.

In a bloody coup de théâtre on the scaffold Mendo chops off his right hand rather than carry out his prescribed duty and execute his prospective son-in-law. In admiration at this magnanimous gesture the peasants rush forward to defend Mendo against the police. Don Luis arrives on horseback, followed by the king, who ennobles Mendo for his heroism and pardons Don Esteban on condition that he marry Inès. The drama ends with the characters stepping out of character to give the play's title and subtitle and announce the sequel.

Inès Mendo ou Le Triomphe du préjugé follows the old Spanish division into three days rather than acts, but the time covered by the action actually extends to several weeks or even months, and the place of action shifts from Don Esteban's château in Estremadura to an inn in Portugal and the Spanish convent of Badajoz. The passage of time is central to the play's psychological theme. After several months of marriage Don Esteban grows increasingly irritated by his wife's uneducated peasant ways and lack of refinement while at the same time resenting his neighbors for snubbing her. Here Mérimée foreshadows midcentury bourgeois comedy of manners, such as Emile Augier's *Le Gendre de M. Poirier* (The Son-in-law of M. Poirier, 1854).

When Esteban's former love, the Duchess Dona Serafina de Montalvan, arrives as a refugee from the Spanish court, accused of complicity in the revolt of Portugal and hunted by the king's troops, she is able to awaken his former passion. The weak and susceptible Esteban is first manipulated into accompanying Serafina in her flight to Portugal, then into deserting his wife and betraying his country. After exhausting her uses of Esteban, whom she despises, the duchess abandons him for the court of Portugal and another lover. Esteban returns to Spain just in time to be pardoned by Inès, who dies in his arms. Aware of his error in previously sparing Esteban's life, Mendo becomes an executioner again in earnest, gripping his pistol in his still intact left hand and shooting the faithless husband dead. In the ironic, distanced epilogue Mendo discloses the title of the play, and Inès rises to her feet to declare that the author has ordered her to come back to life to solicit the audience's indulgence and assure the public it will not have to endure a third part of *Inès Mendo.*

Le Ciel et l'enfer (1825; translated as *Heaven and Hell,* 1825), the last work in the original edition of *Clara Gazul,* is another satire on religious hypocrisy, with details from Lope de Vega and a play by Moratín based on Molière's *Tartuffe* (1664). The drama takes place in Valencia at the time of the Inquisition. While her husband is in the New World, the pious Dona Urraca de Pimentel conducts an adulterous affair with Don Pablo Romero, a handsome young officer of atheistic views whom she hopes to convert to Catholicism. Dona Urraca's confessor is the Machiavellian inquisitor Bartolome. To discover whether her freethinking lover is the author of an impious antigovernment pamphlet, the crafty priest tricks Urraca into believing that Romero has been deceiving her with another woman. In a fit of violent passion the jealous Urraca betrays the young officer.

In a prison of the Inquisition, Urraca confronts her lover with his crime toward her, only to discover he has not been unfaithful. Condemned to die the next day, Romero readily forgives her because without jealousy there can be no love. Full of hatred for her deceitful confessor, Urraca stabs the priest with her dagger as one kills a bull in the ring. Then the beautiful murderess flees with her lover, disguised in the dead inquisitor's robe.

In articles written for the *London Magazine* and *New Monthly Magazine* in 1826, Stendhal emphasized the originality of the *Théâtre de Clara Gazul,* praising the plays for their naturalness, lack of sentimentality, depth of observation, and knowledge of the passions. An anonymously translated edition appeared immediately in English and a later German version was favorably received by Johann Wolfgang von Goethe.

For the second edition of *Théâtre de Clara Gazul* four years later, Mérimée added two new plays, *L'Occasion* (The Occasion, 1830) and *Le Carrosse du Saint-Sacrement* (1830; translated as *The Coach of the Holy Sacrament*, 1917), that display a more subtle technique. Abandoning his earlier combative manner and rapid flow of brutal events, the playwright achieved more-fully defined characters, more-humane situations, and deeper psychological analysis.

L'Occasion is an intimate study of adolescent passion, despair, and the longing for death and oblivion. The entire drama of illicit love and jealousy takes place in colonial Havana within the peaceful garden of a convent school. Maria, a precocious fifteen-year-old pupil, is smoldering with repressed passion for the handsome young director of the convent, Fray Eugenio. Maria is devastated when she discovers that the priest is the lover of her friend Francisca. When, after reading her confession of love, Eugenio hypocritically lectures Maria on her impiety, she confronts him with his affair, forcing the priest to admit that he and Francisca are planning to flee to Jamaica on the proceeds of a book he is writing on the church fathers.

Determined to kill herself after this humiliation, Maria prepares lemonade laced with poison. Just as she is about to drink it and end her life, Francisca appears, complaining of the obstacles to her love for Fray Eugenio. Maria's first impulse is to give Francisca her diamonds to facilitate the lovers' escape. But when her friend asks to use her room as a trysting place with the priest, Maria's generosity turns to jealousy, and she lets the thirsty Francisca drink the poisoned lemonade, and then she drowns herself in the well.

The "occasion" of the title is an ineluctable moment heavy with disastrous consequences that sweeps human characters along with it. In a jarring epilogue Eugenio turns to the audience and, stepping out of the play, makes excuses for the author's errors and begs forgiveness for having caused the deaths of two likable young ladies.

L'Occasion is one of Mérimée's masterpieces. In its artful mixture of lyricism, irony, psychological finesse, and violent passion, it is worthy of a place alongside Alfred de Musset's *On ne badine pas avec l'amour* (No Trifling with Love, 1861). Although the Gothic anticlerical sensationalism, derived from *The Monk*, has been muted, the play still retained its power to shock at least some spectators when in 1948 it entered the repertory of the Comédie-Française with Jeanne Moreau as Maria.

Le Carrosse du Saint-Sacrement is Mérimée's most popular play on the French stage, serving also as the basis of Jacques Offenbach's opera-bouffe *La Périchole* (1868) and Jean Renoir's film *The Golden Coach* (1952). It was premiered by the Théâtre du Vieux Colombier in New York in 1917 and in Paris in 1920, with Valentine Tessier, Jacques Copeau, and Louis Jouvet. The combined total of 179 performances made Mérimée's comedy the most popular play in the Vieux Colombier's repertory. Revived by Jouvet in 1926, it entered the Comédie-Française in 1940 and was staged at the Théâtre National Populaire in 1958 with Maria Casarès and Georges Wilson.

The comedy takes place in eighteenth-century Lima at the residence of the viceroy of Peru, a vain, pompous, and gout-ridden colonial tyrant who is flagrantly deceived by his mistress, the "comédienne" and courtesan Camila Perichole. Mérimée based his play on a well-known anecdote about a celebrated Peruvian actress—who was perhaps an Indian or a half-breed—who had died not long before; Peru itself had been much in the news since 1824 because of Simón Bolívar and the Peruvian War of Independence.

Rumors of Camila's infidelities with a handsome captain and a mulatto matador have made the viceroy jealous, and his secretary Martinez, like an Iago, fans the fires of his suspicions. Without even defending herself, the irrepressible Camila gains the upper hand and compels the doting viceroy to assent to her outrageous request to give her his magnificent new coach. The actress will ride in splendor to mass at the cathedral to humiliate her rivals; then she will give the coach to the church to bring the holy sacrament of extreme unction to the dying. Even the bishop is charmed into accepting an invitation to dinner with the viceroy and Camila, who will sing pious songs for them. Through her histrionic abilities the courtesan-performer vanquishes two powerful institutions, outwitting the state and winning over the church, which will profit from her chicanery.

Le Carrosse du Saint-Sacrement is an ambivalent celebration of theatricality. Camila, a consummate actress onstage and in life, worshiped by the common people and adulated by officials such as the viceroy, enjoys only a marginal social status. Mérimée depicts a culture like his own in which performers, particularly actresses, are sought-after celebrities who are officially excluded from the respectable society they are starting to infiltrate.

The climax of the play is not Camila's tricking of the viceroy but her "blessing" by the bishop. When they first come onstage together, the man of

God gives his hand to the courtesan-actress. The church, fiercest enemy of the stage, has capitulated to the powers of theater. Although the character appears only at the penultimate moments of the play, the brief role of the bishop of Lima is central to the denouement and proved rewarding for an actor of such imposing stage presence as Louis Jouvet. In their final duo the more La Perichole disparages her "questionable profession," the more the bishop defends it. "Mademoiselle," the bishop proclaims, "ce carrosse sera pour vous le chariot d'Eliejil vous mènera droit an ciel" (Mademoiselle, this coach will be for you the chariot of Elijah; it will carry you straight to heaven). It is no wonder that at its premiere in 1850 this delightfully malicious satire was hissed by scandalized conservatives.

Published with *La Jacquerie* (The Jacquerie) in 1828, *La Famille de Carvajal* (The Carvajal Family) was condemned by French critics of the day as sordid and ugly, but Mary Shelley in the January 1829 issue of the *Westminster Review* praised the play as "a tremendous domestic tragedy, founded on the same story as the Cenci," and found that "Each scene transcends the one before in its appalling horror; and the last, in which the miserable girl poignards her father, completes the dark picture, spreading over the canvas the lurid hues of whirlwind and volcano." Unlike Percy Bysshe Shelley's pseudo-Shakespearean five-act blank-verse tragedy *The Cenci* (1819), Mérimée's one-act prose drama is written in the popular idiom of Gothic melodrama. In the violent colonial world of his isolated plantation in seventeenth-century Spanish New Granada (present-day Colombia), José de Carvajal is the brutal landowner who tortures native blacks and Indians; he is also a tyrannical father who abuses his wife, Agustina, and daughter Catalina.

Gripped by incestuous passion for Catalina, José puts a knife to his wife's throat, forcing her to write a letter denying his paternity. But Catalina fights off her father's advances, displaying the same strong-willed temperament. "Nous sommes deux démons aux prises; je veux être le plus fort" (We are two demons fighting it out; I want to be the stronger), José declares; "Ella sera à moi, on je mourrai!" (I'll have her, or I'll die!). The drama rushes headlong to its sensational denouement. While José practices alchemy in his laboratory, Catalina waits to be abducted by her lover, Captain Alonso. Poisoned by her husband, Agustina dies in terrible agony. Although José, maddened by desire, slips an aphrodisiac into his daughter's milk, the scheme fails because the girl is fasting. Catalina stabs her father as he attempts to rape her. Alonso arrives at the head of his party of two hundred Indi-

ans—only to find his fiancée clutching a bloody knife above the corpse of his prospective father-in-law. A young Indian is ready to cut off the head of the murderess. Spared by the chief, Catalina asks to be led into the forest even if it means being devoured by tigers. "Plutôt des tigres que des hommes!" (Better by tigers than by humans!) exclaims the beautiful patricide. The young Indian then steps forward to address the audience: "Ainsi finit cette comédie et la famille de Carvajal. Le père est poignardé, la fille sera mangée; excusez les fantes de l'auteur" (Thus ends this comedy and the Carvajal family. The father has been stabbed, the daughter will be eaten; pardon the faults of the author).

The breakneck tempo, hyperbolic passions, and improbable events have led critics to declare *La Famille de Carvajal* a hilarious parody of melodrama. This view is supported by a deadpan preface consisting of three bogus documents: extracts from a scholarly Spanish source and two letters from readers. The first comes from a Spanish privateer looking for a play his sailors can stage on ship, for whom "rien ne sera trop chaud pour nous, ni trop épicé" (nothing will be too hot or too spicy). The second is a plea from a fifteen-year-old, forbidden by her mother to read Romantic literature, for strong after-midnight reading matter. Having exhausted her father's library, she needs a short drama or *roman noir* full of crimes and love à la George Gordon, Lord Byron that ends badly with the heroine dying unhappily and, if possible, a hero named Alphonse.

Reveling in perverse passions and piling up macabre horrors characterized the "black romanticism" of the late 1820s and colored even Pixérécourt's last plays. These conventions and traditions are as much the subject of Mérimée's pastiche in *La Famille de Carvajal* as are styles and mannerisms of Spanish theater.

Written and published in 1828, *La Jacquerie* is Mérimée's longest and most ambitious and controversial dramatic work: an historical drama in thirty-six scenes about a fourteenth-century peasant revolt named for its anonymous protagonists, "les Jacques." The playwright abandoned Spanish exoticism for French history and the Middle Ages, then coming into vogue. This experiment in the imaginative use of the materials of history served as a transition to Mérimée's first prose narrative, *1572. Chronique du temps de Charles IX* (Chronicle of the Times of Charles IX, 1829), an historical novel largely in dialogue.

For many, *La Jacquerie* seems flawed artistically and historically. Even admirers of its scope—thirty-seven named characters, active roles for the masses, sieges and battles, and dozens of scene changes—are troubled by the play's apparent lack of unity and focus. In her generally favorable review Mary Shelley objected: "We feel the want of one prominent character to concentrate the interest, without which a dramatic composition is never perfect." For others it is Mérimée's dramatic masterpiece and the most original French historical drama of the nineteenth century, anticipating Brechtian epic structure and technique.

La Jacquerie, subtitled "Scènes féodales" (Feudal Scenes), belongs to the category of scènes historiques, a genre intended for reading, not stage performance, developed by Ludovic Vitet and his circle. These scenes, which were read by their authors at the salon of Mérimée's friend Etienne-Jean Delécluze, dealt episodically with historical subjects in dialogue form and strove for a picturesque evocation of a strictly historical past.

Mérimée, who based La Jacquerie on Jean Froissart and other historians, used as his models foreign works admired by the young Romantics: Goethe's Götz von Berlichingen (1773), Walter Scott's Quentin Durward (1823), and William Shakespeare's histories, especially the Cade rebellion in II Henry VI (1594). But unlike most historical drama that includes prominent public figures, all the characters and events and most of the places in La Jacquerie are invented. No reference is made to the actual leaders of the Jacques revolt or any of its events. Instead the playwright chose to re-create the period through fictional characters who exemplify different aspects of the revolt.

Living under the repressive monarchy of Charles X, Mérimée showed daring in choosing as his subject the peasant wars, thereby giving voice to those ignored by official history and treating sympathetically an uprising by oppressed lower classes against the clergy and nobility. In the preface Mérimée explains his goal: "J'ai tâché de donner une idée des moeurs atroces du XIVᵉ siècle, et je crois avoir plutôt adouci que rembruni les couleurs de mon tableau" (I have tried to give an impression of the horrifying mores of the fourteenth century, and I believe that I have lightened rather than darkened the colors of my picture). La Jacquerie paints a bloody and grotesque picture of the savagery, ignorance, and lawlessness of the Middle Ages in deliberate contrast to the idealized image of medieval piety, courtliness, and virtue given by Catholic romantics such as François-René Chateaubriand.

The thirty-six disconnected scenes convey the broad sweep of the peasant revolt in northern France in the spring of 1358. Destitute vassals driven by hunger and despair are pitted against nobles and clergy fighting ruthlessly to defend their property and privileges. Mérimée is not interested in individual heroes but in the collective drama, revealing the fundamental conflict between two classes—serfs and peasants on the one hand and lords and clergy on the other—and the temporary alliances each forms with other social groups. The English mercenaries follow whichever side offers them the greatest opportunities for pillage. As victims of tyranny with a just cause, the peasants are sympathetic but undisciplined and confused. In the end, lacking either solidarity or brains, they are betrayed, outwitted, and defeated.

Various characters come briefly to the fore only to be consumed by treachery and violence. Disgruntled at not being chosen abbot, Frère Jean (a character derived from François Rabelais) betrays the monks to lead the revolt, but, himself a ruthless authoritarian with contempt for the peasants, he is eventually killed by his own followers. The valet Pierre, in love with the daughter of the lord of the castle, is twice a turncoat, betraying his master and then his new friends, the "Jacques." The only man of principle is the outlaw Werewolf, leader of a group of bandits, who hates all of society. A brigand of honor who loves liberty and justice, Werewolf is a primitive being of the sort fascinating to the young Romantics.

Each scene of La Jacquerie has an independent life of its own, serving to illustrate the operation of the social and psychological forces shaping the conflict. For example, in scene 14, when the tyrannical baron of Apremont captures the English soldier of fortune Siward and holds him for ransom in his castle, the prisoner flirts with the nobleman's daughter Isabelle, hoping to persuade her to break her engagement so that he can marry her for her property. Falsely but cunningly Isabelle informs Siward that if she renounces her fiancé she will lose her inheritance. On hearing this news Siward abandons his passionate wooing and beats a hasty retreat. The episode illustrates Mérimée's technique of unmasking the feudal conventions of chivalry and courtly love in order to reveal the real motives of greed and self-interest that lie beneath. Siward later rapes Isabelle.

The brevity and schematic clarity of the scenes give them the sharpness of parable or moral exemplum. In scene 18 Werewolf, temporarily allied with the peasants, storms the convent and kills the abbot as he clutches a reliquary and excommunicates the bandit. Horrified by the sacrilege and fearing divine retribution, the serfs listen in disbelief as Werewolf proclaims the abbott a carcass devoid of power, but their superstitious faith soon crumbles. In the course of a few speeches the timorous peasants go

Eugénie Montijo on the day of her marriage to Louis Napoleon; drawing by Mérimée, who took charge of royal entertainments after the couple became emperor and empress in 1852 (Collection Broglie / J.-L. Charmet)

from pious awe to callous disregard for human decency, leaving the desecrated corpse for others to bury after robbing it of a gold chain, purse, and clothes. In scene 23 the bourgeois merchants of Beauvais, unwilling to meet their workers' demands for higher pay, haggle so long with the local serfs that the town is sacked by the enemy. Mérimée's ironic technique of stripping away moral pretense to expose human cupidity gives many scenes of *La Jacquerie* a theatrical power and incisiveness worthy of Bertolt Brecht. The play received its world premiere in 1921 in the Soviet Union, where it was given several different productions. Vsevolod Meyerhold planned but did not realize a staging in the spring of 1922.

First published in *La Revue de Paris* in 1830, *Les Mécontents* (The Discontented), is an amusing but facile satire on royalist conspirators under the Empire, aiming by extension at the ultras of Mérimée's day. Less an historical drama than a comedy of manners, the long one-act play was well received in liberal salons. The action unfolds in the châteaux of the Count and Countess of Tournelles, where a bumbling group of vain, pretentious, and cowardly aristocrats play at plotting against the emperor to re-

store the monarchy. When a gendarme appears, the would-be conspirators scatter in fear but soon are delighted to learn that the count has been named chamberlain to the empress.

In 1834 Mérimée was appointed inspector general of historical monuments and charged with identifying and preserving the national patrimony. As a writer he turned to the novella, which became his preferred genre and source of lasting fame. Involved in scholarly research and an active social life, the inventor of Clara Gazul abandoned the theater. In 1848 Mérimée began studying Russian, eventually translating the works of Alexander Pushkin, Nikolai Vasilyevich Gogol, and Ivan Turgenev. A government inspector who relished hoaxes, Mérimée made the first French version of Gogol's *The Inspector General* (1836).

In 1850 Mérimée permitted an actress at the Comédie-Française to perform *Le Carrosse du Sacre-Sacrement,* which was greeted with hisses. Shortly thereafter the author gave a salon reading of his new play, *Les Deux Héritages* (The Two Heritages), to see if it was stageworthy, but the reaction was overwhelmingly unfavorable. A highly plotted comedy of manners, this "morality play in six tableaux" dealt with the amorous and political intrigues of the young hero Félix as he tried to win an election. Like George Sand and Alfred de Musset, Mérimée harbored the illusion that he could achieve success in the theater with the sort of moralizing bourgeois drama then coming into vogue.

In 1852, as a prologue to his historical study, *Episode de l'histoire de Russie. Les Faux Démétrius,* (1853; translated as *Demetrius the Impostor: An Episode in the History of Russia,* 1853), Mérimée published *Les Débuts d'un aventurier* (The Debuts of an Adventurer, 1853), "scènes historiques" in dialogue form about the Russian pretender who attempted to overthrow Boris Godunov, which was the subject of Pushkin's play. When in 1859 his friend Emile Augier proposed turning the story of the pretender into "un grand mélodrame," Mérimée again had hopes of a triumph in the theater, but nothing came of it.

As a cultured civil servant interested in archaeology and languages, Merimée traveled widely in France and abroad. Although he had several longlasting love affairs, the author never married, having a deep mistrust of permanent emotional commitment. His long-standing friendship with the family of Eugénie Montijo, who married Louis Napoleon and became the empress of France in 1852, made the writer an intimate of the imperial household, where he served as unofficial literary adviser, helping the emperor write his life of Julius Caesar and assisting the empress in organizing entertainment for guests at the royal residence at Compiègne. Mérimée served as author, actor, and producer of the charades and amateur theatricals at official house parties.

During the last years of his life, Mérimée suffered from asthma. On 23 September 1870 he died of emphysema and heart failure in Cannes, where he is buried in the English cemetery. An atheist, he asked to have a Protestant minister officiate at his funeral.

His dramatic career, after opening brilliantly, ended in unrealized projects and trivial social games. It was when he was out of step with the stage of his time that Mérimée made his most lasting contribution to world drama, not when he attempted to compromise with the popular taste of nineteenth-century theatergoers.

Although he was not appreciated as a playwright in his own time, Mérimée was the true pioneer of Romantic theater in France, creating several years before Hugo or Dumas *père* a radically original form of drama that boldly challenged neoclassical rules of decorum, bienséance, and probability. Putting into practice the theoretical ideas found in Stendhal's *Racine and Shakespeare* (1823) that called for the abolition of the unities, the use of prose, and the presentation of action on the stage, Mérimée produced a small body of work for the stage unlike any other. These cruel, violent, and exotic plays are concise and ironic, devoid of the high-flown sentiments and turgid expansiveness characteristic of Hugo. In the twentieth century they have been recognized for their high theatrical values by such masters of the French stage as Jacques Copeau, Charles Dullin, Georges Pitoëff, and Louis Jouvet.

Letters:

Correspondence générale, edited by Maurice Parturier, volumes I–VI (Paris: Le Divan, 1941–1947); volumes VII–XVII (Toulouse: Privat, 1953–1964).

Bibliographies:

Pierre Trahard and Pierre Josserand, *Bibliographie des oeuvres de Prosper Mérimée* (Paris: Champion, 1929);

Barbara T. Cooper, "Mérimée's Romantic Theater: The Present State of Scholarship," *Nineteenth-Century French Studies,* 6, nos. 1–2 (1977–1978): 72–81;

Natalia Chechel, "Zhakeriya' Prospera Merime v teatri 'Berezil,'" *Ukrainske teatralne vidrodzhennia* (Kiev: Natalia Chechel and the International Renaissance Fund, 1993), pp. 59–82.

Biographies:

Pierre Trahard, *La Jeunesse de Prosper Mérimée (1803–1834),* 2 volumes (Paris: Champion, 1925);

Trahard, *Prosper Mérimée de 1834 à 1853* (Paris: Champion, 1928);

Trahard, *La Vieillesse de Mérimée (1854–1870)* (Paris: Champion, 1930);

Robert Baschet, *Mérimée (1803–1870): Du Romantisme au Second Empire* (Paris: Nouvelles Editions Latines, 1959);

Paul Léon, *Mérimée et son temps* (Paris: Presses Universitaires Françaises, 1962);

Alan W. Raitt, *Prosper Mérimée* (New York: Scribner, 1970);

Jean Freustié, *Prosper Mérimée, le nerveux hautain* (Paris: Hachette, 1982);

Jean Autin, *Prosper Mérimée: écrivain, archéologue, homme politique* (Paris: Perrin, 1983).

References:

Roger Bellet, "Jacques Bonhomme, loup-garou et la lutte de classes dans *La Jacquerie,*" *Europe,* 557 (September 1975): 8–30;

Frank Paul Bowman, *Prosper Mérimée: Heroism, Pessimism and Irony* (Los Angeles: University of California Press, 1962);

P. W. M. Cogman, "The Brother and the Beast: Structure and Meaning of Mérimée's *La Jaquerie*," *French Studies,* 36 (January 1982): 26–36;

Barbara T. Cooper, "Dramatized Prologues: The Space of Aesthetic Reflection in Works by Alexandre Duval and Prosper Mérimée," *Degré Second,* 9 (1985): 33–41;

Cooper, "Mérimée's *La Jacquerie:* Time, History, and the 'Pleating' of the Text," in *L'Hénaurme Siècle: A Miscellany of Essays on Nineteenth-Century Literature,* edited by Will L. McLendon (Heidelberg: Carl Winter Universitätsverlag, 1984), pp. 27–34;

Françoise Court-Perez, *"La Jacquerie," Dictionnaire des Oeuvres Littéraires de la langue française,* volume 2, edited by Jean-Pierre Beaumarchais and Daniel Couty (Paris: Bordas, 1994), pp. 991–992;

Court-Perez, "Théâtre de Clara Gazul," *Dictionnaire des Oeuvres Littéraires de la langue française,* volume 4, edited by Beaumarchais and Couty (Paris: Bordas, 1994), pp. 1888–1890;

Daniel Couty and Dominique Giovacchini, "Mérimée," *Dictionnaire des Littératures de langue française,* volume 2, edited by Beaumarchais, Couty, and Alain Rey (Paris: Bordas, 1984), pp. 1473–1480;

Charles Dédéyan, "Les Nouvelles Pièces de Mérimée," in *Le Drame romantique en Europe* (Paris: Société d'Edition d'Enseignement Supérieur, 1982), pp. 223–226;

Dédéyan, "Le Théâtre de Clara Gazul," in his *Le Drame romantique en Europe* (Paris: Société d'Edition d'Enseignement Supérieur, 1982), pp. 217–219; 223–226;

V. Dynnik, "Dramaturgiya Prospera Merime," *Izbrannye Dramaticheskiye Proizvedeniya* (Moscow: Iskusstvo, 1954), pp. 5–31;

Hassan El Nouty, "Le Jeu de Clara Gazul," in his *Théâtre et pré-cinéma: essai sur le problématique du spectacle au XIXe siècle* (Paris: A.-G. Nizet, 1978), pp. 123–127;

El Nouty, "Spectacle oculaire et bande dessinée—*La Jacquerie* de Mérimée," in his *Théâtre et pré-cinéma: essai sur le problématique du spectacle au XIXe siècle* (Paris: A.-G. Nizet, 1978), pp. 171–186;

W. D. Howarth, "Romantic skirmishes: Mérimée and the 'scène historique,'" in *Sublime and Grotesque: A Study of French Romantic Drama* (London: Harrap, 1975), pp. 110–121;

Russell King, "Prosper Mérimée: Attempts at Romantic Drama," *Nottingham French Studies,* VI (October 1967): 67–76;

Jean Mallon and Pierre Salomon, "Approche de Mérimée," *Théâtre de Clara Gazul: Romans et nouvelles* (Paris: Gallimard, 1978), pp. IX–LVI;

Gérard Milhaud, "Un théâtre sous le masque," *Europe,* 557 (September 1975): 47–59;

Salomon, "Préface," *Théâtre de Clara Gazul, suivi de La famille de Carvajal* (Paris: Garnier-Flammarion, 1968), pp. 19–33;

Maxwell A. Smith, *Prosper Mérimée* (New York: Twayne, 1972);

Gerd Thieltges, *Bürgerlicher Klassizismus und romantisches Theater: Untersuchungen zu den frühen Dramen Prosper Mérimées (1803–1870)* (Geneva: Droz, 1975);

Pierre Valde, *Prosper Mérimée, L'Occasion. Mise en scène et commentaires* (Paris: Le Seuil, 1949).

Papers:

All of Mérimée's papers and books were destroyed when the house he had lived in was burned on 23 May 1871 during the last days of the Paris Commune.

Octave Mirbeau
(16 February 1848 – 16 February 1917)

Julia Przybos
Hunter College of The City University of New York

PLAY PRODUCTIONS: *Vieux ménage,* Paris, Théâtre d'Application, 20 December 1894;

Les Mauvais bergers, Paris, Théâtre de la Renaissance, 14 December 1897;

L'Epidémie, Paris, Théâtre-Libre d'Antoine, 14 May 1898;

Les Amants, Paris, Théâtre du Grand Guignol, 25 May 1901;

Le Portefeuille, Paris, Théâtre de la Renaissance-Gémier, 19 February 1902;

Scrupules, Paris, Théâtre du Grand Guignol, 2 June 1902;

Les Affaires sont les affaires, Paris, Théâtre-Français, 20 April 1903;

Interview, Paris, Théâtre du Grand Guignol, 1 February 1904;

Le Foyer, Paris, Théâtre-Français, 7 December 1908.

BOOKS: *Le Comédien, suivi de: L'Entrefilet de M; Vitu, la Lettre de M. Mirbeau à M. Magnard, l'Ordre du jour du théâtre du Château-d'Eau, C. Coquelin, Les Comédiens par un comédien, réponse à M. Octave Mirbeau* (Paris: Brunox, 1883);

Lettres de ma chaumière (Paris: Evreux, 1886);

L'Abbé Jules (Paris, 1888);

Sébastien Roch (Paris, 1890);

Les Mauvais bergers (Paris: Charpentier et Fasquelle, 1898);

L'Epidémie (Paris: Fasquelle, 1898);

Le Journal d'une femme de chambre (Paris, 1900); translated by Douglas Garman as *The Diary of a Chambermaid* (London: Elek, 1966);

Vieux ménage (Paris: Fasquelle, 1901);

Le Portefeuille (Paris: Fasquelle, 1902);

Les Affaires sont les affaires (Paris: Fasquelle, 1903);

Farces et moralités: L'Epidémie; Vieux ménage; Le Portefeuille; Les Amants; Scrupules; Interview (Paris: Fasquelle, 1908);

Le Foyer (Paris: Fasquelle, 1908);

Oeuvres inédites, 4 volumes (Paris, 1918–1920);

Théâtre, 3 volumes (Paris: Flammarion, 1921–1922);

Octave Mirbeau

Le Jardin des supplices (Paris: G. & A. Mornay, 1923); translated by Raymond Rudorff as *The Garden of Tortures* (London: Tandem, 1969);

Gens de théâtre. Auteurs et critiques; Comédiens et Comédiennes. La Censure. Le Théâtre populaire. Quelques portraits (Paris: Flammarion, 1924);

Théâtre (Paris: Editions nationales, 1936).

SELECTED PERIODICAL PUBLICATIONS— UNCOLLECTED: *Les Affaires sont les affaires, L'Illustration,* supplément au no. 3139, 25 April 1903;

Le Foyer, L'Illustration théâtrale, no. 103, 12 December 1908.

Octave Mirbeau was one of the best-known figures on the journalistic, literary, and artistic scene of France's belle époque. In his youth Mirbeau wrote for the right-wing press and later for the left. His mature journalism championed the oppressed, addressing such issues as poverty, colonialism, child welfare, the death penalty, prostitution, and women's legal rights. His novels presented moral and social problems such as the sexual abuse of boys at Jesuit *collèges,* priests' celibacy, and the sexual hypocrisy of the ruling classes. He became a playwright in the 1890s, expressing leftist views with an anarchist bent. In his plays he attacked the hypocrisy of bourgeois marriage (*Vieux ménage* [Old Couple, 1894]), chastised the corruption of politicians (*L'Epidémie* [The Epidemic, 1898]), condemned the irresponsibility of leaders (*Les Mauvais bergers* [Bad Shepherds, 1897]), criticized the obsessional pursuit of riches (*Les Affaires sont les affaires* [Business Is Business, 1903]), and exposed the dishonesty of philanthropists running charitable institutions (*Le Foyer* [The Shelter, 1908]). Mirbeau's battles with the Comédie-Française, before that bastion of conservatism staged *Les Affaires sont les affaires* and *Le Foyer,* are important events in French theatrical history. His major plays were successful in France and abroad, making him a "red millionaire" who provided Emile Zola with financial support during the Alfred Dreyfus affair. Mirbeau's *engagement* went beyond social, political, and judicial issues, embracing theatrical, literary, and artistic causes. His discovery and promotion of Symbolist playwright Maurice Maeterlinck's *La Princesse Maleine* in 1890 did not diminish his admiration for Henry Becque, often considered the best naturalist playwright in France, nor his taste for such a light comedy as Alexandre Bisson and Antony Mars's *Les Surprises du divorce* (Surprises of Divorce, 1888). His veneration for the writings of the elitist Jules-Amédée Barbey d'Aurevilly did not stifle his enthusiasm for the populist *Marie-Claire* (1910), penned by the ex-seamstress Marguerite Audoux, further attesting to his openness toward new and diverse styles. Similarly, his liking of Puvis de Chavannes did not prevent him from admiring Pierre-Auguste Renoir, Vincent Van Gogh, Paul Cézanne, and Félix Vallotton. "I am lucky to be an eclectic who can maximize the pleasure I get from works of art," he wrote in *Les Eonvains.* His pen helped many, including Jean Grave, for whose anarchist books he wrote prefaces. He befriended Claude Monet, Auguste Rodin, Aristide Maillol, Camille Claudel, and Jean-François Raffaelli, promoting their art in his criticism, which appeared in the widely read press. Mirbeau's celebrity faded after his death. His only work that has remained popular is the novel *Le Journal d'une femme de chambre* (The Diary of a Chambermaid, 1900), thanks to its film adaptations, including one by Luis Buñuel. The recent efforts of a few dedicated scholars, critics, and theater directors have rescued Mirbeau from oblivion. *Les Affaires sont les affaires* has been a great success in Paris and throughout France in 1994 and 1995.

Octave Mirbeau was born on 16 February 1848 at Trévières in Normandy, the son of an *officier de santé* of common origins. At eleven he entered the Collège Saint-François-Xavier, a prestigious Jesuit boarding school catering to sons of the nobility and the wealthy bourgeoisie. Memories of humiliations he endured for four unhappy years found their way into *Sébastien Roch* (1890), a partially autobiographical novel. A mediocre student, he was dismissed under unclear circumstances. His stay with the Jesuits at Vannes seems to have given Mirbeau his militant anticlericalism and a profound distaste for all institutions that limit liberty: boarding schools, military barracks, prisons, and monasteries. He obtained his *baccalauréat* in 1866 and studied law in Paris, according to his father's wishes. He discovered the city's theatrical life, which was dominated by the plays of Emile Augier and Alexandre Dumas *fils.* Mirbeau participated in the Franco-Prussian War of 1870, and the atrocities he witnessed are thought to be the source of his antimilitarism. After a brief stint as a notary clerk in Normandy, he returned to Paris in 1873 as secretary to the editor of *L'Ordre de Paris,* a Bonapartist biweekly.

Mirbeau's literary career began in journalism, which was initially his primary source of income. In "Un Gentilhomme" (A Nobleman), an unfinished, semi-autobiographical novel, he describes the time he slaved for editors of different political convictions as mental prostitution. For the next twenty-five years his theater reviews, art criticism, and columns on current events appeared throughout the political spectrum of the press, from the extremist, anti-Semitic *Grimaces* to the mildly anti-Semitic *Gaulois* and the moderate *Figaro* to the Dreyfusards' leftist *Aurore* and the anarchist *L'En-dehors.* Mirbeau's literary debut in 1886 was *Lettres de ma chaumière* (Letters from my Cottage), a collection of stories previously published in *La France.* He dedicated them to writers as disparate as Zola, Henri Lavedan, and Barbey d'Aurevilly, calling the latter "the master of masters" when d'Aurevilly sent him his first novel, *Le Calvaire* (The Cavalry, 1886). His eclectic tastes led him to Leo Tolstoy and Fyodor Dostoyevsky in the 1880s and Knut Hamsun in the 1890s. Although present with Paul Alexis, Henry Céard, Léon Hennique, and Guy de Maupassant at the famous Trapp dinner celebrating Edmond de Goncourt, Gustave Flaubert, and Zola in 1877, Mirbeau rejected the naturalist label and objected to being counted among Zola's disciples. Goncourt recognized Mirbeau as a kindred spirit and in his will designated him as a founding member of the Académie Goncourt.

The success of Mirbeau's novel *Le Journal d'une femme de chambre,* published in 1900, brought him financial independence and liberated him from slaving for the press. An article refused by the popular *Le Journal,* for which he wrote more than four hundred chronicles, prompted Mirbeau to fight its owner in court. In a May 1902 issue of the satirical *L'Assiette au beurre* he rebuked nationalists and anti-Semites. After this vitriolic farewell to slave journalism, he rarely consented to requests for articles.

In the 1890s the theater became Mirbeau's alternative to the press for the dissemination of his antiestablishment ideas, despite his 1882 *Figaro* article exhibiting distrust of actors as puppets of a society dominated by artifice and philistine taste for operetta, musical reviews, and conventional plays. He despised directors as industrialists motivated by gain who would rather entertain than provoke. He nevertheless became a playwright and married a former actress, Alice Regnault, in 1887.

Mirbeau's stage debut was *Vieux ménage,* a one-act play that opened on 20 December 1894 at the Théâtre d'Application. The characters include a stout, philandering husband of sixty; his half-paralyzed and self-pitying wife; and at the beginning a young maid. First the wife complains that his dalliances with her maids have left her without respectful help; then she warns him of the underage local girls that are damaging his political career. Fearing abandonment, she encourages him to seek the company of their neighbor, an elegant divorced woman who would bring life to their home. The hypocritical husband pretends offense as a Catholic and political leader and walks out. Her last effort to establish contact with her husband having failed, the sick woman wishes for death. In this poignant farce Mirbeau addresses the themes he developed in *Le Journal d'une femme de chambre:* existential suffering, the war between the sexes, and lack of communication between people that characterize a declining society. *Vieux ménage* is the first of six one-act plays published in the 1908 collection *Farces et moralités* (Farces and Morality Plays), whose title suggests Mirbeau's moral intent. The plays feature satirical exaggeration of characters and situations for didactic purposes.

Les Mauvais bergers opened on 15 December 1897 at the Théâtre de la Renaissance with Sarah Bernhardt in the role of Madeleine. It was a great success, one that prompted Henry Becque to declare Mirbeau his artistic superior. The play in five acts reflects Mirbeau's political shift to the anarchist left. It depicts the growth and defeat of a strike, focusing on the life of two families, the working-class Thieuxs and the industrialist Hargands. The main character, Jean Roule, is a disappointed activist who has failed in his effort to organize workers in Brazil and Spain. The Thieux family's struggles and his love for Madeleine lead him to galvanize the oppressed workers. The pregnant Madeleine assists Jean, exhorting the distrustful workers to fight till death. She compares their fate to Christ's, arguing that victory demands blood sacrifice. The toll of her fanatical eloquence is heavy: she and Jean are killed with many others in a confrontation with the army. Hargand's son Robert favors the strike. Hargand's humanity in the face of Robert's death at the barricades makes him more than a stereotype, something that became clear earlier when he admits to his administrators that the workers' demands are just. He blames himself for Robert's death, lamenting over his body. Before dying, Madeleine refuses to deliver Robert's body to Hargand, declaring that he belongs to the workers. The plot of *Les Mauvais bergers* is reminiscent of Zola's *Germinal* (1885). Jean Roule resembles Etienne Lantier, especially in the forest scene when he speaks to unruly strikers. Not content to rely on literary sources, Mirbeau traveled to Creusot to visit Schneider's plants. While the end of *Germinal* optimistically prophesies the birth of new generations of fighters, the deaths of Jean Roule and the pregnant Madeleine send a pessimistic message about the future of the workers' movement. In accordance with Mirbeau's anarchist beliefs, the bad shepherds of the title are both paternalistic industrialists and elected or self-appointed leaders. These include radical and socialist politicians and fanatics like Jean and Madeleine.

L'Epidémie opened at the Théâtre-Libre d'Antoine on 14 May 1898. Its subject mirrors Henrik Ibsen's *An Enemy of the People* (1882), which was performed on 29 March, with Mirbeau's participation, to benefit Alfred Dreyfus and his defender, Zola. Characteristically, Mirbeau had already criticized a city council that ignores an epidemic when it rages in army barracks and slums in his investigative journalism. The councilmen's attitudes change upon hearing that a "respected, fat, pink and happy" bourgeois has died of the disease. This incarnation of Henry Monnier's smug Joseph Prudhomme is proclaimed a hero worthy of an official burial. In a panic the councilmen designate enormous funds to fight the epidemic, which has "mi-

Mirbeau in his study, mid 1890s

raculously" violated class lines. The play's characters are caricatures, with Dr. Triceps's pseudoscientific speeches echoing Flaubert's apothecary, Homais. The stage set's abundance of flags, official portraits, and statuettes of the French Republic enhances the play's confrontational, antigovernmental character. This one-act satirical play soon disappeared from Antoine's realistic repertory.

After this condemnation of the ruling classes Mirbeau returned to the private realm with *Les Amants* (Lovers). In this one-act play that premiered at the Grand Guignol on 25 May 1901 he targets love that is free of marriage's compromises. The play opens with a solemn, black-clad introducer who salutes the audience and describes the romantic set, an old bench in a moonlit park. He announces that all that will happen in the play between lovers conforms to tradition; their words, sighs, silences, cries, and singing exalt "eternal things." This romanticization of love is immediately shattered by a lovers' quarrel. The man's clichéd flattery is answered by the woman's complaints about his indifference to her deepest needs. Their fight dissolves into passionate caresses. The play's dialogue masterfully employs the spontaneous language of argument. Half realism, half parody, the play conveys Mirbeau's Schopenhauerian pessimism about the lack of communication be-

tween the sexes, which condemns men and women to solitude.

Le Portefeuille (The Wallet) opened at the Renaissance-Gémier on 19 February 1902 and is based on a true story Mirbeau published in *Le Journal*. This one-act comedy takes place in a police commissioner's office that features an old sofa. The commissioner complains to his assistant, Jean Maltenu, that theater bores him because it rehashes such shopworn subjects as love and adultery instead of tackling social issues. Maltenu leaves, and the commissioner sits at his desk, ostensibly to work, but strikes a Don-Juanesque pose when he hears a high-pitched female voice. Flora Tambour is dragged in by policemen. She has an arrest record and has been caught again soliciting in front of the police station. The commissioner dismisses the policemen to better grill the prisoner, and Flora sits on her lover's lap. He congratulates himself on their arrangement, which does not compromise his position and provides a foolproof excuse for his wife. He allays her doubts of his love, declaring that "we ask sacrifice of people we love passionately." Flora calls him a pervert upon hearing that he becomes aroused when the police brutalize her. Offstage voices force the lovebirds to resume their charade. The aptly named beggar Jean Guenille (*guenille* means "tattered garment" or "worthless object") enters, insisting on seeing the commissioner. He has found a wallet containing ten thousand francs. The commissioner calls him a hero for returning the money but changes his attitude when he learns that Jean is homeless. Since the law does not reward heroism but punishes crimes and misdemeanors, the commissioner has Jean arrested for breaking the antivagrancy law. Once the lovers are alone, Flora conveys her disapproval and the commissioner orders her arrest. The commissioner locks the wallet in his desk drawer.

Scrupules (Scruples), another one-act play, opened on 2 June 1902 at the Grand Guignol. A man in evening attire enters through the window of a Louis XVI salon, followed by an older man carrying a large suitcase. The gentleman, the prototype of Maurice Leblanc's detective character Arsène Lupin, tells his valet that he got delayed at his club and orders him to pack a collection of precious medals. The intruder finds a bundle of letters from a woman but leaves them behind, explaining that he despises blackmail. While the valet is dreaming aloud about the quiet country life, his master breaks a vase. A man in a nightshirt enters the salon. The burglar asks forgiveness for waking him up and compliments him on his taste in furniture and art. He advises the victim to don a robe out of concern that he will catch cold. The robed man leaves the room, announcing that he will call the police, and the valet urges his master to flee. The robber refuses and orders him to unpack their loot. The victim returns, and the burglar explains that he chose his current profession after much experience and reflection. He has been a merchant, a financier, a politician, and a journalist, but these respectable professions forced him to be a hypocrite. Now that he steals openly his conscience is clear. To prove that theft drives men's actions, he cites the victim's thievery as a stock market speculator, an art collector, and a philanthropist. The burglar's profession offers advantages that make the burglarized man envious; on the job he meets women who like him not for his social position but for himself. When a commissioner arrives, the victim sends him away, explaining the presence of strangers as an art appraisal, then asks the burglar to share his breakfast. Ever a gentleman, the burglar declines because he is not appropriately attired. The burglar prepares to leave through the window, but the victim invites him to exit proudly through the front door.

Les Affaires sont les affaires is Mirbeau's finest long play. He had already written about the power of money in the story "Agronomie," published in *Lettres de ma chaumière*. Mirbeau resurrects a traditional character first made famous by Alain-René

Lesage in *Turcaret* (1709) and later by Honoré de Balzac in *Mercadet* (1851). Mirbeau's ruthless financier of common origins advocates progress; Isidore Lechat is a new man in a new world dominated by financial capitalism, where anything can be bought. Lechat is virtually omnipotent in international business and public affairs. The only person who can resist him is his daughter, who abhors him. Germaine urges her lover, Lucien Garraud, a Lechat employee, to leave Château Vauperdu with her. The castle is a property Lechat acquired after ruining its owner, the marquis de Porcellet. She wants a simple life that reflects her moral standards. Germaine is disgusted by her father's shameful deals that impoverished many and pushed others to suicide. Lechat is revolutionizing French agriculture, launching his political campaign, and planning Germaine's marriage with Porcellet's son to forge a politically valuable alliance with the aristocracy. He appears onstage accompanied by Gruggh and Phinck, two sly engineers who seek capital for a hydroelectric plant. Not even the death of his son Xavier can keep Lechat from catching the engineers in a subversive scheme.

The director of the Comédie-Française, Jules Claretie, found Lechat's callousness outrageous and fought protractedly with Mirbeau. The play finally opened on 20 April 1903 and was a resounding success both at home and abroad. Critics accustomed to tightly crafted plots objected to the play's emphasis on character over action, resenting its form as a throwback to old-fashioned character comedies. Indeed, each act presents a different facet of Lechat's complex personality, building considerable psychological depth. Xavier's death by car crash provides the play with a moral dimension, and for Alfred Jarry it is a modern version of the deus ex machina where, in the absence of God, the machine acts alone in punishing Lechat for his crimes. Some critics stressed the play's tragic aspect, with money replacing the ancient *fatum*.

Interview, a successful one-act farce that is an adaptation of two journalistic pieces, opened at the Grand Guignol on 1 February 1904. In the first scene the audience is introduced to a ruddy, middle-aged bar owner, Chapuzot, and a woman in rags whose face is "marked by alcoholism and extreme poverty." She is sipping a shot of liquor while seeking Chapuzot's advice about her baby's stomachache. He tells her to add some alcohol to the child's milk bottle. She has already lost two sons on whom she had tried this cheap remedy and leaves the bar with a vial of Chapuzot's panacea. The bar owner is guilty of ruining his clients' health and provoking their premature death. At the beginning of scene 2 a pale-faced reporter enters and orders a beer. Without explanation he photographs Chapuzot's tattooed arm, measures his height and girth, and examines his fingers and chin. He explains to the surprised Chapuzot that he is an interviewer for *Mouvement,* a literary journal boasting twelve million readers. He accuses Chapuzot of unpatriotic acts because heavy drinking leads to debauchery and, worse still, brings socialism to the masses. An uproarious misunderstanding ensues: convinced that the bar owner has killed his wife, the reporter resolves to sketch the killer's portrait. Gulping down many jugs of beer, he tries to extricate an interview from Chapuzot, first by promises of financial gain and, when this fails, by blackmail. He repeats clichés about the press: it is a great educator, the conscience of the world, a judge that condemns but knows how to forgive when the price is right. The baffled and suspicious barman refuses to participate in an absurd experiment inspired by Lombroso's theories of the criminal personality. The exasperated journalist shows him a *Petit Journal* article about a bar owner from Montrouge named Chapuzot, who killed his wife. Chapuzot protests that he is from Montmartre, but the reporter refuses to admit his mistake and continues to bombard him with questions about literature, politics, science, and social issues. When asked to pay by the bar owner, who has been keeping count of the drinks, the journalist declares that the press never owes anything. No summary could do justice to this hilarious farce, which exposes the cynicism and arrogance of journalists. Mirbeau addresses a topic that remains relevant in today's world, where the sensationalist press thrives.

The authorship of Mirbeau's last play, *Le Foyer,* was disputed. Generous to artists in need, Mirbeau may have attributed cowriting credit to the beleaguered Thadée Natanson after his friend's *La Revue Blanche* closed in 1903. In an opening scene reminiscent of Becque's *La Parisienne* (The Parisian Woman, 1885), the millionaire of humble origin, Armand Biron, reproaches his onetime mistress, Thérèse Courtin du Hallier, for her coolness. The young and penniless Robert d'Auberval has replaced him in the baroness's heart. Mlle Rambert, the director of Le Foyer, a charitable institution Courtin du Hallier has founded, arrives at his house unexpectedly. She informs him that an unfortunate accident has happened on the eve of the duchess of Saragossa's visit to Le Foyer. A supervisor, Mlle Barandon, has forgotten to liberate a punished girl she locked in a small closet for twenty-four hours. In order that the accident be kept secret, neither a doctor nor the institution's priest, Abbé Laroze, has been

Alice Regnault, the actress Mirbeau married in 1887

called upon to see the girl before she dies. The baron approves the cover-up, saying that "it is less important to do good than to silence evil." His financial situation is dire, and he counts on the duchess's generosity to improve Le Foyer's finances. Through his financial schemes Armand Biron has brought him to the verge of bankruptcy in hopes of winning back Thérèse. The baron fears an investigation and asks the baroness to resume her affair with Armand Biron. When she refuses the arrangement, he confesses that he has appropriated Le Foyer's funds to finance risky deals. Thanks to his wife's prostitution his honor will remain intact. The accommodating Biron agrees to share Thérèse's favors with her husband and her young lover, Robert d'Auberval. The foursome plans pleasure cruising of the Mediterranean on Biron's luxurious yacht.

Mirbeau uses the character of Baron Courtin du Hallier to attack the most respected French institutions: the Assemblée Nationale, the Légion d'Honneur, and the Académie Française. The baron is a leader in the parliamentary opposition and a commander of the Legion of Honor. His moral treatises on Napoleon and charity have won him a seat at the Académie Française.

261

After a long battle with the director of the Comédie-Française, *Le Foyer,* a play in four acts, opened on 7 December 1908, truncated of its second act. The censored act depicts the charitable institution with famished, illiterate, overworked wards and sadistic supervisors. It portrays hypocritical society women for whom the visit to the institution is just another rendezvous with their lovers, the stinginess of the aristocracy's donations, and the overt sexual advances of Mlle Rambert toward rebellious Louisette Lapar, who, unlike other wards, refuses to visit her at night.

In the last twenty years Mirbeau's fiction has been published in French paperback editions, and some recently discovered novels, which originally appeared under pseudonyms, will be republished under his name. His *Dialogues tristes* (Sad Dialogues), a series of *saynètes* (sketches) for *Echo de Paris,* are also slated for publication. In addition to the present-day success of *Le Foyer* and *Les Affaires sont les affaires,* young audiences have acknowledged Mirbeau's relevance with collegiate productions of *L'Epidémie.* Some of his critical writings on theater and the arts have recently been adapted for the stage and produced at experimental theaters, often as one-man or one-woman shows.

Letters:

Correspondance avec Auguste Rodin, edited by Pierre Michel and Jean-François Nivet (Paris: Editions du Lérot, 1988);

Lettres à Alfred Bansard des Bois (1862–1874), edited by Michel and Nivet (Montpellier: Editions du Limon, 1989);

Correspondance avec Camille Pissarro, edited by Michel and Nivet (Paris: Editions du Lérot, 1990);

Correspondance avec Claude Monet, edited by Michel and Nivet (Paris: Editions du Lérot, 1990);

"Lettres à Emile Zola," *Cahiers naturalistes,* 64 (1990).

Biographies:

Martin Schwarz, *Octave Mirbeau, vie et oeuvre* (The Hague: Mouton, 1966);

Jean-François Nivet and Pierre Michel, *Octave Mirbeau: L'imprécateur au coeur fidèle* (Paris: Librairie Séguier, 1990).

References:

Wolfgang Asholt, "*Les Mauvais bergers* et le théâtre anarchiste des années 1890," in *Octave Mirbeau:* *actes du colloque international d'Angers* (Angers: Presses Universitaires d'Angers, 1992), pp. 351–367;

Philippe Baron, "La Technique dramatique d'Octave Mirbeau dans *Les Mauvais bergers, Les Affaires sont les affaires* et *Le Foyer,*" in *Octave Mirbeau: actes du colloque international d'Angers* (Angers: Presses Universitaires d'Angers, 1992), pp. 369–377;

Walter Fähnders and Christoph Knüppel, "Gustav Landauer et *Les Mauvais bergers,*" *Cahiers Octave Mirbeau,* 3 (1996): 73–90;

Joseph Fumet, "Au Nouveau théâtre d'Angers, Octave Mirbeau met le feu aux planches!," *Cahiers Octave Mirbeau,* 3 (1996): 255–257;

Fumet, "Isidore Lechat, le Diable et les jésuites," *Cahiers Octave Mirbeau,* 3 (1996): 91–94;

Robert Helms, "Un Américain découvre Mirbeau," *Cahiers Octave Mirbeau,* 2 (1995): 234–237;

Alain Mercier, "Octave Mirbeau et Maurice Maeterlinck," in *Octave Mirbeau: acte du colloque international d'Angers* (Angers: Presses Universitaires d'Angers, 1992), pp. 419–422;

Pierre Michel, "Les *Farces et moralités,*" in *Octave Mirbeau: actes du colloque international d'Angers* (Angers: Presses Universitaires d'Angers, 1992), pp. 379–392;

Michel, "*Les Mauvais bergers,* et *Le Repas du lion,*" *Cahiers Octave Mirbeau,* 3 (1996): 213–220;

Maxime Revon, *Octave Mirbeau, son oeuvre* (Paris: Nouvelle revue critique, 1924);

Régis Santon, "A props de *Des Artistes,*" *Cahiers Octave Mirbeau,* 1 (1994): 81–83;

Jean-Marie Thomasseau, "Grandeur et décadence du personnage de l'homme d'affaires au XIXE siècle," in *Commerce et Commerçants dans la littérature* (Bordeaux: Presses Universitaires de Bordeaux, 1989), pp. 181–195;

S. J. Turcotte, *Les Gens d'Affaires sur la scène française* (Paris: Nizet, 1936), pp. 155–162.

Papers:

Documents related to Mirbeau's theater are at the Bibliothèque de l'Arsenal, Fonds Rondel, and in several public and private archives, including those of the Théâtre-Français and Sociétés des auteurs et compositeurs dramatiques. Documents donated by Mirbeau's widow to the Académie des Sciences are at the Bibliothèque de l'Institut and are partially available to the public.

Alfred de Musset
(11 December 1810 – 2 May 1857)

David Sices
Dartmouth College

PLAY PRODUCTIONS: *La Nuit vénitienne, ou les noces de Laurette,* Paris, Théâtre de l'Odéon, 1 December 1830;

Un Caprice, Paris, Théâtre-Français, 27 November 1847;

Il faut qu'une porte soit ouverte ou fermée, Paris, Théâtre-Français, 7 April 1848;

Il ne faut jurer de rien, Paris, Théâtre-Français, 22 June 1848;

Le Chandelier, Paris, Théâtre Historique, 10 August 1848; revised version, Paris, Théâtre de la République, 29 June 1850;

André del Sarto, Paris, Théâtre-Français, 21 November 1848;

Louison, Paris, Théâtre-Français, 22 February 1849;

L'Habit vert, by Musset and Emile Augier, Paris, Théâtre des Variétés, 23 February 1849;

On ne saurait penser à tout, Paris, Théâtre-Francais, 30 May 1849;

Les Caprices de Marianne, revised version, Paris, Théâtre-Français, 14 June 1851; original version, Paris, Théâtre Montparnasse, 3 December 1935;

Bettine, Paris, Théâtre du Gymnase, 30 October 1851;

On ne badine pas avec l'amour, revised by Paul de Musset, Paris, Théâtre-Français, 18 November 1861; original version, Paris, Comédie-Française, 1923;

Carmosine, revised by Paul de Musset, Paris, Théâtre de l'Odéon, 7 November 1865; original version, Paris, Théâtre Français, 10 February 1926;

Fantasio, revised by Paul de Musset, Paris, Théâtre-Français, 18 August 1866; original version, Paris, Théâtre des Arts, 1911;

La Nuit d'octobre (dramatic reading from *Poésies nouvelles d'Alfred de Musset*), Paris, Théâtre-Français, 2 May 1868;

La Nuit de mai (dramatic reading from *Poésies nouvelles d'Alfred de Musset*), Paris, Théâtre-Français, 1 April 1876;

Alfred de Musset (portrait by Charles Landelle; from Henry Dwight Sedgwick, Alfred de Musset, *1931)*

L'Ane et le ruisseau, Paris, Conservatoire de Musique, 6 May 1876;

A quoi rêvent les jeunes filles (from *Premières poésies*), Paris, Théâtre des Variétés, 10 April 1881; original version, music by Claude Debussy, Paris, Théâtre-Français, 21 April 1926;

Barberine (revised version of *La Quenouille de Barberine*), Paris, Théâtre-Français, 27 February 1882;

La Coupe et les lèvres (from *Contes d'Espagne et d'Italie*), Paris, Salle Duprez, 12 March 1882;

Les Marrons du feu (from *Contes d'Espagne et d'Italie*), Paris, Salle Duprez, December 1883;

Lorenzaccio (revised by Armand d'Artois), Paris, Théâtre de la Renaissance, 3 December

1896; (revised by Emile Fabre), Paris, Théâtre-Français, 1926; (revised by Gaston Baty), Paris, Théâtre Montparnasse, 1947; original version, Paris, Théâtre National Populaire, 1952;

La Nuit d'août (dramatic reading from *Poésies nouvelles*), Paris, Théâtre-Française, 11 December 1910;

La Nuit de décembre (dramatic reading from *Poésies nouvelles*), Paris, Théâtre-Française, 11 December 1910.

BOOKS: *L'Anglais mangeur d'opium* (Paris: Mame et Dalaunay-Vallée, 1828);

Les Contes d'Espagne et d'Italie (Paris: Urbain Canel, 1830)—includes *La Coupe et les lèvres* and *Les Marrons du feu*;

Un Spectacle dans un fauteuil (Paris: Eugène Renduel, 1833 [i.e. 1832])—comprises *La Coupe et les lèvres*, *A Quoi rêvent les jeunes filles*, and *Namouna*; second series, 2 volumes (Paris: Librairie de la Revue des Deux Mondes, 1834)—comprises *Lorenzaccio*, translated by Edmund Thompson as *Lorenzaccio: A Drama in Five Acts* (New York: E. C. Hill, 1907); *Les Caprices de Marianne*, *André del Sarto*; *Fantasio*, translated by Maurice Baring as *Fantasio: A Comedy in Two Acts* (New York: The Pleiad, 1929) and translated by Eric Bentley as *Fantasio*, in *From the Modern Repertoire*, series one, edited by Bentley (Denver: University of Denver Press, 1949), pp. 1–28; *On ne badine pas avec l'amour*, translated by George Calderon as *Perdican and Camilla*, in *Two plays by Anton Chekhov: The Seagull; The Cherry Orchard; and one by Alfred de Musset: Perdican and Camilla [On ne badine pas avec l'amour]* (London: Grant Richards, 1924); and *La Nuit vénitienne*;

La Confession d'un enfant du siècle, 2 volumes (Paris: Bonnaire, 1836); translated by Kendall Warren as *The Confession of a Child of the Century* (Chicago: C. H. Sergel, 1892?);

Comédies et Proverbes par Alfred de Musset (Paris: Charpentier, 1840)—comprises *La Nuit vénitienne*; *André del Sarto*; *Les Caprices de Marianne*; *Fantasio*; *On ne badine pas avec l'amour*; *Lorenzaccio*; *La Quenouille de Barberine*; *Le Chandelier*; *Il ne faut jurer de rien*, translated by E. de V. Vermont as *Valentine's Wager*, in *Three Novelettes and Valentine's Wager: A Comedy* (New York: Brentano's, 1888); *Un Caprice*, translated by John Oxenford as *A Good Little Wife* (London: T. H. Lacy, 1847?); revised and corrected by Musset, 2 volumes (Paris: Charpentier, 1853)—comprises *André del Sarto* [two-act revision for

Théâtre de l'Odéon production, 1851]; *Lorenzaccio; Les Caprices de Marianne* [three-act revision for Théâtre-Français production, 1851]; *Fantasio; On ne badine pas avec l'amour; La Nuit vénitienne; Barberine* [revision of *La Quenouille de Barberine*, performed by Théâtre-Français, 1850]; *Le Chandelier* [revised for production by Théâtre-Français, 1850], translated by Edmund Burke Thompson as *The Chandler*, in *The Chandler. Prudence Spurns A Wager* (New York: Privately printed, 1908); *Il ne faut jurer de rien* [revised for production by Théâtre-Français, 1848]; *Un Caprice; Il faut qu'une porte soit ouverte ou fermée; Louison; On ne saurait penser à tout; Carmosine;* and *Bettine;* translated by S. L. Gwynn as *Comedies* (London: Walter Scott, 1890)—comprises *Barberine, Fantasio; No Trifling With Love,* and *A Door Must Be Open or Shut;* translated by David Sices as *Comedies & Proverbs of Alfred de Musset* (Baltimore, Md.: Johns Hopkins University Press, 1994)—comprises *What Does Marianne Want?, Fantasio, You Can't Trifle with Love, The Candlestick, You Never Can Tell, A Passing Fancy,* and *A Door Has to Be Either Open or Shut;*

Poésies complètes d'Alfred de Musset (Paris: Charpentier, 1840)—comprises *Contes d'Espagne et d'Italie, Poésies diverses, Un Spectacle dans un fauteuil,* and *Poésies nouvelles;* "La Nuit de mai," "La Nuit d'août," and "La Nuit d'octobre" translated by Walter Herries Pollock as *The Poet and His Muse* (London: R. Bentley, 1880);

Le Chandelier [version presented by Théâtre Historique, 1848] (Paris: Charpentier, 1848);

L'Habit vert, by Musset and Emile Augier (Paris: Michel Lévy, 1849); translated by Barrett H. Clark as *The Green Coat* (New York: S. French, 1915);

Poésies nouvelles d'Alfred de Musset (1840–1849) (Paris: Charpentier, 1850);

Les Caprices de Marianne [version presented by Théâtre-Français, 1851] (Paris: Charpentier, 1851);

André del Sarto [version presented by Théâtre de L'Odéon, 1848] (Paris: Charpentier, 1851);

Premières Poésies, Poésies nouvelles d'Alfred de Musset, 2 volumes (Paris: Charpentier, 1852);

Contes (Paris: Charpentier, 1854)—comprises "La Mouche," "Pierre et Camille," "Mademoiselle Mimi Pinson," "Le Secret de Javotte," "Le Merle blanc," and "Lettres de Dupuis et Cotonet;" translated by E. de V. Vermont as *Tales from Alfred de Musset* (New York: Brentano, 1888);

Oeuvres posthumes d'Alfred de Musset, "*Complément de toutes les éditions des Oeuvres d'Alfred de Musset*"

(Paris: Charpentier, 1860)—includes *L'Ane et le ruisseau;* translated by Walter Creyke as *All Is Fair in Love and War* (New York: Sampson, 1868);

On ne badine pas avec l'amour [revised by Paul de Musset for performance by Théâtre-Français, 1861] (Paris: Charpentier, 1861);

Carmosine (Paris: Charpentier, 1865); translated as *Carmosine* (New York: N.p., 1850);

Oeuvres complètes d'Alfred de Musset, 10 volumes (Paris: Charpentier, 1865–1866)—includes *La Coupe et les lèvres, Comédies et Proverbes, La Nuit vénitienne, André del Sarto, Les Caprices de Marianne, Fantasio, On ne badine pas avec l'amour, Barberine, Lorenzaccio, Le Chandelier, Il ne faut jurer de rien, Un Caprice, Il faut qu'une porte soit ouverte ou fermée, Louison, On ne saurait penser à tout, Bettine,* and *Carmosine;*

Fantasio [revised by Paul de Musset for performance by Théâtre-Français, 1866] (Paris: Charpentier, 1866);

Mélanges de Littérature et de Critique (Paris: Charpentier, 1867);

Oeuvres complètes d'Alfred de Musset, 10 volumes (Paris: Lemerre, 1874);

Comédies et Proverbes, 3 volumes (Paris: Charpentier, 1878);

Oeuvres complètes d'Alfred de Musset, 10 volumes (Paris: Lemerre, 1884–1896);

Théâtre d'Alfred de Musset, 4 volumes, introduction by Jules Lemaître (Paris: Jouaust, 1889–1891);

Lorenzaccio (Paris: Société des Amis des Livres, 1895); revised by Armand d'Artois for performance in Théâtre de la Renaissance, 1896 (Paris: Ollendorf, 1898);

Comédies et Proverbes (Paris: Charpentier, 1905–1906);

Alfred de Musset, Les Caprices de Marianne, edited by G. Michaut (Paris: Société d'Edition française et étrangère, 1908);

Mélanges de Littérature et de Critique (Paris: Garnier, 1909);

Alfred de Musset, oeuvres complémentaires, edited by Maurice Allem (Paris: Mercure de France, 1911);

Oeuvres complètes d'Alfred de Musset, 4 volumes (Paris: Conard, 1922–1923);

Comédies et Proverbes (Paris: E. Flammarion, 1927);

Comédies et Proverbes, 2 volumes, introduction by Jacques Copeau (Paris: La Cité des Livres, 1931);

Les Deux "André del Sarto" de Alfred de Musset, edited by Pierre Gastinel (Rouen: Imprimerie Commerciale du Journal de Rouen, 1933);

Théâtre complet d'Alfred de Musset, edited by Allem [revised performance texts of *André del Sarto, Les*

Caprices de Marianne, Barberine, Il ne faut jurer de rien, and *On ne saurait penser à tout*] (Paris: Gallimard, 1934);

La Genèse de "Lorenzaccio," introduction and notes by Paul Dimoff (Paris: Droz, 1936; revised edition Paris: Librairie Marcel Didier, 1964);

Les Caprices de Marianne, edited by Gaston Baty (Paris: Seuil, 1952);

Textes dramatiques inédites, edited by Jean Richer (Paris: Nizet, 1953);

Comédies et Proverbes, edited by Gastinel (Paris: Belles Lettres, 1952–1957);

Poésies complètes d'Alfred de Musset, edited by Allem (Paris: Gallimard, 1957);

Théâtre complet d'Alfred de Musset, edited by Allem (Paris: Gallimard, 1958); revised Pléiade edition, edited by Simon Jeune (Paris: Gallimard, 1990);

Oeuvres complètes en prose d'Alfred de Musset, edited by Allem and Paul Courant (Paris: Gallimard, 1960);

Oeuvres complètes, edited by Philippe Van Tieghem (Paris: "L'Intégrale," Editions du Seuil, 1963);

Il ne faut jurer de rien, edited by Bernard Masson (Paris: Bordas, 1966);

Gamiani: ou, Deux nuits d'excès (Paris: Filipacchi, 1974);

Les Caprices de Marianne, edited by P.-G. Castex (Paris: Société d'édition d'enseignement supérieur, 1978).

Editions in English: *Barberine and Other Comedies* (Chicago: C. H. Sergel, 1892)—comprises *Barberine, Fantasio, No Trifling With Love, A Door Must Be Either Open or Shut, A Caprice,* and *One Can Not Think of Everything;*

The Complete Writings of Alfred de Musset, 10 volumes, translated by Andrew Lang and others. (New York: E. C. Hill, 1905); volumes 3–5 translated by Raoul Pellissier and Mary H. Dey—comprises *A Venetian Night, André del Sarto, The Follies of Marianne, Fantasio, No Trifling With Love, Barberine, A Caprice, The Door Must Be Either Open or Shut, Louison,* and *One Cannot Think of Everything;*

Three Plays, by Alfred de Musset, translated by Claudine I. Wilson (London & New York: T. Nelson and Son, 1929)—comprises *Fantasio, On ne badine pas avec l'amour,* and *Carmosine;*

Seven Plays, translated by Peter Meyer (New York: Hill & Wang, 1962)—comprises *Marianne, Fantasio, Camille and Perdican, The Candlestick, A Diversion, A Door Must Be Kept Either Open or Shut,* and *Journey to Gotha;*

A Comedy and Two Proverbs, translated by George Gravely (London: Oxford University Press,

1974)—comprises *Caprice, A Door Should Be Either Open or Shut,* and *It's Impossible to Think of Everything*;

Fantasio and Other Plays, translated by Michael Feingold, Richard Howard, Nagle Jackson, and Paul Schmidt (New York: Theater Communications Group, 1993)—comprises *Fantasio, Don't Trifle With Love, Lorenzaccio,* and *You Can't Think of Everything*;

Three Plays by Alfred de Musset, translated by Peter Meyer and Declan Donnellan (Bath, England: Absolute Classics, 1993)—-comprises *Don't Fool With Love, The Candlestick,* and *A Door Must Be Kept Open or Shut*;

Historical Dramas, translated by David Sices (New York: Peter Lang, 1996)—comprises *Andrea del Sarto* and *Lorenzaccio.*

Most great dramatists who have played a major role in the development of their national dramatic traditions—William Shakespeare and Molière spring immediately to mind—were actively involved in the theater of their times, but Alfred de Musset is an exception to the rule. His influence on French playwriting and stagecraft in the later nineteenth and twentieth centuries has been, in retrospect, enormous; yet his career as a dramatist was marked at an early period by his complete withdrawal from the Parisian stage, during which time his best dramatic works were written. The main reason for Musset's absence was the noisy "fiasco" of his play *La Nuit vénitienne, ou les noces de Laurette* (The Venetian Night, or Lauretta's Wedding; translated as *A Venetian Night,* 1907) at the Théâtre de l'Odéon in 1830. When, following a successful production in 1847 of his one-act play, *Un Caprice* (A Passing Fancy), Musset decided to become active in the theater once again, principally in connection with France's national repertory company, the Théâtre-Français, or Comédie-Français, not only did he produce markedly inferior new works in the genre but, in the interest of regularizing earlier plays for the sake of stage convention, he greatly weakened original texts that he had already published as "armchair drama."

During the period from 1833 to 1834, however, while he was still in his early twenties, Musset wrote four strikingly original plays—*Les Caprices de Marianne* (1841; variously translated as *The Whims of Marianne* and *What Does Marianne Want?*), *Fantasio, Lorenzaccio,* and *On ne badine pas avec l'amour* (translated as *No Trifling With Love, Camille and Perdican,* and *You Can't Trifle With Love*)—all of which, unstaged, were published in the second issue of *Un Spectacle dans un fauteuil* (An Armchair Show) in

1834. The originality of these plays lay first in their language, which was a lyrical prose almost unknown in the French theater before Musset, although it owed some debt to Pierre Carlet de Chamblain de Marivaux; second, in their characterization, combining sympathetic portraits of youthful, passionate heroes and heroines with "flat" comic grotesques, usually older characters; and third, in their structure, which, freed from the limitations placed on playwrights by the resources and conventions of an active, popular theater in Musset's time, appealed to their readers' imagination. It was not until increasingly sophisticated machinery and lighting made staging possible, in the twentieth century, that the original versions of these plays were performed satisfactorily. From that time onward Musset's four greatest plays became staples of the repertory theater both at the Théâtre-Français and, to a lesser extent, elsewhere in the world. So, too, did several of Musset's less significant but eminently stageworthy comedies, all of which were first published in periodical form in *La Revue des deux mondes.* These include *Barberine* (1850, a revised version of the 1835 *La Quenouille de Barberine* [Barberine's Distaff]), *Le Chandelier* (1835; translated as *The Chandler,* 1908), *Il ne faut jurer de rien* (1836; translated as *You Never Can Tell,* 1994), and *Un Caprice, Il faut qu'une porte soit ouverte ou fermée* (1845; translated as *A Door Has To Be Either Open or Shut,* 1890).

Alfred de Musset's dramatic works, like most of his literary creations, are notably Parisian, though usually neither realistically nor specifically set in Paris. He was born there on 11 December 1810, the second son of an old though not particularly prominent noble family, which traced its roots to the twelfth century and included soldiers and royal counselors as well as one of the muses who inspired the poet Pierre de Ronsard: this according to his adoring older brother, Paul, whose hagiographic 1877 biography remains an essential source of information. (Paul de Musset later became a man of letters in his own right, the editor and reviser of Alfred's literary oeuvre, and his brother's active literary promoter after his death.) Although there were no theater people in Alfred's immediate background, his father, Victor de Musset-Pathay, wrote *Histoire de la vie et des ouvrages de J.-J. Rousseau* (History of the Life and Works of Jean-Jacques Rousseau, 1821), an author whom he greatly admired and whose presence can be felt in many of Alfred's works. The writer's maternal grandfather, Claude-Antoine Guyot-Desherbiers, by profession a lawyer, loved the theater and was able to recite from memory extensive portions of dramatic works, in particular the *Proverbes* (1768–1787) of Carmontelle

(Louis Carrogis), which would influence Alfred's dramatic production. He is also said to have served as the model for the protagonist's uncle Van Buck in *Il ne faut jurer de rien* (1848). Perhaps most significantly, from childhood on Alfred showed striking natural dramatic propensities that, as his brother later attested, were used by the charming though hypersensitive boy to rule over his doting family, particularly his mother.

After private studies until the age of eight, as was customary for a scion of the nobility, Alfred continued his schooling brilliantly as a day student at the Collège Henri IV, where he made two good friends, the duke of Chartres, the son of future king Louis-Philippe, and Paul Foucher, Victor Hugo's future brother-in-law. There he won a first prize in French composition and, in the 1827 national *concours général,* a second prize in Latin composition. After his baccalaureate Musset, like several other French literary figures of the nineteenth century, undertook and abandoned studies of law and medicine; he then became a clerk in a military-supplies firm. An overactive participant in Paris's "high life," to which he remained devoted for many years, and in the social activities of Victor and Adèle Foucher Hugo's salon, *le Cénacle,* one of French Romanticism's sancta sanctorum, Musset nevertheless found time to write and publish a free translation of Thomas de Quincey's *Confession of an Opium-Eater* (1822), which Musset translated as *L'Anglais mangeur d'opium* in 1828, and, in 1829, at the age of nineteen, a book of verse titled *Contes d'Espagne et d'Italie* (Tales of Spain and Italy). This latter volume achieved considerable notoriety because of its hyper-Romantic poetry, which could also be read as a parody of Romantic clichés, and established Musset's reputation as one of the rising literary stars of his generation. In addition it gave evidence of his theatrical tendencies because two of the poetic works it contained were in part or in whole dramatic dialogues: "Don Paez" and "Les Marrons du feu" (the latter foretells Musset's use of proverbial titles, the French suggesting the English expressions "irons from the fire" or "cat's paw").

"Don Paez," as its title suggests, has a Spanish setting. It is a mixture of lyric, narrative, and dramatic poetry, parts of it in dialogue form. In the quintessential Romantic mode of its time, it combines passion, jealousy, and violent death. "Les Marrons du feu," on the other hand, is both more developed and more completely dramatic in form, divided into nine scenes with a cast of six characters, of whom the major ones are a priest, Annibal Desiderio, who is in love with the actress heroine, La Camargo; she is also loved by a young noble-

The actress Rachel, the lover for whom Musset tried unsuccessfully to write a modern verse tragedy

man, Rafael Garuci. Its plot, set in a stereotyped, romantic Italy, is once again a farrago of passion, jealousy, and murder, with the added spice that one of the lovers—in fact, the murderer—is the priest, who concludes the work on a pirouette typical of the volume's cynical tone: "J'ai tué mon ami, j'ai mérité le feu, / J'ai taché mon pourpoint, et l'on me congédie. / C'est la moralité de cette comédie." (I have killed my friend, I have earned hellfire, / I have stained my doublet, and I have been dismissed. / That is the moral of this comedy)."

Ten months after the publication of *Les Contes d'Espagne et d'Italie,* on 1 December 1830 Musset's one-act comedy, *La Nuit vénitienne, ou Les Noces de Laurette,* was performed at the Théâtre de l'Odéon in Paris. The play was a rather unmemorable satire of the Romantic hero (here, Razetta, a Venetian gentleman), whose planned elopement with the heroine, Laurette, is foiled when she decides to accept the hand of a very unromantic and rational German suitor, the Prince of Eysenach. Once again the play ends on a pirouette as Razetta decides to seek consolation, crying, "Puissent toutes les folies des amants finir aussi joyeusement que la mienne!" (May all lovers' follies end as joyously as mine!) Musset's characteristic wit is evident in this play, as is his ambiguous relationship with the Romantic ethic and aesthetic. But the work's most notable effect came about because it was laughed off the stage. Legend has it that the laughter resulted from the heroine's encounter, in a white dress, with a freshly painted green trellis, but a more likely explanation is that the play was ridiculed by a literary cabal occasioned by the author's refusal to identify himself with either dominant literary school of the time. In any case, the humiliation led Musset to abandon the stage for the next seventeen years, an essential factor in his development as a playwright.

Musset's volume of poetry had had a mixed reception, shocking both Romantics and Neoclassicists. But in the period following its publication he wrote several dramatic works inspired to some extent by critical appreciation of his theatrical bent. One of these, *La Quittance du Diable* (The Devil's Receipt, 1830) was drawn from a Walter Scott novel published in 1824, *Redgauntlet* (with typical Gallic confusion, one character was called "Le Laird [and also: le Sir] de Redgnauntley"). This Gothic story, set in Scotland, involves a midnight visit to the graveyard by its hero, Sténie, to secure a missing receipt for his land fees from the dead former "Laird." Musset evidently wrote it with its accompanying songs for a performance at the Théâtre des Nouveautés that never took place. *La Quittance du Diable,* unlike *La Coupe et les lèvres* (The Cup and the Lip), which appeared in the first volume of *Un Spectacle dans un fauteuil* in 1832, was not published until 1914, years after the author's death. *La Coupe et les lèvres* ("The Cup and the Lip" is another proverbial title), a verse drama set in the Tyrol and northern Italy, is a more consequential work: it provided the libretto for one of Giacomo Puccini's early operas, *Edgar* (1889), among other lyric works. The play embodied one of Musset's enduring personal and artistic themes, the protagonist's inability to shake off the deadly effects of dissipation. Frank, a hunter, driven by ambition to leave his native Tyrol village, commits murder, lives with a courtesan (Belcolore, the mistress of the man he has murdered), and becomes a renowned mercenary soldier; but when boredom prompts him to attempt a return to his earlier life and to Déidamia, the innocent girl who still loves him, she is stabbed to death by the jealous Belcolore.

The same volume of *Un Spectacle dans un fauteuil* contained a second, quite different play: the brief two-act comedy in verse, *A Quoi rêvent les jeunes filles* (What Girls Dream About, 1832). Musset's poetic skill was apparent in the lyrical, conversational alexandrines of his dialogue, and his gift for light comedy is evident in the characterization of the two more-or-less interchangeable young sisters, Ninon and Ninette; their shrewd father, Duke Laertes (who wants to make sure his daughters think their arranged marriages are love matches); the handsome young lover, Silvio; and the grotesque second suitor, Count Irus, who foreshadows the puppets that later figured so importantly in Musset's best comedies, *Les Caprices de Marianne, Fantasio,* and *On ne badine pas avec l'amour.*

The death of Musset's father from cholera in the epidemic of 1832 seems to have had a deep effect on the author's attitude toward his art because of its emotional echoes as well as its financial ones, his family being convinced that the loss of Victor's income would condemn it to drastically straitened circumstances. Although that fear proved to be unfounded (Musset was, however, periodically beset by financial troubles, most of which were allayed by the timely intervention of influential friends), the writer certainly produced his best literary works in the five years following his father's death. In terms of the theater his first major work, *André del Sarto,* was published that same year, in 1832. Although it was less important than the great Renaissance historical tragedy that he wrote the following year—*Lorenzaccio*—it marked a step forward in Musset's mastery of dramaturgy as well as a clear prefiguration of two of his dominant themes, the hero as failure and the conflict between love and art. The painter-hero, Andrea del Sarto, is betrayed by his friend and disciple, Cordiani, who is having an affair with Andrea's beloved wife, Lucrezia, for whom the artist has sacrificed his talent and his personal integrity, misusing funds from King Francis I of France intended for the acquisition of Florentine artworks. In despair at both these events, Andrea commits suicide (Musset, like most of his Romantic confreres, took liberties with truth in his historical dramas), allowing Cordiani and Lucrezia to remain together.

The notorious, legendary love affair between Musset and George Sand, climaxed by their ill-fated trip to Venice (so that they remained thenceforth "Les Amants de Venise" [The Lovers of Venice]), occupied the next two years of the author's life and endured sporadically through most of 1835. Although it probably had a less lasting effect on the author's personal and creative life than was generally thought in the nineteenth century, when it was the subject of several books, there is no doubt that it was a major factor in Musset's development as a man and as an artist. At the very least his relationship with Sand provided him with the basic material for his great historical tragedy, *Lorenzaccio,* as well as some important dialogue exchanges in *On ne badine pas avec l'amour.* Conversely, Musset's self-representation as both the idealist, Coelio, and the hedonist,

Octave, in the somewhat earlier *Les Caprices de Marianne,* is referred to in letters exchanged between the two lovers during their affair. At the least the couple's stormy relationship and breakup featured prominently in what became one of the legendary, exemplary nineteenth-century artistic lives, along with those of some other *poètes maudits* such as Gérard de Nerval and Arthur Rimbaud.

It seems clear that three of Musset's four great plays—*Les Caprices de Marianne, Fantasio,* and *Lorenzaccio*—were finished prior to the lovers' fateful departure for Venice at the end of 1833 (although it was long thought that *Lorenzaccio,* because of its Florentine setting, had to date at least in part from the voyage or after). The fourth, *On ne badine pas avec l'amour,* was begun, evidently as a much "lighter" comedy, before their departure; a clear break is evident, however, in the exchanges of act 2, scene 5 of the play, when the protagonists' amorous "badinage" takes on a far more serious and personal tone. That scene ends with a quotation—curiously, by the hero, Perdican—from a letter from Sand to Musset, dated 12 May 1834; both internal and external evidence points to the play's then having been finished after Musset's return, alone, from Venice.

Like *On ne badine pas avec l'amour, Les Caprices de Marianne,* a two-act play, begins in a light, stylized fashion, contrasting its two heroes by their parallel opening statements. It is set in a very scantily described Naples. Coelio, whose idealistic love has been ignored by the beautiful, devout Marianne, married to the elderly, stupidly rigid Claudio (one of Musset's remarkable puppet-figures, along with his servant, Tibia), reluctantly engages his friend, the drunken rake Octave, to speak in his behalf. During a series of heated exchanges Marianne falls in love with Octave, but her jealous husband arranges an ambush, and Coelio, believing himself to have been betrayed by his friend, goes willingly to his death. The play concludes with a scene in which Marianne offers herself to Octave. He refuses her, replying that he, a sensualist, is not capable of love—it was the idealist Coelio who loved her. The combination of traditional commedia dell'arte stylization and Romantic lyricism makes this one of the most original and viable dramas in the French repertory; Gérard Phillipe, in particular, made a deep impression as Octave in a celebrated 1958 production directed by Jean Vilar at the Théâtre National Populaire.

Fantasio, also in two acts, has led a more problematic life in the theater, both because its hero spends much of his time disguised as an ugly, hunchbacked jester and because the play has no real love interest. The hero, Fantasio (his first name,

Madame Allan-Despréaux, the actress who played Madame de Léry in the April 1848 production of Il faut qu'une porte soit ouverte ou fermée *at the Comédie-Française in Paris*

Henri, is one that Musset often used for his personae), a world-weary young bourgeois from Munich, decides to take the place of the recently deceased court jester, Saint-Jean, in order to escape from his many debts, not to mention his boredom. Once in the court of the king of Bavaria, he offhandedly saves the king's daughter, Elsbeth, from a stultifying marriage of state to the prince of Mantua (a grotesque puppet figure whose tics include, among other things, a scathing parody of Hugo's or Alexandre Dumas *père*'s Romantic heroes) by removing his wig with a fishing line, thus depriving him of his royal dignity. The play ends, inconclusively, with the princess unmarried and the hero free to come and go in his dual roles of burgher and court jester. It is enlivened by some delightful free-form exchanges between Fantasio, as jester, and Princess Elsbeth as well as the comic inanities of the prince of Mantua, for whom the height of daring is, as in a well-worn fairy-tale plot, to exchange clothing with his aide-de-camp in order to see whether the princess will love him for himself.

On ne badine pas avec l'amour, a melodramatic three-act "proverb," was the last of the four great plays to be completed, but resemblances of form,

Illustration for On ne badine pas avec l'amour *in the 1865–1866 edition of Musset's complete works*

language, and tone have led to its usually being associated with the two earlier comedies rather than the intervening *Lorenzaccio*. This is a somber comedy, however, apart from the contributions of its amusing puppets—the hero's father; the baron; the two clerics, Blazius and Bridaine; and the heroine's governess, Dame Pluche, whose roles consist mainly of looking on in horror and puzzlement as the young protagonists vie with one another. Essentially the plot constitutes a "duel of vanities" between the hero, Perdican, and his cousin, Camille, whom the baron has long planned to wed to each other. Perdican defends his role as a charming, free man-about-town; Camille swears that she will return to her convent rather than settle for anything less than a vow of total, lifelong fidelity. The peasant girl Rosette, who evidently is also in love with the young master, becomes a pawn in their ongoing struggle for moral and emotional supremacy. Her death from grief upon hearing the two young nobles finally confess mutual love seals their fate and precludes any hope of their coming together, closing the play suddenly just when a happy ending seems assured.

Lorenzaccio differs markedly from the other three plays that Musset wrote in 1833 and 1834. Rather than a two- or three-act comedy or proverb, it is a generously proportioned historical tragedy in the traditional five acts. Derived from material in Sand's *Une Conspiration en 1537* (A Conspiracy in 1537, [1831])—she used the wrong date, which Musset corrected—inspired in its turn both by Benedetto Varchi's chronicle, *Storia fiorentina* (Florentine Stories, 1721) and Ludovic Vitet's *Scènes historiques* (1829) (which strove to present "real" history in dramatic form), the play deals with the assassination by Lorenzo de'Medici ("Lorenzino" or "Lorenzaccio") of his cousin Alessandro, the duke of Florence, in 1536. Musset makes Lorenzo an antihero who embodies the personal traits that preoccupied him at that time: apparent indecision, inspired to some extent by Shakespeare's Hamlet, as is much of the play's structure; the inability to undo vice's corruption of political idealism and moral virtue; and a deep cynicism as to the possibility of meaningful political action by the individual in the face of mass apathy or selfishness, reflecting disappointment in the aftermath of the 1830 July Revolution in France. Lorenzo carries out his long-meditated assassination although he has warned his idealistic older friend, Filippo Strozzi, that it will not result in Florence's liberation from tyrannical forces, both within and without, and his predictions are realized: Alessandro is replaced by another, weaker Medici duke, who is a puppet of the emperor and the Pope, and Lorenzo is assassinated in his turn by an angry mob in Venice. Important subplots involve Filippo Strozzi and his family, who contemplate action against the duke until Filippo's daughter is poisoned, and Ricciarda Cibo, who vainly attempts to sway the duke from tyranny by means of her sexual charms; in addition, Ricciarda's brother-in-law, Cardinal Cibo, and several other historical or invented figures play significant roles in the action. The more than thirty characters and thirty-seven scenes in Musset's drama present a marked contrast with the sober means that he used in the three comedies. *Lorenzaccio* was long considered impossible to produce and was not actually staged until near the end of the century, when Sarah Bernhardt had it modified and cut by Armand d'Artois so that she could play the role of Lorenzo, whose small stature and ambiguous sexuality suggested such treatment (she had also played Hamlet). Her example seems to have influenced the play's theater productions for the next half-century as revivals cast female actresses as the hero until Gérard Phillipe embodied him in a noted 1952 Théâtre National Populaire staging directed by Jean Vilar.

Lorenzaccio has been the most enduring and, in this century, most successful of all nineteenth-century historical dramas, a genre that Romanticism's leaders saw as crucial to their movement's success. Musset took pains to distinguish himself from the Romantics, who looked on him as a renegade, but that irony has been effaced by passing time, whose perspective suggests considerable artistic unanimity despite the apparent divisions among the era's principal figures. In any case Musset's play differs from Victor Hugo's historical tragedies in being written in prose rather than alexandrine verse; it is considerably less melodramatic and obvious, in both its effects and its language, than Dumas *père*'s plays, and more effective as theater than those of either Alfred de Vigny or such lesser writers as Casimir Delavigne. Recent years have seen increasingly frequent productions of *Lorenzaccio* both in France and elsewhere, despite the difficulties it presents: a 1969 staging by the Za Branou Theater of Prague, in the wake of the 1968 Soviet invasion, was both unusually imaginative as a production and peculiarly relevant as history.

The aftermath of Musset's love affair with Sand was a difficult period for the author, both personally and artistically, although he went on to have many well-documented love affairs, involving the noble Aimée d'Alton; Caroline Jaubert, a "grisette" who inspired one of his short stories; and several well-known actresses. Its principal literary fruit was an autobiographical novel, *La Confession d'un enfant du siècle* (The Confession of a Child of the Century, 1836), and the widely read cycle of four extended poems known as *Les Nuits* (The Nights of May [1835], December [1835], August [1836], and October [1837]; all of these later lent themselves readily to dramatic performances at the Théâtre-Français thanks to their dialogic form, which involved the poet and his muse or, in one case, his double).

When Musset returned to writing for the theater—or, in the beginning at least, to writing in dramatic form—he produced several successful though less-personal and original plays. The first of these, *La Quenouille de Barberine,* dates from 1835, the year following his return from Venice. It dramatized Matteo Bandello's twenty-first tale, which can be traced both to Indian sources and to Giovanni Boccaccio's mid-fourteenth-century *Decameron,* involving an impoverished Bohemian knight, Count Ulric, and his wife, Barberine, who remains faithful to her husband during his lengthy absence from their castle and thereby—unknowingly—wins a wager for him; she locks a boastful would-be seducer, the young Baron Rosemberg, in her tower room with instructions to spin all the wool in it, before she will

Poster by A. M. Mucha for the 1896 production of Musset's Lorenzaccio, starring Sarah Bernhardt

release him. This—for a man of those times—"painless but humiliating punishment" (in the words of Maurice Allem) is communicated to her husband and the queen of Hungary, Beatrice of Aragon, who congratulates the knight on his wife's fidelity. Musset revised the play, as *Barberine,* for the 1851 edition of his complete works, notably modifying it from two acts to three and adding a major character, Barberine's confidant, Kalékairi; but his hopes of seeing it performed by the Comédie-Française at that time were dashed, and the play was not produced, in its revised form, until 1882.

In the same year as *La Quenouille de Barberine* Musset wrote a comedy that has proved quite successful in the theater, *Le Chandelier* (translated as *The Chandler,* 1908) so named because of the French expression for what the British call a "gooseberry," a suitor who serves as the screen for a real lover). In it a young clerk, Fortunio, by his proofs of fidelity and dedication, wins the love of Jacqueline, his master André's wife, from a dashing, boastful officer of the dragoons, Clavaroche, who tries to use him as a screen for their affair. Fortunio's elegant poem in honor of his mistress was set to music by several French composers, including Jacques Offenbach; the entire play was the subject of popular operettas by both Offenbach (1872) and André Messager (1907). When Musset's work was performed for the first time, in August 1848–at the wrong theater by contemporary accounts, the Théâtre Historique on the Boulevard, and with the wrong cast, actors who were used to playing "boulevard du crime" melodramas–its brief series of performances was interrupted by the 1848 Revolution; but in any case the subject was felt to be too shocking for a middle-class audience. The work was revived not long afterward (June 1850) in slightly modified form by the Théâtre-Français and has held the stage ever since.

Il ne faut jurer de rien (1836; translated as *You Never Can Tell*) bears a superficial resemblance to *Le Chandelier* in that its hero, Valentin, sets out to seduce Cécile, who has been suggested to him as a suitable–that is, financially attractive–match by his pragmatic-minded uncle, Van Buck. The uncle and nephew make a wager: if the young man, made wary by his own adulterous successes, can gain Cécile's love, it will prove that she is open to seduction and therefore not a proper wife. Cécile not only thwarts all Valentin's machinations but also wins his heart and hand, thanks to her directness and lack of guile. This play, too, has been one of Musset's most successful comedies, thanks in great part to the excellent comic roles of Van Buck, of Cécile's mother (the baroness), and of the local curate, who add a leavening of sentimental warmth and good sense to the puppet formula of Musset's earlier plays. Indeed, the play's "message" strikes a surprising–and to some critics, alarming–note of reconciliation with middle-class values after the moral and emotional idealism of his four great earlier plays.

In 1837 Musset wrote a one-act comedy, *Un Caprice* (1847; translated as *A Good Little Wife,* 1847?), that was to have a decisive effect on his theatrical career. It was a delightful short play reflecting an event in which the author and his mistress, Aimée d'Alton, had in fact been personally involved and that he later incorporated as well into his short story, "Le Fils du Titien" (Titian's Son, 1838): the heroine's anonymous stitching of an embroidered purse as a gift and an incitement to economy for the man she loves. Mathilde, the young heroine, is afraid that her husband, Monsieur de Chavigny, who is addicted to gambling, has fallen in love with a notorious coquette, Madame de Blainville, and that her present, despite the long hours she has spent working on it, will have arrived too late. Her beautiful, apparently scatterbrained friend, Madame de Léry, makes Chavigny see the error of his ways in a scene of charming flirtation, and it is he who pronounces the comedy's final, proverbial message: "A young preacher gives the best sermons."

Another excellent, theatrically viable one-act comedy, *Il faut qu'une porte soit ouverte ou fermée,* involves only two characters, laconically designated as "the Count" and "the Marquise." Their worldly yet sentimental conversation in her–for once–empty salon on a rainy winter day leads to the Count's declaration of love and ultimate proposal of marriage to the Marquise. Although nothing of great note can be said to happen, the witty quality of the play's dialogue led to a successful performance in Russia by Karatyghina, a friend of the French actress Madame Allan-Despréaux, who then performed it–taking, like her friend, the role of Madame de Léry–to great acclaim at the Théâtre-Française in April 1848.

The success of the play marked a new era in Musset's theatrical career: henceforth he involved himself actively in the production of his plays, including several of his earlier comedies: *Il ne faut jurer de rien* in June 1848; *Le Chandelier* in August 1848; *André del Sarto* in November 1848; and *Les Caprices de Marianne* in June 1851. The author's extensive revisions to the latter two plays to make them conform better to stage and language conventions generally weakened their originality and set the pattern for his brother Paul's revisions to several other plays for presentation after Alfred's death: *On ne badine pas avec l'amour,* November 1861; *Carmosine,* November 1865; and *Fantasio,* August 1866. Paul's attempts to have his revised version of *Lorenzaccio* performed at the Théâtre de l'Odéon in 1864 failed, and the play was not staged until Sarah Bernhardt's 1896 production.

Musset's success with several of his earlier plays changed his attitude toward the theater and led to his writing several comedies directly for the stage, often for specific actresses, with some of whom, such as Madame Allan-Despréaux, he became romantically involved. But in general these plays, the product of a declining level of energy and talent, are inferior to the earlier ones. They are *Louison* (a comedy in verse performed at the Théâtre-Française in 1849); *L'Habit vert* (The Green Coat, 1849, little of whose final text is by Musset), written in collaboration with Emile Augier; *On ne saurait penser à tout* (1849; trans-

Statue of Musset outside the Comédie-Française

lated as *You Can't Think of Everything,* 1905); an adaptation of one of Carmontelle's "proverbs"; the "edifying" *Carmosine,* which the author adapted from a Boccaccio story (the play was published in 1850 but not staged, at the Théâtre de l'Odéon, until 1865); *Bettine* (written for Rose Chéri and produced unsuccessfully at the Théâtre du Gymnase in 1851); and *L'Ane et le ruisseau* (literally, "The Donkey and the Stream," it was translated into English as *All Is Fair In Love and War* in 1868; it was not staged in Paris until 1876).

Musset's writings on the theater include several of his "Revues fantastiques" (Fantastical Reviews), a series of essays published in *Le Temps* between January and June 1831; the *Lettres de Dupuis et Cotonet* (Letters of Dupuis and Cotonet), published first in the *Revue des deux mondes* between September 1836 and May 1837; and several 1838 articles in the *Revue des deux mondes,* primarily concerning the revival of interest in

Neoclassical drama spurred by performances of Jean Racine's work at the Théâtre-Français by the great tragedian Rachel, who carried on a sporadic love affair with the author and whose hopes that he would write a significant modern verse tragedy for her were never realized (several projects, including *Le Comte d'Essex* [The Earl of Essex] and *La Servante du roi* [The King's Serving-maid], were left unfinished at his death). *Lettres de Dupuis et Cotonet,* which purported to be bemused reflections on the state of current Paris literature by two bourgeois art lovers from La Ferté-sous-Jouarre, are a satire on Romanticism that ends with the two provincial amateurs deciding that the movement's aesthetic consists primarily of the overuse of adjectives. Along with his articles on the actress Rachel, these letters had signaled Musset's final break with his erstwhile Romantic colleagues.

The last ten years of Musset's life were marked by physical, emotional, and artistic decline. Although he never stopped writing plays, essays, and verse, none of these works displayed the quality of his earlier ones. His admission to that official constellation of literary greats, the Académie Française, in 1852, was spoiled for him by two previous failed candidacies and by his own realization that his best work lay behind him. The writer's health was sapped by fear of mental illness and by intermittent cardiac episodes, as well as his long-standing tendency to alcoholism (his preferred "cocktail" seems to have been a mixture of cognac, absinthe, and beer), which was common knowledge among his contemporaries and came close to destroying the youthful elegance and good looks that he never completely lost. He spent the latter years of his life being cared for by a governess, Adèle Colin Martellet, whose published memoirs are an important source of information about that period; he died on 2 May 1857. According to his brother Paul, his last words (which, coming from a lifelong insomniac, reassured his brother) were: "Dormir! . . . enfin je vais dormir!" (Sleep! . . . at last I am going to sleep!).

Several of Musset's dramatic and lyric works have inspired musical composers, from shortly after his death until the present. Aside from Offenbach and Messager's operetta versions of *Le Chandelier* and Puccini's opera, *Edgar,* taken from *La Coupe et les lèvres,* there have been operatic treatments of several of the author's plays: Prince de Polignac's, Gustave Canoby's, and E. d'Hervilly's three additional nineteenth-century settings of *La Coupe et les lèvres,* Daniel-Lesur's recent *André del Sarto,* Henri Sauguet's *Les Caprices de Marianne,* Gabriel Pierné's *On ne badine pas avec l'amour,* and Ernest Moret's *Lorenzaccio.* In a different medium Jean Renoir's noted pre–World War II film, *La Règle du jeu* (The Rules of the Game, 1939) was based to a great extent on both *Les Caprices de Marianne* and *On ne badine pas avec l'amour.* Thus it is clear that Musset's influence on theatrical practice extended well beyond the legitimate stage.

Despite the disappointments of his later life, which made Musset one prototype of the *poète maudit*—in his case, the poet whose youthful genius and promise are dissipated by moral and physical weakness—he must nonetheless be viewed as one of the most significant figures of nineteenth-century French writing and, in particular, as the most gifted and influential dramatist of his time. Although his best plays were not staged in their original form until after his death, whereas many of his contemporaries regularly had theirs performed in the lively theatrical hotbed of Paris—notably Hugo, Dumas *père* and Dumas *fils,* Alfred de Vigny, and Eugène Scribe—the enduring presence of Musset's works in contemporary theater is unique for their time. To a great extent, ironically, this can be ascribed to his good luck in avoiding a stage whose aesthetic limitations (primarily those of realist, "boulevard" theater, but also those of the literary drama of the Théâtre-Français) in the long run condemned to mediocrity those playwrights who successfully mastered them. But this longevity can also be traced to Musset's special talent, a dramatic imagination that shone through his poetry as well as his works for the stage and allowed him to conceive of an "impossible" theater years ahead of its time, one that would achieve satisfactory performance only when the theater's stage resources and the public's notion of drama reached the point of which he had dreamed in his armchair shows. The psychological depth, linguistic richness, and theatrical imaginativeness of *Les Caprices de Marianne,* *Fantasio,* and *On ne badine pas avec l'amour* are especially notable. *Lorenzaccio*'s ethical and psychological complexity, as well as the complexity of its dramatic form, on the other hand, transcends its genre, that of the Romantic historical tragedy, as neither Dumas *père*'s *Les Trois Mousquetaires* (The Three Musketeers, 1844) nor Hugo's *Hernani* (1830) does, for example. Such widely varied European dramatists as Maurice Maeterlinck, Edmond Rostand, Hugo von Hofmannsthal, Jean Giraudoux, Jean Anouilh, Fernando Arrabal, Samuel Beckett, Harold Pinter, and Edward Albee can be said to have been strongly influenced, in quite different ways, by the form and language of the theatrical works of Musset.

Letters:

Correspondance de George Sand et d'Alfred de Musset, edited by Félix Decori (Brussels: E. Deman, 1904);

Alfred de Musset. Correspondance (1827–1857), edited by Léon Séché (Paris: Mercure de France, 1907);

Lettres d'amour à Aimée d'Alton (Madame Paul de Musset), edited by Léon Séché (Paris: Mercure de France, 1910);

Correspondance (1827–1857) (Paris: Librairie de France, 1928);

George Sand et Alfred de Musset. Correspondance. Journal intime de George Sand (1834) (Monaco: Editions du Rocher, 1956);

Correspondance d'Alfred de Musset, (1826–1839), volume 1, edited by Marie Cordroch, Roger Pierrot, and Loïc Chotard (Paris: Presses Universitaires de France, 1985);

Sand et Musset: Lettres d'amour, edited by Françoise Sagan (Paris: Hermann, 1985).

Bibliographies:

Charles Victor Maximilien Albert, Vicomte de Spoelberch de Lovenjoul, *Etude critique et biblio-*

graphique des oeuvres d'Alfred de Musset (Paris: R. Pincebourde, 1867);

Héritiers d'Alfred de Musset, *Les Héritiers d'Alfred de Musset contre M. Charpentier, éditeur* (Paris: E. Brière, 1867);

Maurice Clouard, *Bibliographie des oeuvres d'Alfred de Musset et des ouvrages . . .* (Paris: P. Rouquette, 1883);

Spoelberch de Lovenjoul, *Les Lundis d'un chercheur* (Paris: Calmann-Lévy, 1894);

Clouard, *Documents inédits sur Alfred de Musset* (Paris: A. Rouquette, 1900);

Bibliothèque Nationale, *Alfred de Musset 1810–1857; exposition organisée pour le centenaire de sa mort* (Paris: Bibliothèque nationale, 1957);

Patricia Joan Siegel, *Alfred de Musset: A Reference Guide* (Boston: G. K. Hall, 1982).

Biographies:

Alfred Musset, *Lui et elle* (Paris: Naumbourg, 1859);

George Sand, *Elle et lui* (Paris: Hachette, 1859);

Mathurin de Lescure, *Eux et elles: histoire d'un scandale* (Paris: Poulet-Malassis et de Broise, 1860);

Paul de Musset, *Biographie de Alfred de Musset; sa vie et ses oeuvres* (Paris: Fasquelle, 1877);

Caroline Jaubert, *Souvenirs de Madame C. Jaubert: lettres et correspondances* (Paris: J. Hetzel, [1881]);

Arvède Barine [Cécile Vincens], *Alfred de Musset* (Paris: Hachette, 1893);

Paul Marieton, *Une Histoire d'amour; George Sand et A. de Musset, [avec] documents inédits [et] lettres de Musset* (Paris: G. Havard Fils, 1897);

Charles Victor Maximilien Albert, Vicomte de Spoelberch de Lovenjoul, *La Véritable Histoire de "Elle et lui": notes et documents* (Paris: Calmann-Lévy, 1897);

Adèle Colin Martellet, *Dix Ans chez Alfred de Musset* (Paris: Chamuel, 1899);

Octave Teissier, *Alfred de Musset. Documents généalogiques* (Draguignan: Impr. C. & A. Latil, 1903);

Martellet, *Alfred de Musset intime; souvenirs de sa gouvernante,* preface by Georges Montorgueil (Paris: Librairie F. Juven, [1906]);

Léon Séché, *Alfred de Musset,* 2 volumes (Paris: Mercure de France, 1907);

Emile Faguet, *Amours d'hommes de lettres. Pascal–Corneille–Voltaire–Mirabeau–Chateaubriand–Lamartine–Guizot–Mérimée–Sainte-Beuve–George Sand et Musset* (Paris: Société française d'imprimerie et de librairie, 1907);

Maurice Dumoulin, *Les Ancêtres d'Alfred de Musset, d'après des documents inédits* (Paris: Emile-Paul, 1911);

Charles Maurras, *Les Amants de Venise: George Sand et Musset, nouvelle édition augmentée d'une préface* (Paris: Boccard, 1916);

Maurice Donnay, *La Vie amoureuse d'Alfred de Musset* (Paris: E. Flammarion, 1926?);

Anatole Feugère, *Un Grand Amour romantique, George Sand et Alfred de Musset* (Paris: Boivin, 1927);

Emile Henriot, *Alfred de Musset* (Paris: Hachette, 1928?);

Marie-Louise Pailleron, *François Buloz et ses amis; la vie littéraire sous Louis-Philippe* (Paris: Firmin-Didot, 1930);

Henry Dwight Sedgwick, *Alfred de Musset 1810–1857* (Indianapolis: Bobbs-Merrill, 1931);

Pierre Gastinel, *Le Romantisme d'Alfred de Musset* (Paris: Hachette, 1933);

Antoine Adam, *Le Secret de l'aventure vénitienne: la vérité sur Sand et Musset* (Paris: Perrin, 1938);

John Charpentier, *Alfred de Musset* (Paris: Tallandier, 1938);

André Bonnichon, *La Vie privée d'Alfred de Musset* (Paris: Hachette, [1939]);

Henriot, *Alfred de Musset, l'enfant du siècle. Avec une correspondance inédite: lettres de Paul de Musset à Madame Jaubert* (Paris: Amiot-Dumont, [1953]);

Charlotte Haldane, *Alfred: The Passionate Life of Alfred de Musset* (New York: Roy, 1961);

Gilbert Ganne, *Alfred de Musset: sa jeunesse et la nôtre* (Paris: Librairie académique Perrin, 1970);

Henri Guillemin, *La Liaison Musset-Sand* ([Paris]: Gallimard, [1972]).

References:

Charles Affron, *A Stage for Poets: Studies in the Theater of Hugo and Musset* (Princeton: Princeton University Press, 1971);

Maurice Allem, *Alfred de Musset,* revised edition (Grenoble: Arthaud, 1947);

Georges Ascoli, *Le Théâtre romantique* (Paris: "Les Cours de Sorbonne," 1936);

Helen Phelps Bailey, *Hamlet in France: From Voltaire to Laforgue* (Geneva: Droz, 1964);

Ivan Barko and Bruce Burgess, *La Dynamique des points de vue dans le texte de théâtre: analyses de points de vue: "Le Misanthrope," "Le Mariage de Figaro," "Lorenzaccio," "En attendant Godot"* (Paris: Minard, 1988);

Jeanne Bem, "Lorenzaccio entre l'histoire et le fantasme," *Poétique: Revue de Théorie et d'Analyse Littéraires,* 11 (1980): 451–461;

Bem and others, *Musset: "Lorenzaccio," "On ne badine pas avec l'amour,"* "avec la participation de la *Société des études romantiques*" (Paris: SEDES, 1990[?]);

Paul Bénichou, *L'Ecole du désenchantement: Sainte-Beuve, Nodier, Musset, Nerval, Gautier* (Paris: Gallimard, 1992?);

Frank Paul Bowman, "Notes Toward the Definition of the Romantic Theater," *Esprit Créateur*, 5 (1965): 121–130;

Rachel Brownstein, *Tragic Muse: Rachel of the Comédie-Française* (New York: Knopf, 1993);

Auguste Brun, *Deux Proses de théâtre: drame romantique, comédies et proverbes* (Gap: Editions Ophrys, 1954);

Barbara T. Cooper, "Breaking up/down/apart: 'l'éclatement' as a unifying principle in Musset's *Lorenzaccio*," *Philological Quarterly*, 65 (1986): 103–112;

Cooper, "Staging a Revolution: Political Upheaval in *Lorenzaccio* and *Léo Burckart*," *Romance Notes*, 24 (1983): 23–29;

Ceri Crossley, *Musset, "Lorenzaccio"* (London: Grant & Cutler, 1983);

Maurice Descotes, *Le Drame romantique et ses grands créateurs (1827–1839)* (Paris: Presses Universitaires, 1955);

Jean-Jacques Didier, *L'Esprit: stylistique du mot d'esprit dans le théâtre de Musset* (Amsterdam: Rodopi, 1992);

Charlotte Dolder, *Le Thème de l'être et du paraître dans l'itinéraire spirituel d'Alfred de Musset* (Zurich: Juris-Verlag, 1968);

Hassan El-Nouty, "L'Esthétique de *Lorenzaccio*," *Revue des Sciences Humaines*, 108 (1962): 589–611;

David Owen Evans, *Le Drame moderne à l'époque romantique (1827–1850)* (Geneva: Slatkine, 1974);

Angelika Fabig, *Kunst und Künstler im Werk Alfred de Mussets* (Heidelberg: Winter, 1976);

Donald R. Gamble, "Alfred de Musset and the Uses of Experience," *Nineteenth-Century French Studies*, 18 (1989): 78–84;

Gamble, "The Image of Italy and the Creative Imagination of Alfred de Musset," in *Proceedings of the XIIth Congress of the International Comparative Literature Association, II, Space and Boundaries in Literature*, edited by Roger Bauer and others (Munich: Iudicium Verlag, 1990);

Eric L. Gans, *Musset et le "drame tragique"; essai d'analyse paradoxale* (Paris: J. Corti, 1974);

Pierre Gauthiez, *Lorenzaccio: (Lorenzino de Médicis) 1514–1548* (Paris: Fontémoing, 1904);

Théophile Gautier, *Histoire de l'art dramatique en France depuis vingt-cinq ans*, series 1–6 (Paris: Magnin, Blanchard et Cie, 1858–1859);

Jean Giraud, "Alfred de Musset et trois romantiques allemands," *Revue d'Histoire Littéraire*, 18 (1911): 297–334; 19 (1912): 341–375;

Herbert Gochberg, *Stage of Dreams* (Geneva: Droz, 1967);

Maurice Gravier, "Georg Büchner et Alfred de Musset," *Orbis Litterarum*, 9 (1954): 29–44;

Ronald Grimsley, "The Character of Lorenzaccio," *French Studies*, 11 (January 1957): 16–27;

James F. Hamilton, "From *Ricochets* to *Jeu* in Musset's *On ne badine pas avec l'amour*: A Game Analysis," *French Review*, 58 (1985): 820–826;

Hamilton, "Mimetic Desire in Musset's *Lorenzaccio*," *Romance Quarterly*, 32 (1985): 347–357;

Alain Heyvaert, *La Transparence et l'indicible dans l'oeuvre de Musset* (Paris: Klincksieck, 1994);

Robert Horville, *"Lorenzaccio," Musset: analyse critique* (Paris: Hatier, 1972);

W. D. Howarth, "Drama," in *The French Romantics*, edited by D. G. Charlton (Cambridge: Cambridge University Press, 1984), pp. 205–247;

Gianni Iotti, *Il gioco del comico e del serio: saggi sul teatro di Musset* (Naples: Edizioni scientifiche italiane, 1990);

Simon Jeune, *Musset et sa fortune littéraire* (Bordeaux: G. Ducros, 1970);

Louis Jouvet, *Théâtre classique et théâtre du XIXe siècle, extraits des cours de Louis Jouvet au Conservatoire (1939–1940)* (Paris: Gallimard, 1968);

Sarah Kernochan, *Impromptu* (New York: ICM, 1989);

Kenneth Kraus, "Lorenzaccio, Castraccio, Lorenzetta: A Consideration of Who May Play Musset's Lorenzo," *George Sand Studies*, 10 (1990–1991): 18–27;

Léon Lafoscade, *Le Théâtre d'Alfred de Musset* (Paris: Nizet, 1901);

Yves Lainey, *Musset: ou la difficulté d'aimer* (Paris: Société d'édition d'enseignement supérieur, 1978);

André Lebois, *Vues sur le théâtre de Musset* (Avignon: Aubanel, 1966);

Guy Leclerc, *Les Grandes Aventures du théâtre* (Paris: Editeurs français réunis, 1965);

Henri Lefebvre, *Alfred de Musset dramaturge* (Paris: L'Arche, 1955);

Jules Lemaître, *Impressions de théâtre*, volume 10 (Paris: Lecène, Oudin et Cie, 1898);

Henry Lyonnet, *Les "Premières" d'Alfred de Musset* (Paris: Delagrave, 1927);

Jacqueline Machabeis, "Propositions sur la structure de *Lorenzaccio*," *Les Lettres Romanes*, 38 (1984): 99–116;

John W. MacInnes, "*Lorenzaccio* and the Drama of Narration," in *Text and Presentation*, edited by Karelisa V. Hartigan (Lanham, Md.: University Press of America, 1988), pp. 137–145;

Thérèse Malachy, *"Lorenzaccio:* du meurtre politique au sacrifice rituel," *Revue d'Histoire du Théâtre*, 40 (1988): 273–280;

Cecil Malthus and Rex A. Barrell, eds., *Musset et Shakespeare: Etude analytique de l'influence de Shakespeare sur le théâtre d'Alfred de Musset* (New York: Peter Lang, 1988);

Bernard Masson, *Lectures de l'imaginaire* (Paris: Presses universitaires de France, 1993);

Masson, *"Lorenzaccio," ou la difficulté d'être* (Paris: Lettres modernes, 1962);

Masson, *Musset et son double: lecture de "Lorenzaccio"* (Paris: Minard, 1978);

Masson, *Musset et le théâtre intérieur; nouvelles recherches sur "Lorenzaccio"* (Paris: Armand Colin, 1974);

Masson, *Théâtre et langage: essai sur le dialogue dans les comédies de Musset* (Paris: Lettres modernes, 1977);

André Maurois, "Alfred de Musset: Les Comédies," *Revue des Sciences Humaines,* 101 (1958): 17–29;

Robert Mauzi, "Les Fantoches d'Alfred de Musset," *Revue d'Histoire Littéraire,* 66 (1966): 257–283;

Joachim-Claude Merlant, *Le Moment de "Lorenzaccio" dans le destin de Musset* (Athens: N.p., 1955);

Désiré Nisard, *Histoire de la littérature française,* 4 volumes (Paris: Firmin Didot frères, 1844–1861);

Pierre Nordon, "Alfred de Musset et l'Angleterre," *Les Lettres Romanes,* 20 (1966): 319–333; 21 (1967): 28–46, 123–140, 238–256, 354–368;

Pierre Odoul, *Le Drame intime d'Alfred de Musset: étude psychanalytique de l'oeuvre et de la vie d'Alfred de Musset* (Paris: Pensée universelle, 1976?);

Jean Pommier, *Alfred de Musset* (Oxford: Clarendon Press, 1957);

Pommier, *Autour du drame de Venise* (Paris: Nizet, 1958);

Pommier, *Variétés sur Alfred de Musset et son théâtre* (Paris: Nizet, 1966);

Suzanne A. Rothschild, *A Critical and Historical Study of Alfred de Musset's "Barberine"* (Paris: Imprimerie I.A.C., 1965);

Evelyn Schels, *Die Tradition des lyrischen Dramas von Musset bis Hofmannsthal* (Frankfurt am Main & New York: Peter Lang, 1990);

Naomi Schor, "La pérodie: Superposition dans *Lorenzaccio,*" in *Discours et pouvoir,* edited by Ross Chambers (Ann Arbor: Department of Romance Languages, University of Michigan, 1982), pp. 73–86;

Marjorie Shaw, "Deux Essais sur les comédies d'Alfred de Musset," *Revue des Sciences Humaines,* 93 (1959): 47–76;

Shaw, "A Propos du 'Fantasio' d'Alfred de Musset," *Revue d'Histoire Littéraire,* 55 (1955): 319–328;

Maurice Z. Shroder, *Icarus: The Image of the Artist in French Romanticism* (Cambridge, Mass.: Harvard University Press, 1961);

David Sices, "Alfred de Musset," in *Major World Writers: Great Foreign Language Writers* (London: Saint James, 1984);

Sices, "Alfred de Musset," in *European Writers,* edited by W. T. H. Jackson and others, volume 6 (New York: Scribners, 1985), pp. 999–1032;

Sices, *Theater of Solitude: The Drama of Alfred de Musset* (Hanover, N.H.: University Press of New England, 1974);

John K. Simon, "The Presence of Musset in Modern French Drama," *French Review,* 40 (1966): 27–38;

Albert B. Smith, "Musset's *Les Caprices de Marianne:* A Romantic Adaptation of a Traditional Comic Structure," *Nineteenth-Century French Studies,* 20 (1991): 53–64;

Jean Starobinski, "Note sur un bouffon romantique," *Cahiers du Sud,* 61 (1966): 270–275;

Alex Szogyi, "Musset's *Lorenzaccio:* George Sand's Ultimate Gift," in *Woman as Mediatrix: Essays on Nineteenth-Century Women Writers,* edited by Avriel H. Goldberger (Westport, Conn.: Greenwood Press, 1987), pp. 89–98;

Jean-Jacques Thomas, "Les maîtres-mots de Musset: Peuple et pouvoir dans *Lorenzaccio,*" in *Peuple et pouvoir: Etudes de lexicologie politique,* edited by Michel Glatigny and Jacques Guilhaumou (Lille: Presses universitaires de Lille, 1981), pp. 179–196;

Jean-Marie Thomasseau, *Alfred de Musset: "Lorenzaccio"* (Paris: Presses universitaires de France, 1986);

Maurice Toesca, *Alfred de Musset; ou, l'amour de la mort* (Paris: Hachette, 1970);

Frederick Tonge, *L'Art du dialogue dans les Comédies en prose d'Alfred de Musset. Etude de stylistique dramatique* (Paris: Nizet, 1967);

Philippe Van Tieghem, "L'Evolution du théâtre de Musset des débuts à *Lorenzaccio,*" *Revue d'Histoire du Théâtre,* 4 (1952): 261–275;

Van Tieghem, *Musset* (Paris: Hatier, 1944);

Jean Vilar, *De la Tradition théâtrale* (Paris: L'Arche, 1955);

Marie Josephine Whitaker, *Lorenzo ou Lorenzaccio?: misères et splendeurs d'un héros romantique* (Paris: Lettres modernes, 1989);

J. J. White, "Hofmannsthal and Musset," in *Hugo von Hofmannsthal 1874–1929: Commemorative Essays,* edited by W. E. Yuill and Patricia Howe (London: N.p., 1981), pp. 35–49;

Matthew H. Wikander, "The Revolution of the Times: Musset, Büchner, and Brecht," in his *The Play of Truth and State: Historical Drama from Shakespeare to Brecht* (Baltimore: Johns Hopkins University Press, 1986), pp. 197–240.

Papers:

Musset's papers are held in Paris at the Bibliothèque Nationale and the Bibliothèque de l'Arsenal.

René-Charles Guilbert de Pixerécourt
(22 January 1773 – 27 July 1844)

Angela Pao
Indiana University

PLAY PRODUCTIONS: *Sélico, ou les Nègres généreux,* Nancy, Théâtre Molière, 8 January 1793;

Les Petits Auvergnats, Paris, Théâtre de l'Ambigu-Comique, 16 September 1797;

La Nuit Espagnole, ou la Cloison, Paris, Théâtre de l'Ambigu-Comique, 30 September 1797;

Victor, ou l'Enfant de la forêt, Paris, Théâtre de l'Ambigu-Comique, November 1797;

La Forêt de Sicile, Paris, Theatre Montansier, 1798;

Le Château des Apennins, ou les Mystères d'Udolphe, Paris, Théâtre de l'Ambigu-Comique, 27 June 1798;

Blanchette, Paris, Théâtre Louvois, 1798;

La Soirée des Champs Élysées, Paris, Théâtre Montansier, 24 January 1799;

Léonidas, ou le Départ des Spartiates, Paris, Grand Opéra, 1799;

Zozo, ou le mal avisé, performed as comic opera, Paris, Théâtre Montansier, 17 October 1799; performed as a comedy titled *Les Deux Valets,* Paris, Théâtre de la Porte Saint-Martin, 3 March 1803;

L'Auberge du diable, Paris, Théâtre Montansier, 29 January 1800;

Le Petit Page, ou la Prison d'état, Théâtre Feydeau, 14 February 1800;

La Musicomanie, Paris, Théâtre de l'Ambigu-Comique, May 1800;

Rancune, ou les Charcutiers Troyens, Paris, Théâtre des Troubadours, May 1800;

La Jarretière, Paris, Théâtre des Troubadours, 25 July 1800;

Rosa, ou l'Ermitage du Torrent, Paris, Théâtre de la Gaîté, 9 August 1800;

Le Chansonnier de la paix, Paris, Théâtre Feydeau, 18 February 1801;

Flaminius à Corinthe, Paris, Théâtre des Arts, 24 February 1801;

Coelina, ou l'Enfant du mystère, Paris, Théâtre de l'Ambigu-Comique, 6 April 1801;

Quatre Maris pour un, Paris, Théâtre des Jeunes Artistes, 27 April 1801;

René-Charles Guilbert de Pixerécourt

Le Vieux Major, Paris, Théâtre Montansier, 24 August 1801;

L'Homme à trois visages, ou le Proscrit de Venise, Paris, Théâtre de l'Ambigu-Comique, 6 October 1801;

Madame Villeneuve, ou la Tireuse de cartes, Paris, Théâtre de la Gaîté, 23 November 1801;

La Peau de l'ours, Paris, Théâtre Montansier, 1 March 1802;

La Femme à deux maris, Paris, Théâtre de l'Ambigu-Comique, 14 September 1802;

Raymond de Toulouse, ou le Retour de la Terre-sainte, Paris, Théâtre des Jeunes Artistes, 16 September 1802;

Pizarre, ou la Conquête du Pérou, Paris, Théâtre de la Porte Saint-Martin, 27 September 1802;

Le Sac et le portefeuille, ou le Procureur ermite, Paris, Théâtre de la Gaîté, 22 November 1802;

Les Mines de Pologne, Paris, Théâtre de l'Ambigu-Comique, 3 May 1803;

La Chaumière et le trésor, Paris, Théâtre Montansier, 10 September 1803;

Tékéli, ou le Siège de Montgatz, Paris, Théâtre de l'Ambigu-Comique, 29 December 1803;

Les Maures d'Espagne, ou le Pouvoir de l'enfance, Paris, Théâtre de l'Ambigu-Comique, 9 May 1804;

Avis aux femmes, ou le Mari colère, Paris, Théâtre Favart, 27 October 1804;

Le Grand Chasseur, ou l'Ile des palmiers, Paris, Théâtre de l'Ambigu-Comique, 6 November 1804;

La Forteresse du Danube, Paris, Théâtre de la Porte Saint-Martin, 3 January 1805;

Robinson Crusoé, Paris, Théâtre de la Porte Saint-Martin, 2 October 1805;

Le Solitaire de la roche noire, Paris, Théâtre de la Porte Saint-Martin, 14 May 1806;

Koulouf, ou les Chinois, Paris, Opéra-Comique, 18 December 1806;

L'Ange tutélaire, ou le Démon femelle, Paris, Théâtre de la Gaîté, 2 June 1808;

La Citerne, Paris, Théâtre de la Gaîté, 14 January 1809;

La Rose blanche et la Rose rouge, Paris, Opéra-Comique, 20 March 1809;

Marguerite d'Anjou, Paris, Théâtre de la Gaîté, 11 January 1810;

Les Trois Moulins, Paris, Théâtre de la Gaîté, 30 March 1810;

Les Ruines de Babylone, ou le Massacre des Barmécides, Paris, Théâtre de la Gaîté, 30 October 1810;

Le Berceau, Paris, Opéra-Comique, 28 March 1811;

Le Précipice, ou les Forges de Norwège, Paris, Théâtre de la Gaîté, 30 October 1811;

Le Fanal de Messine, Paris, Théâtre de la Gaîté, 23 June 1812;

Le Petit Carillonneur, ou la Tour ténébreuse, Paris, Théâtre de la Gaîté, 24 November 1812;

L'Ennemi des modes, ou la Maison de Choisy, Paris, Théâtre de l'Imperatrice, 7 December 1813;

Le Chien de Montargis, ou la Forêt de Bondy, Paris, Théâtre de la Gaîté, 18 June 1814;

Charles-le-Téméraire, ou le Siège de Nancy, Paris, Théâtre de la Gaîté, 26 October 1814;

Christophe Colomb, ou la Découverte du Nouveau-Monde, Paris, Théâtre de la Gaîté, 5 September 1815;

Le Suicide, ou le Vieux Sergent, Paris, Théâtre de la Gaîté, 20 February 1816;

Le Monastère abandonné, ou la Malédiction paternelle, Paris, Théâtre de la Gaîté, 28 November 1816;

La Chapelle des bois, ou le Témoin invisible, Paris, Théâtre de la Gaîté, 12 August 1818;

Le Belvéder, ou la Vallée de l'Etna, Paris, Théâtre de l'Ambigu-Comique, 10 December 1818;

La Fille de l'exilé, ou Huit mois en deux heures, Paris, Théâtre de la Gaîté, 13 March 1819;

Les Chefs écossais, Paris, Théâtre de la Porte Saint-Martin, 1 September 1819;

Bouton de rose, ou le Pêcheur de Bassora, Paris, Théâtre de la Gaîté, 13 November 1819;

Le Mont sauvage, ou le Duc de Bourgogne, Paris, Théâtre de la Gaîté, 12 July 1821;

Valentine, ou la Séduction, Paris, Théâtre de la Gaîté, 15 December 1821;

Le Pavillon des fleurs, ou les Pêcheurs de Grenade, Paris, Opéra-Comique, 13 May 1822;

Ali-Baba, ou les Quarante voleurs, Paris, Théâtre de la Gaîté, 28 September 1822;

Le Château de Loch-Leven, ou l'Évasion de Marie Stuart, Paris, Théâtre de la Gaîté, 3 December 1822;

La Place du Palais, Paris, Théâtre de la Gaîté, 26 March 1824;

Le Baril d'olives, Paris, Théatre des Variétés, 1 February 1825;

Le Moulin des étangs, Paris, Théâtre de la Gaîté, 28 January 1826;

Les Natchez, ou la Tribu du serpent, Paris, Théâtre de la Gaîté, 21 June 1827;

La Tête de mort, ou les Ruines de Pompeïa, Paris, Théâtre de la Gaîté, 8 December 1827;

La Muette de la forêt, Paris, Théâtre de la Gaîté, 29 January 1828;

Guillaume Tell, Paris, Théâtre de la Gaîté, 3 May 1828;

La Peste de Marseille, Paris, Théâtre de la Gaîté, 2 August 1828;

Polder, ou le Bourreau d'Amsterdam, Paris, Théâtre de la Gaîté, 15 October 1828;

L'Aigle des Pyrénées, Paris, Théâtre de la Gaîté, 19 February 1829;

Les Compagnons du chêne, Paris, Théâtre de la Gaîté, 6 June 1829;

Alice, Paris, Théâtre de la Gaîté, 24 October 1829;

Ondine, ou la Nymphe des eaux, Paris, Théâtre de la Gaîté, 17 February 1830;

Judacin, ou les Filles de la veuve, Paris, Théâtre de la Gaîté, 4 September 1830;

Fénélon, Paris, Théâtre de la Gaîté, 16 September 1830;

Malmaison et Sainte-Hélène, Paris, Théâtre de la Gaîté, 13 January 1831;

L'Oiseau bleu, Paris, Théâtre de la Gaîté, 10 February 1831;

La Lettre de cachet, ou les Abus de l'ancien régime, Paris, Théâtre de la Gaîté, 26 February 1831;

Les Dragonnades, Paris, Théâtre de la Gaîté, 9 April 1831;

L'Abbaye aux bois, ou la Femme de chambre, Paris, Théâtre de la Gaîté, 9 April 1831;

Le Petit homme rouge, Paris, Théâtre de la Gaîté, 19 March 1832;

Six florins, ou la Brodeuse et la Dame, Paris, Théâtre de la Gaîté, 7 July 1832;

L'Allée des veuves, ou la Justice en 1773, Paris, Théâtre de la Gaîté, 16 March 1833;

Les Quatre éléments, Paris, Théâtre de la Gaîté, 10 July 1833;

La Ferme et le château, Paris, Théâtre de la Gaîté, 20 March 1834;

Latude, ou trente-cinq ans de captivité, Paris, Théâtre de la Gaîté, 15 November 1834;

Le Four à chaux, ou l'Auberge de Peyrebelle, Paris, Théâtre du Cirque Olympique, 3 October 1835;

Bijou, ou l'Enfant de Paris, Paris, Théâtre du Cirque Olympique, 31 January 1838.

BOOKS: *La Forêt de Sicile* (Paris: Vogt, 1798);

Les Petits Auvergnats (Paris: Barba, 1799);

Victor, ou l'Enfant de la forêt (Paris: Barba, 1799);

Le Château des Apennins, ou les Mystères d'Udolphe (Paris: Barba, 1799);

Zozo, ou le mal avisé (Paris: Barba, 1799/1800?);

La Soirée des Champs Élysées (Paris: Barba, 1800);

Le Petit Page, ou la Prison d'état (Paris: André, 1800);

Rosa, ou l'Ermitage du Torrent (Paris: Barba, 1800);

Almanach des Spectacles de Paris, ou Calendrier Historique et Chronologique des Théâtres (Paris, 1800);

Coelina, ou l'Enfant du mystère (Paris: Barba, 1801);

Le Chansonnier de la paix (Paris: Huet, 1801);

Flaminius à Corinthe (Paris: Ballard, 1801);

Le Pèlerin blanc, ou les Orphelins du hameau (Paris: André, 1801); translated as *The Wandering Boys* (London, 1830);

Le Vieux Major (Paris: Barba, 1801);

L'Homme à trois visages, ou le Proscrit de Venise (Paris: 1801);

La Peau de l'ours (Paris: Barba, 1802);

La Femme à deux maris (Paris: Barba, 1802); translated by Elizabeth Gunning as *The Wife with Two Husbands* (London: Symonds, 1803);

Raymond de Toulouse, ou le Retour de la Terre-sainte (Paris: Barba, 1802);

Les Deux Valets (Paris: Barba, 1803);

Les Mines de Pologne (Paris: Barba, 1803);

Tékéli, ou le Siège de Montgatz (Paris: Barba, 1804);

Les Maures d'Espagne, ou le Pouvoir de l'enfance (Paris: Barba, 1804);

Avis aux femmes, ou le Mari colère (Paris: Barba, 1804);

Le Grand Chasseur, ou l'Ile des palmiers (Paris: Fages, 1804);

La Forteresse du Danube (Paris: Barba, 1805);

Robinson Crusoé (Paris: Barba, 1805);

Le Solitaire de la Roche Noire (Paris: Barba, 1806);

Koulouf, ou les Chinois (Paris: Barba, 1807);

La Citerne (Paris: Barba, 1809);

La Rose blanche et la Rose rouge (Paris: Barba, 1809);

L'Ange tutélaire, ou le Démon femelle (Paris: Barba, 1810);

Vie de Dalayrac, Chevalier de la Légion d'Honneur et membre de l'Académie royale de Stockholm (Paris: Barba, 1810);

Marguerite d'Anjou (Paris: Barba, 1810);

Les Trois Moulins (Paris: Barba, 1810);

Les Ruines de Babylone, ou le Massacre des Barmécides (Paris: Barba, 1810);

Le Berceau (Paris: Barba, 1811);

Le Précipice, ou les Forges de Norwège (Paris: Barba, 1811);

Le Fanal de Messine (Paris: Barba, 1812);

Le Petit Carillonneur, ou la Tour ténébreuse (Paris: Barba, 1812);

L'Ennemi des modes, ou la Maison de Choisy (Paris: Barba, 1814);

Le Chien de Montargis, ou la Forêt de Bondy (Paris: Barba, 1814);

Charles-le-Téméraire, ou le Siège de Nancy (Paris: Barba, 1814);

Christophe Colomb, ou la Découverte du Nouveau-Monde (Paris: Barba, 1815);

Le Suicide, ou le vieux sergent (Paris: Barba, 1816);

Le Monastère abandonné, ou la Malédiction paternelle (Paris: Barba, 1816);

Le Belvéder, ou la Vallée de l'Etna (Paris: Barba, 1818);

La Chapelle des bois, ou le Témoin invisible (Paris: Barba, 1818);

Des faits opposés à des mensonges . . . (Paris: D'Everat, 1818);

Guerre au Mélodrame!!! (Paris: Delaunay, 1818);

La Fille de l'Exilé, ou Huit mois en deux heures (Paris: Barba, 1819);

Les Chefs écossais (Paris: Barba, 1819);

Bouton de rose, ou le Pêcheur de Bassora (Paris: Barba, 1819);

Le Mont sauvage, ou le Solitaire (Paris: Barba, 1821);

Valentine, ou la Séduction (Paris: Barba, 1822);

Le Pavillon des fleurs, ou les Pêcheurs de Grenade (Paris: Pollet, 1822);

Ali-Baba, ou les Quarante voleurs (Paris: Pollet, 1822);

Le Château de Loch-Leven, ou l'Évasion de Marie Stuart (Paris: Pollet, 1822);

La Place du Palais (Paris: Quoy, 1824);

Le Baril d'olives (Paris: Pollet, 1825);

Le Moulin des étangs (Paris: Duvernois, 1826);

Les Natchez, ou la Tribu du serpent (Paris: Quoy, 1827);

La Tête de mort, ou les Ruines de Pompeïa (Paris: Quoy, 1828);

La Muette de la forêt (Paris: Barba, 1828);

Guillaume Tell (Paris: Lami, 1828);

La Peste de Marseille (Paris: Duvernois, 1828);
Polder, ou le Bourreau d'Amsterdam (Paris: Pollet, 1828);
L'Aigle des Pyrénées (Paris: Barba, 1829);
Alice, ou les Fossoyeurs écossais (Paris: Barba, 1829);
Ondine, ou la Nymphe des eaux (Paris: Barba, 1830);
Judacin, ou les Filles de la veuve (Paris: Pollet, 1830);
Fénélon (Paris: Barba, 1830);
La Lettre de cachet, ou les Abus de l'ancien régime (Paris: Barba, 1831);
L'Oiseau bleu (Paris: Hardy, 1832);
L'Abbaye aux bois, ou la Femme de chambre (Paris: Riga, 1832);
Le Petit homme rouge (Paris: Riga, 1832);
Six Florins, ou la Brodeuse et la Dame (Paris: Riga, 1832);
L'Allée des veuves, ou la Justice en 1773 (Paris: Hardy, 1833);
Les Quatre éléments (Paris: Marchant, 1833);
La Ferme et le château (Paris: Barba, 1834);
Latude, ou Trente-cinq ans de captivité (Paris: Marchant, 1834);
Bijou, ou l'Enfant de Paris (Paris: Ve. Dondey-Dupré, 1838);
Le Jesuite (Paris: Tresse, 1840).

Collections: *Œuvres Complètes* (Paris: Barba, 1796–1838);
Théâtre Choisi, 4 volumes (Paris: Tresse, 1841–1843; Geneva: Slatkine Reprints, 1971).

OTHER: "Le Mélodrame," in *Paris ou le Livre des Cent-et-un,* volume 6 (Paris: Advocat, 1832), pp. 319–352;
"Observations sur l'état où se trouvaient les théâtres avant la Révolution, sur l'effet qu'elle a produit sur eux, sur l'influence que la tyrannie de Robespierre a eue sur les spectacles, et nécessairement de [*sic*] l'influence qu'ils ont à leur tour exercée sur le peuple, enfin sur leur situation actuelle" (1795); in an appendix to Edmond Estève, *Etudes de Littérature préromantique* (Paris: Champion, 1923).

René-Charles Guilbert de Pixerécourt's reputation as one of the most distinguished authors of French classical melodrama has survived to the present day. In addition to fifty-nine melodramas, he composed twenty-one *drames lyriques* (comic operas), seventeen vaudevilles, nine comedies, eight *féeries* (or pantomimes), four dramas, and two tragedies. As one of the most prolific and highly regarded writers for the popular theaters of the early nineteenth century, Pixerécourt was unusual for being able to produce works that appealed to the wide range of spectators who frequented the theaters of the Boulevard du Temple while at the same time retaining the respect of leading literary critics. This situation was a reflection of Pixerécourt's mastery of both the theatrical and literary aspects of his craft, the distinct moral positioning that he brought to his work, and an erudition that in previous generations was uncommon among authors specializing in popular genres. Pixerécourt was designated by many of his contemporaries as the founder or originator of nineteenth-century French melodrama, and he was frequently given appellations such as "le père du mélodrame" (the father of melodrama), "le prince du mélodrame" (the prince of melodrama), "le Corneille des boulevards" (the Corneille of the boulevards), and "le Shakespeare français" (the French Shakespeare). While many nineteenth- and twentieth-century critics have given equal credit to other authors as originators of the form, no one would dispute the claim that Pixerécourt was unsurpassed in his ability to apply the formulas or codes of melodrama with exceptional power, variety, and subtlety.

Pixerécourt was born in Nancy on 22 January 1773 to a family of provincial aristocrats, his great-grandfather having been ennobled at the beginning of the century. In "Souvenirs du jeune âge" (Memories of My Youth), in his *Théâtre Choisi* (1841–1843), Pixerécourt describes a highly disciplined, even rigid, upbringing that included a strong emphasis on religious instruction. He received his formal education first at the Collège de Nancy and then at the Faculté de Nancy, which he entered to study law from 1789 to 1790. His studies were interrupted by the French Revolution, which had a strong impact on the fortunes of his family. In a move to raise the family's status, Pixerécourt's father, Nicolas Charles Georges Guilbert, had sold the *seigneurie* of Pixerécourt in order to purchase the property of Saint-Vallier, which had once conferred the title of marquis on its owner. His plans to petition to have the title restored were thwarted by the 5 August 1789 decree of the Assemblée Nationale, which abolished all feudal rights. In his "Souvenirs de la Révolution" Pixerécourt describes his first experience of violence directly related to the French Revolution. In September 1790 he and his father were apparently confronted on their own lands by peasants armed with scythes, pitchforks, and even some swords and axes. The incident provoked the family's flight from their estate. In June 1791 René-Charles Guilbert left France for Koblenz, where he joined other exiled members of the aristocracy in the *armée des Princes*. There he met a young woman named Clotilde, whom he would later describe as the great love of his life. Sadly, she died of tuberculosis before Pix-

Set design by Gué for Pixerécourt's Le Château de Loch-Leven, *first produced in December 1822 at the Théâtre de la Gaîté in Paris*

erécourt returned to Nancy in 1793. From there he made his way to Paris.

His early years in Paris were characterized by poverty and the constant danger of being arrested and executed because of his aristocratic origins (although during this period he had dropped the "de Pixerécourt" from his name) and more particularly for having left the country illegally to serve in the forces of the *émigrés*. It was during this period that he found the subject for his first play in the work of the novelist and fabulist Jean-Pierre Claris de Florian. The drama, titled *Sélico, ou les Nègres généreux* (Sélico, or The Generous Negroes, 1793), was an adaptation of Florian's short story of the same name and was completed in one week. The play was accepted by the Théâtre Molière. An opera and two comedies followed in rapid succession. An order for universal conscription issued on 17 August 1793 forced Pixerécourt to return to Nancy, where he was assigned to a cavalry regiment, although he later obtained a medical deferment. Unusual circumstances there prompted him to compose his fifth work for the stage. The unpublished play—titled "Marat-Mauger ou le Jacobin en mission" (Marat-Mauger, or the Jacobin on a Mission, 1794) and described as "un fait

historique en un acte, mêlé de vaudevilles" (an historical incident in one act, interspersed with vaudevilles)—was in fact a denunciation of a representative of the *Convention* who had raped several local young women, including one known to the Pixerécourt family. The play was accepted by the Théâtre de Nancy but suppressed by the *Comité de surveillance,* which also ordered the arrest of Pixerécourt. Fortunately, the playwright was able to escape and return to Paris. On 30 September 1795 he married Marie Jeanne Françoise Quinette de la Hogue. Little is known of what Pixerécourt characterized as his "premature" marriage other than that the early years—during which the couple had one child, Anne-Françoise Guilbert—were financially difficult and unhappy.

Between 1795 and 1797 Pixerécourt wrote about ten works that were accepted by various theaters but never actually performed. It was on 16 September 1797 that Pixerécourt achieved his first success with a comic opera called *Les Petits Auvergnats* (The Little Auvergnats), which ran for seventy-three performances at the Théâtre de l'Ambigu-Comique. Two months later he surpassed this achievement with *Victor, ou l'Enfant de la forêt*

(Victor, or The Child of the Forest), which had a run of almost four hundred performances at the Théâtre de l'Ambigu-Comique. From then until 1835 Pixerécourt would regularly have three to five, and occasionally as many as ten, new works being produced on the stages of Paris in any given year. Between their performances in Paris and those in the provinces, the most successful works had a total of more than one thousand performances. The plays in this category included *Coelina, ou l'Enfant du mystère* (Coelina, or the Child of Mystery, 1801); *Le Pèlerin blanc, ou les Orphelins du hameau* (The White Pilgrim, or the Orphans of the Hamlet, 1801); *L'Homme à trois visages, ou le Proscrit de Venise* (The Man with Three Faces, or the Outlaw of Venice, 1801); *La Femme à deux maris* (The Wife with Two Husbands, 1802); *Tékéli, ou le Siège de Montgatz* (Tékéli, or the Siege of Montgate, 1803); and *Le Chien de Montargis, ou la Forêt de Bondy* (The Dog of Montargis, or the Forest of Bondy, 1814). Other popular works that ran for several hundred performances included *La Musicomanie* (Musicomania, 1800); *Les Mines de Pologne* (The Mines of Poland, 1803); *La Forteresse du Danube* (The Fortress on the Danube, 1805); *Robinson Crusoé* (1805); *L'Ange tutélaire, ou le Démon femelle* (The Guardian Angel, or the Female Demon, 1808); *La Citerne* (The Cistern, 1809); *Marguerite d'Anjou* (1810); *Les Ruines de Babylone, ou le Massacre des Barmécides* (The Ruins of Babylon, or the Massacre of the Barmacides, 1810); *Charles-le-Téméraire, ou le Siège de Nancy* (Charles the Bold, or the Siege of Nancy, 1814); *Le Monastère abandonné, ou la Malédiction paternelle* (The Abandoned Monastery, or the Father's Cause, 1816); *La Fille de l'Exilé, ou Huit mois en deux heures* (The Exile's Daughter, or Eight Months in Two Hours, 1819); and *Latude, ou trente-cinq ans de captivité* (Latude, or Thirty-five Years in Captivity, 1834). Except for *La Musicomanie,* a comic opera, and *Charles-le-Téméraire,* described as a *drame héroïque,* all the works listed above were melodramas.

In "Dernières réflexions . . . sur le mélodrame" (Final Reflections . . . on Melodrama), written in 1843 and published in the fourth volume of his *Théâtre Choisi,* Pixerécourt gives a retrospective account of his purpose and principles for developing melodrama into the dominant dramatic form of the first half of the nineteenth century. He notes that the genres of classical tragedy and comedy had been perfected over the previous two centuries. His conclusion was that "Il fallait donc inventer un nouveau théâtre" (It was therefore necessary to invent a new theater). For Pixerécourt it was important that this new theater be shaped by religious ideals and moral sentiments. He found models in the *drames bourgeois* of Louis-Sébastien Mercier (1740–1814)

and Michel-Jean Sedaine (1719–1797). In his estimation the success of these authors lay in their choice of subject matter that was both dramatic and moral; dialogue that was natural, direct, and true to life; the portrayal of generous sentiments and refined sensibilities; and finally, the consistent rewarding of virtue and punishment of crime. Making an argument for increased realism, Pixerécourt found fault with his immediate predecessors for making all characters speak in the same manner (a manner of speaking, moreover, which resembled that of a professor of rhetoric), regardless of their station in life. He called instead for a theater that would be "une représentation exacte et véridique de la nature" (an accurate and truthful representation of nature). Working in a genre that would frequently be criticized for its reliance on visual spectacle, Pixerécourt held that the longevity of any work depended on the author's words and the actors' delivery of those words. It was therefore essential, in his mind, that the author also be the one to rehearse and stage his own works and that he impose a strict discipline on himself and on all those with whom he worked. Only by occupying such a central position of authority could an author attend fully to the smallest details in all aspects of composition and production that would ensure success. Unlike many of his contemporaries, Pixerécourt resisted collaborating with other writers, believing that only the unified vision provided by a single author could produce effective final results. In fact, he blamed the mediocrity of many of his later works on his having succumbed to pressures to work with collaborators. During the latter part of his career Pixerécourt's involvement in theater included the exercise of administrative authority: he served as director of the Théâtre de la Gaîté from 1825 to 1835 and was also named director of the Théâtre Royal de l'Opéra-Comique in 1827.

Pixerécourt defended melodrama as a genre against its detractors in an 1818 pamphlet titled "Guerre au Mélodrame!!!" (War on Melodrama!!!) and signed "Le Bonhomme du Marais" (The Good Fellow of the Marais). To those who criticized melodrama for mixing genres, he replied that this sort of merging had been commonplace from the time of the ancient Greeks through the French Renaissance and even up to Pierre Corneille. In response to those who charged that melodrama contributed to the degeneration of the dramatic arts by catering to the less educated segments of society, he answered that such people were no less deserving of diversion. He maintained that those who did not constitute the most enlightened portion of the nation, which he pointed out included the majority of the population, should have pleasures suited "à leurs goûts, à leur éducation, à leur

The Théâtre de la Gaîté, the Paris playhouse where Pixerécourt served as director from 1825 until the building was destroyed by fire in 1835

état et surtout à leurs moyens pécuniaires" (to their tastes, to their education, to their station and above all to their financial means). Pixerécourt continued his defense in a second article, "Le Mélodrame," which appeared under his own name in 1832 in a collection of essays called *Paris ou le Livre des Cent-et-un* (Paris, or the Book of the Hundred and One). This piece took the form of a dialogue between the author and a pedantic gentleman he meets at a glittering soiree. In addition to the arguments already advanced, the author points out that ever since melodrama had been banished from the national theaters and relegated to the secondary theaters of the boulevards, both professional newspaper critics and public opinion had preferred the new productions of the popular theaters to those presented at the Comédie-Française on more than one occasion.

Pixerécourt believed the popular theater could be morally and socially useful by providing sound examples for public and private behavior. This moral concern, combined with a sure sense of what would be dramatically and theatrically effective, governed Pixerécourt's adaptations of his original sources. Sources have been identified for forty-three of his melodra-

mas. Approximately half were taken from French, English, or German novels; one-third were based on historical events; and the remainder were drawn from other dramatic works. Whatever the source, Pixerécourt skillfully transformed the material into an engaging three-act melodrama.

In Pixerécourt's first successful play strong connections to eighteenth-century drama remain evident. *Victor, ou l'Enfant de la forêt* (1797) was a close adaptation of the novel by François-Guillaume Ducray-Duminil, published in 1796. The plot revolves around the dilemmas of the central character, Victor. Believed to be an orphan, Victor was taken in and raised by a baron, whose daughter Clémentine he is now about to marry. Victor's true identity, however, is revealed when the baron's castle is attacked by brigands: he is in fact the son of Roger, the chief of the bandits, whose life he has just spared. In the eyes of everyone except Clémentine, the revelation of Victor's origins seemed to present an insurmountable obstacle to his marriage with the baron's daughter until Roger is fatally wounded by soldiers sent to hunt down the band of outlaws. In his dying moments Roger entreats the baron to consider Victor's life and character rather than his blood and so find him worthy of Clémentine. The play is an affirmation of the importance of the paternal role celebrated by the bourgeois dramas of Denis Diderot and Michel-Jean Sedaine: the baron, who made it possible for Victor to lead a virtuous and honest life, is seen to be more worthy of the title of father than the young man's biological parent, whose example might have led him into a life of crime.

Pixerécourt's next significant work, *Coelina, ou l'Enfant du mystère,* was likewise based on a Ducray-Duminil novel published in 1798. Written three years after *Victor, Coelina* also centered on crises arising from discoveries concerning the parentage of the title character. In this case Coelina is believed to be an orphaned member of the Dufour family. She has been raised under the guardianship of her paternal uncle, M. Dufour, and a mutual attraction has grown between Coelina and her cousin Stéphany. As the play opens, however, another potential suitor is introduced. This is the son of Coelina's maternal uncle, M. Truguelin. It is soon revealed that Truguelin (who became one of the archetypal villains of French classical melodrama) is motivated purely by avarice. By marrying Coelina to his son, he intends to gain control over the fortune she has inherited from her parents. Truguelin's evil character is exposed when he is overheard plotting the murder of a vagabond, Francisque Humbert, to whom Dufour has given shelter. Once a painter, Francisque has fallen into destitution following a vicious attack by two assailants who beat him and cut out his tongue. In an act of revenge Truguelin reveals that Coelina is not a Dufour after all but the illegitimate daughter of Francisque Humbert. Unable to forgive the insult to his dead brother, Dufour promises to help support the Humberts but, over his son's protests, orders them to leave his house forever. Further discoveries, however, prove that Truguelin and his servant were the perpetrators of the attack on Francisque. They had hoped to conceal the fact that Francisque had in fact been secretly married to Coelina's mother two months before she met Dufour's brother. It was Truguelin, unwilling to forgo the lucrative alliance, who had nevertheless forced his sister to go through with the second wedding. Truguelin's attempt to escape his inevitable punishment for villainy culminated in a celebrated chase over mountainous terrain and a leap into a torrential waterfall that set the early-nineteenth-century standard for spectacular action.

Victor and *Coelina* were strongly marked by the popular ideals of postrevolutionary French society. The challenges to paternal authority and values in both works paralleled the recent rejection of patriarchal feudalism in France. In declining to follow their fathers and to reject the person they loved when that person's questionable origins were discovered, Clémentine and Stéphany represented a new generation that placed individual merit and inherent worth, guaranteed by a virtuous upbringing and generous nature, above high birth.

Le Pèlerin blanc, ou les Orphelins du hameau, Pixerécourt's next major success, continued to feature orphans as central characters, but with a twist. The two brothers, Paul and Justin, age fourteen or fifteen, were to be played by young women. The "trousers roles" were said to be one of the primary attractions of the production, along with the sets that appealed to prevailing Romantic sensibilities by depicting a picturesque village and a partially ruined Gothic castle. The play also introduced one of the notable villainesses of early French melodrama, the Baroness of Castelli, who rivaled Truguelin in her greed and capacity for evil. Her hopes of inheriting the property and wealth of her uncle, the Count of Castelli, had been destroyed when he married and his wife Laurence bore him twin sons. The baroness therefore set fire to the castle; Laurence was killed in the blaze, and her two infant sons were reported to have died with her. Mad with grief, the count quit the region to wander abroad, leaving his niece the baroness in control. Rumors persisted, however, that a faithful servant had rescued the boys and sent them to be raised far from the castle. As the play begins, the villagers are preparing for a wedding celebration. Two boys, Paul and Justin, whose mother has just died, arrive and are promptly adopted by the villagers, who are charmed by their innocence and generosity. They are now penniless because they have given the money from the sale of their mother's goods to the church and to the poor. Over the years the baroness, mindful of the rumors, has examined any boys new to the region who would be the age of her uncle's children. After Paul and Justin are brought to her castle, she discovers papers revealing the twins' true identity and orders her steward Roland to poison them. He is thwarted by a recently hired servant, whom everyone believed to be a deaf and harmless old man. This servant turns out to be the count himself, who has returned in disguise after years of traveling in Europe and in Africa. The count resumes his rightful place, and his reunion with his sons is celebrated amid the festivities of the village wedding.

L'Homme à trois visages, ou le Proscrit de Venise dealt more directly with the question of preserving legitimized authority. Here the issues were addressed not through the bringing to light of an obscured lineage but through the linking of family and individual honor with patriotic sentiment. Here disguise becomes not just a dramatic device, as it was in *Coelina,* but the focus of the action. Eight years earlier Vivaldi and his father were banished from their native Venice after being falsely accused of a crime by Count Orsani. The senior Vivaldi died in exile. Vivaldi now has the opportunity to expose a conspiracy led by Orsani to overthrow the doge and assassinate thirty loyal members of the Venetian senate. He carries out his plan by assuming two identities other than his own: that of Edgar, a heroic foreign officer who has led Venetian troops to victory over their enemies and gained the confidence of the doge; and that of Abélino, a criminal and assassin whom Orsani believes to be a coconspirator. Vivaldi reveals his true identity only to a trusted friend, the senator Alfieri, and eventually to the doge's daughter Rosemonde, who is actually Vivaldi's wife. Just before Vivaldi was sent into exile, he and Rosemonde had been secretly married. Among Rosemonde's long-standing admirers is the Count Orsani, whose jealousy was a chief factor in motivating him to falsely denounce the Vivaldis. Alternating adroitly among his various identities, Vivaldi is able to gain knowledge of the conspirators' plans, alert the doge, and protect Rosemonde. The conspirators are exposed; Vivaldi's true identity is revealed; and his father's name is cleared. Only after ensuring the security of the state and restoring the honor of his family name is Vivaldi free to enjoy the personal rewards of love and friendship.

Seven years later Pixerécourt wrote what was in effect a companion piece to *L'Homme à trois visages*. *L'Ange tutélaire, ou le Démon femelle* (1808) was set in Ferrara in the mid sixteenth century. The plot was similar to that of the Venetian melodrama in that it revolved around an attempt to overthrow the rightful prince. The action, however, was modified to accommodate a woman in the central virtuoso role. The title character is Flora, a young noblewoman: she acts as guardian angel to the rightful duke of Ferrara, Alphonse, at the same time that she is the demon who plagues his ambitious brother, Amaldi. Betrothed to Amaldi, she uses her position to obtain information on the conspiracy to assassinate the noble and generous duke, who cannot be convinced of his brother's perfidy. In the process of protecting Alphonse and spying on Amaldi, she disguises herself as a seductive gypsy, a young page, and an old man. Unlike most heroines of melodrama, Flora was motivated not by romantic love or filial affection but above all by a desire to serve her country by preserving for it a good and just prince, who was also an honest and decent man.

In their clear condemnation of conspiracies aimed at overthrowing a legitimate government, *L'Homme à trois visages* and *L'Ange tutélaire* presented no problems for the ever vigilant official censors in-

stalled under Napoleonic rule. This was not the case with Pixerécourt's most widely performed historical melodrama, *Tékéli, ou le Siège de Montgatz,* first produced in 1803. The play recounted the adventures of a seventeenth-century Hungarian ruler, Tékéli, who was deposed but is eventually restored to his throne. *Tékéli* was being performed during a period of political instability created by a series of royalist plots designed to restore the Bourbon monarchy. Certain scenes concerning the harboring of a political refugee were thought to present an unfavorable comment on a similar situation where a suspect in hiding was betrayed to the authorities by informers. Since the play had been in performance for a month before the occurrence of the incident in question, Pixerécourt undoubtedly had no intention of making an allusion to the affair; but the fact remained that certain members of the audience insisted on making the application of their own accord. There were, moreover, certain remarks that were judged to be directed at the emperor himself. One monologue, in act 1, scene 2, exhorted:

O vous, êtres privilégiés que le hasard, la naissance ou les talents ont placé à la tête des nations; montrez-vous toujours justes et bons envers les peuples qui vous sont soumis: sachez par des bienfaits sagement répartis, gagner les coeurs de ceux qui vous entourent; au milieu de votre gloire peut-être un revers un vous attend, vous trouverez un ami dans chacun des heureux que vous aurez faits.

(Oh you privileged beings, whom chance, birth or talent has placed at the head of nations; always show yourself to be just and good to the peoples who are your subjects: through generous deeds wisely meted out, learn to win the hearts of those who surround you; in the midst of your glory, a reversal may await you; you will find a friend in each of those whom you have made happy.)

In act 1, scene 6 another character offers the observation: "La renommée grossit les objets et fait souvent à un général une très grande réputation, aux dépens de tel ou tel de ses officiers ou même de ses soldats, qui a contribué, plus que lui, à ses succès" (Fame magnifies objects and often creates a great reputation for a general, at the expense of one or another of his officers or even his soldiers, who has contributed, more than he, to his successes). Rumors of the provocative content of the melodrama had apparently circulated and prompted the attendance of two government officials at the forty-eighth performance. The fact that the objectionable passages were uttered by actors playing the naïfs of the cast failed to distract the government agents. On their recommendation the play was closed as of the following evening. Some compromise was evidently

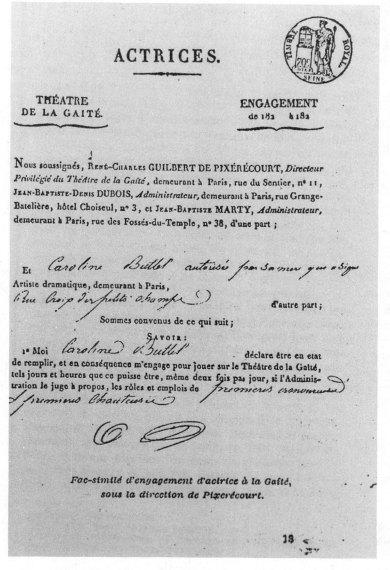

Contract prepared by Pixerécourt while he was the director at the Théâtre de la Gaîté

reached, as the play eventually ran for 904 performances in Paris alone, and no subsequent play of Pixerécourt's encountered any objections from the censors.

Pixerécourt's most overtly patriotic gesture can be found in his drame héroïque, *Charles-le-Téméraire, ou le Siège de Nancy* (1814), which was also a tribute to his native region. Although Pixerécourt chose to distinguish this piece from his other dramatic works, some critics persisted in seeing it as a unique melodrama in which there was no ballet and heroism substituted for romance. The historical event being reenacted with dramatic embellishments was the Battle of Nancy of 1477, in which the forces of Charles, Duke of Burgundy, invaded Lorraine and laid siege to the town of Nancy. The duke's imperialistic designs, along with his life, came to an end when René, Duke of Lorraine, returned with reinforcements provided by his Swiss allies. When the text of the play was published in Charles Nodier's edition of *Théâtre Choisi*, the prefatory material included strategic analyses of the battle by two army officers and a topographical map indicating troop positions. This concern for historical precision was not fully matched by Pixerécourt's treatment of the material in the play itself. In this dramatization Charles meets his death at the hands of the governor's daughter Léontine, whose husband was executed upon Charles's orders. This transpires only after she has infiltrated the enemy camp to effect a daring rescue of her young son and devised a strategy to defeat the invading forces. In the manner of Jeanne d'Arc, Léontine dons full armor to defend her homeland and strikes down Charles le Téméraire in hand-to-hand combat.

While women might have moments of glory in historical dramas, in domestic melodrama they were most often consigned to the passive role of the virtuous victim who must be saved by a father, brother, fiancé, or husband. *La Femme à deux maris* was notable for creating a female protagonist, Eliza Werner, who had indeed been victimized in her youth but who then managed to assert a degree of control over her life. She later served as one of the prototypes for "the woman with a past" who remained highly visible in popular theater and film over the next 150 years. Pixerécourt took the basic plot for *La Femme à deux maris* from another Ducray-Duminil novel, *Paul, ou la Femme abandonnée.* The novel was intended primarily as a warning to young women who would see passionate attraction rather than duty and obligation as the basis for marriage. Pixerécourt altered the plot and characters sufficiently to present a broader comment on justice and familial relations. While a young woman living with her father in Munich, Eliza fell in love with a soldier, Isidore Fritz, whose handsome appearance and charming manner concealed a depraved and cruel nature. Faced with paternal opposition, he persuaded Eliza to flee with him. Fritz's intention was to seduce and abandon her, but she defended her honor and insisted that he marry her. After the ceremony Fritz's true character was revealed as he abused Eliza and fell into a life of debauchery and dissipation. They had a son, Jules, before Eliza finally left him after six years. An attempt at reconciliation with her father failed, but she nevertheless managed to help care for him from a distance as he lost his sight. Eventually, Eliza was notified of the death of her estranged husband. She then consented to marry Edouard, Count of Fersen and a colonel in the Imperial Army, who proves to be an ideal husband. He alone knows of Eliza's past; everyone else, including Jules himself, believes the boy is an orphan whom Eliza has raised. All this is recounted by Eliza in the opening scene of *La Femme à deux maris* when she learns that her first husband is in fact alive: the documents attesting to his death were forgeries. Fritz threatens to expose her as a bigamist and accuse her of falsifying the documents in order to deceive the count. His threats prove impotent, however, because Eliza has the complete confidence of her husband. To save Eliza from being censured by society, the count vows to live apart from her despite the emotional distress this move costs him. He also adopts Jules to save him from the claims of his biological father. The latter is offered a large sum of gold on the condition that he will leave the region and never return. Instead, Fritz attempts to have the count murdered; the plot, of course, backfires, and it is Fritz himself who is slain, leaving the true family free to reunite.

The emphasis on the family as the foundational unit of society could already be seen in the eighteenth century with the growing dominance of the bourgeoisie. As this group consolidated its power over the nineteenth century, theater joined other forms of cultural representation in featuring the integrity of the family unit as emblematic of the cohesion of society. This theme was played out in a wide variety of settings, the original European domestic melodrama being recast to fit historical periods and exotic locations. *Les Ruines de Babylone, ou le Massacre des Barmécides* exemplified both Pixerécourt's approach to historical sources and his adaptation of the central themes of domestic melodrama to an exotic setting. The story is that of Haroun al-Raschid, caliph of Baghdad from 786 to 809, and his chief minister, Giafar, of the powerful Barmacide family, who was not only the caliph's chief adviser but also his closest companion. An incident that contributed to the fall from grace of Giafar and his family was immortalized in the *Tales of the 1001 Nights,* a collection that became widely known in France in the eighteenth century. According to this story, the caliph had married his sister Abassa to his chief minister on the condition that the marriage not be consummated. This condition was not respected, and a son was born to Giafar and Abassa. In the Arabic versions Giafar and the Barmécides were sacrificed as part of Haroun's revenge; the unfortunate Abassa was spared only to live out her life in humiliation and misery. In his version Pixerécourt replaced the original tragic outcome with the happier resolution demanded by melodramatic form. Here, Haroun is dissuaded from taking revenge by his own son, Hassan, who speaks with the purity and generosity that consistently characterize the youth of the genre. Several sentimental scenes create intimate family portraits of Giafar, Zaïde (the renamed Abassa), and their young son, which are differentiated from similar scenes in domestic settings only by the Orientalist decor and costumes.

In addition to maintaining the focus on the family, *Les Ruines de Babylone* repeats the call to support the legitimate ruler and the established order. At the end of the play, when Haroun is about to be set upon by Bedouins, Giafar comes to his aid. The prescribed remedy for unjust rule is reform rather than the forceful overthrow of the regime. As always, the audience is reassured that the morally and ethically inspired will prevail. What subversive elements there are are benignly introduced in the form of a character named

Raymond, who was included for comic leavening. The only French character in the play, Raymond is Giafar's guardian angel. Raymond and his counterparts in other plays are theatrical rather than dramatic characters in that the relationship they establish with the audience is perhaps more important than their contributions to the narrative. The comic figures do not appear in the earliest melodramas. As can be seen from the examples above, the role of the confidant and aide was a serious rather than a humorous one, fully integrated into the fiction of the performance. The shift to a comic mode for this or other characters marked an increasing mix of genres that was strongly condemned by the severest critics of melodrama. Authors such as Pixerécourt who recognized the value of inserting lighter elements were responding to changing or developing audience tastes. The variety provided by the obligatory festival or ballet was no longer always sufficient. Pixerécourt, in fact, attributed the disappointing reception of an earlier historical melodrama *Les Maures d'Espagne, ou le Pouvoir de l'enfance* (The Moors of Spain, or the Power of Childhood)—61 performances in Paris and 163 in the provinces as compared to 318 and 594, respectively, for *Les Ruines de Babylone*—to its uniformly serious tone.

Pixerécourt's other excursions into the Middle or Far East—*Koulouf, ou les Chinois* (Koulouf the Chinese) in 1806 and *Ali-Baba, ou les Quarante voleurs* (Ali Baba, or the Forty Thieves) in 1822—met with only moderate success. The same was true for his experiments with material from the Americas: *Pizarre, ou la Conquête du Pérou* (Pisarro, or the Conquest of Peru, 1802); *Christophe Colomb, ou la Découverte du Nouveau-Monde* (Christopher Columbus, or the Discovery of the New World, 1815); and *Les Natchez, ou la Tribu du serpent* (The Natchez, or the Tribe of the Snake, 1827). *Robinson Crusoé* (1805) proved an exception, perhaps because of the extraordinary popularity of Daniel Defoe's novel. The conversion of the tale of Robinson Crusoe into a stage version presented particular challenges that no dramatist prior to Pixerécourt had been able to meet. To a large extent the appeal of the novel lay in the detailed accounts of Robinson's ingenious inventions and schemes to conquer his natural environment, accompanied by only a dog and a parrot until the arrival of Friday. This was not promising material for a full-length melodrama. Pixerécourt solved the problem by having his Vendredi present from the outset. By scene 5 of act 1 they are joined by a band of Caribbean natives who are about to execute Iglou, Vendredi's father. Robinson comes to the rescue. Interestingly, while Vendredi speaks a fractured, agrammatical French that transforms him into a comic figure, Iglou's French is not only grammatically correct

but often eloquent. This phenomenon is explained by the fact that Iglou has had extensive dealings with European traders, a position that has also resulted in his being chosen to be chief of his nation. Immediately following the rescue, the traditional elements for a melodramatic situation arrive via a ship with an international crew. The ship belongs to a Portuguese armorer, Don Diego. Among the other passengers is an Englishwoman, Emma, who is accompanied by her nineteen-year-old son Isidor and her old governess, Béatrix. Also aboard are an unscrupulous petty officer, Atkins, and his cohorts, Ocroly and James. Atkins, disciplined for making unwanted advances to Emma, has schemed to have Diego, Emma, Isidor, and Béatrix put ashore and abandoned to the appetites of cannibals and wild beasts. Their mutinous intentions are foiled, and in the process Robinson is reunited with his family—for Emma is his wife, and Isidor his son.

The theatrical and moral heart of *Robinson Crusoé* is located in act 2. Theatrically, the designers had the occasion to break out from the usual limitations of a desert-island setting and create an ingeniously furnished grotto—testimony to Robinson's resourcefulness. This resourcefulness also provided the theme for an extended monologue by Robinson on the usefulness of the mechanical arts and the benefits of human industry—lessons that his father had tried to teach him and that he had failed to heed. In addition to this affirmation of paternal wisdom and authority, one of the leading dramatic and literary critics of the day, Julien-Louis Geoffroy, saw in Pixerécourt's adaptation a confirmation of the original message of Defoe's novel. According to Geoffroy, the novel presented an argument in favor of the benefits of society for human beings. In a preface to the play prepared for Nodier's *Théâtre Choisi* Geoffroy maintained that the story of Robinson Crusoe countered the antisocial ideas of Jean-Jacques Rousseau and his Romantic followers, who portrayed society as corrupt and advocated a return to nature. The fact that Geoffroy could so readily use one of Pixerécourt's melodramas to mount a defense of the social order reflected the latter's essentially conservative social and political positioning and, according to many critics, the inherently conservative nature of classical (as opposed to social) melodrama itself.

If any single play could be said to exemplify the form and function of French classical melodrama, a strong candidate would be *Le Chien de Montargis, ou la Forêt de Bondy* (1814). The actual incident that justified the classification of the play as a *mélodrame historique* was the notorious murder of Aubri de Montdidier, whose assassin was said to have been identified by the dead man's faithful dog. In

Pixerécourt's version, set in the fifteenth century, Aubri is a young soldier whose courage has attracted the favor of both the captain of his company and the king himself. Among his many rewards are a lieutenant's commission and the hand in marriage of the captain's daughter. His good fortune excites the envy of another member of the company, Macaire, who is also in love with the captain's daughter. Macaire forces Aubri to fight a duel; Aubri gains the upper hand but spares his rival's life, thereby exciting Macaire's hatred all the more. Encouraged by his perfidious friend Landry, Macaire kills Aubri as he journeys through the depths of the forest of Bondy on an important mission and buries his body at the foot of a tree. Aubri's dog, Dragon, witnesses the murder and calls attention to his master's grave. Initially, blame for the crime falls on a young mute, Eloi. Dragon, however, signals Eloi's innocence by licking his hand and points to the true culprit by attacking Macaire. Dragon is slain by Macaire, but not before his behavior has been remarked upon. Additional evidence against Macaire is soon produced. Confronted with the signs of his guilt, Macaire confesses and willingly accepts his punishment. In his final speech he reminds himself and the audience:

> Je n'étais pas né pour le crime. Une passion insensée et des conseils perfides m'ont égaré au point de me faire commettre un double meurtre. . . . Le ciel est juste: il sauve l'innocent et frappe deux coupables à la fois. Je lui rends grâce de m'ôter une existence que je ne pouvais supporter, chargé de l'épouvantable fardeau d'un tel crime.

> (I was not born to commit crimes. A mad passion and perfidious advice led me astray to the point of committing a double murder. . . . Heaven is just: it saves the innocent and strikes down two criminals at once. I thank heaven for ending a life that would be unbearable, weighed down by the fearsome burden of such a crime.)

Even though he has been unable to defend himself with words, the silent Eloi has been exonerated in a convincing demonstration of the workings of divine justice.

By the end of the first decade of the nineteenth century, Pixerécourt had begun to test the restrictions of the three-act form. The first to break the standard pattern was the highly successful melodrama *La Citerne,* which required a fourth act to develop the convoluted plot, with its profusion of unexpected incidents—more, one critic noted, than would be found in the combined works of Pierre Corneille, Jean Racine, and Voltaire. The play was set on the island of Majorca off the coast of Spain. A

violent storm (impressively staged with thunder, lightning, rain, hail, and distressed boats) wrecks the ship of Don Rafael and his daughter Clara and deposits them onto the rocky coast. Also forced ashore by the storm are a band of pirates, who seek refuge in their old hideout—a vast subterranean cistern. It is revealed that fifteen years ago Don Rafael and Clara were kidnapped and sold into slavery in Algiers. In their absence Don Fernand, guardian of Don Rafael's younger daughter, Séraphine, has been conniving to gain control of her fortune by forcing her to marry him. His plans, however, have been jeopardized by Séraphine's impending marriage to the governor's son, Don Alvar. To avert the marriage Fernand convinces the scoundrel Picaros to impersonate her father, whom Séraphine has not seen since she was six years old. Picaros, however, intends to take advantage of the situation to abduct Séraphine and make her his own bride. An encounter in the cistern with the band of pirates, whom he has betrayed in the past, puts an end to Picaros's hopes. Undergoing a change of heart, he instead helps reunite Séraphine with her father and sister. The climax of the performance was the terrifying and much-applauded collapse of the underground chamber in the final act. In *La Citerne* only the vestiges of the filial and familial bonds that had driven Pixerécourt's earlier melodramas remain in evidence; when they do surface, it is only to be submerged in suspense and spectacle. In this work the rewarding of goodness and the punishment of evil are accomplished without open moralizing and the evocation of sentimental emotions.

Ten years later in 1819 Pixerécourt formally breached the traditional rules of dramatic composition with *La Fille de l'exilé.* The nature of that breach is advertised by the play's subtitle—*ou Huit mois en deux heures.* Several years before Stendhal challenged the unities of time and place in his celebrated pamphlets *Racine et Shakespeare* (1823, 1825), Pixerécourt was putting these principles into practice. While recognizing the risks of setting such a precedent, Pixerécourt noted that he had preserved the essential unity—that of action. In his preface to *La Fille de l'exilé* in *Théâtre Choisi* Pixerécourt further defends his decision by arguing that the subject matter of the play must govern its composition. In this case the source was the novel *Elisabeth* (1806) by Madame Sophie Cottin. The title character journeyed across Russia on foot, making her way through vast forests, impenetrable swamps, and icy wastelands all in the hope of obtaining a pardon for her father, a victim of political intrigues who was unjustly exiled from court. In his version Pixerécourt consecrated one act to each of three sites: Siberia, a ferry crossing on the banks of the Kama River just west of the mountains dividing Asia and Europe, and finally Moscow. On the way Elisabeth saves an old ferryman from a hoard of marauding Tartars; the man turns out to be Ivan, her father's old enemy, now repentant. While Elisabeth is generous in her forgiveness, nature exacts its revenge, and Ivan is drowned in the torrential waters of the river as it overflows its banks. Elisabeth survives the flood to continue on to Moscow, where the czar grants her father a pardon. Pixerécourt's ultimate justification for stretching the Aristotelian unities was the benefits to be derived from portraying a worthy and noble action in a manner that would reach the largest possible audience.

Valentine, ou la Séduction (1821) was classified as a melodrama but, as some critics noted, more closely resembled a bourgeois tragedy. *Valentine* represented a radical departure from the typical melodrama in its tragic ending. The virtuous daughter of an elderly, blind soldier, Valentine attracted the eye of Edouard, the son of the powerful count of Noralberg. Following the suggestion of his despicable friend, Ernest, Edouard disguised himself as a painter named Adrien and courted and married Valentine. The morning after their wedding night Valentine accidentally learns of Adrien's true identity. At the same time, she learns that Edouard is already married to the Countess Honora; her own marriage ceremony was a sham, with the priest and all Adrien's relatives being played by Ernest's friends. This is the moment where the action of the play commences, but the situation is not unveiled gradually in a carefully crafted exposition–Pixerécourt's normal practice. Instead, the curtain rises on a piercing cry emanating from inside a house, immediately followed by Valentine rushing out and crying "Grand Dieu! Je ne suis point mariée!" (Good God! I am not married!). The theatrical impact of this moment was considerable and matched only by the effectiveness of the final tableau. Valentine, unable to live with her shame and assured by the generosity of the Countess Honora that her father will be cared for, leaps from a bridge into the flowing river. As darkness falls, a sailboat illuminated by torches brings back her lifeless body. Her death is mourned on the shore by her grief-stricken father, a remorseful Edouard, and the count, who promises that Ernest will suffer the consequences of his evil counsel. Aside from its unhappy ending the play was something of an anomaly in that it represented only an average success for Pixerécourt in France but under the title *Adeline, or, The Victim of Seduction* was one of his best-received plays in England and the United States.

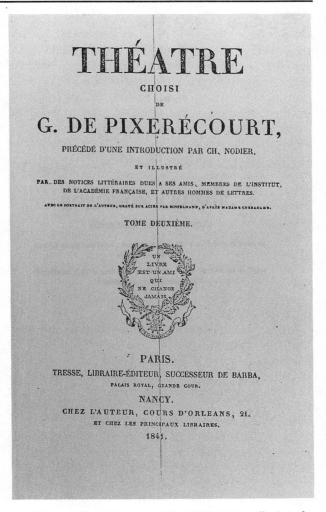

Title page for volume two of the 1841–1843 collection of Pixerécourt's plays

Pixerécourt's last great success was *Latude, ou trente-cinq ans de captivité*, performed in 1834. The title character was in fact an historical figure who had come to represent the abuses of power and gross injustices that had characterized the Ancien Régime. Latude was a twenty-two-year-old indigent veteran of the 1747–1748 campaigns in Flanders, who came up with a scheme to advance himself by placing Louis XV's powerful mistress in his debt. He sent an attractive package filled with small bottles containing a powder to Madame de Pompadour. Under separate cover he sent a note claiming to have overheard a plot to poison her and warned her to beware of a package she was about to receive. Unfortunately, the powder was analyzed and found to be harmless, and the handwriting on the package was easily determined to match that on the letter of warning. Furious at having been targeted as a dupe, Mme de Pompadour had Latude thrown into the Bastille. He managed to escape to Holland but was recaptured. Over the next thirty-five years Latude was moved several times and at one point was incarcerated in Charenton, the asylum for the mentally ill. His case was finally brought to the attention of Louis XVI, who obtained his release. Many of the most distinguished members of the court contributed to a fund for his maintenance. Latude lived for twenty-one years after his release and died in 1805 at the age of eighty. Pixerécourt's melodrama followed the historical sequence of events but substituted a more appealing motive for Latude's desire to attract Mme de Pompadour's attention: he had fallen hopelessly in love with her. While Pixerécourt claimed artistic license on several other points as well, the play's grounding in reality was signaled as soon as the spectators entered the lobby of the Théâtre de la Gaîté, where various artifacts from Latude's imprisonment were displayed. These included the ladder made from unraveled linen that Latude used to escape from the Bastille and various other tools ingeniously fashioned from the limited materials or objects at his disposal. The five-act structure of *Latude* reflected the evolution of melodramatic form. Audiences had come to expect more-involved plots and greater variety in settings than could be accommodated by the original three-act format.

While Pixerécourt was not averse to judicious modifications of melodramatic form, at the end of his life he deplored what he saw as the general degeneration of the genre as the century progressed. In his "Dernières Réflexions . . . sur le mélodrame" a now infirm and elderly Pixerécourt notes that once melodrama portrayed only positive subjects. To his mind the theaters were now filled with "des crimes monstrueux qui révoltent la morale et la pudeur" (monstrous crimes that offend morality and any sense of decency). He condemned the new romantic drama—which he equated with the incessant depiction of adultery, rape, incest, parricide, prostitution, and the most shameless and disgusting vices—for driving "la bonne société" from the theaters of the boulevards. He pointed to the success of his final masterpiece, *Latude,* as an indication that a public hungry for morally uplifting fare still existed and needed only to be lured back into the theaters by writers willing to follow the example of Pixerécourt's own career. Pixerécourt's final assessment of the state of the dramatic arts was not optimistic. He wrote:

> J'ai vu, pendant plus de trente ans, toute la France accourir aux représentations multipliées de mes ouvrages. Hommes, femmes, enfants, riches et pauvres, tous venaient rire et pleurer aux mélodrames bien faits. Hélas! ce temps est passé. Le théâtre est abandonné pour tou-

> jours. Grâce au progrès, on a privé la société d'un grand plaisir bien innocent et que l'on ne retrouvera plus . . .

(For over thirty years, I have watched all France flock to the repeated performances of my works. Men, women, children, the rich and the poor, all came to laugh and cry at well-made melodramas. Alas! These times have passed. The theater has been abandoned forever. Thanks to progress, society has been deprived of an important source of innocent pleasure, which it will never have again . . .)

As melodrama disappeared from the stages of Europe and America, critical interest in Pixerécourt waned. Over the past twenty years, however, there has been a renewed acknowledgment of the significance of his work. This renewal of interest can be attributed largely to developments in the fields of cultural history and criticism in general and the publication of Peter Brooks's *The Melodramatic Imagination: Balzac, Henry James, Melodrama, and the Mode of Excess* (1976) in particular. Unprecedented in its sophisticated analysis of melodramatic forms, this study placed Pixerécourt's work alongside the fiction of Honoré de Balzac and Henry James. It would surely have pleased Pixerécourt to know that the power and appeal of his melodramas would one day be understood in ways he could never have imagined.

Biographies:

Charles Nodier, *Catalogue des livres de la bibliothèque de G. de Pixerécourt* (Paris: Crozet, 1838);

E. Desnues, "Guilbert de Pixerécourt," in *Nouvelle Biographie générale* (Paris: Firmin Didot, 1858), pp. 584–589;

Jules Janin, "Guilbert de Pixerécourt," *Journal des Débats* (19 August 1844, 1 February 1862);

Nodier, *Réflexions à propos de la vente de la bibliothèque de G. de Pixerécourt* (Paris, 1846);

René Alby, article on Pixerécourt in *Biographie Universelle* (Paris: Michaud, 1857);

André Virely, *René Charles Guilbert de Pixerécourt* (Paris: Edouard Rahir, Librairie de la Société des Bibliophiles français, 1909);

Willie Gustave Hartog, *Guilbert de Pixerécourt: sa vie, son mélodrame, sa technique et son influence* (Paris: Champion, 1913).

References:

William H. Akins Jr., Introduction to *Three Melodramas by Pixerécourt,* translated by Akins (Ann Arbor: UMI, 1971)—includes translations of *Coelina, L'Homme à trois visages,* and *Le Chien de Montargis;*

André Billaz, "Mélodrame et littérature: le cas de Pixerécourt," *Revue des sciences humaines,* 41 (April–June 1976): 231–245;

Oscar G. Brockett, "The Function of Dance in the Melodramas of Guilbert de Pixerécourt," *Modern Philology,* 56 (February 1959): 154–161;

Brockett, "Pixerécourt and Unified Production," *Educational Theater Journal,* 9 (1959–1960): 181–187;

Peter Brooks, *The Melodramatic Imagination: Balzac, Henry James, Melodrama, and the Mode of Excess* (New Haven: Yale University Press, 1976);

Pierre Carral, "Recherches pour une physionomie du mélodrame au temps de Guilbert de Pixerécourt," *Revue d'histoire du théâtre,* 4 (1984): 386–391;

Arsène Chassang, "Approches du mélodrame et Guilbert de Pixerécourt," *Mémoires de l'Académie de Stanislas,* volume 2, seventh series (1972–1973), pp. 181–186;

Chassang, "Ficelles et trucs du mélodrame d'après Guilbert de Pixerécourt," in *Mémoires de l'Académie de Stanislas,* volume 2, seventh series (Nancy, 1972–1973), pp. 193–214;

Barbara T. Cooper, "Up in Arms: Defending the Patriarchy in Pixerécourt's *Charles le Téméraire,*" *Symposium,* 47 (Fall 1993): 171–187;

Jean Delume, "*Coelina ou l'Enfant du mystère.* Un mélodrame alpin," in *Recherches et travaux* (Grenoble: Université de Grenoble, 1982);

Edmond Estève, *Etudes de littérature préromantique* (Paris: Champion, 1923);

Europe, special issue on "Le Mélodrame," 703–704 (November/December 1987);

Daniel Gerould, ed., *Melodrama,* includes anonymous adaptation into English of *The Forest of Bondy, or, The Dog of Montargis* as performed in London and New York in 1816 (New York: New York Literary Forum, 1980);

Paul Ginisty, *Le Mélodrame* (Paris: Michaud, 1910);

Clover Holly Gutling, *The Strange, Surprising Adventures of Robinson Crusoe "chez" Pixerécourt,* dissertation, University of South Carolina (Ann Arbor: University of Michigan, 1979);

Charles-Nicolas Alexandre Haldat, *Discours sur la tombe de M. Guilbert de Pixerécourt* (Nancy: L. Vincenot, 1844);

Franz (Joseph Georg Ferdinand) Heel, *Guilbert de Pixerécourt* (Erlangen: Buchdr. von Junge & sohn, 1912);

Charles Hequet, *Notice sur G. de Pixerécourt* (Bitsch: Vitry le Français, 1865);

William D. Howarth, "Word and Image in Pixerécourt's melodramas: the dramaturgy of the strip-cartoon," in *Performance and Politics in Popular Drama,* edited by David Bradby, Louis James, and Bernard Sharratt (Cambridge: Cambridge University Press, 1980), pp. 17–32;

Gabrielle Hyslop, "Deviant and Dangerous Behavior: Women in Melodrama," *Journal of Popular Culture,* 19 (Winter 1985): 65–77;

Hyslop, "Pixerécourt and the French Melodrama Debate: Instructing Boulevard Theatre Audiences," in *Themes in Drama 14: Melodrama,* edited by James Redmond (Cambridge: Cambridge University Press, 1992), pp. 61–85;

Alexander Lacey, *Pixerécourt and the French Romantic Drama* (Toronto: University of Toronto Press, 1928);

Marie-Pierre Le Hir, "La Représentation de la famille dans le mélodrame du début du dix-neuvième siècle de Pixerécourt à Ducange," *Nineteenth Century French Studies,* 18 (Fall-Winter 1989–1990): 15–24;

Le Hir, *Le Romantisme aux enchères: Ducange, Pixerécourt, Hugo,* Purdue University monographs in Romance languages, volume 42 (Amsterdam & Philadelphia: Benjamins, 1992);

Thierry Leroux, "A propos de *Coelina ou l'Enfant du mystère* de Pixerécourt," *Connaissance des hommes,* 109 (March–April 1985): 15–16;

Thérèse Marcilly-Memdith, "Le Mélodrame de Pixerécourt aux Etats-Unis," *Le Pays lorrain,* 15 (1974): 83–93;

J. Paul Marcoux, *Guilbert de Pixerécourt: French Melodrama in the Early Nineteenth Century,* includes translation and adaptation for the modern stage of *Coelina* and *The Dog of Montargis* (New York: P. Lang, 1992);

Marcoux, "Guilbert de Pixerécourt: The People's Conscience," in *Themes in Drama 14: Melodrama,* edited by Redmond (Cambridge: Cambridge University Press, 1992), pp. 47–59;

James Frederick Mason, *The Melodrama in France from the Revolution to the Beginning of Romantic Drama, 1791–1830* (Baltimore: Furst, 1912);

Roger Mathe, "Le Père du mélodrame, R.-C. Guilbert de Pixerécourt: Sa Jeunesse Mélodramatique," *Bulletin de l'Association des professeurs de lettres* (June 1979): 15–19;

Bruce A. McConachie, "Pixerécourt's Early Melodramas and the Political Inducements of Neoplatonism," in *Themes in Drama 14: Melodrama,* edited by Redmond (Cambridge:

Cambridge University Press, 1992), pp. 87–103;

Jane H. Moss, "Mérimée et Pixerécourt," *Revue d'histoire littéraire de la France,* 80 (1973): 87–89;

Norma Perry, ed., *Guilbert de Pixerécourt, Coelina ou l'enfant du mystère* (Exeter: Exeter University Press, 1972);

Frank Rahill, *The World of Melodrama* (University Park: Pennsylvania State University Press, 1967);

J. de Ravinel, "Guilbert de Pixerécourt," *Terre lorraine,* facsimile 11 (1977): 25–29;

Revue des sciences humaines, special issue on "Le Melodrame," 162 (1976);

James L. Smith, *Melodrama: The Cultural Idiom* (London: Methuen, 1973);

Chantal Tatu, "Pixerécourt ou les malheurs du texte," *Sujet, texte, histoire, (colloque du 28 avril 1977), Annales littéraires de l'Université de Besançon,* series 2, no. 259 (Paris, 1981);

Themes in Drama 14: Melodrama, edited by Redmond (Cambridge: Cambridge University Press, 1992);

Jean-Marie Thomasseau, *Le Mélodrame* (Paris: Presses Universitaires de France, 1984);

Thomasseau, *Le Mélodrame sur les scènes parisiennes: de Coelina (1800) à l'Auberge des Adrets (1823)* (Lille: Service de reproduction des thèses, 1974);

Rodrigue Villeneuve, "Coelina, ou l'anti-Justine," in *Etudes littéraires,* volume 11 (Quebec: Université Laval, 1978), pp. 403–439.

Papers:
Pixerécourt's letters, along with his manuscripts and personal papers, are collected in the Fonds Pixerécourt of the Musée ducal de Nancy.

François Ponsard
(1 June 1814 – 7 July 1867)

Marcia G. Parker
University of Wisconsin–Stevens Point

PLAY PRODUCTIONS: *Lucrèce,* Paris, Theâtre de l'Odéon, 22 April 1843;

Agnès de Méranie, Paris, Theâtre de l'Odéon, 22 December 1846;

Charlotte Corday, Paris, Théâtre-Français, 23 March 1850;

Horace et Lydie, Paris, Théâtre-Français, 19 June 1850;

Ulysse, music by Charles Gounod, Paris, Théâtre-Français, 18 June 1852;

L'Honneur et l'argent, Paris, Theâtre de l'Odéon, 11 March 1853;

La Bourse, Paris, Theâtre de l'Odéon, 6 May 1856;

Ce qui plaît aux femmes, Paris, Théâtre du Vaudeville, 30 July 1860;

Harmonie (Arme au nid), Compiègne, Palais de Compiègne, 15 December 1863;

Le Lion amoureux, Paris, Théâtre-Français, 18 January 1866;

Galilée, Paris, Théâtre-Français, 7 March 1867;

Le Mariage d'Angélique, Paris, Theâtre de l'Odéon, 15 January 1902; staged as *Molière à Vienne* (original title), Paris, Théâtre-Français, 1910.

BOOKS: *Lucrèce* (Paris: Furne et Cie, 1843); translated by Sir A. Rumbold as *Lucretia* (London, 1848);

Agnès de Méranie (Paris: Furne et Cie, 1847);

Charlotte Corday (Paris: Blanchard, 1850);

Horace et Lydie (Une Ode d'Horace) (Paris: Blanchard, 1850); translated as *Horace and Lydia* (New York: Darcie & Corbyn, 1855);

Théâtre complet (Paris: Michel Lévy frères, 1851)—comprises *Lucrèce, Agnès de Méranie, Charlotte Corday,* and *Horace et Lydie;*

Ulysse (Paris: Michel Lévy frères, 1852);

Choeurs d'Ulysse (Paris: Michel Lévy frères, 1852);

Etudes antiques: Homère, Ulysse (Paris: Michel Lévy frères, 1852);

Homère, poème (Paris: Michel Lévy frères, 1853);

L'Honneur et l'argent (Paris: Michel Lévy frères, 1853);

François Ponsard (courtesy of the Lilly Library, Indiana University)

Discours prononcé à sa réception à l'Académie française, le 4 décembre 1856 (Paris: Michel Lévy frères, 1856);

La Bourse (Paris: Michel Lévy frères, 1856);

Ce qui plaît aux femmes (Paris: Michel Lévy frères, 1860);

Harmonie (Arme au nid) (Paris: Imprimerie Impériale, 1863);

Oeuvres complètes (Paris: Michel Lévy frères, 1865–1876)—volume 1 comprises *Discours de réception à l'Académie française, Discours de M. Désiré Nisard en réponse à M. Ponsard, Lucrèce, Agnès de Méranie, Charlotte Corday,* and *Horace et Lydie;* volume 2 comprises *Etudes antiques, Homère, Ulysse, L'Honneur et l'argent, La Bourse,* and *Ce qui plaît aux femmes;* volume 3 comprises *Le Lion amoureux, Galilée, Molière à Vienne,* and variation on the fifth act of *Charlotte Corday;*

Le Lion amoureux (Paris: Michel Lévy frères, 1866);
Galilée (Michel Lévy frères, 1867);
Le Mariage d'Angélique (Paris: Calmann-Lévy, 1902).

With the success of his first play, *Lucrèce* (1843; translated as *Lucretia,* 1848), François Ponsard was immediately accepted into the most prestigious literary circles in Paris. The supporters of Classicism welcomed Ponsard's play as the beginning of a revival of classical theater in France. With the failure of Victor Hugo's *Les Burgraves* (1843) just a few weeks earlier, those seeking to destroy the Romantic school of theater used *Lucrèce* as their standard and prepared the public and critics for its success even before opening night. When viewed closely, Ponsard's play, and others of his that followed, contain elements from both the Classical and Romantic styles of writing. Nevertheless, the playwright's advocates from the Classical school chose to ignore the Romantic qualities of his work, while the enemies of the Classicists pointed out the inconsistencies in Ponsard's plays. After creating three tragedies Ponsard turned to writing comedies that explored the moral issues of his contemporary French society. He remained an important figure in the theater throughout his life, and each of his new plays received close scrutiny by both critics and the public. Critics and audiences did not always agree about the merits of his plays, but whether they deemed a particular play worthy of its creator or not, the interest in Ponsard's work did not diminish in his lifetime.

Today some theater historians credit Ponsard only with providing a successful but ephemeral opposition to Romantic drama by producing works considered to represent the *école du bon sens* (school of good sense), which decried the excesses of the Romantic playwrights and included among its members the popular Emile Augier. These critics feel that interest in Romantic drama was waning without outside assistance and point out the mediocrity of Ponsard's dramaturgy. Others admit that Ponsard was not an exceptional playwright but insist that he and other playwrights from this period must be examined in the context of their society and in how they fit into the phases of transition from one literary school to another, for example, from Romanticism to realism. In fact, differences of opinion about the importance of Ponsard's work emerged soon after he began his career as a playwright in 1843, and those differences continue to the present.

Joseph-François Ponsard was born on 1 June 1814 in Vienne, France, a community in the Dauphiné, to Jean-Marie Hercule and Françoise-Joséphine-Modeste Bruant Ponsard. An only child, he studied law in Paris and began to practice law in Vienne, as his fa-

ther had done. Ponsard's interest in the literary world preceded his career in the theater; as a young man he translated George Gordon, Lord Byron's *Manfred* (1817), composed poems, and wrote literary articles for a local newspaper, *Revue de Vienne.* Upon seeing the rising new star, Rachel, perform in a revival of Classical plays in Lyon, Ponsard began to write his tragedy *Lucrèce,* which was based on a Roman character. When Ponsard had completed the tragedy, his friend and fellow poet Charles Reynaud accompanied him to Paris to find a theater to produce the play. The Theâtre de l'Odéon, under the directorship of Auguste Lireux, accepted Ponsard's work. In the midst of the continuing battle between the Romanticists and the Classicists for dominance in the French theater in the 1840s, advocates of Classicism greeted Ponsard's play with energetic enthusiasm.

Two Parisian literary salons soon became important in Ponsard's personal life and influential in the direction of his career. It was in Mme d'Agoult's circle that the actor Bocage first read Ponsard's play in the presence of the poet Alphonse de Lamartine. The latter is reported to have pronounced the arrival of a genuine and unforgettable young poet. Critic Jules Janin introduced Ponsard to the salon of Mme de Lamartine, establishing the beginning of a close relationship between Ponsard and Lamartine. The salons provided him immediate influential contacts, an indispensable step for an unknown talent. His affiliation with Lamartine also led the playwright beyond theater into politics. Ponsard worked with Lamartine during his political career and ran for public office himself in 1848, 1849, and 1857. Ponsard was unsuccessful as a political candidate, but his republican beliefs found their way into several of his plays.

More successful in the literary world than in politics, Ponsard in 1845 received the prize for the best tragedy for *Lucrèce* from the Académie Française. This prestigious body also elected Ponsard to its society in 1855 to fill the seat of the poet Pierre Baour-Lormian. In addition to his career in the theater Ponsard wrote poems and coedited *Le Spectateur Républicain* with Augier. The Légion d'Honneur admitted him into its ranks in 1845.

But a seven-year period of gambling, love affairs, traveling, and living beyond his means led to the playwright's becoming increasingly plagued by severe financial problems, and his debts eventually forced him to sell the land that he had inherited from his parents. In 1863, at the age of forty-nine, Ponsard finally settled into marriage with the young Marie Dormoy and lived a quieter lifestyle in Vienne. With the money he earned from his writing, which was encouraged by his small family and his friends, he managed eventually to pay his creditors. His financial status improved further when Napoleon III revoked the ban censors had placed on his tragedies in 1852 and awarded Ponsard additional monetary support.

Lucrèce, Ponsard's first play and his first tragedy, premiered at the Odéon in Paris on 22 April 1843. This play fits into the Classical category by being set in Roman times and by portraying the tragedy of Lucretia, who kills herself in front of her husband, father, and friend after informing them that the king's son has raped her. Her suicide prompts an overthrow of the Roman government, a political act foreshadowed by Lucretia's misunderstood friend, Junius, also known as Brute. Another Classical feature in this tragedy is Ponsard's use of alexandrine verse, a form he favored in almost all his work. But admiring such Romantics as Hugo, he also employed characteristic devices from their school, which included the use of local color, detailed scenic instructions, simplified language, and scenes of private daily life. *Lucrèce* proved to be a brilliant success with the public and most critics. It played for 50 performances in 1843, then a total of 111 performances between 1843 and 1870 (21 of which took place at the Comédie-Française).

Ponsard understood the difficulty of repeating such a success but nonetheless attempted to please the public with a second tragedy, *Agnès de Méranie,* which opened at the Odéon on 22 December 1846. This play was eagerly anticipated, but it disappointed the audiences and received only twenty performances. For this play Ponsard had chosen a topic from medieval French history, a quarrel between King Philippe Augustus and the Catholic Church. The new Pope, Innocent III, reverses his predecessor's decision to annul the King's previous marriage. The Pope commands Philippe to repudiate his present wife, Agnès, the daughter of the duke of Méran. Philippe refuses and asks his people to choose between allegiance to the king or to the Pope. Agnès averts the crisis by poisoning herself. As she dies, she asks her husband to reconcile with the church and pleads with the church representative to legitimize her children. Arguments in the play condemn intervention by the church in governmental affairs, but the conclusion proposes a peace between these two powers. Although spectators were polite in their reception of the play, critics attacked *Agnès de Méranie* with energy. Some of these critics may have avoided expressing disapproval of Ponsard's first play because of its overwhelmingly enthusiastic reception, and may now have felt freer to express negative views of Ponsard's work.

After the failure of his second play Ponsard began to lose confidence in his abilities as a playwright. Deciding to write one more tragedy, this time using the French Revolution as the background for his action, Ponsard based his new plot on his friend Lamartine's recently published history of the Girondin party, a political faction that was more moderate than either the Montagnards or the Jacobins, who directed the Reign of Terror. *Charlotte Corday* (1850) dramatizes the story of Corday, a young woman from Caen, Normandy, who travels to Paris to assassinate Jean-Paul Marat, one of the triumvirate who had proposed the execution of all Girondins. Corday kills Marat in his bath and is captured, tried, and then executed after a rapid trial.

The renowned actress Rachel encouraged the director Arsène Houssaye to persuade Ponsard to withdraw *Charlotte Corday* from the Théâtre de la Porte Saint-Martin because she planned to play the title role at the prestigious Théâtre-Français, where she worked. Ponsard agreed, only to learn later that Rachel changed her mind and decided not take the part. Another possible obstacle to the production of the play arose in the government, where a group of political reactionaries in the assembly was working toward the censorship of the play. Hugo then stepped forward and persuaded these officials to approve the play; his action began the friendship between him and Ponsard.

Charlotte Corday opened on 23 March 1850 at the Théâtre-Français. It elicited a chorus of favorable reviews in the press, including authoritative praise from Alfred de Musset, Gérard de Nerval, and Hugo. But the public did not join in the approbation of these voices, and the play closed after thirty-eight performances. Some critics, such as Jules Claretie, claimed the play was hampered by a mediocre performance by Mlle Judith (Julie Bernat), the actress who played the title role. Other critics believed that playing Corday pushed this actress ahead in her career. Eventually the government's decision to censor all Ponsard's tragedies negated the significance of the critics' responses to this and his other plays. *Charlotte Corday* was revived in later years both at the Odéon and the Théâtre-Français and was performed 128 times before the end of the century; it was then revived again in 1921. Earlier, in 1876, the play had inspired the composer Benoît to transform it into an opera.

Although Rachel had refused the role of Charlotte Corday, she asked Ponsard to create another play specifically for her, which he did. *Horace et Lydie* (1850; translated as *Horace and Lydia,* 1855), is a one-act comedy in verse about jealousy and reconciliation, involving a poet and his lover. The comedy enjoyed an immediate success when it opened at the Théâtre-Français on 19 June, and by 1910 the Théâtre-Français had presented this short play 218 times.

Ponsard turned to one of his passions, Greek antiquity, for his final tragedy, *Ulysse* (1852). This is the only play for which he wrote a preface, because he believed that a play should succeed or fail on its own merit without authorial explanations. His excuse here is that the work is not truly his own; he is serving as a translator who wishes to present the great Homer to modern audiences. In this preface, which provides a rare insight into Ponsard's thoughts about his own work and his reactions to criticism, he defends his manner of developing his characters and defends the lack of action in his plays. He argues that a playwright must choose between creating a series of peripeteias constructed solely to amuse spectators and, by contrast, developing the feelings and the individuality of his characters. He argues, furthermore, that a detailed representation of the historical period should take precedence over plot construction. His preface also points out his admiration both for Molière and Pierre Corneille and the work of such nineteenth-century writers as Hugo, Lamartine, and Musset.

The Théâtre-Français produced *Ulysse* on 18 June 1852 at great expense and included choruses written by Charles Gounod, then in the early stages of his career. The theater director Houssaye pronounced the work a success, although he himself was criticized for including music in the play. As in his other tragedies, Ponsard combined Classical and Romantic features. Once again, critics praised the play, but it failed in the public's eyes, playing only for twenty-six performances. It had brief revivals in 1854 and 1901.

Discouraged by the discrepancy between the critics' praise and the spectators' lack of enthusiasm for his tragedies, and influenced also by the recent censorship of his tragic works because of their perceived political messages, Ponsard turned his attention to comedy. His first attempt, *L'Honneur et l'argent* (Honor and Money), proved a resounding success at the Odéon, where it opened on 11 March 1853. Further productions over the years helped this work become Ponsard's most popular play, with critics as well as audiences. By 1910 the Odéon and the Théâtre-Français had produced 537 performances of *L'Honneur et l'argent,* with revivals continuing into 1936. Historians who pass over *Charlotte Corday* as Ponsard's best play typically select *L'Honneur et l'argent,* and it was this comedy that assured Ponsard lasting recognition as a great playwright during his lifetime. It also provided the sustained success necessary for him to be elected to the Académie Française in 1855. Now, rather than being called "the new Corneille," Ponsard began to be called "the new Molière."

Both *L'Honneur et l'argent* and Ponsard's second comedy, *La Bourse* (The Stock Market, 1856), attack the middle class's worship of money generally and the fanatical practices of speculation in particular. In Ponsard's treatment of the popular subjects of greed and avariciousness the public appreciated finding positive characters with whom they could identify; audiences were also receptive to the admonitions not to become like the characters who made unfortunate choices. In both these plays it is clear that fathers should aspire for their daughters to marry men of honor rather than men who are simply wealthy; furthermore, men should guard carefully against allowing themselves to become addicted to the stock market. Basically, just as Ponsard expressed a predilection for a path between the Classicists and the Romantics in the theater and in politics espoused a republicanism that was neither socialistic nor democratic, so in his comedies he proposes the middle path for his positive characters and, by extension, the audience. Money, in Ponsard's comedies, is not necessarily bad in itself, if used judiciously, but it should not become the sole motivation in life.

La Bourse premiered at the Odéon on 6 May 1856 with the Emperor Napoleon III in attendance. Believing that this comedy would be a triumph just as *L'Honneur et l'argent* had been, the public clamored for tickets on the street that were well above the usual opening-night price. Both critics and audiences praised the play, and it closed the season with seventy-nine performances. However, its success did not endure. It was revived the next year for only nine performances and then two performances in 1861.

The one major work by Ponsard ignored in most reviews of his plays is *Ce qui plaît aux femmes* (Women's Pleasures), his only play not performed at the Odéon or the Théâtre-Français. This work opened at the Théâtre du Vaudeville on 30 July 1860 and had a successful beginning, but the government censored the play because of its social criticism. This play in three acts, one act in verse and two in prose, condemns women of wealth who waste their time in frivolous activities instead of concerning themselves with less fortunate members of society. Again Ponsard depicts a character the audience can admire and emulate, a countess who is truly compassionate and who changes her behavior in order to assist the poor.

Ponsard's last successful play was a comedy set in the French Revolution. *Le Lion amoureux* (The Amorous Lion) opened at the Théâtre-Français on 18 January 1866, again with the emperor in attendance. During the Directory, the government is executing emigrants accused of plotting against the Republic. Humbert, a Republican, falls in love with the Marquise de Maupas, who uses her influence with Humbert to save her father. Torn between duty to her father and her love for Humbert, the marquise finally chooses love and a new beginning in an era of equality. The two main characters in this play represent different social classes; their ultimate resolution of their differences allows Ponsard to underline the importance of harmony and understanding between divergent groups and the importance of a united France. By 1910 the Théâtre-Français and the Odéon had performed this play 224 times; it was revived again in 1930 and once more in 1939 for the 150th anniversary of the storming of the Bastille.

A final play performed just before Ponsard's death originated in a poem he had begun earlier; *Galilée,* dedicated to Napoleon III, opened at the Théâtre-Français on 7 March 1867. In this play religious leaders treat the scientist Galileo as a heretic because of his claims regarding the Earth and its relationship to the sun. Galileo resists all attempts to force him to recant his teachings, including the threat of being burned at the stake, until his daughter pleads with him to stay alive. The play conveys Ponsard's political views concerning the importance of the separation of church and state. Despite the fact that critics claimed that this play did not measure up to Ponsard's best work, they and the public received it warmly, perhaps because they knew the physical condition of the ailing author, perhaps because they respected his other works. Ponsard was not well enough to attend the play and died four months later on 7 July 1867.

At his death Ponsard left his spouse of four years, Marie, and a young son, François. He succumbed to a long-term illness that had begun before his marriage, yet he wrote his two final plays during the last two years of his life, when he was in considerable physical pain. Both critics and the public, who had continued to pay attention to each new play by Ponsard, mourned his death. Vienne prepared a memorial for its celebrated son, including a statue inscribed, *A François Ponsard, ses compatriotes, ses amis* (To François Ponsard from his compatriots, his friends). Among those presenting eulogies were the playwright Augier and Edouard Thierrey, the administrator of the Théâtre-Français. In later years the Théâtre-Français and the Odéon continued to produce Ponsard's plays well into the twentieth century.

Ponsard's work is no longer produced in theaters or studied in university courses, but his name continues to appear in theater history books, where he is identified either as the playwright who struck the final blow to the popularity of Romantic drama or as a representative of plays that reflected the bourgeois concerns of his period. His so-called école du bon sens often drew ridicule from later critics, but it exercised a marked influence on the French theater of the second half of the nineteenth century. During that time Ponsard enjoyed periods of great popularity. Audiences anticipated each of his plays with curiosity or impatience, and his reputation extended beyond France when his plays were translated into German and Spanish and performed in other European countries. Perhaps his work is less compelling today because it does not reflect any extreme view but rather a compromise between opposing viewpoints, a desire for harmony.

One of the criticisms lodged against his plays in his own time, that they did not contain enough action, would probably be echoed by contemporary theater audiences. Despite the interest that his plays stirred in his own lifetime, it seems likely that Ponsard will remain an interesting but comparatively peripheral figure in the annals of theater history.

Letters:

Camille Latreille, *La Fin du théâtre romantique et François Ponsard d'après des documents inédits* (Paris: Hachette, 1899);

Jacques Vier, *La Comtesse d'Agoult et François Ponsard d'après une correspondance inédite, 1843–1867,* volume 1 (Paris: Armand Colin, 1960).

Biographies:

Paulin Blanc, *Ponsard, biographie* (Vienne: Savigné, 1870);

Jules Janin, *F. Ponsard: 1814–1867* (Paris: Librairie des Bibliophiles, 1872);

Siegbert Himmelsbach, *Un Fidèle reflet de son époque: Le Théâtre de François Ponsard* (Frankfurt am Main: Peter Lang, 1980).

References:

Patrick Berthier, *Le Théâtre au XIXe siècle* (Paris: Presses Universitaires de France, 1986), pp. 54–55, 57–60, 82, 84–85;

Marvin Carlson, *The French Stage in the Nineteenth Century* (Metuchen, N.J.: Scarecrow Press, 1972);

Jules Claretie, *La Vie moderne au théâtre: Causeries sur l'art dramatique* (Paris: G. Barba, 1869), pp. 61–68;

Siegbert Himmelsbach, "François Ponsard, poète du juste milieu," *Revue d'histoire littéraire de la France,* 81, no. 1 (1981): 99–108;

Arsène Houssaye, *Behind the Scenes of the Comédie Française,* translated by Albert D. Vandam (New York: Benjamin Blom, 1971);

Fernand Letessier, "Lamartine, François Ponsard et la famille Duréault," *Bulletin de l'Association Guillaume Budé,* 4, no. 3 (1964): 377–386;

Christopher R. McRae, "François Ponsard," in *Critical Survey of Drama: Foreign Language Series,* volume 4, edited by Frank N. Magill (Eaglewood Cliffs, N.J.: Salem Press, 1986), pp. 1488–1493;

Albert Sonnenfeld, "Théâtre de moeurs: A Reappraisal," *Kentucky Foreign Language Quarterly,* 13, no. 3 (1966): 156–164;

Pierre Aimé Touchard, *Grandes heures de théâtre à Paris* (Paris: Librairie Académique Perrin, 1965), pp. 230–234, 240, 255;

Jean Valmy-Baysse, *Naissance et vie de la Comédie-Française* (Paris: Librairie Floury, 1945), pp. 228–230, 242, 250, 258–261.

Rachilde
(Marguerite Eymery Vallette)
(11 February 1860 – 4 April 1953)

Melanie C. Hawthorne
Texas A&M University

and

Frazer Lively
University of Pittsburgh

See also the Rachilde entry in *DLB 123: Nineteenth-Century French Fiction Writers: Naturalism and Beyond, 1860–1900.*

PLAY PRODUCTIONS: *La Voix du sang,* Paris, Salle Duprez, 10 November 1890;
Madame la Mort, Paris, Théâtre Moderne, 20 March 1891;
L'Araignée de cristal, Paris, Bouffes du Nord, 13 February 1894;
Les Fils d'Adam, Paris, Théâtre d'Application, 29 April 1894;
Le Vendeur de soleil, Paris, Théâtre de Montparnasse, 8 June 1894;
Volupté, Paris, Athénée-Comique, 4 May 1896;
La Panthère, Paris, Théâtre Sarah Bernhardt, 25 February 1899;
Le Char d'Apollon, Paris, Théâtre Antoine, 11 September 1913;
La Poupée transparente, Paris, Art et Action, 9 December 1919;
Le Rôdeur, Paris, Théâtre Fémina, 23 February 1928;
Terreur, by Rachilde and G. Kamke, Paris, Grand Guignol, 30 September 1933;
En deuil d'amour, by Rachilde and Kamke, Paris, Théâtre Potinière, 1 October 1933;
La Tour d'amour, adapted by Marcelle-Maurette, Paris, Grand Guignol, January 1935;
Monsieur Vénus, by Rachilde, adapted by Pierre Spivakoff, Paris, Théâtre des Mathurins, 10 February 1988.

BOOKS: *Monsieur de la Nouveauté* (Paris: Dentu, 1880);
Monsieur Vénus (Brussels: Brancart, 1884; revised edition, Paris: Brossier, 1889); translated by

Rachilde, circa 1890

Madeleine Boyd (New York: Covici, Friede, 1929);
Histoires bêtes pour amuser les petits enfants d'esprit (Paris: Brissy, 1884);
Queue de poisson (Brussels: Brancart, 1885);
Nono (Paris: Monnier, 1885);
La Virginité de Diane (Paris: Monnier, 1886);
A mort (Paris: Monnier, 1886);

La Marquise de Sade (Paris: Monnier, 1887);

Le Tiroir de Mimi-Corail (Paris: Monnier, 1887);

Madame Adonis (Paris: Monnier, 1888);

L'Homme roux (Paris: Librairie Illustrée, 1888);

Minette (Paris: Librairie Française et Internationale, 1889);

Le Mordu (Paris: Brossier, 1889);

Théâtre (Paris: Savine, 1891);

La Sanglante Ironie (Paris: Genonceaux, 1891);

L'Animale (Paris: H. Simonis Empis, 1893);

La Princesse des Ténèbres (Paris: Calmann-Lévy, 1896);

Les Hors nature (Paris: Mercure de France, 1897);

L'Heure sexuelle (Paris: Mercure de France, 1898);

La Tour d'amour (Paris: Mercure de France, 1899);

La Jongleuse (Paris: Mercure de France, 1900); translated, with an introduction, by Melanie C. Hawthorne as *The Juggler* (New Brunswick, N.J. & London: Rutgers University Press, 1990);

Contes et nouvelles suivis du Théâtre (Paris: Mercure de France, 1900);

L'Imitation de la mort (Paris: Mercure de France, 1903);

Le Dessous (Paris: Mercure de France, 1904);

Le Meneur de louves (Paris: Mercure de France, 1905);

Son printemps (Paris: Mercure de France, 1912);

La Terre qui rit (Paris: Maison du Livre, 1917);

Dans le puits, ou, La Vie inférieure (Paris: Mercure de France, 1918);

La Découverte de l'Amérique (Geneva: Kundig, 1919);

La Maison vierge (Paris: Ferenczi, 1920);

Les Rageac (Paris: E. Flammarion, 1921);

La Souris japonaise (Paris: E. Flammarion, 1921);

Le Grand Saigneur (Paris: E. Flammarion, 1922);

L'Hôtel du Grand Veneur (Paris: E. Flammarion, 1922);

Le Parc du mystère, by Rachilde and Francisco de Homem-Christo (Paris: E. Flammarion, 1923);

Le Château des deux amants (Paris: E. Flammarion, 1923);

Au seuil de l'enfer, by Rachilde and Homem-Christo (Paris: E. Flammarion, 1924);

La Haine amoureuse (Paris: E. Flammarion, 1924);

Le Théâtre des bêtes (Paris: Les Arts et le Livre, 1926);

Refaire l'amour (Paris: Ferenczi, 1927);

Alfred Jarry, ou, Le Surmâle de lettres (Paris: Grasset, 1928);

Madame de Lydone, assassin (Paris: Ferenczi, 1928);

Le Prisonnier, by Rachilde and André David (Paris: Editions de France, 1928);

Pourquoi je ne suis pas féministe (Paris: Editions de France, 1928);

Portraits d'hommes (Paris: Mornay, 1929);

Le Val sans retour, by Rachilde and Jean-Joë Lauzach (Paris: Fayard, 1929);

La Femme aux mains d'ivoire (Paris: Editions des Portiques, 1929);

L'Homme aux bras de feu (Paris: Ferenczi, 1930);

Les Voluptés imprévues (Paris: Ferenczi, 1931);

Notre-Dame des rats (Paris: Querelle, 1931);

L'Amazone rouge (Paris: Lemerre, 1931);

Jeux d'artifices (Paris: Ferenczi, 1932);

Mon étrange plaisir (Paris: Baudinière, 1934);

La Femme Dieu (Paris: Ferenczi, 1934);

L'Aérophage, by Rachilde and Lauzach (Paris: Les Ecrivains Associés, 1935);

L'Autre Crime (Paris: Mercure de France, 1937);

Les Accords perdus (Paris: Editions Corymbes, 1937);

Pour la lumière (Paris: Imprimerie la Technique du Livre, 1938);

La Fille inconnue (Paris: Imprimerie la Technique du Livre, 1938);

L'Anneau de Saturne (Paris: Ferenczi, 1939);

Face à la peur (Paris: Mercure de France, 1942);

Duvet d'ange (Paris: Messein, 1943);

Survie (Paris: Messein, 1945);

Quand j'étais jeune (Paris: Mercure de France, 1947);

A l'auberge de l'Aigle (Rheims: A l'Ecart, 1977).

Collection: *Le Démon de l'absurde* (Paris: Mercure de France, 1893)—comprises *L'Araignée de cristal, Volupté,* and *Le Rôdeur.*

Editions in English: "The Crystal Spider," translated by Daniel Gerould in *Doubles, Demons, and Dreamers, an International Collection of Symbolist Drama,* edited by Daniel Gerould (New York: Johns Hopkins PAJ Publications, 1985);

"The Crystal Spider," translated by Kiki Gounaridou and Frazer Lively in *Modern Drama by Women,* edited by Katherine E. Kelly (London: Routledge, 1996);

Madame La Mort, translated by Lively and Gounaridou in *"Madame La Mort" and Other Plays by Rachilde* (New York: Johns Hopkins PAJ Publications, forthcoming).

SELECTED PERIODICAL PUBLICATIONS—UNCOLLECTED: "Un Siècle après!," *L'Union Nontronnaise,* 47 (21 November 1880);

"Le Char d'Apollon," *Comœdia* (11 December 1913);

"La Délivrance," *Mercure de France* (1 July 1915): 447–455;

"La Poupée transparente," *Le Monde Nouveau* (20 March 1919);

"La Femme peinte," *Mercure de France* (1 August 1921): 642–652;

"A l'auberge de l'Aigle," *L'Age Nouveau* (17 July 1939).

OTHER: F. A. Cazals, *Le Jardin des ronces,* preface by Rachilde (Paris: Editions de la Plume, 1902);

Marie Huot, *Le Missel de Notre-Dame des Solitudes,* preface by Rachilde (Paris: Sansot, 1908);

Alfred Machard, *Petits romans parisiens; Souris l'Arpète,*
preface by Rachilde (Paris: Mercure de
France, 1914);

André David, *L'Escalier de velours,* preface by Rachilde (Paris: E. Flammarion, 1922);

Lucien Aressy, *La Dernière Bohème. Verlaine et son milieu,* preface by Rachilde (Paris: Jouve, 1923);

Jean Rogissart, *Au chant de la grive et du coq,* preface
by Rachilde (Mézières: Editions de la Grive,
1930);

Claude Kamme, *Le Message des jours,* preface by Rachilde (Paris, 1934);

Alfred Vallette, *Roman d'un homme sérieux,* preface by
Rachilde (Paris: Mercure de France, 1942).

Rachilde had a major role in the first Symbolist theaters in Europe, where she was instrumental in getting Alfred Jarry's *Ubu Roi* produced as well as serving as a voice of encouragement for directors, playwrights, and actors. She herself wrote over twenty plays that were produced in Paris, Saint Petersburg, Tunis, Germany, and Scandinavia. Rachile helped form the Symbolist aesthetic in drama.

Rachilde was born Marguerite Eymery in the provincial city of Périgueux on 11 February 1860. An only child, she suffered rejection from her parents, who wanted a boy, and endured a lonely and troubled childhood marked by her father's military career and the 1870 Franco-Prussian War. She began writing as a teenager, publishing mostly in local newspapers, and adopted the pseudonym Rachilde, which gradually replaced her given name. As soon as she was old enough to live independently she moved to Paris and continued working as a journalist and writer until her breakthrough with the controversial novel *Monsieur Vénus* in 1884. She was involved in many bohemian literary circles and was at the forefront of the Symbolist and Decadent movements. In 1889 she married Alfred Vallette, a cofounder of the *Mercure de France* review, where she maintained a high profile as a literary critic, enjoyed a prestigious reputation as a novelist, and presided over a celebrated literary salon. A prolific writer, she published many works of literature (novels, plays, and even poetry), literary criticism, and memoirs. Her reputation declined somewhat after the turn of the century, and, although she enjoyed renewed popularity in some circles in the 1920s and 1930s, she never regained her position in the avant-garde and died all but forgotten in 1953.

Rachilde's most significant involvement with the theater coincided with what one critic has called the Golden Age of French Symbolism, the decade 1890 to 1900. In French theater, too, this decade marked a historic moment. By the end of the nine-teenth century theater had become principally a form of entertainment dominated by bourgeois values and tastes. The Symbolists aspired to reclaim theater as an art form by reasserting its poetic qualities. Their challenge was facilitated by the 1887 founding of André Antoine's Naturalist theater, the Théâtre Libre, which created a sensation in Paris with its new, superrealistic staging. Using the breach in conventions opened by the Théâtre Libre, the Symbolist theater pursued a program of innovation and extensive experimentation that transformed French theater and laid the foundations for the avant-garde in twentieth-century drama. Through her involvement with the Théâtre d'Art, founded by Paul Fort in 1890, and the Théâtre de l'Oeuvre, founded by Aurélien Lugné-Poe in 1893, Rachilde played a significant role in this period of transition.

The staple of Antoine's repertoire was the short, gritty play that showed a slice of life in fifteen minutes, but he also introduced Henrik Ibsen to Paris with the production of *Ghosts* in 1890. The Naturalist plays and production style at the Théâtre Libre breathed fresh air into a tired medium, yet the Symbolists rejected Antoine's emphasis on sordid reality in favor of attempts to convey a hidden level of reality that could not be depicted directly, only suggested. An evening might include several plays and poetry recitations—and often ended with a noisy brawl over literary style, a far cry from Stéphane Mallarmé's desire for a reverent audience that would treat the theater like a temple. Lights were dim; pauses were long (Maurice Maeterlinck theorized that in the spaces between the words, the supernatural could enter). To heighten the desired atmosphere of the unknown, a gauze curtain sometimes separated the audience from the stage. One of the standard conventions of performance today—the dimming of houselights during a play—became common practice in France thanks to the Symbolists.

Mallarmé and Maeterlinck theorized that a personal response to poetry eclipsed any attempt at physical realization on a stage and that reading plays at home was consequently preferable to seeing them performed. Realistic sets and even the bodies and voices of live actors could interfere with achieving a state of reverie. Consequently, Symbolist actors did not strive for realism in their performance but instead adopted a declamatory form of delivery and a stylized form of movement most often described as hieratic and intended to heighten poetic effect.

Synesthesia—the notion that phenomena in one sensory register corresponded to those in another—suggested that theater could and should mobilize all the senses (not just sight and sound) to provide a full aesthetic experience. One of the most interesting illustrations of this theory was offered by Paul-Napoleon Roinard's production at the Théâtre d'Art in 1891 of the *Song of Songs,* a landmark in Symbolist theater. Each segment of the performance featured a backdrop of a certain color that corresponded to music in a certain key as well as to a certain perfume wafted among the audience to accompany the drama.

This agenda of experimentation and innovation formed the backdrop to Rachilde's dramatic career. She participated in the Symbolist movement from the beginning, and although she may be remembered today principally as a novelist, her contributions to French drama were notable. Rachilde was involved with the first Symbolist theater, the Théâtre d'Art, from its inception. The Théâtre d'Art originated in June 1890 when Paul Fort offered the first production of what was then called the Théâtre Mixte. By November of that year the theater had changed its name, and it gave its first performance as the Théâtre d'Art on Wednesday, 10 November, in the Salle Duprez. Featured that night were *Sur la lisière d'un bois* (At the Edge of a Word) and *Les Gueux* (The Tramps; scenes taken from Victor Hugo's short plays collected in *Théâtre en Liberté* [1886]), which began and ended the evening; Jules Méry's Breton mystery, *Morized;* Alexis Martin's "Le Débat du coeur et de l'estomac" (The Debate Between the Heart and the Stomach), a medieval-flavored farce; and Rachilde's first production, *La Voix du sang* (Voice of Blood, 1880).

Between 1890 and 1892 the Théâtre d'Art presented eight programs. The theater never had its own home; Fort rented a separate hall for each production, which usually ran no more than two evenings. The programs generally involved at least two plays and several recitations of poems. The Théâtre d'Art produced more than twenty plays in the course of seventeen months, each play different from the last; if there was a particular Symbolist aesthetic, it was difficult to define. The performance sometimes lasted until the early morning hours (Percy Bysshe Shelley's *Cenci* [1819] in January 1891 lasted from eight in the evening until two in the morning). The Théâtre d'Art faced many difficulties: a shortage of money, neophyte actors, grandiose plans, and largely hostile criticism from the mainstream press, which tended to vilify everything that did not fit preconceived notions of theater. The biggest problem, however, was the lack of a new repertory. Fort had founded his theater with the promise to produce plays by *les jeunes* (young people), but in fact there was not a host of scripts

waiting to be staged, and his friends had to scramble to write some. New styles of performance had yet to evolve. Nevertheless, Fort found visionary artists and writers. Pierre Bonnard, (Jean-) Edouard Vuillard, Maurice Denis, Paul Sérusier, Odilon Redon, and Paul Gauguin painted scenery and made program drawings. The Théâtre d'Art became the first theater to produce Maeterlinck. Other writers for the theater included Pierre Quillard, Charles Morice, Rémy de Gourmont, Charles van Lerberghe, Catulle Mendès, and Rachilde. Ambitious productions of supposedly "unplayable" works included Shelley's *Cenci,* a portion of the *Iliad,* and "The Song of Songs." After 1892, when the theater could no longer sustain itself financially and Fort decided to concentrate on his own poetry, Lugné-Poe shouldered the Symbolist project, founded the Théâtre de l'Oeuvre, and went on to produce Ibsen, August Strindberg, Bjørnstjerne Martinius Bjørnson, and Alfred Jarry, but it was the Théâtre d'Art that pioneered the Symbolist experiment in theater.

Rachilde's first play, *La Voix du sang,* coincided with the first production of the Théâtre d'Art in 1890 (it was also later performed in Tunis on 21 December 1928). Rachilde was at this time already a well-known and even notorious novelist (her reputation having been established in 1884 with the gender-bending novel *Monsieur Vénus*); thus, her name was a drawing card for the Théâtre d'Art (along with the free letter openers offered to critics) and helped establish a following among the avant-garde. Since the Théâtre d'Art (like the Théâtre Libre) relied on subscriptions rather than receipts at the door for its financing, it traded heavily on reputation and promise rather than popular, long-running crowd pleasers.

Several critics thought that *La Voix du sang* belonged at the Naturalist Théâtre Libre rather than at the Théâtre d'Art, no doubt because the one-act play is set in a bourgeois living room and depicts an event the critics read literally. The play concerns a smug husband and wife who are sitting in the living room after supper when they hear a scream for help outside. They convince themselves that it is none of their business, only to discover that it is their own son, whom they thought safely at home, who has been murdered. The play can certainly be read as the kind of Naturalist "slice of (brutal) life" drama the critics took it for, but the anonymous couple also represents the established bourgeois order that rationalizes its own complacency. The generational difference is not only chronological but also ideological, but the older generation has failed to notice what has been happening: the younger generation has been acting independently and quietly rebelling

Alfred Jarry, Rachilde, and costume designer
Marie-Thérèse Collière

end this did not come to pass, but the statement highlighted the close connection between Symbolist theater, particularly the Théâtre d'Art, and a group of painters known as the Nabis (from the Hebrew for prophet), as though the synesthesia promoted by Symbolism were paralleled by the interdisciplinarity of the Théâtre d'Art, in which novelists (such as Rachilde) wrote plays, poets directed, and painters supplied scenery and backdrops. The Nabis group included Paul Sérusier, who supplied sets, and Denis, whose article in *Art et Critique* (23 August 1890) suggesting that painting was less a matter of representation than a matter of a flat surface covered with colors that form a certain pattern was one of the first aesthetic statements challenging the representational importance of art and shifting the focus to its formal qualities.

The Nabis collaborated on the next production of the Théâtre d'Art, on Friday, 20 March 1891. This program featured, among other things, Pierre Quillard's "passion play," *La Fille aux mains coupées* (The Girl with Severed Hands; with set by Sérusier), which served as a short curtain-raiser before Rachilde's *Madame la Mort* (Madame Death), the central piece of the evening. The author called the play a *drame cérébrale,* but the first and third acts were essentially realistic. Rachilde's innovation was to try to show a subjective inner truth by locating the second act inside the protagonist's mind. In the first act Paul Dartigny, a neurasthenic, bored, decadent type, despises ordinary existence and longs for death, whom he imagines as a beautiful woman. Paul evades the prosaic company of his mistress Lucie and his best friend, Jacques, who has come to borrow money, and smokes a poisoned cigar in an effort to commit suicide. Act 2 takes place in a mysterious garden where two women—the Lady Death of the title, veiled in gray, and the incarnation of Life, played by Lucie in a fashionable evening gown—struggle for possession of Paul. Act 3 returns to the realistic smoking room as Jacques and Lucie discover Paul's body, arrange his possessions, and console each other while the doctor who provided the poison washes his hands.

The play's fusion of domestic drama, melodrama, and heavy-handed allegory might today seem ridiculous, but the second-act attempt to show the soul onstage fascinated many of Rachilde's contemporaries. Of the more than twenty reviews of the production, only two condemned the second act. The audience responded with two curtain calls and called out Rachilde's name with frenzy. The theme of suicide was a popular one for Symbolism. It was widely feared at the end of the nineteenth century that suicide had reached epidemic proportions in

against authority. Many people, Rachilde implies, may one day look up from their newspapers and find that while they were preoccupied with banalities, the world outside has changed. Despite this symbolic undercurrent, the production of *La Voix du sang* retained the stylistic qualities of a *quart d'heure* (fifteen-minute play) from the Théâtre Libre. The performers attempted a literal, realistic rendition (in fact, reviewers criticized the play for not being sufficiently believable, finding that the man who played the son executed too cautious a fall and failed to bleed enough, and that the actress who played the wife was too tall for the tiny set). A Symbolist playing style had yet to be discovered at this early stage.

In January of the following year (1891) Rachilde joined the play selection committee of the Théâtre d'Art. Other committee members included Adrien Remacle, Jules Méry, Saint-Pol-Roux, and Jules Renard. At the end of that month Fort announced in the *Echo de Paris* that henceforth each performance of the Théâtre d'Art would close with a viewing of a painting while music played. In the many European countries, a fear emblematized by the Mayerling affair (the suicide of the Hapsburg crown prince Rudolf in 1889). Symbolism contributed to this fashion not by advocating literal suicide but by offering a more allegorical interpretation within the Symbolist framework. The acceptance of death signifies a detachment from physical existence, sometimes in an explicitly mystical perspective, and a readiness to perceive a deeper reality. The theme is best exemplified in Villiers de l'Isle Adam's classic play *Axël,* which circulated widely in written form before it was produced onstage in 1894. *Madame la Mort* fits squarely within this tradition of viewing suicide as a form of higher reality, the crowning achievement of Paul Dartigny's failure as an artist. The fact that his loved ones remain ignorant of his success on another plane underscores the limitations of reality, which makes it difficult for these characters to see what really matters. The audience, on the other hand, shares Paul's vision in the second act and is in a more privileged position than Paul's friends. The play appealed to audiences outside France: Franz Kafka saw a production in Germany in May 1912, and the innovative director Vera Komissarzhevskaya produced it in Saint Petersburg in 1908.

In the Théâtre d'Art production (at the Théâtre Moderne), the role of Madame la Mort was played by Camée, one of the most celebrated of Symbolist actresses. Georgette Camée had been known simply as Camm when she began her career at the Théâtre Mixte while still an acting student at the Conservatoire de Paris, but when the Mixte changed its name to the Théâtre d'Art, she changed her name as well. She was the first performer to develop a specifically Symbolist acting style of hieratic movements and gestures, incantatory voice, and stylized poses. Cameé's vocal technique may have been partly based on the monotone declamatory style with which the Symbolists read their poetry aloud, but her physical gestures and presence offered something new to the Symbolist theater. Her portrayal of Madame la Mort apparently had a strong influence on Rachilde's playwriting. When Rachilde revised the acting manuscript of the play for publication, her changes in the stage directions and physical description for the Veiled Woman reflected Camée's successful interpretation of the role. Camée, the acknowledged star of the early Symbolist theater, created several roles for the Théâtre d'Art and later played the role of Sara in Villiers de L'Isle Adam's *Axël* before leaving Paris in 1895.

The most renowned artist associated with the Nabis group was Paul Gauguin. Along with Sérusier

he had designed the program for *Madame la Mort,* and his work was displayed in the theater during the benefit held jointly for him and for Paul Verlaine on 21 May 1891. He also supplied an illustration for the publication in 1891 of Rachilde's plays (*Théâtre*), which contained *La Voix du sang, Madame la Mort,* and *Le Vendeur de soleil* (The Sun Vendor; not performed until 8 June 1894) along with a *dossier critique* that reproduced the critical notices from the contemporary press. (Unfortunately this edition is rare, and the later edition of the plays in *Contes et Nouvelles suivis du Théâtre* [Short Stories followed by Plays, 1900] omits the dossier.)

Despite its impact on the history of French theater, the Théâtre d'Art was not long-lived; its last production was in 1892. Work had begun on a new production (Maeterlinck's *Pelléas et Mélisande* [1892]) when Fort was obliged to abandon his efforts. The work was taken over by Aurélien Lugné-Poe, who founded the Théâtre de l'Oeuvre the following year, making Maeterlinck's play the inaugural offering on 17 May. Lugné-Poe had trained at the Paris Conservatoire as well as at Antoine's Théâtre Libre; he was thus the first Symbolist director who was also a practical man of the theater. Although he ended his association with Symbolism in 1897, he went on to achieve great renown in his theatrical career. In the few years he directed the Symbolist Théâtre de l'Oeuvre he changed the face of French drama through his introduction of Scandinavian dramatists such as Ibsen and his landmark staging in 1896 of Jarry's *Ubu Roi.* Rachilde was an important impetus of this theatrical movement, encouraging Lugné-Poe to stage innovative productions such as *Pelléas et Mélisande* and *Ubu Roi.* She left an important book of memoirs of Jarry (*Alfred Jarry, ou, Le Surmâle de lettres* [Alfred Jarry, or the Superman of Letters, 1928]), though her role in presenting a mythologized version of the opening night of *Ubu Roi* has been analyzed by Frantisek Deak. She also served as a buffer between the irascible director and the many artists and playwrights whom he offended (in later years Lugné-Poe admitted that he had been "aggressive" during his early career, an attitude he blamed on the emptiness in his stomach during decades of poverty). Rachilde involved herself in details behind the scenes, had plays copied, helped with publicity, suggested actors, and searched for French playwrights.

The first French work performed by the Oeuvre was Rachilde's one-act play *L'Araignée de cristal* (translated as "The Crystal Spider," 1985), staged on 13 February 1894 at the Bouffes du Nord theater and taken on tour the following fall to Antwerp, Copenhagen, Christiana, Brussels, and The Hague. The play concerns a young man, the terror-stricken Sylvius (played by Lugné-Poe), who is afraid of mirrors and

Rachilde in 1930 (photograph by Harlingue-Viollet)

by extension any other reflective surface, especially the eyes of women. At the insistence of his mother (played by Berthe Bady), he keeps her company at dusk. Although the son's obsession seems bizarre, the play suggests that his madness has a mystical dimension: mirrors reflect a hidden level of the self. A true Symbolist hero, Sylvius fears mirrors because of what they reveal to him of the monstrous deeper reality of human existence. He is also a character with modern appeal: the psychoanalyst Jacques Lacan's explanation of the role of mirrors in identity formation gives new resonance to Sylvius's childhood trauma of seeing a mirror shatter as he gazes at his own reflection.

L'Araignée de cristal originally appeared in print in 1892 in the *Mercure de France* and was republished in 1893 in the collection *Le Démon de l'absurde* (The Demon of the Absurd). The anthology contains some of Rachilde's finest short stories, prose poems, and plays, including the notable Symbolist one-acts *Volupté* (Pleasure) and *Le Rôdeur* (The Prowler). Even though both plays had been printed in the *Mercure de France* by 1893, neither was ever produced by the Théâtre de l'Oeuvre. *Volupté* was performed on 4 May 1896 at the

Athénée Comique; *Le Rôdeur* did not receive its first performance until the Théâtre Fémina's version of 23 February 1928. *L'Araignée de cristal* was the only one of Rachilde's works to appear on the stage of the theater she championed.

Rachilde's plays are nevertheless more interesting to a modern reader than many of those written by her protégés. An atmosphere of dread and a fascination with death were common elements in Symbolist dramaturgy (Maeterlinck's early plays such as *L'Intruse* [The Intruder, 1891] and *Les Aveugles* [The Blind, 1891] helped define the style); but Rachilde's plays expand the genre to include a focus on sexuality and a macabre irony. *Volupté* places two adolescents by a mysterious pool in the woods where they play an unpleasant presexual game: she tells him the things that give her pain; he tells her what gives him pleasure. The imperious Girl negates most of the Boy's statements and calls him an insensitive animal. His pleasures are physical and aggressive: scraping his fingernail on glass; drinking wine to get a headache; grabbing for a mouse that almost bites. She talks more metaphysically of passive pain: of the smell of hyacinths and of the intense sound of a single note on the piano, of drinking milk from a lily and weeping for the children who have no milk. She will not allow him to caress her body, but she lets him touch the water in the pool where they can see her reflection. As she leans over the water, she sees a corpse. She faints, and her lover, finally terrified by the unknown, carries her away without daring to look into the pool.

In *Le Rôdeur* three maidservants gradually become infected with their mistress's dread in much the same way the mother catches her son's fear in *L'Araignée de cristal*. The servants laugh at first, but when Madame orders them to shut all three doors to keep out a possible prowler, they stumble over themselves in panic. The youngest and most suggestible servant, repelled and attracted by the notion of a strange man in the house, fumbles the bolt of the second door, hides her mistake, and convinces herself and the others that she has felt an arm reaching up her skirt. Certain that the prowler is now somewhere inside, Madame leads the group to the last door, and the four women run out into the dark countryside, leaving a candle to burn on the threshold of the abandoned house.

Not all of Rachilde's plays of the 1890s fit the Symbolist mold, and indeed she claimed not to know her own aesthetic style. *Les Fils d'Adam* (Adam's Sons), produced by an amateur society at the Théâtre d'Application on 29 April 1894, shows no hypersensitive anguish. An unpretentious comedy, the play deals with men's solidarity on the subject of adultery. A married daughter comes home in hysterics, convinced that her husband is seeing another woman. Her father interrogates the son-in-law, but his long tale of seduction piques the father's memories of his own escapades. When the daughter and her mother return to the room, they find the men laughing together. The father lies, gives his word of honor that there is no cause for jealousy, and sends his daughter back home with her straying husband.

The year 1894 was an active one in Rachilde's theater career. In addition to the productions of *L'Araignée de cristal* and *Les Fils d'Adam*, *Le Vendeur de soleil* was performed on 8 June by the Théâtre de la Rive Gauche at the Théâtre de Montparnasse. The play had already been performed in other European cities, according to one review, and it was performed at the private atelier of the Futurist Valentine de Saint-Point in April 1912 and directed by Georges Pitoëff in Notre Théâtre, Saint Petersburg, in July 1913. The one-act dark comedy satirizes bourgeois artistic values and crass commercialism. A starving artist cannot make money selling his art but suddenly becomes legitimate by drawing the attention of the crowd to the beauty of the setting sun. Rachilde suggests both the failure of the bourgeoisie to recognize artistic talent and the ease with which they can be duped into paying for an experience that is already free to all with eyes to see.

By 1897 the Symbolist movement in French theater had run its course, and Lugné-Poe wrote an open letter severing his connection with his Symbolist supporters. Rachilde joined eleven other writers in repudiating Lugné-Poe—a mere actor had no right to concern himself with judgments on literary merit—but renewed her friendship with Lugné-Poe a few years later, and he thanked her for the encouragement that had made him believe in his abilities and in the Théâtre de l'Oeuvre. Rachilde had helped assure the existence of the first "art theaters" in Europe, but she was never again closely associated with the workings of any one company. Her interest in theater continued well after interest in Symbolism had waned, however.

In several of her plays written after World War I Rachilde speaks with a more personal voice, and these works complement her fictional preoccupations. *La Femme peinte* (The Painted Woman), published in the *Mercure de France* in 1921, was apparently never performed although the play gives one of Rachilde's most intriguing commentaries on sexual relationships. It is one of her few plays to deal directly with World War I, and it introduces themes taken up in the novel *Le Grand Saigneur* (The Great Bloodletter, 1922). As in *L'Araignée de cristal* and *Volupté*, a mirror forms an essential part of the physical and metaphorical decor. A soldier harangues his mistress in her bedroom while she puts on makeup; for most of the play the audience cannot see her face. He resists her desire to know him better, since for him the incognito in love is the essence of desire. He wants her to help him forget; she wonders who it is that she reminds him of. Finally, in a monologue during which he demands that she not look at him, he confesses his complicity in the execution of a prostitute during the war. As he describes the appearance of the corpse, his mistress applies makeup with feverish gestures. When she turns around she has painted herself to look like the grotesque face he described. He kneels and begs his lover's forgiveness. She gives it, in the name of "all the tortured women."

La Poupée transparente (The Transparent Doll), first staged on 9 December 1919, had several productions; the play evidently moved contemporary audiences as well as actresses, such as Louise Lara, who became emotionally involved with the leading role. A young wife, alone in a somewhat bare room in an asylum, talks to her imaginary son and insists to a doctor that he lives "fed by my mind, the *cerebral* cord was never severed." The doctor is attracted by her beauty and her evident intelligence but cannot join the fantasy and gives up, convinced that "one cannot cure fools who speak reason."

"Répulsion" was written in the early 1920s, but the setting and many of the stage directions echo the Symbolist garden scene in *Madame la Mort*. The play focuses on the trauma of a young woman's first sexual experience after her marriage. In a park by moonlight a young, phantomlike woman rushes to a bench, as if she is escaping something. Eva thinks that her handsome young husband has gone insane, that the wedding music offstage comes from hell. A black form glides toward the bench: it is her father, drunk on American cocktails, who, not recognizing his daughter at first, expresses sexual interest in her. Eva—for whom love is what one feels for a father, a brother, or a friend—despairs of the incomprehensible behavior of her husband and her father. The husband runs in, searching for his wife; falls at her feet; and asks her forgiveness (in an image similar to that in the final moment in *La Femme peinte*). The father, concerned about the possibility of scandal, orders Eva to go back to her room with the husband, but she is afraid to be alone with him. She asks the two men if she is free to leave on her own. Hesitating, they agree that she may go. A servant covers Eva's torn wedding dress in "a black coat of mourning which makes her seem taller," and she says goodbye to husband and father.

"Répulsion" was adapted by Georges Kamke in 1933 and performed on 1 October of that year at the Théâtre Potinière under the title *En deuil de l'amour* (In Mourning for Love). Kamke's version added a female character, a friend who takes Eva in when she leaves the two men, and this alteration must have diluted the sense of Eva's power and her isolation. The play was not a success onstage; reviewers complained that the material was too dated and quaint to appeal to a modern audience, and *En deuil d'amour* was taken off the bill after only a few performances. It was the last of Rachilde's plays to be produced during her lifetime. In 1928 the minister of education, Edouard Herriot, suggested to Rachilde the plot of a play based on the assumption that Napoleon Bonaparte had escaped from exile and was running a bar in the United States, which she turned into the drama *A l'auberge de l'Aigle* (At the Eagle Inn). This play remained unpublished until 1977 and was never performed.

In addition to the plays she wrote, some of Rachilde's prose was adapted for stage; for example, the prose poem "La Panthère" was recited at the Théâtre Sarah Bernhardt in 1899. A stage adaptation of her novel *La Tour d'amour* (The Tower of Love, 1899) appeared in January 1935. An opera was begun based on her novel *Le Meneur de louves* (The Leader of the She-Wolves, 1905), but although parts of it received performances at Rachilde's Tuesday salon, it seems not to have been completed beyond the first act. As part of the late-twentieth-century revival of interest in Rachilde's work, there has been a stage adaptation of her novel *Monsieur Vénus*. In this production the adapter Pierre Spivakoff played the role of the heroine Raoule de Vénérande and framed the novel by presenting it as the bedtime reading of the mad king Ludwig II of Bavaria. In the United States *Le Rôdeur* was produced at the University of Pittsburgh Studio Theater on 3 February 1994.

The enormous significance of the Symbolists to theater and cultural history has been well documented, most recently by Deak in *Symbolist Theater: The Formation of an Avant-Garde* (1993). Earlier works, such as John Henderson's *The First Avant-Garde* (1971) and Jacques Robichez's *Le Symbolisme au théâtre* (Symbolism in the Theater, 1954), mention Rachilde; but the authors are interested neither in gender studies nor in Rachilde's strange place in an otherwise masculine environment. Many articles about her fiction have appeared in the 1980s and 1990s, and her theatricalized persona has been gaining increasing attention among feminists, literary scholars, and cultural historians. What has not been sufficiently noted is that Rachilde's plays are among the most interesting of the Symbolist experiments in theater, and that her influence on this watershed movement, which sparked the beginning of the modern theater, was decisive.

Letters:

Auriant, "9 lettres inédites de Rachilde au père Ubu," *Le Bayou,* 20 (1956): 42–51;

Pierre Lambert, "Trois lettres de Rachilde à J.-K. Huysmans," *Bulletin de la Société J.-K. Huysmans,* 41 (1961): 250–254;

Organographes du Cymbalum Pataphysicum, 18 (8 September 1982): 1–51;

Will L. McLendon, "Autour d'une lettre inédite de Rachilde à Huysmans," *Bulletin de la Société J.-K. Huysmans,* 20 (1983): 21–24.

Bibliographies:

Melanie C. Hawthorne, "Rachilde," in *Critical Bibliography of French Literature: The Nineteenth Century* (Syracuse, N.Y.: Syracuse University Press, 1993), pp. 78–84;

Christian Soulignac, "Bibliographie des oeuvres de jeunesse de Rachilde, 1877–1889," *Revue Frontenac,* 10–11 (1993–1994): 198–218.

Biographies:

Ernest Gaubert, *Rachilde: Biographie critique* (Paris: Sansot, 1907);

André David, *Rachilde, homme de lettres* (Paris: Editions de la Nouvelle revue critique, 1924);

Claude Dauphiné, *Rachilde* (Paris: Mercure de France, 1991).

References:

Frantisek Deak, *Symbolist Theater: The Formation of an Avant-Garde* (Baltimore: Johns Hopkins University Press, 1993);

Daniel Gerould, ed., *Doubles, Demons, and Dreamers: An International Collection of Symbolist Drama* (New York: PAJ Publications, 1985);

John Henderson, *The First Avant-Garde* (London: Harrap, 1971);

Christine Kiebuzinska, "Behind the Mirror: Madame Rachilde's *The Crystal Spider,*" *Modern Language Studies,* 24 (Summer 1994): 28–43;

Frazer Lively, "Rachilde, the Actor's Spectre, and Symbolist Dramaturgy: the Staging of *Madame la Mort,*" *Nineteenth Century Theater,* 231–232 (Summer/Winter, 1995): 33–66;

Aurélien Lugné-Poe, *La Parade: Souvenirs et impressions de théâtre* (Paris: Gallimard, 1930–1933);

Jacques Robichez, *Le Symbolisme au théâtre: Lugné-Poe et les débuts de l'Oeuvre* (Paris: L'Arche, 1957).

Papers:

The main collection of Rachilde's papers is in the Bibliothèque Littéraire Jacques Doucet at the Bibliothèque de la Sorbonne, Paris. The Harry Ransom Humanities Research Center at the University of Texas at Austin has the largest collection of papers, mostly correspondence, in the United States. Other documents are preserved in private collections.

Jean Richepin
(14 February 1849 – 12 December 1926)

Julia Przybos
Hunter College of The City University of New York

PLAY PRODUCTIONS: *L'Etoile,* by Richepin and André Gill, Paris, Théâtre de la Tour d'Auvergne, 9 August 1873;

Mesdames et Messieurs, Paris, Théâtre de la Tour d'Auvergne, 28 August 1873;

La Glu, Paris, Théâtre de l'Ambigu-Comique, 27 January 1883;

Pierrot Assassin, Paris, Trocadéro, 28 April 1883;

Nana-Sahib, Paris, Théâtre de la Porte Saint-Martin, 20 December 1883;

Le Machiniste, Paris, Théâtre de la Porte Saint-Martin, 27 March 1884;

Macbeth, Paris, Théâtre de la Porte Saint-Martin, 21 May 1884;

La Sulamite, Paris, Concerts Lamoureux, 15 March 1885;

Monsieur Scapin, Paris, Théâtre-Français, 27 October 1886;

Le Flibustier, Paris, Théâtre-Français, 14 May 1888;

Prologue, Paris, Galerie Vivienne, 3 April 1889;

Le Chien de garde, Paris, Théâtre des Menus-Plaisirs, 21 May 1889;

A Emile Augier, Paris, Théâtre-Français, 5 November 1889;

Le Mage, music by Jules Massenet, Paris, Académie Nationale de Musique (Opéra), 16 March 1891;

Par le Glaive, Paris, Théâtre-Français, 8 February 1892;

Vers la Joie!, Paris, Théâtre-Français, 13 October 1894;

Résurrection, Paris, Théâtre de l'Odéon, 5 November 1896;

Le Chemineau, Paris, Théâtre de l'Odéon, 16 February 1897; translated by Louis Napoleon Parker as *Ragged Robin,* Adelphi Theater, London, July 1898; *The Harvester,* prose adaptation by Charles Skinner, New York, Lyric Theater, 10 October 1904;

Les Deux Avrils, Paris, Académie Nationale de Musique (Opéra), 14 April 1897;

La Rose du Pauvre, Paris, Théâtre de l'Odéon, 16 April 1897;

Jean Richepin (courtesy of the Lilly Library, Indiana University)

La Marjolaine, Paris, Théâtre de la Porte Saint-Martin, 20 April 1897;

La Martyre, Paris, Théâtre-Français, 18 April 1898;

Les Chansons de Miarka, music by Alexandre Georges, Paris, Salle du *Journal,* 25 May 1898;

Les Truands, Paris, Théâtre de l'Odéon, 22 March 1899;

La Gitane, Paris, Théâtre Libre (Antoine), 22 January 1900;

Prologue pour la réouverture de la Comédie Française, Paris, Théâtre-Français, 29 December 1900;

L'Impératrice, ballet with music by Paul Vidal, Paris, Théâtre Olympia, 6 April 1901;

Don Quichotte, Paris, Théâtre-Français, 16 October 1905;

Miarka, music by Georges, Paris, Opéra-Comique, 6 November 1905;

Zino Zina, ballet-pantomime with music by Vidal, Montecarlo, 14 December 1906;

Soléa, Cologne, Stadttheater, 12 December 1907;

Le Chemineau, music by Xavier Leroux, Paris, Opéra-Comique, 6 November 1907;

La Belle au bois dormant, by Richepin and Henri Cain, music by Francis Thomé, Paris, Théâtre Sarah-Bernhardt, 25 December 1907;

La Route d'émeraude, Paris, Théâtre du Vaudeville, 4 March 1909;

Rômi-Tchavé, music by Tiarko Richepin, Paris, Folies-Bergère, 4 September 1909;

La Glu [opera], by Richepin and Cain, music by Gabriel Dupont, Nice, Opéra, 26 January 1910;

La Beffa, Paris, Théâtre Sarah-Bernhardt, 2 March 1910;

Le Carillonneur, music by Leroux, Paris, Opéra-Comique, 20 March 1913;

Le Tango, by Richepin and Mme Richepin, Paris, Athénée, 30 December 1913;

La Plus forte, by Richepin and Paul Choudens, music by Leroux, Paris, Opéra-Comique, 11 January 1924.

BOOKS: *Les Etapes d'un réfractaire. Jules Vallès* (Paris, 1872);

L'Etoile, by Richepin and André Gill (Paris: Lemerre, 1873);

La Chanson des gueux (Paris: Librairie illustrée, 1876);

Les Morts bizarres (Paris: G. Decaux, 1876);

Les Caresses (Paris: M. Dreyfous, 1882);

Quatre Petits Romans (Paris: M. Dreyfous, 1882);

La Glu (Paris: M. Dreyfous, 1883);

Nana-Sahib (Paris: M. Dreyfous, 1883);

Le Pavé (Paris: M. Dreyfous, 1883);

Les Blasphèmes (Paris: M. Dreyfous, 1884);

La Sulamite: Poésie de Jean Richepin, musique d'Emmanuel Chabrier (Paris: Enoch, 1885);

Brave gens (Paris: M. Dreyfous, 1886);

La Mer (Paris: M. Dreyfous, 1886);

Monsieur Scapin (Paris: M. Dreyfous, 1886; revised, 1888);

Césarine (Paris: M. Dreyfous, 1888);

Le Flibustier (Paris: M. Dreyfous, 1888);

Contes de la décadence romaine (Paris: E. Fasquelle, 1889);

Le Cadet (Paris: Charpentier et Cie, 1890);

Les Débuts de César Borgia (Paris: Société des bibliophiles contemporains, 1890);

Le Mage: Poème de Jean Richepin, musique de Jules Massenet (Paris: G. Hartmann, 1891);

Truandailles (Paris: Bibliothèque-Charpentier, 1891);

Cauchemars (Paris: Charpentier et Fasquelle, 1892);

Par le glaive (Paris: Charpentier et Fasquelle, 1892);

L'Aimé (Paris: Charpentier et Fasquelle, 1893);

La Miseloque, choses et gens de théâtre (Paris: Charpentier et Fasquelle, 1893);

Le Flibustier: Poème de Jean Richepin, musique de César Cui (Paris: Heugel, 1893);

Mes Paradis (Paris: Charpentier et Fasquelle, 1894);

Vers la Joie! (Paris: Charpentier et Fasquelle, 1894);

Flamboche (Paris: Bibliothèque-Charpentier, 1895);

Grandes Amoureuses (Paris: Charpentier et Fasquelle, 1896);

Théâtre chimérique: vingt-sept actes de pantomime, à-propos, sotie, proverbe, pastorale, comédie, farce, conférence-mime en prose et en vers (Paris: E. Fasquelle, 1896);

Le Chemineau (Paris: Charpentier et Fasquelle, 1897); translated by Frederick H. Martens as *The Vagabond* (New York: G. Schirmer, 1917);

La Martyre (Paris: Charpentier et Fasquelle, 1898);

Le Chien de garde (Paris: Charpentier et Fasquelle, 1898);

La Bombarde (Paris: Bibliothèque-Charpentier, 1899);

Les Truands (Paris: Charpentier et Fasquelle, 1899);

Mam'selle Napoleon, adapted from the French by Joseph W. Herbert, music by Gustav Luders (New York: Witmark, 1903);

Miarka: Poème de Jean Richepin, musique d'Alexandre Georges (Paris: Enoch, 1905);

Soléa: Poème et musique d'Isidore de Lara, mise en vers français par Jean Richepin (Paris: Choudens, 1907);

La Belle au bois dormant, par Jean Richepin et Henri Cain, musique de scène par Francis Thomé (Paris: Fasquelle, 1908);

La Glu (Paris: Heugel, 1910);

La Beffa, de Sem Benelli; transposition en vers français de Jean Richepin (Paris: Fasquelle, 1910);

L'Aile (Paris: P. Lafitte et Cie, 1911);

L'Ame athénienne, volume 1—comprises *De l'Olympe à l'Agora;* volume 2 comprises *D'Eschyle à Aristophane* (Paris: Fayard, 1912);

Le Carillonneur, d'après le roman de G. Rodenbach. Poème de Jean Richepin, musique de Xavier Leroux (Paris: Choudens, 1913);

Macbeth: version française, vers et prose (Paris: Charpentier et Fasquelle, 1914);

A travers Shakespeare: conférences faites à l'Université des Annales (Paris: Fayard, 1914);

Prose de guerre (Paris: E. Flammarion, 1915);

La Clique, 1915–1916 (Paris: E. Flammarion, 1916);

La Guerre et l'amour (Paris: Charpentier, 1918);

Poèmes durant la guerre: 1914–1918 (Paris: E. Flammarion, 1919);

Théâtre en vers, 4 volumes (Paris: E. Flammarion, 1919–1924);

Le Coin des fous, histoires horribles (Paris: E. Flammarion, 1921);

Contes sans morales (Paris: E. Flammarion, 1922);

Les Glas (Paris: E. Flammarion, 1922);

Interludes (Paris: E. Flammarion, 1923);

La Plus forte, by Richepin and Paul de Choudens (Paris: Choudens, 1924);

Choix de poésies (Paris: Bibliothèque-Charpentier, 1926).

SELECTED PERIODICAL PUBLICATIONS–
UNCOLLECTED: "Don Quichotte: drame héroïcomique, en trois parties et huit tableaux," *L'Illustration théâtrale,* 16 (21–28 October 1905);

"La Belle au bois dormant: féerie lyrique en vers, par Jean Richepin et Henri Cain, musique de scène par Francis Thomé," *L'Illustration théâtrale,* 79 (25 January 1908): 1–32;

"La Route d'émeraude: drame en cinq actes, en vers, d'après le roman d'Eugène Demolder," *L'Illustration théâtrale,* 114 (20 March 1909);

"La Beffa: drame italien en quatre actes, en vers, de Sem Benelli. Transposition en vers français de Jean Richepin," *L'Illustration théâtrale,* 142 (19 March 1910);

"Le Tango (with Mme Richepin): comédie en quatre actes," supplement to *La Vie heureuse* (5 and 20 January 1914).

Known today only to specialists, Jean Richepin was a significant figure on the literary scene during the last three decades of the nineteenth century. The publications of the poems, plays, and fiction of this prolific writer were considered important literary events. The press informed readers about his private life and gave details about his liaison with Sarah Bernhardt. Even before the publication of *La Chanson des gueux* (Beggar's Song) in 1876, his exuberance, affability, good looks, and flamboyant dress made him popular with his fellow bohemians, who congregated in the cafés of the Latin Quarter. Richepin's poems about the urban poor, vagabonds, prostitutes, and street urchins were an important step in the evolution of French poetry. They challenged the dominant aesthetics of the Parnassians, who advocated emotional restraint and wrote perfectly crafted verses rooted in history and legend. Richepin's thematic and linguistic boldness—he used argot in his poems—was not matched by his formal innovations: he used traditional verse forms to express irreverent thoughts. Often consid-

ered as poetic equivalents of naturalistic fiction, *La Chanson des gueux* and *Les Blasphèmes* (Blasphemies, 1884) established Richepin's reputation as a rebel without respect for traditional values.

Richepin wrote plays in several theatrical genres, including drama, comedy, and pantomime, which were performed at the Comédie-Française, the Théâtre de l'Odéon, the Théâtre de l'Ambigu-Comique, the Théâtre de la Porte Saint-Martin, the Théâtre de l'Athénée, and the Théâtre du Vaudeville. These plays made him a luminary of the theater by the turn of the century. In some plays he depicts the unconstrained life of vagrants, Gypsies, and other social outcasts, such as François Villon, who appears as a character in *Les Truands* (Swindlers, 1899). But psychology and social issues are absent from his plays, and he distanced himself from the realism of Aurélien Lugné-Poë and André Antoine's Théâtre Libre. Usually written in sonorous alexandrines, his plays are examples of a now extinct genre popular in France until 1914, the heroic *drame en vers.* Although Edmond Rostand is most often associated with this style, Richepin was also a major writer of plays in verse.

The majority of Richepin's dramas are loosely connected tableaux that resemble traditional operas in their absence of verisimilitude. Indeed, he rewrote some of his plays as librettos that were staged at the Opéra and the Opéra-Comique in Paris. Best known as a poet and dramatist, Richepin also wrote nineteen volumes of novels, many short stories, and novellas. His novels often depict life on the fringes of society, while some of his short stories, set in late antiquity, feature themes popular with Decadent writers. Richepin's eclectic and diversified work has many characteristics in common with Naturalism, late Romanticism, and Decadence. However, he was not affected by new developments in the theater. He appears today as a writer full of contradictions: his early poetry is innovative, while his plays are Hugoesque.

Jean Richepin was born on 14 February 1849 at Médéa, Algeria, to Jules-Auguste, the son of a French military physician, and Rose-Pauline Beschepoix. He claimed to be of Gypsy descent but was actually of peasant stock. After an itinerant childhood in Algeria and France he received his *baccalauréat* at sixteen as a student of the Lycée Charlemagne in Paris. At the Ecole Normale, which he attended for two years, he studied foreign languages, including Latin and Spanish.

Richepin's literary career began in journalism. Shortly before the Franco-Prussian War he was assigned to eastern France. He spent the period of the Commune in Paris. Before the publication of *La Chanson des gueux* he led a bohemian life in the Latin Quarter, supporting himself with private lessons and occasional articles placed in reviews. His friends included such writers as Paul Bourget, Maurice Bouchor, and Raoul Ponchon. Together they founded a new literary movement in 1874, the Vivants, wishing to distinguish themselves from the Parnassian poets, known as the Impassibles, with whom Richepin associated at the salon of the marquise de Ricard. Charles Cros, Maurice Rollinat, and Gabriel Vicaire joined the Vivants. Their aesthetic advocates the rendering of humorous or pathetic scenes from the life of the common people. Richepin also knew such poets as Germain Nouveau, Arthur Rimbaud, and Paul Verlaine. He attended the animated soirees of Nina de Villard in Montmartre, whose salon attracted leading figures in literature and the arts. Plays of the habitués were performed in Nina's salon, the forerunner of the *Chat Noir,* the celebrated café-cabaret in Montmartre. Among them only *Le Moine bleu* (The Blue Monk), a burlesque written by the hostess, Richepin, Nouveau, and perhaps Jean-Marie Mathias Phillipe-Auguste, Comte de Villiers de l'Isle-Adam, was published and included in Nina de Villard's *Feuillets parisiens* (Parisian Book Leaves).

Richepin's official debut in theater was *L'Etoile* (The Star), written with the artist André Gill and performed at the Théâtre de la Tour d'Auvergne on 9 August 1873 before an invited audience. Richepin played Sir Richard, who goes mad when his wife, Bella, leaves him for another man. He believes his wife dead and that stars are candles carried across the sky by mothers who died without kissing their children. This strange one-act play set in William Shakespeare's England involves an infanticide when Sir Richard slits his son's throat so that his dead wife's ghost can rest in peace. It already contains aspects of Richepin's mature work. The action is spirited, though extravagant; the characters seem unreal; and the verses are vigorous yet uniform.

In 1876 *La Chanson des gueux* brought Richepin instant fame and the charge of an offense against public morals. He was tried and sentenced to a month in prison, where he wrote *Les Morts bizarres* (Bizarre Deaths), a collection of short stories published the same year. His imprisonment led the younger generation of writers to celebrate him as a champion of freedom of thought and expression. In 1891 a group of young writers called their satirical journal *Le Gueux,* attesting to the enduring popularity that Richepin gained from his life and charisma rather than his writing.

In the years following his first literary successes Richepin traveled across France, sailed on a merchant vessel, and is said to have joined Gypsies, living up to the legend of his origins. On his visits to Paris he frequented the literary circles of the Left Bank, including the "Club des Hydropathes" of Emile Goudeau. His marriage in 1879 to Eugénie Constant, a talented pianist, put a stop to his wanderings but not to his intense social life. His love affair with Sarah Bernhardt began during rehearsals of his *La Glu* (The Glue, 1883), a play in prose derived from his successful 1883 novel and memorable chiefly for Réjane's triumphant debut. This new star played the title role of a femme fatale who is killed with an ax at the end of the fifth act by Marie-des-Anges, the mother of the seduced Breton adolescent, Marie-Pierre. The *fête des sardinières* (Sardine-fishers' feast) enlivened the Théâtre de l'Ambigu-Comique production, providing vivid local color. The play was praised by Théodore de Banville, who compared the young Richepin to Aeschylus. Its 1909 revival at the Théâtre de la Porte Saint-Martin was met with less enthusiasm. A year later an opera based on *La Glu* with Gabriel Dupont's music attracted little attention and was never performed in Paris.

Pierrot Assassin (Pierrot the Assassin, 1883), a pantomime in three tableaux, was the second play staged during Richepin's liaison with Sarah Bernhardt. Réjane played Colombine, and Sarah Bernhardt, coached by the mime Paul Legrand, played the murderous Pierrot. Paul Vidal wrote the musical accompaniment. The third play, *Nana-Sahib,* was a sumptuous production that opened at the Théâtre de la Porte Saint-Martin on 20 December 1883, with Sarah Bernhardt in the leading role of Princess Djamma. The hero, an Indian raja and the leader of the Sepoy revolt of 1857 against the British, is a patriotic leader reminiscent of Victor Hugo's Hernani. The play boasted spectacular sets and wildly colorful moments, including the unpredictable actions of Nana-Sahib, the coveting of his fiancée Djamma by the pariah Çimrou, the final reunion of lovers climbing a flaming pyre, as well as a dungeon and a cave full of treasures. With the exception of a journalist writing for *Grimaces* who could hear in Richepin's language "the murmur of waterfalls and the humming of birds," the flowery alexandrines did not impress contemporary critics. They decried Richepin's lack of originality, citing both highbrow and lowbrow influences, including Sully-Prudhomme and Chevalier Charles Victor-Prévost, Vicomte d'Arlincourt, whose popular novel *Le Solitaire* was adapted for stage by René-Charles Guilbert de Pixerécourt.

Richepin's next work for the stage was a poem inspired by the biblical *Song of Solomon* called *La Sulamite,* a cantata for mezzo-soprano and women's chorus composed by Emmanuel Chabrier. The cantata's first performance at the Concert Lamoureux on 15 March 1885 was praised by some for its harmonic audacity but was unpopular when performed again on 28 February 1892.

The opening of *Monsieur Scapin* on 27 October 1886 at the Comédie-Française marked Richepin's arrival as a playwright. This three-act play with its complex plot is a sequel to Molière's farce *Les Fourberies de Scapin* (The Cheats of Scapin, 1671), with borrowings from Mathurin Régnier, Jean-François Regnard, Paul Scarron, Pierre Corneille's *L'Illusion comique* (The Theatrical Illusion, 1635), and Jean Racine's *Les Plaideurs* (The Litigants, 1668). Scapin is a wealthy bourgeois who insists on being addressed as "Monsieur." His wife Dorine has retained her spirit and mocks her pompous husband. Scapin's daughter, Suzette, loves Florisel, a poor musician well served by his impertinent valet, Tristan, who aspires to surpass the exploits of Scapin's youth. Monsieur Scapin plans to marry Suzette to Antoine, son of the notary Barnabé, but Tristan informs Scapin that the youth is under the spell of a dangerous courtesan, Rafa, and that Barnabé has gambled away his fortune. Scapin disguises himself as the chief of police to uncover the truth. He exposes the villains, and the disguised Tristan obtains his signature on Suzette's and Florisel's marriage document. *Monsieur Scapin* begins as a farce but ends as a moralistic play with a message dear to Richepin's heart: respectable people are often hypocrites and knaves, while social outcasts are honest and noble at heart. The Comédie-Française production featured Coquelin *aîné,* later immortalized in the role of Rostand's Cyrano de Bergerac.

One of Richepin's most popular plays, *Le Flibustier* (The Buccaneer), was a success from its first performance at Théâtre-Français on 14 May 1888 and remained in its repertoire until 1934. This three-act comedy about seamen and their families is set in Brittany at the end of the seventeenth century. François Legoëz, a retired sailor living in Saint-Malo, worships the sea even though his four sons and three sons-in-law have drowned. He hopes for the return of his only remaining grandson, Pierre, who left home at the age of ten as a ship hand and from whom he has not heard for eight years. His granddaughter Janik, Pierre's childhood bride, shares his enthusiasm for the sea, but Marie-Anne, Janik's mother, who is of peasant stock, does not. Pierre's companion, Jacquemin, finds Marie-Anne home alone and tells her that his friend was killed by Spanish buccaneers. Fearing that the weakhearted Legoëz might die of shock, Marie-Anne convinces Jacquemin to pose as Pierre during his visit in Saint-Malo. The real Pierre returns to find that Jacquemin has taken his place in the family and in Janik's heart. The old Legoëz is furious at first but soon realizes that he prefers the impostor to his grandson. Whereas the latter is a gold prospector in America,

Jacquemin has remained loyal to the sea. Legoëz transfers his affection to Jacquemin. Pierre returns to his gold mines in Mexico, and Jacquemin marries Janik. The characters lack psychological depth: Legoëz is an idealized seaman; the young men are noble and generous; and the widow Marie-Anne is patience and resignation incarnate. Only the innocent Janik shows complexity when she encourages the reluctant Jacquemin to confess his love for her (act 2, scene 4). Written only four years after the incendiary *Les Blasphèmes,* this unoriginal idyll of the sea disappointed the critics, who noted the clichéd theme of the absent lover's return. Ten years later *Le Flibustier* was set to music by a Russian composer of French descent, César Cui.

Le Chien de garde (The Watch-Dog) opened on 21 May 1889 at the Théâtre des Menus-Plaisirs. This prose drama in five acts has a sensational plot that includes theft, political conspiracy, betrayal, and murder. The prologue is set during the French retreat from Leipzig in 1813. A dying general of Napoleon, Count d'Olmutz, asks his honest orderly, Sergeant Férou, to become the moral guardian of his illegitimate son, Paul. Férou tries but ultimately fails to make the weak Paul a virtuous patriot. The young man is a gambler who "borrows" a large sum from the bank of his godfather, Baron Mouriez. The baron's untimely death prevents Paul from returning the money he hoped to win. When the theft is discovered, Férou takes the blame and goes to prison in place of his charge. On escaping from prison, he is pleased to discover that Paul is conspiring against Louis XVIII. When the police uncover this Bonapartist plot, Paul's mistress turns over the list of conspirators to save her lover's life. Férou cannot tolerate Paul's refusal to commit suicide in the face of such dishonor and shoots the young man himself when encouraged by an apparition of Count d'Olmutz. *Le Chien de garde* was rejected by the *comité de lecture* of the Comédie-Française, which was accustomed to more-literary plays. Richepin borrows his material from many sources. The prologue is lifted from Pierre Alexis, Vicomte de Ponson du Terrail's popular novel *L'Héritage mystérieux* featuring *Rocambole* (1858), and the heroic killing is a distant echo of both Prosper Mérimée's "Mateo Falcone" (1829) and *Antony* (1831) by Alexandre Dumas *père.* Despite its melodramatic overtone, the play's vivid language distinguishes it from standard lowbrow works.

Richepin's next work for the stage was the libretto for Jules Massenet's *Le Mage* (The Magus), which opened on 16 March 1891. Critics remarked on its affinity with Giuseppe Verdi's *Aïda* (1871), Ludovic Halévy's *La Juive* (The Jewess, 1835), and Massenet's *Le Roi de Lahore* (The King of Lahore, 1877). The action takes place in Bactria, a satrapy of ancient Persia. Zarastra, the conqueror of the Turanians, loves their captive queen, Anahita. The king consents to Zarastra's marriage, but Vahreda, daughter of the priest of Ahriman, produces witnesses who swear that Zarastra is betrothed to her. Zarastra flees to a mountain, communes with the god Ormazd, and founds Zoroastrianism. Upon learning that Anahita must marry the king against her will, Zarastra returns to the capital to find that the captive Turanians rebelled and liberated their queen. The god Ormazd helps the reunited lovers flee the burning city while Vahreda dies with a cry of hatred. Massenet's undramatic music was criticized for not living up to the opera's grandiose scenes. The special effects, lavish costumes, and spectacular production received acclaim.

Richepin returned to the Théâtre-Français with *Par le Glaive* (By the Sword), which opened on 8 February 1892. The play was wildly successful and praised by critics who had on other occasions derided the faulty construction of Richepin's plays. A drama in verse, it is set in fourteenth-century Ravenna, ruled nominally by a child, Rizzo da Pollenta. Guido da Pollenta, Rizzo's older brother, is believed to have been assassinated by orders of Conrad le Loup, a ruthless condottiere. Guido's life was saved by his illegitimate half-brother Strada, who goes in rags playing the guitar but, not unlike Alfred de Musset's Lorenzaccio, is plotting to overthrow Conrad to bring Guido back to power. Once Guido has disappeared, his fiancée, the patriotic Rinalda, marries Conrad, wishing to improve the conditions of the oppressed populace. Before the overthrow of Conrad, Strada wants Guido to marry the commoner Bianca to gain popular support for Pollenta's cause. Guido dresses as a monk and meets Rinalda with the intent to kill her for betrayal. Rinalda explains her motives, and their mutual love is renewed. Guido, like Saint-Mégrin in *Henri III et sa cour* (Henry III and His Court, 1829) by Dumas *père,* hides in Rinalda's chapel, just before the jealous husband's untimely arrival. When Conrad demands the chapel key, Rinalda throws it out the window. After the defeat of Conrad the conspirators liberate Guido, but his happiness is cut short when Rinalda impales herself on Strada's sword. She intends to free Guido to marry Bianca and thus bring peace and harmony to Ravenna. Rinalda's patriotic sacrifice prompted critics to call Richepin's play a neo-Cornelian tragedy.

Vers la Joie! (Toward Joy!) opened at the Théâtre-Français on 13 October 1894, only to close after fifteen performances. With its elements of comedy, pastoral, operetta, and farce, this eclectic play was dismissed by critics as puerile, linguistically bizarre, and occasionally vulgar. Set in an imaginary kingdom, it concerns a young and meek prince suffering from boredom. At the advice of an old shepherd, he abandons the affairs of state to a regent and leaves his court for the country. He grows strong and confident working the soil and soon falls in love with a young beauty. When his kingdom is invaded by a foreign army, he regains control of the capital and vanquishes the enemy. The prince marries the peasant girl in a rustic ceremony, thus bridging the gap between royalty and commoners.

Although originally rejected by Comédie-Française, Richepin's five-act alexandrine play *Le Chemineau* (1897; translated as *The Vagabond,* 1917) was a great success. It opened at the Odéon on 16 February 1897 and was performed 158 times within the year. The play was revived at the Gymnase in 1900, at the Théâtre Sarah-Bernhardt in 1908, and finally by the Théâtre-Français in 1929. Arguably Richepin's best play, it is set in contemporary Burgundy. A nameless, happy vagabond of thirty who despises material possessions and cherishes his freedom above all else works occasionally to avoid the humiliations of mendacity. The wanderer has gained mysterious powers from his deep understanding of nature. In the opening scene he sings offstage to encourage the harvesters he is supervising. The song is the background to a conversation between Toinette, an orphaned farm girl, and François, an aging farm worker, who is proposing marriage. Toinette rejects François, but her hope that the wanderer, father of her unborn child, will stay is shattered when he forgoes a job offer from Maître Pierre. Unaware of Toinette's pregnancy and fearing the entrapment of love, the vagabond leaves her his wages and takes to the road. Toinette marries François in despair. The second act takes place twenty-two years later, when the vagabond happens to pass by the Burgundian village. Toinette is a devoted wife to her paralyzed husband and an excellent mother to her hardworking son, Toinet, who is in love with Maître Pierre's daughter Aline. The rich man will not consent to the young couple's marriage. Aline refuses to eat, and Toinet becomes a suicidal drunkard. Toinette tells the vagabond everything, and he takes action. He sings sorcerer's curses to the superstitious Maître Pierre, threatening to blight the farm. The rich man surrenders and approves the marriage. After the ceremony the vagabond stays with the family to teach his secrets to Toinet. On Christmas eve, when everybody is at church, he is nursing the dying François, who suddenly recovers speech and urges him to marry Toinette. When the vagabond learns that Maître Pierre suspects him of wishing François dead, he leaves the comforts of sedentary life to continue his wanderings.

In *Le Chemineau,* as in other plays, Richepin rejects Realism and espouses the lofty ideals of freedom and magnanimity. To Jules Lemaître, the play is as conventional as an opéra comique and "must be judged by the beauty of its poetry and the nobility of the sentiments." The ease with language, skillful versification, and propensity to a grandiloquence inherited from Hugo are typical of Richepin. His poetry is in sharp contrast with Paul Verlaine's contemporaneous prescriptions found in his poem "L'Art poétique" (1874), which bans eloquence and warns against rhyming for rhyme's sake. Shortened to four acts and with its verses adapted for music, *Le Chemineau* became the libretto for Xavier Leroux's opera of 1907, which was considered to be that composer's best work.

Le Chemineau marks the high point in Richepin's theatrical career; none of his subsequent plays received such an enthusiastic reception. By the turn of the century, after twenty-five years of prolific writing, Richepin's inspiration seemed to show signs of fatigue. His output for the stage was less abundant than in the past, consisting mainly of opera, ballet, and pantomime librettos, adaptations of past and contemporary novels (including his own), and translations of English and Italian repertory.

La Martyre (The Martyr), with Sarah Bernhardt in the title role, exemplifies Richepin's diminishing creativity. It opened at the Comédie-Française on 18 April 1898 but closed after eighteen performances despite its star power and sumptuous production. *La Martyre* belongs to a subgenre popular at the end of the century, the religious play set in antiquity. Other examples are Rodolphe Darzens's *L'Amante du Christ* (The Lover of Christ, 1888), Edmond Haraucourt's *La Passion* (1890), and Edmond Rostand's *La Samaritaine* (The Samaritan Woman, 1897), all exhibiting a mixture of religiosity and eroticism found in the prose writings of Jules Amédée Barbey d'Aurevilly, Joris-Karl Huysmans, Léon Bloy, and Rémy de Gourmont. Flammeola is a jaded Roman in love with the apostle Johannès, who is unaware of her lust for him. She wants to convert to Christianity to be reunited with the object of her love. The apostle and Flammeola are denounced by her slaves and die martyrs' deaths. In the final scene the crucified Johannès baptizes Flammeola with blood oozing from his wounds. Unlike the fate of Corneille's character Polyeucte, Flammeola's death is not a result of inner motivation but of external events.

Les Truands is another play of Richepin's declining years notable for a freer verse form: besides alexandrines, it is written in lines of four, seven, eight, and ten syllables. Like Hugo's novel *Notre-Dame de Paris* (1831), it is set in fifteenth-century Paris, complete with cathedral, narrow streets, taverns, and brothels. It boasts a large cast of characters typical of Richepin: Gypsies, thieves, vagrants, prostitutes, and, in the first act, the rebellious François Villon, a student of theology arguing in Latin with his professor. The author seems to have borrowed from Rostand, his former protégé. The ballad of Robin, the leader of vagabonds, echoes the passage about Cyrano's nose in *Cyrano de Bergerac* (1897). *Les Truands* opened at the Théâter de l'Odéon on 22 March 1899 and was forced to close after twenty-nine performances. *La Gitane* (The Gypsy Woman), an unpublished prose melodrama in four acts, was even less successful, in spite of Antoine's skillful production. It opened on 22 January 1900 at the Théâtre Libre and disappeared from the repertory after a few performances. Richepin's election to the Académie Française in 1909 was a bright point in his fading career.

Written in collaboration with his wife, Richepin's last original work for the stage, *Le Tango,* opened on 30 December 1913 at the Athénée in Paris. An unsympathetic critic summarized its plot as the story of a dowager princess pushing her grandchildren to consummate their marriage. After many fruitless attempts to secure the continuation of Lusignan's line the princess's goal is reached at last, thanks to the aphrodisiac properties of tango dancing. The play contains derogatory comments about Symbolist poets and Cubist painters, indicating how out of touch with his times Richepin had become. At the dress rehearsal *Le Tango* was laughed at by an audience of invited guests. Modern readers of Richepin's prolific theatrical oeuvre would be more inclined to indulgence than sarcasm. Even his best plays seem dated, but, like many works of the past, they can exude an old-fashioned charm.

Biography:

Howard Sutton, *The Life and Work of Jean Richepin* (Geneva: Librairie Droz, 1961).

References:

Emile Faguet, *Notes sur le théâtre contemporain—1888* (Paris: Lecène et Oudin, 1889);

Jules Lemaître, *Impressions de théâtre,* third series (Paris: Lecène et Oudin, 1889), pp. 253–273;

Lemaître, *Impressions de théâtre,* tenth series (Paris: Lecène et Oudin, 1900), pp. 113–123;

Octave Mirbeau, "Jouets de Paris," in *Les Ecrivains (1884–1894),* first series (Paris: Ernest Flammarion, 1925–1927), pp. 13–20;

Francisque Sarcey, *Quarante ans de théâtre,* volume 7 (Paris: Bibliothèques des Annales politiques et littéraires, 1902);

Jean-Marie Mathias Phillipe-Auguste, Comte de Villiers de l'Isle-Adam, "Une Soirée chez Nina de Villard," in *Oeuvres complètes,* volume 2 (Paris: Gallimard, Bibliothèque de la Pléiade, 1986), pp. 410–415.

Edmond Rostand
(1 April 1868 – 2 December 1918)

Juliette M. Rogers
University of New Hampshire

PLAY PRODUCTIONS: *Les Romanesques,* Paris, Comédie-Française, 21 March 1894;

La Princesse Lointaine, Paris, Théâtre de la Renaissance, 5 April 1895;

La Samaritaine, Paris, Théâtre de la Renaissance, 14 April 1897;

Cyrano de Bergerac, Paris, Théâtre de la Porte Saint-Martin, 28 December 1897;

L'Aiglon, Paris, Théâtre Sarah-Bernhardt, 15 March 1900;

Chantecler, Paris, Théâtre-Français, 7 February 1910;

La Dernière Nuit de Don Juan, Paris, Théâtre-Français, 1922.

BOOKS: *Les Musardises* (Paris: Lemerre et Fasquelle, 1890; revised edition, Paris: Fasquelle, 1911);

Les Deux Pierrots ou le souper blanc (Paris: Charpentier et Fasquelle, 1891);

Les Romanesques (Paris: Charpentier et Fasquelle, 1895); translated by Henderson Daingerfield Norman as *The Romantics,* in *Plays of Edmond Rostand,* volume 1 (New York: Macmillan, 1921), pp. 1–58;

Cyrano de Bergerac (Paris: Charpentier et Fasquelle, 1898); translated by Norman as *Cyrano de Bergerac,* in *Plays of Edmond Rostand,* volume 1, pp. 207–360; translated by Anthony Burgess as *Cyrano de Bergerac* (London: Hutchinson, 1985);

La Princesse Lointaine (Paris: Charpentier et Fasquelle, 1898); translated by Norman as *The Princess Far Away* (New York: Stokes, 1899); translated by Norman in *Plays of Edmond Rostand,* volume 1, pp. 59–140;

La Samaritaine (Paris: Charpentier et Fasquelle, 1900); translated by Norman as *The Woman of Samaria,* in *Plays of Edmond Rostand,* volume 1, pp. 141–206;

L'Aiglon (Paris: Charpentier et Fasquelle, 1900); translated by Louis N. Parker (New York: R. H. Rusell, 1900); translated by Norman as

Edmond Rostand

The Eaglet, in *Plays of Edmond Rostand,* volume 2 (New York: Macmillan, 1921), pp. 1–204;

Un Soir à Hernani (Paris: Charpentier et Fasquelle, 1902);

Le Cantique de l'aile (Paris: Charpentier et Fasquelle, 1910);

Chantecler (Paris: Charpentier et Fasquelle, 1910); translated by Gertrude Hall (New York: Duffield, 1910); translated by Norman as *Chanticleer,* in *Plays of Edmond Rostand,* volume 2, pp. 205–370;

Le Vol de la Marseillaise (Paris: Charpentier et Fasquelle, 1914);

La Dernière Nuit de Don Juan (Paris: Charpentier et Fasquelle, 1921); translated by T. Lawrason

Riggs as *The Last Night of Don Juan* (Yellow Springs, Ohio: Kahoe, 1929).

Collections: *Oeuvres complètes illustrées de Edmond Rostand,* 7 volumes (Paris: P. Lafitte et Cie, 1905–1923);

Théâtre complet, 10 volumes (Paris: Charpentier et Fasquelle, 1921–1926);

Plays of Edmond Rostand, translated by Norman (New York: Macmillan, 1921)—includes *Les Romanesques, Cyrano de Bergerac, La Princesse Lointaine, La Samaritaine, L'Aiglon,* and *Chantecler.*

If Edmond Rostand is known throughout the world today, it is for his play *Cyrano de Bergerac* (1897; translated, 1921). Although he wrote a total of seven plays and three volumes of poetry, he has been remembered through the years for the "panache" and poetry of his heroic character Cyrano. Rostand wrote at the end of the nineteenth century and was influenced both by early-nineteenth-century Romantic playwrights such as Alfred de Musset and by late-nineteenth-century literary figures such as the Decadents, who emphasized ennui and extravagance. He is notable as one of the last dramatists in France to write his plays in verse. It is often his brilliant use of language, in combination with his winning heroes and heroines, that has been responsible for the praise and continued popularity of Rostand's work.

Born in Marseilles on 1 April 1868, Rostand came from a literary and cultural family. His aunt Victorine Rostand wrote poetry; his uncle Alexis Rostand was a composer and music critic; and his father, Eugène Rostand, was a part-time poet and translator of Catullus, even though his appointment at the Académie des Sciences Politiques et Morales de Marseilles was in the department of economics. It is therefore perhaps not surprising that Edmond was recognized for his talent as a translator and poet as early as the age of sixteen, while studying at the Lycée Marseilles. When he continued his studies at the Collège Stanislas in Paris from 1884 to 1886, he was considered the best student in French composition, history, and philosophy. Following his brilliant academic career, Edmond made efforts to please his father by studying law in Paris for two years. However, these attempts to prepare for the legal profession were only secondary to his growing literary interests. During the time of his legal studies Rostand won the 1887 literary essay competition held by the Marseilles Academy for an essay that he had written on Honoré d'Urfé and Guy de Maupassant. He also began to write a collection of poetry that he published in 1890 under the title *Les Musardises* (Daydreams).

In 1890 Rostand married Rosemonde Gérard, to whom he dedicated *Les Musardises.* Rosemonde, herself a poet, was a great and harmonious influence on Rostand. Her collection of poems, *Les Pipeaux* (Fibs), dates from 1889, one year before their marriage; it received special mention from the Académie Française. After the wedding, however, Rosemonde dedicated herself to her husband's career and often helped him work through difficult passages, lending her poetic sensibilities to his. Many years after Rostand's death Rosemonde wrote a memoir-biography of her beloved husband, *Edmond Rostand* (1935), in which she recalled fondly their early days of marriage.

The decade of the 1890s was a period of great success, both personal and professional, for Rostand. During a four-year period beginning in 1893 he wrote and produced an incredible succession of dramatic works: *Les Romanesques* (1894; translated as *The Romantics,* 1921), *La Princesse Lointaine* (1895; translated as *The Princess Far Away,* 1921), *La Samaritaine* (1897; translated as *The Woman of Samaria,* 1921), and *Cyrano de Bergerac.* Shortly after *La Samaritaine* premiered Rostand began a passionate affair with Sarah Bernhardt, his favorite actress, for whom he had written *La Princesse Lointaine, La Samaritaine,* and the role of Roxane in *Cyrano de Bergerac,* which she never performed. He was never faithful to his loving wife Rosemonde again, moving from his affair with Bernhardt to the poetess Anna de Noailles, then to the actresses Simone Marquet and Mary Marquet during the next fifteen years. Rosemonde suffered in silence for many years but finally began an open love affair with Tiarko Richepin, her eldest son's best friend, in 1911. Despite these marital infidelities, the Rostands remained united throughout Edmond's life.

Rostand's first play, *Les Romanesques,* premiered on 21 May 1894 at the Comédie-Française. It was praised both by the public and the drama critics and was honored with the Prix Toirac by Académie Française members later that year. The play begins with a young couple in love, Sylvette and Percinet, who are reading lines of William Shakespeare's *Romeo and Juliet* (1594) to each other, separated by a wall that divides their feuding fathers' properties. In their romantic view of themselves they compare their situation to that of Romeo and Juliet. Later in the first act their two fathers, Bergamin and Pasquinot, arrive at the wall and reveal to the audience the fact that they are only feigning their animosity. They have always wanted to combine their two properties through an arranged marriage between their two children but realize that their romantic offspring ("les romanesques") would never agree to an arranged marriage. The fathers plan a staged kidnapping of Sylvette for that night so that Percinet can romantically rescue her and thus provide a noble excuse for the fathers to "agree to" their children's desire to marry each other.

In the second act Bergamin and Pasquinot, annoyed by their children's repetitive recounting of the remarkable event that brought them together, finally admit to Sylvette that they had feigned their hatred and arranged her kidnapping. Soon after, Percinet also discovers the bill that the hired swordsman and kidnapper, Straforel, has left for the fathers to pay. Both lovers are offended by the scam, and Percinet leaves for a "real" life of adventure and pleasure on his own. During the third act Straforel schemes again to get Sylvette and Percinet back together so that he will finally be paid for his work. As he knows that Sylvette has been claiming that she, like Percinet, wants a life of real adventure, he disguises himself as a marquis and pressures her into running away with him. At the moment she is about to leave, Percinet returns home and the couple is happily reunited, deciding that their love was real even if their parents' hatred and scheming were false.

Les Romanesques, written in alexandrine verse, displays Rostand's talent for spirited language, rich plays on words, and charming ironic passages. In act 1, scene 2, for example, Bergamin discovers his son by the wall and accuses him of daydreaming and idleness. Percinet, to defend himself, states that he finds that the wall is "adorable," "admirable," and has "de bien beaux yeux" (very beautiful eyes), to his father's mock astonishment. When Bergamin announces that he has found the true reason why Percinet always spends his days by the wall, Percinet and Sylvette are frightened that their secret rendezvous spot has been discovered. But Bergamin picks up the volume of *Romeo and Juliet* that he has plucked from Percinet's pocket and continues:

Tu viens lire en cachette! . . . Et du théâtre! . . . En vers!
Des vers! Voilà pourquoi, la cervelle à l'envers.
Vous rêvez, vous errez, évitant les approches,
Pourquoi vous me venez parler d'aristoloches,
Et pourquoi vous voyez des yeux bleus à ce mur!
Un mur n'a pas besoin d'être joli,—mais sûr!

(You come to read in secret!
[He takes the book that is sticking out of Percinet's pocket and looks at the cover.]

Plays!
[He opens the book and lets it drop, horrified.]
In verse!
Poetry! That's why you get worse and worse.
Mooning! And hiding! It's enough to shock you,—
Your grown son talks about 'aristolochia.'
—And blue eyes of a wall. You go along!
Walls ain't for pretty, but they must be strong.)

This short tirade by Bergamin on the terrible effects of reading drama in verse is a perfect example of the comic self-irony that Rostand offered for his audience's enjoyment in his theatrical works. The play's tone in general is lighthearted, despite the opening reference to the tragic and sorrowful Romeo and Juliet. The conclusion offers another interesting theatrical device: the characters join hands and address the audience directly. Sylvette explains: "Et Maintenant, nous quatre,—et Monsieur Straforel— / Excusons ce que fut la pièce, en un rondel" (And now, we four and Master Straforel / Make for an Epilogue a rare rondel). They indeed sing the remaining lines of the play, Percinet proclaiming:

Un repos naïf des pièces amères,
Un peu de musique, un peu de Watteau,
Un spectacle honnête et qui finit tôt,
Un vieux mur fleuri,—deux amants,—deux pères[.]

(Home, a harbor from hateful times,
A little music, a scene Watteau,
A pretty playlet, not long nor slow,
Sires,—lovers,—a wall where sweet-brier climbs . . .
    Sylvette
Dainty dresses and rippling rhymes[.])

Rostand, speaking through his characters, thus ends his first work with a simple and direct appeal to the audience about the type of play ("Un Spectacle honnête") and the type of effect ("Un repos naïf") that he wanted to create. Rostand's dramatic verve, displaying both his trademark panache and finesse, assured the success of *Les Romanesques* with both the critics and the French public, and it established Rostand as a major playwright of his time.

In the following year Rostand wrote another successful play, *La Princesse Lointaine,* for Sarah Bernhardt, with whom he collaborated often during the next ten years. In contrast to *Les Romanesques,* which takes place "où l'on voudra, pourvu que les costumes soient jolis" (wherever the director wishes, provided that the costumes are pretty), *La Princesse Lointaine* has a more specific time, the twelfth century, and setting, Tripoli. The entire first act, however, takes place on the boat of a Provençal troubadour and prince, Joffroy de Rudel, who has embarked on a long and dangerous voyage across the Mediterranean to meet Mélissinde, princess of the Orient and countess of Tripoli. She has been promised to Manuel, emperor of Byzantium, but has learned of Joffroy de Rudel's love for her and desires to meet this French prince and poet.

Rudel and his entire crew have fallen ill during the voyage, and after sighting the port of Tripoli at the end of act 1 it is clear that Joffroy cannot make the trip himself and must send his friend Bertrand to fetch the princess and bring her back to the boat. In act 2 the Princess's guard, the Chevalier aux Armes Vertes (The Knight in Emerald Mail), has redoubled his surveillance of the castle. When Bertrand lands on shore, he fights off the guards one by one, even killing the chevalier in order to arrive at the princess's door. Mélissinde mistakes Bertrand for Joffroy and falls in love with him after learning of his courageous battles with the chevalier and his soldiers. After she has revealed her love and they decide not to return to Joffroy's boat, they are both filled with regret when they hear that a boat in the harbor has raised a black sail—a sign of death. Soon after, however, Mélissinde discovers that the black sail is for her guard, the chevalier, and that Joffroy is still alive. They immediately repent and go to the boat, where in act 4 Joffroy dies joyously in her arms. Mélissinde announces that "Mount Carmel's path shall know my climbing feet," and to begin her life of asceticism she throws all her jewels to Bertrand and his sailors and sends them off on a mission in the Crusades.

Rostand's interpretation of courtly narratives of the medieval period is simultaneously modern, original, and yet faithful to the tone and content of troubadour legends. The courtly hero Joffroy loves a perfect beauty whom he has never met. His love is pure and idealistic, as is his vision of the princess whom he seeks on his voyage. On the other hand, in a much more modern tone, the princess is not merely an idealized figure for whom the brave knight writes epic poems and sings his high praises. Mélissinde is an outspoken, active, and feeling individual, one who falls in love with the "wrong" man, struggles with her physical attraction to Bertrand, and finally decides to seek a higher destiny with her spiritual love, Joffroy. The Mélissinde character is a totally modern personage, divided and confused, and the plot and tone of the play center around her human vibrancy. In the following discussion with her lady-in-waiting, Sorismonde, the audience is able, in act 3, scene 6, to understand the battles going on in Mélissinde's mind:

> Ah! il y a pourtant bien des mélanges troubles!
> Il y a bien des coeurs désespérément doubles!
> Celui dont si longtemps mes rêves furent pleins,
> Celui qui meurt pour moi, je l'aime, je le plains.
> Et l'autre, je l'adore! et ma souffrance est telle
> Qu'il me semble, mon âme, entre eux, qu'on écartèle!

> ('Tis their commingling that makes all our trouble,
> So many hearts are desperately double!
> One held so long the cup of dreams a-brim,
> He who lies sick,—I love and pity him.
> The other I adore! Both loves I rue!
> My heart between them has been riven in two!)

Bertrand, in his singular devotion to Joffroy, is completely unaware of Mélissinde's feelings for him. After much inner struggle Mélissinde decides to tell Bertrand about her desires, and only then does Bertrand announce that he will betray his friend and master. They shut the window that has a view on Joffroy's ship waiting in the harbor and try to justify their decisions until the wind blows the window back open and they hear valets and pages announcing the arrival of a boat with black sails.

The conclusion of *La Princesse Lointaine* is pious but satisfying. Rostand's third play, *La Samaritaine,* written in early 1897 and produced for the first time during Easter week, also has a strong moral and religious message for the reader or spectator. This work recounts the biblical story of the Samaritan woman, Photine, who welcomed Jesus and his apostles and who singlehandedly convinced the rest of the inhabitants of Samaria to recognize him as their savior. Again, Rostand wrote this play with Sarah Bernhardt in mind, and Photine is the central character of the work rather than Jesus. This deviation from the biblical story caused much concern among the more conservative critics of the period, and it is still considered one of the faults of the play. The Jesus character is flat and static, hardly moving around on the stage at all. In contrast, Photine is energetic, full of life, movement, and song. Her entrance on stage is bold and insouciant, as she sings a love song dedicated to her current lover. Her recognition of Christ and conversion to his gospel is likewise a stunning event, as she falls to her knees, then bursts into the same song again, this time for her love of Christ. When she recognizes the blasphemy that she has just committed, Photine is horrified but is assured by Christ, in act 1, scene 5, that she has done him no harm:

> Grand Dieu! Qu'ai-je fait? Que disais-je?
> Pour lui! le même chant! le même, ô sacrilège!
> Pour lui, les même mots qui me servirent pour . . .
>
> 　　　Jesus
> Je suis toujours un pen dans tous les mots d'amour.
>
> . . . Maître, pour t'adorer, j'ai dit ce que j'ai su!
>
> 　　　Jésus
> Et ton hommage me fut doux. Je l'ai reçu.

> (My God! What have I done?
> For Him the same song, Oh the very one!
> Oh, sacrilege! The idle words and free!
> 　　　Jesus
> All words of love must speak at last of Me.
> 　　　Photine
> . . . Master, adoring, I could but repeat
> The words I knew . . .

        Jesus
I know. The gift was sweet.
I have received it.)

Like their exchange cited above, the play takes a serious theme and story line but once again modernizes the female character and allows her a much greater range of emotions and actions.

Her ability to cite passages from the Bible to her fellow townsmen develops into another brilliant and striking scene for the Photine character. At first the villagers ignore her and go about their marketing as usual. But her eloquence draws the people to listen to her words and finally believe her when she tells them that Christ has come to Samaria. It is not Christ himself who shines in this crucial scene but the common prostitute, Photine, who has been transformed and who is transformative.

Cyrano de Bergerac, the best-known and most-loved of Rostand's plays, was created during the same year that *La Samaritaine* was enjoying success on the stage, 1897, and it was produced for the first time at the end of that year, on 28 December. As was now expected from a Rostand play, the main character was based on an historical figure, this time in the form of the seventeenth-century nobleman, Savinien de Cyrano de Bergerac. Born in 1619, Cyrano de Bergerac left his hometown of Mauvières at age twelve to study at the Collège de Beauvais in Paris. Here he was greatly influenced by his cousin Madeleine Robineau, who married the nobleman Christophe de Neuvillette in 1635 and thus left behind the bourgeoisie for an exciting life among the aristocracy in Paris. In 1638 Cyrano left school and became a cadet in the company of the Gascon Guards and then in the Count's Army, but after a serious injury in battle at the Siege of Arras in 1640, he moved back to Paris and studied with the renowned philosopher and mathematician, Pierre Gassendi. During his life he wrote a variety of works, including treatises on the sun and the moon and two plays, a tragedy and a comedy, both of which were unsuccessful. After a roof beam fell on his head, he lingered for a year, then died in July 1655 at the young age of thirty-six. In the nineteenth century his military prowess, courage, wit, and intelligence were all celebrated in Théophile Gautier's *Les Grotesques* (1844). It was also in Gautier's text that explicit references to the unusual size of Cyrano's nose are found. Gautier went so far as to compare Cyrano's nose to the Himalayan mountains in the preface to his biography.

Rostand followed faithfully many of the biographical details of Cyrano de Bergerac's life but embroidered on some and invented other aspects to create a typical Rostandian character. Rostand's plot is as follows: Cyrano is a brilliant poet and courageous swordsman who, in act 1, bullies a ridiculous actor, Montfleury, off the stage during a public performance because he detests his bad acting. The crowd is at first shocked at Cyrano's outrageous behavior, but when he duels the Viscount de Valvert and simultaneously composes a poem, they are thrilled and become an admiring audience. At the end of the first act Cyrano goes to the Porte de Nesles, where a hundred men are waiting to attack his friend, the poet Lignière. Cyrano goes in Lignière's place and defeats all one hundred assassins.

During the second act Cyrano meets with his cousin, Roxane, whom he loves, at Ragueneau, the baker-poet's pastry shop. He discovers sadly that Roxane secretly loves another man—the handsome young Christian de Neuvillette, who is going to join Cyrano's Gascon Cadets that day. She worries that Christian will be mistreated as a new recruit and asks that Cyrano watch over him. While Cyrano is disappointed that Roxane loves another man, he considers her request to take care of Christian very seriously. When he finds out that the basically illiterate Christian also loves Roxane, Cyrano decides to combine their "talents": he is intelligent but ugly, and Christian is handsome but tongue-tied. Cyrano thus offers to write beautiful poems and letters to Roxane for Christian. He even speaks on Christian's behalf: during act 3 Christian and Cyrano find themselves under Roxane's balcony, and, remaining in the shadows, Cyrano speaks to Roxane of love. He must then watch Christian climb up the trellis and give Roxane a kiss. She and Christian are secretly married that night, in direct opposition to the wishes of her guardian, the count de Guiche. After being delayed by Cyrano in the street the count arrives just after Roxane and Christian have finished taking their vows. De Guiche's anger is so great that he sends both Christian and Cyrano, along with the entire Gascon Cadets, to the Siege of Arras.

Act 4 takes place entirely at the siege, where Christian discovers that Cyrano has been writing letters twice daily to Roxane under Christian's name, without even telling him. Roxane suddenly appears at the siege, and Christian realizes that she now loves the spiritual and intellectual qualities of the composer of the letters more than any physical beauty that he has. When the battle finally begins, he commits a daring gesture of bravery and is mortally wounded. Roxane finds one last love letter in his pocket and saves it for herself.

Act 5 takes place fifteen years later at the convent where Roxane has been living since she was widowed. Cyrano comes to visit her every Saturday evening but has never revealed his love for her or the fact that he wrote all the letters signed with Christian's name. However, on this particular Saturday, he arrives late, having been mortally wounded by a beam that fell on his head. Because he realizes that this will be his last chance to speak with her, he confesses his love and his letters to a confused and anguished Roxane. At the end of the play he dies nobly and with panache.

Rostand disregarded many of the historical and biographical details of the original Cyrano de Bergerac and altered other facts to mold his Cyrano to his own ideal of a romantic hero. First, he stated that Cyrano was actually from the Gascogne region in France, even though the historical figure was from the countryside surrounding Paris. This slight alteration was perhaps related to the legendary bravado and panache that Gascogne gentlemen cultivated. And while the historical Cyrano learned much about sophistication and wit from his cousin Madeleine Robineau in Paris, there is no evidence that he was in love with her, as Rostand's character is. The historical Cyrano also helped out a fellow soldier during the 1640 Siege of Arras by writing a few poetic letters to the man's newlywed wife, but the man was the count de Canvoye, not Madeleine Robineau's husband, Christian de Neuvillette. Furthermore, the historical Cyrano did go once to visit his cousin Madeleine in the convent, soon after she had retired there following her husband's tragic death at the Siege of Arras. But Cyrano was supposedly so upset by her face of mourning that he left and swore that he would never return to a convent again (he never did). Madeleine Robineau finally came to visit him when he had his head injury from the beam accident. However, he was apparently not pleased by her presence, because he asked another friend to take him away so that he could die by himself.

Some critics and historians from the turn-of-the-century period were dismayed by Rostand's liberal adaptations of the historical figure Cyrano, and they criticized several historical inaccuracies that they found in the play, as well. For example, in act 5 Cyrano's friend Ragueneau claims that the previous evening he heard some of Cyrano's lines in a performance of Molière's *Les Fourberies de Scapin* (Trickeries of Scapin). However, act 5 is supposed to take place in 1655, while Molière did not write or produce *Les Fourberies de Scapin* until seventeen years later in 1672. In general, however, the public and the press overlooked these historical details and loved the Rostandian hero who represented French honor, courage, wit, and dignity. At the close of the

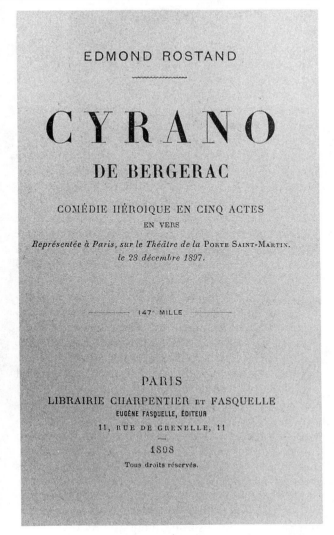

Title page for Rostand's best-known play, based on the life of a seventeenth-century French nobleman

tumultuous nineteenth century, France was in need of a hero like Cyrano. Although he was occasionally a troublemaker and even sometimes pretentious in his wordiness, he was also a devoted friend, faithful and humble to the point of saintliness and motivated only by honor and dignity. He was also good-natured and inspiring. The combination of these admirable qualities brought audiences to their feet in the Théâtre de la Porte Saint-Martin, where the standing ovation on opening night lasted almost one hour and called the actors back on stage forty times.

In addition to his courageous and faithful personality, Cyrano represents a well-rounded human being with qualities that appeal to all types of audiences: his physical abilities to engage in and excel at military maneuvers and fencing duels are matched by his mental ability to compose delightful poetry and to express himself in refined and intelligent verse. This double ability is best represented by the duel scene in act 1. Amid thrusts, parries, and blows Cyrano composes a ballad that, as he calmly explains to a stunned Valvert, is a poem of "three stanzas of eight lines" plus "an envoy of four [lines.]" Built into the poem's verses are mocking descriptions of Valvert's weakness, possible targets on Valvert's body for Cyrano's sword, and Cyrano's repeated and growing menace that "à la fin de l'envoi je touche" (at the end of the envoy, I touch). Indeed, at the end of the poem he does strike a final wounding blow to Valvert, and his men must carry the viscount away from the scene of the duel in defeat. The audiences who flocked to see *Cyrano de Bergerac* came for a variety of interests, and, from schoolchildren to society women to military fans, they were all pleased by the heroic character Cyrano.

For all these reasons Rostand's Cyrano became the fin-de-siècle superhero—both a literary and a military hero. An instant success, Cyrano has remained one of France's, and one of the world's, most beloved characters. However, it was not only the heroic character that drew crowds and critical acclaim; Rostand's linguistic virtuosity delighted audiences. In the area of meter Rostand used traditional alexandrine verse, usually divided into two equal hemistiches by a strong caesura. But he also interjected uneven alexandrine verses, divided into smaller groups of two or three syllables each. This strategy avoided any possibility of an annoying or repetitive sound in the verse, yet his frequent return to the traditional format of the alexandrine couplet reinforced the play's underlying discursive rhythm. In the area of rhyme Rostand created many refreshingly new ones by inventing words, rediscovering archaic words, rearranging words from common sayings, and adding unusual endings to words (verb tenses or arcane suffixes, for example). The result is certainly Rostand's most skillfully written play.

Rostand's *Cyrano de Bergerac* was well received in Paris and especially throughout the provinces. It is said that by the time they were celebrating the one-thousandth performance of *Cyrano de Bergerac* in Paris, it had been performed more than two thousand times in the provinces. Another sign of its popular success was indicated by the fact that the first parody version of the play, *Cyraunez de Blairgerac*, appeared in February 1898, only two months after the original play debuted in Paris. Two more parodies were produced before the end of 1898.

Cyrano de Bergerac was also well loved abroad and translated into several languages by the end of 1898. However, in the United States the play was banned from 1902 to 1920. A Chicago businessman,

Samuel Eberly Gross, believed that Rostand had plagiarized his own unpublished play, *The Merchant Prince of Cornville,* which he wrote in the 1870s and brought to Paris in 1889 and again in 1896, looking for a theater willing to produce it. Gross had left the manuscript with Benoît-Constant Coquelin's theater in 1889, where eight years later *Cyrano de Bergerac* was performed for the first time, and Gross believed that Rostand had read his manuscript and stolen ideas and lines from it. Included in the 1902 judgment were fifteen noted similarities between Gross's play and Rostand's *Cyrano de Bergerac,* including:

> In each the heroine has a suitor who cannot frame his lovemaking in acceptable language and is rebuffed for his stupidity. In each the stupid lover has a friend more ready with language than himself with whom he arranges to act for him as his unrecognized proxy in furthering the lovemaking. In each the proposition to act as such proxy comes from the one of more ready wit. In each the proxy gives specific instructions to the stupid suitor. In each these directions provide that the proxy shall station himself in the darkness below the heroine's balcony. In each it was arranged that the suitor would stand in the dim but partial view while the proxy should remain concealed near him and prompt him with the words to be used.

Although there were several scenes in common (a balcony scene that includes the two suitors and a duel scene that uses language in addition to arms, for examples), the main protagonist of the Gross play was not the witty "proxy" but rather the "stupid suitor." The balcony scene has been used in many plays and operas, including Pierre-Augustin Caron de Beaumarchais's *Le Barbier de Séville* (1775; translated as *The Barber of Seville*) and Wolfgang Amadeus Mozart's *Don Juan* (1787). Further, Gross's balcony scene is rather comical and ends with six people on the balcony (four men and two women), while Rostand's balcony scene is touching and romantic and is confined to three people (two men and one woman). In regard to the language duels, these two scenes also remain completely different, because Gross's duelists do not use any military arms at all. They both pick up dictionaries and scream the worst insults that they can find at each other until one falls over in defeat. In contrast, Rostand's duelists engage in a traditional sword fight while Cyrano composes a poem about their battle as he fights. These obvious differences were finally used in conjunction with the opinions published by Columbia University professor A. G. H. Spiers. In 1918 Spiers declared that the most obvious source for Rostand's *Cyrano de Bergerac* was the 1836 play *Roquelaure ou l'homme le plus laid de France* (Roquelaure or the Ugliest Man in France) by Adolphe de Leuven, Charles de

Livry, and L. L. Lhérie, which had had a revival in Paris in 1872. Following this new information and a closer look at the similarities between the two plays, the 1920 decision overturned the 1902 ban on *Cyrano de Bergerac* in the United States and allowed its performance by Edward Vroom in New York that year.

Throughout the twentieth century there have been many performances of the play, which has also inspired a ballet, a lyric opera, and several film adaptations. In the 1980s actors Gerard Depardieu and Steve Martin both took on the title role in French and American film versions of the play. The 1989 French version, titled *Cyrano de Bergerac,* is set in seventeenth-century France and adheres strictly to the script of the Rostand play. The 1987 American version, titled *Roxanne,* is set in late-twentieth-century America and has several feminist and postmodern twists in the plot, although many of the best-known scenes are still included. In *Roxanne,* for example, the main character, C. D. Bales, lists twenty inventive ways to describe his enormous nose (as in Rostand's act 1, scene 4). Bales also helps a handsome younger man, Chris McConnell, to woo Roxane with letters; Bales also whispers lines to Chris under a balcony at night (as in Rostand's act 3, scene 7). Although he duels with a tennis racket rather than a sword, Bales also insults his foe poetically while engaging in a mock battle (as in Rostand's act 1, scene 4). The film's main character also falls out of a tree and then claims that he has just returned from a trip to outer space (as in Rostand's act 3, scene 11), but with different intentions than those of Cyrano de Bergerac in Rostand's play. The popular and critical success of both these recent films attests to the universal appeal of the Cyrano character that Rostand created.

Following the overwhelming success of *Cyrano de Bergerac* Rostand wished to create a new type of hero for the stage. He thus created *L'Aiglon* in 1900 (translated as *The Eaglet,* 1921), based on the historical figure Franz, Duke of Reichenstadt and king of Rome. Franz was the son of Napoleon Bonaparte and Napoleon's second wife, Marie-Louise of Austria, and he spent most of his brief life (1811–1832) in exile in Austria, even though there were several political movements in France during that time to bring him back to the throne as Napoleon II. This tragic hero of the Romantic era was a familiar figure for Rostand, because a portrait of the exiled youth had hung over Rostand's bed during his childhood in Marseilles.

The play is structured in a series of tableaux rather than acts, each one in a separate mood and space. During the first act, which takes place at Marie-Louise's villa in Baden, all precautions have

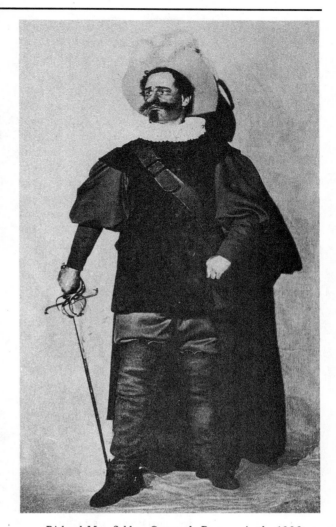

Richard Mansfield as Cyrano de Bergerac in the 1898 American production of Rostand's most popular play

been taken by Metternich, the chancellor of Austria, and by Marie-Louise herself, to assure that nothing French is mentioned in the presence of Franz. Marie-Louise, enjoying her "exile" in her native homeland, does not want to stir up dreams of power and the French throne in her son, because these types of ambitions would upset her own life of pleasures and ease. Metternich, of course, does not want to see France rise up and take over Europe as it had under the control of Napoleon. For him, Austrian power must be preserved at all costs. Marie-Louise's only exceptions to this anti-French rule in her home are a French tailor and a seamstress, whom she has smuggled in from Paris so that she and her son Franz may wear the latest French fashions. In spite of the severe censorship, however, Franz demonstrates to his tutors much knowledge about his father's political strategies and the history of France, both of which have been rigorously omitted from his education. At the end of act 1 the audience discovers the source of his knowledge: Fanny Elssler, who is both Franz's lover and his tutor in French and Napoleonic history.

Acts 2 through 6 take place one year later, at the Schoenbrunn Palace and Park in Vienna. At first Franz is disappointed with his supporters, thinking that they have abandoned him and his plans for a glorious return to France as emperor. His friend, the Chevalier de Prokesch-Osten, boosts his spirits and tells him that his allies are working secretly, that he should not despair. In the third act Franz disguises himself as a shepherd and appears before Emperor Franz of Austria, his grandfather. Although he convinces his grandfather that he should become emperor of France, Metternich enters and persuades the grandfather to invoke many restrictions and conditions on the duke's power, thus rendering him a mere figurehead, a puppet of the Austrian empire. Undeterred, Franz later that day leaves one of Napoleon's black hats on a map of Europe, signaling to the conspirators that he wishes to go ahead with their plans for an escape to Paris. In a stunning scene Metternich discovers the black hat and lets loose a long soliloquy against Napoleon's power and fame. When Franz enters during this diatribe, he appears so weak and sickly that Metternich gleefully scorns the duke, telling him that he will never become Napoleon II. During the costume ball in act 4 Franz appears briefly, even though his pride has been wounded by Metternich's harsh statements about his inferiority to his father.

Despite this moral setback his allies plan an escape, and at the outset of act 5 he meets with his conspirators on a plain outside Vienna to begin the journey to Paris. However, at the moment of their departure Franz discovers that his cousin and ally, the Countess Camarata, who is currently disguised as the duke to distract the police from his escape, has been threatened by murderers. He refuses to leave without first helping her, and his chivalrous delay causes the entire trip to fail; he is arrested soon after by the Viennese chief of police. The defeat is too much for the duke's fragile health, and the final act takes place at the duke's deathbed, where he receives publicly the last rites, then asks that his "Austrian family" leave him. He requests that French folk songs be sung and that General Hartmann read aloud from a history book about his proclamation as king of Rome by the Emperor Napoleon. Franz then dies and the curtain falls.

Rostand's portrayal of this Romantic hero cleverly combines the *mal de siècle* of the Romantic era and the ennui and decadence of the fin-de-siècle era. For example, in act 1, when the anonymous French tailor reveals to Franz the secret plans that he and the "seamstress" (actually the Countess Camarata, Franz's cousin) have devised to help him escape to France, Franz wants to know who the tailor is. His response in act 1, scene 10, typifies not only the lost and wandering youth of the Romantic era but also the bored extravagance of fin-de-siècle decadence:

> Ce que je suis? Je ne sais pas. Voilà mon mal.
> Suis-je? Je voudrais être,—et ce n'est pas commode.
> Je lis Victor Hugo. Je récite son Ode
> A la Colonne. Je vous conte tout cela
> Parce que tout cela, mon Dieu, c'est toute la
> Jeunesse! Je m'ennuie avec extravagance;
> Et je suis, Monseigneur, artiste et Jeune France.

> (What am I? I know not. There's nothing real.
> Am I? I would be, were the charges light!
> I read from Hugo, loving to recite
> Ode to the Column . . . all this, I declare,
> Because . . . Lord, Lord! It's Youth! It's in the air!
> I bore myself, Oh with extravagance;
> I am an artist, Highness, and Young France.)

This young man's confused state of ennui appeals to a deep-rooted feeling in the duke's soul, and he continues the tailor's lament, claiming that he too suffers from "le malaise dont souffre en ce moment la jeunesse française" (the malaise that French youth are suffering at this moment), that is: 'l'inquiétude sourde" (worry), "la mauvaise fierté" (false pride), and "le dédain de ceux qui peuvent vivre satisfaits" (disdain for those who are able to live satisfied). Even though he begins to take more-decisive actions, the character of Franz does not develop much from this original position. His basic outlook is that the world needs a new emperor, Napoleon II, and that as long as he remains in exile both doubt and unease will reign in the souls of Europe's youth.

Beginning in 1830, for the play by Eugène Sue and Philippe Auguste Alfred Pittaud de Forges titled *Le Fils de l'homme* (The Son of Man), the young Duke Franz was traditionally played by a cross-dressed actress. For Rostand's *L'Aiglon* the title role was rendered by none other than Sarah Bernhardt, his favorite actress. *L'Aiglon* was Rostand's last great popular success, and although the critics generally enjoyed the beautiful lyrical poetry of the verse, they were severe about his "deviations" from historical truth. In particular René Doumic (Rostand's literature teacher at the Collège Stanislas from 1884 to 1886) and Frédéric Masson, both in 1900, wrote that Rostand had taken too much literary license and did not respect historical details. In 1927, however, historian Gaston-Louis Malécot published a study titled *Les Sources de "l'Aiglon"* that proved that Rostand meticulously followed a variety of historical sources and produced a work that was simultaneously an accurate history and a piece of creative fiction.

At the turn of the century Rostand's health began to decline as he suffered the onset of a pulmonary congestion, yet he still created his well-received *L'Aiglon* and was awarded the prestigious Légion d'Honneur. In 1901 he was again honored by being the youngest member ever elected to the Académie Française, but the official ceremony and reception were postponed until 1903 because of his failing health. After several prolonged stays in the Pyrenean spa town of Cambo he produced *Chantecler* in 1910 (translated as *Chanticleer*, 1921). He also published in 1910 his second collection of poems, *Le Cantique de l'aile* (The Canticle of the Wing).

In *Chantecler*, written ten years after the first production of *L'Aiglon*, Rostand produced a drama about the mighty cock and his duty to usher in each new morning with his call "cocorico!" Chantecler worships the sun and light above all else. In act 1 he meets the exotic and beautiful Pheasant Hen, who has flown into the barnyard to escape a hunting dog who chased her out of the forest where she lives. Chantecler is attracted to her beauty, but she is unimpressed with him. At the end of act 1 and the beginning of act 2 the night animals (owls, cat, mole, and others) reveal their hatred of the cock, since he brings about the daylight that blinds them. They conspire to kill Chantecler through a special plot with the Peacock, who has agreed to bring a variety of specially bred cocks to the socialite Guinea Hen's party the following day. Included in the amazing array of cocks will be a champion gamecock named White Pile, who has killed roosters in the United States and Europe.

In act 3 the Guinea Hen's party begins peacefully, but Chantecler arrives and engages in a fight with White Pile, who almost kills Chantecler. However, during the battle a hawk circles overhead, causing White Pile and all the other birds to run for cover under Chantecler's wings. After his brave act Chantecler's strength is recovered, and White Pile injures himself and limps off defeated. In act 4 Chantecler has agreed to go live in the forest with the Pheasant Hen, but she is jealous of his continuing devotion to the sun and light. One night, when he is mourning the Nightingale's death, she comforts him under her wing until after the dawn has arrived to prove to him that he is not needed to make the sun rise. Chantecler cannot bear this announcement and returns to the farm to

Franz, Duke of Reichenstadt, the subject of Rostand's play L'Aiglon

continue his "true calling." However, as he is leaving, the Woodpecker spots a poacher hunting nearby, and the Pheasant Hen, in a heroic gesture, uses herself as a distraction so that Chantecler might live. She is caught in a snare and must sacrifice her life so that Chantecler may continue to usher in the sun and the light. She dies happy with the thought that he will be able to go on.

Chantecler did not enjoy the same critical and popular acclaim that Rostand's earlier plays had received. The barnyard setting and animal costumes were perhaps too unusual, or the symbolic nature of the play may have been too obvious for audiences to appreciate. For example, Rostand's critique of Parisian high society, rather openly displayed during the Guinea Hen's party in act 3, does appear exaggerated, superficial, and very farcical. *Chantecler* was also the first nonhistorical play that Rostand wrote, and the lack of historical characters may have also contributed to its less enthusiastic reception. Linguistically, however, it is probably one of Rostand's richest pieces, with exquisite plays on words and versification and poems at the beginning of each act to set the mood for the following scenes. Yet it was not often studied until recently, when in 1987 a new English translation was published in the United States by Kay Nolte Smith.

In 1910 Rostand also wrote his last play, *La Dernière Nuit de Don Juan* (translated as *The Last Night of Don Juan*, 1929). Unpublished and unperformed until after his death, this play, like *Chantecler,* did not become either a critical or popular success. Its plot is rather simple: ten years after making a pact with the devil, Don Juan is supposed to give up his life of seduction and abandon his soul to the devil. While waiting in Venice for the trip to Hell, Don Juan begins detailing his art of seduction. As he speaks, he throws his list of names of the 1,003 women that he has seduced into the Adriatic Sea, and they return as gondolas filled with the ghosts of the women. The devil tauntingly asks him to name some of these masked ghosts, and each time that Don Juan tries he is wrong. After a series of tests it becomes obvious that Don Juan's life has not been the successful adventure of which he had originally boasted but rather a life without true love or connections with other human souls. In the end the devil turns Don Juan into a puppet for eternity, requiring him to beat other puppets with his stick and play the fool.

In this play, as with *Chantecler,* the symbolism was obvious and heavy, but to weigh down the play further, the poetry is also sometimes ponderous and even obscure. The following example from part 1, scene 6, illustrates the lack of fluidity and invention in his poetry that sometimes flaws this last play:

Don Juan
J'ai serré contre moi leurs âmes toutes nues.
Pas un ne lisait mieux dans leur jeu! Qui Lauzun?
Richelieu? . . . Des enfants qui me singeaient! Pas un
Ne leur a fait pétrir, par sa vision clair,
Tant de petits mouchoirs en tampons de colère!
Ah! Je peux déchirer la liste!
                    Diable
                              Oui c'est la.
Déchirons-la!
              Don Juan
              Je sais les noms!
              Diable
                              Dechirons-la!

(*Don Juan*
            I grasped their naked souls.
Who understood them better? Richelieu?
Lauzun? Bah, they were children aping me!
No piercing gaze ever made women twist
So many little, lacy handkerchiefs
To wads of rage! I can tear up the list!
              The Devil
Yes, let us tear it up!
              Don Juan
              I know the names!
              The Devil
                              Let's tear it up!)

In Rostand's last two works, *Chantecler* and *La Dernière Nuit de Don Juan,* two very new types of main characters appear. Chantecler, the rooster (symbolizing France), is proud, superstitious, and content with his humble surroundings. The Pheasant Hen takes him on an adventure to the forest, but Chantecler's thoughts continually return to his familiar barnyard setting while he is on this brief and only trip away from the farm. Even when the Pheasant Hen demonstrates that his crow is not necessary for the sunrise, Chantecler stubbornly insists that it is his duty to usher in the sun every morning. As he is about to fight the dangerous White Pile, he encourages all the Guinea Hen's guests to laugh at him, claiming that mockery will make him a better fighter. All these characteristics—pride, stubbornness, base humility—are quite different from the typical Rostandian traits of humor, intelligence, and dignity that are found in most of his main characters, such as Cyrano, the Eaglet, or the Romantics. In Don Juan one finds even more pride, more stubborn behavior, and more overt ineptness. This new character type is not as easily admired or even criticized; it leaves the reader or spectator distanced from the personality.

After a pulmonary embolism in 1910 and a car accident in 1911 Rostand's health continued to decline. He had nevertheless managed to finish *La Dernière Nuit de Don Juan* in 1910. During World War I Rostand was unable to fight but went to the battlefields and then came home to write long dramatic poems describing what he had witnessed there. This experience resulted in his third and last collection of poems, *Le Vol de la Marseillaise* (The Flight of the Marseillaise, 1914). Rostand died in 1918 at the age of fifty, several weeks after the war ended.

Although his last two plays may not have inspired audiences or readers, the majority of Rostand's plays have exhilarated audiences worldwide. After a century of productions, translations, adaptations, and readings of *Cyrano de Bergerac,* this play continues to move spectators. Moreover, Rostand's work has influenced twentieth-century culture through its emphasis on noble and courageous characters and its artistic use of language. Although he is mainly known for *Cyrano de Bergerac,* Rostand's renown is international, and his characters are considered quintessentially "French" throughout the world, for their bravado and their finesse.

However, though Rostand's popular appeal has continued, the critical reception of his work has declined throughout the twentieth century. For example, the centennial year of the first performance of *Cyrano de Bergerac* (1897–1997) passed by with relatively little notice from the critical and scholarly press. Although there were several productions of the play in 1997, few publications or conferences were devoted to the study of Rostand and his work during the year. Thus one must conclude that Rostand's achievements in the literary world have been perhaps unfairly forgotten by twentieth-century scholars of French literature, since his plays and his characters symbolize French culture in many aspects.

Bibliographies:

Caroline de Margerie, *Edmond Rostand ou le baiser de la gloire* (Paris: Grasset, 1997);

Roland Dargeles and Carole Garcia, *Edmond Rostand: panache et tourments* (Helette: Jean Curutchet, 1997).

Biographies:

Julius Haraszti, *Edmond Rostand* (Paris: Fontemoing, 1913);

J. Edmond Karsenty, *Rostand* (Marseilles, 1919);

Jean Suberville, *Edmond Rostand* (Paris: Etienne Chiron, 1921);

Pierre Apestuguy, *La Vie profonde d'Edmond Rostand* (Paris: Charpentier et Fasquelle, 1929);

Rosemonde Gérard, *Edmond Rostand* (Paris: Charpentier et Fasquelle, 1935);

Emile Ripert, *Edmond Rostand, sa vie, son oeuvre* (Paris: Hachette, 1968);

Marc Andry, *Edmond Rostand: Le panache et la gloire* (Paris: Plon, 1986).

References:

Alba della Fazia Amoia, *Edmond Rostand* (Boston: Twayne, 1978);

J. W. Grieve, *L'Oeuvre dramatique d'Edmond Rostand* (Paris: Les Oeuvres Représentatives, 1931);

Samuel Gross, *The Merchant Prince of Cornville* (Chicago: R. R. Donnelly and Sons, 1896);

Louis Haugmard, *Edmond Rostand* (Paris: E. Sansot, 1910);

André Lautier and Fernand Keller, *Edmond Rostand: son oeuvre* (Paris: La Nouvelle revue critique, 1924);

Adolphede Leuven, Charles de Livrey, and L. L. Lhérie, *Roquelaure ou l'homme le plus laid de France* (Paris: Magasin Théâtral, 1836);

Gaston-Louis Malécot, *Les Sources de "l'Aiglon"* (Paris: Bureau Général de Traductions et de Recherches Documentaires, 1927);

Dorothy Page, *Edmond Rostand et la legende napoléonienne dans "l'Aiglon"* (Paris: H. Champion, 1928);

Hobart Ryland, *The Sources of the Play* Cyrano de Bergerac (New York: Institute of French Studies, 1936);

A. G. H. Spiers, "Introduction," in *Cyrano de Bergerac,* by Rostand (New York: Oxford University Press, 1938), pp. vii–xxvi;

Spiers, "Rostand as Idealist," *Columbia University Quarterly,* 20 (1918): 155–169.

George Sand
(Armantine-Aurore-Lucile Dupin)
(1 July 1804 – 8 June 1876)

Gay Smith (Manifold)
Wesleyan University

See also the Sand entry in *DLB 119: Nineteenth-Century French Fiction Writers: Romanticism and Realism, 1800–1860.*

PLAY PRODUCTIONS: *Cosima,* Paris, Comédie-Française, 29 April 1840;

Le Roi attend, Paris, Comédie-Française, 6 April 1848;

François le champi, Paris, Théâtre de l'Odéon, 23 November 1849;

Claudie, Paris, Théâtre de la Porte Saint-Martin, 11 January 1851;

Molière, Paris, Théâtre de la Gaîté, 10 May 1851;

Le Mariage de Victorine, Paris, Théâtre du Gymnase, 26 November 1851;

Les Vacances de Pandolphe, Paris, Théâtre du Gymnase, 3 March 1852;

Le Démon du Foyer, Paris, Théâtre du Gymnase, 1 September 1852;

Le Pressoir, Paris, Théâtre du Gymnase, 13 September 1853;

Mauprat, Paris, Théâtre de l'Odéon, 28 November 1853;

Flaminio, Paris, Théâtre du Gymnase, 31 October 1854;

Maître Favilla, Théâtre de l'Odéon, 15 September 1855;

Lucie, Paris, Théâtre du Gymnase, 15 February 1856;

Françoise, Paris, Théâtre du Gymnase, 3 April 1856;

Comme il vous plaira, Paris, Comédie-Française, 12 April 1856;

Marguerite de Sainte-Gemme, Paris, Théâtre du Gymnase, 23 April 1859;

Le Pavé, Paris, Théâtre du Gymnase, 18 March 1862;

Le Marquis de Villemer, Paris, Théâtre de l'Odéon, 29 February 1864;

Le Lis du Japon, Paris, Théâtre du Vaudeville, 14 August 1866;

George Sand, 1864 (photograph by Nadar)

L'Autre, Paris, Théâtre de l'Odéon, 25 February 1870;

Un Bienfait n'est jamais perdu, Paris, Théâtre de Cluny, 7 November 1872.

BOOKS: *Rose et Blanche,* by Sand and Jules Sandeau, 5 volumes (Paris: Renault, 1831);

Indiana, 2 volumes (Paris: Roret et Dupuy, 1832); translated by George B. Ives (Philadelphia: Barrie & Son, 1900);

Valentine, 2 volumes (Paris: Dupuy, 1832); translated by Ives (Philadelphia: Barrie & Son, 1900);

Lélia, 2 volumes (Paris: Dupuy, 1833); revised edition, 1 volume (Paris: Bonnaire, 1839); translated by Maria Espinosa (Bloomington: Indiana University Press, 1978);

Jacques (Paris: Bonnaire, 1834);

Leone Leoni (Paris: Bonnaire, 1835); translated by Ives (Philadelphia: Barrie & Son, 1900);

André (Paris: Bonnaire, 1835);

Simon (Paris: Bonnaire, 1836);

Lettres d'un voyageur (Brussels: Scribe, Tecmen & Compagnie, 1837); translated by Eliza A. Ashurst as *Letters of a Traveller,* edited by Matilda M. Hays (London: E. Churton, 1847); translated by Sacha Rabinovitch and Patricia Thomson (Harmondsworth, U.K.: Penguin, 1987);

Mauprat (Paris: Bonnaire, 1837); translated by Stanley Young (London: Heinemann, n.d.); translated by Hays (London: E. Churton, 1847);

Spiridion (Paris: Bonnaire, 1839; revised edition, Paris: Perrotin, 1842);

Les Sept Cordes de la lyre (Paris: Bonnaire, 1840); translated by George A. Kennedy in *A Woman's Version of the Faust Legend: The Seven Strings of the Lyre* (Chapel Hill: University of North Carolina Press, 1989);

Gabriel (Paris: Bonnaire, 1840); translated by Gay Smith Manifold in *George Sand's Gabriel* (Westport, Conn. & London: Greenwood Press, 1992);

Le Compagnon du Tour de France, 2 volumes (Paris: Perrotin, 1841); translated by Hays as *The Companion of the Tour of France* (London: Churton, 1847);

Horace (Paris: L. de Porter, 1842);

Consuelo (Paris: L. de Porter, 1843); translated by Francis G. Shaw, 2 volumes (Boston: Ticknor, 1846); translated by Fayette Robinson (Greenwich, Conn.: Fawcett, 1961);

Teverino (Paris: Calmann-Lévy, n.d.; Brussels: Société Belge de Librairie, 1845);

La Comtesse de Rudolstadt (Paris: L. de Porter, 1844); translated by Shaw (Boston: Ticknor, 1847);

Jeanne (Brussels: Hauman, 1844);

Le Meunier d'Angibault (Paris: Desessart, 1845); translated by Mary E. Dewey as *The Miller of Angibault* (Boston: Roberts, 1863);

Isidora (Paris: Souverain, 1846);

Le Péché de Monsieur Antoine (Brussels: Lebèque et Sacré fils, 1846);

La Mare au diable (Paris: E. Proux, [1846?]); translated by Antonia Cowan as *Devil's Pool* (London: Blackie, 1966); translated by Frank Porter as *The Haunted Pool* (Berkeley, Cal.: Shameless Hussy Press, 1976);

Lucrezia Floriani (Paris: E. Proux, 1846);

François le champi (Brussels: Meline, Cans & Compagnie, 1848); translated by Eirene Collis as *The Country Waif* (Lincoln: University of Nebraska Press, 1977);

La Petite Fadette, 2 volumes (Paris: Michel Lévy, 1849); translated as *Little Fadette. A Domestic Story* (London: G. Slater, 1849); translated by Hays as *Fadette. A Domestic Story* (New York: Putnam, 1851); translated by Eva Figes as *Little Fadette* (London: Blackie, 1967);

Le Château des désertes (Paris: Michel Lévy, 1851);

Les Maîtres sonneurs (Paris: Cadot, 1853); translated by Katherine Wormeley as *The Bagpipers* (Boston: Little, Brown, 1890);

Histoire de ma vie, 4 volumes (Paris: Lecou, 1854–1855); excerpts translated by Maria E. McKaye as *My Convent Life* (Chicago: Academy Chicago, 1977); excerpts translated by Dan Hofstadter as *My Life* (New York: Harper & Row, 1979); translated and edited by Thelma Jurgrau as *Story of My Life* (Binghamton, N.Y.: SUNY Press, 1991);

La Daniella (Paris: Librairie nouvelle, 1857);

Elle et lui (Paris: Hachette, 1859); translated by Ives as *She and He* (Philadelphia: Barrie & Son, 1900);

Le Marquis de Villemer (Paris: Naumbourg et Paetz, 1860–1861);

Valvèdre (Paris: Michel Lévy, 1861);

Tamaris (Paris: Michel Lévy, 1862);

Mademoiselle la Quintinie (Paris: Michel Lévy, 1863);

Le Marquis de Villemer [play] (Paris: Michel Lévy, 1864);

La Confession d'une jeune fille (Paris, 1865);

Le Dernier Amour (Paris: Michel Lévy, 1867);

Mademoiselle Merquem (Paris: Michel Lévy, 1868);

Les Mississippiens (Paris: Michel Lévy, 1869);

L'Autre (Paris: Michel Lévy, 1870);

Pierre qui roule (Paris: Michel Lévy, 1870).

Césarine Dietrich (Paris: Michel Lévy, 1871);

Nanon (Paris: Michel Lévy, 1872);

Contes d'une grand-mère, volume 1 (Paris: Michel Lévy, 1873); volume 2 (Paris: Calmann-Lévy, 1876); translated by Margaret Bloom (Philadelphia & London: Lippincott, 1930);

Ma Soeur Jeanne (Paris: Michel Lévy frères, 1874); translated by R. S. Crocker as *My Sister Jeannie* (Boston: Roberts, 1874);

La Laitière et le pot au lait, in *Journal le Temps* (Paris: Schiller, 1875), pp. 65–80;

Une Conspiration en 1537, in *La Genese de Lorenzaccio,* edited by Paul Dimoff (Paris: Droz, 1936).

Editions and Collections: *Œuvres complètes de George Sand,* 24 volumes (Paris: Bonnaire, 1836–1840); 1 volume (Paris: Magen et Comon, 1841); 2 volumes (Paris: Souverain, 1842);

Œuvres complètes de George Sand, 16 volumes, revised by Sand (Paris: Perrotin, 1842–1844; Paris: Garnier, 1847);

Œuvres complètes de George Sand illustrées par Tony Johannot et Maurice Sand, 9 volumes (Paris: Hetzel, 1851–1856);

Œuvres de George Sand, 109 volumes (Paris: Hetzel-Lecou, 1852–1855; Paris: Michel Lévy, 1856–1857);

Théâtre complet, 4 volumes (Paris: Calmann-Lévy, 1866)—volume 1 comprises *Cosima, Le Roi attend, François le champi, Claudie,* and *Molière;* volume 2 comprises *Le Mariage de Victorine, Les Vacances de Pandolphe, Le Demon du foyer,* and *Le Pressoir;* volume 3 comprises *Mauprat, Flaminio, Maître Favilla,* and *Lucie;* volume 4 comprises *Françoise, Comme il vous plaira,* and *Marguerite de Sainte-Gemme;*

Théâtre de Nohant: Le Drac, Plutus, Le Pavé, La Nuit de Noel, Marielle (Paris: Michel Lévy, 1865);

Questions d'art et de littérature (Paris: Calmann-Lévy, 1878);

Questions politiques et sociales (Paris: Calmann-Lévy, 1879);

Masterpieces of George Sand, 20 volumes, translated by George B. Ives (Philadelphia: Barrie & Son, 1900–1902);

Voyage en Auvergne, in *Œuvres autobiographiques,* 2 volumes, edited by Georges Lubin (Paris: Gallimard, 1970–1971);

Œuvres complètes, 33 volumes, edited by Lubin (Paris: Aujourd'hui/Les Introuvables, 1976–1979);

George Sand: In Her Own Words, translated and edited by Joseph Barry (Garden City, N.Y.: Doubleday, 1979).

George Sand (Armantine-Aurore-Lucile Dupin) is often remembered for her work as a novelist, but she devoted much of her abundant energy to drama and the theater as well, producing twenty-one plays for the professional theaters in Paris and at least ninety plays and scenarios for her private theater at her home in Nohant. From Sand's twenty-five volumes of correspondence emerges a detailed chronicle of her extensive work in both the professional theater and her private, experimental one. Indeed, several of her more than one hundred novels were written as plays but published as closet or armchair dramas. Several novels use the theater as their settings. One, *Pierre qui roule* (Rolling Stone, 1870), focuses on the training of professional actors, and the other, *Le Château des désertes* (Castle in the Wilderness, 1851), explores the education of young adults in a private theater at home. Many of Sand's essays and reviews relate specifically to drama and theater. Her playwriting career spanned forty years, from the early 1830s, when she wrote *Une Conspiration en 1537* (1936), to 1872, when the last of her twenty-one Paris premieres was produced, appropriately titled *Un Bienfait n'est jamais perdu* (A Good Deed Is Never Lost).

Interest in Sand's life and works waned in the first three quarters of the twentieth century and then revived after the centennial of her death, with a major retrospective at the Bibliothèque Nationale marking that occasion. Since 1976 many biographies and studies about Sand and her work have appeared, along with new editions of many of her novels and a few of her plays, as well. Even so, Sand's reputation as a literary giant of nineteenth-century France, while acknowledged in her own day, albeit reluctantly by her politically conservative enemies, has yet to be fully appreciated. She is considered too idealistic, even moralistic, for late-twentieth-century taste; only two or three of her novels appear on academic reading lists. Even less attention has been given to her dramas.

Sand readily acknowledged that she wrote for her contemporaries about issues that were of immediate concern to them. Her plays were not conservative reinforcements of the status quo but radical efforts to reform society and include the working classes in her audience. Sand created new heroes for the stage that included socialist democrats, abolitionists, artists, highly educated women, proletariat poets, and migrant workers. Their impact was immediate and strong. Sand participated in the movement to reform the theater and in some instances paved the way for major changes in dramatic form and theater practice, such as the shifts from Romanticism to realism and from melodrama's huge public theaters to the more experimental small-theater movement. She was admired by her peers and emulated by her successors. Between the revolutions of 1830 and 1848, the apex and demise of French Romanticism, Sand became an admired colleague of Victor Hugo and Alexandre Dumas *père.* Later, between the revolutions of 1848 and 1870, she pioneered realism on the stage and became an inspiration to Gustave Flaubert and Alexandre Dumas *fils,* who called her "Mon Maître" (My Teacher).

George Sand was pleased to claim that she had no bourgeois blood, being the daughter of a patrician father, Maurice Dupin, and a bohemian mother, Sophie Delaborde (whose father had been a bird seller along the quais of the Seine). Sand's parents were married one month before she, Aurore Dupin, was born in Paris on 1 July 1804. Four years later when Maurice died tragically young (his neck was broken when he was thrown from his horse), Sand's paternal grandmother and namesake negotiated guardianship of the young Sand and raised her at her Nohant country house in Berry, with private tutors and a convent school (a Scottish order). Sand at seventeen lost her grandmother and was reclaimed by her mother, who took her to Paris. A year later Sand married and subsequently bore two children, Maurice and Solange. She ended her eight-year marriage by a costly legal separation (divorce remained illegal in France during Sand's entire lifetime) but retained the estate left her by her grandmother. The Nohant manor house passed to Sand's own granddaughter, the third Aurore, who willed it to France upon her death in 1962. It now stands as a national treasure and contains Sand's little theater intact.

Sand's career as a playwright began and ended with revolution in France. The failure of the 1830 revolution coincided with the failure of Sand's marriage, and in her disillusionment with both events she wrote her first play, about an assassination. In her correspondence Sand, the would-be anarchist, not yet thirty, admits to hating all political factions and wishes she had the power to harm them. She speculates that had she been born a man she would be dangerous. Instead she wrote a play, *Une Conspiration en 1537,* about such an anarchist, the Renaissance prince Lorenzaccio, who assassinated Duke Alexander de Medici. The character Lorenzo acts out Sand's passion and rage, making the culminating scene, the assassination, a violent consummation of "betrothal," with no other goal than the act itself. Lorenzo admits that if, as a result of the assassination, he were to be made duke, he would do good without any pleasure and maybe evil without any remorse. His rebellion, like Sand's, turns to the gall of disenchantment. Written in 1831 and not published until 1936, the manuscript of *Une Conspiration en 1537* was given to Alfred de Musset as a lover's gift in 1833, when the couple began their two-year affair. That same year Musset took the play and rewrote it into his full-length masterpiece, *Lorenzaccio,* keeping the same principal characters and events as Sand's and ending with the spectacular assassination scene. Musset's piece was first staged in 1896 with Sarah Bernhardt in the principal role. In a 1977 production of Musset's *Lorenzaccio,* French director Pierre Vielhescase chose to stage de-

Actor-director Pierre Bocage, who contributed to Sand's success as a playwright (photograph by Delbarre)

tails from Sand's assassination scene from *Une Conspiration en 1537,* where Duke Alexander bites his assassin's thumb and will not let loose, chewing it as Lorenzo stabs him. With Sand's dramatization of a revolutionary's embitterment, she contributed to the creation of one of the theater's great antiheroes, Lorenzaccio, contemporary with Georg Buchner's Danton and Woyczek.

Sand's second play, *Aldo le rimeur* (Aldo the Rhymer), was published in 1833 in *La Revue des deux monde* and though never staged probably gave rise to the celebrated staircase scene in Alfred de Vigny's *Chatterton,* performed by Sand's close friend, Marie Dorval, in 1835. The set designer for *Chatterton* credited Dorval with the inspiration for the staircase, and decades later Emile Zola recalled the impact of Dorval's use of the staircase, which became for Zola a character in and of itself. The innovative design element originates in *Aldo le rimeur:* the poor poet living in a garret sleeps fitfully while his sick mother attempts to descend the staircase but falls in a heap, dead, at the bottom. Dor-

Sand's private theater at her country house in Nohant ("Recueil de principaux types créés avec leur costumes sur le Théâtre de Nohant," Bibliothèque Nationale, Départment des Estampes, Réserves, Tb471; 1: 195)

val enacts the same staircase stage business while performing the role of Kitty Bell, who loves Thomas Chatterton; when she comes to the top of the stairs, distraught and terrified at having just discovered Chatterton dead, a suicide by poisoning, she recoils, her back to the banister, and weightlessly slides to the bottom like a wounded bird. This highly charged and admired theatrical moment appears to have been another of Sand's gifts to a lover, this one to Dorval.

The life of Aldo the Rhymer, unlike Chatterton's, does not end in suicide, though Aldo makes two attempts. The first act ends with Aldo's plan to drown himself; the second begins with the queen and her entourage fishing him out of the river. Aldo becomes the queen's consort, but failing to amuse her sufficiently, he contemplates suicide again. This time the court astrologer persuades him to wait until he has seen the lunar eclipse that night. So the play ends with Aldo and the astrologer retreating from society to a mountaintop to view the moon, all the while engaged in a lively debate about the merits of art and science, and ultimately agreeing that they are the same—truth.

Aldo le rimeur represents Sand's earliest experiment with what she came to call *drame fantastique* in an essay of that title published in 1839. The scenes alternate between monologues and dialogues: Aldo's monologues reveal his interior world; the dialogues dramatize Aldo's conflicts with external characters, some of whom are realistic and others of whom represent Aldo's interior psychological oppositions. In her essay about drame fantastique Sand argued that George Gordon, Lord Byron, in *Manfred* (1817), Johann Wolfgang von Goethe in *Faust* (1808, 1832), and Adam Mickiewicz in *Konrad* (1828) developed this new kind of play.

Sand's third play, *Les Sept Cordes de la lyre* (The Seven Strings of the Lyre, 1840; translated by

George A. Kennedy in *A Woman's Version of the Faust Legend: The Seven Strings of the Lyre,* 1989), comes even closer to her effort to dramatize the metaphysical. Written and published in the first year of Sand's celebrated liaison with Frédéric Chopin in 1838, the play uses music to evoke the fantastic. Harp music and singing associated with the principal character Hélène, a muse-priestess, alternate with dry and skeptical discourse, decidedly unmusical, associated with the philosopher-teacher Albertus. Mephistopheles emerges from an extinguished lamp in act 1 to try to get the lyre. Not being able to touch it because of its magic, he brings in a troupe of artists who in turn can neither make music on the lyre nor carry it away. It plays beautifully and mysteriously only when held by Hélène and without her touching the strings. Through the course of the remaining four acts Albertus tries to discover its mystery by eliminating two strings at a time (there are seven total). In act 2, when Hélène is in a garden, the lyre plays full harmony until Albertus breaks the two gold strings, which represent faith and contemplation of the infinite. In act 3 the lyre plays a song about "resigned hearts" while Hélène sits on a riverbank; then Albertus breaks the two silver strings, which symbolize hope and nature's beauties. In act 4, with Hélène atop a church spire sitting on the pedestal of the archangel's statue, the harp plays with the last three strings of man's industry, but Hélène answers with man's destruction and throws the lyre from her perch. When Albertus recovers the lyre he breaks the two steel strings that stand for man's inventiveness. Act 5 shows Hélène silently staring out a window in her room where she herself breaks the one last bronze string, which represents love, and dies. At that moment Albertus recognizes his love for Hélène and is liberated from his false philosophy and dreams, acknowledging that love is the only thing that can be infinite in the heart of humanity. He returns to his students saying that the lyre is broken, but its harmony has passed into his soul, and it is time to get to work. This poetic drama was not produced on the stage, so one must imagine the music that might accompany it. With its correspondence of visual and aural images *Sept Cordes de la lyre* was the culmination of Sand's efforts to write a metaphysical *drame fantastique.* To appease her critics, especially her editor, she tried in her next play to be less philosophical and more romantic.

Gabriel, written in Marseilles following Sand and Chopin's sojourn in Majorca in 1839, appealed more to the public taste for adventure. But it also explores the controversial subject of women's education and equality. Born a woman but raised as a Renaissance prince, Gabriel can fight and reason with the best of men. But when she discovers that her grandfather has disguised her in order to prevent her male cousin from inheriting the family estate, out of a sense of justice she goes in search of the rightful heir, Astolphe. Gabriel keeps her male persona, saves Astolphe's life in a barroom brawl by killing his attacker, and shares a prison cell with him where their deep attachment to one another grows. Gabriel "disguises" herself as a woman in order to go to one of Astolphe's stag parties, and when they return to their quarters and Astolphe stumbles upon Gabriel undressing, his fantasies of Gabriel being a real woman are fulfilled, and they fall in love. But when Gabriel dresses as a woman to please Astolphe, he is jealous and possessive; and when she departs to act as a male prince, he chafes at her independence. In the end she escapes to Rome, prevails on the Pope to change the inheritance in Astolphe's favor, sees Astolphe, who has followed, with his old mistress, and finally falls prey to her grandfather's hired killer. Honoré de Balzac considered *Gabriel* a Shakespearean drama and encouraged Sand to get it produced onstage. Some years later she revised the text with that intention. The 1850s revision, renamed *Julia,* a more moralistic and convoluted play, came close to being produced in Paris, but the actors wrangled over roles and squelched the project. Paul Meurice wrote a revision in the 1860s, but his stage version met the same fate. *Gabriel* was reedited in French in 1988 and translated into English in 1992 by Gay Smith Manifold with extensive notes on the *Julia* adaptation, which remains in manuscript.

Sand's fifth play, *Cosima,* received a full production in 1840 in the national theater of France, the Comédie-Française. *Cosima* portrays a Renaissance woman who is the obverse to Gabriel. Cosima has received a girl's education in domestic arts and married well. The play shows her as the wife of a wealthy and kindly Florentine businessman, supervising the household servants and spending hours at her spinning wheel. Feeling confined and bored, she entertains the flirtations of a young and handsome dandy. Entrapped and almost raped in the seducer's stifling bedroom, Cosima escapes home, where she tells her good husband everything and then kills herself in shame. With this domestic drama Sand expressed the intent to create a new genre, a psychological drama that analyzes intimate thought, foreshadowing Henrik Ibsen, especially his *A Doll's House* (1879). Marie Dorval played Cosima, and according to reliable critics such as Théophile Gautier, the production and especially Dorval had its appeal. But other critics found the piece morally offensive, especially objecting to Cosima's ingratitude to her husband and to Sand's efforts to reha-

Sand as the title character in the 1850 Nohant production of her play Claudie *(illustration by Maurice Sand; "Recueil de principaux types crées avec leur costumes sur le Théâtre de Nohant," Bibliothèque Nationale, Départment des Estampes, Réserves, Tb471; 1: 161)*

bilitate women who fall into temptation. As for the audience at large, Sand's enemies organized a claque that booed and hissed the piece night after night, interfering with the performances and making a long run all but impossible: *Cosima* closed after seven performances. The experience both in the rancorous rehearsal hall with arrogant actors and ineffectual directors and then with her enemies in the audience discouraged Sand from writing for the theater. She waited almost a decade before being persuaded to try again.

In 1840 Sand published a play she had written for the stage just before the *Cosima* debacle. *Les Mississippiens* (1869) was to have starred her friend and lead-

ing tragedian, Pierre Bocage, in the principal role. Set in the last years of Louis XIV's long reign (1702), the play exposes the greed and distortion of values brought about by wild capitalist speculative schemes and marrying for money. The hero of the piece immigrates to America and becomes a well-known abolitionist, returning to France in 1720 to clean up the mess begun a generation earlier. Once spiritual peace and order are restored for those he has loved, George Freeman, his name as author of antislavery books, returns to America to continue his good works there.

Les Mississippiens marks the turning point in Sand's dramatic focus, similar to what Ibsen would undergo almost thirty years later when he abandoned Romanticism's large-scale dramas and began a series of smaller-scale realist dramas. Sand's *Les Mississippiens* points toward the realistic plays she wrote in the 1850s and 1860s with many of the same concerns: women, love and marriage, and monetary concerns. No more suicidal melancholics and isolated individuals of *Aldo le rimeur* and *Les Sept Cordes de la lyre*. Sand's new heroes, like George Freeman, were those who work with and for other people to get things done and set things right. She clearly observes the change in a letter:

> I no longer like that severity and tension of heroes who live only in legends, because I don't believe in them anymore. . . . I am more touched by the true than the beautiful and by the good than by the grand. I am more touched in direct proportion to my getting older and to my measuring the abyss of human weakness (*Correspondance* 9:222).

In 1846 Sand resumed writing for the theater, not for the Parisian public she had come to mistrust but rather for her family and private guests in her country house in the little village of Nohant. The Berrichon countryside in central France, where Sand's Nohant Château theater is located, looks like parts of Scotland and Ireland, a resemblance that extends to kindred Celtic folk customs and bagpipe music. Several of Sand's admired pastoral novels and plays take place in these environs. The little theater of Nohant began in Sand's living room, or salon, with her grown children performing scenarios Sand wrote for them. For the first winter season, which lasted two months, Sand wrote scenarios for twenty-one performances, variously scripted for her son, daughter, and two or three of their friends. The season opened with *Le Druide peu délicat* (The Indelicate Druid) on 8 December and closed with *Riquet à la houppe* on 30 January. On 31 December they acted a version of *Don Juan* that Sand adapted from Molière, Wolfgang Amadeus Mozart, and Lord Byron, an experience that she soon afterward fictionalized in her novel *Le Château des désertes*. This novel provides insights into Sand's theories on acting and how valuable theater can be in the education and self-development of young people.

Cut short by the Revolution of 1848 and Sand's return to the public stage in Paris, the Nohant theater season of 1847–1848 featured only two performances, *Barbe bleue* (Blue Beard) on Christmas day and *L'Auberge du crime* (The Inn of Crime) on New Year's Eve. Nohant was dark the winter of 1848–1849. But activity intensified during the winter of 1849–1850 with Sand composing at least fourteen pieces for the little theater, which included adaptations of William Shakespeare (*Much Ado About Nothing* and *Henry IV*) and a fully scripted full-length play, *Lélio,* performed at Nohant on 10 February 1850 and published as *Marielle* (1851) in Sand's collected theater. With *Cinderella* on 12 November 1849 the company inaugurated its new permanent quarters, a southeast bedroom on the ground floor of the mansion with direct access to the entrance foyer. Here, the following July, Sand performed the principal role in her full-length drama *Claudie* so that her director, Bocage, could see it before taking it to Paris in 1851 for a successful professional production.

Sand and her partner, Alexandre Manceau, remodeled the theater during the winter of 1850–1851, removing a wall to create an auditorium in the adjoining room that could seat their audience, which had grown to forty or fifty people. Other improvements included light stands and ceiling lights, which replaced the footlights, the dimming of lights over the audience seating, a drop curtain, and professionally painted scenery. These innovations and experiments fueled Sand's playwriting for the professional theater. And while there were relatively few Nohant theater performances between 1851 and 1856, the ones they did do significantly aided Sand's professional theater work by giving at least some of her plays a trial run in the private theater before moving them to Paris.

Experimentation with commedia dell'arte vigorously resumed at Nohant with twenty-one performances during the fall seasons of 1856 and 1857. Excited by the rediscovery of an Italian Renaissance dramatist-performer, Ruzzante, Sand translated and performed his pieces in an analogous French-peasant dialect and gave them to the actors at the Comédie-Française in hopes of a professional revival, but to no avail. Sand's efforts to revive commedia dell'arte would have to wait fifty years before Jacques Copeau, acknowledging his debt to Sand and her son, Maurice (whose illustrations are published in their collection *Masques et bouffons* [1860]), revived commedia dell'arte on the professional stage in the 1920s. After 1857 the Nohant theater continued with four to six new performances each fall, including previews of two Paris productions, until its final closing in 1862 with a performance of *Daphnis et Chloé*. Sand's little handkerchief theater, with its small space, intimacy, modern lighting, and actors who moved and spoke naturally onstage, foreshadowed the little-theater movement of the late 1890s and early twentieth century.

Sand's return to the public stage came about when she wrote a piece to help celebrate the 1848 Revolution. *Le Roi attend* (The King Awaits), a short

A scene from the second act of the 1851 Paris production of Claudie, *with Charles Fechter as Sylvain at left and Pierre Bocage as Ronciat at center (Bibliothèque Spoelberch de Lovenjoul [Institut de France], Chantilly)*

play she wrote expressly to rededicate the old Comédie-Française as the new Théâtre de la République on 6 April 1848, was performed once and later published in the collection of Sand's works for the theater. Sand describes *Le Roi attend* as a sort of pastiche in which the author expresses her own good intentions by attaching them to some of the most renowned dramatic masters. Molière, the principal character, has called together his actors to devise a play for the king (as in his *L'Impromptu du Versailles* [Improvisation at Versailles, 1663]). After the actors exit, Molière falls asleep, and, as if in a dream, he is visited by celebrated writers: Aeschylus, Sophocles, Euripides, Shakespeare, Voltaire, and Pierre-Augustin Caron de Beaumarchais, who appear one by one on a cloud to tell the sleeping dramatist about liberty, equality, and the rich and the poor. One of the actors then returns to awaken Molière and hurry him to the awaiting king. Molière walks to the edge of the stage, peers out looking for the king, smiles, and says, "I can see the king very well now, but he's not Louis XIV, his name is 'the people'! The sovereign people, words as great as eternity." The audience saluted this with tumultuous

applause. Spurred on by this success, Sand returned to writing for the stage, especially to writing plays for "the people."

In her next play Sand chose to dramatize the people she knew well in the province of Berry, the farmers and sheepherders and their folkways. Already in 1847 Sand had written a popular novel set in the countryside around Nohant that some actors at the Comédie-Française now encouraged her to adapt for them. She quickly responded and sent her play manuscript of *François le champi* (Francois the Foundling) off to the national theater. But the new, more conservative government's appointees heading the theater proved unreceptive to the play and its author, who, after all, had been the minister of public information during the 1848 Revolution and had written several radical pamphlets addressed to the people. So Sand sent *François le champi* to her actor and director friend Bocage, who was holding on to the directorship of the Théâtre de l'Odéon. There on the Left Bank in a poor quarter made up of workers and students, the play received a tumultuous welcome in 1849, running for 140 performances from November 1849 to April 1850, a record. *François le champi* would receive several revivals in Sand's lifetime, with Sarah Bernhardt beginning her professional acting career in the 1856 revival.

As France's first realistic folk play *François le champi* appealed to audiences for a variety of reasons. The play's action begins late in the novel's story, when the champi, a foundling (*champi* means *foundling* in Berrichon patois), returns to his foster home after spending his adolescent years away working on a distant farm. He comes back to his adoptive mother, Madeleine, who is recently widowed, convalescent, and burdened with debts. In the course of the play François, now about twenty years old, helps Madeleine get out of debt and recover her health and spirits. At the same time he falls in love with her. The novel gives Madeleine's earlier history when she had been unhappily married to an alcoholic flour-mill owner who abused and beat her. François's first arrival as a child of eight or so exacerbated an already unhappy marriage, for the husband was jealous of the boy. Perhaps the popularity of the novel assured that the theater audience would have known this background since Sand chose not to dramatize it.

Critical response to the drama varied widely, reflecting the oppositions in aesthetic and moral opinion prevalent during Sand's theater career. The François and Madeleine relationship appalled Pierre-Joseph Proudhon: he found offensive Sand's representation of a bastard child as a model of filial devotion and unconscionable that the bastard boy marries his foster mother in what amounted to "spiritual incest." Emile Zola, on the other hand, writing much later in the century, commended Sand for her generous and tolerant treatment of this delicate subject and for her refusal to see immorality where others saw incest. Zola only wished that Sand had made Madeleine less passive and would have liked to have seen the older woman fall in love with François in the course of the play the way he does with her. Gautier focused on the play's visual innovations, the set's rustic interior with windows that showed the changing season from winter to spring. He felt he was looking at an authentic thatched cottage from the Berrichon countryside and folk costumes of rare exactitude. Sand's correspondence reveals how much she was responsible for that exactitude, supervising every detail in the furniture and costume selection, even sending actual headdresses to Bocage with careful instructions on how they should be worn.

Sand's language for the Berrichon peasants succeeded with her first audiences, but by the end of the century it had become outmoded. Sand did not write the dialogue entirely in Berrichon patois because it would have been incomprehensible to Parisian audiences. Instead, she did what John Millington Synge would later do for his Irish peasants, utilizing Berrichon expressions and rhythms to suggest Berrichon speech. However, the playwright was disappointed with the actors' delivery of her lines in that premiere production, finding their delivery too distinct and academic, not natural enough. A critic who went to the 1849 premiere of *François le champi* reported that the dialogue offered a truthful and unaffected study of peasant language. Gautier, too, was impressed with the peasant dialect he heard onstage, which he described as patois employed with art. But a generation later both Francisque Sarcey and Zola commented negatively. Sarcey thought that the country people had changed more in the preceding twenty-five years (he was writing in 1876) than in the six hundred years prior to Sand's dramatization, so that the piece was no longer a realistic representation, and he judged the play's language as too eloquent for peasantry in general. Zola, writing at the end of the century, found in *François le champi* language pretentiously naive and mannered, but he praised Sand for the simplicity and natural development of her characters and sentiments. He imagined that *François le champi* must have been a "delicious repose for the public in the middle of the complicated abominations of romantic melodrama."

Encouraged by her audience and Bocage to write another rustic drama, Sand followed up with *Claudie* (1851), a play "simple as a *bonjour,*" she announced to Bocage when she finished it in the summer of 1850. *Claudie* shows how the hard work and goodness of a young woman, a migrant worker and unwed mother, reward her in the end with love and marriage to the most desirable young man in the countryside. This quiet and industrious woman stoically treks several miles each day to come to work in the fields with the men and then into the kitchen with the women, and because she is a woman receives less pay. She takes care of her aging grandfather, who accompanies her and does what he can in the fields. Sand's play shows Claudie silently working onstage: at the end of her day in the fields harvesting wheat she goes to the well and draws a heavy bucket of water, then washes dishes, sorts laundry, and in a later scene appears at an ironing board with a series of old-fashioned irons heating up at the fireplace. In contrast to Claudie's quiet work, Ronciat, the bourgeois scoundrel who seduced and abandoned her five years previous to the play's action, does nothing but talk. Vain and egotistical, he makes promises he never intends to keep, and he lies and slanders for the sake of appearance, his

Scenes from the 1853 Paris production of **Mauprat** *(Bibliothèque Spoelberch de Lovenjoul [Institut de France], Chantilly)*

own. He proves himself useless to this working community, so in the end he is driven out. Sylvain, the man who marries Claudie in the end, is the laboring son of the foreman on the farm, which is owned by a coquettish bourgeois woman.

Thus Sand's play achieves its diatribe against the bourgeoisie and an idealization of the workers. No wonder the government censors prevailed upon the playwright to prune out references to the poor people and the evil rich. Sand complied in order that it be produced. This workers' play, with its Berrichon harvest festival and authentic bagpipes, drums, and fiddles, achieved her goal to celebrate "the people"; now she had to get the people into the audience to achieve her ultimate goal of creating a people's theater. That was difficult because the government dropped Bocage from the Odéon directorship about the same time Sand finished the play, so playwright and director had to look elsewhere for a suitable theater. The play opened at the Théâtre de la Porte Saint-Martin in January 1851 and played to mostly bourgeois audiences. There were other disappointments for the author. The lead actress who played Claudie was weak though the ensemble was strong, and Charles Fechter, who played Sylvain, gave a highly charismatic performance (he went on the next year to star in the premiere of Alexandre Dumas *fils*'s *La Dame aux camelias* [1852]). Bocage himself was a problem; he did not honor Sand's instructions on how to stage the harvest festival authentically, with the Berrichon singing and dancing beginning in a solemn, almost sad manner, like chanting vespers, to be followed by a burst of madness, as if drunk for an instant, then calm again. Instead, the staged music and dancing at the theater were altered to conform to current Parisian taste. Bocage also prevailed upon Sand to write an overly long speech for him as the old man at the end of the play, and critics complained about its superfluity.

But the critics were generally enthusiastic in their responses to *Claudie,* however divided on the morality and politics of the play. P. Busoni compared Sand to Demeter and her play to Virgil's first-century A.D. *Georgics.* Gautier called Claudie a rustic Antigone and Sylvain an Apollo. Years later, in 1872, Hippolyte Taine wrote to Sand asking her to write plays again, comparing her talent to the old Greek poets. Jules Janin applauded the play's ensemble acting but took offense at the play's ostensible immorality; he rejected Sand's rehabilitation of the unwed and therefore unchaste mother, claiming that the personification of chastity and charm was Sylvain, the true *fille* of the play, Claudie the *garçon.* Another critic who shared Janin's moral outrage condemned Sand for the scene in with Claudie ap-

peared on the stage in the company of both of the men who had possessed her, or rather the one who had, on one side, and the one who would, on the other. In a long and sympathetic review that ran fifteen pages Gustave Planche (a friend who had years earlier fought a duel to protect Sand's honor) argues in favor of Sand's rehabilitation of a fallen woman, citing the case of Mary Magdalen.

Two English adaptations of *Claudie* by Charles Reade were produced in London, *The Village Tale* in 1852 and *Rachel the Reaper* in 1874, the latter featuring Ellen Terry in the principal role. Terry complained that the stage set was far too real: it included live pigs. By the 1890s critics viewed *Claudie* as more idealistic than realistic. In 1904, when an early biographer of Sand, the Russian Vladimir Karénine (Varvara Komarova), attended a revival of *Claudie* at the Comédie-Française, she found the language and characterization comparable to those of Leo Tolstoy and the play a hymn to work and the glorification of laborers, observing that the audience gained new courage to continue their work. This socialist response was not without precedent: a production of *Claudie* in the city of Nantes in 1851 was so popular with the workers that the city officials shut it down, fearing a popular uprising as a possible result of the play's socialist ideas. The story of Claudie, who was born in a period of national crisis, was again performed in France in 1942 during World War II.

François le champi and *Claudie* established Sand as the dramatic voice of the new movement called *réalisme.* Champfleury (Jules Husson) in his seminal essay "Du realisme: une lettre à George Sand" (1855) identified Sand as the leading artist of realism in drama, Gustave Courbet of realism in painting, and Richard Wagner of realism in music. A third rustic folk play called *Le Pressoir* (The Winepress), staged in 1853, was Sand's last effort in that particular kind of rustic realism. She had grown disheartened by the absence of the people, or working classes, attending her plays. And so, accepting the inevitability of middle-class audiences, Sand wrote a series of plays addressed to them. The first of these, *Le Mariage de Victorine* (The Marriage of Victorine, 1851) features the daughter of a petit-bourgeois clerk who marries into the upper-middle-class family of a kindly businessman. It was produced at the Théâtre du Gymnase. Sand had been reluctant to give it to the Gymnase initially, regarding the audience there as a "constipated public" that did not want to laugh too much and only wanted to cry a little. But the quality of the production and the reception by the audience changed her mind, and she had eight more of her play productions staged there be-

First page of Sand's manuscript for the prologue to Bilora, *one of the plays by Italian dramatist
Ruzzante that Sand translated and performed at Nohant in 1856–1857 (from Gay Manifold,*
George Sand's Theatre Career, *1985)*

tween 1851 and 1862. At the Gymnase, known as the "House of Scribe," the manager, Adolphe Lemoine-Montigny, has been credited with introducing stage reforms associated with realism and the new generation of realistic playwrights. Significantly, *La Dame aux camélias* opened at the Gymnase in 1852, and most of Dumas *fils's* subsequent pieces played there. During the run of Sand's *Le Mariage de Victorine* at the Gymnase, in December 1851, Napoleon III staged his coup d'état, and soldiers patrolled the streets. Sand wrote to Montigny that it would no longer be the socialists and their ideas that would disturb society but the capitalists, the middle class, with their material greed and needs.

Writing for the middle-class audience at the Gymnase meant that Sand would have to narrow the range of characters to family, friends, and business associates, placing them in the confines of a bourgeois sitting room or tended garden, where they would talk about making money and good marriages. But even though Sand dulled her political edge, she never lost it, for she attempted to educate and gently satirize the bourgeoisie and consequently continued to provoke the ire of her more-conservative critics. *Les Vacances de Pandolphe* (The Vacation of Pandolphe, 1852) creates an amusing picture of a celibate, middle-class professor on vacation at his Alpine cottage, sitting under his linden tree—"my tree," "my house," "my garden." The greedy gentry and its materialistic courtesans cheat and lie to get the loot left in Pandolphe's will. Audience and critics were more aghast than amused. More appealing was *Flaminio* (1854), which pits an artist against haute-bourgeois interests, with both good and bad bourgeois types. The artist is himself transformed into a prospering architect-engineer who builds monuments of industry rather than the puppets of former days.

Maître Favilla (1855) played at the Odéon rather than the Gymnase, though it too features another bourgeois businessman, Keller, who combines Tartuffe-like hypocrisy with the calculated profit motive of a Lopakhin-like character from Anton Chekhov's *The Cherry Orchard* (1904) in his efforts to manage an estate in a modern, moneymaking manner. Favilla, a foolish and lovable old musician, receives the audience's sympathies even though his claims on the estate are clearly ridiculous. In an obituary of the actor, Rouvière, who played the part of Favilla, Charles Baudelaire remembered how surprised everyone was to see the actor's customarily ferocious nature transformed into the paternal Favilla who loves utopia, revolutionary idylls, and the cult of Jean-Jacques Rousseau. More outraged than surprised, the conservative critic Janin called *Maître*

Favilla a demonstration of a systematic hatred for the bourgeoisie. Sand retorted that she did not hate the whole class but the speculators who were the enemy of the ideal, those profitmakers who play the big game that has become the soul of modern society at the expense of the artists, philosophers, and moralists. She chooses to reclassify the honest bourgeois workers, those who don't play at the stock market, who count out each evening the modest profits of a day's work, as members of "the people." She called on Janin to wake up to the new categories because times were changing and he was too lost in his books of the past.

Françoise, which opened at the Gymnase in 1856, is another gentle satire of a *bourgeois gentilhomme,* in which an egotistical young dandy, Henri, chooses to marry a rich woman rather than Françoise, the strong and virtuous young woman who loves him. Henri's bride is the daughter of two masterfully satirized parvenus, the Dubuissons, former innkeepers. Ridiculously overdressed, Monsieur Dubuisson, now become the most successful banker in Berry, and his wife, the most determined of social climbers, have a daughter who is a pretty, petulant, badly raised enfant terrible. Gautier reported that Sand's creation of Henri in *Françoise* heralded a new type of character in drama, a weak and odious protagonist under the guise of a lighthearted youth.

During the 1850s when Sand wrote plays for and about the new middle class, she never gave up entirely on writing Romanticist dramas for a larger stage and audience. After *Le Roi attend* Sand wrote two more plays about actors in the seventeenth century, one about a somewhat imaginary commedia dell'arte traveling troupe, the other a more biographical piece on Molière's troupe, and especially about his wife, Armande Béjart. With the first, *Marielle,* Sand wanted to show the serious business of true actors creating commedia dell'arte and satirizing not just the commoners but the powerful as well. Begun in 1850 as *Lélio,* a partially scripted, partially improvised piece performed in the private theater at Nohant, the play went through three drafts to accommodate Bocage, who directed and played the lead role. He feared the newness in the piece, and Sand replied that the only thing new was that Pierrot was played by a woman. While Bocage hesitated, another play quite similar to Sand's received a successful production, and she had to let a year's work come to nothing.

Following their success with *Claudie* in 1851, Bocage persuaded Sand to write the real historical story of Molière and his troupe, and he directed and played the principal role in this play, titled *Molière,* at the Théâtre de la Gaîté. Sand wrote the historical drama rather reluctantly, considering it a profanation to embellish Molière's life, but then became impassioned with creating a new interpretation of the character of Armande, Molière's wife. Sand's Armande loves no one; she is intelligent, ambitious, proud, mocking, vain, dry, ungrateful, fascinating, and repellent, all at the same time. Sand believed that historical accounts of Armande's infidelities were false, that Molière would have lost interest in her if she had actually been unfaithful or become a courtesan. The playwright wanted to show how Armande inspired Molière and at the same time destroyed him. When well-wishers separated Molière from his tormenting wife, his obsession only worsened, consuming him with jealous fantasies. Working out the production details for *Molière* did not go smoothly: Sand had engaged her friend, the composer Charles-François Gounod, to arrange some of Jean-Baptiste Lully's music, but the Théâtre de la Gaîté's orchestra conductor insisted upon doing it himself. Sand was unable to engage the actors she wanted. And Bocage made changes without consulting Sand, going so far as to cut the entire fourth act, which had important revelations about the psychology of Armande and Molière's relationship. The twelve performances in May 1851 received tepid responses, leaving critics wondering why Sand wanted to sanitize the character of Armande when the playwright should have accepted that Molière's wife was an actress, after all, a daughter of the theater. Gautier wondered if Armande is only a flirt, not actually unfaithful to Molière, why is she humiliated and ostracized? At least the critics were focusing on Armande, which is what Sand wanted.

In addition to writing plays about Berrichon folk and commedia dell'arte actors, Sand wanted to revive larger-scale Romantic melodrama. She tried again to get her revision of *Gabriel* produced, but to no avail. But with play adaptations of other of her novels Sand was able to revive some of the adventure and excitement of Romanticism. With a new ally in the triumvirate of directors at the Odéon, Gustave Vaez (who wrote libretti for Gaetano Donizetti operas), Sand produced her adaptation of *Mauprat*. First published as a novel in 1837, the stage production in 1853 preserved enough cliff-hanging excitement to assure its success, but some observers felt it may have lost its literary quality in the transference to the stage.

Sand adapted a Shakespeare play for the Comédie-Française in 1856, titled *Comme il vous plaira,* the first production of *As You Like It* in French. A reading of this text shows how radically she altered the original by focusing on Celia and Jacques as the main romantic duo and relegating Rosalind to the background. Of course similar tidyings up and new, happier endings to Shakespeare's plays had been going on in England for more than two hundred years. But when Charles Dickens attended Sand's adaptation in Paris, he walked out after the second act, complaining that all he saw were actors with nothing to do but sit down on roots and trees every chance they got.

Sand also adapted many other of her novels for the stage, two of which succeeded and were successful financially, both at the Théâtre de l'Odéon. In 1864 the premiere of *Le Marquis de Villemer* (after the novel's publication in 1860–1861) proved to be Sand's greatest commercial success in the theater. The play itself, charming but rather inconsequential in terms of innovations, does not explain that success. It was more the timing of having something by the renowned author go up on the boards. Sand had just published an attack on the church clergy in her novel *Mademoiselle la Quintinie* (1863), which scandalized some and roused support in others, especially the students of the Odéon quarter, where *Le Marquis de Villemer* was staged. Huge crowds of these students and other supporters gathered outside the theater, assembling as early as ten in the morning, to cheer their heroine, Sand, a sixty-year-old novelist and playwright who regarded this display of devotion with quizzical amusement. Inside they shouted and stamped with approval, and even the imperial family and the emperor joined in. But Sand's play adaptation of *Mademoiselle la Quintinie,* the attack on the clergy, was censored and delayed. It never played in Paris during Sand's lifetime but was produced in Brussels in 1879, after her death.

Sand's last full-length play to premiere in her lifetime, in 1870 at the Odéon, was another adaptation of a novel, her *La Confession d'une jeune fille* (Confession of a Young Woman), published in 1865 and retitled *L'Autre* (The Other) for the stage. Finding the director at the Odéon, Duquesnel, incompetent, Sand reluctantly took over all the rehearsals with the actors and the arrangements for lighting, sets, and costumes. She reports in her letters that the actors would not work when she turned her back although she liked the actress Sarah Bernhardt, who was playing the lead role, a charming character, who was perhaps a bit jejune, and Sand was glad to have rehearsal time to revise the script. This last play dramatizes the conflict of two young men, one a pragmatist, close to becoming an egotistical cynic, pitted against the other, a romantic idealist. Bernhardt played the young female goad who brings these two men to a new awareness that each has within himself the opposite type. The goad forgives and rehabilitates, Sand's dramatic watchwords to the end. *L'Autre* succeeded with the public and earned Sand Fr 12,000 before it was forced to close by the outbreak of the 1870 Revolution, when barricades and gunshots again disrupted Paris streets.

In addition to her theater experiments in Romanticism, realism, commedia dell'arte, and folk plays, Sand tried new approaches to the one-act play structure. The one-act structure had been taken seriously by Pierre Carlet de Chamblain de Marivaux, Johann Wolfgang von Goethe, and Musset, and now Sand added the new realism in stage settings and character psychology. She first reworked the form in a published one-act tract about socialism, *Père va-tout-seul* (Old Man Go It Alone, 1844), about an old tramp who refuses to live in a shelter for the homeless, preferring instead to live off the kindness of the country folk who take turns feeding and housing him. She later staged a realistic and sober one-act play, *Lucie,* at the Gymnase in 1856. More one-act performances followed and received acclaim on the Parisian stages.

Le Pavé (The Pavement), which opened at the Gymnase in 1862, is a well-observed depiction of a middle-aged naturalist working on fossils in his study, attended by a bright young woman and an awkward but lovable serving boy. The older man sees a romance developing between these youngsters and decides he wants the young woman for himself, only recognizing his folly in the end. The original manuscript of *Le Pavé* (performed privately at Nohant) has a scene with the two young people alone onstage hearing the master of the house ringing for his valet, neither of them wishing to answer. In a later published but unproduced one-act play by Sand, *La Laitière et le pot au lait* (The Milkmaid and the Pot of Milk, 1875), the playwright used the scene again but made the master more severe. Later still in the century August Strindberg staged the same scene in his short naturalist play *Miss Julie* (1889).

Sand's next one-act, *Le Lis du Japon* (The Japanese Lily), featured stylish, Marivaux-like dialogue combined with an O. Henry–type story; it opened in 1866 at the Vaudeville. The innovative setting shows an artist's basement studio where the audience sees only the pedestrians' lower legs and feet through the windows facing the street. The penniless artist paints flowers for his meager living. When he is about to be evicted for not paying his rent, he turns to the one treasure he has in his small apartment, a rare and expensive Japanese lily, which he cuts from its roots and presents to his upper-class landlady, whom he secretly loves.

The last of Sand's one-acts to be produced, actually the last of all of her play premieres, *Un Bienfait*

n'est jamais perdu (A Good Deed's Never Lost), played at the little Théâtre de Cluny in 1872, four years before her death. Sand indicates in her correspondence that this piece was buried in an old manuscript box; it harks back to her earlier experiments in Carmontelle-like proverbs, with the same swift and bright repartee.

Completing her retirement from Paris theater life after 1872, Sand continued making multifarious contributions to her son's highly skilled puppet theatre at Nohant, sewing and storytelling for her son's puppets to entertain her two granddaughters and an entourage of visitors that included Gustave Flaubert and Ivan Turgenev. In the end, suffering from a stomach ailment now suspected of having been cancer, Sand died in her bedroom in the Berrichon country house of Nohant on 8 June 1876.

Looking at Sand's body of dramatic work as a whole it is easy to see how extraordinarily expansive and inclusive her contributions were to nineteenth-century genres and innovations in theater. From her earliest Romantic dramas of the 1830s to her trailblazing Realist plays of the 1850s, Sand anticipated and created new forms and subjects for the professional stage, especially new representations of women. *Cosima* and *Claudie* feature such women: Cosima a romanticized Renaissance *maîtresse de la maison* (mistress of the house) trapped in domestic boredom, who anticipates Gustave Flaubert's *Madame Bovary* (1856) and Ibsen's Nora of *A Doll's House;* and Claudie, an unwed mother and migrant worker shown onstage doing the field work of a man and the domestic labors of a woman. One scene with Claudie at an ironing board precedes by a hundred years the better-known one in John Osborne's *Look Back in Anger* (1956). Sand's one-act plays anticipate Strindberg and J. M. Synge in subject matter and staging techniques. And Sand's experiments with commedia dell'arte in her private Théâtre de Nohant directly inspired Copeau's twentieth-century revival of that improvisational art. Sand's socialist-democrat politics and the Revolution of 1848 inspired her to write plays for "the people," that is, the lower classes of artisans and laborers. However, in practice she had to resign herself to audiences of mostly bourgeois and aristocratic classes. Sand found that to continue working in the theater meant the compromise and censorship of many of her ideals; government officials censored and directors and actors altered her work with or without her consent. Even so, Sand succeeded in getting her work produced, and she became one of the most successful dramatists of her time. After her death in 1876 Sand's reputation suffered: her plays began to seem outmoded, and her detractors, whether motivated by gender bias, professional or personal jealousy, or genuine aesthetic and/or political distaste (and there is evidence for all such motivations), gained ground in minimizing and diminishing her accomplishments. The work of historians and critics of the last twenty years has somewhat righted that imbalance, but a history of the process by which Sand's theater career was vilified and eclipsed has yet to be written.

Letters:

Correspondance, 26 volumes, edited by Georges Lubin (Paris: Garnier, 1964–1991).

Bibliographies:

Vicomte Charles Spoelberch de Lovenjoul, *George Sand: Etude bibliographique sur ses œuvres* (Paris: Leclerc, 1914);

Annarosa Poli, *George Sand vue par les Italiens: Essai de bibliographie critique* (Paris: Didier, 1965);

Robert A. Keane and Natalie Datlof, "George Sand and the Victorians: Bibliography," *George Sand Newsletter,* 1 (1978): 5–6;

Gaylord Brynolfson, "Works on George Sand, 1964–1980: A Bibliography," in *George Sand Papers: Conference Proceedings, 1978,* edited by Datlof (New York: AMS, 1982), pp. 189–233;

Gay Smith Manifold, *George Sand's Theatre Career* (Ann Arbor: VMI Press, 1985);

David A. Powell, "Selected Bibliography," in *The World of George Sand,* edited by Datlof, Jeanne Fuchs, and Powell (New York: Greenwood Press, 1991), pp. 271–278.

Biographies:

Vladimir Karénine, *George Sand: Sa vie et ses œuvres,* 4 volumes (Paris: Ollendorff et Plon, 1899–1926);

André Maurois, *Lélia, ou la vie de George Sand* (Paris: Hachette, 1952); translated by Gerard Hopkins as *Lélia: The Life of George Sand* (New York: Harper, 1953);

Pierre Salomon, *George Sand* (Paris: Hatier-Boivin, 1953);

Curtis Cate, *George Sand* (Boston: Houghton Mifflin, 1975);

Francine Mallet, *George Sand* (Paris: Grasset, 1976);

Joseph Barry, *Infamous Woman: The Life of George Sand* (Garden City, N.Y.: Doubleday, 1977);

Renee Winegarten, *The Double Life of George Sand, Woman and Writer: A Critical Biography* (New York: Basic Books, 1978);

Donna Dickenson, *George Sand: A Brave Man—The Most Womanly Woman* (Oxford: Berg, 1988).

References:

Joseph-Marc Bailbé, "Le Théâtre et la vie dans *Le Château des Desertes,*" *Revue d'Histoire Littéraire de la France,* 79 (1979): 600–612;

Germain Bapst, *Essai sur l'histoire du théâtre: La Mise en scène, le décor, le costume, l'architecture, l'éclairage, l'hygiène* (Paris: Hachette, 1893);

Jules Barbey d'Aurevilly, *Les Bas-bleus* (1877, Geneva: Slatkine, 1968);

Barbey d'Aurevilly, *Le Théâtre contemporain (1866–1868)* (Paris: Stock, 1908);

Nicole Belmont, "L'Académie celtique et George Sand: Les Débuts des recherches folkloriques en France," *Romantisme,* no. 9 (1975): 29–39;

Antoine Benoist, *Essais de critique dramatique* (Paris: Hachette, 1898);

Bibliothèque Nationale, *George Sand: Visages du romantisme,* 1977 Exposition Catalogue (Paris: Bibliothèque Nationale, 1977);

Bibliothèque Nationale, *Lorenzaccio: Mises en scène d'hier et d'aujourd'hui* (Paris: Bibliothèque Nationale, 1979);

Paul G. Blount, *George Sand and the Victorian World* (Athens: University of Georgia Press, 1979);

Blount, "George Sand's Misquotation of Shakespeare," *American Notes and Queries,* 12 (1973): 34–35;

Patrice Boussel, "George Sand et la technique dramatique," *L'Europe* (June–July 1954): 68–78;

George Brandes, *L'Ecole romantique en France,* translated into French by A. Topin (Paris: Michalon, 1902);

F. Brunetière, *Les Epoques du théâtre français: 1636–1850* (Paris: Hachette, 1892);

Ross Chambers, *L'Ange et l'automate: Variations sur le mythe de l'actrice de Nerval à Proust* (Paris: Archives de Lettres Modernes, 1971);

Chambers, *La Comédie au château* (Paris: Corti, 1971);

Champfleury [Jean Husson], *Du réalisme: correspondance, Champfleury, George Sand* (Paris: Editions des Cendres, 1991);

Champfleury, *Le Réalisme* (Paris: Hermann, 1973);

A. David-Sauvageot, *Le Réalisme et le naturalisme* (Paris: Calmann-Lévy, 1889);

Nancy Dersofi, *Arcadia and the Stage: An Introduction to the Dramatic Art of Angelo Beolco called Ruzzante* (Madrid: Turanzas, 1978);

Maurice Descotes, *Le Drame romantique et ses grands créateurs* (Paris: Presses Universitaires, n.d.);

Descotes, *Le Public de théâtre et son histoire* (Paris: Presses Universitaires, 1964);

Paul Dimoff, *La Genèse de Lorenzaccio* (Paris: Droz, 1936);

Edouard Dolléans, *Féminisme et mouvement ouvrier: George Sand* (Paris: Editions Ouvriers, 1951);

Alexandre Dumas *père, Souvenirs dramatiques,* 2 volumes (Paris: Calmann Lévy, n.d.);

Dorrya Fahmy, *George Sand: Auteur dramatique* (Paris: Droz, 1935);

Julia Bloch Frey, "Theatre in an Armchair," *Friends of George Sand Newsletter,* Hofstra University (Spring 1979): 20–22;

Théophile Gautier, *Histoire de l'art dramatique en France depuis vingt-cinq ans,* 6 volumes (Paris: 1858–1859; Geneva: Slatkine, 1968);

William T. Hammond, "Analysis of the Plot and Character Drawing in the Theatre of George Sand," *Birmingham-Southern College Bulletin,* 22 (May 1929): 45–54;

H. Hostein, *Souvenirs d'un homme de théâtre* (Paris: Dentu, 1878);

Arsène Houssaye, *Behind the Scenes of the Comédie-Française,* translated by Albert D. Vandam (London: Chapman and Hall, 1889);

Armand Kahn, *Le Théâtre social en France de 1870 à nos jours* (Paris: Fischbacher, 1907);

C. Latreille, *George Sand et Shakespeare* (Macon: Protat, 1901);

Renée Lelièvre, "Un Prologue inédit de George Sand imité de Ruzzante," *Revue de Littérature Comparée,* 42 (1968): 572–583.

Lelièvre, *Le Théâtre dramatique italien en France, 1855–1940* (Paris: Colin, 1959);

Hippolyte Lucas, *Histoire philosophique et littéraire du théâtre français* (Paris: Gosselin, 1843);

Gay Manifold [Gay Smith], "George Sand et l'acteur," *Présence de George Sand Grenoble,* 19 (February 1984): 22–29

Manifold, *George Sand's Gabriel* (Westport, Conn: Greenwood Press, 1992);

Manifold, *George Sand's Theatre Career* (Ann Arbor: UMI Research, 1985);

Thérèse Marix, "Les Débuts de George Sand critiqué dramatique," *Revue du Berry et du Centre* (March–April 1934): 26–33; (July–August 1934): 57–65;

Edith Melcher, *Stage realism in France Between Diderot and Antoine* (New York: Russell and Russell, 1976);

Théodore Muret, *L'Histoire par le théâtre: 1789–1851* (Paris: Amyot, 1865);

Marie-Louise Pailleron, *François Buloz et ses amis: La Revue des Deux Mondes et la Comédie-Française* (Paris: Firmin-Didot, 1930);

Pailleron, *François Buloz et ses amis: Les Derniers Romantiques* (Paris: Perrin, 1923);

Valentine Petoukhoff, "George Sand et le drame philosophique: *Aldo le rimeur, Les Sept Cordes de la lyre, Gabriel, Les Mississipiens, Le Diable aux champs,*" dissertation, University of Pennsylvania (1975);

Jean Pommier, *Les Ecrivains devant la Révolution de 1848* (Paris: Presses Universitaires, 1948);

Jean Rousset, "Le Comédien et son spectateur: Don Juan," *Ecriture: Cahier de Littérature et de Poésie,* 13 (1977): 132–143;

Rousset, *L'Intérieur et l'extérieur* (Paris: Corti, 1968);

C. A. Sainte-Beuve, *Causeries du lundi,* volume 1 (Paris: Garnier, 1850);

Maurice Sand, *Masques et bouffons: Comédie italienne,* 2 volumes (Paris: A. Lévy fils, 1860);

Sand, *Plays for Marionettes,* translated by Babette Hughes and Glenn Hughes (New York: Samuel French, 1931);

Francisque Sarcey, *Quarante ans de théâtre,* volume 4 (Paris: Bibliothèque des Annales, 1901);

Gerald Schaeffer, *Espace et temps chez George Sand* (Neuchatel: A la Baconniere, 1981);

Charles Séchan, *Souvenirs d'un homme de théâtre 1831–1855* (Paris: Calmann-Lévy, 1883);

Enid M. Standring, "The Lélio's of Berlioz and George Sand," *The George Sand Papers,* Conference Proceedings at Hofstra University (New York: AMS, 1976);

Robert Storey, *Pierrot: A Critical History of a Mask* (Princeton: Princeton University Press, 1978);

Isaïa Sully-Lévy, "Souvenirs du doyen des Comédiens Français: Une Représentation à Nohant," *Revue de Française* (30 October 1913): 486–495;

Hippolyte Taine, *Derniers Essais de critique et d'histoire* (Paris: Hachette, 1903);

Taine, "Lettres de George Sand et H. Taine," *Revue des Deux Mondes* (15 January 1933): 335–351;

Debra Linowitz Wentz, *Les Profils du théâtre de Nohant de George Sand* (Paris: Nizet, 1978);

Emile Zola, *Le Naturalisme au théâtre* (Paris: Charpentier, 1893);

Zola, *Nos auteurs dramatiques* (Paris: Charpentier, 1889).

Papers:

Sand's papers are held in the Bibliothèque de l'Arsenal, Paris; the Bibliothèque Historique de la Ville de Paris, France; the Bibliothèque Municipale, Chateauroux, France; the Bibliothèque Municipale, La Chatre, France; Bibliothèque Nationale, Paris; and the Spoelberch de Lovenjoul Collection, Institut de France, Chantilly, France.

Victorien Sardou
(5 September 1831 – 8 November 1908)

Mario Hamlet-Metz
James Madison University

PLAY PRODUCTIONS: *La Taverne,* Paris, Théâtre de l'Odéon, 1 April 1854;

Les Premières Armes de Figaro, by Sardou and Emile Vanderbuch, Paris, Théâtre Déjazet, 27 September 1859;

Les Gens nerveux, by Sardou and Théodore Barrière, Paris, Palais Royal, 4 November 1859;

Les Pattes de mouche, Paris, Théâtre du Gymnase, 15 May 1860;

Monsieur Garat, Paris, Théâtre Déjazet, 31 May 1860;

Les Femmes fortes, Paris, Théâtre du Vaudeville, 31 December 1860;

L'Ecureuil, Paris, Théâtre du Vaudeville, 9 February 1861;

L'Homme aux pigeons, by Sardou and Jules Pélissié, Paris, Théâtre du Vaudeville, 12 May 1861;

Onze Jours de siège, Paris, Théâtre du Vaudeville, 1 June 1861;

Piccolino, Paris, Théâtre du Gymnase, 18 July 1861;

Nos Intimes!, Paris, Théâtre du Vaudeville, 16 November 1861;

Chez Bonvalet, by Sardou, Henri Lefebvre, and Pélissié, Paris, Théâtre Déjazet, 15 December 1861;

La Papillonne, Paris, Comédie-Française, 11 April 1862;

La Perle noire, adapted from Sardou's novel *La Perle noire,* Paris, Théâtre du Gymnase, 12 April 1862;

Les Prés Saint-Gervais, Paris, Théâtre Déjazet, 24 April 1862;

Les Ganaches, Paris, Théâtre du Gymnase, 29 October 1862;

Bataille d'amour, by Sardou and Karl Daclin, music by Auguste Emmanuel Vaucorbeil, Paris, Opéra-Comique, 13 April 1863;

Les Diables noirs, Théâtre du Vaudeville, 28 November 1863;

Le Dégel, Paris, Théâtre Déjazet, 12 April 1864;

Don Quichotte, Paris, Théâtre du Gymnase, 25 June 1864; rearranged by Sardou and Charles Nuitter, music by Maurice Renaud, Paris, Châtelet, 9 February 1895;

Victorien Sardou

Les Pommes du voisin, Paris, Palais Royal, 15 October 1864;

Le Capitaine Henriot, by Sardou and Gustave Vaez, music by François Auguste Gevaert, Paris, Opéra-Comique, 29 December 1864;

Les Vieux Garçons, Paris, Théâtre du Gymnase, 21 January 1865;

Les Ondines au Champagne, by Sardou, Pélissié, and Lefebvre, Paris, Folies Dramatiques, 5 September 1865;

La Famille Benoîton, Paris, Théâtre du Vaudeville, 4 November 1865;

Les Cinq Francs d'un bourgeois de Paris, by Sardou, Antoine Gadon Dunan-Mousseux, and Pélissié, Paris, Folies Dramatiques, 26 February 1866;

Nos Bons Villageois, Paris, Théâtre du Gymnase, 3 October 1866;

Maison neuve, Paris, Théâtre du Vaudeville, 4 December 1866;

Séraphine, Paris, Théâtre du Gymnase, 29 December 1868;

Patrie!, Paris, Théâtre de la Porte Saint-Martin, 18 March 1869; revised as *Patrie!,* by Sardou and Louis Gallet, music by Emile Paladilhe, Paris, Théâtre de l'Opéra, 20 December 1886;

Fernande, Paris, Théâtre du Gymnase, 8 March 1870;

Le Roi Carotte, by Sardou, music by Jacques Offenbach, Paris, Théâtre de la Gaîté, 15 January 1872;

Les Vieilles Filles, by Sardou and Charles de Courcy, Paris, Théâtre du Gymnase, 14 August 1872;

Andréa, Paris, Théâtre du Gymnase, 17 March 1873;

L'Oncle Sam, Paris, Théâtre du Vaudeville, 6 November 1873; translated as *Uncle Sam,* New York, Grand Opera House, 17 March 1873;

Les Merveilleuses, by Sardou, music by Félix Hugo, Théâtre des Variétés, 16 December 1873;

Le Magot, Paris, Palais Royal, 14 January 1874;

La Haine, by Sardou, music by Offenbach, Paris, Théâtre de la Gaîté, 3 December 1874;

Ferréol, Paris, Théâtre du Gymnase, 17 December 1875;

L'Hôtel Godelot, by Sardou and Henri Crisafulli, Paris, Théâtre du Gymnase, 13 May 1876;

Dora, Paris, Théâtre du Vaudeville, 22 January 1877;

Les Exilés, by Sardou, Gregorij Lubomirski, and Eugène Nus, Théâtre de la Porte Saint-Martin, 2 March 1877;

Les Bourgeois de Pont-Arcy, Paris, Théâtre du Vaudeville, 1 March 1878;

Les Noces de Fernande, by Sardou and Emile de Najac, music by Louis-Pierre Deffès, Paris, Opéra-Comique, 18 November 1878;

Daniel Rochat, Paris, Comédie-Française, 16 February 1880;

Divorçons!, by Sardou and Najac, Paris, Palais Royal, 6 December 1880; translated as *Cyprienne,* New York, Thalia Theater, 2 February 1882;

Odette, Paris, Théâtre du Vaudeville, 17 November 1881;

Fédora, Paris, Théâtre du Vaudeville, 12 December 1882;

Théodora, Paris, Théâtre de la Porte Saint-Martin, 26 December 1884; revised by Sardou and P. Ferrier, music by Xavier Leroux, Monte Carlo, Opéra Monte-Carlo, 19 March 1907;

Georgette, Paris, Théâtre du Vaudeville, 9 December 1885;

Le Crocodile, music by Jules Massenet, Paris, Théâtre de la Porte Saint-Martin, 21 December 1886;

La Tosca, Paris, Théâtre de la Porte Saint-Martin, 24 November 1887; revised by Sardou, Giuseppe Giacosa, and Luigi Illica as the libretto for Giacomo Puccini's opera *Tosca,* Rome, Theatro Costanzi, 14 January 1900;

Marquise, Paris, Théâtre du Vaudeville, 12 February 1889;

Belle-Maman, by Sardou and Raymond Deslandes, Paris, Théâtre du Gymnase, 15 March 1889;

Cléopâtre, by Sardou and Emile Moreau, music by Leroux, Paris, Théâtre de la Porte Saint-Martin, 23 October 1890;

Thermidor, Paris, Comédie-Française, 24 January 1891;

Madame Sans-Gêne, by Sardou and Moreau, Paris, Théâtre du Vaudeville, 27 October 1893;

Gismonda, Paris, Théâtre de la Renaissance, 31 October 1894;

Marcelle, Paris, Théâtre du Gymnase, 21 December 1895;

Spiritisme, Paris, Théâtre de la Renaissance, 8 February 1897;

Paméla, Paris, Théâtre du Vaudeville, 11 February, 1898;

Robespierre, English translation by Laurence Irving, London, Royal Lyceum Theater, 15 April 1899;

La Fille de Tabarin, by Sardou and Paul, music by Gabriel Pierné, Paris, Opéra-Comique, 20 February 1901;

Les Barbares, by Sardou and Pierre Barthélemy Gheusi, music by Camille Saint-Saëns, Théâtre de l'Opéra, Paris, 23 October 1901;

Dante, by Sardou and Emile Moreau, London, Drury Lane Theatre, 30 April 1903;

La Sorcière, Théâtre Sarah-Bernhardt, 15 December 1903;

Fiorella, by Sardou and Gheusi, music by Amherst Webber, London, Waldorf Theater, 7 June 1905;

L'Espionne, Paris, Théâtre de la Renaissance, 6 December 1905;

La Piste, Paris, Théâtre des Variétés, 15 February 1906;

L'Affaire des poisons, by Sardou and Pélissié, Paris, Théâtre de la Porte Saint-Martin, 7 December 1907.

BOOKS: *La Taverne* (Paris: D. Giraud, 1854);
Les Premières Armes de Figaro, by Sardou and Emile Vanderbuch (Paris: Librairie théâtrale, 1859);

Les Gens nerveux, by Sardou and Théodore Barrière (Paris: Michel Lévy frères, 1860);

Monsieur Garat (Paris: Michel Lévy frères, 1860);

Les Pattes de mouche (Paris: Michel Lévy frères, 1860); translated by J. Palgrave Simpson as *A Scrap of Paper* (London: Lacy, 1861?; New York: French, 1861?);

L'Homme aux pigeons, by Sardou and Jules Pélissié (Paris: Michel Lévy frères, 1861);

Piccolino (Paris: Michel Lévy frères, 1861);

Les Femmes fortes (Paris: Michel Lévy frères, 1861);

Chez Bonvalet, by Sardou, Henri Lefebvre, and Pélissié (Paris: Michel Lévy frères, 1862?);

Nos Intimes! (Paris: Michel Lévy frères, 1862); translated by Horace Wigan as *Friends or Foes?* (London: T. H. Lacy, 186–); translated by George March as *Our Friends* (London: S. French, 1872);

La Papillonne (Paris: Michel Lévy frères, 1862); translated by Augustin Daly as *Taming of a Butterfly* (N.p., 1864);

Les Prés Saint-Gervais (Paris: Michel Lévy frères, 1862); translated and adapted by Robert Reece (London, 1875);

La Perle noire [novel] (Paris: Michel Lévy frères, 1862);

Les Diables noirs (Paris: Michel Lévy frères, 1862);

La Perle Noire [play] (Paris, Michel Lévy, 1862); translated by Henry Bedlow as *The Black Pearl* (New York, 1887);

Bataille d'amour, by Sardou and Karl Daclin, music by Auguste Emmanuel Vaucorbeil (Paris: Michel Lévy frères, 1863);

Les Ganaches (Paris: Michel Lévy frères, 1863); translated and adapted by Thomas W. Robertson as *Progress* (London, 1869);

Le Dégel (Paris: Michel Lévy frères, 1864); translated by Vincent Amcotts as *Adonis Vanquished* (London: T. H. Lacy, 186–);

Don Quichotte (Paris: Michel Lévy frères, 1864);

Le Capitaine Henriot, by Sardou and Gustave Vaez, music by François Auguste Gevaert (Paris: Michel Lévy frères, 1865);

L'Ecureuil (Paris: Michel Lévy frères, 1865);

Les Ondines au Champagne, by Sardou, Pélissié, and Lefebvre (Paris: E. Dentu, 1865);

Les Pommes du voisin (Paris: Michel Lévy frères, 1865);

Les Vieux Garçons (Paris: Michel Lévy frères, 1865);

Les Cinq Francs d'un bourgeois de Paris, by Sardou, Dunan-Mousseux, and Pélissié (Paris: E. Dentu, 1866);

La Famille Benoîton (Paris: Michel Lévy frères, 1866);

Maison neuve (Paris: Michel Lévy frères, 1867); translated and adapted by A. W. Pinero as *Mayfair* (London, 1869);

Nos Bons Villageois (Paris: Michel Lévy frères, 1867); translated by Daly as *Hazardous Ground* (London & New York: S. French, 1868);

Patrie! (Paris: Michel Lévy frères, 1869); translated by Barrett H. Clark (Garden City, N.Y.: Doubleday, Page, 1915);

Séraphine (Paris: Michel Lévy frères, 1869);

Fernande (Paris: Michel Lévy frères, 1870); translated and adapted by Henri L. Williams Jr. as *Fernanda; or, Forgive and Forget* (New York: R. M. De Witt, 1870);

Rabagas (Paris: Michel Lévy frères, 1872);

Le Roi Carotte, music by Jacques Offenbach (Paris: Michel Lévy frères, 1872);

Andréa (Paris: Michel Lévy frères, 1875);

Les Prés Saint-Gervais, by Sardou and Ph. Gille, music by Ch. Lecocq (Paris: Michel Lévy frères, 1875);

La Haine, by Sardou, music by Offenbach (Paris: Michel Lévy frères, 1875);

L'Oncle Sam (Paris: Michel Lévy frères, 1875);

L'Hôtel Godelot, by Sardou and Henri Crisafulli (Paris: Les Auteurs, 1875);

Piccolino, by Sardou and Charles Nuitter, music by E. Guiraud (Paris: Calmann Lévy, 1875);

L'Heure du spectacle (Paris: Charpentier, 1878);

Discours prononcé à l'Académie française, pour la réception de Victorien Sardou, le 23 mai 1878 (par le récipiendaire et M. Charles Blanc) (Paris: Firmin-Didot, 1878);

Daniel Rochat (Paris: Calmann Lévy, 1880); translated by J. V. Prichard (London & New York: S. French, 1880);

Mes Plagiats! (Paris: Librairie universelle, 1882);

Divorçons!, by Sardou and Emile de Najac (Paris: Calmann Lévy, 1883); English translation (New York: F. Rullman, 1885); translated by Herman Merivale as *The Queen's Proctor* (London: Chiswick Press, 1896); translated by M. Mayo as *Cyprienne* (New York: S. French, 1941);

Patrie!, by Sardou and Louis Gallet, music by Emile Paladilhe (Paris: Calmann Lévy, 1886);

Les Barbares, by Sardou and Pierre Barthélemy Gheusì, music by Camille Saint-Saens (Paris: Calmann Lévy, 1901);

La Fille de Tabarin, by Sardou and P. Ferrier, music by G. Pierné (Paris: Choudens, 1901);

La Sorcière (Paris: Calmann Lévy, 1904); translated by Charles Alfred Byrne as *The Sorceress* (New York: F. Rullman, 1905?);

Fiorella, by Sardou and Gheusi (Paris: Enoch, 1905);

La Piste (Paris: Illustration théâtrale, 1906);

The Merveilleuses, English translation by Basil Hood and Adrian Ross (London: Chappell, 1906);

Thermidor (Paris: Illustration théâtrale, 1907);

Madame Sans-Gêne, by Sardou and Emile Moreau (Paris: Illustration théâtrale, 1907);

Théodora (Paris: Illustration théâtrale, 1907);

L'Affaire des Poisons (Paris: Illustration théâtrale, 1908);

Belle-Maman, by Sardou and Raymond Deslandes (Paris: Illustration théâtrale, 1908);

Fédora (Paris: Illustration théâtrale, 1908); translated by John R. Coryell (New York: Street & Smith, 1890);

La Tosca (Paris: Illustration théâtrale, 1909);

Carlin (Paris: A. Michel, 1932).

Collections: *Oeuvres complètes,* 21 volumes (Paris: Michel Lévy frères, 1861–1871);

Oeuvres complètes, 15 volumes (Paris: A. Michel, 1934–1961).

OTHER: Preface to *Oeuvres de William Shakespeare,* translated by Jules Lermina (Paris: Boulanger, 1898);

Preface to *Le Théâtre français et anglais,* by Charles Hastings (Paris: Firmin-Didot, 1900);

Preface to *Hommes et choses de théâtre,* by Adolphe Aderer (Paris: Calmann Lévy, 1905);

Foreword to *Casimir Delavigne d'après des documents inédits,* edited by Marcelle Fauchier-Delavigne (Paris: Société Française d'Imprimerie et de Librairie, 1907).

Soon after the death in 1861 of Eugène Scribe, founder and master of the so-called well-made play, Victorien Sardou, Scribe's disciple in many ways, became the reigning playwright of the Parisian Boulevard stages. His knowledge of the prevailing frivolity of his time, in particular of the audiences for whom he was writing, as well as his vast erudition, his ability to detect dramatic potential (serious or comic) in whatever he read or heard, and to transform or adapt for the stage already existing materials and make them his own, are largely accountable for his enormous success. His sixty-odd plays include vaudevilles, comedies, melodramas, historical dramas, and *féeries*—fantastic plays requiring colossal stagings. A Sardou play as typically a tightly knit, straightforward, often melodramatic series of events leading in rapid succession to a climax followed by a happy ending. Lacking confusing subplots and psychological depth in its characters, its emphasis is on the visual aspects and the captivating presence of a strong female protagonist. Until his death in 1908 Sardou enjoyed popularity. Emile Fa-

guet, not the most generous of the French literary critics, ranked Sardou as one of the three most truly talented dramatists in French literature, while the sharp-tongued Bernard Shaw coined the word *sardoodledom* to describe the madness about Sardou's plays in London. In the New World audiences awaited anxiously each of his premieres, especially after he became associated with the famous Sarah Bernhardt, for whom he wrote many of his dramas.

Victorien Sardou was the oldest child of Léandre Sardou, a teacher, and Eveline Viard, a devoted wife and caring mother. Because of their precarious financial situation the Sardous changed residences frequently while Victorien was growing up, from the Marais, where Victorien spent his early childhood; to Léandre's native Cannes; and then back to Paris again, first to the Saint-Sulpice Quarter, then to the rue des Postes, the site of the highly reputable but short-lived "Pension Sardou." Victorien's intelligence and intellectual curiosity were soon detected by his father, who initially wanted him to follow his footsteps in teaching but later decided that his gifted son would have a more lucrative career if he became a doctor. Shortly after beginning his medical studies, however, Victorien turned rebellious and decided to leave not only medical school but his paternal home as well, establishing himself in a garret on the rue de Royer-Collard, near the Luxembourg. There, living on a near-starvation budget that at one point drove him to contemplate suicide, he was finally able to do as he pleased. This independence nearly brought about a rupture in his once-close relationship with his father, a relationship that would have its ups and downs until their final reconciliation in the mid 1870s, when the successful Victorien could prove to the elder Sardou that the world of the arts was morally and financially safe.

But the lessons in discipline and the sense of responsibility that he had learned at home did not go to waste; instead of becoming a bohemian Sardou worked hard from the beginning, spending his time reading history voraciously (he was particularly fond of the Renaissance and of the Revolutionary period), giving private lessons, and writing: an entry on the sixteenth century for a biographical dictionary was followed by a few articles for *L'Europe Artiste* and his first, never-to-be-performed plays. *Othon,* in verse and five acts, was a mere exercise in versification in the classical style, and the author himself was dissatisfied with its ending; *La Poudre d'Or* (Gold Dust) seemed quite dangerous because its main character, Pougnasse, a declared criminal who laughed at crime, was reminiscent of the infamous Robert Macaire; *La Reine d'Ulfra* (The Queen of Ulfra) was unsuccessful, first because of the renowned actress Rachel, who liked the script but disliked Sweden, and later because her rival, Mlle Desfossés, mysteriously disappeared right before opening night. The production of *Paris à l'enverse* (Paris Upside Down) was aborted when Eugène Scribe called it "horrible"; *Candide* was refused twice, first by Jean Hyppolite Cogniard, the director of the Théâtre des Variétés, who found it too offensive, and then by the censors themselves. Sardou also sketched the libretto for the production of *Hamlet* by Jacques Meyerbeer, who liked it but never used it.

The failure of Sardou's first performed play, *La Taverne,* at the Théâtre de l'Odéon in 1854 was a bitter pill to swallow; the overconfident author had anticipated a favorable reception and celebrated its success in advance. But this play had caught the attention of Gustave Vaez, the theater's director, and of the popular actor Boudeville, both of whom saluted Sardou as a true playwright in the making.

Determined to succeed and eager to learn the mechanics of playwriting, Sardou frequently attended performances of Scribe's comedies, rushed home, and rewrote the comedy in his own words, simply as an exercise in playwriting. By 1858 he had become somewhat known in the theatrical milieu, and things were beginning to look better for him, especially after meeting a few important people, such as Vaez and Cogniard, Charles Gounod (who recognized Sardou's talent at once), and Emile Goujon, who initiated him to spiritism. He had also moved to more comfortable quarters on the Quai Voltaire, and, most important, he had happily married Léontine Brécourt. His wife, an aspiring actress turned couturiere, introduced him to Virginie Déjazet, the renowned actress who became his artistic "godmother" and agreed to perform in *Les Premières Armes de Figaro* (Figaro's First Arms, 1859), the Sardou play she also chose for the opening of her own theater. The story about the popular hero struggling for his survival as a man of letters revisited in the vivacious Sardou style brought the playwright his first moments of satisfaction despite the cold reception by the press.

The real turning point in Sardou's career came in 1860 with *Les Pattes de mouche* (translated as *A Scrap of Paper,* 1861?), the first in a series of well-written humorous comedies that made him the most popular author of this genre. In it Sardou's ability to construct a plot and keep the audience interested in the situation (however implausible) and in the characters (however thin psychologically) came across admirably. *Les Pattes de mouche* also contained at least one element that played a central role in many of his later works—the introduction of a letter on which

the happiness or honor of the characters depends. Critics often condemned Sardou for resorting to this simple artifice to solve sometimes serious domestic dramas, but here, given the title of the comedy, the odyssey of the letter seems fully justified. In the beginning it is just there; but then, as the plot thickens, it is taken away, is partially burned, and falls into the wrong hands; it is burned again but not completely, thrown out of a window, and picked up; a message is added to it for another character to whom it is secretly sent; and it falls into the wrong hands again, is misread, intercepted, and finally destroyed, to the relief and delight of the two couples affected by its text.

With the death of Scribe in 1861 Sardou became the most popular playwright in Paris. In December of that year he gained more notoriety when *Nos Intimes!* (Our Intimates!), a comedy with serious undertones that suggests that the people closest to one are not necessarily his friends, was performed for Napoleon III and his court at Compiègne. Sardou recovered from a disappointing debut at the Comédie-Française with *La Papillonne* (The Butterfly, 1862) by later scoring two huge successes, the first with *Les Prés Saint-Gervais* (1862), in which Déjazet played *in travesti* the part of the prince of Conti, and immediately after with *Les Ganaches* (Easy Chairs, 1862), his first political play, dealing with the conflict between tradition and progress. By this time, decorated with the Légion d'Honneur and out of debt, he was able to choose freely both the subjects and the performers for his plays. Among his favorites were Déjazet, Rose Chéri, the faithful Mlle Fargueil, to whom he dedicated the controversial *Maison neuve* (1866), Marie Laurent, and, of course, Sarah Bernhardt and Réjane.

With success came material wealth and social prominence. During the summer of 1863 Sardou visited and subsequently bought the elegant estate of Mme De Béthune at Marly-le-Roi, with its old château that had once belonged to the Montmorency family; at Le Verduron he spent long periods of time with his family, wrote five hours each day during the five months it took him to complete a play, and did extensive reading in philosophy, sociology, political science, and jurisprudence. He also did painstaking research in history and archaeology; collected antiques and books; designed houses, gardens, and sets and costumes; and showed a genuine interest in agriculture and in the overall modernization of the region. He became, too, a gracious host of notable artists and intelligent socialites, especially Jacques Offenbach and Princess Mathilde, with whom he developed a close friendship. But trying times awaited Sardou just as he was becoming accustomed to this fulfilling life. The loss of his wife in 1867 was soon followed by the events that surrounded the fall of Napoleon III and the Paris Commune, which he witnessed and vividly described in his journal. A liberal monarchist, Sardou had been honored by the emperor but never fully supported him. Whatever Sardou might have thought of the Empire, he agreed even less with the politics of the Third Republic but shared his personal opinions only with his closest friends and refrained from making political statements in public–these he made forcefully enough in his plays. In fact, aside from his active involvement in the struggles during the occupation of Paris after Sedan and a short term as mayor of Marly, he did not participate again in public matters until the Dreyfus Affair, during which he openly joined forces with the French intelligentsia and became a most outspoken Dreyfussard.

He also found happiness again in his second marriage, in 1872, to Anne Soulié, daughter of the curator of the museum at Versailles. The disappointments following the initial failure of *La Haine* (Hatred, 1874), the interdiction of his *Thermidor* (1891) after its second performance, and the deaths of a few friends (Offenbach's especially, in 1880) and of his parents were practically the only clouds that darkened the otherwise serene life of the aging Sardou. He began entertaining again at Marly on Sundays. He became a member of the Académie Française in 1878, bought a second residence on the Mediterranean, and kept an apartment in Paris on the Boulevard de Courcelles. He was also appointed to the commission on Old Paris and elected president of an association of French playwrights. He continued to write regularly for the theater on a large variety of subjects, keeping alive the interest of his faithful audiences until the end of his long and productive life.

As a dramatist Sardou was the natural heir of Scribe. He assimilated and perfected the author's "well-made play" and became an unequaled master in constructing easy to understand serious and comic plots that constantly grow in complexity and tension but leave nothing unclear or unresolved at the end. If Scribe had contributed enormously to the triumph of French grand opera earlier in the century, Sardou's own libretti had the same effect on Opéra-Bouffe, the favorite musical genre during the Second Empire, and on some of the naturalistic operas that were produced in the late 1800s and at the beginning of the twentieth century. Sardou's first libretto was written rather early in his career in collaboration with François Auguste Gevaert (*Le Capitaine Henriot,* 1864). Later he collaborated with, among others, Camille Saint-Saëns (*Les Barbares* [1901]), Gabriel Pierné (*La Fille de Tabarin* [1901]), and Charles Lecocq (*Les Prés Saint-Gervais*).

With his friend Offenbach, who had written the incidental music for *La Haine,* he produced *Le Roi Carotte* (King Carrot, 1872), a subtle satire of the Second Empire; with Jules Massenet, who had volunteered to compose the accompaniment for *Théodora* (1884), he collaborated in the production of *Le Crocodile* (1886), which was misjudged by a press that did not understand that the harmless piece was simply created for the amusement of Sardou's young child. He was also credited as one of the librettists of Giacomo Puccini's opera *Tosca* (1900) and was consulted by Umberto Giordano during the composition of the opera *Fedora* (1908). Xavier Leroux readily agreed to write music for the playwright's *Cléopâtre* (1890) and *Dante* (1903).

But this and other similarities between Scribe and Sardou covered only some basic ground, for the masterful elder playwright was clearly surpassed by a highly cultivated disciple, who was much more conscious of linguistic and stylistic matters and who could therefore be infinitely more versatile in the choice of subjects and more accurate when it came to plots and characters taken directly from history. Versatility and diversity characterize Sardou's works for the theater–ninety-odd plays that comprise several types of comedies (vaudevilles, political comedies, historical comedies, comedies of manners, and comedies of character), historical and contemporary social dramas, opéra-bouffes, operettas, operas, féeries, and *pièces* (a part-drama, part-comedy hybrid genre). In his plays he takes his spectators from sixth-century Byzantium (*Théodora*) all the way to contemporary France (urban and rural) and the New World (*L'Oncle Sam* [1873]), via the colorful Renaissance period in Athens (*Gismonda* [1894]), Italy (*La Haine*), the Netherlands (*Patrie!* [1869]), and Spain (*La Sorcière* [1903]).

Sardou's comedies are full of verve, clever dialogue, and relatively believable situations. Only in his comedies of character does the author purposely resort to exaggeration, and here he evidently follows the example of Molière: Séraphine, in the homonymous play of 1868, is a fanatically devout woman, reminiscent of Tartuffe, whose statements are as outrageous as her behavior and lifestyle. Her salon is like a chapel in a boudoir, a mixture of austerity and comfort; there, only pious conversations are permitted, only *L'Abeille mystique* can be read. As a candidate for the presidency of the Society of Devout Women, Séraphine, more concerned with the spiritual than with the physical, gives alms while making the most uncharitable remarks about the needy. Her husband, a recent convert, too, has no personality and is not allowed to smoke during Lent because it is a sign of joy. And the loyal but dishonest servant, Sulpice, has gone to the theater only once, to see a performance of Jean Racine's *Athalie* (1691). Also as in Molière, both a vic-

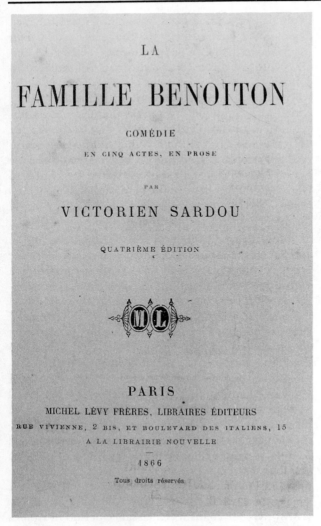

LA

FAMILLE BENOITON

COMÉDIE

EN CINQ ACTES, EN PROSE

PAR

VICTORIEN SARDOU

QUATRIÈME ÉDITION

PARIS

MICHEL LÉVY FRÈRES, LIBRAIRES ÉDITEURS

RUE VIVIENNE, 2 BIS, ET BOULEVARD DES ITALIENS, 15

A LA LIBRAIRIE NOUVELLE

1866

Tous droits réservés

Title page for Sardou's comedy about the family of a man who has become wealthy by manufacturing bedsprings

tim and a savior intervene in the name of nature and common sense. Yvonne, Séraphine's daughter, is being forced to enter a convent, and Henri de Montignac, Séraphine's former lover whom she thought dead and who also happens to be Yvonne's real father, returns just in time to avoid this disaster. All ends well: Montignac rejoins the army; Yvonne is engaged to marry her secret admirer; and Séraphine is elected president of her society.

Nos Bons Villageois (Our Good Villagers, 1867) presents the conflict between two different types of characters: the educated Parisian versus the uncivilized villagers of Bouzy-le-Têtu, who feel invaded and want to catch the intruders in their village in any wrongdoing. The rivalry starts when Morrison takes the native Grinchu's fishing spot on the river. At the town's ball the market-gardener, the grocer, and the pharmacist swear to defend the independence of their

land, just as "those famous three Swiss did," a satirical reference to the three Canton scenes in Friedrich von Schiller's *William Tell* (1804). The scenes are humorous but expose all the pettiness and prejudices of the country folk as well as the presumptiveness of others who have and know more. There is a love story in the play, and the honor of both the baron and his wife is at risk momentarily, but again all ends well. Floupin, the pharmacist, is a true caricature, the communal Homais: he is outspoken and insolent; he knows it all; he lectures; he is on the town council; and he is a churchwarden and sergeant firefighter. He is also cowardly and vindictive and must lose in the end, naturally.

Rabagas (1872) is a comedy of character that introduces the figure of the modern lawyer-politician, a true demagogue, an opportunist who is able to turn every event to his advantage. His ambition is to upset the princely regime at Monaco, establish a republic, and become the first president. He subsequently abandons his revolutionary designs and forgets his background and his former associates when he is tricked by a woman who uses flattery to disarm him; he triumphs for a day when he is appointed minister but is outsmarted and defeated and finds himself abandoned by everyone. When he finally resigns from his position, he declares that he is expatriating himself to France, the only country where people of his kind are truly appreciated. The subject is rather grim for a comedy, but it is lightened by subplots and by the outrageousness of most of Rabagas's remarks about himself, people, and politics in general.

Among Sardou's comedies of characters *Les Exilés* (1877) also deserves attention. In it Schelm, chief of police, loves Nadège, who in turn loves Max de Lussières; the dramatic interest here lies in the novelty of giving the villain a truly prominent part in the plot. Indeed, Schelm's ruthlessness and cruelty make him appear as a forerunner of that most sadistic of all Sardou's characters, Baron Scarpia in *La Tosca*, which premiered ten years later.

Isolating and exaggerating the physical or psychological traits of characters serves a purpose (usually moralizing) in the comedy of characters, but if used in the comedy of manners it risks making the plot and the characters unrealistic; this happened in quite a few of Sardou's plays. *La Famille Benoîton* (The Benoîton Family, 1865) was one of the earliest successful comedies by Sardou. The characters, the situations, the language, and the philosophy of life of the Benoîtons are truly amusing. The wealthy Monsieur Benoîton, a former bedspring maker, is now involved in real estate and construction and has embraced the fashionable positivist ideology: instead of playing with soldiers, which awaken useless warrior instincts, his children must think in positive, productive, lucrative, practical terms. As a result his family is completely dehumanized and divided. Little Didier, the oldest son, is always busy and has no spare time for his wife, Martha, and their child, which will cause a serious problem in his life as Martha starts going out alone (to gamble, not to betray him, as he thought). The youngest, Fanfan, knows how to get into his father's safe; Théodulphe leads a dissolute life and thinks that being arrested is chic and that work is good only for those who have an empty stomach. His frivolous, brainless daughters, Camille and Jeanne, are very elegant; one of them gambles, the other pretends to be an artist: she sings, paints, uses only slang ("the language of the future"), and is opinionated. As for Mme Benoîton, she is always gone. This is indeed a family without a family life and without family values. Around them Clotilde, a wealthy widow, is in the business of marrying off other people; she advises the spinster Adolphine not to be so demanding; and Formichel, a materialistic iron-structure builder, has a son, Prudent, a dishonest rascal who courts one of the Benoîton girls and tells all about his recent trip to Italy ("You see one museum, you have seen them all"; "Venice? Full of water, no people; one should fill in the Grand Canal and pave it").

Sardou criticized materialism, greed, luxury, vanity, social insensitivity, and lack of moral values in a much more serious and sharper way in *Maison neuve*. René and Claire live in an old house and work at their uncle Genevoix's shop, "A la Vieille Cocarde." Claire is bored with her modest life and convinces René to move to a luxurious new house and open a more modern shop, "Le Bouton d'Or." There they try to disregard their past and lead the frivolous life of the nouveaux riches. "Vanity is puerile, ridiculous, but it brings happiness" is their motto. Genevoix, a firm believer in traditional bourgeois values, is horrified at all this and invites the couple back to their old quarters, where they belong. They return after their illusionary world crumbles: financial ruin, social disgrace, and humiliation bring them back to their senses.

Sardou also touched upon other social issues or activities that were fashionable during the latter part of the nineteenth century. In *Divorçons!* (1880; translated as *Cyprienne,* 1882) several characters discuss the law of divorce that was being voted in the legislature. With the exception of Mme de Valfontaine, who foresees the end of the institution of marriage if the law is approved, the rest of the characters seem in favor of it. Indeed, with divorce lawfully established there would be no more need for duels or murders caused by passion or jealousy, no more sexual abstinence for betrayed wives. For them marriage is a blind alley and

divorce an exit road. Cyprienne, the protagonist, does not approve of the four-year waiting period before being able to remarry: What will she do between the time she leaves her first husband, who is no longer her husband, and her second one, who is not her husband yet? A false telegram stating that the law had actually passed inspires the rest of the hilarious dialogues and some highly dramatic confrontations before the happy finale. The entire play is built on the contradiction between an appealing idea and its unpleasantness when it becomes a reality.

In *Spiritisme* (1897) Sardou dealt with a topic he knew intimately. Mme d'Aubenas is in a train accident on her way to see her lover and is believed dead; then she appears as a spirit before her husband, who practices spiritism, tells him about her adultery and is forgiven because M. d'Aubenas believes in the doctrine of the purification of souls. This is a deceptive piece because spiritism is used here only as a gimmick for the happy solution of the central problem, which really is adultery. *Fernande* (1870) is about gambling, another fashionable activity whose popularity was reaching epidemic proportions in Paris during the second half of the nineteenth century. Again, Sardou dealt with the topic superficially. In a house where meals are served officially and gambling is done clandestinely by a group of vicious customers, the heroine manages to keep her purity and virtue intact. Her mother, a decent woman who has lost her fortune and is cruelly exploited by M. Roqueville, runs this house but is saved with her Fernande by M. Pomérol. He takes them away and helps get the two women installed in a small garden house at the residence of the wealthy Clotilde under false names. Things get complicated as Fernande's suitor, who does not know the girl's true identity or her background, happens to be the same André whom Clotilde loves. The scorned woman wants to avenge herself by destroying Fernande's life and André's happiness; an explanatory letter by Fernande never reaches André, but at the end she reads it aloud, and because of the sincerity of her sad tone he forgives her, and they embrace. Most likely, the predominantly melodramatic aspects of this pièce are the cause of its huge popularity, especially outside France.

Daniel Rochat (1880), a beautifully written play too serious for a comedy, is about two young people who love each other deeply and sincerely but are separated by an insuperable barrier: religion. Rochat is a brilliant speaker, an honest politician (diametrically opposed to Rabagas), and a declared atheist; the woman he loves is a charming person of Anglo-American descent and a practicing Anglican. At the beginning there is no disagreement: both are liberal minded; both are anti-Catholic. The conflict begins after they are legally married by the mayor. No priest is acceptable to both, but she will not consider herself married until there is a religious ceremony. Daniel makes an eloquent defense of the atheist, who is able to concentrate all his energy and love on his wife or children rather than on God. Lea argues that his love is finite while hers is infinite. Finally, Daniel yields, accepting the religious marriage provided they do it secretly, which she refuses. At that point there is no reconciliation possible: he is speaking passionately in the name of love while she reacts coldly in the name of reason; divorce is the only viable solution. *Daniel Rochat* and *Odette* (1881), a play about the aristocratic, sex-driven adulteress whose guilt prevails at the end, are the only Sardou comedies with unhappy finales.

The visit at Marly of the American Elliott Burnett, who had been acquitted of the murder of his daughter's seducer and had traveled to Europe with an extremely negative memory of the customs of his country, inspired *L'Oncle Sam* (1873; translated as *Uncle Sam*), one of Sardou's best comedies of manners. In it the author wanted to contradict the idealizations of Alexis de Tocqueville through a humorous description of the ignorance of the pragmatic Americans and of some of the flaws of their democratic system. Mme Bellamy, an adventurous, clever French woman, is determined to make a fortune in America; she fails in the beginning but succeeds when she outsmarts the shrewd Sam in the purchase and resale of worthless land. In the meantime she observes the ridiculous world around her attentively. People, customs, and institutions are scrutinized and mocked with pointed, witty *gaulois* remarks about the religious meetings in camps; the frequency and ease of divorce; the independence and shamelessness of young girls before their marriage; the racial intolerance; the excessive number of religious sects, some of which exist for sexual activities only; the unscrupulousness of commercial transactions and political deals; the impersonal relationship between parents and children; the calculating, business-minded women who treat their love affairs like "bank accounts that are easily opened and closed"; the constant mobility of the people, who do not know what a real home is (even the wealthy but miserly Sam lives in a hotel on Fifth Avenue); and the justice system, used for political purposes. While Mme Bellamy triumphs in the end but refuses to marry Sam, her friend and compatriot Robert de Rochemore falls in love and marries Sam's niece, Sarah. Sardou uses all sorts of well-known clichés and stereotypes here, but in general his criticism is harmless and the ending quite conciliatory: the French have the virtues and vices of old age and the Americans those of youth, but they can learn from each other's

experience and live together in peace and harmony. The French authorities, afraid of offending the American community, did not approve of the contents of this play, and its Parisian premiere was cancelled; it was first performed in New York, where it scored an instant success.

The intriguing milieu of diplomats and spies constituted another rich theatrical theme that Sardou used in his *Dora* (1877) and in its rearranged version (*L'Espionne* [The Female Spy, 1905]). In this case Sardou was delighted by the fact that spying was an almost exclusively female profession. But instead of making spying the central theme, the playwright made it secondary to a love story between André and the innocent Dora, falsely accused of espionage by the real spy, the jealous Countess Zicka.

Maison neuve can, in a different context, be considered an antigovernment statement, but Sardou was much more direct in expressing his political sentiments elsewhere in his works. *Patrie!* (Fatherland) and *Le Roi Carotte* precede and succeed immediately the events of 1870. The first is a spectacular historical drama in five acts whose action takes place in the Netherlands during the Spanish rule of the duke of Alba; patriotism is glorified and treason execrated. Even Victor Hugo, still in exile, praised this play, stating that its grandeur awakened noble feelings and profound thoughts. The latter work, an opéra-bouffe written in collaboration with Offenbach, is a clever satire of the weakness of a fallen regime. It is about a prince who, trusting the unwise advice of his prime minister, declares war against his better-prepared neighbor. And *L'Affaire des poisons* (The Poisoning Case), his last play, first performed on 7 December 1907, a year before his death, served as eloquent proof of the alertness of his mind and of his civic concerns: he conceived this interesting historical drama after learning about the unjust accusation of Solange d'Ormoize in the poisoning of Mlle De Fontanges, the official mistress of Louis XIV. At the time Sardou's message was loud and clear: for the villainous Colbert, lying is perfectly admissible if it is in the best interest of the state, whereas for the Abbé Griffard, the hero, there should be no higher interest among humans than that of justice itself.

Sardou and Sarah Bernhardt, two authentic "bêtes de théâtre" (theater monsters), met in the early 1880s and immediately formed a perfect and lasting artistic partnership. Bernhardt found in the plays of her "Maître Chéri" (Dear Master) the ideal vehicles for her acting talents; indeed, it was said that when performing Sardou her sometimes annoyingly affected movements and tone of voice disappeared completely to give way to naturalness, spontaneity, and sincerity. In turn Sardou found in "La divine Sarah" the ideal performer; for her he created historical plays in which the strong female protagonist practically never leaves a center-stage position. Having sensed from the beginning that Bernhardt was primarily a tragedienne, Sardou strayed away from his customary comedy-drama mixture, keeping the tone and the mood of the plays written for her at a consistently serious level. Moreover, Sardou made her appear in a variety of settings in which her magnetic personality and her regal stage presence would stand out most strikingly. In each one of them she seemed to become the character she was portraying: in *Cléopâtre*, the unhappy Egyptian Queen; in *Fédora*, a contemporary Russian Princess; in *Gismonda*, which takes place during the Renaissance, the duchess of Athens; in *La Tosca*, a roman diva during the time of Queen Caroline (about 1800); in *Théodora*, her greatest Parisian triumph in a Sardou play, she impersonated the publicly imposing but domestically weary Byzantine empress whose incognito escapades lead her to adultery, treason, and death; in *La Sorcière*, their final and universally acclaimed collaboration, she is Zoraya, a Moorish sorceress who is willing to sacrifice herself for the man she loves and who eventually poisons herself with him.

While still in his teens, living with his parents at the rue des Postes, Sardou met Henriette Lebas, a fascinating survivor of 1789 (and sister of Joseph Lebas, a close associate of Maximilien Robespierre during the Reign of Terror). She triggered his fascination with the revolutionary period, particularly with Robespierre, whom he initially admired and subsequently abhorred. Throughout his life Sardou studied and researched the French Revolution and used it as setting for his plays: *Monsieur Garat* (1860) was followed by *Les Merveilleuses* (1873), *Thermidor*, *Madame Sans-Gêne* (1893), *Paméla* (1898) and *Robespierre* (1899). The most notorious of them premiered one century after the Revolution and created a scandal known in literary circles as "La Bataille de Thermidor" (The Battle of Thermidor). After an auspicious opening at the Comédie-Française, the third performance was cancelled by order of Georges Clemenceau, who argued that the French Revolution must be judged as a whole and that for reasons of prestige its significance should not be diminished by the actions of individuals, however atrocious or regrettable. The interdiction of the play was lifted five years later, when it reopened at the Théâtre de la Porte Saint-Martin. It was a spectacular production with more than three hundred people on stage, in which the author wanted to give a vivid account of the cruelty and irrationality that characterized the last days of the Reign of Terror. Charles Labussière, the hero, is an actor, fired and replaced at the Mareux because he destroyed Jean Marat's bust; he is now a civil servant at the Comité de Sécurité Publique, where he poses as a weakling and saves victims from the guillotine by burning their files. Labussière laments the sad outcome of the initially noble intentions of the convention and blames it all on Robespierre and his cohorts, especially Louis-Antoine-Léon de Saint-Just. A realistic dramatization of the judgment and indictment of the person known as the Incorruptible is followed by the gruesome description of the departure of the last group of passengers with the frightful executioner, Sanson.

Madame Sans-Gêne, another of the plays inspired by the French Revolution, is Sardou's finest comedy. The action of the prologue takes place on 10 August 1792, that most violent day of the revolutionary period. The laundress Cathérine pays little attention to cannons and bullets and delivers a basket of clean laundry as usual—her fearlessness and carefree attitude win her the nickname of Sans-Gêne. Her shop is the meeting point of interesting beginners including Fouché and a brave Corsican soldier who is called "Timoléon Bouna . . . , Boura . . . , Buonaparte" and is always short of money to pay his bills. The three acts that follow are about Cathérine's gaffes, now that she has become the wife of Field-Marshall Lefebvre and duchess of Danzig. She dresses inappropriately, and her uncouth language and manners embarrass the emperor, who wants Lefebvre to divorce her; her sharp tongue and outrageous sallies astound the emperor himself and make her two influential enemies, Elise and Caroline, Napoleon's two patronizing sisters, with whom she is constantly at odds. But she is an honest, sensitive, attractive, and intelligent woman whose mediation is indispensable in the happy solution of all the problems afflicting herself and her former customers at the laundry shop. A charming, truly funny play worthy of Molière and Pierre-Augustin Caron de Beaumarchais, it shows Sardou's verve, wit, and inventiveness at their best.

Sardou not only put his incredible erudition to good use in his plays but also called upon it when defending himself from those who denounced him as a plagiarist. Accused by Mario Uchard of plagiarizing his *Fiammina* (1857) in *Odette*, Sardou wrote a brilliant booklet in which he not only ridiculed Uchard but also categorically refuted those who had made similar accusations against him from the earliest time of his career. In general terms his response to his accusers was quite clear and consisted of two basic arguments: first, that in the late nineteenth century it is practically impossible to be totally original, which means that, thematically, every new piece must at a given mo-

Madame Réjane as Cathérine in Madame Sans-Gêne, *Sardou's 1893 comedy about the French Revolution*

ment resemble an older one; second, that the author, any author, writes exclusively from the memory of what he has seen or read and that it is style and plot development that make a new work different from earlier ones.

The best proof of Sardou's erudition, however, came after some reviewers denounced a few anachronisms in *Théodora*. He demonstrated the ignorance and amateurism of his critics by explaining, one by one, the elements of his production, including the blue glass in Justinian's place, the myrtle branches that indicate the presence of Théodora, and the appropriate use of a fork by the empress, an argument that became known among art critics and historians as "la fourchette de Théodora" (the fork of Theodora). Only once did Sardou have to stand corrected, and this was during the preparation of Puccini's *La Tosca,* whose action takes place in Rome. For dramatic effect he wanted the Tiber (into which the heroine leaps at the end) to flow between the Sant'Angelo fortress and Saint Peter's, a geographical mistake that the composer and his Italian librettists detected immediately and would not ac-

cept, mainly because they (rightly) feared the adverse reaction of the opening-night Roman audience.

Were it not for the operas *La Tosca* and *Fédora* and for an occasional revival of *La Famille Benoîton* and *Madame Sans-Gêne,* the works of this popular playwright of the nineteenth century would now be practically forgotten. Unfortunately Sardou was writing for his day and looking for immediate success only; as a consequence many of his works have not withstood the passage of time. This is especially true with his comedies of manners: the "dreadful" railroads, positivism, the Second Empire, the ignorance and ferocity of the Communards, matters of common law, and so many other timely concerns that amused two generations of theatergoers became totally uninteresting and irrelevant to the third.

As for the historical dramas, they are praiseworthy for their accuracy and suitability for lavish productions rather than for their intrinsic literary value. Indeed, *Théodora, Patrie!,* and *Thermidor* are historically and physically correct to the point of being almost documentary pieces, while, in strictly literary terms, they are only a couple of notches above the level of melodrama. *La Haine* is an honorable exception. This was Sardou's own favorite play. The action is set in Siena during the fourteenth century, in the midst of the bitter struggle between Guibelins and Guelfs. The merit of *La Haine* lies in the fact that in it Sardou offers much more than his customary scholarly reproduction of an historical period for spectacle or for the glory of the female protagonist; instead he creates a drama in which everything looks and sounds right and true: the action is consistently plausible, and the characters have strong feelings and convictions but are vulnerable and much more humane in their reactions than those of his other plays. For once, Sardou made an extra effort and succeeded in making a perfect fusion of history and art, in the best Shakespearean manner. Cordelia, a noble Guibelin, has been raped by Orso, chief of the Guelfs. She hates him, as does Uberta, her nurse, whose child Orso has killed in battle; they both want him dead, but Cordelia's compassion is stronger than her hatred, and she saves his life. She also persuades Uberta to forgive him, saying that pardon is nobler than vengeance. Without betraying her Guibelin family, the heroine now loves and admires Orso's idealism, rejoicing at his victory over Emperor Charles, the foreign ally of the Guibelins. Orso returns triumphant and wants Guibelins, Guelfs, the rich and the poor, the patricians and the craftsmen to form a single, united, and free Siena. He also wants to marry Cordelia, but she is poisoned, and his wounds reopen. They both die. Like their cousins from Verona, these young lovers are the victims of a cruel, inhuman civil war.

The mixing of genres, in particular drama and comedy, did not contribute to the literary value of Sardou's works. Too many times his plays start out as comedies and suddenly turn into serious dramas only to return to their light beginning in the final scene. Finally, there is the question of artifice. In spite of the facility with which Sardou conceived and constructed plots and subplots, and the clever twists that helped increase the suspense until the moment of crisis (usually highly dramatic, violent scenes at the end of the penultimate act), the basic conflict is too often created by lost, misinterpreted, falsified, intercepted letters or telegrams, hidden identities, withheld information, or simple lack of communication, as in *Daniel Rochat* and *Fédora*. People at the beginning of the century laughed at a troublemaking, thieving magpie; fifty years later, in Sardou's *Les Bons Villageois,* they could laugh at a hat on which everyone's happiness or honor depended.

Sardou was seventy-five years old when his farce *La Piste* (The Trace, 1906) won unanimous acclaim of public and press, who praised with equal enthusiasm the playwright's inexhaustible energy and imagination. His popularity was also picking up in the provinces, where it had a slow start. At the beginning of his career Sardou refused to have his plays printed for fear the texts would be mutilated; in time he not only allowed them to be printed in France but also made profitable deals for their adaptations and translations into other languages, especially English. In New York several of his plays were adapted and produced by Augustin Daly in the 1870s and 1880s. Later, *tournées* of Sarah Bernhardt maintained Sardou's popularity and prestige in the New World. Death took the industrious seventy-seven-year-old Sardou while he was at work on two more dramas—"Madame Talien" and "De Batz." As commandeur of the Légion d'Honneur he was entitled to official funeral rites, which took place on 11 November 1908. A mass was said at the church of Saint François de Sales, and the remains of the man recognized as "l'homme-théâtre" were laid to rest at Marly-le-Roi.

Posterity has not been kind to Sardou, the prolific and imaginative playwright who knew better than any of his contemporaries how to entertain audiences with the dramatization of the fashions, vices, and concerns of the society of his day as well as with grandiose productions of historical plays. Had he been born in the twentieth century, his fate might have been different—his privileged eye for the typical and the unusual, his sense of humor, his unambiguous style, and particularly his cinematographic approach to producing and directing would have undoubtedly ensured him a prominent place in the world of movies alongside such entertainers as Frank Capra, Billy Wilder, and Cecil B. de Mille.

Biographies:

Jules Clarétie, *Victorien Sardou, portraits contemporains* (Paris: Librairie Illustrée, 1865);

Blanche Roosevelt, *Victorien Sardou* (London: Kegan Paul, 1892);

Hugues Rebell, *Victorien Sardou* (Paris: Jouven, 1903);

Jerome A. Hart, *Sardou and the Sardou Plays* (Philadelphia: Lippincott, 1913);

Georges Mouly, *Vie prodigieuse de Victorien Sardou (1831–1908)* (Paris: Albin Michel, 1931).

References:

Henri Becque, *Souvenirs d'un auteur dramatique* (Paris: Bibliothèque Artistique, 1895);

Sarah Bernhardt, *Mes Mémoires* (Paris: Fasquelle, 1923);

A. Brisson, *Le Théâtre et les moeurs* (Paris: E. Flammarion, 1905);

René Doumic, *Victorien Sardou,* in his *Portraits d'écrivains* (Paris: Delaplane, 1892), pp. 97–125;

Marvin Felheim, *The Theater of Augustin Daly* (Cambridge, Mass.: Harvard University Press, 1956);

Robert de Flers, "Sardou et le Théâtre Lyrique," *Musica,* 9 (November 1910): 63;

P. B. Gheusi, *Les Chefs* (Paris: E. Flammarion, 1913);

Léopold Lacour, *Trois Théâtres. Emile Augier. Alexandre Dumas fils. Victorien Sardou.* (Paris: Calmann-Lévy, 1880);

Jules Lemaître, *Impressions de théâtre* (Paris: Librairie Lecène, 1888);

Octave Mirbeau, *Gens de théâtre* (Paris: E. Flammarion, 1924);

Emile Moreau, *Thermidor, compte rendu analytique* (Paris: Librairie Nilson, 1892);

Georges Mouly, *Les Papiers de Victorien Sardou* (Paris: Albin Michel, 1934);

Armand Praviel, "Victorien Sardou," *Le Correspondant* (25 August 1931), pp. 514–528;

Jean Selz, "La Technique de l'immortalité chez Victorien Sardou," *Lettres Nouvelles,* 57 (February 1958): 278–282;

J. Weiss, *Le Théâtre et les moeurs* (Paris: Calmann-Lévy, 1889);

Emile Zola, *Nos Auteurs dramatiques,* in *Oeuvres complètes,* volume 35 (Paris: Fasquelle, n.d.), pp. 153–192.

Papers:

Sardou's papers are at the Bibliothèque Nationale in Paris.

Eugène Scribe

(24 December 1791 – 20 February 1861)

Douglas Cardwell
Salem College

PLAY PRODUCTIONS: *Les Dervis,* by Scribe and Germain Delavigne, Paris, Théâtre du Vaudeville, 2 September 1811;

L'Auberge, ou les Brigands sans le savoir, by Scribe and Delavigne, Paris, Théâtre du Vaudeville, 19 May 1812;

Thibaut, Comte de Champagne, by Scribe and Delavigne, Paris, Théâtre du Vaudeville, 27 September 1812;

Le Bachelier de Salamanque, by Scribe, Jean Henri Dupin, and Delavigne, Paris, Théâtre des Variétés, 18 January 1815;

La Mort et le bûcheron, by Scribe and Charles-Delestre Poirson, Paris, Théâtre du Vaudeville, 4 November 1815;

Une Nuit de la Garde Nationale, by Scribe and Poirson, Paris, Théâtre du Vaudeville, 4 November 1815;

Encore une Nuit de la Garde Nationale, ou le Poste de la barrière, by Scribe and Poirson, Paris, Théâtre de la Porte Saint-Martin, 15 December 1815;

Flore et Zephyre, by Scribe and Poirson, Paris, Théâtre du Vaudeville, 8 February 1816;

Le Valet de son rival, by Scribe and Delavigne, Paris, Théâtre de l'Odéon, 19 March 1816;

Farinelli, ou la Pièce de circonstance, by Scribe and Dupin, Paris, Théâtre du Vaudeville, 25 July 1816;

Gusman d'Alfarach, by Scribe and Dupin, Paris, Théâtre du Vaudeville, 22 October 1816;

Les Montagnes russes, ou le Temple à la mode, by Scribe, Poirson, and Dupin, Paris, Théâtre du Vaudeville, 31 October 1816;

La Jarretière de la mariée, by Scribe and Dupin, Paris, Théâtre des Variétés, 12 November 1816;

Le Comte Ory, anecdote du XIᵉ siècle, by Scribe and Poirson, Paris, Théâtre du Vaudeville, 16 December 1816;

Le Nouveau Pourceaugnac, by Scribe and Poirson, Paris, Théâtre du Vaudeville, 18 February 1817;

Eugène Scribe

Le Solliciteur, ou l'Art d'obtenir des places, by Scribe, J. G. Ymbert, and François-Antoine Varner, Paris, Théâtre des Variétés, 17 April 1817;

Wallace, ou la Barrière Montparnasse, by Scribe, Dupin, and Poirson, Paris, Théâtre du Vaudeville, 8 May 1817;

Les Deux Précepteurs, ou l'Asinus Asinum, by Scribe and Jean-Victor Moreau, Paris, Théâtre des Variétés, 19 June 1817;

Le Combat des montagnes, ou la Folie-Beaujon, by Scribe and Dupin, Paris, Théâtre des Variétés, 12 July 1817;

Le Café des Variétés, by Scribe and Dupin, Paris, Théâtre des Variétés, 5 August 1817;

Tous les Vaudevilles, ou Chacun chez soi, by Scribe, Marc-Antoine-Madeleine Désaugiers, and Poirson, Paris, Théâtre du Vaudeville, 18 September 1817;

Le Petit Dragon, by Scribe, Poirson, and Charles Mélesville, Paris, Théâtre du Vaudeville, 18 September 1817;

Les Comices d'Athènes, ou les Femmes Agricoles, by Scribe and Varner, Paris, Théâtre du Vaudeville, 7 November 1817;

Les Nouvelles Danaïdes, by Scribe and Dupin, Paris, Théâtre des Variétés, 3 December 1817;

La Fête du mari, ou Dissimulons, by Scribe and Dupin, Paris, Théâtre de la Gaîté, 24 December 1817;

Chactas et Atala, by Scribe and Dupin, Paris, Théâtre des Variétés, 9 March 1818;

Les Dehors Trompeurs, ou Boissy chez lui, by Scribe, Poirson, and Mélesville, Paris, Théâtre des Variétés, 6 April 1818;

Une Visite à Bedlam, by Scribe and Poirson, Paris, Théâtre du Vaudeville, 23 April 1818;

Les Vélocipèdes, ou la Poste aux chevaux, by Scribe, Dupin, and Varner, Paris, Théâtre des Variétés, 2 May 1818;

La Volière de Frère Philippe, by Scribe, Poirson, and Mélesville, Paris, Théâtre du Vaudeville, 15 June 1818;

Le Nouveau Nicaise, by Scribe and Dupin, Paris, Théâtre des Variétés, 15 October 1818;

L'Hôtel des Quatre-Nations, by Scribe, Dupin, and Nicholas Brazier, Paris, Théâtre des Variétés, 7 November 1818;

Le Fou de Péronne, Paris, Théâtre du Vaudeville, 18 January 1819;

Les Deux Maris, by Scribe and Varner, Paris, Théâtre des Variétés, 3 February 1819;

Le Mystificateur, by Scribe, Poirson, and Alphonse Cerfbeer, Paris, Théâtre du Vaudeville, 22 February 1819;

Caroline, by Scribe and Ménisser, Paris, Théâtre du Vaudeville, 15 March 1819;

Les Frères invisibles, by Scribe, Mélesville, and Poirson, Paris, Théâtre de la Porte Saint-Martin, 10 June 1819;

Les Bains à la Papa, by Scribe, Dupin, and Varner, Paris, Théâtre du Vaudeville, 9 October 1819;

Les Vêpres siciliennes, by Scribe and Mélesville, Paris, Théâtre du Vaudeville, 17 November 1819;

La Somnambule, Paris, Théâtre du Vaudeville, 6 December 1819;

L'Ennui, ou le Comte Derfort, by Scribe, Dupin, and Mélesville, Paris, Théâtre des Variétés, 2 February 1820;

L'Ours et le pacha, by Scribe and Xavier Saintine, Paris, Théâtre des Variétés, 10 February 1820;

Le Spleen, by Scribe and Poirson, Paris, Théâtre des Variétés, 20 March 1820;

Marie Jobard, by Scribe, Dupin, and Pierre-Frédéric Carmouche, Paris, Théâtre des Variétés, 11 April 1820;

Le Chat botté, by Scribe, Mélesville, and Poirson, Paris, Théâtre du Vaudeville, 19 April 1820;

L'Homme automate, by Scribe, Varner, and Ymbert, Paris, Théâtre des Variétés, 10 May 1820;

Le Vampire, Paris, Théâtre du Vaudeville, 15 June 1820;

L'Eclipse totale, by Scribe and Dupin, Paris, Théâtre des Variétés, 6 September 1820;

Le Témoin, by Scribe, Mélesville, and Saintine, Paris, Théâtre des Variétés, 28 September 1820;

Le Déluge, ou les Petits Acteurs, by Scribe, Mélesville, and Saintine, Paris, Théâtre des Variétés, 12 October 1820;

L'Homme noir, by Scribe and Dupin, Paris, Théâtre du Vaudeville, 18 November 1820;

L'Hôtel des Bains, by Scribe and Dupin, Paris, Théâtre des Variétés, 22 November 1820;

Le Beau Narcisse, Paris, Théâtre de la Porte Saint-Martin, 9 December 1820;

Le Boulevard Bonne-Nouvelle, by Scribe, Moreau, and Mélesville, Paris, Théâtre du Gymnase, 28 December 1820;

L'Amour platonique, by Scribe and Mélesville, Paris, Théâtre du Gymnase, 18 January 1821;

Le Secrétaire et le cuisinier, by Scribe and Mélesville, Paris, Théâtre du Gymnase, 18 January 1821;

Frontin Mari-Garçon, by Scribe and Mélesville, Paris, Théâtre du Vaudeville, 18 January 1821;

Le Colonel, by Scribe and Delavigne, Théâtre du Gymnase, 29 January 1821;

L'Intérieur de l'étude, ou le Procureur et l'avoué, by Scribe and Dupin, Paris, Théâtre des Variétés, 1 February 1821;

Le Gastronome sans argent, by Scribe and Brulay, Paris, Théâtre du Gymnase, 10 March 1821;.

Le Parrain, by Scribe, Poirson, and Mélesville, Paris, Théâtre du Gymnase, 23 April 1821;

Le Ménage de garçon, by Scribe and Dupin, Paris, Théâtre du Gymnase, 27 April 1821;

La Campagne, by Scribe, Dupin, and Mélesville, Paris, Théâtre des Variétés, 7 May 1821;

La Petite Soeur, by Scribe and Mélesville, Paris, Théâtre du Gymnase, 6 June 1821;

Le Mariage enfantin, by Scribe and Delavigne, Paris, Théâtre du Gymnase, 16 August 1821;

Les Petites Misères de la vie humaine, by Scribe and Mélesville, Paris, Théâtre du Gymnase, 20 October 1821;

L'Amant bossu, by Scribe, Mélesville, and Vandière, Paris, Théâtre du Gymnase, 22 October 1821;

L'Artiste, by Scribe and Adrien Perlet, Paris, Théâtre du Gymnase, 23 November 1821;

Michel et Christine, by Scribe and Dupin, Paris, Théâtre du Gymnase, 3 December 1821;

Philibert Marié, by Scribe and Moreau, Paris, Théâtre du Gymnase, 26 December 1821;

Le Plaisant de société, by Scribe and Mélesville, Paris, Théâtre du Gymnase, 18 February 1822;

Mémoires d'un Colonel de Hussards, by Scribe and Mélesville, Paris, Théâtre du Gymnase, 21 February 1822;

La Demoiselle et la dame, ou Avant et après, by Scribe, Dupin, and F. de Courcy, Paris, Théâtre du Gymnase, 11 March 1822;

La Petite Folle, by Scribe and Mélesville, Paris, Théâtre du Gymnase, 6 May 1822;

Le Vieux Garçon et la petite fille, by Scribe and Delavigne, Paris, Théâtre du Gymnase, 24 May 1822;

Les Nouveaux Jeux de l'amour et du hasard, by Scribe and Delavigne, Paris, Théâtre du Gymnase, 21 June 1822;

Les Eaux du Mont-Dore, by Scribe, de Courcy, and Saintine, Paris, Théâtre du Gymnase, 25 July 1822;

La Veuve du Malabar, by Scribe and Mélesville, Paris, Théâtre du Gymnase, 19 August 1822;

La Nouvelle Clary, ou Louise et Georgette, by Scribe and Dupin, Paris, Théâtre du Gymnase, 11 November 1822;

L'Ecarté, ou un Coin du salon, by Scribe, Mélesville, and Jules-Henri de Saint-Georges. Théâtre du Gymnase, 14 November 1822;

Le Bon Papa, ou la Proposition de mariage, by Scribe and Mélesville, Paris, Théâtre du Gymnase, 2 December 1822;

Valérie, by Scribe and Mélesville, Paris, Théâtre-Français, 21 December 1822;

La Loge du portier, by Scribe and Mazères, Paris, Théâtre du Gymnase, 14 January 1823;

L'Intérieur d'un bureau, ou la Chanson, by Scribe, Ymbert, and Varner, Paris, Théâtre du Gymnase, 25 February 1823;

Trilby, ou le Lutin d'Argail, by Scribe and Pierre-Frédéric-Adophe Carmouche, Paris, Théâtre du Gymnase, 13 March 1823;

Le Plan de campagne, by Scribe, Dupin, and Mélesville, Paris, Théâtre du Gymnase, 14 April 1823;

Le Menteur véridique, by Scribe and Mélesville, Paris, Théâtre du Gymnase, 24 April 1823;

La Pension bourgeoise, by Scribe, Dupin, and Dumersan, Paris, Théâtre du Gymnase, 27 May 1823;

La Maîtresse au logis, Paris, Théâtre du Gymnase, 9 June 1823;

Partie et revanche, by Scribe, Francis, and Nicholas Brazier, Paris, Théâtre du Gymnase, 16 June 1823;

L'Avare en goguettes, by Scribe and Delavigne, Paris, Théâtre du Gymnase, 12 July 1823;

Les Grisettes, by Scribe and Dupin, Paris, Théâtre du Gymnase, 8 August 1823;

La Vérité dans le vin, by Scribe and Edouard Mazères, Paris, Théâtre du Gymnase, 10 October 1823;

Le Retour, ou la Suite de Michel et Christine, by Scribe and Dupin, Paris, Théâtre du Gymnase, 17 October 1823;

Un Dernier Tour de fortune, by Scribe and Louis Emmanuel Félicité Charles Dupaty, Paris, Théâtre du Gymnase, 11 November 1823;

Rodolphe, ou Frère et soeur, Paris, Théâtre du Gymnase, 20 November 1823;

Rossini à Pâris, ou le Grand Dîner, by Scribe and Mazères, Paris, Théâtre du Gymnase, 29 November 1823;

L'Héritière, by Scribe and Delavigne, Paris, Théâtre du Gymnase, 20 December 1823;

Le Coiffeur et le perruquier, by Scribe and Mazères, Paris, Théâtre du Gymnase, 15 January 1824;

Le Fondé de pouvoirs, by Scribe and Carmouche, Paris, Théâtre du Gymnase, 18 February 1824;

La Mansarde des artistes, by Scribe, Dupin, and Varner, Paris, Théâtre du Gymnase, 2 April 1824;

Les Trois Genres, Paris, Théâtre de l'Odéon, 27 April 1824;

Le Leicester du Faubourg, ou l'Amour et l'ambition, by Scribe, Saintine, and Carmouche, Paris, Théâtre du Gymnase, 1 May 1824;

Le Baiser au porteur, by Scribe, Justin Gensoul, and de Courcy, Paris, Théâtre du Gymnase, 9 June 1824;

Le Dîner sur l'herbe, by Scribe and Mélesville, Paris, Théâtre du Gymnase, 2 July 1824;

Les Adieux au comptoir, by Scribe, Dupin, and Varner, Paris, Théâtre de Madame, 9 August 1824;

Le Château de la poularde, by Scribe, Dupin, and Varner, Paris, Théâtre de Madame, 4 October 1824;

Le Bal champêtre, ou les Grisettes à la campagne, by Scribe and Dupin, Paris, Théâtre de Madame, 21 October 1824;

Coraly, ou la Soeur et le frère, by Scribe and Mélesville, Paris, Théâtre de Madame, 19 November 1824;

Monsieur Tardif, by Scribe and Mélesville, Paris, Théâtre de Madame, 1 December 1824;

La Haine d'une femme, ou le Jeune Homme à marier, Paris, Théâtre de Madame, 14 December 1824;

Vatel, ou le Petit-fils d'un grand homme, by Scribe and Mazères, Paris, Théâtre de Madame, 18 January 1825;

La Quarantaine, by Scribe and Mazères, Paris, Théâtre de Madame, 3 February 1825;

Le Plus Beau Jour de la vie, by Scribe and Varner, Paris, Théâtre de Madame, 22 February 1825;

La Charge à payer, ou la Mère intrigante, by Scribe and Varner, Paris, Théâtre de Madame, 13 April 1825;

Les Inséparables, by Scribe and Dupin, Paris, Théâtre de Madame, 2 May 1825;

Le Charlatanisme, by Scribe and Mazères, Paris, 10 May 1825;

Les Empiriques d'autrefois, by Scribe and Alexandre, Paris, Théâtre de Madame, 11 June 1825;

Le Mauvais Sujet, by Scribe and Camille, Paris, Théâtre du Gymnase, 16 July 1825;

Les Premières Amours, ou les Souvenirs d'enfance, Paris, Théâtre de Madame, 12 November 1825;

Le Médecin des dames, by Scribe and Mélesville, Paris, Théâtre de Madame, 17 December 1825;

Le Confident, by Scribe and Mélesville, Paris, Théâtre de Madame, 5 January 1826;

La Demoiselle à marier, ou la Première Entrevue, by Scribe and Mélesville, Paris, Théâtre de Madame, 18 January 1826;

Le Testament de Polichinelle, by Scribe, Moreau, and A. M. Lafortelle, Paris, Théâtre de Madame, 17 February 1826;

Les Manteaux, by Scribe, Varner, and Dupin, Paris, Théâtre de Madame, 20 February 1826;

La Belle-Mère, by Scribe and Jean-François-Alfred Bayard, Paris, Théâtre de Madame, 1 March 1826;

L'Oncle d'Amérique, by Scribe and Mazères, Paris, Théâtre de Madame, 14 March 1826;

La Lune de miel, by Scribe, Mélesville, and Carmouche, Paris, Théâtre de Madame, 31 March 1826;

Simple histoire, by Scribe and de Courcy, Paris, Théâtre de Madame, 26 May 1826;

L'Ambassadeur, by Scribe and Mélesville, Paris, Théâtre de Madame, 10 July 1826;

Le Mariage de raison, by Scribe and Varner, Paris, Théâtre de Madame, 10 October 1826;

La Chatte métamorphosée en femme, by Scribe and Mélesville, Paris, Théâtre de Madame, 3 March 1827;

Les Elèves du conservatoire, by Scribe and Saintine, Paris, Théâtre de Madame, 28 March 1827;

Le Diplomate, by Scribe and Delavigne, Paris, Théâtre de Madame, 23 October 1827;

La Marraine, by Scribe, M. Lockroy, and Chabot, Paris, Théâtre de Madame, 27 November 1827;

Le Mariage d'argent, Paris, Théâtre-Français, 3 December 1827;

Le Mal du pays, ou la Batelière de Brienz, by Scribe and Mélesville, Paris, Théâtre de Madame, 28 December 1827;

Le Prince Charmant, ou les Contes de fée, by Scribe, Poirson, and Dupin, Paris, Théâtre de Madame, 14 February 1828;

Yelva, ou l'Orpheline russe, by Scribe, Devilleneuve and Desvergiers, Paris, Théâtre de Madame, 18 March 1828;

Le Vieux Mari, by Scribe and Mélesville, Paris, Théâtre de Madame, 2 May 1828;

La Manie des places, ou la Folie du siècle, by Scribe and Bayard, Paris, Théâtre de Madame, 19 June 1828;

Avant, pendant, et après, by Scribe and Baron de Rougemont, Paris, Théâtre de Madame, 28 June 1828;

Le Baron de Trenck, by Scribe and Delavigne, Paris, Théâtre de Madame, 14 October 1828;

Les Moralistes, by Scribe and Varner, Paris, Théâtre de Madame, 22 November 1828;

Malvina, ou un Mariage d'inclination, Paris, Théâtre de Madame, 8 December 1828;

Théobald, ou le Retour de Russie, by Scribe and Varner, Paris, Théâtre de Madame, 12 February 1829;

Madame de Sainte-Agnès, by Scribe and Varner, Paris, Théâtre de Madame, 20 February 1829;

Aventures et voyages du Petit Jonas, by Scribe and Dupin, Paris, Théâtre des Nouveautés, 28 February 1829;

La Bohémienne, ou l'Amérique en 1775, by Scribe and Mélesville, Paris, Théâtre du Gymnase, 1 June 1829;

Les Héritiers de Crac, by Scribe and Mélesville, Paris, Théâtre de Madame, 21 August 1829;

La Famille du baron, by Scribe and Mélesville, Paris, Théâtre de Madame, 21 August 1829;

Les Actionnaires, by Scribe and Bayard, Paris, Théâtre de Madame, 22 October 1829;

Louise, ou la Réparation, by Scribe, Mélesville, and Bayard, Paris, Théâtre de Madame, 16 November 1829;

Les Inconsolables, Paris, Théâtre-Français, 8 December 1829;

La Cour d'Assises, by Scribe and Varner, Paris, Théâtre de Madame, 28 December 1829;

La Seconde Année, ou à qui la faute?, by Scribe and Mélesville, Paris, Théâtre de Madame, 12 January 1830;

Zoé, ou l'Amant prêté, by Scribe and Mélesville, Paris, Théâtre de Madame, 16 March 1830;

Philippe, by Scribe, Mélesville, and Bayard, Paris, Théâtre de Madame, 19 April 1830;

Le Foyer du Gymnase, Paris, Théâtre du Gymnase, 17 August 1830;

Une Faute, Paris, Théâtre du Gymnase, 17 August 1830;

La Protectrice, by Scribe and Varner, Paris, Théâtre du Gymnase, 2 November 1830;

Jeune et Vieille, ou le Premier et le dernier chapitre, by Scribe, Mélesville, and Bayard, Paris, Théâtre du Gymnase, 18 November 1830;

La Famille Riquebourg, ou le Mariage mal assorti, Paris, Théâtre du Gymnase, 1 January 1831;

Les Trois Maîtresses, ou une Cour d'Allemagne, by Scribe and Bayard, Paris, Théâtre du Gymnase, 24 January 1831;

Le Budget d'un jeune ménage, by Scribe and Bayard, Paris, Théâtre du Gymnase, 4 March 1831;

Le Quaker et la danseuse, Paris, Théâtre du Gymnase, 28 March 1831;

La Favorite, Paris, Théâtre du Gymnase, 16 May 1831;

Le Comte de Saint-Ronan, ou l'Ecole et le château, by Scribe and Dupin, Paris, Théâtre du Palais Royal, 21 June 1831;

Le Suisse de l'Hôtel: Anecdote de 1816, by Scribe and de Rougemont, Paris, Théâtre du Gymnase, 14 November 1831;

Le Soprano, by Scribe and Mélesville, Paris, Théâtre du Gymnase, 30 November 1831;

Le Luthier de Lisbonne, by Scribe and Bayard, Paris, Théâtre du Gymnase, 7 December 1831;

La Vengeance italienne, ou le Français à Florence, by Scribe, Poirson, and Desnoyers, Paris, Théâtre du Gymnase, 23 January 1832;

Le Chaperon, by Scribe and Paul Duport, Paris, Théâtre du Gymnase, 6 February 1832;

Le Savant, by Scribe and Monvel, Paris, Théâtre du Gymnase, 22 February 1832;

Schahabaham II, ou les Caprices d'un autocrate, by Scribe and Saintine, Paris, Théâtre du Gymnase, 2 March 1832;

Dix Ans de la vie d'une femme, ou les Mauvais Conseils, by Scribe and Terrier, Paris, Théâtre de la Porte Saint-Martin, 17 March 1832;

L'Apollon du Réverbère, ou les Conjectures du Carrefour, by Scribe, Mélesville, and Saintine, Paris, Théâtre des Variétés, 21 March 1832;

Le Premier Président, by Scribe and Mélesville, Paris, Théâtre du Gymnase, 21 August 1832;

Une Monomanie, by Scribe and Duport, Paris, Théâtre du Gymnase, 31 August 1832;

Le Paysan amoureux, by Scribe and Bayard, Paris, Théâtre du Gymnase, 17 September 1832;

La Grande Aventure, by Scribe and Varner, Paris, Théâtre du Gymnase, 2 November 1832;

Toujours, ou l'Avenir d'un fils, by Scribe and Varner, Paris, Théâtre du Gymnase, 13 November 1832;

Camilla, ou la Soeur et le frère, by Scribe and Bayard, Paris, Théâtre du Gymnase, 12 December 1832;

Le Voyage dans l'appartement, ou l'Influence des localités, by Scribe and Duport, Paris, Théâtre des Variétés, 18 January 1833;

Les Malheurs d'un Amant heureux, Paris, Théâtre du Gymnase, 29 January 1833;

Le Gardien, by Scribe and Bayard, Paris, Théâtre du Gymnase, 11 March 1833;

Le Moulin de javelle, by Scribe and Mélesville, Paris, Théâtre du Gymnase, 8 July 1833;

Jean de Vert, by Scribe, Mélesville, and Carmouche, Paris, Théâtre du Vaudeville, 19 August 1833;

Un Trait de Paul I, ou le Czar et la Vivandière, by Scribe and Duport, Paris, Théâtre du Gymnase, 12 September 1833;

La Dugazon, ou le Choix d'une maîtresse, by Scribe and Duport, Paris, Théâtre du Gymnase, 30 October 1833;

Bertrand et Raton, ou l'Art de conspirer, Paris, Théâtre-Français, 14 November 1833;

Le Lorgnon, Paris, Théâtre du Gymnase, 21 December 1833;

La Chanoinesse, by Scribe and Francis-Cornu, Paris, Théâtre du Gymnase, 31 December 1833;

La Passion secrète, Paris, Théâtre-Français, 13 March 1834;

Salvoisy, ou l'Amoureux de la reine, by Scribe, de Rougemont, and Alexis de Camberousse, Paris, Théâtre du Gymnase, 18 April 1834;

La Frontière de Savoie, by Scribe and Bayard, Paris, Théâtre du Gymnase, 20 August 1834;

Estelle, ou le Père et la fille, Paris, Théâtre du Gymnase, 7 November 1834;

L'Ambitieux, Paris, Théâtre-Français, 27 November 1834;

Etre aimé, ou, Mourir, Paris, Théâtre du Gymnase, 10 March 1835;

Une Chaumière et son coeur, Paris, Théâtre du Gymnase, 12 May 1835;

La Pensionnaire mariée, by Scribe and Varner, Paris, Théâtre du Gymnase, 3 November 1835;

Valentine, by Scribe and Mélesville, Paris, Théâtre du Gymnase, 4 January 1836;

Chut!, Paris, Théâtre du Gymnase, 26 March 1836;

Sir Hugues de Guilfort, by Scribe and Bayard, Paris, Théâtre du Gymnase, 3 October 1836;

Avis aux Coquettes, ou l'Amant singulier, by Scribe and de Camberousse, Paris, Théâtre du Gymnase, 29 October 1836;

Le Fils d'un agent de change, by Scribe and Dupin, Paris, Théâtre des Variétés, 30 November 1836;

Les Dames patronnesses, ou à quelque-chose malheur est Bon, by Scribe and Arvers, Paris, Théâtre du Gymnase, 15 February 1837;

César, ou le Chien du château, by Scribe and Varner, Paris, Théâtre du Gymnase, 4 March 1837;

L'Etudiant et la Grande Dame, by Scribe and Mélesville, Paris, Théâtre des Variétés, 30 March 1837;

Le Bout de l'an, ou les Deux Cérémonies, by Scribe and Varner, Paris, Théâtre du Palais Royal, 2 June 1837;

La Camaraderie, ou la Courte-échelle, Paris, Théâtre-Français, 19 June 1837;

Les Indépendants, Paris, Théâtre-Français, 20 November 1837;

Clermont, ou une Femme d'artiste, by Scribe and Vander-Burch, Paris, Théâtre du Gymnase, 30 March 1838;

La Calomnie, Paris, Théâtre-Français, 20 February 1840;

La Grand'mère, ou les Trois Amours, Paris, Théâtre du Gymnase, 14 March 1840;

Japhet, ou la Recherche d'un père, by Scribe and Vander-Burch, Paris, Théâtre-Français, 20 July 1840;

Le Verre d'eau, ou les Effets et les causes, Paris, Théâtre-Français, 17 November 1840;

Cicily, ou le Lion amoureux, Paris, Théâtre du Gymnase, 8 December 1840;

Le Veau d'or, by Scribe and Dupin, Paris, Théâtre du Gymnase, 26 February 1841;

Une Chaîne, Paris, Théâtre-Français, 29 November 1841;

Oscar, ou le Mari qui trompe sa femme, by Scribe and Joseph Duveyrier, Paris, Théâtre-Français, 21 April 1842;

Le Fils de Cromwell, ou une Restauration, Paris, Théâtre-Français, 20 November 1842;

La Tutrice, ou l'Emploi des richesses, by Scribe and Duport, Paris, Théâtre-Français, 29 November 1843;

Les Surprises, by Scribe and Roger, Paris, Théâtre du Gymnase, 31 July 1844;

Babiole et Joblot, by Scribe and Saintine, Paris, Théâtre du Gymnase, 1 October 1844;

Rebecca, Paris, Théâtre du Gymnase, 2 December 1844;

L'Image, by Scribe and Sauvage, Paris, Théâtre du Gymnase, 17 April 1845;

Jeanne et Jeanneton, by Scribe and Varner, Paris, Théâtre du Gymnase, 29 April 1845;

La Loi salique, Paris, Théâtre du Gymnase, 30 December 1845;

Geneviève, ou la Jalousie paternelle, Paris, Théâtre du Gymnase, 30 March 1846;

La Protégée sans le savoir, Paris, Théâtre du Gymnase, 5 December 1846;

Maître Jean, ou la Comédie à la cour, by Scribe and Dupin, Paris, Théâtre du Gymnase, 14 January 1847;

Irène, ou le Magnétisme, by Scribe and Lockroy, Paris, Théâtre du Gymnase, 2 February 1847;

D'Aranda, ou les Grandes Passions, Paris, Théâtre du Gymnase, 6 April 1847;

Une Femme qui se jette par la fenêtre, by Scribe and Gustave Lemoine, Paris, Théâtre du Gymnase, 19 April 1847;

La Déesse, by Scribe and Saintine, Paris, Théâtre du Gymnase, 30 October 1847;

Le Puff, ou Mensonge et vérité, Paris, Théâtre-Français, 22 January 1848;

O Amitié! ou les Trois Epoques, by Scribe and Varner, Paris, Théâtre du Gymnase, 14 November 1848;

Les Filles du docteur, ou le Dévouement, by Scribe and Michael Masson, Paris, Théâtre du Gymnase, 10 February 1849;

Adrienne Lecouvreur, by Scribe and Emile Legouvé, Paris, Théâtre-Français, 14 April 1849;

Héloïse et Abélard, ou à quelque-chose malheur est bon, by Scribe and Masson, Paris, Théâtre du Gymnase, 22 April 1850;

Les Contes de la Reine de Navarre, ou la Revanche de Pavie, by Scribe and Legouvé, Paris, Théâtre-Français, 15 October 1850;

La Bataille de dames, ou un Duel en amour, by Scribe and Legouvé, Paris, Théâtre-Français, 17 March 1851;

Madame Schlick, by Scribe and Varner, Paris, Théâtre du Gymnase, 9 February 1852;

Mon Etoile, Paris, Théâtre-Français, 6 February 1854;

La Czarine, Paris, Théâtre-Français, 15 January 1855;

Feu Lionel, ou Qui vivra verra, by Scribe and Charles Potron, Paris, Théâtre-Français, 23 January 1858;

Les Doigts de fée, by Scribe and Legouvé, Paris, Théâtre-Français, 29 March 1858;

Les Trois Maupin, ou la Veille de la régence, by Scribe and Boisseaux, Paris, Théâtre du Gymnase, 23 October 1858;

Rêves d'amour, by Scribe and Etienne de Biéville, Paris, Théâtre-Français, 1 March 1859;

La Fille de trente ans, by Scribe and Emile de Najac, Paris, Théâtre du Vaudeville, 15 December 1859;

La Frileuse, Paris, Théâtre du Vaudeville, 6 September 1861.

BOOKS: *Une Nuit de la Garde-Nationale* (Paris: Gages, 1815);

L'Ours et le pacha (Paris: J. Didot l'aîné, 1820);

Valérie (Paris: Ladvocat, 1822);

Rodolphe, ou Frère et soeur (Paris: Pollet, 1823);

Le Mariage d'argent (Paris: J. Didot, 1827?);

La Bohémienne, ou L'Amérique en 1775 (Paris: Pollet, 1829);

Dix Ans de la vie d'une femme, ou Les Mauvais Conseils (Paris: J. N. Barba, 1832);

Bertrand et Raton, ou L'Art de conspirer (Paris: J. N. Barba, 1833);

La Passion secrète (Paris: J. N. Barba, 1834);

L'Ambitieux (Paris: André, 1835);

Les Indépendants (Brussels, 1837);

La Camaraderie, ou La Courte-échelle (Paris: J. N. Barba, 1837);

Oeuvres complètes, 5 volumes (Paris: Furne, 1840–1841).

Oeuvres complètes, 8 volumes (Paris: Furne, 1840–1858);

La Calomnie (Brussels, 1840);

Le Verre d'eau, ou Les Effets et les causes (Paris: Calmann-Lévy, n.d. [1840s?]);

Une Chaîne (Paris: Beck, 1841?);

Le Fils de Cromwell, ou une Restauration (Paris: Tresse, 1842);

Oscar, ou le Mari qui trompe sa femme (Paris: Beck, 1842?);

La Tutrice, ou l'Emploi des richesses (Paris, 1844);

Le Puff, ou Mensonge et vérité (Paris: Beck, 1848?);

Adrienne Lecouvreur (Paris: Beck, 1849);

Les Contes de la reine de Navarre, ou la Revanche de Pavie (Paris, 1850);

La Bataille de dames (Paris: Calmann-Lévy, 1851);

Mon étoile (Paris: Beck, 1854);

Oeuvres complètes, 17 volumes (Paris: Lebigre-Duquesne, 1854–1858);

La Czarine (Paris: Michel Lévy frères, 1855);

Les Trois Maupin, ou la Veille de la régence (Paris: Charlieu, 1858);

Feu Lionel, ou Qui vivra verra (Paris: Michel Lévy frères, 1858);

Les Doigts de fée (Paris: Calmann-Lévy, [1858–1859?]);

Rêves d'amour (Paris: Michel Lévy frères, 1859);

La Fille de trente ans (Paris: Michel Lévy frères, 1860);

La Frileuse (Paris, 1861);

Oeuvres complètes de Eugène Scribe, 76 volumes (Paris: E. Dentu, 1874–1885).

OTHER: "Discours de M. Scribe prononcé dans la séance publique du 28 janvier 1836 en venant prendre séance à la place de M. Arnault," in *Recueil des discours, rapports et pièces diverses lus dans les séances publiques et particulières de l'Académie française, 1830–1839* (Paris: Firmin Didot frères, 1841).

Augustin-Eugène Scribe was the first French playwright to make a fortune solely by writing plays. He was proud to acknowledge the source of his income and went so far as to have inscribed over the gate of his country estate: "Le théâtre a payé cet asile champêtre / Vous qui passez, merci! Je vous le dois peut-être." (The theater funded this rustic retreat. Thanks, traveler! I may owe it to you.) He was so much in demand that he could negotiate good royalties for his plays, and he helped impose the rules that brought similar benefits to his fellow authors. His name on the playbill virtually assured a successful run, and his inventive mind and quick pen kept his name constantly in the public eye and brought them back regularly to the theaters he supplied. He was as versatile as he was prolific; in the E. Dentu edition of his complete works, which may not be complete because he used several pseudonyms, there are, according to the editors' classification, 35 plays, 216 vaudevilles, 86 comic operas, and 37 operas and ballets as well as a few undistinguished works of prose fiction. His fame waned only gradually after his death in 1861, and by 1920 the Théâtre-Français had performed the twenty-four plays he contributed to its repertory more than three thousand times. It would be foolhardy even to guess the total number of performances of all his works, but it is easy to see to what extent Scribe dominated the stage both during and after his lifetime and thus to understand the basis for the resentment many of his competitors and successors felt. He was even accused of driving Gérard de Nerval to suicide, a charge that led to a successful suit for libel. He was widely imitated by playwrights as different as Henrik Ibsen, Bernard Shaw, Emile Augier, and Georges Feydeau, to name but a few, many of whom denied their debt to him and joined his detractors, who had almost from the beginning loudly proclaimed his supposed faults. Such sustained criticisms and a vogue for new forms led to his eventual eclipse. A few of his plays have been produced in modern times, but today few among the theatergoing public even know his name although the techniques he used so masterfully continue to permeate the theater and made their way into the cinema and eventually into television.

Scribe was the perfecter of the well-made play, taking forms and devices from the theater of earlier periods and combining them in inventive and systematic ways that constituted a new type of play adaptable to various styles and genres, which, by its clarity, logic, and intriguing combination of inevitability and surprise, seldom failed to please the public. His less talented imitators reduced his practice to a formula that grew tiresome, but a reading of his plays yields more of an impression of variety than of similarity, with a wide range of characters, situations, events, time periods, places, and settings.

Scribe rejuvenated each genre to which he set his hand, adapting both form and subject matter to suit his own concepts, finding in each genre audiences receptive to his new ways, and leaving on each an imprint that can still be seen. It is a rare author who can so dominate the stage of his time that he could have successful productions running concurrently in several theaters of Paris and in genres as varied as those represented by the Théâtre de l'Opéra, the Théâtre de l'Opéra-Comique, the Théâtre du Gymnase (headquarters for the *comédie-vaudeville,* thanks to Scribe), and the Théâtre-Français and do so year after year.

This master of the stage was born in Paris on 24 December 1791. His father, a silk merchant, died when Eugène was an infant but left enough for his widow to raise their son without financial worries. She was able to send him to good schools, and he was a brilliant student at the Collège Sainte-Barbe, where he finished with first prize in his last year. He received his prize under the dome of the Académie Française and, coincidentally, from the hands of Vincent-Antoine Arnault, whose seat at the Académie he eventually inherited. His mother then placed him with a prominent lawyer, expecting him to demonstrate his talents in the field of law, but young Eugène had developed a passion for the theater, and neither his mother's nor his employer's efforts could keep him away. When his mother died in 1807, his inheritance provided him an adequate living, and there was nothing to prevent him from devoting himself fully to the theater. He soon graduated from watching plays to writing them in collaboration with his former classmate, Germain Delavigne, and others.

The first play to be staged, on 13 January 1810, was *Le Prétendu par hasard; ou l'Occasion fait le larron* (The Accidental Suitor; or, Opportunity Makes the Thief), which did not make it through its first performance. Over the next five years there followed more plays, none of which could be counted a success. After several failures Delavigne gave up, but Scribe struggled on, and eventually his persistence was rewarded. In November 1815 he achieved his first hit with *Une Nuit de la Garde Nationale* (A Night at the National Guard), which opened a vein he would mine for the rest of his career. It broke with the pastoral tradition of the comédie-vaudeville to deal realistically with a contemporary subject. He also achieved the right tone, finding humor in particular situations rather than in mocking his characters, which meant that even members of the guard could laugh rather than take offense.

Although there were more failures, it did not take long for the successes to mount as Scribe's prolific pen churned out more than a dozen works a year. Many were written with collaborators, which was a frequent practice at the time, and he was always generous with his colleagues, sharing both credit and profits even though in many cases he did more than his share of the work. Indeed, there are many stories of people who brought him ideas or drafts of works that he turned into successful plays; when Scribe invited such people to the premieres, they did not recognize their paternity and were amazed to hear themselves named as an author at the end of the performance. It is noteworthy that his collaborators always remained his friends.

The opening of the Théâtre du Gymnase in 1820 demonstrated and added to the prominence of Scribe. He provided its first play and was bound to it by a long-term contract. Over the next decade he wrote more than a hundred plays for the Théâtre du Gymnase, which did not keep him from filling other theaters with more than forty more. His production included not only vaudevilles but also full-length dramas for the Théâtre-Français and librettos for the Opéra-Comique and the Opéra. He showed that he could be serious as well as funny and that he understood the special needs of the musical genres, which made him much in demand as a librettist. He worked with the outstanding composers of the day, including Esprit Auber, Fromental Halévy, Giacomo Meyerbeer, François-Adrien Boïeldieu, Gioacchino Rossini, and Giuseppe Verdi.

His popularity made him an invaluable member of the Société des Auteurs et Compositeurs Dramatiques, which he helped found in 1827. Writers had little leverage in dealing with theater managers and often had to settle for nominal payments for their work even if it went on to make a fortune for the theater. The new organization was able to establish fairer practices that set minimum payments and allowed those in great demand, such as Scribe, to negotiate upward from the base payments.

In 1834 Scribe entered the Académie Française, replacing Arnault in the seat that had once belonged to Jean Racine. His election was by no means universally acclaimed, for many critics, especially those associated with the Romantic movement, had long decried his "lack of style," as Théophile Gautier put it. They placed primary emphasis on the literary value of dramatic works, and they could forgive him neither for his preference for realistic dialogue, including the catchwords of the day and unfinished sentences, nor the commercial success he enjoyed and that was denied the authors they favored. There were also comments about his collaborators by those who unwittingly, or perhaps willfully, ignored the preponderant share of labor that Scribe took upon himself. Scribe, following his usual practice when he was attacked, did not bother to respond.

Although many critics and playwrights recognized Scribe's mastery of dramatic construction and technique, few made more than a cursory attempt to explain it even though they attributed his success to nothing else. Such an omission may result from disdain since for some the phrase "well-made play" was not a compliment, but it may also have been from a lack of a full understanding of that term as exemplified by Scribe. The technique is impossible to explain fully, and certainly impossible to reduce to a formula, because its most important characteristic is its inventiveness. It is only possible to describe the results of that inventiveness and to list the principles that appeared to guide the development of a new play by Scribe.

The first of those principles was to please the public, and everything else derived from that. If spectators prefer to understand what is going on, and, what is more, to understand its significance, then it is important to give them a clear and complete exposition. Scribe may withhold some details until they are needed, or to prepare a surprise, but there is at least an allusion to every event or fact that is needed to explain or to prepare for the action. To hold the spectators' interest during the exposition, there must be some action that draws them into the play and brings the necessary information out naturally. Often an action illustrates or reinforces the exposition: when an unexpected visitor shows up for breakfast in the first act of *Les Trois Maupin* (The Three Maupins, 1858), the tip he gives the servant is used to buy the groceries needed to feed him, which graphically demonstrates the poverty of the family. Long monologues and dialogues with confidants are excluded in favor of a succession of scenes with different combinations of characters who pass on information that the others do not know but have a reason or a need to know. Often the main character involved in the exposition is young, good-looking, and in love so that a good actor or actress in the role would not fail to gain the sympathy of the audience. Once it cares about the young lovers, it will care about other plots that affect their happiness, and Scribe made sure that virtually all of the subplots do. The main plot, and the real subject of the play, might involve events and themes from history, politics, or various social issues of the day, but there were no dry dissertations or somniferous sermons. Any lessons to be learned were presented so that they could be absorbed almost subliminally because the audience tended to favor or disfavor actions or ideas or values according to their impact on the young lovers, or by virtue of the example set by them or by those who help them.

Secrets play a large role in Scribe's plays, and he usually divulges to the audience almost all the secrets that help determine the outcome of the play. Octave Feuillet, in the speech he gave when taking Scribe's seat at the Académie Française, quoted him as saying:

> Le public m'aime parce que j'ai soin de le mettre toujours dans ma confiance; il est dans le secret de la comédie; il a dans les mains les fils qui font jouer mes personnages; il connaît les surprises que je leur ménage, et il croit les leur ménager 'lui-même; bref, je le prends pour collaborateur; il s'imagine qu'il a fait la pièce avec moi, et naturellement il l'applaudit.

> (The public likes me because I am always careful to take them into my confidence; they know the secrets of the play; they hold the strings which control my characters; they know the surprises I am preparing, and believe they themselves prepare them; in short, I take them as my collaborators; they believe they have helped me create the play, so naturally they applaud it.)

This explanation may indeed illustrate one reason for this practice, but there is also more potential for drama and suspense when the audience knows the secret than when it does not because then it is constantly aware of what is at stake. Sometimes, though, Scribe has a character hold back a secret from the audience, as when it learns only at the end of *Oscar* (1842) the identity of the woman with whom the title character has had a rendezvous, after two other candidates have been implicated, then cleared. The woman turns out to be the character's wife. If she had revealed herself any earlier, there would have been no suspense. Such a twist is quite infrequent for plays whose outcome nearly always hinges on information—the revelation or continued concealment of a secret, the receipt of certain information by the correct person, or the prevention of its discovery by the wrong person. In the course of the play information may be communicated, withheld, distorted, falsified, or invented, causing the many ups and downs in the action. One visible indication of the importance of communication in Scribe's plays is the constant use of letters and various documents and papers, which can go astray or arrive at just the right time or just the wrong time. Another type of secret is the *quiproquo* (misunderstanding), of which Scribe makes generous use, sometimes as the basis for the main action. Usually the misunderstanding is an accident, with nobody aware of it but the audience, but sometimes it arises out of an intent to deceive, and often someone discovers and exploits it.

In many of Scribe's plays the structure centers around a single character whose actions and decisions vitally affect the lives of the other characters. Often this character makes a decision and then changes it several times, provoking appropriate reactions from the other characters before the final decision brings about the denouement. The reversals do not really take the action forward until the end. In other plays the action is essentially linear, with a steady progression from beginning to end. In *Rêves d'amour* (Dreams of Love, 1859), for example, Jeanne flees from Henri throughout the play while Henri overcomes obstacle after obstacle before finally catching her in the last scene.

Whatever the basic structure, Scribe obviously believed that the audience wanted the action to keep moving. Each scene makes a definite contribution to the development of the action. Lyrical interludes and development of character beyond what is needed for the plot or for engaging the interest of the audience are considered superfluous; they interrupt the flow of the action, so they are kept to a minimum, if not eliminated entirely. Since the flow of information is such an essential part of the action, the combination of characters who are onstage at any given moment is determined mainly by the potential for its transfer. Some transfer or failure to transfer, some act or failure to act, some decision or indecision marks every scene. A major element of the construction of the well-made play is the arrangement of the entrances and exits and the onstage combinations that result. The scenes are usually tightly linked together, as each prepares the next; Scribe makes sure that each scene has a combination of characters that will permit the action to move forward according to plan. He avoids, however, certain necessary combinations as long as possible or, even more tantalizingly, permits and then interrupts them before finally satisfying the carefully cultivated desire of the audience to witness the expected confrontation or outcome. He also avoids excessive and increasingly hard-to-justify entrances and exits by any of the characters. Major characters typically stay onstage for several scenes at a time, sometimes even for a whole act. There are usually only a few characters onstage at a time—often two or three—to control the flow of information, but Scribe often brings on most or all of the main characters for the last scene, for the long-awaited revelation of the facts that will make possible the happy ending or that will give certain characters (and the audience) some anxious moments before the danger of a fatal revelation is dissipated, often by means of the artful lie. At the end of *Le Verre d'eau* (The Glass of Water, 1840) disastrous scandal threatens the queen when she invites Masham, a young officer, to her apartments and is discovered by her enemies. Bolingbroke saves her and brings about the desired marriage of Masham to Abigail by falsely asserting that he sent Masham there to see his wife, Abigail.

Since Scribe often linked a love interest to the principal plot, most plays have at least one subplot, and there may be as many as seven, usually solidly linked to the main plot. In *Le Verre d'eau* the love plot of Masham and Abigail and the struggle of Bolingbroke to overthrow the duchess become interdependent when the first three characters join forces. Two plots may be more nearly parallel, as in *Les Trois Maupin,* where Henri's success at court is independent of his sister's rise to fortune while masquerading as a celebrated singer, also at Versailles, although their contemporaneous presence there also leads to some exciting complications in the action. The subplot may be minor or nearly as important as the main plot, and it may stretch from beginning to the end of the play or just occupy a part of it, but it must be satisfactorily resolved before the final curtain. There can be no loose ends in a well-made play.

The dénouement is always swift, complete, and plausible. There are several ways of bringing about the final reversal, but it usually comes at a moment when all hope seems lost, when a solution seems either impossible or too late to prevent a catastrophe. The reversal must be unpredictable, and much of the art of the well-made play lies in the preparation of its elements in such a way that the audience will not be able to put them together before the right moment but will quickly recognize the logic of the solution once it is presented to them.

To this structural description must be added an observation about content. Scribe chose a wide variety of subjects for his plays. Many are linked to historical events in various times and places, including England, Russia, France, and even the United States during the American Revolution. They are only in a limited sense historical plays, for they tend to emphasize private lives against an historical backdrop rather than to portray political history for its own sake. Scribe sometimes illustrates historical arguments, such as the thesis that big events stem from little causes in *Le Verre d'eau* and the study of the effects of ambition in *L'Ambitieux* (1834), but the emphasis is still on the personal, rather than the national or international, implications of the events. The latter text exemplifies plays that hinge on the effects of certain character traits on the happiness of the individual and of others, and a variety of character traits figure in other plays. There are also comedies of manners in which Scribe holds up the foibles, values, and manias of contemporary society for gentle satire. Only in *La Calomnie* (The Calumny, 1840) is the criticism harsh and the punishment of the guilty relatively severe, for Scribe's desire to please and to entertain remains paramount. The values he expresses consistently but without belaboring them include the standard virtues and values that are generally called bourgeois. He opposes the old aristocratic prejudices against earning a living and favors individual merit above class origin. He shows the consequences of gambling, adultery, and a variety of character weaknesses. His characters speak constantly of money, reflecting its importance in society, but he repeatedly shows in an unfavorable light those who are excessively concerned about it, especially those who sacrifice their happiness, or that of others, to it. His most frequent form of happiness is a good marriage, one in which there is enough money for a modicum of comfort and a genuine affection between the partners. He is distrustful of passion and prefers a quieter, more lasting form of love. He had no illusions about correcting the views or the behavior of his audience, as did the practitioners of the *pièce à thèse* (thesis play), who criticized Scribe for not teaching lessons to his public.

Scribe's philosophy of the theater included the belief that spectators do not come to look for the realities they left at home; they come looking for fiction. It is fiction that entertains them, but, paradoxically, the fiction must have the ring of truth. Whether looking to history or purely to his imagination for characters, situations, and events,

Scribe sought the uncommon, the extraordinary, because he judged it more interesting to the audience, as long as he could maintain a certain plausibility. To hold their interest Scribe tried to present characters with whom the audience could identify and to construct a plot that would keep them in suspense. He carefully prepared any coincidences or other apparent interventions of chance so that the audience accepted them as perfectly justified or even natural. If the heroine is to be poisoned in the fifth act (*Adrienne Lecouvreur*, 1849), the poison will be seen and its potency described in the first act, and in a different scene will appear the bouquet on which it will be delivered. If a character appears at a particularly dramatic moment, the possibility of his arrival will have been established well before, and it is only the timing of the entrance that is unforeseen. Indeed, the most consistent characteristic of the well-made play is the thoroughness with which every action, every event, even every entrance and exit is prepared, explained, and justified. The spectator becomes caught up in a tightly linked, logical chain of events that does not permit him time or reason to doubt.

Beyond the concatenation of the events, Scribe imbues his fictions with the trappings of reality and actually represents a new degree of realism in the theater. His plays include contemporary manners, lifestyle, and surroundings and the presence, and especially the manipulation, of an abundance of stage properties which are, to all appearances, real and whose significance in the action and variety of uses represent an important innovation in stagecraft. Even his much-criticized style, by corresponding closely to the actual spoken language of the day, is part of the reality he transfers to the stage to help maintain the plausibility of his plots and thus to permit him to hold the interest of the spectator.

Scribe's first real success was a vaudeville, *Une Nuit de la Garde Nationale,* which, as the title indicates, shows one night at a post of the National Guard. The rather thin plot involves the attempt of Saint-Léon to get Versac in trouble with his wife by making it seem that he has spent the night with a former love. A mysterious visitor and an unknown guardsman independently arrive and spend the night at the post, without seeing each other. When morning comes, it turns out that the visitor is Versac and the guardsman is his wife in disguise. They are of course amazed to see each other. They endure their mutual embarrassment good-naturedly as all break into the final song. Around this plot are tucked scenes that combine humor with respect for the guard and for patriotism. Scribe pokes some fun at individual members and makes use of humorous situations and jokes to amuse the audience without insulting the institution, and there were reports of guardsmen who went to see the comedy again and again.

Another very successful vaudeville was *L'Ours et le pacha* (The Bear and the Pasha, 1820), in which two animal trainers who have lost all their menagerie in the desert arrive at the court of a pasha who loves trained animals. His beloved polar bear has just died, and no one dares tell him, for he is very quick to cut off people's heads when he is angry. There follow scenes of men disguised as bears to please the pasha but who frighten each other and even end up unknowingly exchanging heads, to everyone's amusement. Once again the plot is minimal and simply serves as an excuse for the comic elements.

It did not take long for Scribe to expand his work into higher dramatic forms. After several one- and three-act plays he moved up to a full five-act drama performed at the Théâtre-Français. *Le Mariage d'argent* (Marrying for Money, 1827) puts primary emphasis on a theme that appears as a secondary consideration in many of his plays—the role of money in society and, more particularly, in marriage. Two longtime friends wish to marry the same lovely widow. Poligni has the prior claim since the woman loved him before she heroically married someone else, but his determination to have riches at any cost eventually leads him to choose the rich ward of Dorbeval, a banker friend. This causes the widow to turn to Olivier, an artist whose industry and economy have given him a modest living. Olivier's loyalty and unselfishness throughout the play are eventually rewarded not only with the lady's love but also with a considerable fortune.

Scribe constructed both the plot and the characters to demonstrate that the love of money destroys happiness—Poligni vacillates between love and fortune, and fortune ultimately wins. He knows his marriage will be a disaster and chooses it anyway. Dorbeval's preoccupation with money has already created serious problems for his marriage, and his self-satisfaction from his riches makes it unlikely that Mme Dorbeval's lot will ever improve. The two characters who are capable of being happy with limited resources will be the only happy couple, and the money they receive at the end is a reward that will not prevent that happiness. In Scribe's world good character is more important than passion and far more important than money. Money is a constant theme, but he consistently emphasizes the problems of excess greed as much as the problems of having too little.

Other plays are based on various aspects of contemporary society. *La Camaraderie, ou la Courte échelle* (Camaraderie, or, A Hand up the Ladder, 1837) deals with a group of mediocrities who, by supporting one another, temporarily gain influence beyond their merits. The only person to gain real success refuses to go along with their schemes. *Une Chaîne* (A Ball and Chain, 1841) features a young man who nearly ruins his chance for happiness by his difficulties separating from his mistress, a condition set by his prospective father-in-law for his marriage. *Le Puff* (The Puff, 1848) shows how people get ahead by starting false rumors or by exaggerating their accomplishments. Ultimately, some of them find failure or ridicule while the earnest and honest young man ends up with the most desirable match. And in *Les Doigts de fée* (Magic Fingers, 1858) a young couple must overcome their aristocratic family's prejudice against earning a living so that the couple can find happiness. The obstacle is all the more formidable because it is the young woman who is working as a fashionable dressmaker.

La Bohémienne, ou l'Amérique en 1775 (The Gypsy, or America in 1775, 1829) was Scribe's first attempt at historical drama, but the setting was simply a backdrop for a plot that could easily have been placed elsewhere. His second effort was much more successful. *Bertrand et Raton, ou l'Art de conspirer* (Bertrand and Raton; or, How to Conspire, 1833) is a political drama set in Denmark in 1772 that serves to illustrate Jean La Fontaine's fable "Bertrand et Raton" as the Count Bertrand de Rantzau gains from the risks taken by merchant Raton Burkenstaff. Rantzau takes advantage of a power struggle between the queen and the queen mother to manipulate characters on both sides while avoiding any involvement himself. The climax of the political intrigue corresponds with the scheduled execution of Eric Burkenstaff, whose love for a minister's daughter has caused him to be mistaken for a conspirator. At the last minute he is saved and united with Christine, while Raton reads the king's proclamation naming Rantzau prime minister and Raton official supplier to the royal house, which, in effect, he already was. So Raton has spent a fortune and almost lost his son for the benefit of Rantzau. Though Scribe uses the love plot to heighten the interest of the audience, Rantzau is clearly the central character, and the political intrigue is primary. The message is not profound, but the events are well orchestrated to illustrate Rantzau's subtlety and opportunism along with Raton's blustery blundering.

The next year Scribe used the English court for a character study on the love of power in *L'Ambitieux* and a few years later chose the same locale for what is probably his best-known play, *Le Verre d'eau*. It improves on *Bertrand et Raton* by opposing two antagonists who are equally matched and who alternate performing tricks against each other, leaving the outcome in doubt until the last card is played. The duchess of Marlborough is the queen's favorite and, with the aid in Parliament of her party, wields great power to the benefit of her husband, who is engaged in a war against France. Her rival for power is Bolingbroke, who favors an end to the war and thus automatically gains the favor of French audiences. The pawns in their conflict are two young lovers—Masham, a new officer at court, and Abigail, ironically a cousin of the duchess. After several swings in the action Bolingbroke discovers that the duchess and the queen are both interested in Masham and that both want him to come to see them at the same time. He plays on the duchess's jealousy to gain a concession from her in exchange for the coded message by which an unnamed lady of the court will signal that Masham is to come that evening. When it is the queen who asks Masham for a glass of water, the duchess cannot contain her jealous anger and makes a scene that culminates in her spilling the water on the queen and consequently resigning. This results in a change of government and a change of policy, as Bolingbroke desired, but the duchess soon seeks revenge by bringing many witnesses to find the queen alone with Masham (Abigail apparently does not count), and it is only Abigail's claim that Masham came to see her, backed up by Bolingbroke's announcement that Abigail is Masham's wife, that finally confounds the duchess, saves the queen, allows the lovers to marry while earning the queen's undying gratitude rather than her jealousy, and confirms the end of the war and the beginning of peace negotiations. All of this for a glass of water, remarks Bolingbroke as the curtain drops, thus illustrating his thesis, asserted several times during the play, that great events arise from small causes.

Scribe used historical characters and events as the background for several other plays, including *Le Fils de Cromwell, ou une Restauration* (Son of Cromwell, or, a Restoration, 1842), in which Richard Cromwell decides not to oppose the Restoration, and *Les Contes de la Reine de Navarre, ou la Revanche de Pavie* (The tales of the Queen of Navarre; or, The Revenge for Pavia, 1850), in which Marguerite de Navarre matches wits with the emperor in one scheme after the other and finally gains the release of Francis I. *La Czarine* (1855) takes place in Russia,

and *Les Trois Maupin* is set mostly at the court of Louis XIV, but in all of these plays personal relationships rather than political intrigue dominate the plot. The history merely provides some local color and atmosphere, as when members of the court escape the gloom imposed by Madame de Maintenon by going off in secret to have a wild party. It is in *Adrienne Lecouvreur* that one finds the most unusual historical character—the title character, also the most sympathetic character, is an actress who sacrifices her fortune to free her lover even though she believes him to be unfaithful. Her rival is the princess of Bouillon, who poisons Adrienne when it becomes clear that her lover, Maurice, is abandoning her for the actress. As usual the plot is tightly constructed and full of suspense, and Scribe takes advantage of the theater environment to put apt quotes from Racine and Pierre Corneille in the mouths of several characters, leading up to the literally dramatic confrontation scene in which Adrienne uses a scene from Jean Racine's *Phèdre* (1677) to publicly humiliate the princess. That and the death scene gave the actress Rachel ample opportunity to display her talents. This is the only play by Scribe in which an innocent victim dies at the end, and it is the only play that provides an instance of cold-blooded murder; although there are threats of violence in other plays, it is rare for it actually to take place, and death onstage is rare indeed. Scribe presents a world in which words do whatever damage is done, and even evildoers are only punished by shame and by the failure of their schemes.

Another play in which a major character dies at the end is unusual for several reasons. *Dix Ans de la vie d'une femme, ou les Mauvais conseils* (Ten Years in the Life of a Woman, or Bad Advice, 1832) is divided into five acts and nine tableaux, and one might be justified in saying that it is actually a nine-act play, with the action spread over the ten years of the title. Adèle has a good family, a loving and considerate husband, and a comfortable life, but she falls in with the wrong crowd, takes a lover, and ends up running away with him. During the ten years she goes from lover to lover, moving ever lower both socially and morally, at one time even trying to dishonor her sister, who has continued to try to help her. Finally, as she lies dying of consumption, a charitable woman comes to visit her, and each woman recognizes the other as her sister, lending added poignancy to the death scene. In his portrayal of her fall Scribe includes scenes of a raw brutality not often seen before the works of the Naturalists. The moral is clear and not different from that presented more gently in other plays, but the treatment is different and not satisfying because Scribe's depiction of lowly characters and their milieu is not particularly successful.

Scribe remained single until he was forty-eight, when he married a Madame Biollay, the widow of a wine merchant. It appears that she managed to do what his mother could not—get him to think at least occasionally about something other than the theater. His production after his marriage decreased by about half. It was apparently the ideal bourgeois marriage that he favored so consistently in his plays—comfortable and harmonious. He continued to work up until his death, which claimed him without warning on 20 February 1861 as he rode home in his carriage after a meeting. He was sixty-nine years old. Thousands turned out to watch his funeral cortege pass.

Scribe's natural tendencies led him to advocate virtue, love, honesty, loyalty, generosity, industry, and self-reliance, but those bourgeois values are not, so to speak, pushed on the spectator. They underlie Scribe's plays, but his choice of characters and plots and the way he weaves them into a play make him an entertainer, not a preacher. Alexandre Dumas *fils* and his fellow practitioners of the pièce à thèse copied Scribe's techniques, but they used them to far different purposes. In the final analysis one might well argue that it was Scribe, rather than his successors and detractors, who was the purer practitioner of the theater.

References:

Louis Allard, *La Comédie de moeurs en France au dix-neuvième siècle,* 2 volumes (volume 1, Cambridge, Mass.: Harvard University Press, 1923; volume 2, Paris: Hachette, n.d.);

Neil Cole Arvin, *Eugène Scribe and the French Theater (1815–1860)* (Cambridge, Mass.: Harvard University Press, 1924);

Théodore de Banville, *Mes Souvenirs* (Paris: Charpentier, 1882);

Antoine Benoist, "Le Théâtre de Scribe: les comédies historiques," *Revue des cours et conférences,* 3 (14 February 1895): 417–422; (21 February 1895): 449–464;

Paul Bonnefon, "Scribe sous l'Empire et sous la Restauration d'après des documents inédits," *Revue d'histoire littéraire de la France,* 27 (July–September 1920): 321–370;

Bonnefon, "Scribe sous la Monarchie de juillet d'après des documents inédits," *Revue d'histoire littéraire de la France,* 28 (January–March 1921): 60–99; (April–June 1921) 241–260;

Ferdinand Brunetière, *Les Epoques du théâtre français, (1636–1850)* (Paris: Calmann-Lévy, 1899);

Brunetière, *Etudes critiques sur l'histoire de la littérature française* (Paris: Hachette, 1880);

Walter Douglas Cardwell Jr., "The Dramaturgy of Eugène Scribe," dissertation, Yale University, 1971;

Cardwell, "The Role of Stage Properties in the Plays of Eugène Scribe," *Nineteenth-Century French Studies,* 16 (Spring–Summer 1988): 290–309;

Cardwell, "The Well-Made Play of Eugène Scribe," *French Review,* 56 (May 1983): 876–884;

Charles Marc Des Granges, *La Comédie et les moeurs sous la Restauration et la monarchie de juillet (1815–1848)* (Paris: A. Fontemoing, 1904);

René Doumic, *De Scribe à Ibsen: Causeries sur le théâtre contemporain* (Paris: Perrin, 1896);

Colin Duckworth, "Comment Scribe composait *le Verre d'eau," Revue d'histoire du théâtre,* 4 (1959): 315–326;

Duckworth, "The Historical and Dramatic Sources of Scribe's *Verre d'eau,*" *French Studies,* 12 (January 1958): 30–43;

Alexandre Dumas *père, Souvenirs dramatiques,* 2 volumes (Paris: Calmann-Lévy, 1881);

Emile Faguet, *Propos de théâtre,* 5 volumes (Paris: Société française d'imprimerie et de librairie, 1903–1910);

Octave Feuillet, "Discours de M. Octave Feuillet, prononcé dans la séance publique du 26 mars 1863, en venant prendre séance à la place de M. Scribe," in *Recueil des discours, rapports, et pièces diverses lus dans les séances publiques et particulières de l'Académie française, 1860–1869. Première partie* (Paris: Firmin Didot frères, Fils et Cie, 1866);

Théophile Gautier, *Histoire de l'art dramatique en France depuis vingt-cinq ans,* 6 volumes (Paris: Magnin, Blanchard, 1858–1859);

Gautier, *Les Maîtres du théâtre français de Rotrou à Dumas fils* (Paris: Payot, 1929);

Patti P. Gillespie, *The Well-Made Plays of Eugène Scribe* (Ann Arbor, Mich.: University Microfilms, 1971);

Jules Janin, *Critique dramatique,* 4 volumes (Librairie des Bibliophiles, 1875–1877);

Janin, *Histoire de la Littérature dramatique,* 6 volumes (Paris: Michel Lévy frères, 1853–1858);

Helen Koon and Richard Switzer, *Eugène Scribe* (Boston: Twayne, 1980);

Gustave Larroumet, *Etudes de littérature et d'art,* 4 volumes (Paris: Hachette, 1893–1896);

Ernest Legouvé, *Eugène Scribe* (Paris: Didier, 1874);

Legouvé, *Soixante Ans de souvenirs,* 2 volumes (Paris: J. Hetzel, n.d.);

Jules Lemaître, *Les Contemporains: Etudes et portraits littéraires*, 8 volumes (Paris: Société Française d'imprimerie et de librairie, n.d.);

Charles Lenient, *La Comédie en France au XIXe siècle*, volume 2 (Paris: Hachette, 1898);

J. Brander Matthews, *French Dramatists of the Nineteenth Century* (New York: Scribners, 1881);

Matthews, "Pleasant Land of Scribia," *Yale Review*, 8 (1919): 836–844;

Eugène de Mirecourt, *Les Contemporains: Scribe*, volume 3 (Paris: Gustave Havard, 1856);

Allardyce Nicoll, *A History of Early 19th Century Drama, 1800–1850*, 2 volumes (Cambridge: Cambridge University Press, 1930);

Nicoll, *A History of Late Nineteenth Century Drama, 1850–1900*, 2 volumes (Cambridge: Cambridge University Press, 1946);

Pierre Petit de Julleville, *Le Théâtre en France: Histoire de la Littérature dramatique* (Paris: Librairie Armand Colin, 1927);

Gustave Planche, *Nouveaux Portraits littéraires*, 2 volumes (Paris: Amyot, 1854);

Joachim Rolland, *Les Comédies historiques et politiques d'Eugène Scribe* (Paris: Bibliothèque d'histoire du théâtre, 1933);

Rolland, *Les Comédies politiques d'Eugène Scribe* (Paris: Sansot, 1912);

Francisque Sarcey, *Quarante ans de théâtre. (Feuilletons dramatiques)*, 8 volumes (Paris: Bibliothèque des "Annales politiques et littéraires," 1900–1902);

Sarcey, "Théâtre de Scribe.–Le Verre d'eau," *Revue des cours et conférences*, 4 (12 March 1896): 795–809;

Stephen Sadler Stanton, *English Drama and the Well-Made Play, 1815–1915* (Ann Arbor, Mich.: University Microfilms, 1958);

Stanton, "Shaw's Debt to Scribe," *PMLA*, 76 (December 1961): 575–585.

Anthony John Visconti, *Eugène Scribe: Bourgeois Dramatist* (Ann Arbor, Mich.: University Microfilms, 1973);

Wolfgang von Wurzbach, "Notice," in his *Les Doigts de fée. Oeuvres de Scribe et Legouvé*, Bibliotheca Romanica, Bibliothèque Française, nos. 201–202 (Strasbourg: Heitz, 1913);

Wurzbach, "Notice," in *Le Verre d'eau. Théâtre d'Eugène Scribe*, Bibliotheca Romanica, Bibliothèque Française, nos. 125–126 (Strasbourg: Heitz, 1911).

Papers:

Scribe's papers are located at the Bibliothèque Nationale in Paris.

Germaine de Staël
(Anne-Louise-Germaine de Staël-Holstein)
(22 April 1766 – 14 July 1817)

John Claiborne Isbell
Indiana University at Bloomington

See also the Staël entry in *DLB 119: Nineteenth-Century French Fiction Writers: Romanticism and Realism, 1800–1860.*

PLAY PRODUCTIONS: *Les Inconvénients de la vie de Paris,* Saint-Ouen [Paris], salon performance, September 1778;

Agar dans le désert, Geneva, Théâtre du Molard, 11 March 1806;

Geneviève de Brabant, Château de Coppet, salon performance, 26 November 1807;

La Sunamite, Coppet, salon performance, 2 November 1808;

La Signora Fantastici, Geneva, salon performance, 28 November 1808;

Le Capitaine Kernadec, ou, Les Sept Années, Château de Coppet, salon performance, 11 February 1811;

Le Mannequin, Château de Coppet, salon performance, 18 February 1811.

BOOKS: *Lettres sur les ouvrages et le caractère de J.-J. Rousseau* (Paris, 1788); translated anonymously as *Letters on the Works and Character of Jean-Jacques Rousseau* (London: Robinson, 1789);

Sophie, ou, Les Sentiments secrets (Paris, 1790);

Jane Grey (Paris: Desenne, 1790);

Refléxions sur la paix addressées à M. Pitt et aux Français (Paris, 1794);

Réflexions sur la paix intérieure (Paris, 1795);

Recueil de morceaux détachés (Lausanne: Durand, Ravanel et comp^e / Paris: Fuchs, 1795)—comprises *Epître au malheur; Essai sur les fictions;* and *Trois nouvelles: Mirza, ou Lettre d'un voyageur, Adelaïde et Théodore, Histoire de Pauline;*

De l'influence des passions sur le bonheur des individus et des nations (Lausanne: J. Mourer, 1796); translated anonymously as *A Treatise on the Influence of the Passions upon the Happiness of Individuals and of Nations* (London, 1798);

Germaine de Staël (portrait by Baron Gerald, Musée de Versailles)

De la littérature considérée dans ses rapports avec les institutions sociales (Paris: Maradan, 1800); translated anonymously as *A Treatise on Ancient and Modern Literature* (London: G. Cawthorn, 1803);

Delphine (Geneva: J. J. Paschoud, 1802); translated anonymously as *Delphine* (London, 1803);

Corinne, ou, l'Italie (Paris: Nicolle, 1807); translated by D. Lawler as *Corinne, or Italy* (London: Corri, 1807); translated by Avriel Goldberger as *Corinne, or Italy* (New Brunswick, N.J.: Rutgers University Press, 1987);

373

De l'Allemagne, 3 volumes (Paris: Nicolle, 1810; London: John Murray); translated anonymously as *Germany* (London: John Murray, 1813);

Réflexions sur le suicide (Stockholm: C. Delén, 1813);

Considérations sur les principaux événemens de la Révolution française, 3 volumes (Paris: Delaunay, 1818);

Dix années d'exil (Paris: Treuttel et Würtz, 1821); translated anonymously as *Ten Years' Exile; or, Memoirs of That Interesting Period of the Life of the Baroness de Staël-Holstein, Written by Herself* (London, 1821);

Des circonstances actuelles qui peuvent terminer la Révolution et des principes qui doivent fonder la république en France (Paris: Fischbacher, 1906).

Editions and Collections: *Œuvres complètes,* 17 volumes, edited by Auguste de Staël (Paris: Treuttel et Würtz, 1820–1821);

Les Carnets de voyage de Madame de Staël, edited by Simone Balayé (Geneva: Droz, 1971);

Des circonstances actuelles qui peuvent termine la Révolution et des principes qui doivent fonder la république en France, edited by Lucia Omancini (Geneva: Droz, 1979);

Madame de Staël: Ecrits retrouvés, edited by John Isbell *Cahiers staëliens,* 46 (Paris: Touzot, 1995);

Dix années d'exil, edited by Simone Balayé and Mariella Vianello Bonifacio Fayard (Paris: Fayard, 1996).

Editions in English: *Madame de Staël on Politics, Literature, and National Character,* translated and edited by Morroe Berger (Garden City, N.Y.: Doubleday, 1964);

An Extraordinary Woman. Selected Writings of Germaine de Staël, edited by Vivian Folkenlik (New York: Columbia University Press, 1987).

Anne-Louise-Germaine de Staël-Holstein's impact on nineteenth-century theater comes above all from *De l'Allemagne* (1810–1813; translated as *Germany,* 1813), to which later Romantic drama theory (Stendhal's *Racine et Shakspeare* [1823] and Victor Hugo's *Préface de Cromwell* [1827]) owes profound debts. Other intellectual sources for Romantic theater, Benjamin Constant, A. W. Schlegel, and J. C. L. Simonde de Sismondi, wrote under Staël's roof at Coppet, her home in Switzerland, and indeed, almost the entire intellectual framework of French Romantic theater may be found in the works of this group Staël led. The translators for Jean-Baptiste Ladvocat's *Chefs-d'oeuvre des théâtres étrangers* (Masterpieces of Foreign Theaters, 1822–1825) were Coppet intimates, and their enterprise answers the call of *De l'Allemagne* to renovate French literature

by translating nonclassical drama. Romantic France's pantheon of German models again follows Staël's lead: Friedrich von Schiller, Zacharias Werner, and Johann Wolfgang von Goethe, whose *Faust* she transformed in introducing it to France. Hector Berlioz and Charles Gounod echo her choices. The scope of this influence, which seems to fade after 1848, deserves study. *Corinne, ou, l'Italie* (1807; translated as *Corinne, or Italy,* 1807) may stand next among Staël's works in its impact on French theater. Gioacchino Antonio Rossini borrowed Corinne's name, companions, and parts of her story for *Il viaggio a Reims* (The Voyage to Rheims) in 1824; the Bibliothèque Nationale has a manuscript of *Corinne, ou, La Fatalité,* a manscript prose *drame* with songs; *Corinne ressuscitée* (1815); and *Corinne* (1830), a verse drame by Monier de La Sizeranne that offers Corinne not death but a nunnery.

A dozen copies each of *Sophie, ou les sentiments secrets* and *Jane Grey* were published in 1790; seven other plays appeared in 1821, and five remained in manuscript. Four are now at last in publication: *Thamas* (1789?), *La Mort de Montmorenci* (1791), *Rosamonde* (1791), and *Jean de Witt* (fragments, 1797). Clearly Staël's theater was all but invisible before 1821, though her own performances of her work, in Geneva, Vienna, Moscow, Stockholm, and London, caused some stir. Two Romantic authors, nonetheless, owe debts to Staël's theater. First, in E. T. A. Hoffmann's *Der Sandmann* (1815), which opens his *Nachtstücke* (Night Pieces), and Jacques Offenbach's *Les Contes d'Hoffmann* (Tales of Hoffmann, 1880), the hero falls in love with an artist's dummy, as in Staël's *Le Mannequin* (1811; translated as *The Mannequin,* 1987). Hoffmann's friend Adelbert von Chamisso was at Coppet as Staël wrote the play. Second, on 20 July 1822 Henri de Latouche staged *Le Vieillard malgré lui* (The Old Man Despite Himself) at the Panorama-Dramatique; the comedy is an egregious plagiarism of Staël's *Le Capitaine Kernadec, ou, Les Sept Années* (1811), including even the characters' names. In short, Staël's theater missed its rendezvous with a century she heavily influenced elsewhere.

The first obstacle to Staël's success was her own decision not to publish: only in recent years has the arguable center of her oeuvre, four Voltairean tragedies, at last begun publication. Second, her other plays were buried in the posthumous *Œuvres complètes* (1820–1821), though Latouche spotted her art. In the 1820s her dramatic innovations may have been lost in the scuffle; by the 1830s their novelty was superseded. Publication before 1821 might have meant a different impact: Staël's revolutionary theater was streamlined and up-to-date, while her Empire theater was avant-garde. But as Staël told

Château de Coppet, Staël's estate in Switzerland

Benjamin Constant for *Wallstein* (1809), success in the theater is the result mainly of luck and sweat: she may have felt unable to guarantee her plays' success while exiled from Paris, given the political climate. She may also have felt a name as a dramatist was unfitting to the "private" persona she cultivated in answer to the endless charges of her political influence. All this is ironic, since theater lies at the heart of her thought about France's moral and political regeneration. Nor did Staël's theater deserve oblivion: the homage of Latouche is a fitting compliment to her comedic skill; *Le Mannequin* is a fine comedy; and *Jane Grey* is equal to many post-Voltairean tragedies, with twists that whet one's appetite for the tragedies still in manuscript. Staël's current reputation as a dramatist is thus in transition. The influences reviewed here are previously uncited; the dozen studies listed below are most of what exists. None of Staël's fourteen plays has been republished this century; her manuscript tragedies should do much to open a window on an unexplored past.

Staël's life and works are grounded in the transformations of a Europe in revolution and in Staël's awareness of her sex. She was heavily involved in European politics from 1786 to her death in 1817, and her art reflects that engagement; except for the busy years from 1805 to 1808 theater was not Staël's principal concern, and her plays must be seen against her much longer novels and treatises.

Within this sweep Staël's dramatic output also divides into two periods: 1778 to 1791 and 1805 to 1811. Two lost works lie outside this divide: the Voltairean tragedy *Jean de Witt,* 1797, of which fragments survive, and the short plays in 1814 that are based on the works of George Gordon, Lord Byron. Martine de Rougemont reviews Staël's performances, where a similar divide appears between 1777–1794 and 1803–1814, though records may be lacking.

Staël was born in Paris on 22 April 1766. She loved theater from childhood and built a puppet theater to perform tragedies; she had acting lessons from Claire Clairon with Jean-François de La Harpe and Jean-François Marmontel supporting and Denis Diderot present. In 1778 Friedrich Melchior von Grimm praised her *Les Inconvénients de la vie de Paris* (Inconveniences of Parisian Life, 1778) to the crowned heads of Europe: the work was a short *comédie larmoyante* (sentimental comedy) in prose, starring the author. She performed endings of tragedies with her cousin and in 1785 starred in La Harpe's *Mélanie* (1778), which resembles her novel *Delphine* (1802; translated, 1803), in her mother's salon.

Sophie and *Jane Grey* frame Staël's marriage in 1786 to Eric Magnus, Baron de Staël-Holstein. *Sophie,* a comédie larmoyante in verse echoing Pierre-Claude Nivelle de La Chaussée's *La Gouvernante* (The Governess, 1747), has a governess and her married employer who, as in Charlotte Brontë's

Jane Eyre (1847), discover and renounce their mutual love. Sophie then rejects her other suitor and leaves for England. The play is set in an English garden, where the count's locked pavilion hides Sophie's bust, decked in flowers. The frequent use of the terms *père* (father) and *mère* (mother) in the play solicits a Freudian reading: extremely close to her father, Staël refused a marriage to William Pitt the Younger to stay in Paris. Skillful verse, dramatic irony, and private affect add merit to this meditation on love in marriage, which has two picturesque touches: the erotic denouement, where the mother finds the count at Sophie's feet in the unlocked pavilion, and Sophie's romance, sung to her pupil while the count eavesdrops.

Jane Grey, a sound Voltairean tragedy, shows Jane in England and married off by an ambitious father, a villain who goes to the scaffold seeking the crowd's hate. Reference to Sigmund Freud again seems apt, since Staël's father, Jacques Necker, profited from his daughter's marriage. Politics, intrigue, promises, and misunderstanding swirl around the resolute heroine, proclaimed queen in act 1 and a prisoner of Bloody Mary in act 3. Written by a Genevan in 1787, the year Louis XVI restored the Protestant civil rights that Louis XIV had revoked, the play is built on a Protestantism in vogue since Voltaire. Performance might easily have brought success; several scenes are superb, notably Jane's arguments with Northumberland and Pembroke, where her heroic virtue triumphs, and the trial, where Jane and her husband, Guilfort, each refuse to say the word that would save them: their complex pretrial discussions distill to one-word replies and silence, matching the officious speed of this kangaroo court. Time is nicely managed, notably in act 4's confessor scenes, set in prison. Besides William Shakespeare's history plays, *Romeo and Juliet* (1594) stands behind the young leads, but odd echoes of Jean Racine also add baroque local color: "Faudra-t-il donc, seigneur, regretter votre haine?; J'espère le néant et redoute le ciel" (Must I then, Sire, regret your hatred?; I fear Heaven and hope for the void). Racine's question-answer hemistiches are reworked, and some baroque detail verges on excess, in Romantic fashion: "Ah! viens, viens sur mon sein reposer cette tête, / Qu'à faire, hélas! tomber un barbare s'apprête" (Ah! come, come rest on my breast this head, / That a barbarian is preparing, alas! to remove). Staël wrote this tragedy at twenty-one.

Staël's return to dramaturgy after 1805 was anchored in performance. François-Joseph Talma, whose acting *De l'Allemagne* superbly analyzes, was an old friend; he talked of playing Jean Racine's *Iphigénie* (1674) with her. Staël had detailed, concrete knowledge of the theater, as society actress and director alike. She staged Carmontelle, Alexandre Duval, Philippe Destouches, Michel Sedaine, and Bernard-Joseph Saurin; also Jean-Jacques Rousseau's *Pygmalion* (1770), Pierre de Marivaux's *Le Legs* (The Legacy, 1736), Pierre-Augustin Beaumarchais's *Le Barbier de Séville* (The Barber of Seville, 1775), and some friends' works. She staged Voltaire ten times, Jean Racine nineteen times, and her own plays sixteen times, all with herself as heroine (she also played soubrettes, a rare combination in contemporary theater). She staged one Molière, *Les Femmes savantes* (1672), and one drame, La Harpe's *Mélanie.* Eight of eleven dramatists were recent comic authors. In 1808 she staged her son Auguste's *Gustave Vasa:* this is Alexandre Duval's *Edouard en Ecosse* (Edward in Scotland, 1802) with the names changed to appease Napoleon Bonaparte's police, a sign of the publicity Staël's society theater generated. Racine seems her favorite playwright: she declaims from *Phèdre* (1677) in 1803–1805 and in 1813, staging it again in 1806 and 1807; declaims from *Athalie* (1691) in 1804 and 1813; and recites from *Andromaque* (1667) in 1804 and stages it in 1807. Staël declaims scenes from Voltaire's *Tancrède* (1760) and *Adélaïde du Guesclin* (1734) in 1793 and 1794; in 1805 and 1806 she stages his *Mérope* (1743), *Mahomet* (1742), *Alzire* (1736), and *Zaïre* (1732); then *Sémiramis* (1748) in 1807. August Wilhelm von Schlegel ran stage design for her theater, grounded in superb theory, while Staël as actress seems to have combined a professional skill with an intense meditation on her art. Two productions close this cycle of performances at Geneva and Coppet: Constant's *Wallstein,* adapted from Friedrich von Schiller, with stage design complete before cancellation in 1808, and Werner's *24. Februar* (1815), staged in 1809. Staël writes to Mme. Récamier, "what took me a little time was arranging a play by Werner."

In addition to her performance of works by others, Staël again began composing for the theater in 1805, writing *Agar dans le désert* (1806), *Geneviève de Brabant* (1807), and *La Sunamite* (1808), three religious drames. Agar is African, dark like Corinne; Staël's art does much to launch the Romantic blonde/brunette opposition, drawing on her self-image as not white enough. But these drames are also experiments in nonclassical technique. In 1806 Staël told Henri Meister that her dramatic experiments continued, giving her the type of ideas she wanted, as *De l'Allemagne* and these drames attest. In them Staël abandons verse despite her talent for it, and her new plays all share dreams and masks. Discussing *Agar dans le désert* (1806), Staël's son Auguste mentions debts to Mme. de Genlis and to

Népomucène Lemercier; Staël follows Genlis throughout, borrowing Ishmael, the spilt jug, and Hagar's comments on her rival Sarah, all absent from Genesis 16. Above all, Staël brings simplicity to the subject. Genlis's tendentious prose yields to the silence underlying Staël's "scène lyrique," or lyric scene: after Abraham expels his wife's handmaid Hagar and their child, Ishmael, an angel succors them. As in Staël's other drames, sustained dramatic poetry is replaced by Sophoclean lyric interludes, an experiment echoing new developments both in opéra comique, with its spoken dialogue, and in the German theater since Schiller, who was much discussed at Coppet. Music and the divine move onstage.

Geneviève de Brabant answers Johann Ludwig Tieck's sprawling Romantic manifesto, *Leben und Tod des heiligen Genoveva* (Life and Death of Saint Genevieve, 1802–1811). Sigefroi finds his innocent queen and their daughter sheltered by a forest hermit, years after ordering their death. It is no accident that Staël writes *Geneviève de Brabant* just before *De l'Allemagne;* there, German Romantic theater is roundly rejected in favor of Schiller and Goethe, with a sharp review of Tieck's *Genoveva* as a "roman dialogué" (dialogue romance). Staël thus answers Tieck outside *De l'Allemagne,* as she bans Heinrich von Kleist from its text to attack him in her 1813 *Réflexions sur le suicide.* Since Staël's main thesis is that recent German drama is unperformable, theater "dans un fauteuil" (in an armchair), as Alfred de Musset called it, *Geneviève de Brabant* has the special interest of a project taken onward to performance. Staël submits Tieck's chronicle to the unities, leaping ten years of events to his conclusion, the arid Sigefroi's return. Tieck's presence is hinted at by elements less present in the folk legend: Sigefroi's hunting horns and Geneviève's veil. The French Empire public had seen religious decor in melodrama, even animals onstage, such as Staël's doe, but this is a leap from her Voltairean tragedies and a far cry from what Diderot called a drame. Every object is charged with affect: "Où donc est-il le poignard qui soulagerait mon coeur?" (Where then is the dagger that could soothe my heart?). Again life and art combine: Staël calls Sigefroi's son Adolphe, the name of Constant's hero, and Geneviève's ten years of exile parallel her own autobiography's title.

La Sunamite turns once more to the Old Testament: II Kings 4, Elisée (Elisha or Elysium) and the Shunamite. As in *Geneviève,* Staël replaces the biblical son with a daughter—a role performed by her own daughter, Albertine. In II Kings the aging Shunamite is blessed with a son who dies abruptly at the harvest; the prophet Elisha then performs the Old

Staël's son Auguste (portrait by Anne Louis Girodet Roucy Trioson; Château de Coppet)

Testament's only resurrection. Staël embroiders: promised to God, Semida dies at the feast her proud mother insists on despite a sister's warnings. The scenario speaks to Staël's biographers. As in *Geneviève de Brabant,* flowers, dreams, music, and religion add local color, part of Romantic theater's early history; after horns, a flute and a harp appear onstage. Sémida performs the veil dance Mme. Récamier taught Albertine, combining music, dance, and theater as Jean-Baptiste Lully had done with Molière's work. Light and music mark an onstage resurrection. These three dramas have a permanent place in Romantic theater; Staël's religion, local color, and lyric interludes mark a reasoned break with Neoclassical and Boulevard traditions alike.

Staël's three short *proverbes* of 1808 to 1811, her next dramatic works, are a world apart. *La Signora Fantastici* (1808) stars a comic Corinne, bringing theater with her daughter to Rousseau's placid Geneva. The opening scenes anticipate Eugène Ionesco as Staël skewers the vapid dialogue of a loveless household: the Germanic M. de Kriegschenmahl (with pipe) and his English wife (with tea) have appropriate accents for local color. This couple and their two sons clearly meant more to Staël's circle, for the play is full of just-intelligible private jokes: Licidas recites *Phèdre,* as Staël had, and the stuttering *commissaire* comes like Napoleon's prefects to order the heroine out of town but ends by joining the converted Kriegschenmahls in her troupe instead.

Le Capitaine Kernadec may be Staël's best pure theater, a well-oiled machine to which each crisp character contributes. Captain Kernadec wants his daughter Rosalba to marry a sailor, not the artistic Derval. That night, during his drunken sleep, the others work to create the illusion that the household has aged seven years. Kernadec's faithful Sabord, with a fake wooden leg, presents the maid Nérine as his wife. Derval enters mustachioed, in navy uniform, and swearing quietly, using navy jargon so absurd the captain reacts; they explain that with the new regulations the maneuver has changed considerably. Finally Mme. de Kernadec enters, and her husband remarks so strongly on the way that she has aged that she reveals the fraud. Lovely moments echo Schlegel's thesis of gratuitous comedy: Sabord's lament that before losing his leg he never came in through the door, but "toujours par la fenêtre, monsieur, toujours par la fenêtre" (always through the window, Sir, always through the window); Rosalba's comment that seven years on from sixteen, one has so little time left that marriage would hardly be worth it. Naming the captain's ship the Belle-Poule, the model for Louis XVI *coiffures à la frégate* after its sinking by the English, is another effective touch.

Le Mannequin is set in a Huguenot household in Berlin, where M. de La Morlière's daughter Sophie prefers the poor painter Hoffmann to her father's choice, the Parisian comte d'Erville, an echo of Erfeuil in *Corinne*. Erville finds silent women less of a threat to his vanity. Sophie therefore presents a tailor's dummy, behind curtains, as her rich cousin, and Erville quickly proposes marriage, struck by the dummy's modest silence and other qualities: the dummy does not read, draw, sing, or dance, and never interrupts. This striking image precisely expresses the gender dispensation of postrevolutionary France and the ideology of silence and submission *Corinne* attacks: indeed, the image is larger than its vehicle, a perfect window on nineteenth-century gender roles and one of Staël's great mythic symbols. Within this fabric there is much of Molière, in the two men's rival vanities, for instance, or in M. de La Morlière's dialogue; but the enduring image is of the Frenchman and his puppet wife.

Remarkably, Staël wrote these comedies amid despair: Constant's abandonment and departure after 1808, the pulping of *De l'Allemagne* by Napoleon in 1810, and Staël's virtual house arrest at Coppet, which was ended by her flight to England via Moscow weeks before the city burned. To some extent

Staël's comedies transpose her great dilemmas to a comic universe as Schlegel felt Aristophanes did; but as 1810 ended, Staël also met John Rocca, her second husband, and his devotion was something new. Moreover, Staël always had a gift for joy and despair together; thus, 1811 also brought *Sappho,* which ends in suicide. *Sappho* shares the two heroines, one brilliant, one submissive, who are central to Staël's fiction but oddly absent elsewhere in her theater except in *Agar.* The theme of Sappho was much in vogue in Europe, and Staël had written a romance based on the poetess by 1785. In her 1811 play Phaon abandons Sappho for Cléone's beauty; Sappho, "une femme qui ne craignait point la tempête" (a woman who did not fear the storm), blasphemes Apollo after being crowned his priestess, preferring Venus; she then persuades Cléone to marry Phaon and after a final hymn leaps into the sea at their wedding. Staël enjoys this Racinian telescoping of ceremonies, where altars serve for marriage, God, or sacrifice. In another innovation the lyric interludes in *Sappho* feature an actual lyre, as Staël continues her Romantic search for Greek authenticity. This play has drawn excellent biographical analysis as the reflection of another self-image of Staël's.

In *De l'Allemagne* and her other treatises Staël offers a history and theory of drama: in *Lettres sur les ouvrages et le caractère de J.-J. Rousseau* (1788; translated as *Letters on the Works and Character of Jean-Jacques Rousseau,* 1789) she prefers *Pygmalion* to the *Devin du village* (The Village Soothsayer, 1752). *De la littérature considérée dans ses rapports avec les institutions sociales* (1800; translated as *A Treatise on Ancient and Modern Literature,* 1803) covers the Greeks and Romans, Shakespeare's tragedies, and French Classicism; and *Corinne* reviews Vittorio Alfieri and Metastasio. Corinne's improvisations and her triumph remind one, like the constant lyric interludes in Staël's dramas, that the separation of theater, music, improvisation, and other public ceremony was drawn differently around 1800 and that Staël put considerable effort into the project Victor Hugo and Richard Wagner inherited, that of breaking down the barriers to a total aesthetic continuity. The rigidity of the form of the French theater in her era offers perhaps a final word on why Staël the experimenter chose, if not a *théâtre dans un fauteuil,* at least a *théâtre dans un salon* to perfect her art.

Letters:

Mme de Staël, *Correspondance générale,* edited by Béatrice W. Jasinski (Paris: Pauvert, Hachette, Klincksieck, 1960–).

Bibliographies:

F.-C. Lonchamp, *L'Oeuvre imprimé de Madame Germaine de Staël* (Geneva: Cailler, 1949);

Karyna Szmurlo, "Madame de Staël," in *A Critical Bibliography of French Literature, V: The Nineteenth Century,* edited by David Baguley (Syracuse, N.Y.: Syracuse University Press, 1994), pp. 51–69.

Biographies:

Pierre Kohler, *Madame de Staël et la Suisse* (Lausanne: Payot, 1916);

J. Christopher Herold, *Mistress to an Age: A Life of Madame de Staël* (Indianapolis: Bobbs-Merrill, 1958).

References:

Simone Balayé, *Madame de Staël, Lumières et liberté* (Paris: Klincksieck, 1979);

Jean-Daniel Candaux, "Le théâtre de Mme de Staël au Molard (1805–6)," *Cahiers staëliens,* 14 (1972): 19–32;

Joan DeJean, *Fictions of Sappho, 1546–1937* (Chicago: University of Chicago Press, 1989), pp. 167–197;

Michel Delon, "La Métaphore théâtrale dans les *Considérations sur la Révolution française*," in *Le Groupe de Coppet et la Révolution française* (Lausanne & Paris: Touzot, 1988), pp. 163–173;

Madelyn Gutwirth, *Madame de Staël, Novelist: The Emergence of the Artist as Woman* (Urbana: University of Illinois Press, 1978);

John Isbell, *The Birth of European Romanticism: Truth and Propaganda in Staël's* De l'Allemagne (Cambridge: Cambridge University Press, 1994);

Isbell, "The Painful Birth of the Romantic Heroine: Staël as Political Animal, 1786–1818," *Romantic Review,* 87 (January 1996): 59–67;

Danielle Johnson-Cousin, "La société dramatique de Mme de Staël de 1803 à 1816," *Studies on Voltaire and the XVIIIth Century,* 296 (1992): 207–242;

Johnson-Cousin, "Une source italienne inconnue du drame de *Sapho* (1811) par Mme de Staël: *L'Avventura di Saffo, poetessa di Mitilene,* d'Alessandro Verri," *Studies on Voltaire and the XVIIIth Century,* 266 (1989): 499–511;

Comtesse Jean de Pange, *Auguste-Guillaume Schlegel et Madame de Staël* (Paris: Payot, 1938);

Martine de Rougemont, "L'Activité théâtrale dans le Groupe de Coppet: la dramaturgie et le jeu," in *Le Groupe de Coppet* (Geneva: Slatkine, 1977), pp. 263–284;

De Rougemont, "Pour un répertoire des rôles et des représentations de Mme de Staël," *Cahiers staëliens,* 19 (1974): 79–92;

Jean Starobinski, "Suicide et mélancolie chez Mme de Staël," in *Madame de Staël et l'Europe* (Paris: Klincksieck, 1970), pp. 242–252.

Papers:

Staël's papers are in private hands or dispersed throughout Europe and the United States. Significant manuscript holdings are in the Bibliothèque Nationale in Paris and in the Berg Collection of the New York Public Library in New York City.

Alfred de Vigny

(27 March 1797 – 17 September 1863)

Robert T. Denommé
University of Virginia

See also the Vigny entry in *DLB 119: Nineteenth-Century French Fiction Writers: Romanticism and Realism, 1800–1860.*

PLAY PRODUCTIONS: *Le More de Venise,* Paris, Comédie-Française, 24 October 1829;
La Maréchale d'Ancre, Paris, Théâtre de l'Odéon, 25 June 1831;
Quitte pour la peur, Paris, Opéra (Salle Garnier), 30 May 1833;
Chatterton, Paris, Comédie-Française, 12 February 1835;
Shylock, Le Marchand de Venise, Paris, Comédie-Française, 7 April 1905.

BOOKS: *Poèmes,* anonymous (Paris: Pelicier, 1822); enlarged as *Poèmes antiques et modernes* (Paris: Urbain Canel, 1826);
Eloa, ou, La Sœur des anges, mystère (Paris: Boulland, 1824);
Cinq-Mars, ou, Une Conspiration sous Louis XIII, 2 volumes (Paris: Urbain Canel, 1826); translated by William Hazlitt as *Cinq-Mars: A Conspiracy under Louis XIII* (London: D. Bogue, 1847);
Othello, ou, Le More de Venise (Paris: Levasseur, 1830);
La Maréchale d'Ancre (Paris: Gosselin Barba, 1831);
Stello: Les Consultations du Docteur-Noir (Paris: Gosselin, 1832); translated by Irving Massey as *Stello: A Session with Doctor Noir* (Montreal: McGill University Press, 1963);
Quitte pour la peur, in *Revue des Deux Mondes* (1 June 1833): 533–564;
Chatterton (Paris: Souverain, 1835); translated by William Hazlitt (London: D. Bogue, 1847); translated by Philip A. Fulvi (New York: Griffon House, 1990);
Servitude et grandeur militaires (Paris: Bonnaire et Magen, 1835); translated by F. W. Huard as *Military Servitude and Grandeur* (New York: Doran, 1919);
Discours prononcés dans la séance publique tenue par l'Académie française pour la réception de M. le comte

Alfred de Vigny, circa 1860 (photograph by Nadar)

Alfred de Vigny, le 26 janvier 1846 (Paris: Didot, 1846);
Les Destinées (Paris: Michel Lévy frères, 1864);
Journal d'un poète, edited by Louis Ratisbonne (Paris: Michel Lévy frères, 1867);
Daphné, edited by Frenand Gregh (Paris: Delagrave, 1913);
Oeuvres complètes, 8 volumes, edited by Fernand Baldensperger (Paris: Conard, 1914–1935);
Oeuvres complètes, 2 volumes, edited by Baldensperger (Paris: Gallimard, Bibliothèque de la Pléiade, 1948);
Mémoires inédits, fragments et projets, edited by Jean Sangnier (Paris: Gallimard, 1958);
Chatterton, edited by Liano Petroni (Bologna: Pàtron, 1962);

Oeuvres complètes, edited by Paul Viallaneix (Paris: Seuil, 1965);

Chatterton, Quitte pour la peur (Paris: Garnier-Flammarion, 1968);

Oeuvres complètes, 2 volumes, edited by François Germain and Alphonse Bouvet (Paris: Gallimard, Bibliothèque de la Pléiade, 1986, 1993).

Alfred de Vigny, poet, novelist, and dramatist, was an influential figure in the Romantic movement, particularly as it developed in the late 1820s and 1830s. His influence on the direction of French theater was profound, despite the fact that his dramatic output was relatively small. He completed only three original plays, each of which he saw produced and published, and a translation-adaptation of William Shakespeare's *Othello* (1604), which was the first of Vigny's plays to be produced. His three-act version of Shakespeare's *The Merchant of Venice* (1596), titled *Shylock, Le Marchand de Venise* (Shylock, The Merchant of Venice), was not published during his lifetime and not produced until after his death, when it was staged at the Comédie-Française on 7 April 1905. Although he worked on dramatic adaptations of the anonymous twelfth-century *Chanson de Roland* (The Song of Roland) and Shakespeare's *Antony and Cleopatra* (1606), he abandoned such ambitions in 1832 during a bout with cholera, relegating his unfinished manuscripts to the fire.

Vigny's interest in the reform of the French theater was set off by the publication of such manifestos as François Guizot's *Sur la vie et les oeuvres de Shakespeare* (Concerning the Life and Works of Shakespeare) in 1821, Stendhal's *Racine et Shakespeare* in 1823 and 1825, and Victor Hugo's *Préface de Cromwell* in 1827. It was then clinched by two decisive events: Vigny's encouragement by Baron Taylor, the newly appointed director of the Comédie-Française, and the arrival in Paris in 1828 of the Penley Players, an English company that performed Shakespeare's representative plays in English. As early as 1823, Vigny admired Shakespeare's adroit synthesis of styles that allowed him to capture both the prosaic and lyrical aspects of the totality of human expression and aspiration. He found such attributes to be conspicuously absent in the virtually moribund Neoclassical dramas of the period. He became convinced that Shakespearean drama could serve as a model for the reform and modernization of French theater.

Vigny's sporadic career as a dramatist began precisely at the time the Shakespeare controversy erupted in France during the 1820s. When his collaboration in 1827 with Emile Deschamps on a French adaptation of *Romeo and Juliet* (1594) was nei-

ther produced nor subsequently published, he set to work alone to translate *Othello* as *Le More de Venise* (The Moor of Venice), first performed at the Comédie-Française on 24 October 1829. Vigny wanted his adaptation to serve as a point of mediation between the Neoclassical factions that resisted all change and the Romantic innovators who advocated a complete revamping of the French stage. His translation endeavored to show that a new style, crucially informed by a different worldview, could triumph over the arbitrary limitations imposed by Neoclassicism. His adaptation of *Othello* in 1829 succeeded in softening the diehard resistance of opponents of Shakespeare and may be justifiably credited with preparing the atmosphere that enabled the success of Hugo's *Hernani* in 1830 and other daring dramas afterward.

Chatterton, Vigny's celebrated play based on the life of the English poet Thomas Chatterton, received its first performance in 1835. A three-act drama, it is a dramatic elaboration of the second narrative of Vigny's three-part novel *Stello: Les Consultations du Docteur-Noir* (translated as *Stello: A Session with Doctor Noir,* 1963), published three years earlier in 1832. *Chatterton,* usually considered the masterpiece of Vigny's dramatic work, constitutes a thesis play that decries the plight of the poet in a callous and indifferent society. The play might strike one in some ways as an example of dated dramaturgy, were it not for the effective infusion of Vigny's philosophical statements in it and the felicitously crafted portrait of Kitty Bell. This modest and gracious heroine harbors a chaste love for the besieged poet. Although she plays no strictly necessary role in the narrow elucidation of the play's thesis, the reticence that characterizes Kitty Bell's presence in the drama communicates intensely felt emotions that confer upon key scenes a certain delicate yet tragic grandeur. As such, her role prefigures those that have been subsequently elaborated in the modern theater of silence. Vigny's adaptation of *Othello* and his drama *Chatterton* have thus imprinted, each in their own way, their mark on the development of modern French drama.

Alfred de Vigny was born in Loches in southern Touraine on 27 March 1797. As the only surviving child of a retired captain from the Seven Years War and a mother whose father was a former naval officer, the young boy was raised virtually as a former aristocrat at the requisitioned palace of the Elysée-Bourbon, where the Vignys moved when Alfred was eighteen months old. He lived there until he was four years old. His mother took charge of his early education, instructing her son in painting, music, and mathematics while his enfeebled father re-

LA MARÉCHALE D'ANCRE

La Maréchale. — Regardez bien cet homme là. (Acte V, Scène dernière)

Illustration from the first edition of La Maréchale d'Ancre, *set during the final years of the regency of Marie de Medicis*

galed his son's imagination with tales of his military exploits. When he was ten, Alfred enrolled in Monsieur Hix's school, a somewhat militaristic establishment, where he was taunted by the other students for the particule *de* in his family name. His parents had impressed on him from an early age the importance of cultivating and maintaining a feudal and moral sense of honor. By and large, the education Vigny received as a young child led him to consider surviving members of the aristocracy as the pariahs of the new society. The young boy listened to the elegant conversations of his parents and their friends in which they recollected the extinguished glorious past, contrasting it with the humiliation of their present situation.

From 1811 until 1813 Vigny attended the Lycée Bonaparte (now Condorcet), where he excelled at mathematics and delighted in hearing accounts of Napoleon Bonaparte's great army by enthusiastic teachers. These stories, coupled with tales of his ancestors' exploits, whetted his appetite for more excitement. At seventeen years of age he opted for a military career. His mother obtained for him a commission as second lieutenant in the First Regiment of the King's Royal Guard in July 1814. In March 1815 he was ordered with others of his regiment to accompany the fleeing Louis XVIII to

Ghent as Napoleon returned to France for the Hundred Days return to power. Vigny quickly suffered bitter disillusionment with his army career. After the restoration of the Bourbons in 1815, he managed to have himself transferred to the sixth regiment of the Royal Guard. From 1816 until 1823 he experienced firsthand the boredom of barracks life in a peacetime army. It was during this period that he undertook to reeducate himself; he read widely in the Scriptures, in literature, and in mathematics to fill in his many hours of leisure. He was especially impressed by the works of George Gordon, Lord Byron; André Chénier; and René de Chateaubriand. Byron's denunciation of the present and his pessimism concerning the future coincided with Vigny's own attitude in 1820. No small wonder, then, that his first published article should be a study of the English writer up to that time.

In 1820 Vigny renewed his acquaintance with Emile Deschamps, an employee at the Ministry of Finance, whom he had known as a child when he lived at the Elysée Bourbon. The two became steadfast friends; they shared similar interests in the arts and the Parisian literary scene. Deschamps introduced Vigny to Victor Hugo, who took an immediate liking to the young military officer and invited him to contribute to the new legitimist journal, *Le*

Conservateur littéraire, which he had founded the previous year. Besides the article he wrote on Byron, Vigny contributed in the December 1820 issue a poem titled "Le Bal" (The Ball), describing a waltz whose joyous sounds and movements are triggered by an undertone of melancholy. More important, Vigny's relationships with Hugo and Deschamps helped dislodge the budding poet from the isolation in which he kept himself because of his military obligations.

Hugo's warm encouragement unleashed Vigny's enthusiasm for poetry. With Hugo he soon saw himself searching for ways to restore the French lyric to its original vigor. Hugo encouraged him to frequent the literary salon of Virginie Ancelot at the Hôtel de la Rochefoucauld on the rue de Seine in Paris. Jacques and Ancelot were so impressed by Vigny's demeanor that they struck up a lasting friendship with him. The latter, at his death, bequeathed his personal estate to their daughter, Louise-Edmée, who was born in 1825. Vigny met the budding poet Delphine Gay in Madame Ancelot's salon. She fell immediately in love with the soldier-turned-poet; whether Vigny returned her love is not known. Vigny's mother, a pragmatic woman, voiced her disapproval by reminding her son that the family's wretched financial situation would not allow him to marry for love alone.

Vigny's first collection of poetry, *Poèmes* (Poems), was published anonymously in March 1822. The volume consisted of three cantos of "Helena" followed by three sets of poems, each appearing under the three following rubrics: *Poèmes antiques* (poems of antiquity), *Poèmes judaïques* (Judaic poems), and *Poèmes modernes* (modern poems). The collection garnered only scant attention in the French press. Vigny reworked some of the poems and added six new poems to fit under slightly altered rubrics for a more definitive edition, *Poèmes antiques et modernes,* in 1826.

In 1822 the French decided to intervene in the Spanish war to ensure Ferdinand VII's return to the throne as absolute monarch. Vigny's hopes for a glorious military career were momentarily buoyed when he was named captain and assigned to the Fifty-fifth Infantry Regiment at Strasbourg. He and his regiment had reason to believe that they would be sent to Spain to take part in combat. While waiting in southwestern France, presumably to cross the Pyrenees into Spain, he whiled away the time by working on a major poem, "Eloa, ou La Soeur des anges" (Eloa, or Sister of the Angels). At this stage Vigny was beginning to evolve a grand scheme of poems, *mystères* (mysteries), that would address religious and philosophical questions that continued to perplex him. But he never managed to complete the series.

While in Bordeaux, Edouard Delprat, a cousin of Deschamps, introduced Vigny to the literary salon of Mme Paul Nairac, which was frequented by Edmond Géraud, editor of a regional journal and unofficial head of the local literati. Marceline Desbordes-Valmore, an author of plaintive elegies, corresponded with Sophie Gay and spread rumors of Vigny's alleged romance with Delphine Gay. Such gossip about the young military officer elicited as much attention as his readings of sections of "Eloa." Vigny's hopes for a glorious military career were dashed when he and his regiment were ordered to the province of Béarn instead of Spain in December 1823. If Vigny encountered only a sense of boredom in performing the monotonous tasks of a peacetime soldier while at Orloron, Pau, and Navareux, the leisure at his disposal enabled him to undertake excursions that would prove significant to his blossoming career as a writer. He drew up plans for his first historical novel, *Cinq-Mars, ou, Une Conspiration sous Louis XIII* (1826; translated as *Cinq-Mars: A Conspiracy under Louis XIII,* 1847). He also completed "Eloa," his first major poem, for publication.

"Eloa" is an epic poem in three cantos that relates how a young virgin, transformed by a tear shed by Christ over the death of Lazarus, attempts, in vain, to redeem the fallen Lucifer. The 778-line poem describes, as its major theme, the grandeur and beauty of human compassion. The poem succeeds in fashioning striking portraits of the virgin-turned-angel and Lucifer. "Eloa" gets its primary inspiration not from the account of the Fall of Man in Genesis but from John Milton's *Paradise Lost* (1667) and from Vicomte François-René de Chateaubriand's *Les Martyrs* (Martyrs, 1809). Vigny's development of Satan's personality, that of seducer and comforter to mankind, conjures up Byron's Lucifer in *Cain* (1821). Critical reaction to "Eloa" was for the most part approving, if not entirely enthusiastic. Vigny had begun to evolve his moral philosophy, emphasizing in "Eloa" the themes of doubt, pity, and fraternal commiseration.

When Vigny rejoined his regiment at Bayonne and was subsequently given an assignment in Pau in June 1824, he met and fell deeply in love with a "blonde Antigone," Lydia Bunbury. After considerable maneuvering on the young officer's part, Sir Hugh Bunbury grudgingly consented some months later to his daughter's marriage to Vigny. The nuptials in February 1825 gradually led to another disappointment for the young poet. Lydia adjusted poorly to wedded life and after two miscarriages grew obese and became noticeably awkward. She understood nothing of her husband's writing, spoke little French, and even forgot the idioms of her native language. By 1826 she had become virtually a chronic invalid. All of this prompted Vigny gradually to distance himself from Deschamps and Hugo, as well as other friends. Eventually, many took his reticence for aloofness and affectation. In April 1825 Vigny requested extended military leave and thus, practically speaking, brought his military career to a close.

Once in Paris, he gathered the poems associated with his military experience into the collection *Poèmes antiques et modernes* (1826). This time he divided the poems according to their inspiration into three categories: The Mystical Book, The Book of Antiquity, and The Modern Book. In The Mystical Book he placed "Eloa," "Moïse" (Moses), and "Le Déluge." "Moïse," the most successful of the three, is a symbolic representation of the suffering and isolation endured by all superior beings, and in the author's estimation, by all superior poets. "Le Déluge" reveals a God who punishes, without distinguishing, the innocent along with the guilty. Except for "Le Cor" (The Horn) in The Modern Book, where Vigny evokes his recollections as a soldier in a reverie concerning the exploits of Roland and Charlemagne in the Pyrenees, the other poems are of questionable quality. The main objective of the collection was to advance philosophical ideas and attitudes in short poems that assumed either a dramatic or an epic dimension. Vigny's conception of the epic as a short poem was considered innovative in the 1820s. "Eloa," "Moïse," and "Le Déluge" can be said to be worthwhile realizations toward such an achievement. The originality of some of the pieces in *Poèmes antiques et modernes* stems from the poet's use of anecdotes and fables to convey philosophically certain individual confrontations with destiny. Vigny thus attempts to bring out, through the symbolic employment of fables or anecdotes, essential aspects of the human condition. In such a poem as "Moïse," for example, the anecdotal ingredient tends to become overwhelmed by the urgency of the moral or metaphysical issues in question. The *Poèmes antiques et modernes* met with mixed reactions in the popular and critical press. Whatever their shortcomings, the poems attested to the accomplishment of a talented poet whose verse remained intricately connected to the most urgent problems of the new civilization being elaborated in the aftermath of the French Revolution.

Vigny resided in Paris from 1826 to 1830, where he regularly attended the literary cénacle of Charles Nodier, whom he had known since 1823. In 1826 Vigny saw himself as a man of noble birth increasingly interested in articulating his ideas on the trajectory of French history. Discussions at the cénacle focused on the historical novel and the historical drama as emerging genres capable of capturing popular support for the Romanticists' campaign to rejuvenate and modernize French literature. He began to gather documentation for his novel *Cinq-Mars*. His original aim was to write a huge historical novel, a kind of epic of the French nobility, in the form of complementary tableaux. He planned other historical tableaux on Louis XIV, on the French Revolution, and on the Napoleonic Empire. He completed only *Cinq-Mars*.

In an essay written in 1827, which he subsequently inserted as a preface to succeeding editions of *Cinq-Mars*, Vigny defined what he thought the historical novel should be. Titled "Réflexions sur la vérité dans l'art" (Reflections on Truth in Art), the treatise attempts to illustrate how *Cinq-Mars* reverses the manner in which Sir Walter Scott had dealt with his historical characters. Rather than relegate historical personalities to minor roles as Scott had done, Vigny made them the principals in *Cinq-Mars*. "Réflexions sur la vérité dans l'art" tackled the problematics of the historical novel, whose subject involves both history and art. The essay distinguished in history between two elements considered to be true, but true in significantly different ways. Vigny concluded that since the aim of art is idealistic, the historical novel should endow its author with the necessary freedom to invent what he senses to approximate the ideal in order to relate more than simple factual truths. The essay goes on to claim: "L'art ne doit jamais être considéré que dans ses rapports avec la *beauté idéale* . . . la vérité dont il doit se nourrir est la vérité sur la *nature humaine* et non l'authenticité du fait" (Art must be considered only in its relationship with *ideal beauty* . . . the truth that underpins it is the truth of the observation of *human nature,* and not that of the authenticity of facts). The argument of his justificatory essay constitutes a formula for transmuting historical fact into legend. Just as Vigny had previously altered the image of Moses to have him meet the pressing requirements of his viewpoint in the poem, Vigny resorts to several historical distortions to assert his thesis more forcefully in *Cinq-Mars*.

In his novel he meant to portray the gradual weakening of the French nobility in the seventeenth century and to warn of the evil awaiting the nation in the event of its collapse. Vigny wished to hold Cardinal Armand-Jean du Plessis Richelieu accountable since his policies sought to undermine the fabric of the French feudal system. To realize such ob-

*Frontispiece for the first edition of Vigny's play about British poet
Thomas Chatterton*

jectives in *Cinq-Mars* he resorted to the fictionalization of historical personages such as Louis XIII, Cardinal Richelieu, Father Joseph, and Henri d'Effiat de Cinq-Mars. The novelist utilized the history of the failed conspiracy of Cinq-Mars and his friend, de Thou, against Cardinal Richelieu to elucidate his thesis concerning the latter's systematic weakening of the French nobility. Vigny even suggests that the cardinal's policies prepared the way for the French Revolution. *Cinq-Mars* proved to be a great popular success. A second printing appeared in June 1826, and by 1827 Vigny could count a total of thirteen printings of the novel in various formats.

Between 1826 and 1830 Vigny lived in Paris and became increasingly active in Nodier's cénacle, where the young Romantic writers discussed literary questions. He grew more intimate with Hugo, Ancelot, Alexandre Soumet, Henri Latouche, and the brothers Emile and Antony Deschamps. During this time Vigny became more disenchanted with the Bourbon regime and aligned himself with dissatisfied aristocrats who began to press for greater secularization in the structure of the Restoration. In September 1826 his wife Lydia became seriously ill, and he devoted much of his time to caring for her. He requested a military discharge for reasons of health, which was granted in May 1827. There were discernible signs that same year that a political revolution was about to occur within the shadows of the Romantic revolution, which focused most of its attention on the reform of the French theater. At the same time Baron Taylor, the new director of the Comédie-Française, encouraged members of Nodier's cénacle to write plays for his national theater. In February Hugo invited his friends to readings of the five acts of his new drama, *Cromwell* (1827), and its manifesto preface. Hugo's conceptualization of the unity of opposites, the sublime and the grotesque, which he presented in the *Préface,* proposed a positive definition of the new Romantic drama. Hugo's *Cromwell* and its accompanying *Préface* emboldened Vigny to write for the theater.

Vigny's recently deceased cousin, Baron Bruguière de Sorsum, had bequeathed him the translations of four of Shakespeare's plays that he entrusted to the poet Charles Lioult de Chênedollé for their publication. Shakespeare was in the limelight in 1827 when the English troupe of Charles Kemble and Charles Abbott, along with Harriet Smithson, arrived in September 1827 at the Théâtre de l'Odéon and the Salle Favart (now the Opéra Comique) for performances of Shakespeare in English. Vigny attended some of their performances and was won over to the cause of Shakespeare, declaring that the English bard had demonstrated that the liberating freedom in art constituted a precondition for progress. Vigny was now eager to make Shakespeare better known to French audiences.

By the end of 1827 Vigny joined Deschamps, already at work on a verse translation of *Romeo and Juliet.* The two collaborators—Deschamps was to translate the first three acts, Vigny the last two acts—voiced their common ambition: to shake the French theater out of its stagnation with a translation faithful to the spirit of Shakespeare. The reading committee at the Comédie-Française approved the translation-adaptation on 15 April 1828, but its performance was postponed indefinitely, partly because the leading lady, Mlle Mars, forty-nine years old, refused to assume the role of Juliet, and partly because Fréderic Soulié's adaptation of *Roméo et Juliette* was already in rehearsal and scheduled to open at the Théâtre de l'Odéon on 10 June. Deschamps and Vigny's *Roméo et Juliette* was never performed. Be that as it may, Vigny, in an 1856 entry to his *Journal d'un poète* (Diary of a Poet, 1867), admitted that the two acts he had translated were *mauvais et incorrect* (bad and incorrect). Deschamps later undertook another translation of *Roméo et Juliette* on his own.

Undaunted, Vigny embarked on a translation-adaptation of *Othello,* which he titled *Le More de Venise.* The completed script was accepted by the Comédie-Française on 17 July 1829, and the play went into rehearsal at the end of the same month.

Meanwhile, Hugo worked feverishly to complete his drama *Hernani,* after his play, *Un Duel sous Richelieu* (A Duel under Richelieu), retitled *Marion de Lorme,* had been rejected by the censors. Hugo's *Hernani* was accepted by the reading committee on 30 September. He felt strongly that an original drama and not a literal translation of Shakespeare would serve more convincingly as a proving ground for the future of the French Romantic theater. But Vigny proved to be adamant, and Hugo conceded to him on the matter. *Le More de Venise* premiered at the Comédie-Française on 24 October 1829. It ran for thirteen performances and was considered, on the whole, a significant critical success.

Vigny did not intend his *Le More de Venise* to be a literal translation of *Othello.* His "Lettre à Lord***" (Letter to Lord***) is an explanation of his translation-adaptation of *Othello* and constitutes his preface to the tragedy. If a modern tragedy portraying the crucial issues of existence could win French audiences, then the rejuvenation of the theater could be undertaken with confidence and enthusiasm. Vigny defined the "new" drama in terms of the final impression it left with the theatergoer rather than by any rules or prescriptions to which it should adhere. "Ecoutez ce soir le langage que je pense devoir être de la tragédie moderne; dans lequel chaque personnage parlera selon son caractère, et dans l'art comme dans la vie, passera de la simplicité habituelle à l'éxaltation passionnée" (Listen, tonight, to the language which I believe to be that of modern tragedy; in which each personage will speak according to his character, and in art as it is also in life, will gravitate at times, from a customary simplicity to occasional bursts of passionate exaltation). Vigny's translation of *Othello,* while faithful to its spirit, enabled all the power of the original text to come through to French audiences in an indelible fashion. The truth of the matter was that *Le More de Venise* attempted to blend the best features of classicism with modernism. Far from trying to illustrate, in his translation, the superiority of one system of drama over the other, *Le More de Venise* sought to graft Shakespearean tragedy to the possibilities of modern drama. Unless the plays of Shakespeare could be so modernized, they would be incapable of contributing to the cause of progress and reform in the nineteenth-century French theater.

To avoid upsetting the Neoclassicists who would likely constitute a part of his audience, Vigny edited certain puns, coarse language, and double entendres that risked unduly irritating conservative spectators. For example, he cut part of the scene between Iago and Desdemona in act 2, scene 1; the clown scenes in act 3, scene 1; and act 4, scene 1. Act

2 ends with a dialogue between Iago and Roderigo. But by and large, Vigny's alterations and omissions do not betray seriously the tone and temper of Shakespeare's script. His translations are from the Bathurst text of the First Folio edition of *Othello*. In several instances Vigny succeeded handsomely in finding an exact correspondence between French and English terms. A case in point occurs in Iago's soliloquy in act 3, just after he has planted the seed of jealousy in Othello's heart:

> Look where he comes! Not poppy nor mandragora,
> Not all the drowsy syrup of the world
> Shall ever medicine thee to that sweet sleep
> Which thou owedst yesterday[.]

becomes in Vigny's romantic alexandrine verse:

> Va déchire ton coeur! Va, ni le feu ni l'eau,
> Les boissons de pavots, d'opium, de mandragora
> Ne pourront te guérir et te donner encore
> Ce paisible sommeil que tu goûtas hier.

Vigny's particularly adept handling of the alexandrine enabled him to capture the majestic rendering of Othello's well-known farewell scene to his past military exploits. There occur in *Le More de Venise* several alterations that derive from the translator's imperfect comprehension of the English language. But these are relatively few, and they never detract seriously from the overall sense of *Othello*. Overall, one comes away with the impression that *Le More de Venise* is the work of a first-rate translator and adaptor. General critical reaction to Vigny's work made it clear that the battle to popularize Shakespeare in France had been won and that the example of the English bard would provide useful directions for the needed reform of the French theater.

Vigny's translation of *The Merchant of Venice* as *Shylock, Le Marchand de Venise,* although undertaken in the same spirit as *Othello* and completed in 1830, reveals the same lack of care that marred the two last acts of his *Roméo et Juliette*. Vigny shows himself in the verse adaptation of *Le Marchand de Venise* to be tentative with respect to the observance of the unities. There are instances when whole scenes remind one of remnants of Neoclassical tragedy. Given the additions, suppressions, and mistranslations that punctuate the three acts of *Le Marchand de Venise,* one understands the reticence of the Comédie-Française to pit it against several adaptations of the play available on the Parisian stages. Even the title of Vigny's adaptation underwent a puzzling metamorphosis in 1858 when it was published as *Shylock, Marchand de Venise*. This title is baffling since the merchant in the play is Antonio and not Shylock. *Le Marchand de*

Venise received its first performance at the Comédie-Française on 7 April 1905.

With the advent of the July Revolution of 1830 Vigny's faith in the structure of France's political institutions was visibly shaken. He registered expressions of shocked resignation in the entries in the *Journal d'un poète* concerning the fateful days of July 27 to July 29. Despite the apprehension he experienced concerning his own safety as well as that of his sick wife during the days of violent conflict, he could not refrain from expressing admiration for the struggling people who displayed the same type of courage and tenacity he had encountered in the Imperial Guard. He volunteered to serve in the National Guard that Louis-Philippe had established to quash disorders and riots and to restore order to the various Parisian neighborhoods. Yet, despite his outward cooperation with the new regime, he refrained from rallying openly to the king and his political agenda. Vigny's lingering aristocracy was still too entrenched for him to endorse Louis-Philippe's despoliation of the throne's rightful heir, the duke of Bordeaux. He chose, instead, to maintain a neutral and skeptical position during the years of the July Monarchy (1830–1848), which he felt lacked an acceptable mandate.

Vigny had already begun to question his own values and beliefs during the waning years of the Bourbon Restoration. He was now skeptical about the efficacy of all institutions, and he was increasingly perturbed by organized religions, which he found hopelessly congealed by dogmas that made them blind to any appreciable notion of progress. Taken with Benjamin Constant's monumental treatise, *De la religion* (On Religion, 1824–1831), among others, he reflected on the capital distinction made by Constant between religious sentiment and religious forms or dogmas. He was particularly struck by the discernible separation that occurred between the two whenever religious sentiment outgrew its outward form. The divorce between the two usually resulted in periods of moral decay and social upheaval. Of the nature of this opposition Vigny concluded in his *Journal d'un poète* in 1829: "Les formes religieuses ne peuvent absorber ni une tête puissante ni un coeur passionné. Le philosophe veut passer au-delà, l'amant sentir davantage, aimer plus violemment, avec moins d'égoisme" (Religious forms can neither absorb a powerful mind nor a passionate heart. The philosopher wants to go beyond cults and dogmas, and the lover wants to feel more intensely and to love more violently with less egoism). Liberation from such constraints would enable the philosopher to pursue goals that transcended those trapped within the contingencies of time and

Page from the manuscript for Chatterton *(Bibliothèque Nationale)* space. Vigny's comment explains to a considerable degree the motivation that underpinned his subsequent quest after *l'esprit pur* (pure spirit) that informs all his future writing. His unfinished novel, *Scènes du désert: L'Alméh* (Scenes from the Desert: L'Alméh), published in the April 1831 issue of the *Revue des Deux Mondes,* investigates the problem of the fragility of religious forms and institutions. Vigny developed the thesis that the exterior forms of religious belief inevitably succumb to the passage of time.

In 1830 Vigny met the actress Marie Dorval at a time when his wife suffered from the lymphatism that turned her into a helpless invalid. Vigny had seen the actress perform at the Théâtre de la Porte Saint-Martin and asked Alexandre Dumas *père,* who knew her well, to introduce him to her. He was immediately taken with her and asked her to play the leading role in a drama he was writing. He arranged for a reading of his new play, *La Maréchale d'Ancre* (The Wife of the Marshall d'Ancre) at Dorval's apartment on 5 and 7 October 1830. Prior commitments prevented her from playing the role intended for her when the drama was scheduled to open at the Théâtre de l'Odéon on 22 June 1831. This mutual disappointment did not prevent them from entering into a passionate and stormy liaison that lasted until 1838. Mlle George assumed the leading role, but the actual premiere of *La Maréchale d'Ancre* took place three days later, on 25 June.

The outstanding success of Hugo's *Hernani* (1830) and an avid interest in the acting career of Dorval ended Vigny's reluctance to write an original drama. His own adaptation of *Othello* and its prefatory essay purported to demonstrate how the example of Shakespeare could serve in the ongoing rejuvenation of the French stage. *La Maréchale de'Ancre* focuses on the last year of Louis XIII's regency. Vigny pinpoints the plot in a prefatory essay dated July 1831: "La minorité de Louis XIII finit comme elle avait commencé, par un assassinat. Concini et la Galigaï régnèrent entre ces deux crimes" (Louis XIII regency ended as it had begun, by an assassination. Concini and [Leonora] Galigaï governed between these two crimes). Concini and the former Leonora Galigaï, the marshalls of Ancre, exercised enormous influence over Louis XIII's mother, Marie de Medicis, during her regency. If they enjoyed great power after the assassination of Henri IV in 1610, they also incurred the wrath of the Prince Condé and other dissidents at court. The drama's specific action takes place in 1617. It is revealed that the fates of the marshalls of Ancre have been sealed. Their enemies have convinced the sixteen-year-old king to order the executions of the marshall and his wife and to banish his mother to

exile. To underline the idea that these new assassinations are meant to expiate Henri IV's murder, Vigny makes considerable alterations concerning historical facts. In the drama the Baron de Vitry shoots down Concini at exactly the same spot in the rue de la Ferronnerie where Ravaillac had previously assassinated the king.

Vigny chooses to distort historical facts to accentuate more forcefully the sense of fatality that hovers over the lives of the marshall and his wife. The latter's outcries concerning her fate surface several times, constituting a veritable leitmotiv. In act 4 she cries bitterly: "Ah! Je sens que je suis perdue: j'ai eu beau lutter, le destin a été le plus fort. Ah, je sens que ju suis perdue! perdue!" (Alas, I know that I am a doomed woman. What is the use of fighting! Fate is stronger than I am! Oh, I sense that I am lost, lost!). Vigny deliberately ascribes all responsibility for the assassination of Henri IV to the marshall of Ancre. Ravaillac, who actually plunged his knife into the king's heart, is reduced in the drama to little more than Concini's accomplice, who acted solely on orders from the latter. Thus, the marshall emerges both as an ambitious man, which history records, and as the assassin of the king, for which act he will be justly punished. To situate the event indelibly in the mind of his audience Vigny has him meet his fate at the same boundary stone, marking the spot where Ravaillac killed Henri IV, rather than on the block in the courtyard of the Louvre. Vigny distorts historical fact again by having the marshall's wife meet her fate on the same day, burned at the stake for sorcery in front of the Châtelet.

Fired up by the trials of Charles X's former ministers during the early years of Louis-Philippe's monarchy, Vigny wrote *La Maréchale d'Ancre* to argue for the abolition of capital punishment for political crimes. At her trial for high treason and sorcery at the Bastille, the marshall's wife admonishes her judges: "Regardez-y à deux fois avant de déshonorer le Parlement; c'est tout ce que je puis vous dire. Quel coupable politique a-t-on tué jamais sans l'avoir regretté un an après? J'ai vu un jour le feu roi Henri pleurer M. le maréchal de Biron. Bientôt il en serait de même pour moi" (Think twice before you bring dishonor on the Parliament; that is all I can tell you. Can you name a man, guilty of a political crime for which he was put to death, who did not cause consternation and regret afterward? One day, I saw the late King Henri mourn the death of Marshall Biron [executed for conspiring with Spain and Savoy against the French throne]. Soon, it will be the same for me). Despite the timeliness of its thesis, *La Maréchale d'Ancre* proved only a tepid success.

The drama has really only one important role, that of the marshall's wife. The other characters, by comparison, appear dramatically underdeveloped. Only the Maréchale sustains attention and interest. Vigny succeeds in portraying her as an intelligent, sensitive, and charming woman who used her influence reluctantly with the queen to appease the man who is the father of her children. Despite her kindness and compassion, she enlists the audience's sympathy only up to a point, because her inherent passivity leads her to surrender too quickly to her fate, early in the third act. The last two acts depict her slowly slipping to her doom.

If *La Maréchale d'Ancre* was meant to illustrate what, after Shakespeare, could be achieved in the French theater, then Vigny's first original drama could only be considered a disappointing effort. Despite certain outside influences—Borgia's portrait suggests that of Othello; Concini acts occasionally in ways that recall Iago; and there is some commingling of comic and tragic elements—this historical drama emerges as too Neoclassically oriented and didactic for it to qualify as a genuine tragedy in the Shakespearean manner. *La Maréchale d'Ancre* resembles an historical treatise. The plot is too contrived and centers on a single event that is insufficiently weighted to carry the drama. Despite its limitations, *La Maréchale d'Ancre* was revived by the Comédie-Française in 1840 with Dorval in the principal role.

When a serious cholera epidemic broke out in Paris, both Vigny and his wife suffered severe attacks that caused them to be bedridden. Dorval also became seriously ill during the dreaded epidemic. The actress began to assume a greater importance for Vigny almost in proportion to the increasing personal malaise he experienced in 1832. Perhaps motivated by his denunciation by the Ministry of Interior for remaining a legitimist Carlist, while at the same time the Palais Royal suspected him of being a republican sympathizer, Vigny reveals in *Journal d'un poète* a steadfast preoccupation with the plight of the individual in the frustrating social and political environment of his time. His 1832 narrative, *Stello: Les Consultations du Docteur-Noir,* emerges as the fictional expression of this concern.

Loosely taken, *Stello* is a novel that intermingles fact with fiction to convey the wretchedness experienced by poets in the societies in which they attempt to exercise their function as artists. Stello, a young poet given to fits of depression, consults Doctor Noir, who relates the stories of the pathetic demises of three poets: Nicholas Gilbert, Thomas Chatterton, and André Chénier. All three were either ignored or abused by their respective governments and societies: Gilbert by the monarchy of Louis XV, Chatterton by the English constitutional state, and Chénier by the revolutionary government. When Stello reacts with dismay to the situation of the poets, Doctor Noir dispenses the following prescription: "Séparer la vie poétique de la vie politique" (Keep the poetical life separate from the political life). Doctor Noir's advice to Stello reflects Vigny's own attempts to elaborate his personal poetics during the 1830s.

Vigny's energies were severely taxed in March 1833 when he had to assume full responsibility for the care of his ailing wife and also of his mother, who had recently moved into his apartment after suffering a disabling stroke. During his occasional evening visits to Dorval he was repeatedly reproached for having done little to advance her theatrical career. In fact, he proved to be her staunchest advocate, and in his articles on the French dramatic scene he frequently pointed out that the actress's unusual talents should be put to better use in the renewal of the theater. To overcome the opposition by members of the Comédie-Française to admit her to their prestigious ranks, Vigny wrote a playlet, initially called a *proverbe,* to show off Dorval's talent before the distinguished audience that was expected to attend the benefit for the Opéra. Reportedly completed in a single day, *Quitte pour la peur* (Getting Off with a Fright, 1833) recalled the *proverbes dramatiques* of Carmontelle (Louis Carrogis) of the eighteenth century and the genre later exploited by Alfred de Musset. The playlet dramatizes an anecdote recounted to Vigny by the princess de Béthune. It was performed as one of two short bills for a single performance at the Opéra on 30 May 1833. Dorval played the leading role as well as that in the one-act play of Nicolas Pradon's *Phédre* (Phaedra, 1677).

Quitte pour la peur is set in 1778 during the reign of Louis XVI. The plot revolves around a young duchess who has been abandoned by her husband for a marquise who has become his mistress. The duchess in turn takes a lover by whom she becomes pregnant. The duke learns of the pregnancy and returns home one night. The young duchess thinks that he has returned to kill her. The duke suspects as much and makes sport of frightening her at first. He eventually informs her that he has returned to spend the night with her for the sake of their reputations: "Dans une société qui se corrompt et se dissout chaque jour comme la nôtre, tout ce qui reste encore de possible, c'est le respect des convenances. . . . Je vous ai dit que je tenais à notre nom. . . . En voici la preuve: vos gens et les miens m'ont vu entrer, ils me verront sortir, et, pour le monde, c'est tout qu'il faut" (In a society such as ours, which grows more corrupt and dissolute each day, all that is left possible, is the respect of proprieties. . . . I told you that I wanted to ensure our good reputation. . . . Both your servant and mine have seen me enter your room and they will see me leave it. As far as people are concerned, that is all that is necessary to restore our good name). The theme of adultery in *Quitte pour la peur* raises questions, some of which Vigny attempts to answer. He suggests that during times of decadence or moral disarray such as that of 1778–and, by implication, that of 1833–the individual can find no better guide than one's own sense of honor or of fair play. The duchess's adultery is thus justified by the playwright, who establishes a distinction between the rights of love and the obligations of marriage. *Quitte pour la peur* met with mixed critical reaction. Some hailed it as a witty and delicious comedy, while others decried it as the mistake of a talented writer. The one-act play was banned by the censors in 1847 because of its immorality. It was revived more successfully in 1849.

Vigny's relationship with Dorval deteriorated after *Quitte pour la peur*. Their rendezvous in her apartment often disintegrated into scenes of mutual recrimination, and she went on tour in the provinces for an extended period. Meanwhile, Vigny worked diligently on a dramatization of the second narrative of *Stello,* which became his 1835 play, *Chatterton*. In August 1834 he read the completed manuscript of his drama to a committee that accepted it for eventual production at the Comédie-Française. After considerable manipulation Vigny succeeded in getting the role of Kitty Bell for Dorval. *Chatterton* opened on 12 February 1835.

Chatterton dramatizes the plight of the poet as a victim or pariah in modern historical times. The drama appeared at a period when France was undergoing a sweeping transformation from a feudal to an industrial system. The parallelisms that are implied between the 1770 London setting in the play and the conditions that characterized the new French industrial society under Louis-Philippe endow *Chatterton* with a pertinent topicality. Along with Hugo, Vigny studies the repercussions wrought by the cataclysmic French Revolution. Vigny amplifies the thesis elucidated in *Stello* by pitting the greedy materialism of a newly industrialized society against such wary victims as a defenseless woman, hapless workers, and an unappreciated poet. *Chatterton* becomes a powerful comment on the revolution's failure to realize its dream of an ideal republic. More than a portrait of the poet's plight because he or she has no appreciable role to play in a utilitarian society, the drama also provides a disconcerting view of the modern individual in a fragmented social structure, devoid of any meaningful direction. Even if Thomas

Marie Dorval as Kitty Bell in the 1835 Paris production of Chatterton *(engraving by Edme Hedouin; Collection of the Comédie-Française)*

Chatterton's mind may be unbalanced, one can see that the alienation that he experiences in the play catapults him into an environment that is bereft of any hierarchical or providential order. The disintegration of values that results from the social materialism of the time dissuades the young poet from his heroic mission and from total dedication to a society that no longer attaches importance to the values he espouses. The uneasiness he feels under such circumstances compels him to live isolated in a garret that he rents in the home of the manufacturer, John Bell.

There Chatterton leads, in his imagination if not in reality, the life of a tenth-century monk, whom he has named Thomas Rowley. He cuts himself off as completely as possible from all communication with the bourgeois society that exemplifies to him all that is negative. It is only in the purely contrived context that Chatterton is able to discover truth and satisfy his appetite for that kind of beauty that his society rejects. In a real sense Chatterton, as the poet-protagonist, seeks to resolve his own identity as a heroic personage who is in conflict with the unheroic historical time in which he lives.

The quiet words and gestures of a Quaker and Kitty Bell and her small daughter, Rachel, usher in the drama's critical moment with a touching effectiveness in the first scene of act 1. In their opening dialogue they allude to John Bell and to Chatterton, both of whom are offstage. One can hear the strident voice of the industrialist reprimanding one of his workers in the rear workshop while the poet's presence in the house is evoked by an allusion to the Bible he had given to Rachel as a gift. As commentator on the action that takes place, the Quaker informs the audience almost immediately that it will be confronted by characters with completely antithetical attitudes. He establishes a striking analogy between Kitty Bell's simple and tormented heart and the humiliating situation of the wretched poet. The angry voice of John Bell emerges in sharp contrast to the virtually imperceptible sobbing of Chatterton in his room. When the Quaker, speaking of Kitty's husband, informs Kitty simply: "Cet homme-là vous tuera . . . C'est une espèce de vautour qui écrase sa couvée" (That man will kill you. He's a kind of vulture that crushes his own brood), he is letting the audience understand by extension that the arrogant and brutal attitudes of the new industrialist will also stifle the voice of the poet.

John Bell, who embodies the power of money in society, declares with the pride and cynicism of the parvenu that everything for him must yield a profit. And when the Quaker, a rather misanthropic observer of the ways of the world, begs him not to fire Tobie, the injured worker, Bell belts out the creed of the new utilitarian positivism: "Ce qui est fait est fait.—Que n'agissent-ils tous comme moi!—Tobie est un ouvrier habile, mais sans prévoyance.—Un calculateur véritable ne laisse rien subsister d'inutile autour de lui—Tout doit rapporter, les choses animées et inanimées" (What's done is done.—Why don't they all act as I do!—Tobie is a skilled worker, but without foresight.—One who truly works things out does not let anything that is useless subsist around him.—Everything must yield a profit, what is animate and inanimate). In Vigny's drama John Bell becomes the spokesman for a democracy that prizes the tyranny of capitalism above all else. But when he dares to proclaim: "Je suis juste selon la loi" (I am a just man according to the law), the Quaker quickly replies: "Et ta loi, est-elle juste selon Dieu?" (And is your law just according to God?). Vigny highlights the differences between divinely inspired laws and laws that are simply politically and socially inspired. In this respect he is revealing suspicion and even hostility toward the latter.

The Quaker's reaction points out Chatterton's dilemma. If John Bell, whose attitude represents the utilitarianism of industrial society, exhibits no compassion for the fate of a worker whose labor contributed to the expansion of that utilitarian society, he will certainly pay no attention to the poet's situation, because the poet's work serves no ostensible or useful purpose. Society refuses to acknowledge that Chatterton even is a poet.

To a large extent most protagonists in Romantic drama appear bent on affirming their authentic personalities through their respective revolts against the societies of their time. When the audience encounters Chatterton for the first time, it sees that he suffers from his self-imposed isolation. He admits to the Quaker the antipathy he nurtures for an environment that neither understands nor appreciates his role as a poet. He alludes to his mysterious election that sets him apart from ordinary mortals, and he complains bitterly about not being able to achieve his destiny in a world that has no use for heroism or idealism. He dismisses outright any possibility of a compromise; he can never settle by becoming a professional writer, an "Homme de lettres." He protects the integrity and purity of his poems by setting them in an imaginary medieval past: "j'ai écrit comme le roi Harold au duc Guillaume, en vers à demi-saxons et francs; et ensuite, cette muse du dixième siècle, cette muse religieuse, je l'ai placée dans un châsse comme une sainte" (I have written, like King Harold to Duke William, in verses which are half-Saxon and half-Frankish. Then, I placed this muse of the tenth century, this religious muse, in a reliquary like the remains of a saint). Chatterton's complaints against society are more general and perhaps contradictory. He ardently hopes that his work will be accepted and appreciated by a society that he knows only nurses antipathy and contempt for art and the artist. He blurts out reproachfully to the Quaker: "Et cependant n'ai-je pas quelque droit à l'amour de mes frères, moi qui travaille pour eux nuit et jour; . . . moi qui veut ajouter une perle de plus à la couronne d'Angleterre, et qui plonge dans tant de mers et des fleuves pour la chercher?" (And, do I not have some right to the esteem of my fellow men, I who labor night and day for them; . . . I who wish to add another pearl to the English crown, and who have plunged into so many rivers and oceans to find it?). On the whole Chatterton only succeeds in defining his role as a poet in negative terms in opposition to the society he confronts in this dialogue.

He nonetheless feels intuitively that only the woman who is beloved can understand his predicament and appreciate the role he has undertaken. Chatterton loves Kitty Bell chastely, and he would like to believe that she nurtures love for him, for Chatterton understands love as a kind of transforming force. Indeed, the love he feels for John Bell's wife surfaces as the very symbol of the ideal universe he would like to achieve in his lyrical verse.

Early in the play Chatterton appeals by letter to the lord mayor for financial aid rather than appealing to his friend, the likable Lord Talbot, who stands ready to give him monetary support. Chatterton reveals his egotism when he insists: "Le Lord-maire est à mes yeux le gouvernement, et le gouvernement est l'Angleterre, milord; c'est sur l'Angleterre que je compte" (The Lord-Mayor, in my eyes, is the government, and the government is England, milord; I am counting upon England). The confrontation between Chatterton and Lord Bedford, the mayor of London, brings out dramatically the hostility and indifference of the new society toward the plight of the artist. When the poet proclaims, in elaborating his metaphor of England, that "... nul n'est inutile dans la manoeuvre de notre glorieux navire" (... no one is useless in the maneuvering of our glorious ship"), Beckford booms: "Que diable peut faire le Poète dans la manoeuvre?" (What the devil can the Poet do in the maneuvering?). When Chatterton retorts: "Il lit dans les astres la route que nous montre le doigt du Seigneur" (He reads in the stars the direction shown by the Lord), the government official states brutally: "Imagination, mon cher! Ou folie, c'est la même chose; Vous n'êtes bon à rien, et vous vous êtes rendu tel par ces billevesées" (Pure imagination, my dear fellow! Or nonsense; it is all the same thing; you are good for nothing, and you got that way by all these stupid ideas). What Vigny noted earlier in an 1830 entry to his *Journal,* using the same metaphor that he exploits in *Chatterton,* reveals his innermost thoughts concerning the possible reconciliation of the poet with society: "L'équipage d'un vaisseau et son obéissance à un seul est un miracle de l'esprit social" (The crew of a ship and its obedience to a single being is a miracle of the social mind). The lord-mayor's cynical and disdainful reaction, in his rejection of Chatterton's metaphorical invention, allows the audience to perceive a world that is deprived of the type of authority that should have ascendency over each individual, for a society without laws or principles other than those of money imposes a horrible constraint upon the poet. Chatterton despairs of being able to achieve his personal destiny within such social contexts.

In his eagerness to identify his protagonist with the thesis he expounds, Vigny does not entirely succeed in creating a complex character in Chatterton. It is the reader's or viewer's power of deduction that locates the poet's authentic identity somewhere in the wings of the stage. Chatterton's expressed despair manages only to evoke the tragic reality of many disillusioned artists in the 1830s. Indeed, the suicide in February of the young poet Emile Boullaud intensified the public's interest in Vigny's thesis play. But his protagonist fails to project any appreciable positive image of his situation, because he remains essentially isolated from the social system under attack. Even as Chatterton never questions his vocation as a poet, he never communicates any detailed scheme of his poetic universe.

Chatterton enjoyed a resounding success in 1835. The winding staircase situated almost at center stage dismayed a few critics at first, but Dorval's sensational fall down the steps in the final scene more than justified the presence of such an unusual prop in the minds of the gasping audience. Dorval's portrayal of Kitty Bell won the critics by her touching performances of a modest and gracious heroine weighted down by a tragic grandeur. Indeed, the drama's outstanding attribute was the stunningly simple but effective manner in which Vigny had crafted the role of Kitty Bell. Her subtle reticence and her mostly silent presence on the stage prefigure some of the techniques later exploited in the modern theater of silence. But the notoriety that Vigny achieved through *Chatterton* did little to improve his deteriorating relationship with his mistress.

If *Chatterton* focused on the plight of the poet, *Servitude et grandeur militaires* (1835; translated as *Military Servitude and Grandeur,* 1919) addressed the plight of the soldier in the French army, yet another pariah of French society. The three fictional narratives in this book pay handsome tribute to the selfless devotion of officers and ordinary soldiers in the peacetime army. Vigny perceived a touching grandeur in their quiet obedience and in their unquestioning respect of duty. In *Servitude et grandeur militaires* honor emerges as a kind of religion capable of replacing the outworn codes and as a reliable aid placed in the service of social institutions. For many *Servitude et grandeur militaires* is Vigny's literary masterpiece.

In 1836 Vigny worked on a three-part series of narratives about Julian the Apostate, Philipp Melanchthon, and Jean-Jacques Rousseau, men of three different epochs who confronted the conflict between religious sentiment and religious forms. By October 1837 he had completed only the first part of this philosophical novel. Titled *Daphné,* the frag-

Costume by Perrier for Iago in Vigny's Le More de Venise, *based on*
William Shakespeare's Othello *(watercolor by de Maleuvre;*
Collection of the Comédie-Française)

ment was published posthumously in 1913. *Daphné* recounts the destiny of Julian, the nephew of Constantine, who renounced his Christian faith after studying Greek philosophy. As in *L'Alméh, Daphné* studies the crucial moment when a dying religion confronts a nascent one.

In August 1837 Vigny's relationship with Dorval worsened to the point that he ended it. In the same period his wife's condition continued to deteriorate, and he experienced financial difficulties. In 1838 he inherited a modest family property at Blanzac in the Maine-Giraud. By the summer he slipped into a life of semiretirement there, assuming the preoccupations of a country gentleman. His mother's death, though expected, left him seriously depressed, and he produced almost no writing. To distract himself he tried to resume his relationship with Dorval, but that proved futile because their rendezvous nearly always erupted into emotional scenes of mutual recrimination. In Paris he met Julia and Maria Dupré, sisters from Charleston, South Carolina, and became romantically involved with Julia. By November 1838 Vigny had written little but the major parts of the poem "La Mort du loup" (The Death of the Wolf). But his stay at his property in Maine-Giraud proved therapeutic: his minor restorations relieved his depression. He returned to Paris with Lydia in 1839.

Toward the end of 1841 Vigny was officially invited to present his candidacy for election to the Académie Française. Rejected five times, presumably because of his lack of new publications, he won election on his sixth attempt in May 1845 after publishing in the *Revue des Deux Mondes* such poems as "La Flûte" (The Flute), "La Sauvage" (The Savage Woman), "La Mort du loup," and "Le Mont des Oliviers" (The Mount of Olives). Vigny's studied aloofness in politics probably accounted for the hesitation by the academicians to admit him to their ranks. In February 1848 he rallied to the revolution and was optimistic that a republican constitution, similar to that of the United States, could be drawn up for France. He ran for election as a delegate from the Charente area of Maine-Giraud. He declined, however, to wage a campaign, and the results at the polls were abysmal. The bloody reprisals of the June days in 1848 convinced him that he should leave Paris with Lydia to return to their country cottage. There he devoted his energies to repairing the house and exploiting the land for the lucrative production of wine and brandy.

Vigny openly declared himself in favor of Napoleon III after the coup d'état on 2 December 1851. He considered Louis-Napoleon the lesser of the evils confronting France. In the Maine-Giraud, Vigny dedicated himself to the betterment of his neighbors; he was instrumental in getting a municipal library established in Blanzac. He engaged in correspondence with his niece, Alexandria, the vicomtesse du Plessis, as well as with Mme Louise Ancelot-Lachaud. He admitted to his niece that Lydia's sustained illness prevented him from working during the day. He wrote at night to console himself but made little headway. Back in Paris in 1854, where he remained except for a few brief trips in Charente, Vigny became involved with Louise Colet, to whom he had been introduced by the sculptor James Pradier. But that relationship soon proved abortive. In December 1858 he met Augusta Froustey Bouvard, the daughter of Baron Poupart de Wilde. Although she was forty years his younger, they entered into a passionate relationship that lasted until his death. Lydia died of a seizure on 22 December 1862. Vigny, who had been suffering from stomach cancer, was too ill to attend the funeral. When he died on 17 September 1863, Augusta was eight months pregnant; she gave birth to a son a little more than a month after Vigny's death.

Entries in his *Journal* during the closing weeks of his life point to a man preoccupied with metaphysical questions. There are reflections on doubt as distinguished from skepticism as well as on the possibility of a supernatural world. He struggled to put the finishing touches on his eleven poems known as *Les Destinées* (The Fates), published posthumously in 1864. These philosophical poems focus on the individual's struggle with the forces of destiny, identified variously, during different epochs, as Fate, Providence, or Predestination. The collection recounts the poet's efforts to achieve a measure of freedom from an overpowering fate in order to accede to the ennobling status of pure spirit. In the crowning poem, "La Maison du berger" (The Shepherd's Hut), Vigny states that the poet's function is to distinguish for the masses between activity that improves the human lot and the futile gestures that merely impede human progress. Among the themes Vigny developed in *Les Destinées* are that the individual finds no solace in nature ("La Maison du berger"), nor in the love of woman ("La Colère de Samson" [Samson's Anger]), nor in God's silence ("Le Mont des Oliviers" [The Mount of Olives]). In the end the poet adopts a stoic attitude ("La Mort du loup") and places his hope in the ultimate triumph of mind over matter ("La Bouteille à la mer" [The Bottle in the Sea]). "L'Esprit pur" concludes the collection on a conditionally optimistic tone.

The ringing affirmation of a new religion, celebrated in the last poem of *Les Destinées,* is informed by the dramatic opposition that predicts the ultimate victory of the human spirit in a materialist universe. The dramatic tension between the individual and society that Vigny explored and rehearsed in *La Maréchale d'Ancre, Quitte pour la peur,* and *Chatterton,* and in his translations of Shakespeare, finds its crowning pronouncement in the posthumously published *Les Destinées.*

Letters:

Correspondance (1816–1863), edited by Emma Sakellaridès (Paris: Calmann-Lévy, 1905);

Correspondance (1822–1863), 2 volumes, edited by Léon Séché (Paris: Renaissance du Livre, 1913);

Lettres inédites d'Alfred de Vigny au marquis de La Grange, edited by Albert de Luppé (Paris: Conard, 1914);

Correspondance entre Sainte-Beuve et Alfred de Vigny, lettres inédites, edited by Louis Gillet (Paris: Kra, 1929);

Correspondance 1816–1835, edited by Fernand Baldensperger (Paris: Conard, 1933);

Lettres d'un dernier amour: Correspondance inédite avec 'Augusta' [Froustey Bouvard], edited by V.-L. Saulnier (Geneva: Droz, 1952);

Les plus belles lettres d'Alfred de Vigny, edited by Francis Ambrière (Paris: Calmann-Lévy, 1963);

Correspondance d'Alfred de Vigny (1816-juillet 1830), volume 1, edited by Madeleine Ambrière (Paris: Presses universitaires de France, 1989); *Correspondance d'Alfred de Vigny (août 1830–septembre 1835),* volume 2, edited by Ambrière (Paris: Presses universitaires de France, 1991); *Corre-

spondance d'Alfred de Vigny (septembre 1835–avril 1839), volume 3, edited by Ambrière (Presses universitaires de France, 1994).

Bibliography:

François Germain, *L'Imagination d'Alfred de Vigny* (Paris: Corti, 1961), pp. 548–582.

Biographies:

Ernest Séché, *Alfred de Vigny,* 2 volumes (Paris: Mercure de France, 1913);

Ernest Dupuy, *Alfred de Vigny: La vie et l'oeuvre,* 2 volumes (Paris: Hachette, 1915);

Pierre Flottes, *Alfred de Vigny* (Paris: Perrin, 1925);

Robert de Traz, *Alfred de Vigny* (Paris: Hachette, 1928);

Arnold Whitridge, *Alfred de Vigny* (London & New York: Oxford University Press, 1933);

Ernest Lauvrière, *Alfred de Vigny,* 2 volumes (Paris: Grasset, 1945);

Maurice Toesca, *Vigny, ou La Passion de l'honneur* (Paris: Hachette, 1972);

Nicole Casanova, *Alfred de Vigny, sous le masque de fer* (Paris: Calmann-Lévy, 1990);

Gonzaque Saint-Bris, *Alfred de Vigny ou la volupté et l'honneur* (Paris: Grasset, 1997).

References:

Madeleine Ambrière and Nathalie Basset, eds., *Alfred de Vigny et les siens: documents inédits* (Paris: Presses universitaires de France, 1989);

Fernande Bassan, "Les Débuts dramatiques d'Alfred de Vigny: *Roméo et Juliette* et *Le More de Venise,*" *Bulletin de L'Association des Amis d'Alfred de Vigny,* 9 (1979–1980): 56–62;

Bassan, "Un Drame historique d'Alfred de Vigny: *La Maréchale d'Ancre,*" *Studia Neophilologica,* 51 (1979): 115–124;

Bassan, "Les Représentations de *Chatterton* en dehors de La Comédie-Française," *Bulletin de L'Association des Amis d'Alfred de Vigny,* 11 (1981–1982): 70–80;

Bassan, "Vigny, auteur comique: *Quitte pour la peur,*" *Revue d'Historire du Théâtre* (1980): 53–80;

Paul Bénichou, *Les Mages romantiques* (Paris: Gallimard, 1988);

George Bonnefoy, *Le Pensée religieuse et morale d'Alfred de Vigny* (Paris: Hachette, 1944);

Frederick Brown, *Theater and Revolution: The Culture of the French Stage* (New York: Viking, 1980);

Robin Buss, *Chatterton* (London: Grant & Cutler, 1984);

Barbara T. Cooper, "Exploitation of the Body in Vigny's *Chatterton:* The Economy of Drama and the Drama of Economics," *Theatre Journal,* 32 (1982): 20–26;

Barry Daniels, "*Chatterton* et *La Maréchale d'Ancre* à La Comédie-Française: documents inédits," *Bulletin de L'Association des Amis d'Alfred de Vigny,* 20 (1991): 60–67;

Daniels, *Revolution in the Theatre: French Romantic Theories of Drama* (Westport, Conn.: Greenwood Press, 1983);

Daniels, "Sur les décors du *More de Venise,*" *Bulletin de L'Association des Amis d'Alfred de Vigny,* 7 (1976–1977): 21–30;

Robert T. Denommé, "*Chatterton,* ou le dilemme du héros dans un monde non-héroïque," *Cahiers de L'Association Internationale des Etudes Françaises,* 35 (1983): 141–154;

Denommé, "French Theatre Reform and Vigny's Translation of *Othello* in 1829," in *Symbolism and Literature,* edited by Marcel Tetel (Durham, N.C.: Duke University Press, 1978), pp. 81–102;

Anne S. de Fabry, *Vigny et le rayon intérieur ou la permanence de Stello* (Paris: La Pensée universelle, 1978);

François Germain, *L'Imagination d'Alfred de Vigny* (Paris: Corti, 1961);

André Jarry, "*Roméo et Juliette:* de Shakespeare à Vigny et Deschamps, en passant par les traductions Letourneur," *Bulletin de l'Association des Amis d'Alfred de Vigny,* 6 (1974–1975): 40–54;

Jean Jourdheuil, "Les Enjeux de *Chatterton,*" *Europe, revue littéraire mensuelle,* 589 (May 1978): 100–107;

Liano Petroni, "Notes sur *Chatterton,*" *Bulletin de l'Association des Amis d'Alfred de Vigny,* 6 (1974–1975): 55–59;

Jean-Pierre Richard, *Etudes sur le romantisme* (Paris: Editions du Seuil, 1970);

Jacques-Philippe Saint-Gérand, *L'Intelligence et l'émotion: Fragments d'une esthétique vignyenne* (Paris: Société pour L'Information Grammaticale, 1988);

Emma Sakellarides, *Alfred de Vigny, auteur dramatique* (Paris: Editions de la Plume, 1902).

Papers:

Vigny's papers and manuscripts are on deposit in the Fonds Ratisbonne at the Bibliothèque Nationale in Paris. Notebook D-631 can be found at the Bibliothèque Spoelberch de Lovenjoul at Chantilly, France.

Jean-Marie Mathias Philippe-Auguste, Comte de Villiers de l'Isle-Adam

(7 November 1838 – 18 August 1889)

John Blaise Anzalone
Skidmore College

See also the entry on Villiers de l'Isle-Adam in *DLB 123, Nineteenth-Century French Fiction Writers: Naturalism and Beyond, 1860–1900.*

PLAY PRODUCTIONS: *La Révolte,* Paris, Théâtre du Vaudeville, 6 May 1870;
Le Nouveau Monde, Paris, Théâtre des Nations, 19 February 1883;
L'Evasion, Paris, Théâtre-Libre, 13 October 1887;
Axël, Paris, Théâtre de la Gaîté, 26 February 1894;
Elën, Paris, Théâtre-Libre, 1895;
Le Prétendant, performed as a televised play, 31 December 1965.

BOOKS: *Deux essais de poésie* (Paris: L. Tinterlin, 1858);
Premières poésies (Lyons: N. Scheuring, 1859);
Isis (Paris: E. Dentu, 1862);
Elën (Paris: Poupart-Davyl, 1865);
Morgane (St. Brieuc: Guyon Francisque, 1866);
La Révolte (Paris: Lemerre, 1870); translated by Theresa Barkley as *The Revolt* (London: Duckworth, 1901);
Le Nouveau Monde (Paris: Richard, 1880);
Maison Gambade, père et fils, Srs (Paris: La Comédie humaine, 1882);
Contes cruels (Paris: Calmann-Lévy, 1883); translated by Robert Baldick as *Cruel Tales* (London: Oxford University Press, 1966);
L'Eve future (Paris: Brunhoff, 1886); translated by Robert Martin Adams as *Tomorrow's Eve* (Chicago: University of Illinois Press, 1982); translated by Marilyn Gaddis Rose as *Eve of the Future Eden* (Kansas: Coronado Press, 1982);
Akëdysséril (Paris: Brunhoff, 1886);
L'Amour suprême (Paris: Brunhoff, 1886);
Tribulat Bonhomet (Paris: Tresse et Stock, 1887);
Histoires insolites (Paris: Quantin, 1888);
Nouveaux contes cruels (Paris: Librairie illustrée, 1888);
Chez les passants (Paris: Comptoir d'édition, 1890);

Jean-Marie Mathias Philippe-Auguste, Comte de Villiers de l'Isle-Adam (photograph by Nadar)

Axël (Paris: Quantin, 1890); translated by H. P. R. Finberg (London: Jarrolds, 1925); translated by June Guicharnaud (Englewood Cliffs, N.J.: Prentice-Hall, 1970); translated by Rose (Dublin: Dolmen Press, 1970);
L'Evasion (Paris: Tresse et Stock, 1891); translated by Barkley as *The Escape* (London: Duckworth, 1901);
Nouveaux contes cruels et Propos d'au delà (Paris: Calmann-Lévy, 1893);
Trois portraits de femmes (Paris: Bernard, 1929);
Reliques (Paris: Corti, 1954);

Le Prétendant (Paris: Corti, 1965);

Nouvelles Reliques (Paris: Corti, 1968);

Sonnet (Paris: Fata Morgana, 1990).

Collections: *Oeuvres complètes,* 11 volumes (Paris: Mercure de France, 1914–1931);

Oeuvres complètes, 2 volumes, edited by Alan Raitt and Pierre-Georges Castex, with the collaboration of Jean-Marie Bellefroid (Paris: Gallimard, Bibliothèque de la Pléiade, 1986).

By conventional standards Jean-Marie Mathias Philippe-Auguste, Comte de Villiers de l'Isle-Adam was an utter failure as a dramatist in his lifetime. His first plays were issued in editions so small in number that almost no one knew they existed. Of the three plays staged before his death, two were complete flops; the third, a minor work, is memorable only for having been performed at André Antoine's innovative Théâtre-Libre. *Morgane* (1866), one of Villiers's first plays, has never been performed at all; he produced a splendid revision of it called *Le Prétendant* (The Pretender), which was not staged until 1965, and then only on French television. The story of Villiers's tragicomic relationship to the world of the theater is a tale of gigantic ambition and repeated, bitter frustration. But despite all the disappointments he suffered, Villiers did have one great moment in the theater; it came only after his death, with the 1894 *récitation,* or recital, at the Théâtre de la Gaîte, of *Axël* (1890), his lasting legacy to the theater.

On the strength of only two sold-out performances in this modified form, *Axël* became a seminal work and Villiers a central figure in the evolution of French theater at the end of the nineteenth century. The changing intellectual climate of the 1890s, and a more widespread rejection of the positivism Villiers had fought throughout his career, contributed to the consecration of *Axël* as the bible of dramaturgy as well as of ideology for the Symbolist generation. The play presaged the outright rejection of Naturalist scenic conventions that would soon distinguish early avant-garde theater even as it posited a world of symbols where, as the author noted in the *Contes cruels:* (1883; translated as *Cruel Tales,* 1966) "les idées sont des êtres vivants" (ideas are living beings). Villiers would soon be acknowledged as a precursor of genius by writers as diverse as Maurice Maeterlinck and Paul Claudel and was an important influence on William Butler Yeats, whose attendance at the 1894 recital was to remain a vivid memory until the end of his life. By his attitude toward theater as well as by his work, Villiers succeeded in strongly marking the renewal in drama he had always sought to lead. Yet despite an impact that marked the course of twentieth-century French drama, *Axël* soon disappeared from the theater until a daring, full theatrical staging in 1962 that is to date the only one ever attempted. As influential as the play has been, it receives relatively little attention compared to Villiers's other writings. In effect it continues to survive more as an historical reference than as a dramatic creation of considerable complexity and vitality.

There are several reasons for the paradoxical situation of Villiers's theater today, when this engaging author seems more appreciated than perhaps at any time since his death. The life of a play is on the stage, and Villiers's plays have been only rarely performed. For too long a time their texts were also entirely inaccessible to readers as well. All were republished in the Mercure de France edition of Villiers's complete works during the 1920s, but this set soon went out of print, and except for *Axël,* no play by Villiers appeared, from World War I until the mid 1960s, in a separate edition.

Villiers's reputation as a storyteller has also contributed to his obscurity as a dramatist. What literary success he attained in his day depended to a great extent on his brilliant narrative gifts. Initially he exercised them in the frequent, and by all accounts captivating, performances that he gave in the brasseries he haunted throughout his life. This ability to act out his writing using Parisian cafés as the stage for extemporaneous renditions played an important part in his early reputation as a genius. Subsequent publication of the tales in various journals and reviews over the years exposed his talents for irony and the fantastic to the public at large. And over the years Villiers wrote more and more short fiction as he became aware that his theatrical ambitions had ever smaller chances for success. During these years he began to assume an almost mythical status in literary circles. When in the 1880s he finally began to achieve a modicum of success, it came because of the combination of his matchless personal prestige and the publication in 1883 of the *Contes cruels.* But few in his day thought of him as a dramatist.

For posterity as well Villiers has survived especially as an author of short, striking narrative works that paint nineteenth-century materialist society with a corrosive brush. But neither his standing as a writer of fiction nor his repeated failures to have his plays performed to public acclaim ever prompted Villiers to renounce his youthful ambition to become a great dramatist. Any serious consideration of him as a writer must take into account that desire and the effect upon it of the repeated rebuffs and rejections to which the plays themselves were subjected. It is true that in recent years the accepted image of Villiers has begun to change. Renewed scholarly assessment of his brilliant novel *L'Eve future* (1886; translated as *Tomorrow's Eve,* 1982) has been under way since the 1980s and constitutes an important step away from the nearly exclusive attention paid the tales. But the theater has not benefited similarly from this promise of critical and scholarly revision. In a curious twist a contributing cause may be the exalted status *Axël* has enjoyed since even before it was published. Almost immediately it was (rightly) interpreted as Villiers's "literary testament," but over the years its special claim as a splendid and emblematic work may also have contributed to the progressive disappearance of the rest of Villiers's theater, which remains unplayed, unread, and unknown. In recent years even the brilliance of *Axël* has receded into the shadow of the more accessible and disturbing narrative works. The impetus among scholars to return to the dramatic corpus seems accordingly less compelling, even though Villiers's theater still has much to offer. Indeed, the very tenacity with which Villiers constantly returned to writing for the theater long after it had become clear to him that his plays would not be performed underscores the importance the genre had for him.

Villiers was born in Saint Brieuc, Brittany, on 7 November 1838, the heir to a name of ancient nobility, but the scion of a family already burdened by material hardship and mental eccentricity. Though he probably descended from a minor branch of the Villiers family, he held the unshakable conviction that he was the latest member of the legendary Villiers de l'Isle-Adam line, among whom could be counted the founder of the Order of the Knights of Malta and a marshal of France. His fierce attachment to the splendor of the Villiers name and his rejection of its social destitution after the Revolution of 1789 formed the cornerstone for a poetics of nobility and race: in the fallen world into which he came, only one activity held the promise of redemption—literature.

It seems that from an early age Villiers destined himself for literary greatness. An only child, he was supported in this ambition by his indulgent family: his father, the Marquis Joseph-Toussaint, penniless and obsessed by fabulous wealth; Marie-Françoise Le Nepvou de Carfort, his retiring mother; and his maternal aunt and godmother, Marie-Félix Daniel de Kérinou, whose small fortune provided for a time the only material stability the family ever experienced. As the artistically inclined Villiers reached the end of a sheltered, provincial childhood, the promise of a career in literature grew

more immediate: beginning in the late 1850s and over several years the small family relocated to the capital to facilitate the marquis's frequent harebrained moneymaking schemes. But the move had the additional effect of introducing the gifted son—the family's great hope for future distinction—to the Paris literary milieu, to the cafés and theaters he restlessly haunted for much of his life. As the decade drew to a close, Villiers's earliest writing began to appear in print.

From his earliest literary stirring Villiers was powerfully attracted to the theater. By temperament and by intellect he was drawn to vast syntheses, to expansive ruminations suited to the lengthy, discursive genres. By the age of seventeen he had plotted plays of epic proportion based on the Faust and Don Juan legends. Soon after arriving in Paris he had begun to frequent the theaters and submit his plays to their reading committees. A letter from 1855 shows him already dreaming of the time, perhaps ten years away, when he would reign over the world of drama. He confides in the letter to his friend Lemercier de Neuville, who was later to have a reputation in puppet theater, his ambition to erect "un édifice dramatique qui bouleverse le théâtre" (a dramatic edifice that will revolutionize the theater) and to climb upon the throne vacated by Victor Hugo. The reference to Hugo is telling, for it points in the direction of the Romantic models that Villiers never entirely abandoned; it suggests that he could not look forward without looking back. "Il y a les Romantiques et les imbéciles" (There are Romantics and there are imbeciles), he was fond of saying, and early in his career he borrowed extensively, though not always effectively, from the conventions of Romantic melodrama. He had also practiced music and verse before coming to Paris, and it was with poetry that his literary career began.

The *Premières poésies* (First Poems, 1859), despite Villiers's subsequent disclaimers, were clearly intended to make his mark in the literary world by demonstrating his affiliations with Alphonse de Lamartine, Hugo, Alfred de Musset, and Alfred de Vigny. Considering Villiers's preoccupation with his lineage, it is no exaggeration to claim that this first significant publication represents an attempt to claim a place in the genealogy of Romanticism. The attempt fell short. *Premières poésies* is a collection of undistinguished juvenile verse that displays little beyond its author's espousal of the themes and attitudes of a literature that by 1859 was entirely outdated. But Villiers was especially attracted to the strains of Romanticism that implied revolt and rejection so that, even after he abandoned poetry as unsuited to his particular genius, he clung stubbornly in his early dramatic creations to a Romantic rhetoric that signaled his rejection of the modern society that had already dispossessed and disowned the Villiers de l'Isle-Adams.

In effect a paradigm begins to take shape at this time that drove Villiers's lifelong indictment of what Léon Daudet called "le stupide dix-neuvième siècle" (the stupid nineteenth century). It consists of a distinctly personal fusion of Romantic ideology, Idealist philosophy, and occult doctrine, all of which came together during the 1860s to reinforce Villiers's superstitious Catholicism. From his first novel, *Isis* (1862), to his first plays, *Elën* (1865) and *Morgane* (1866), Villiers's literary output during this decade bore the stamp of this heterogeneous fusion. It colored his first short stories. It accounted in part for the impression of genius he created in person, as well as the incomprehension his writing regularly generated among noninitiates.

Isis, Villiers's next published work, is the first of only two novels he wrote. It appeared in 1862, in an edition of only two hundred copies, the first and only installment of a projected seven-volume literary work of speculative metaphysics. *Isis* was to prove to materialists that the realities of the spirit were all the more exigent for being trampled by a heedless society. This strange work, combining sonorous cadence and abstruse speculation, is especially noteworthy for its lyric creation of a female magus named Tullia Fabriana, the ancestor of Stéphane Mallarmé's *Hérodiade* (1876–1887), and the first in a series of strong, even dominant female characters that inhabit Villiers's universe and provide one of its most salient and singular features.

Tullia Fabriana, a Florentine princess of great beauty and powerful intellect, lives in ascetic isolation in her castle, where she languishes in the knowledge that the world of 1788 holds little interest for her. Her study of occult doctrine has revealed to her, however, that transcendent power can be attained through the mystical union of souls. To this end she undertakes to seduce young Count Wilhelm de Strally d'Anthas, with whom she will plot to take over the kingdom of Naples. The seduction, essentially a prelude to the plot of the planned but never executed subsequent installments, barely begins as the first volume draws to a close. But by introducing to the plot the idea, common in occultist doctrine, of a hierogamy, or sacred marriage, Villiers adds a human dimension to Tullia's otherwise abstract situation, one that anticipates the major thematic axes of the two plays he was perhaps already writing at the time *Isis* was published.

Indeed, this quest for transcendence by an elite couple, before whom "les forces réunies de l'or et de l'amour tomberaient positivement" (the combined forces of gold and love would positively fail), links the novel to Villiers's first plays and sets in motion a theme of purity and transcendence, of temptation and fall, that echoes in Villiers's subsequent dramatic production until it culminates in the double suicide of *Axël*. In these early works the initiator of the relationship is always the woman. In contrast with her the male character seems weak, immature, or indecisive. In *Isis* Wilhelm de Strally is clearly to be molded to suit Tullia's project. In *Elën* the young student leader Samuel Wissler falls prey to the charms of the countess Elën, a femme fatale whose identity as a rich courtesan hides a profound thirst for the absolute that Samuel is unable to satisfy. In *Morgane* the adventurer Morgane de Poleastro initiates a conspiratorial political alliance with the rebel Sergius d'Albamah. Their plot to conquer the throne of the Two Sicilys is thwarted, and they realize too late that it has also cost them an ideal love. In the quest for creating a perfect couple that is the common theme of all three works, the bitter lesson seems to be that spiritual aspirations and material fulfillment can never coexist.

Villiers had high hopes for these first plays. He sought to resurrect the glory of Hugo's early triumphs with a resounding success in the theater that would also bring him fortune by trumpeting his name across literary Paris. But in fact, like the *Premières poésies* and *Isis,* the works were unknown to the public of the 1860s. They too had been published in extremely small editions, intended as actors' scripts or as introductions to theatrical agents, and were never republished during Villiers's lifetime. Closely related, though in different ways, to *Isis, Elën* and *Morgane* emphasize different features of the novel and point to conflicting tendencies in Villiers's writing for the stage. Briefly stated, the conflict involves the tension between Villiers's metaphysical temptations and the practical demands of the theater. The occultism to which Villiers was drawn early in his career can be seen in the figure of the magus in *Isis* and *Elën.* The fall of the magus is only glimpsed in the novel, but it actually occurs in *Elën* as Samuel Wissler's ascetic ascension is compromised when he yields to the temptation of sensuality. And the drive for the conquest of a spiritual realm that underlies Tullia Fabriana's quest has its material counterpart in the lust for power that motivates both the Florentine princess and the beautiful Countess Morgane de Poleastro and dooms them both.

The description of these works points to the melodramatic trappings that made them less-than-compelling prospects for theater directors in the mid 1860s. But if both *Morgane* and *Elën* demonstrate the

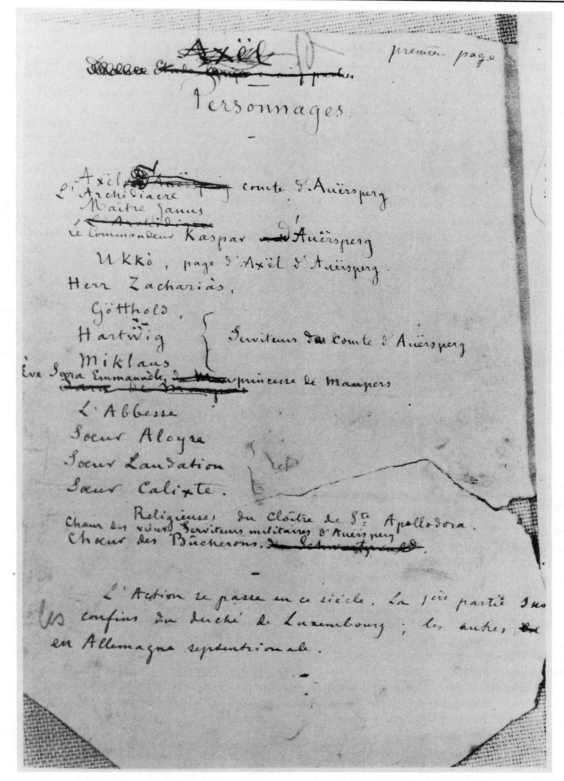

First page from the manuscript for Axël *(from Jacques-Henry Bornecque,* Villiers de l'Isle-Adam, créateur et visionnaire, *1974)*

difficulties Villiers experienced by clinging to an outdated aesthetic, they also show the direction in which he was headed. Pronounced tendencies toward a poetic theater that would come to fruition in *Axël* are already apparent in the well-known "opium dream" at the end of *Elën* (in act 3, scene 2), when the drug the countess slips Samuel to rid herself of this now tiresome suitor inspires Samuel with a series of premonitory hallucinations. Long cited as the most remarkable passage of the play, this extended prose poem provides an intimation of the theater of shadows and dreams that was to evolve among the Symbolists, thanks to Villiers's influence. The opium dream did much to solidify his standing among his contemporaries, who by then included the awestruck young Mallarmé. They saw him as a "poète absolu," in Paul Verlaine's apt expression, a creator already dreaming of a theater that had not yet been invented.

Despite his best efforts, however, these first plays in the end became part of a repertory that Villiers eventually called, with characteristic irony, his "théâtre lisible" (readable plays). By the mid 1860s he was thus in the paradoxical position of having written two plays, a novel, and a collection of poetry that warranted him a reputation for genius in poetic circles even as he was virtually unknown to the general reading public. The admiration of his friends in the literary world helped soften this nearly total lack of general recognition. Most crucial to the course of Villiers's career as a writer during these years was his friendship with Charles Baudelaire, whom he probably met at the Brasserie des Martyrs in 1860 and with whom he seems to have been in occasional contact until the poet's desperate final years. As Alan W. Raitt has claimed, "there can be no doubt that Baudelaire altered the whole course of Villiers's life" in many subtle ways. *Les Fleurs du mal* (Flowers of Evil, 1857), of course, as well as the elder poet's unconditional enthusiasm for Edgar Allan Poe and Richard Wagner, did much to redirect Villiers's aesthetic preferences away from an exclusive allegiance to the Romantics and closer to the modern spirit of bizarre beauty that Baudelaire had heralded. It was from his contact with the works of Poe in Baudelaire's translations that Villiers was drawn to the art of the short story. And Baudelaire's enthusiasm for Wagner found a ready reply in the musically gifted Villiers. These exciting new models clearly prompted Villiers to redirect his energies away from his early preoccupation with the theater, where his ambitions had been so painfully unfulfilled.

But there were other pressing reasons for Villiers to extend his writer's range in an attempt to live by his pen. Material woes were beginning to dog the family: in March 1864 the Marquis de Villiers de l'Isle-Adam declared bankruptcy in Paris. Later that year Villiers set out to Lyons in search of a rich heiress to marry, in the first of several such attempts to secure a fortune. All would fail, and increasingly they took on cruel and tragicomic overtones that are reflected in his later works. But to achieve a more stable financial situation had become a very pressing matter. Thus it was that in 1867 Villiers cofounded the *Revue des lettres et des arts* as a way of securing a regular outlet for his writing. Though only twenty-five weekly issues appeared, the *Revue* was notable for its publication of the new Parnassian writing. Villiers republished *Elën* in its pages in February 1868. More important, however, it was there that Villiers published his first two tales, "Claire Lenoir" and "L'Intersigne" (The Sign). The first introduced one of his most memorable satirical creations, Dr. Tribulat Bonhomet, the incarnation of the self-sufficient debility and spiritual opacity of the century for Villiers. *L'Intersigne,* on the other hand, is a tightly crafted tale of the supernatural in which the pacing, the seeming monomania of the narrator, and the hallucinations of which he is victim all point to Poe's influence. But the story is also faithful to the preoccupations with metaphysics and spiritual realities apparent in Villiers's early theater.

In 1869 Villiers traveled to Germany with his friends Catulle Mendès and Judith Gautier, ostensibly as newspaper correspondents to the Munich *Exposition universelle* but in fact so that they could visit Richard Wagner. This was a great moment for Villiers, who was himself an unusually talented amateur musician, singer, and composer. He revered Wagner as the initiator of a great synthesis in the art of dramatic musical composition. The lessons of Wagnerism deeply marked Villiers's attempt in *Axël* to write a drama he hoped would transform the French stage. But while in Triebschen he read Wagner his latest play, *La Révolte* (1870; translated as *The Revolt,* 1901), a work markedly different from his earliest plays.

The difficulty of having his Romantic dramas staged led him to attempt a play with contemporary resonances and setting. *La Révolte* is situated in the bourgeois drawing rooms of the banker Felix and Elisabeth, his young associate and wife, who are the play's only characters. One night Felix returns home to discover Elisabeth ready to leave him. Calmly she tells him that she can no longer share his exclusively materialist life, that she aspires to a deeper fulfillment. He listens in utter incomprehension and faints when she actually walks out the door. But soon Elisabeth returns, a broken woman. Three years of life with Felix have made her incapable of acting on her dream of a different life. Worse, her ability to dream has been destroyed.

Beneath its contemporary decor *La Révolte* conceals a poetic drama. It is at once a tragic and grotesque allegory of modern spiritual distress, as Villiers indicated in describing Elisabeth as a "Prométhée femelle dont le foie est dévoré par une oie" (a female Prometheus whose liver is devoured by a goose). With this strangely compelling play Villiers understood that he had written something new; for the first time the practical expectations he had for a play seemed justified to him. Though Wagner had reacted with incomprehension to *La Révolte,* Villiers took great encouragement from the very occasion of a reading in the presence of the composer. Early in 1870 a provocative journal article by Alexandre Dumas *fils* prompted the Théâtre du Vaudeville to schedule *La Révolte.* It lasted for all of five performances. The middle-class theatergoing public was not at all sympathetic to Villiers's portrayal of Felix's brutal response to the lofty concerns of the play's heroine. Years before Henrik Ibsen would triumph on the Paris stage with *En dukkehjem* (A Doll's House, 1879), Villiers's thesis that a woman might deem middle-class material comfort an obstacle to inner truth provoked little but scorn. This was especially so for the critics of the theater establishment. They sensed, as P.-G. Castex and Raitt so astutely suggest, that Villiers had created something "dangerously subversive" without their being able to understand exactly what; they reacted by savaging the play in the press, thereby hastening its departure from the Vaudeville's stage.

Villiers was deeply stung by the failure of *La Révolte.* By 1870 he no longer held out any hope that *Elën* or *Morgane* could convey his dramatic ambition to the world. A great deal had thus been at stake in the performance of *La Révolte,* and the incomprehension of the establishment critics aroused his anger and his pride. Their hostility reinforced Villiers's conviction that theater, in the hands of a great artist, was the means of bringing certain truths before men and that he was that artist. The experience of failure, as it crystallized around *La Revolte,* was to establish once and for all in Villiers an antagonistic reflex to the theatrical world of his day and to confirm his belief that the French stage needed reforming. Both antagonism and ambition are recorded in the preface he wrote to answer the play's detractors. He proclaims his lineage by likening the failure of *La Révolte* to that of Hugo's *Les Burgraves* (1843), a play too grandiose to be accomodated by a theater in which "Etre ou ne pas être est une longueur" (To be or not to be is considered longwinded):

Villiers late in life (portrait by Guth; from Pierre-Georges Castex, ed., Contes cruels, Nouveaux Contes cruels, *1968)*

Le Théâtre de France, qui nous avait été laissé en bon état par Poquelin de Molière et Pierre Corneille, est devenu l'opprobre de l'art moderne.

Toute pensée impartiale, jetée pantelante, devant la Foule est une source de colères si elle ne sort pas du moule breveté. Le dédain des moyens connus, des gesticulations et de parades, est consideré par les critiques en vogue comme la plus haute preuve de l'inhabilité scenique. *La Révolte* est la première tentative, le premier essai, risqués sur la scène française pour briser ces soi-disant règles déshonorantes!

(French Theater, which was handed down to us in good shape by Poquelin de Molière and Pierre Corneille, has become the opprobrium of modern art.

Any impartial thought thrown, gasping, before the Mob, is a pretext for fury if it breaks the accepted mold. The least disdain for conventionality, for gesticulation or ostentation, is considered by the critics in power as the utmost proof of dramatic ineptitude. *The Revolt* is the first attempt, the first essay on the French stage to risk breaking these so-called rules which so dishonor it!)

The repercussions of this event made themselves felt in their eventual effect on the composition of *Axël*. Villiers's deeply nonconformist nature was reinforced. He worked from then on with the conviction that an entire reinvention of the dramatic genre was needed. Already at work on *Axël,* he began to shape this immense drama to constitute the magnum opus of a new theater. Once "Le Monde Religieux" (The Religious World), the play's first part, had been published in 1872, he set about broadening the play's scope, accumulating its many philosophical dimensions and debates, and indulging his bent for didacticism and predication. In short he made it ever more unplayable, a tendency further exaggerated after the cruel debacle of the staging of *Le Nouveau Monde* (The New World, 1883) eleven years later.

The 1870s would be, in Raitt's succinct description, Villiers's "years of darkness." The social upheaval of the Franco-Prussian War and the Paris Commune, followed by the death in August 1871 of Tante Kérinou, left the family nearly destitute. Villiers by no means abandoned writing for the theater. Indeed, at around the same time that *La Révolte* demonstrated the considerable gulf separating his lofty goals from the standard practices of the day, he wrote a one-act play titled *L'Evasion* (translated as *The Escape,* 1901) that seems much in the spirit of the times. Composed rapidly—supposedly in one night, on a bet—it is the story of a criminal's awakening to morality and is modeled on the conversion of Jean Valjean in Hugo's *Les Misérables* (1862). Its two performances at André Antoine's Théâtre Libre in 1887 remain its principal claim to distinction. But in 1870 the luxury of waiting for another chance at imposing his own vision of a new theater on his contemporaries was out of the question. Even as he published the first installments of *Axël* (1872), rewrote *Morgane* as *Le Prétendant,* and completed *Le Nouveau Monde* he had to resort increasingly to writing tales for any journal that would pay, however poorly, for his copy.

Throughout the 1870s Villiers wrote extensively. Parts of major works appeared sporadically in the papers, yet nothing was published in book form from *La Révolte* in 1870 to *Le Nouveau Monde* in 1880. Villiers seemed at times to have disappeared almost entirely from view. Only an improved commercial climate finally led the publishing firm of Calmann-Lévy to accept an anthology of short stories for publication in February 1883 under the title *Contes cruels.* The acceptance had come none too soon. Villiers had had a son, Victor, in 1881 by Marie Dantine, the illiterate charwoman he lived with until his death. He also had to support his increasingly demented father. A book contract was nothing short of a godsend. This landmark collection of twenty-eight short pieces had cost Villiers years of tremendous effort; he sold it outright to the publisher for a mere Fr 375. But at last a book of his tales was available to a readership increasingly interested in what he had to say. Villiers is in full possession of his multifaceted genius in these tales, many of which had been revised extensively over the years. By turns the satirist, the social critic, the poet, the visionary, and the spellbinder each take the narrative stage with equal conviction. Several of the tales (for example, "La Machine à gloire" [The Glory Machine] or "Sombre récit, conteur plus sombre" [Dark Tale, Darker Teller]) convey in a fantastic or sardonic mode Villiers's harsh assessment of the theater of the times.

Also in February 1883 the staging of *Le Nouveau Monde* ended in the greatest fiasco of Villiers's career in the theater. He had written the play between April and October 1875 as an entry in a contest celebrating the American Centennial. When the appointed panel of judges declared themselves unable to choose among the three final entries, Victor Hugo was called upon to cast the deciding vote. He pronounced them all of equal merit, with an evenhandedness that has been interpreted to mean that he never read any of them, and the prize money was shared. *Le Nouveau Monde* was created around the time Villiers was finishing *Le Prétendant,* and these plays resemble one another more than they do *Elën* or *Axël.* Both stage a passionate love affair complicated by jealousy and framed by an historical struggle between an established power and a political rebellion. Like *Le Prétendant, Le Nouveau Monde* is a costume drama filled with local color and an extravagant decor that was to cause enormous production difficulties. But it was a solidly crafted work that had considerable appeal, thanks to attractive characters, a complex but intelligible plot, and a topicality that promised interest and recognition among potential viewers. If ever one of Villiers's plays had realistic chances for material success, it was *Le Nouveau Monde.*

Over the next seven years Villiers attempted repeatedly to have the play performed; he came tantalizingly close more than once. But by the time the play opened at the Théâtre des Nations on 19 February 1883, some eight years had passed since the contest, and the pretext for its creation, the celebration of American independence, had lost much of its topical appeal. From the start the production was plagued with serious difficulties; indeed, Villiers himself created some of the most drastic problems by his stubborn insistence on trying to control every aspect of the

Playbill for the premiere of Villiers's most influential play, which was staged in Paris nearly five years after his death

staging. It is easy enough to understand his action. After so many false starts, here at last were backers, a serious theater, and apparently reputable actors. In the end, however, the huge expenditures associated with the decor and the many intractable conflicts among the actors, between them and Villiers, and between the producers and almost everyone else combined to bring the play down after seventeen performances. As he watched the warring actors sabotage the play night after night, a furious and devastated Villiers ended up leading the booing himself.

But this final setback in the theater occurred just as his *Contes cruels* launched Villiers's reputation as a prose writer unlike that of anyone else then at work in France. This work made it easier for him to place his copy, and in the six years from the appearance of *Contes cruels* to his death, Villiers took maximum advantage of his newfound celebrity. To judge by the praise Joris-Karl Huysmans lavished on the *Contes cruels* in *A Rebours* (1884; translated as *Against the Grain,* 1922) in giving the volume a prominent place in the library of his character des Esseintes, its violent mood swings sent an electrical jolt through a new readership.

A specific polarity carries the charge of these stories and most of Villiers's writing in his final years. It consists of a current alternating between idealistic longing and grinding satire that Villiers succinctly de-

fined in dedicating his novel *L'Eve future* (1886; translated as *Tomorrow's Eve,* 1982) "aux rêveurs, aux railleurs" (to dreamers, to deriders). Inspired by his failed arranged marriage to an English heiress in 1874, the work tells of what transpires when, to repay a moral debt, the scientist-inventor Thomas Edison undertakes to rescue his friend Lord Celian Ewald from that most drastic of fictional disasters, a love affair with the wrong woman. Edison proposes to create for Ewald the perfect replica of Alicia Clary, Ewald's beloved, in the form of an android named Hadaly. Unable to distinguish her from Alicia, Ewald falls in love with the robot and resolves to live in seclusion with her on his estate in Scotland. But the novel ends with a catastrophic shipwreck that destroys Hadaly forever. In *L'Eve future* the android replaces the female partner in the perfect couple that had obsessed Villiers since *Elën, Morgane,* and *La Révolte.* This strangely moving novel is one of Villiers's greatest and most personal works, all of which abound in similar leaps toward the unattainable, in the refusal of human imperfections, and, in the end, the refusal of life itself. Such is the lesson of Villiers's posthumous dramatic masterwork, *Axël.*

Over the years the long-awaited *Axël* had become invested by Villiers himself and by many of his new admirers with the magical power to make his reputation by restoring to the theater the poetry and imagination lost for many since the heyday of Romantic drama. From 1886 to 1888 Villiers brought out important new collections of tales, such as *L'Amour suprême* (The Supreme Love, 1886), *Tribulat Bonhomet* (1887), and *Nouveaux contes cruels et Propos d'au delà* (New Cruel Tales and Matters of the Beyond, 1893). But much of his energy was devoted to the vast play he had been meditating, writing, and revising for nearly twenty years. That energy was now waning fast. His harsh life had aged him prematurely, and from 1886 on, his health declined steadily. Though seriously ill, Villiers traveled in early 1888 to Belgium to lecture on *Axël* and his ambition for a new theater. The warmth of the reception of the literary community there confirmed for him a sense that the tide was turning in his favor; he was planning a return engagement when at the end of the year his illness worsened. Within a few months his destitution had reached alarming proportions, leading Mallarmé to arrange a subscription among Villiers's friends to support him—without his knowledge—in his distress. In the summer of 1889 his now terminal cancer forced him into a hospice. There he died, on 18 August, after an in extremis marriage to Marie Dantine that finally legitimized his beloved son, Victor, affectionately known as "Totor."

Axël was published by Quantin in 1890. Few works proclaim with such bitter conviction, born of harsh experience, the pessimism that emerges in the play's extraordinary conclusion. Sara de Maupers and Axël d'Auërsperg have both rejected initiation, she into Catholic vows, he into occult apprenticeship with his teacher, the magus Maître Janus, to pursue a treasure hidden by Axël's father during the Napoleonic Wars. They discover one another and fall in love in the burial crypt of Axël's castle, where Sara has come on Easter morning following a clue that enables her to discover the treasure. With limitless wealth literally at their feet, the young lovers realize that the world can only corrupt the perfect union they now share, and they commit suicide before life can imprison them in its illusions.

By their suicide Axël and Sara refuse to affirm the Creation so as to avoid the degradation of the Spirit, which is not of the world. Their renunciation of the treasure and of life represents a total break with a world that has been recognized as false and fallen. Although Villiers intended to revise *Axël* so as to give it a more religiously orthodox conclusion, the play's power derives specifically from the defiant gesture of renunciation of its protagonists. The end of *Axël* proposes, in effect, a rigorously anti-Christian message that underscores the many intellectual temptations Villiers's work as a whole portrays. As Henri Roujon, one of his earliest biographers, so aptly noted, Villiers

"avait gardé tant bien que mal la foi bretonne de son enfance, non sans laisser des lambeaux de dogme à tous les buissons de l'hérésie" (more or less kept the Breton faith of his childhood, but not without leaving shreds of dogma on all the bushes of heresy).

But Villiers's belief in the possibility of a transcendent spirituality also appears in its fullest form in *Axël,* through the symbolic character of Maître Janus. The magus has arranged for the meeting and the suicide of these last surviving members of two ancient noble families in order to create "un signe nouveau" (a new sign). In a profound sense that sign is dual. Suicide is typically associated with despair; here, as a consequence of philosophic idealism, it seems to point to the integral nihilism that literary history has identified as Villiers's legacy. At the same time the triumph of transcendence allows for a positive reading of the suicide. What Axël and Sara achieve by rejecting the treasure is a form of mastery. They conquer the "double illusion of gold and love" that the narrator of *Isis* identified as the obstacle to spiritual regeneration. By their mystical union of opposites Axël and Sara celebrate the sacred marriage that was the implicit ambition of Villiers's earliest plays.

The resplendent poetry and complex metaphysics of *Axël* resonated deeply in the young Symbolists of the 1890s. In its themes the play mirrored their own pessimism and their own turning away from the world in favor of the supremacy of imagination and dream. For later critics *Axël* provided the evidence that Villiers was the worthy successor to the greatness of Romantic drama, the intermediary figure between the grandiose plays of expiation and reconciliation of Hugo's latter years as a dramatist and a new attempt at a kind of total theater that became a major focus of twentieth-century avant-garde drama.

Few writers of the late nineteenth century in France bear so deeply the imprint of the exalted place of theater in the literary hierarchy of the period as Villiers de l'Isle-Adam. His dreams of success in the theater were imperial dreams; but as they collided with harsh realities, Villiers began to espouse a commitment to a freedom in the theater so total as to foreordain the repeated failures he experienced. In this, too, he resembled Hugo: his failures confirmed for him the validity of the enterprise of writing for the theater at all. Remarkably successful stagings, some utilizing new scenic technologies, like that of *Le Nouveau Monde* by Jean-Louis Barrault in 1977 or of *La Révolte* at the Petit Odéon in 1981, suggest that, as in so many arenas of his difficult existence, Villiers may simply have been ahead of his time. If he failed as a dramatist in that time, it was in part the price he paid for making the quest for a new theater in society his own.

Moreover, theatrical adaptations of the *Contes cruels* and of *L'Eve future* at the Festival d'Avignon during the 1980s point to the fundamental dramatic qualities of much of Villiers's work and remind one of his theatrical gifts as an actor-interpreter of his tales. To proceed to a useful reassessment of Villiers's dramatic writing and art, it may first be necessary to acknowledge—as some scholars have indeed already begun to do—that the distance separating his narrative works from his plays is far less great than traditional generic boundaries might suggest. Meanwhile, lovers of theater will not have to look far to discover in the varied works of Villiers de l'Isle-Adam an opulent imagination possessed of intrinsically dramatic qualities.

Letters:

Villiers de l'Isle-Adam, *Correspondance générale*, 2 volumes, edited by Joseph Bollery (Paris: Mercure de France, 1962).

Bibliographies:

Joseph Bollery, *Biblio-iconographie de Villiers de l'Isle-Adam* (Paris: Mercure de France, 1936);

Bertrand Vibert, "Villiers de l'Isle-Adam et 'I'mpossible théâtre' au XIXe siècle," *Romantisme,* no. 99 (1998): 71–87.

Biographies:

Robert du Pontavice de Heussey, *Villiers de l'Isle-Adam* (Paris: Savine, 1893);

Henri Roujon, *La Galérie des Bustes* (Paris: Rueff, 1909);

Edouard de Rougemont, *Villiers de l'Isle-Adam* (Paris: Mercure de France, 1910);

Alan W. Raitt, *The Life of Villiers de l'Isle-Adam* (Oxford: Clarendon Press, 1981).

References:

John Anzalone, "The First English Translation of *Axël*," *Bulletin du bibliophile,* 2 (1980): 149–161;

Anzalone, "Victor's Throne: The Shade of Hugo in the Theater of Villiers de l'Isle-Adam," *Les Cahiers du CERLI,* new series 2 (February 1993): 123–131;

Jacques-Henry Bornecque, *Villiers de l'Isle-Adam, créateur et visionnaire* (Paris: Nizet, 1974);

Peter Bürgisser, *La Double Illusion de l'or et de l'amour chez Villiers de l'Isle-Adam* (Bern: Peter Lang, 1969);

Pierre-Georges Castex, "Villiers de l'Isle-Adam et sa cruauté," in *Le Conte fantastique en France de Nodier à Maupassant* (Paris: Corti, 1962);

Castex, *Villiers de l'Isle-Adam, 1838–1889,* Catalogue de l'Exposition, Bibliothèque historique de la ville de Paris, 1989;

Castex and Alan W. Raitt, eds., *Villiers de l'Isle-Adam, Le Prétendant* (Paris: Corti, 1965);

Fernando Cipriani, "La Révolte, dramma di Villiers de l'Isle-Adam, note con frammenti inediti," *Annali della facoltà di di Lettere e Filosofia dell'Università degli Studi di Milano* (September–December 1975);

William T. Conroy, *Villiers de l'Isle-Adam* (Boston: G. K. Hall, 1978);

Michel Crouzet and Raitt, eds., *Actes du Colloque Villiers de l'Isle-Adam* (Paris: SEDES, 1990);

Max Daireaux, *Villiers de l'Isle-Adam, l'homme et l'oeuvre* (Paris: Desclée de Brouwer, 1936);

Emile Drougard, "Le Vrai sens d'*Axël*," *La Grande Revue* (April 1931): 262–284;

Jean-Paul Gourévitch, *Villiers de l'Isle-Adam* (Paris: Seghers, 1971);

Dorothy Knowles, *La Réaction idéaliste au théâtre depuis 1890* (Geneva: Droz, 1934);

André Lebois, *Villiers de l'Isle-Adam, révélateur du verbe* (Neuchâtel: Messeiller, 1952);

Alain Néry, *Les Idées politiques et sociales de Villiers de l'Isle-Adam* (Paris: Diffusion Université Culture, 1984);

Jacques Noiray, *Le Romancier et la machine,* volume 2: *Jules Verne et Villiers de l'Isle-Adam* (Paris: Corti, 1982);

Rodolphe Palgen, *Villiers de l'Isle-Adam, auteur dramatique* (Paris: Champion, 1925);

Alan W. Raitt, "Les Déboires d'un auteur dramatique: Villiers de l'Isle-Adam à l'Ambigu," *Cahiers d'histoire et de folklore,* 1 (1955): 14–20;

Raitt, *Villiers de l'Isle-Adam et le mouvement symboliste* (Paris: Corti, 1965);

Jacques Robichez, *Le Symbolisme au théâtre: Lugné-Poë et les débuts de L'Œuvre* (Paris: L'Arche, 1957);

Sylvain Simon, *Le Chrétien malgré lui, ou la religion de Villiers de l'Isle-Adam* (Paris: Association Découvrir, 1995);

Bertrand Vibert, *Villiers l'inquiéteur* (Toulouse: Presses Universitaires du Mirail, 1995).

Papers:

Significant holdings of Villiers's papers belong to the Bibliothèque Nationale in Paris and the Bibliothèque municipale de La Rochelle, but many of his manuscripts are in private hands. Many extremely important pieces having belonged to Pierre-Georges Castex, among others, were sold at auction in November 1991 by Maître Thierry Bodin. The sale catalogue, titled *Villiers de l'Isle-Adam et son siècle,* provides historical data as well as full descriptions of this extraordinary collection, one unlikely ever to be equaled.

Checklist of Further Readings

The following list includes books in English and French that treat the history, aesthetics, or analysis of French drama and theater in the nineteenth century, either in part or as their sole subject. While by no means an exhaustive survey of recent writings on nineteenth-century French theater, many of these studies reflect or constitute the most up-to-date scholarship in the area. The reader wishing to locate other bibliographical resources (both old and new) may consult, among others, Otto Klapp, *Bibliographie der französischen Literaturwissenschaft* (Frankfurt: Klosterman, 1960–); the two volumes of the *Critical Bibliography of French Literature: The Nineteenth Century* (Syracuse, N.Y.: Syracuse University Press, 1993), edited by David Baguley; and the bibliographies published in such journals as the *Revue d'Histoire Littéraire de la France, Revue d'Histoire du Théâtre, Theatre Journal, Nineteenth-Century Theatre,* and *Theatre Research International.*

Arsac, Louis. *Le Théâtre français du XIXe siècle.* Paris: Ellipses-Marketing, 1996.

Autrand, Michel, ed. *Les Derniers Feux du théâtre en vers de Hugo à Cocteau.* (Special issue of the *Revue d'histoire du théâtre,* nos. 2–3 [1993].)

Autrand, ed. *Mouvement et statisme au théâtre.* Poitiers: Publications de *La Licorne,* 1995.

Bafaro, Georges, and others. *Etude sur le drame romantique.* Paris: Ellipses, 1996.

Berthier, Patrick. *La Presse littéraire et dramatique au début de la monarchie de Juillet.* Villeneuve-d'Ascq: Presses Universitaires du Septentrion, 1997.

Bird, Charles George. *The Role of the Family in Melodrama, 1797–1827.* Chico, Cal.: C. G. Bird, 1976.

Block, Haskell M. *Mallarmé and the Symbolist Drama.* Detroit: Wayne State University Press, 1963.

Brady, David, and others. *Performance and Politics in Popular Drama.* New York: Cambridge University Press, 1980.

Brooks, Peter. *The Melodramatic Imagination: Balzac, Henry James and the Mode of Excess.* New Haven & London: Yale University Press, 1976; revised, 1995.

Brown, Frederick. *Theater and Revolution. The Culture of the French Stage.* New York: Viking, 1980.

Carlson, Marvin. *The French Stage in the Nineteenth Century.* Metuchen, N.J.: Scarecrow Press, 1972.

Comeau, Paul T. *Diehards and Innovators. The French Romantic Struggle, 1800–1830.* New York: Lang, 1988.

Cox, Jeffrey N. *In the Shadows of Romance: Romantic Tragedy in Germany, England, and France.* Athens: Ohio University Press, 1987.

Daniels, Barry V., ed. *Revolution in the Theatre: French Romantic Theories of Drama.* Westport, Conn.: Greenwood Press, 1983.

Daudet, Alphonse. *Pages inédites de critique dramatique: 1874–1880.* Paris: L'Harmattan, 1993.

Deak, Frantisek. *Symbolist Theater: The Formation of the Avant-Garde.* Baltimore: Johns Hopkins University Press, 1993.

Descotes, Maurice. *Le Drame romantique et ses grands créateurs (1827–1839)*. Paris: Presses Universitaires de France, 1955.

Descotes. *Histoire de la critique dramatique en France*. Tübingen: G. Narr / Paris: Place, 1980.

Fournier, Nathalie. *L'Aparté dans le théâtre français du XVIIIeme siècle au XXe siècle: Etude linguisitique et dramaturgique*. Louvain: Peeters, 1991.

Fulcher, Jane. *The Nation's Image: French Grand Opera as Politics and Politicized Art*. Cambridge: Cambridge University Press, 1987.

Ganz, Arthur. *Realms of the Self: Variations on a Theme in Modern Drama*. New York: New York University Press, 1980.

Gascar, Pierre. *Le Boulevard du crime*. Paris: Hachette-Massin, 1980.

Gengembre, Gérard. *Premières Leçons sur le drame romantique*. Paris: Presses Universitaires de France, 1996.

Gerould, Daniel, ed. *Melodrama*. Special issue of *New York Literary Forum*, 7 (1980).

Gould, Evlyn. *Virtual Theater from Diderot to Mallarmé*. Baltimore: Johns Hopkins University Press, 1989.

Hallays-Dabot, Victor. *Histoire de la censure théâtrale en France*. Geneva: Slatkine Reprints, 1970 (reprint of the Paris edition of 1862).

Hays, Michael. *The Public and Performance: Essays in the History of French and German Theatre, 1871–1900*. Ann Arbor: University of Michigan Institute Research Press, 1981.

Hays and Anatasia Nickolopoulou. *Melodrama: The Cultural Emergence of a Genre*. New York & London: St. Martin's Press, 1996.

Hemmings, Frederick William John. *Theatre and State in France, 1760–1905*. Cambridge: Cambridge University Press, 1994.

Hemmings. *The Theatre Industry of Nineteenth-Century France*. Cambridge: Cambridge University Press, 1993.

Henderson, John A. *The First Avant-Garde, 1887–1894. Sources of the Modern French Theatre*. London: Harrap, 1971.

Hillery, David. *The Théâtre des Variétés in 1852*. Durham, U.K.: University of Durham Press, 1996.

Hobson, Harold. *French Theatre Since 1830*. London: J. Calder / Dallas: Riverrun Press, 1970.

Howarth, William Driver. *Sublime and Grotesque: A Study of French Romantic Drama*. London: Harrap, 1975.

Issacharoff, Michael. *Le Spectacle du discours*. Paris: Corti, 1985; translated by Issacharoff as *Discourse as Performance*. Stanford, Cal.: Stanford University Press, 1989.

Jomaron, Jacqueline de, and others. *Le Théâtre en France, volume 2: De la Révolution à nos jours*. Paris: A. Colin, 1989.

Jones, Michèle H. *Le Théâtre national en France de 1800 à 1830*. Paris: Klincksieck, 1975.

Kennedy, Emmet, and others. *Theatre, Opera, and Audiences in Revolutionary Paris: Analysis and Repertory*. Westport, Conn.: Greenwood Press, 1995.

Krakovitch, Odile. *Hugo censuré: La Liberté au théâtre au XIXe siècle.* Paris: Calmann-Lévy, 1985.

Krakovitch. *Les Pièces de Théâtre soumises à la censure (1800–1830).* Paris: Archives Nationales, 1982.

Kruger, Loren. *The National Stage: Theatre and Cultural Legitimation in England, France, and America.* Chicago: University of Chicago Press, 1992.

Le Hir, Marie-Pierre. *Le Romantisme aux enchères: Ducange, Pixerécourt, Hugo.* Amsterdam & Philadelphia: John Benjamins, 1992.

Lioure, Michel. *Le Drame de Diderot à Ionesco.* Paris: A. Colin, 1963.

Marie, Gisèle. *Le Théâtre symboliste: ses origines, ses sources. Pionniers et réalisateurs.* Paris: Nizet, 1973.

McCormick, John. *Popular Theatres of Nineteenth-Century France.* London & New York: Routledge, 1993.

Métayer, Léon. *La Représentation des rôles et des status de la femme dans le mélodrame en France et en Angleterre, de 1830 à 1870.* Dissertation, Université de Reims, 1981 (microfiches).

Pao, Angela. *The Orient of the Boulevards: Exoticism, Empire, and 19th-Century French Theatre.* Philadelphia: University of Pennsylvania Press, 1998.

Przybos, Julia. *L'Entreprise mélodramatique.* Paris: José Corti, 1987.

Redmond, James, ed. *Melodrama,* volume 14 in *Themes in Drama.* Cambridge: Cambridge University Press, 1992.

Roubine, Jean-Jacques. *Théâtre et mise en scène, 1880–1980.* Paris: Presses Universitaires de France, 1980.

Thomasseau, Jean-Marie. *Drame et tragédie.* Paris: Hachette, 1995.

Thomasseau. *Le Mélodrame sur les scènes parisiennes de "Coelina" à "L'Auberge des Adrets."* Lille: Service de reproduction de thèses, 1976.

Thomasseau, ed. Special issue on melodrama, *Europe,* vol. 65, nos. 703–704 (1987).

Ubersfeld, Anne. *Le Dialogue de théâtre.* Paris: Belin, 1996.

Ubersfeld. *Le Drame romantique.* Paris: Belin, 1993.

Ubersfeld. *L'Ecole du spectateur.* Paris: Editions sociales, 1981.

Ubersfeld. *Les Termes clés de l'analyse de théâtre.* Paris: Seuil, 1996.

Wicks, Charles Beaumont. *The Parisian Stage,* 5 volumes. University: University of Alabama Press, 1948–1979.

Wild, Nicole. *Décors et costumes du XIXe siècle,* 2 volumes. Paris: Bibliothèque Nationale, 1987, 1993.

Contributors

John Blaise Anzalone ....*Skidmore College*

Janice Best ....*Acadia University*

Douglas Cardwell...*Salem College*

Marvin Carlson ....*The Graduate School and University Center, The City University of New York*

Barbara T. Cooper ....*University of New Hampshire*

John A. Degen ....*Florida State University*

Robert T. Denommé..*University of Virginia*

Daniel Gerould .....*The Graduate School and University Center, The City University of New York*

Diana R. Hallman ....*University of Kentucky*

Mario Hamlet-Metz...*James Madison University*

Melanie C. Hawthorne ....*Texas A&M University*

Marie-Pierre Le Hir ....*Case Western Reserve University*

John Claiborne Isbell...*Indiana University at Bloomington*

John J. Janc...*Mankato State University*

Rhona Justice-Malloy...*Central Michigan University*

Bettina L. Knapp ....*Hunter College of The City University of New York*

Frazer Lively ....*University of Pittsburgh*

John McCormick ....*Trinity College, Dublin*

Binita Mehta..........*The Graduate School and University Center, The City University of New York*

Judith Graves Miller..*University of Wisconsin—Madison*

Denise R. Mjelde..*University of Wisconsin—Madison*

Angela Pao ....*Indiana University*

Marcia G. Parker ....*University of Wisconsin—Stevens Point*

Julia Przybos...*Hunter College of The City University of New York*

Juliette M. Rogers ....*University of New Hampshire*

Norman R. Shapiro ....*Wesleyan University*

David Sices...*Dartmouth College*

Gay Smith (Manifold) ....*Wesleyan University*

Lynn R. Wilkinson ....*University of Texas, Austin*

Cumulative Index

Dictionary of Literary Biography, Volumes 1-192
Dictionary of Literary Biography Yearbook, 1980-1997
Dictionary of Literary Biography Documentary Series, Volumes 1-16

Cumulative Index

DLB before number: *Dictionary of Literary Biography*, Volumes 1-192
Y before number: *Dictionary of Literary Biography Yearbook*, 1980-1997
DS before number: *Dictionary of Literary Biography Documentary Series*, Volumes 1-16

A

B

G

H

J

L

M

N

V